STREET ATLAS

Cardiff, Swansea and the Valleys

ATLAS STRYDOEDD

Caerdydd, Abertawe a'r Cymoedd

www.philips-maps.co.uk

First published in 1995 as *'Cardiff, Swansea and Glamorgan'* by

Philip's, a division of
Octopus Publishing Group Ltd
www.octopusbooks.co.uk
2-4 Heron Quays, London E14 4JP
An Hachette Livre UK Company
www.hachettelivre.co.uk

Third colour edition 2007
Second impression 2008
CSVCA

ISBN 978-0-540-09165-2 (spiral)

Printed and bound in China by Toppan

Contents

III **Administrative and Postcode boundaries**

IV **Key to map symbols**

VI **Key to map pages**

VIII **Route planning**

1 **Street maps** at 3½ inches to 1 mile

218 **Street maps** at 1¾ inches to 1 mile

232 **Street maps of Cardiff and Swansea city centres** at 7 inches to 1 mile

234 **Index** of towns, villages, streets, hospitals, industrial estates, railway stations, schools, shopping centres, universities and places of interest

Digital Data

The exceptionally high-quality mapping found in this atlas is available as digital data in TIFF format, which is easily convertible to other bitmapped (raster) image formats.

The index is also available in digital form as a standard database table. It contains all the details found in the printed index together with the National Grid reference for the map square in which each entry is named.

For further information and to discuss your requirements, please contact victoria.dawbarn@philips-maps.co.uk

On-line route planner

For detailed driving directions and estimated driving times visit our free route planner at www.philips-maps.co.uk

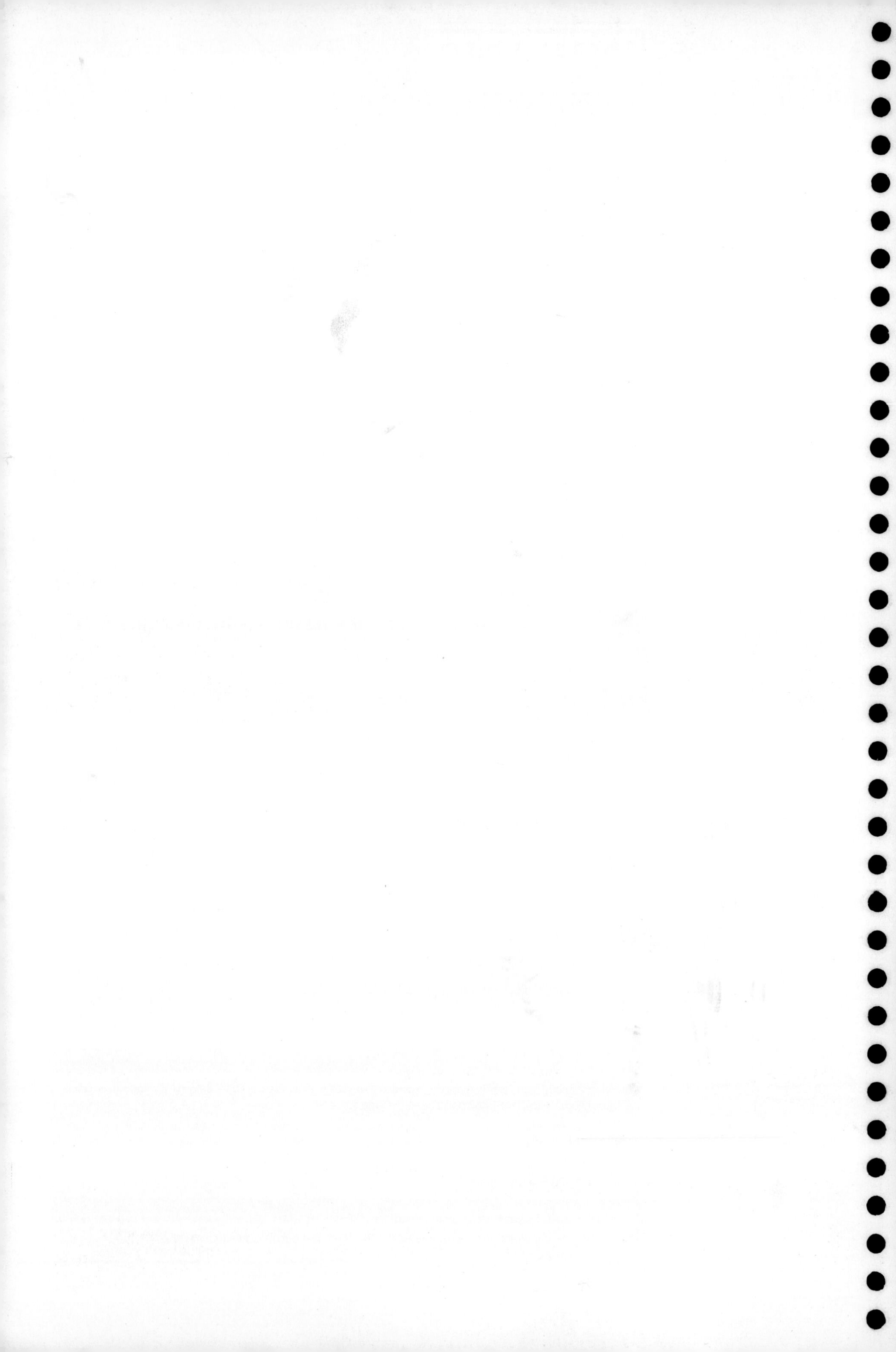

Major administrative and Postcode boundaries

Allwedd i symbolau'r map

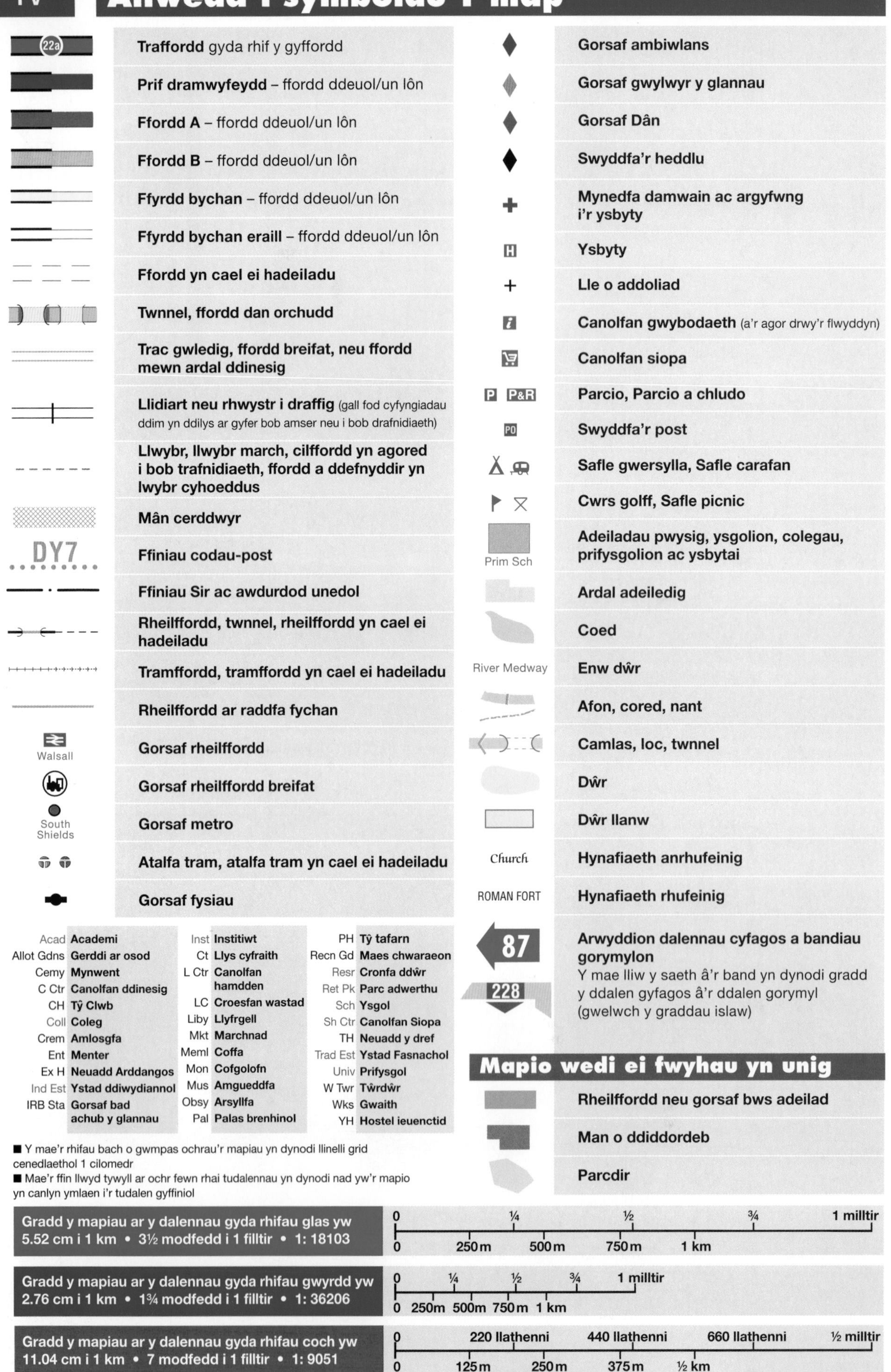

Traffordd gyda rhif y gyffordd

Prif dramwyfeydd – ffordd ddeuol/un lôn

Ffordd A – ffordd ddeuol/un lôn

Ffordd B – ffordd ddeuol/un lôn

Ffyrdd bychan – ffordd ddeuol/un lôn

Ffyrdd bychan eraill – ffordd ddeuol/un lôn

Ffordd yn cael ei hadeiladu

Twnnel, ffordd dan orchudd

Trac gwledig, ffordd breifat, neu ffordd mewn ardal ddinesig

Llidiart neu rhwystr i draffig (gall fod cyfyngiadau ddim yn ddilys ar gyfer bob amser neu i bob drafnidiaeth)

Llwybr, llwybr march, cilffordd yn agored i bob trafnidiaeth, ffordd a ddefnyddir yn lwybr cyhoeddus

Mân cerddwyr

Ffiniau codau-post

Ffiniau Sir ac awdurdod unedol

Rheilffordd, twnnel, rheilffordd yn cael ei hadeiladu

Tramffordd, tramffordd yn cael ei hadeiladu

Rheilffordd ar raddfa fychan

Gorsaf rheilffordd

Gorsaf rheilffordd breifat

Gorsaf metro

Atalfa tram, atalfa tram yn cael ei hadeiladu

Gorsaf fysiau

Gorsaf ambiwlans

Gorsaf gwylwyr y glannau

Gorsaf Dân

Swyddfa'r heddlu

Mynedfa damwain ac argyfwng i'r ysbyty

Ysbyty

Lle o addoliad

Canolfan gwybodaeth (a'r agor drwy'r flwyddyn)

Canolfan siopa

Parcio, Parcio a chludo

Swyddfa'r post

Safle gwersylla, Safle carafan

Cwrs golff, Safle picnic

Adeiladau pwysig, ysgolion, colegau, prifysgolion ac ysbytai

Ardal adeiledig

Coed

Enw dŵr

Afon, cored, nant

Camlas, loc, twnnel

Dŵr

Dŵr llanw

Hynafiaeth anrhufeinig

Hynafiaeth rhufeinig

Arwyddion dalennau cyfagos a bandiau gorymylon
Y mae lliw y saeth â'r band yn dynodi gradd y ddalen gyfagos â'r ddalen gorymyl (gwelwch y graddau islaw)

Acad	**Academi**	Inst	**Institiwt**	PH	**Tŷ tafarn**
Allot Gdns	**Gerddi ar osod**	Ct	**Llys cyfraith**	Recn Gd	**Maes chwaraeon**
Cemy	**Mynwent**	L Ctr	**Canolfan hamdden**	Resr	**Cronfa ddŵr**
C Ctr	**Canolfan ddinesig**	LC	**Croesfan wastad**	Ret Pk	**Parc adwerthu**
CH	**Tŷ Clwb**	Liby	**Llyfrgell**	Sch	**Ysgol**
Coll	**Coleg**	Mkt	**Marchnad**	Sh Ctr	**Canolfan Siopa**
Crem	**Amlosgfa**	Meml	**Coffa**	TH	**Neuadd y dref**
Ent	**Menter**	Mon	**Cofgolofn**	Trad Est	**Ystad Fasnachol**
Ex H	**Neuadd Arddangos**	Mus	**Amgueddfa**	Univ	**Prifysgol**
Ind Est	**Ystad ddiwydiannol**	Obsy	**Arsyllfa**	W Twr	**Tŵrdŵr**
IRB Sta	**Gorsaf bad achub y glannau**	Pal	**Palas brenhinol**	Wks	**Gwaith**
				YH	**Hostel ieuenctid**

■ Y mae'r rhifau bach o gwmpas ochrau'r mapiau yn dynodi llinelli grid cenedlaethol 1 cilomedr

■ Mae'r ffin llwyd tywyll ar ochr fewn rhai tudalennau yn dynodi nad yw'r mapio yn canlyn ymlaen i'r tudalen gyffiniol

Mapio wedi ei fwyhau yn unig

Rheilffordd neu gorsaf bws adeilad

Man o ddiddordeb

Parcdir

Gradd y mapiau ar y dalennau gyda rhifau glas yw
5.52 cm i 1 km • 3½ modfedd i 1 filltir • 1: 18103

0 – ¼ – ½ – ¾ – 1 milltir
0 – 250 m – 500 m – 750 m – 1 km

Gradd y mapiau ar y dalennau gyda rhifau gwyrdd yw
2.76 cm i 1 km • 1¾ modfedd i 1 filltir • 1: 36206

0 – ¼ – ½ – ¾ – 1 milltir
0 – 250m – 500m – 750m – 1 km

Gradd y mapiau ar y dalennau gyda rhifau coch yw
11.04 cm i 1 km • 7 modfedd i 1 filltir • 1: 9051

0 – 220 llathenni – 440 llathenni – 660 llathenni – ½ milltir
0 – 125 m – 250 m – 375 m – ½ km

Key to map symbols

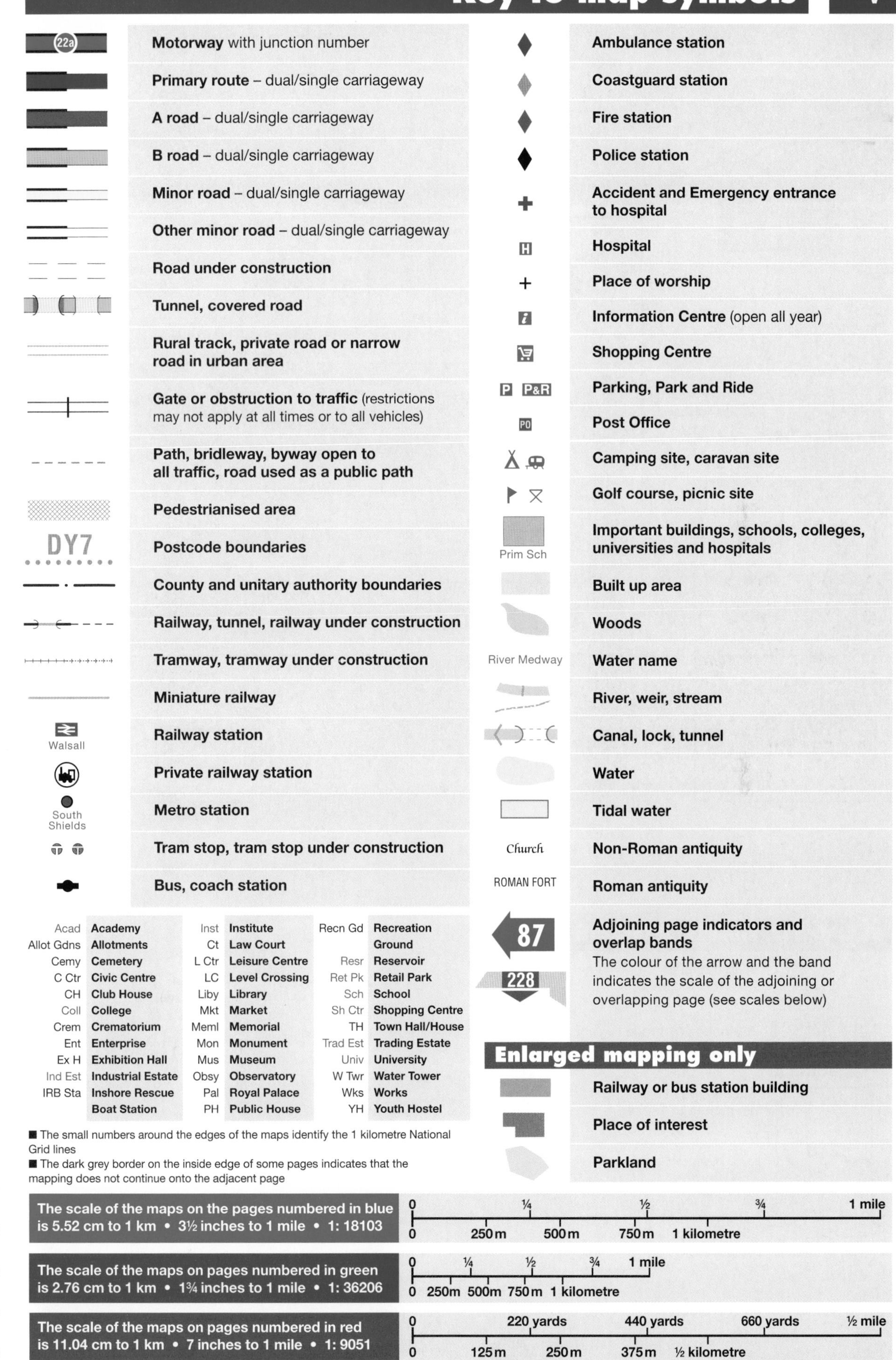

Acad	Academy	Inst	Institute	Recn Gd	Recreation Ground
Allot Gdns	Allotments	Ct	Law Court	Resr	Reservoir
Cemy	Cemetery	L Ctr	Leisure Centre	Ret Pk	Retail Park
C Ctr	Civic Centre	LC	Level Crossing	Sch	School
CH	Club House	Liby	Library	Sh Ctr	Shopping Centre
Coll	College	Mkt	Market	TH	Town Hall/House
Crem	Crematorium	Meml	Memorial	Trad Est	Trading Estate
Ent	Enterprise	Mon	Monument	Univ	University
Ex H	Exhibition Hall	Mus	Museum	W Twr	Water Tower
Ind Est	Industrial Estate	Obsy	Observatory	Wks	Works
IRB Sta	Inshore Rescue Boat Station	Pal	Royal Palace	YH	Youth Hostel
		PH	Public House		

■ The small numbers around the edges of the maps identify the 1 kilometre National Grid lines

■ The dark grey border on the inside edge of some pages indicates that the mapping does not continue onto the adjacent page

The scale of the maps on the pages numbered in blue is 5.52 cm to 1 km • 3½ inches to 1 mile • 1: 18103

0 ¼ ½ ¾ 1 mile
0 250 m 500 m 750 m 1 kilometre

The scale of the maps on pages numbered in green is 2.76 cm to 1 km • 1¾ inches to 1 mile • 1: 36206

0 ¼ ½ ¾ 1 mile
0 250m 500m 750m 1 kilometre

The scale of the maps on pages numbered in red is 11.04 cm to 1 km • 7 inches to 1 mile • 1: 9051

0 220 yards 440 yards 660 yards ½ mile
0 125 m 250 m 375 m ½ kilometre

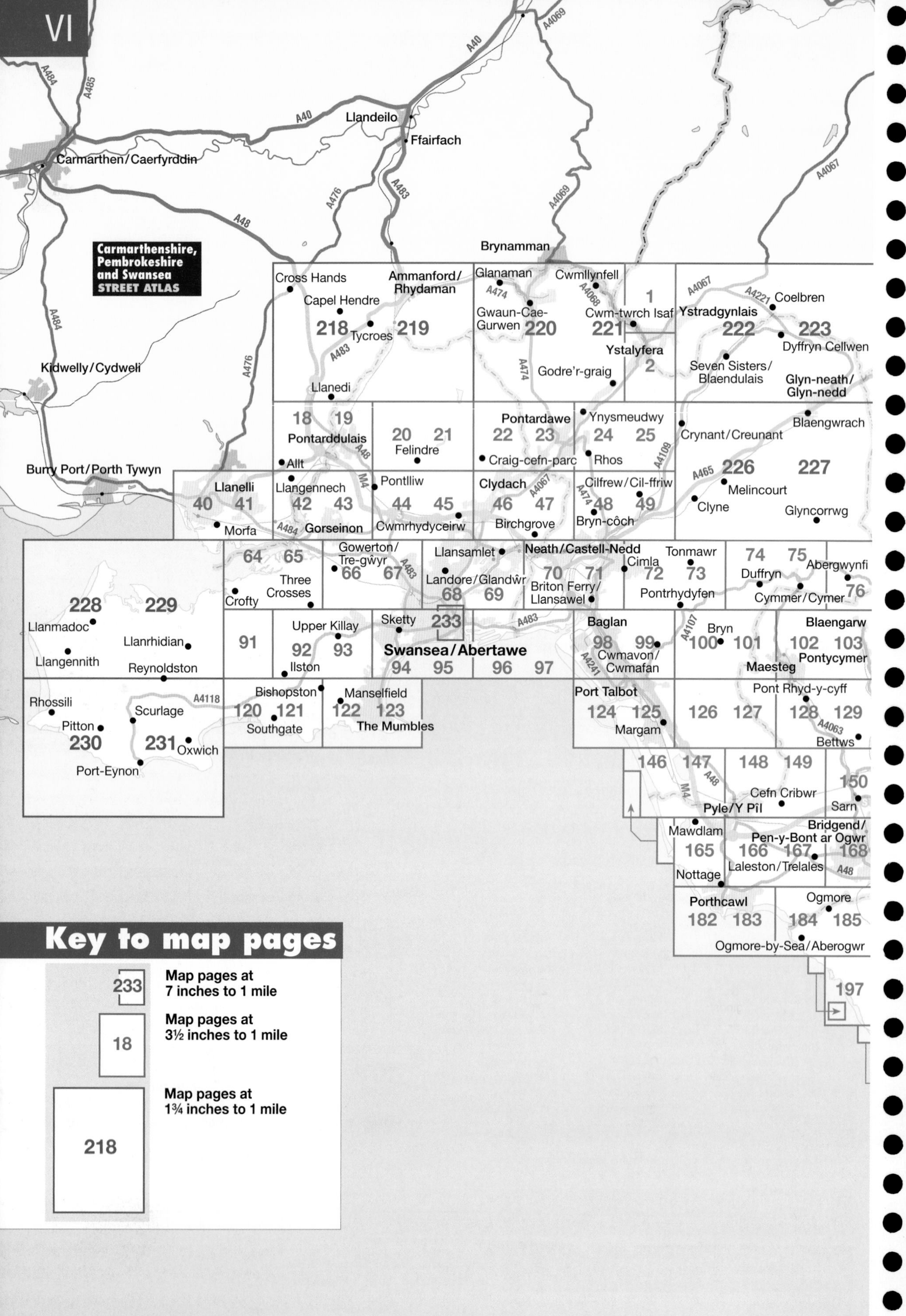

Key to map pages

233	Map pages at 7 inches to 1 mile
18	Map pages at 3½ inches to 1 mile
218	Map pages at 1¾ inches to 1 mile

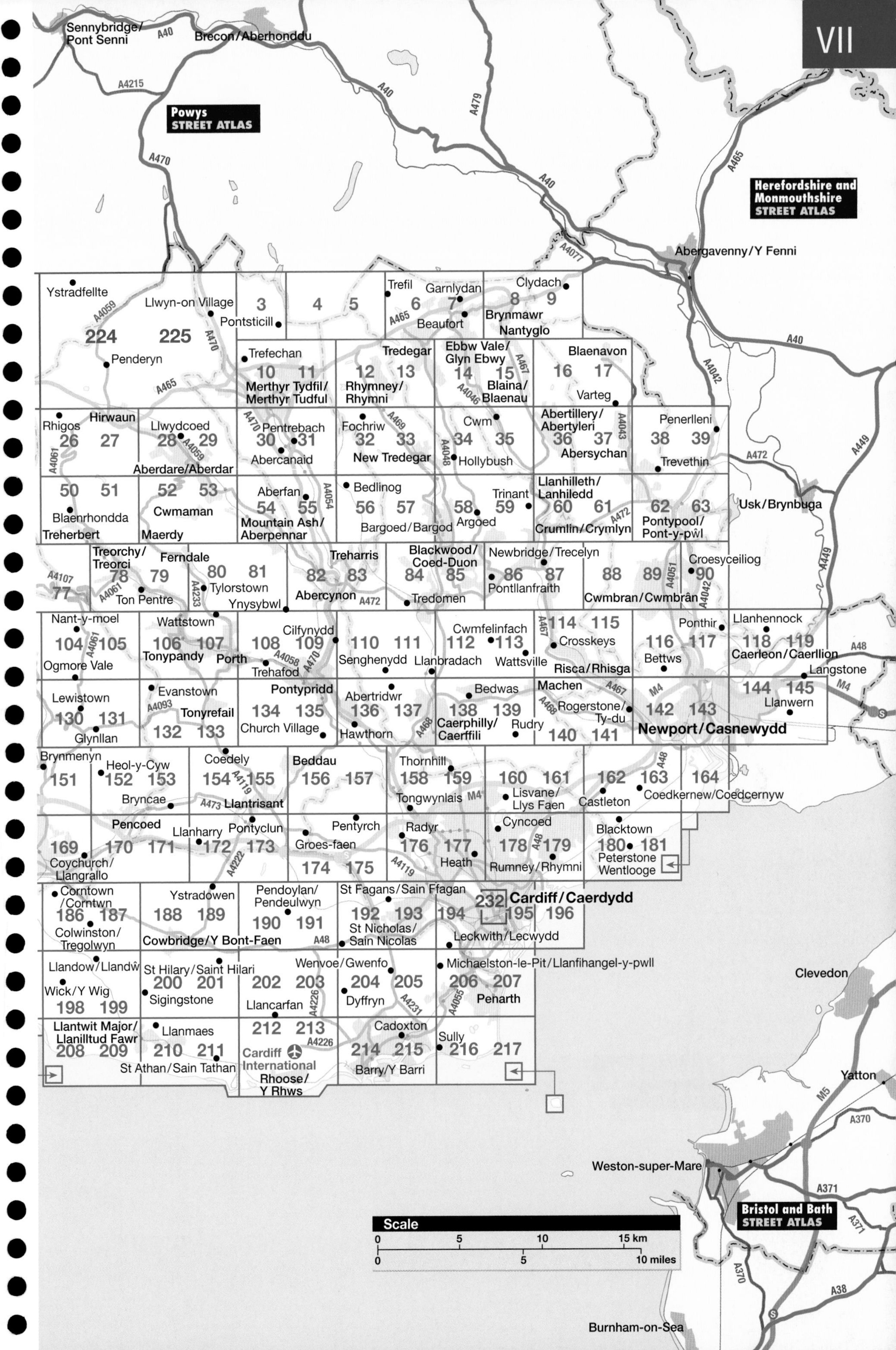

Sennybridge/Pont Senni
Brecon/Aberhonddu
Powys STREET ATLAS
Herefordshire and Monmouthshire STREET ATLAS
Abergavenny/Y Fenni
Ystradfellte
Llwyn-on Village
Pontsticill
Penderyn
224
225
3
4
5
Trefil
Garnlydan
Clydach
6
7
8
9
Beaufort
Brynmawr
Nantyglo
Trefechan
10
11
Merthyr Tydfil/Merthyr Tudful
Tredegar
12
13
Rhymney/Rhymni
Ebbw Vale/Glyn Ebwy
14
15
Blaina/Blaenau
Blaenavon
16
17
Varteg
Rhigos
Hirwaun
26
27
Llwydcoed
28
29
Aberdare/Aberdar
Pentrebach
30
31
Abercanaid
Fochriw
32
33
New Tredegar
Cwm
34
35
Hollybush
Abertillery/Abertyleri
36
37
Abersychan
Penerlleni
38
39
Trevethin
50
51
Blaenrhondda
Treherbert
52
53
Cwmaman
Maerdy
Aberfan
54
55
Mountain Ash/Aberpennar
Bedlinog
56
57
Bargoed/Bargod
58
Argoed
Trinant
59
Llanhilleth/Lanhiledd
60
61
Crumlin/Crymlyn
62
63
Pontypool/Pont-y-pŵl
Usk/Brynbuga
77
Treorchy/Treorci
78
79
Ferndale
Ton Pentre
80
81
Tylorstown
Ynysybwl
Treharris
82
83
Abercynon
Blackwood/Coed-Duon
84
85
Tredomen
Newbridge/Trecelyn
86
87
Pontllanfraith
88
89
Croesyceiliog
90
Cwmbran/Cwmbrân
Nant-y-moel
104
105
Ogmore Vale
Wattstown
106
107
Tonypandy
Porth
108
Cilfynydd
109
Trehafod
110
111
Senghenydd
Llanbradach
Cwmfelinfach
112
113
Wattsville
114
115
Crosskeys
Risca/Rhisga
Ponthir
116
117
Bettws
Llanhennock
118
119
Caerleon/Caerllion
Langstone
Lewistown
130
131
Glynllan
Evanstown
Tonyrefail
132
133
Pontypridd
134
135
Church Village
Abertridwr
136
137
Hawthorn
Bedwas
138
139
Caerphilly/Caerffili
Rudry
Machen
Rogerstone/Ty-du
140
141
142
143
Newport/Casnewydd
144
145
Llanwern
Brynmenyn
151
Heol-y-Cyw
152
153
Bryncae
Coedely
154
155
Llantrisant
Beddau
156
157
Thornhill
158
159
Tongwynlais
160
161
Lisvane/Llys Faen
162
163
Castleton
164
Coedkernew/Coedcernyw
169
Coychurch/Llangrallo
Pencoed
170
171
Llanharry
Pontyclun
172
173
Groes-faen
Pentyrch
174
175
Radyr
176
177
Heath
Cyncoed
178
179
Rumney/Rhymni
Blacktown
180
181
Peterstone Wentlooge
Corntown/Corntwn
186
187
Colwinston/Tregolwyn
Ystradowen
188
189
Cowbridge/Y Bont-Faen
Pendoylan/Pendeulwyn
190
191
St Fagans/Sain Ffagan
192
193
St Nicholas/Sain Nicolas
194
232
Cardiff/Caerdydd
195
196
Leckwith/Lecwydd
Llandow/Llandŵ
Wick/Y Wig
198
199
St Hilary/Saint Hilari
200
201
Sigingstone
202
203
Llancarfan
Wenvoe/Gwenfo
204
205
Dyffryn
Michaelston-le-Pit/Llanfihangel-y-pwll
206
207
Penarth
Llantwit Major/Llanilltud Fawr
208
209
Llanmaes
210
211
St Athan/Sain Tathan
212
213
Cardiff International
Rhoose/Y Rhws
Cadoxton
214
215
Barry/Y Barri
Sully
216
217
Clevedon
Yatton
Weston-super-Mare
Bristol and Bath STREET ATLAS
Burnham-on-Sea
Scale
0
5
10
15 km
0
5
10 miles
A40
A4215
A470
A479
A465
A4077
A4042
A449
A472
A48
M4
M5
A370
A371
A38
A4059
A4061
A4046
A467
A469
A4048
A4043
A4054
A4107
A4233
A4051
A4058
A4093
A468
A4119
A473
A4222
A4055
A4226
A4231

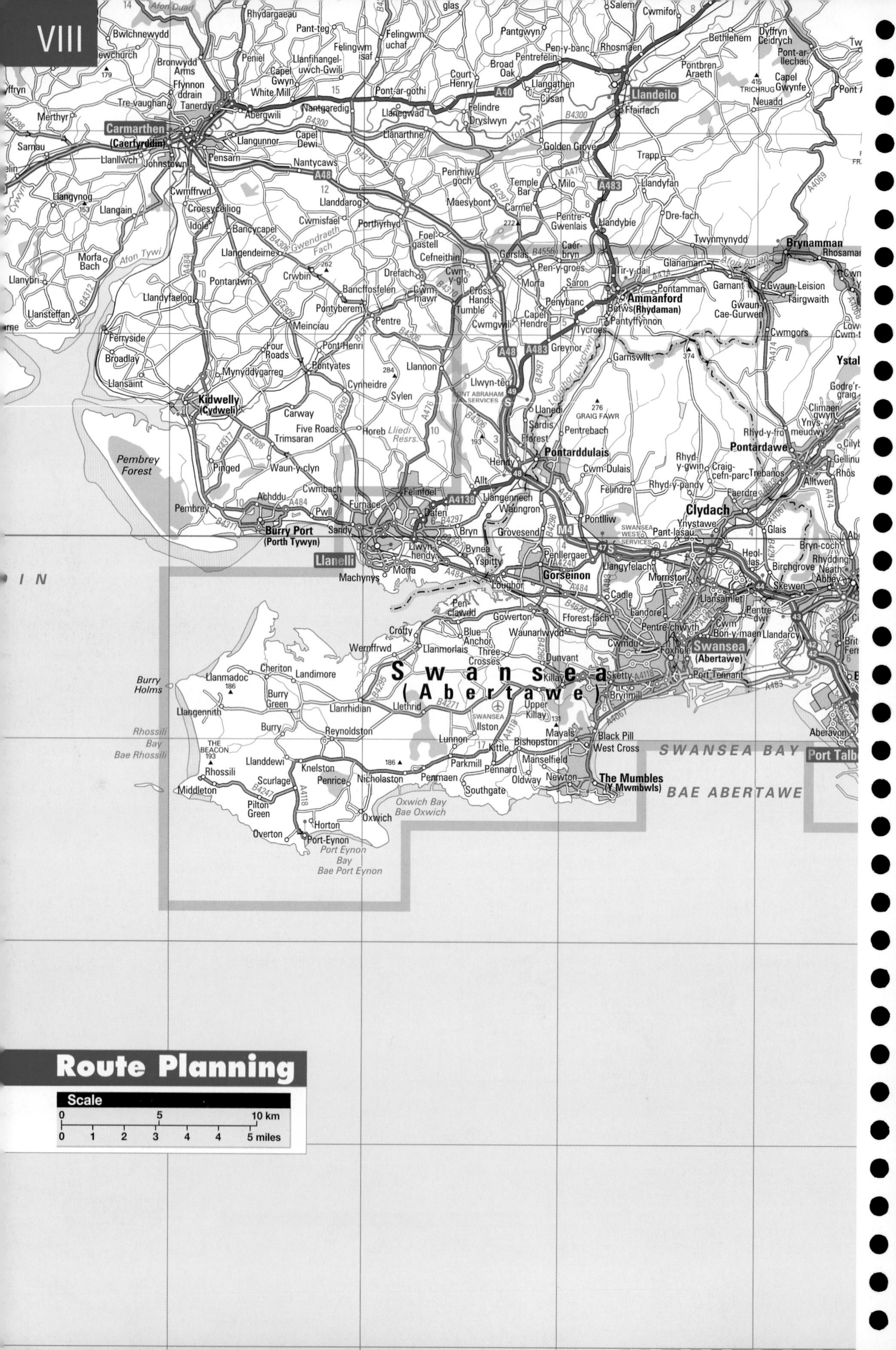
Carmarthen
(Caerfyrddin)
Llandeilo
Ammanford
(Rhydaman)
Brynamman
Kidwelly
(Cydweli)
Burry Port
(Porth Tywyn)
Llanelli
Pontarddulais
Gorseinon
Clydach
Pontardawe
Swansea
(Abertawe)
Swansea
(Abertawe)
The Mumbles
(Y Mwmbwls)
Port Talb
SWANSEA BAY
BAE ABERTAWE
Pembrey Forest
Burry Holms
Rhossili Bay
Bae Rhossili
Oxwich Bay
Bae Oxwich
Port Eynon Bay
Bae Port Eynon
Afon Tywi
Gwendraeth Fach
Lliedi Resrs.
Loughor (Llwchwr)
Afon Aman
A40
A48
A483
A484
A4138
A476
A474
A4118
M4
B4300
B4297
B4309
B4306
Nantgaredig
Pensarn
Llangunnor
Johnstown
Llanllwch
Llangain
Llangynog
Llansteffan
Ferryside
Llandyfaelog
Pontantwn
Llangendeirne
Bancycapel
Idole
Croesyceiliog
Cwmffrwd
Porthyrhyd
Llanddarog
Nantycaws
Cwmisfael
Foel-gastell
Cefneithin
Cross Hands
Tumble
Gorslas
Drefach
Crwbin
Bancffosfelen
Pontyberem
Meinciau
Pont-Henri
Pontyates
Four Roads
Mynyddygarreg
Llansaint
Broadlay
Carway
Five Roads
Trimsaran
Cynheidre
Sylen
Llannon
Horeb
Pinged
Waun-y-clyn
Pembrey
Achddu
Pwll
Cwmbach
Furnace
Felinfoel
Dafen
Sandy
Bryn
Llwynhendy
Bynea
Yspitty
Morfa
Machynys
Loughor
Llangennech
Waungron
Hendy
Allt
Llanedi
Sardis
Fforest
Pentrebach
Cwm-Dulais
Felindre
Garnswllt
Grovesend
Pontlliw
Penllergaer
Llangyfelach
Morriston
Llansamlet
Cadle
Landore
Fforest-fach
Cwmdu
Sketty
Brynmill
Killay
Dunvant
Gowerton
Penclawdd
Crofty
Wernffrwd
Llanmorlais
Blue Anchor
Three Crosses
Waunarlwydd
Upper Killay
Mayals
Black Pill
West Cross
Bishopston
Kittle
Manselfield
Newton
Oldway
Pennard
Southgate
Parkmill
Ilston
Lunnon
Penmaen
Nicholaston
Penrice
Knelston
Reynoldston
Llethrid
Llanrhidian
Burry
Burry Green
Landimore
Cheriton
Llanmadoc
Llangennith
Rhossili
Middleton
Llanddewi
Scurlage
Pilton Green
Overton
Horton
Port-Eynon
Oxwich
THE BEACON
Tycroes
Pantyffynnon
Betws
Saron
Penybanc
Capel Hendre
Cwmgwili
Pen-y-groes
Morfa
Llandybie
Pentregwenlais
Milo
Temple Bar
Carmel
Maesybont
Penrhiw-goch
Golden Grove
Ffairfach
Trapp
Llandyfan
Dre-fach
Twynmynydd
Glanaman
Garnant
Pontamman
Gwaun-Cae-Gurwen
Gwaun-Leision
Tairgwaith
Cwmgors
Tir-y-dail
Ynystawe
Pant-lasau
Rhyd-y-pandy
Craig-cefn-parc
Rhyd-y-gwin
Trebanos
Alltwen
Glais
Skewen
Birchgrove
Heol-las
Bryn-coch
Neath Abbey
Llandarcy
Pentre-dwr
Bon-y-maen
Foxhole
Port Tennant
Aberavon
SWANSEA
SWANSEA WEST SERVICES
PONT ABRAHAM SERVICES
GRAIG FAWR
TRICHRUG
Rhydargaeau
Bwlchnewydd
Bronwydd Arms
Peniel
Pant-teg
Felingwm isaf
Felingwm uchaf
Llanfihangel-uwch-Gwili
Capel Gwyn
White Mill
Ffynnon ddrain
Tre-vaughan
Tanerdy
Abergwili
Merthyr
Sarnau
Pont-ar-gothi
Court Henry
Broad Oak
Llangathen
Cilsan
Felindre
Dryslwyn
Llanegwad
Llanarthne
Capel Dewi
Pentrefelin
Pen-y-banc
Rhosmaen
Pantgwyn
Cwmifor
Salem
Bethlehem
Dyffryn Ceidrych
Pont-ar-llechau
Capel Gwynfe
Pontbren Araeth
Neuadd
Morfa Bach
Llanybri
Pentre
Llwyn-teg
Route Planning
Scale
0 5 10 km
0 1 2 3 4 4 5 miles

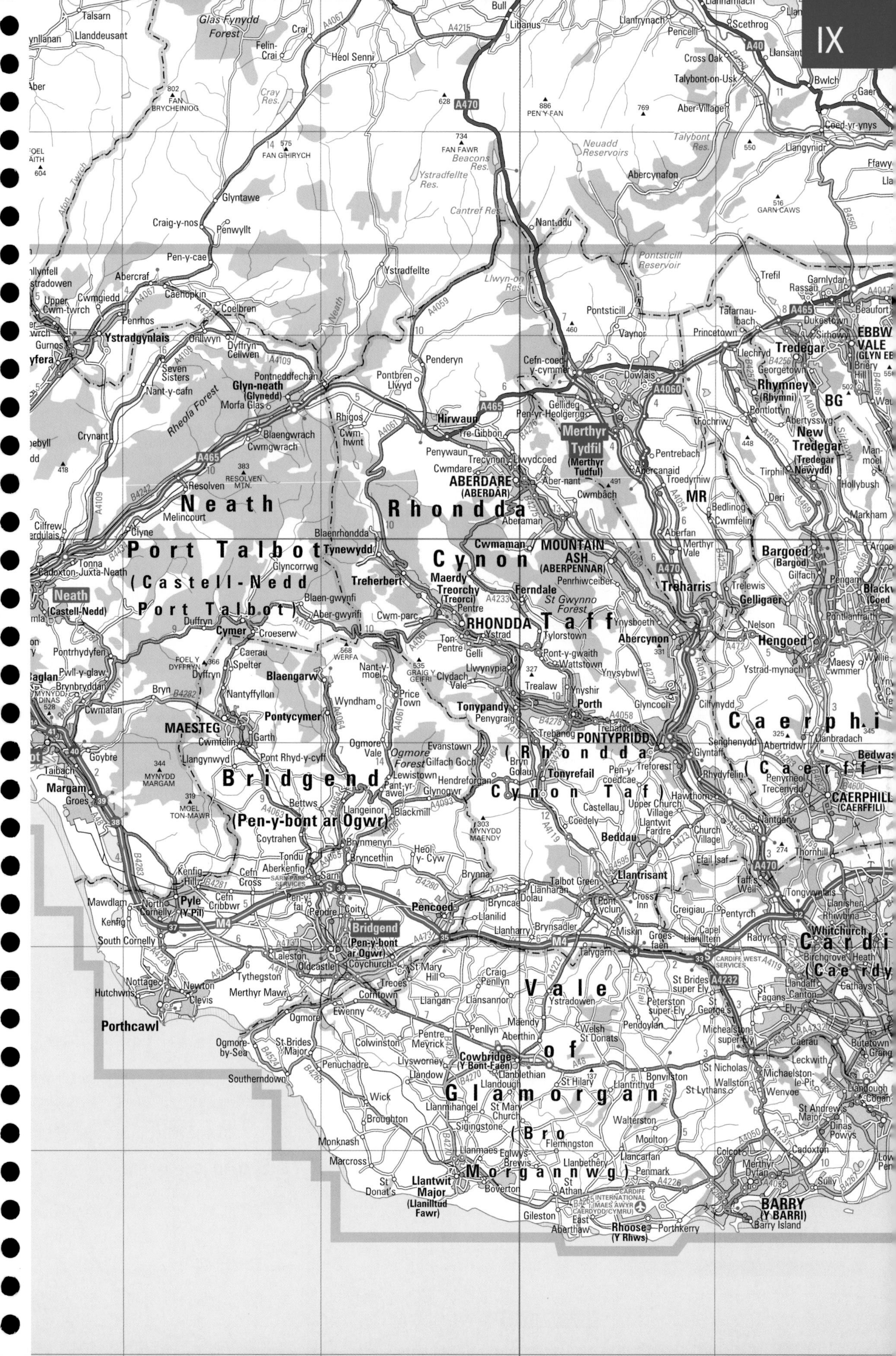
Talsarn
Llanddeusant
Glas Fynydd Forest
Crai
Felin-Crai
Heol Senni
Bull
Libanus
Llanfrynach
Pencelli
Scethrog
Llanhamlach
Cross Oak
Talybont-on-Usk
Bwlch
Llansantffraed
Aber-Village
Coed-yr-ynys
Llangynidr
Talybont Res.
Neuadd Reservoirs
Abercynafon
FAN BRYCHEINIOG
PEN Y FAN
FAN FAWR
FAN GIHIRYCH
Beacons Res.
Ystradfellte Res.
Cantref Res.
Cray Res.
GARN CAWS
Glyntawe
Craig-y-nos
Penwyllt
Nant-ddu
Pen-y-cae
Pontsticill Reservoir
Abercraf
Cwmgiedd
Caehopkin
Coelbren
Ystradfellte
Llwyn-on Res.
Pontsticill
Vaynor
Trefil
Rassau
Garnlydan
Beaufort
Tafarnau-bach
Princetown
Dukestown
Sirhowy
EBBW VALE
Tredegar
Georgetown
Rhymney (Rhymni)
Ystradgynlais
Onllwyn
Dyffryn Cellwen
Seven Sisters
Nant-y-cafn
Penderyn
Pontbren Llwyd
Cefn-coed-y-cymmer
Dowlais
Gellideg
Pen-yr-Heolgerrig
Glyn-neath (Glynedd)
Pontneddfechan
Morfa Glas
Rheola Forest
Rhigos
Hirwaun
Tre-Gibbon
Merthyr Tydfil (Merthyr Tudful)
Pontlottyn
Abertysswg
New Tredegar (Tredegar Newydd)
Fochriw
Pentrebach
Blaengwrach
Cwmgwrach
Crynant
Cwm-hwnt
Penywaun
Trecynon
Llwydcoed
Cwmdare
ABERDARE (ABERDÂR)
Aber-nant
Abercanaid
Troedyrhiw
Cwmbach
Tirphil
Hollybush
RESOLVEN MTN.
Resolven
Neath
Rhondda
Melincourt
Aberaman
Deri
Bedlinog
Cwmfelin
Markham
Clyne
Cilfrew
Aberfan
Merthyr Vale
Blaenrhondda
Tynewydd
Cwmaman
MOUNTAIN ASH (ABERPENNAR)
Bargoed (Bargod)
Gilfach
Pengam
Blackwood (Coed Duon)
Tonna
Cadoxton-Juxta-Neath
Port Talbot
Glyncorrwg
Treherbert
Cynon
Maerdy
Treorchy (Treorci)
Pentre
Ferndale
Penrhiwceiber
Treharris
Trelewis
Gelligaer
Neath (Castell-Nedd)
(Castell-Nedd Port Talbot)
Blaen-gwynfi
Aber-gwynfi
Cwm-parc
St Gwynno Forest
Duffryn
Cymer
Croeserw
RHONDDA
Ystrad
Taff
Ynysboeth
Abercynon
Nelson
Hengoed
Pontllanfraith
Pontrhydyfen
Ton-Pentre
Gelli
Tylorstown
Ront-y-gwaith
Wattstown
Ynysybwl
Ystrad-mynach
Maesycwmmer
Caerau
Spelter
FOEL Y DYFFRYN
Dyffryn
WERFA
Nant-y-moel
GRAIG Y GEIFR
Clydach Vale
Llwynypia
Trealaw
Ynyshir
Baglan
Pwll-y-glaw
Bryn
Blaengarw
Porth
Glyncoch
Cilfynydd
Bryn-bryddan
Cwmafan
Nantyffyllon
Wyndham
Price Town
Tonypandy
Penygraig
Trehafod
Trebanog
PONTYPRIDD
Caerphilly
MAESTEG
Cwmfelin
Garth
Pontycymer
Ogmore Vale
Evanstown
Senghenydd
Abertridwr
Llanbradach
Goytre
Llangynwyd
Pont Rhyd-y-cyff
Ogmore Forest
Gilfach Goch
Glyntaff
Treforest
Rhydyfelin
Penyrheol
Trecenydd
Taibach
MYNYDD MARGAM
Bridgend
Lewistown
Hendreforgan
Bryn Golau
Tonyrefail
Pen-y-coedcae
Margam
Groes
MOEL TON-MAWR
Bettws
Pant-yr-awel
Glynogwr
Cynon Taf
Castellau
Upper Church Village
Hawthorn
CAERPHILLY (CAERFFILI)
(Pen-y-bont ar Ogwr)
Llangeinor
Blackmill
MYNYDD MAENDY
Coedely
Llantwit Fardre
Church Village
Nantgarw
Coytrahen
Brynmenyn
Beddau
Thornhill
Tondu
Aberkenfig
Bryncethin
Heol-y-Cyw
Efail Isaf
Kenfig Hill
Cefn Cross
SARN PARK SERVICES
Sarn
Brynna
Talbot Green
Llantrisant
Taff's Well
Tongwynlais
Mawdlam
North Cornelly
Pyle (Y Pîl)
Cefn Cribbwr
Pen-y-fai
Pendre
Coity
Pencoed
Bryncae
Llanharan
Dolau
Llanilid
Pont-y-clun
Cross Inn
Creigiau
Pentyrch
Llanishen
Rhiwbina
Kenfig
South Cornelly
Bridgend (Pen-y-bont ar Ogwr)
Llanharry
Brynsadler
Miskin
Groes-faen
Capel Llanilltern
Radyr
Whitchurch
Cardiff (Caerdydd)
Laleston
Oldcastle
Coychurch
St Mary Hill
Craig Penllyn
Talygarn
CARDIFF WEST SERVICES
Birchgrove
Heath
Nottage
Newton
Tythegston
Merthyr Mawr
Treoes
Corntown
Llangan
Llansannor
Vale
Ystradowen
Ely (Elai)
St Brides super Ely
Peterston super-Ely
St George's
Llandaff
Canton
Cathays
St Fagans
Hutchwns
Clevis
Porthcawl
Ogmore
Ewenny
Maendy
Penllyn
Aberthin
Welsh St Donats
Pendoylan
Michaelston-super-Ely
Ely
Caerau
Butetown
Grangetown
Ogmore-by-Sea
St Brides Major
Colwinston
Pentre Meyrick
Cowbridge (Y Bont-Faen)
of
St Nicholas
Leckwith
Michaelston-le-Pit
Wenvoe
Southerndown
Penuchadre
Llysworney
Llandow
Llanblethian
Llandough
St Hilary
Llantrithyd
Bonvilston
Wallston
St Lythans
Llandough
Cogan
Wick
Glamorgan
Llanmihangel
St Mary Church
Broughton
Sigingstone
Walterston
St Andrew's Major
Dinas Powys
(Bro Morgannwg)
Flemingston
Moulton
Monknash
Llanmaes
Eglwys-Brewis
Llanbethery
Llancarfan
Colcot
Cadoxton
Marcross
Penmark
Merthyr Dyfan
St Donat's
Llantwit Major (Llanilltud Fawr)
Boverton
St Athan
Sully
CARDIFF INTERNATIONAL MAES AWYR CAERDYDD CYMRU
BARRY (Y BARRI)
Barry Island
Gileston
East Aberthaw
Rhoose (Y Rhws)
Porthkerry
A40
A470
A4215
A4067
A465
A4059
A4060
A4109
A4061
A4233
A4058
A4054
A4107
A4063
A4064
A4093
A4119
A473
A4222
A48
A4232
A4226
A4050
A4231
A4055
B4282
B4281
B4283
B4280
B4270
B4265
B4524
B4595
B4278
B4275
B4256
B4257
B4255
B4254
B4560
B4558
M4
Aber
Sirhowy
Neath river
Afon Twrch

X
Monmouthshire
(Sir Fynwy)
Torfaen
(Tor-faen)
Caerphilly
(Caerffili)
Newport
(Casnewydd)
Cardiff
(Caerdydd)
North
Somerset
ABER HAFREN
MOUTH OF THE SEVERN
Abergavenny
(Y Fenni)
Monmouth
(Trefynwy)
Cwmbran
(Cwmbrân)
Newport
(Casnewydd)
CARDIFF
(CAERDYDD)
Weston-super-Mare
Weston Bay
PONTYPOOL
(PONT-Y-PWL)
Griffithstown
EBBW VALE
(GLYN EBWY)
Tredegar
Rhymney
(Rhymni)
New Tredegar
(Tredegar Newydd)
Brynmawr
Nantyglo
Blaina
Blaenavon
Abertillery
(Abertyleri)
Abersychan
Llanhilleth
(Llanhiledd)
Crumlin
(Crymlyn)
Blackwood
(Coed Duon)
Oakdale
Bargoed
(Bargod)
Gelligaer
Hengoed
Abercarn
Crosskeys
Risca
(Rhisga)
Pontnewydd
Usk
(Brynbuga)
Caerleon
(Caerllion)
CAERPHILLY
(CAERFFILI)
Machen
Bedwas
Whitchurch
Rumney
PENARTH
BARRY
(Y BARRI)
Barry Island
Portishead
Redcliff Bay
Clevedon
Nailsea
Yatton
Wrington
Avonmouth
Caldicot
Crickhowell
Raglan
SECOND SEVERN CROSSING
Severn Beach
Chepstow Pk. Wood
M4
M48
A40
A465
A4042
A449
TOLL
Scale
0 5 10 km
0 1 2 3 4 5 miles

221
222

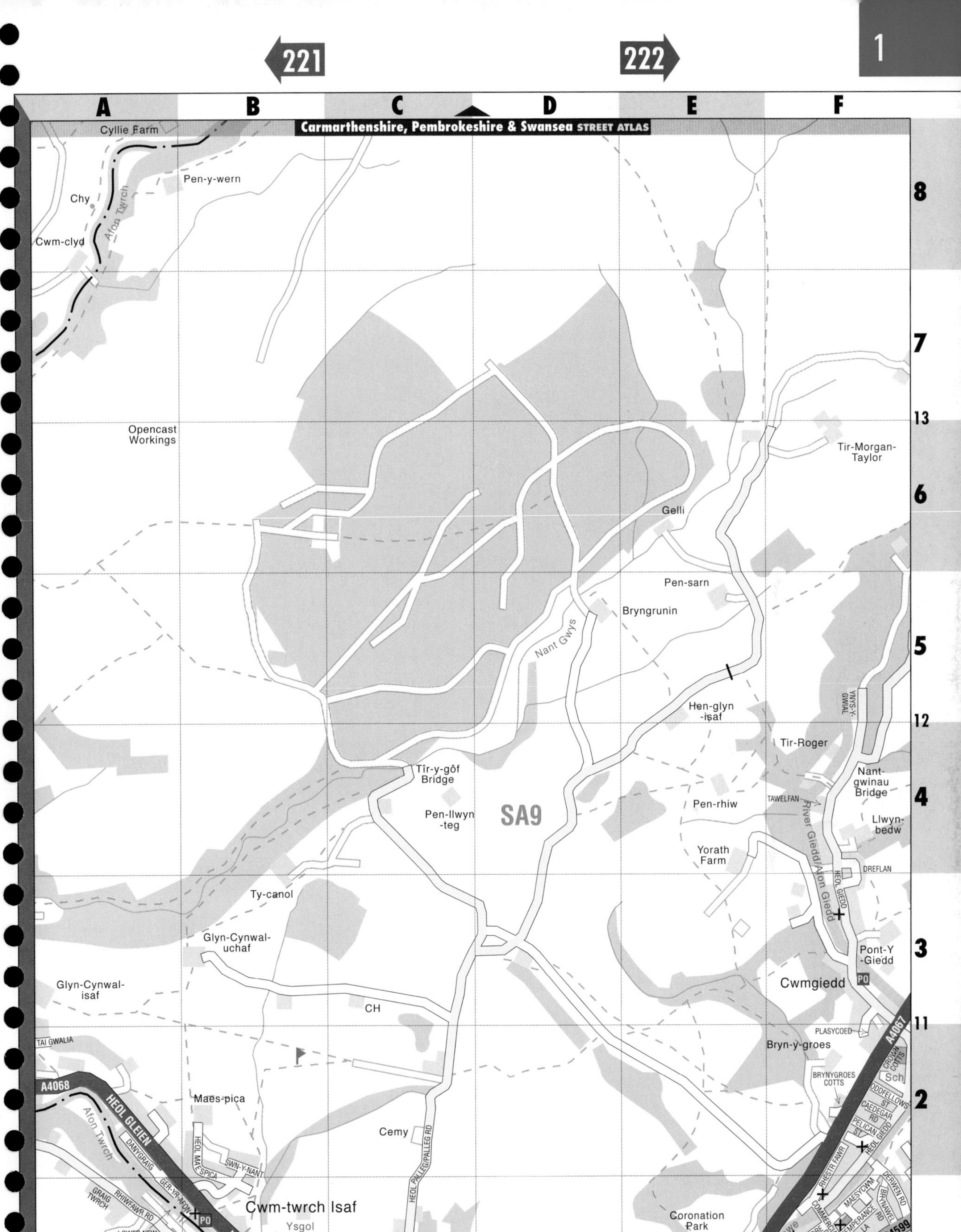

221
2
222

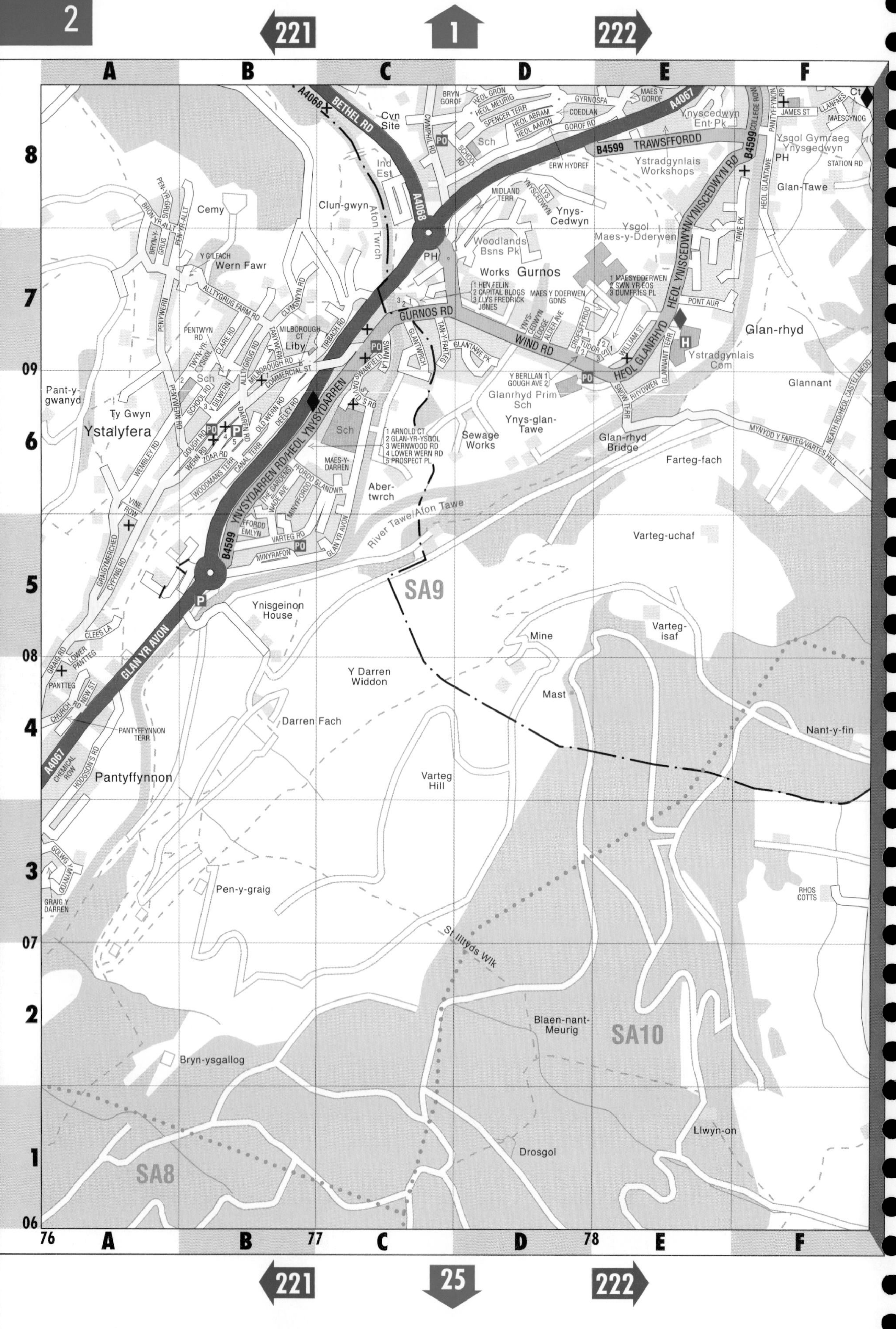
221
1
222
A
B
C
D
E
F
8
7
09
6
5
08
4
3
07
2
1
06
76
77
78
A4068
BETHEL RD
Cvn Site
Ind Est
Clun-gwyn
Afon Twrch
BRYN GOROF
HEOL GRON
HEOL MEURIG
SPENCER TERR
HEOL ABRAM
HEOL AARON
GYRNOSFA
COEDLAN
GOROF RD
MAES Y GOROF
A4067
Ynyscedwyn Ent Pk
B4599
TRAWSFFORDD
Ystradgynlais Workshops
ERW HYDREF
Sch
SCHOOL RD
CWMPHIL RD
PO
PANTYFFYNNON RD
JAMES ST
LLANFAES
Ct
MAESCYNOG
Ysgol Gymraeg Ynysgedwyn
PH
STATION RD
Glan-Tawe
COLLEGE ROW
HEOL GLANTAWE
TAWE PK
HEOL YNISCEDWYN/YNISCEDWYN RD
MIDLAND TERR
YNYSCEDWYN
LLYS
Ynys-Cedwyn
Ysgol Maes-y-Dderwen
Woodlands Bsns Pk
Works
Gurnos
1 MAESYDDERWEN
2 SWN YR EOS
3 DUMFRIES PL
1 HEN FELIN
2 CAPITAL BLDGS
3 LLYS FREDRICK JONES
MAES Y DDERWEN GDNS
PONT AUR
Glan-rhyd
GURNOS RD
WIND RD
HEOL GLANRHYD
CROESFFYRDD
TUDOR ST
WILLIAM ST
GLANNANT TERR
H
Ystradgynlais Com
Glannant
NEATH RD/HEOL CASTELL-NEDD
MYNYDD Y FARTEG/VARTEG HILL
Y BERLLAN
GOUGH AVE
Glanrhyd Prim Sch
Ynys-glan-Tawe
Sewage Works
Glan-rhyd Bridge
Farteg-fach
RHYDWEN
SNOW TERR
PEN-YR-GRUG
BRON YR ALLT
PEN-YR-ALLT
BRYN-Y-GRUG
Cemy
Y GILFACH
Wern Fawr
ALLTYGRUG FARM RD
CLYNSWYN RD
TIRBACH RD
PENYWERN
PENTWYN RD
TWYN-YR-YSGOL
CLARE RD
MILBOROUGH CT
Liby
TANYWERN LA
MILBOROUGH RD
COMMERCIAL ST
ALLTYGRUG RD
Sch
SCHOOL RD
Y GILWERN
PENYWERN RD
DARREN RD
OLD WERN RD
DEELEY RD
Pant-y-gwanyd
Ty Gwyn
Ystalyfera
WEMBLEY RD
GOUGH RD
WERN RD
ZOAR RD
CANAL TERR
WOODMANS TERR
P
YNYSYDARREN RD/HEOL YNYSYDARREN
SWANFIELD
SWAN LA
DAVID'S RD
GLANTWRCH
TAN-Y-FARTEG
GLANTAWE PK
Sch
1 ARNOLD CT
2 GLAN-YR-YSGOL
3 WERNWOOD RD
4 LOWER WERN RD
5 PROSPECT PL
MAES-Y-DARREN
Aber-twrch
FFORDD GLANDWR
THE GARDENS
WADE AVE
MINYFFORDD
FFORDD EMLYN
VARTEG RD
GLAN YR AVON
MINYRAFON
VINE ROW
River Tawe/Afon Tawe
Varteg-uchaf
GRAIGYMERCHED
CYFYNG RD
SA9
Ynisgeinon House
Mine
Varteg-isaf
CLEES LA
GRAIG RD
LOWER PANTTEG
PANTTEG
CHURCH ST
NEW ST
GLAN YR AVON
Y Darren Widdon
Mast
Darren Fach
PANTYFFYNNON TERR
Nant-y-fin
A4067
CHEMICAL ROW
HODGSON'S RD
Pantyffynnon
Varteg Hill
GOLWG Y MYNYDD
GRAIG Y DARREN
Pen-y-graig
RHOS COTTS
St Illtyds Wlk
Blaen-nant-Meurig
SA10
Bryn-ysgallog
Llwyn-on
Drosgol
SA8
221
25
222

225
4

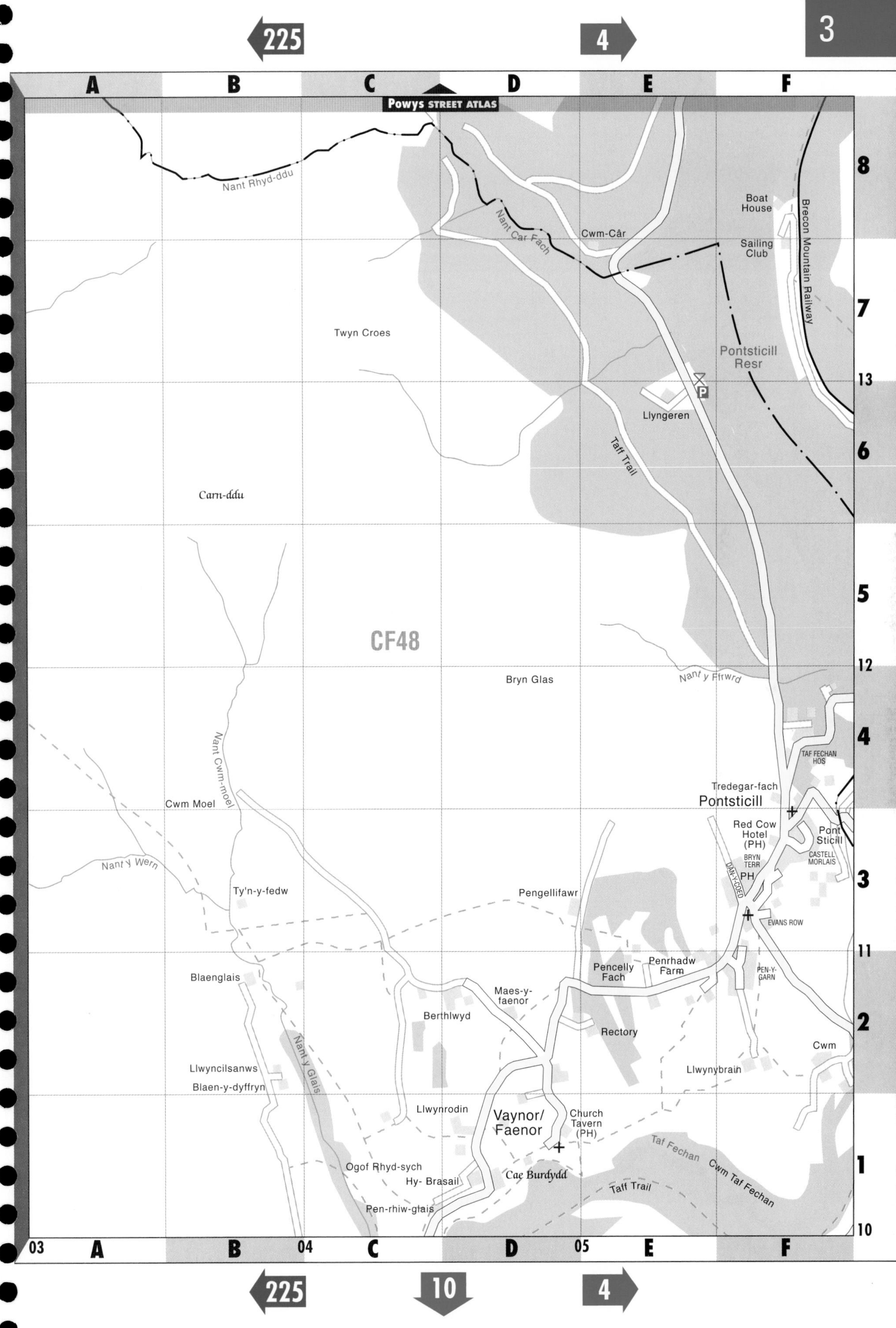
A
B
C
D
E
F
Powys STREET ATLAS
Nant Rhyd-ddu
Nant Car Fach
Cwm-Câr
Boat House
Sailing Club
Brecon Mountain Railway
Twyn Croes
Pontsticill Resr
Llyngeren
Taff Trail
Carn-ddu
CF48
Bryn Glas
Nant y Ffrwrd
TAF FECHAN HOS
Tredegar-fach
Pontsticill
Cwm Moel
Nant Cwm-moel
Red Cow Hotel (PH)
Pont Sticill
BRYN TERR
CASTELL MORLAIS
DAN-Y-COED
PH
Nant y Wern
Ty'n-y-fedw
Pengellifawr
EVANS ROW
Blaenglais
Pencelly Fach
Penrhadw Farm
PEN-Y-GARN
Maes-y-faenor
Berthlwyd
Rectory
Cwm
Nant y Glais
Llwyncilsanws
Blaen-y-dyffryn
Llwynybrain
Llwynrodin
Vaynor/ Faenor
Church Tavern (PH)
Taf Fechan
Cwm Taf Fechan
Ogof Rhyd-sych
Hy- Brasail
Cae Burdydd
Taff Trail
Pen-rhiw-glais
8
7
13
6
5
12
4
3
11
2
1
10
03
04
05

225
10
4

3

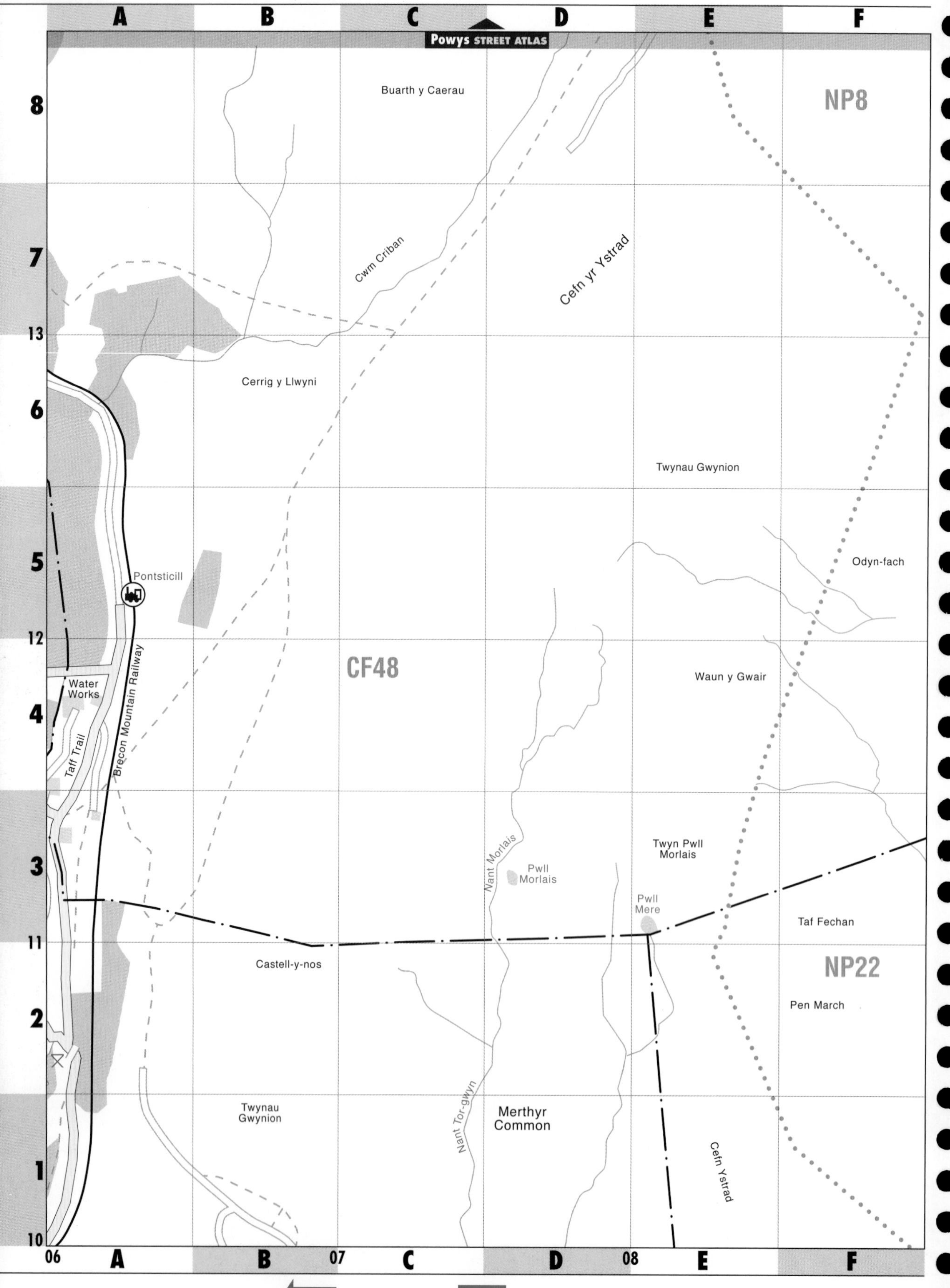
A
B
C
D
E
F
Powys STREET ATLAS
8
7
13
6
5
12
4
3
11
2
1
10
06
07
08
Buarth y Caerau
NP8
Cwm Criban
Cefn yr Ystrad
Cerrig y Llwyni
Twynau Gwynion
Odyn-fach
Pontsticill
CF48
Waun y Gwair
Water
Works
Brecon Mountain Railway
Taff Trail
Nant Morlais
Twyn Pwll
Morlais
Pwll
Morlais
Pwll
Mere
Taf Fechan
Castell-y-nos
NP22
Pen March
Twynau
Gwynion
Nant Tor-gwyn
Merthyr
Common
Cefn Ystrad

3
11

6

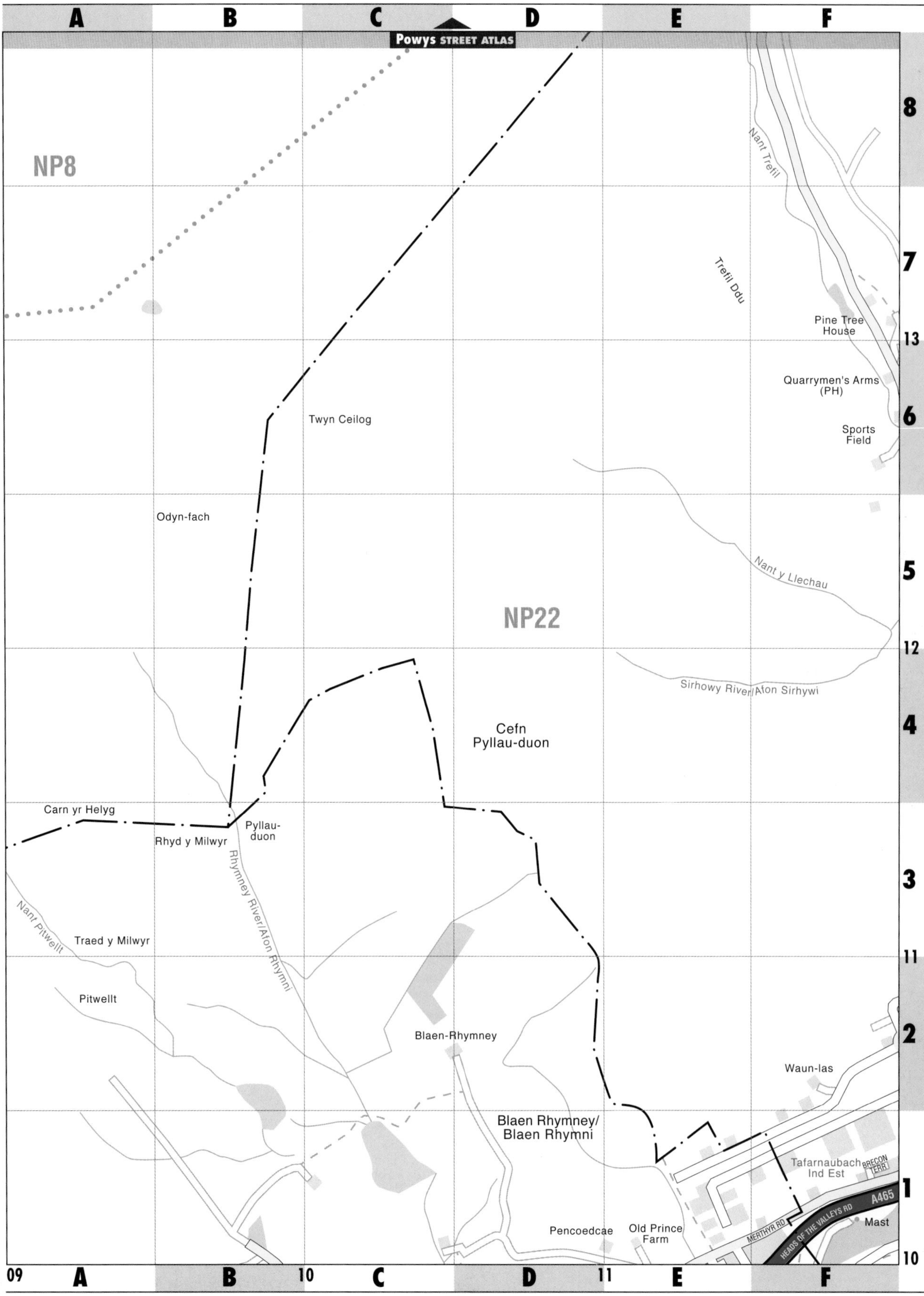

A
B
C
D
E
F
Powys STREET ATLAS
NP8
NP22
Nant Trefil
Trefil Ddu
Pine Tree House
Quarrymen's Arms (PH)
Sports Field
Twyn Ceilog
Odyn-fach
Nant y Llechau
Sirhowy River/Afon Sirhywi
Cefn Pyllau-duon
Carn yr Helyg
Rhyd y Milwyr
Pyllau-duon
Rhymney River/Afon Rhymni
Nant Pitwellt
Traed y Milwyr
Pitwellt
Blaen-Rhymney
Waun-las
Blaen Rhymney/ Blaen Rhymni
Tafarnaubach Ind Est
BRECON TERR
A465
HEADS OF THE VALLEYS RD
MERTHYR RD
Mast
Pencoedcae
Old Prince Farm
8
7
13
6
5
12
4
3
11
2
1
10
09
10
11

12
6

5

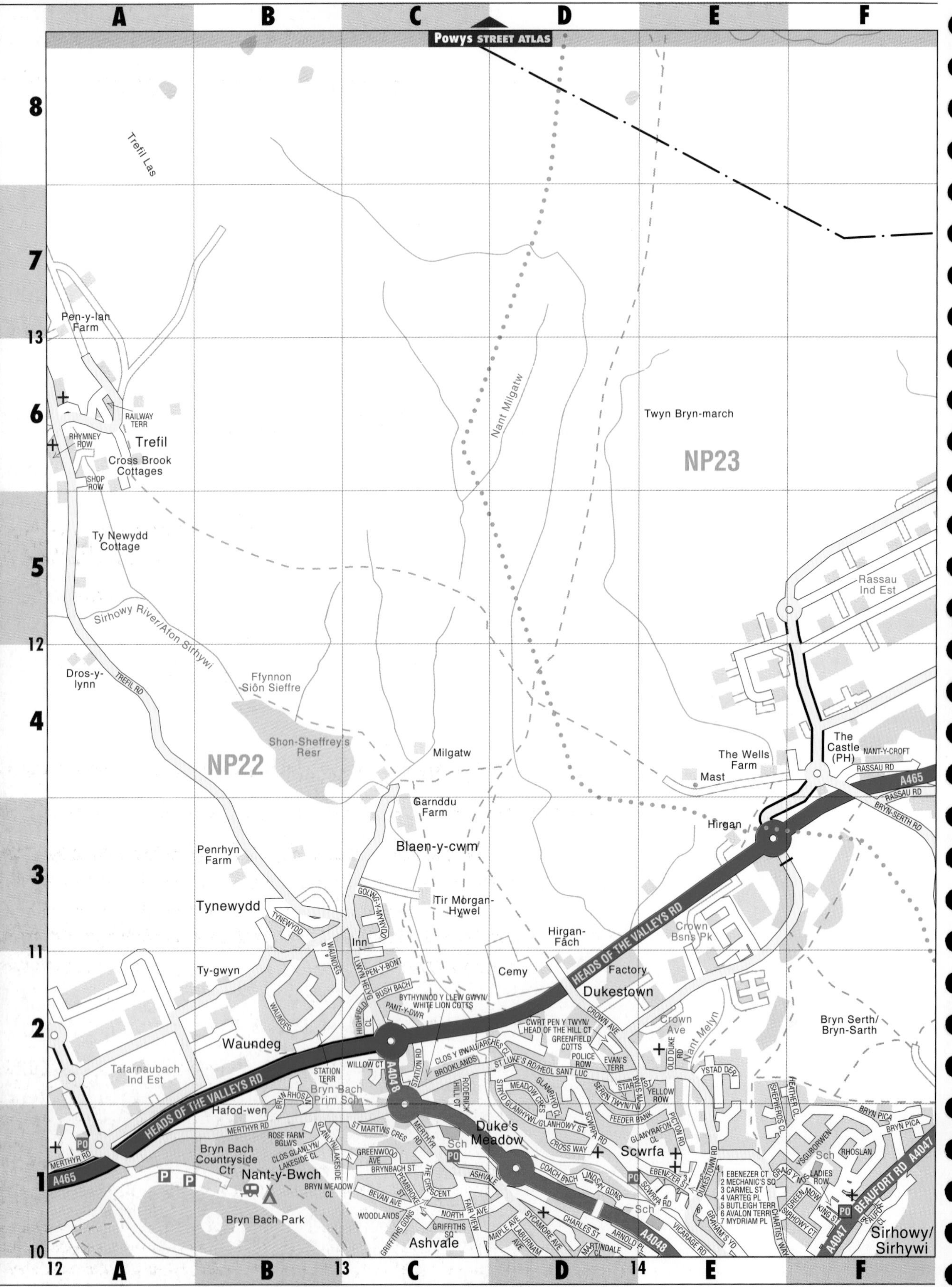
A
B
C
D
E
F
Powys STREET ATLAS
8
7
6
5
4
3
2
1
13
12
11
10
14
Trefil Las
Pen-y-lan Farm
RAILWAY TERR
RHYMNEY ROW
Trefil
Cross Brook Cottages
SHOP ROW
Ty Newydd Cottage
Nant Milgatw
Twyn Bryn-march
NP23
Rassau Ind Est
Sirhowy River/Afon Sirhywi
Dros-y-lynn
TREFIL RD
Ffynnon Siôn Sieffre
Shon-Sheffrey's Resr
NP22
Milgatw
Garnddu Farm
Blaen-y-cwm
Penrhyn Farm
The Wells Farm
Mast
The Castle (PH)
NANT-Y-CROFT
RASSAU RD
A465
BRYN-SERTH RD
Hirgan
Tir Morgan-Hywel
Tynewydd
Inn
Hirgan-Fach
Crown Bsns Pk
HEADS OF THE VALLEYS RD
Ty-gwyn
Cemy
Factory
Dukestown
Waundeg
Tafarnaubach Ind Est
Crown Ave
Nant Melyn
Bryn Serth/ Bryn-Sarth
Bryn Bach Prim Sch
Hafod-wen
Bryn Bach Countryside Ctr
Nant-y-Bwch
Duke's Meadow
Scwrfa
Bryn Bach Park
Ashvale
A4048
A4047
BEAUFORT RD
Sirhowy/ Sirhywi
1 EBENEZER CT
2 MECHANIC'S SQ
3 CARMEL ST
4 VARTEG PL
5 BUTLEIGH TERR
6 AVALON TERR
7 MYDRIAM PL
12
A
B
13
C
D
14
E
F

5
13

8

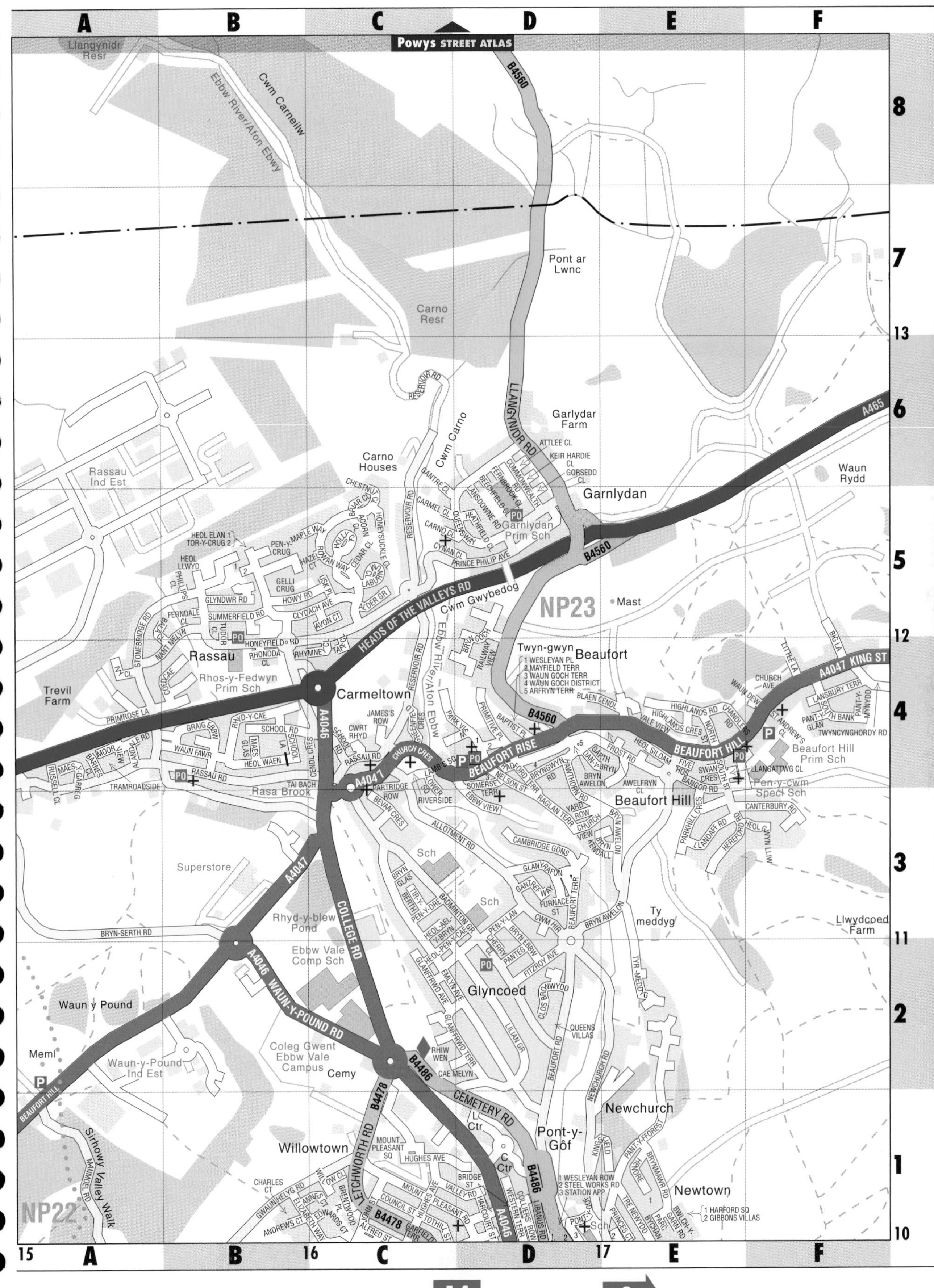

A
B
C
D
E
F
Powys STREET ATLAS
Llangynidr Resr
Ebbw River/Afon Ebwy
Cwm Carneilw
B4560
8
7
Pont ar Lwnc
Carno Resr
13
RESERVOIR RD
LLANGYNIDR RD
Garlydar Farm
6
A465
Cwm Carno
Carno Houses
ATTLEE CL
KEIR HARDIE CL
GORSEDD CL
Waun Rydd
Rassau Ind Est
Garnlydan
Garnlydan Prim Sch
B4560
HEOL ELAN 1
TOR-Y-CRUG 2
PEN-Y-CRUG
MAPLE WAY
HEOL LLWYD
GELLI CRUG
PRINCE PHILIP AVE
5
GLYNDWR RD
HOWY RD
CLYDACH AVE
AVON CT
ALDER GR
Cwm Gwybedog
NP23
Mast
HEADS OF THE VALLEYS RD
FERNDALE CL
SUMMERFIELD RD
STONEBRIDGE RD
NANT MELYN
TUDOR CT
HONEYFIELD RD
RHONDDA CL
RHYMNEY
12
Rassau
Rhos-y-Fedwyn Prim Sch
Twyn-gwyn
Beaufort
1 WESLEYAN PL
2 MAYFIELD TERR
3 WAUN GOCH TERR
4 WAUN GOCH DISTRICT
5 ARFRYN TERR
Trevil Farm
Carmeltown
JAMES'S ROW
BLAEN CENDL
CHURCH AVE
A4047 KING ST
PRIMROSE LA
RHYD-Y-CAE
SCHOOL RD
CWRT RHYD
B4560
HIGHLANDS RD
4
GRAIG EBBW
A4046
BAPTIST PL
VALE VIEW
LANSBURY TERR
PANT-Y-GLAN
TWYNCYNGHORDY RD
WAUN FAWR
HEOL WAEN
RASSAU RD
CHURCH CRES
BEAUFORT RISE
FROST RD
HEOL SILOAM
BEAUFORT HILL
Beaufort Hill Prim Sch
LLANGATTWG CL
MAES-Y-GARREG
RUSSELL CL
TRAMROADSIDE
TAI BACH
Rasa Brook
A4047
PARTRIDGE ROW
BEVAN CRES
LOWER RIVERSIDE
SOMERSET TERR
NELSON ST
RAGLAN TERR
EBBW VIEW
BRYN AWELON
Beaufort Hill
AWELFRYN CL
FIVE HOS
SWAN CRES
BANGOR RD
Pen-y-cwm Specl Sch
CANTERBURY RD
ALLOTMENT RD
CAMBRIDGE GDNS
PARKHILL CRES
LLANDAFF RD
HEREFORD RD
HEOL GWYN LLIW
Superstore
Sch
3
A4047
COLLEGE RD
Rhyd-y-blew Pond
Sch
BADMINTON GR
FURNACE ST
BEAUFORT TERR
BRYN AWELON
Ty meddyg
Llwydcoed Farm
BRYN-SERTH RD
11
A4046
Ebbw Vale Comp Sch
FITZROY AVE
TYR-MEDDYG
Waun y Pound
WAUN-Y-POUND RD
Glyncoed
NWYDD
2
Meml
LILIAN GR
QUEENS VILLAS
Coleg Gwent Ebbw Vale Campus
RHIW WEN
Waun-y-Pound Ind Est
Cemy
B4486
CAE MELYN
BEAUFORT RD
NEWCHURCH RD
P
BEAUFORT HILL
CEMETERY RD
Newchurch
Ctr
Sirhowy Valley Walk
LETCHWORTH RD
B4478
Pont-y-Gôf
MOUNT PLEASANT SQ
Willowtown
HUGHES AVE
C Ctr
B4486
PANT-Y-FFOREST
1
CHARLES CT
BRIDGE ST
1 WESLEYAN ROW
2 STEEL WORKS RD
3 STATION APP
Newtown
1 HARFORD SQ
2 GIBBONS VILLAS
NP22
COUNCIL ST
B4478
ALFRED ST
A4046
Sch
10
15
A
B
16
C
D
17
E
F

14

8

7

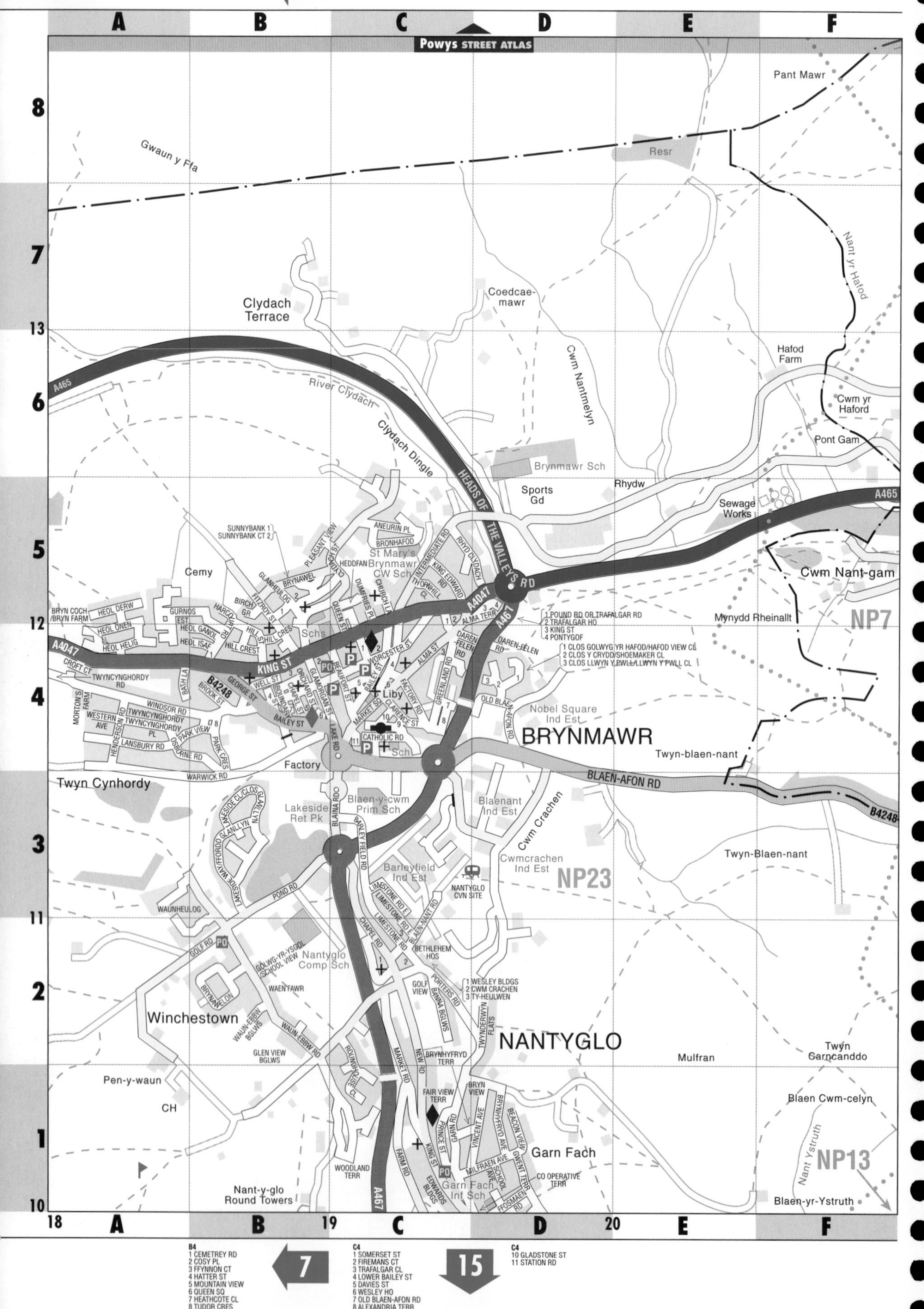

B4
1 CEMETREY RD
2 COSY PL
3 FFYNNON CT
4 HATTER ST
5 MOUNTAIN VIEW
6 QUEEN SQ
7 HEATHCOTE CL
8 TUDOR CRES

7

C4
1 SOMERSET ST
2 FIREMANS CT
3 TRAFALGAR CL
4 LOWER BAILEY ST
5 DAVIES ST
6 WESLEY HO
7 OLD BLAEN-AFON RD
8 ALEXANDRIA TERR
9 CURZON ST

15

C4
10 GLADSTONE ST
11 STATION RD

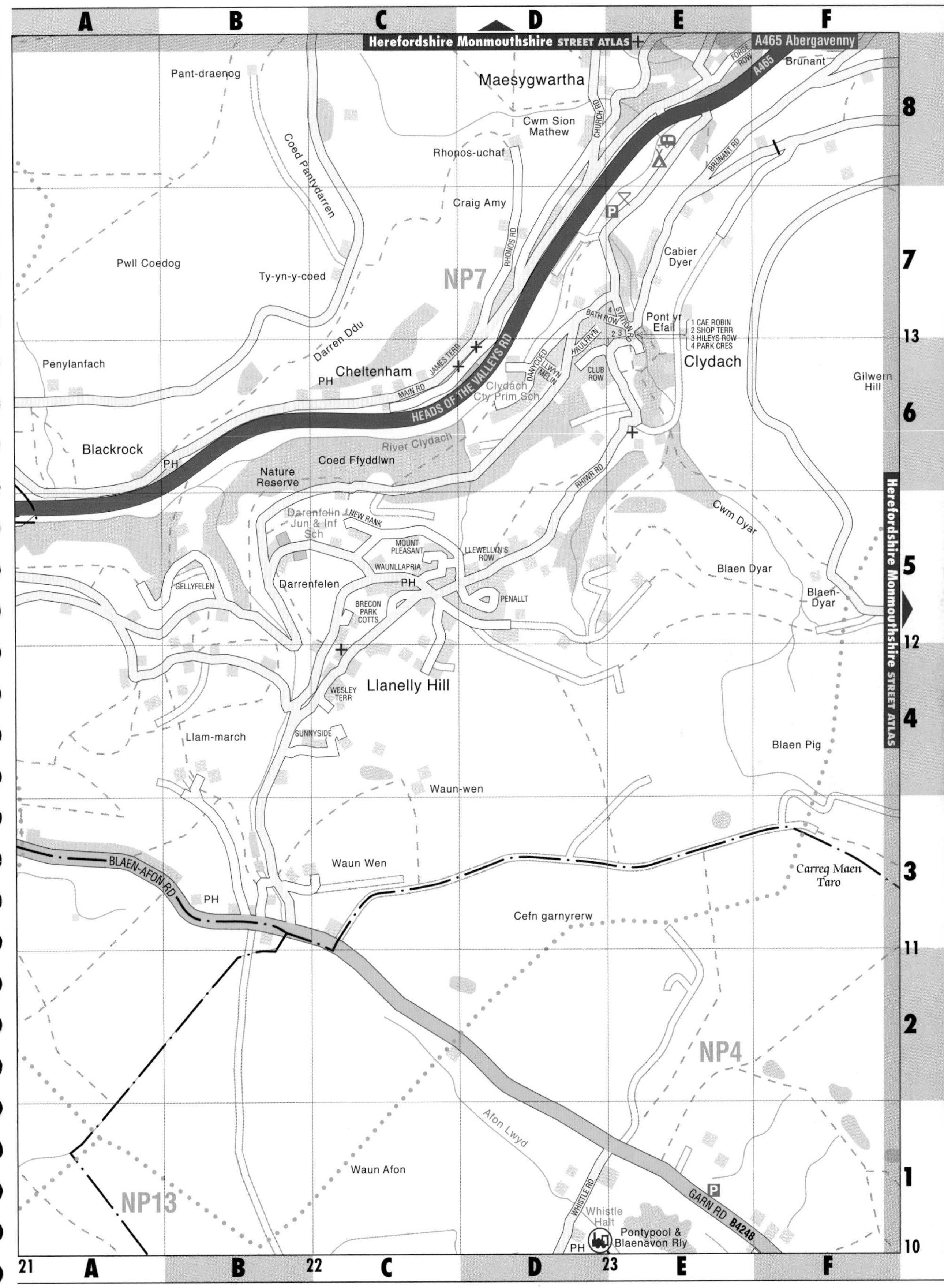

Herefordshire Monmouthshire STREET ATLAS
A465 Abergavenny
Pant-draenog
Maesygwartha
Brunant
FORGE ROW
A465
Cwm Sion Mathew
CHURCH RD
Coed Pantydarren
Rhonos-uchaf
BRUNANT RD
Craig Amy
RHONOS RD
Pwll Coedog
Ty-yn-y-coed
NP7
Cabier Dyer
BATH ROW
STATION RD
Pont yr Efail
1 CAE ROBIN
2 SHOP TERR
3 HILEYS ROW
4 PARK CRES
Darren Ddu
Penylanfach
Cheltenham
JAMES TERR
HAULFRYN
DANYCOED
LLWYN MELIN
Clydach
CLUB ROW
PH
MAIN RD
HEADS OF THE VALLEYS RD
Clydach Cty Prim Sch
Gilwern Hill
Blackrock
River Clydach
Coed Ffyddlwn
Nature Reserve
RHIWR RD
Cwm Dyar
Darenfelin Jun & Inf Sch
NEW RANK
MOUNT PLEASANT
LLEWELLYN'S ROW
WAUNLLAPRIA
Blaen Dyar
GELLYFELEN
Darrenfelen
PENALLT
Blaen-Dyar
BRECON PARK COTTS
Llanelly Hill
WESLEY TERR
Blaen Pig
SUNNYSIDE
Llam-march
Waun-wen
BLAEN-AFON-RD
Waun Wen
Carreg Maen Taro
Cefn garnyrerw
NP4
Afon Lwyd
Waun Afon
NP13
WHISTLE RD
GARN RD
B4248
Whistle Halt
Pontypool & Blaenavon Rly
A
B
C
D
E
F
8
7
13
6
5
12
4
3
11
2
1
10
21
22
23

225 3

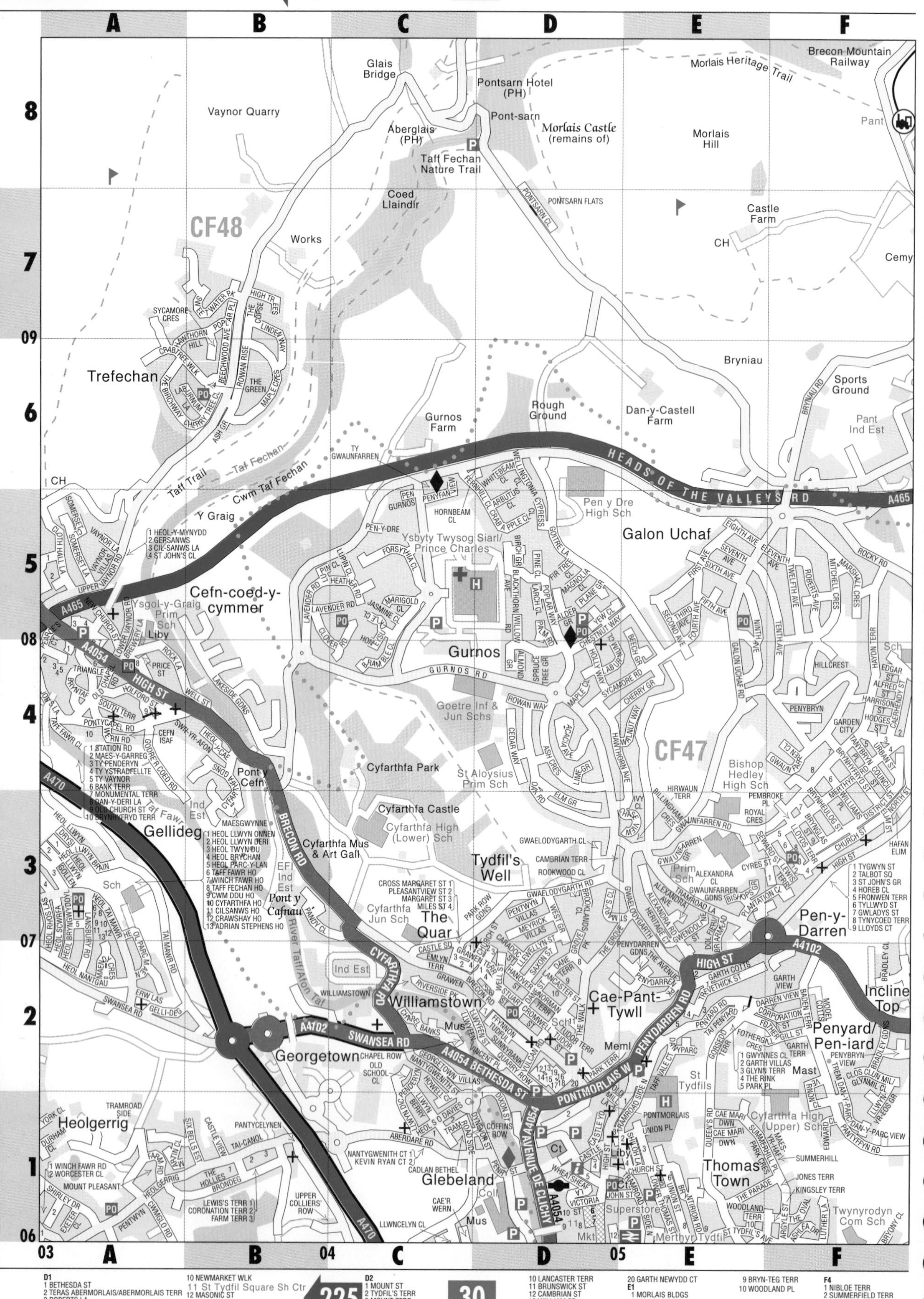

D1
1 BETHESDA ST
2 TERAS ABERMORLAIS/ABERMORLAIS TERR
3 ROBERTS LA
4 POST OFFICE LA
5 GLEBELAND ST
6 MARKET SQ
7 GRAHAM ST
8 GRAHAM WAY
9 RIVER WLK
10 NEWMARKET WLK
11 St Tydfil Square Sh Ctr
12 MASONIC ST

225

D2
1 MOUNT ST
2 TYDFIL'S TERR
3 MOUNT TERR
4 MORGAN ST
5 CROSS MORGAN ST
6 TAIR GRAWEN
7 BRYCHAN PL
8 KING EDWARD VILLAS
9 LANCASTER VILLAS

30

10 LANCASTER TERR
11 BRUNSWICK ST
12 CAMBRIAN ST
13 WILLIAM ST
14 SAND ST
15 LOWER EDWARD ST
16 DAVID ST
17 MORIAH ST
18 GARTH ST
19 UPPER EDWARD ST
20 GARTH NEWYDD CT

E1
1 MORLAIS BLDGS
2 NEW CASTLE ST
3 UPPER THOMAS ST
4 TRAMROAD TERR
5 LIBRARY LA
6 UNION TERR
7 SOMERSET PL
8 TERAS TIR Y LLYS/COURTLAND TERR
9 BRYN-TEG TERR
10 WOODLAND PL

F4
1 NIBLOE TERR
2 SUMMERFIELD TERR
3 AMBERTON PL
4 BRYNMAIR TERR
5 BRYN-ONEN TERR
6 BRYNMORLAIS ST
7 AWELFRYN TERR
8 PENYBRYN VILLAS

4
12

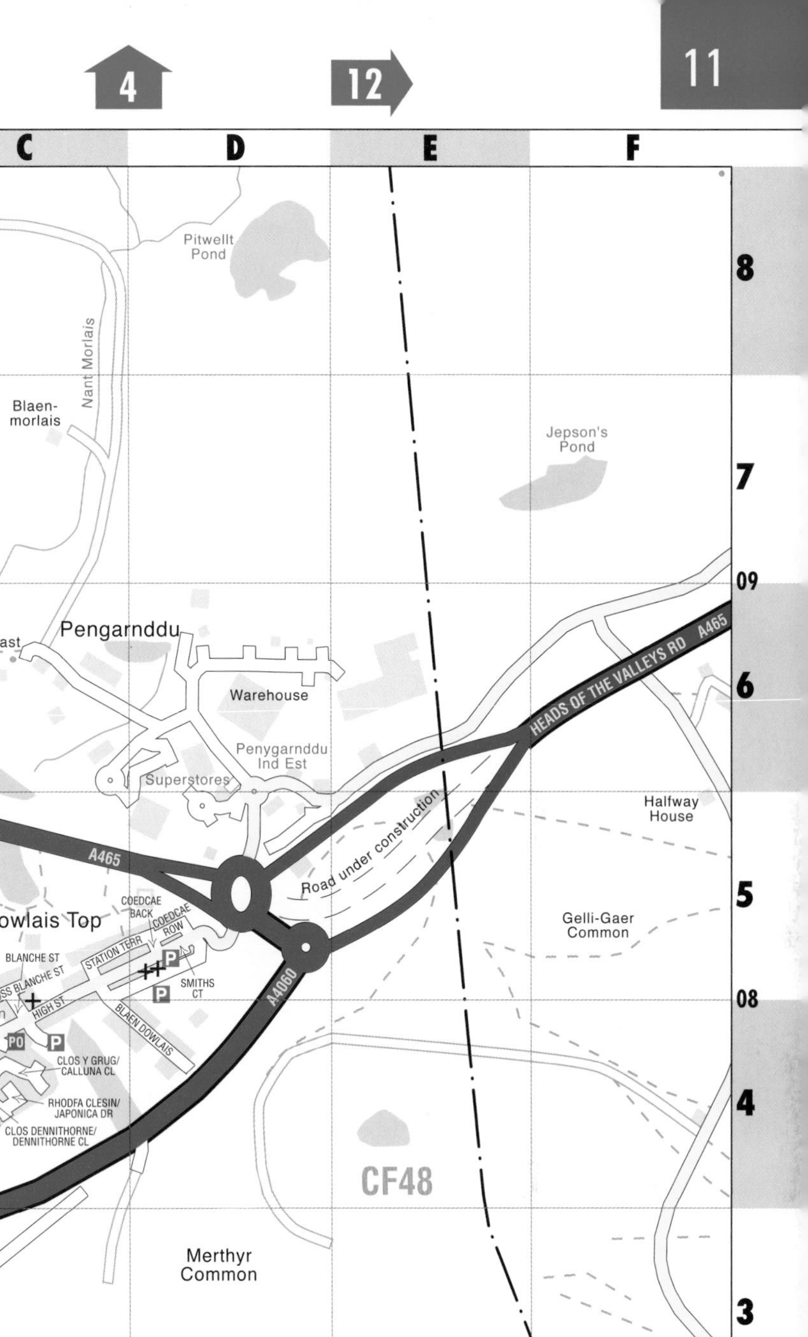
A
B
C
D
E
F
8
7
09
6
5
08
4
3
07
2
1
06
Blaen-y-garth
Garth
Pantcerddinen
Pantcadifor
Caeracca
Pitwellt Pond
Nant Morlais
Blaen-morlais
Jepson's Pond
Mast
Pengarnddu
Pantysgallog Prim Sch
Rhyd-y-Bedd
Pant
Ind Est
Warehouse
Penygarnddu Ind Est
Superstores
HEADS OF THE VALLEYS RD
A465
Halfway House
Road under construction
Dowlais Top
Gelli-Gaer Common
Pen-y-wern
Gwernllwyn Jun Sch
Dowlais Inf Sch
A4060
St Illtyd's Prim Sch
Liby
Factories
Dowlais
CF48
Merthyr Common
Phoenix Ind Est
MERTHYR TYDFIL/
MERTHYR TUDFUL
Tair Carreg
CF47
GOAT MILL RD A4102
Mountain Hare
Isaac Morgan Cottages
LC
A4060
1 ALPHONSO ST
2 CROSS HOULSON ST
3 HOULSON ST
4 DAVIES ST
5 GUEST COTTS
6 WERN ST
7 CROSS ST
1 GLENDOWER ST
2 CROSS FRANCIS ST
3 LIBANUS ST
4 ALMA TERR
5 WIMBORNE ST
6 BRYNTIRION ST
7 MORLAIS ST
8 OVERTON ST
9 WALTER ST
10 CROSS MORLAIS ST
1 BODALAW
2 STABLES CT
3 DOWLAIS STABLES
4 CHURCH ST
5 COMMERICAL ST
6 MAES-Y-FFYNNON
7 CHARLOTTE ST
8 MENELAUS SQ
9 LOWER UNION ST
1 WYNDHAM ST
2 MARY ST
3 MORGAN ST
4 GWERNLLWYN CL
5 Y GANOLFAN
1 PRIMROSE CL
2 HEDDWCH CL
HAFOD COTTS
BEACONS VIEW
CROSS IVOR TERR
PANT TERR
CWM GRAIG BGLWS
THOMAS TERR
ROCKY RD
BARRACKS ROW
UPPER ROW
LOWER ROW
WERN ISAF
MURIEL TERR
BLANCHE ST
CROSS BLANCHE ST
STATION TERR
COEDCAE BACK
COEDCAE ROW
SMITHS CT
BLAEN DOWLAIS
HIGH ST
STATION RD
CHARLOTTE GDNS
GWERNLLWYN UCHAF
CLOS Y GRUG/ CALLUNA CL
RHODFA CLESIN/ JAPONICA DR
CLOS DENNITHORNE/ DENNITHORNE CL
PARC ASALEAS/ AZALEA PK
NEW RD
GOAT MILL RD
MANSFIELD TERR
MARDY ST
BRYN TERR
CROSS MARDY ST
PENHEOL FERTHYR
BOGEY RD
MOUNT VIEW
PANTYSGALLOG TERR
KING ST
QUEEN ST
HEOL BONYMAEN
HEOL RHYD-Y-BEDD
TAI-YR-EFAIL
THE HAWTHORNS
AMELIA CL
TAI'R TWYNAU
RHIW ABERHONDDU
EDWARD ST
GLANMORLAIS
TYDFIL VILLAS
WINDSOR PL
NEW HOS
THE HAFOD
PANT RD
CAERACCA VILLAS
NANT MORLAIS
REES ST
JONES ST
BRYNWERN ST
WINIFRED ST
FRANCIS ST
WHITE ST
SPRING ST
ODESSA ST
MOUNT PLEASANT ST
REGENT ST
VAUGHAN ST
BALACLAVA RD
RUSSELL ST
UPPER ELIZABETH ST
HERMON CL
VICTORIA ST
NORTH ST
IVOR ST
CHURCH ROW
UPPER UNION ST
EAST ST
MARKET ST
BRYN MAWR
BRYN-CARNW
GARDEN ST
RECTORY
GWERNLLWYN RD
GREENFIELD TERR
GELLIFAELOG TERR
GELLIFAELOG OLD RD
HIGH ST

31
12

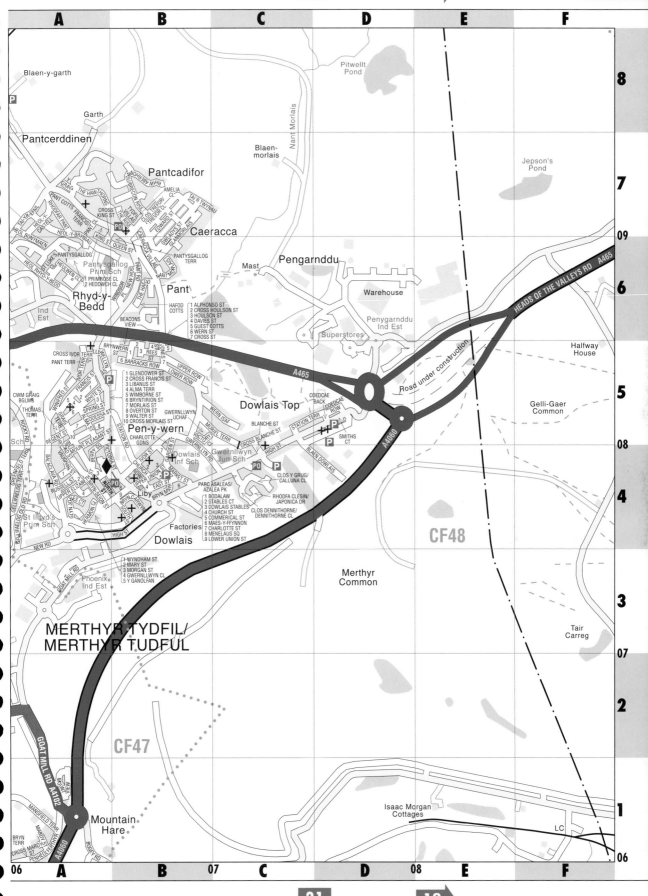

11
5

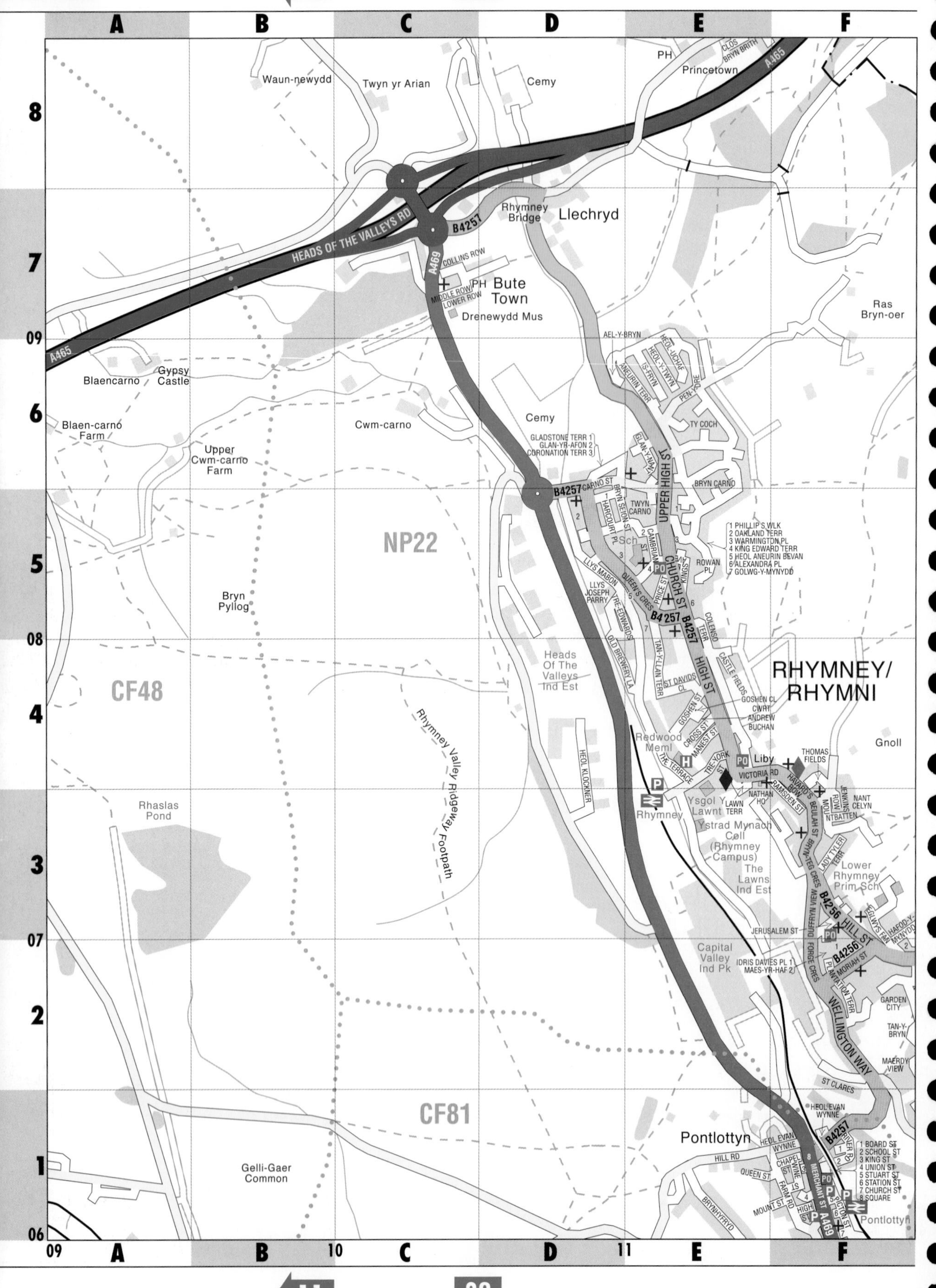
Waun-newydd
Twyn yr Arian
Cemy
Princetown
A465
HEADS OF THE VALLEYS RD
Rhymney Bridge
Llechryd
B4257
A469
COLLINS ROW
Bute Town
MIDDLE ROW
LOWER ROW
Drenewydd Mus
Ras Bryn-oer
Blaencarno
Gypsy Castle
Blaen-carno Farm
Cwm-carno
Cemy
Upper Cwm-carno Farm
GLADSTONE TERR 1
GLAN-YR-AFON 2
CORONATION TERR 3
UPPER HIGH ST
TY COCH
BRYN CARNO
TWYN CARNO
NP22
1 PHILLIP'S WLK
2 OAKLAND TERR
3 WARMINGTON PL
4 KING EDWARD TERR
5 HEOL ANEURIN BEVAN
6 ALEXANDRA PL
7 GOLWG-Y-MYNYDD
ROWAN PL
CHURCH ST
Bryn Pyllog
LLYS MABON
LLYS JOSEPH PARRY
QUEEN'S CRES
HIGH ST
Heads Of The Valleys Ind Est
CF48
RHYMNEY/
RHYMNI
Rhymney Valley Ridgeway Footpath
Redwood Meml
Liby
THOMAS FIELDS
Gnoll
HEOL KLOCKNER
Rhaslas Pond
Rhymney
Ysgol Y Lawnt
Ystrad Mynach Coll (Rhymney Campus)
The Lawns Ind Est
Lower Rhymney Prim Sch
JERUSALEM ST
HILL ST
B4256
Capital Valley Ind Pk
IDRIS DAVIES PL 1
MAES-YR-HAF 2
WELLINGTON WAY
GARDEN CITY
TAN-Y-BRYN
MAERDY VIEW
ST CLARES
HEOL EVAN WYNNE
CF81
Pontlottyn
HILL RD
QUEEN ST
1 BOARD ST
2 SCHOOL ST
3 KING ST
4 UNION ST
5 STUART ST
6 STATION ST
7 CHURCH ST
8 SQUARE
Gelli-Gaer Common
MOUNT ST
Pontlottyn
A B C D E F
8 7 6 5 4 3 2 1
09 08 07 06
09 10 11

11
32

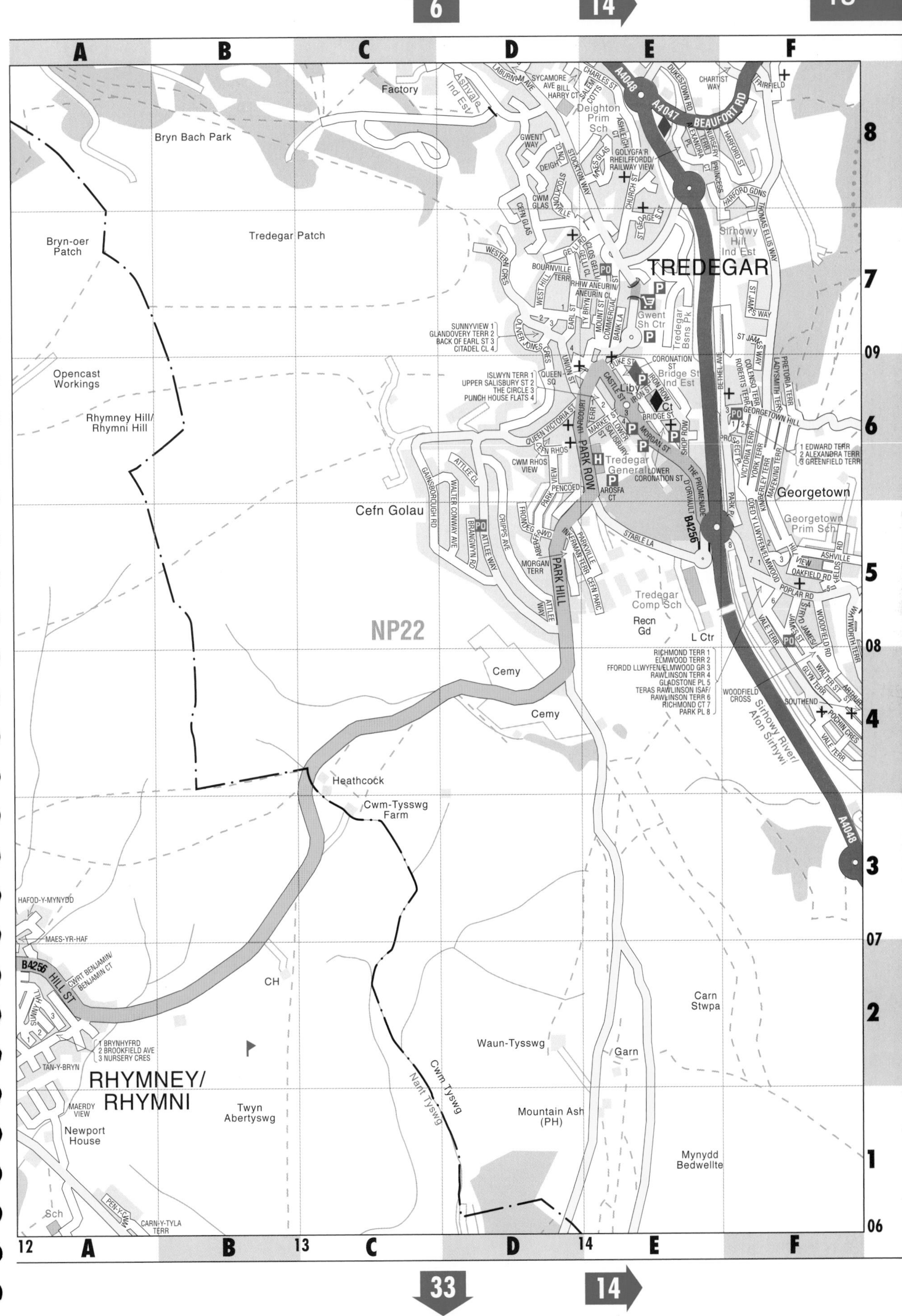
6
14
TREDEGAR
Bryn Bach Park
Tredegar Patch
Bryn-oer Patch
Opencast Workings
Rhymney Hill/ Rhymni Hill
Cefn Golau
NP22
Heathcock
Cwm-Tysswg Farm
Cemy
Georgetown
Tredegar Comp Sch
Recn Gd
L Ctr
Carn Stwpa
Waun-Tysswg
Garn
Mountain Ash (PH)
Mynydd Bedwellte
Twyn Abertyswg
RHYMNEY/ RHYMNI
Newport House
Sirhowy River/ Afon Sirhywi
Cwm Tysswg
Nant Tysswg
A4048
A4047
B4256
33
14

13
7

D6
1 WOODVILLE PL
2 RODERICK PL
3 BETHESDA PL
4 ZION PL
5 REDWOOD PL
6 SARON PL
7 BRYN EGLWYS CT
8 HEOL Y MWYN CT
9 FARM FIELDS RD
10 BRIERY CT
11 MAEN MOEL
12 DOMEN CT
13 PLAS NEWYDD
14 CWRT YR GOLLEN

D8
1 WESTERN TERR
2 BEULAH PL
3 AYNHO PL
4 COLLIERS ROW
5 LIBANUS RD
6 STATION RD
7 WILLIAM ADAMS CT
8 GEORGE PARRY CT

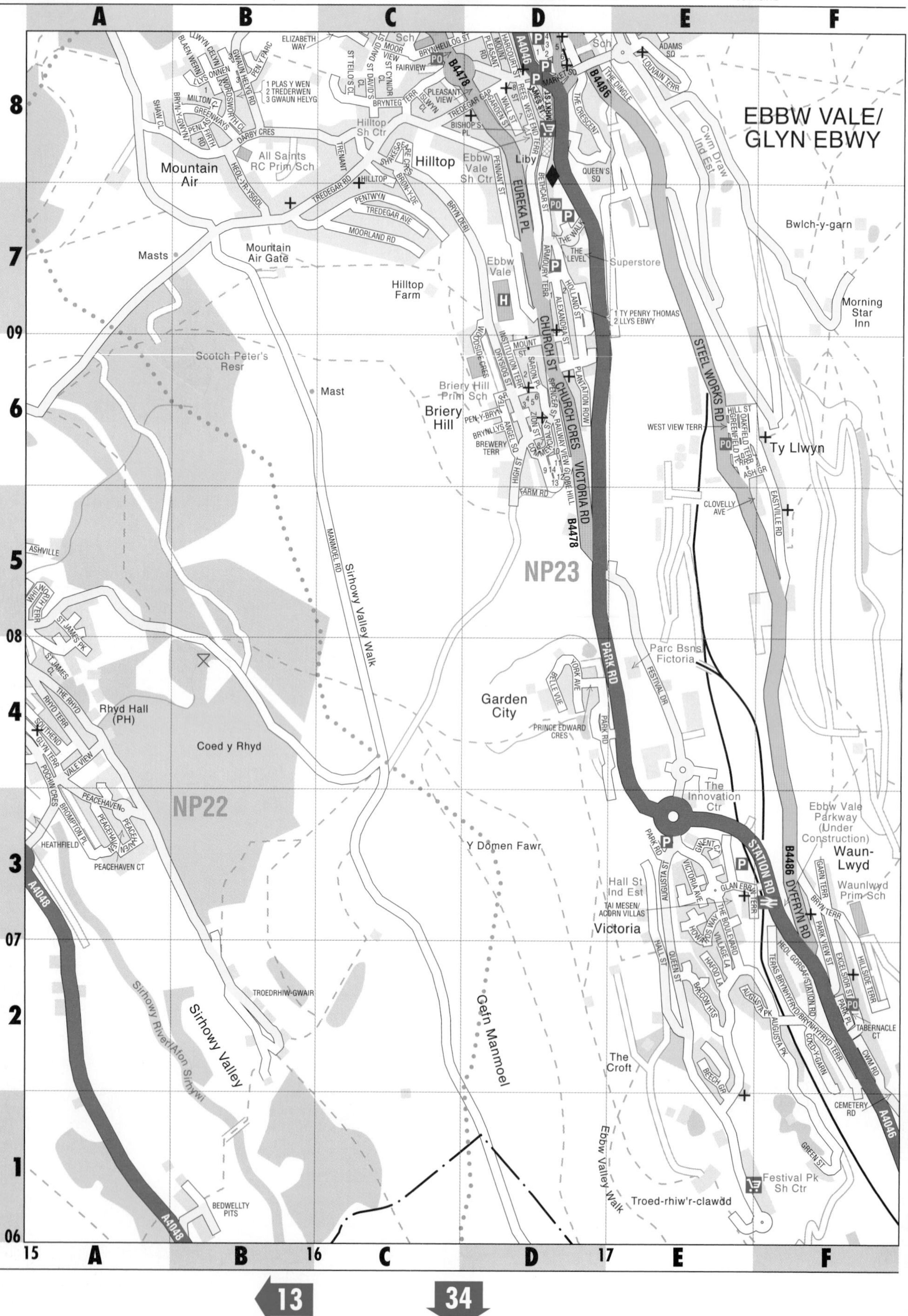

A B C D E F

8 7 6 5 4 3 2 1
09 08 07 06
15 16 17

13
34

A B C D E F

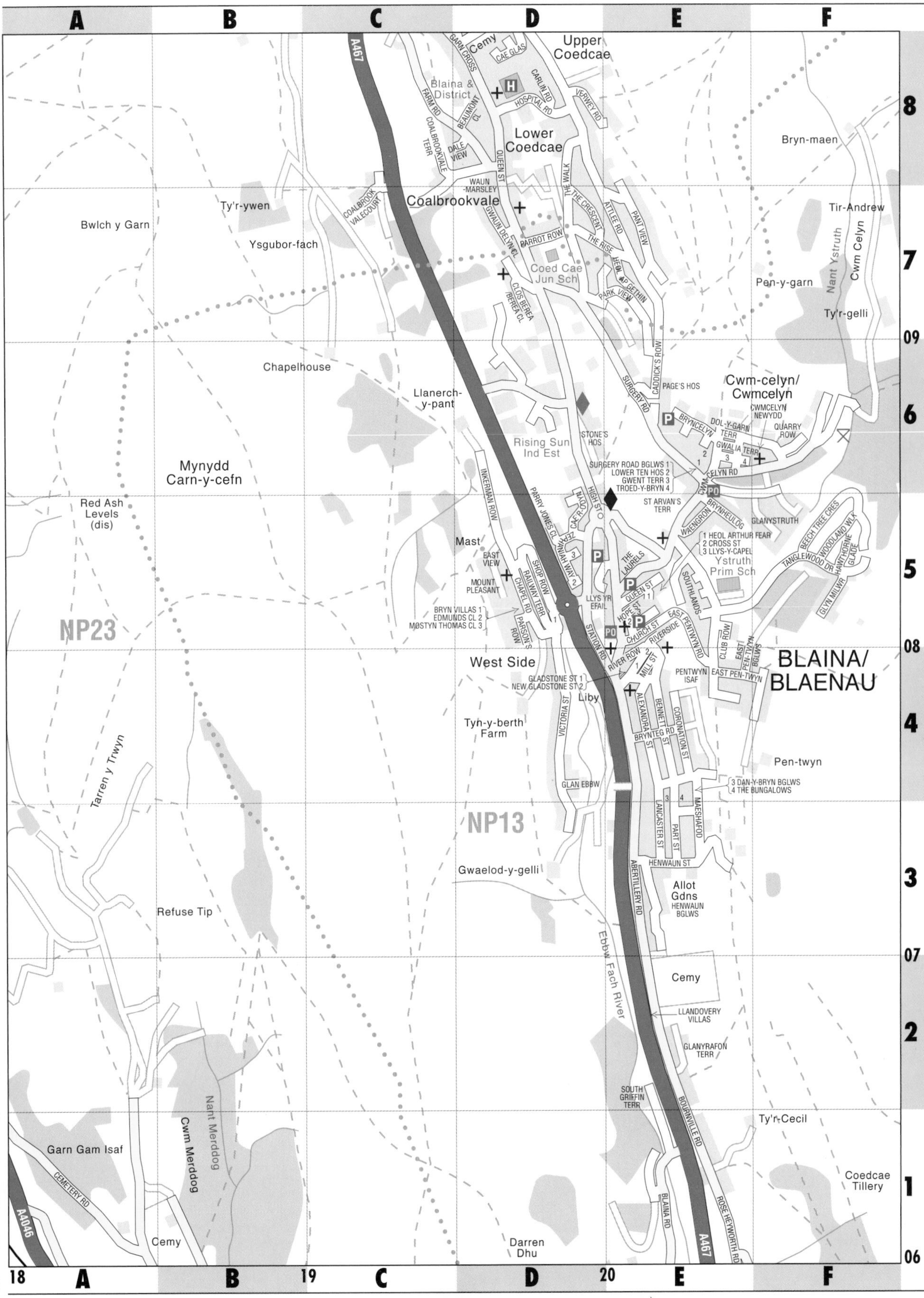

8
Cemy
Upper Coedcae
Blaina & District
H
GARN CROSS
CAE GLAS
CARLIN RD
HOSPITAL RD
VERWEY RD
FARM RD
BEAUMONT CL
COALBROOKVALE TERR
DALE VIEW
Lower Coedcae
QUEEN ST
WAUN -MARSLEY
Coalbrookvale
COALBROOK VALECOURT
A467
Ty'r-ywen
Bwlch y Garn
Ysgubor-fach
GWAUN DELYN CL
PARROT ROW
THE WALK
THE CRESCENT
ATTLEE RD
PANT VIEW
THE RISE
HEOL AP GETHIN
PARK VIEW
Coed Cae Jun Sch
CLOS BEREA /BEREA CL
Bryn-maen
Tir-Andrew
Nant Ystruth
Cwm Celyn
Pen-y-garn
Ty'r-gelli
7
09
Chapelhouse
Llanerch-y-pant
SURGERY RD
CADDICK'S ROW
PAGE'S HOS
Cwm-celyn/ Cwmcelyn
CWMCELYN NEWYDD
QUARRY ROW
P
BRYNCELYN
DOL-Y-GARN TERR
GWALIA TERR
6
Rising Sun Ind Est
STONE'S HOS
Mynydd Carn-y-cefn
SURGERY ROAD BGLWS 1
LOWER TEN HOS 2
GWENT TERR 3
TROED-Y-BRYN 4
CWM-CELYN RD
PO
Red Ash Levels (dis)
INKERMAN ROW
PARRY JONES CL
CAE-R-GOF
HIGH ST
ST ARVAN'S TERR
BRYNHEULOG
GLANYSTRUTH
WAENGRON
BEECH TREE CRES
WOODLAND WLK
HAWTHORNE GLADE
1 HEOL ARTHUR FEAR
2 CROSS ST
3 LLYS-Y-CAPEL
Mast
EAST VIEW
JEREMIAH WAY
THE LAURELS
Ystruth Prim Sch
TANGLEWOOD DR
GLYN MILWR
5
MOUNT PLEASANT
SHOP ROW
RAILWAY TERR
CHAPEL RD
SOUTHLANDS
QUEEN ST
LLYS YR EFAIL
HOPE ST
BRYN VILLAS 1
EDMUNDS CL 2
MOSTYN THOMAS CL 3
PARSON'S ROW
NP23
CHURCH ST
EAST PENTWYN RD
RIVERSIDE
CLUB ROW
EAST PEN-TWYN BGLWS
STATION RD
RIVER ROW
MILL ST
08
West Side
BLAINA/ BLAENAU
GLADSTONE ST 1
NEW GLADSTONE ST 2
PENTWYN ISAF
EAST PEN-TWYN
Liby
VICTORIA ST
ALEXANDRA ST
BENNETT ST
CORONATION ST
BRYNTEG RD
Tyn-y-berth Farm
4
Tarren y Trwyn
Pen-twyn
GLAN EBBW
3 DAN-Y-BRYN BGLWS
4 THE BUNGALOWS
MAESHAFOD
LANCASTER ST
PART ST
NP13
HENWAUN ST
Gwaelod-y-gelli
ABERTILLERY RD
3
Allot Gdns
HENWAUN BGLWS
Refuse Tip
Ebbw Fach River
07
Cemy
LLANDOVERY VILLAS
2
GLANYRAFON TERR
Nant Merddog
Cwm Merddog
SOUTH GRIFFIN TERR
BOURNVILLE RD
Ty'r-Cecil
Garn Gam Isaf
CEMETERY RD
1
Coedcae Tillery
BLAINA RD
ROSE HEYWORTH RD
A4046
Cemy
Darren Dhu
A467
06

18 A B 19 C D 20 E F

15
9

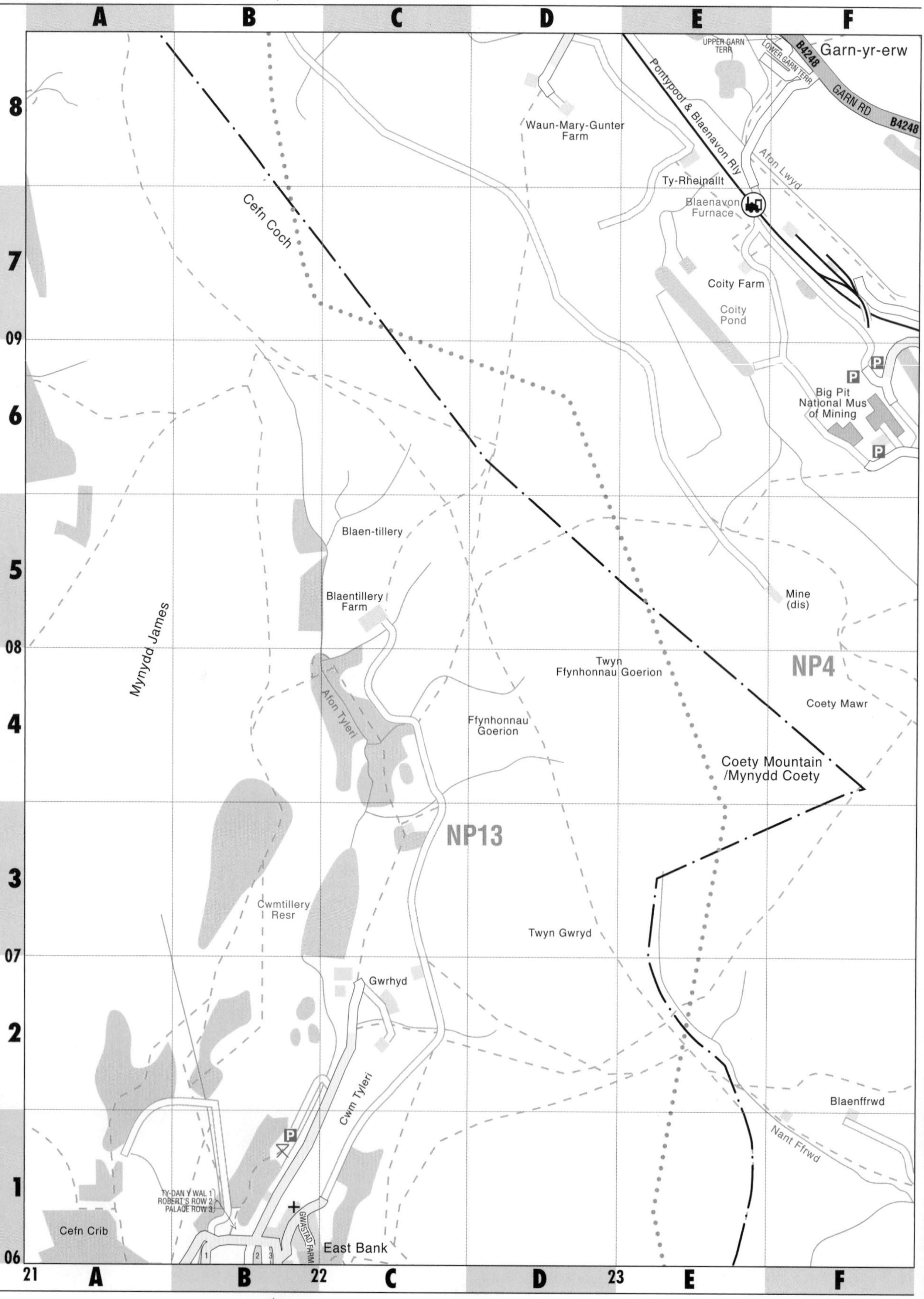

A B C D E F

8
7
09
6
5
08
4
3
07
2
1
06

Garn-yr-erw
B4248
GARN RD
B4248
UPPER GARN TERR
LOWER GARN TERR
Pontypool & Blaenavon Rly
Waun-Mary-Gunter Farm
Afon Lwyd
Ty-Rheinallt
Blaenavon Furnace
Cefn Coch
Coity Farm
Coity Pond
Big Pit National Mus of Mining
P
Blaen-tillery
Blaentillery Farm
Mine (dis)
Mynydd James
NP4
Twyn Ffynhonnau Goerion
Coety Mawr
Afon Tyleri
Ffynhonnau Goerion
Coety Mountain /Mynydd Coety
NP13
Cwmtillery Resr
Twyn Gwryd
Gwrhyd
Cwm Tyleri
Blaenffrwd
Nant Ffrwd
TY-DAN Y WAL 1
ROBERT'S ROW 2
PALACE ROW 3
GWASTAD FARM
Cefn Crib
East Bank

21 A B 22 C D 23 E F

15
36

C6
1 LION CT
2 LION ST/HEOL Y LLEW
3 NEW QUEEN ST
4 BURFORD ST/STRYD BURFORD
5 DUKE ST
6 BOOT LA
7 ANNE ST
8 GEORGE ST
9 CHURCH VIEW
10 COMMERCIAL ST
11 OLD JAMES ST
12 BAKER STREET HO
13 OLD WILLIAM ST
14 MARY ST
15 LOWER HILL ST
16 SOUTHVIEW TERR
17 NEW WILLIAM ST
18 BRIDGE ST
19 BRYNAVON

C7
1 MAXWORTHY RD
2 RIFLE GN
3 CLIFTON TERR/TERAS CLIFTON
4 ELGAM GN
5 ALMA ST
6 STACK SQ
7 VINCENT ST

D6
1 GLADSTONE TERR
2 NEW JAMES ST
3 CAPEL NEWYDD RD
4 COED TERR
5 FRANCIS MORRIS EST
6 BRIGHTS LA
7 MIDDLE COEDCAE/COEDCAE GANOL

D7
1 BLORENGE TERR
2 NEVILL TERR
3 GARN DYRUS MOUNT
4 LLANFOIST CRES
5 COURT RISE
6 MORRIS RISE
7 MORGAN RISE
8 GWAUNFELIN WLK
9 GILCHRIST WLK
10 CARADOC WLK
11 LOWER WOODLAND ST

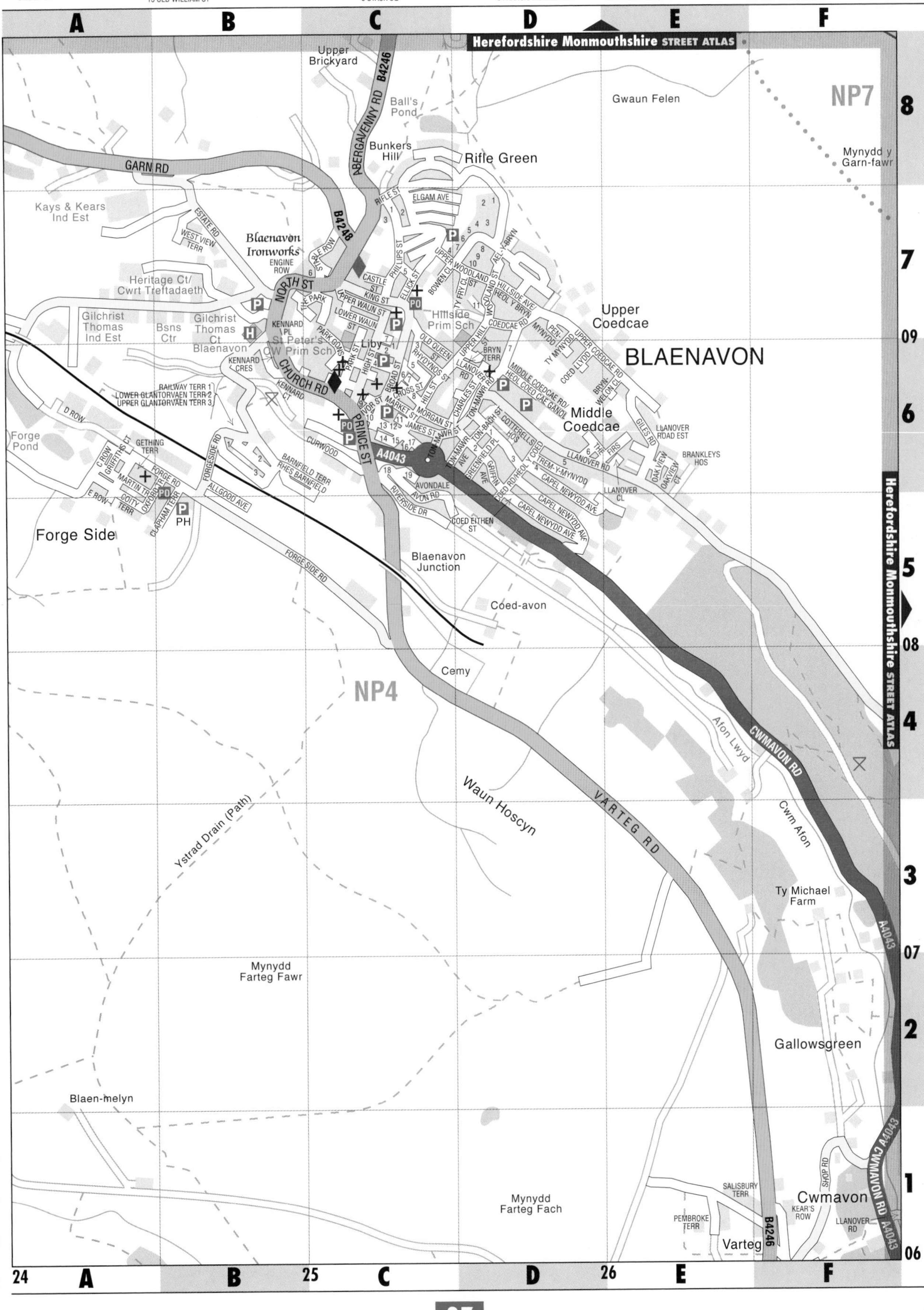

A B C D E F

Herefordshire Monmouthshire STREET ATLAS

Upper Brickyard
B4246
ABERGAVENNY RD
Ball's Pond
Gwaun Felen
NP7
8
Bunkers Hill
Rifle Green
Mynydd y Garn-fawr
GARN RD
Kays & Kears Ind Est
Blaenavon Ironworks
B4248
7
Heritage Ct/ Cwrt Treftadaeth
NORTH ST
Gilchrist Thomas Ind Est
Bsns Ctr
Gilchrist Thomas Ct Blaenavon
Hillside Prim Sch
Upper Coedcae
St Peter's CW Prim Sch
Liby
09
BLAENAVON
CHURCH RD
Middle Coedcae
6
Forge Pond
PRINCE ST
A4043
Forge Side
PH
Blaenavon Junction
5
Coed-avon
08
Cemy
NP4
4
Afon Lwyd
CWMAVON RD
Waun Hoscyn
VARTEG RD
Cwm Afon
Ystrad Drain (Path)
3
Ty Michael Farm
07
Mynydd Farteg Fawr
2
Gallowsgreen
Blaen-melyn
1
Mynydd Farteg Fach
SALISBURY TERR
PEMBROKE TERR
B4246
Cwmavon
KEAR'S ROW
LLANOVER RD
Varteg
06

24 A B 25 C D 26 E F

37

218

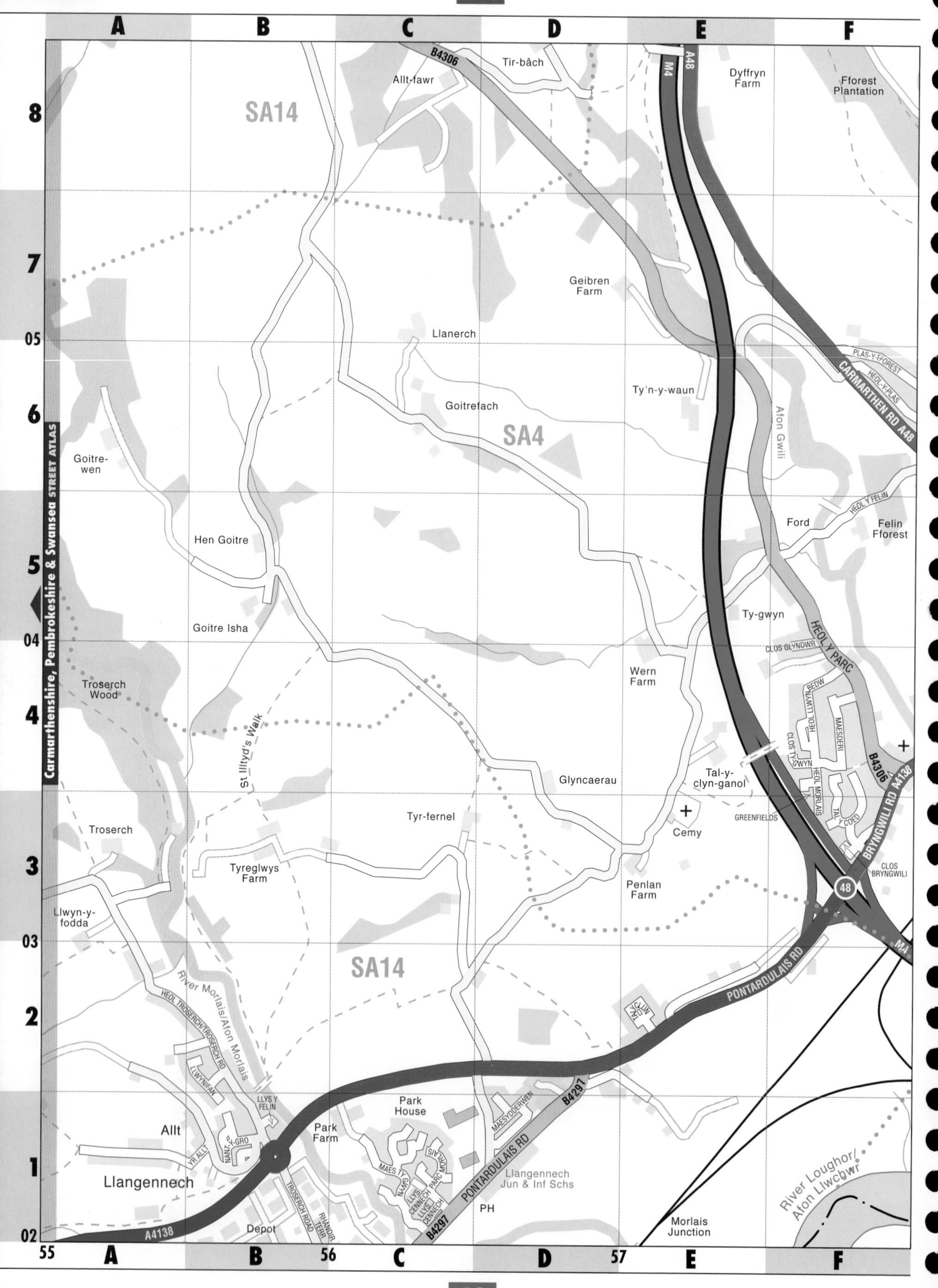

A
B
C
D
E
F
8
7
05
6
5
04
4
3
03
2
1
02
55
56
57
SA14
SA4
SA14
Carmarthenshire, Pembrokeshire & Swansea STREET ATLAS
B4306
Allt-fawr
Tir-bâch
M4
A48
Dyffryn Farm
Fforest Plantation
Geibren Farm
Llanerch
Goitrefach
Ty'n-y-waun
PLAS-Y-FFOREST
HEOL-Y-PLAS
CARMARTHEN RD A48
Afon Gwili
Goitre-wen
Hen Goitre
Ford
HEOL Y FELIN
Felin Fforest
Goitre Isha
Ty-gwyn
HEOL Y PARC
CLOS GLYNDWR
Troserch Wood
Wern Farm
HEOL LLWYN BEDW
MAESDERI
CLOS TY'S WYN
HEOL MORLAIS
B4306
A4138
St Illtyd's Walk
Glyncaerau
Tal-y-clyn-ganol
Troserch
Tyr-fernel
Cemy
GREENFIELDS
TAL Y COED
BRYNGWILI RD
CLOS BRYNGWILI
Tyreglwys Farm
Penlan Farm
48
Llwyn-y-fodda
M4
River Morlais/Afon Morlais
PONTARDULAIS RD
HEOL TROSERCH/TROSERCH RD
LLWYNIFAN
LLYS Y FELIN
Park House
MAESYDDERWEN
B4297
Allt
Park Farm
NANT-Y-GRO
YR ALLT
MAES TY GWYN
PARC MENAI
LLYS CENNECH
PONTARDULAIS RD
Llangennech Jun & Inf Schs
Llangennech
TROSERCH ROAD
RHANDIR TERR
PH
B4297
River Loughor/ Afon Llwchwr
Morlais Junction
A4138
Depot

42

A B C D E F

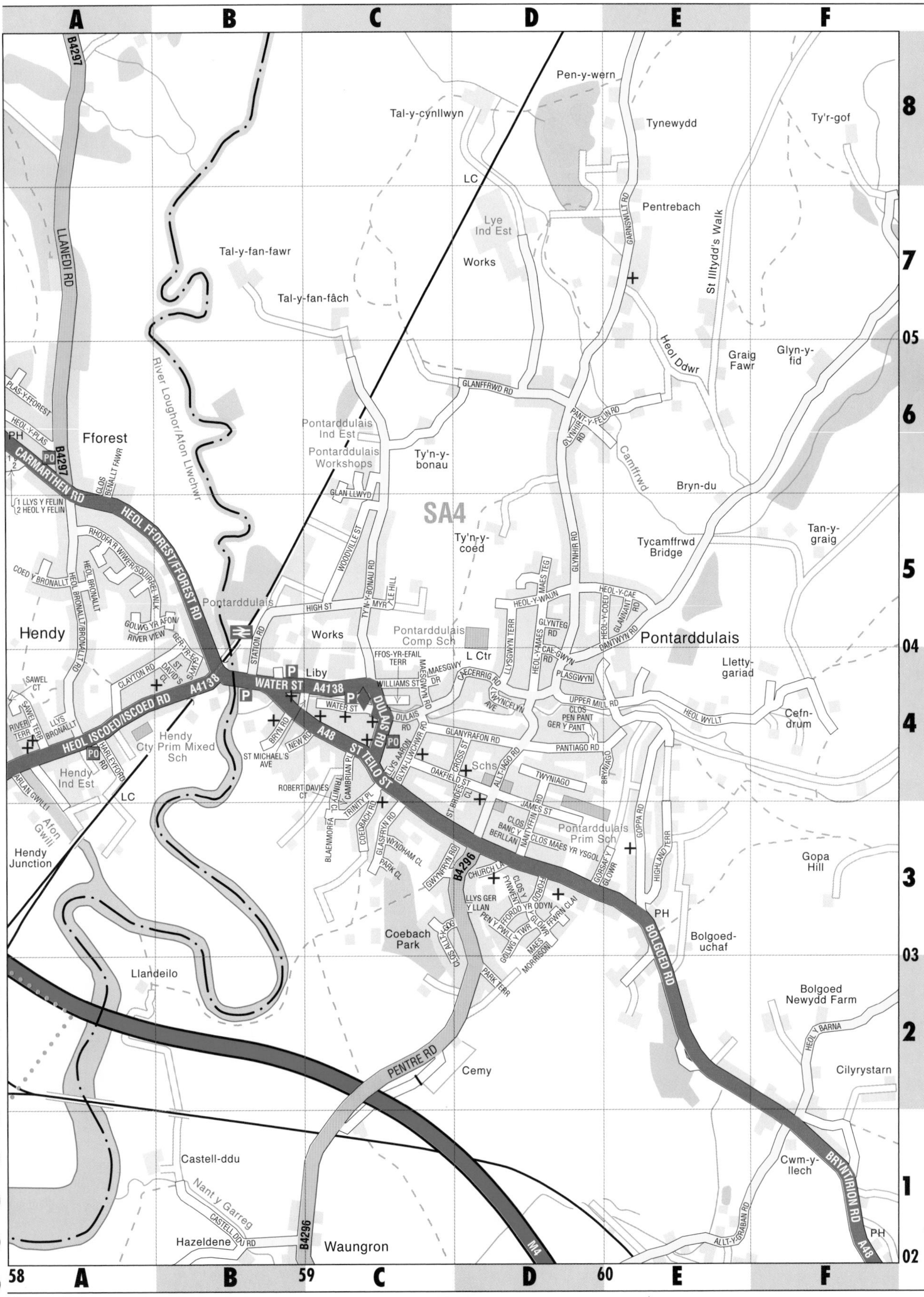

8
7
05
6
5
04
4
3
03
2
1
02

Pen-y-wern
Tal-y-cynllwyn
Tynewydd
Ty'r-gof
LC
Pentrebach
Lye Ind Est
Works
Tal-y-fan-fawr
Tal-y-fan-fâch
LLANEDI RD
B4297
GARNSWLLT RD
St Illtyd's Walk
Heol Ddwr
Graig Fawr
Glyn-y-fid
GLANFFRWD RD
PANT-Y-FELIN RD
GLYNHIR RD
River Loughor/Afon Llwchwr
Pontarddulais Ind Est
Pontarddulais Workshops
Ty'n-y-bonau
Camffrwd
Bryn-du
PLAS-Y-FFOREST
HEOL-Y-PLAS
PH
Fforest
PO
CARMARTHEN RD
CLOS BENALLT FAWR
1 LLYS Y FELIN
2 HEOL Y FELIN
HEOL FFOREST/FFOREST RD
GLAN LLWYD
SA4
Ty'n-y-coed
Tycamffrwd Bridge
Tan-y-graig
RHODFA'R WIWER/SQUIRREL WALK
COED Y BRONALLT
HEOL BRONALLT
HEOL BRONALLT/BRONALLT RD
WOODVILLE ST
TY'N-Y-BONAU RD
LE HILL
MYR
MAES TEG
HEOL-Y-WAUN
HEOL-Y-CAE
HEOL-Y-COED
GLANNANT RD
Pontarddulais
HIGH ST
GOLWG YR AFON/RIVER VIEW
GER-YR-EFAIL
Hendy
STATION RD
Works
Pontarddulais Comp Sch
LLYSGWYN TERR
GLYNTEG RD
HEOL-Y-MAES
CAE-GWYN
CAE RD
DANTWYN RD
Pontarddulais
Lletty-gariad
FFOS-YR-EFAIL TERR
L Ctr
ST DAVID'S CL
MAESGWYN RD
MAESGWY DR
CAECERRIG RD
PLASGWYN
SAWEL CT
CLAYTON RD
P
Liby
WATER ST
A4138
WILLIAMS ST
DULAIS
A4138
UPPER MILL RD
HEOL WYLLT
LLWYNCELYN AVE
CLOS PEN PANT
GER Y PANT
Cefn-drum
SAWEL TERR
RIVER TERR
LLYS BRONALLT
HEOL ISCOED/ISCOED RD
WATER ST
DULAS RD
BRYN RD
NEW RD
A48
GLANYRAFON RD
PANTIAGO RD
HARLEYFORD RD
Cty Hendy Prim Mixed Sch
ST MICHAEL'S AVE
ST TEILO ST
LLYS AARON
GLYN-LLWCHWR RD
CROSS ST
Schs
ALLT-IAGO RD
TWYNIAGO
BRYNIAGO
Hendy Ind Est
LC
ARLAN GWILI
ROBERT DAVIES CT
CAMBRIAN PL
TRINITY PL
OAKFIELD ST
ST BRIDGET CL
JAMES ST
GOPPA RD
Afon Gwili
Hendy Junction
BLAENMORFA
COEDBACH RD
GLASFRYN RD
WYNDHAM CL
PARK CL
CLOS BANC Y BERLLAN
NANTYFFIN RD
Pontarddulais Prim Sch
CLOS MAES YR YSGOL
HIGHLAND TERR
Gopa Hill
GWYNFRYN RD
B4296
CHURCH LA
CLOS Y FYNWENT
FFORDD
GORSAFY GLOWR
PH
LLYS GER Y LLAN
PEN Y PWLL
FFORDD YR ODYN
GLOWR
FFWRN CLAI
Coebach Park
CLOS ALLT-Y-BOG
GOLWG Y TWR
MAES MORRISON
BOLGOED RD
Bolgoed-uchaf
Llandeilo
PARK TERR
Bolgoed Newydd Farm
HEOL Y BARNA
Cilyrystarn
PENTRE RD
Cemy
Castell-ddu
Cwm-y-llech
BRYNTIRION RD
Nant y Garreg
CASTELL DDU RD
ALLT-Y-GRABAN RD
Hazeldene
B4296
Waungron
M4
PH
A48

58 A B 59 C D 60 E F

19
219

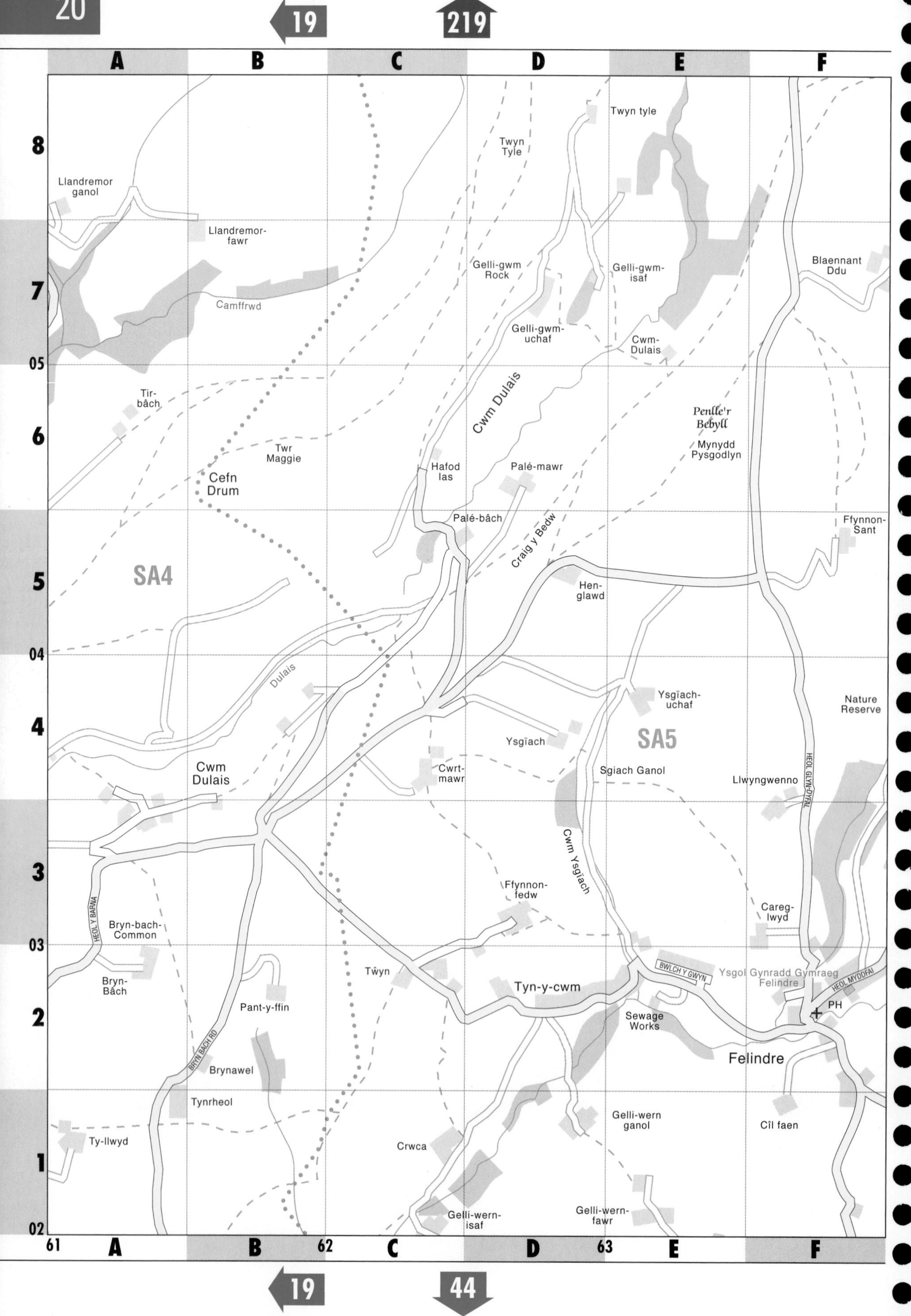
A
B
C
D
E
F
8
7
05
6
5
04
4
3
03
2
1
02
61
62
63
Twyn tyle
Twyn
Tyle
Llandremor
ganol
Llandremor-
fawr
Gelli-gwm
Rock
Gelli-gwm-
isaf
Blaennant
Ddu
Camffrwd
Gelli-gwm-
uchaf
Cwm-
Dulais
Tir-
bâch
Cwm Dulais
Penlle'r
Bebyll
Mynydd
Pysgodlyn
Twr
Maggie
Cefn
Drum
Hafod
las
Palé-mawr
Palé-bâch
Ffynnon-
Sant
Craig y Bedw
SA4
Hen-
glawd
Dulais
Ysgïach-
uchaf
Nature
Reserve
Ysgïach
SA5
Cwm
Dulais
Cwrt-
mawr
Sgiach Ganol
Llwyngwenno
HEOL GLYN-DYFAL
Cwm Ysgïach
HEOL Y BARNA
Ffynnon-
fedw
Bryn-bach-
Common
Careg-
lwyd
Bryn-
Bâch
Twŷn
Tyn-y-cwm
BWLCH Y GWYN
Ysgol Gynradd Gymraeg
Felindre
HEOL MYDDFAI
PH
Pant-y-ffin
Sewage
Works
Felindre
BRYN BACH RD
Brynawel
Tynrheol
Gelli-wern
ganol
Cîl faen
Ty-llwyd
Crwca
Gelli-wern-
isaf
Gelli-wern-
fawr

19
44

219
22

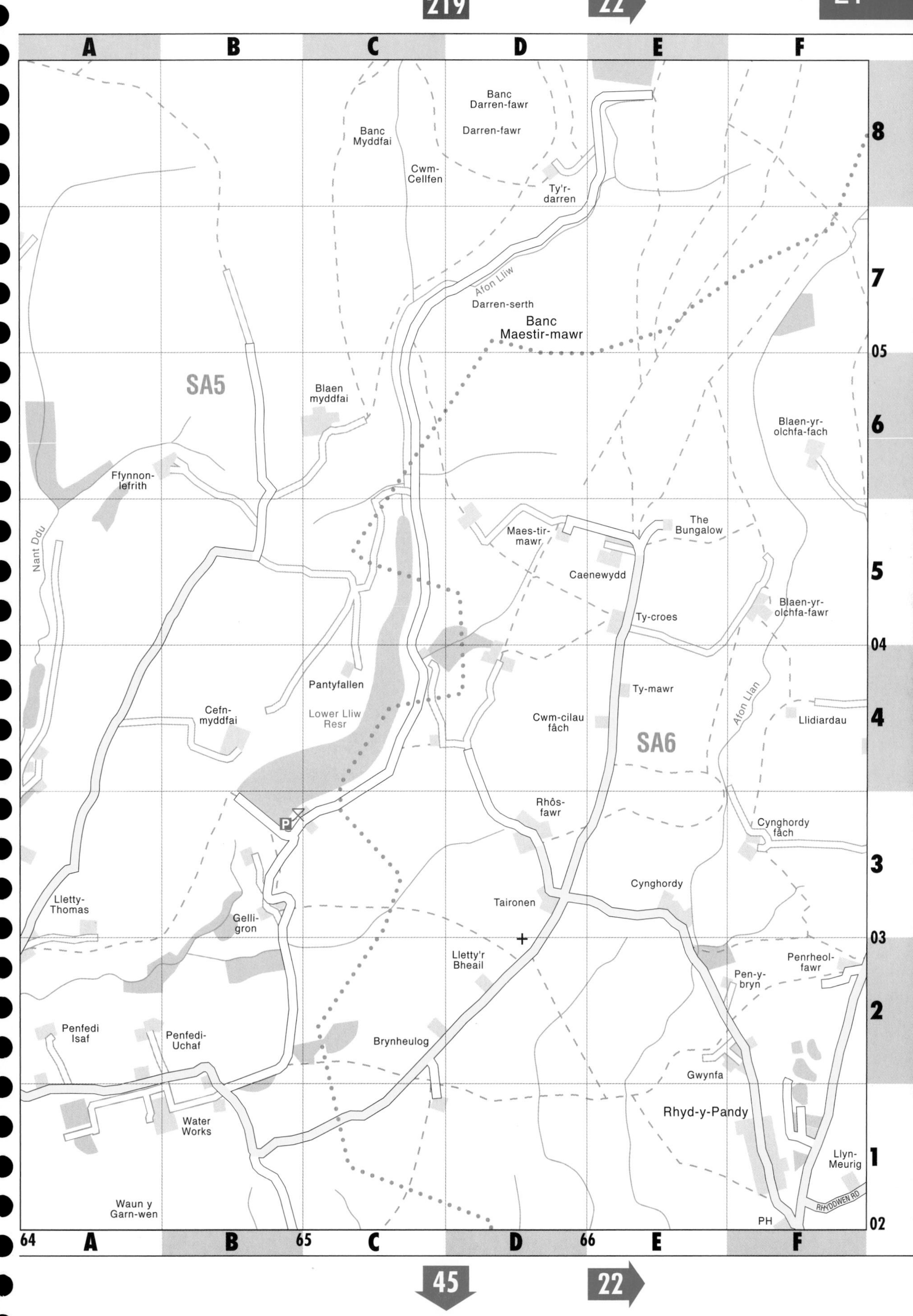

A B C D E F
8
7
05
6
5
04
4
3
03
2
1
02
64 65 66
Banc Darren-fawr
Darren-fawr
Banc Myddfai
Cwm-Cellfen
Ty'r-darren
Afon Lliw
Darren-serth
Banc Maestir-mawr
SA5
Blaen myddfai
Blaen-yr-olchfa-fach
Ffynnon-lefrith
Nant Ddu
Maes-tir-mawr
The Bungalow
Caenewydd
Blaen-yr-olchfa-fawr
Ty-croes
Ty-mawr
Pantyfallen
Cefn-myddfai
Lower Lliw Resr
Cwm-cilau fâch
SA6
Afon Llan
Llidiardau
Rhôs-fawr
Cynghordy fâch
P
Cynghordy
Lletty-Thomas
Gelli-gron
Taironen
Lletty'r Bheail
Penrheol-fawr
Pen-y-bryn
Penfedi Isaf
Penfedi-Uchaf
Brynheulog
Gwynfa
Water Works
Rhyd-y-Pandy
Llyn-Meurig
RHYDDWEN RD
Waun y Garn-wen
PH

45
22

21
220

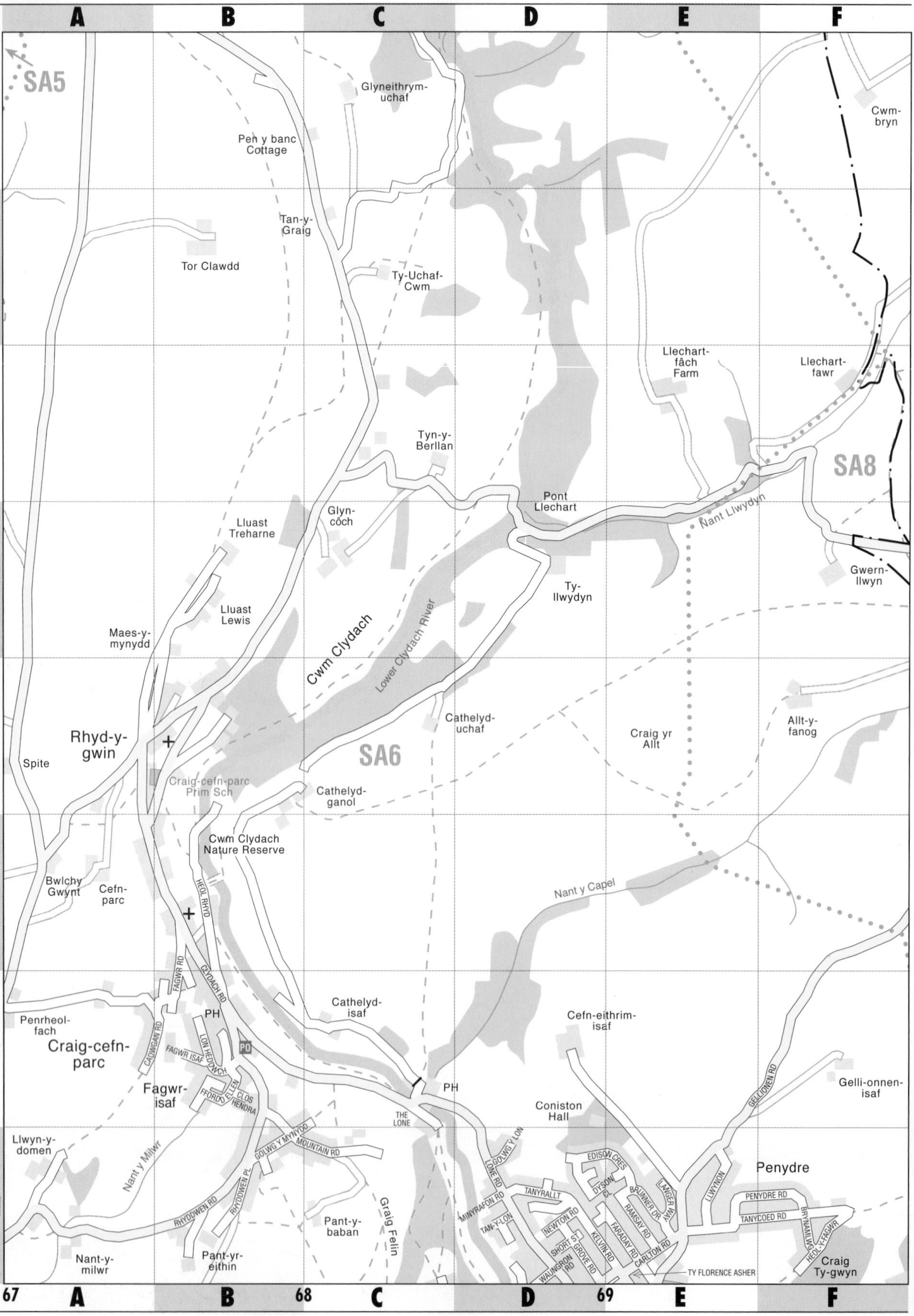

A B C D E F
8
7
05
6
5
04
4
3
03
2
1
02
SA5
SA6
SA8
Glyneithrym-
uchaf
Cwm-
bryn
Pen y banc
Cottage
Tan-y-
Graig
Tor Clawdd
Ty-Uchaf-
Cwm
Llechart-
fâch
Farm
Llechart-
fawr
Tyn-y-
Berllan
Pont
Llechart
Nant Llwydyn
Lluast
Treharne
Glyn-
côch
Gwern-
llwyn
Ty-
llwydyn
Lluast
Lewis
Maes-y-
mynydd
Cwm Clydach
Lower Clydach River
Cathelyd-
uchaf
Craig yr
Allt
Allt-y-
fanog
Rhyd-y-
gwin
Spite
Craig-cefn-parc
Prim Sch
Cathelyd-
ganol
Cwm Clydach
Nature Reserve
Bwlchy
Gwynt
Cefn-
parc
HEOL RHYD
Nant y Capel
FAGWR RD
CLYDACH RD
Cathelyd-
isaf
Cefn-eithrim-
isaf
Penrheol-
fach
PH
Craig-cefn-
parc
CADWGAN RD
FAGWR ISAF
LON HEDDWCH
PO
Fagwr-
isaf
FFORDD ELLEN
CLOS HENDRA
PH
Coniston
Hall
GELLIONEN RD
Gelli-onnen-
isaf
THE
LONE
Llwyn-y-
domen
Nant y Milwr
GOLWG Y MYNYDD
MOUNTAIN RD
RHYDDWEN PL
RHYDDWEN RD
GOLWG Y LON
LONE RD
EDISON CRES
DYSON CL
BRUNNER DR
LANGER WAY
LLWYNON
Penydre
PENYDRE RD
TANYCOED RD
BRYNAMLWG
HEOL-Y-FAGWR
TANYRALLT
MINYRAFON RD
TAN-Y-LON
NEWTON RD
SHORT ST
GROVE RD
KELVIN RD
FARADAY RD
RAMSAY RD
CARLTON RD
WAUNGRON RD
TY FLORENCE ASHER
Craig
Ty-gwyn
Pant-y-
baban
Craig Felin
Nant-y-
milwr
Pant-yr-
eithin
67 A B 68 C D 69 E F

21
46

220
24

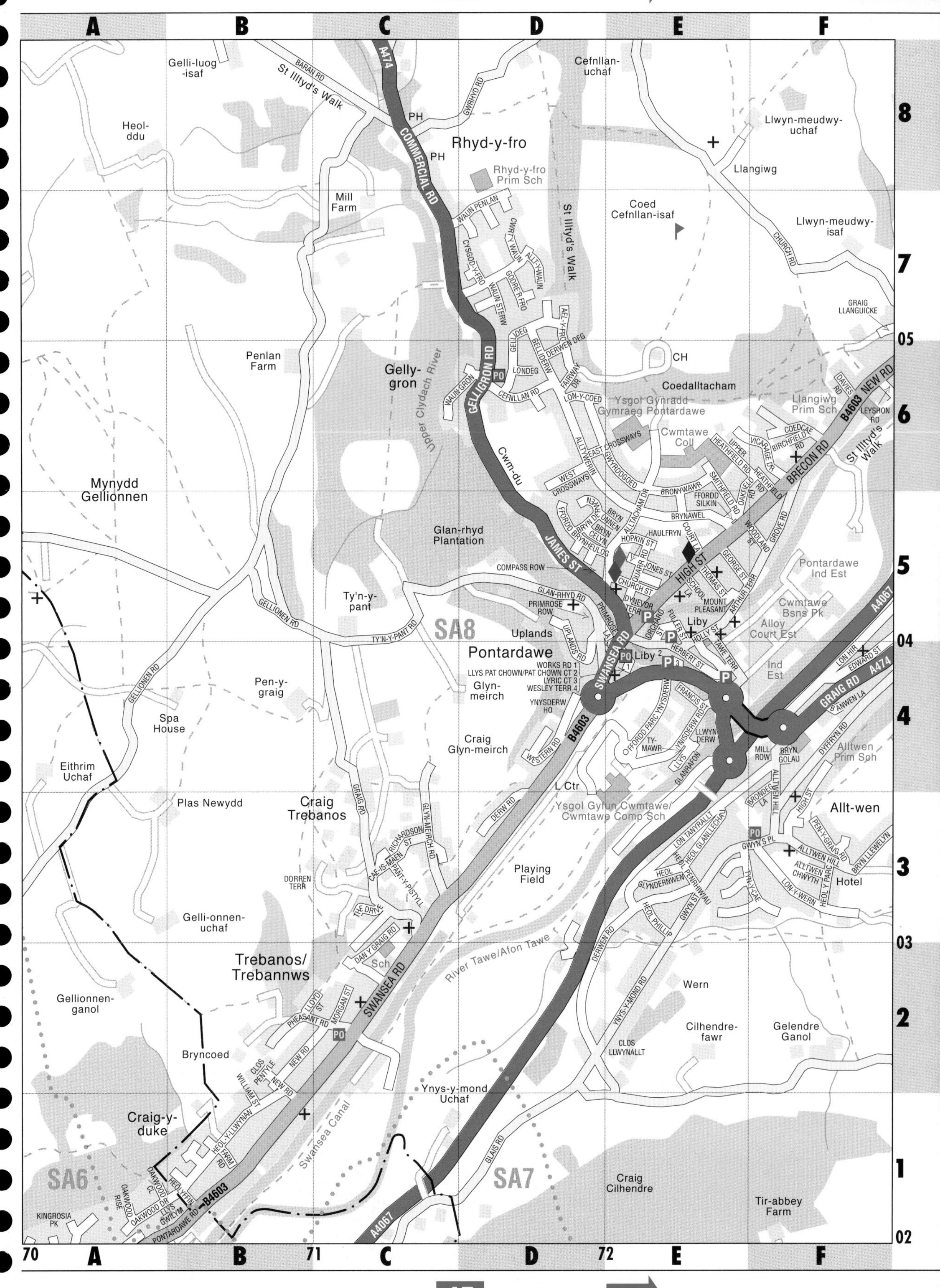
Rhyd-y-fro
Pontardawe
Gelly-gron
Cwm-du
Glan-rhyd Plantation
Mynydd Gellionnen
Uplands
Glyn-meirch
Craig Glyn-meirch
Craig Trebanos
Trebanos/ Trebannws
Allt-wen
Coedalltacham
Cwmtawe Coll
Ysgol Gyfun Cwmtawe/ Cwmtawe Comp Sch
Playing Field
River Tawe/Afon Tawe
Swansea Canal
Craig Cilhendre
Craig-y-duke
Bryncoed
Wern
Cilhendre-fawr
Gelendre Ganol
Tir-abbey Farm
Ynys-y-mond Uchaf
Pontardawe Ind Est
Cwmtawe Bsns Pk
Alloy Court Est
Llangiwg
Llwyn-meudwy-uchaf
Llwyn-meudwy-isaf
Coed Cefnllan-isaf
Cefnllan-uchaf
Heol-ddu
Gelli-luog-isaf
Mill Farm
Penlan Farm
Ty'n-y-pant
Pen-y-graig
Spa House
Eithrim Uchaf
Plas Newydd
Gelli-onnen-uchaf
Gellionnen-ganol
SA8
SA7
SA6
COMMERCIAL RD
GELLIGRON RD
JAMES ST
SWANSEA RD
HIGH ST
BRECON RD
GRAIG RD
A474
A4067
B4603
70
71
72
02
03
04
05
8
7
6
5
4
3
2
1
A
B
C
D
E
F

47
24

23 221

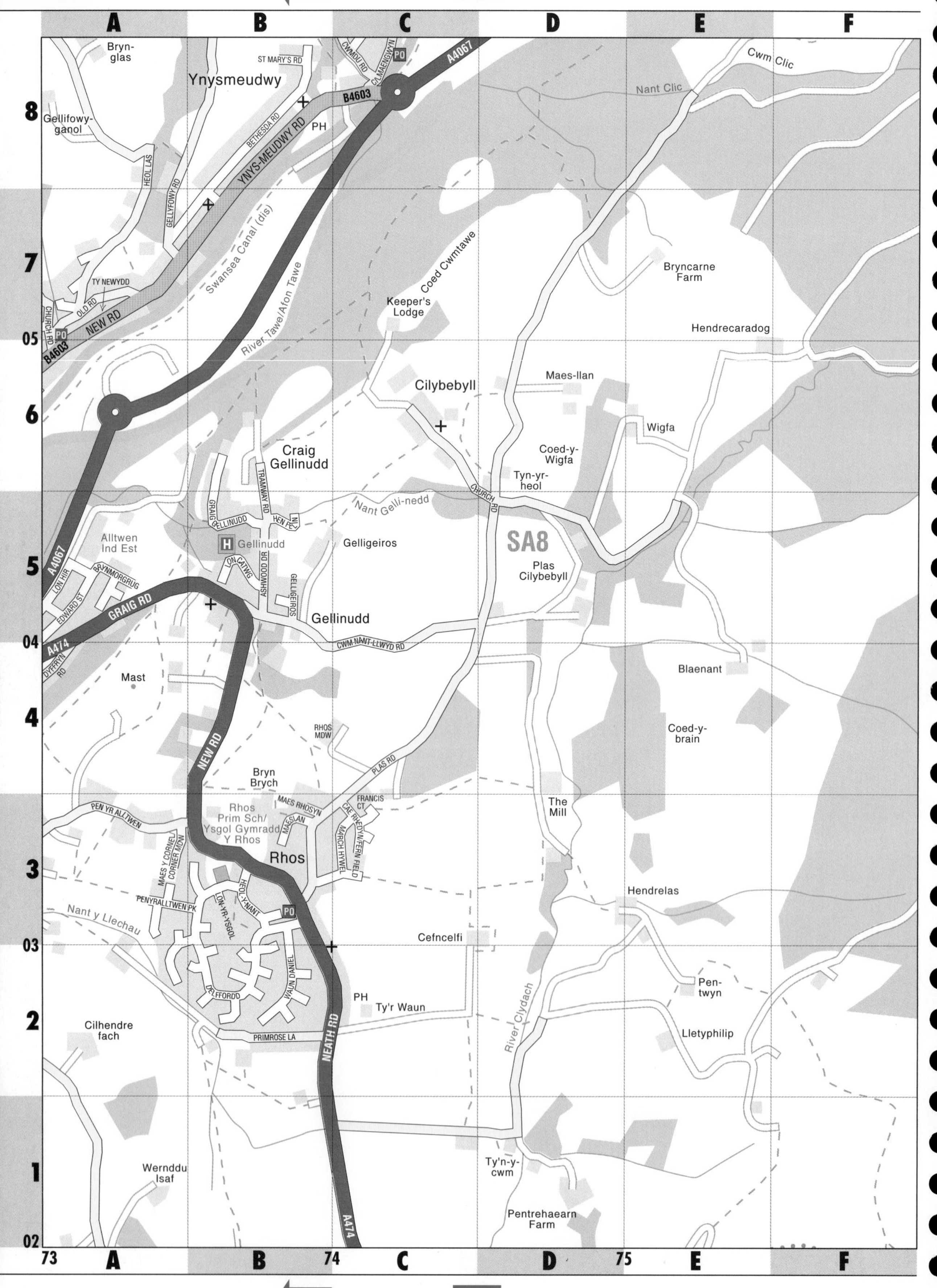
A B C D E F
8
7
05
6
5
04
4
3
03
2
1
02
73 A B 74 C D 75 E F
Bryn-glas
Ynysmeudwy
ST MARY'S RD
CWMDU RD
CL MAENGWYN
PO
A4067
B4603
Cwm Clic
Nant Clic
Gellifowy-ganol
BETHESDA RD
YNYS-MEUDWY RD
PH
HEOL LAS
GELLYFOWY RD
Swansea Canal (dis)
River Tawe/Afon Tawe
Coed Cwmtawe
Bryncarne Farm
TY NEWYDD
OLD RD
CHURCH RD
NEW RD
B4603
Keeper's Lodge
Hendrecaradog
Maes-llan
Cilybebyll
Wigfa
Craig Gellinudd
Coed-y-Wigfa
Tyn-yr-heol
TRAMWAY RD
CHURCH RD
Nant Gelli-nedd
GRAIG GELLINUDD
HEN FFD
Alltwen Ind Est
Gellinudd
Gelligeiros
SA8
Plas Cilybebyll
A4067
LON HIR
BRYNMORGRUG
LON CATWG
ASHWOOD DR
GELLIGEIROS
GRAIG RD
EDWARD ST
Gellinudd
A474
CWM-NANT-LLWYD RD
DYFFRYN RD
Mast
Blaenant
Coed-y-brain
RHOS MDW
NEW RD
PLAS RD
Bryn Brych
FRANCIS CT
The Mill
PEN YR ALLTWEN
MAES RHOSYN
Rhos Prim Sch/ Ysgol Gymradd Y Rhos
MAESLAN
CAE RHEDYN
FERN FIELD
MARCH HYWEL
MAES Y CORNEL
CORNER MDW
Rhos
Hendrelas
PENYRALLTWEN PK
LON-YR-YSGOL
HEOL-Y-NANT
PO
Nant y Llechau
Cefncelfi
DELFFORDD
WAUN DANIEL
PH
Ty'r Waun
River Clydach
Pen-twyn
Cilhendre fach
PRIMROSE LA
NEATH RD
Lletyphilip
Wernddu Isaf
Ty'n-y-cwm
Pentrehaearn Farm
A474

23 48

2
226

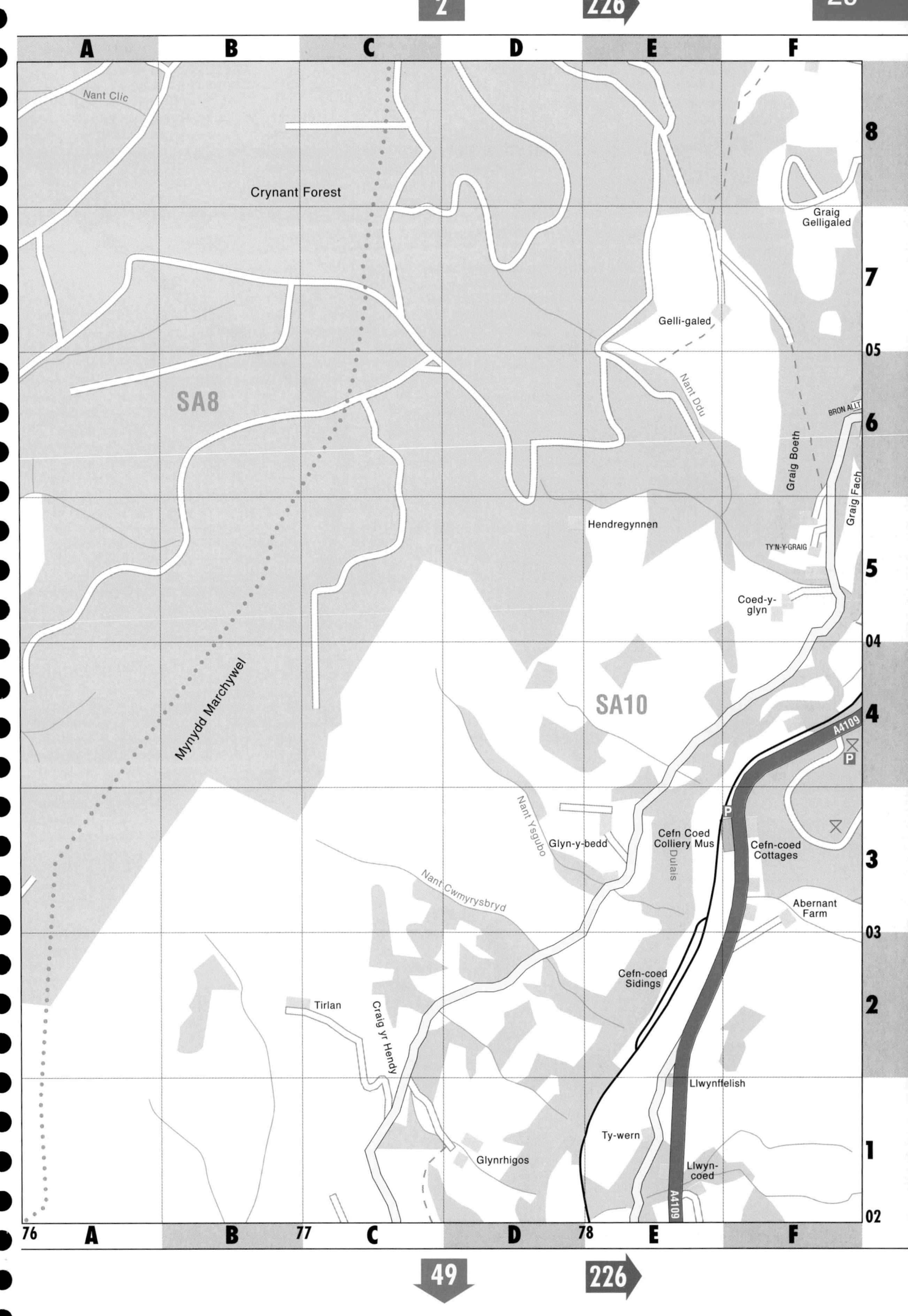
A
B
C
D
E
F
8
7
05
6
5
04
4
3
03
2
1
02
76
77
78
Nant Clic
Crynant Forest
SA8
Mynydd Marchywel
Graig
Gelligaled
Gelli-galed
Nant Ddu
BRON ALLT
Graig Boeth
Graig Fach
Hendregynnen
TY'N-Y-GRAIG
Coed-y-
glyn
SA10
A4109
Nant Ysgubo
Glyn-y-bedd
Cefn Coed
Colliery Mus
Dulais
Cefn-coed
Cottages
Nant Cwmyrysbryd
Abernant
Farm
Cefn-coed
Sidings
Tirlan
Craig yr Hendy
Llwynffelish
Ty-wern
Glynrhigos
Llwyn-
coed

49
226

227
224

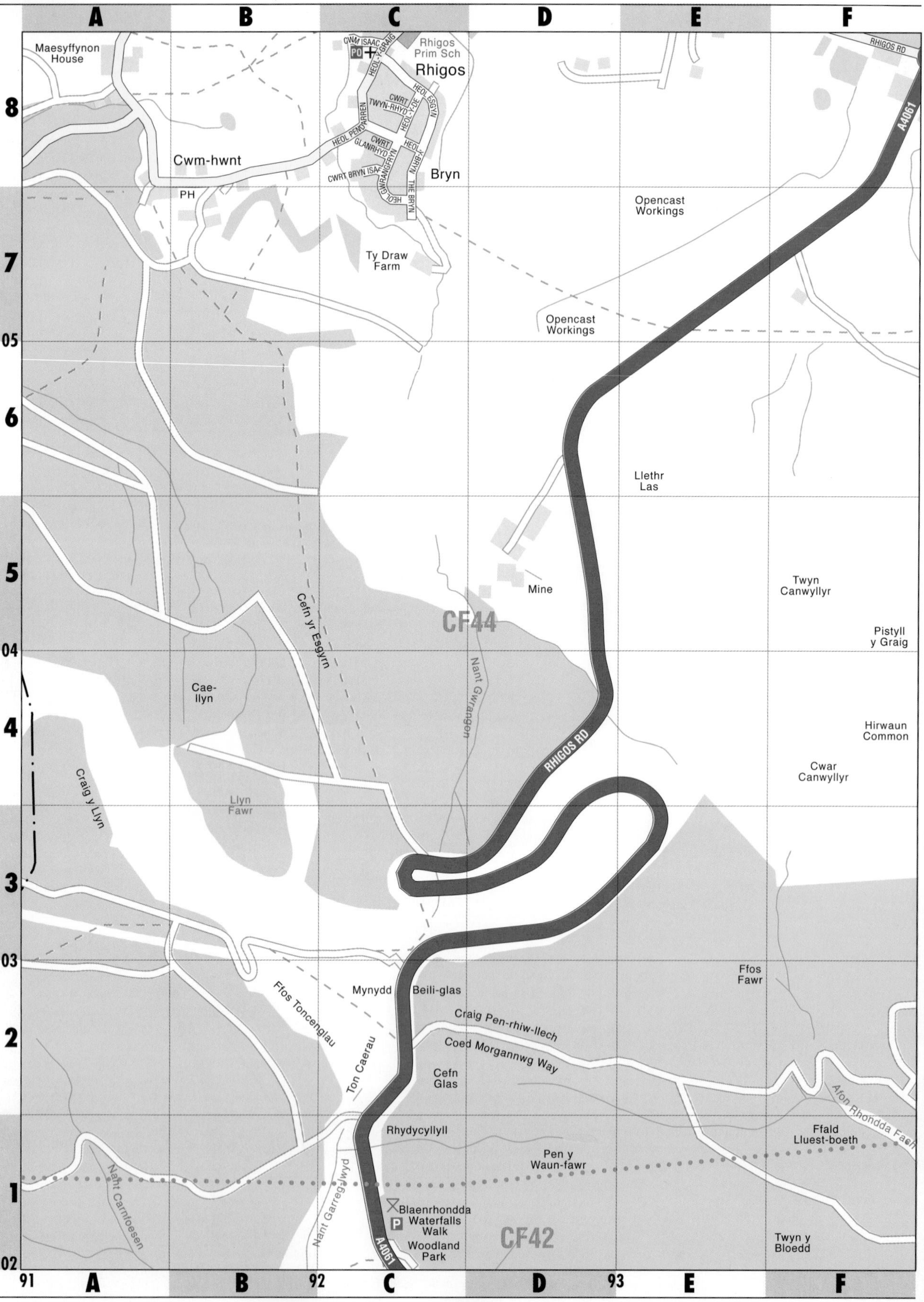

227
50

224

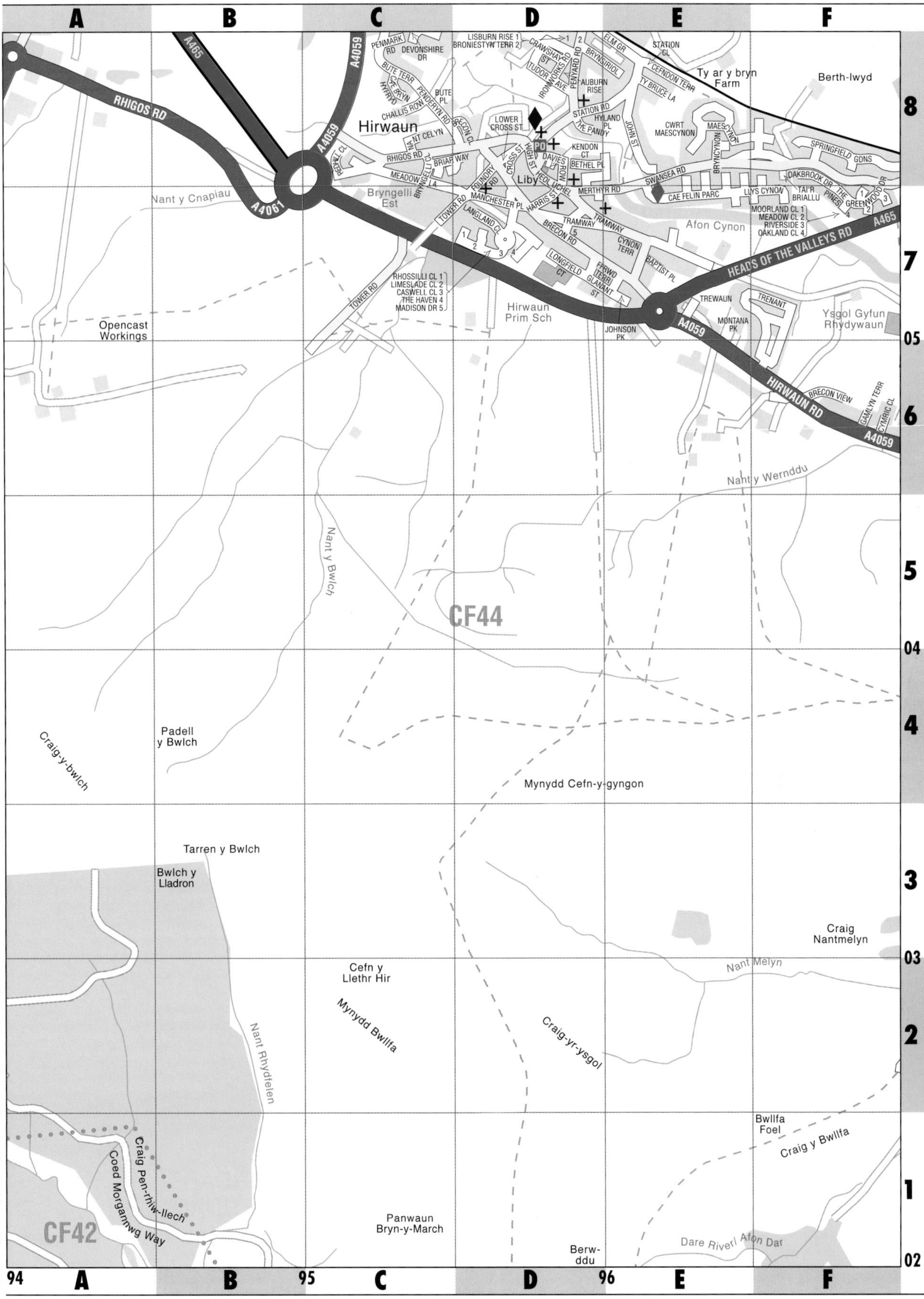

A B C D E F

8 7 05 6 5 04 4 3 03 2 1 02

RHIGOS RD
A465
A4059
A4061
Hirwaun
PENMARK RD
DEVONSHIRE DR
BUTE TERR
CAE BRYN
HYFRYD
BUTE PL
PENDERYN RD
CHALLIS ROW
BRECON CL
NANT CELYN
RHIGOS RD
BRIAR WAY
MEADOW LA
BRYNGELLI CL
Bryngelli Est
LISBURN RISE 1
BRONIESTYN TERR 2
CRAWSHAY ST
TUDOR AVE
IRONWORKS RD
PENYARD RD
BRYNSIRIOL
ELM GR
AUBURN RISE
STATION RD
LOWER CROSS ST
HYLAND PL
THE PANDY
JOHN ST
PO
KENDON CT
DAVIES ROW
BETHEL PL
CROSS ST
HIGH ST
Liby
HEOL UCHEL
FOUNDRY RD
MANCHESTER PL
HARRIS ST
MERTHYR RD
TOWER RD
LANGLAND CL
TRAMWAY
BRECON RD
CYNON TERR
LONGFIELD CT
FFRWD TERR
GLANANT ST
BAPTIST PL
RHOSSILLI CL 1
LIMESLADE CL 2
CASWELL CL 3
THE HAVEN 4
MADISON DR 5
TOWER RD
Hirwaun Prim Sch
JOHNSON PK
STATION CL
CEFNDON TERR
TY BRUCE LA
Ty ar y bryn Farm
Berth-Iwyd
CWRT MAESCYNON
MAESCYNON
BRYNCYNON
SWANSEA RD
CAE FELIN PARC
LLYS CYNON
TAI'R BRIALLU
SPRINGFIELD GDNS
OAKBROOK DR
THE PINES
GREENWOOD DR
MOORLAND CL 1
MEADOW CL 2
RIVERSIDE 3
OAKLAND CL 4
Afon Cynon
HEADS OF THE VALLEYS RD
A465
TREWAUN
TRENANT
MONTANA PK
A4059
Ysgol Gyfun Rhydywaun
HIRWAUN RD
BRECON VIEW
GAMLYN TERR
CYMRIC CL
A4059
Nant y Cnapiau
Opencast Workings
Nant y Wernddu
Nant y Bwlch
CF44
Craig-y-bwlch
Padell y Bwlch
Mynydd Cefn-y-gyngon
Tarren y Bwlch
Bwlch y Lladron
Craig Nantmelyn
Cefn y Llethr Hir
Nant Melyn
Mynydd Bwllfa
Craig-yr-ysgol
Nant Rhydfelen
Bwllfa Foel
Craig y Bwllfa
Craig Pen-rhiw-llech
Coed Morgannwg Way
CF42
Panwaun Bryn-y-March
Berw-ddu
Dare River/ Afon Dar

94 A B 95 C D 96 E F

51

28

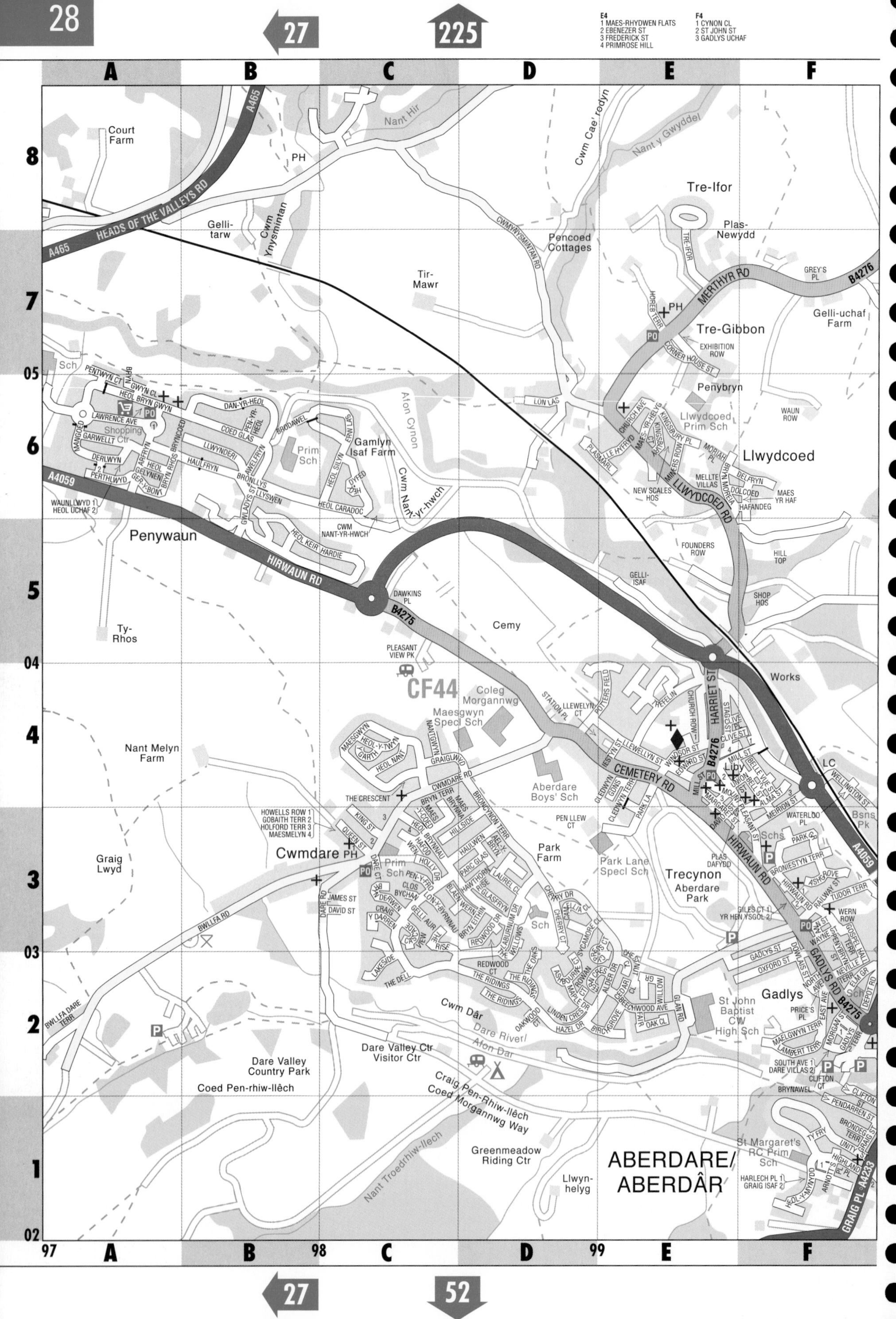
27
225
E4
1 MAES-RHYDWEN FLATS
2 EBENEZER ST
3 FREDERICK ST
4 PRIMROSE HILL
F4
1 CYNON CL
2 ST JOHN ST
3 GADLYS UCHAF
A
B
C
D
E
F
8
7
05
6
5
04
4
3
03
2
1
02
97
98
99
Court Farm
A465
HEADS OF THE VALLEYS RD
PH
Nant Hir
Cwm Cae'rodyn
Nant y Gwyddel
Tre-Ifor
Gelli-tarw
Cwm Ynysmintan
CWMYNYSMINTAN RD
Pencoed Cottages
Plas-Newydd
TRE-IFOR
MERTHYR RD
B4276
GREY'S PL
Tir-Mawr
HOREB TERR
Tre-Gibbon
Gelli-uchaf Farm
EXHIBITION ROW
CORNER HOUSE ST
Sch
PENTWYN CT
GWYN CL
HEOL BRYN GWYN
LAWRENCE AVE
Shopping Ctr
MANGOED
GARWELLT
DERLWYN
PERTHLWYD
GER-Y-BONT
DAN-YR-HEOL
COED GLAS
PEN-YR-HEOL
LLWYNDERI
HAULFRYN
BRONLLYS
LLYSWEN
GWLADYS ST
BRODAWEL
ERW LAS
HEOL SILYN
DYFED
Prim Sch
Gamlyn Isaf Farm
Afon Cynon
Cwm Nant-yr-hwch
LON LAS
Penybryn
Llwydcoed Prim Sch
CHURCH AVE
MAES-YR-HELYG
KINGSBURY PL
PLASMARL
MINERS ROW
MORIAH PL
Llwydcoed
BRYN MORIA
DELFRYN
DOLCOED
HAFANDEG
MELLTE VILLAS
NEW SCALES HOS
LLWYDCOED RD
MAES YR HAF
WAUN ROW
A4059
WAUNLLWYD 1
HEOL UCHAF 2
HEOL CARADOC
CWM NANT-YR-HWCH
Penywaun
HEOL KEIR HARDIE
HIRWAUN RD
FOUNDERS ROW
HILL TOP
GELLI-ISAF
DAWKINS PL
B4275
SHOP HOS
Cemy
Ty-Rhos
PLEASANT VIEW PK
Works
CF44
Coleg Morgannwg
STATION PL
LLEWELYN CT
POTTERS FIELD
CHURCH ROW
HARRIET ST
Maesgwyn Specl Sch
MAESGWYN
HEOL-Y-TWYN
Y-GARTH
HEOL NANT
NANTGWYN
GRAIGWYN
LLEWELLYN ST
WINDSOR ST
EDWARD ST
CLIVE ST
MILL ST
Nant Melyn Farm
CWMDARE RD
THE CRESCENT
BRYN TERR
BRONCYNON TERR
Aberdare Boys' Sch
CEMETERY RD
CLEDWYN TERR
PARK LA
PEN LLEW CT
Llby
LC
WELLINGTON ST
Bsns Pk
HOWELLS ROW 1
GOBAITH TERR 2
HOLFORD TERR 3
MAESMELYN 4
KING ST
QUEEN ST
Cwmdare
HILLSIDE
HAULWEN
MEIRION ST
WATERLOO PL
Schs
PARK GR
Graig Llwyd
Prim Sch
PARC GLAS
HAWTHORN RISE
GLASFRYN
LAUREL CL
Park Farm
Park Lane Specl Sch
Trecynon
Aberdare Park
PLAS DAFYDD
BRONIESTYN TERR
ASHGROVE
TUDOR TERR
RAILWAY ST
WERN ROW
GILES CT 1
YR HEN YSGOL 2
JAMES ST
DAVID ST
DARE RD
BWLLFA RD
CRAIG Y DARREN
CHERRY DR
CHERRY CT
SYCAMORE CL
Sch
GADLYS ST
OXFORD ST
DOWLAIS ST
GADLYS RD
LAKESIDE
THE DELL
REDWOOD CT
THE RIDINGS
THE OAKS
ROWAN CT
ALDER DR
CEDAR GR
BEECHWOOD AVE
OAK CL
GLAN RD
Gadlys
BWLLFA DARE TERR
Cwm Dâr
Dare River/
Afon Dâr
OAKWOOD CT
HAZEL DR
LINDEN CRES
BIRCH GROVE
St John Baptist CW High Sch
PRICE'S PL
MAELGWYN TERR
LAMBERT TERR
Dare Valley Ctr
Visitor Ctr
Dare Valley Country Park
Coed Pen-rhiw-llêch
Craig Pen-Rhiw-llêch
Coed Morgannwg Way
SOUTH AVE 1
DARE VILLAS 2
CLIFTON CT
BRYNAWEL
CLIFTON ST
PENDARREN ST
Greenmeadow Riding Ctr
Nant Troedrhiw-llech
ABERDARE/
ABERDÂR
Llwyn-helyg
St Margaret's RC Prim Sch
HARLECH PL 1
GRAIG ISAF 2
TY FRY
HEOL-Y-MYNYDD
GRAIG PL
A4233
52

225
30

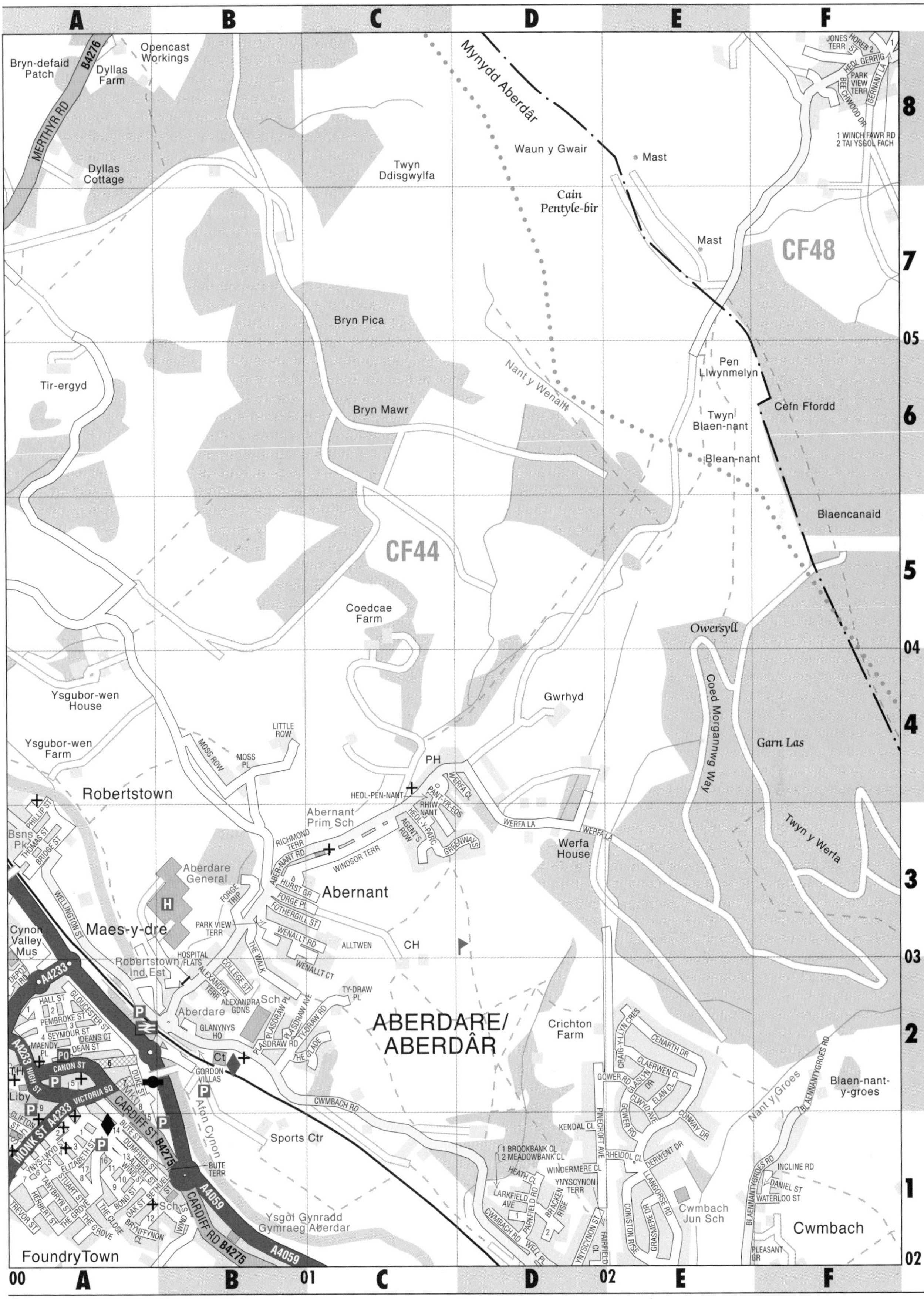

A B C D E F

Bryn-defaid Patch
Dyllas Farm
Opencast Workings
B4276
MERTHYR RD
Dyllas Cottage
Mynydd Aberdâr
Waun y Gwair
Mast
Twyn Ddisgwylfa
Cain Pentyle-bir
Mast
CF48
JONES TERR
HOREB ST
HEOL GERRIG
PARK VIEW TERR
BEE CWMWOOD DR
GERNANT LA
1 WINCH FAWR RD
2 TAI YSGOL FACH

8
7
05
6
5
04
4
3
03
2
1
02

Bryn Pica
Tir-ergyd
Bryn Mawr
Nant y Wenallt
Pen Llwynmelyn
Twyn Blaen-nant
Cefn Ffordd
Blean-nant
Blaencanaid
CF44
Coedcae Farm
Owersyll
Coed Morgannwg Way
Ysgubor-wen House
Ysgubor-wen Farm
Gwrhyd
Garn Las
LITTLE ROW
MOSS ROW
MOSS PL
PH
Robertstown
HEOL-PEN-NANT
WERFA CL
PANT-YR-EOS
RHIW NANT
HEOL-Y-PARC
AGENT'S ROW
GREENWAYS
WERFA LA
Twyn y Werfa
Abernant Prim Sch
RICHMOND TERR
ABER-NANT RD
WINDSOR TERR
Werfa House
Bsns Pk
PHILLIPS ST
THOMAS ST
BRIDGE ST
Aberdare General
H
HURST GR
FORGE PL
FOTHERGILL ST
FORGE TRIP
Abernant
WELLINGTON ST
Cynon Valley Mus
Maes-y-dre
PARK VIEW TERR
WENALLT RD
ALLTWEN
CH
WENALLT CT
THE WALK
HOSPITAL FLATS
Robertstown Ind Est
COLLEGE ST
ALEXANDRA TERR
ALEXANDRA GDNS
TY-DRAW PL
A4233
HALL ST
GLOUCESTER ST
PEMBROKE ST
SEYMOUR ST
DEANS CT
DEAN ST
MAENDY PL
PO
CANON ST
Aberdare
Sch
GLANYNYS HO
PLASDRAW PL
PLASDRAW AVE
PLASDRAW RD
TY-DRAW RD
THE GLADE
ABERDARE/ ABERDÂR
Crichton Farm
CRAIG-Y-LLYN CRES
CENARTH DR
CLAERWEN CL
GLASLYN DR
ELAN CL
CLWYD AVE
CONWAY DR
GOWER RD
Nant y Groes
BLAENNANTYGROES RD
Blaen-nant-y-groes
TH
Liby
HIGH ST
A4233
VICTORIA SQ
DUKE ST
Ct
GORDON VILLAS
CWMBACH RD
CLIFTON ST
MONK ST A4233
Sch
BUTE ST
CARDIFF ST B4275
Afon Cynon
Sports Ctr
KENDAL CL
PINECROFT AVE
RHEIDOL CL
DERWENT DR
YNYS-LWYD ST
ELIZABETH ST
DUMFRIES ST
ALBERT ST
WIND ST
BETHEL ST
BUTE TERR
1 BROOKBANK CL
2 MEADOWBANK CL
HEATH CL
WINDERMERE CL
YNYSCYNON TERR
LANGORSE RD
Cwmbach Jun Sch
INCLINE RD
DANIEL ST
WATERLOO ST
BLAENNANTYGROES RD
A4059
TANYBRYN ST
STUART ST
HERBERT ST
THE GROVE
BOND ST
OAK ST
THE CLOSE
BRYNFFYNON CL
CARDIFF RD B4275
Ysgol Gynradd Gymraeg Aberdar
LARKFIELD AVE
PARKFIELD RD
BRACKEN RISE
CWMBACH RD
WELL PL
YNYSCYNON ST
FAIRFIELD CL
CONISTON RISE
GRASMERE DR
Cwmbach
PLEASANT GR
TREVOR ST
FoundryTown
A4059

00 A B 01 C D 02 E F

A1
1 GRIFFITH ST
2 PRICE ST
3 RACHEL ST
4 JENKIN ST
5 CATHERINE ST
6 MARY ST
7 JOHN ST
8 GLANNANT ST
9 LITTLE WIND ST
10 UPPER REGENT ST
11 DAVID PRICE ST
12 HAWTHORNE TERR
13 NITH ST
14 CROSS ST
15 MERCHANT ST
16 NANT ROW
17 ST MARGARETS CWRT

A2
1 GADLYS GDNS
2 BANKES ST
3 WHITCOMBE ST
4 WEATHERAL ST
5 CHURCH ST
6 COMMERCIAL ST
7 MARKET ST
8 STATION ST
9 CHAPEL ROW

53
30

29

E8
1 GILAR ST
2 COURT ST
3 TRAMROAD SIDE N
4 COBDEN PL
5 CROSS THOMAS ST
6 WINDSOR TERR

10

7 MILTON TERR
8 MILTON PL
9 NEWTON TERR
10 FOUNDRY PL
11 TWYNYRODYN RD
12 COURT TERR
13 COEDCAE'R CWRT
14 DAVIES TERR
15 BAILLIE GLAS CT
16 CATHERINE'S CT
17 RUSSELL TERR
18 DYKE ST
19 WILLIAM ST
20 ALEXANDRA TERR
21 JENKINS PL
22 MORRELL ST
23 JAMES ST
24 ST JOHN'S GDNS
25 PHILIPS TERR
26 HAMPTON PL
27 PATRICIA CL
28 LINCOLN TERR
29 THE ARCHES

F8
1 PENUEL ST
2 PARFITT TERR
3 BRYONY CL
4 AERON TERR
5 WILLIAMS TERR
6 EVANS TERR
7 ARFRYN TERR
8 DALTON CL

D8
1 PORTAL HO
2 WILSON CT
3 ATTLEE HO
4 KAMSLEY HO
5 BUCKLAND HO
6 TREVETHICK HO
7 GLYNDWR HO
8 JOSEPH PARRY CT
9 HYWEL HO
10 ST TYDFIL'S CT
11 MORLAIS CT
12 BROAD ST
13 MASONIC ST

ANN'S CL 1
GLYNCOED TERR 2
DAVID ST 3
EASTBOURNE PL 4
WESTBOURNE PL 5
GWYNFAN PL 6
PEASE LA 7
MARDY TERR 8
GLADSTONE TERR 9
GWILYM TERR 10
EASTFIELD TERR 11
HANKEY TERR 12
HANKEY PL 13

1 LEWIS SQ
2 CHAPEL SQ
3 QUAY ROW

STANFIELD CL 1
CANAL ROW 2
HOPKINS CL 3
RIVER ROW 4
JENKIN HOUSES 5
CHURCH VIEW 6
GETHIN PL 7

MERTHYR TYDFIL/
MERTHYR TUDFUL

Heolgerrig
Heolgerrig Prim Sch
Ynys-fach
Cae-Draw
Twynyrodyn
Rhydycar Bsns Pk
Rhyd-y-car
Ysgubor Newydd
CF47
Cwm Glo
Blaen-canaid
CF48
Abercanaid Ind Est
Glyndyrus House
Upper Abercanaid
Waunwyllt
Coed Morgannwg Way
Taff Trail
River Taff/Afon Taf
Parc Busnes Y Triongl/Triangle Bsns Pk
GLYNMIL CVN SITE
Pentrebach
Twyn Gwersyllfa
Gethin Woodland Park
Nant Graig
Abercanaid
Gethin
Pen-y-lan Hill
Graig Gethin
Craig Gilfach
Carn Castellymeibion
CF44
Penwaun Iago
Twyn Ddisgwylfa Fawr
Tyle Robert
Gwaun Helen
CF45
Mynydd Gethin
Tarren y Gafr
Bryn Pica
Gnoll
Cefn-pennar-uchaf
Cefn Pennar
A470
A4054
A4102
A4060
PLYMOUTH ST
PENTREBACH RD
MERTHYR RD

29

54

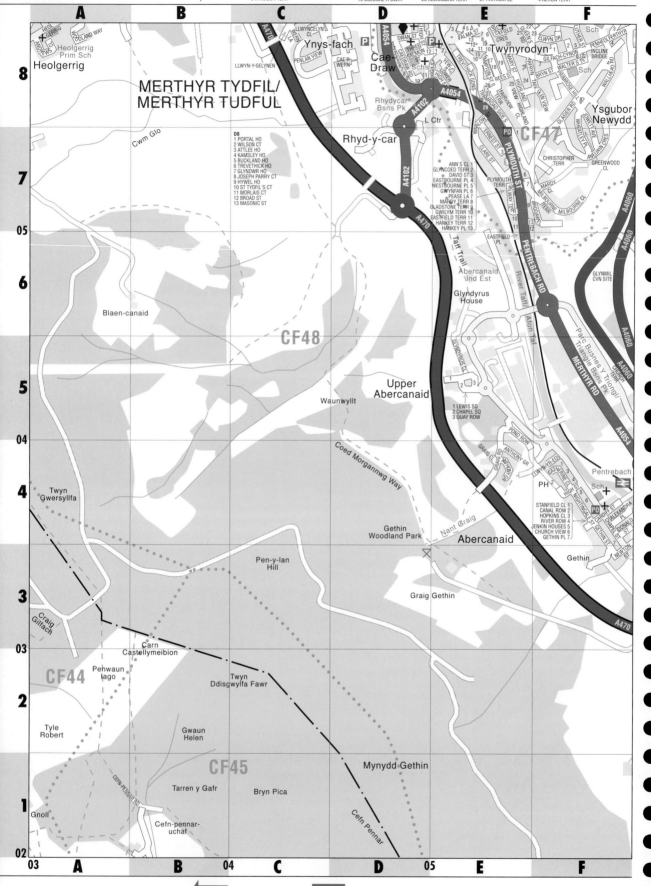

11
32

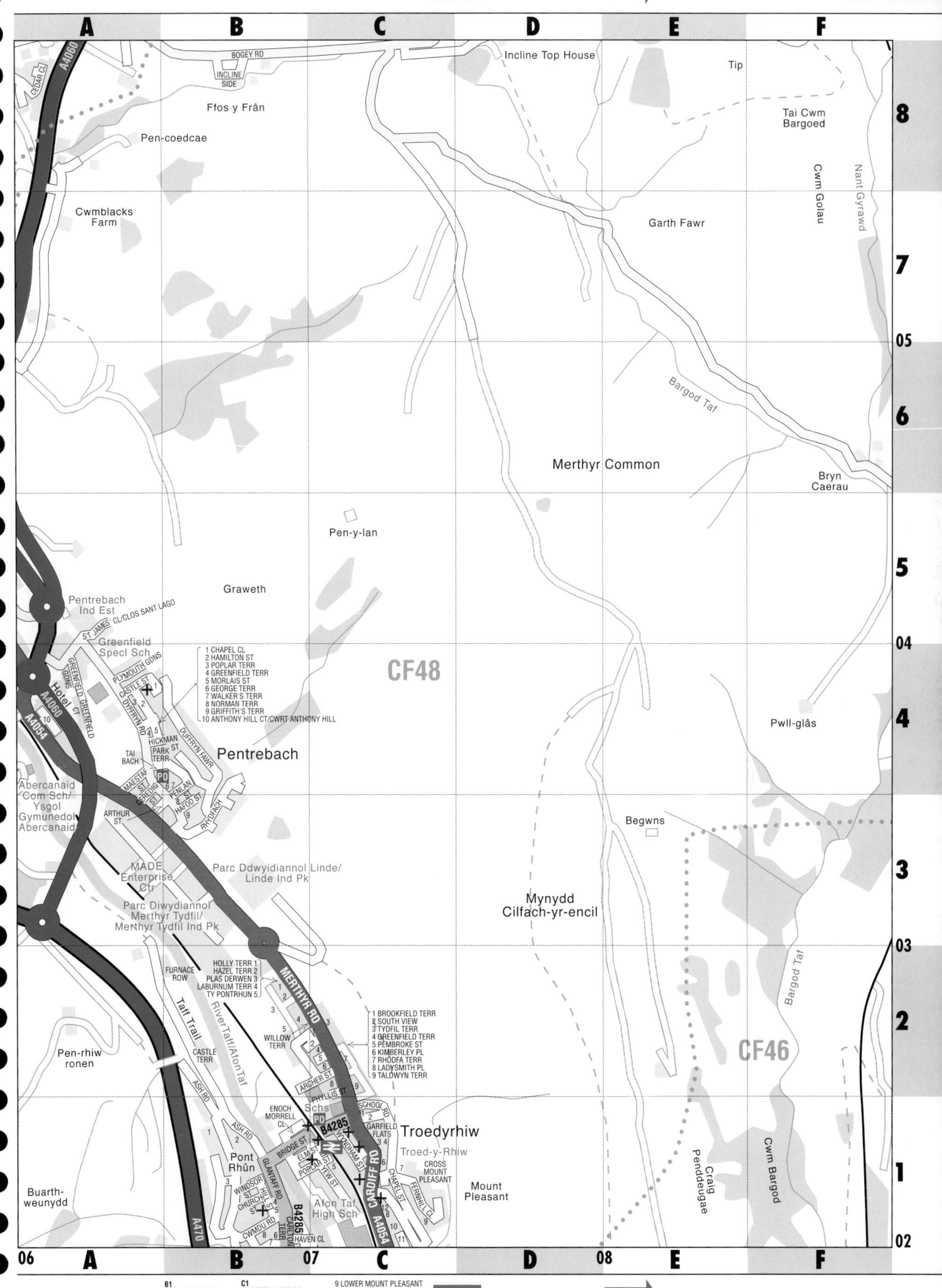

B1
1 PLANTATION SQ
2 HARRIET TOWN
3 NANT-Y-COED
4 WESTBOURNE PL
5 GLYNTAFF CT
6 HAWARDEN PL
7 ANGUS ST
8 LLANRHYD

C1
1 VICTORIA BLDGS
2 TYNTALDWYN RD
3 INDUSTRIAL TERR
4 MORGAN JONES SQ
5 POPLAR MEWS
6 THOMAS JONES SQ
7 UPPER MOUNT PLEASANT
8 ASH VILLAS
9 LOWER MOUNT PLEASANT
10 PLEASANT VIEW
11 HENRY RICHARD ST
12 ZION CL

55
32

31
12

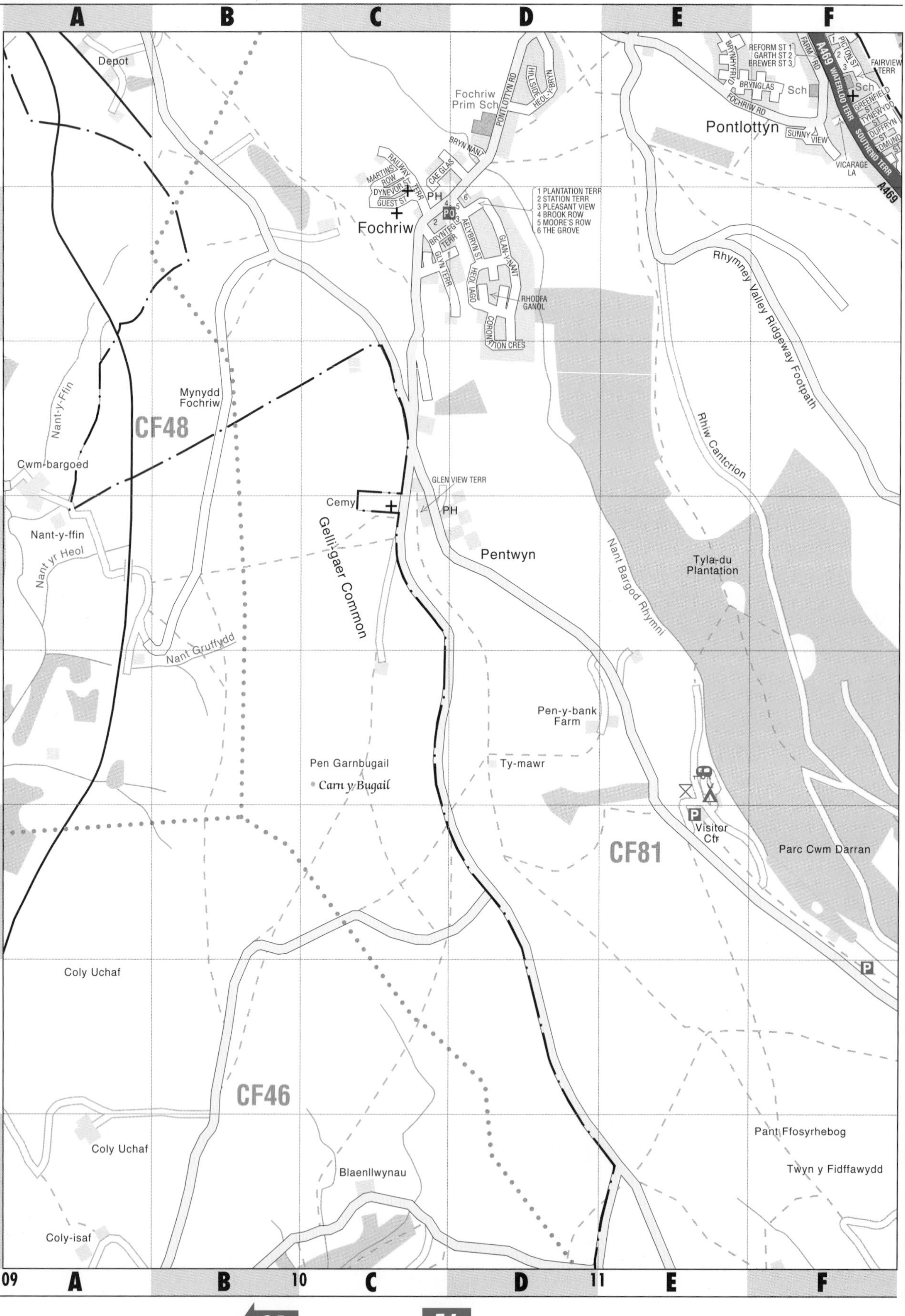

A
B
C
D
E
F
8
7
05
6
5
04
4
3
03
2
1
02
09
10
11
Depot
Fochriw
Prim Sch
PONTLOTTYN RD
HILLSIDE
HEOL-Y-BRYN
BRYN NANT
RAILWAY
TERR
MARTINS
ROW
DYNEVOR ST
GUEST ST
CAE GLAS
PH
PO
Fochriw
BRYNTEG
TERR
GLYN TERR
AELYBRYN ST
GLAN-Y-NANT
HEOL IAGO
RHODFA
GANOL
CORONATION CRES
1 PLANTATION TERR
2 STATION TERR
3 PLEASANT VIEW
4 BROOK ROW
5 MOORE'S ROW
6 THE GROVE
BRYNHYFRYD
REFORM ST 1
GARTH ST 2
BREWER ST 3
FARM RD
BRYNGLAS
Sch
FOCHRIW RD
Pontlottyn
SUNNY VIEW
A469
WATERLOO TERR
SOUTHEND TERR
PICTON ST
FAIRVIEW
TERR
Sch
GREENFIELD
ST
TYNEWYDD
ST
DUFFRYN
ST
EDMUND
ST
VICARAGE
LA
Rhymney Valley Ridgeway Footpath
Nant-y-Ffin
Mynydd
Fochriw
CF48
Cwm-bargoed
Nant-y-ffin
Nant yr Heol
Nant Gruffydd
Cemy
Gelligaer Common
GLEN VIEW TERR
PH
Pentwyn
Rhiw Cantcrion
Nant Bargod Rhymni
Tyla-du
Plantation
Pen-y-bank
Farm
Ty-mawr
Pen Garnbugail
Carn y Bugail
Visitor
Cfr
CF81
Parc Cwm Darran
P
Coly Uchaf
CF46
Coly Uchaf
Pant Ffosyrhebog
Twyn y Fidffawydd
Blaenllwynau
Coly-isaf

31
56

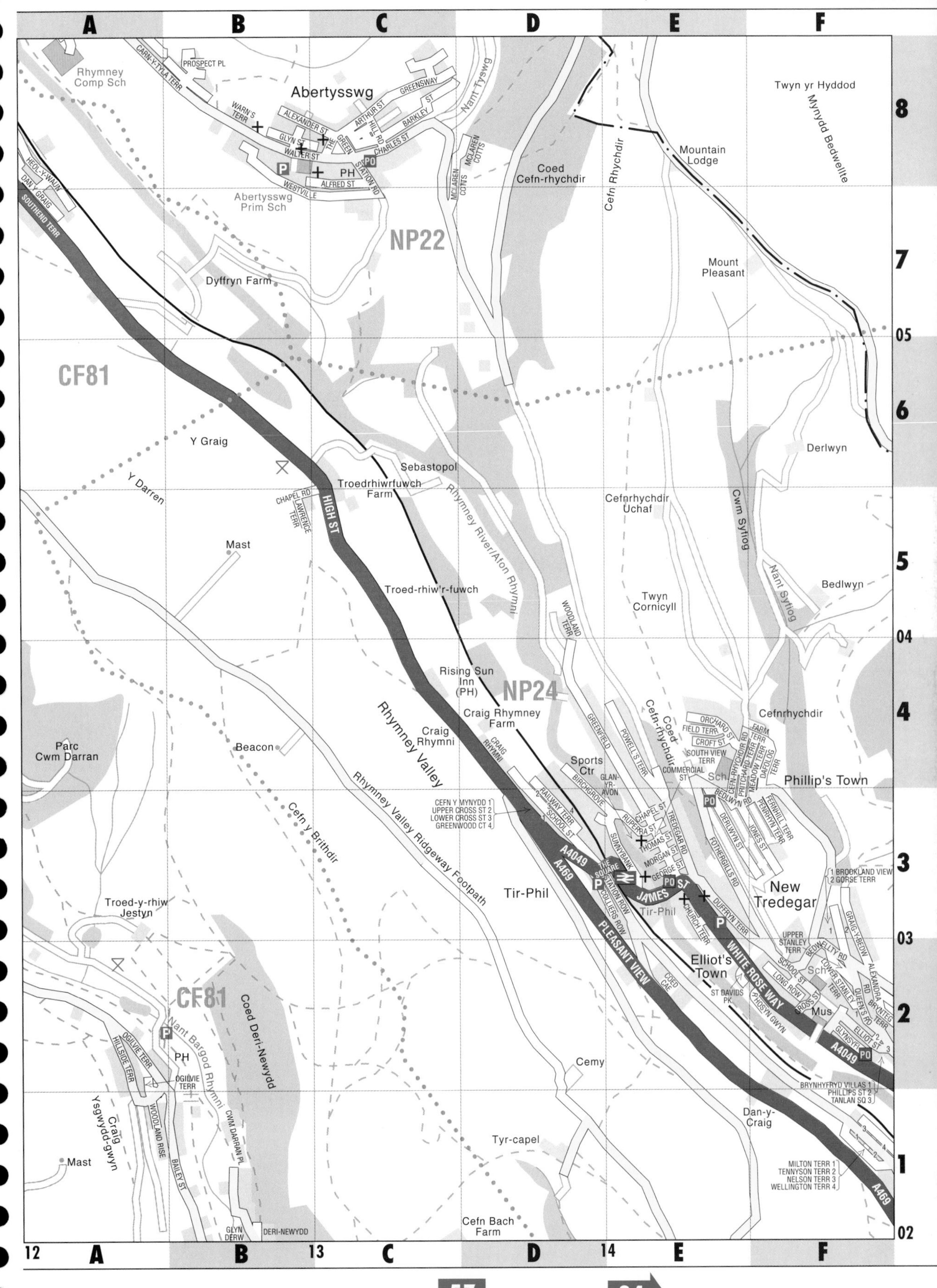
13
34
A
B
C
D
E
F
Rhymney Comp Sch
PROSPECT PL
CARN-Y-TYLA TERR
Abertysswg
GREENSWAY
ALEXANDER ST
ARTHUR ST
HILL RD
BARKLEY ST
GLYN ST
WALTER ST
CHARLES ST
STATION RD
ALFRED ST
WESTVILLE
Abertysswg Prim Sch
HEOL-Y-WAUN
DAN-Y-GRAIG
SOUTHEND TERR
Nant Tyswg
MCLAREN COTTS
Coed Cefn-rhychdir
Cefn Rhychdir
Mountain Lodge
Twyn yr Hyddod
Mynydd Bedwellte
NP22
Dyffryn Farm
Mount Pleasant
CF81
Y Graig
Y Darren
Sebastopol
Troedrhiwrfuwch Farm
CHAPEL RD
LAWRENCE TERR
HIGH ST
Rhymney River/Afon Rhymni
Derlwyn
Cefnrhychdir Uchaf
Cwm Syfiog
Mast
Troed-rhiw'r-fuwch
Twyn Cornicyll
Nant Syfiog
Bedlwyn
WOODLAND TERR
Rising Sun Inn (PH)
NP24
Craig Rhymney Farm
Craig Rhymni
Rhymney Valley
Parc Cwm Darran
Beacon
Coed Cefn-rhychdir
Cefnrhychdir
Phillip's Town
Sports Ctr
Rhymney Valley Ridgeway Footpath
Cefn y Brithdir
CEFN Y MYNYDD 1
UPPER CROSS ST 2
LOWER CROSS ST 3
GREENWOOD CT 4
RAILWAY TERR
SCHOOL ST
A4049
A469
Tir-Phil
JAMES ST
PLEASANT VIEW
New Tredegar
1 BROOKLAND VIEW
2 GORSE TERR
Troed-y-rhiw Jestyn
Elliot's Town
WHITE ROSE WAY
Coed Deri-Newydd
Nant Bargod Rhymni
PH
OGILVIE TERR
HILLSIDE TERR
Cemy
BRYNHYFRYD VILLAS 1
PHILLIPS ST 2
TANLAN SQ 3
Dan-y-Craig
Craig Ysgwydd-gwyn
Mast
WOODLAND RISE
BAILEY ST
CWM DARRAN PL
Tyr-capel
MILTON TERR 1
TENNYSON TERR 2
NELSON TERR 3
WELLINGTON TERR 4
Cefn Bach Farm
GLYN DERW
DERI-NEWYDD
12
13
14
05
04
03
02
57
34

33
14

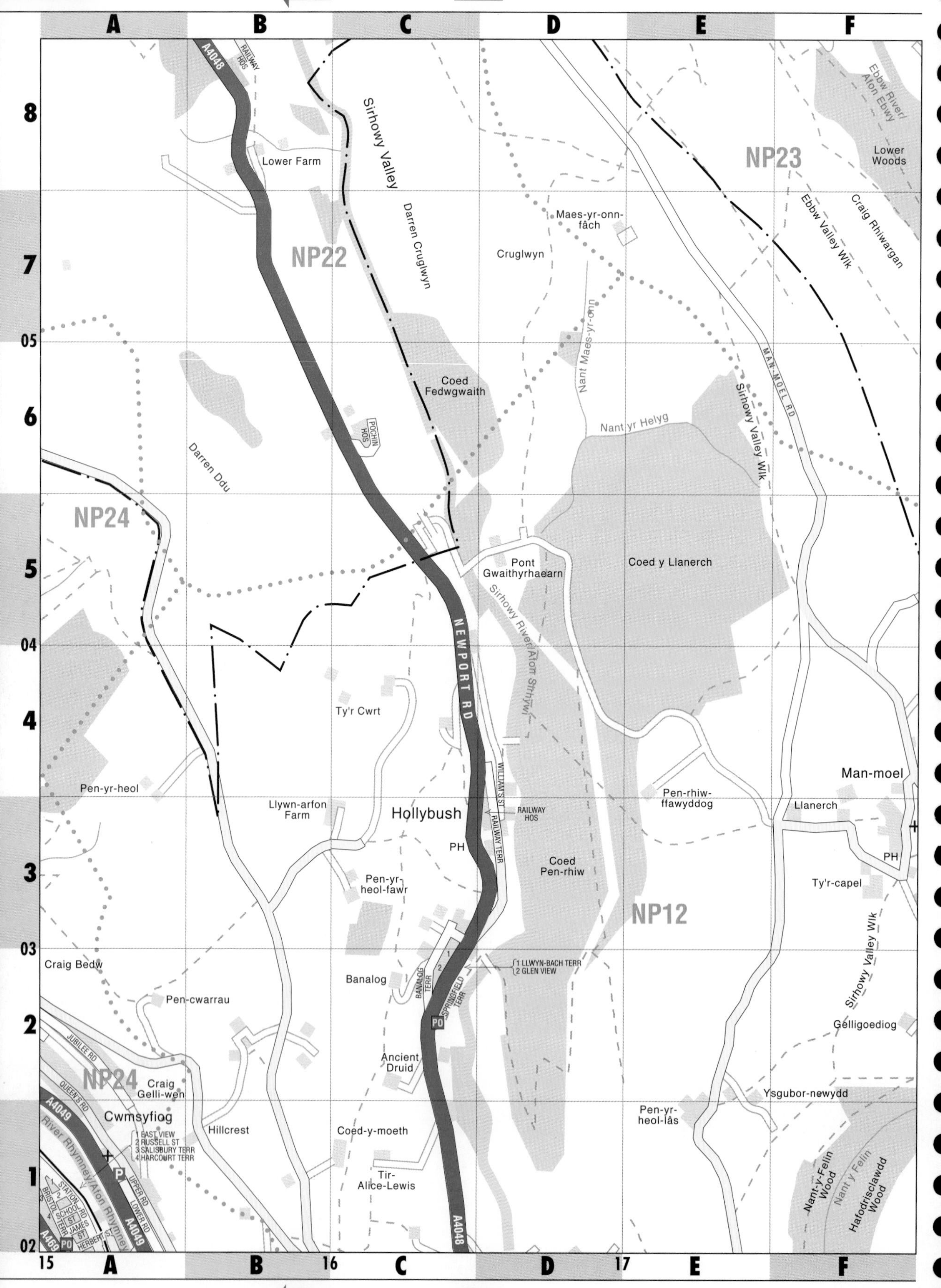
A4048
Lower Farm
Sirhowy Valley
Darren Cruglwyn
NP22
Maes-yr-onn-fâch
Cruglwyn
NP23
Lower Woods
Ebbw River/Afon Ebwy
Ebbw Valley Wlk
Craig Rhiwargan
Coed Fedwgwaith
Nant Maes-yr-onn
Nant yr Helyg
Sirhowy Valley Wlk
MAN-MOEL RD
Darren Ddu
NP24
Pont Gwaithyrhaearn
Coed y Llanerch
NEWPORT RD
Sirhowy River/Afon Sirhywi
Ty'r Cwrt
Pen-yr-heol
Llwyn-arfon Farm
Hollybush
WILLIAM ST
RAILWAY HOS
RAILWAY TERR
Pen-rhiw-ffawyddog
Llanerch
Man-moel
PH
Coed Pen-rhiw
Pen-yr-heol-fawr
Ty'r-capel
NP12
Craig Bedw
1 LLWYN-BACH TERR
2 GLEN VIEW
Banalog
BANALOG TERR
SPRINGFIELD TERR
Pen-cwarrau
Gelligoediog
PO
JUBILEE RD
Ancient Druid
NP24
Craig Gelli-wen
QUEEN'S RD
Ysgubor-newydd
Cwmsyfiog
Hillcrest
Coed-y-moeth
Pen-yr-heol-lâs
1 EAST VIEW
2 RUSSELL ST
3 SALISBURY TERR
4 HARCOURT TERR
River Rhymney/Afon Rhymni
A4049
UPPER RD
LOWER RD
STATION RD
BRISTOL TERR
SCHOOL ST
JAMES ST
HERBERT ST
A469
Tir-Alice-Lewis
Nant-y-Felin Wood
Nant y Felin
Hafodrisclawdd Wood
A B C D E F
8 7 05 6 5 04 4 3 03 2 1 02
15 16 17

33
58

15
36

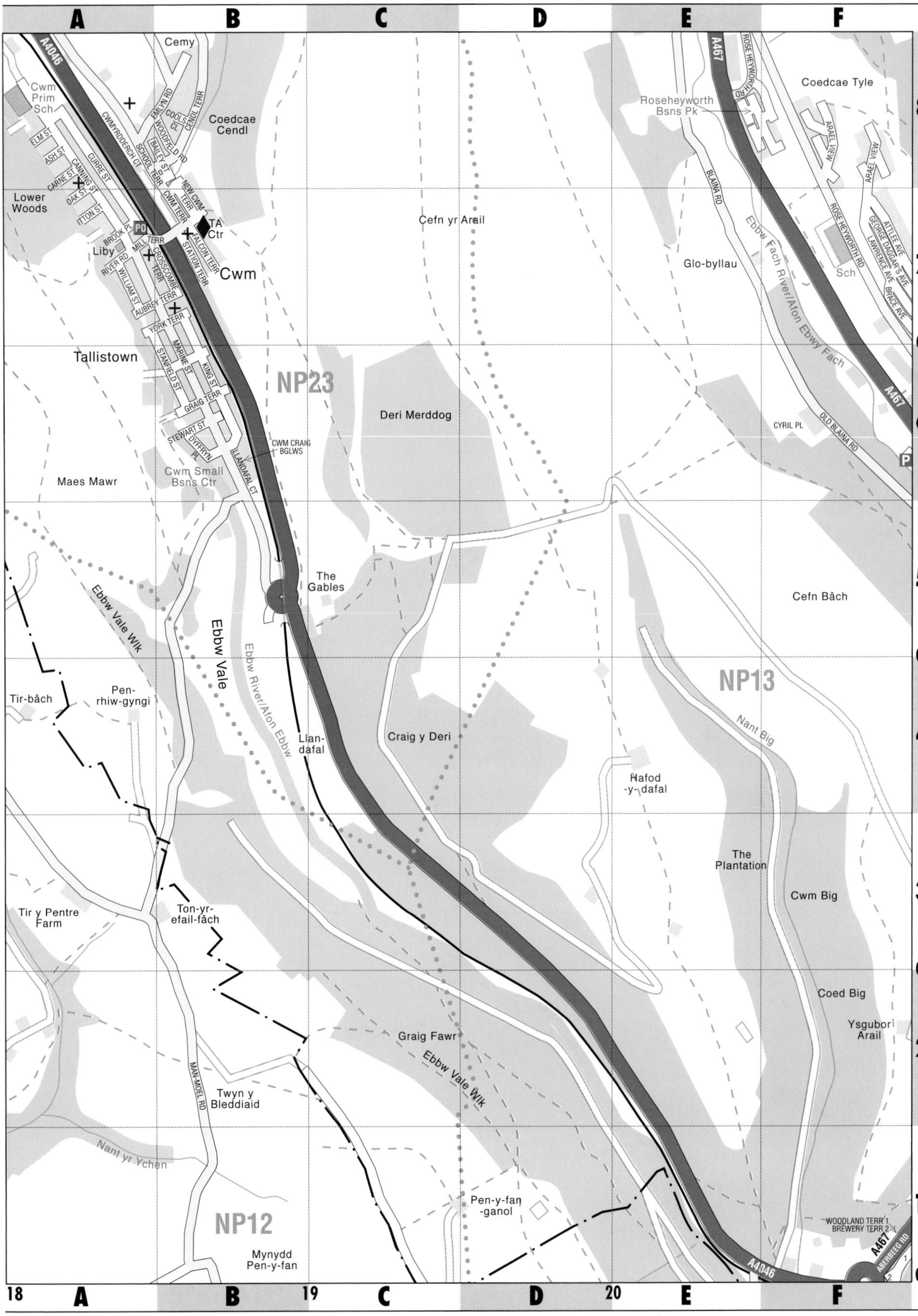

A B C D E F

Cemy
A4046
Cwm Prim Sch
Coedcae Cendl
EMLYN RD
COOLS CL
CENDL TERR
WOODFIELD RD
BAILEY ST
SCHOOL TERR
CWMYRDDERCH CT
ELM ST
ASH ST
CURRE ST
CARNE ST
CANNING ST
OAK ST
ITTON ST
Lower Woods
NEW CWM TERR
CWM TERR
PO
TA Ctr
BROOK PL
MILL TERR
FALCON TERR
STATION TERR
Liby
RIVER RD
CROSSCOMBE TERR
Cwm
WILLIAM ST
AUBREY TERR
YORK TERR
Tallistown
MARINE ST
KING ST
STANFIELD ST
GRAIG TERR
STEWART ST
DYFFRYN PL
LLANDAFAL CT
CWM CRAIG BGLWS
Cwm Small Bsns Ctr
Maes Mawr
NP23
Cefn yr Arail
Deri Merddog
The Gables
Ebbw Vale Wlk
Ebbw Vale
Ebbw River/Afon Ebbw
Tir-bâch
Pen-rhiw-gyngi
Llan-dafal
Craig y Deri
Ton-yr-efail-fâch
Tir y Pentre Farm
Graig Fawr
Ebbw Vale Wlk
MAN-MOEL RD
Twyn y Bleddiaid
Nant yr Ychen
NP12
Mynydd Pen-y-fan
Pen-y-fan -ganol
A467
ROSE HEYWORTH RD
Roseheyworth Bsns Pk
Coedcae Tyle
ARAEL VIEW
ARAEL VIEW
BLAINA RD
Ebbw Fach River/Afon Ebwy Fach
ROSE HEYWORTH RD
ATTLEE AVE
GEORGE DAGGAR'S AVE
LAWRENCE AVE
BRACE AVE
Sch
Glo-byllau
A467
CYRIL PL
OLD BLAINA RD
P
Cefn Bâch
NP13
Nant Big
Hafod -y- dafal
The Plantation
Cwm Big
Coed Big
Ysgubor Arail
WOODLAND TERR 1
BREWERY TERR 2
A467
ABERBEEG RD
A4046

8 7 05 6 5 04 4 3 03 2 1 02

18 A B 19 C D 20 E F

59
36

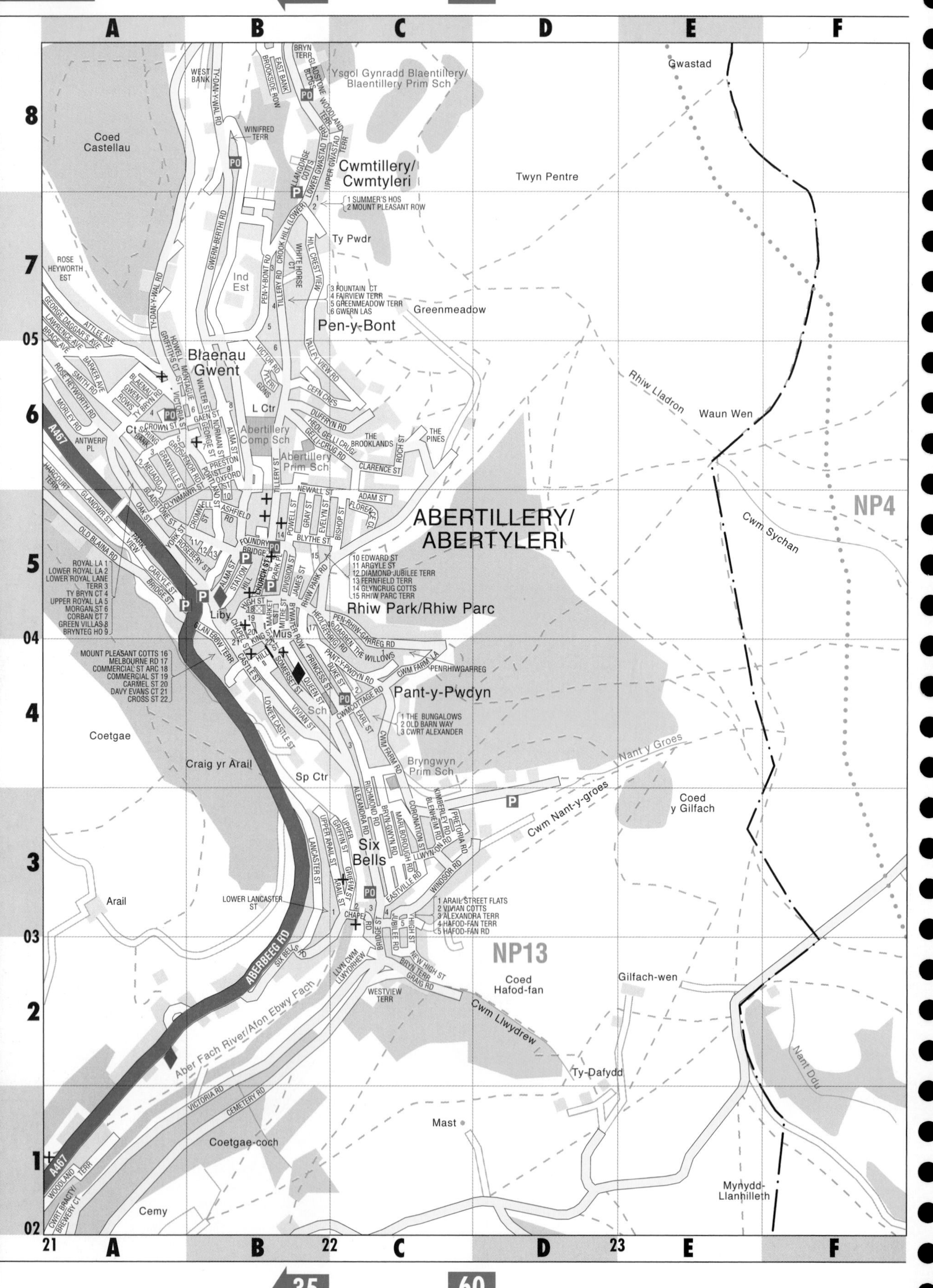
ABERTILLERY/
ABERTYLERI
Blaenau
Gwent
Cwmtillery/
Cwmtyleri
Pen-y-Bont
Rhiw Park/Rhiw Parc
Pant-y-Pwdyn
Six
Bells
Coed
Castellau
Twyn Pentre
Gwastad
Ty Pwdr
Greenmeadow
Rhiw Lladron
Waun Wen
Cwm Sychan
NP4
NP13
Coetgae
Craig yr Arail
Arail
Coed
y Gilfach
Coed
Hafod-fan
Cwm Llwydrew
Gilfach-wen
Ty-Dafydd
Mast
Coetgae-coch
Cemy
Mynydd-
Llanhilleth
Nant Ddu
Aber Fach River/Afon Ebwy Fach
Cwm Nant-y-groes
Nant y Groes
ABERBEEG RD
A467
Ysgol Gynradd Blaentillery/
Blaentillery Prim Sch
Abertillery
Comp Sch
Abertillery
Prim Sch
Bryngwyn
Prim Sch
Ind
Est
L Ctr
Liby
Mus
Sch
Sp Ctr
1 SUMMER'S HOS
2 MOUNT PLEASANT ROW
3 FOUNTAIN CT
4 FAIRVIEW TERR
5 GREENMEADOW TERR
6 GWERN LAS
10 EDWARD ST
11 ARGYLE ST
12 DIAMOND JUBILEE TERR
13 FERNFIELD TERR
14 GLYNCRUG COTTS
15 RHIW PARC TERR
ROYAL LA 1
LOWER ROYAL LA 2
LOWER ROYAL LANE TERR 3
TY BRYN CT 4
UPPER ROYAL LA 5
MORGAN ST 6
CORBAN CT 7
GREEN VILLAS 8
BRYNTEG HO 9
MOUNT PLEASANT COTTS 16
MELBOURNE RD 17
COMMERCIAL ST ARC 18
COMMERCIAL ST 19
CARMEL ST 20
DAVY EVANS CT 21
CROSS ST 22
1 THE BUNGALOWS
2 OLD BARN WAY
3 CWRT ALEXANDER
1 ARAIL STREET FLATS
2 VIVIAN COTTS
3 ALEXANDRA TERR
4 HAFOD-FAN TERR
5 HAFOD-FAN RD
A B C D E F
8 7 6 5 4 3 2 1
05 04 03 02
21 22 23

Craig-ddu Wood
Cwmavon
Rose Cotts
Snail Creep Terr/ Teras Llsyg Falwen
A4043
B4246
Shop Rd
8
Twyn Du
Varteg Waste
Ysgol Bryn Onnen
Heol Varteg/Varteg Rd
Gladstone Terr
Rhodfa Samson/ Samson's Ave
Greenfield Terr
Craig Wen
Balance Mdws
Cilgant Gwyn Cres
Cwmavon Rd
Rock Villa
Rock Villa Cl
Balance Rd
7
Carnau British Wood
Cwm Ffrwd
Blaengaefog Brook
The Bungalows
Trem Craigddu/ Craigddu View 1
Trem y Goedlan/ Woodland View 2
Heol Newydd/New Rd
Heol Pen-y-lan
Heol Is Ty Gwyn/ Lower Ty Gwyn Rd
Rhos-r-Gwyn
Pen-y-lan Wood
A4043
05
Herbert's Cl
Herbert's Rd
Butler's Ct
Ty'r-beili Wood
Hillcrest
Severn View
Emlyn Rd
Bethel Ct
Stryd Bailey/Bailey St
Lewis Cl
The Avenue
Gelli Rhwy Rd
6
Garndiffaith
Garnteg Prim Sch
Top Rd
Stanley Rd
Cross St
Neville St
Ty'r-beili Farm
Golynos Waste
Teras Trem y Graig/ Craig View Terr
Bailey Cres 1
Empire Terr 2
Chapel Cl 3
Earl Cl 4
High St
Earl St
Green Way
Golynos
New Rd
Emlyn Terr
Clos Pisgah/ Pisgah Cl
Pisgah Rd
Heol Albert/ Albert Rd
Castle Wood
3 Sid Griffiths Ct
4 Griffiths Way
Jubilee Pl 1
Victoria Pl 2
Talywain Ho
Lower Stoney Rd
Heol Harper
Harper's Rd
Bryn Garreg
Winstone Cotts
Lhynam Pl
Stony Rd
5
Cwm Sychan
Cwm Sychan Brook
Farm Rd
Commercial Rd
Commercial Cl
Ambleside
Fairview Terr
Viaduct Rd
Bluetts La
Vicarage
Hillrise
Co-operative Terr 1
The Woodlands 2
Bluetts Cl
St Thomas Cl
Talywain
Victoria Village
Victoria Rd
Sch
04
School La
NP4
Waterloo
Heol Waun
Waterloo Pl
Works
Coed Terr
Coronation Terr
Saxons Hos
Manor Way
Incline Rd
L Ctr
British
British Rd
Raglan Cl
Heol Waterloo/Waterloo Rd
Fairfield
Gordon Rd
Wellington Rd
Ffordd Wellington/Wellington Rd
Heol yr Eglwys/Church Rd
British School Cl
Picton Rd
Prospect Place
Abersychan Comp Sch
Pleasant View
4
Mount Pleasant
Heol y Plas/Manor Rd
Lewis St
Glansychan La
Glansychan Hos
Byrgwm
The Barracks
St Francis RC Prim Sch
Brynteg
Ffrwd Rd
Lodge Rd
Chy
Elizabeth Row/ Rhes Elizabeth
Pant-Glas
Maes Dyfnaint/ Devon Pl
The Promenade
Foundry Rd
Cleeves Terr
Exeter Pl
High St/Stryd Fawr
Stryd yr Undeb/Union St
Liby
Station St
Broad St
Abersychan
Neath Villas
Pentwyn Prim Sch
B4246
Lon y Gelli/ Lock-up La 1
Old Rd 2
Pentwyn Hts
Caradoc St
Acorn Cl
Pentwyn La
Oaks Cl
North Rd
3
A4043
Pen-twyn
03
Pant-glâs Slip
Red Lion Flats 3
Bell La 4
Lethbridge Terr 5
Severn View Terr 6
Pentwyn Terr 7
Heol Pentwyn/Pentwyn Rd
Snatchwood Terr 1
Holyoake Terr 2
Owendale Terr 3
Oaks Rd
Club Row
Snatchwood Rd
Snatchwood
2
Cooper's Hos
Coedlan-y-West End/ West End Ave
Brynhyfryd
Snatchwood Ct
A4043
Freehold Land
Charlesville
NP13
Pistyll-gwyn
1
Cwm Du
Pentre-Piod/ Pentrepiod
Pentrepiod Rd
Maes Prospect/ Prospect Pl
Highfield Cl
Lodge View
Lewis Wood
Tan-y-Coed Grove
Gypsy La
02

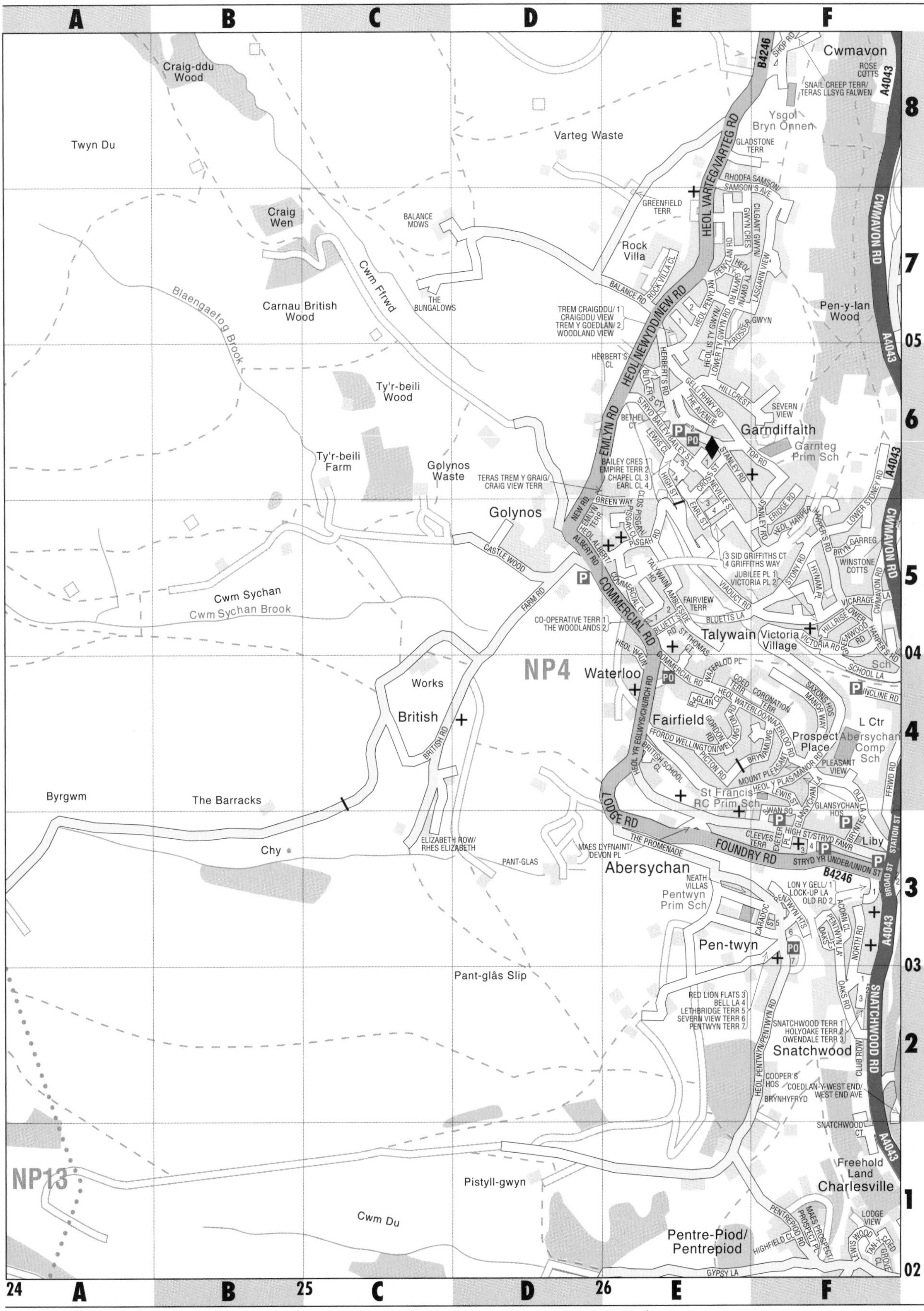

37

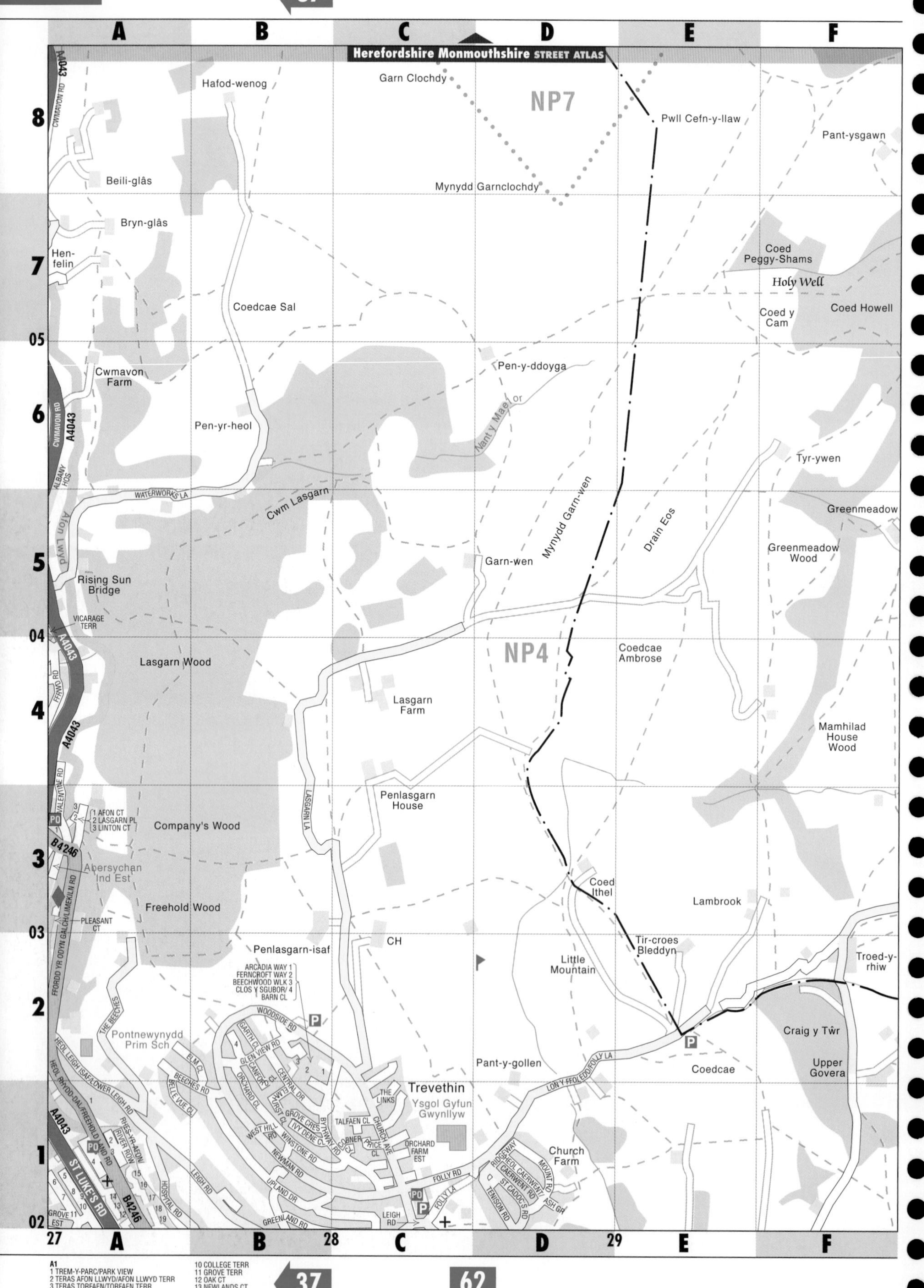

37
62

A1
1 TREM-Y-PARC/PARK VIEW
2 TERAS AFON LLWYD/AFON LLWYD TERR
3 TERAS TORFAEN/TORFAEN TERR
4 DOL BEIRIANT/MACHINE MDW
5 MITCHELL TERR
6 ROCHDALE TERR
7 PARK TERR
8 CHURCH TERR
9 GROVESIDE VILLAS
10 COLLEGE TERR
11 GROVE TERR
12 OAK CT
13 NEWLANDS CT
14 BELLE VIEW CT
15 BELGRAVE CT
16 CAPEL CT
17 WEST BANK CT
18 HARDY CT
19 PARKSIDE CT

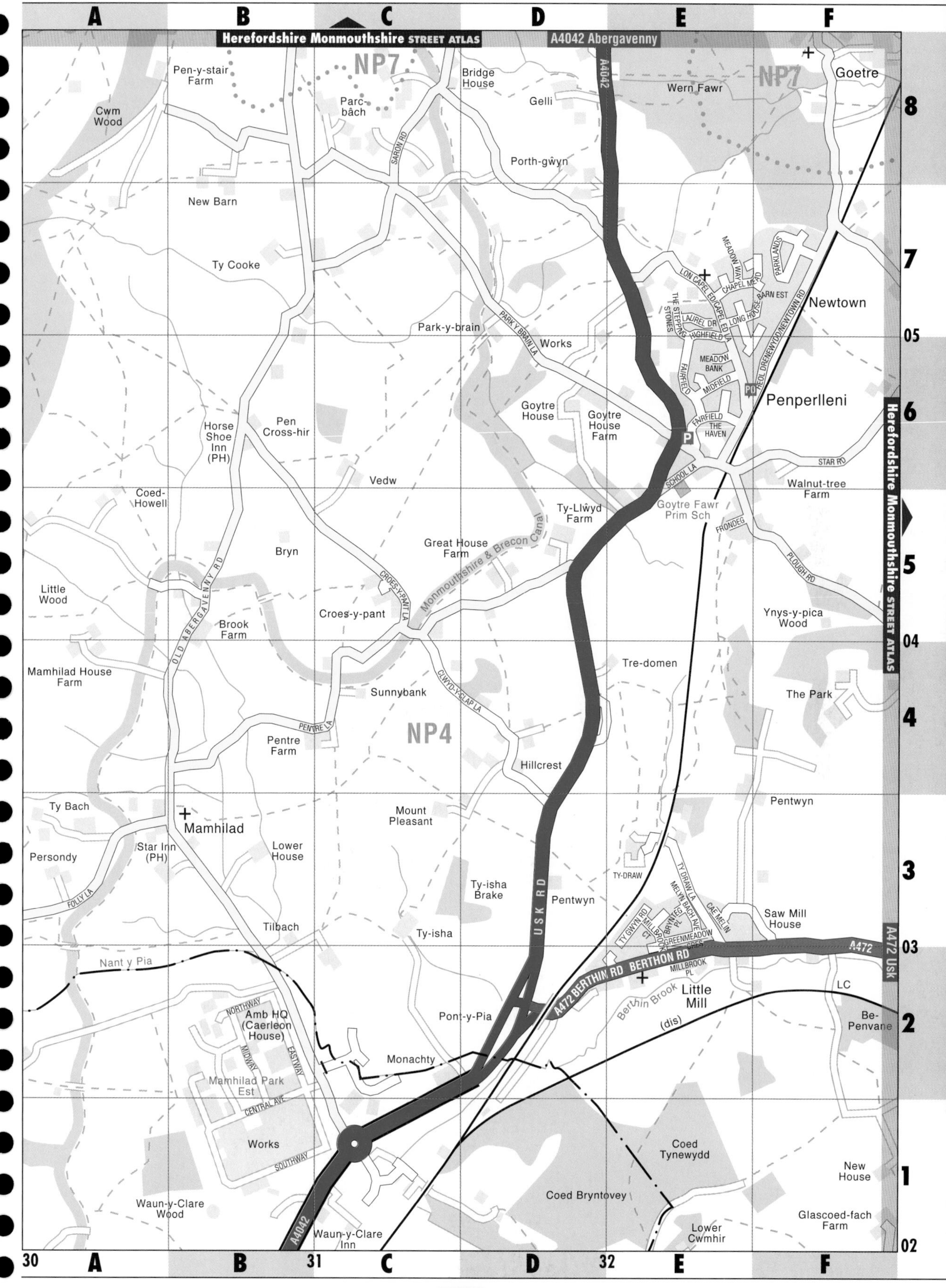
Herefordshire Monmouthshire STREET ATLAS
A4042 Abergavenny
NP7
Pen-y-stair Farm
Cwm Wood
Parc bâch
Bridge House
Gelli
Wern Fawr
Goetre
Porth-gŵyn
New Barn
Ty Cooke
Newtown
Park-y-brain
Works
Penperlleni
Goytre House
Goytre House Farm
Horse Shoe Inn (PH)
Pen Cross-hir
Vedw
Walnut-tree Farm
Coed-Howell
Ty-Llŵyd Farm
Goytre Fawr Prim Sch
Bryn
Great House Farm
Monmouthshire & Brecon Canal
Little Wood
Brook Farm
Croes-y-pant
Ynys-y-pica Wood
Mamhilad House Farm
Tre-domen
Sunnybank
The Park
NP4
Pentre Farm
Hillcrest
Ty Bach
Mamhilad
Mount Pleasant
Pentwyn
Persondy
Star Inn (PH)
Lower House
Ty-isha Brake
Pentwyn
Saw Mill House
Tilbach
Ty-isha
Nant y Pia
Little Mill
Amb HQ (Caerleon House)
Pont-y-Pia
Be-Penvane
Monachty
Mamhilad Park Est
Works
Coed Tynewydd
Coed Bryntovey
New House
Waun-y-Clare Wood
Waun-y-Clare Inn
Lower Cwmhir
Glascoed-fach Farm
A4042
A472 BERTHIN RD
BERTHON RD
USK RD
OLD ABERGAVENNY RD
A472 Usk

C7
1 THE LOWER DELL
2 CWM TERR
3 STRADEY CT
4 LUTON TERR

D5
1 ARCADE
2 FREDERICK ST
3 STEPNEY ST
4 STEPNEY PREC
5 UPPER PARK ST
6 PARK EYNON
7 STRYD Y CROCHENDY/POTTERY ST
8 COWELL PREC
9 UPPER INKERMAN ST
10 RICHARD ST
11 UPPER ROBINSON ST
12 COLUMBIA ROW
13 CROWN PREC
14 PUGH BLDGS
15 LLYS CAEGLAS

D6
1 COBBLERS CT
2 MOUNT PLEASANT BLDGS
3 SWANFIELD PL
4 FALCON CHAMBERS
5 LLYS YR HEN FELIN

E5
1 UPPER WILLIAM ST
2 LAWRENCE TERR
3 DAVIES SQ
4 CWRT ELUSENDY
5 PLEASANT ROW

E6
1 CAE-DU-BACH
2 FRANSHAM ST
3 CLOS ANDREAS

F6
1 BRADFORD ST
2 CLIFTON TERR
3 BOX TERR
4 LLYS PENALLT

A476 Cross Hands, Llandeilo

A484 Burry Port, Kidwelly

Pentre-Iago, Stradey Wood, Stradey Castle, Pen-y-fai, Furnace, Furnace Prim Sch, Ysgol Gyfun Y Strade, Stradey Pk Llanelli Scarlets RUFC, Sandy, Sandy Water Park, Millennium Coastal Park, Breakwater, Millennium Quay, North Dock, Discovery Ctr, Cefn Padrig, The Flats, Seaside, Craig Wen, Pentre-Poeth, Parc Howard, Parc Howard Mus & Art Gall, Cemy Mount Pleasant, SA15, Tyrfran, Llanerch, Ysgol Heol Goffa, Ysgol Gymraeg Dewi Sant, SA14, Pen-y-Gaer-Isaf, Box, Penallt, Marble Hall, Coedcae Comp Sch, Bigyn, Wern, Pen-y-Fan, Ty-Isaf, Llanelli, Works, Morfa, Morfa CP Jun Mix Sch, Trostre Ind Pk, Llanelli Ent Workshops, Millennium Coastal Park, Machynys, Machynys Peninsular Golf Club

CWRT MYRDDIN 1
CWRT PANDORA 2
CWRT AFON LLIEDI 3
PENTRE DOC Y GOGLEDD 4
CWRT CAMBRIA 5
CWRT NAIAD 6
CWRT CLARA NOVELLO 7

F4
1 BRYCHAN
2 PYNTWS TERR
3 LLWYNWHILWG TERR

1 GLANDAFEN RD
2 RHES GWAITH TYN
3 HAFAN-Y-MORFA

49 A B 50 C D 51 E F

C3
1 BRYN TERR
2 LLYS GLAN Y MOR
3 CAROLINE ST
4 LLYSNEWYDD

C4
1 ST PETERS TERR
2 GLANMOR TERR
3 GLANMOR PL
4 SEASIDE CRES
5 CAMBRIAN PL
6 BRYN PL
7 LLYS YR ORSAF
8 FFORDD Y WAGEN/RAILWAY PL
9 RHES YR ORSAF/RAILWAY TERR

229

D3
1 GREAT WESTERN TERR
2 TERAS CAERSALEM/CAERSALEM TERR
3 CINEMA BLDGS
4 STANLEY RD
5 PRESWYLFA ROW

D4
1 LAKEFIELD CL
2 CWRT NEVILLE
3 CWRT WADDL
4 HAFAN
5 CLOS SANT PEDR
6 TY ELIZABETH
7 TY HOWARD
8 TY MERIEL
9 TY STAFFORD
10 TY CYDWEL
11 GATHEN TERR
12 FFORDD DELABECHE/DELABECHE ST
13 STRYD EMMA/EMMA ST
14 STRYD LLEWELLYN/LLEWELLYN ST
15 HEOL MANSEL/MANSEL ST

42

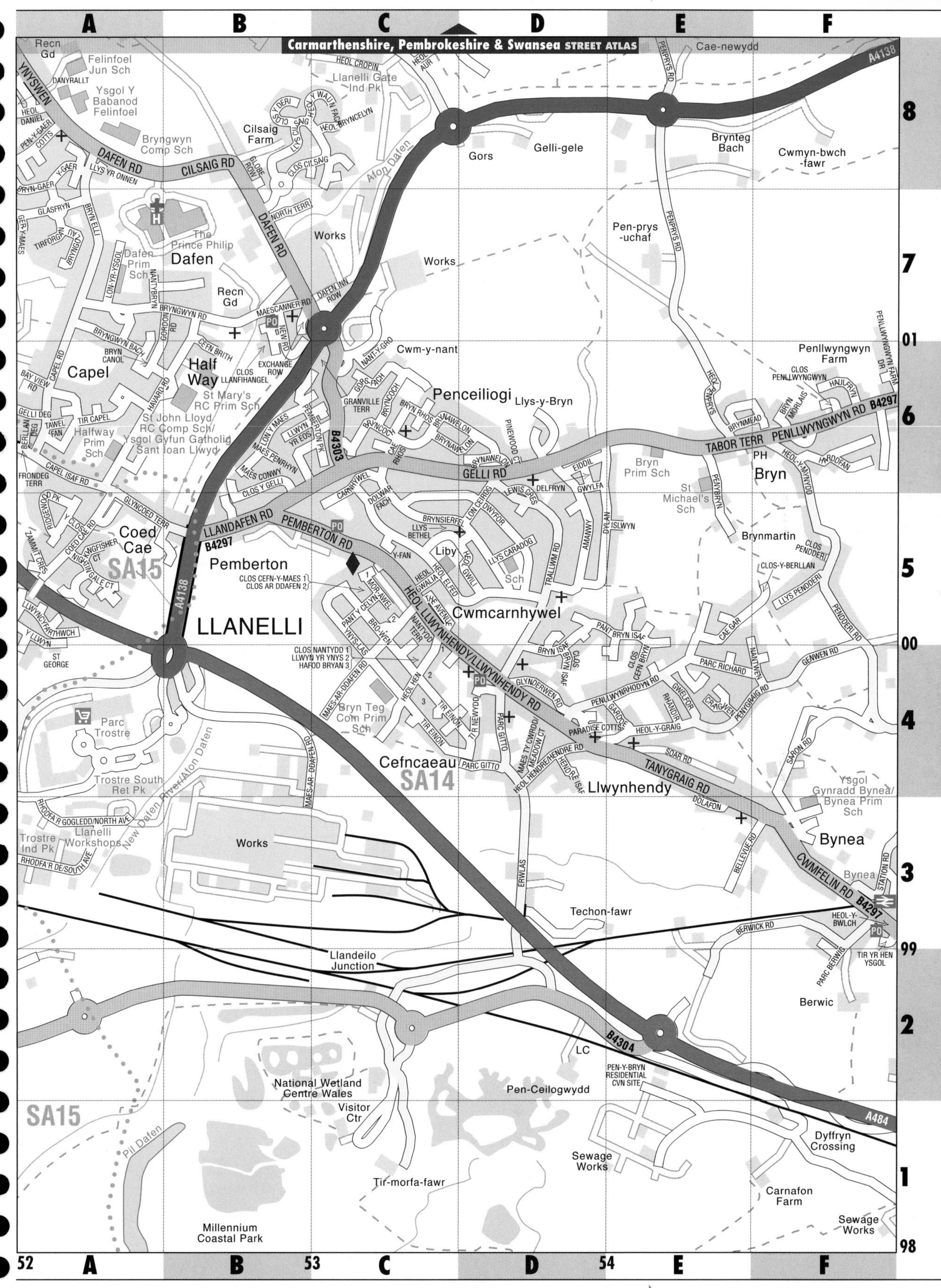

A
B
C
D
E
F
Carmarthenshire, Pembrokeshire & Swansea STREET ATLAS
Recn Gd
Felinfoel Jun Sch
DANYRALLT
Ysgol Y Babanod Felinfoel
Bryngwyn Comp Sch
YNYSWEN
HEOL DANIEL
PEN-Y-GAER COTTS
DAFEN RD
CILSAIG RD
LLYS YR ONNEN
Y-GAER
BRYN-GAER
GLASFRYN
GER-Y-MAES
TIRFORGAN
BRYN ELLI
Cilsaig Farm
HEOL CROPIN
Llanelli Gate Ind Pk
HEOL AUR
HEOL-BRYNCELYN
CLOS CILSAIG
Afon Dafen
NORTH TERR
GLOBE ROW
The Prince Philip
Dafen Prim Sch
Dafen
LON-YR-YSGOL
NANTYBRYN
Recn Gd
Works
Works
DAFEN INN ROW
MAESCANNER RD
BRYNGWYN RD
BRYNGWYN BACH
GORDON RD
CEFN BRITH
NEW RD
CLOS LLANFIHANGEL
EXCHANGE ROW
BRYN CANOL
Capel
Half Way
CAPEL RD
BAY VIEW RD
HAVARD RD
St Mary's RC Prim Sch
St John Lloyd RC Comp Sch/ Ysgol Gyfun Gatholig Sant Ioan Llwyd
TIR CAPEL
GELLI DEG
TAWEL FAN
Halfway Prim Sch
FRONDEG TERR
CAPEL ISAF RD
GLYNCOED TERR
Coed Cae
SA15
Pemberton
A4138
LLANDAFEN RD
B4297
PEMBERTON RD
LLANELLI
ST GEORGE
Parc Trostre
Trostre South Ret Pk
New Dafen River/Afon Dafen
RHODFA'R GOGLEDD/NORTH AV
Trostre Ind Pk
Llanelli Workshops
RHODFA'R DE/SOUTH AVE
Works
Llandeilo Junction
National Wetland Centre Wales
Visitor Ctr
SA15
Pil Dafen
Millennium Coastal Park
Tir-morfa-fawr
Gors
Gelli-gele
Cwm-y-nant
NANT-Y-GRO
GRANVILLE TERR
BRYNCOCH
B4303
Penceiliogi
Llys-y-Bryn
PINEWOOD CT
GELLI RD
BRYNAWELON
DELFRYN
GWYLFA
EIDDIL
LEWIS CRES
LON CEIRIOG
DWYFOR
BRYNSIERFEL
LLYS BETHEL
Liby
LLYS CARADOG
Sch
TRALLWM RD
AMANWY
DYFAN
ISLWYN
HEOL LLWYNHENDY/LLWYNHENDY RD
Cwmcarnhywel
CLOS CEFN-Y-MAES 1
CLOS AR DDAFEN 2
CLOS NANTYDD 1
LLWYN YR YNYS 2
HAFOD BRYAN 3
MAES-AR-DDAFEN RD
Bryn Teg Com Prim Sch
TIR EINON
PARC GITTO
Cefncaeau
SA14
GLYNDERWEN RD
PARADISE COTTS
HEOL-Y-GRAIG
TANYGRAIG RD
SOAR RD
Llwynhendy
DOLAFON
ERWLAS
Techon-fawr
LC
B4304
PEN-Y-BRYN RESIDENTIAL CVN SITE
Pen-Ceilogwydd
Sewage Works
Cae-newydd
PENPRYS RD
A4138
Brynteg Bach
Cwmyn-bwch -fawr
Pen-prys -uchaf
Penllwyngwyn Farm
CLOS PENLLWYNGWYN
PENLLWYNGWYN FARM DR
TABOR TERR
PENLLWYNGWYN RD
B4297
PH
Bryn
Bryn Prim Sch
St Michael's Sch
Brynmartin
CLOS PENDDERI
CLOS-Y-BERLLAN
LLYS PENDDERI
PENDDERI RD
PANT BRYN ISAF
CAE GAR
PARC RICHARD
GENWEN RD
PENLLWYNRHODYN RD
PENYGRAIG RD
SARON RD
Ysgol Gynradd Bynea/ Bynea Prim Sch
Bynea
BELLEVUE RD
CWMFELIN RD
Bynea
STATION RD
HEOL-Y-BWLCH
BERWICK RD
TIR YR HEN YSGOL
PARC BERWIG
Berwic
A484
Dyffryn Crossing
Carnafon Farm
Sewage Works
8
7
01
6
5
00
4
3
99
2
1
98
52
53
54

64

42

41
18

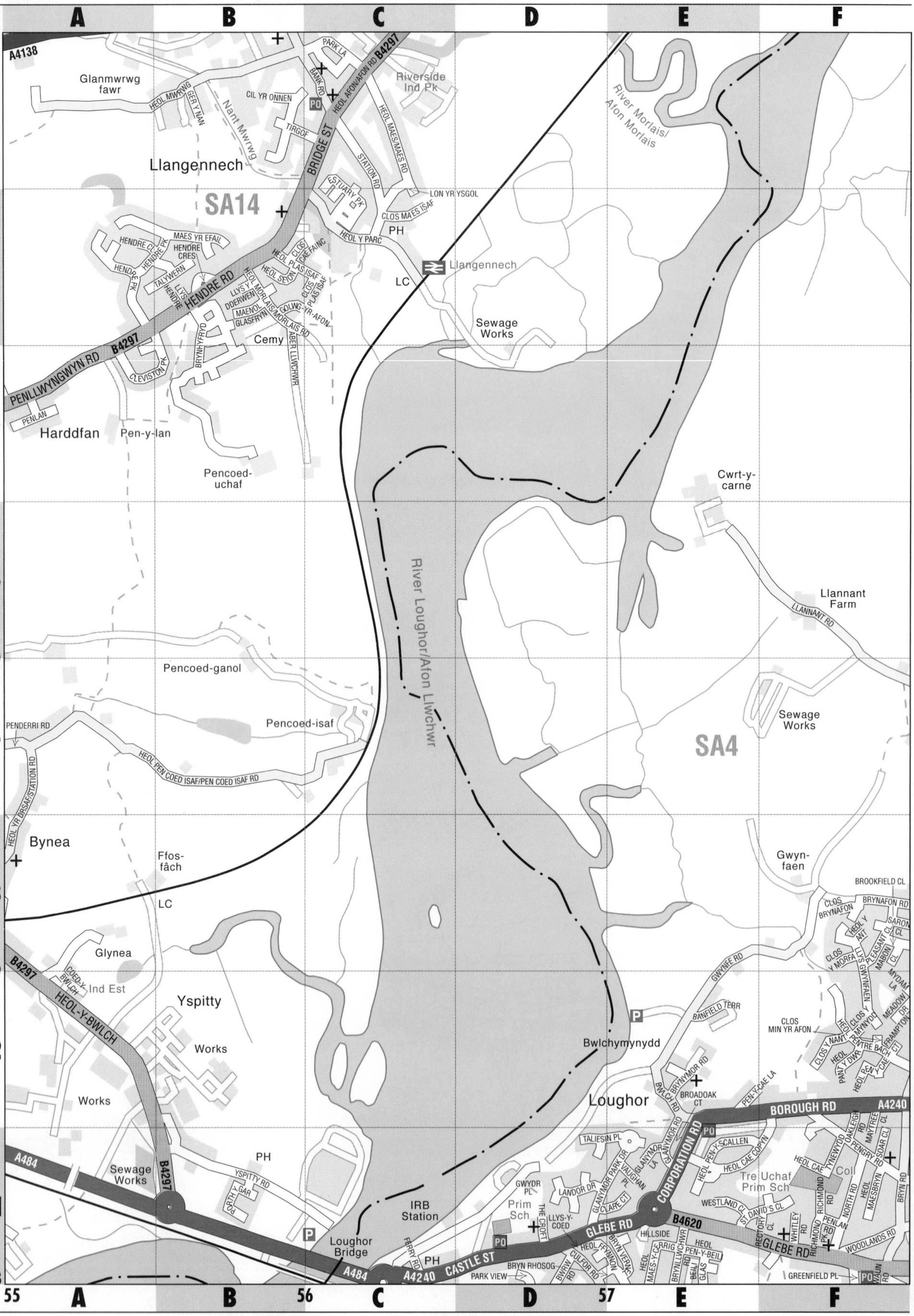

A B C D E F

8
7
01
6
5
00
4
3
99
2
1
98

Glanmwrwg fawr
Llangennech
SA14
Nant Mwrwg
Riverside Ind Pk
River Morlais/ Afon Morlais
Llangennech
LC
PH
Sewage Works
Cemy
Harddfan
Pen-y-lan
Pencoed-uchaf
Cwrt-y-carne
River Loughor/Afon Llwchwr
Llannant Farm
Pencoed-ganol
Pencoed-isaf
Sewage Works
SA4
Bynea
Ffos-fâch
LC
Gwyn-faen
Glynea
Ind Est
Ysplitty
Works
Works
Bwlchymynydd
Loughor
PH
Sewage Works
IRB Station
Loughor Bridge
PH
Prim Sch
Tre Uchaf Prim Sch
Coll

A4138
B4297
BRIDGE ST
HENDRE RD
PENLLWYNGWYN RD
PENDERRI RD
HEOL PEN COED ISAF/PEN COED ISAF RD
HEOL YR ORSAF/STATION RD
HEOL-Y-BWLCH
A484
A4240
CASTLE ST
GLEBE RD
B4620
CORPORATION RD
BOROUGH RD
LLANNANT RD

55 A B 56 C D 57 E F

41
65

19
44

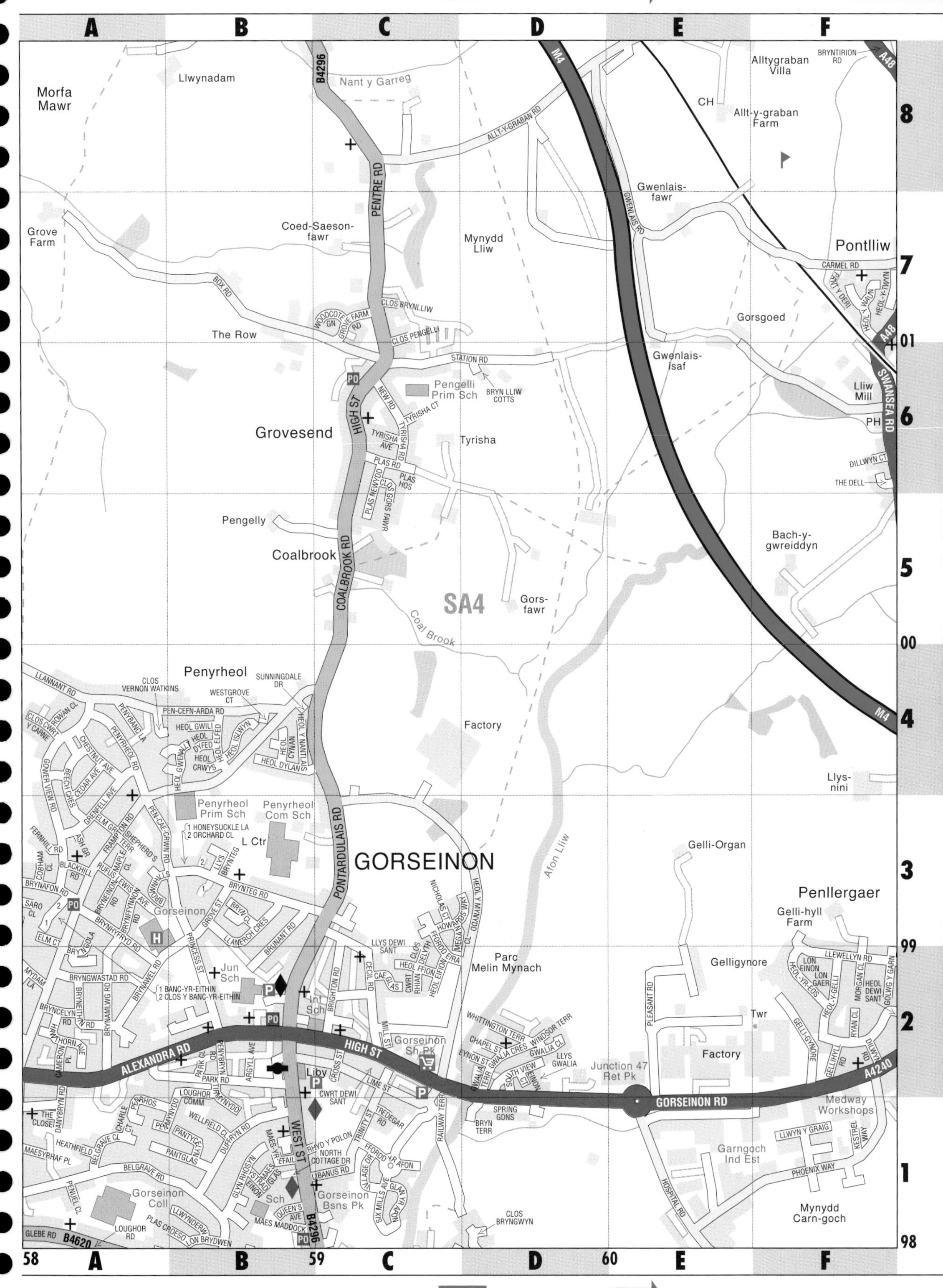
Morfa Mawr
Llwynadam
Nant y Garreg
Alltygraban Villa
Allt-y-graban Farm
Grove Farm
Coed-Saeson-fawr
Mynydd Lliw
Gwenlais-fawr
Pontlliw
The Row
Gorsgoed
Gwenlais-isaf
Pengelli Prim Sch
Lliw Mill
Grovesend
Tyrisha
Pengelly
Coalbrook
Bach-y-gwreiddyn
SA4
Gors-fawr
Coal Brook
Penyrheol
Factory
Llys-nini
Penyrheol Prim Sch
Penyrheol Com Sch
L Ctr
GORSEINON
Gelli-Organ
Penllergaer
Gelli-hyll Farm
Gorseinon
Parc Melin Mynach
Gelligynore
Jun Sch
Inf Sch
Twr
Gorseinon Sh Pk
Factory
Liby
Junction 47 Ret Pk
Medway Workshops
Garngoch Ind Est
Gorseinon Coll
Gorseinon Bsns Pk
Sch
Mynydd Carn-goch
M4
A48
B4296
A4240
B4620
PENTRE RD
HIGH ST
COALBROOK RD
PONTARDULAIS RD
WEST ST
ALEXANDRA RD
GORSEINON RD
SWANSEA RD
ALLT-Y-GRABAN RD
GWENLAIS RD
BOX RD
STATION RD
HOSPITAL RD
PLEASANT RD
Afon Lliw
A B C D E F
58 59 60
8 7 01 6 5 00 4 3 99 2 1 98

66
44

43
20

Gwenlais-fâch
Nant y Crimp
Gwenlais-uchaf
Clordir
Pontlliw Prim Sch
Aber-gwenlais
Glan-lliw-uchaf
Pontlliw
Brynawel
Fforest-newydd
Coed-cae-croes
Glan-Lliw
Penllergaer Forest
Pen-y-waun
Cefnfforest-fawr
SA4
Craig Tyle-du
SA5
The Poplars
Tircoed
Llwyn-y-beech Covert
Coed-Tremig
Green Plantation
Ty'rheol
Motel
Tredegar-fawr
Pen-deri-fawr
Swansea West Service Area
Penllergaer Forest Walks
Afon Llan
Melin -llan
Tir-ffordd
Cwm Tir-fford Wood
Penllergaer Prim Sch
Coedwig-Hywel
C Ctr
Penllergaer Bsns Pk
Cil-fwnwr
PH
Penllergaer
Parc Penllergaer
Valley Wood
Parc-mawr
Gelli-aur
Clawdd-y-duon Wood
Y Bwthyn
SA5
SWANSEA RD
PONTARDULAIS RD
GORSEINON RD
BRYNTIRION RD
M4
A48
A483
A4240

43
67

21
46

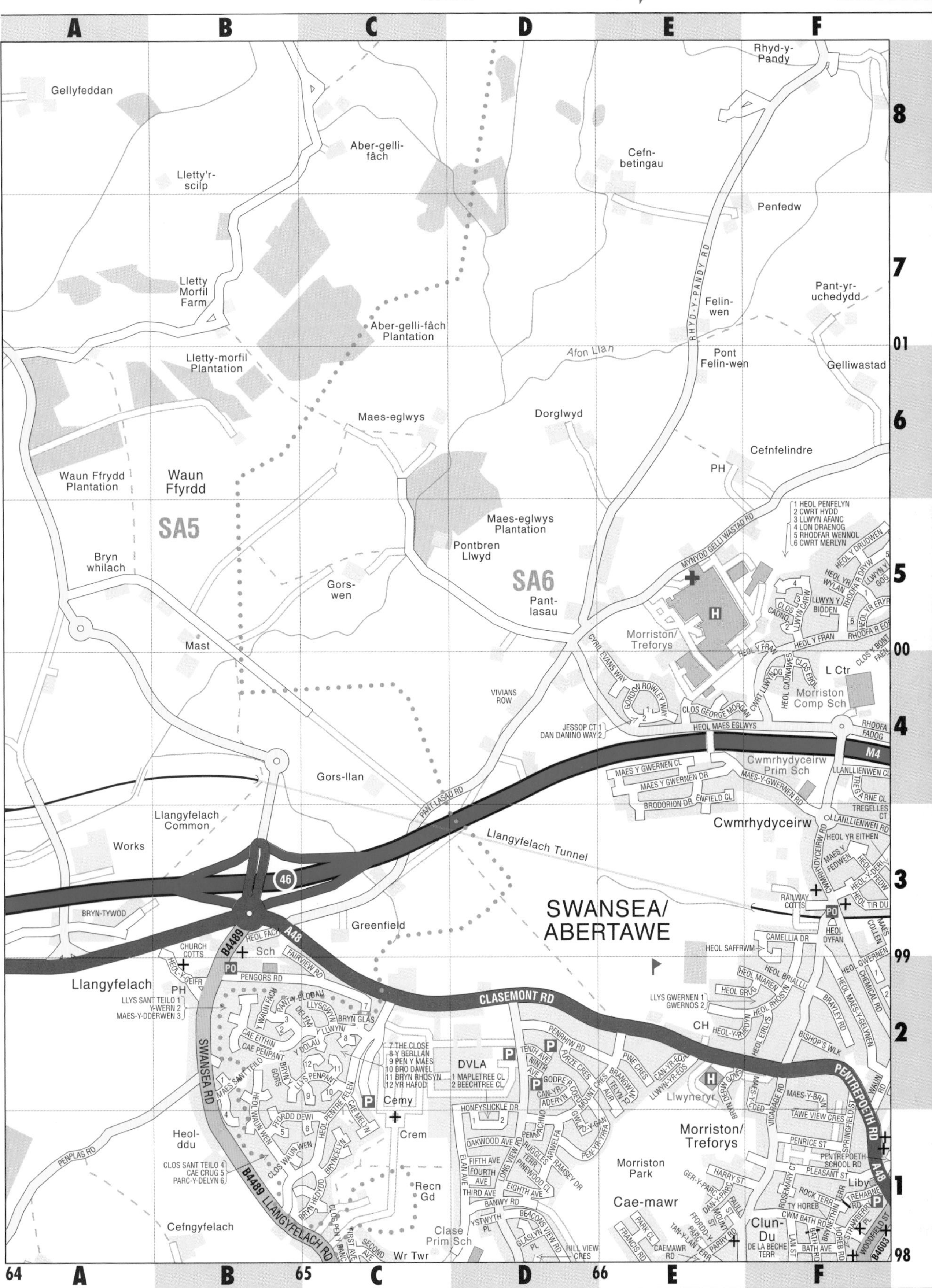
A B C D E F
8 7 01 6 5 00 4 3 99 2 1 98
64 65 66
Gellyfeddan
Aber-gelli-fâch
Lletty'r-scilp
Cefn-betingau
Rhyd-y-Pandy
Penfedw
Llety Morfil Farm
Aber-gelli-fâch Plantation
RHYD-Y-PANDY RD
Felin-wen
Pant-yr-uchedydd
Afon Llan
Pont Felin-wen
Gelliwastad
Lletty-morfil Plantation
Maes-eglwys
Dorglwyd
Cefnfelindre
PH
Waun Ffrydd Plantation
Waun Ffyrdd
SA5
Maes-eglwys Plantation
Pontbren Llwyd
SA6
Bryn whilach
Gors-wen
Pant-lasau
Morriston/Treforys
Mast
Mynydd Gelli Wastad Rd
1 HEOL PENFELYN
2 CWRT HYDD
3 LLWYN AFANC
4 LON DRAENOG
5 RHODFAR WENNOL
6 CWRT MERLYN
HEOL Y DRUDWEN
HEOL YR WYLAN
CLOS CADNO
LLWYN CARW
LLWYN Y BIODEN
HEOL Y FRAN
L Ctr
Morriston Comp Sch
CYRIL EVANS WAY
GORDON ROWLEY WAY
CLOS GEORGE MORGAN
CWRT LLWYNOG
HEOL CADNAWES
VIVIANS ROW
JESSOP CT 1
DAN DANINO WAY 2
HEOL MAES EGLWYS
RHODFA FADOG
M4
Gors-llan
MAES Y GWERNEN CL
MAES Y GWERNEN DR
BRODORION DR
ENFIELD CL
Cwmrhydyceirw Prim Sch
MAES-Y-GWERNEN RD
LLANLLIENWEN CL
TREGELLES CT
Cwmrhydyceirw
PANT-LASAU RD
Llangyfelach Common
Works
Llangyfelach Tunnel
HEOL YR EITHEN
46
SWANSEA/ABERTAWE
RAILWAY COTTS
PO
HEOL DYFAN
BRYN-TYWOD
Greenfield
A48
B4489
HEOL FACH
CHURCH COTTS
Sch
CAMELLIA DR
HEOL SAFFRWM
PENGORS RD
FAIRVIEW RD
Llangyfelach
PH
LLYS SANT TEILO 1
Y-WERN 2
MAES-Y-DDERWEN 3
CLASEMONT RD
HEOL BRIALLU
HEOL GRUG
LLYS GWERNEN 1
GWERNOS 2
CH
BISHOP'S WLK
SWANSEA RD
7 THE CLOSE
8 Y BERLLAN
9 PEN Y MAES
10 BRO DAWEL
11 BRYN RHOSYN
12 YR HAFOD
DVLA
1 MAPLETREE CL
2 BEECHTREE CL
Cemy
Crem
PENRHIW RD
FORZE CRES
PINE CRES
Llwyneryr
PENTREPOETH RD
HONEYSUCKLE DR
OAKWOOD AVE
Morriston/Treforys
Heol-ddu
CLOS SANT TEILO 4
CAE CRUG 5
PARC-Y-DELYN 6
PENPLAS RD
Recn Gd
FIFTH AVE
FOURTH AVE
THIRD AVE
ELAN AVE
LONG VIEW RD
EIGHTH AVE
RAMSEY DR
Morriston Park
HARRY ST
PENRICE ST
PENTREPOETH SCHOOL RD
PLEASANT ST
Liby
Cae-mawr
ROCK TERR
TY HOREB
CWM BATH RD
B4489 LLANGYFELACH RD
Cefngyfelach
Clase Prim Sch
BANWY RD
YSTWYTH PL
BEACONS VIEW RD
GLASLYN PL
HILL VIEW CRES
PARK CL
FRANCIS RD
CAEMAWR RD
Clun-Du
DE LA BECHE TERR
BATH AVE
Wr Twr
SECOND AVE
FIRST AVE
B4603

68
46

45
22

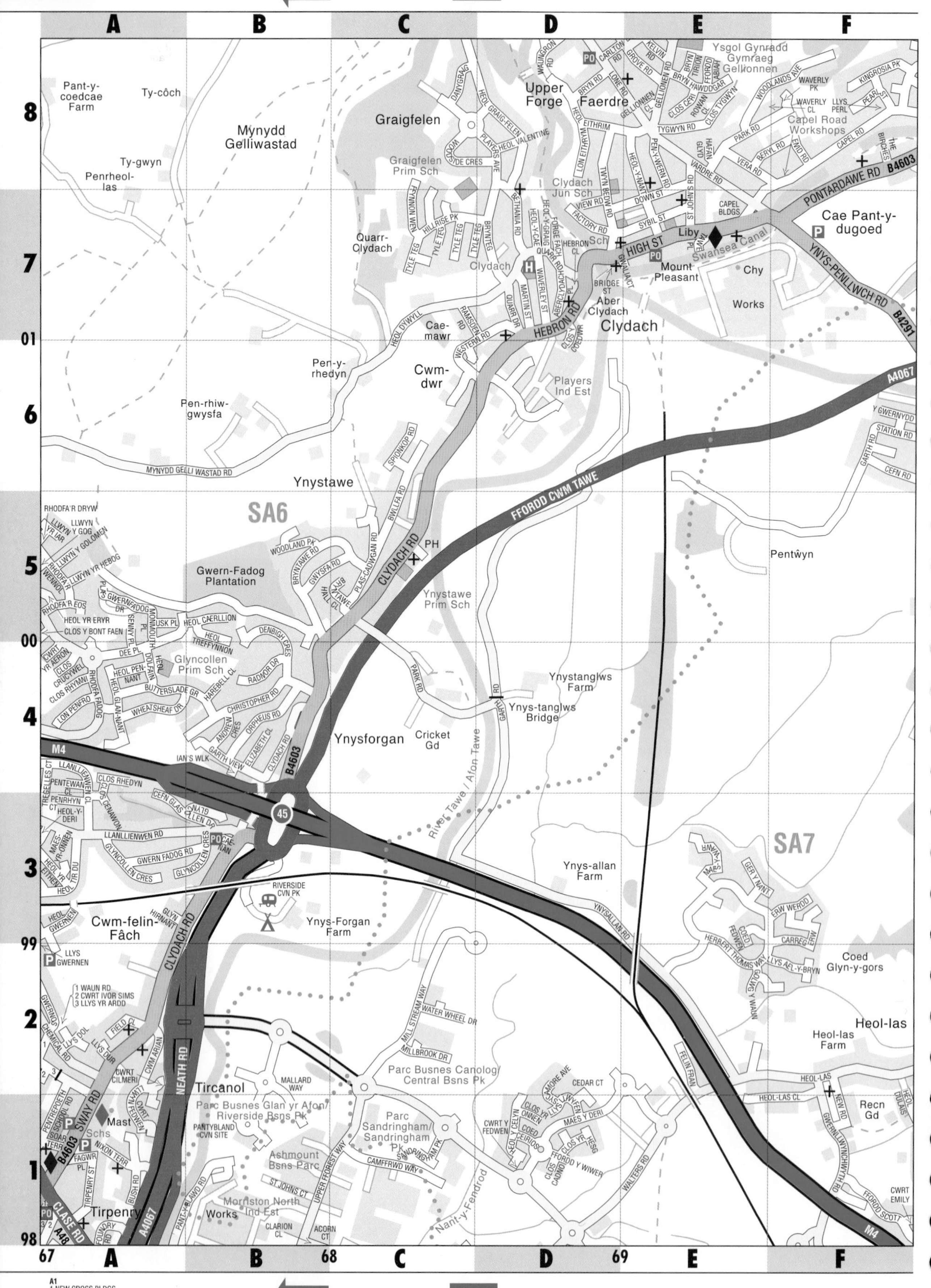

A1
1 NEW CROSS BLDGS
2 GLANTAWE ST
3 TY FFOREST

45
69

23
48

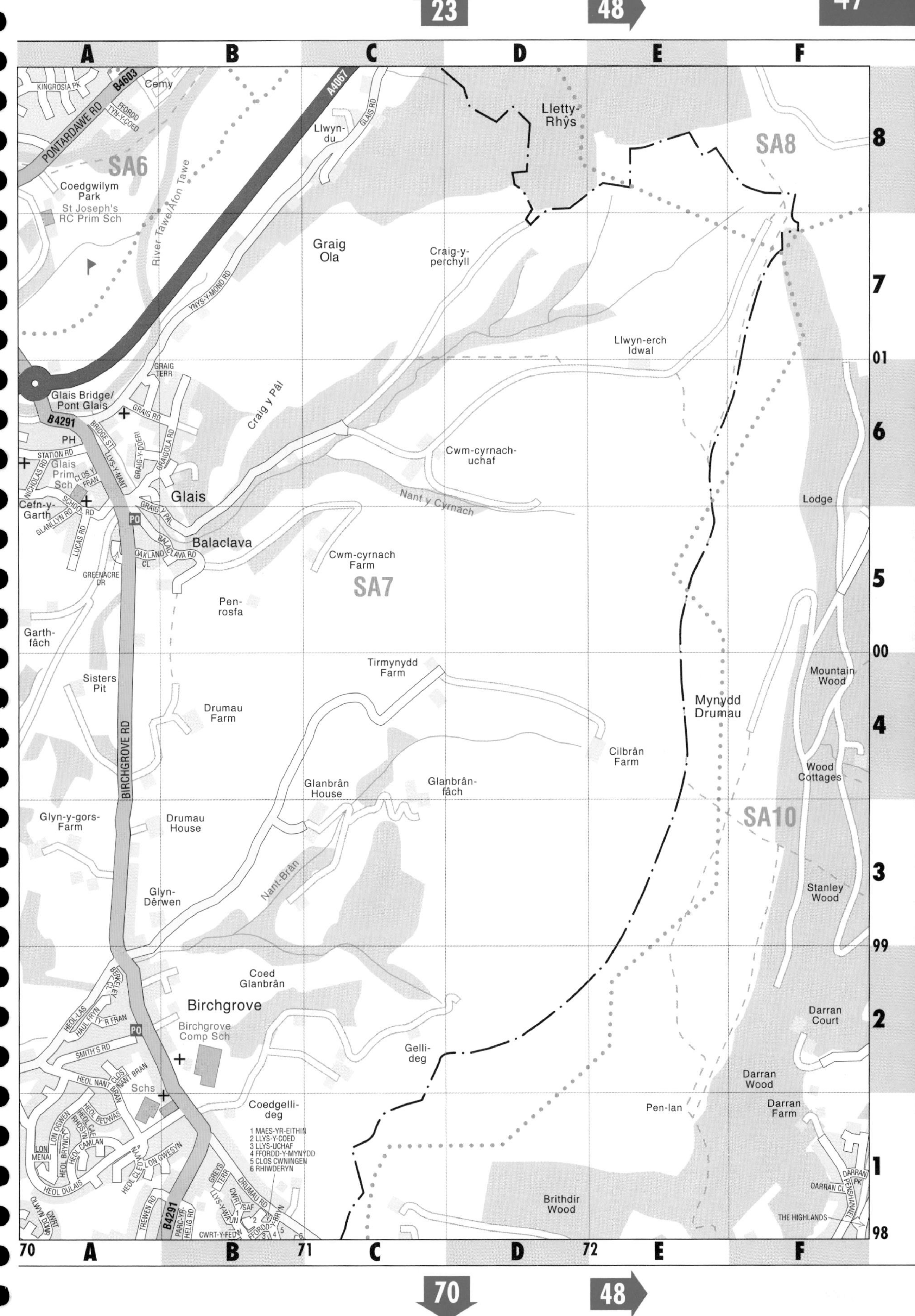
A
B
C
D
E
F
KINGROSIA PK
B4603
Cemy
PONTARDAWE RD
FFORDD TYN-Y-COED
SA6
A4067
GLAIS RD
Llwyn-du
Lletty-Rhŷs
SA8
Coedgwilym Park
St Joseph's RC Prim Sch
River Tawe/Afon Tawe
Graig Ola
Craig-y-perchyll
YNYS-Y-MOND RD
Llwyn-erch Idwal
GRAIG TERR
Glais Bridge/ Pont Glais
B4291
GRAIG RD
Craig y Pâl
PH
STATION RD
Glais Prim Sch
CLOS Y FRAN
NICHOLAS RD
SCHOOL RD
Cefn-y-Garth
GLANLLYN RD
LUCAS RD
BRIDGE ST
LLYS-Y-NANT
GRAIG-Y-DDERI
GRAIGOLA RD
Glais
GRAIG Y PAL
PO
Balaclava
BALACLAVA RD
OAKLAND CL
GREENACRE DR
Cwm-cyrnach-uchaf
Nant y Cyrnach
Lodge
Cwm-cyrnach Farm
SA7
Pen-rosfa
Garth-fâch
Tirmynydd Farm
Sisters Pit
Drumau Farm
BIRCHGROVE RD
Mynydd Drumau
Mountain Wood
Cilbrân Farm
Wood Cottages
Glanbrân House
Glanbrân-fâch
Glyn-y-gors-Farm
Drumau House
SA10
Nant-Brân
Glyn-Dêrwen
Stanley Wood
Coed Glanbrân
BERKELEY CL
Birchgrove
Birchgrove Comp Sch
HEOL-LAS
HAUL FRYN
TY'R FRAN
PO
Darran Court
SMITH'S RD
Gelli-deg
HEOL NANT BRAN
CLOS NANT BRAN
Schs
Darran Wood
Coedgelli-deg
Pen-lan
Darran Farm
HEOL BEDWAS
LON OGWEN
HEOL BRYNCYN
RHOSYN
HEOL CAE
HEOL CAMLAN
LON MENAI
HEOL DULAIS
LON GWESYN
HEOL CLEDAN
1 MAES-YR-EITHIN
2 LLYS-Y-COED
3 LLYS-UCHAF
4 FFORDD-Y-MYNYDD
5 CLOS CWNINGEN
6 RHIWDERYN
GREYS TERR
DRUMAU RD
CWRT-Y-SAF
LLYS-Y-WAUN
FFORDD-Y-BRYN
CWRT-Y-FEDW
PARC-YR-HELIG RD
TREWEN RD
B4291
OLWYN DOWN
CWRT
Brithdir Wood
DARRAN PK
DARRAN CL
PENSHANNEL
THE HIGHLANDS
8
7
01
6
5
00
4
3
99
2
1
98
70
71
72

70
48

47
24

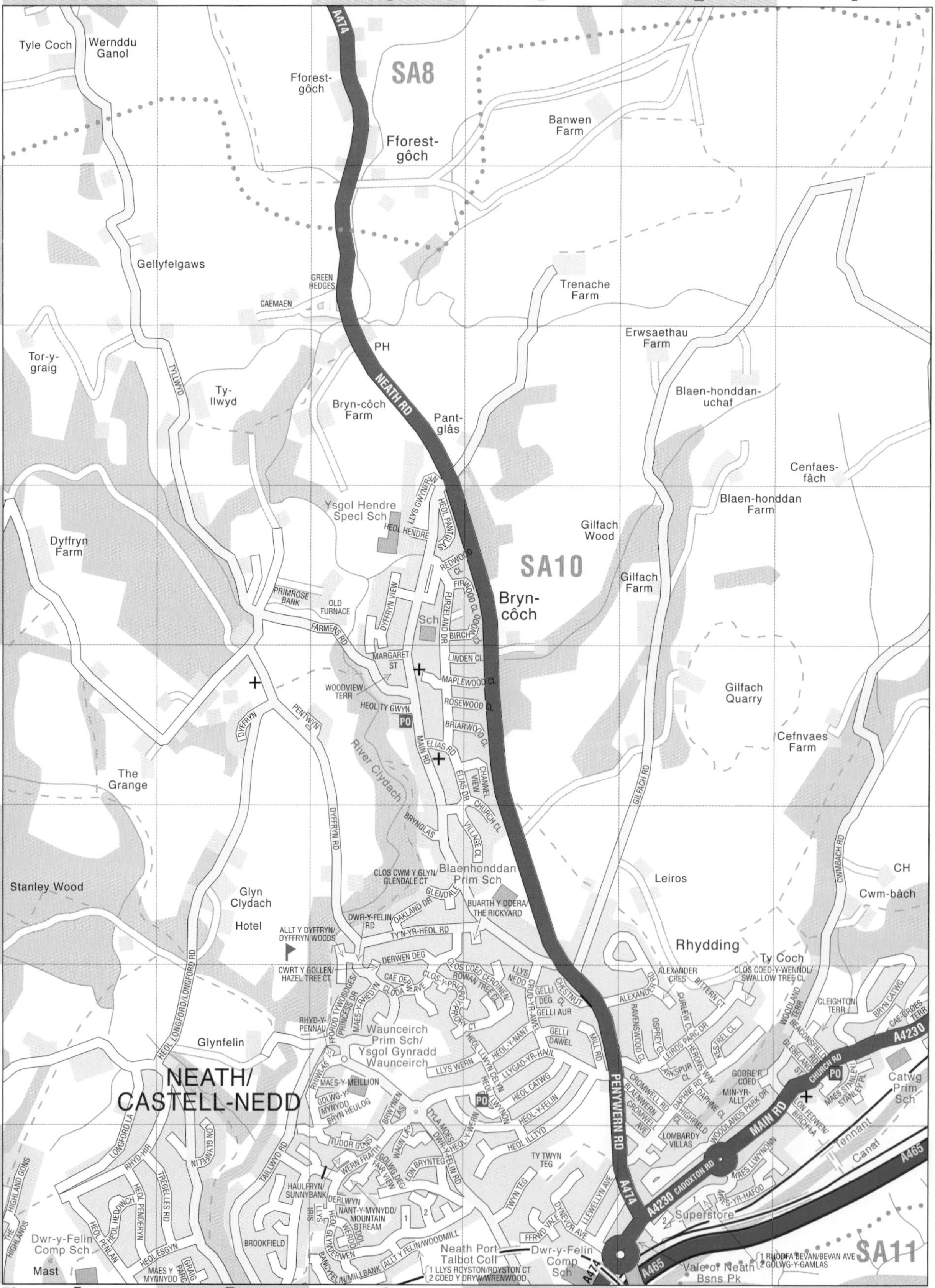

A B C D E F

8
7
01
6
5
00
4
3
99
2
1
98

Tyle Coch
Wernddu Ganol
Fforest-gôch
SA8
Fforest-gôch
Banwen Farm
Gellyfelgaws
GREEN HEDGES
CAEMAEN
Trenache Farm
Erwsaethau Farm
Tor-y-graig
PH
TYLLWYD
Ty-llwyd
Bryn-côch Farm
NEATH RD
Pant-glâs
Blaen-honddan-uchaf
Cenfaes-fâch
Ysgol Hendre Specl Sch
LLYS GWYNFA
HEOL PANTGLAS
HEOL HENDRE
Blaen-honddan Farm
Gilfach Wood
Dyffryn Farm
REDWOOD CL
SA10
Gilfach Farm
PRIMROSE BANK
OLD FURNACE
DYFFRYN VIEW
FIRWOOD CL
FURZELAND DR
Sch
Bryn-côch
BIRCHWOOD CL
FARMERS RD
LINDEN CL
MARGARET ST
MAPLEWOOD CL
WOODVIEW TERR
ROSEWOOD CL
Gilfach Quarry
HEOL TY GWYN
PO
DYFFRYN
PENTWYN
BRIARWOOD CL
Cefnvaes Farm
MAIN RD
ELIAS RD
River Clydach
CHANNEL VIEW
ELIAS DR
The Grange
CHURCH CL
GILFACH RD
BRYNGLAS
VILLAGE CL
DYFFRYN RD
CWMBACH RD
CH
CLOS CWM Y GLYN/ GLENDALE CT
Blaenhonddan Prim Sch
Leiros
Stanley Wood
Glyn Clydach Hotel
GLENDALE
BUARTH Y DDERA/ THE RICKYARD
Cwm-bâch
DWR-Y-FELIN RD
OAKLAND DR
ALLT Y DYFFRYN/ DYFFRYN WOODS
TY'N-YR-HEOL RD
Rhydding
Ty Coch
CWRT Y GOLLEN/ HAZEL TREE CT
DERWEN DEG
CLOS COED CERDIN/ ROWAN TREE CL
LLYS NEDD
ALEXANDER CRES
BITTERN CT
CLOS COED-Y-WENNOL/ SWALLOW TREE CL
FFORDD TYWYSOGES/ PRINCESS DR
CAE DERWEN AVE
CLOS-Y-PRIORDY/ PRIORY CT
CRUD-YR-AWEL
GELLI DEG
CHESTNUT CL
ALEXANDER
CLEIGHTON TERR
BRYN CATWG
CAE-GROES TERR
MAES-Y-WHEDYN
CLOS-Y-DAEA
GELLI AUR
RAVENSWOOD CL
CURLEW CL
OSPREY CL
WOODLAND TERR
A4230
RHYD-Y-PENNAU
Wauncierch Prim Sch/ Ysgol Gynradd Wauncierch
HEOL-Y-NANT
GELLI DAWEL
MILL RD
LEIROS PARC DR
HERONS WAY
KESTREL CL
BEACONSFIELD RD
HEOL LONGFORD/LONGFORD RD
Glynfelin
LLYS WERN
LLYGAD-YR-HAUL
LARKSPUR CL
GLEBELAND ST
CHURCH RD
NEATH/ CASTELL-NEDD
RHIWLAS
MAES-Y-MEILLION
HEOL LLWYN CELYN
HEOL CATWG
CROMWELL RD
GODRE'R COED
MAES STANLEY/ STANLEY PL
Catwg Prim Sch
GOLWG-Y-MYNYDD/ BRYN HEULOG
PO
HEOL LLWYNON
HEOL-Y-FELIN
BLAENWERN
CROMWELL AVE
DAPHNE RD
DAPHNE CL
MIN-YR-ALLT
WOODLANDS PARK DR
MAIN RD
PO
LON FEDWEN/ BIRCH LA
LON GLYNFELIN
BRYNWEN LAS
TYLA MOESS
DWR-Y-FELIN RD
HEOL ILLTYD
HIGHFIELD
LOMBARDY VILLAS
Tennant
LONGFORD LA
RHYD-HIR
TUDOR GONS
WERN FRAITH
WAUN LAS
TY TWYN TEG
PENTWERN RD
CADOXTON RD
MAES LLWYNON
Canal
A465
HEOL PENDERYN
TREGELLES RD
TAILLWYD RD
GOLWG DEG/ FAIR VIEW
LON BRYNTEG
THE HIGHLAND GDNS
HAULFRYN/ SUNNYBANK
DERLWYN
TWYN TEG
LLEWELLYN AVE
A474
HEOL-S-YR-HAFOD
HEOL HEDDWCH
LLYS IRIS
NANT-Y-MYNYDD/ MOUNTAIN STREAM
1 2
DYNEVOR AVE
A4230
Superstore
THE HIGHLANDS
Dwr-y-Felin Comp Sch
HEOL PENLAN
HEOL ESGYN
BROOKFIELD
HEOL GLYNDERWEN
WERDD
ALLT Y FELIN/ WOODMILL
Neath Port Talbot Coll
FFRWD VALE
Dwr-y-Felin Comp Sch
SA11
1 RHODFA BEVAN/BEVAN AVE
2 GOLWG-Y-GAMLAS
Mast
MAES Y MYNYDD
GRAIG PARC
BANCYFELIN/MILLBANK
1 LLYS ROYSTON/ROYSTON CT
2 COED Y DRYW/WRENWOOD
A474
A465
Vale of Neath Bsns Pk

73 A B 74 C D 75 E F

47
71

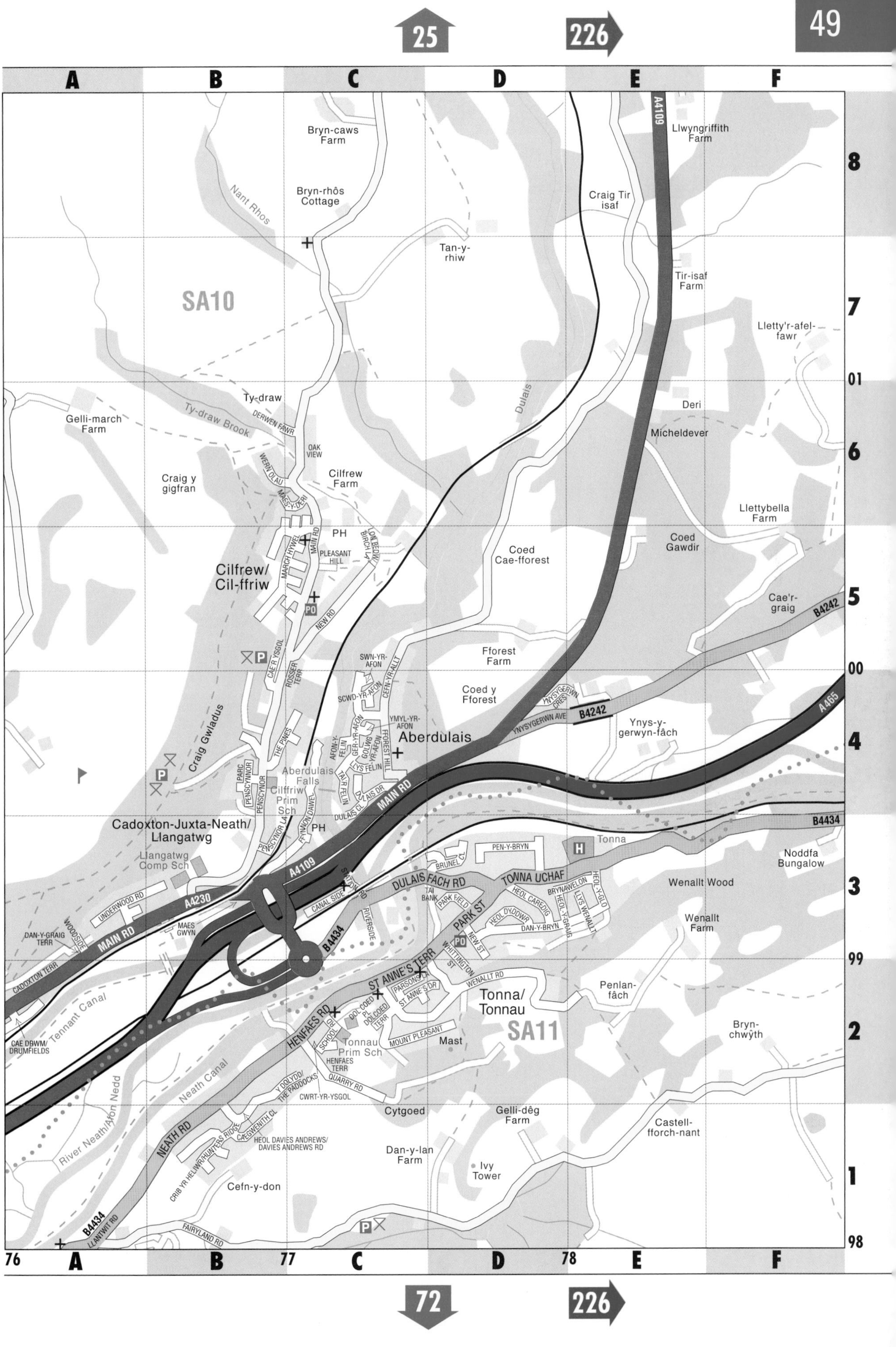

25
226

A B C D E F

Bryn-caws Farm
Llwyngriffith Farm
A4109
8
Nant Rhos
Bryn-rhôs Cottage
Craig Tir isaf
Tan-y-rhiw
Tir-isaf Farm
SA10
7
Lletty'r-afel-fawr
01
Ty-draw
Gelli-march Farm
Ty-draw Brook
DERWEN FAWR
Deri
Micheldever
OAK VIEW
Dulais
6
WERN OLAU
Craig y gigfran
Cilfrew Farm
MAES-Y-DERI
Llettybella Farm
PH
MARCH HYWEL
MAIN RD
PLEASANT HILL
LON BEDW
BIRCH LA
Coed Cae-fforest
Coed Gawdir
Cilfrew/ Cil-ffriw
PO
NEW RD
5
Cae'r-graig
B4242
CAE'R YSGOL
P
ROSSER TERR
Fforest Farm
SWN-YR-AFON
CEFN-YR-ALLT
00
Coed y Fforest
YNYSYGERWN CRES
SCWD-YR-AFON
YNYSYGERWN AVE
B4242
A465
Craig Gwladus
THE PINES
YMYL-YR-AFON
Ynys-y-gerwyn-fâch
AFON-Y-FELIN
GER-YR-AFON
GOLWG-YR-AFON
FFOREST HILL
Aberdulais
4
PARC PENSCYNOR
PENSCYNOR
LLYS FELIN
P
Aberdulais Falls
TAL'R FELIN
Cilffriw Prim Sch
LAIS DR
DULAIS CL
MAIN RD
B4434
Cadoxton-Juxta-Neath/ Llangatwg
PENSCYNOR LA
FFYNNON DAWEL
PH
PEN-Y-BRYN
H
Tonna
Noddfa Bungalow
Llangatwg Comp Sch
A4109
BRUNEL CL
STATION RD
DULAIS FACH RD
TONNA UCHAF
BRYNAWELON
HEOL-Y-GLO
UNDERWOOD RD
A4230
CANAL SIDE
TAI BANK
PARK FIELD
HEOL CAREDIG
HEOL-Y-GRAIG
Wenallt Wood
3
LLYS WENALLT
PARK ST
HEOL DYDDWR
Wenallt Farm
DAN-Y-GRAIG TERR
WOODSIDE
MAES GWYN
RIVERSIDE
DAN-Y-BRYN
MAIN RD
PO
B4434
NEW ST
WHITTINGTON ST
99
CADOXTON TERR
ST ANNE'S TERR
WENALLT RD
Penlan-fâch
Tennant Canal
PARSONS CL
ST ANNE'S DR
Tonna/ Tonnau
HENFAES RD
DOL COED PL
DOLCOED TERR
CAE DRWM/ DRUMFIELDS
SCHOOL RD
SA11
Bryn-chwŷth
2
Mast
Tonnau Prim Sch
MOUNT PLEASANT
HENFAES TERR
Neath Canal
Y DOLYDD/ THE PADDOCKS
QUARRY RD
River Neath/Afon Nedd
CWRT-YR-YSGOL
Cytgoed
Gelli-dêg Farm
Castell-fforch-nant
CAEGWENITH CL
NEATH RD
HUNTERS RIDGE
HEOL DAVIES ANDREWS/ DAVIES ANDREWS RD
Dan-y-lan Farm
CRIB YR HELIWR
Ivy Tower
1
Cefn-y-don
B4434
LLANTWIT RD
FAIRYLAND RD
P
98

76 A B 77 C D 78 E F

72
226

227
26

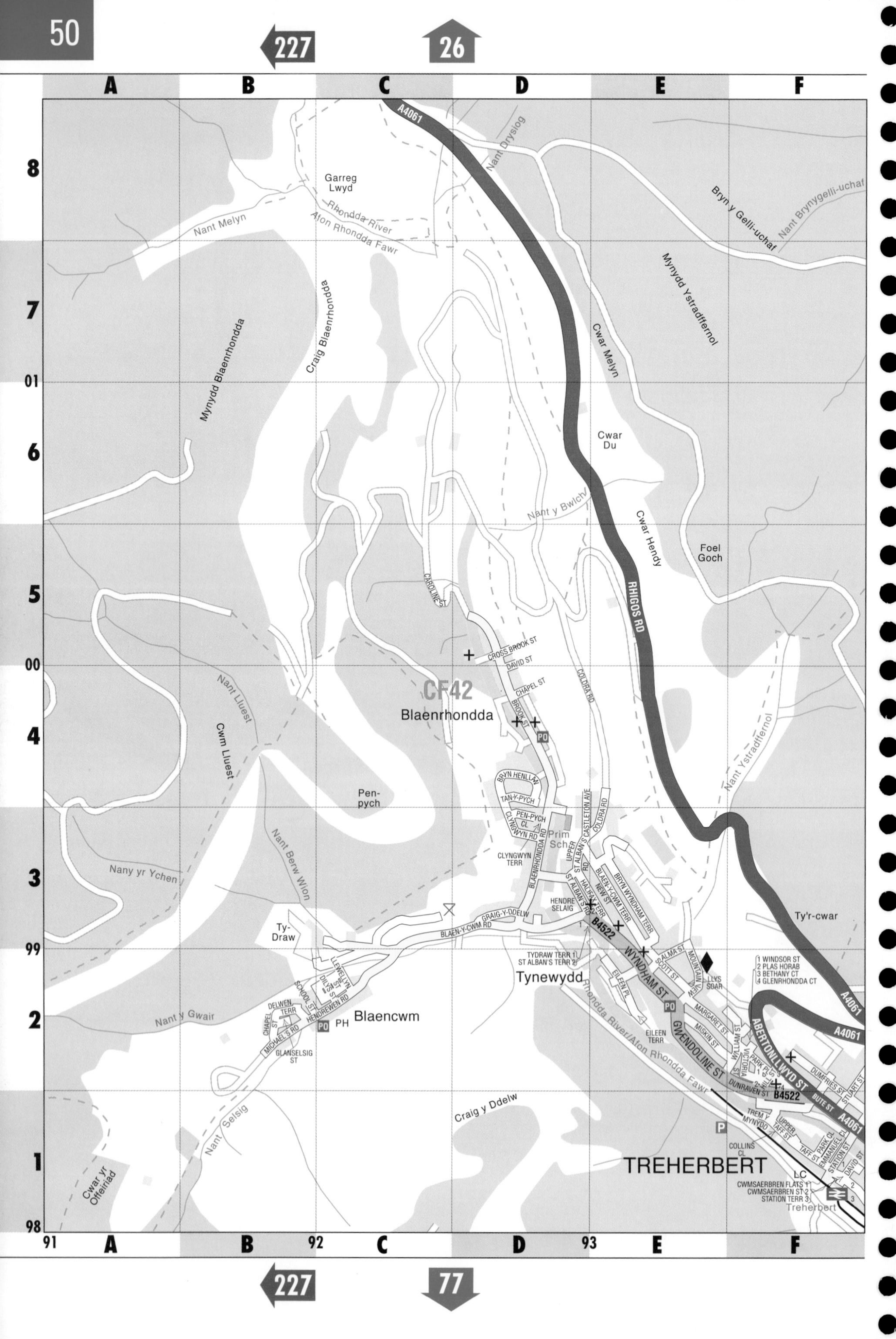
A
B
C
D
E
F
8
7
01
6
5
00
4
3
99
2
1
98
91
92
93
A4061
Garreg
Lwyd
Nant Drysiog
Rhondda River
Afon Rhondda Fawr
Nant Melyn
Bryn y Gelli-uchaf
Nant Brynygelli-uchaf
Mynydd Ystradffernol
Craig Blaenrhondda
Mynydd Blaenrhondda
Cwar Melyn
Cwar
Du
Nant y Bwlch
Cwar Hendy
Foel
Goch
RHIGOS RD
CAROLINE ST
CROSS BROOK ST
DAVID ST
CHAPEL ST
CF42
Blaenrhondda
BROOK ST
PO
COLDRA RD
Nant Lluest
Cwm Lluest
Nant Ystradffernol
Pen-
pych
BRYN HENLLAN
TAN-Y-PYCH
PEN-PYCH
CL
CLYNGWYN RD
UPPER
ST ALBAN'S CASTLETON AVE
COLDRA RD
Prim
Sch
CLYNGWYN
TERR
BLAENRHONDDA RD
RD
HALIFAX TERR
BLAEN-Y-CWM TERR
NEW ST
BRYN WYNDHAM TERR
Nany yr Ychen
Nant Berw Wlon
HENDRE
SELAIG
B4522
Ty'r-cwar
Ty-
Draw
GRAIG-Y-DDELW
BLAEN-Y-CWM RD
TYDRAW TERR 1
ST ALBAN'S TERR 2
ALMA ST
SCOTT ST
MOUNTAIN
LLYS
SOAR
1 WINDSOR ST
2 PLAS HORAB
3 BETHANY CT
4 GLENRHONDDA CT
LLEWELLYN ST
DILYS ST
SCHOOL ST
Tynewydd
EILEEN PL
WYNDHAM ST
DELWEN
TERR
HENDREWEN RD
Blaencwm
Nant y Gwair
CHAPEL ST
MICHAEL'S RD
PH
GLANSELSIG
ST
Rhondda River/Afon Rhondda Fawr
EILEEN
TERR
GWENDOLINE ST
MARGARET ST
MISKIN ST
WILLIAM ST
VICTORIA ST
PARK PL
DUNRAVEN ST
ABERTONLLWYD ST
A4061
DUMFRIES ST
STUART ST
BUTE ST
Craig y Ddelw
Nant Selsig
TREM Y MYNYDD
UPPER TAFF ST
PARK CL
TAFF ST
EMMANUEL CL
STATION ST
DAVID ST
P
COLLINS
CL
TREHERBERT
LC
Cwar yr
Offeiriad
CWMSAERBREN FLATS 1
CWMSAERBREN ST 2
STATION TERR 3
Treherbert

227
77

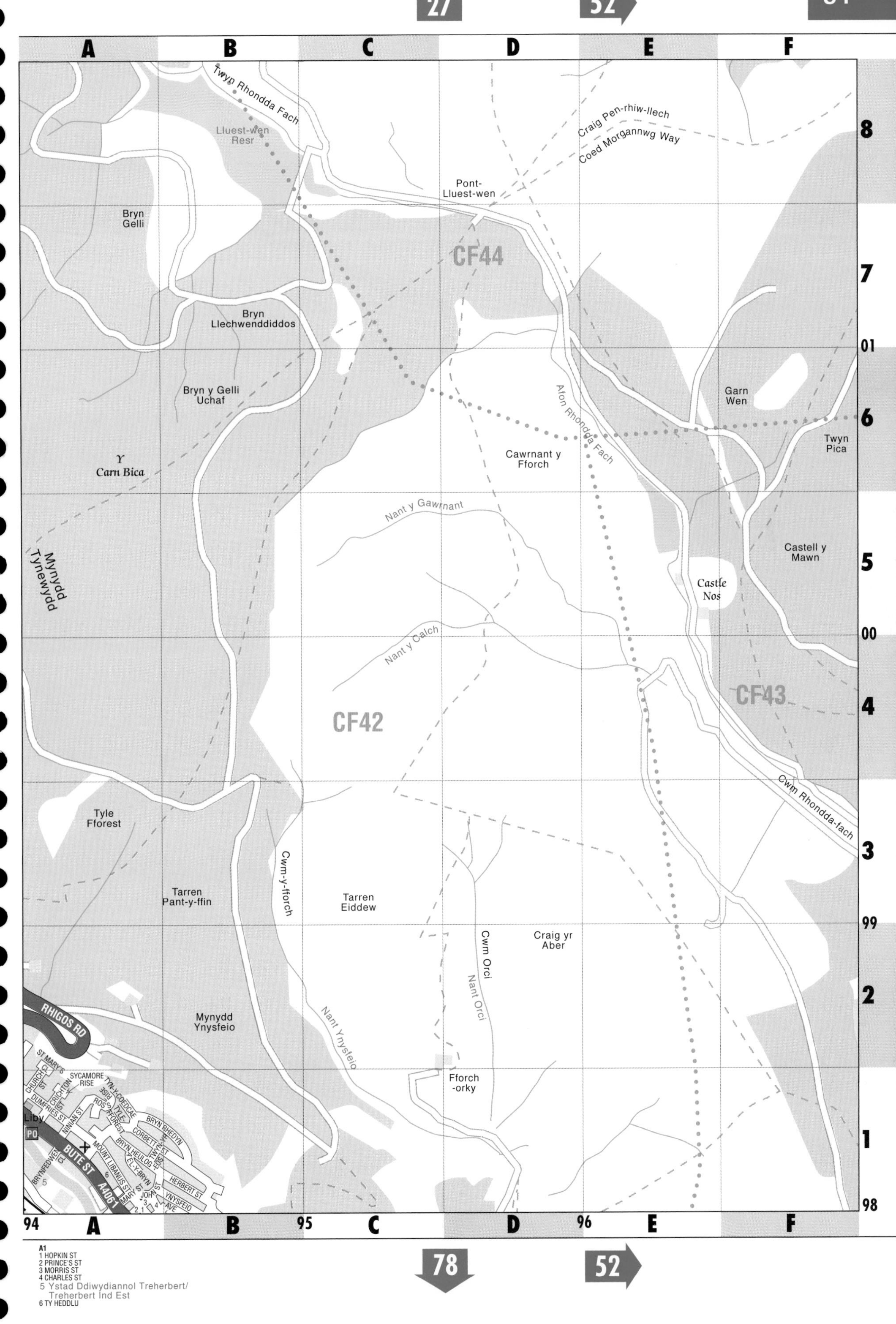

A1
1 HOPKIN ST
2 PRINCE'S ST
3 MORRIS ST
4 CHARLES ST
5 Ystad Ddiwydiannol Treherbert/ Treherbert Ind Est
6 TY HEDDLU

51
28

A B C D E F
8
7
01
6
5
00
4
3
99
2
1
98
97 98 99
A4233
Dumfries Park
Craig Rhiw-ddu
Graig Rhiwmynach
Troedrhiw lech Foel
MAERDY RD
Cefnrhos-gwawr
Fire Tower
P
Hafod-wen
Panwen Garreg-wen
Rhos-gwawr
Nant Aman Fach
CF44
Pen Foel Aman
Coed Blaenaman-fach
Craig Fforchaman
Bryn Du
Nant Aman Fawr
Glynhafod Jun Sch
GLYNHAFOD ST
GLANRHYD ST
BRYNHYFRYD
KINGSBURY PL
GLANAMAN RD
Cwm Aman
Twyn Croesffordd
PWLLFA PL
CF43
Afon Rhondda Fach
Craig Bedwlwyn
Craig Tirllaethdy
Bedwlwyn
Cefn Craig Amos
SPRINGFIELD RD
WRIGHT PL
MONA PL
WOOD ST
PARK PL
JAMES ST
PARK RD
GRIFFITH ST
NORTH TERR
EDWARD ST
Liby
STATION RD
STATION TERR
INSTITUTE ST
Maerdy Farm
Mynydd y Ffaldau
SUNNY HILL
CHURCH ST
THOMAS ST
PO
Maerdy
MAERDY CT
MILES ST
HILL ST
SCHOOL ST
PENTRE RD
WILSON PL
OXFORD ST
MAERDY RD FLATS
ROWLEY TERR
BROOK ST
Maerdy Inf Sch
MAERDY RD
A4233
Cwm Rhondda-fach
Craig y Gilwern
ROYAL COTTS
CAIRN CT

51
79

D7
1 GLANCYNON TERR
2 LOWER STATION ST
3 BRECON ST
4 GLAMORGAN CT
5 ABERAMAN HOS
6 CLIFTON CRES

29

D7
7 WYNDHAM CRES
8 GER-YR-AFON

54

E8
1 THIRLEMERE TERR
2 CARDINEN TERR
3 PIT PL
4 CWRT GLANWERN
5 CHAPEL ROW

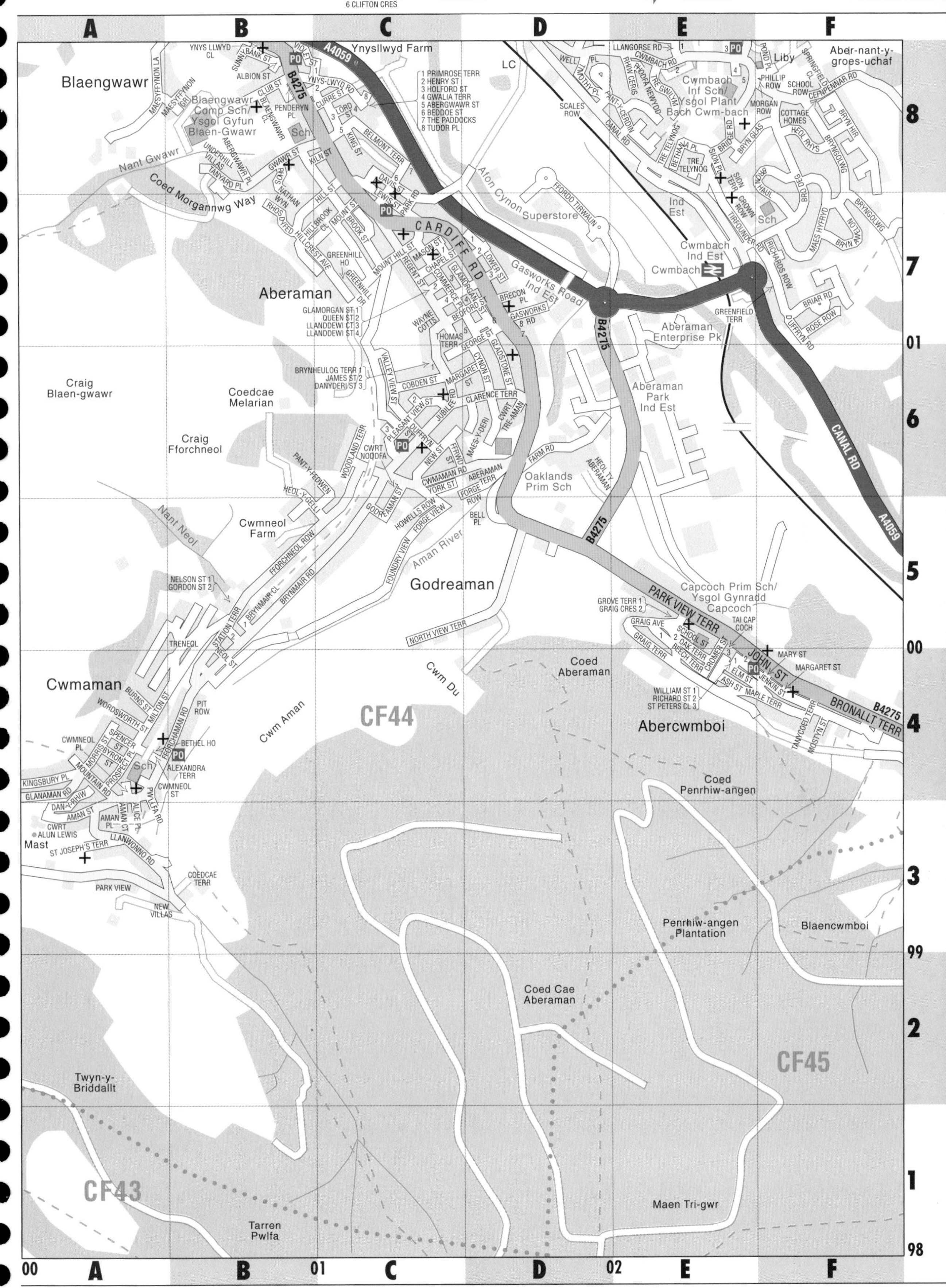

80

54

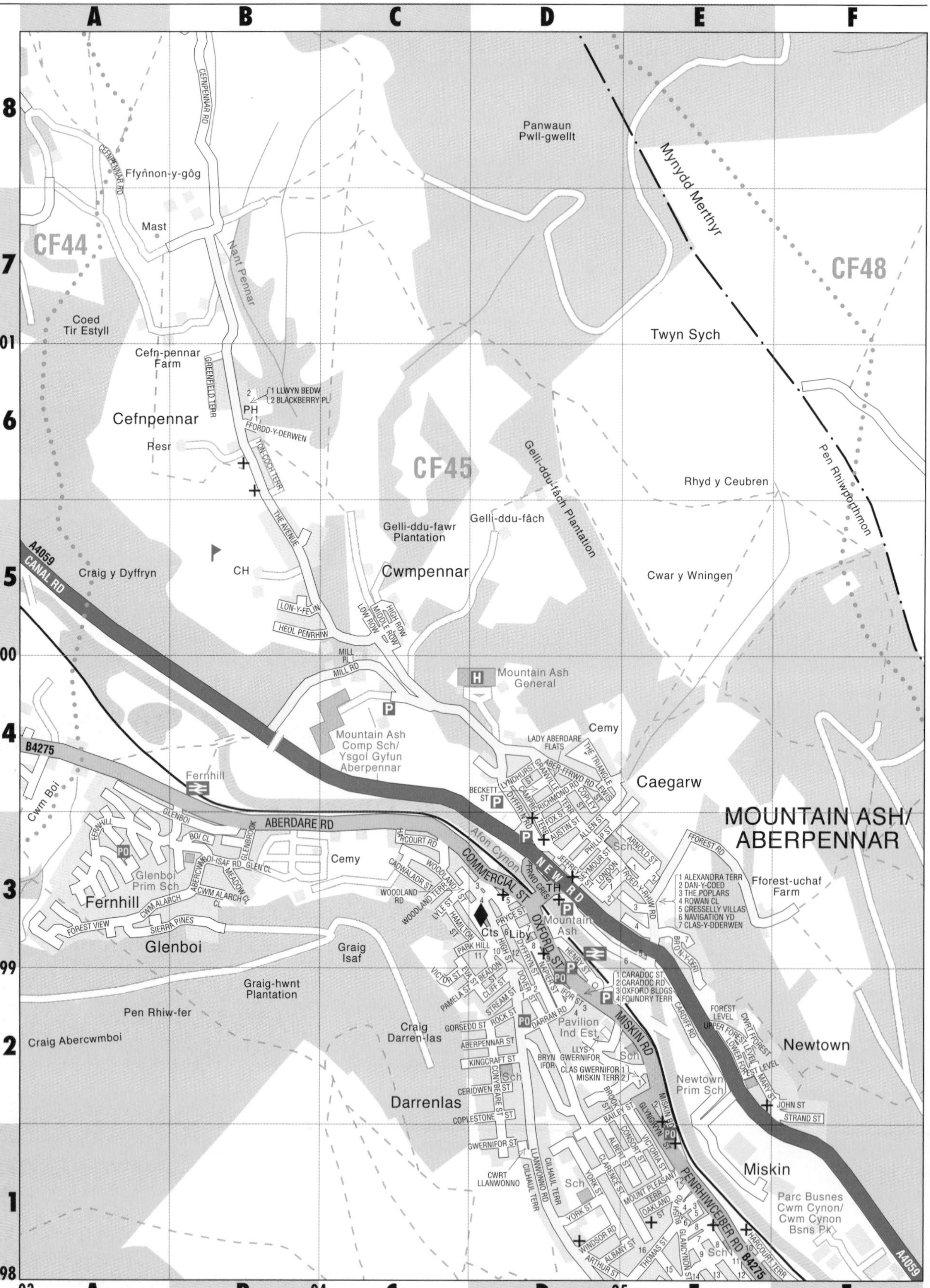

53 30

A B C D E F

8 7 01 6 5 00 4 3 99 2 1 98

Ffynnon-y-gôg
Mast
CF44
Coed Tir Estyll
Cefn-pennar Farm
Cefnpennar
Resr
Nant Pennar
Panwaun Pwll-gwellt
Mynydd Merthyr
CF48
Twyn Sych
CF45
Gelli-ddu-fâch Plantation
Rhyd y Ceubren
Pen Rhiwporthmon
Gelli-ddu-fawr Plantation
Gelli-ddu-fâch
Craig y Dyffryn
CH
Cwmpennar
Cwar y Wningen
A4059 CANAL RD
Mountain Ash General
Cemy
Mountain Ash Comp Sch/ Ysgol Gyfun Aberpennar
B4275
Fernhill
Cwm Boi
Caegarw
MOUNTAIN ASH/ ABERPENNAR
ABERDARE RD
Afon Cynon
COMMERCIAL ST
NEW RD
OXFORD ST
Mountain Ash
Glenboi Prim Sch
Fernhill
Glenboi
Graig Isaf
Fforest-uchaf Farm
1 ALEXANDRA TERR
2 DAN-Y-COED
3 THE POPLARS
4 ROWAN CL
5 CRESSELLY VILLAS
6 NAVIGATION YD
7 CLAS-Y-DDERWEN
1 CARADOC ST
2 CARADOC RD
3 OXFORD BLDGS
4 FOUNDRY TERR
Graig-hwnt Plantation
Pen Rhiw-fer
Craig Abercwmboi
Craig Darren-las
Pavilion Ind Est
MISKIN RD
Newtown
Newtown Prim Sch
Darrenlas
Miskin
Parc Busnes Cwm Cynon/ Cwm Cynon Bsns Pk
PENRHIWCEIBER RD
A4059

03 A B 04 C D 05 E F

53 81

D3
1 NAVIGATION ST
2 THE POPLARS
3 FOUNTAIN ST
4 GRAIG ST
5 UNION ST
6 TY SEION
7 CHANCERY LA
8 KNIGHT ST
9 BRUCE ST
10 QUARRY RD
11 QUARRY COTTS
12 ST DAVID'S PL

E1
1 MOUNT PLEASANT COTTS
2 NAVAGATION VILLAS
3 JONES ST
4 HUGHES ST
5 JAMES ST
6 MOUNT PLEASANT PL
7 EDWARDS ST
8 PROSSER ST
9 MORGAN ST
10 HILL HO
11 PARK HILL
12 WOODFIELD TERR
13 PARK ST
14 TY'RFELIN ST
15 GLADSTONE ST
16 GLADSTONE TERR

56

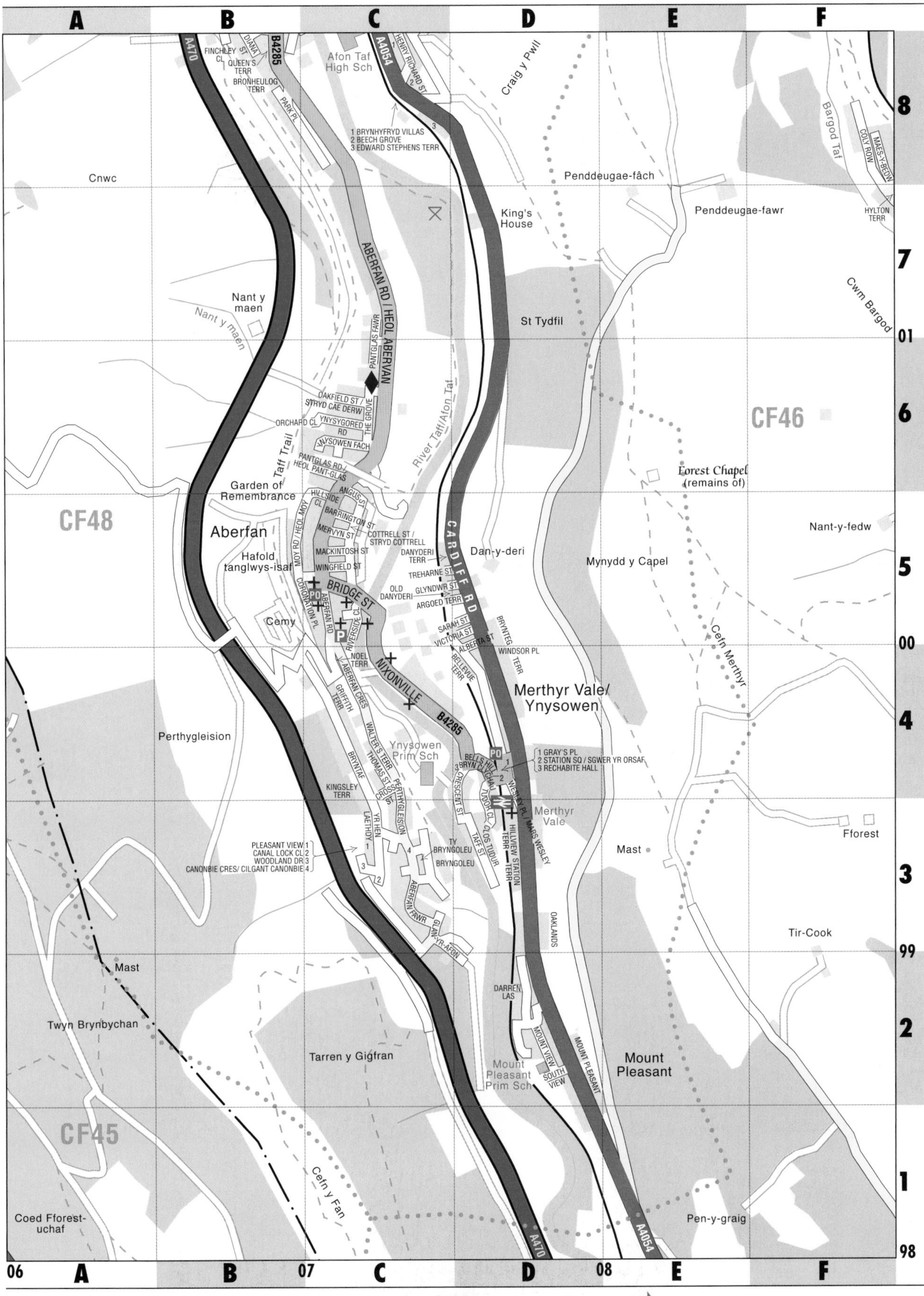

A B C D E F

8
7
01
6
5
00
4
3
99
2
1
98

Afon Taf High Sch
Craig y Pwll
Bargod Taf
Cnwc
Penddeugae-fâch
Penddeugae-fawr
King's House
Cwm Bargod
Nant y maen
St Tydfil
CF46
CF48
Forest Chapel (remains of)
Garden of Remembrance
Aberfan
Hafold tanglwys-isaf
Nant-y-fedw
Dan-y-deri
Mynydd y Capel
Cemy
Cefn Merthyr
Merthyr Vale/ Ynysowen
Perthygleision
Ynysowen Prim Sch
Merthyr Vale
Fforest
Mast
Tir-Cook
Mast
Twyn Brynbychan
Tarren y Gigfran
Mount Pleasant Prim Sch
Mount Pleasant
CF45
Cefn y Fan
Coed Fforest-uchaf
Pen-y-graig

A470
B4285
A4054
A4054
A470
B4285
FINCHLEY CL
DIANA ST
QUEEN'S TERR
BRONHEULOG TERR
PARK PL
HENRY RICHARD ST
1 BRYNHYFRYD VILLAS
2 BEECH GROVE
3 EDWARD STEPHENS TERR
COLY ROW
MAES-Y-BEDW
HYLTON TERR
ABERFAN RD / HEOL ABERVAN
PANTGLAS FAWR
OAKFIELD ST / STRYD CAE DERW
ORCHARD CL
YNYSYGORED RD
THE GROVE
YNYSOWEN FACH
PANTGLAS RD / HEOL PANT-GLAS
Taff Trail
River Taff/Afon Taf
HILLSIDE CL
ANGUS ST
BARRINGTON ST
MERVYN ST
COTTRELL ST / STRYD COTTRELL
MACKINTOSH ST
DANYDERI TERR
MOY RD / HEOL MOY
WINGFIELD ST
TREHARNE ST
CARDIFF RD
BRIDGE ST
CORONATION PL
ABERFAN RD
OLD DANYDERI
GLYNDWR ST
ARGOED TERR
RIVERSIDE CL
SARAH ST
VICTORIA ST
ALBERTA ST
BRYNTEG TERR
WINDSOR PL
NOEL TERR
BELLEVUE TERR
NIXONVILLE
ABERFAN CRES
GRIFFITH TERR
WALTER'S TERR
THOMAS ST
BRYNTAF
CROSS ST
PERTHYGLEISION
KINGSLEY TERR
1 GRAY'S PL
2 STATION SQ / SGWER YR ORSAF
3 RECHABITE HALL
BELL'S HILL
BRYN CLYCHAU
CRESCENT ST
TUDOR CL
CLOS TUDUR
WESLEY PL / MAES WESLEY
HILLVIEW TERR
STATION TERR
YR HEN LAETHDY
PLEASANT VIEW 1
CANAL LOCK CL 2
WOODLAND DR 3
CANONBIE CRES/ CILGANT CANONBIE 4
TY BRYNGOLEU
BRYNGOLEU
TAFF ST
ABERFAN FAWR
GLAN-YR-AFON
OAKLANDS
DARREN LAS
MOUNT VIEW
SOUTH VIEW
MOUNT PLEASANT

06 A B 07 C D 08 E F

82

56

55
32

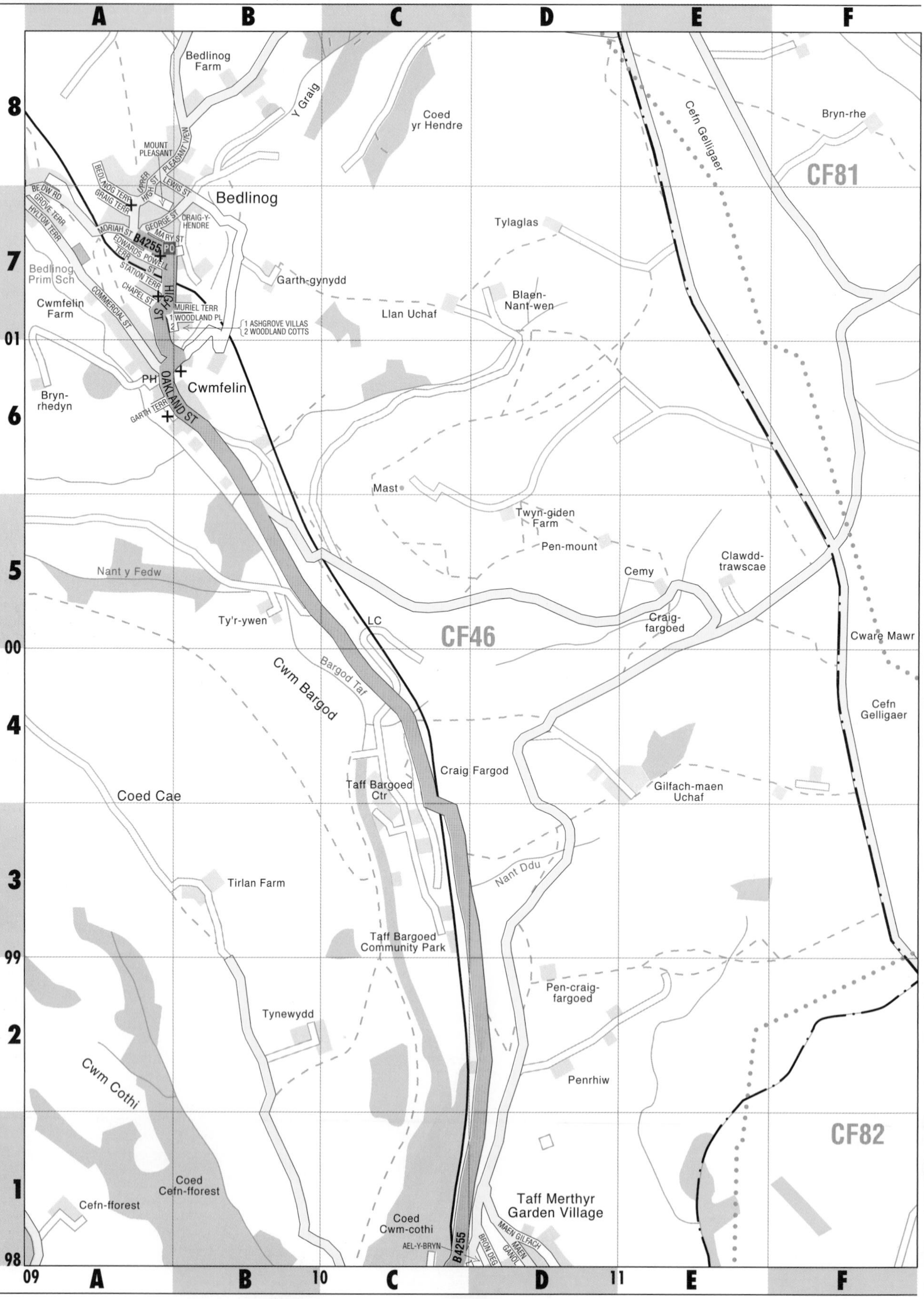

A
B
C
D
E
F
8
7
01
6
5
00
4
3
99
2
1
98
09
10
11
Bedlinog Farm
Y Graig
Coed yr Hendre
Cefn Gelligaer
Bryn-rhe
CF81
MOUNT PLEASANT
PLEASANT VIEW
BEDLINOG TERR
UPPER HIGH ST
LEWIS ST
BEDW RD
GROVE TERR
HYLTON TERR
GRAIG TERR
Bedlinog
GEORGE ST
CRAIG-Y-HENDRE
MORIAH ST
MARY ST
B4255
PO
EDWARDS TERR
POWELL ST
STATION TERR
CHAPEL ST
HIGH ST
COMMERCIAL ST
MURIEL TERR
1 WOODLAND PL
1 ASHGROVE VILLAS
2 WOODLAND COTTS
Tylaglas
Bedlinog Prim Sch
Cwmfelin Farm
Garth-gynydd
Blaen-Nant-wen
Llan Uchaf
PH
OAKLAND ST
Cwmfelin
Bryn-rhedyn
GARTH TERR
Mast
Twyn-giden Farm
Pen-mount
Clawdd-trawscae
Cemy
Nant y Fedw
Ty'r-ywen
LC
Craig-fargoed
CF46
Cware Mawr
Bargod Taf
Cwm Bargod
Cefn Gelligaer
Craig Fargod
Taff Bargoed Ctr
Gilfach-maen Uchaf
Coed Cae
Nant Ddu
Tirlan Farm
Taff Bargoed Community Park
Pen-craig-fargoed
Tynewydd
Cwm Cothi
Penrhiw
CF82
Coed Cefn-fforest
Taff Merthyr Garden Village
Cefn-fforest
Coed Cwm-cothi
AEL-Y-BRYN
B4255
BRON DEG
MAEN GILFACH
MAEN GANOL

55
83

33
58

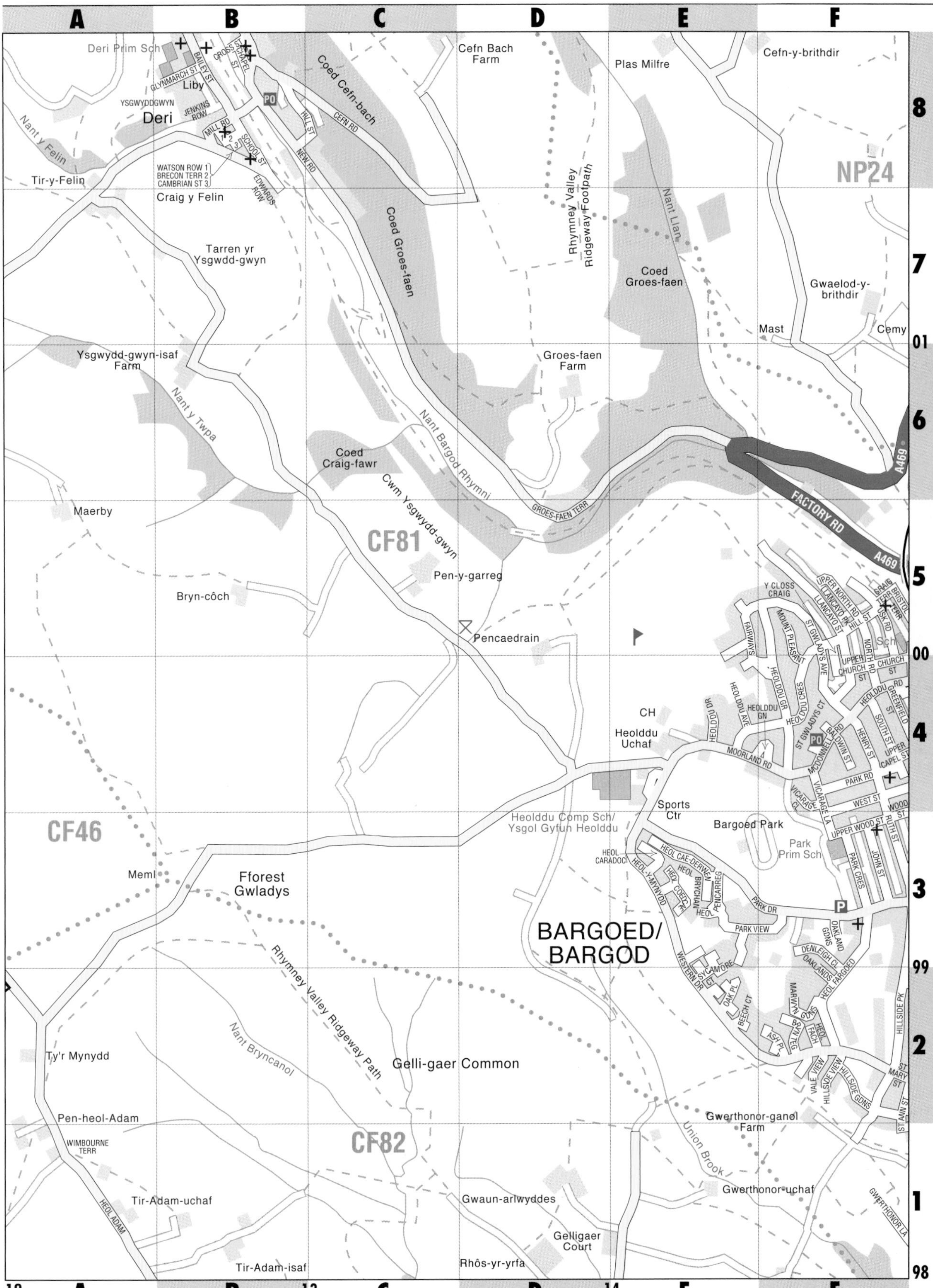

Deri Prim Sch
Liby
Deri
Nant y Felin
Tir-y-Felin
Craig y Felin
Coed Cefn-bach
Cefn Bach Farm
Plas Milfre
Cefn-y-brithdir
NP24
Rhymney Valley Ridgeway Footpath
Nant Llan
Coed Groes-faen
Tarren yr Ysgwdd-gwyn
Gwaelod-y-brithdir
Mast
Cemy
Ysgwydd-gwyn-isaf Farm
Groes-faen Farm
Nant y Twpa
Nant Bargod Rhymni
Coed Craig-fawr
Cwm Ysgwydd-gwyn
Maerby
FACTORY RD
A469
CF81
Pen-y-garreg
Bryn-côch
Pencaedrain
CH
Heolddu Uchaf
Sports Ctr
Bargoed Park
Park Prim Sch
Heolddu Comp Sch/ Ysgol Gyfun Heolddu
CF46
Meml
Fforest Gwladys
BARGOED/ BARGOD
Rhymney Valley Ridgeway Path
Nant Bryncanol
Gelli-gaer Common
Ty'r Mynydd
Pen-heol-Adam
WIMBOURNE TERR
CF82
Gwerthonor-ganol Farm
Union Brook
Gwerthonor-uchaf
Tir-Adam-uchaf
Gwaun-arlwyddes
Gelligaer Court
Tir-Adam-isaf
Rhôs-yr-yrfa
HEOL ADAM
GWERTHONOR LA
MOORLAND RD
PARK DR
PARK VIEW
WESTERN DR
12
13
14
98
99
00
01
A B C D E F
1 2 3 4 5 6 7 8

57
34

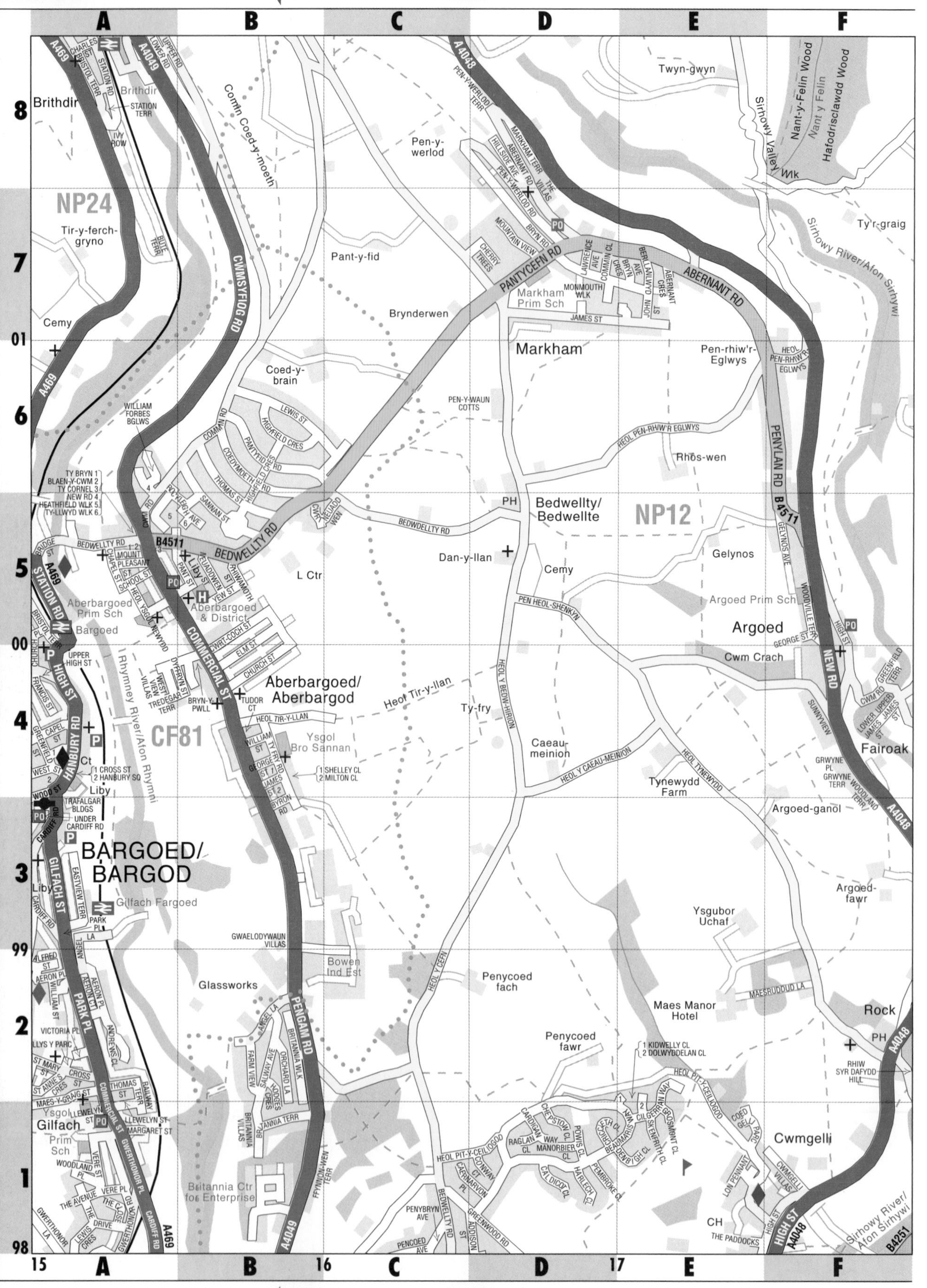
A
B
C
D
E
F
Brithdir
NP24
Tir-y-ferch-gryno
Cemy
Comin Coed-y-moeth
CWMSYFIOG RD
Pen-y-werlod
Pant-y-fid
Brynderwen
Twyn-gwyn
Nant-y-Felin Wood
Hafodrisclawdd Wood
Sirhowy Valley Wlk
Ty'r-graig
Sirhowy River/Afon Sirhywi
PANTYCEFN RD
ABERNANT RD
Markham Prim Sch
JAMES ST
Markham
Pen-rhiw'r-Eglwys
Coed-y-brain
PEN-Y-WAUN COTTS
HEOL PEN-RHIW'R EGLWYS
Rhos-wen
PENYLAN RD
B4511
PH
Bedwellty/ Bedwellte
NP12
BEDWDELLTY RD
BEDWELLTY RD
Dan-y-llan
Gelynos
L Ctr
Cemy
PEN HEOL-SHENKYN
Argoed Prim Sch
Argoed
Aberbargoed Prim Sch
Aberbargoed & District
Bargoed
COMMERCIAL ST
Cwm Crach
NEW RD
Aberbargoed/ Aberbargod
Heol Tir-y-llan
Ty-fry
Rhymney River/Afon Rhymni
CF81
Ysgol Bro Sannan
Caeau-meinion
HEOL Y CAEAU-MEINION
HEOL TYNEWYDD
Fairoak
Tynewydd Farm
Argoed-ganol
A4048
BARGOED/ BARGOD
Gilfach Fargoed
Argoed-fawr
Ysgubor Uchaf
GWAELODYWAUN VILLAS
Bowen Ind Est
Glassworks
Penycoed fach
PENGAM RD
Maes Manor Hotel
Rock
Penycoed fawr
PH
HEOL PIT-Y-CEILIOGOD
Ysgol Gilfach Prim Sch
Cwmgelli
Britannia Ctr for Enterprise
A4049
A469
CH
THE PADDOCKS
HIGH ST
B4251
15
16
17
98
99
00
01
1
2
3
4
5
6
7
8

57
85

35
60

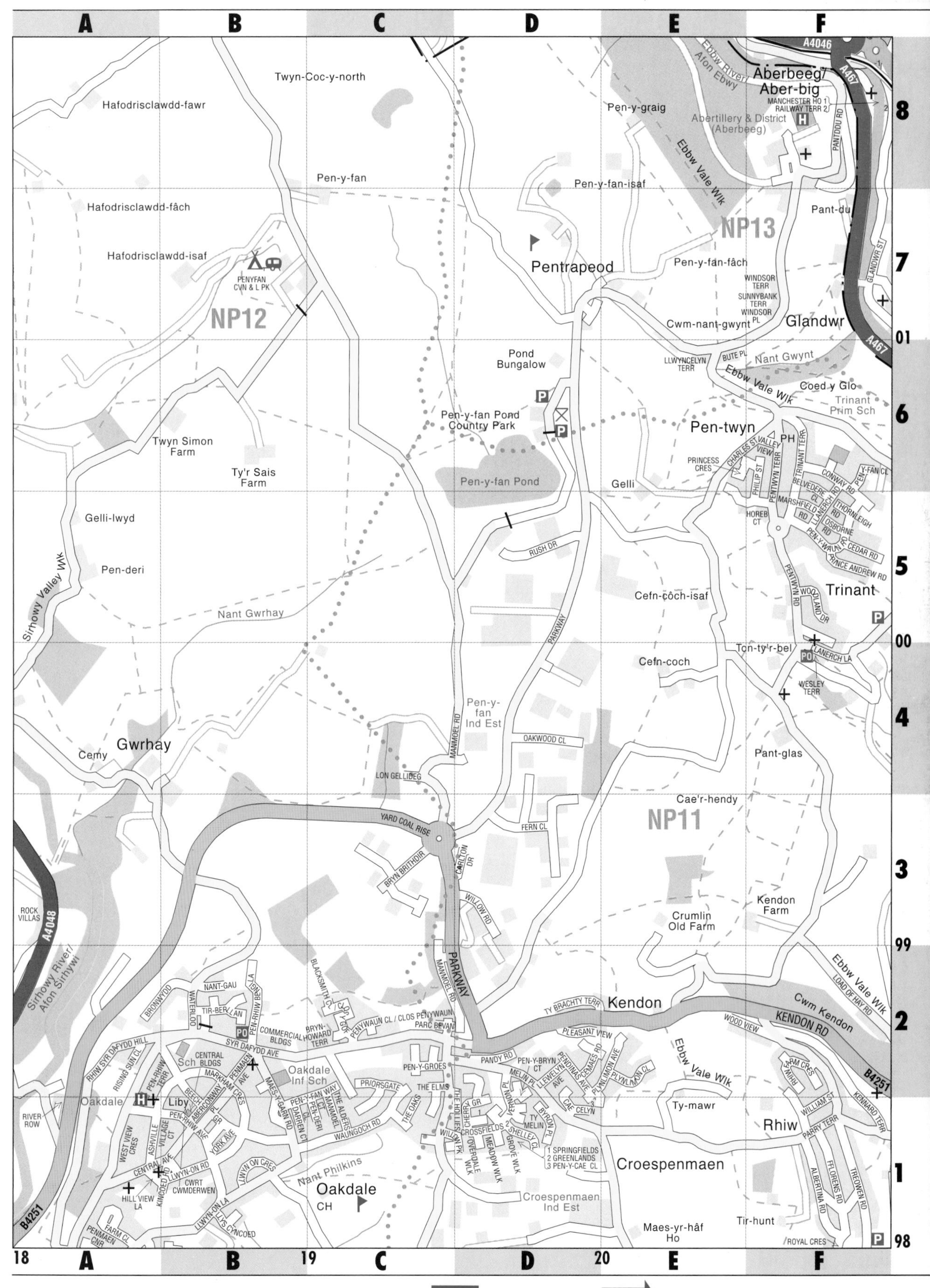

Twyn-Coc-y-north
Hafodrisclawdd-fawr
Pen-y-fan
Hafodrisclawdd-fâch
Hafodrisclawdd-isaf
PENYFAN CVN & L PK
NP12
Twyn Simon Farm
Ty'r Sais Farm
Gelli-lwyd
Pen-deri
Sirhowy Valley Wlk
Nant Gwrhay
Cemy
Gwrhay
Aberbeeg/ Aber-big
A4046
A467
Ebbw River/ Afon Ebwy
Pen-y-graig
MANCHESTER HO
RAILWAY TERR
Abertillery & District (Aberbeeg)
PANTDDU RD
Ebbw Vale Wlk
Pen-y-fan-isaf
Pant-du
NP13
Pentrapeod
Pen-y-fan-fâch
WINDSOR TERR
SUNNYBANK TERR
WINDSOR PL
Cwm-nant-gwynt
Glandwr
GLANDWR ST
Pond Bungalow
LLWYNCELYN TERR
BUTE PL
Nant Gwynt
Coed y Glo
Trinant Prim Sch
Pen-y-fan Pond Country Park
Pen-y-fan Pond
Pen-twyn
PH
PRINCESS CRES
CHARLES ST
VALLEY VIEW
PHILIP ST
PENTWYN TERR
TRINANT TERR
CONWAY RD
Y-FAN CL
BELVEDERE CL
MARSHFIELD RD
LLANERCH RD
THORNLEIGH
HOREB CT
OSBORNE RD
PEN-Y-WAUN RD
CEDAR RD
PRINCE ANDREW RD
Gelli
RUSH DR
Cefn-côch-isaf
PENTWYN RD
WOODLAND DR
Trinant
PARKWAY
Cefn-coch
Ton-ty'r-bel
LLANERCH LA
WESLEY TERR
Pen-y-fan Ind Est
MANMOEL RD
OAKWOOD CL
Pant-glas
LON GELLIDEG
Cae'r-hendy
NP11
YARD COAL RISE
FERN CL
CARLTON DR
BRYN BRITHDIR
WILLOW RD
ROCK VILLAS
A4048
Sirhowy River/ Afon Sirhywi
Crumlin Old Farm
Kendon Farm
Ebbw Vale Wlk
LOAD OF HAY RD
Cwm Kendon
KENDON RD
Kendon
TY BRACHTY TERR
PLEASANT VIEW
WOOD VIEW
BRONWYDD
WATERLOO
NANT-GAU
TIR-BERLLAN
PEN-RHIW BEILI LA
COMMERCIAL BLDGS
BRYN-Y-GOF TERR
BLACKSMITH CL
PENYWAUN CL / CLOS PENYWAUN
PARC BEVAN
SYR DAFYDD AVE
RHIW SYR DAFYDD HILL
RISING SUN CL
CENTRAL BLDGS
Sch
PENMAEN AVE
MARKHAM CRES
Oakdale Inf Sch
PEN-Y-GROES
PANDY RD
PEN-Y-BRYN CT
MELIN PL
LLEWELYN AVE
PENDINAS AVE
CEMAES RD
PLYNLIMON AVE
PLYNLIMON CL
Ebbw Vale Wlk
B4251
Oakdale
Liby
PEN-RHIW TERR
ABERCONWAY PL
BEECH GR
MAES-Y-GARN RD
PEN-Y-FAN WAY
DARREN CT
PEN-DERI CT
MANMOEL CT
THE ALDERS
PRIORSGATE
THE ELMS
THE OAKS
WAUNGOCH RD
THE HOLLIES
CHERRY GR
CROSSFIELDS
WILLOW PK
OVERDALE WLK
MEADOW WLK
GROVE WLK
SHELLEY CL
TY MELIN
BYRON PL
CAE CELYN
Ty-mawr
Rhiw
FARM CRES
WILLIAM ST
KENNARD TERR
RIVER ROW
WEST VIEW CRES
ASHVILLE
VILLAGE CT
PEN-RHIW AVE
YORK AVE
CENTRAL AVE
KINCOED RD
LLWYN-ON RD
CWRT CWMDERWEN
LLWYN ON CRES
Nant Philkins
1 SPRINGFIELDS
2 GREENLANDS
3 PEN-Y-CAE CL
Croespenmaen
Croespenmaen Ind Est
PARRY TERR
ALBERTINA RD
FFLORENS RD
TREOWEN RD
HILL VIEW LA
LLWYN-ON LA
LLYS CYNCOED
Oakdale
CH
Maes-yr-hâf Ho
Tir-hunt
ROYAL CRES
PENMAEN CNR
FARM CL
18
19
20
98
1
99
2
3
4
00
5
6
01
7
8
A
B
C
D
E
F

86
60

59
36

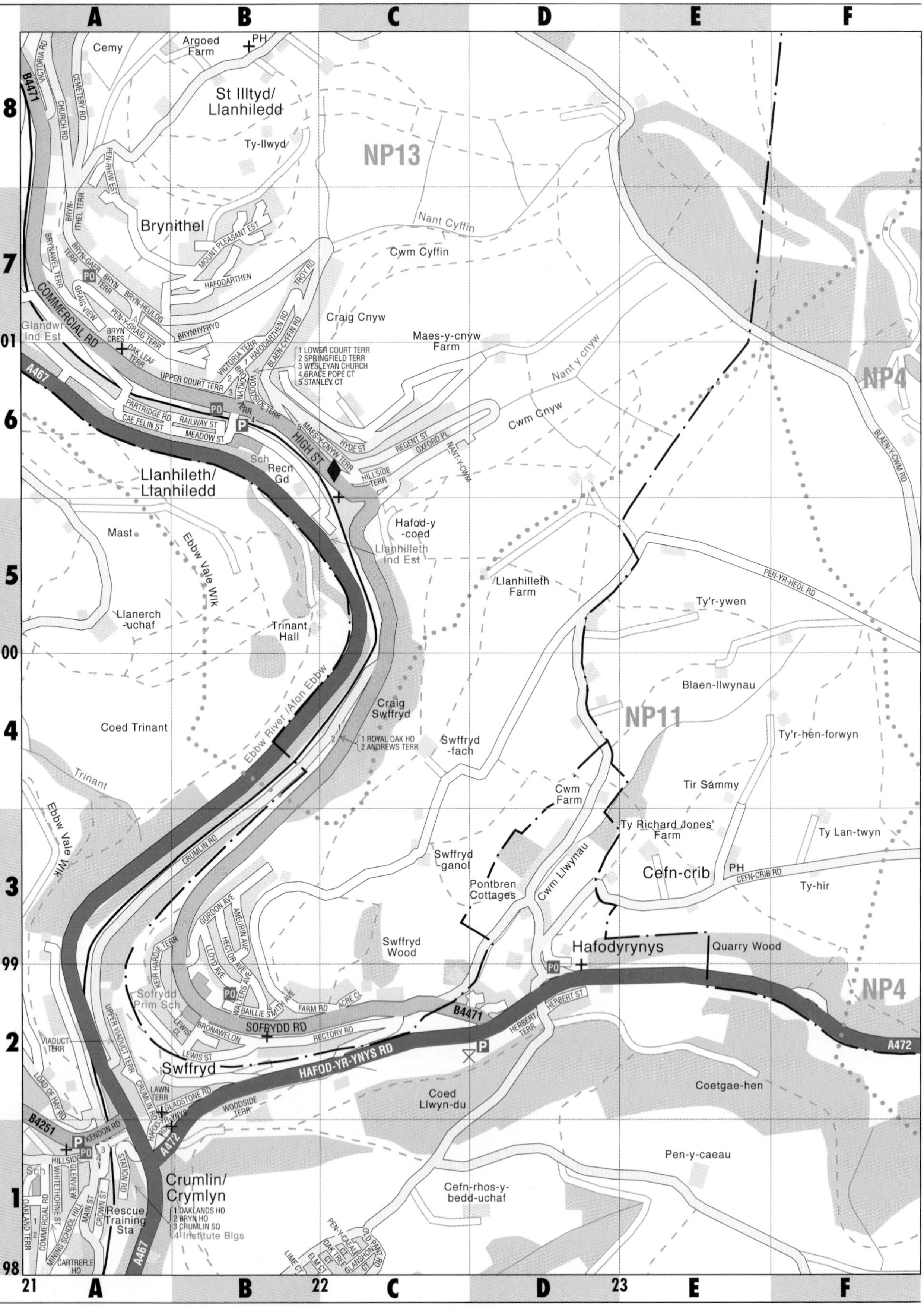
A
B
C
D
E
F
8
7
01
6
5
00
4
3
99
2
1
98
21
22
23
Cemy
Argoed
Farm
PH
St Illtyd/
Llanhiledd
Ty-llwyd
NP13
Brynithel
Nant Cyffin
Cwm Cyffin
MOUNT PLEASANT EST
HAFODARTHEN
Craig Cnyw
Maes-y-cnyw
Farm
Nant y cnyw
Cwm Cnyw
NP4
B4471
VICTORIA RD
CEMETERY RD
CHURCH RD
PEN-RHIW EST
BRYN-ITHEL TERR
BRYNAWEL TERR
BRYN-GAER TERR
BRYN TERR
BRYN-HEULOG
GRAIG VIEW
PEN-Y-GRAIG TERR
BRYNHYFRYD
COMMERCIAL RD
Glandwr
Ind Est
BRYN CRES
OAK LEAF TERR
TROY RD
HAFODARTHEN RD
BLAEN-CYFFIN RD
VICTORIA TERR
1 LOWER COURT TERR
2 SPRINGFIELD TERR
3 WESLEYAN CHURCH
4 GRACE POPE CT
5 STANLEY CT
A467
UPPER COURT TERR
BROOKLYN TERR
WOODSIDE TERR
PO
P
PARTRIDGE RD
RAILWAY ST
CAE FELIN ST
MEADOW ST
HIGH ST
MAES-Y-CNYW TERR
HYDE ST
REGENT ST
OXFORD PL
NANT-Y-CWM
HILLSIDE TERR
BLAEN-Y-CWM RD
Sch
Recn
Gd
Llanhileth/
Llanhiledd
Hafod-y
-coed
Llanhilleth
Ind Est
Mast
Ebbw Vale Wlk
Llanhilleth
Farm
PEN-YR-HEOL RD
Ty'r-ywen
Llanerch
-uchaf
Trinant
Hall
Blaen-llwynau
NP11
Craig
Swffryd
Ebbw River/Afon Ebbw
Coed Trinant
1 ROYAL OAK HO
2 ANDREWS TERR
Swffryd
-fach
Ty'r-hen-forwyn
Tir Sammy
Trinant
Cwm
Farm
Ebbw Vale Wlk
Ty Richard Jones'
Farm
Ty Lan-twyn
CRUMLIN RD
Swffryd
-ganol
Cwm Llwynau
Pontbren
Cottages
Cefn-crib
PH
CEFN-CRIB RD
Ty-hir
GORDON AVE
ANEURIN AVE
HECTOR AVE
KEIR HARDIE TERR
LLOYD AVE
Swffryd
Wood
Hafodyrynys
Quarry Wood
Sofrydd
Prim Sch
WALTERS AVE
BAILLIE SMITH AVE
FARM RD
ACRE CL
B4471
HERBERT ST
HERBERT TERR
A472
LEWIS CL
BRONAWELON
SOFRYDD RD
RECTORY RD
VIADUCT TERR
UPPER VIADUCT TERR
LEWIS ST
Swffryd
HAFOD-YR-YNYS RD
LOAD OF HAY RD
LAWN TERR
CRUMLIN RD
GLADSTONE RD
WOODSIDE TERR
Coed
Llwyn-du
Coetgae-hen
B4251
KENDON RD
HAFOD-YR-YNYS RD
A472
HILLSIDE
GLENVIEW
Sch
WHITETHORNE ST
MINING SCHOOL HILL
MAIN ST
CROWN ST
STATION RD
Crumlin/
Crymlyn
Pen-y-caeau
Cefn-rhos-y-
bedd-uchaf
Rescue
Training
Sta
1 OAKLANDS HO
2 BRYN HO
3 CRUMLIN SQ
4 Institute Blgs
OAKLAND TERR
COMMERCIAL RD
CARTREFLE HO
PEN-Y-CAEAU
OAK TREE CT
GLANSHON CT
OLD PANT RD
LIME CT
ELM CT

59
87

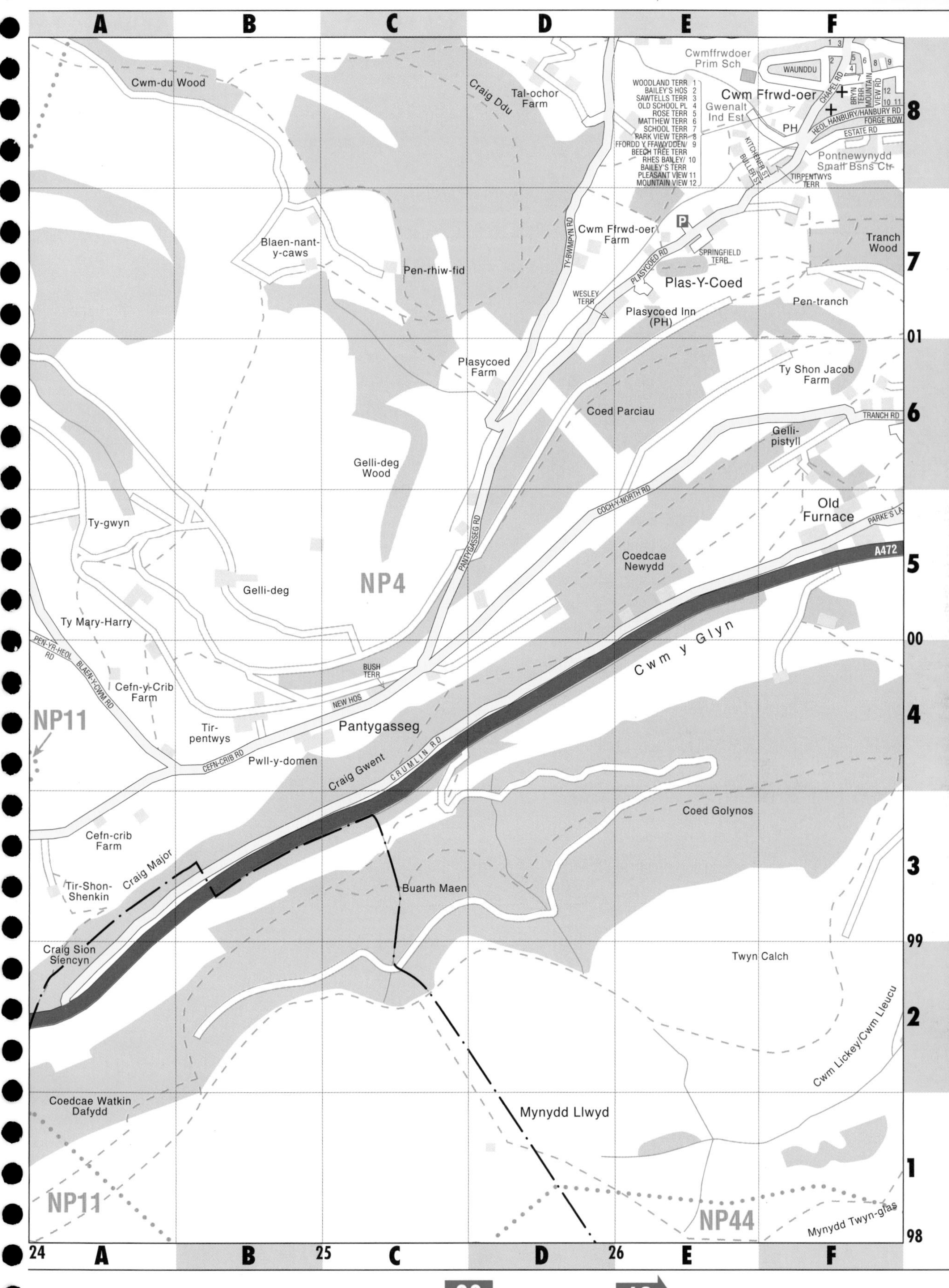
37
62
A B C D E F
Cwm-du Wood
Craig Ddu
Tal-ochor Farm
Cwmffrwdoer Prim Sch
WAUNDDU
WOODLAND TERR 1
BAILEY'S HOS 2
SAWTELLS TERR 3
OLD SCHOOL PL 4
ROSE TERR 5
MATTHEW TERR 6
SCHOOL TERR 7
PARK VIEW TERR 8
FFORDD Y FFAWYDDEN/ 9
BEECH TREE TERR
RHES BAILEY/ 10
BAILEY'S TERR
PLEASANT VIEW 11
MOUNTAIN VIEW 12
Cwm Ffrwd-oer
Gwenalt Ind Est
PH
CHAPEL RD
HEOL HANBURY/HANBURY RD
FORGE ROW
ESTATE RD
Pontnewynydd Small Bsns Ctr
KITCHENER ST
BULLER ST
TIRPENTWYS TERR
Blaen-nant-y-caws
Pen-rhiw-fid
TY-BWMPYN RD
Cwm Ffrwd-oer Farm
PLASYCOED RD
SPRINGFIELD TERR
Plas-Y-Coed
Tranch Wood
WESLEY TERR
Plasycoed Inn (PH)
Pen-tranch
Plasycoed Farm
Ty Shon Jacob Farm
Coed Parciau
TRANCH RD
Gelli-pistyll
Gelli-deg Wood
COCH-Y-NORTH RD
PANTYGASSEG RD
Old Furnace
PARKE'S LA
Ty-gwyn
Coedcae Newydd
A472
Gelli-deg
NP4
Ty Mary-Harry
Cwm y Glyn
PEN-YR-HEOL RD
BLAEN-Y-CWM RD
BUSH TERR
Cefn-y-Crib Farm
NEW HOS
NP11
Tir-pentwys
Pantygasseg
CEFN-CRIB RD
Pwll-y-domen
Craig Gwent
CRUMLIN RD
Coed Golynos
Cefn-crib Farm
Craig Major
Tir-Shon-Shenkin
Buarth Maen
Craig Sion Siencyn
Twyn Calch
Cwm Lickey/Cwm Lleucu
Coedcae Watkin Dafydd
Mynydd Llwyd
NP11
NP44
Mynydd Twyn-glas
8 7 01 6 5 00 4 3 99 2 1 98
24 25 26
88
62

61
38

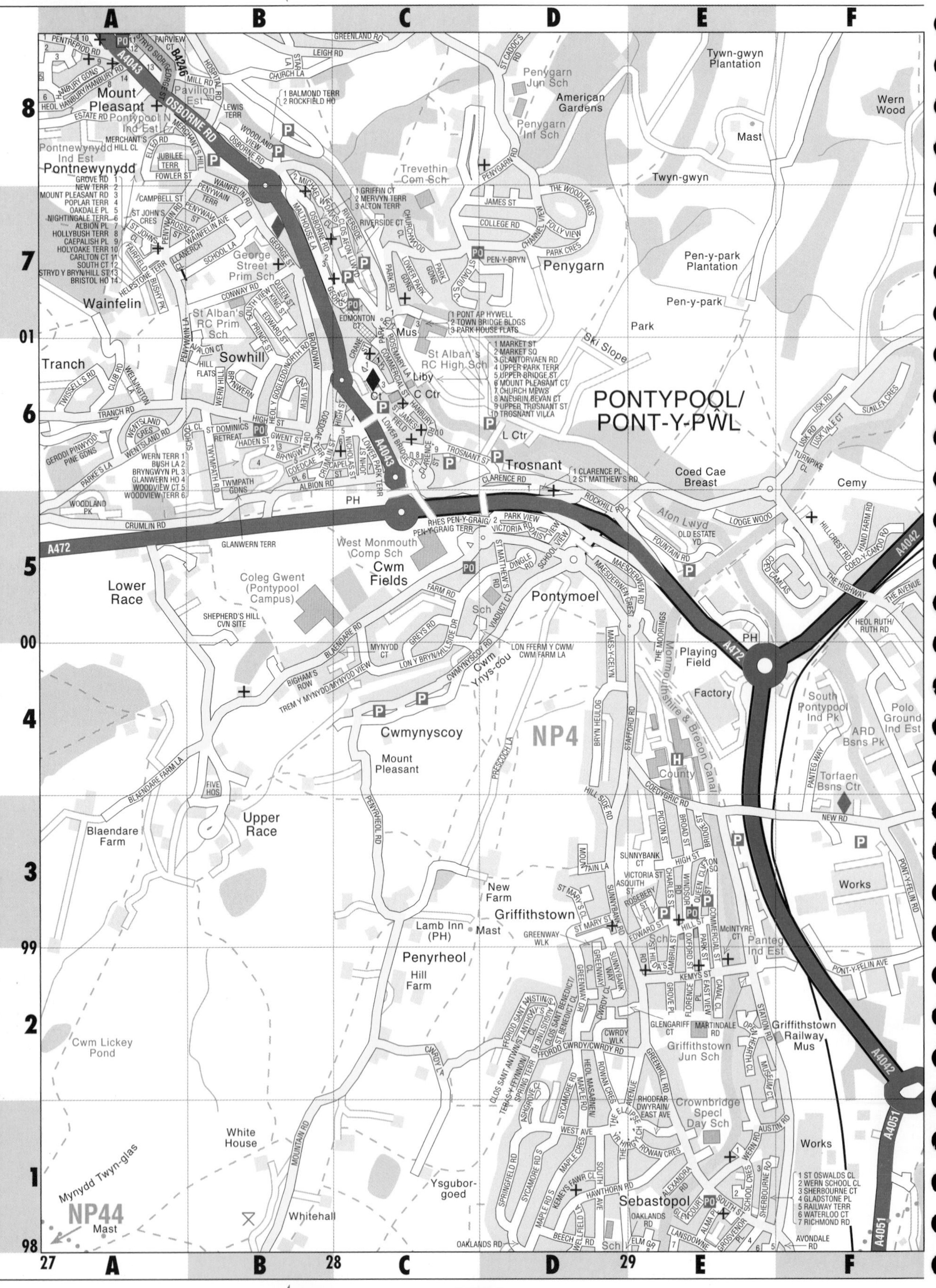
A B C D E F
Mount Pleasant
Pontnewynydd
Wainfelin
Tranch
Sowhill
Pontypool N Ind Est
Pontnewynydd Ind Est
George Street Prim Sch
St Alban's RC Prim Sch
Trevethin Com Sch
Penygarn Jun Sch
Penygarn Inf Sch
American Gardens
Tywn-gwyn Plantation
Twyn-gwyn
Wern Wood
Mast
Penygarn
Pen-y-park Plantation
Pen-y-park
Park
Ski Slope
PONTYPOOL/
PONT-Y-PŴL
St Alban's RC High Sch
Mus
Liby
C Ctr
L Ctr
Trosnant
Coed Cae Breast
Cemy
Afon Lwyd
West Monmouth Comp Sch
Cwm Fields
Lower Race
Coleg Gwent (Pontypool Campus)
Pontymoel
Playing Field
Factory
South Pontypool Ind Pk
Polo Ground Ind Est
ARD Bsns Pk
Torfaen Bsns Ctr
Cwm Ynys-cou
Cwmynyscoy
Mount Pleasant
NP4
County
Monmouthshire & Brecon Canal
Upper Race
Blaendare Farm
New Farm
Griffithstown
Lamb Inn (PH)
Mast
Penyrheol
Hill Farm
Panteg Ind Est
Works
Griffithstown Railway Mus
Griffithstown Jun Sch
Crownbridge Specl Day Sch
Cwm Lickey Pond
White House
Whitehall
Ysgubor-goed
Sebastopol
Mynydd Twyn-glas
NP44
A472
A4043
A4042
A4051
B4246
27 28 29
8 7 6 5 4 3 2 1
01 00 99 98

61
89

39

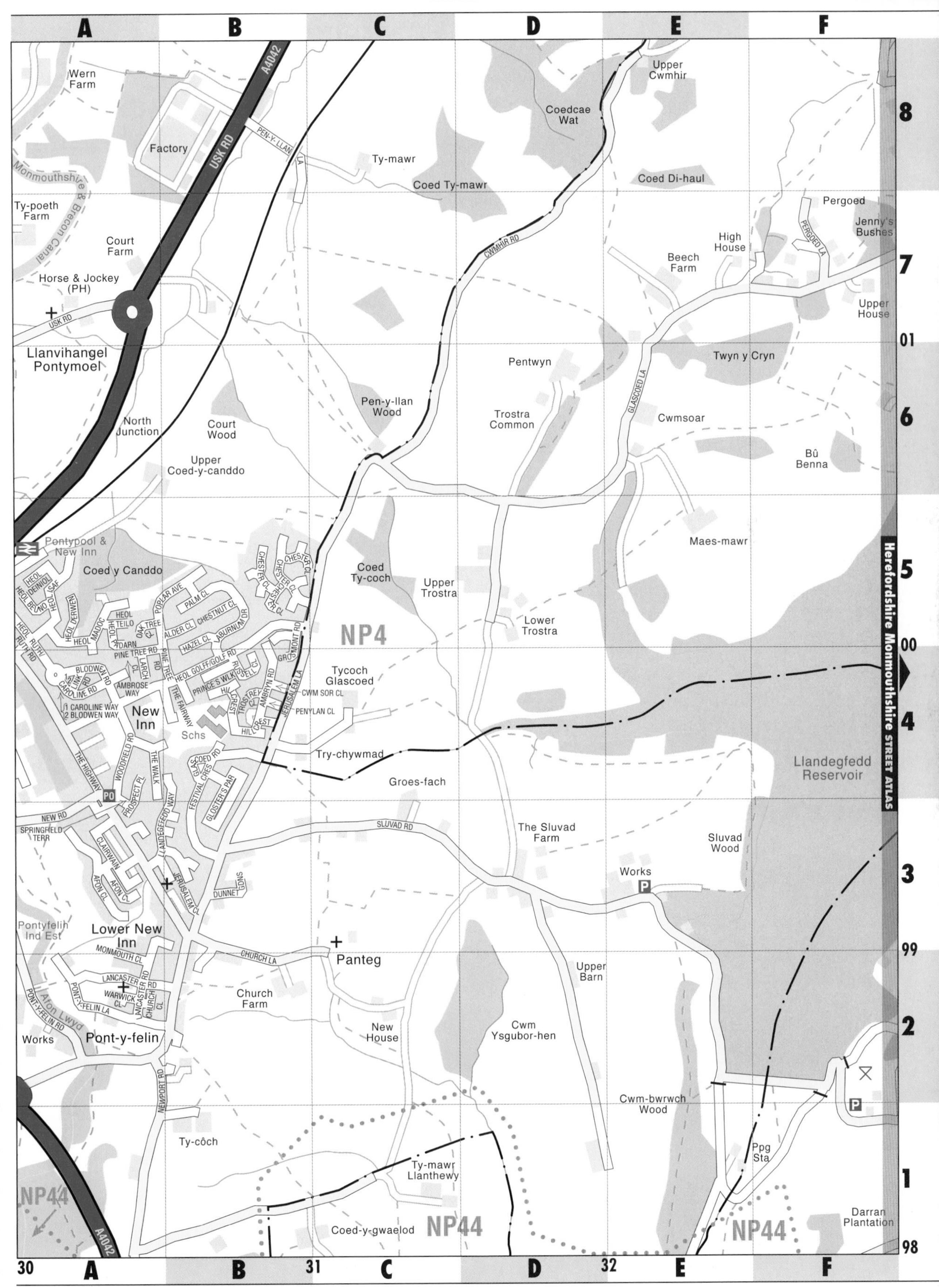

A
B
C
D
E
F
Wern Farm
Factory
A4042
USK RD
PEN-Y-LLAN LA
Ty-mawr
Coed Ty-mawr
Upper Cwmhir
Coedcae Wat
Coed Di-haul
Monmouthshire & Brecon Canal
Ty-poeth Farm
Court Farm
Horse & Jockey (PH)
USK RD
CWMHIR RD
Pergoed
Jenny's Bushes
PERGOED LA
High House
Beech Farm
Upper House
Llanvihangel Pontymoel
Pentwyn
Twyn y Cryn
GLASCOED LA
Pen-y-llan Wood
Trostra Common
Cwmsoar
North Junction
Court Wood
Upper Coed-y-canddo
Bû Benna
Pontypool & New Inn
Coed y Canddo
Maes-mawr
Coed Ty-coch
Upper Trostra
Lower Trostra
NP4
Tycoch Glascoed
New Inn
Schs
Try-chywmad
Groes-fach
Llandegfedd Reservoir
SLUVAD RD
The Sluvad Farm
Sluvad Wood
Works
Pontyfelin Ind Est
Lower New Inn
CHURCH LA
Panteg
Church Farm
Upper Barn
New House
Cwm Ysgubor-hen
Works
Pont-y-felin
Afon Lwyd
Cwm-bwrwch Wood
Ty-côch
Ppg Sta
Ty-mawr Llanthewy
NP44
Coed-y-gwaelod
Darran Plantation
8
7
01
6
5
00
4
3
99
2
1
98
30
31
32
Herefordshire Monmouthshire STREET ATLAS

90

229
41

A B C D E F

Millennium Coastal Park
SA14
Morfa-Bacas
8
7
97
6
River Loughor/Afon Llwchwr
5
Dalton's Point
Sewage Farm
96
4
GLANMOR TERR
PH
1 BELLE VUE
2 BLODWEN TERR
WEST END
BEACH RD
SEA VIEW
PO
B4295
STATION RD
HALL LA
GREENACRES
GRAIG-Y-COED
THE PROMENADE
CWRT Y CASTELL
CAE FOLLAND
TRINITY LA
PARK RD
Sch
BETHEL LA
BANC BACH
DUNRAVEN CL
MAES-YR-HAF
BENSON RD
BENSON STATION TERR
BURRY PL
PEN-Y-LAN
TAN-Y-BRYN TERR
NURSES CNR
MILL ST
GOLWG Y MOR
AEL-Y-BRYN
GOWER TERR
HENDY RD
Parc-hendy
Sewage Works
Salthouse Point
Crofty Ind Est
Pen y Gaer
MYRTLE HILL
BENSON TERR 1
BRYNFA TERR 2
VICTORIA ROW 3
VICTORIA RD
Pen-y-Lan
PARC HENDY CRES
Crofty
PENCAERFENNI CT
PENCAERFENNI PK
PENCAERFENNI LA
SALTHOUSE CL
Pen-caer-fenny
Llottrog
Pen-clawdd
3
Salthouse Pill
Cemy
BLAENCEDI
BLUE ANCHOR RD
CABAN ISAAC RD
RHYD Y FENNI
NEW RD
PO
95
Cefn-bychan
LLAN-YR-NEWYDD
CHURCH LA
FORGE RD
PH
CHAPEL RD
HAZELTREE COPSE
Gelli-orllwyn
SA4
2
RIVERSIDE
Llanmorlais
OSBORNE PL
TREM Y MOR
STATION RD
Morlais River
WERN RD
Wern Fabian Farm
Pwll-y-froga
Llanmorlais Prim Sch
1
Cwm-cynnar
Cerrig Man
B4295
Llwyndyris Farm
94
52 A B 53 C D 54 E F

229
91

42
66

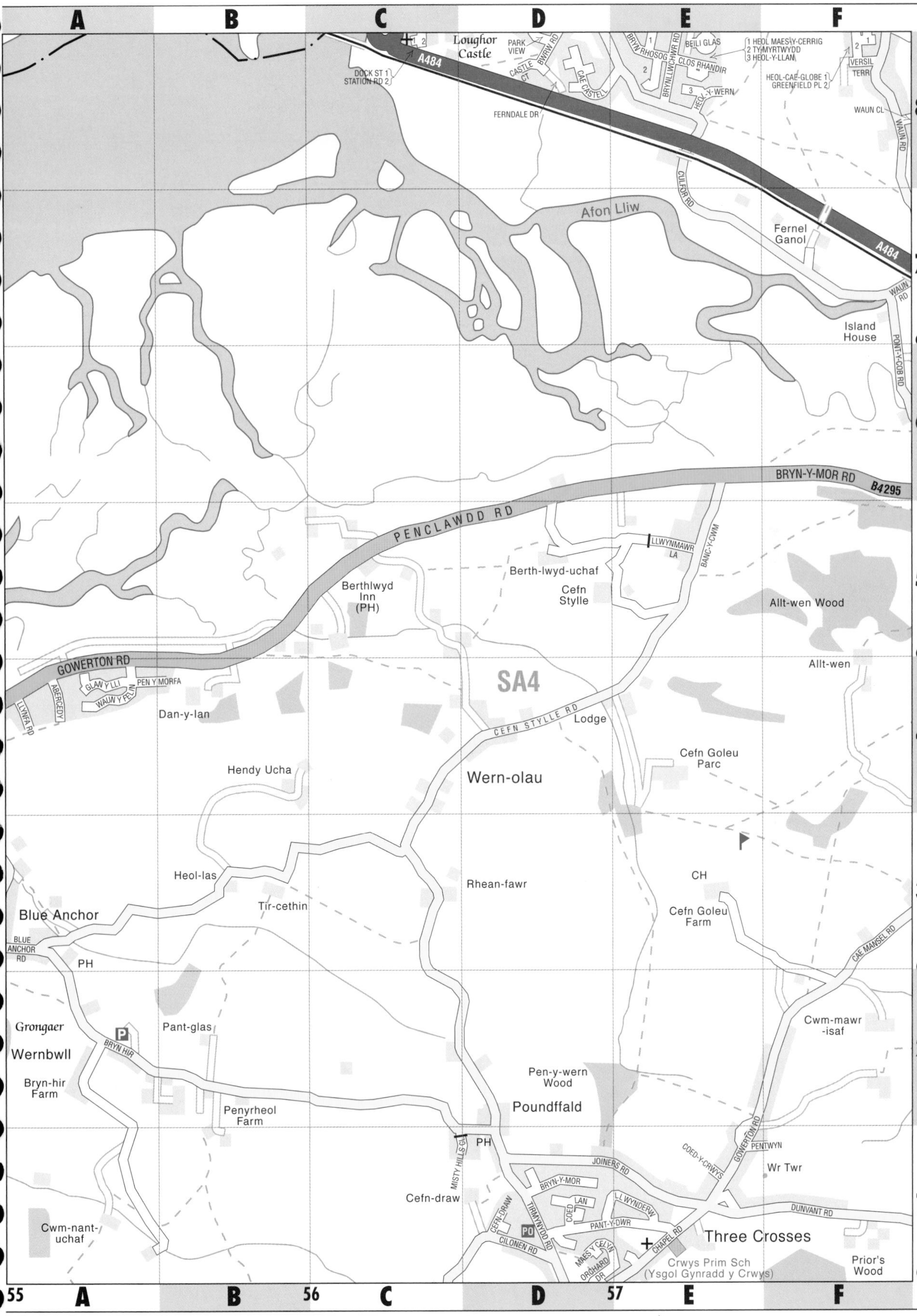

A B C D E F

Loughor Castle
PARK VIEW
BWRW RD
CASTLE CT
CAE CASTELL
DOCK ST 1
STATION RD 2
A484
FERNDALE DR
BRYN RHOSOG
BRYNLLWCHWR RD
BEILI GLAS
CLOS RHANDIR
HEOL-Y-WERN
1 HEOL MAES-Y-CERRIG
2 TY MYRTWYDD
3 HEOL-Y-LLAN
HEOL-CAE-GLOBE 1
GREENFIELD PL 2
VERSIL TERR
WAUN CL
WAUN RD
CULFOR RD
Afon Lliw
Fernel Ganol
WAUN RD
Island House
PONT-Y-COB RD
BRYN-Y-MOR RD
B4295
PENCLAWDD RD
LLWYNMAWR LA
BANC-Y-CWM
Berth-lwyd-uchaf
Cefn Stylle
Berthlwyd Inn (PH)
Allt-wen Wood
Allt-wen
GOWERTON RD
GLAN Y LLI
PEN Y MORFA
WAUN Y FELIN
ABERCEDY
LLYNFA RD
Dan-y-lan
SA4
CEFN STYLLE RD
Lodge
Cefn Goleu Parc
Hendy Ucha
Wern-olau
Heol-las
Rhean-fawr
CH
Blue Anchor
Tir-cethin
Cefn Goleu Farm
BLUE ANCHOR RD
PH
CAE MANSEL RD
Grongaer
Wernbwll
Pant-glas
P
BRYN HIR
Cwm-mawr -isaf
Bryn-hir Farm
Pen-y-wern Wood
Poundffald
Penyrheol Farm
PH
MISTY HILLS CL
JOINERS RD
COED-Y-CRWYS
GOWERTON RD
PENTWYN
Wr Twr
BRYN-Y-MOR
Cefn-draw
CEFN-DRAW
TIRMYNYDD RD
COED LAN
LLWYNDERW
DUNVANT RD
Cwm-nant-uchaf
PO
PANT-Y-DWR
CHAPEL RD
Three Crosses
CILONEN RD
MAES Y CELYN
ORCHARD DR
Crwys Prim Sch (Ysgol Gynradd y Crwys)
Prior's Wood

8 7 97 6 5 96 4 3 95 2 1 94

55 A B 56 C D 57 E F

92
66

65 43

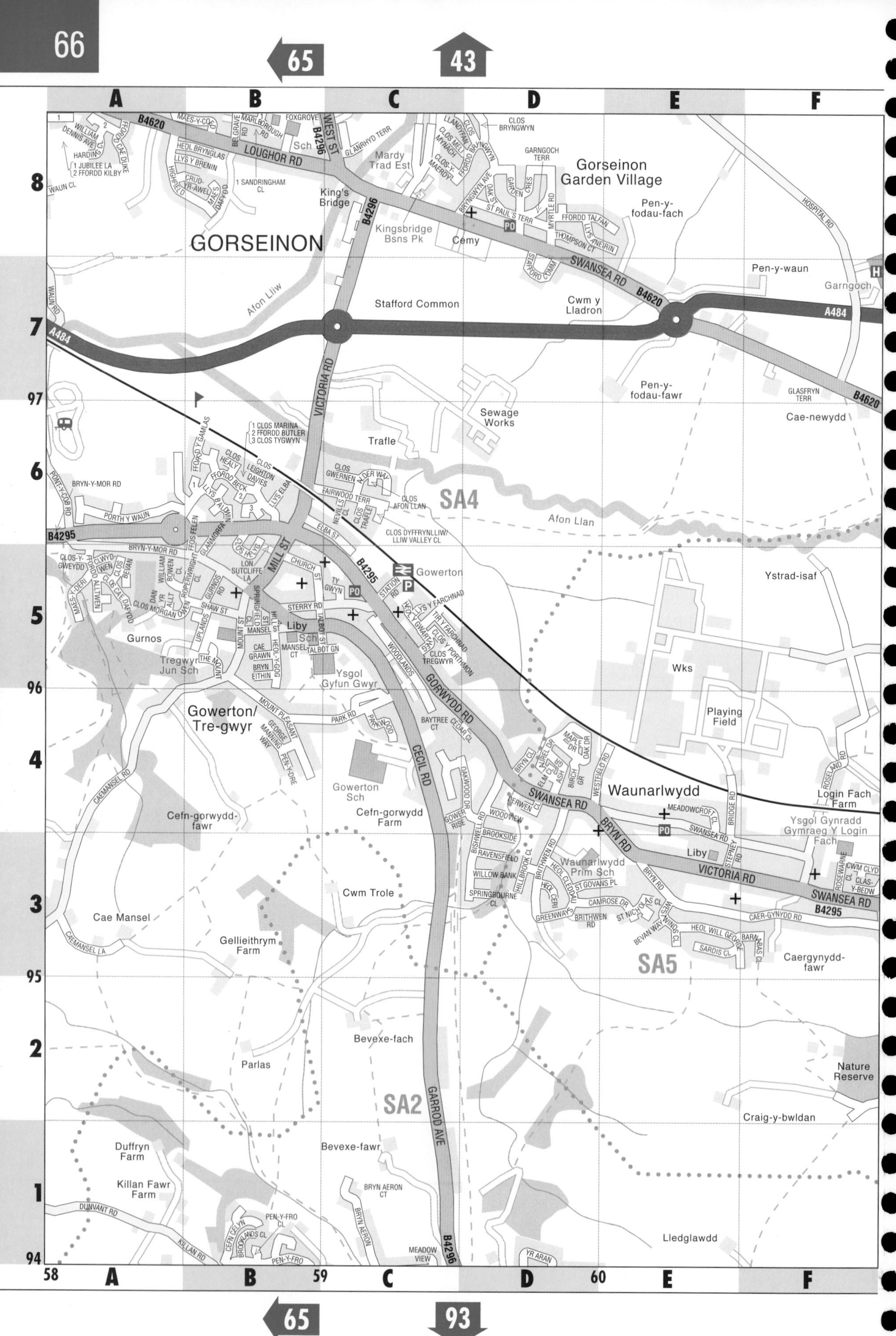
A B C D E F
8
7
97
6
5
96
4
3
95
2
1
94
58 59 60
GORSEINON
Gorseinon Garden Village
Pen-y-fodau-fach
Kingsbridge Bsns Pk
Mardy Trad Est
King's Bridge
Cemy
Pen-y-waun
Garngoch
Stafford Common
Cwm y Lladron
Afon Lliw
Pen-y-fodau-fawr
Cae-newydd
Sewage Works
Trafle
SA4
Afon Llan
Gowerton
Ystrad-isaf
Gurnos
Tregwyr Jun Sch
Ysgol Gyfun Gwyr
Gowerton/ Tre-gwyr
Wks
Playing Field
Gowerton Sch
Cefn-gorwydd Farm
Cefn-gorwydd-fawr
Waunarlwydd
Login Fach Farm
Ysgol Gynradd Gymraeg Y Login Fach
Waunarlwydd Prim Sch
Cwm Trole
Cae Mansel
Gellieithrym Farm
SA5
Caergynydd-fawr
Bevexe-fach
Parlas
SA2
Nature Reserve
Craig-y-bwldan
Duffryn Farm
Bevexe-fawr
Killan Fawr Farm
Lledglawdd
B4620
LOUGHOR RD
SWANSEA RD
A484
B4296
VICTORIA RD
B4295
GORWYDD RD
CECIL RD
GARROD AVE
BRYN RD
WEST ST
MILL ST
HOSPITAL RD
DUNVANT RD
KILLAN RD
CAEMANSEL RD
CAEMANSEL LA

65 93

44 68

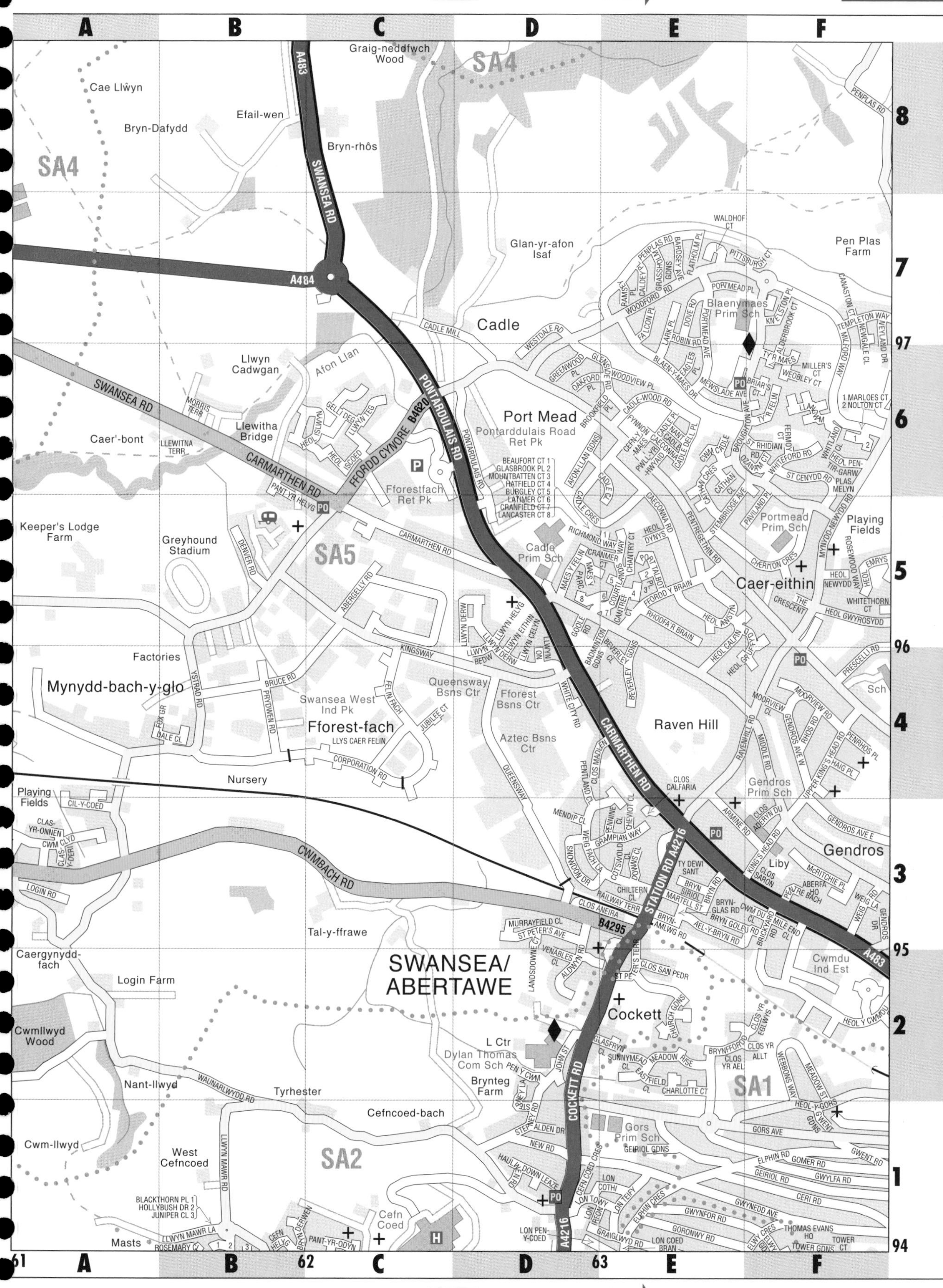
A B C D E F
8 7 6 5 4 3 2 1
97 96 95 94
61 62 63
SA4
SA5
SA1
SA2
Cae Llwyn
Bryn-Dafydd
Efail-wen
Graig-neddfwch Wood
Bryn-rhôs
SWANSEA RD
A483
A484
Glan-yr-afon Isaf
Pen Plas Farm
Cadle
Llwyn Cadwgan
Afon Llan
Llewitha Bridge
Caer'-bont
Port Mead
Pontarddulais Road Ret Pk
PONTARDDULAIS RD
CARMARTHEN RD
FFORDD CYNORE
B4620
Fforestfach Ret Pk
Keeper's Lodge Farm
Greyhound Stadium
Cadle Prim Sch
Blaenymaes Prim Sch
Portmead Prim Sch
Playing Fields
Caer-eithin
Factories
Mynydd-bach-y-glo
Swansea West Ind Pk
Queensway Bsns Ctr
Fforest Bsns Ctr
Fforest-fach
Aztec Bsns Ctr
Raven Hill
Gendros Prim Sch
Gendros
Nursery
Playing Fields
CWMBACH RD
STATION RD A4216
B4295
Tal-y-ffrawe
Caergynydd-fach
Login Farm
SWANSEA/ ABERTAWE
Cwmllwyd Wood
Cockett
Cwmdu Ind Est
L Ctr
Dylan Thomas Com Sch
Brynteg Farm
Nant-llwyd
Tyrhester
Cefncoed-bach
Cwm-llwyd
West Cefncoed
Gors Prim Sch
COCKETT RD
A4216
Cefn Coed
Masts

94 68

67
45

F8
1 LAN AVE
2 STAPLETON PL
3 BEDFORD HO
4 MARKET MEWS
5 MARKET ST
6 LOWER BANWELL ST
7 HEN ORSAF YR HEDDLU

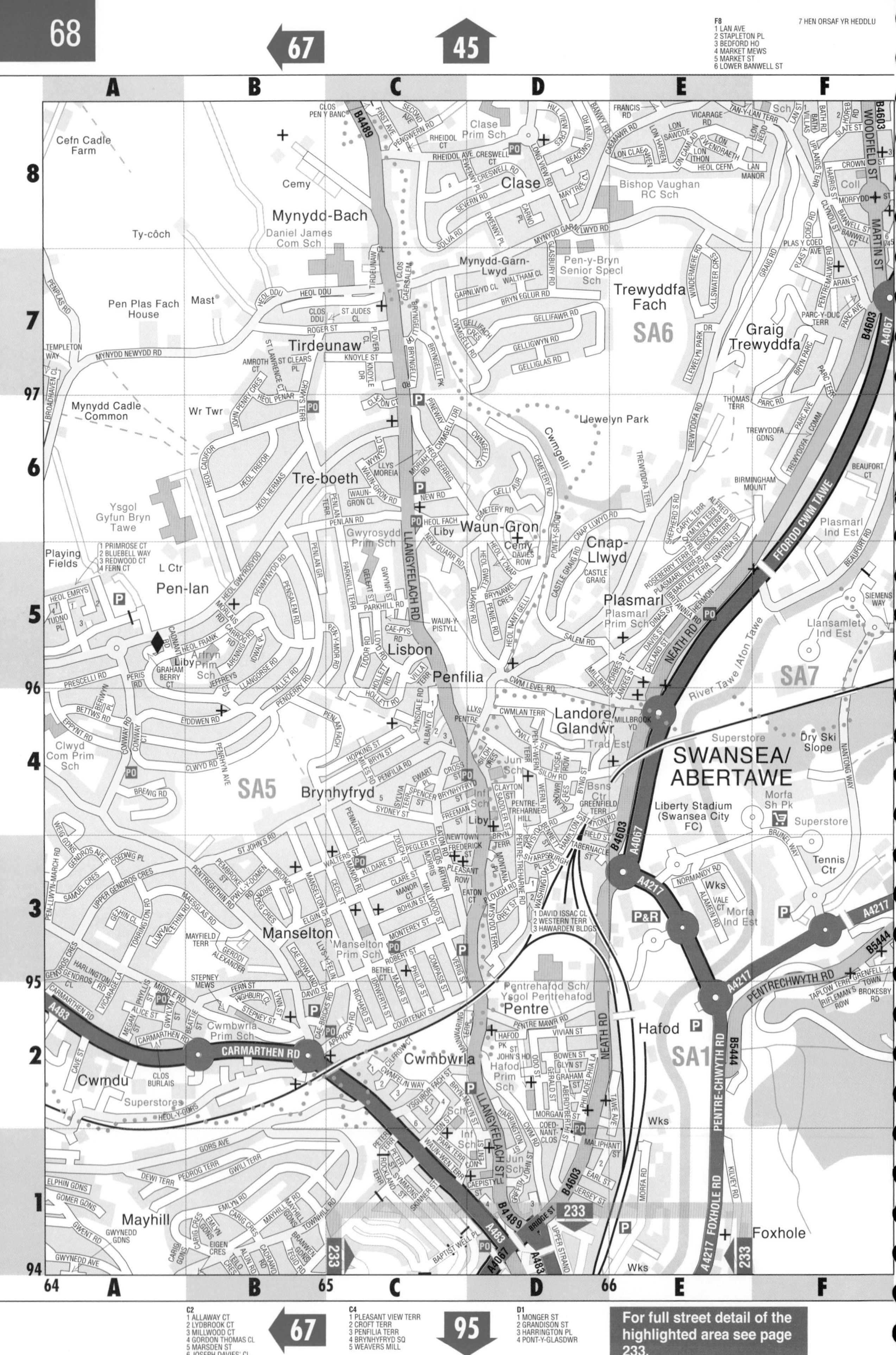

C2
1 ALLAWAY CT
2 LYDBROOK CT
3 MILLWOOD CT
4 GORDON THOMAS CL
5 MARSDEN ST
6 JOSEPH DAVIES' CL
7 CHRIS THOMAS HO

C4
1 PLEASANT VIEW TERR
2 CROFT TERR
3 PENFILIA TERR
4 BRYNHYFRYD SQ
5 WEAVERS MILL

D1
1 MONGER ST
2 GRANDISON ST
3 HARRINGTON PL
4 PONT-Y-GLASDWR

67
95
For full street detail of the highlighted area see page 233.

A8
1 GLOBE ST
2 DAVIES ST
3 MORFYDD ST
4 PHILADELPHIA CT
5 JIM HARVARD CT
6 LIME TREE GR
7 MORRIS ST
8 MARKET ST
9 CLOS YR ORSAF
10 CLOS CAMLAS

46
70

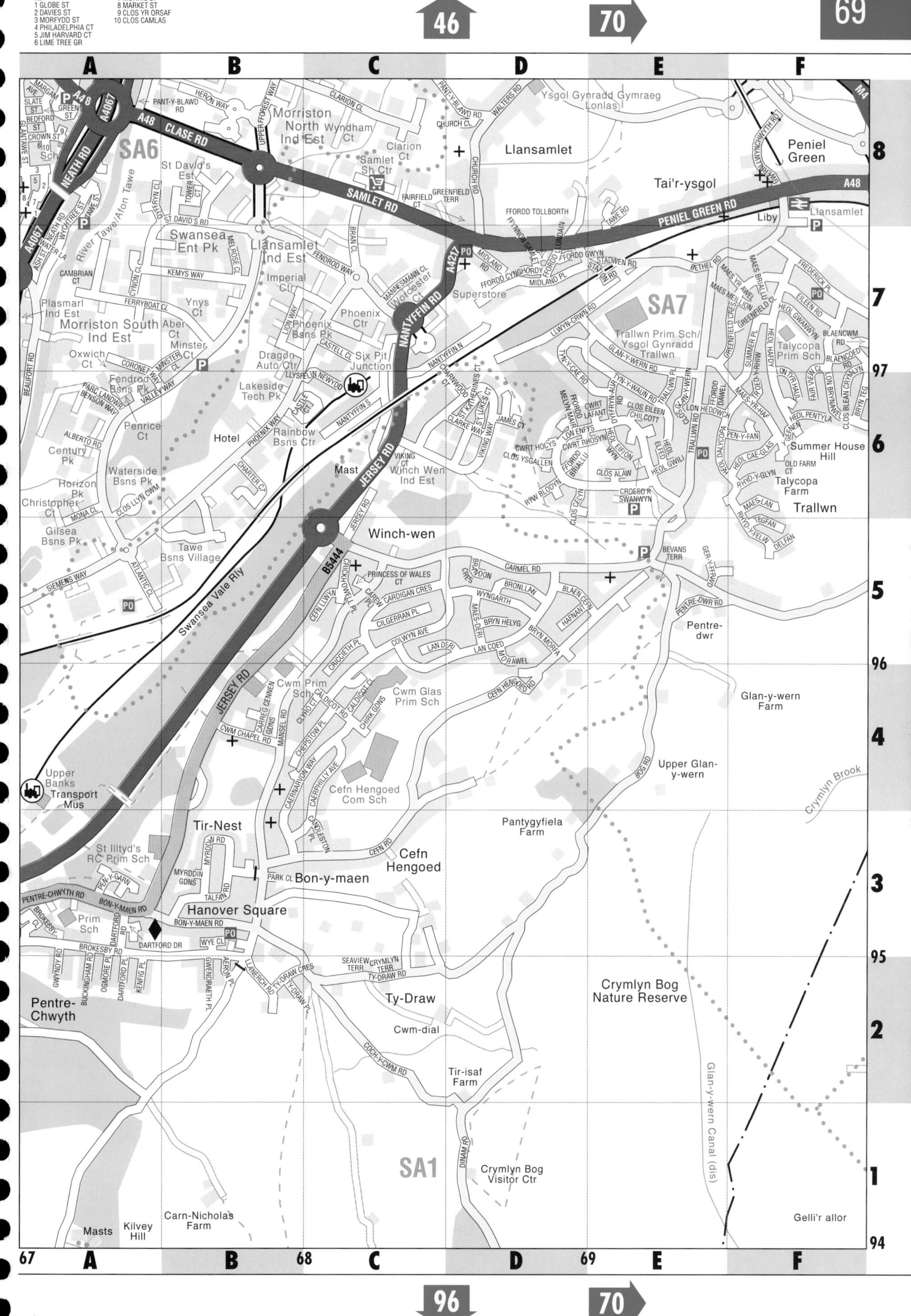

69 47

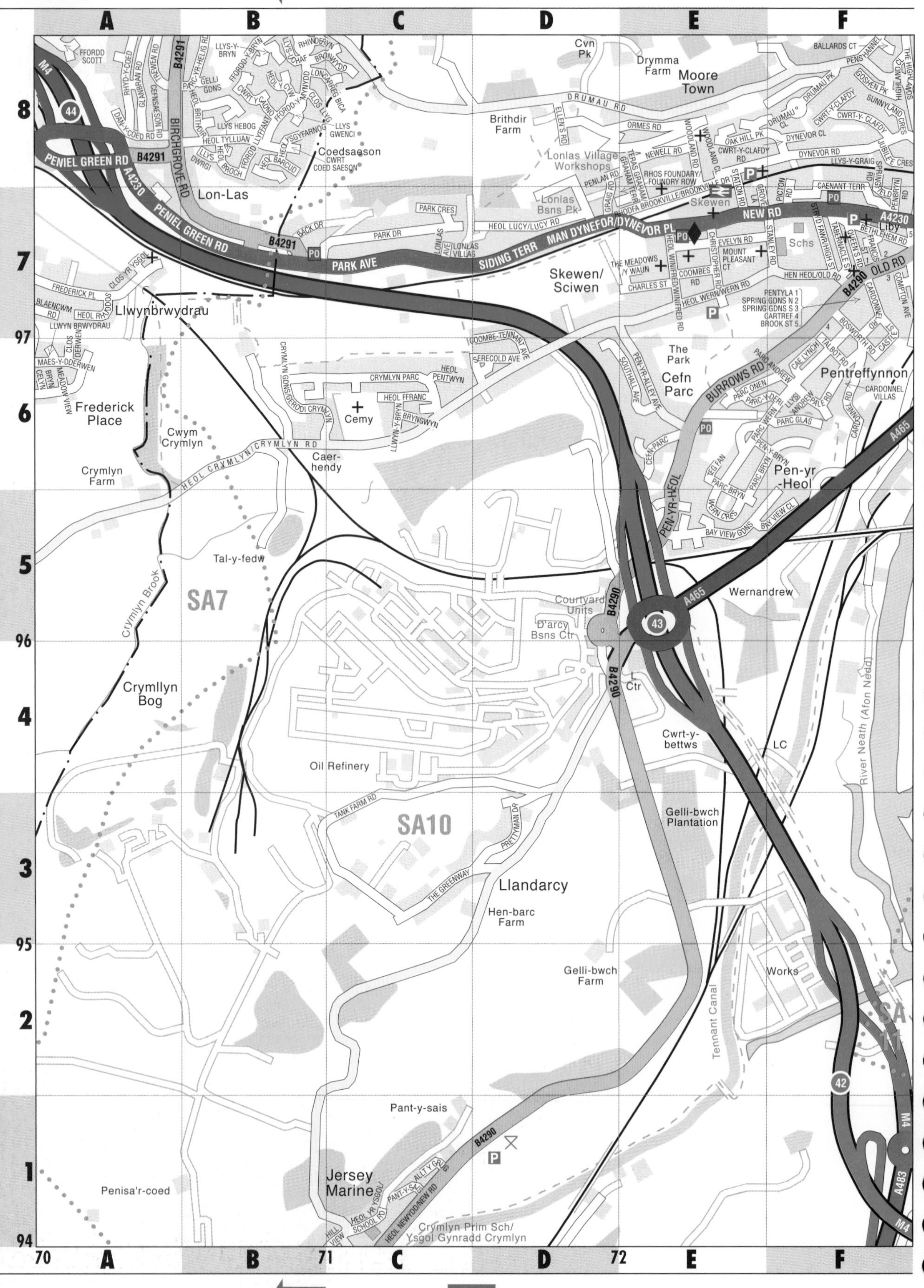

Skewen/
Sciwen
Llandarcy
Jersey
Marine
Oil Refinery
SA7
SA10
Lon-Las
Llwynbrwydrau
Frederick
Place
Crymllyn
Bog
Cefn
Parc
Pentreffynnon
Pen-yr
-Heol
Moore
Town
Coedsaeson
Wernandrew
Cwrt-y-
bettws
Gelli-bwch
Plantation
Gelli-bwch
Farm
Hen-barc
Farm
Pant-y-sais
Penisa'r-coed
Crymlyn
Farm
Cwym
Crymlyn
Tal-y-fedw
Caer-
hendy
Brithdir
Farm
Drymma
Farm
Crymlyn Brook
River Neath (Afon Nedd)
Tennant Canal
PENIEL GREEN RD
PARK AVE
SIDING TERR
MAN DYNEFOR/DYNEVOR PL
NEW RD
BURROWS RD
PEN-YR-HEOL
HEOL CRYMLYN
CRYMLYN RD
DRUMAU RD
BIRCHGROVE RD
M4
A4230
A465
A483
B4290
B4291
Crymlyn Prim Sch/
Ysgol Gynradd Crymlyn

D6
1 PAYNE ST
2 TAYLOR'S ROW
3 LOMBARD ST
4 NEW HENRY ST
5 EMANUEL PL

E6
1 FLORENCE ST
2 STOCKHOLM CNR HO
3 EVA ST
4 TY'R POBYDD
5 WILMOT ST
6 FREDERICK CT
7 EDWARD JARVIS CT
8 SPRINGFIELD TERR
9 LLYS PABI/POPPY CT
10 MAES-Y-FFYNNON CL
11 THOMAS'S CT
12 BURROWS RD

E7
1 STATION SQ
2 SUMMERFIELD PL
3 QUEEN ST BACK RD
4 TY IFOR
5 ALLISTER ST
6 WESLEY PL
7 LLYS BARTLETT
8 CHARLES ST
9 THE MEWS
10 WINDSOR CT
11 MAY'S CT
12 DUDLEY ST
13 RICHMOND ST
14 REES PL
15 MARY ST
16 HENRY ST
17 BROOKDALE ST
18 GEOFFREY ST

E8
1 BANK SIDE
2 CRIBB'S ROW
3 COMMERCIAL ST
4 MAES-YR-HAF RD
5 ZOAR RD
6 BRICKYARD COTTS
7 ANGEL ST
8 ANGEL PL
9 GOLWG Y CASTELL/ CASTLE VIEW
10 CHURCH PL
11 THE SQUARE
12 OLD MARKET ST
13 FAIRFIELD WAY
14 STRYD CASTELL/ CASTLE ST
15 CHARLESVILLE PL

48
72

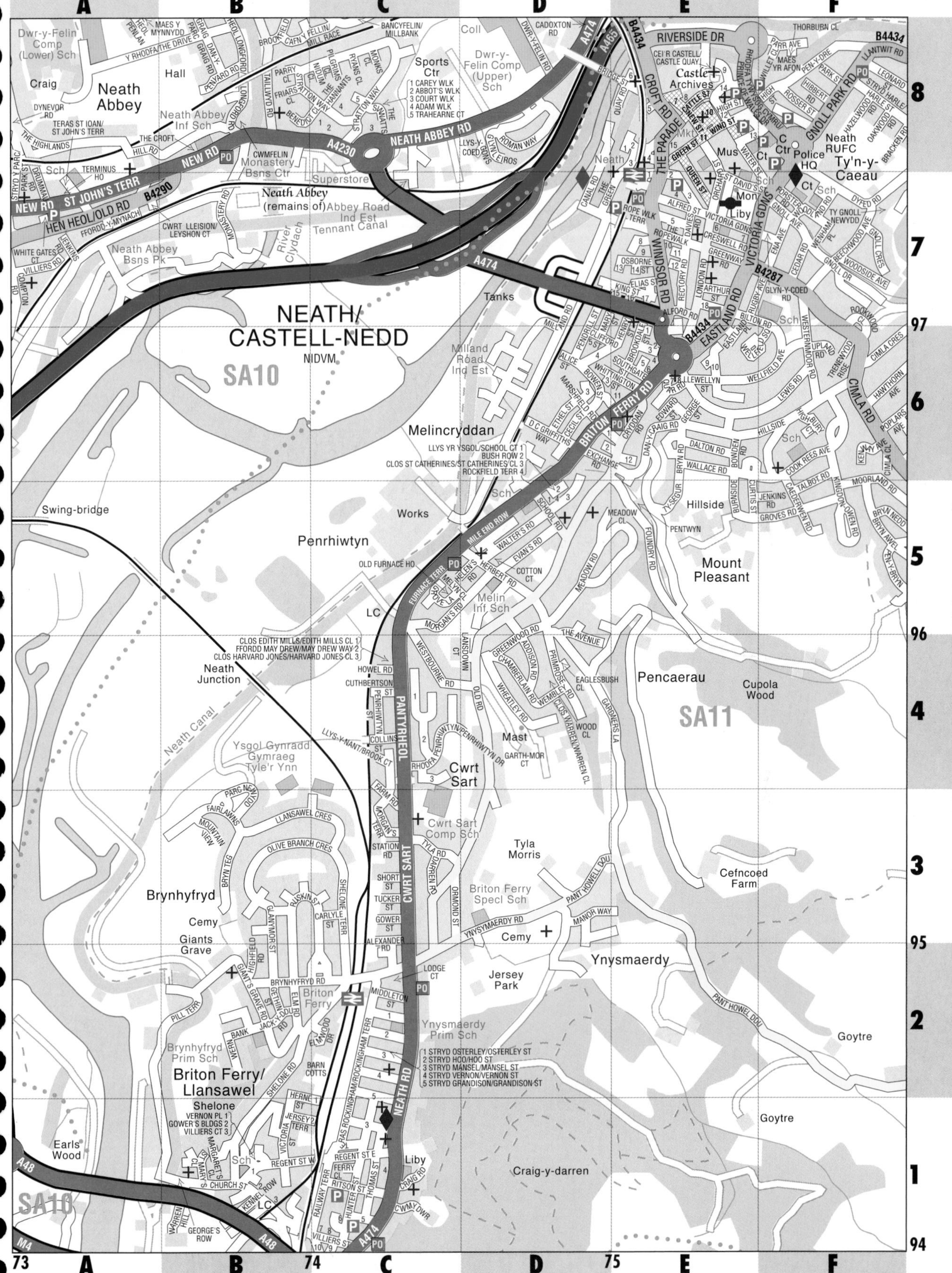

C1
1 PARK VIEW CL/CLOS GOLWG Y PARC
2 WOOD VIEW CL/CLOS GOLWG Y COED
3 STRYD CAROLINE/CAROLINE ST
4 VISCOUNT CT
5 HILL ST
6 TY-LLANSAWEL
7 LLANSAWEL
8 TY BRUNEL
9 SAND LA
10 BETHEL ST

98
72

71 49

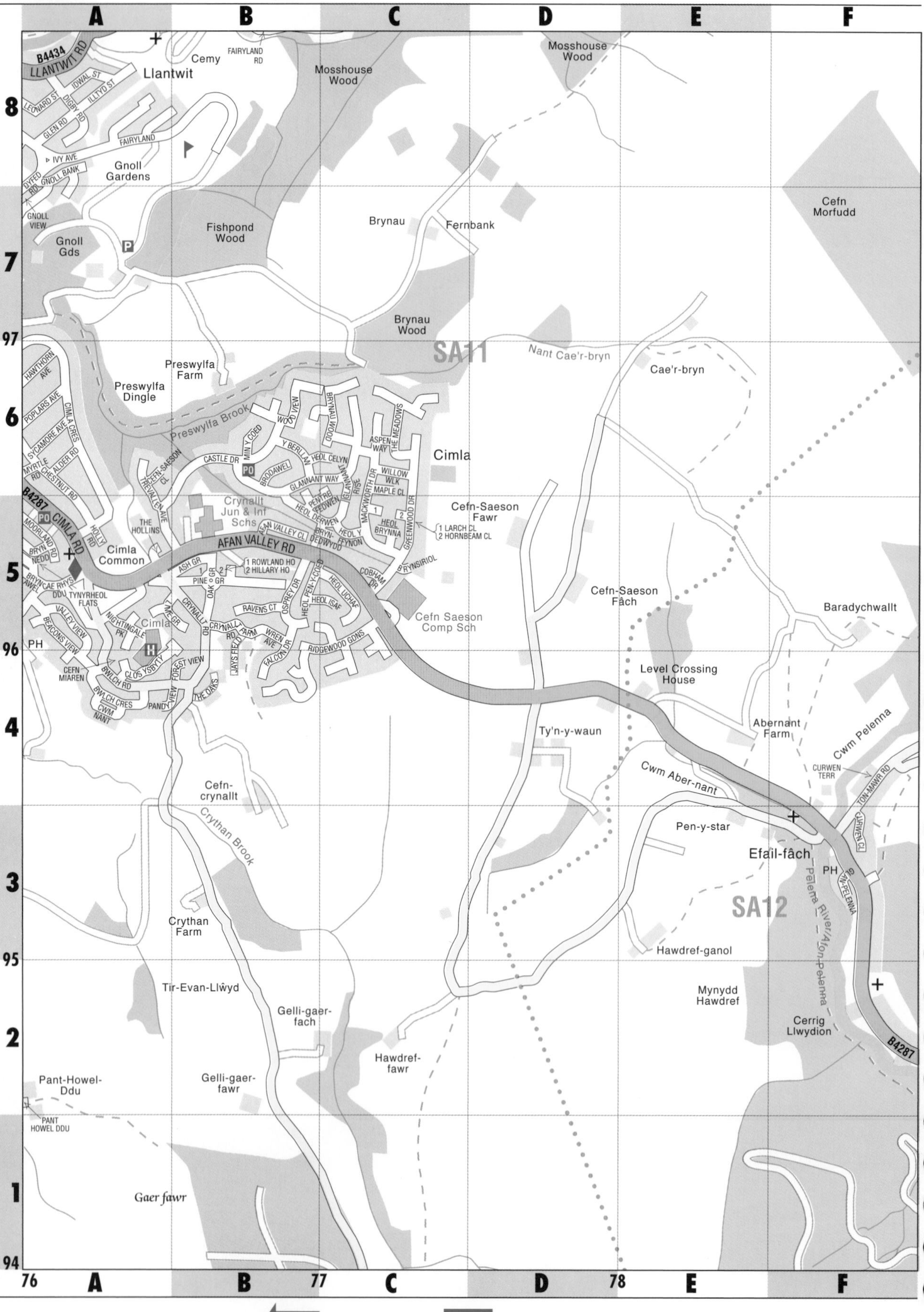

A B C D E F

8 7 97 6 5 96 4 3 95 2 1 94

B4434 LLANTWIT RD
Cemy
FAIRYLAND RD
Llantwit
Mosshouse Wood
Mosshouse Wood
IDWAL ST
ILLTYD ST
LEONARD ST
DIGBY RD
GLEN RD
FAIRYLAND
IVY AVE
GNOLL BANK
DYFED RD
Gnoll Gardens
GNOLL VIEW
Gnoll Gds
Fishpond Wood
Brynau
Fernbank
Cefn Morfudd
Brynau Wood
SA11
Nant Cae'r-bryn
Cae'r-bryn
Preswylfa Farm
Preswylfa Dingle
HAWTHORN AVE
POPLARS AVE
CIMLA CRES
SYCAMORE AVE
ALDER RD
MYRTLE RD
CHESTNUT RD
Preswylfa Brook
WOOD VIEW
BRYNAU WOOD
THE MEADOWS
ASPEN WAY
MIN Y COED
Y BERLLAN
HEOL CELYN
CASTLE DR
CEFN SAESON CL
BRODAWEL
GLANNANT WAY
WILLOW WLK
MAPLE CL
Cimla
B4287 CIMLA RD
MOORLAND RD
PENTRE FEDWEN
GLANNANT RISE
MACKWORTH DR
Crynallt Jun & Inf Schs
HEOL DERWEN
HEOL Y FFYNON
HEOL BRYNNA
GREENWOOD DR
Cefn-Saeson Fawr
1 LARCH CL
2 HORNBEAM CL
TREVALLEN AVE
THE HOLLINS
HOLLY RD
IFAN VALLEY CL
BRYN-DEDWYDD
BRYNSIRIOL
BRYN NEDD
Cimla Common
AFAN VALLEY RD
ASH GR
1 ROWLAND HO
2 HILLARY HO
COBHAM DR
BRYN AWEL
CAE RHYS DDU
TYNYRHEOL FLATS
PINE GR
OAK GR
OSPREY DR
HEOL PEN-Y-COED
HEOL UCHAF
HEOL ISAF
Cefn-Saeson Fâch
Baradychwallt
VALLEY VIEW
NIGHTINGALE PK
Cimla
CRYNALLT RD
RAVENS CT
Cefn Saeson Comp Sch
BEACONS VIEW
PH
CRYNALLT RD
FARM
WREN AVE
RIDGEWOOD GDNS
CLOS YSBYTY
FOREST VIEW
JAYS FIELD
FALCON DR
Level Crossing House
CEFN MIAREN
BWLCH RD
THE OAKS
BWLCH CRES
PANDY VIEW
CWM NANT
Ty'n-y-waun
Abernant Farm
Cwm Pelenna
Cefn-crynallt
Cwm Aber-nant
CURWEN TERR
TON-MAWR RD
Crythan Brook
Pen-y-star
CURWEN CL
Efail-fâch
PH
CWM-PELENNA
SA12
Crythan Farm
Pelena River/Afon Pelenna
Hawdref-ganol
Tir-Evan-Llŵyd
Mynydd Hawdref
Gelli-gaer-fach
Cerrig Llwydion
B4287
Hawdref-fawr
Pant-Howel-Ddu
Gelli-gaer-fawr
PANT HOWEL DDU
Gaer fawr

76 A B 77 C D 78 E F

71 99

226
74

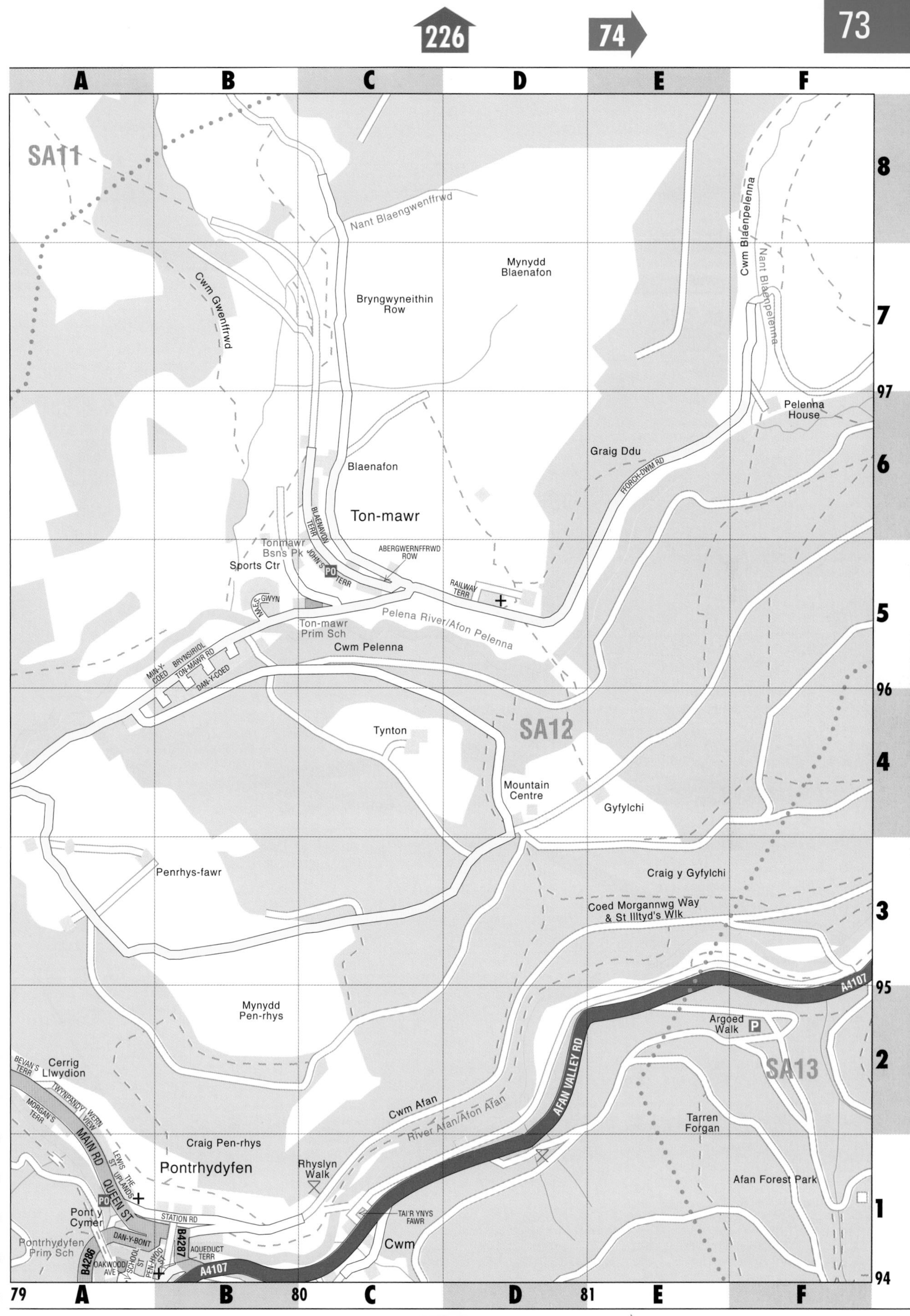
A
B
C
D
E
F
SA11
Nant Blaengwenffrwd
Mynydd Blaenafon
Cwm Gwenffrwd
Bryngwyneithin Row
Cwm Blaenpelenna
Nant Blaenpelenna
Pelenna House
Graig Ddu
FFORCH-DWM RD
Blaenafon
Ton-mawr
BLAENAVON TERR
Tonmawr Bsns Pk
Sports Ctr
JOHN'S TERR
PO
ABERGWERNFFRWD ROW
RAILWAY TERR
MAES GWYN
Ton-mawr Prim Sch
Pelena River/Afon Pelenna
Cwm Pelenna
MIN-Y-COED
BRYNSIRIOL
TON-MAWR RD
DAN-Y-COED
Tynton
SA12
Mountain Centre
Gyfylchi
Penrhys-fawr
Craig y Gyfylchi
Coed Morgannwg Way & St Illtyd's Wlk
A4107
Argoed Walk
P
SA13
Mynydd Pen-rhys
AFAN VALLEY RD
BEVAN'S TERR
Cerrig Llwydion
TWYNPANDY VIEW
WERN
MORGAN'S TERR
MAIN RD
Cwm Afan
River Afan/Afon Afan
Tarren Forgan
Craig Pen-rhys
LEWIS ST
THE UPLANDS
Pontrhydyfen
Rhyslyn Walk
Afan Forest Park
QUEEN ST
PO
STATION RD
TAI'R YNYS FAWR
Pont y Cymer
DAN-Y-BONT
B4287
AQUEDUCT TERR
Cwm
Pontrhydyfen Prim Sch
B4286
OAKWOOD AVE
SCHOOL ST
PEN-HYDD ST
A4107
8
7
97
6
5
96
4
3
95
2
1
94
79
80
81

100
74

73
226

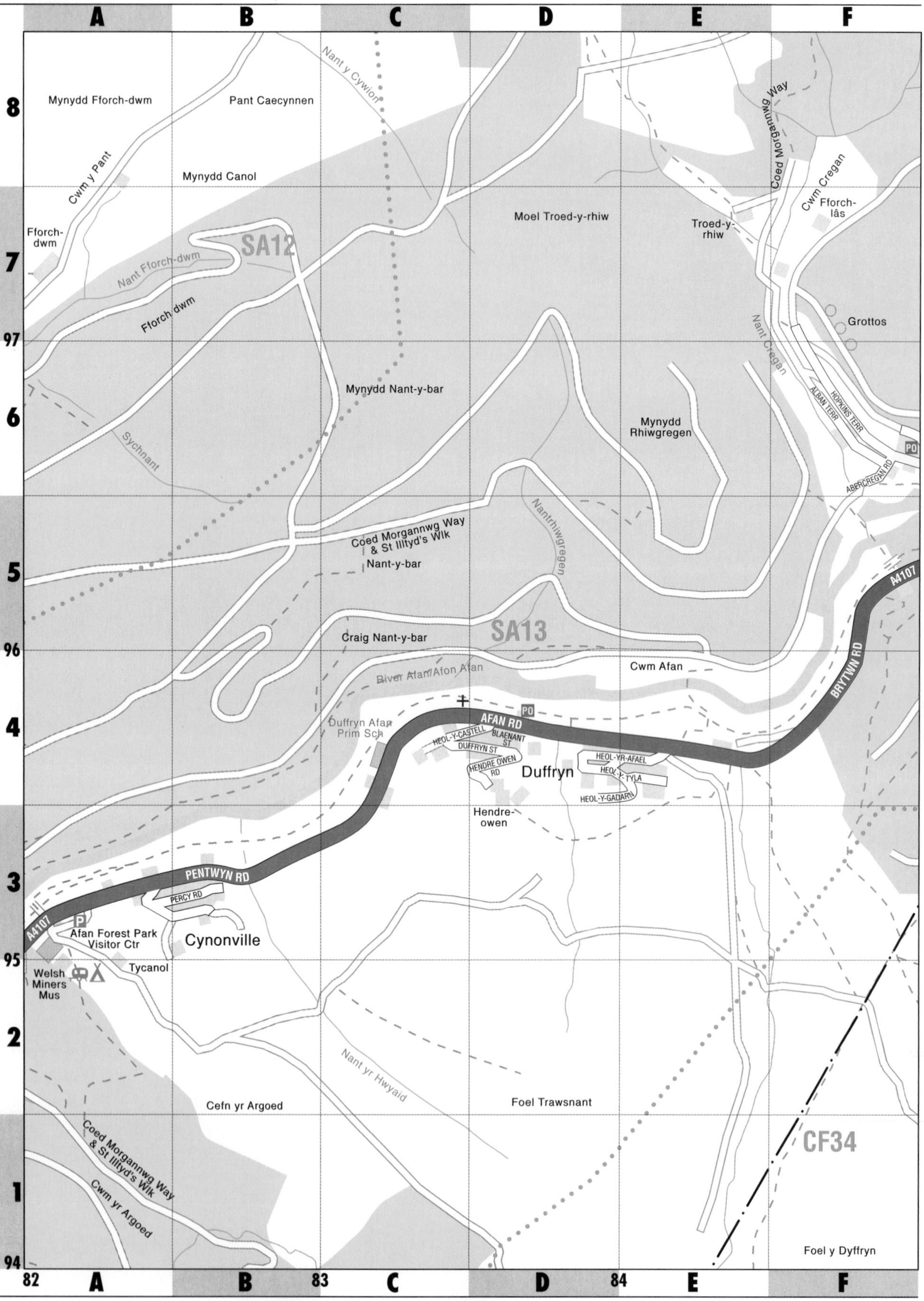

Mynydd Fforch-dwm
Pant Caecynnen
Nant y Cywion
Coed Morgannwg Way
Cwm y Pant
Mynydd Canol
Cwm Cregan
Fforch-lâs
Fforch-dwm
SA12
Moel Troed-y-rhiw
Troed-y-rhiw
Nant Fforch-dwm
Fforch dwm
Grottos
Nant Cregan
Mynydd Nant-y-bar
HOPKINS TERR
ALBAN TERR
Sychnant
Mynydd Rhiwgregen
PO
ABERCREGAN RD
Nantrhiwgregen
Coed Morgannwg Way & St Illtyd's Wlk
Nant-y-bar
A4107
SA13
Craig Nant-y-bar
BRYTWN RD
Cwm Afan
River Afan/Afon Afan
AFAN RD
Duffryn Afan Prim Sch
HEOL-Y-CASTELL
BLAENANT ST
DUFFRYN ST
HENDRE OWEN RD
Duffryn
HEOL-YR-AFAEL
HEOL-Y-TYLA
HEOL-Y-GADARN
Hendre-owen
PENTWYN RD
PERCY RD
A4107
P
Afan Forest Park Visitor Ctr
Cynonville
Welsh Miners Mus
Tycanol
Nant yr Hwyaid
Cefn yr Argoed
Foel Trawsnant
Coed Morgannwg Way & St Illtyd's Wlk
CF34
Cwm yr Argoed
Foel y Dyffryn
A B C D E F
8 7 97 6 5 96 4 3 95 2 1 94
82 83 84

73
101

227
76

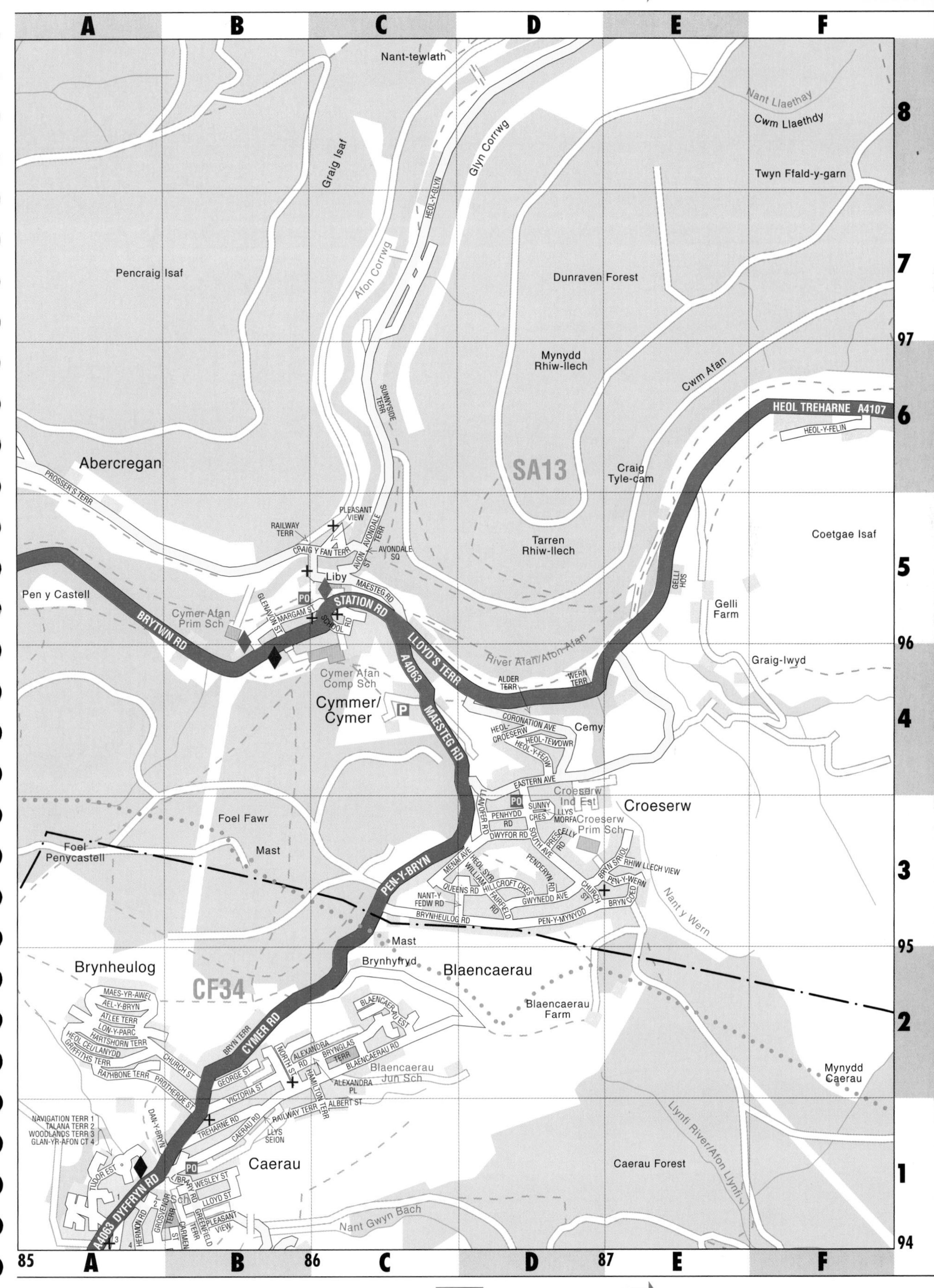
A
B
C
D
E
F
8
7
97
6
5
96
4
3
95
2
1
94
85
86
87
Nant-tewlath
Nant Llaethay
Cwm Llaethdy
Twyn Ffald-y-garn
Graig Isaf
Glyn Corrwg
HEOL-Y-GLYN
Afon Corrwg
Pencraig Isaf
Dunraven Forest
Mynydd
Rhiw-llech
Cwm Afan
SUNNYSIDE
TERR
HEOL TREHARNE A4107
HEOL-Y-FELIN
Abercregan
PROSSER'S TERR
SA13
Craig
Tyle-cam
PLEASANT
VIEW
RAILWAY
TERR
CRAIG Y FAN TERR
AVONDALE
TERR
AVON
ST
AVONDALE
SQ
Tarren
Rhiw-llech
Coetgae Isaf
Pen y Castell
Liby
MAESTEG RD
GELLI
HOS
Gelli
Farm
GLENAVON ST
MARGAM ST
SCHOOL RD
STATION RD
Cymer Afan
Prim Sch
BRYTWN RD
LLOYD'S TERR
River Afan/Afon Afan
Graig-lwyd
A4063
Cymer Afan
Comp Sch
ALDER
TERR
WERN
TERR
Cymmer/
Cymer
MAESTEG RD
CORONATION AVE
HEOL-
CROESERW
HEOL-TEWDWR
HEOL-Y-FEDW
Cemy
EASTERN AVE
Croeserw
Ind Est
Croeserw
LLANWONNO RD
SUNNY
CRES
LLYS
MORFA
PENHYDD
RD
Croeserw
Prim Sch
Foel Fawr
DWYFOR RD
SOUTH AVE
PRESELLY
RD
Foel
Penycastell
Mast
PEN-Y-BRYN
MENAI AVE
HEOL SYR
WILLIAM
QUEENS RD
HILLCROFT CRES
FAIRFIELD
RD
PENDERYN RD
GWYNEDD AVE
CHURCH
ST
BRYN SIRIOL
RHIW LLECH VIEW
PEN-Y-WERN
BRYN COED
Nant y Wern
NANT-Y
FEDW RD
BRYNHEULOG RD
PEN-Y-MYNYDD
Mast
Brynheulog
Brynhyfryd
Blaencaerau
CF34
MAES-YR-AWEL
AEL-Y-BRYN
ATLEE TERR
LON-Y-PARC
HARTSHORN TERR
HEOL CEULANYDD
GRIFFITHS TERR
RATHBONE TERR
CHURCH ST
PROTHEROE ST
BRYN TERR
CYMER RD
BLAENCAERAU EST
Blaencaerau
Farm
ALEXANDRA
RD
NORTH ST
BRYNGLAS
TERR
BLAENCAERAU RD
Blaencaerau
Jun Sch
GEORGE ST
VICTORIA ST
HAMILTON TERR
ALEXANDRA
PL
Mynydd
Caerau
NAVIGATION TERR 1
TALANA TERR 2
WOODLANDS TERR 3
GLAN-YR-AFON CT 4
DAN-Y-BRYN
TREHARNE RD
CAERAU RD
RAILWAY TERR
ALBERT ST
LLYS
SEION
Llynfi River/Afon Llynfi
TUDOR EST
Caerau
Caerau Forest
WESLEY ST
LLOYD ST
A4063 DYFFRYN RD
GROSVENOR
TERR
GREENFIELD
TERR
PLEASANT
VIEW
CARMEN
HERMON RD
Nant Gwyn Bach

102
76

75
227

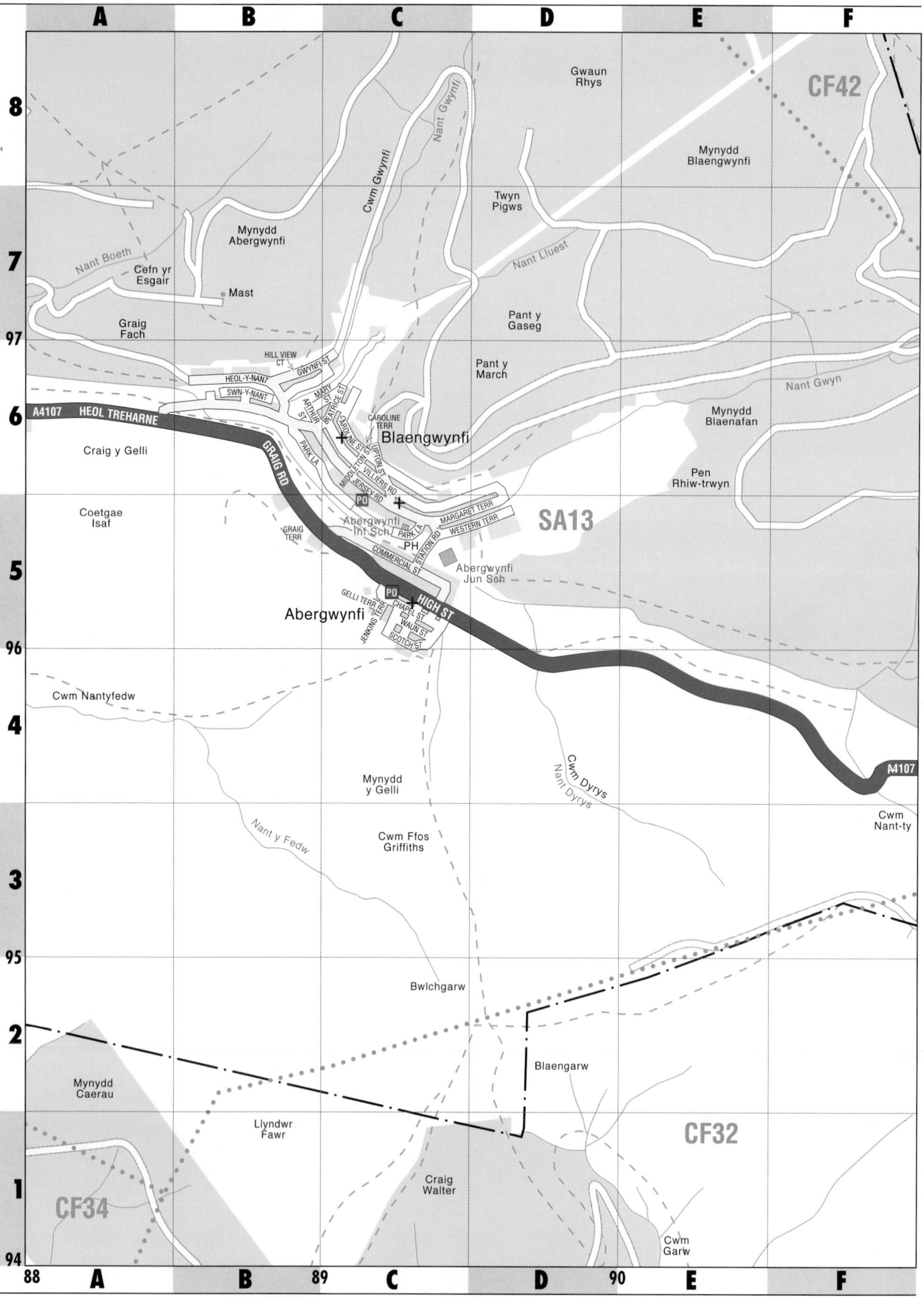

A
B
C
D
E
F
8
7
97
6
5
96
4
3
95
2
1
94
88
89
90
Gwaun Rhys
CF42
Mynydd Blaengwynfi
Nant Gwynfi
Cwm Gwynfi
Twyn Pigws
Mynydd Abergwynfi
Nant Boeth
Cefn yr Esgair
Mast
Nant Lluest
Pant y Gaseg
Graig Fach
Pant y March
HILL VIEW CT
GWYNFI ST
HEOL-Y-NANT
SWN-Y-NANT
MARY ST
ARTHUR ST
BEATRICE ST
CAROLINE TERR
Nant Gwyn
Mynydd Blaenafan
A4107
HEOL TREHARNE
Blaengwynfi
PARK LA
Craig y Gelli
GRAIG RD
MIDDLETON ST
UPTON ST
VILLIERS RD
JERSEY RD
Pen Rhiw-trwyn
PO
MARGARET TERR
WESTERN TERR
SA13
Coetgae Isaf
GRAIG TERR
Abergwynfi Inf Sch
PARK LA
STATION RD
PH
COMMERCIAL ST
Abergwynfi Jun Sch
GELLI TERR
HIGH ST
CHAPEL ST
Abergwynfi
JENKINS TERR
WAUN ST
SCOTCH ST
Cwm Nantyfedw
A4107
Cwm Dyrys
Nant Dyrys
Mynydd y Gelli
Cwm Nant-ty
Nant y Fedw
Cwm Ffos Griffiths
Bwlchgarw
Blaengarw
Mynydd Caerau
Llyndwr Fawr
CF32
Craig Walter
CF34
Cwm Garw

75
103

50
78

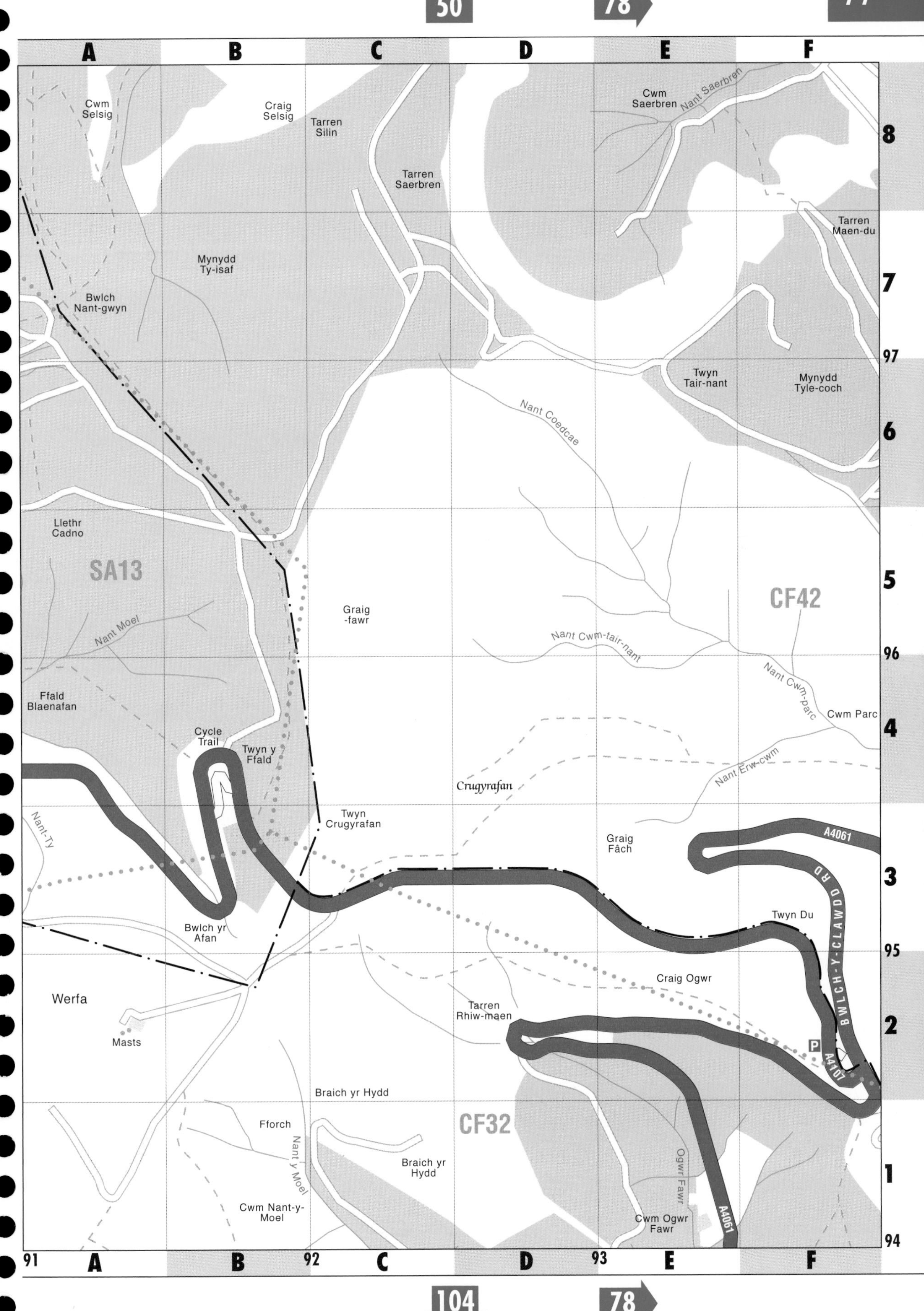
A
B
C
D
E
F
Cwm Selsig
Craig Selsig
Tarren Silin
Tarren Saerbren
Cwm Saerbren
Nant Saerbren
Tarren Maen-du
Mynydd Ty-isaf
Bwlch Nant-gwyn
Twyn Tair-nant
Mynydd Tyle-coch
Nant Coedcae
Llethr Cadno
SA13
Graig -fawr
CF42
Nant Moel
Nant Cwm-tair-nant
Nant Cwm-parc
Ffald Blaenafan
Cwm Parc
Cycle Trail
Twyn y Ffald
Nant Erw-cwm
Crugyrafan
Nant-Ty
Twyn Crugyrafan
Graig Fâch
A4061
Twyn Du
BWLCH-Y-CLAWDD RD
Bwlch yr Afan
Craig Ogwr
Werfa
Tarren Rhiw-maen
Masts
P
A4107
Braich yr Hydd
Fforch
CF32
Nant y Moel
Braich yr Hydd
Ogwr Fawr
Cwm Nant-y-Moel
Cwm Ogwr Fawr
A4061
8
7
97
6
5
96
4
3
95
2
1
94
91
92
93

104
78

77
51

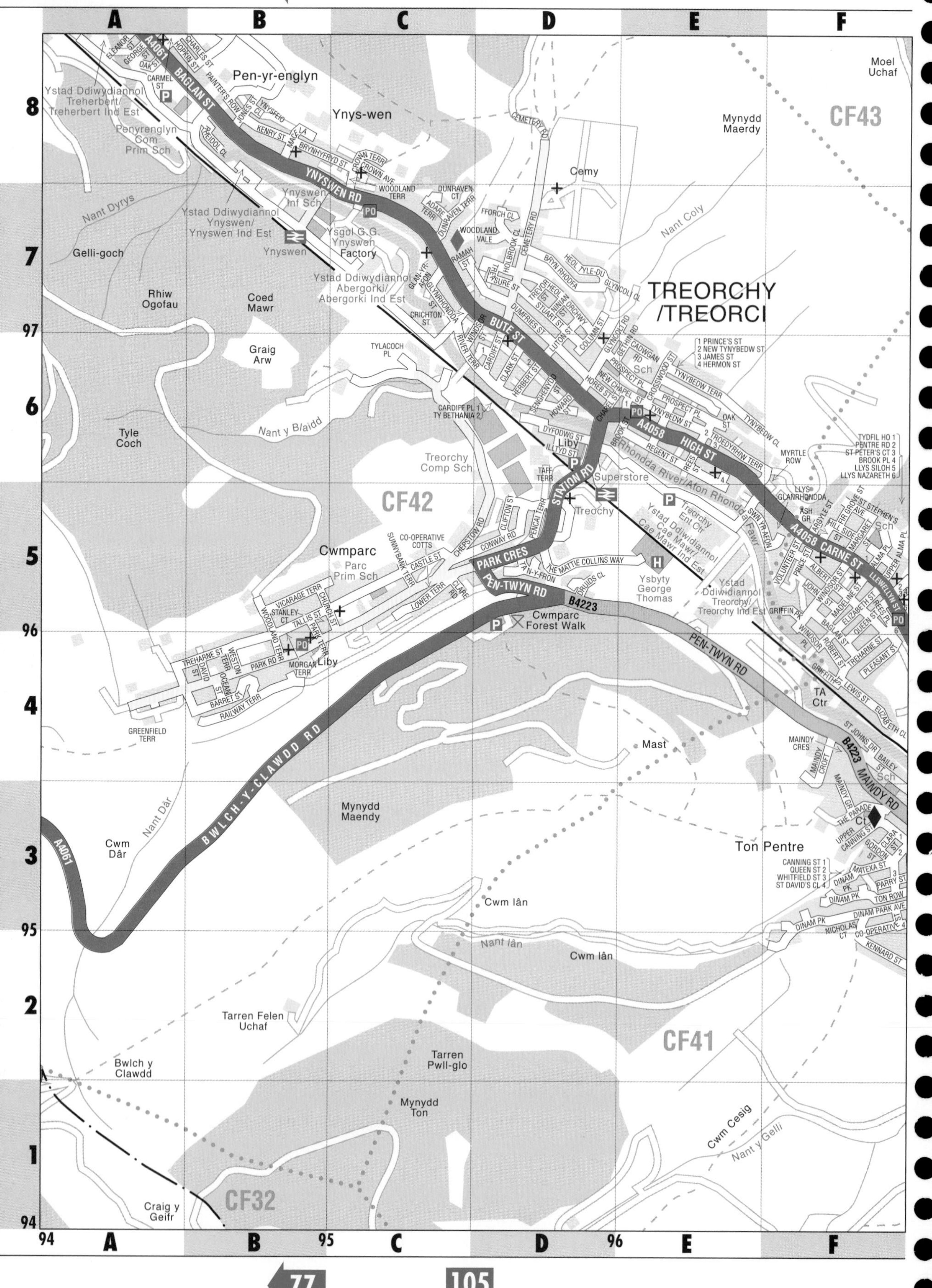
A
B
C
D
E
F
8
7
97
6
5
96
4
3
95
2
1
94
95
96
Pen-yr-englyn
Ynys-wen
Ystad Ddiwydiannol Treherbert/ Treherbert Ind Est
Penyrenglyn Com Prim Sch
BAGLAN ST
YNYSWEN RD
Ynyswen Inf Sch
Ystad Ddiwydiannol Ynyswen/ Ynyswen Ind Est
Ynyswen
Ysgol G.G. Ynyswen
Factory
Ystad Ddiwydiannol Abergorki/ Abergorki Ind Est
Nant Dyrys
Gelli-goch
Rhiw Ogofau
Coed Mawr
Graig Arw
Tyle Coch
Nant y Blaidd
Cemy
Nant Coly
Mynydd Maerdy
Moel Uchaf
CF43
TREORCHY /TREORCI
BUTE ST
HIGH ST
A4058
CARNE ST
STATION RD
Superstore
Treochy
Rhondda River/Afon Rhondda Fawr
Treorchy Comp Sch
CF42
Liby
Cwmparc
Parc Prim Sch
PARK CRES
PEN-TWYN RD
B4223
Cwmparc Forest Walk
Ysbyty George Thomas
Ystad Ddiwidianol Cae Mawr/ Cae Mawr Ind Est
Ystad Ddiwidianol Treorchy/ Treorchy Ind Est
Treorchy Ent Ctr
1 PRINCE'S ST
2 NEW TYNYBEDW ST
3 JAMES ST
4 HERMON ST
TYDFIL HO 1
PENTRE RD 2
ST PETER'S CT 3
BROOK PL 4
LLYS SILOH 5
LLYS NAZARETH 6
CANNING ST 1
QUEEN ST 2
WHITFIELD ST 3
ST DAVID'S CL 4
TA Ctr
Mast
MAINDY RD
Ton Pentre
BWLCH-Y-CLAWDD RD
A4061
Cwm Dâr
Nant Dâr
Mynydd Maendy
Cwm lân
Nant lân
Tarren Felen Uchaf
Tarren Pwll-glo
CF41
Bwlch y Clawdd
Mynydd Ton
Cwm Cesig
Nant y Gelli
CF32
Craig y Geifr

77
105

52
80

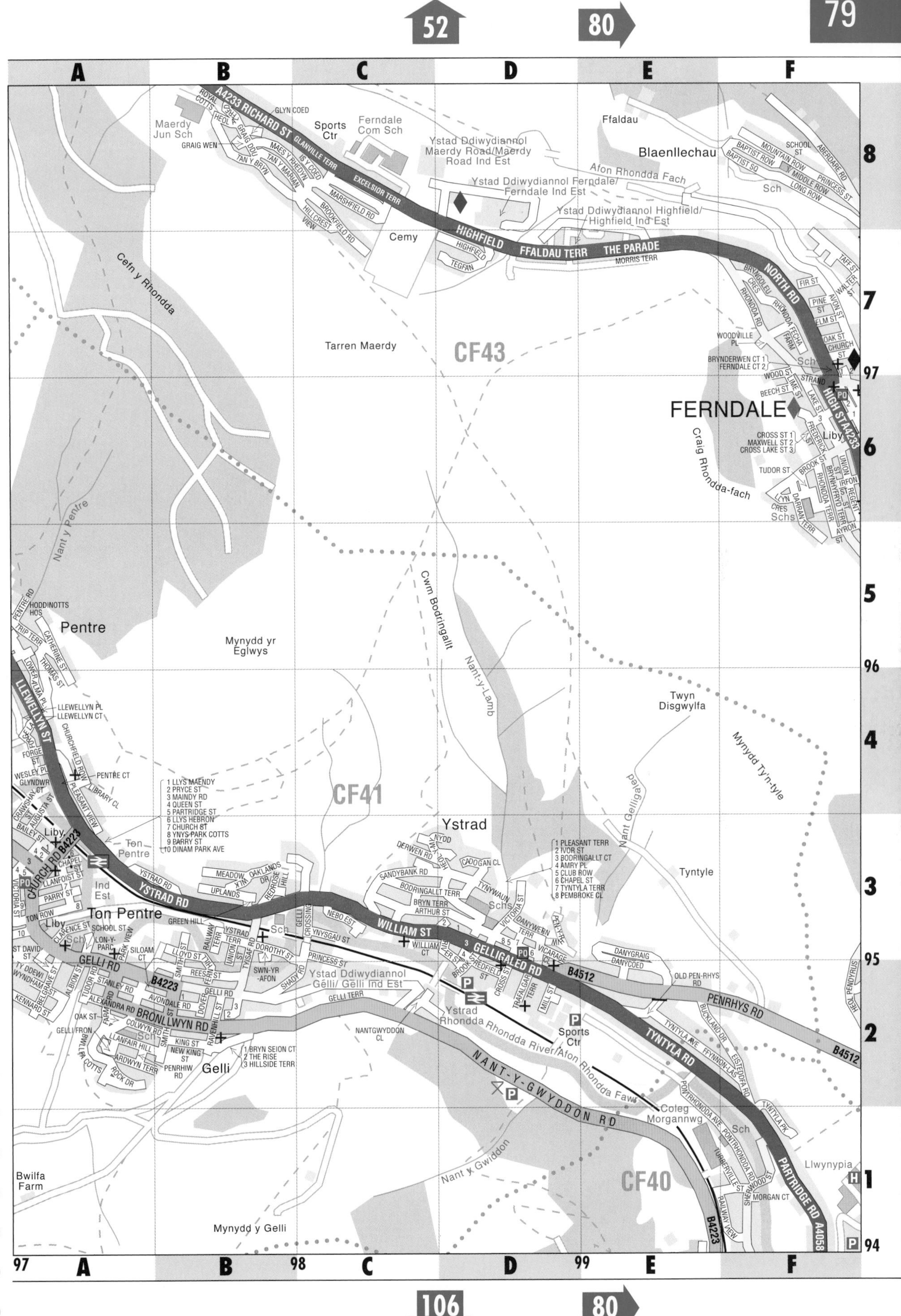
A
B
C
D
E
F
8
7
6
5
4
3
2
1
97
96
95
94
98
99
A4233 RICHARD ST
GLYN COED
Sports
Ctr
Ferndale
Com Sch
Maerdy
Jun Sch
GRAIG WEN
GLANVILLE TERR
EXCELSIOR TERR
MARSHFIELD RD
BROOKFIELD RD
HILLCREST VIEW
Ystad Ddiwydiannol
Maerdy Road/Maerdy
Road Ind Est
Ffaldau
Blaenllechau
Afon Rhondda Fach
Ystad Ddiwydiannol Ferndale/
Ferndale Ind Est
Ystad Ddiwydiannol Highfield/
Highfield Ind Est
Cemy
HIGHFIELD
FFALDAU TERR
THE PARADE
MORRIS TERR
TEGFAN
SCHOOL ST
ABERDARE RD
MOUNTAIN ROW
BAPTIST ROW
BAPTIST SQ
MIDDLE ROW
LONG ROW
PRINCESS ST
Sch
NORTH RD
TAFF ST
FIR ST
PINE ST
ELM ST
OAK ST
CHURCH ST
WOODVILLE PL
BRYNDERWEN CT 1
FERNDALE CT 2
WOOD ST
BEECH ST
STRAND
HIGH ST A4233
FERNDALE
Craig Rhondda-fach
CROSS ST 1
MAXWELL ST 2
CROSS LAKE ST 3
TUDOR ST
Liby
Schs
Cefn y Rhondda
Tarren Maerdy
CF43
Nant y Pentre
Cwm Bodringallt
Nant-y-Lamb
PENTRE RD
HODDINOTTS HOS
Pentre
Mynydd yr
Eglwys
Twyn
Disgwylfa
Mynydd Ty'n-tyle
LLEWELLYN ST
LLEWELLYN PL
LLEWELLYN CT
CHURCHFIELD ROW
PENTRE CT
LIBRARY CL
PLEASANT VIEW
CF41
1 LLYS MAENDY
2 PRYCE ST
3 MAINDY RD
4 QUEEN ST
5 PARTRIDGE ST
6 LLYS HEBRON
7 CHURCH ST
8 YNYS-PARK COTTS
9 BARRY ST
10 DINAM PARK AVE
Ystrad
1 PLEASANT TERR
2 IVOR ST
3 BODRINGALLT CT
4 AMRY PL
5 CLUB ROW
6 CHAPEL ST
7 TYNTYLA TERR
8 PEMBROKE CL
Nant Gelligaled
Tyntyle
Ton Pentre
Ind Est
YSTRAD RD
CHURCH RD B4223
Liby
Ton Pentre
MEADOW
OAKLANDS
UPLANDS
DERWEN RD
SANDYBANK RD
BODRINGALLT TERR
BRYN TERR
ARTHUR ST
CADOGAN CL
WILLIAM ST
GELLIGALED RD
B4512
DANYGRAIG
DANYCOED
OLD PEN-RHYS RD
PENRHYS RD
GELLI RD
B4223
BRONLLWYN RD
Ystad Ddiwydiannol
Gelli/ Gelli Ind Est
GELLI TERR
SWN-YR-AFON
Ystrad
Rhondda
Sports
Ctr
Rhondda River/Afon Rhondda Fawr
NANT-Y-GWYDDON RD
NANTGWYDDON CL
TYNTYLA RD
1 BRYN SEION CT
2 THE RISE
3 HILLSIDE TERR
Gelli
Coleg
Morgannwg
Sch
PARTRIDGE RD A4058
Llwynypia
Nant y Gwiddon
CF40
Bwllfa
Farm
Mynydd y Gelli
B4223
MORGAN CT

106
80

79
53

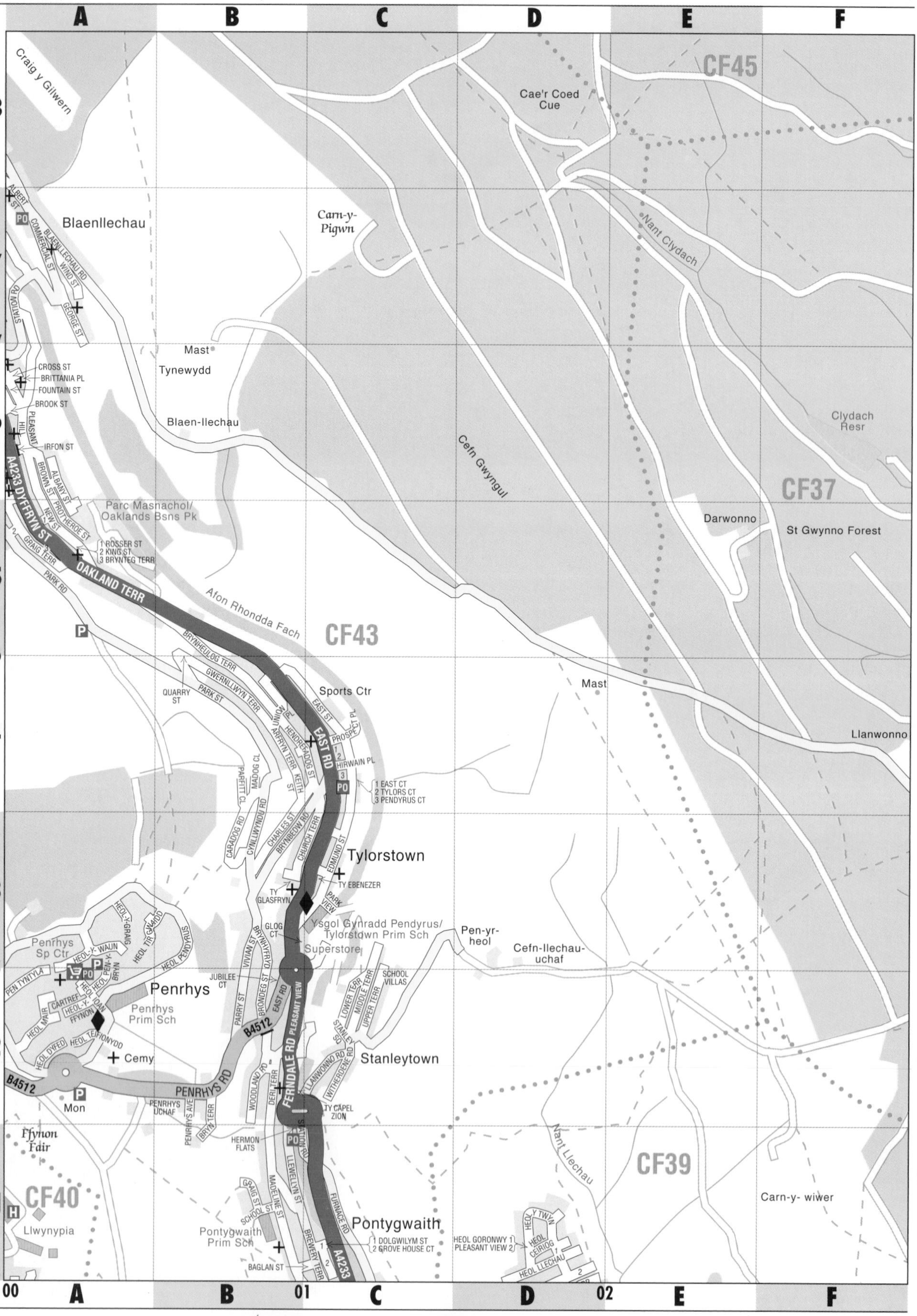

A B C D E F

8
7
97
6
5
96
4
3
95
2
1
94

Craig y Gilwern
CF45
Cae'r Coed
Cue
Carn-y-
Pigwn
Nant Clydach
Blaenllechau
ALBERT ST
PO
COMMERCIAL ST
BLAENLLECHAU RD
WIND ST
GEORGE ST
STATION RD
Mast
Tynewydd
CROSS ST
BRITTANIA PL
FOUNTAIN ST
BROOK ST
HILL
PLEASANT
IRFON ST
Blaen-llechau
Cefn Gwyngul
Clydach
Resr
CF37
A4233 DYFFRYN ST
BROWN ST
ALBANY ST
PROTHEROE ST
NEW ST
Parc Masnachol/
Oaklands Bsns Pk
1 ROSSER ST
2 KING ST
3 BRYNTEG TERR
GRAIG TERR
OAKLAND TERR
PARK RD
Darwonno
St Gwynno Forest
Afon Rhondda Fach
P
CF43
BRYNHEULOG TERR
GWERNLLWYN TERR
QUARRY
ST
PARK ST
Sports Ctr
Mast
EAST ST
PROSPECT PL
UNION ST
HENDREWADOG ST
EAST RD
ARFRYN TERR
KEITH ST
HIRWAIN PL
PO
1 EAST CT
2 TYLORS CT
3 PENDYRUS CT
Llanwonno
MADOG CL
PARFITT CL
CARADOG RD
CYNLLWYNDU RD
CHARLES ST
BRYNBEDW RD
CHURCH TERR
EDMUND ST
Tylorstown
TY EBENEZER
TY
GLASFRYN
PARK VIEW
HEOL-Y-GRAIG
HEOL TIR GWYDD
HEOL PENDYRUS
VIVIAN ST
BRYNHYFRYD
GLOG
CT
Ysgol Gynradd Pendyrus/
Tylorstown Prim Sch
Superstore
Pen-yr-
heol
Cefn-llechau-
uchaf
Penrhys
Sp Ctr
HEOL-Y-WAUN
HEOL PEN-Y-BRYN
PO
P
PEN TYNTYLA
HEOL IOAN
CARTREF
HEOL-Y-FFYNON
Penrhys
Penrhys
Prim Sch
JUBILEE
CT
PARRY ST
BRONDEG ST
EAST RD
SCHOOL
VILLAS
LOWER TERR
MIDDLE TERR
UPPER TERR
HEOL MAIR
HEOL DYFED
HEOL TEIFIONYDD
Cemy
B4512
FERNDALE RD
PLEASANT VIEW
STANLEY SQ
LLANWONNO RD
WITHEROWE RD
Stanleytown
B4512
P
Mon
PENRHYS RD
PENRHYS
UCHAF
PENRHYS AVE
BRYN TERR
WOODLAND RD
DERI TERR
TY CAPEL
ZION
Ffynon
Fair
HERMON
FLATS
PO
STATION RD
Nant Llechau
CF39
CF40
H
Llwynypia
GRAIG ST
SCHOOL ST
MADELINE ST
LLEWELLYN ST
FURNACE RD
Carn-y- wiwer
Pontygwaith
Prim Sch
Pontygwaith
1 DOLGWILYM ST
2 GROVE HOUSE CT
HEOL GORONWY 1
PLEASANT VIEW 2
HEOL Y TWYN
HEOL CEIRIOG
HEOL LLECHAU
BAGLAN ST
BREWERY ST
A4233

00 A B 01 C D 02 E F

79
107

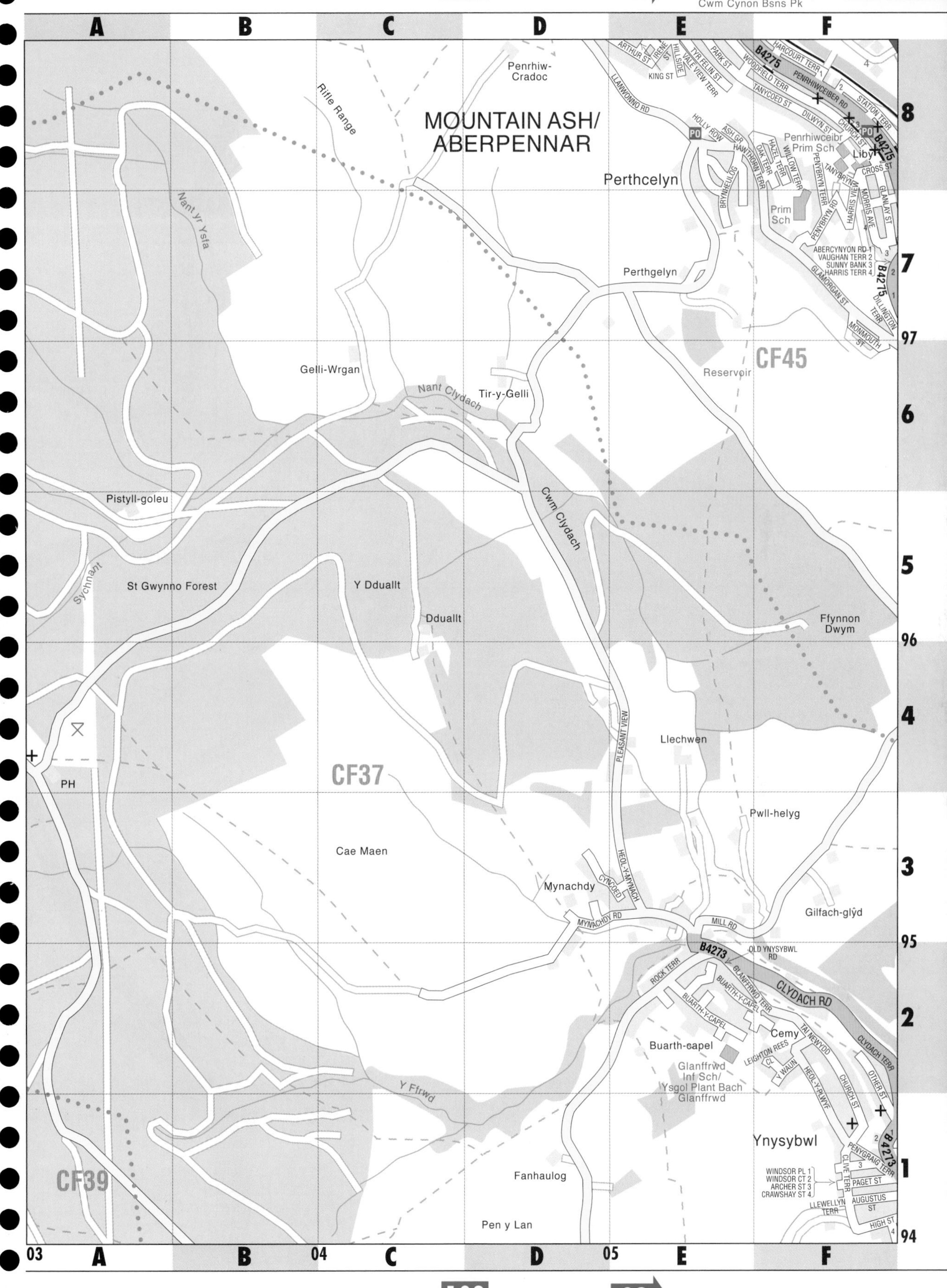
MOUNTAIN ASH/
ABERPENNAR
Penrhiw-
Cradoc
Rifle Range
Perthcelyn
Perthgelyn
Penrhiwceibr
Prim Sch
Prim
Sch
Liby
CF45
Reservoir
Gelli-Wrgan
Nant Clydach
Tir-y-Gelli
Nant yr Ysfa
Pistyll-goleu
St Gwynno Forest
Sychnant
Y Dduallt
Dduallt
Cwm Clydach
Ffynnon
Dwym
Llechwen
PLEASANT VIEW
CF37
PH
Pwll-helyg
Cae Maen
Mynachdy
CYNCOED
HEOL-Y-MYNACH
MYNACHDY RD
MILL RD
Gilfach-glŷd
B4273
OLD YNYSYBWL
RD
CLYDACH RD
ROCK TERR
GLANFFRWD TERR
BUARTH-Y-CAPEL
Cerny
Buarth-capel
Glanffrwd
Inf Sch/
Ysgol Plant Bach
Glanffrwd
Y Ffrwd
Ynysybwl
Fanhaulog
Pen y Lan
CF39
B4275
ARTHUR ST
KING ST
HILLSIDE
VALE VIEW TERR
TYR FELIN ST
PARK ST
WOODFIELD TERR
HARCOURT TERR
PENRHIWCEIBER RD
STATION TERR
TANYCOED ST
DILWYN ST
CHURCH ST
LLANWONNO RD
HOLLY ROW
ASH GR
HAWTHORN TERR
BRYNHEULOG
OAK TERR
HAZEL TERR
WILLOW TERR
PENYBRYN TERR
PENYBRYN RD
TANYBRYN
CROSS ST
HARRIS VIEW
MORRIS AVE
GLANLAY ST
ABERCYNYON RD 1
VAUGHAN TERR 2
SUNNY BANK 3
HARRIS TERR 4
GLAMORGAN ST
DILLINGTON TERR
MONMOUTH ST
TAI NEWYDD
CLYDACH TERR
LEIGHTON REES CL
Y WAUN
HEOL-Y-PLWYF
CHURCH ST
OTHER ST
PENYGRAIG TERR
WINDSOR PL 1
WINDSOR CT 2
ARCHER ST 3
CRAWSHAY ST 4
CLIVE TERR
PAGET ST
LLEWELLYN TERR
AUGUSTUS ST
HIGH ST
A B C D E F
03 04 05
8 7 97 6 5 96 4 3 95 2 1 94

81
55

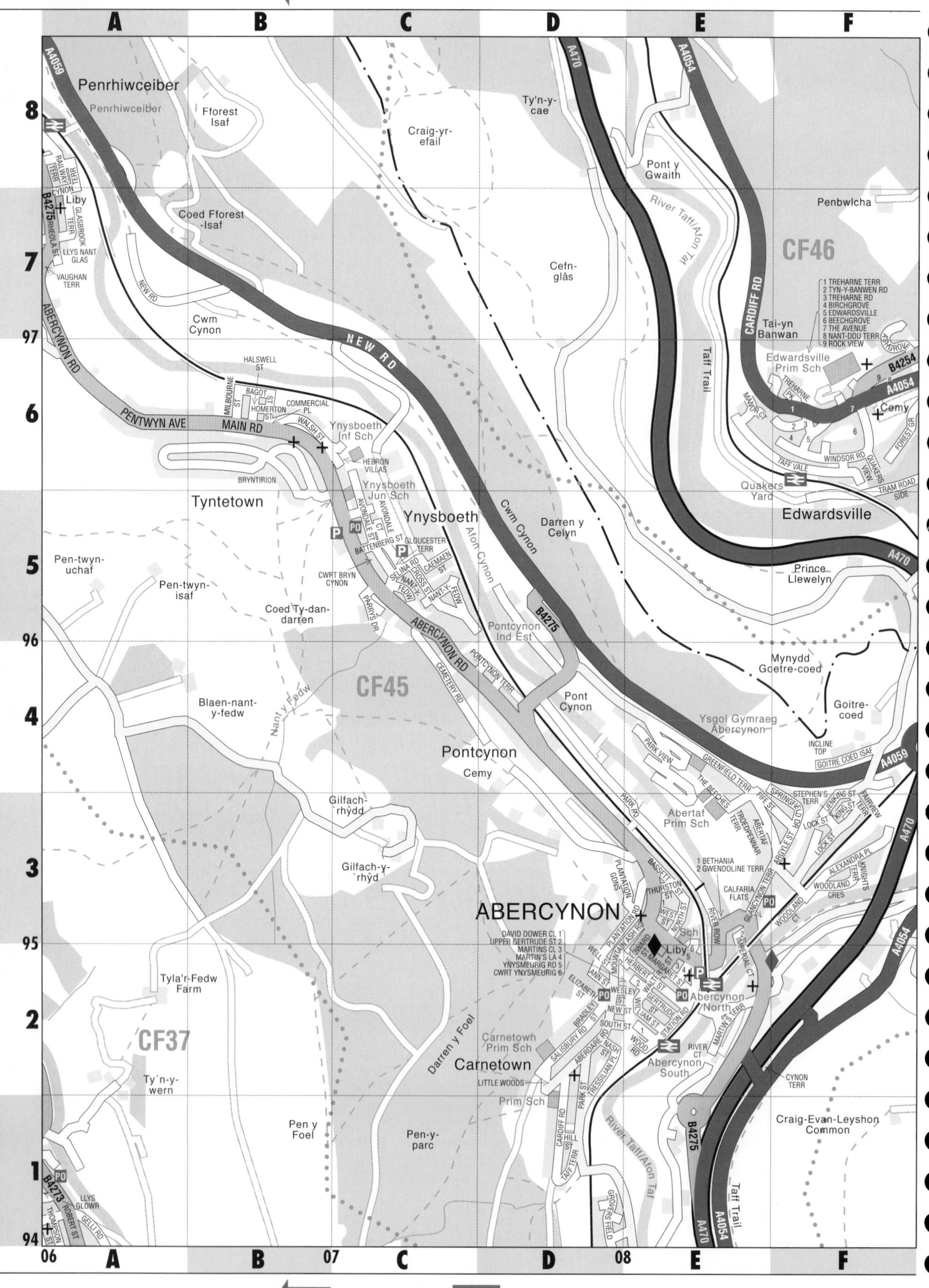
Penrhiwceiber
Fforest Isaf
Craig-yr-efail
Ty'n-y-cae
Pont y Gwaith
Coed Fforest -Isaf
Cefn-glâs
Penbwlcha
CF46
Cwm Cynon
Tai-yn Banwan
Edwardsville Prim Sch
Ynysboeth Inf Sch
Tyntetown
Ynysboeth Jun Sch
Ynysboeth
Darren y Celyn
Quakers Yard
Edwardsville
Pen-twyn-uchaf
Pen-twyn-isaf
Coed Ty-dan-darren
Prince Llewelyn
Pontcynon Ind Est
Mynydd Goetre-coed
CF45
Blaen-nant-y-fedw
Pont Cynon
Goitre-coed
Ysgol Gymraeg Abercynon
Pontcynon
Gilfach-rhydd
Abertaf Prim Sch
Gilfach-y-rhŷd
ABERCYNON
Tyla'r-Fedw Farm
Abercynon North
CF37
Carnetown Prim Sch
Carnetown
Abercynon South
Ty'n-y-wern
Craig-Evan-Leyshon Common
Pen y Foel
Pen-y-parc
Taff Trail
River Taff/Afon Taf
A470
A4054
A4059
B4275
B4254
B4273

81
109

B6
1 PROSSER ST
2 OLD STATION YD
3 VICTORIA ST
4 GLENVIEW VILLAS
5 EDWARD ST

56
84

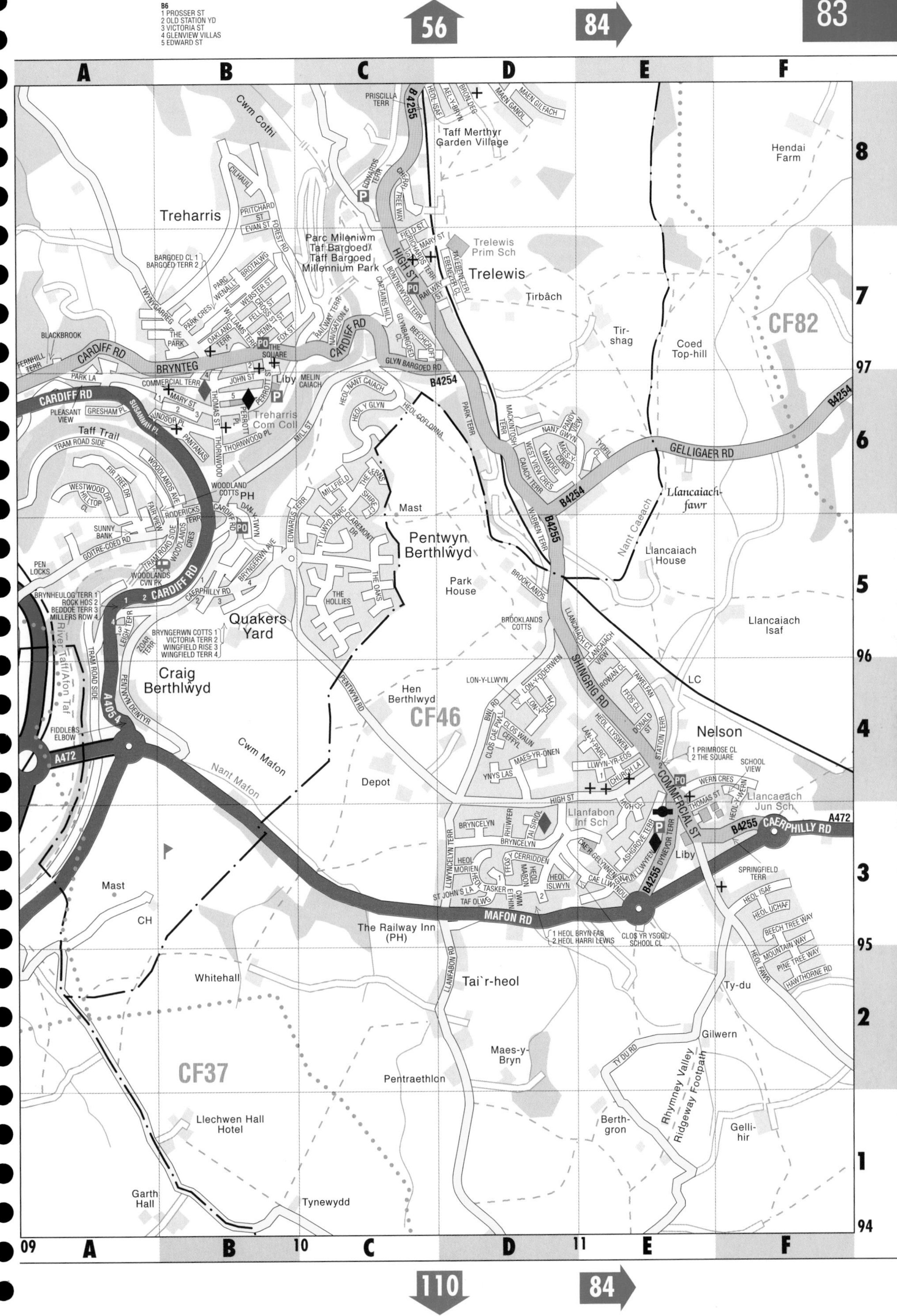

110
84

83
57
A
B
C
D
E
F
8
7
97
6
5
96
4
3
95
2
1
94
12
13
14
Llwyn-goleu
Tir-y-rhen
Maen Cattwg
Rhymney Valley Ridgeway Footpath
PH
Pen-pedair-heol
Cascade House
CF81
PENGAM RD
B4254
Berllan-lwyd
NP12
Tophill
GELLIGAER RD
Green Acres
Greenhill Prim Sch
CHURCH RD
Cemy
Glyn Gaer Prim Sch
Tir Jack Farm
Gelliargwellt Uchaf Farm
Gelligaer
Glyn Gaer
Nant Cylla
Penybryn
Waun Rydd
Penallta Ind Est
CF82
Sch
Cefn Hengoed
Waun Rydd
Cefn-llwynau
Penallta Community Park/ Parc Cymunedol Penallta
Hengoed Prim Sch
PH
A472
CAERPHILLY RD
Wern-ganol
Penalltau-isaf
Pont y Saeson
CF46
Wern-isaf
Ton-teilwr
Parc Tredomen/ Tredomen Pk
Pen-y-waun
Tredomen
Tredomen
Ystrad Mynach
Tir-Twyn Farm
Trinity Fields Sch
Liby
Schs
Sports Ctr
YSTRAD MYNACH
Lewis Girls' Comp Sch
A469
83
111

58
86

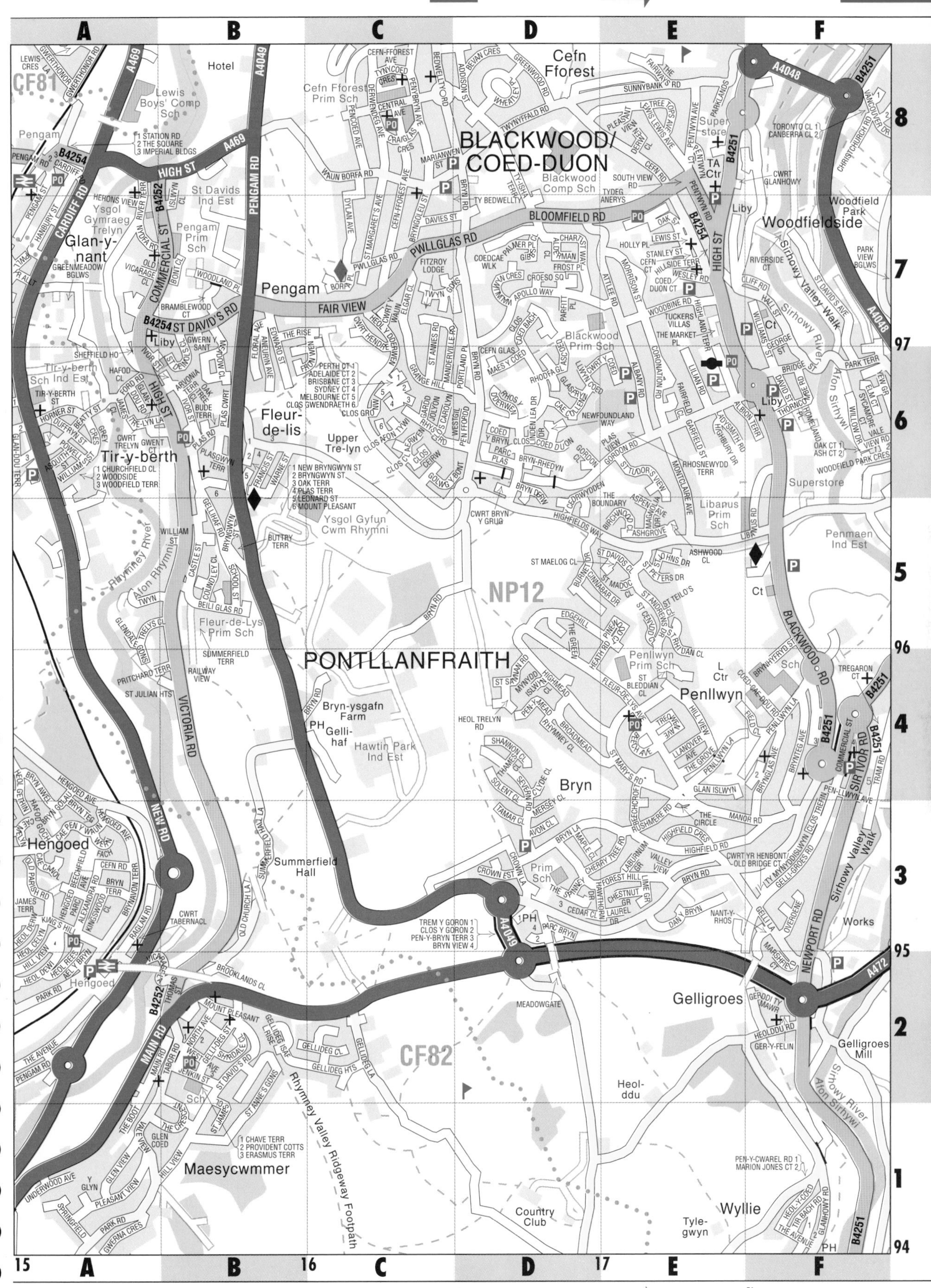

112
86

F4
1 PENLLWYN TERR
2 BRYNGOLEU TERR
3 STATION BLDGS
4 PLAZA CT
5 Tram Rd Ind Est

85 59

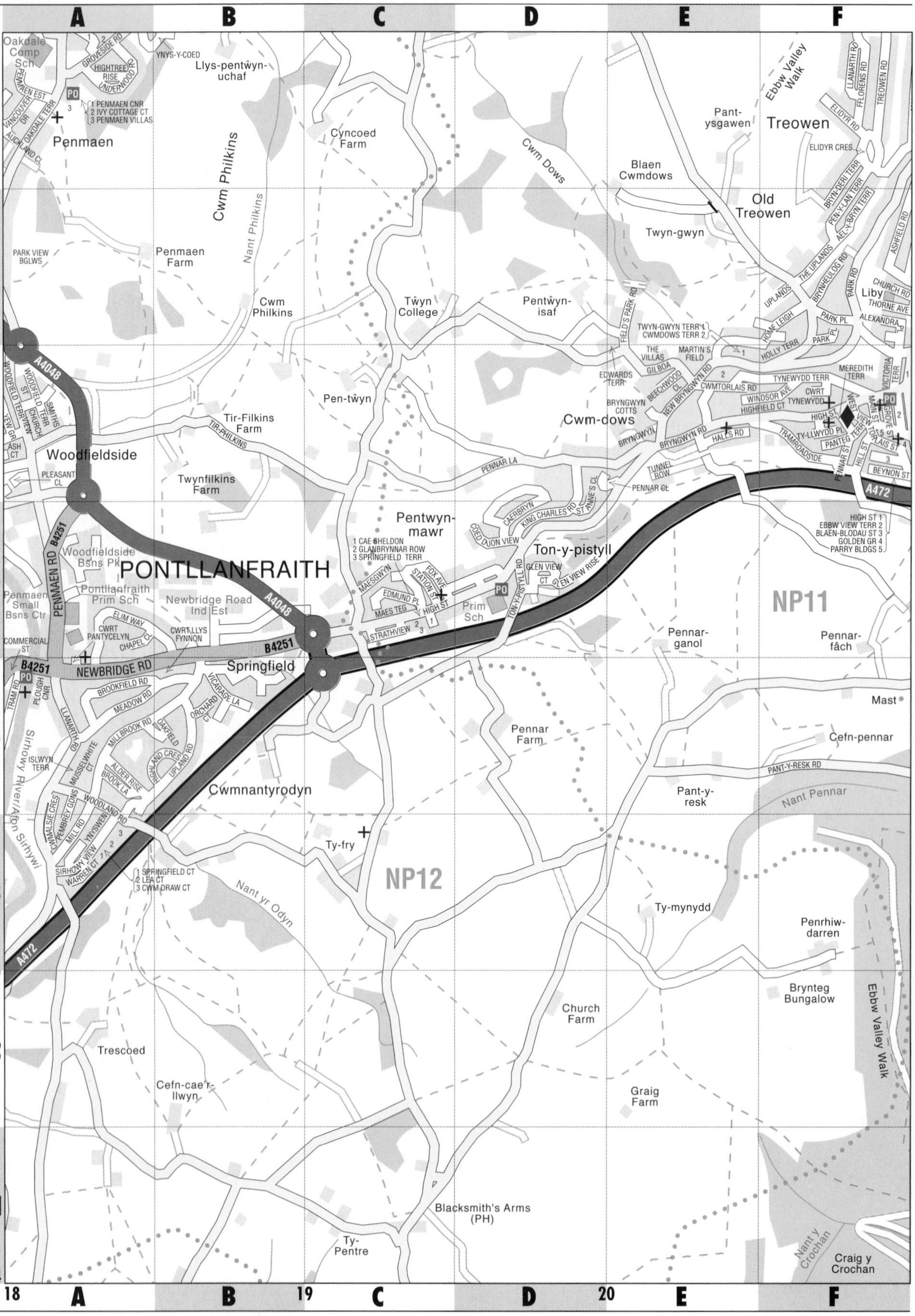

A B C D E F

8 7 97 6 5 96 4 3 95 2 1 94

Oakdale Comp Sch
Llys-pentŵyn-uchaf
Penmaen
Cwm Philkins
Nant Philkins
Cyncoed Farm
Cwm Dows
Pant-ysgawen
Treowen
Ebbw Valley Walk
Blaen Cwmdows
Old Treowen
Twyn-gwyn
Penmaen Farm
Cwm Philkins
Twyn College
Pentŵyn-isaf
Liby
Pen-twyn
Tir-Filkins Farm
Woodfieldside
Cwm-dows
Twynfilkins Farm
Pentwyn-mawr
Ton-y-pistyll
Woodfieldside Bsns Pk
PONTLLANFRAITH
Penmaen Small Bsns Ctr
Pontllanfraith Prim Sch
Newbridge Road Ind Est
Prim Sch
Springfield
NP11
Pennar-ganol
Pennar-fâch
Mast
Pennar Farm
Cefn-pennar
Cwmnantyrodyn
Pant-y-resk
Nant Pennar
Sirhowy River/Afon Sirhywi
Ty-fry
NP12
Nant yr Odyn
Ty-mynydd
Penrhiw-darren
Brynteg Bungalow
Church Farm
Trescoed
Cefn-cae'r-llwyn
Graig Farm
Blacksmith's Arms (PH)
Ty-Pentre
Nant y Crochan
Craig y Crochan
A4048
B4251
A472

18 A B 19 C D 20 E F

85 113

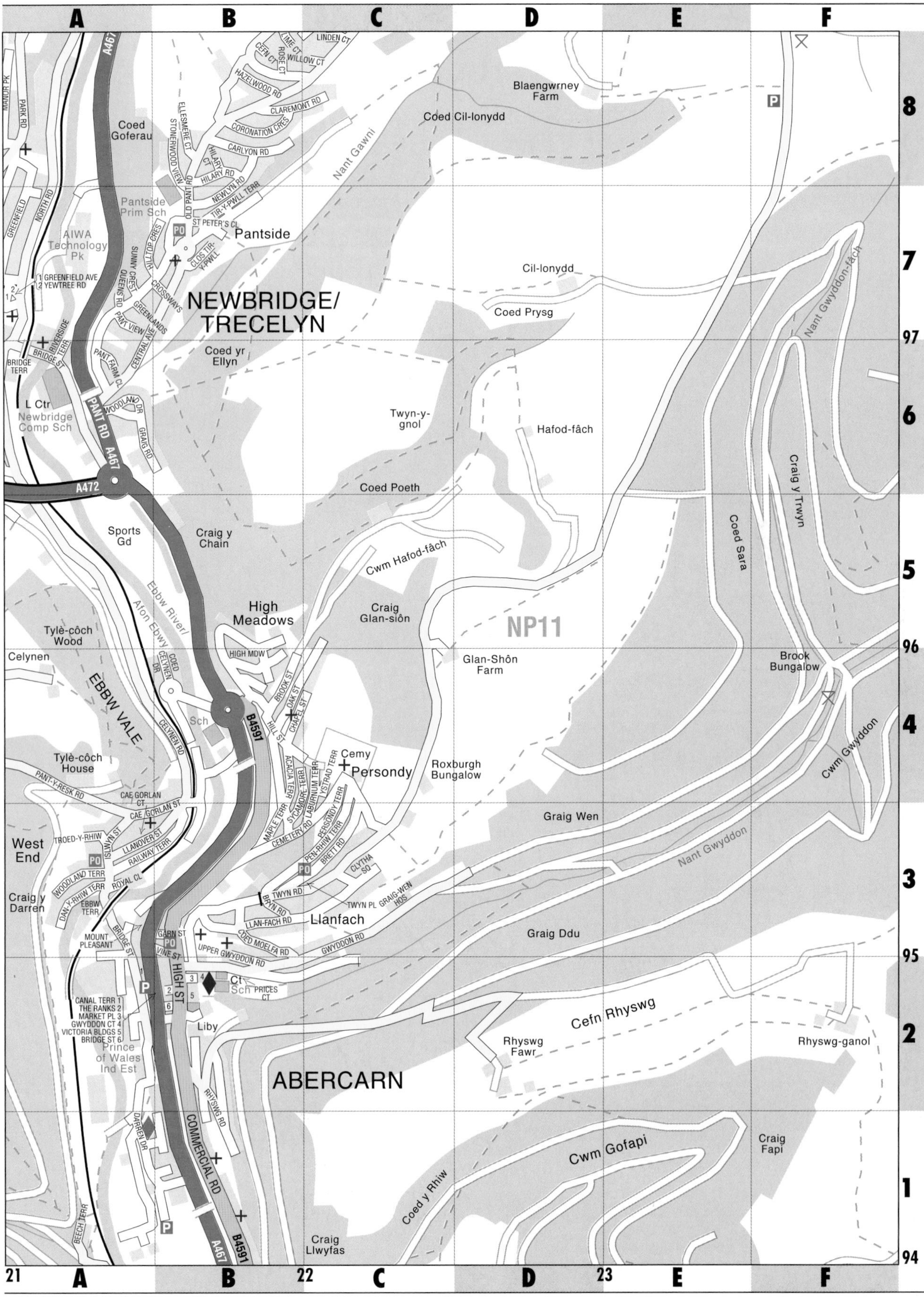

60
88

A B C D E F

8 7 97 6 5 96 4 3 95 2 1 94

21 A B 22 C D 23 E F

114
88

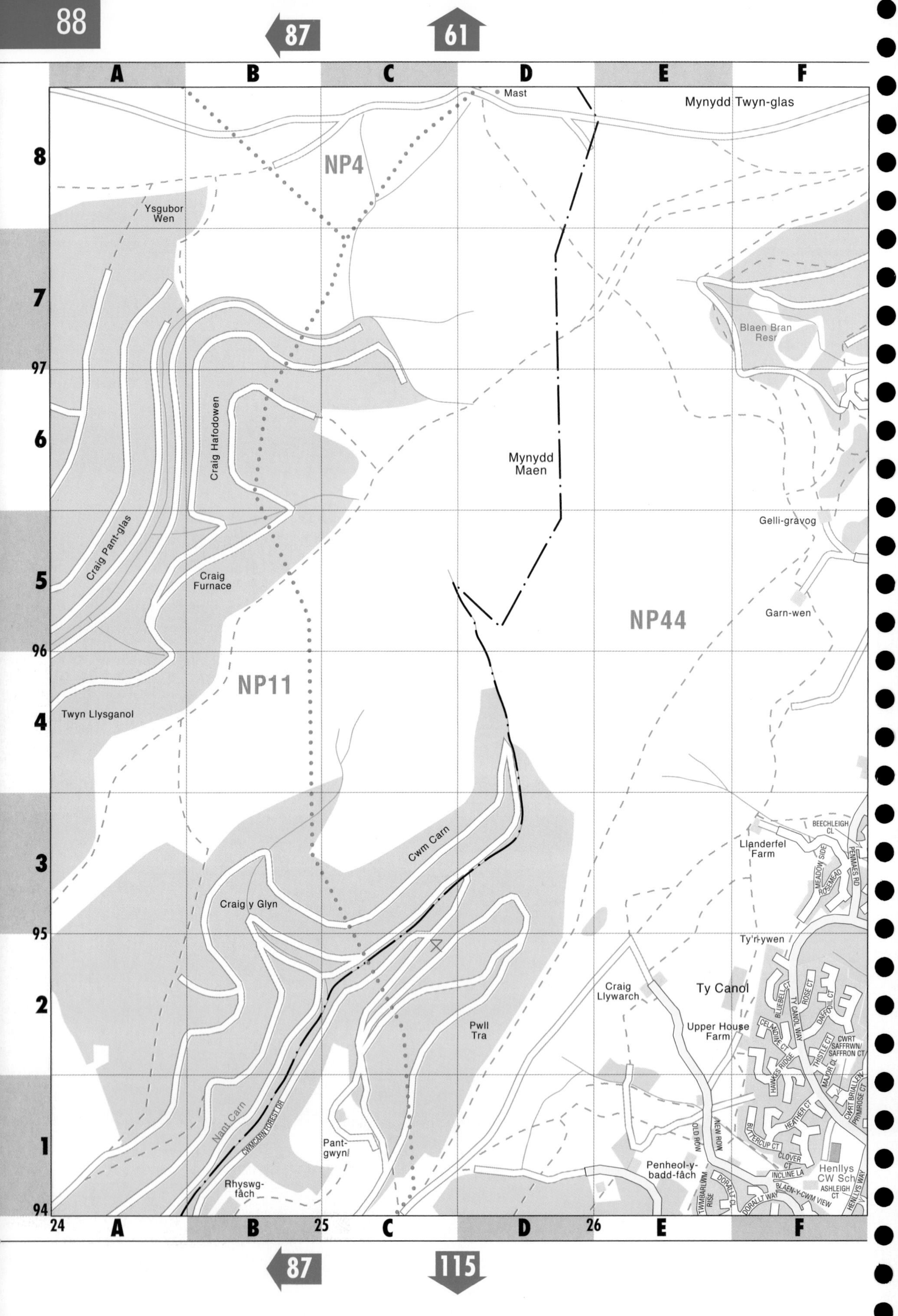
87
61
A
B
C
D
E
F
8
7
97
6
5
96
4
3
95
2
1
94
24
25
26
Mast
Mynydd Twyn-glas
NP4
Ysgubor Wen
Blaen Bran Resr
Craig Hafodowen
Mynydd Maen
Gelli-gravog
Craig Pant-glas
Craig Furnace
NP44
Garn-wen
NP11
Twyn Llysganol
BEECHLEIGH CL
Llanderfel Farm
MEADOW SIDE
ROSEMEAD
PENMAES RD
Cwm Carn
Craig y Glyn
Ty'r-ywen
Craig Llywarch
Ty Canol
BLUEBELL CT
ROSE CT
TY CANOL WAY
DAFFODIL CT
Upper House Farm
CELANDINE CT
THISTLE CT
CWRT SAFFRWN/ SAFFRON CT
Pwll Tra
HAWKES RIDGE
MAJOR CL
CWRT BRIALLEN
PRIMROSE CT
Nant Carn
CWMCARN FOREST DR
HEATHER CT
OLD ROW
NEW ROW
BUTTERCUP CT
Pant-gwynl
CLOVER CT
Penheol-y-badd-fâch
INCLINE LA
Henllys CW Sch
Rhyswg-fâch
TWMBARLWM RISE
DORALLT CL
DORALLT WAY
BLAEN-Y-CWM VIEW
ASHLEIGH CT
HENLLYS WAY
87
115

A3
1 BEECHLEIGH CL
2 BEDFORD CL/
CLOS RHYDWELY
3 ARUNDEL CL/
CLOS ARUNDEL
4 EDINBURGH CL
5 NORFOLK CL/
CLOS NORFOLK
6 MAES-Y-RHIW CT/
CWRT MAES-Y-RHIW

D2
1 ASHTON HO
2 MILFORD HO
3 LYSTEP HO
4 BURNS LA/
LON BURNS
5 BYRON PL
6 WORDSWORTH CL/
CLOS WORDSWORTH
7 MILTON CL/CLOS MILTON
8 THE BEECHES/Y FAWYDD
9 ORCHARD PL/CAE BERLLAN

E2
1 SCHOOL CT
2 ST DIALS CT
3 COUNCIL HOS
4 BROADWEIR RD/HEOL BROADWEIR

62

5 WATERSIDE CT/
CWRT GLANDWR
6 BELLEVUE GDNS
7 MALPAS ST
8 OAK ST/
STRYD Y DDERWEN
9 OLDBURY RD/FFORDD OLDBURY

90

E5
1 RICHMOND ST
2 BROOKLAND HO
3 STATION TERR
4 RUSSELL ST
5 TY-NEWYDD HO
6 COMMERCIAL PL
7 HAROLD ST
8 STANLEY PL
9 PADARN PL
10 CROMWELL PL/
MAN CROMWELL
11 PLAS TROSNANT

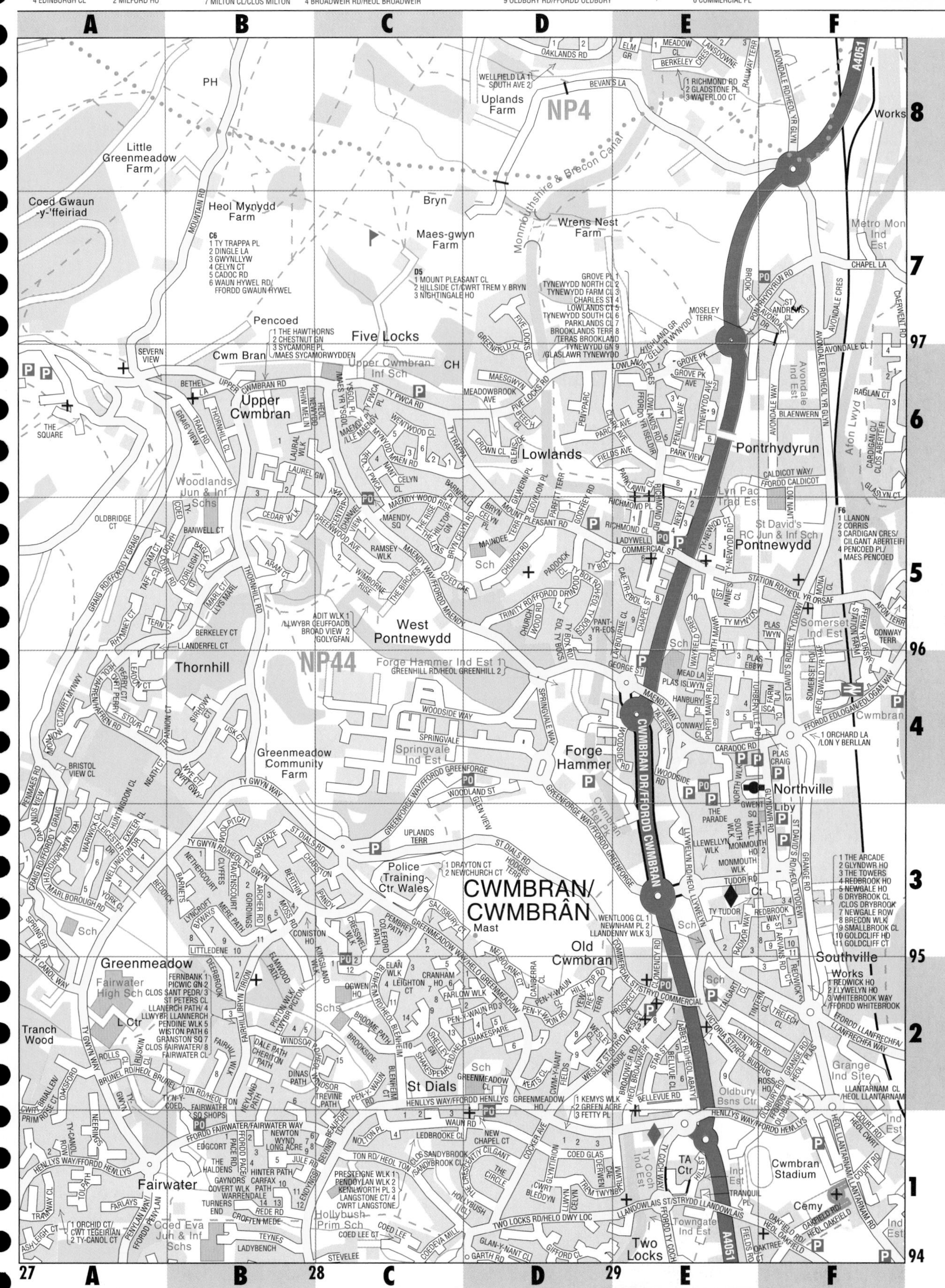

B1
1 HAYSWAYN
2 WALKDENS
3 MAYNES
4 HASSOCKS LEA
5 MOLESCOMBE
6 FIELDINGS
7 POSTERN
8 BETWYNS
9 KINGSLEA
10 FALLOWFIELD
11 TEWENDS
12 INGLES
13 THE WADES
14 MINORIES

B3
1 RUSHBROOK
2 MARLOES PATH
3 PENNYFIELDS
4 CROFTS CNR
5 BADGERS MEDE
6 MANOR GATE
7 EARLSMEDE
8 THE TWININGS
9 THE COURTLANDS
10 HOLMDALE
11 MAYBURY HO

C2
1 RANNOCH HO
2 BALA HO
3 CAMROSE WLK
4 CHARWOOD HO
5 OAKDALE PATH
6 GILESTON WLK
7 SHAWLEY CT
8 HANLEY PATH
9 ROMSLEY CT

C2
10 NORBURY HO
11 MARSTON PATH/
LLWYBR MARSTON
12 BLENHEIM SQ/
SGWAR BLENHEIM
13 COLERIDGE GN/
MAES COLERIDGE
14 AMROTH WLK/RHODFA AMROTH
15 STEYNTON PATH/LLWYBR STEYNTON

E4
1 HEOL TRUSSEL/TRUSSEL RD
2 LONG HOLLOW/PANT HIR
3 RHODFA PONTNEWYDD/PONTNEWYDD WLK
4 ST WOOLOS GN
5 LLANDAFF GN
6 GRANGE LA
7 FORGESIDE/GER-YR-EFAIL

A5
1 HAWTHORN CT
2 ST MARY'S RD/HEOL SANTS FAIR
3 BRONLLYS PL
4 WOODLAND VIEW/GOLYGFA'R GOEDWIG
5 FIELD VIEW/FFORDD GWEL Y CAEAU

89

A6
1 CHEPSTOW RISE/ CEFNEN CAS-GWENT
2 HARLECH CL/ CLOS HARLECH
3 CARDIGAN CRES/ CILGANT ABERTEIFI

63

4 GOWER GN/MAES GWR
5 GARW WOOD DR/LON COED GARW
6 HAZEL WLK/RHOOFA HELYS
7 STREEPFIELD/CAE SERTH
8 GREENCOURT/CWRT GWYRRD

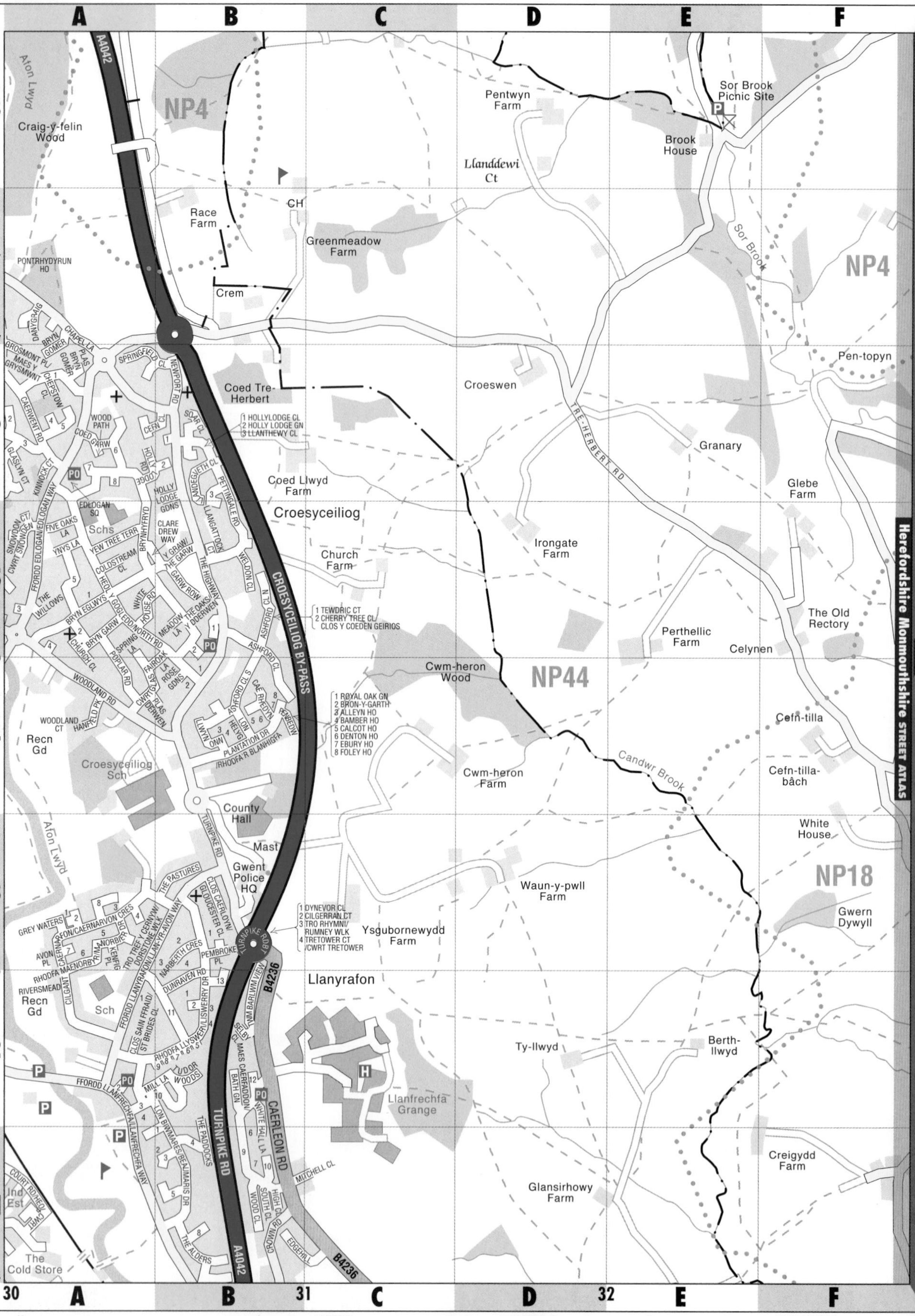

Craig-y-felin Wood
Afon Llwyd
NP4
Race Farm
CH
Greenmeadow Farm
Crem
Pentwyn Farm
Llanddewi Ct
Sor Brook Picnic Site
Brook House
Sor Brook
PONTRHYDYRUN HO
Coed Tre-Herbert
Croeswen
Tre-Herbert Rd
Pen-topyn
Granary
Glebe Farm
Coed Llwyd Farm
Croesyceiliog
Church Farm
Irongate Farm
Croesyceiliog By-Pass
Perthellic Farm
Celynen
The Old Rectory
Cwm-heron Wood
NP44
Cefn-tilla
Cefn-tilla-bâch
Cwm-heron Farm
Candwr Brook
Recn Gd
Croesyceiliog Sch
County Hall
Mast
Gwent Police HQ
White House
Waun-y-pwll Farm
NP18
Gwern Dywyll
Ysguborneywdd Farm
Llanyrafon
Ty-llwyd
Berth-llwyd
Llanfrechfa Grange
Turnpike Rd
Caerleon Rd
Creigydd Farm
Glansirhowy Farm
Ind Est
The Cold Store

1 HOLLYLODGE CL
2 HOLLY LODGE GN
3 LLANTHEWEY CL

1 TEWDRIC CT
2 CHERRY TREE CL/ CLOS Y COEDEN GEIRIOS

1 ROYAL OAK GN
2 BRON-Y-GARTH
3 ALLEYN HO
4 BAMBER HO
5 CALCOT HO
6 DENTON HO
7 EBURY HO
8 FOLEY HO

1 DYNEVOR CL
2 CILGERRAN CT
3 TRO RHYMNI/ RUMNEY WLK
4 TRETOWER CT /CWRT TRETOWER

Herefordshire Monmouthshire STREET ATLAS

A2
1 CLOS CYDWELI /KIDWELLY CL
2 LLAN-YR-AVON SQ
3 LLANGORSE RD/FFORDD LLANGORS
4 LLANGORSE PATH /LLWYBR LLAN-GORS

A3
1 MISKIN HO
2 MAES MEISGYN/MISKIN GN
3 LLWYBR CAERWRANGON/WORCESTER PATH
4 CLOS DIMBYCH-Y-PYSGOD/TENBY CL

89

5 ROATH CT
6 RHODFA'R MELINYDD/ MILLERS RIDE
7 CLOS HENSOL/HENSOL CL
8 WORCESTER CL/ CLOS CAERWRANGON

B1
1 OLWAY CL/CLOS OLWAY
2 LLYS-WEN/LLYSWEN WLK
3 CLOS LLWYDLO/LUDLOW CL

117

4 PADDOCK RISE
5 CWRT PENARTH/PENARTH CT
6 NEWBARN PATH
7 GRANGE PATH/LLWYBR Y PLASTY
8 FRIARS GDN/GERDDI'R BRODYR
9 CROWN RISE/TARDDIAD Y GORON
10 WHITE HALL LA/LON Y NEUADO WEN

B2
1 GOODRICH CT
2 LISWERRY CL/CLOS LLYSWERI
3 NEVERN WLK
4 STOWE PATH/LLYWYBR STOWE
5 RHODRI PL/MAES RHODRI
6 CEREDIG CT
7 ST DONATS PL/CLOS SANT DUNWYD
8 OGMORE PL
9 PENRICE GN
10 BEAUMARIS HO
11 KIDWELLY RD/HEOL CYDWELI
12 WEST BK/GLAN Y GORLLEWIN
13 HAWARDEN GN/MAES HAWARDEN

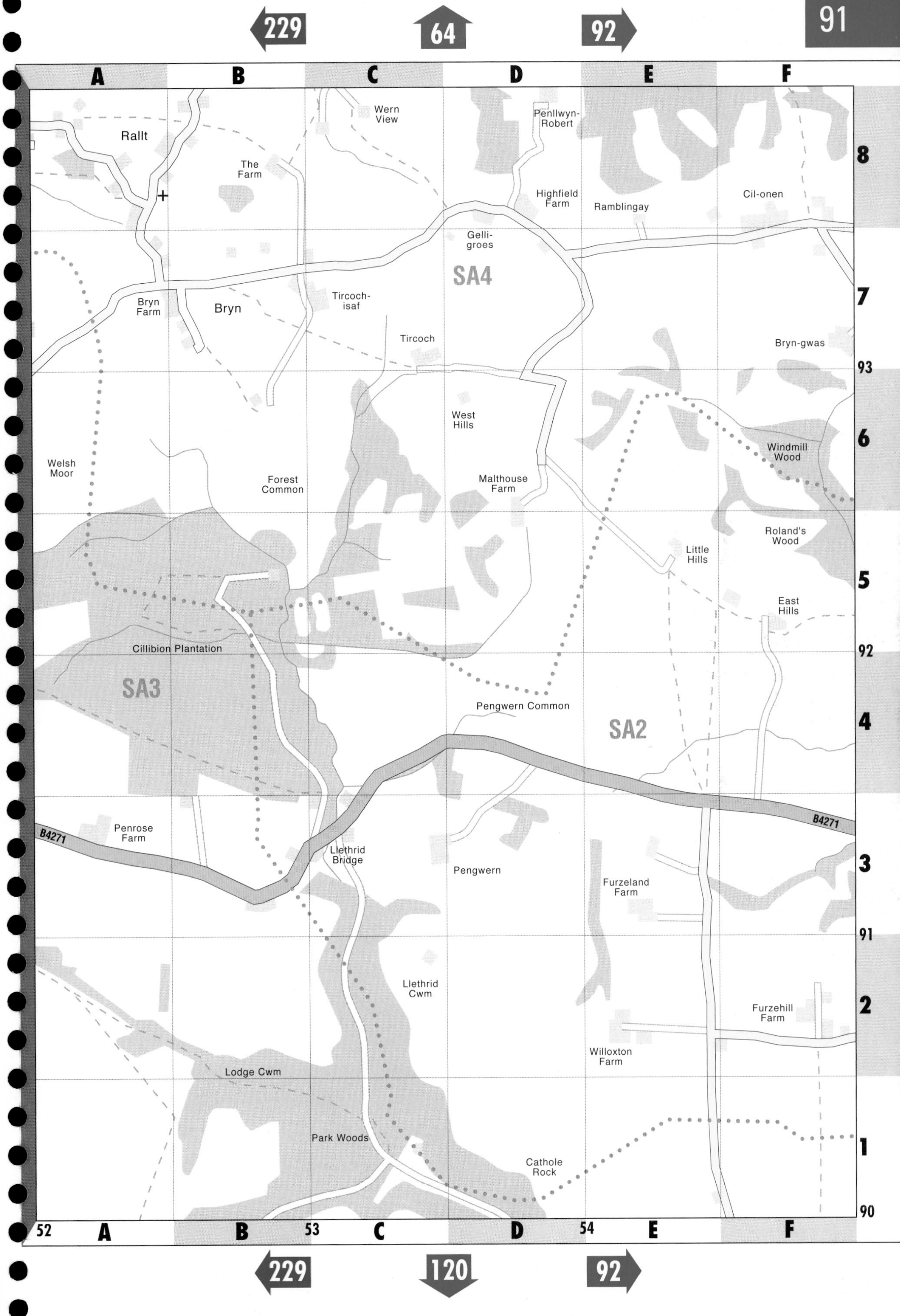
229
64
92
A
B
C
D
E
F
Rallt
Wern View
Penllwyn-Robert
The Farm
Highfield Farm
Ramblingay
Cil-onen
Gelli-groes
SA4
Bryn Farm
Bryn
Tircoch-isaf
Tircoch
Bryn-gwas
West Hills
Windmill Wood
Welsh Moor
Forest Common
Malthouse Farm
Roland's Wood
Little Hills
East Hills
Cillibion Plantation
SA3
Pengwern Common
SA2
B4271
Penrose Farm
Llethrid Bridge
Pengwern
Furzeland Farm
Llethrid Cwm
Furzehill Farm
Willoxton Farm
Lodge Cwm
Park Woods
Cathole Rock
8
7
93
6
5
92
4
3
91
2
1
90
52
53
54
229
120
92

91
65

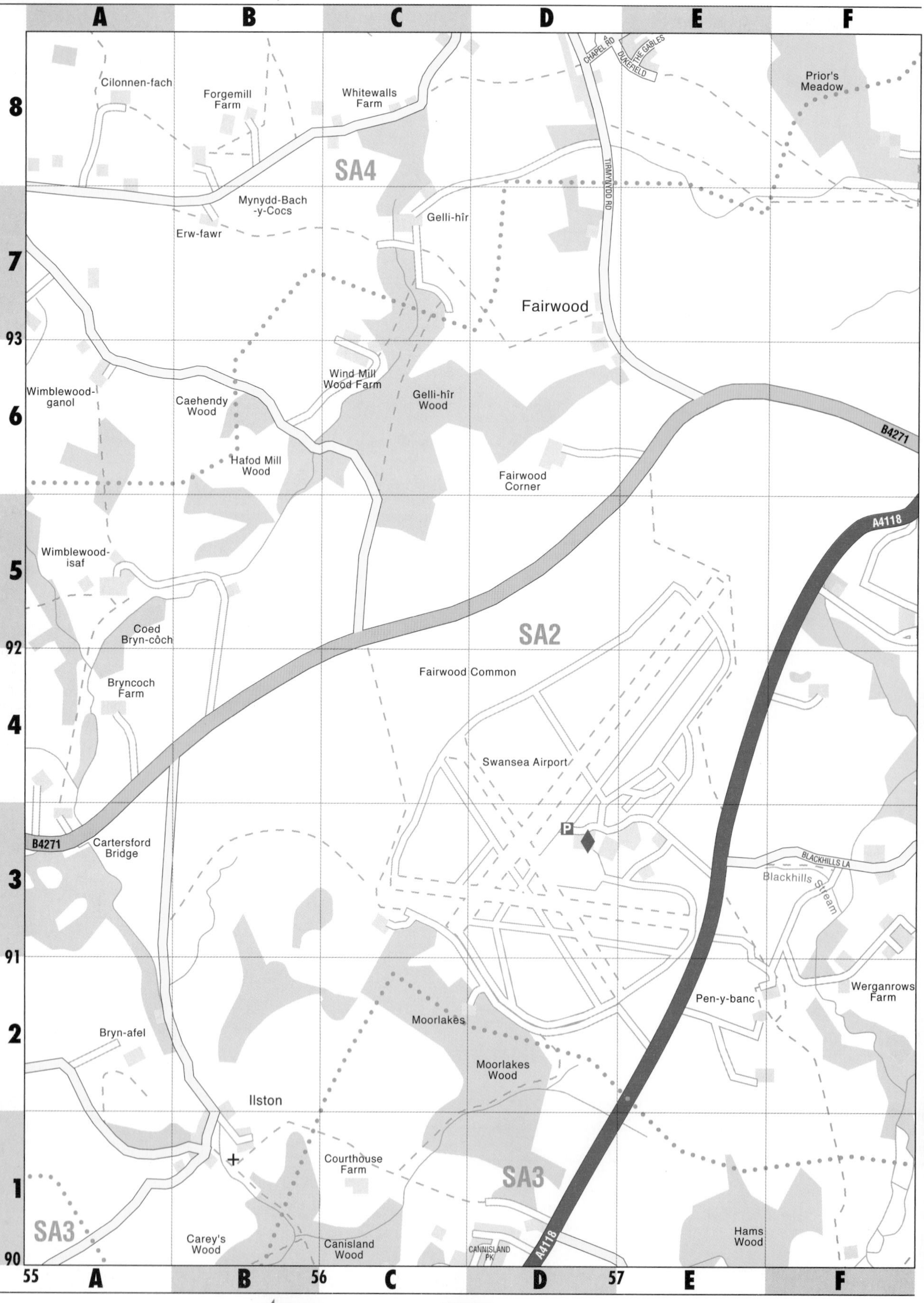

A B C D E F
8 7 93 6 5 92 4 3 91 2 1 90
Cilonnen-fach
Forgemill Farm
Whitewalls Farm
CHAPEL RD
THE GABLES
DUKEFIELD
Prior's Meadow
SA4
Mynydd-Bach -y-Cocs
Erw-fawr
Gelli-hîr
TIRMYNYDD RD
Fairwood
Wind Mill Wood Farm
Wimblewood-ganol
Caehendy Wood
Gelli-hîr Wood
B4271
Hafod Mill Wood
Fairwood Corner
A4118
Wimblewood-isaf
SA2
Coed Bryn-côch
Fairwood Common
Bryncoch Farm
Swansea Airport
P
B4271
Cartersford Bridge
BLACKHILLS LA
Blackhills Stream
Werganrows Farm
Pen-y-banc
Moorlakes
Bryn-afel
Moorlakes Wood
Ilston
Courthouse Farm
SA3
SA3
Carey's Wood
Canisland Wood
CANNISLAND PK
A4118
Hams Wood
55 A B 56 C D 57 E F

91
121

66
94

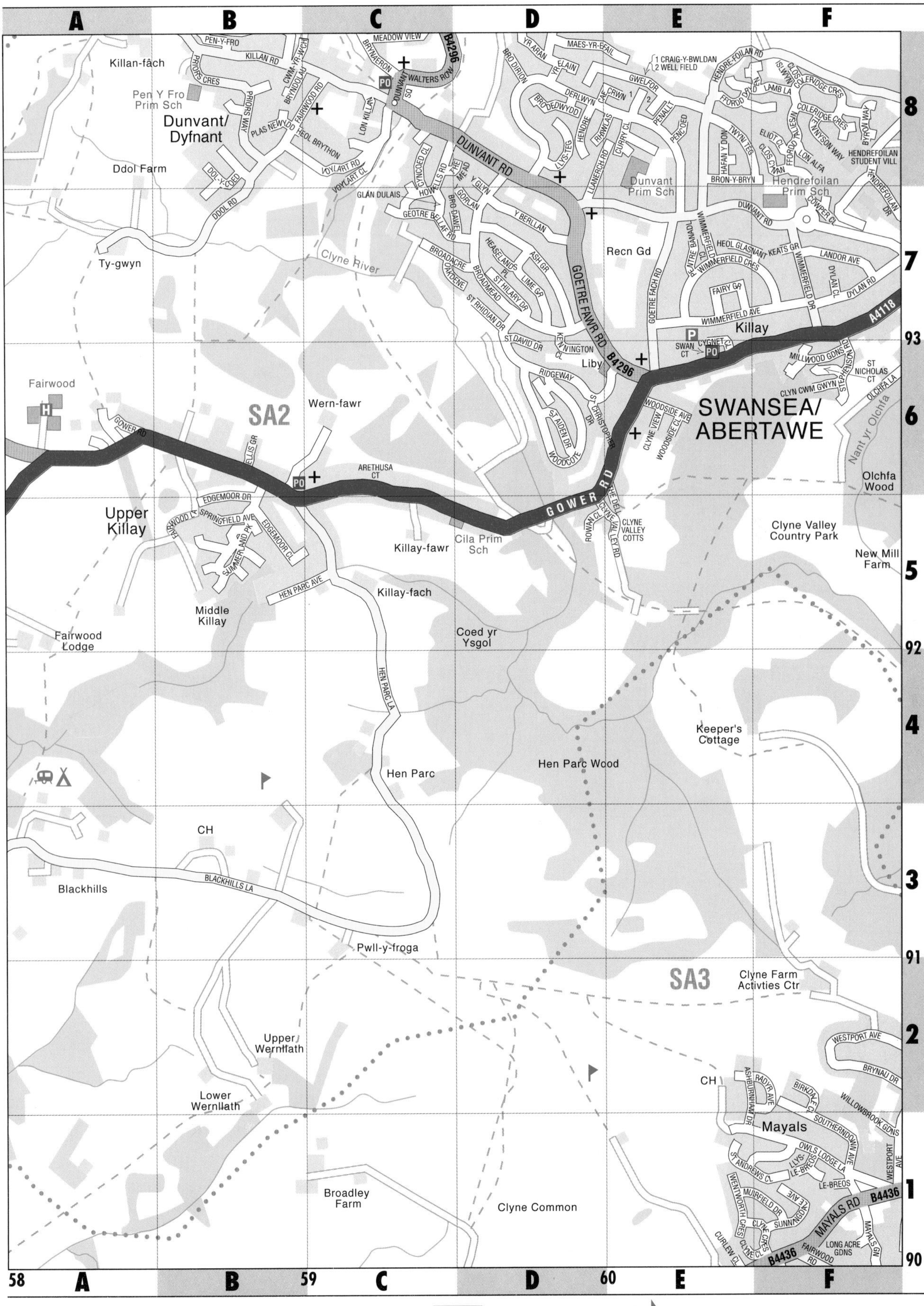

A
B
C
D
E
F
Killan-fâch
Pen Y Fro Prim Sch
Dunvant/ Dyfnant
Ddol Farm
Ty-gwyn
Clyne River
Dunvant Prim Sch
Hendrefoilan Prim Sch
Hendrefoilan Student Vill
Recn Gd
Killay
Liby
Fairwood
SA2
Wern-fawr
SWANSEA/ ABERTAWE
Olchfa Wood
Upper Killay
Cila Prim Sch
Killay-fawr
Clyne Valley Country Park
New Mill Farm
Killay-fach
Middle Killay
Coed yr Ysgol
Fairwood Lodge
Keeper's Cottage
Hen Parc Wood
Hen Parc
CH
Blackhills
Pwll-y-froga
SA3
Clyne Farm Activties Ctr
Upper Wernllath
Lower Wernllath
Mayals
Broadley Farm
Clyne Common
Dunvant Rd
Gower Rd
Goetre Fawr Rd
B4296
A4118
B4436
Mayals Rd
Blackhills La
Hen Parc La
Hen Parc Ave
1 Craig-y-Bwldan
2 Well Field
58
59
60
8
7
93
6
5
92
4
3
91
2
1
90

122
94

93
67

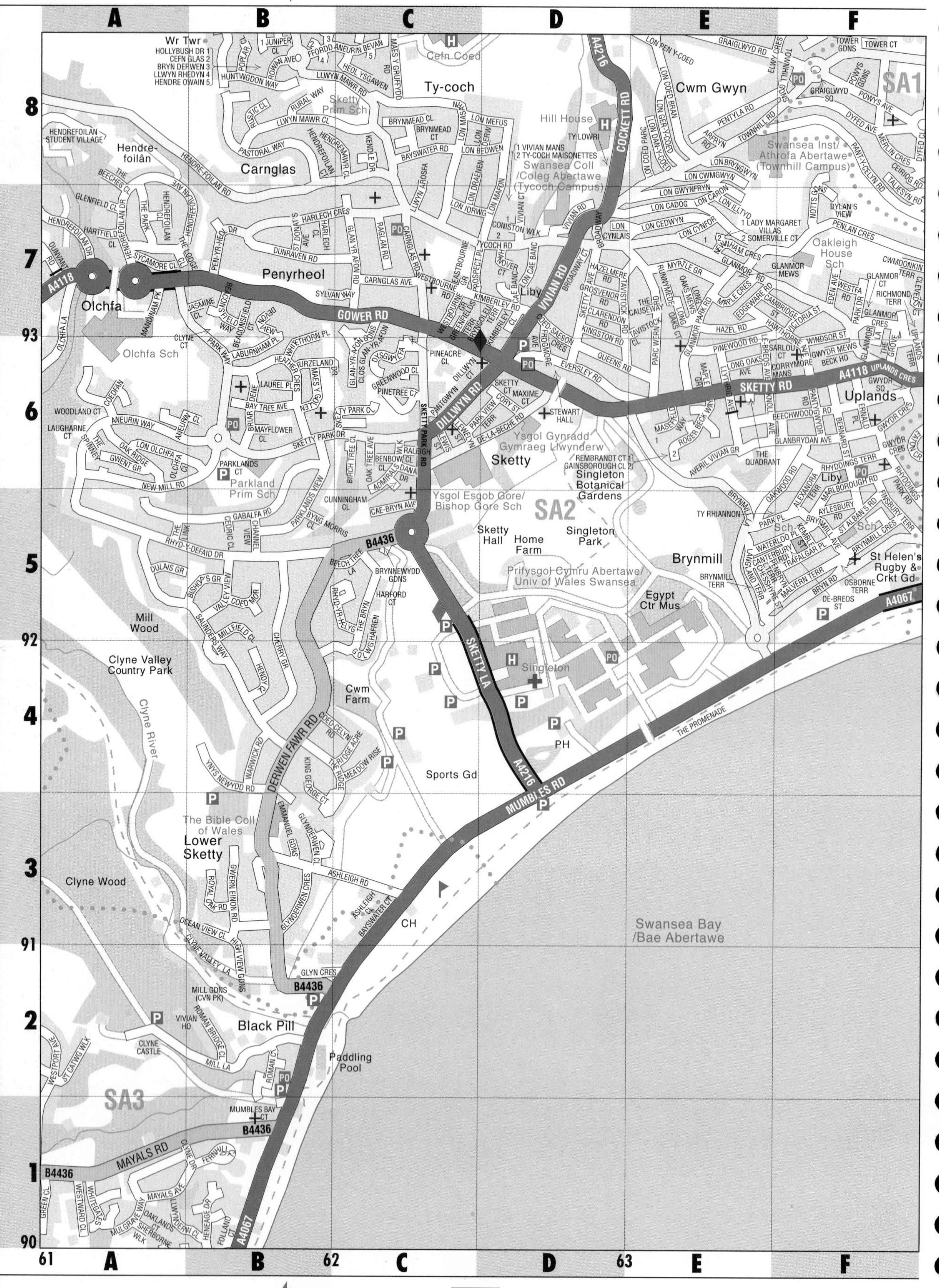
A
B
C
D
E
F
Ty-coch
Cwm Gwyn
SA1
Hendre-foilân
Carnglas
Penyrheol
Olchfa
Olchfa Sch
Sketty
SA2
Uplands
Brynmill
Sketty Hall
Home Farm
Singleton Park
Singleton Botanical Gardens
Prifysgol Cymru Abertawe/ Univ of Wales Swansea
Egypt Ctr Mus
Mill Wood
Clyne Valley Country Park
Clyne River
Cwm Farm
Sports Gd
The Bible Coll of Wales
Lower Sketty
Clyne Wood
Swansea Bay /Bae Abertawe
Black Pill
Paddling Pool
SA3
GOWER RD
SKETTY RD
DILLWYN RD
VIVIAN RD
COCKETT RD
SKETTY LA
MUMBLES RD
DERWEN FAWR RD
MAYALS RD
THE PROMENADE
A4118
A4216
B4436
A4067
Swansea Inst/ Athrofa Abertawe (Townhill Campus)
Swansea Coll /Coleg Abertawe (Tycoch Campus)
Ysgol Esgob Gore/ Bishop Gore Sch
Ysgol Gynradd Gymraeg Llwynderw
Parkland Prim Sch
Sketty Prim Sch
Oakleigh House Sch
St Helen's Rugby & Crkt Gd
Hill House
Cefn Coed
Singleton
8
7
93
6
5
92
4
3
91
2
1
90
61
62
63

93
123

A6
1 RICHMOND MEWS
2 BELGRAVE GDNS
3 ST JAMES CT
4 DUMBARTON HOUSE CT
5 OSCAR CHESS HO

B7
1 CHADDESLEY TERR
2 TY MAWR
3 Celtic Bsns Pk
4 CALVERT TERR
5 BRUNEL CT

For full street detail of the highlighted area see page 233.

68

96

B8
1 CADRAWD RD
2 WAUN-WEN RD
3 TEGID RD
4 CADWALADR CIR

SWANSEA/
ABERTAWE

Swansea Bay/
Bae Abertawe

Townhill
Mount Pleasant
St Thomas
Swansea Castle
Prince of Wales Dock
South Dock
Ferryport
West Pier
Eastern Breakwater

96

95

69

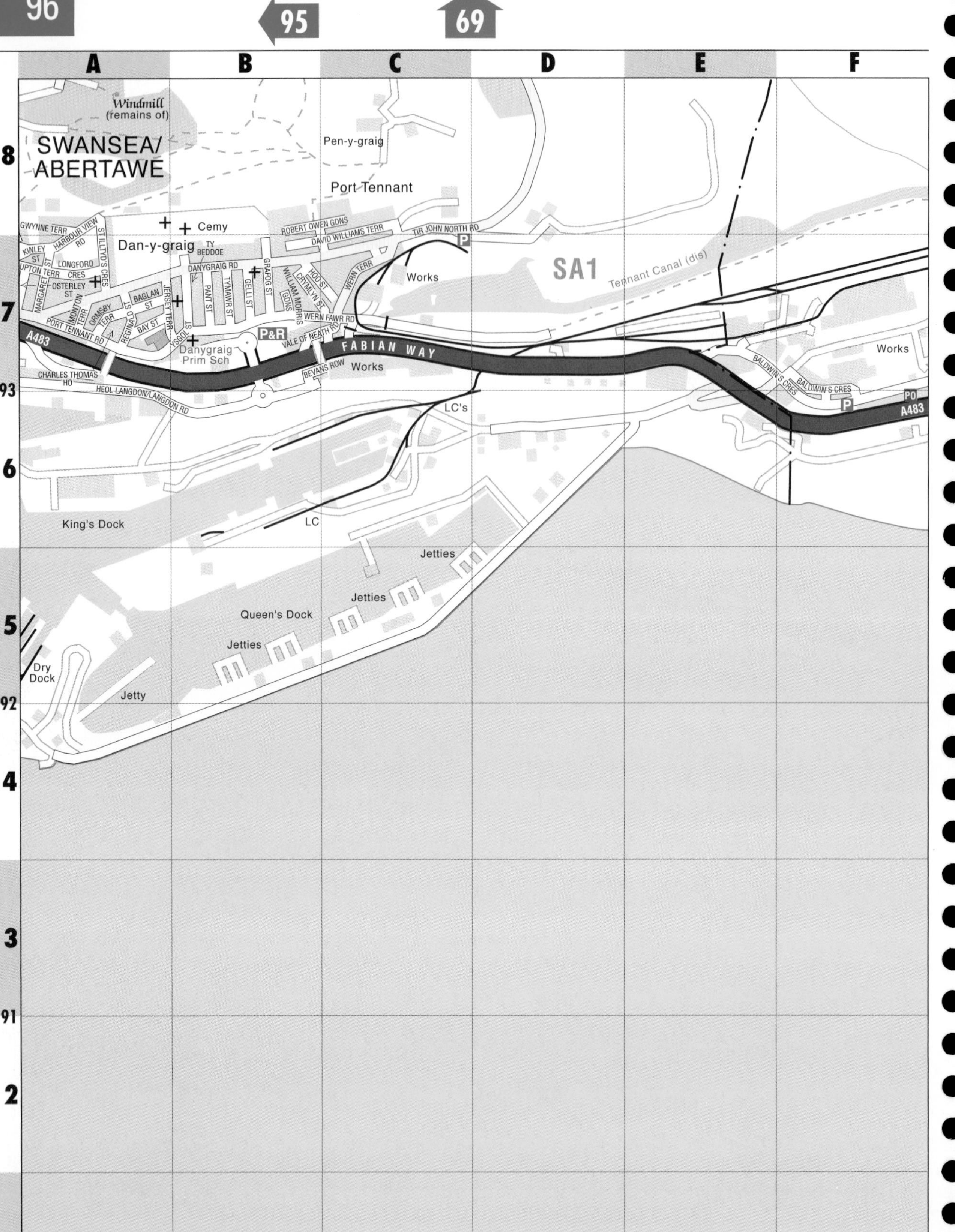

Windmill (remains of)
SWANSEA/ ABERTAWE
Pen-y-graig
Port Tennant
Cemy
Dan-y-graig
SA1
Tennant Canal (dis)
Works
FABIAN WAY
A483
Danygraig Prim Sch
P&R
LC's
LC
King's Dock
Queen's Dock
Jetties
Jetty
Dry Dock
BALDWIN'S CRES
PO

95

70
98

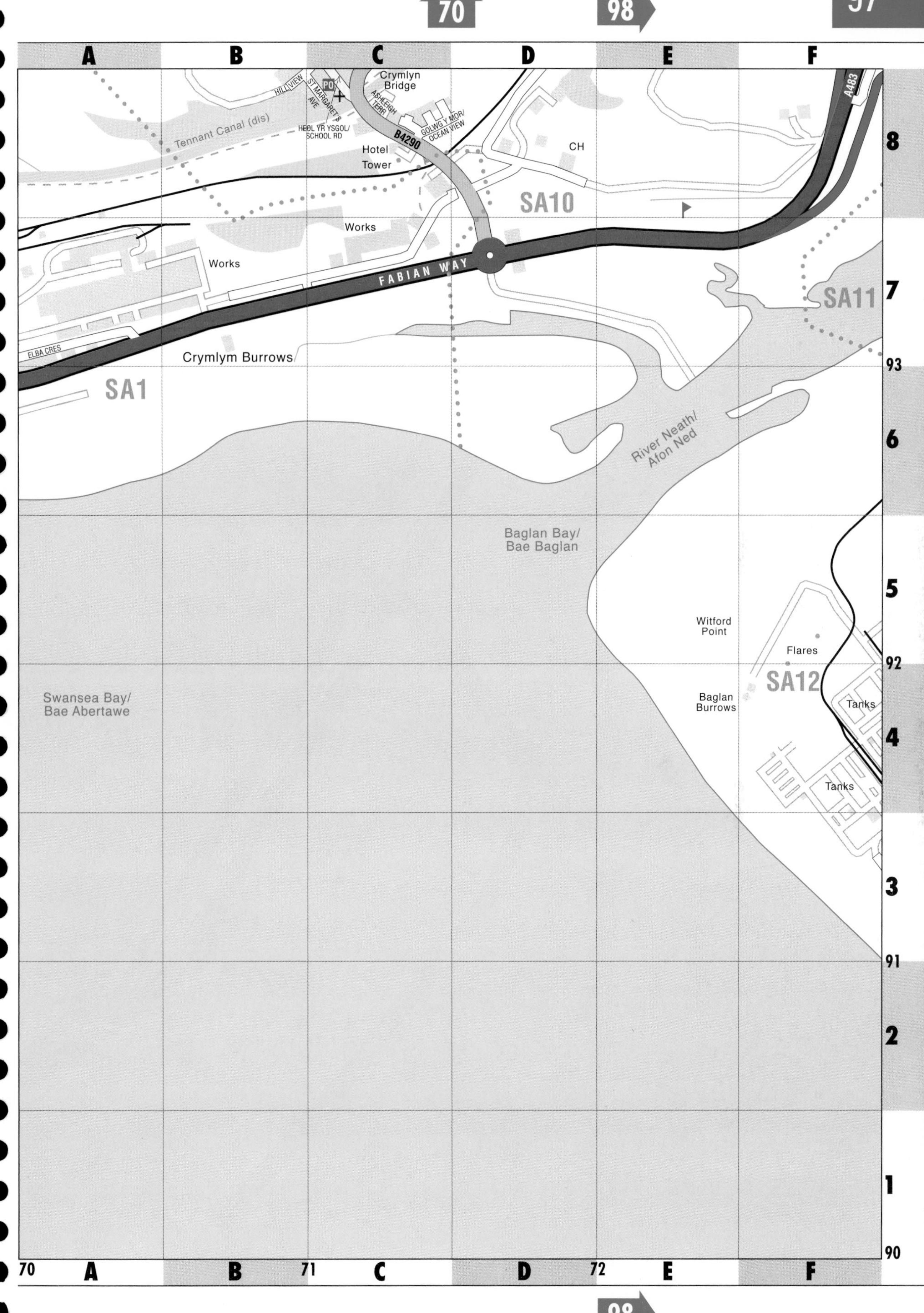
A
B
C
D
E
F
Crymlyn Bridge
HILLVIEW
ST MARGARET'S AVE
PO
ASHLEIGH TERR
GOLWG Y MOR/ OCEAN VIEW
HEOL YR YSGOL/ SCHOOL RD
Tennant Canal (dis)
B4290
Hotel
Tower
CH
A483
SA10
Works
Works
FABIAN WAY
SA11
ELBA CRES
Crymlym Burrows
SA1
River Neath/ Afon Ned
Baglan Bay/ Bae Baglan
Witford Point
Flares
SA12
Baglan Burrows
Tanks
Tanks
Swansea Bay/ Bae Abertawe
8
7
93
6
5
92
4
3
91
2
1
90
70
71
72

98

B3
1 IRVING HO
2 KEMP HO
3 GARRICK HO
4 HEOL CHOPIN/CHOPIN RD
5 ROBERTSON HO
6 KEAN HO

97

7 HEOL BACH/BACH RD
8 CLOS GREIG/GREIG CL
9 MARLOWE HO
10 HEOL WAGNER/WAGNER RD
11 PHELPS HO
12 CWRT GREIG/GREIG CT

71

13 MOZART MEWS
14 SILVER CT
15 CLOS ARIAN/SILVER CL

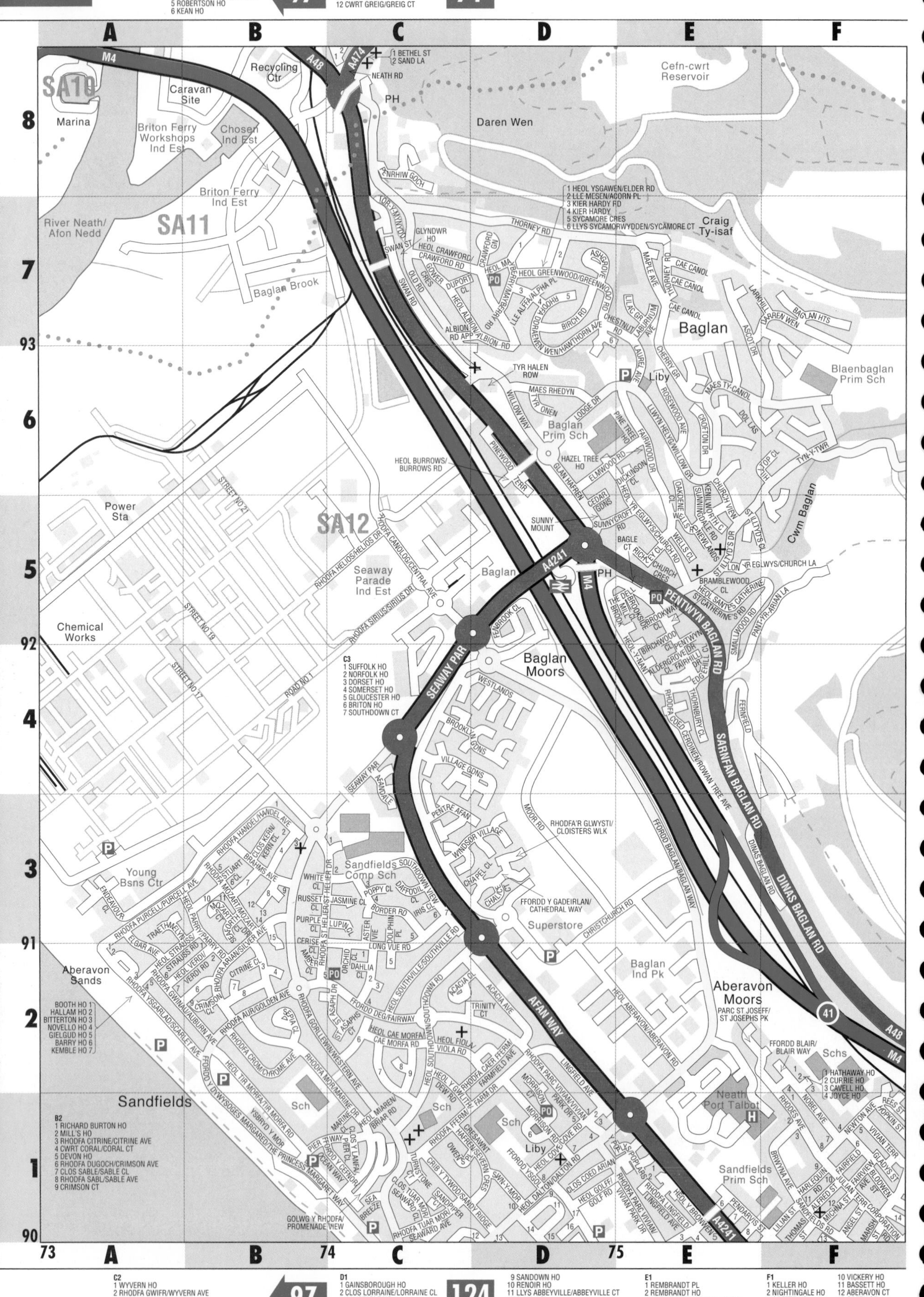

C2
1 WYVERN HO
2 RHODFA GWIFR/WYVERN AVE
3 MAN Y COED/TIMBRE PL
4 CORNWALL HO
5 MAN ST KITTS/ST KITTS PL
6 HEOL GORDON/GORDON RD
7 CRESAWNT GORDON/GORDON CRES
8 FFORDD CROES Y DE/SOUTH CROSS WAY
9 HEOL CROES Y DE/SOUTH CROSS RD

97

D1
1 GAINSBOROUGH HO
2 CLOS LORRAINE/LORRAINE CL
3 CONSTABLE HO
4 RAPHAEL HO
5 COVE HO
6 CRESAWNT MORRISON/ MORRISON CRES
7 MORRISON HO
8 DALTON HO

124

9 SANDOWN HO
10 RENOIR HO
11 LLYS ABBEYVILLE/ABBEYVILLE CT
12 SANDY CL
13 CLOS DALTON/DALTON CL
14 HEOL ROMNEY/ROMNEY RD
15 ABBEYVILLE HO
16 RHODFA ABBEYVILLE/ ABBEYVILLE AVE
17 HEOL SANDOWN/SANDOWN RD

E1
1 REMBRANDT PL
2 REMBRANDT HO
3 HEOL MORFA/MOORLAND RD
4 ADDISON RD
5 Port Talbot Workshops
6 CATHERINE ST
7 CLARICE ST
8 STAIR ST

F1
1 KELLER HO
2 NIGHTINGALE HO
3 ODETTE HO
4 BONDFIELD HO
5 AYLWARD HO
6 LISTER AVE
7 BRONTE HO
8 PATTI HO
9 WOOLLER HO
10 VICKERY HO
11 BASSETT HO
12 ABERAVON CT
13 GREEN ST
14 LESLIE ST

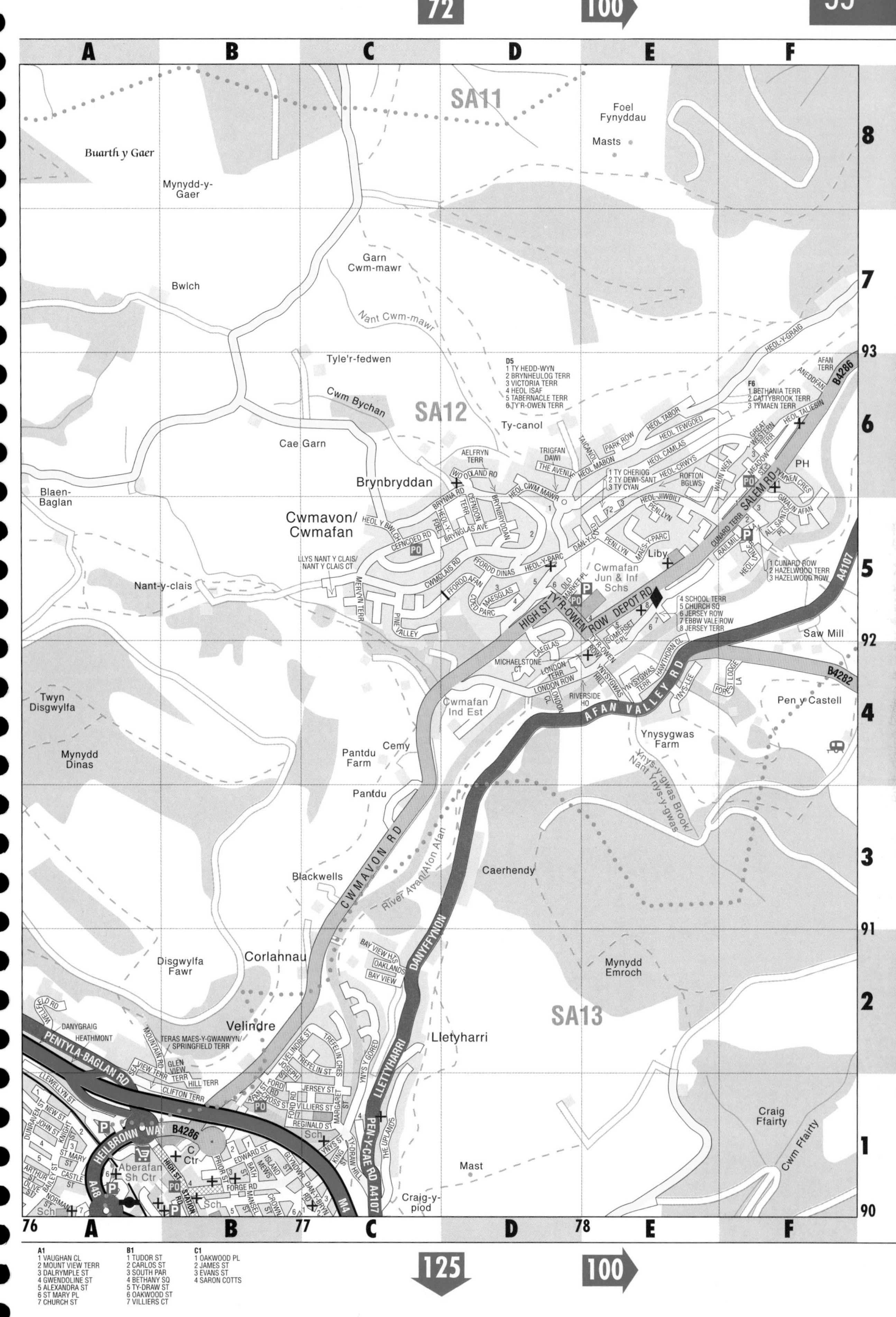
72
100
A
B
C
D
E
F
8
7
93
6
5
92
4
3
91
2
1
90
76
77
78
SA11
SA12
SA13
Buarth y Gaer
Mynydd-y-Gaer
Foel Fynyddau
Masts
Garn Cwm-mawr
Bwlch
Nant Cwm-mawr
Tyle'r-fedwen
Cwm Bychan
Cae Garn
Ty-canol
Blaen-Baglan
Brynbryddan
Cwmavon/Cwmafan
Nant-y-clais
D5
1 TY HEDD-WYN
2 BRYNHEULOG TERR
3 VICTORIA TERR
4 HEOL ISAF
5 TABERNACLE TERR
6 TY'R-OWEN TERR
F6
1 BETHANIA TERR
2 CATTYBROOK TERR
3 TYMAEN TERR
1 TY CHERIOG
2 TY DEWI-SANT
3 TY CYAN
1 CUNARD ROW
2 HAZELWOOD TERR
3 HAZELWOOD ROW
4 SCHOOL TERR
5 CHURCH SQ
6 JERSEY ROW
7 EBBW VALE ROW
8 JERSEY TERR
LLYS NANT Y CLAIS/ NANT Y CLAIS CT
Cwmafan Jun & Inf Schs
Liby
PH
Saw Mill
B4286
B4282
A4107
HIGH ST
TY'R-OWEN ROW
DEPOT RD
SALEM RD
AFAN VALLEY RD
Cwmafan Ind Est
Pen y Castell
Ynysygwas Farm
Nant Ynys-y-gwas
Ynys-y-gwas Brook
Twyn Disgwylfa
Mynydd Dinas
Pantdu Farm
Cemy
Pantdu
Blackwells
CWMAVON RD
River Avan/Afon Afan
Caerhendy
DANYFFYNON
Disgwylfa Fawr
Corlannau
Mynydd Emroch
Velindre
Lletyharri
LLETYHARRI
PENTYLA-BAGLAN RD
HEILBRONN WAY
Aberafan Sh Ctr
Craig Ffairty
Cwm Ffairty
Mast
Craig-y-piod
PEN-Y-CAE RD A4107
M4
A48
125
100
A1
1 VAUGHAN CL
2 MOUNT VIEW TERR
3 DALRYMPLE ST
4 GWENDOLINE ST
5 ALEXANDRA ST
6 ST MARY PL
7 CHURCH ST
B1
1 TUDOR ST
2 CARLOS ST
3 SOUTH PAR
4 BETHANY SQ
5 TY-DRAW ST
6 OAKWOOD ST
7 VILLIERS CT
C1
1 OAKWOOD PL
2 JAMES ST
3 EVANS ST
4 SARON COTTS

99
73

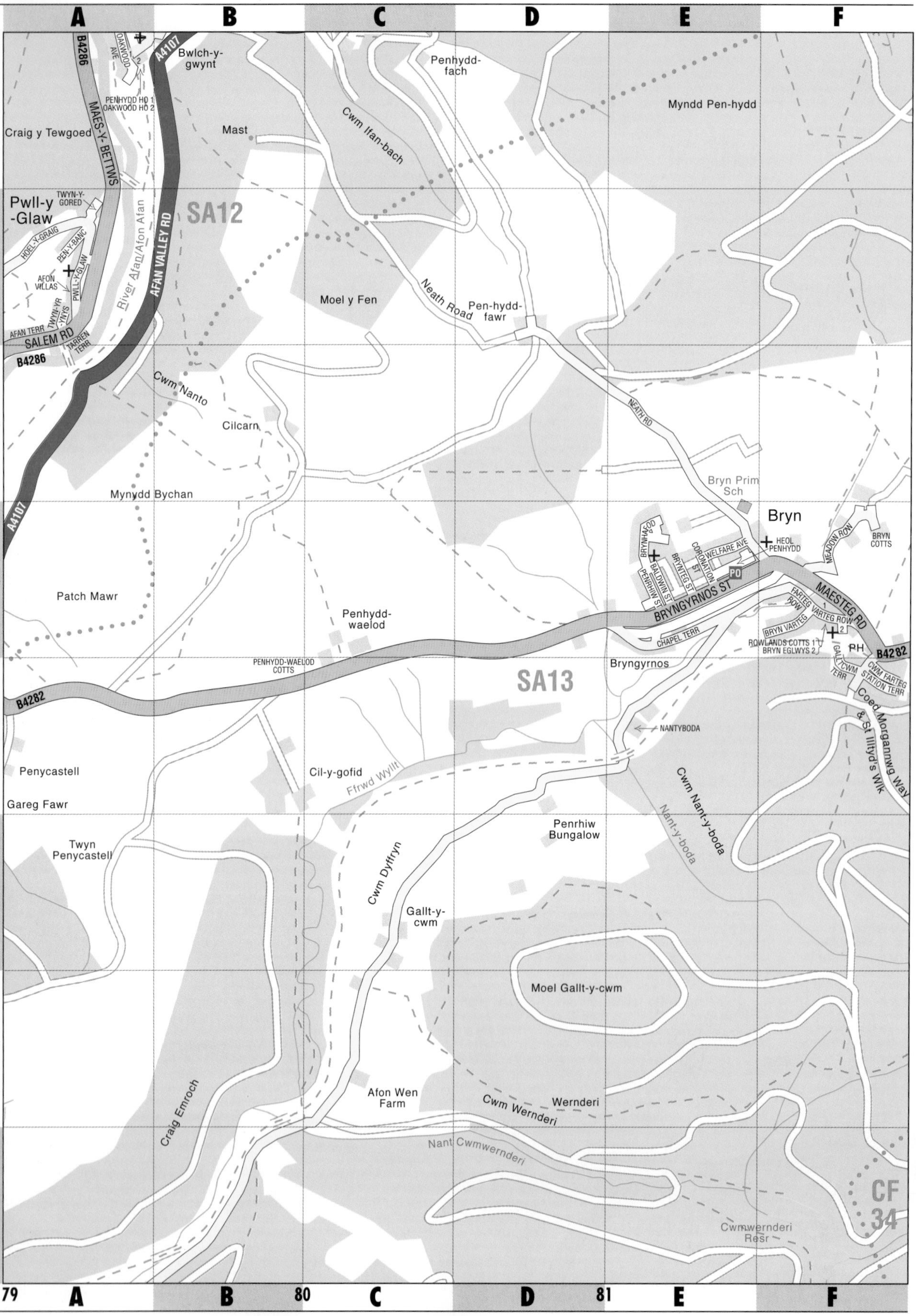

A B C D E F

8
7
93
6
5
92
4
3
91
2
1
90

Craig y Tewgoed
Pwll-y -Glaw
TWYN-Y-GORED
HOEL-Y-GRAIG
PEN-Y-BANC
AFON VILLAS
PWLL-Y-GLAW
TWYN-YR-YNYS
AFAN TERR
SALEM RD
TARREN TERR
B4286
MAES-Y-BETTWS
OAKWOOD AVE
PENHYDD HO 1
OAKWOOD HO 2
River Afan/Afon Afan
AFAN VALLEY RD
A4107
Bwlch-y-gwynt
Mast
SA12
Cwm Nanto
Cilcarn
Mynydd Bychan
Patch Mawr
Penhydd-fach
Cwm Ifan-bach
Moel y Fen
Neath Road
Pen-hydd-fawr
Myndd Pen-hydd
NEATH RD
Bryn Prim Sch
Bryn
HEOL PENHYDD
BRYNHAFOD
BALDWIN ST
PENRHIW ST
BRYNTEG ST
CORONATION ST
WELFARE AVE
PO
BRYNGYRNOS ST
MEADOW ROW
BRYN COTTS
MAESTEG RD
FARTEG ROW
VARTEG ROW
BRYN VARTEG
ROWLANDS COTTS 1
BRYN EGLWYS 2
PH
GALLT CWM TERR
CWM FARTEG
STATION TERR
B4282
CHAPEL TERR
Bryngyrnos
SA13
Penhydd-waelod
PENHYDD-WAELOD COTTS
B4282
NANTYBODA
Coed Morgannwg Way & St Illtyd's Wlk
Penycastell
Gareg Fawr
Cil-y-gofid
Ffrwd Wyllt
Cwm Nant-y-boda
Nant-y-boda
Twyn Penycastell
Penrhiw Bungalow
Cwm Dyffryn
Gallt-y-cwm
Moel Gallt-y-cwm
Craig Emroch
Afon Wen Farm
Cwm Wernderi
Wernderi
Nant Cwmwernderi
Cwmwernderi Resr
CF 34

79 A B 80 C D 81 E F

99
126

74
102

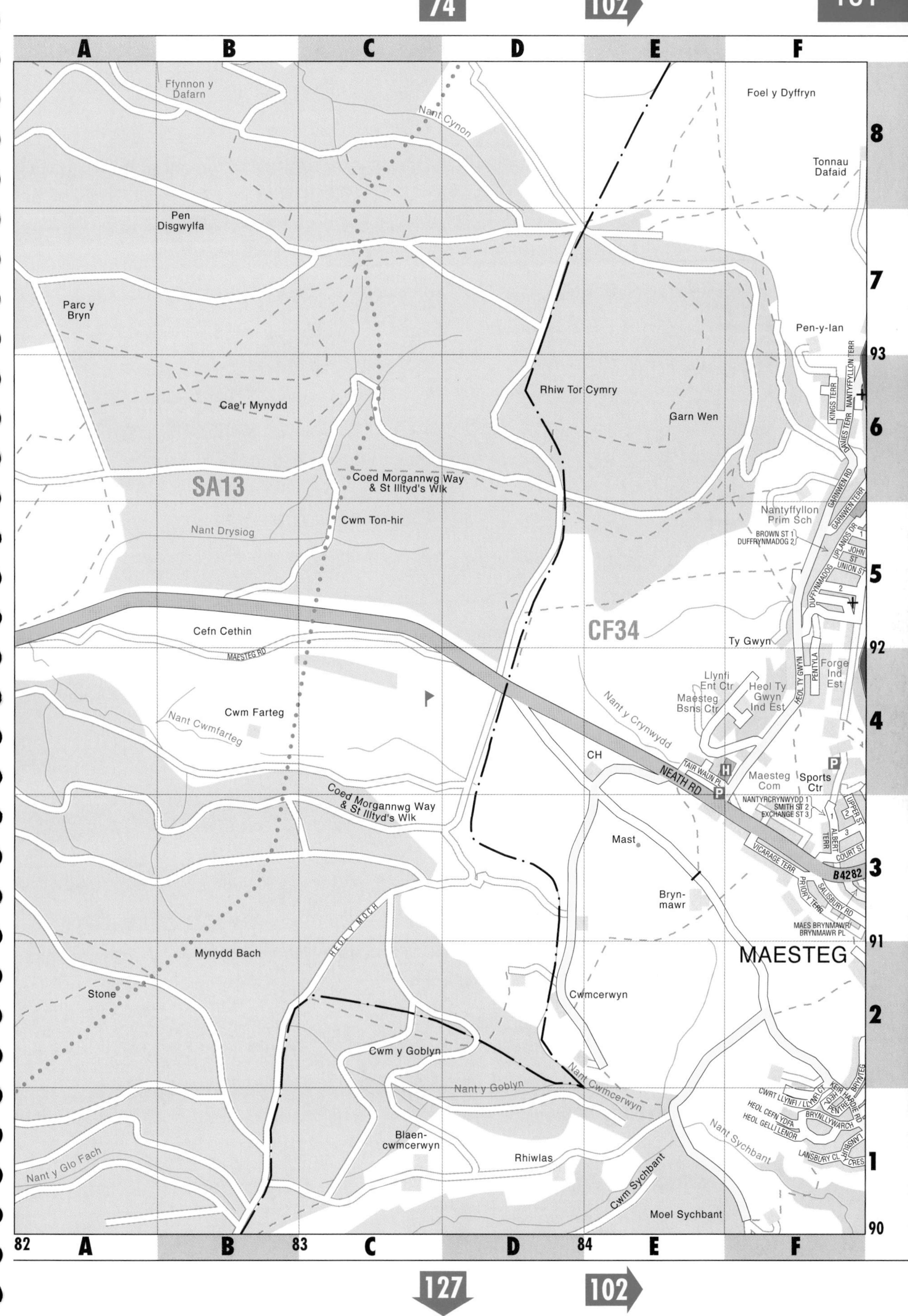

127
102

101
75

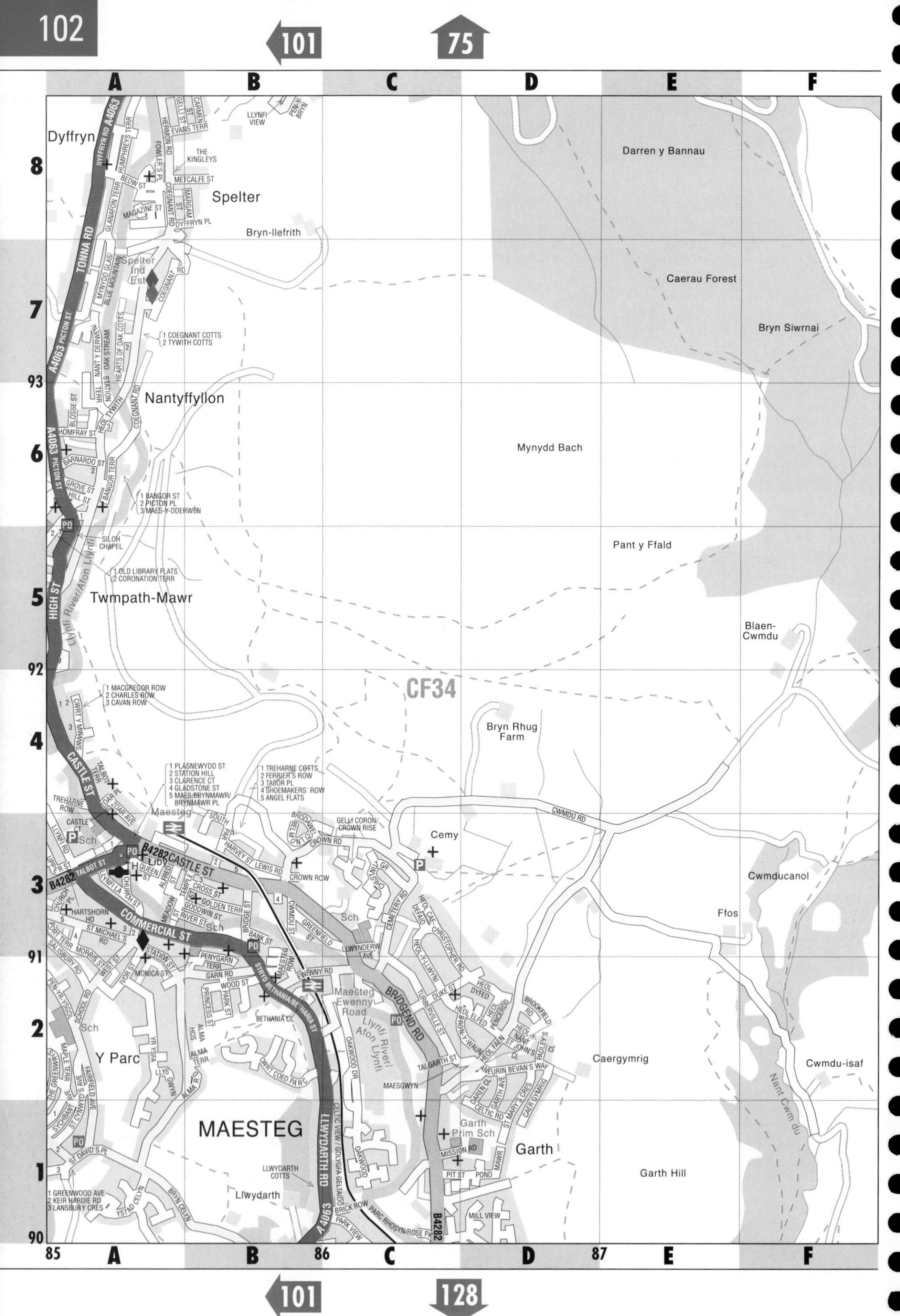

101
128

76
104

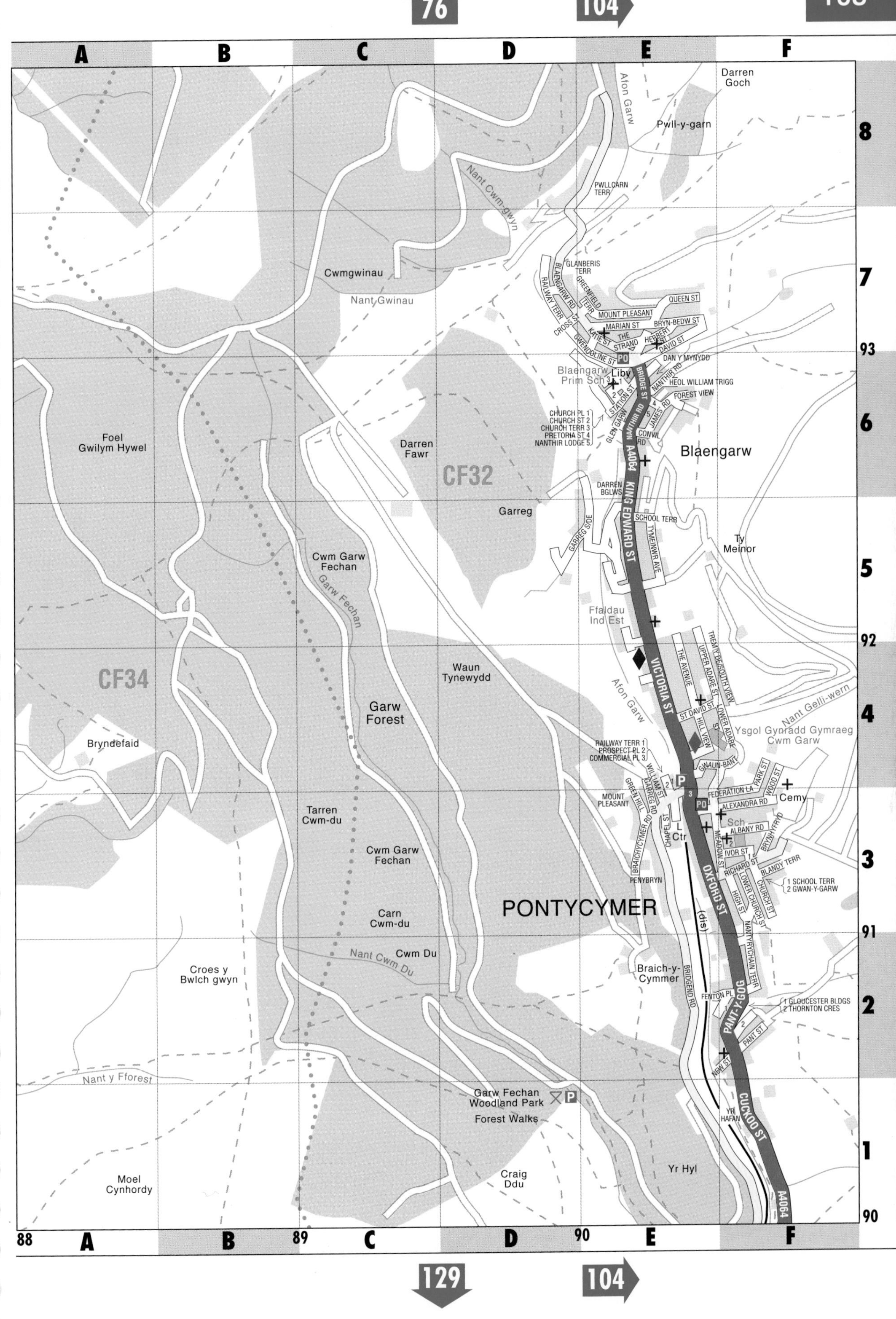

129
104

103 77

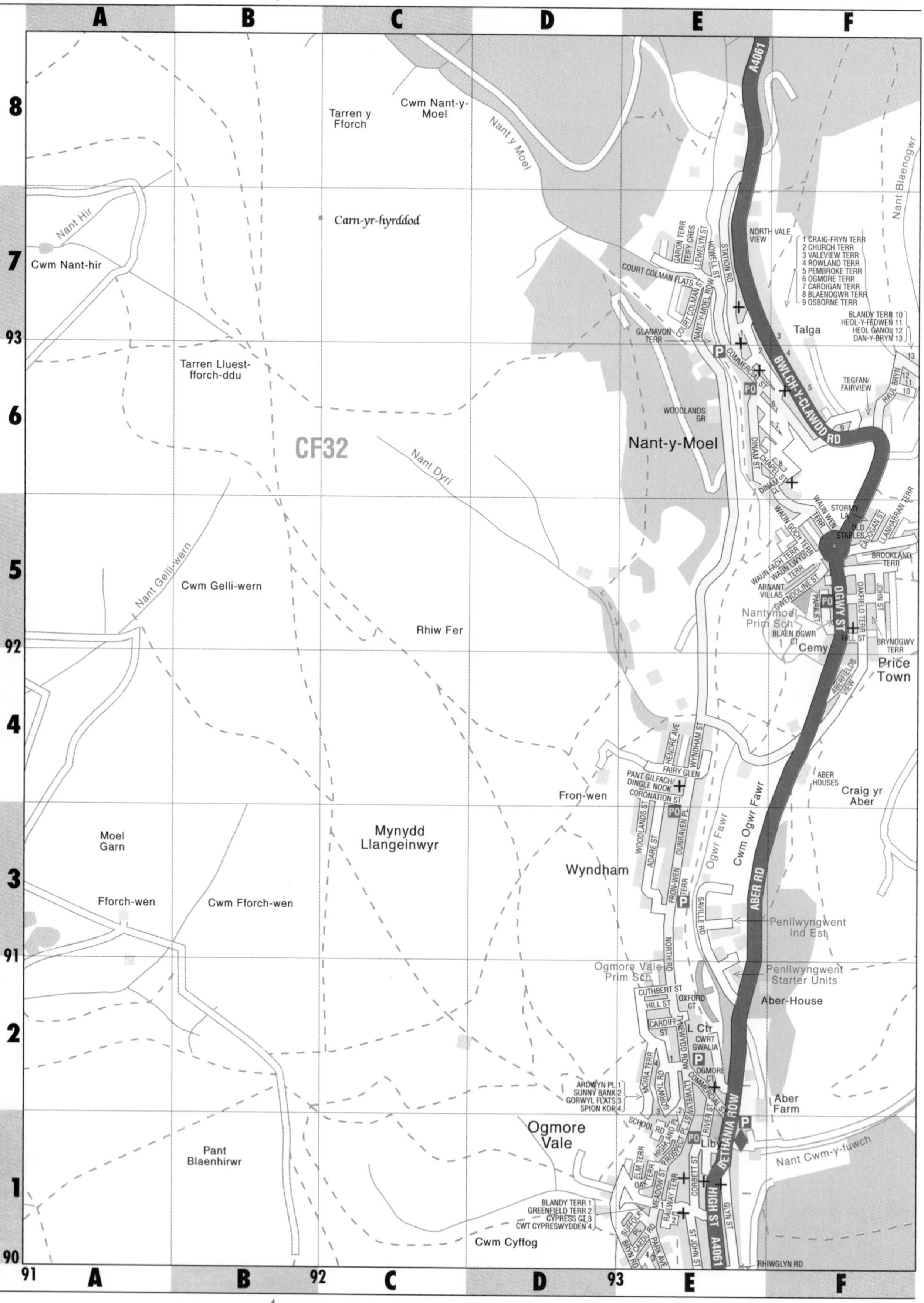

A B C D E F

8 7 93 6 5 92 4 3 91 2 1 90

Tarren y Fforch
Cwm Nant-y-Moel
Nant y Moel
Carn-yr-hyrddod
Nant Hir
Cwm Nant-hir
Nant Blaenogwr
Talga
Tarren Lluest-fforch-ddu
CF32
Nant Dyri
Nant-y-Moel
Nant Gelli-wern
Cwm Gelli-wern
Rhiw Fer
Nantymoel Prim Sch
Cemy
Price Town
Fron-wen
Craig yr Aber
Moel Garn
Mynydd Llangeinwyr
Wyndham
Cwm Ogwr Fawr
Ogwr Fawr
Fforch-wen
Cwm Fforch-wen
Penllwyngwent Ind Est
Ogmore Vale Prim Sch
Penllwyngwent Starter Units
Aber-House
Aber Farm
Ogmore Vale
Pant Blaenhirwr
Nant Cwm-y-fuwch
Cwm Cyffog

1 CRAIG-FRYN TERR
2 CHURCH TERR
3 VALEVIEW TERR
4 ROWLAND TERR
5 PEMBROKE TERR
6 OGMORE TERR
7 CARDIGAN TERR
8 BLAENOGWR TERR
9 OSBORNE TERR

BLANDY TERR 10
HEOL-Y-FEDWEN 11
HEOL GANOL 12
DAN-Y-BRYN 13

ARDWYN PL 1
SUNNY BANK 2
GORWYL FLATS 3
SPION KOP 4

BLANDY TERR 1
GREENFIELD TERR 2
CYPRESS CT 3
CWT CYPRESWYDDEN 4

A4061, BWLCH-Y-CLAWDD RD, OGWY ST, ABER RD, BETHANIA ROW, HIGH ST A4061, NORTH VALE VIEW, GARON TERR, TEIFY CRES, LLEWELYN ST, HOWELL ST, STATION RD, COURT COLMAN FLATS, COURT COLMAN ST, NANT-Y-MOEL ROW, GLANAVON TERR, COMMERCIAL ST, WOODLANDS GR, DINAM ST, CHAPEL ST, DINAM CL, TEGFAN/FAIRVIEW, HAUL BRYN, STORMY LA, WAUN WEN TERR, WAUN GOCH TERR, OLD STABLES, CADOGAN ST, LLANHARRAN TERR, BROOKLAND TERR, WAUN FACH TERR, WAUN LWYDI TERR, ARNANT VILLAS, GWENDOLINE ST, PARK ST, OAKFIELD TERR, JOHN ST, BLAEN OGWR CT, HILL ST, BRYNOGWY TERR, ABERFIELDS VIEW, HENDRE AVE, WYNDHAM ST, FAIRY GLEN, PANT GILFACH/DINGLE NOOK, CORONATION ST, ABER HOUSES, WOODLANDS PL, ADARE ST, DUNRAVEN PL, FRON-WEN TERR, SAVILLE RD, NORTH RD, CUTHBERT ST, HILL ST, OXFORD CT, CARDIFF ST, NEWYDD ROW, L Ctr, CWRT GWALIA, NOIRA TERR, GARNYL RD, LLEWELYN ST, COMMERCIAL ST, OGMORE CT, SCHOOL RD, HIGHLAND PL, PROSPECT PL, RIVER ST, Liby, ELM TERR, OAK, MEADOW ST, RAILWAY TERR, CORBETT ST, GLYN ST, SUFFOLK PL, CAEDU RD, BRYN RD, PARK AVE, ST JOHN ST, RHIWGLYN RD

91 A B 92 C D 93 E F

103 130

78
106

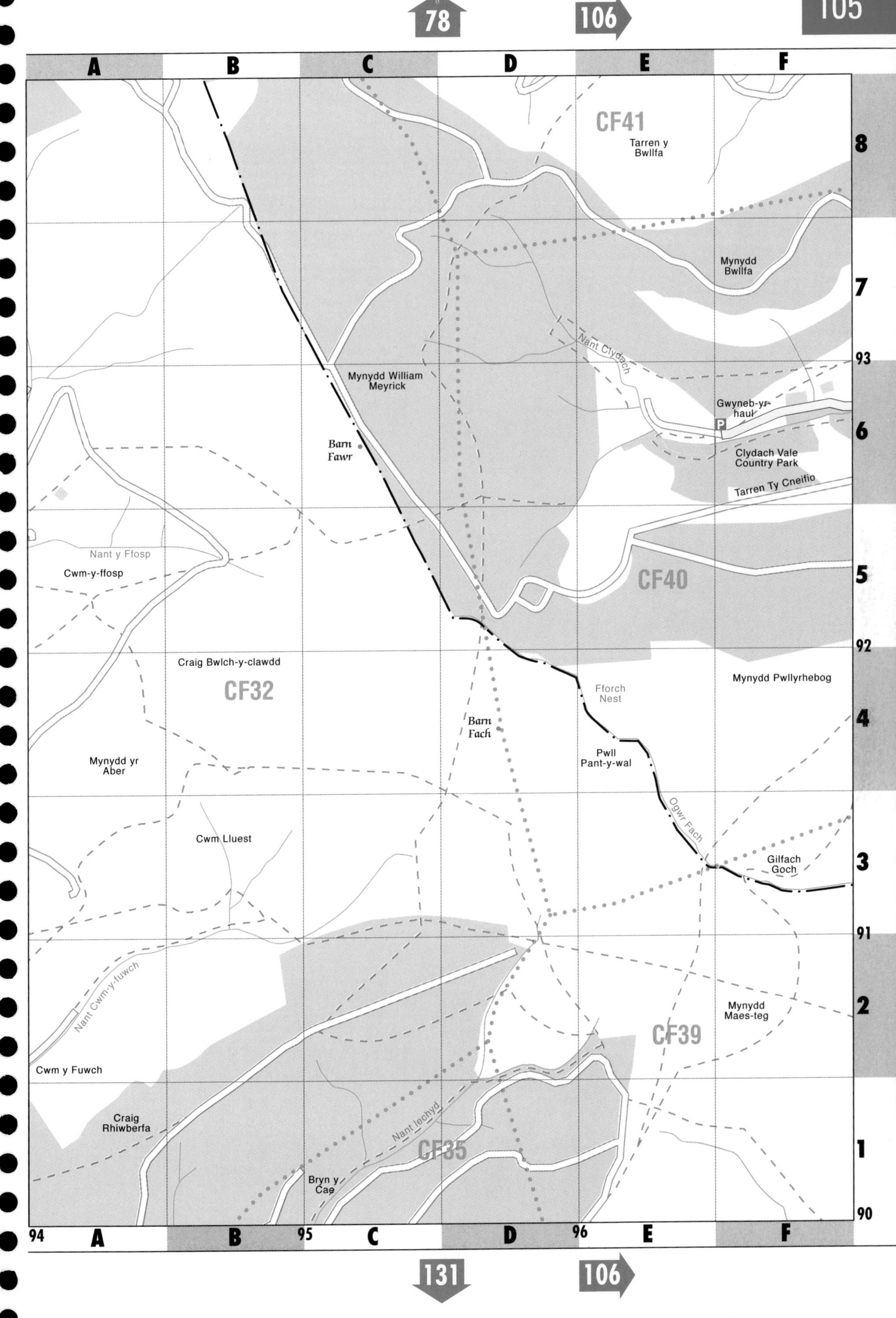

131
106

105
79

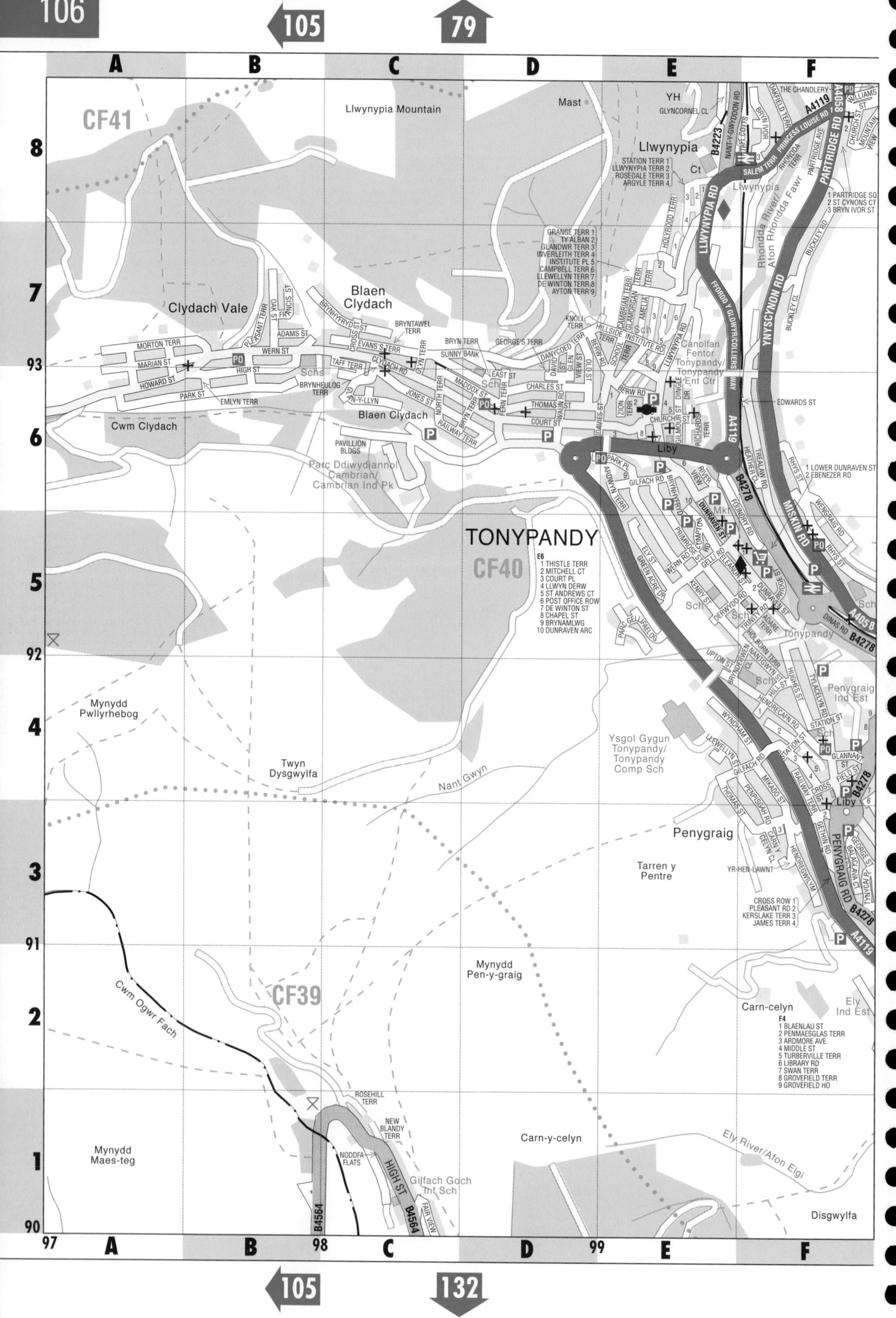

105
132

80 108

133 108

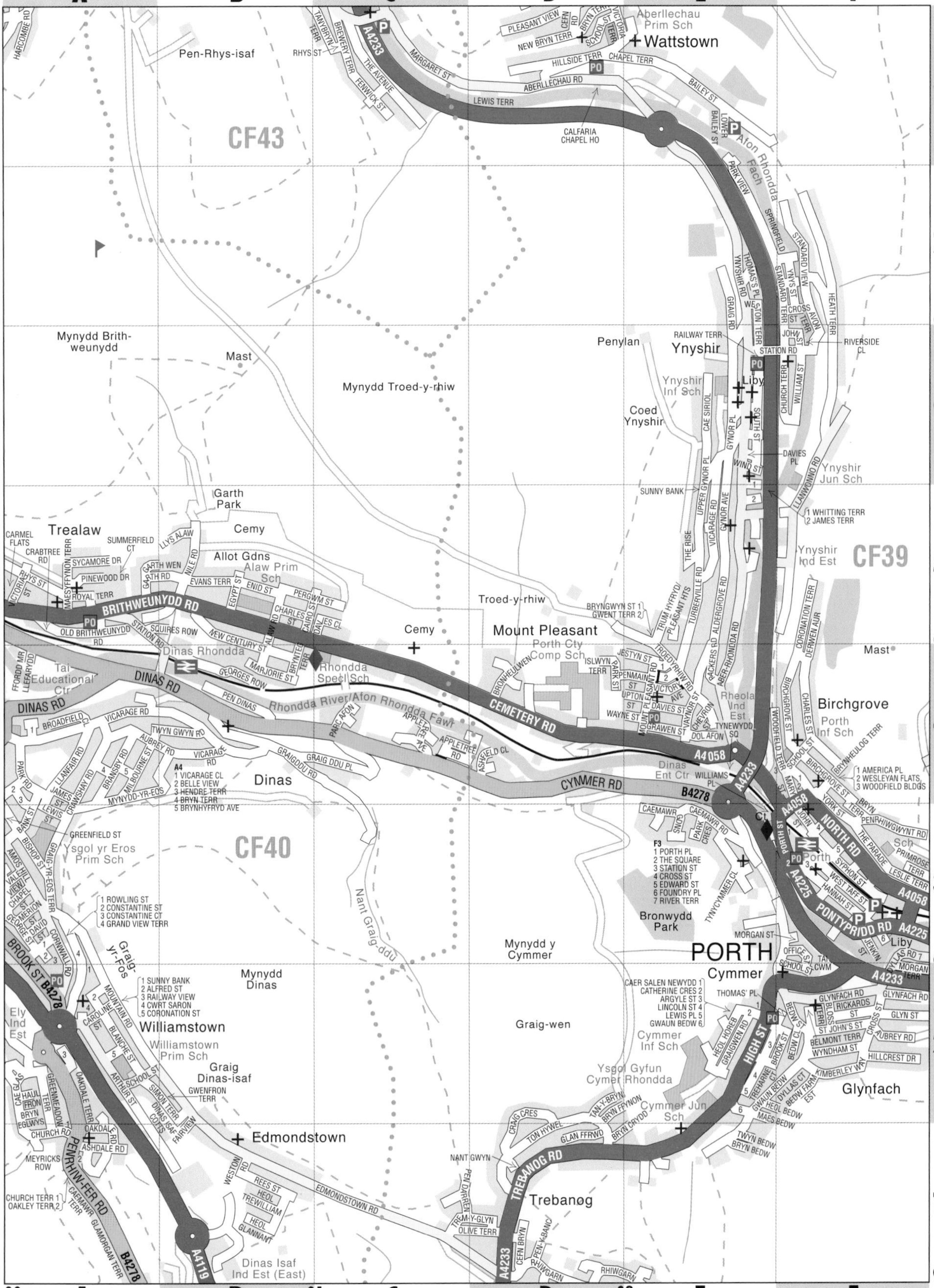

107
81

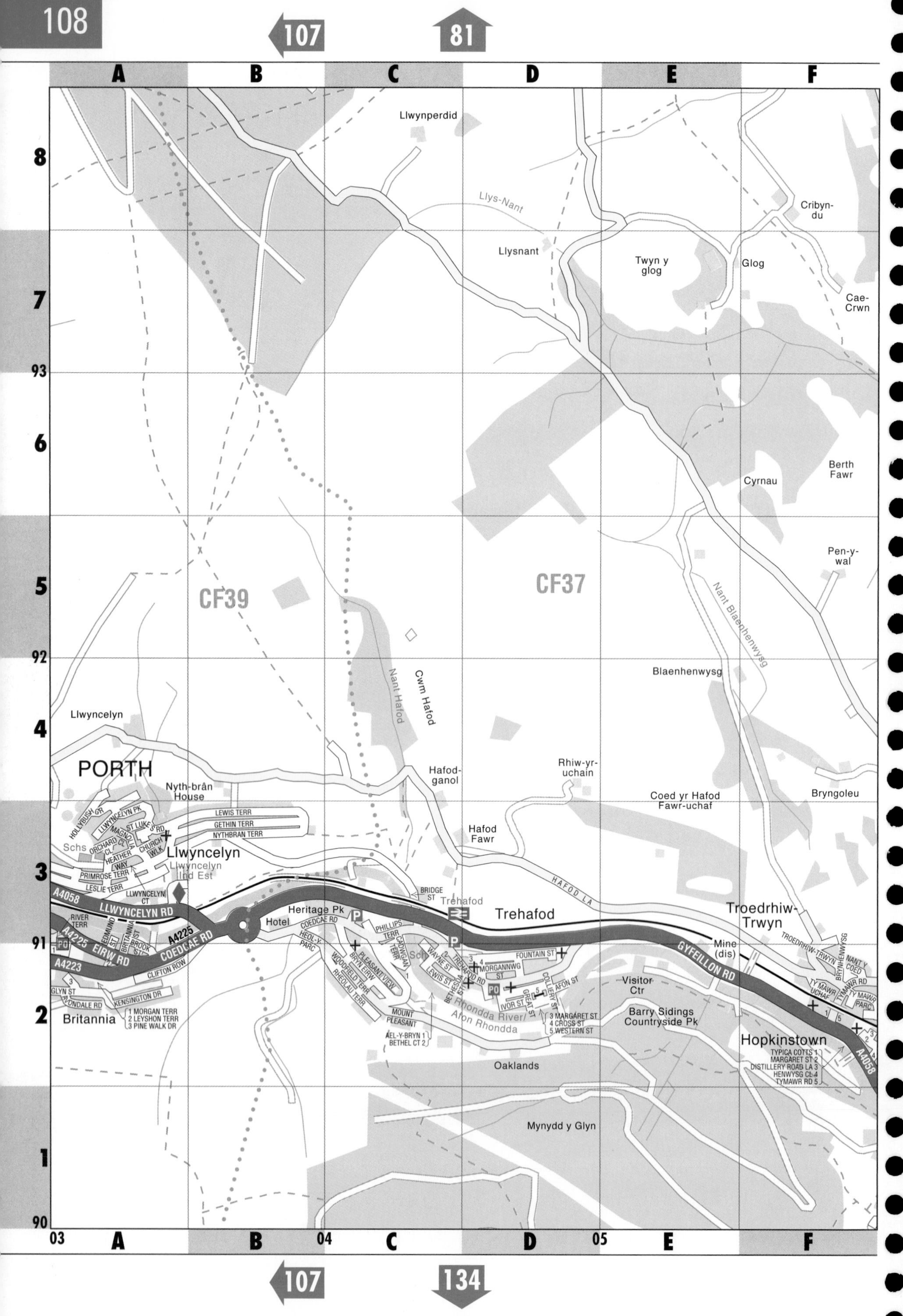

107
134

82
110

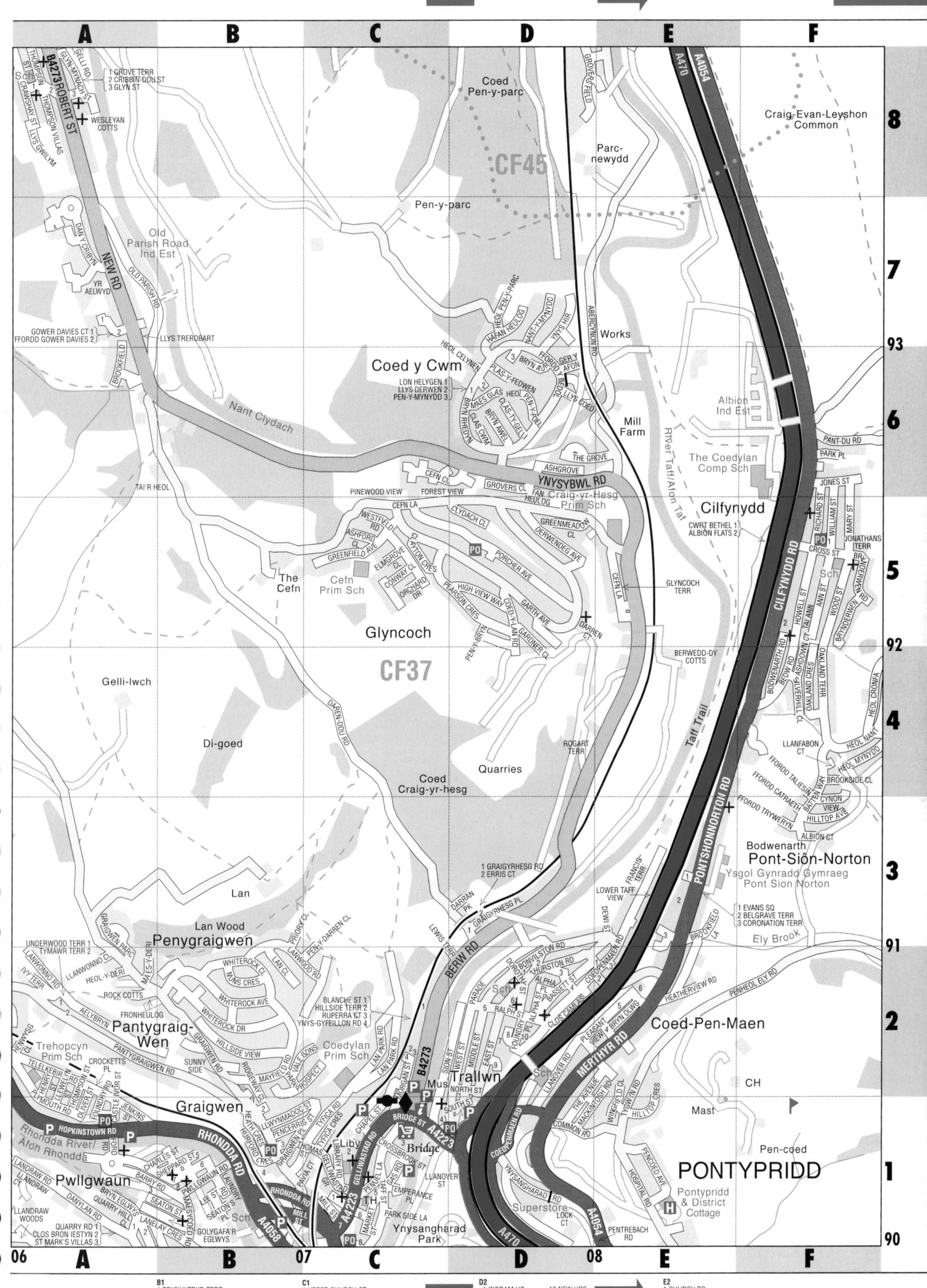

B1
1 BRYNHYFRYD TERR
2 HIGHFIELD TERR
3 LLANBRADACH ST
4 HEATH TERR
5 ROSE COTTS
6 VAUGHAN ST
7 UPPER VAUGHAN ST
8 MERLIN CL

C1
1 UPPER CHURCH ST
2 GELLIWASTAD CT
3 TAFF VALE PREC
4 FISH LA
5 FRATERNAL PAR
6 CHURCH ST
7 CATHERINE ST
8 MILL ST

135

D2
1 INGRAM HO
2 CROSSWAYS ST
3 BONVILSTON TERR
4 CROSS ST
5 CENTRAL SQ
6 PLAS YR EGLWYS
7 CHANDLERS CT
8 NEWBRIDGE CT
9 BAKERS WHARF
10 NEW HOS

110

E2
1 CHURCH RD
2 DODINGTON PL
3 JONES PL
4 FRON TERR
5 SCARBOROUGH RD
6 LLYS TY GWYN

109
83

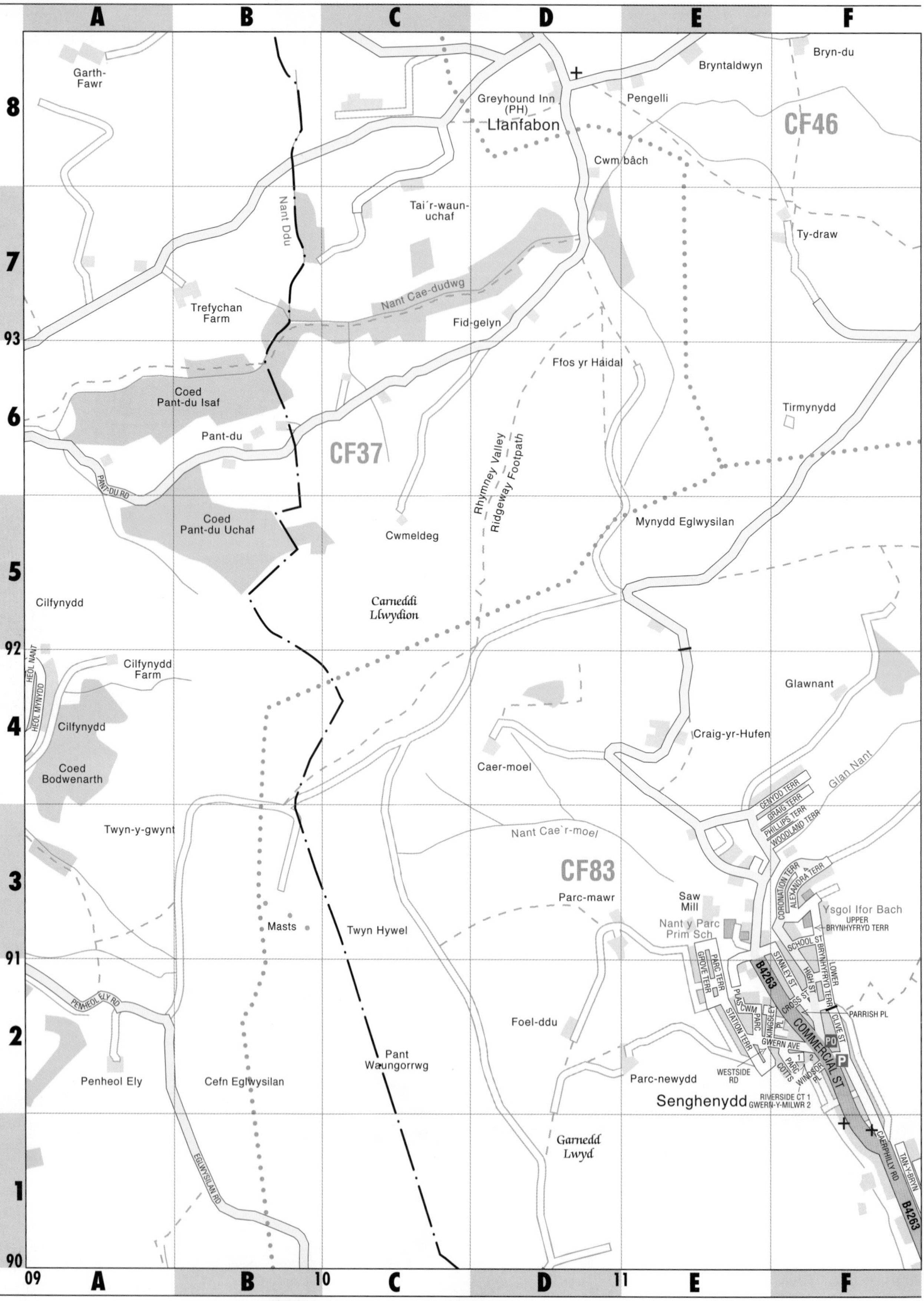

109
136

84
112

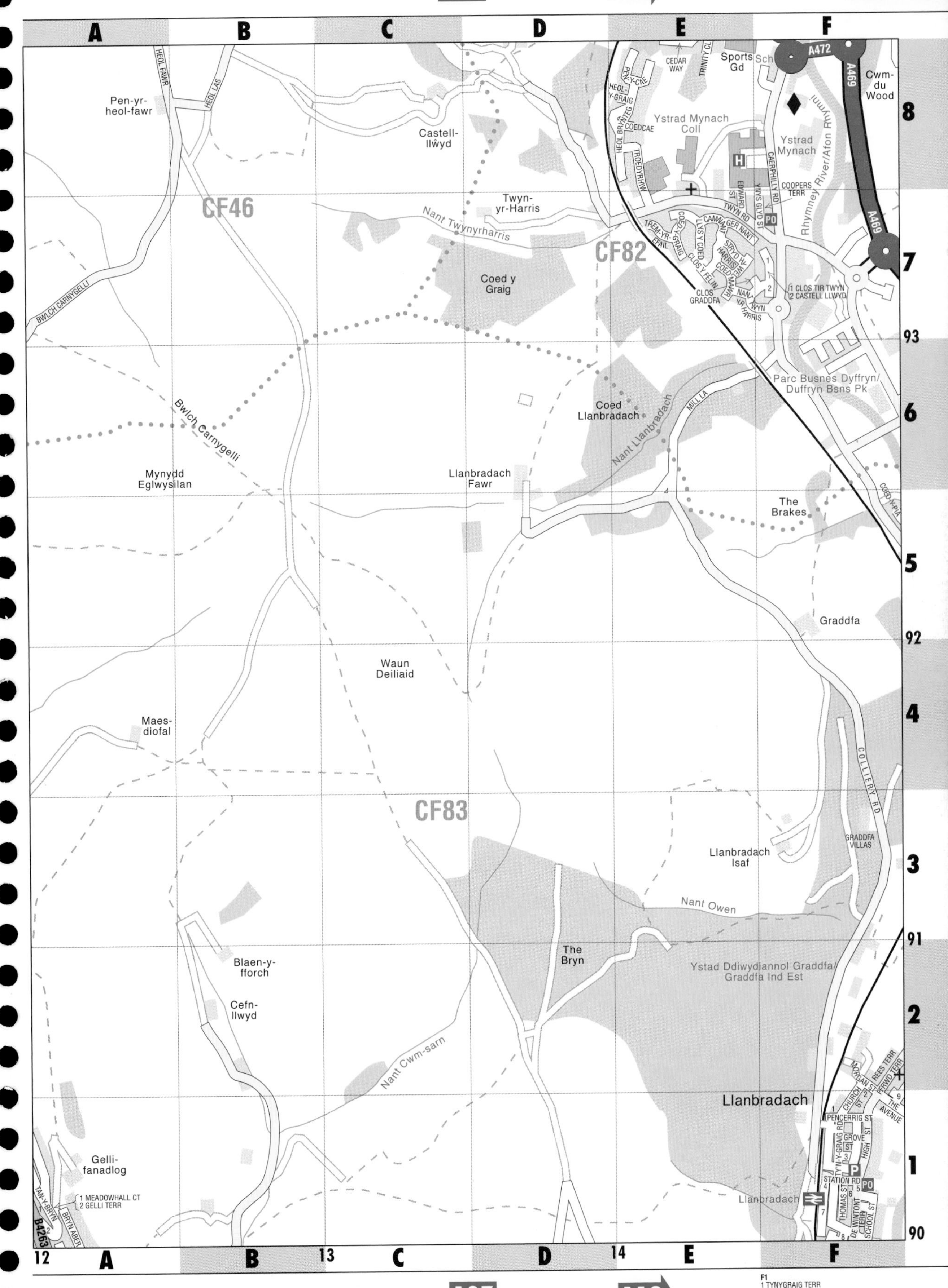

137
112

F1
1 TYNYGRAIG TERR
2 PARK VIEW
3 JAMES ST
4 WOODLAND FLATS
5 OAK TERR
6 LEWIS TERR
7 PLAS CAE LLWYD
8 RICHMOND CL
9 GARDEN ST

111
85

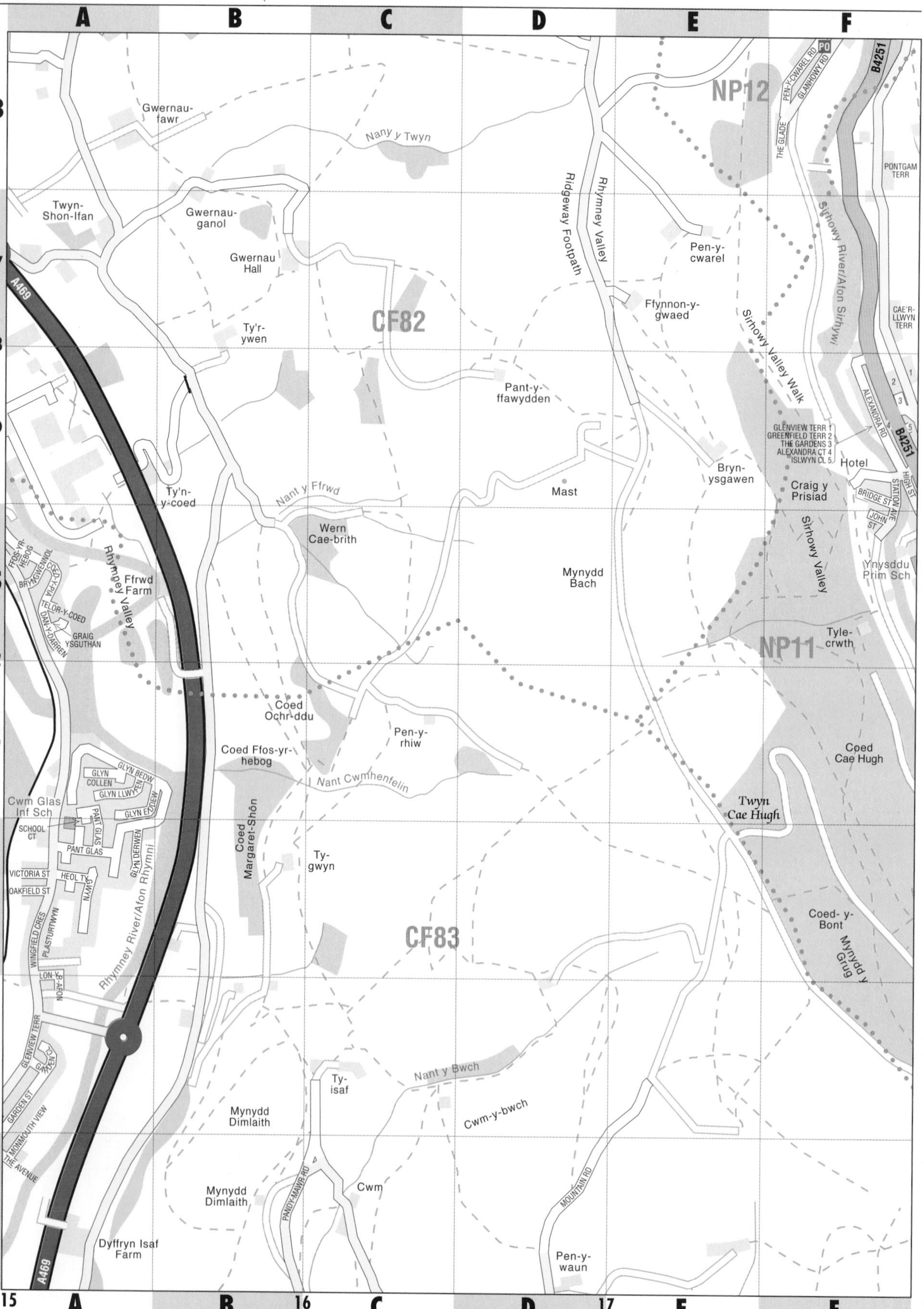

A B C D E F

8
7
93
6
5
92
4
3
91
2
1
90

Gwernau-fawr
Nany y Twyn
NP12
PEN-Y-CWAREL RD
GLANHOWY RD
PO
B4251
THE GLADE
PONTGAM TERR
Twyn-Shon-Ifan
Gwernau-ganol
Gwernau Hall
Ridgeway Footpath
Rhymney Valley
Pen-y-cwarel
Sirhowy River/Afon Sirhywi
A469
CF82
Ffynnon-y-gwaed
Sirhowy Valley Walk
CAE'R-LLWYN TERR
Ty'r-ywen
Pant-y-ffawydden
ALEXANDRA RD
GLENVIEW TERR 1
GREENFIELD TERR 2
THE GARDENS 3
ALEXANDRA CT 4
ISLWYN CL 5
Hotel
Ty'n-y-coed
Nant y Ffrwd
Mast
Bryn-ysgawen
Craig y Prisiad
BRIDGE ST
STATION AVE
HIGH ST
JOHN ST
Wern Cae-brith
FFOS-YR-HEBOG
BRYNGWENNOL
COED-Y-PIA
TELOR-Y-COED
DAN-Y-DARREN
GRAIG YSGUTHAN
Rhymney Valley
Ffrwd Farm
Mynydd Bach
Sirhowy Valley
Ynysddu Prim Sch
Tyle-crwth
NP11
Coed Ochr-ddu
Pen-y-rhiw
Coed Ffos-yr-hebog
Nant Cwmhenfelin
Coed Cae Hugh
GLYN BEDW
GLYN COLLEN
GLYN LLWYFEN
GLYN ENDEW
Cwm Glas Inf Sch
SCHOOL CT
PANT GLAS
GLYN DERWEN
Twyn Cae Hugh
Coed Margaret-Shôn
Ty-gwyn
VICTORIA ST
HEOL TY GWYN
OAKFIELD ST
Rhymney River/Afon Rhymni
Coed-y-Bont
WINGFIELD CRES
PLASTURTWYN
CF83
Mynydd y Grug
LON-Y-AFON
GLENVIEW TERR
GARDEN CL
GARDEN ST
MONMOUTH VIEW
Ty-isaf
Nant y Bwch
Mynydd Dimlaith
Cwm-y-bwch
THE AVENUE
PANDY-MAWR RD
Cwm
MOUNTAIN RD
Mynydd Dimlaith
Dyffryn Isaf Farm
Pen-y-waun

15 A B 16 C D 17 E F

111
138

86
114

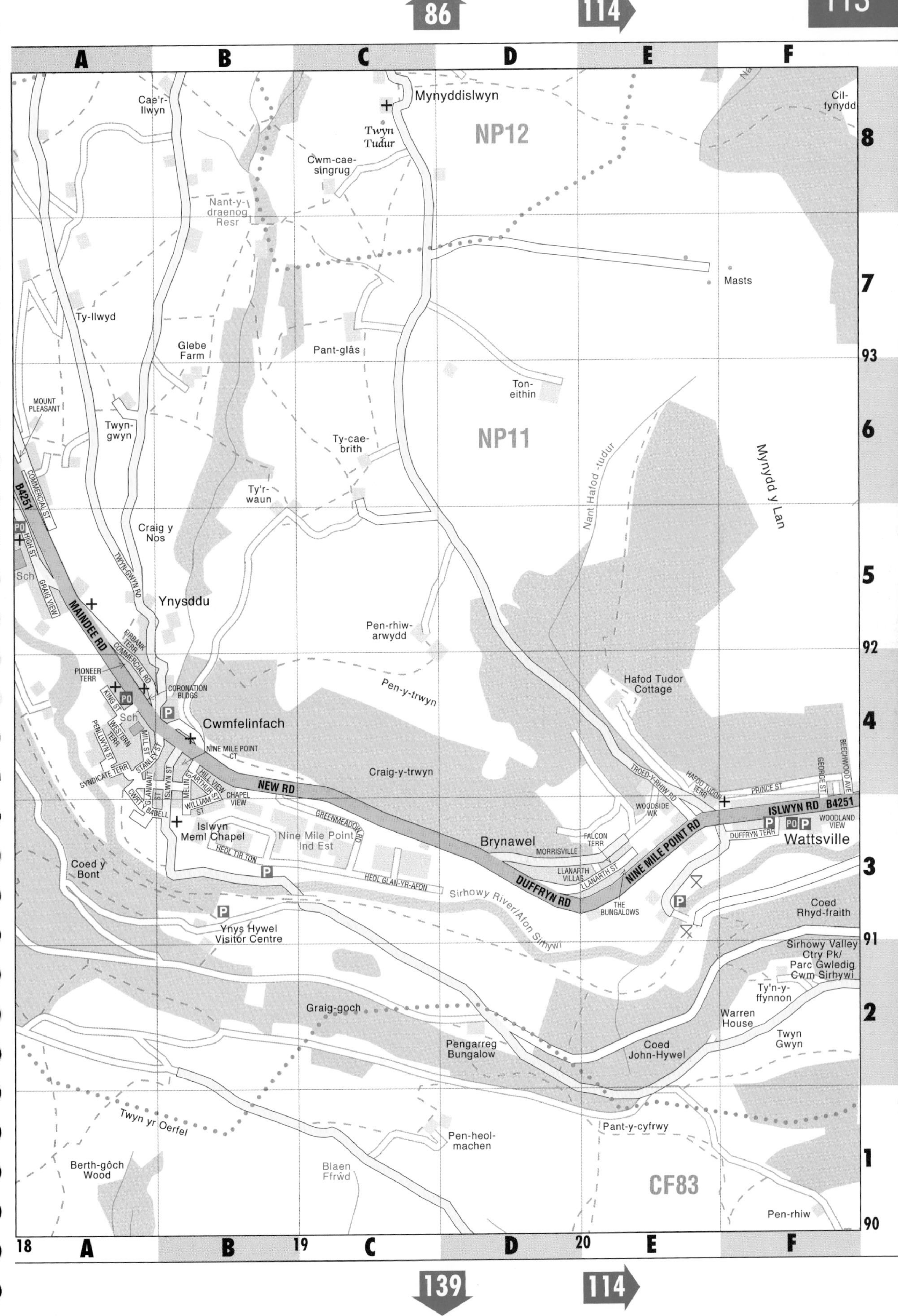

139
114

113
87

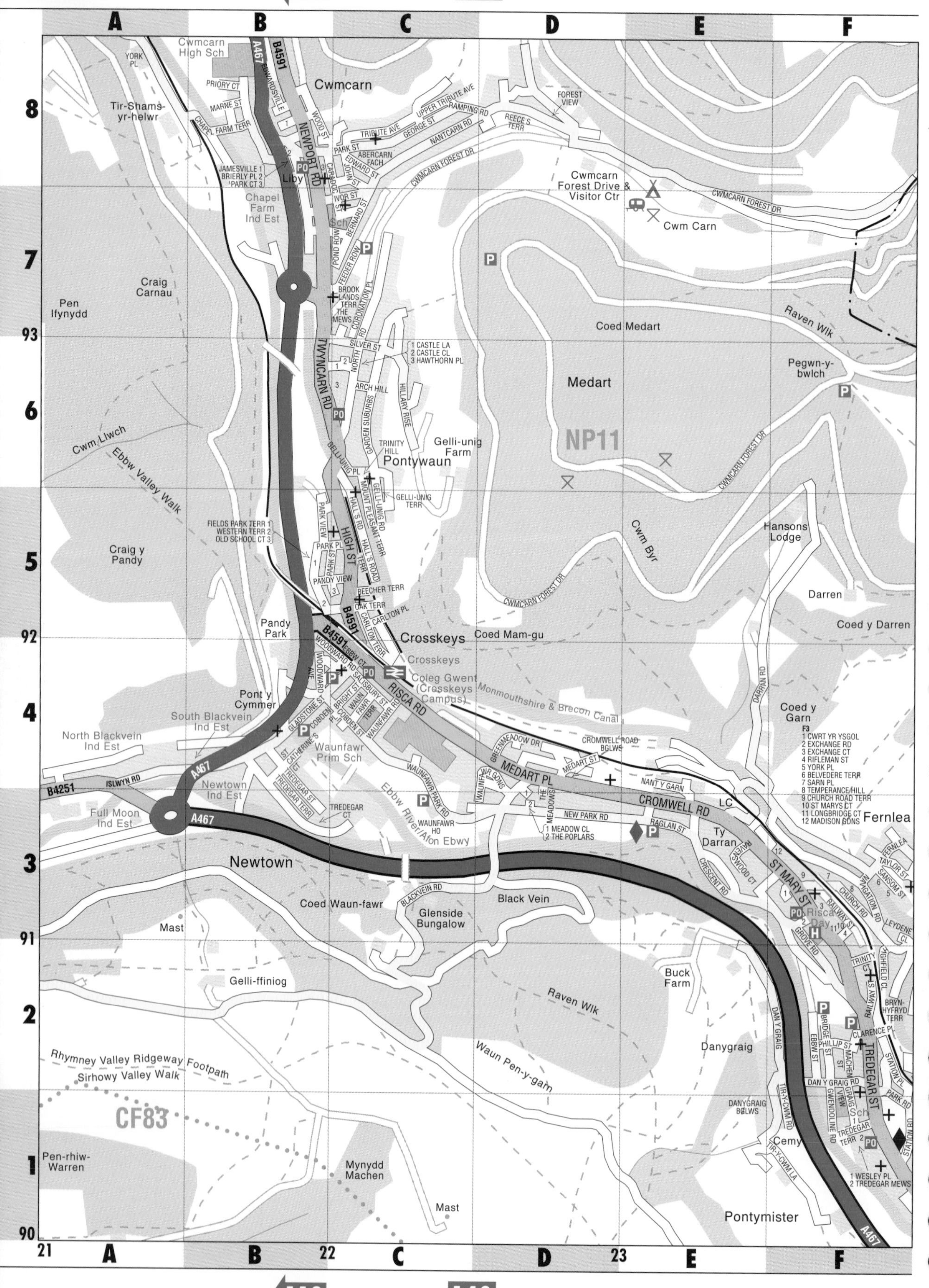

113
140

88

116

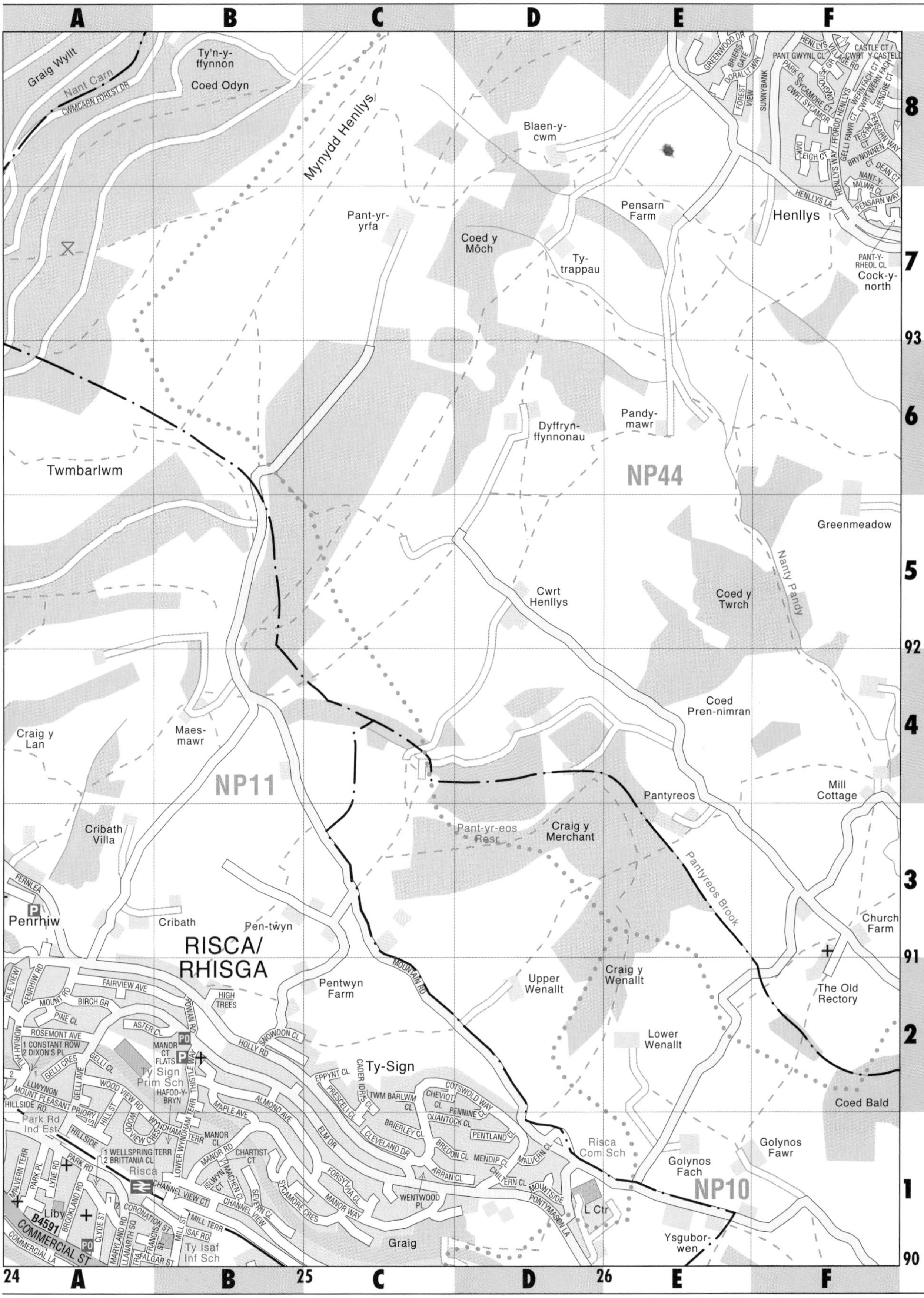

A B C D E F

8

Graig Wyllt
Nant Carn
CWMCARN FOREST DR
Ty'n-y-ffynnon
Coed Odyn
Mynydd Henllys
Blaen-y-cwm
GREENWOOD DR
BRIERS GATE
DORALLT WAY
FOREST VIEW
SUNNYBANK
PANT GWYNL CL
HENLLYS VILLAGE RD
CASTLE CT / CWRT Y CASTELL
PARK CL
SYCAMORE CT
CWRT SYCAMOR
LOCKSLEY GR
OAKLEIGH CT
HENLLYS WAY / FFORDD HENLLYS
GELLI FAWR CT
WERN FACH CT
CWRT WERN FACH
HENDRE CT
TEGFAN
PENSARN WAY
BRYNONNEN CT
DEAN CT
NANT-Y-MILWR CL
HENLLYS LA
PENSARN WAY

7

Pant-yr-yrfa
Coed y Môch
Ty-trappau
Pensarn Farm
Henllys
PANT-Y-RHEOL CL
Cock-y-north

93

6

Dyffryn-ffynnonau
Pandy-mawr
Twmbarlwm
NP44
Greenmeadow

5

Nanty Pandy
Cwrt Henllys
Coed y Twrch

92

4

Coed Pren-nimran
Craig y Lan
Maes-mawr
NP11
Pantyreos
Mill Cottage

3

Cribath Villa
Pant-yr-eos Resr
Craig y Merchant
Pantyreos Brook
FERNLEA
Penrhiw
Cribath
Pen-twyn
Church Farm

91

RISCA/ RHISGA
Pentwyn Farm
MOUNTAIN RD
Upper Wenallt
Craig y Wenallt
The Old Rectory
VALE VIEW
PENRHIW RD
FAIRVIEW AVE
MOUNT RD
BIRCH GR
PINE CL
HIGH TREES
ROSEMONT AVE
1 CONSTANT ROW
2 DIXON'S PL
MORIAH HILL
ASTER CL
ROWAN RD
MANOR CT FLATS
GELLI CRES
GELLI CL
GELLI AVE
HOLLY RD
SNOWDON CL

2

Lower Wenallt
Ty Sign Prim Sch
HAFOD-Y-BRYN
THISTLE WAY
Ty-Sign
EPPYNT CL
CADER IDRIS CL
PRESCELI CL
TWM BARLWM CL
CHEVIOT CL
COTSWOLD WAY
PENNINE CL
QUANTOCK CL
LLWYNON
WOOD VIEW RD
MOUNT PLEASANT RD
HILLSIDE RD
PRIORY
HILL ST
DOON VIEW CRES
WYNDHAM ST
LOWER WYNDHAM TERR
MAPLE AVE
ALMOND AVE
BRIERLEY CL
CLEVELAND DR
PENTLAND CL
Coed Bald
Park Rd Ind Est
HILLSIDE
1 WELLSPRING TERR
2 BRITTANIA CL
MANOR CL
MANOR RD
CHARTIST CT
ELM DR
BREDON CL
MENDIP CL
MALVERN CL
Risca Com Sch
Golynos Fawr
Golynos Fach
Risca
ISLWYN CT
MACHEN CL
SEVERN CL
SYCAMORE CRES
FORSYTHIA CL
ARRAN CL
CHILTERN CL
MOUNTSIDE

1

MALVERN TERR
PARK PL
LYNE RD
PARK RD
BROOKLAND RD
CHANNEL VIEW CT
CHANNEL VIEW
MANOR WAY
WENTWOOD PL
PONTYMASON LA
NP10
L Ctr
Liby
B4591
COMMERCIAL ST
COMMERCIAL LA
CLYDE ST
CORONATION ST
MARYLAND RD
LLANARTH SQ
TRAFALGAR ST
FRANCIS ST
MILL ST
MILL TERR
ISAF RD
Ty Isaf Inf Sch
Graig
Ysgubor-wen

90

24 A B 25 C D 26 E F

141

116

115
89

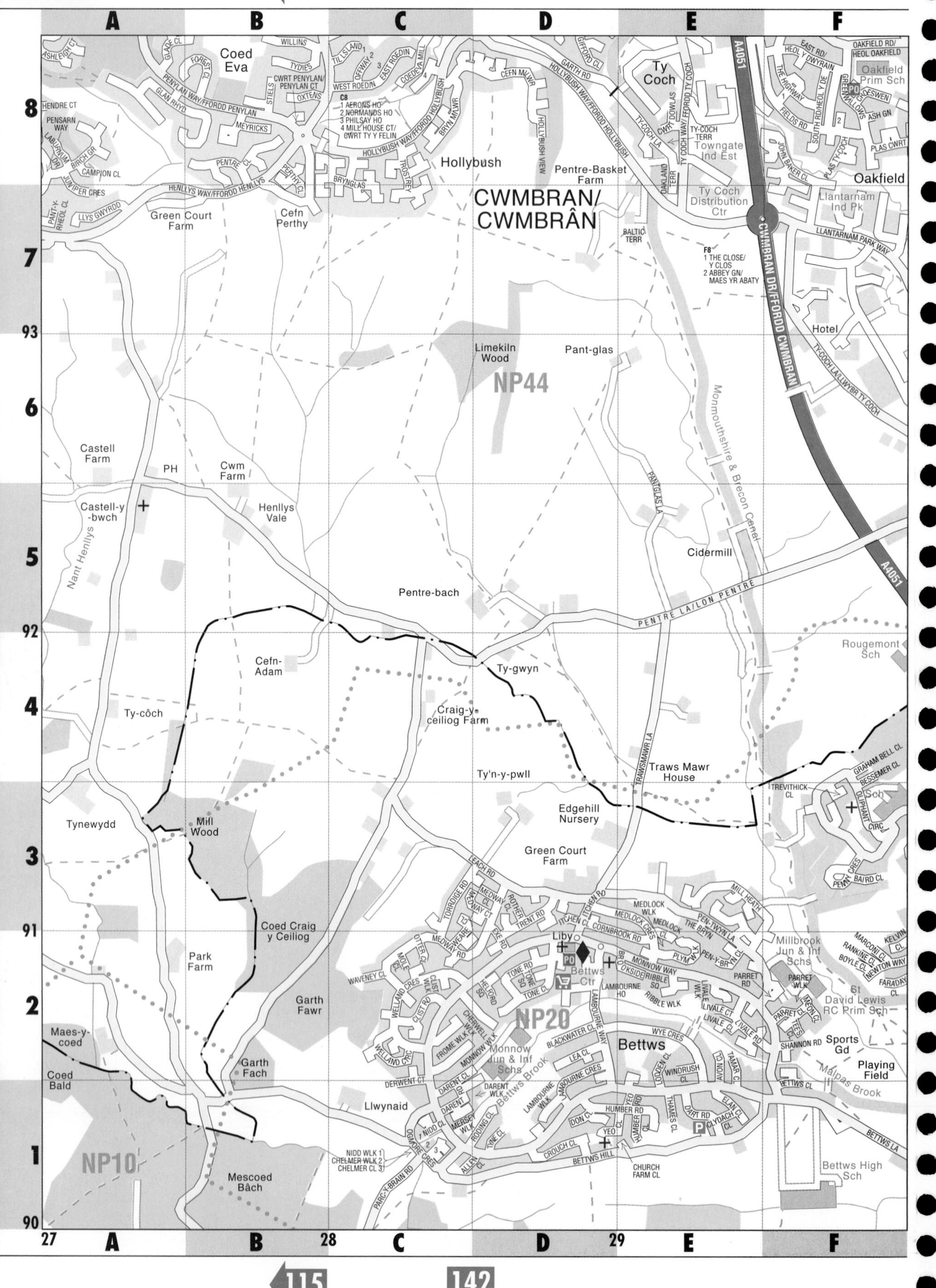

115
142

90 118

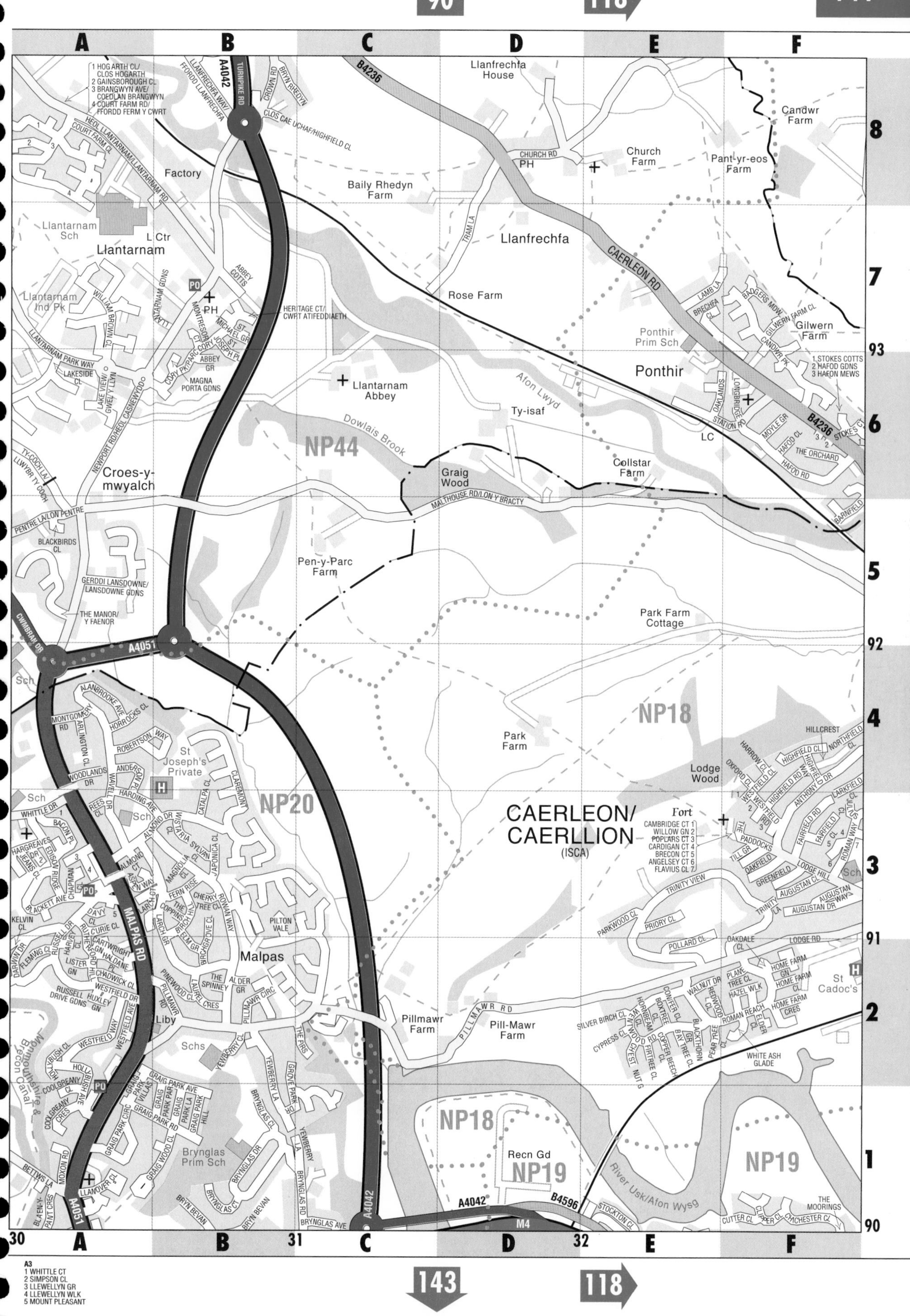

A3
1 WHITTLE CT
2 SIMPSON CL
3 LLEWELLYN GR
4 LLEWELLYN WLK
5 MOUNT PLEASANT

143 118

117

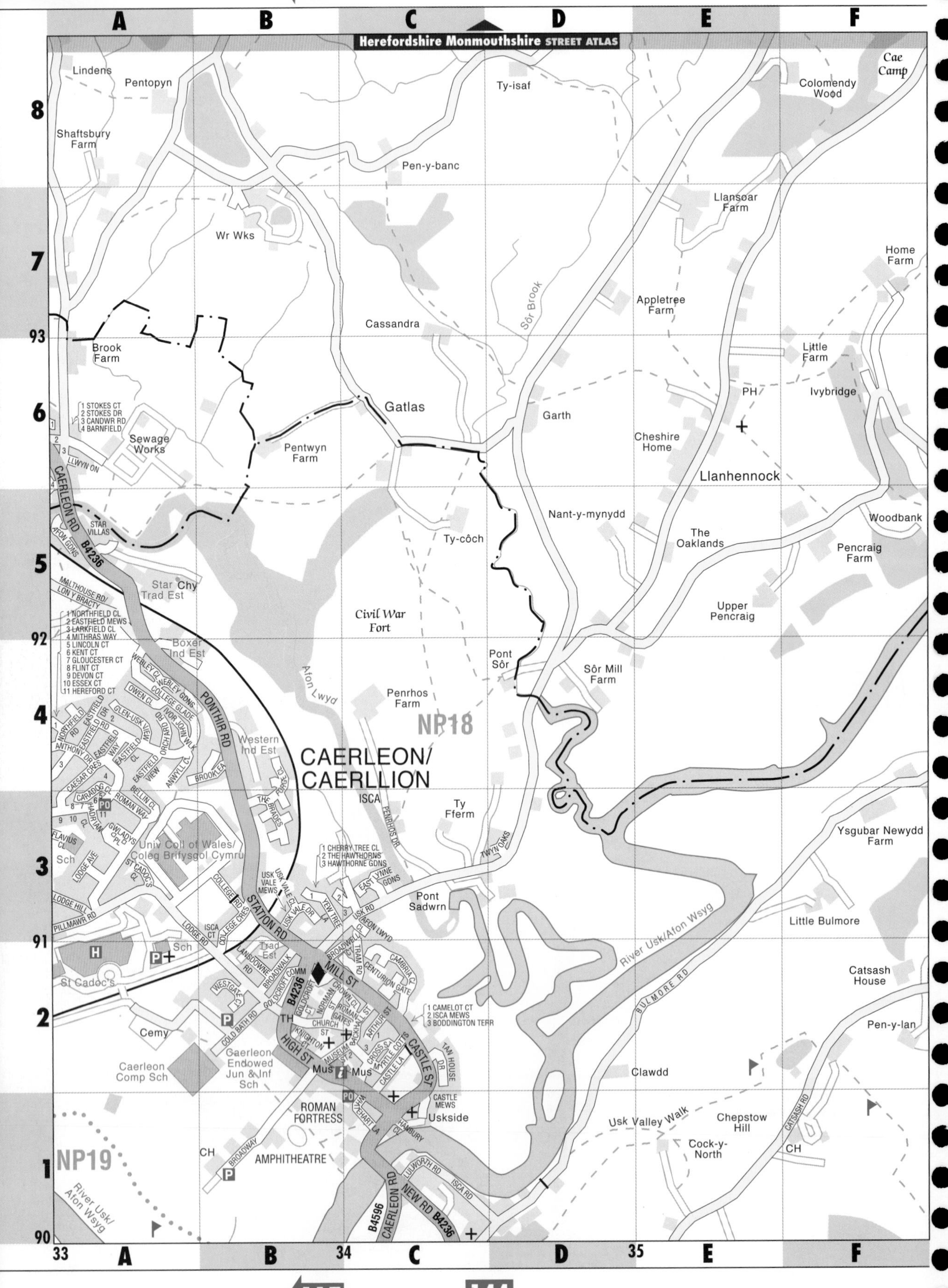
Herefordshire Monmouthshire STREET ATLAS
Lindens
Pentopyn
Shaftsbury Farm
Ty-isaf
Colomendy Wood
Cae Camp
Pen-y-banc
Llansoar Farm
Wr Wks
Home Farm
Sôr Brook
Appletree Farm
Cassandra
Brook Farm
Little Farm
Gatlas
PH
Ivybridge
Garth
Sewage Works
Pentwyn Farm
Cheshire Home
Llanhennock
Nant-y-mynydd
Woodbank
Ty-côch
The Oaklands
Pencraig Farm
Star Trad Est
Chy
Civil War Fort
Upper Pencraig
Boxer Ind Est
Pont Sôr
Sôr Mill Farm
Afon Lwyd
Penrhos Farm
NP18
Western Ind Est
CAERLEON/ CAERLLION
ISCA
Ty Fferm
Univ Coll of Wales/ Coleg Brifysgol Cymru
Ysgubar Newydd Farm
Sch
Pont Sadwrn
River Usk/Afon Wsyg
Little Bulmore
Trad Est
Sch
St Cadoc's
Catsash House
Cemy
Pen-y-lan
Caerleon Comp Sch
Caerleon Endowed Jun & Inf Sch
Mus
Clawdd
ROMAN FORTRESS
Usk Valley Walk
Chepstow Hill
Uskside
CH
Cock-y-North
NP19
AMPHITHEATRE
River Usk/ Afon Wsyg
1 STOKES CT
2 STOKES DR
3 CANDWR RD
4 BARNFIELD
1 NORTHFIELD CL
2 EASTFIELD MEWS
3 LARKFIELD CL
4 MITHRAS WAY
5 LINCOLN CT
6 KENT CT
7 GLOUCESTER CT
8 FLINT CT
9 DEVON CT
10 ESSEX CT
11 HEREFORD CT
1 CHERRY TREE CL
2 THE HAWTHORNS
3 HAWTHORNE GDNS
1 CAMELOT CT
2 ISCA MEWS
3 BODDINGTON TERR
CAERLEON RD
B4236
PONTHIR RD
STATION RD
MILL ST
HIGH ST
CASTLE ST
NEW RD
B4596
BULMORE RD
CATSASH RD
USK RD
A B C D E F
8 7 93 6 5 92 4 3 91 2 1 90
33 34 35

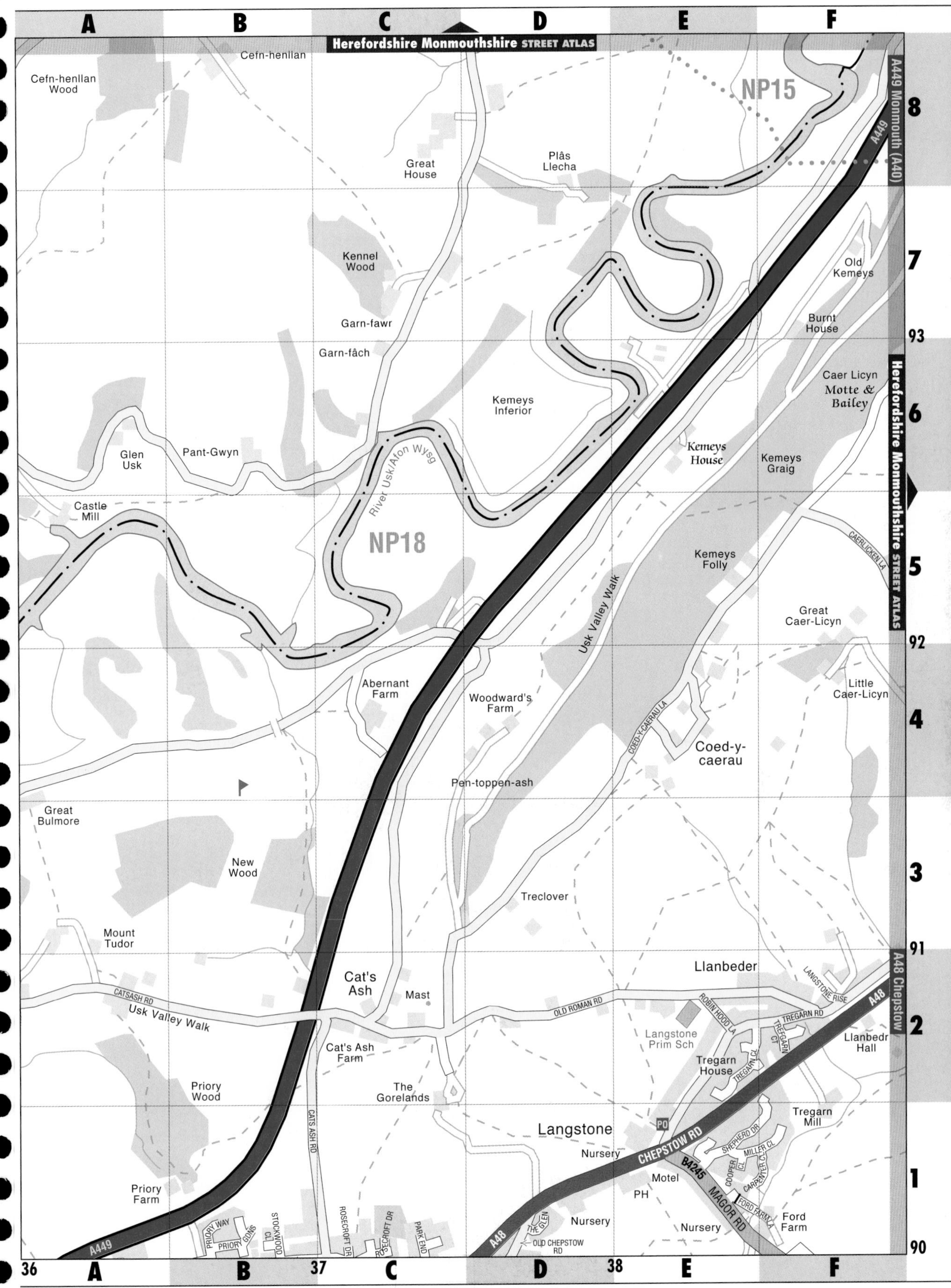

A
B
C
D
E
F
Herefordshire Monmouthshire STREET ATLAS
A449 Monmouth (A40)
Herefordshire Monmouthshire STREET ATLAS
A48 Chepstow
8
7
93
6
5
92
4
3
91
2
1
90
36
37
38
Cefn-henllan
Cefn-henllan Wood
NP15
Great House
Plâs Llecha
Kennel Wood
Old Kemeys
Garn-fawr
Burnt House
Garn-fâch
Caer Licyn
Motte & Bailey
Kemeys Inferior
Glen Usk
Pant-Gwyn
Kemeys House
Kemeys Graig
River Usk/Afon Wysg
Castle Mill
NP18
CAERLICKEN LA
Kemeys Folly
Usk Valley Walk
Great Caer-Licyn
Abernant Farm
Woodward's Farm
Little Caer-Licyn
COED-Y-CAERAU LA
Coed-y-caerau
Pen-toppen-ash
Great Bulmore
New Wood
Treclover
Mount Tudor
Llanbeder
Cat's Ash
Mast
LANGSTONE RISE
CATSASH RD
OLD ROMAN RD
ROBIN HOOD LA
TREGARN RD
A48
Usk Valley Walk
Langstone Prim Sch
TREFGARN CT
Llanbedr Hall
Cat's Ash Farm
Tregarn House
TREGARN CL
The Gorelands
Priory Wood
Tregarn Mill
CATS ASH RD
Langstone
PO
SHEPHERD DR
MILLER CL
Nursery
CHEPSTOW RD
B4245
COOPER CL
Motel
CARPENTER CL
Priory Farm
PH
MAGOR RD
FORD FARM LA
Ford Farm
Nursery
Nursery
PRIORY WAY
PRIORY GDNS
STOCKWOOD CL
ROSECROFT DR
ROSECROFT DR
PARK END
THE GLEN
A48
OLD CHEPSTOW RD
A449
A449

231
91

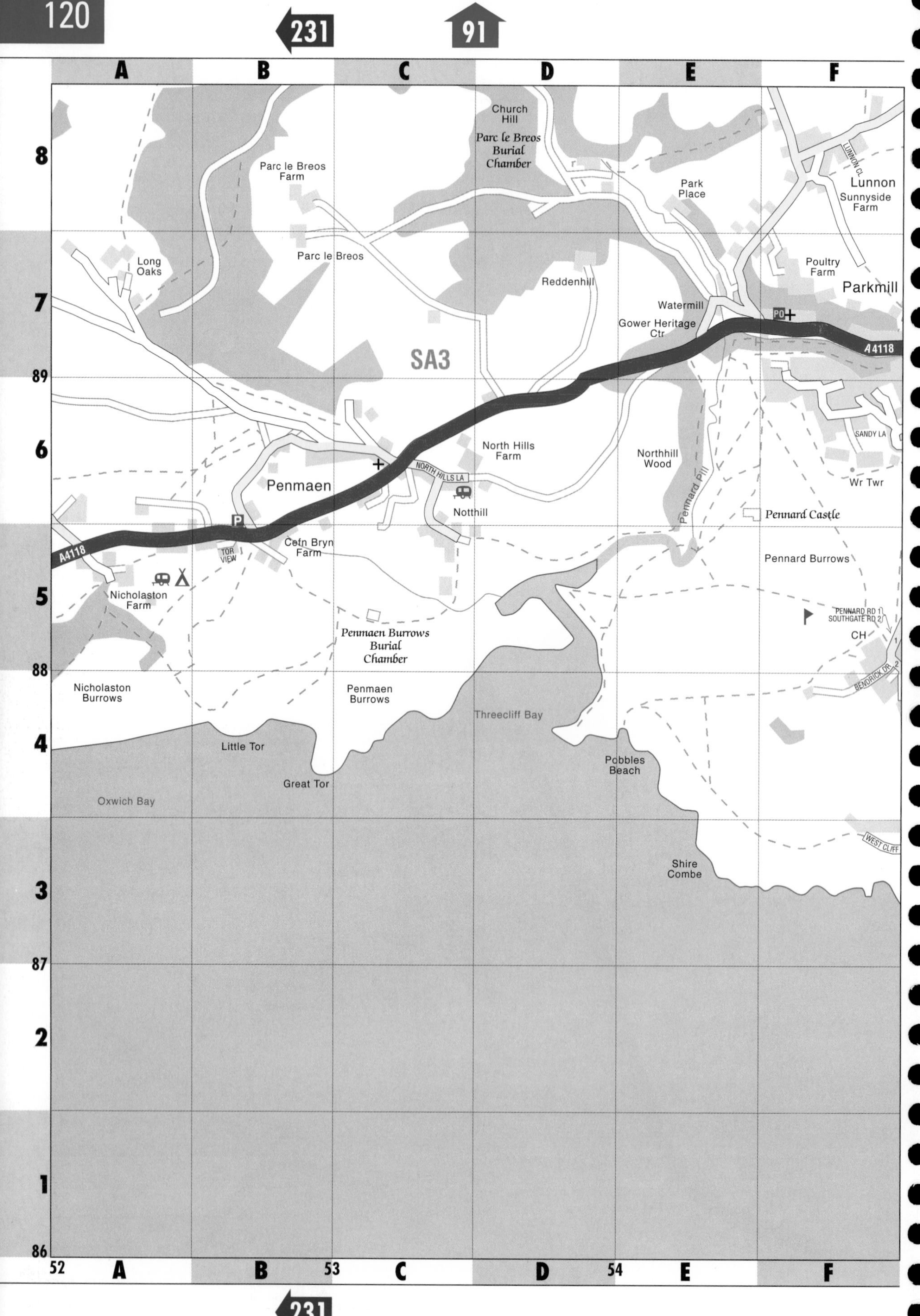
A
B
C
D
E
F
8
7
89
6
5
88
4
3
87
2
1
86
52
53
54
Church Hill
Parc le Breos Burial Chamber
Parc le Breos Farm
Park Place
Lunnon
LUNNON CL
Sunnyside Farm
Long Oaks
Parc le Breos
Reddenhill
Poultry Farm
Parkmill
Watermill
Gower Heritage Ctr
PO
A4118
SA3
SANDY LA
North Hills Farm
Northhill Wood
Penmaen
NORTH HILLS LA
Wr Twr
Notthill
Pennard Pill
Pennard Castle
P
A4118
TOR VIEW
Cefn Bryn Farm
Pennard Burrows
Nicholaston Farm
PENNARD RD 1
SOUTHGATE RD 2
CH
Penmaen Burrows Burial Chamber
BENDRICK DR
Nicholaston Burrows
Penmaen Burrows
Threecliff Bay
Little Tor
Pobbles Beach
Great Tor
Oxwich Bay
WEST CLIFF
Shire Combe

231

92
122

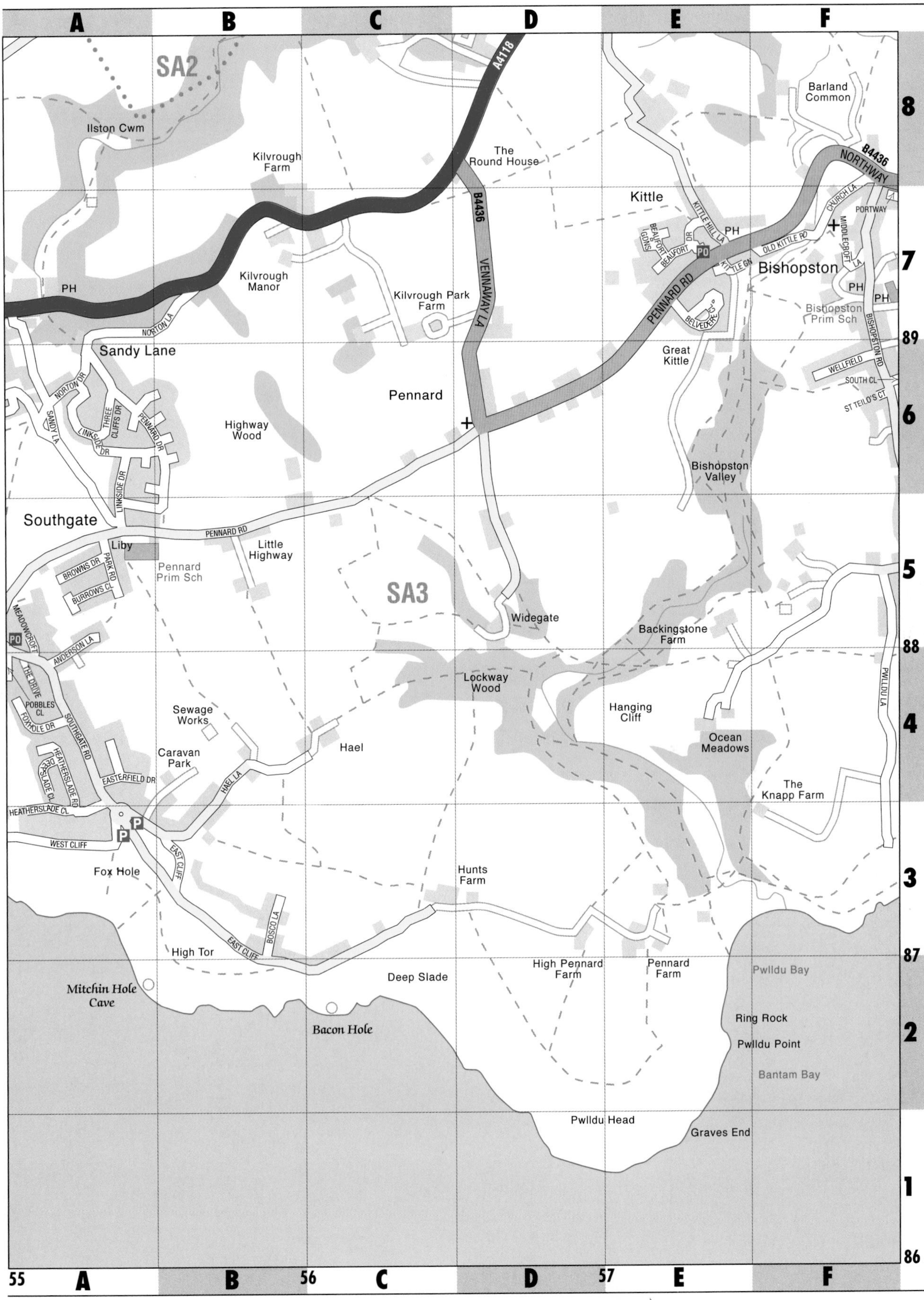

A B C D E F

SA2
Ilston Cwm
Kilvrough Farm
A4118
The Round House
Barland Common
B4436
NORTHWAY
8
Kittle
KITTLE HILL LA
BEAUFORT GDNS
BEAUFORT DR
PH
PO
OLD KITTLE RD
CHURCH LA
PORTWAY
MIDDLECROFT LA
B4436
VENNAWAY LA
Kilvrough Manor
PH
7
KITTLE GN
Bishopston
PH
PH
Kilvrough Park Farm
PENNARD RD
BELVEDERE
Bishopston Prim Sch
BISHOPSTON RD
NORTON LA
Sandy Lane
89
Great Kittle
WELLFIELD
SOUTH CL
ST TEILO'S CT
NORTON DR
Pennard
SANDY LA
THREE CLIFFS DR
PENNARD DR
LINKSIDE DR
Highway Wood
6
Bishopston Valley
LINKSIDE DR
Southgate
PENNARD RD
Liby
Little Highway
Pennard Prim Sch
BROWNS DR
PARK RD
SA3
5
BURROWS CL
MEADOWCROFT
Widegate
PO
Backingstone Farm
ANDERSON LA
88
THE DRIVE
Lockway Wood
PWLLDU LA
POBBLES CL
Sewage Works
Hanging Cliff
FOXHOLE DR
SOUTHGATE RD
4
Caravan Park
Hael
Ocean Meadows
HEATHERSLADE RD
DEEPSLADE CL
EASTERFIELD DR
HAEL LA
The Knapp Farm
HEATHERSLADE CL
P
P
WEST CLIFF
EAST CLIFF
Fox Hole
Hunts Farm
3
BOSCO LA
High Tor
EAST CLIFF
87
High Pennard Farm
Pennard Farm
Pwlldu Bay
Mitchin Hole Cave
Deep Slade
Bacon Hole
Ring Rock
2
Pwlldu Point
Bantam Bay
Pwlldu Head
Graves End
1
86

55 A B 56 C D 57 E F

122

121
93

A B C D E F

8
7
89
6
5
88
4
3
87
2
1
86

B4436
MAYALS RD
WHITESTONE CL
FAIRWOOD RD
LILAC CL
MAYALS GN 1
THE GLADE 2
GONHILL 1
NORTHERON 2
BETTSLAND 3
BROADPARKS 4
LEYSHAN WLK 5
CROSS ACRE 6
WHITE GR 7
YALTON 8
Sunnybank
MULBERRY AVE
SUNNYBANK CL
CYPRES OLIVE RD
CEDAR CRES
ELMGROVE RD
CHESTNUT AVE
BIRCHFIELD RD
YEWTREE CL
GREEN BANK RD
MAYTREE AVE
WOODLAND AVE
BROOKVALE RD
MOORSIDE RD
REDWOOD RD
ALDER WAY
GOLDEN CL
EASTMOOR PARK CL
WESTLAND AVE
CASTLAND
SILVER CL
LARKSPUR DR
WALNUT CL
WESTCROSS LA
Ryeground Farm
B4436
PORTWAY
NORTHWAY
Craig y nos Sch
Campion Gardens
WILLOW CT
Clyne Common
THE GLEBE
NORTHWAY CT
NORTHLANDS PK
Murton Green
Mansel Green
COPLEY LODGE
COPLEY CL
Bishopston Comp Sch
Bishopston Prim Sch
PROVIDENCE LA
EASTLANDS PK
PH
Murton
Whitestone Prim Sch
OSPREY CL
HAWKSTONE CL
HUNTSMANS COVE
LUNDY DR
DRUSLYN RD
BELLEVUE RD
RUSHWIND MEWS
BUTTERCUP CT
FULMAR CL
RUSHWIND CL
RAVENS WLK
SOUTHLANDS DR
GLEN RD
RIVERSDALE RD
THE CLOSE
OAKLANDS
SOUTH CL
TUDOR CT
LONG ACRE CT
LONG ACRE
OLDWAY
MANSELFIELD RD
Manselfield
REIGIT LA
SA3
OAK TREE CL
ORCHID CT
HEOL Y GARREG WEN
FFORDD DRAENEN DDU
CORMORANT WAY
SHEARWATER CL
PO
PROSPECT TERR
HEATH CT
HEATH CL
SLADE GDNS
Colts Hill
VENSLAND
LIME KILN LA
MANSEL DR
MILES LA
ALONE
HILLAND DR
Oldway
WITHY PK
RIDLEY WAY
WOODSIDE CL
GERRETS CL
PYLE CT
PYLE RD
BISHOPSTON RD
KILFIELD RD
HOLTS FIELD
DAWLISH CL
BURNHAM DR
LYNTON CT
MOORLAND AVE
HIGHMEAD CL
HIGHMEAD AVE
CLOVELLY PL
APPLEDORE PL
DUNSTER CL
LAMBOURNE DR
BRAMLEY DR
CHALLACOMBE PL
HATHERLEIGH DR
THE ORCHARD
SHERRINGHAM DR
Cemy
LADY HOUSTY AVE
HIGHPOOL CL
HIGHPOOL LA
BRYNCERDIN RD
CREST ACRE CL
WHITESTONE LA
Newton Prim Sch
WAVERLEY DR
MURTON LA
WHITESTONE AVE
CASWELL BAY RD
HEADLAND RD
HEADLAND CL
BRANDY COVE RD
WHITESTONE RD
PO
Pyle
1 DOUGLAS CT
2 PWLLDU LA
Herberts Lodge Farm
Lady Housty House
BRIARWOOD GDNS
WOOLACOTT MEWS
WOOLACOTT DR
MAYLANDS CL
PICKET MEAD RD
Newton
SLADE RD
MIXEN CL
CALLENCROFT CT
COLTSHILL DR
NEW WELL LA
NEWTON RD
NEWTON VILLAS
BROOKLYN TERR
SUMMERLAND LA
ST PETER'S RD
CROFTFIELD CRES
MELCORN DR
NOTTAGE RD
SOUTHWARD LA
Sewage Wks
Bishop's Wood Nature Reserve
HAVERGAL CL
CASWELL DR
LONG SHEPHERDS DR
CASWELL AVE
VICTORIA CT
NOTTAGE MEWS
OVERLAND RD
CLIFFLANDS CL
LANGLAND RD
B4593
HIGHER LA
Hareslade
CASWELL RD
REDCLIFFE
CASWELL BAY CT
B4593
CASWELL RD
MORFA MAWR
HILLGROVE
MARY TWILL LA
LANGLAND COURT RD
LANSDOWN GROVES AVE
BRYNFIELD CT
SOUTHWARD LA
GILBERTSCLIFFE
ROTHERSLADE RD
Caswell
Caswell Bay
Bishop's Wood Countryside Ctr
SUMMERCLIFFE CHALET PK
LINKSIDE
SEASHELL DR
BRYNFIELD RD
Langland
HIGHCLIFFE CT
WOODRIDGE CT
CRAWSHAY CT
LANGLAND BAY RD
WESTWINDS
LINKS CT
AEL-Y-DON
ST LEONARDS
Brandy Cove
CH
Langland Bay
Newton Cliff
Snaple Point
Whiteshell Point

58 A B 59 C D 60 E F

121

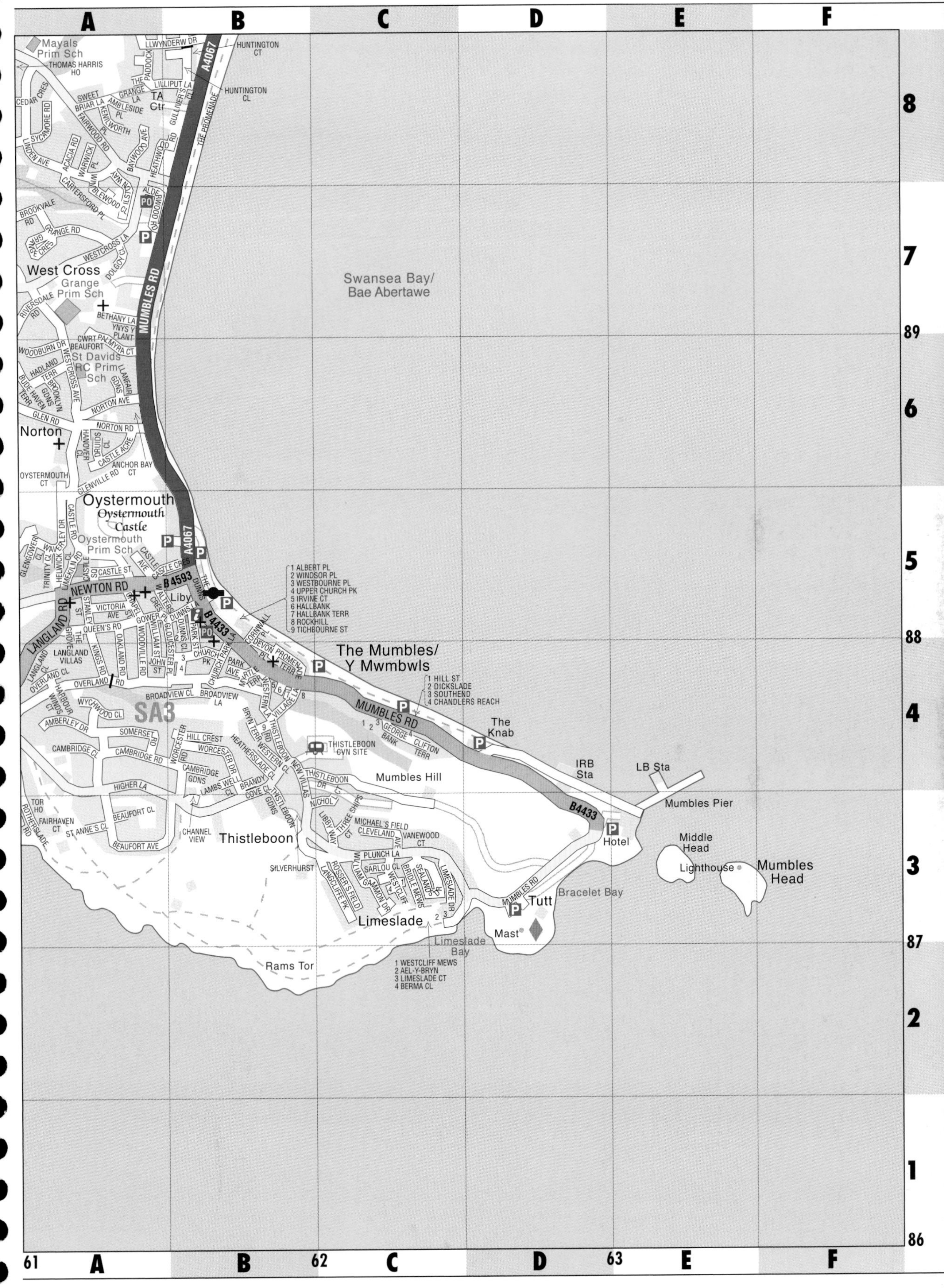
A
B
C
D
E
F
8
7
89
6
5
88
4
3
87
2
1
86
61
62
63
Mayals Prim Sch
West Cross
Grange Prim Sch
St Davids RC Prim Sch
Norton
Oystermouth
Oystermouth Castle
Oystermouth Prim Sch
TA Ctr
Liby
Swansea Bay/
Bae Abertawe
The Mumbles/
Y Mwmbwls
MUMBLES RD
A4067
B4593
B4433
NEWTON RD
LANGLAND RD
SA3
The Knab
IRB Sta
LB Sta
Mumbles Pier
Mumbles Hill
Thistleboon
THISTLEBOON CVN SITE
Limeslade
Limeslade Bay
Rams Tor
Hotel
Tutt
Bracelet Bay
Mast
Middle Head
Lighthouse
Mumbles Head
1 ALBERT PL
2 WINDSOR PL
3 WESTBOURNE PL
4 UPPER CHURCH PK
5 IRVINE CT
6 HALLBANK
7 HALLBANK TERR
8 ROCKHILL
9 TICHBOURNE ST
1 HILL ST
2 DICKSLADE
3 SOUTHEND
4 CHANDLERS REACH
1 WESTCLIFF MEWS
2 AEL-Y-BRYN
3 LIMESLADE CT
4 BERMA CL
HUNTINGTON CT
HUNTINGTON CL
THE PROMENADE

98

E8
1 SEABROOK PL
2 RHODFA WHEATLEY/WHEATLEY AVE
3 HEOL DEWI SANT/ST DAVID'S RD
4 Port Talbot Workshops

F8
1 FREDERICK ST
2 STATION TERR
3 THOMAS ST
4 LADY JANE ST
5 GERALD ST
6 PENDARVIS TERR
7 GREEN ST
8 SANDFIELDS RD
9 MARSH ST
10 PEMBROKE TERR
11 WELLINGTON PL
12 STRYD GLENAFON/GLENAVON ST
13 VICTORIA RD

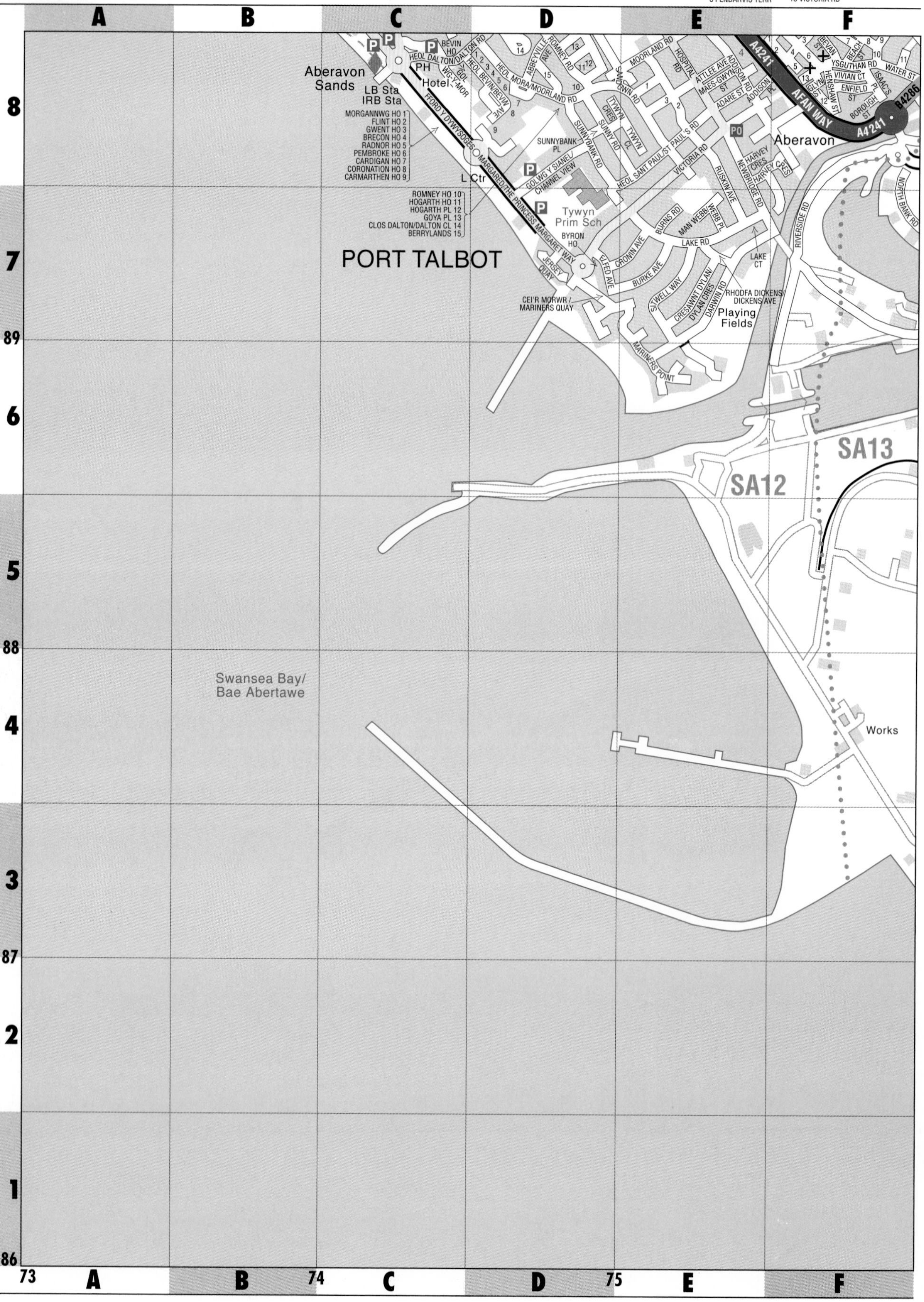

A B C D E F

8
Aberavon Sands
LB Sta
IRB Sta
PH
Hotel
MORGANNWG HO 1
FLINT HO 2
GWENT HO 3
BRECON HO 4
RADNOR HO 5
PEMBROKE HO 6
CARDIGAN HO 7
CORONATION HO 8
CARMARTHEN HO 9
L Ctr
ROMNEY HO 10
HOGARTH HO 11
HOGARTH PL 12
GOYA PL 13
CLOS DALTON/DALTON CL 14
BERRYLANDS 15
Tywyn Prim Sch
BYRON HO
Aberavon
A4241
AFAN WAY
B4286

7
PORT TALBOT
LAKE CT
RHODFA DICKENS/DICKENS AVE
Playing Fields
CEI'R MORWR / MARINERS QUAY

89

6
SA13
SA12

5

88
Swansea Bay/
Bae Abertawe

4
Works

3

87

2

1

86
73 A B 74 C D 75 E F

A8
1 CORPORATION RD
2 GWYN TERR
3 GWYN CT
B8
1 STRYD TYDRAW/TY-DRAW ST
2 COURTLAND BLDGS

C6
1 LOWER WEST END
2 UPPER WEST END
3 CHAPEL TERR
4 FFRWDWYLLT COTTS
5 LIBRARY LA
6 ST ALBAN'S TERR
7 WOODFIELD ST
C7
1 LUCANIA BLDGS
2 MAYFIELD ST
3 PARK HO
4 COUND TERR
5 MAES-Y-CWRT TERR
6 WYNDHAM ST
7 CWRT-UCHA TERR
C8
1 JAMES ST
2 BRIDGE TERR
3 BRIDGE ST
4 HILLVIEW TERR

99

C8
5 BRYNHEULOG ST
6 BRYNHEULOG PL
D5
1 LADY CHARLOTTE LA
2 RHODFA BRYMBO/BRYMBO AVE
3 RHODFA WILDEN/WILDEN AVE

126

D5
4 LON GROESWEN/GROES-WEN LA
5 STRYD DONNEN/DONNEN ST
6 MAESMELYN ST
7 STRYD RHANALLT/RHANALLT ST
8 RHODFA PHOENIX/PHOENIX AVE

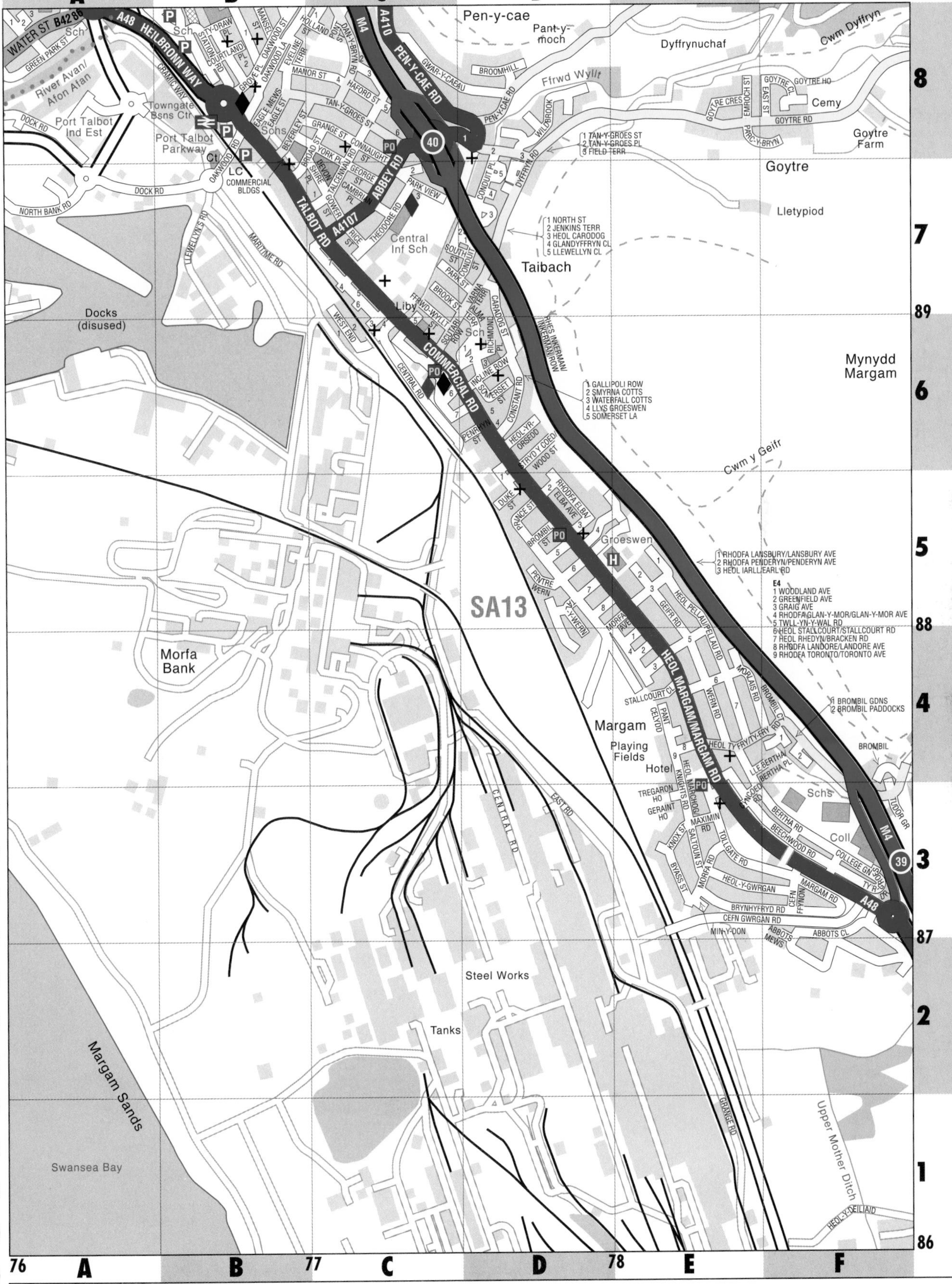

146
126

125
100

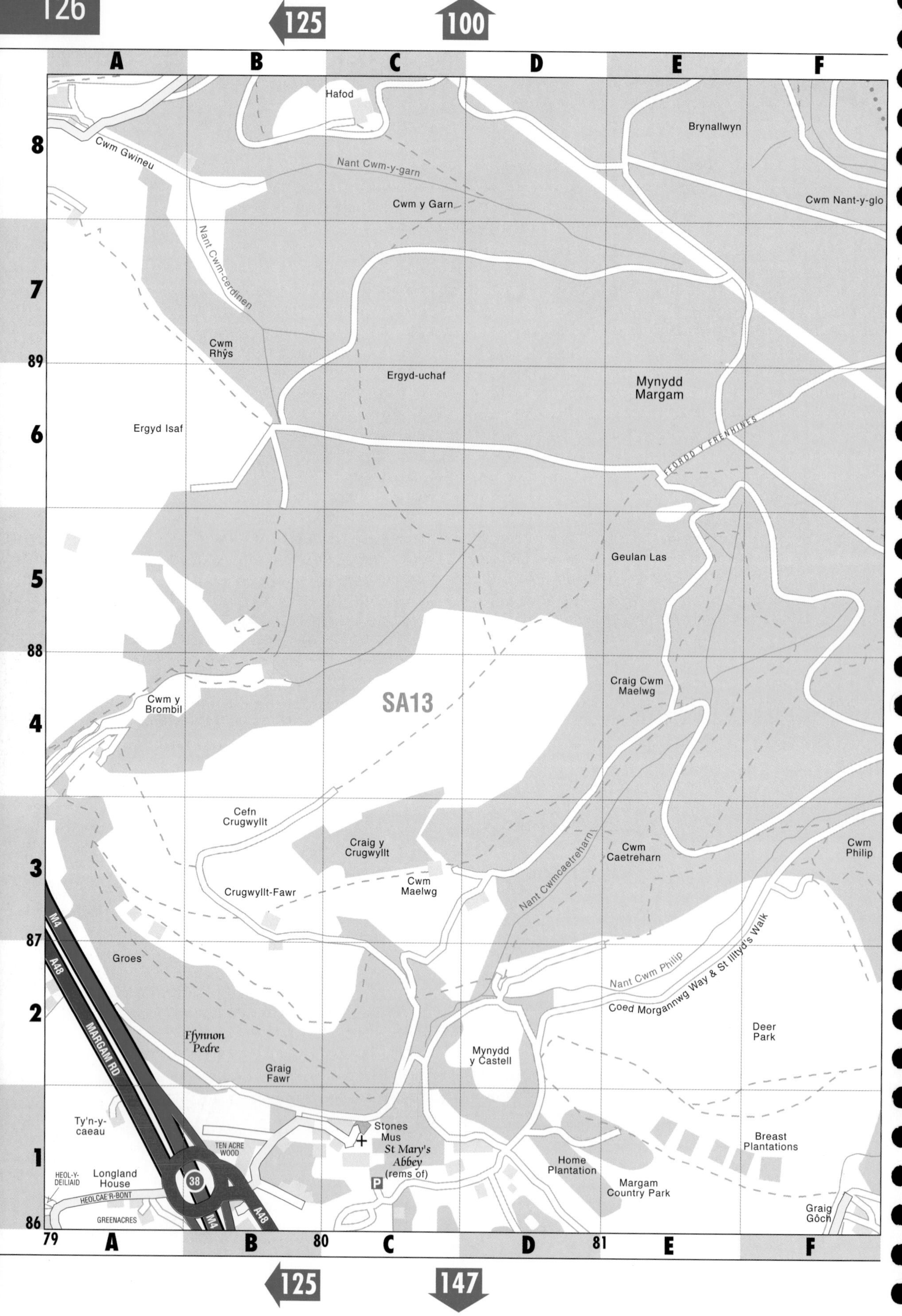

125
147

101
128

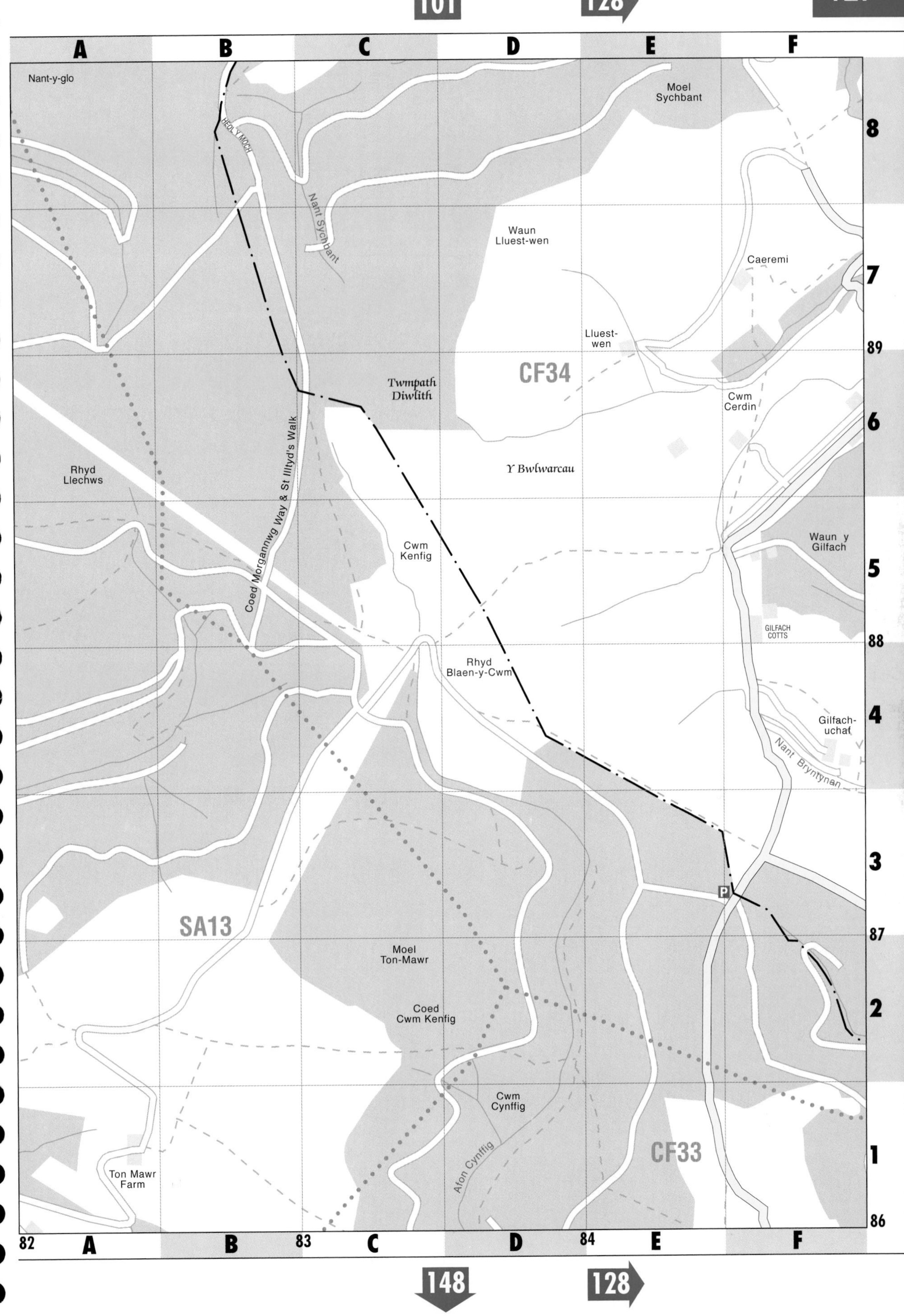

148
128

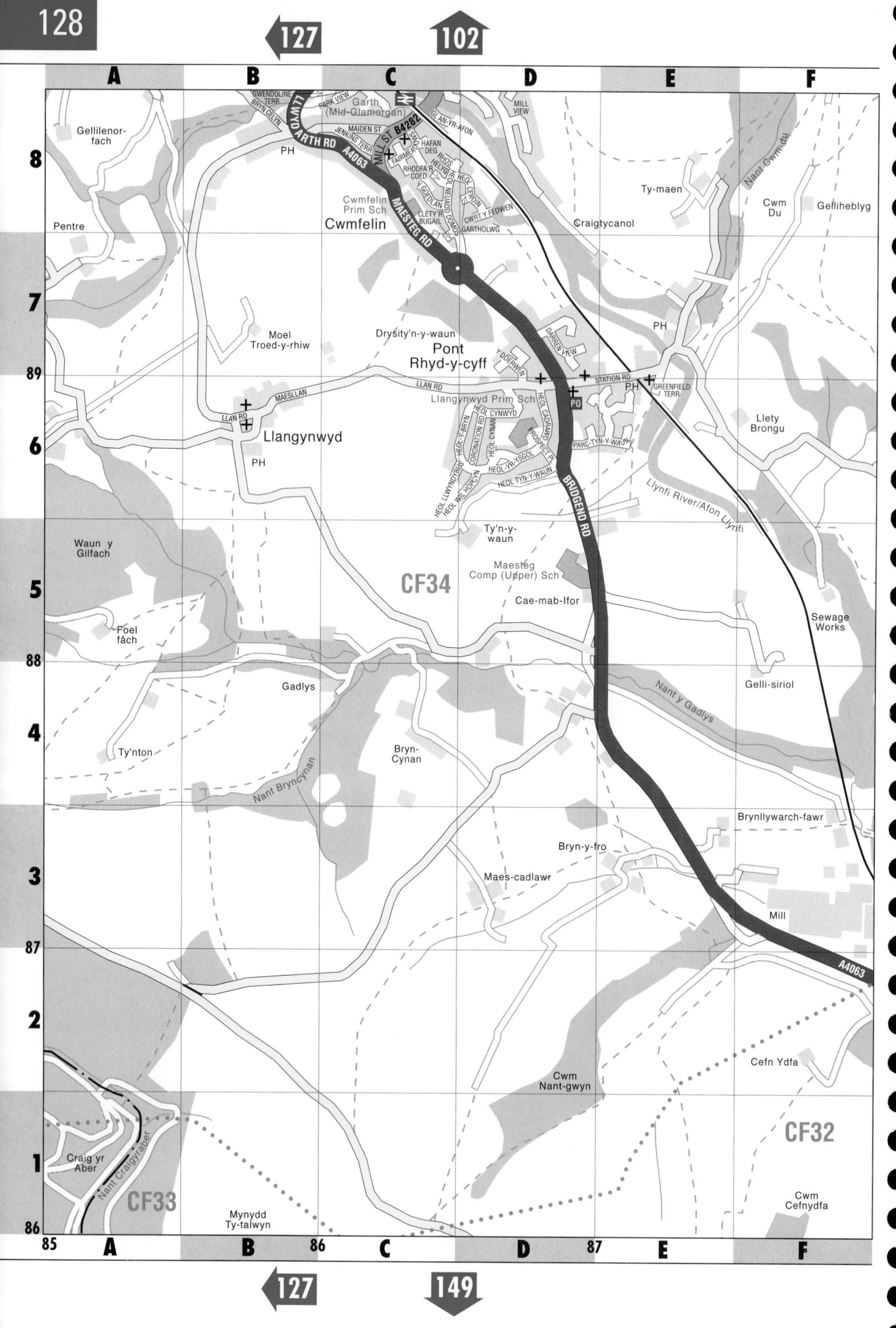

127
102
A
B
C
D
E
F
8
7
89
6
5
88
4
3
87
2
1
86
85
86
87
GWENDOLINE TERR
BRYN CELYN
LLWYDARTH RD
PARK VIEW
Garth (Mid-Glamorgan)
MAIDEN ST
JENKINS TERR
MILL ST
B4282
GLAN-YR-AFON
MILL VIEW
Gellilenor-fach
PH
A4063
FAIRMEAD
HAFAN DEG
RHODFA'R COED
Y GOEDLAN
LLETY'R BUGAIL
HEOL CERDIN
CWRT Y FEDWEN
GARTHOLWG
Cwmfelin Prim Sch
Cwmfelin
MAESTEG RD
Ty-maen
Nant Cwm-du
Cwm Du
Gelliheblyg
Pentre
Craigtycanol
Moel Troed-y-rhiw
Drysity'n-y-waun
Pont Rhyd-y-cyff
DARREN VIEW
Y DDERWEN
PH
STATION RD
GREENFIELD TERR
LLAN RD
MAESLLAN
Llangynwyd Prim Sch
HEOL CYNWYD
HEOL CADRAWD
PO
Llety Brongu
Llangynwyd
PH
CORONATION RD
HEOL-Y-BRYN
HEOL CYNAN
PROSPECT PL
PARC-TYN-Y-WAUN
HEOL-YR-YSGOL
HEOL TYN-Y-WAUN
HEOL LLWYNDYRUS
HEOL WIL HOPCYN
BRIDGEND RD
Llynfi River/Afon Llynfi
Ty'n-y-waun
Waun y Gilfach
Maesteg Comp (Upper) Sch
CF34
Cae-mab-Ifor
Sewage Works
Foel fâch
Gelli-siriol
Gadlys
Nant y Gadlys
Ty'nton
Bryn-Cynan
Nant Bryncynan
Brynllywarch-fawr
Bryn-y-fro
Maes-cadlawr
Mill
A4063
Cefn Ydfa
Cwm Nant-gwyn
CF32
Craig yr Aber
Nant Craigyraber
CF33
Mynydd Ty-talwyn
Cwm Cefnydfa
127
149

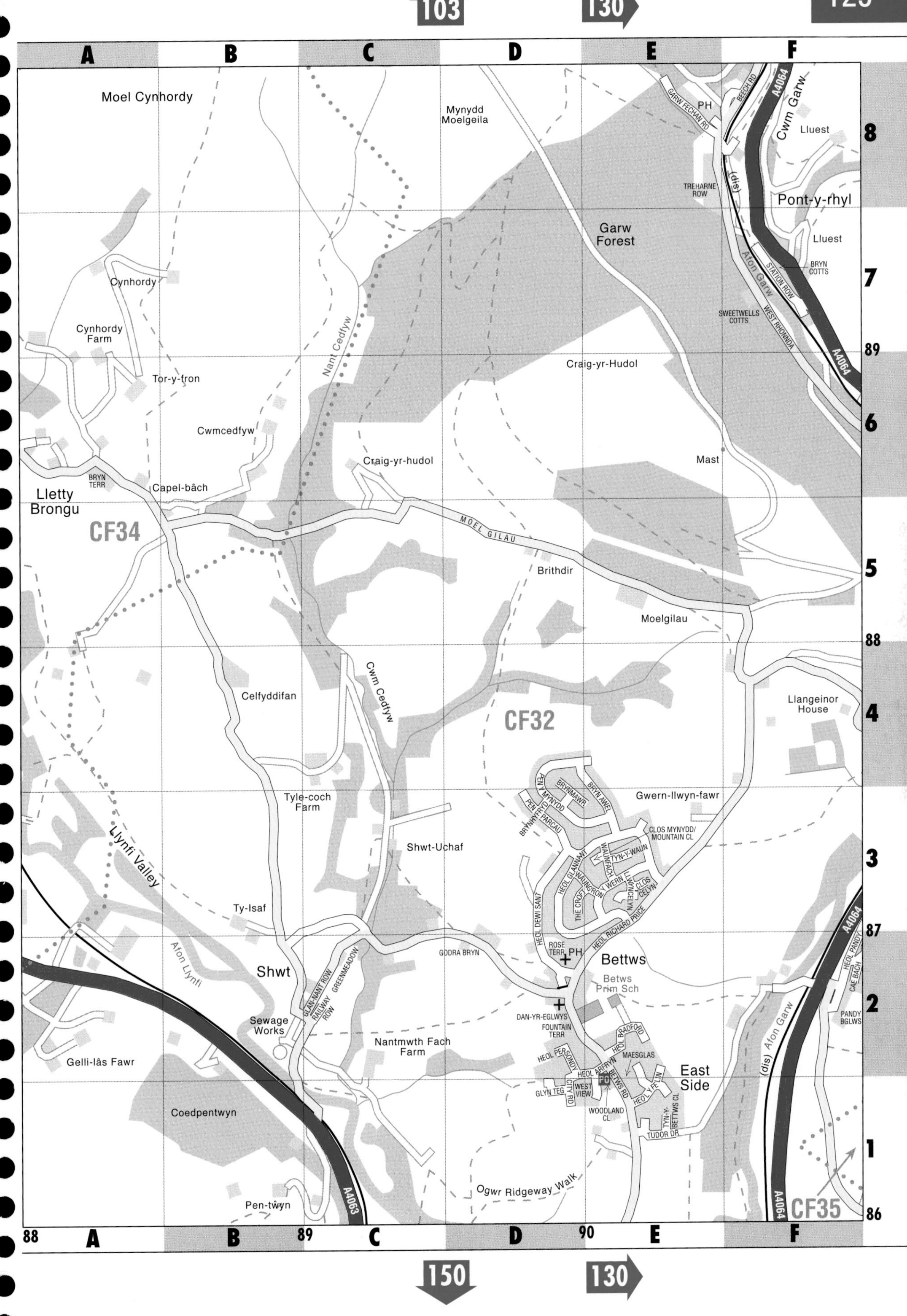
103
130
Moel Cynhordy
Mynydd Moelgeila
Garw Forest
Cwm Garw
Lluest
Pont-y-rhyl
Lluest
TREHARNE ROW
BRYN COTTS
STATION ROW
Afon Garw
SWEETWELLS COTTS
WEST RHONDDA
A4064
GARW FECHAN RD
BEECH RD
PH
(dis)
Cynhordy
Cynhordy Farm
Tor-y-fron
Nant Cedfyw
Craig-yr-Hudol
Cwmcedfyw
Craig-yr-hudol
Mast
BRYN TERR
Capel-bâch
Lletty Brongu
CF34
MOEL GILAU
Brithdir
Moelgilau
Celfyddifan
Cwm Cedfyw
CF32
Llangeinor House
Gwern-llwyn-fawr
Tyle-coch Farm
Shwt-Uchaf
Llynfi Valley
CLOS MYNYDD/ MOUNTAIN CL
BRYNMAWR
BRYN AWEL
PEN Y MYNYDD
PEN Y PARCAU
BRYNHYFRYD
TYN-Y-WAUN
HEOL GLANNANT
WAUNFACH
WAUNGRON
THE CROFT
WERN
LLWYNCELYN
CLOS CELYN
HEOL DEWI SANT
HEOL RICHARD PRICE
Ty-Isaf
GODRA BRYN
ROSE TERR
PH
Bettws
Betws Prim Sch
Afon Llynfi
Shwt
GLAN-NANT ROW
RAILWAY ROW
GREENMEADOW
Sewage Works
Nantmwth Fach Farm
DAN-YR-EGLWYS
FOUNTAIN TERR
HEOL PERSONDY
HEOL BRADFORD
MAESGLAS
HEOL ARFRYN
BETWS RD
GLYN TEG
CITY RD
WEST VIEW
PO
HEOL Y FELIN
WOODLAND CL
TYN-Y-BETWS CL
TUDOR DR
East Side
Afon Garw
(dis)
HEOL PANDY
CAE BACH
PANDY BGLWS
Gelli-lâs Fawr
Coedpentwyn
A4063
Ogwr Ridgeway Walk
Pen-twŷn
A4064
CF35
A B C D E F
8 7 89 6 5 88 4 3 87 2 1 86
88 89 90
150
130

129
104

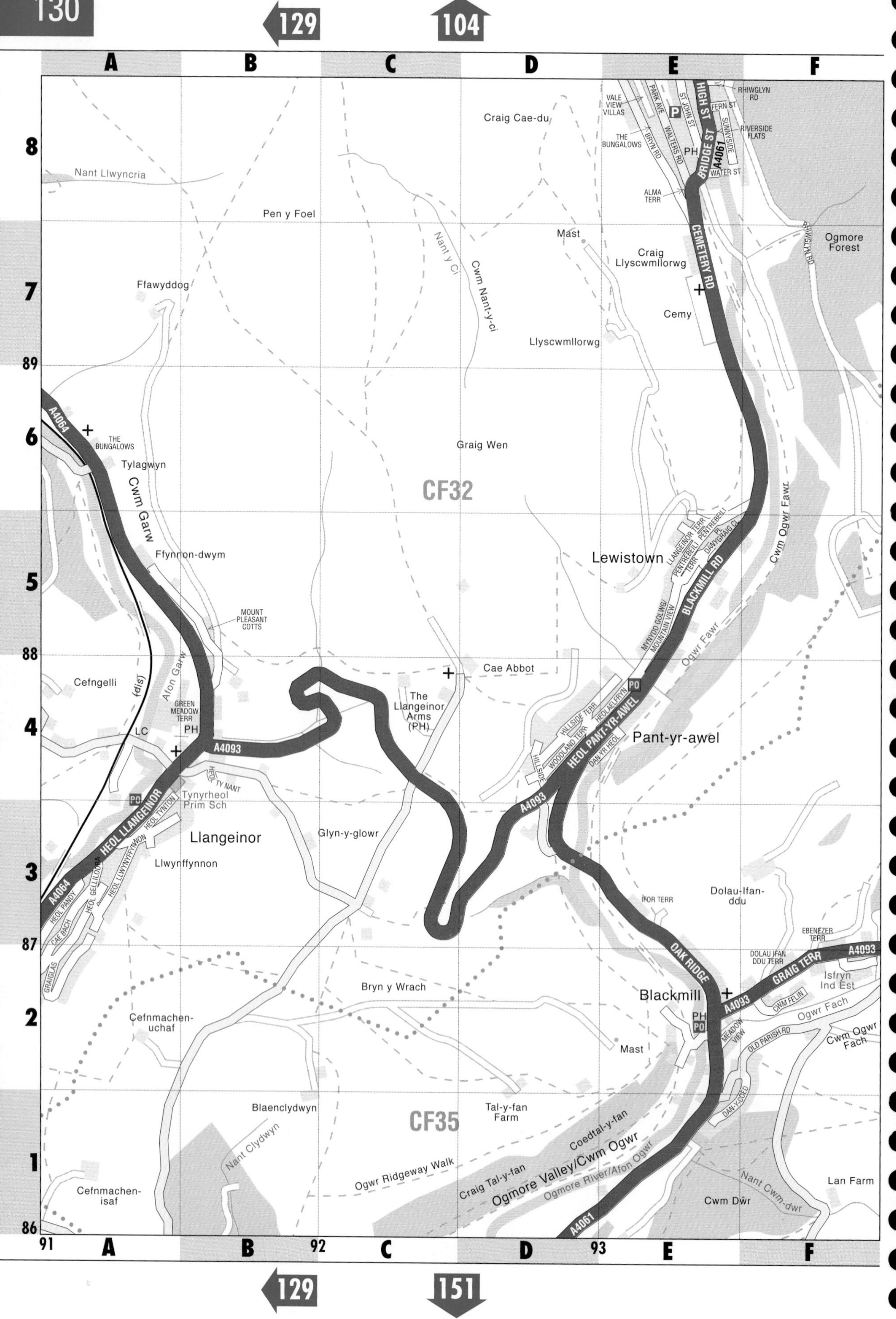

129
151

105
132

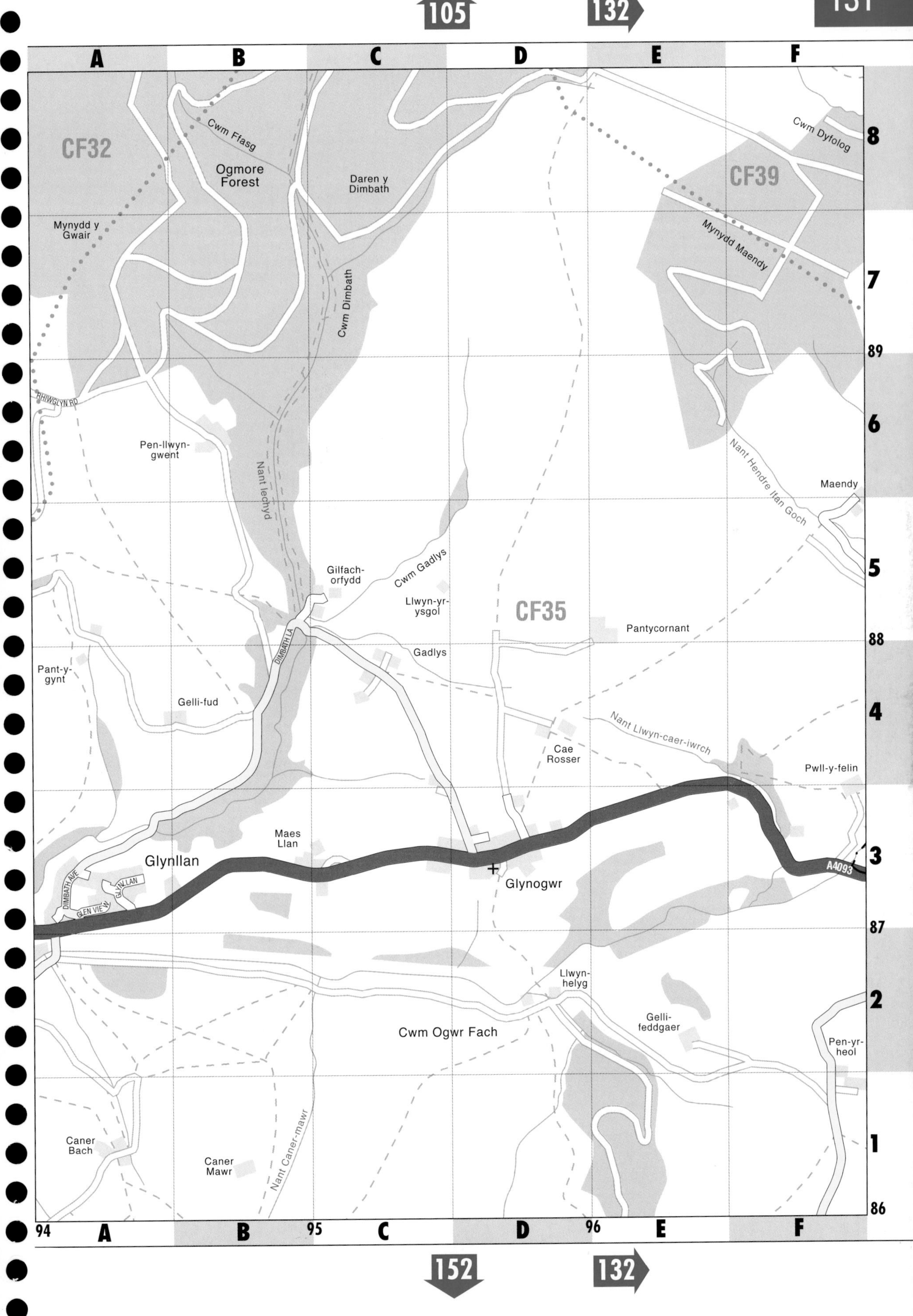

152
132

131
106

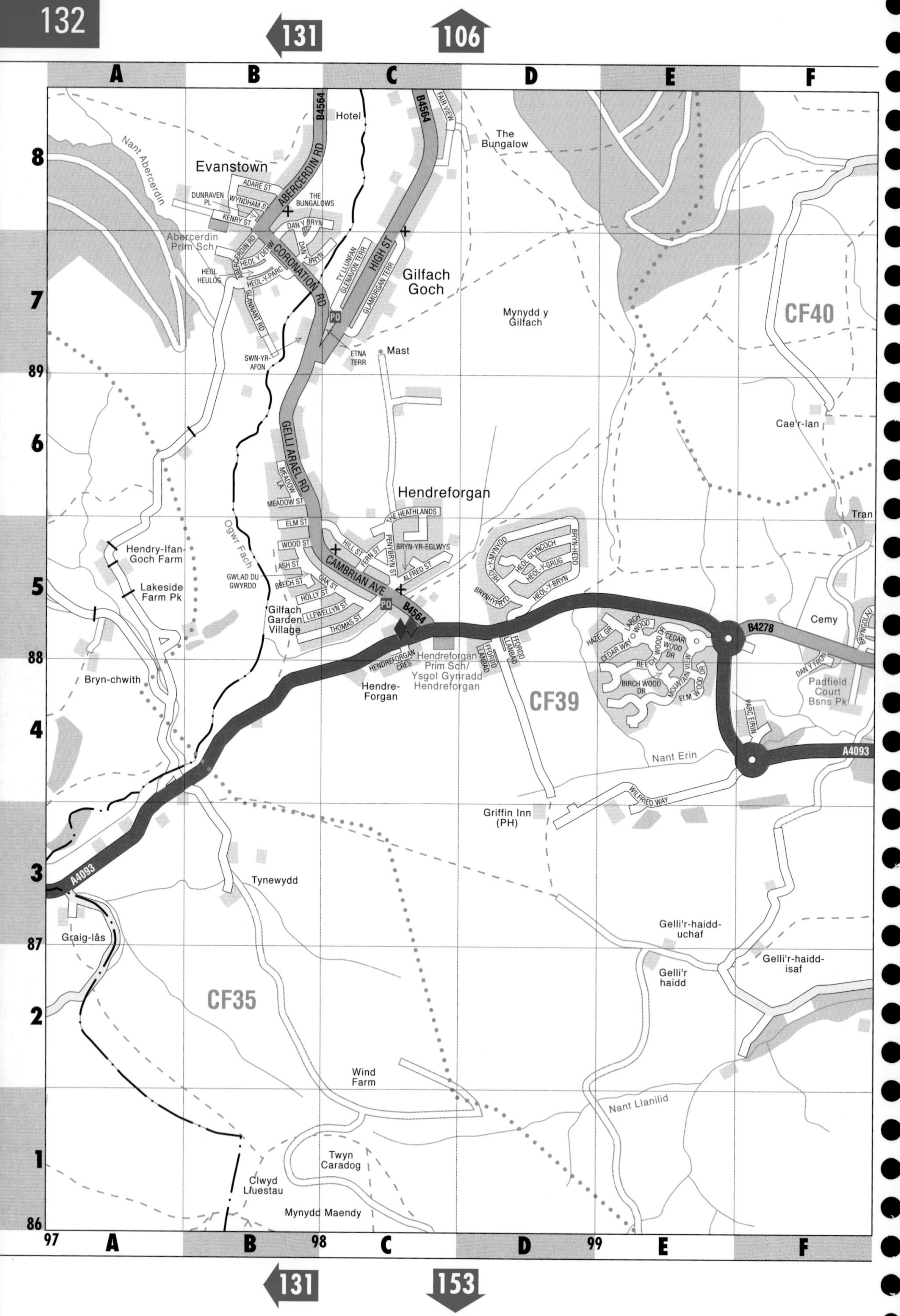

131
153

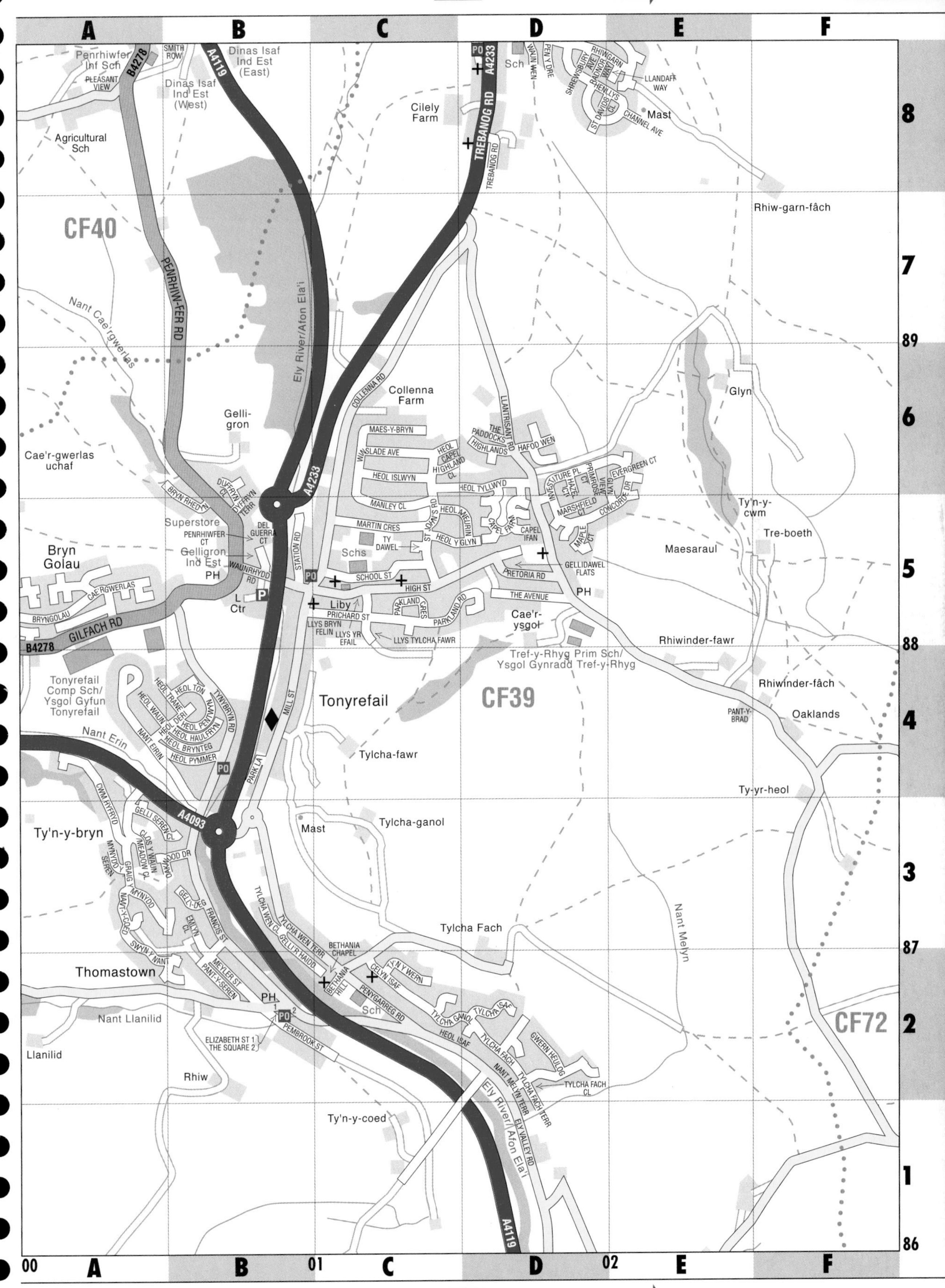

107
134
154
Penrhiwfer Inf Sch
Pleasant View
Smith Row
Dinas Isaf Ind Est (East)
Dinas Isaf Ind Est (West)
Agricultural Sch
Cilely Farm
Sch
Trebanog Rd
Llandaff Way
Mast
Channel Ave
Rhiw-garn-fâch
CF40
Penrhiw-fer Rd
Nant Cae'r-gwerlas
Ely River/Afon Ela'i
Collenna Farm
Gelli-gron
Cae'r-gwerlas uchaf
Superstore
Gelligron Ind Est
Bryn Golau
Gilfach Rd
Tonyrefail Comp Sch/ Ysgol Gyfun Tonyrefail
Tonyrefail
Schs
Liby
Cae'r-ysgol
Glyn
Ty'n-y-cwm
Tre-boeth
Maesaraul
Rhiwinder-fawr
Tref-y-Rhyg Prim Sch/ Ysgol Gynradd Tref-y-Rhyg
Rhiwinder-fâch
Oaklands
CF39
Tylcha-fawr
Ty-yr-heol
Nant Erin
Ty'n-y-bryn
Mast
Tylcha-ganol
Tylcha Fach
Nant Melyn
Thomastown
Nant Llanilid
Llanilid
Rhiw
Ty'n-y-coed
CF72
Bethania Chapel
Pembrook St
Elizabeth St 1
The Square 2
A
B
C
D
E
F
8
7
89
6
5
88
4
3
87
2
1
86
00
01
02

133
108

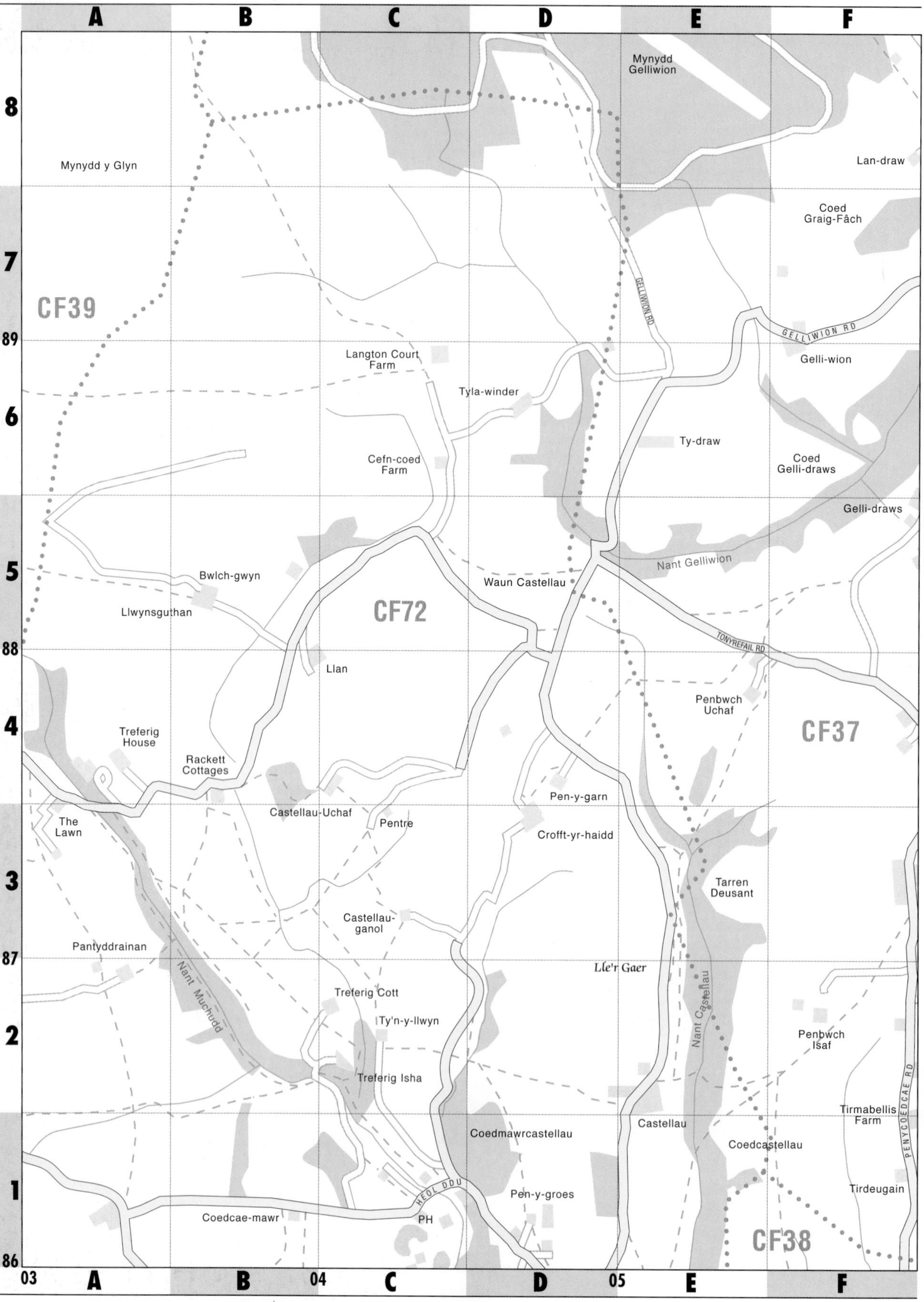

A B C D E F

8
7
89
6
5
88
4
3
87
2
1
86

Mynydd Gelliwion
Mynydd y Glyn
Lan-draw
Coed Graig-Fâch
CF39
Gelliwion Rd
Gelli-wion
Langton Court Farm
Tyla-winder
Ty-draw
Coed Gelli-draws
Cefn-coed Farm
Gelli-draws
Nant Gelliwion
Bwlch-gwyn
Waun Castellau
CF72
Llwynsguthan
Tonyrefail Rd
Llan
Penbwch Uchaf
Treferig House
CF37
Rackett Cottages
Pen-y-garn
The Lawn
Castellau-Uchaf
Pentre
Crofft-yr-haidd
Tarren Deusant
Castellau-ganol
Pantyddrainan
Lle'r Gaer
Nant Muchudd
Treferig Cott
Nant Castellau
Ty'n-y-llwyn
Penbwch Isaf
Treferig Isha
Tirmabellis Farm
Penycoedcae Rd
Castellau
Coedmawrcastellau
Coedcastellau
Heol Ddu
Tirdeugain
Pen-y-groes
Coedcae-mawr
PH
CF38

03 A B 04 C D 05 E F

133
155

109

136

E7
1 CAMBRIAN PL
2 NEW PARK CRES
3 BRIDGE ST
4 HEATHFIELD VILLAS
5 CASTLE ST

F6
1 CAENANT
2 SPRINGFIELD TERR
3 GELLIDAWEL RD
4 MOUNTAIN VIEW

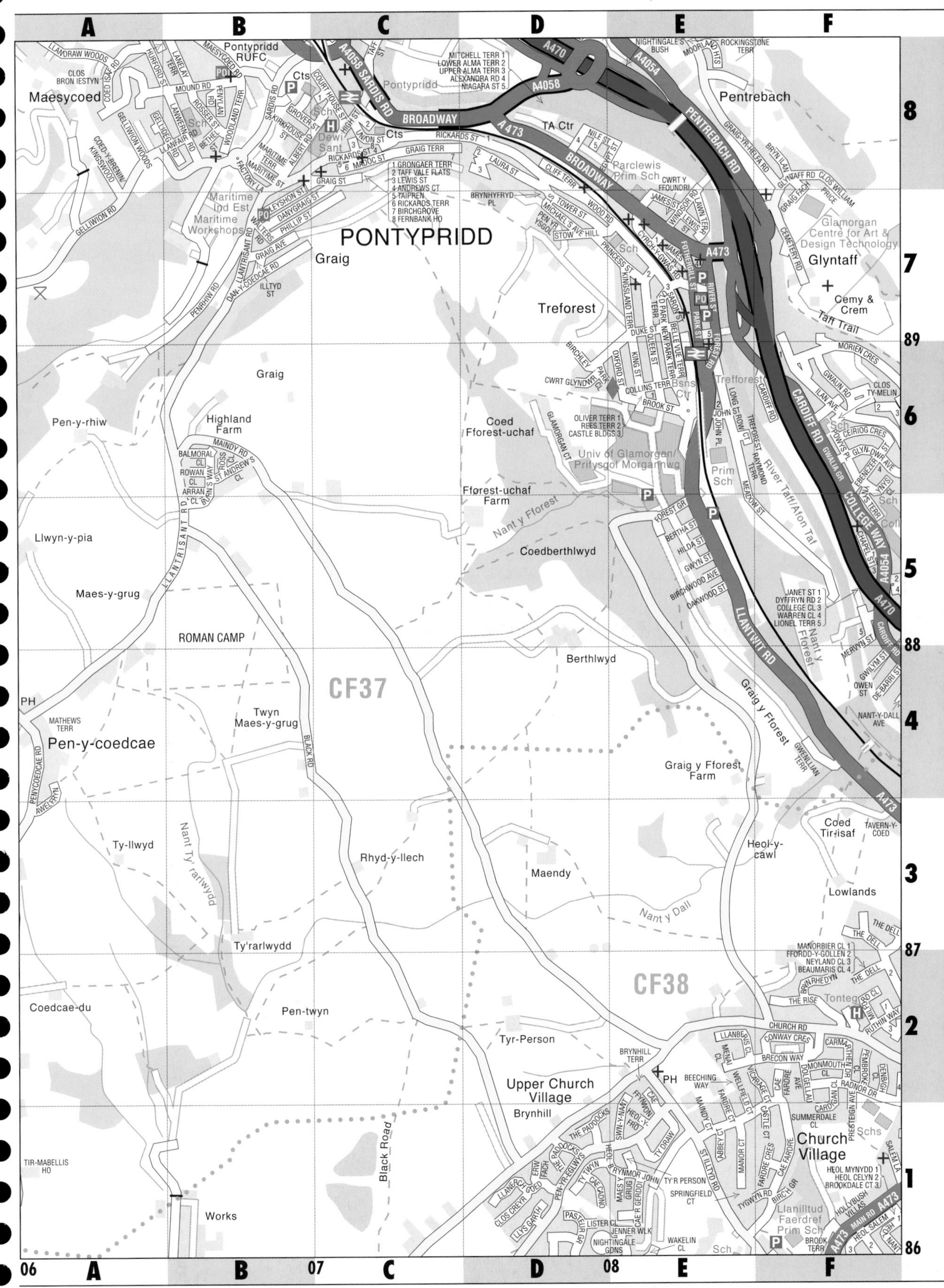

156

136

135 110

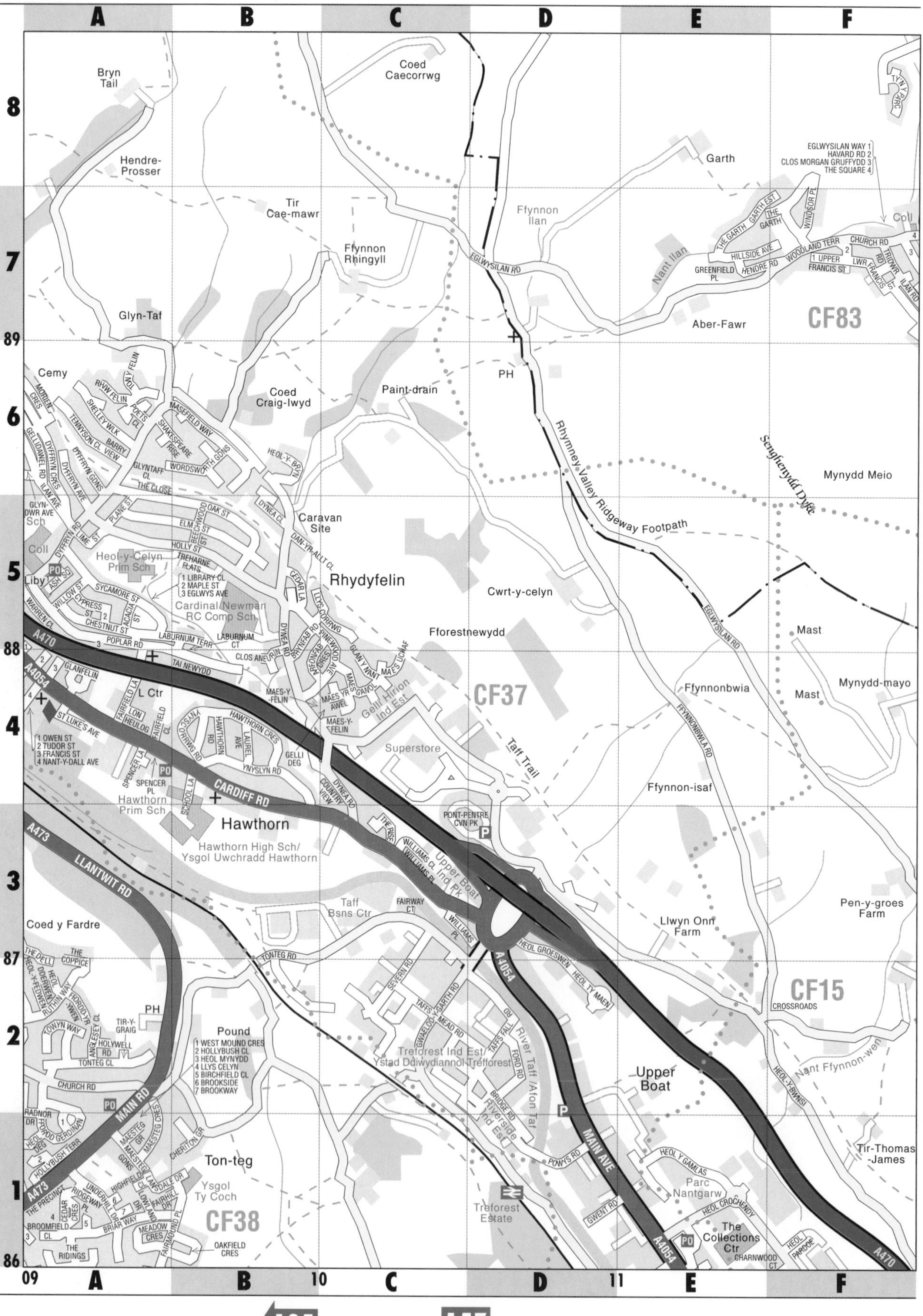

A B C D E F

8 7 89 6 5 88 4 3 87 2 1 86

Bryn Tail
Hendre-Prosser
Tir Cae-mawr
Coed Caecorrwg
Ffynnon Rhingyll
Glyn-Taf
Cemy
Coed Craig-lwyd
Paint-drain
Ffynnon Ilan
Garth
EGLWYSILAN WAY 1
HAVARD RD 2
CLOS MORGAN GRUFFYDD 3
THE SQUARE 4
Aber-Fawr
CF83
PH
Rhymney Valley Ridgeway Footpath
Caravan Site
Rhydyfelin
Cwrt-y-celyn
Fforestnewydd
Mynydd Meio
Mast
Mynydd-mayo
Heol-y-Celyn Prim Sch
Cardinal Newman RC Comp Sch
1 LIBRARY CL
2 MAPLE ST
3 EGLWYS AVE
Liby
Coll
L Ctr
1 OWEN ST
2 TUDOR ST
3 FRANCIS ST
4 NANT-Y-DALL AVE
CF37
Gelli Hirion Ind Est
Superstore
Ffynnonbwia
Ffynnon-isaf
Taff Trail
Hawthorn Prim Sch
Hawthorn
Hawthorn High Sch/
Ysgol Uwchradd Hawthorn
PONT-PENTRE CVN PK
Upper Boat Ind Pk
Taff Bsns Ctr
Coed y Fardre
Llwyn Onn Farm
Pen-y-groes Farm
CF15
CROSSROADS
Pound
1 WEST MOUND CRES
2 HOLLYBUSH CL
3 HEOL MYNYDD
4 LLYS CELYN
5 BIRCHFIELD CL
6 BROOKSIDE
7 BROOKWAY
Treforest Ind Est/
Ystad Ddiwydiannol Trefforest
River Taff/Afon Taf
Riverside Ind Est
Upper Boat
Nant Ffynnon-wen
Tir-Thomas-James
Ton-teg
Ysgol Ty Coch
CF38
Treforest Estate
Parc Nantgarw
The Collections Ctr
A470
A4054
A473
LLANTWIT RD
CARDIFF RD
MAIN RD
MAIN AVE
EGLWYSILAN RD
FFYNNONBWLA RD

09 A B 10 C D 11 E F

135 157

F5
1 ENERGLYN CRES
2 STANLEY DR
3 PANTYCELYN DR
4 HERBERT DR

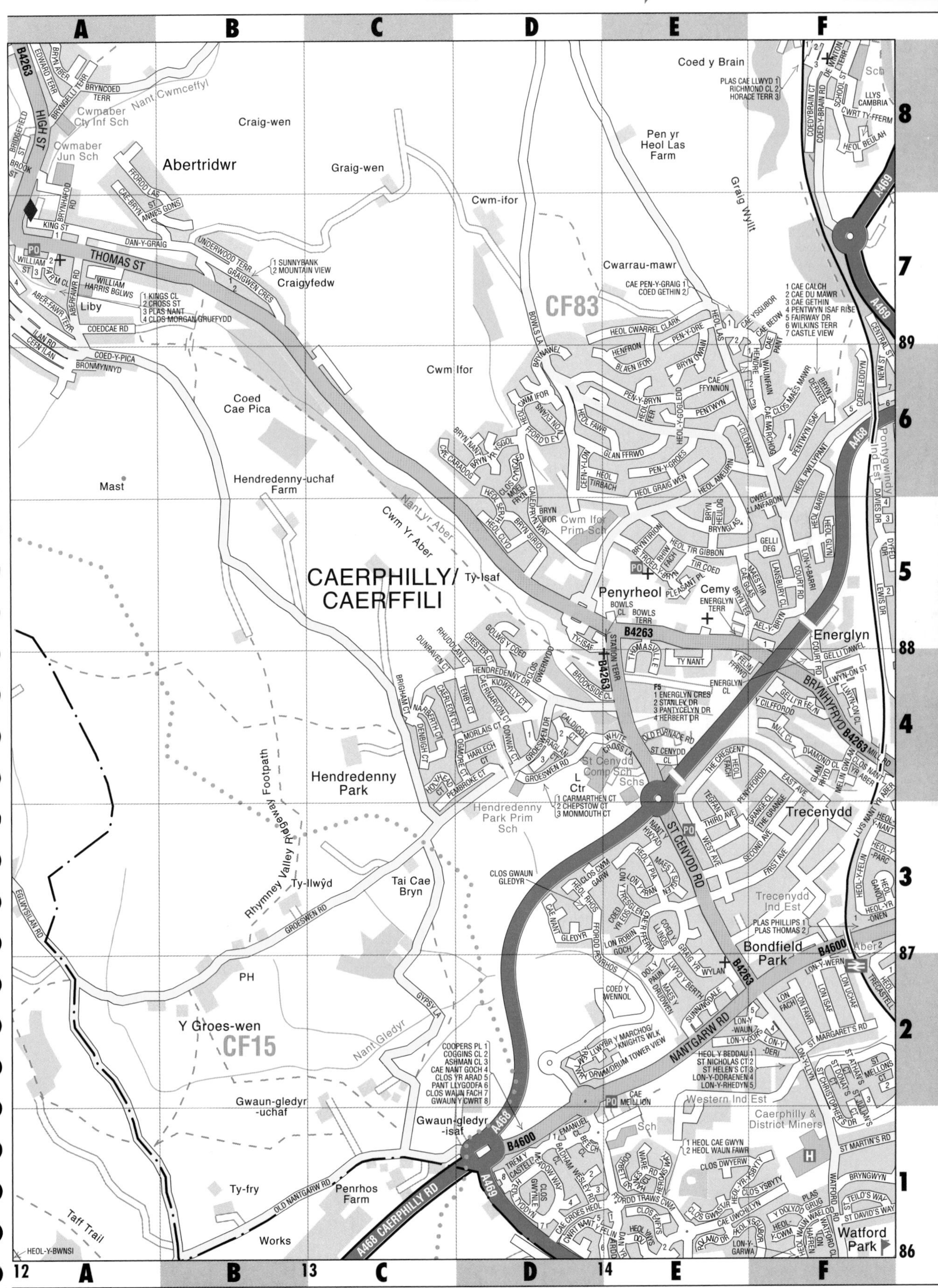

137
112

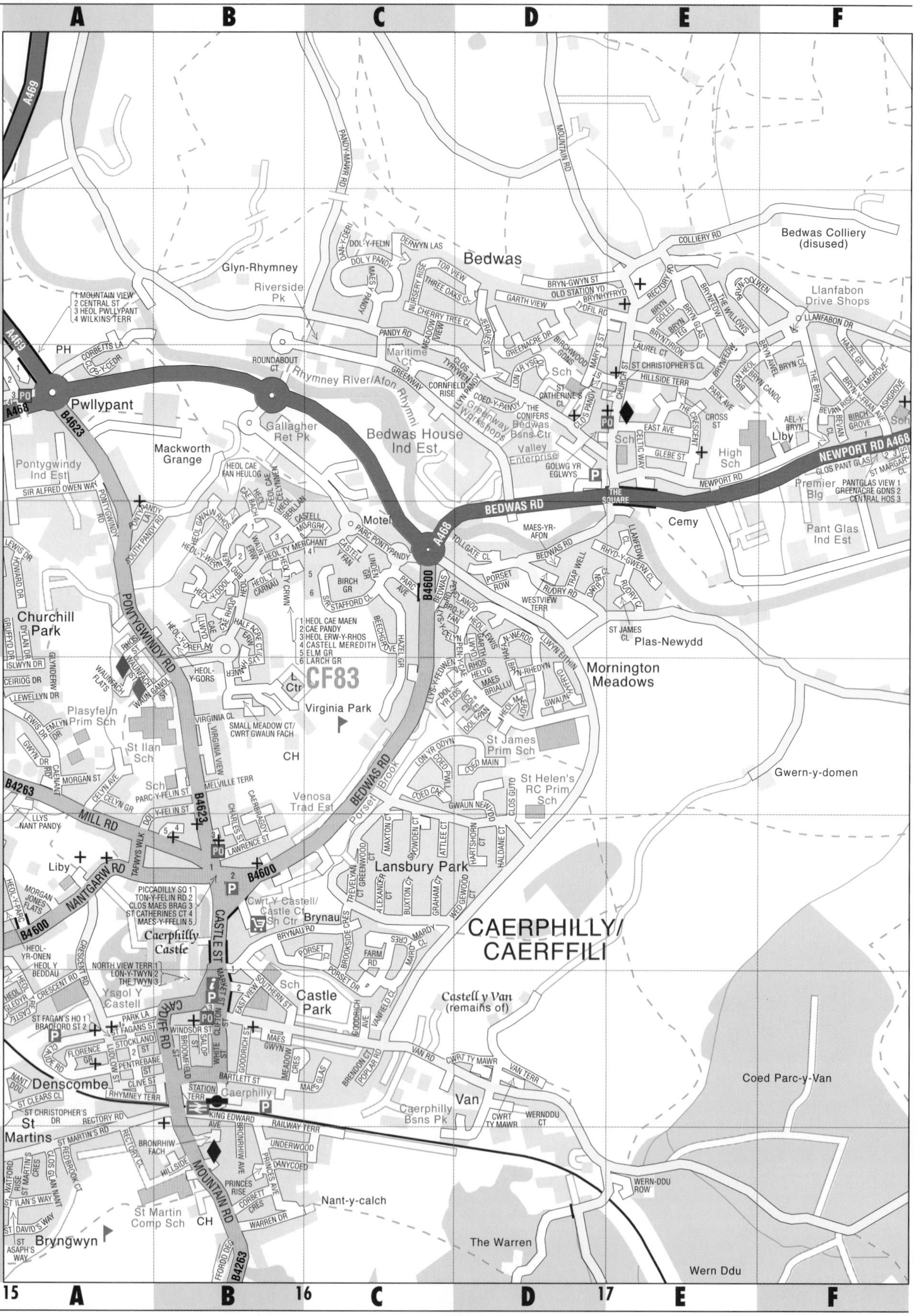

A B C D E F

8
7
89
6
5
88
4
3
87
2
1
86

A469
PANDY-MAWR RD
MOUNTAIN RD
Bedwas Colliery (disused)
COLLIERY RD
DAN-Y-DERI
DOL-Y-FELIN
DERWYN LAS
DOL Y PANDY
MAES Y PANDY
Bedwas
Glyn-Rhymney
Riverside Pk
TOR VIEW
THREE OAKS CL
NURSERY RISE
BRYN-GWYN ST
OLD STATION YD
GARTH VIEW
BRYNHYFRYD
TYDFIL RD
RECTORY RD
BRYN GOLEU
BRYN TEG
BRYN GLAS
BRYNTIRION
BRYNFEDW
THE WILLOWS
BRYN-DOLWEN
Llanfabon Drive Shops
LLANFABON DR
CHERRY TREE CL
MEADOW VIEW
JERRETTS LA
1 MOUNTAIN VIEW
2 CENTRAL ST
3 HEOL PWLLYPANT
4 WILKINS TERR
PANDY RD
Maritime Ct
GREENACRE DR
BIRCHWOOD GDNS
MARY ST
LAUREL CT
ST CHRISTOPHER'S CL
HILLSIDE TERR
BRYN AWEL
BRYN CL
HAZEL GR
ELMGROVE
ASHGROVE
BRYN-Y-FRAN AVE
A469
PH
CORBETTS LA
CLOS-Y-CEDR
PO
A468
Pwllypant
ROUNDABOUT CT
Rhymney River/Afon Rhymni
GREENWAY
CLOS TYRWEN
CORNFIELD RISE
LLYN PANDY
COED-Y-PANDY
LON YR YSGOL
Sch
ST CATHERINE'S CL
CLOS PANDY
CHURCH ST
THE CONIFERS
Bedwas Bsns Ctr
Greenway Workshops
Valley Enterprise
GOLWG YR EGLWYS
PO
Sch
EAST AVE
GLEBE ST
CELTIC WAY
THE CRESCENT
CROSS ST
PARK AVE
BRYN HEOL
BRYN CANOL
High Sch
AEL-Y-BRYN
THE BRYN
BEVAN RISE
BEVAN
BIRCH GROVE
Liby
Sch
NEWPORT RD A468
CLOS PANT GLAS
ST MARGARET'S CL
Premier Blg
PANTGLAS VIEW 1
GREENACRE GDNS 2
CENTRAL HOS 3
NEWPORT RD
THE SQUARE
Cemy
Pant Glas Ind Est
B4623
Gallagher Ret Pk
Bedwas House Ind Est
Mackworth Grange
Pontygwindy Ind Est
SIR ALFRED OWEN WAY
PONTYGWINDY RD
HEOL CAE FAN HEULOG
HEOL CELYNNEN
CAE BACH
HEOL ERW
BERLLAN
CASTELL MORGRAIG
Motel
PARC PONTYPANDY
BEDWAS RD
MAES-YR-AFON
TOLLGATE CL
BEDWAS RD
PORSET ROW
LLANFEDW CL
RHYD-Y-GWERN CL
RUDRY CL
RUDRY RD
TRAP WELL
DARREN VIEW
WESTVIEW TERR
PONTYPANDY LA
SOUTH PANDY RD
HEOL GWAUN RHOS
HEOL-Y-WERN
HEOL TY MERCHANT
CASTELL Y FAN
LINDEN GR
PARC AVE
B4600
A468
LEWIS DR
HOWARD DR
Churchill Park
HEOL-Y-DDOL
HEOL Y CARNAU
HEOL TY CRWN
BIRCH GR
SIR STAFFORD CL
BEDWAS CL
PONT-Y-CLAWDD
BRO-Y-FAN
HEOL LEWIS
HEOL-Y-CELYN
LLWYN EITHIN
ST JAMES CL
Plas-Newydd
GRUFFYD DR
DYLAN DR
GLYNDERW
ISLWYN DR
CEIRIOG DR
LLEWELLYN DR
RHOS
WAUNFACH ST
WAUNFACH FLATS
WAUN GANOL
HEOL-Y-DREFLAN
LLWYD CAE
HALF ACRE CL
1 HEOL CAE MAEN
2 CAE PANDY
3 HEOL ERW-Y-RHOS
4 CASTELL MEREDITH
5 ELM GR
6 LARCH GR
BEECHGROVE
HAZEL GR
HEOL-Y-GORS
L Ctr
CF83
LLYS-Y-FEDWEN
DOL YR EOS
CAE COLE
GARTH
HELYG
MAES BRIALLU
HEOL-Y-RHEDYN
HEOL MAERDY
GWAUN
Mornington Meadows
Plasyfelin Prim Sch
LEWIS DR
EMLYN DR
GWYN DR
CAENANT RD
VIRGINIA CL
SMALL MEADOW CT/ CWRT GWAUN FACH
Virginia Park
St James Prim Sch
LON YR ODYN
COED PWLL
COED MAIN
St Ilan Sch
VIRGINIA VIEW
CH
B4263
MORGAN ST
CELYN AVE
CELYN GR
Sch
PARC-Y-FELIN ST
MELVILLE TERR
Venosa Trad Est
Porset Brook
COED CAE
GWAUN NEWYDD
CLOS GUTO
St Helen's RC Prim Sch
Gwern-y-domen
LLYS NANT PANDY
MILL RD
TAFWYS WLK
DOL-Y-FELIN ST
CHARLES ST
CAERBRAGDY
LAWRENCE ST
PO
B4623
TREVELYAN CT
GREENWOOD CT
MAXTON CT
SNOWDEN CT
ATTLEE CT
HARTSHORN CT
HALDANE CT
Liby
NANTGARW RD
B4600
Lansbury Park
ALEXANDER CT
BUXTON CT
GRAHAM CT
WEDGEWOOD CT
HEOL-Y-PARC
MORGAN JONES PARC
PICCADILLY SQ 1
TON-Y-FELIN RD 2
CLOS MAES BRAG 3
ST CATHERINES CT 4
MAES-Y-FFELIN 5
P
Cwrt Y Castell/ Castle Ct Sh Ctr
Brynau
BRYNAU RD
BROOKSIDE CRES
MARDY CL
MARDY CRES
FARM RD
PORSET CL
PORSET DR
CAERPHILLY/ CAERFFILI
B4600
Caerphilly Castle
CASTLE ST
HEOL-YR-ONEN
HEOL Y BEDDAU
CRESCENT RD
NORTH VIEW TERR 1
LON-Y-TWYN 2
THE TWYN 3
MARKET ST
EAST VIEW
SOUTHERN ST
Sch
Castle Park
GOODRICH AVE
VANFIELD CL
Castell y Van (remains of)
HEOL GLEDYR
CRESCENT RD
Ysgol Y Castell
ST FAGAN'S HO 1
BRADFORD ST 2
PARK LA
ST FAGANS ST
CLIFTON ST
PO
CARDIFF RD
P
STOCKLAND ST
FLORENCE GR
LUDLOW ST
PENTREBANE ST
WINDSOR ST
BROOMFIELD ST
SALOP ST
WHITE ST
GOODRICH ST
MAES GWYN
MEADOW CRES
MAES GLAS
BRENDON CT
POPLAR RD
VAN RD
CWRT TY MAWR
VAN TERR
Coed Parc-y-Van
NANT DDU
Denscombe
ST CLEARS CL
CLIVE ST
RHYMNEY TERR
BARTLETT ST
STATION TERR
Caerphilly
P
Van
Caerphilly Bsns Pk
CWRT TY MAWR
WERNDDU CT
ST CHRISTOPHER'S DR
RECTORY RD
KING EDWARD AVE
RAILWAY TERR
St Martins
ST MARTIN'S RD
RECTORY CL
BRONRHIW FACH
BRONRHIW AVE
UNDERWOOD
DANYCOED
WATFORD RISE
ST MARTIN'S CRES
CLOS GLAN NANT
REDBROOK CT
HILLSIDE
MOUNTAIN RD
PRINCES RISE
PRINCES AVE
CORBETT CRES
WERN-DDU ROW
ST ILAN'S WAY
ST DAVID'S WAY
St Martin Comp Sch
CH
Nant-y-calch
WARREN DR
ST ASAPH'S WAY
Bryngwyn
FFORDD DEG
B4263
The Warren
Wern Ddu

15 A B 16 C D 17 E F

137
159

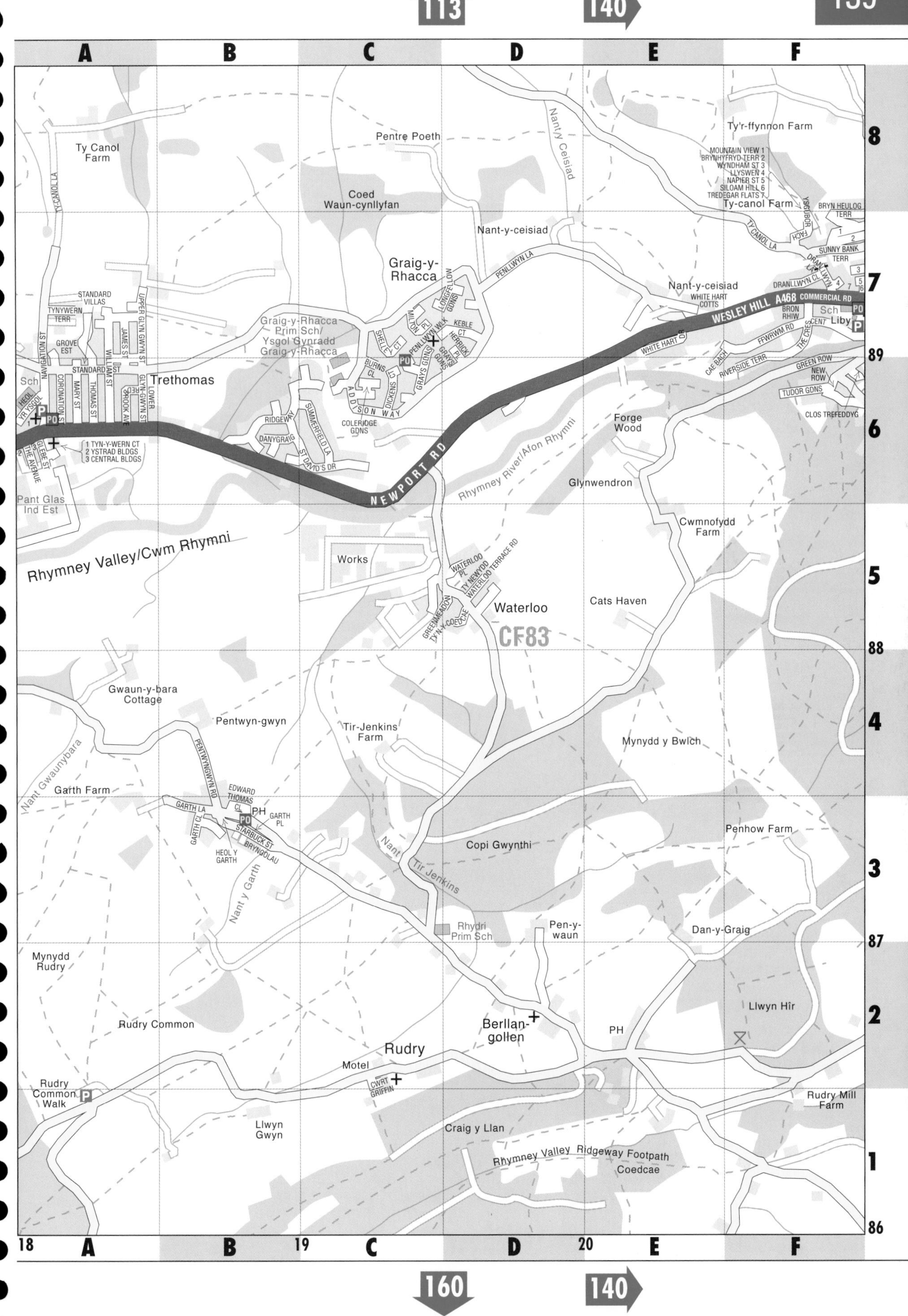
113
140
A B C D E F
8
7
89
6
5
88
4
3
87
2
1
86
18 19 20
Ty Canol Farm
Pentre Poeth
Coed Waun-cynllyfan
Nant y Ceisiad
Ty'r-ffynnon Farm
MOUNTAIN VIEW 1
BRYNHYFRYD TERR 2
WYNDHAM ST 3
LLYSWEN 4
NAPIER ST 5
SILOAM HILL 6
TREDEGAR FLATS 7
Ty-canol Farm
BRYN HEULOG TERR
SUNNY BANK TERR
Nant-y-ceisiad
Graig-y-Rhacca
PENLLWYN LA
WHITE HART COTTS
WESLEY HILL A468 COMMERCIAL RD
DRANLLWYN CL
BRON RHIW
Sch
Liby
STANDARD VILLAS
TYNYWERN TERR
GROVE EST
NAVIGATION ST
UPPER GLYN GWYN ST
JAMES ST
WILLIAM ST
STANDARD ST
Graig-y-Rhacca Prim Sch/ Ysgol Gynradd Graig-y-Rhacca
LONGFELLOW GDNS
MILTON PL
KEBLE CT
SHELLEY CT
PENLLWYN WLK
HERRICK PL
BURNS CL
DICKENS CT
GRAYS GDNS
ADDISON WAY
COLERIDGE GDNS
WHITE HART DR
FFWRWM RD
THE CRES
CENT
CAE BACH
RIVERSIDE TERR
GREEN ROW
NEW ROW
TUDOR GDNS
CLOS TREFEDDYG
Sch
Trethomas
CORONATION ST
MARY ST
THOMAS ST
BROOK AVE
LOWER GLYN GWYN ST
HEOL YR YSGOL
RIDGEWAY
DANYGRAIG
SUMMERFIELD LA
ST DAVID'S DR
1 TYN-Y-WERN CT
2 YSTRAD BLDGS
3 CENTRAL BLDGS
THE AVENUE
GLEBE ST
Forge Wood
Rhymney River/Afon Rhymni
NEWPORT RD
Glynwendron
Pant Glas Ind Est
Cwmnofydd Farm
Rhymney Valley/Cwm Rhymni
Works
WATERLOO PL
TY NEWYDD
WATERLOO TERRACE RD
Waterloo
Cats Haven
GREENMEADOW
TY-N-Y-COEDCAE
CF83
Gwaun-y-bara Cottage
Pentwyn-gwyn
Tir-Jenkins Farm
Mynydd y Bwlch
Nant Gwaunybara
Garth Farm
PENTWYNGWYN RD
EDWARD THOMAS CL
GARTH LA
PH
GARTH PL
GARTH CL
STARBUCK ST
BRYNGOLAU
HEOL Y GARTH
Nant Tir Jenkins
Copi Gwynthi
Penhow Farm
Nant y Garth
Rhydri Prim Sch
Pen-y-waun
Dan-y-Graig
Mynydd Rudry
Llwyn Hîr
Rudry Common
Berllan-gollen
PH
Rudry
Motel
CWRT GRIFFIN
Rudry Common Walk
Llwyn Gwyn
Craig y Llan
Rudry Mill Farm
Rhymney Valley Ridgeway Footpath
Coedcae
160
140

139
114

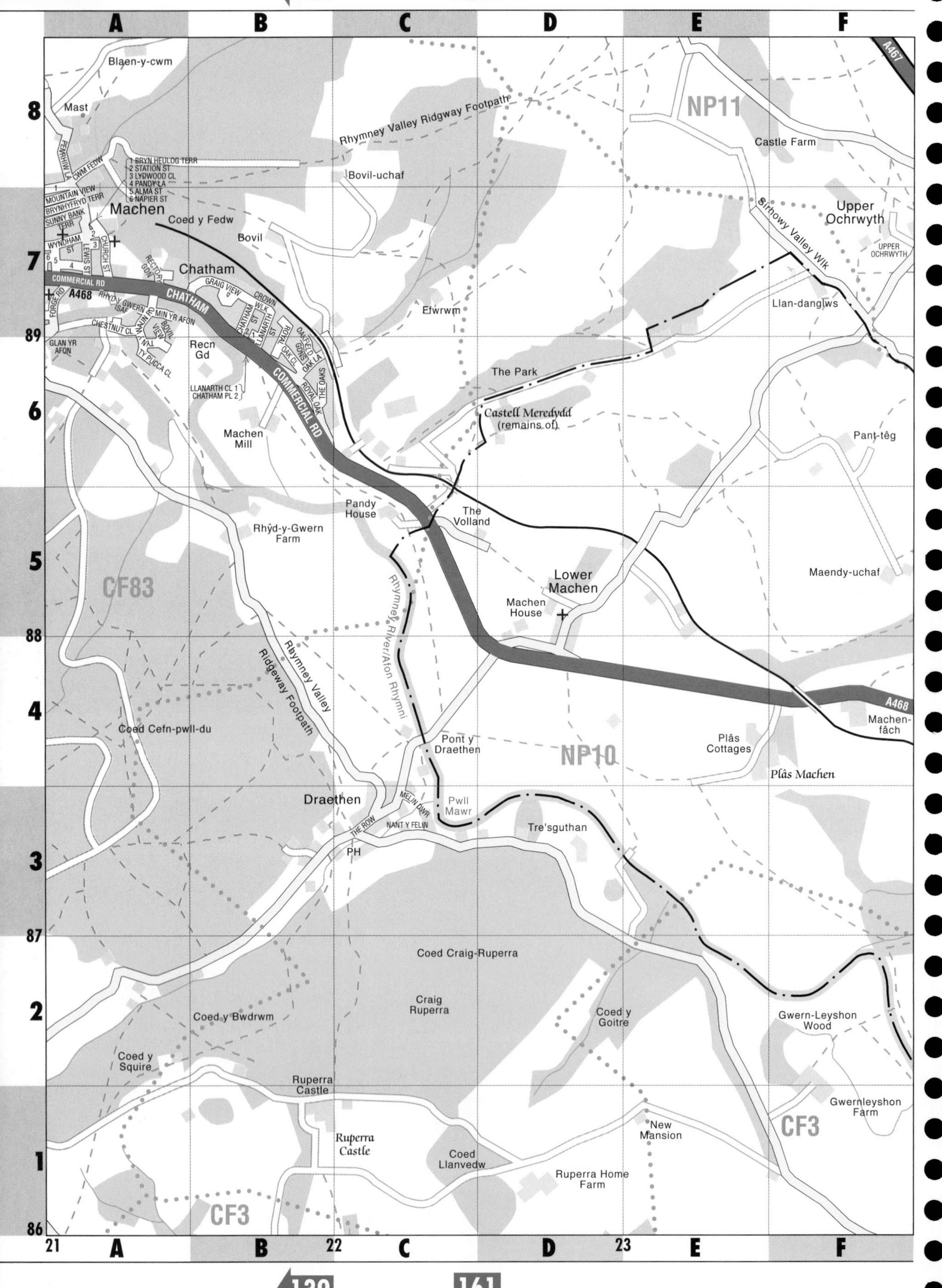

139
161

115
142

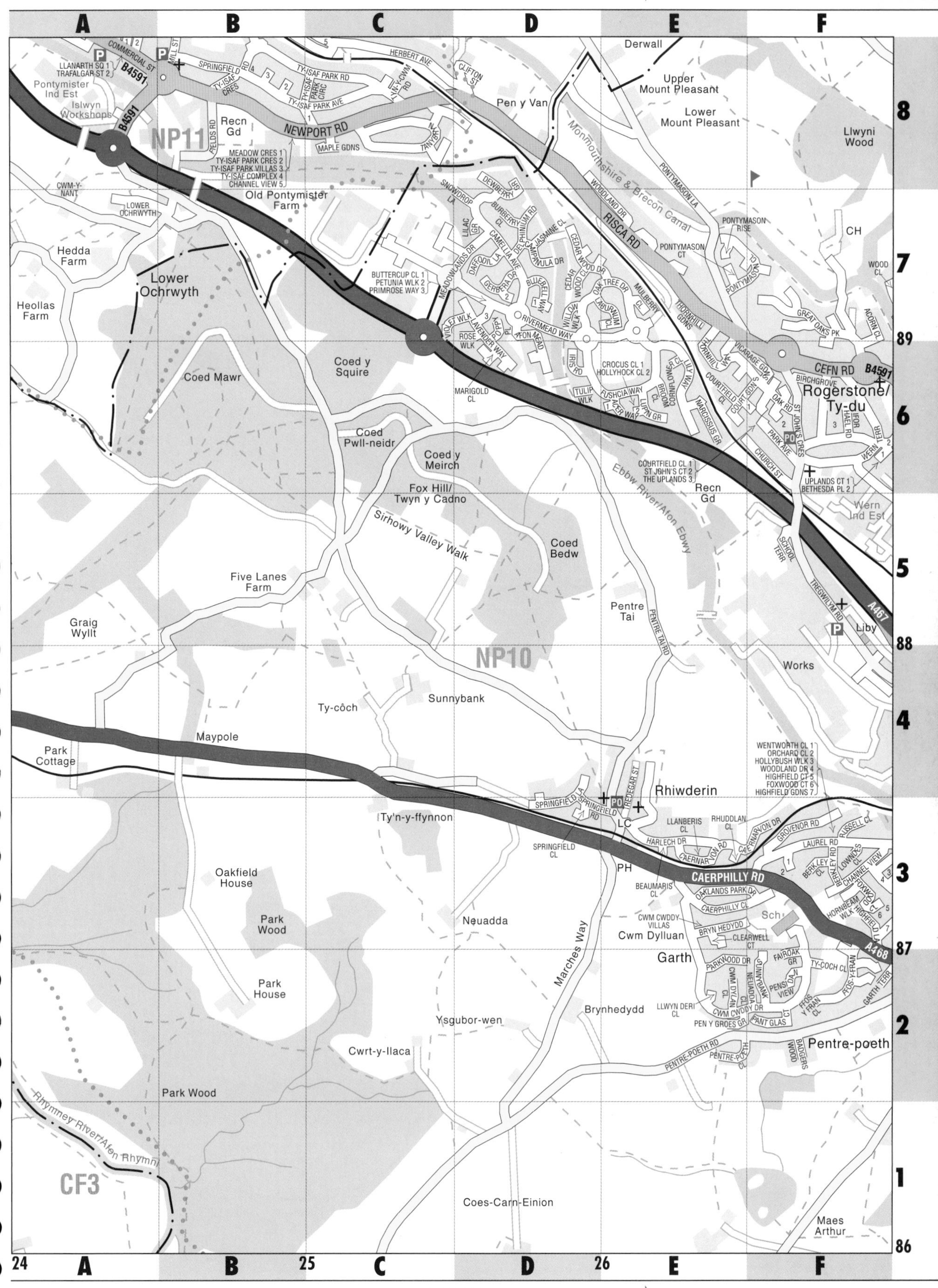

162
142

141
116

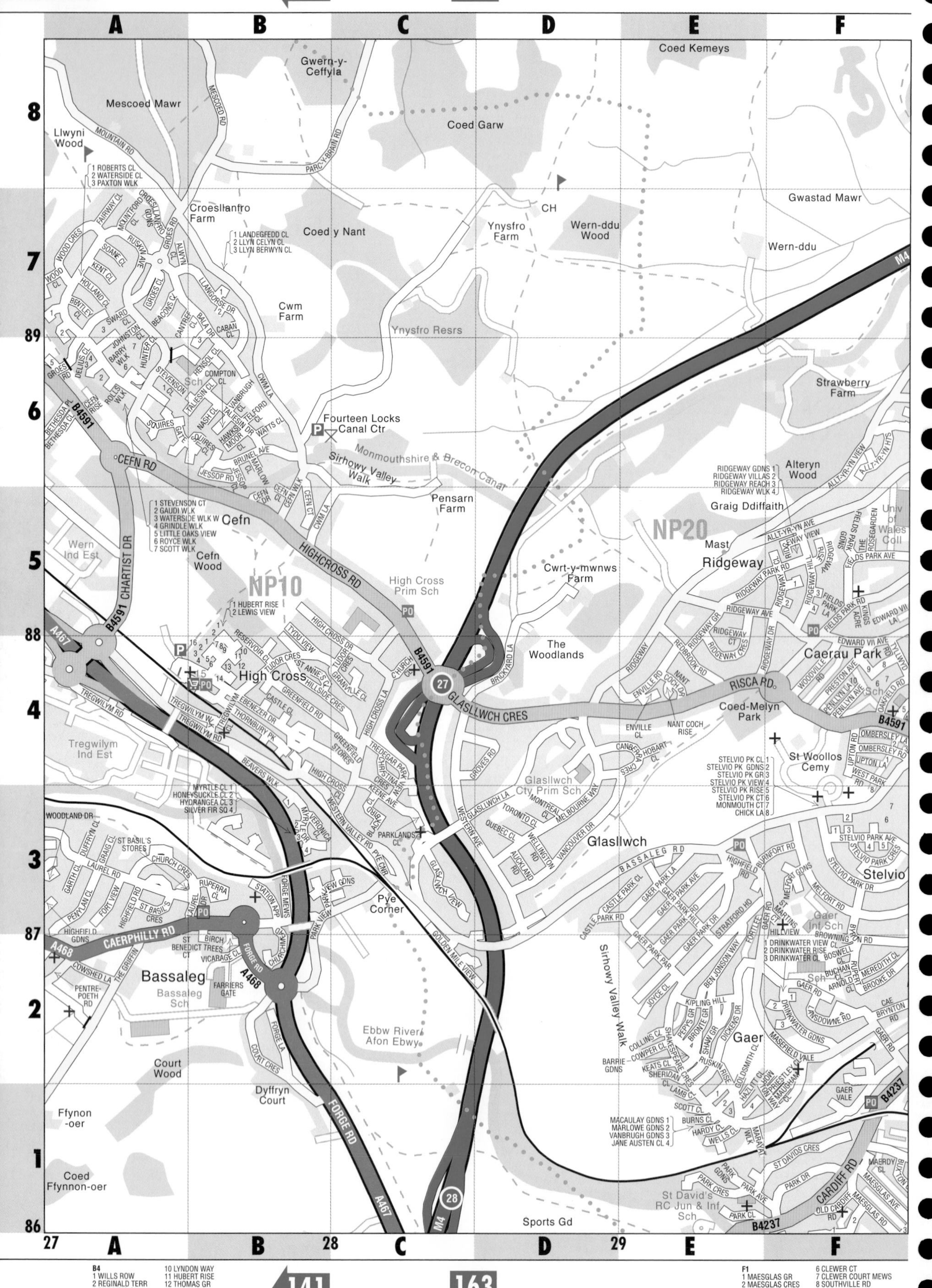

B4
1 WILLS ROW
2 REGINALD TERR
3 PHILLIP'S GN
4 WINDSOR PL
5 WATKINS WLK
6 HAROLD WLK
7 BENSON AVE
8 STEPHEN WLK
9 DAVID WLK
10 LYNDON WAY
11 HUBERT RISE
12 THOMAS GR
13 LESLIE TERR
14 ALAN CL
15 Thornbury Pk Sh Ctr
16 CECIL LA

141
163

F1
1 MAESGLAS GR
2 MAESGLAS CRES
3 MAESGLAS ST
F4
1 WEST PARK LA
2 WATKINS LA
3 PROSSER LA
4 HOMEVALLEY HO
5 BRYNGWYN RD
6 CLEWER CT
7 CLEWER COURT MEWS
8 SOUTHVILLE RD
9 WESTVILLE RD
10 CHAPMAN CT

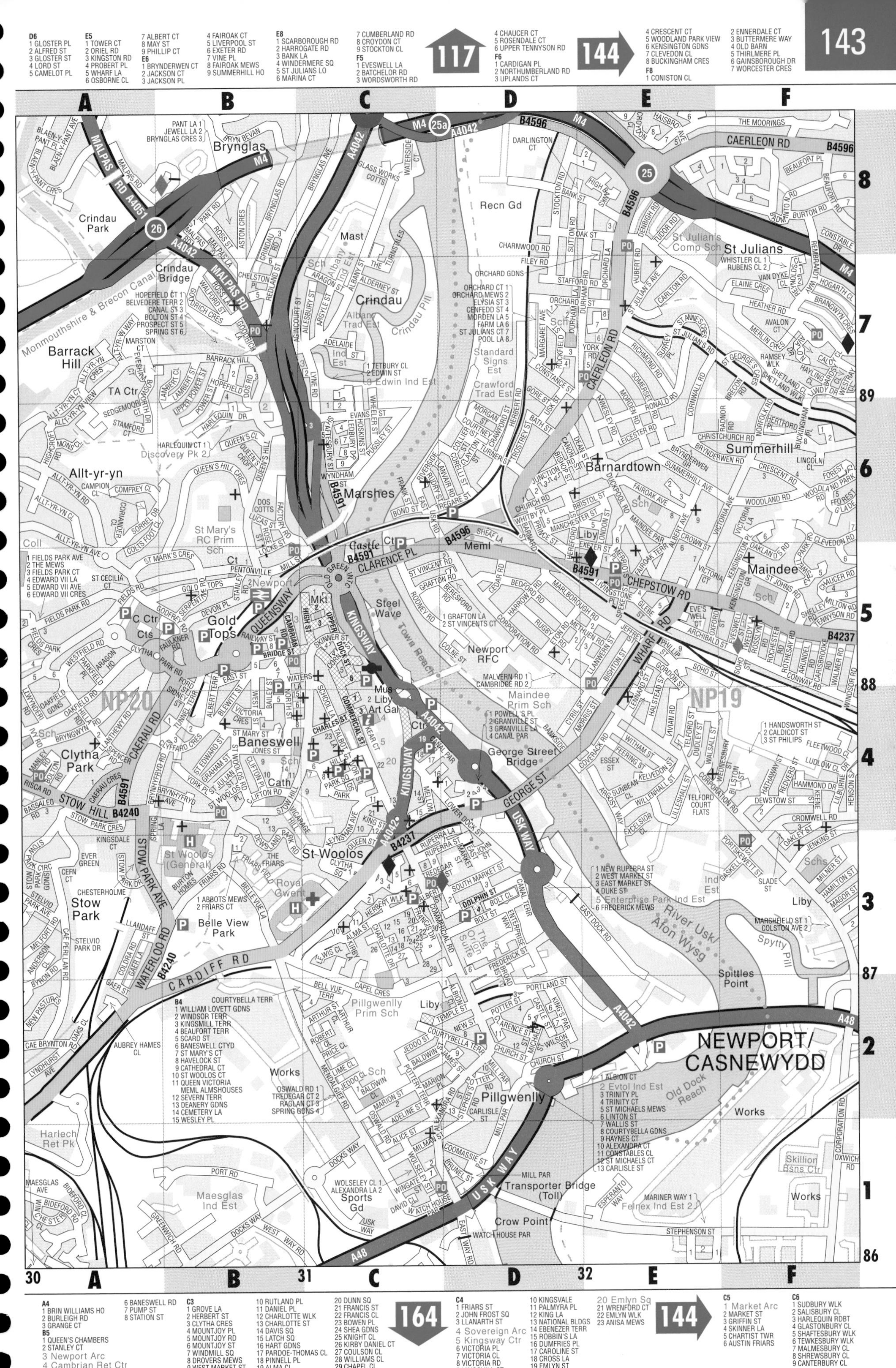

D6
1 GLOSTER PL
2 ALFRED ST
3 GLOSTER ST
4 LORD ST
5 CAMELOT PL
E5
1 TOWER CT
2 ORIEL RD
3 KINGSTON RD
4 PROBERT PL
5 WHARF LA
6 OSBORNE CL
7 ALBERT CT
8 MAY ST
9 PHILLIP CT
E6
1 BRYNDERWEN CT
2 JACKSON CT
3 JACKSON PL
4 FAIROAK CT
5 LIVERPOOL ST
6 EXETER RD
7 VINE PL
8 FAIROAK MEWS
9 SUMMERHILL HO
E8
1 SCARBOROUGH RD
2 HARROGATE RD
3 BANK LA
4 WINDERMERE SQ
5 ST JULIANS LO
6 MARINA CT
7 CUMBERLAND RD
8 CROYDON CT
9 STOCKTON CL
F5
1 EVESWELL LA
2 BATCHELOR RD
3 WORDSWORTH RD
117
4 CHAUCER CT
5 ROSENDALE CT
6 UPPER TENNYSON RD
F6
1 CARDIGAN PL
2 NORTHUMBERLAND RD
3 UPLANDS CT
144
4 CRESCENT CT
5 WOODLAND PARK VIEW
6 KENSINGTON GDNS
7 CLEVEDON CL
8 BUCKINGHAM CRES
F8
1 CONISTON CL
2 ENNERDALE CT
3 BUTTERMERE WAY
4 OLD BARN
5 THIRLMERE PL
6 GAINSBOROUGH DR
7 WORCESTER CRES
A B C D E F
8 7 89 6 5 88 4 3 87 2 1 86
30 31 32
Bryngas
Crindau Park
Crindau Bridge
Barrack Hill
Allt-yr-yn
Crindau
Marshes
Recn Gd
St Julians
Summerhill
Barnardtown
Maindee
Gold Tops
Newport RFC
Clytha Park
Baneswell
St Woolos
Stow Park
Belle View Park
Pillgwenlly
George Street Bridge
Transporter Bridge (Toll)
Crow Point
NEWPORT/ CASNEWYDD
Maesglas Ind Est
Harlech Ret Pk
River Usk/ Afon Wysg
Spittles Point
Old Dock Reach
NP20
NP19
CARDIFF RD
CHEPSTOW RD
CAERLEON RD
USK WAY
KINGSWAY
QUEENSWAY
GEORGE ST
CLARENCE PL
STOW HILL
B4
1 WILLIAM LOVETT GDNS
2 WINDSOR TERR
3 KINGSMILL TERR
4 BEAUFORT TERR
5 SCARD ST
6 BANESWELL CTYD
7 ST MARY'S CT
8 HAVELOCK ST
9 CATHEDRAL CT
10 ST WOOLOS CT
11 QUEEN VICTORIA MEML ALMSHOUSES
12 SEVERN TERR
13 DEANERY GDNS
14 CEMETERY LA
15 WESLEY PL
A4
1 BRIN WILLIAMS HO
2 BURLEIGH RD
3 GRANGE CT
B5
1 QUEEN'S CHAMBERS
2 STANLEY CT
3 Newport Arc
4 Cambrian Ret Ctr
5 CAXTON PL
6 BANESWELL RD
7 PUMP ST
8 STATION ST
C3
1 GROVE LA
2 HERBERT ST
3 CLYTHA CRES
4 MOUNTJOY PL
5 MOUNTJOY RD
6 MOUNTJOY ST
7 WINDMILL SQ
8 DROVERS MEWS
9 WEST MARKET ST
10 RUTLAND PL
11 DANIEL PL
12 CHARLOTTE WLK
13 CHARLOTTE ST
14 DAVIS SQ
15 LATCH SQ
16 HART GDNS
17 PARDOE-THOMAS CL
18 PINNELL PL
19 ALMA CL
20 DUNN SQ
21 FRANCIS ST
22 FRANCIS CL
23 BOWEN PL
24 SHEA GDNS
25 KNIGHT CL
26 KIRBY DANIEL CT
27 COULSON CL
28 WILLIAMS CL
29 CHAPEL CL
30 DOLPHIN CT
164
C4
1 FRIARS ST
2 JOHN FROST SQ
3 LLANARTH ST
4 Sovereign Arc
5 Kingsway Ctr
6 VICTORIA PL
7 VICTORIA CL
8 VICTORIA RD
9 KINGSHILL CT
10 KINGSVALE
11 PALMYRA PL
12 KING LA
13 NATIONAL BLDGS
14 EBENEZER TERR
15 ROBBIN'S LA
16 DUMFRIES PL
17 CAROLINE ST
18 CROSS LA
19 EMLYN ST
20 Emlyn Sq
21 WRENFORD CT
22 EMLYN WLK
23 ANISA MEWS
144
C5
1 Market Arc
2 MARKET ST
3 GRIFFIN ST
4 SKINNER LA
5 CHARTIST TWR
6 AUSTIN FRIARS
C6
1 SUDBURY WLK
2 SALISBURY CL
3 HARLEQUIN RDBT
4 GLASTONBURY CL
5 SHAFTESBURY WLK
6 TEWKESBURY WLK
7 MALMESBURY CL
8 SHREWSBURY CL
9 CANTERBURY CL

143
118

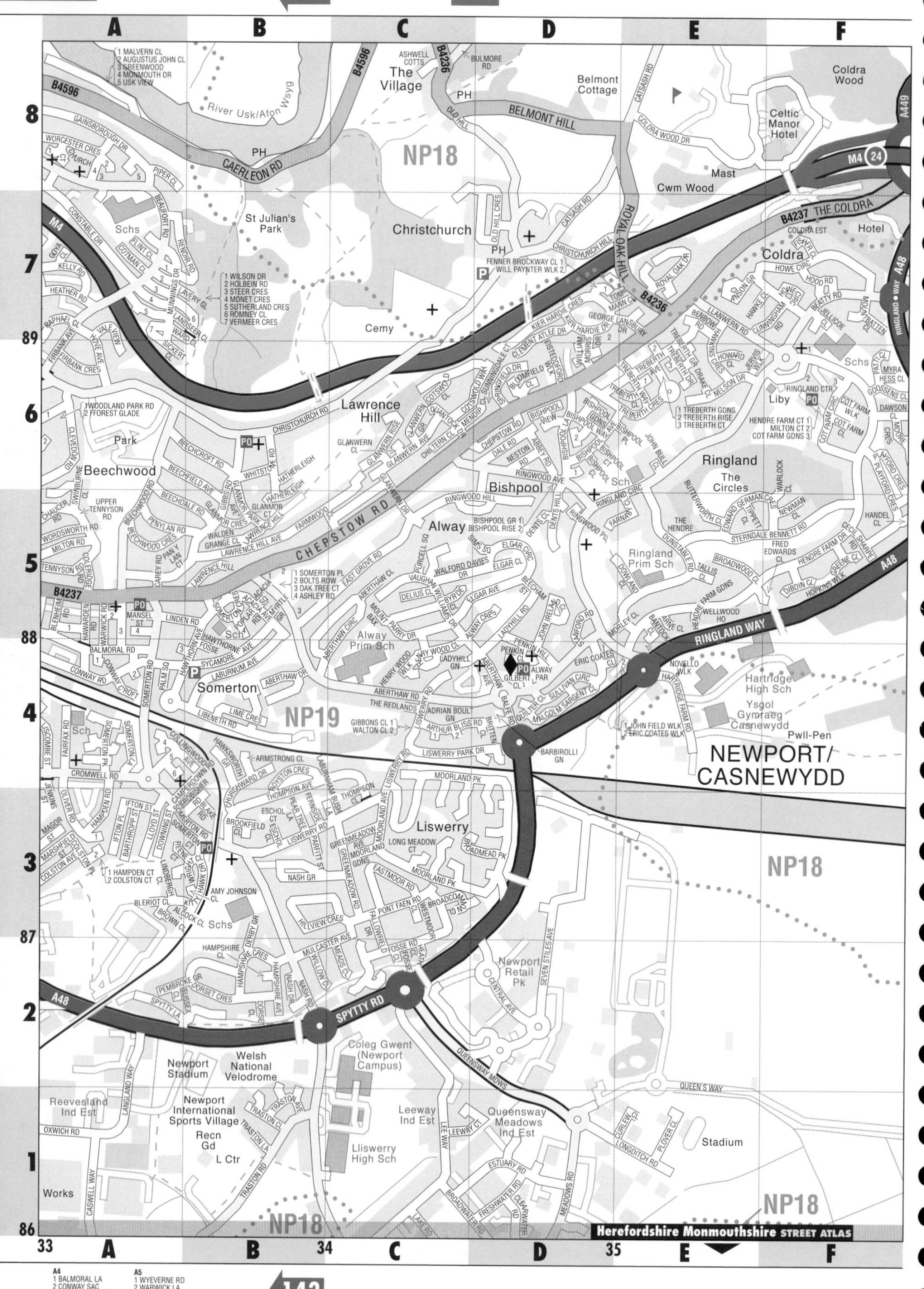

A4
1 BALMORAL LA
2 CONWAY SAC
3 HAWTHORNE SQ
4 COLLINGWOOD CRES
5 COLLINGWOOD RD
6 COLLINGWOOD CL
7 CROMWELL CT

A5
1 WYEVERNE RD
2 WARWICK LA
3 KENILWORTH RD
4 LLEWELLIN ST

143

119

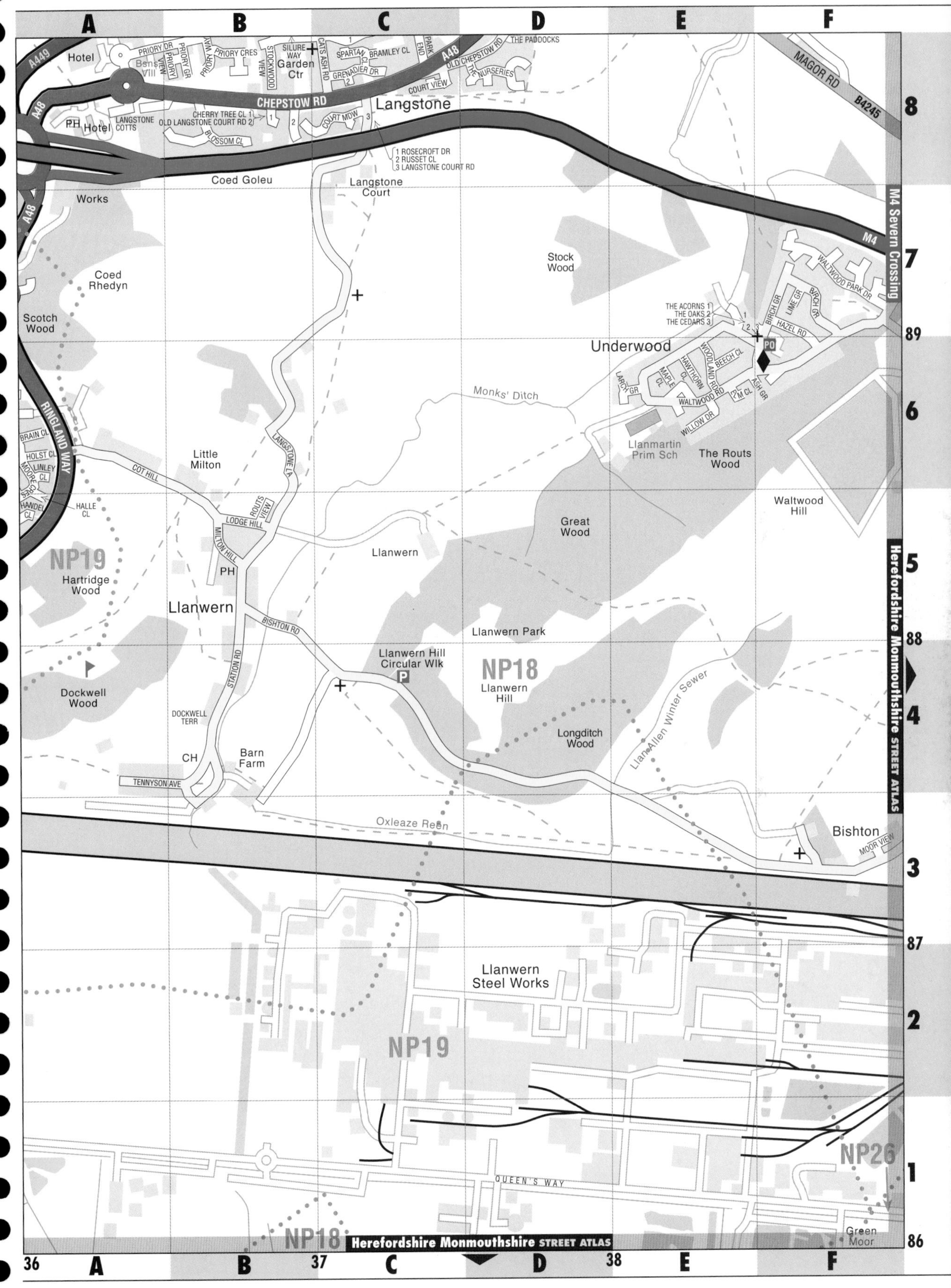

A
B
C
D
E
F
Hotel
PRIORY DR
PRIORY CRES
STOCKWOOD VIEW
SILURE WAY
Garden Ctr
CATS ASH RD
SPARTAN CL
BRAMLEY CL
GRENADIER DR
PARK END
A48
OLD CHEPSTOW RD
THE PADDOCKS
THE NURSERIES
COURT VIEW
MAGOR RD
B4245
A449
A48
CHEPSTOW RD
Langstone
PH
Hotel
LANGSTONE COTTS
CHERRY TREE CL 1
OLD LANGSTONE COURT RD 2
BLOSSOM CL
COURT MDW
1 ROSECROFT DR
2 RUSSET CL
3 LANGSTONE COURT RD
Coed Goleu
Langstone Court
Works
A48
M4
M4 Severn Crossing
Stock Wood
Coed Rhedyn
Scotch Wood
WALTWOOD PARK DR
BIRCH GR
LIME GR
HAZEL RD
THE ACORNS 1
THE OAKS 2
THE CEDARS 3
PO
Underwood
LARCH GR
MAPLE CL
HAWTHORN CL
WOODLAND RD
BEECH CL
WALTWOOD RD
ASH GR
WILLOW DR
Monks' Ditch
RINGLAND WAY
BRAIN CL
HOLST CL
LINLEY CL
MOORE CRES
HANDEL CL
HALLE CL
Little Milton
COT HILL
LANGSTONE LA
ROUTS VIEW
LODGE HILL
MILTON HILL
Llanmartin Prim Sch
The Routs Wood
Waltwood Hill
Great Wood
Llanwern
NP19
Hartridge Wood
PH
Llanwern
BISHTON RD
Llanwern Park
Llanwern Hill Circular Wlk
P
NP18
Llanwern Hill
Dockwell Wood
STATION RD
DOCKWELL TERR
Llan-Allen Winter Sewer
Longditch Wood
CH
Barn Farm
TENNYSON AVE
Oxleaze Reen
Bishton
MOOR VIEW
Llanwern Steel Works
NP19
NP26
QUEEN'S WAY
NP18
Green Moor
36
37
38
8
7
89
6
5
88
4
3
87
2
1
86

125

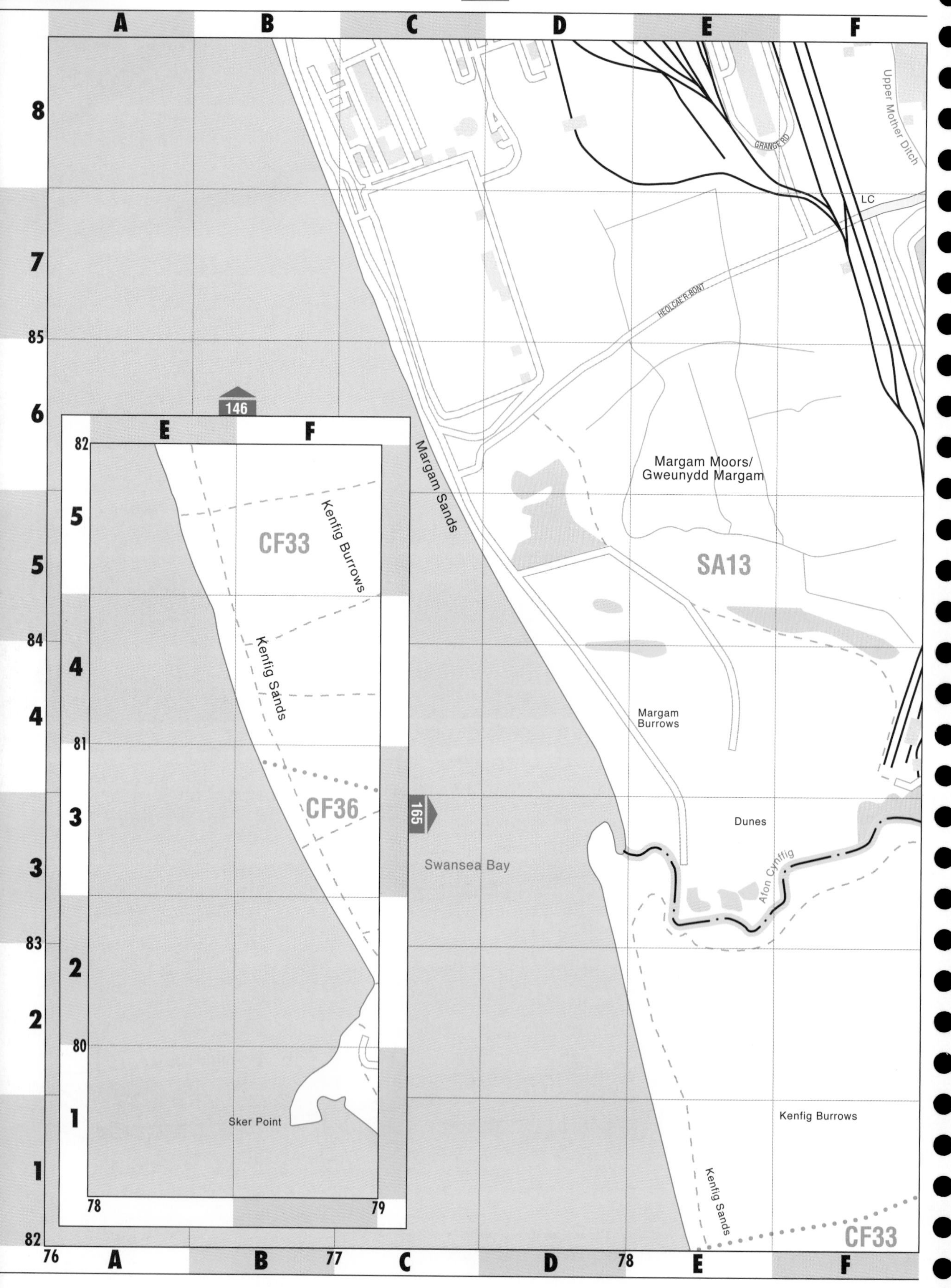

A
B
C
D
E
F
8
7
85
6
5
84
4
3
83
2
1
82
76
77
78
Upper Mother Ditch
GRANGE RD
LC
HEOLCAE'R-BONT
Margam Sands
Margam Moors/
Gweunydd Margam
SA13
Margam
Burrows
Dunes
Afon Cynffig
Swansea Bay
Kenfig Burrows
Kenfig Sands
CF33
146
165
82
81
80
79
CF33
Kenfig Burrows
Kenfig Sands
CF36
Sker Point

126
148

165
148

147 127

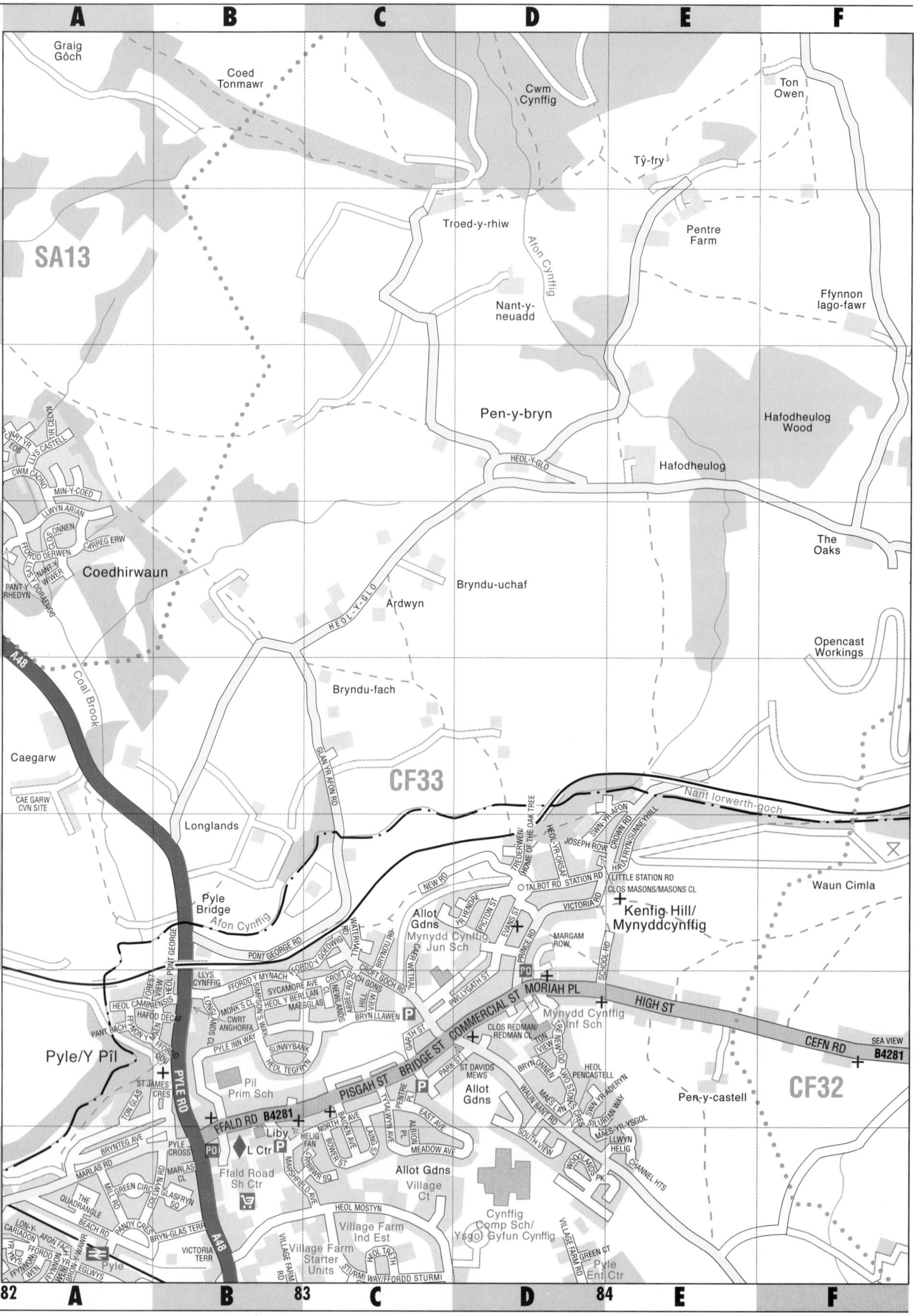
A B C D E F
8 7 85 6 5 84 4 3 83 2 1 82
Graig Gôch
Coed Tonmawr
Cwm Cynffig
Ton Owen
Tŷ-fry
Troed-y-rhiw
Pentre Farm
SA13
Afon Cynffig
Nant-y-neuadd
Ffynnon Iago-fawr
Pen-y-bryn
Hafodheulog Wood
HEOL-Y-GLO
Hafodheulog
Coedhirwaun
The Oaks
Bryndu-uchaf
Ardwyn
A48
Coal Brook
Opencast Workings
Bryndu-fach
Caegarw
CF33
CAE GARW CVN SITE
Nant Iorwerth-goch
Longlands
Pyle Bridge
Waun Cimla
Kenfig Hill/ Mynyddcynffig
Allot Gdns
Mynydd Cynffig Jun Sch
HIGH ST
MORIAH PL
COMMERCIAL ST
Mynydd Cynffig Inf Sch
Pyle/Y Pîl
CEFN RD
B4281
CF32
Pil Prim Sch
PISGAH ST
BRIDGE ST
Allot Gdns
Pen-y-castell
FFALD RD B4281
Liby
L Ctr
PYLE RD
Allot Gdns
Village Ct
Ffald Road Sh Ctr
Cynffig Comp Sch/ Ysgol Gyfun Cynffig
Village Farm Ind Est
Village Farm Starter Units
Pyle
Pyle Ent Ctr
82 A B 83 C D 84 E F

147 166

A B C D E F

Mynydd Ty-talwyn
Mynydd Baedan
Cwm Cefnydfa
8
Craig yr Aber
Nant Craigyraber
Nant Fadog
Ogwr Ridgeway Wlk
Mast
CF33
Craig Fadog
7
Pentitla
Cefn-y-gelli
Baiden Farm
85
Ton Phillip Farm
Nanty-y-gedd
FFORDD-Y-GYFRAITH
6
Ffordd-y-gyfraith Farm
Cwmrisca
Cefn Parc
Ty Gwalia
Aberbaiden Farm
NEW RD
Park Slip Nature Park
Park Farm
5
CF32
Ffordd-y-Gyfraith
Opencast Workings
84
LAW ST
4
Parc Bedford Country Park
Nant Iorwerth-goch
Cefn Junction
Cwm-ffos
PH
BEDFORD RD
Bankers Hill House
COURT TERR
BANKERS HILL
3
Ty Cribbwr Farm
83
B4281
Cefn Cribwr
Dan-y-Bryn
BLACKFIELD ROW
TYCRIBWR HILL
CAE PENTRE
BEDFORD CL
HEOL NEWYDD
WEST AVE
EAST AVE
MAES GLAS
PLEASANT VIEW
JOHN ST
BRYN GLAS
CWM FFOES
DALE VIEW
THE GRAIG
GWELFOR
HEOL SHON
HEOL CASTELL
CEFN RD
Bryn-Bach
FARM RD
2
PO
BRYN TERR
Ballarat
PH
PH
TY FRY RD
Cefn Cribwr Prim Sch
HEOL GOEDOG
GREENMEADOW
Recn Gd
Cefn Cross
Rockfield Farm
M4
TY-ISAF RD
Cefncribwr Wood
Ty'n-y-caeau
Ty'n-y-caeau
1
Tyfry Farm
Pren-Pêr
Tir-Hir
M4
Lluest Fawr
82

85 A B 86 C D 87 E F

149
129

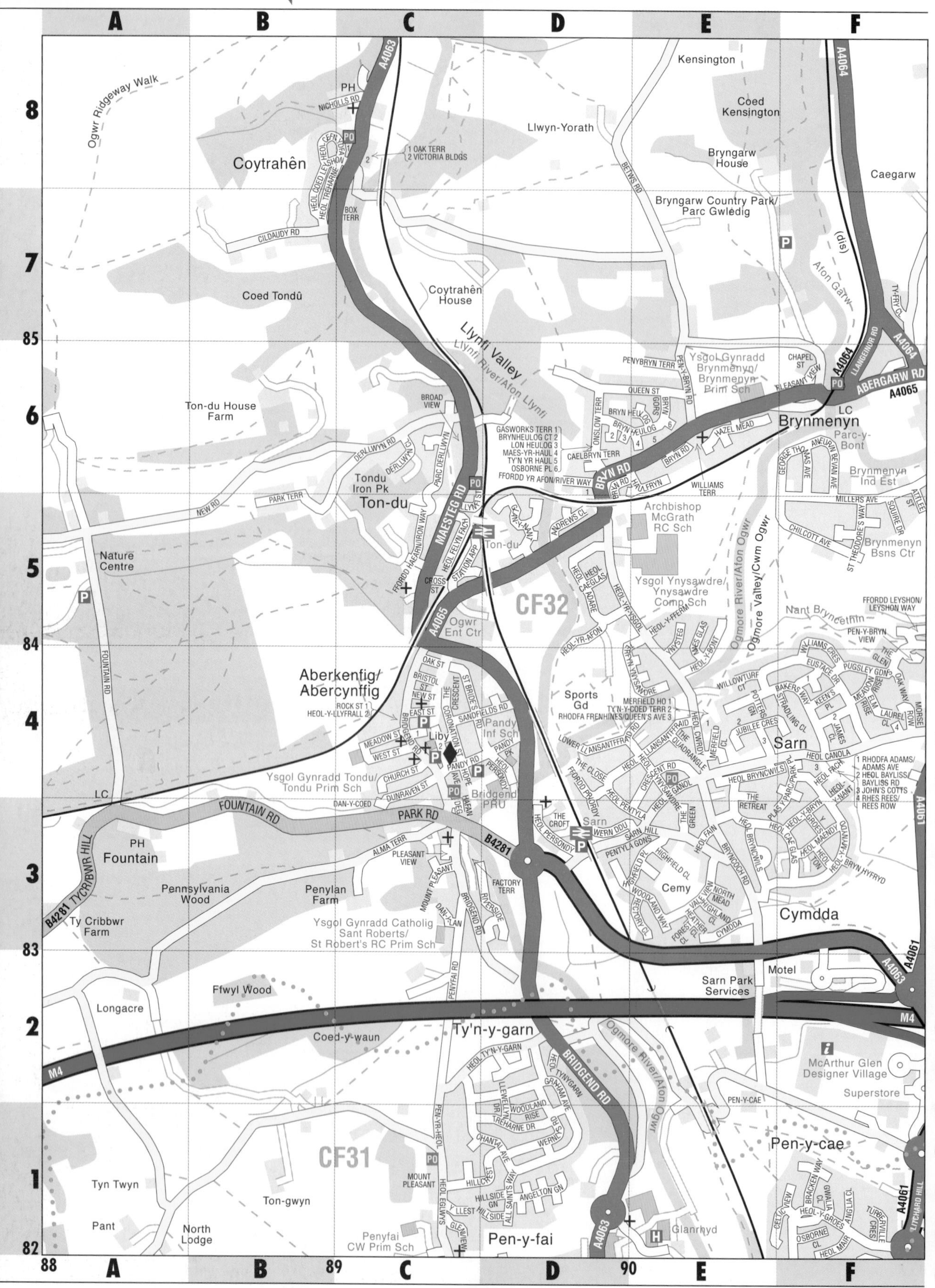

149
168

130
152

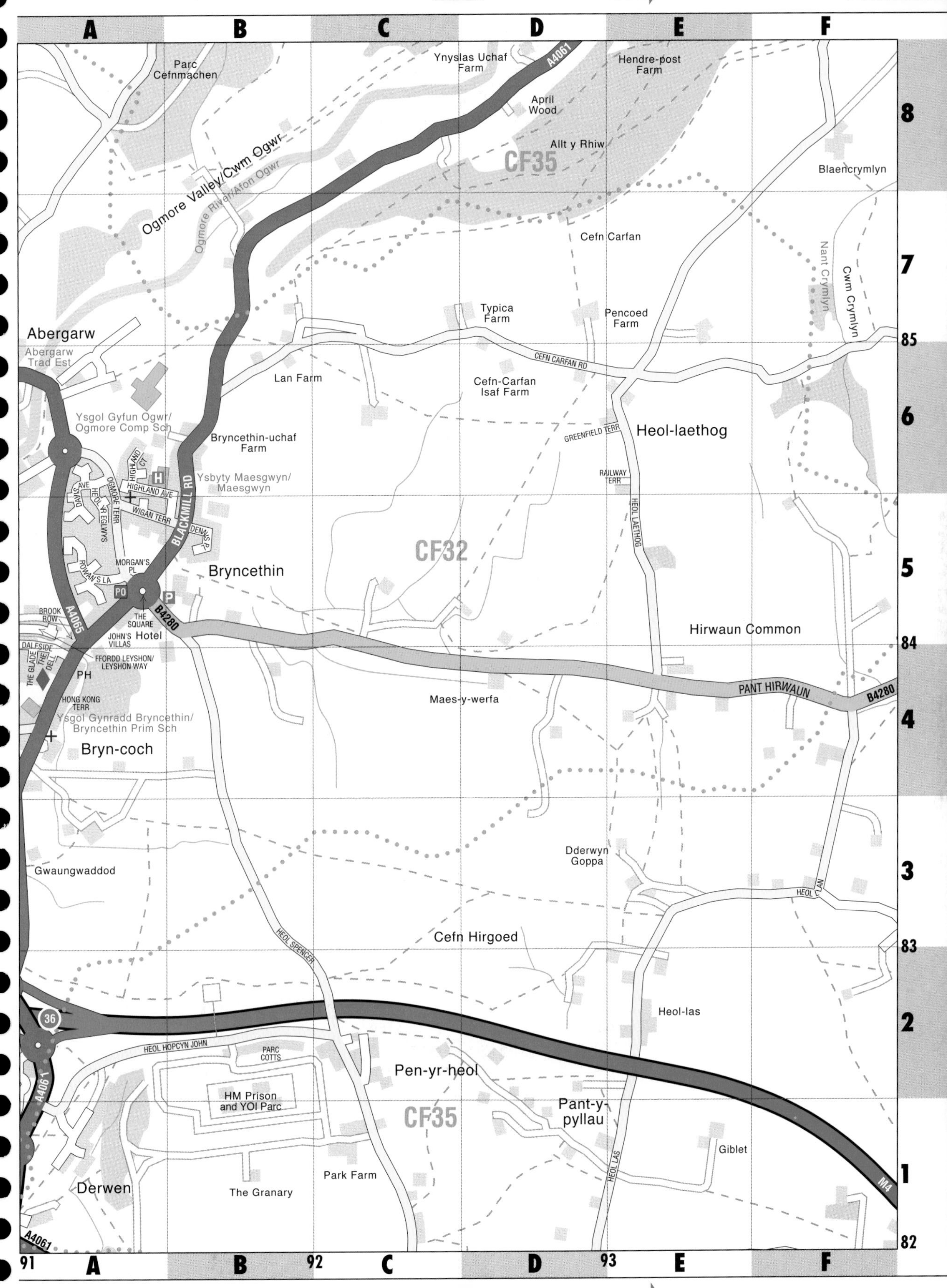

169
152

151
131

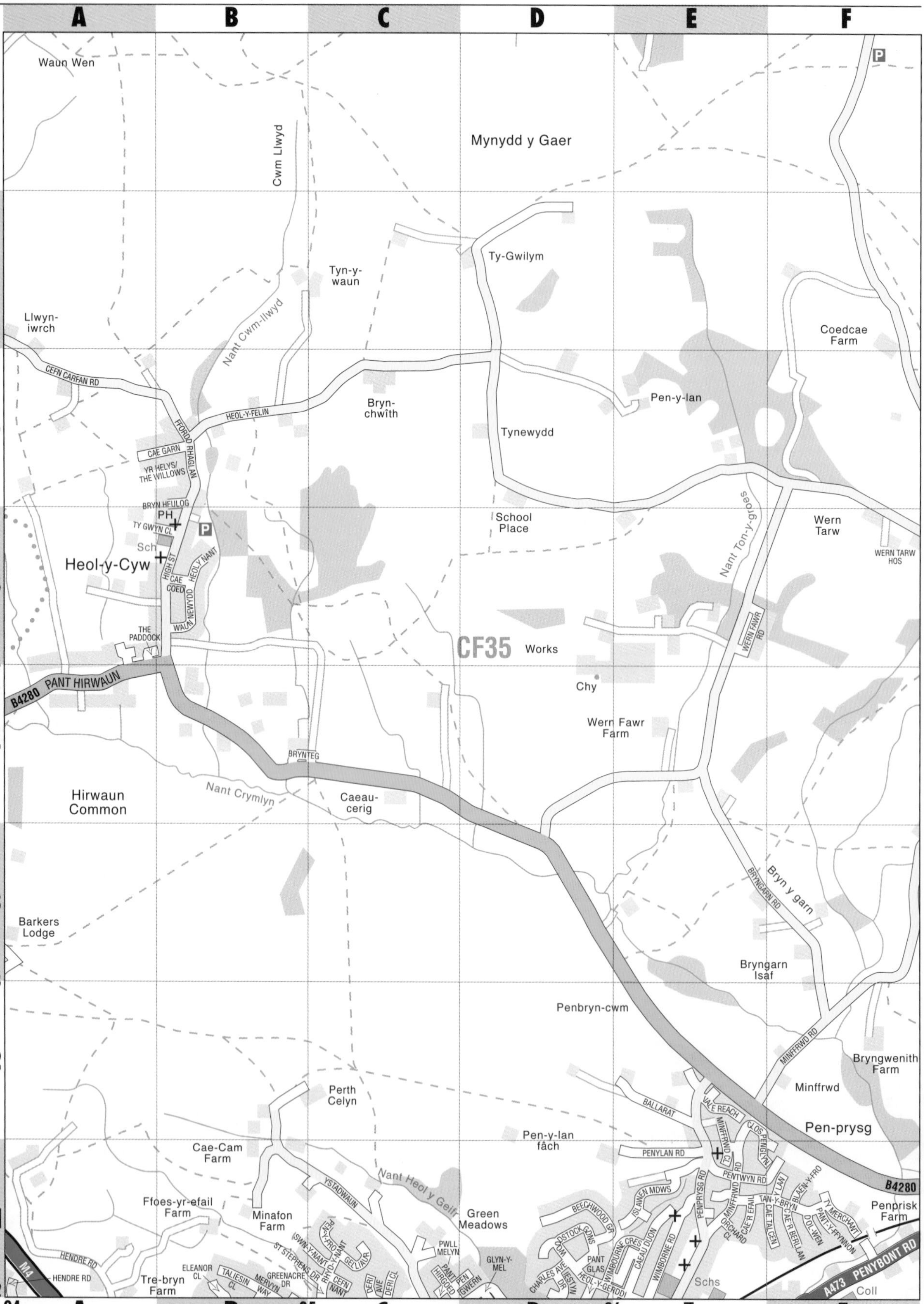

151
170

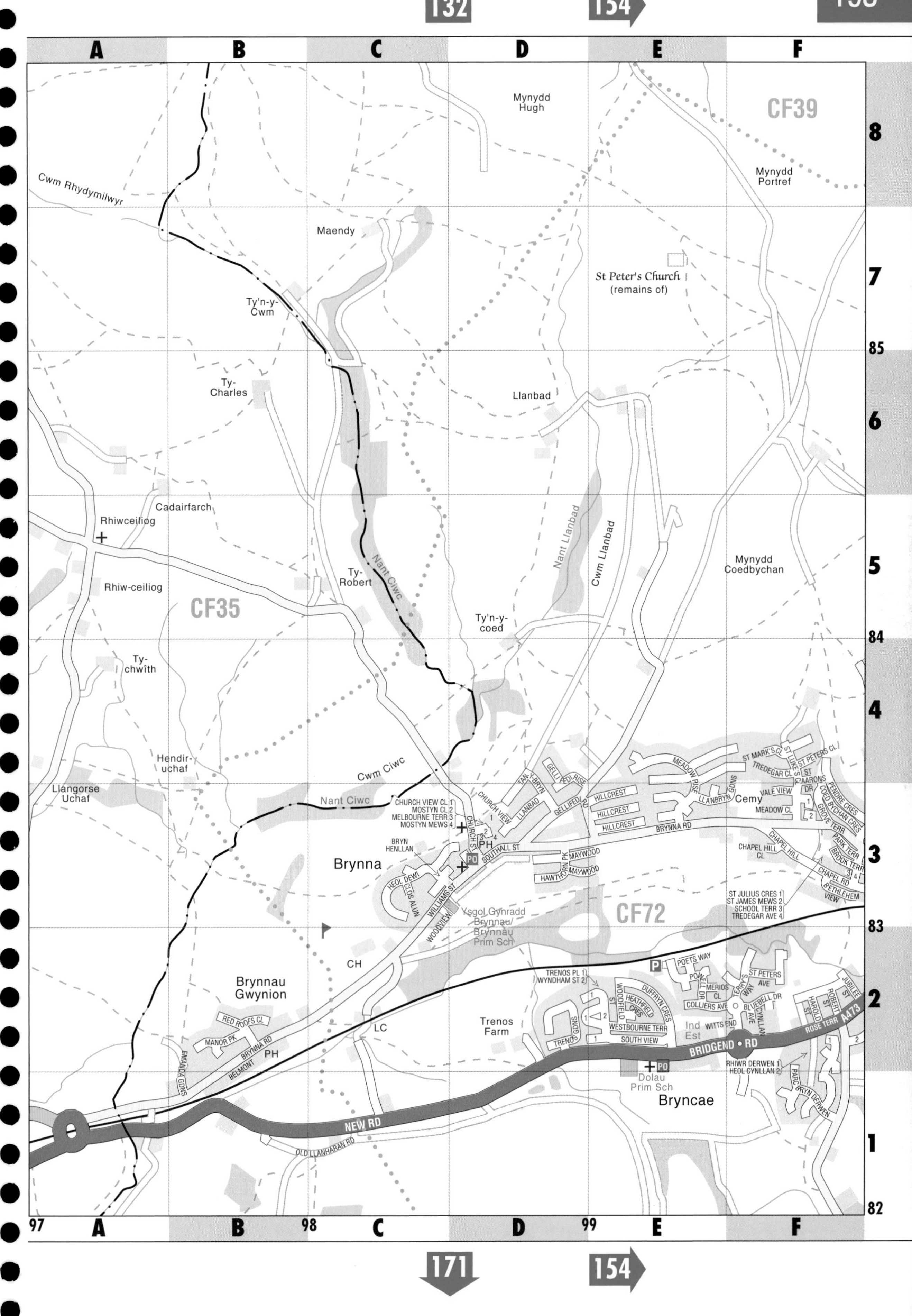
132
154
A
B
C
D
E
F
Mynydd Hugh
CF39
Mynydd Portref
Cwm Rhydymilwyr
Maendy
St Peter's Church (remains of)
Ty'n-y-Cwm
Ty-Charles
Llanbad
Cadairfarch
Rhiwceiliog
Nant Llanbad
Cwm Llanbad
Mynydd Coedbychan
Ty-Robert
Nant Ciwc
Rhiw-ceiliog
CF35
Ty'n-y-coed
Ty-chwith
Hendir-uchaf
Cwm Ciwc
Llangorse Uchaf
Nant Ciwc
Brynna
Cemy
CF72
Ysgol Gynradd Brynnau/ Brynnau Prim Sch
CH
Brynnau Gwynion
Trenos Farm
Ind Est
LC
PH
BRIDGEND RD
NEW RD
OLD LLANHARAN RD
Dolau Prim Sch
Bryncae
A473
ROSE TERR
HILLCREST
BRYNNA RD
MEADOW RISE
SOUTHALL ST
MAYWOOD
HAWTHORN PK
WILLIAMS ST
WOODVIEW
HEOL DEWI
CLOS ALUN
CHURCH VIEW CL 1
MOSTYN CL 2
MELBOURNE TERR 3
MOSTYN MEWS 4
BRYN HENLLAN
ST JULIUS CRES 1
ST JAMES MEWS 2
SCHOOL TERR 3
TREDEGAR AVE 4
TRENOS PL 1
WYNDHAM ST 2
POETS WAY
WESTBOURNE TERR
SOUTH VIEW
RHIWR DERWEN 1
HEOL CYNLLAN 2
RED ROOFS CL
MANOR PK
BELMONT
EMANDA GDNS
CHAPEL HILL CL
VALE VIEW
MEADOW CL
TREDEGAR CL
ST MARK'S CL
8
7
85
6
5
84
4
3
83
2
1
82
97
98
99
171
154

153
133

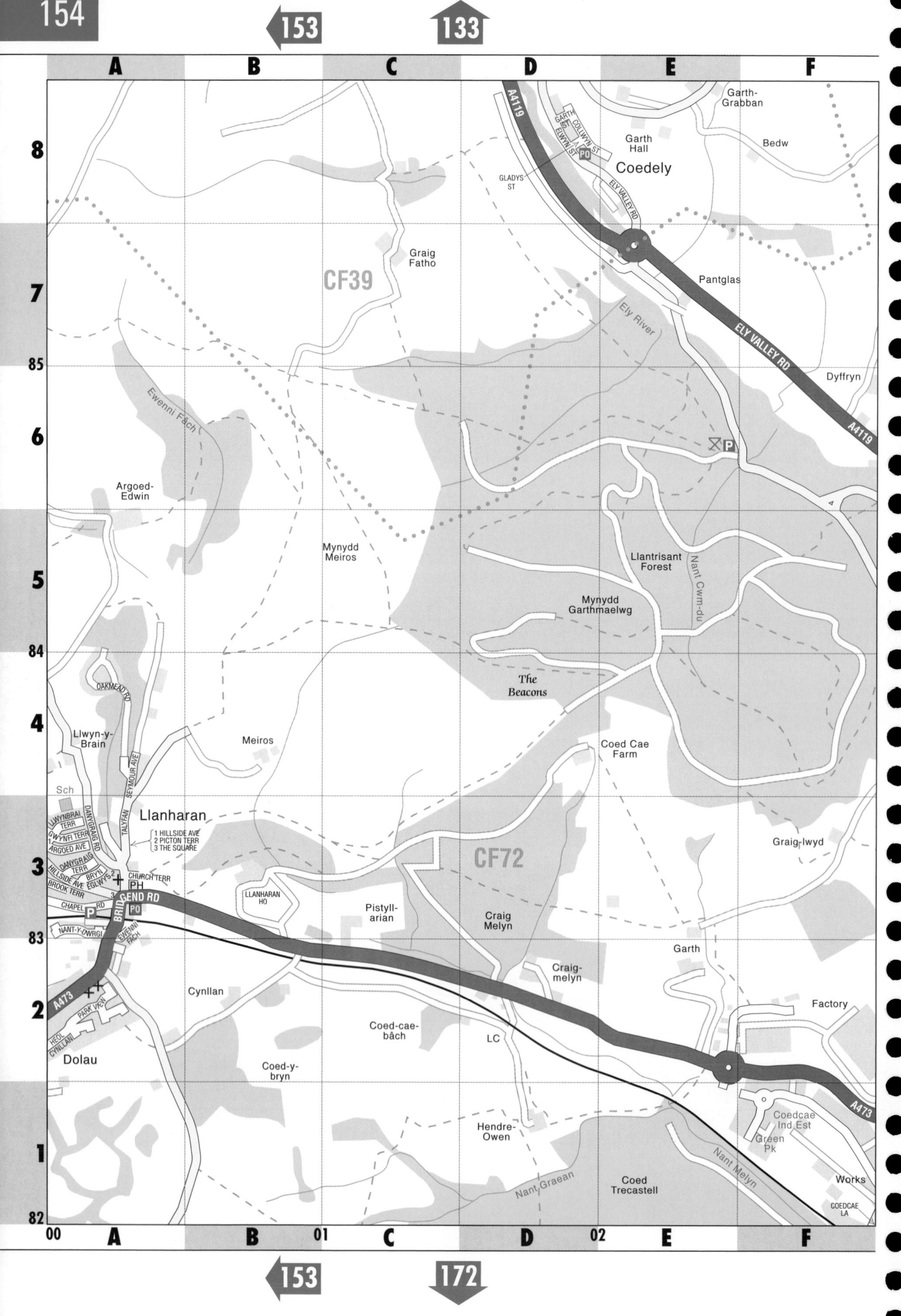
A
B
C
D
E
F
8
7
85
6
5
84
4
3
83
2
1
82
00
01
02
A4119
GARTH ST
COLWYN ST
ELWYN ST
PO
Garth-
Grabban
Garth
Hall
Bedw
Coedely
GLADYS ST
ELY VALLEY RD
Graig
Fatho
CF39
Pantglas
Ely River
ELY VALLEY RD
Dyffryn
A4119
Ewenni Fach
P
Argoed-
Edwin
Mynydd
Meiros
Llantrisant
Forest
Nant Cwm-du
Mynydd
Garthmaelwg
The
Beacons
OAKMEAD RD
Llwyn-y-
Brain
Meiros
Coed Cae
Farm
SEYMOUR AVE
Sch
Llanharan
TALYFAN
LLWYNBRAI TERR
DANYGRAIG RD
GWYNFI TERR
ARGOED AVE
DANYGRAIG TERR
HILLSIDE AVE
BRYN EGLWYS
BROOK TERR
CHAPEL RD
1 HILLSIDE AVE
2 PICTON TERR
3 THE SQUARE
CHURCH TERR
PH
BRIDGEND RD
PO
CF72
Graig-lwyd
LLANHARAN HO
Pistyll-
arian
Craig
Melyn
NANT-Y-DWRGI
EWENNI FACH
Garth
Craig-
melyn
A473
PARK VIEW
Cynllan
Factory
HEOL CYNLLAN
Coed-cae-
bâch
LC
Dolau
Coed-y-
bryn
Coedcae
Ind Est
Green
Pk
A473
Hendre-
Owen
Nant Melyn
Nant Graean
Coed
Trecastell
Works
COEDCAE LA

134
156

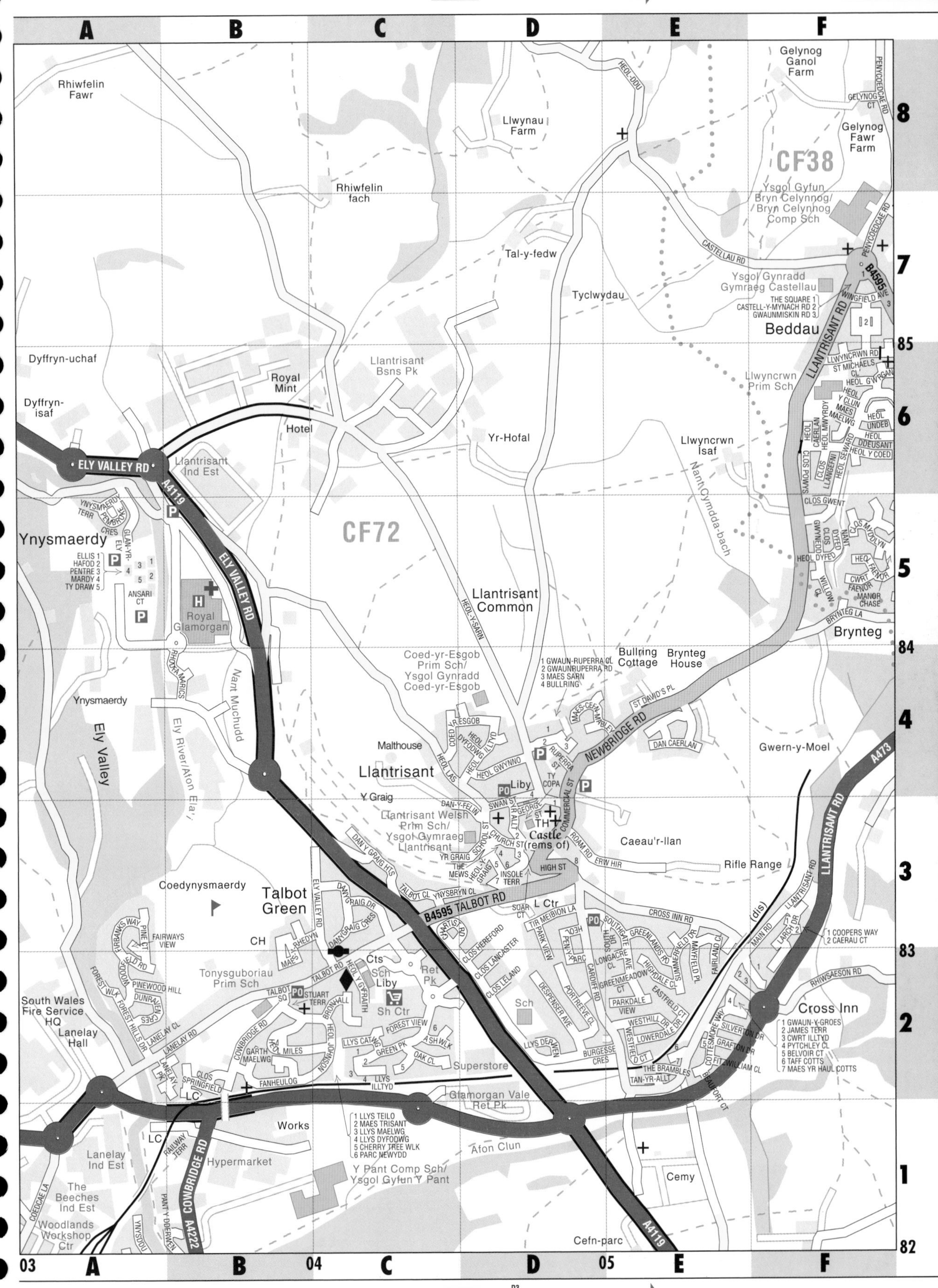

D3
1 HIGH ST
2 CASTLE ST
3 HEOL PENMAEN
4 SUNNY BANK
5 HEOL-Y-BEILIAU
6 CERIDWEN TERR
7 HEOL STICIL-Y-BEDDAU
8 LLANTRISANT HOS

173
156

155
135

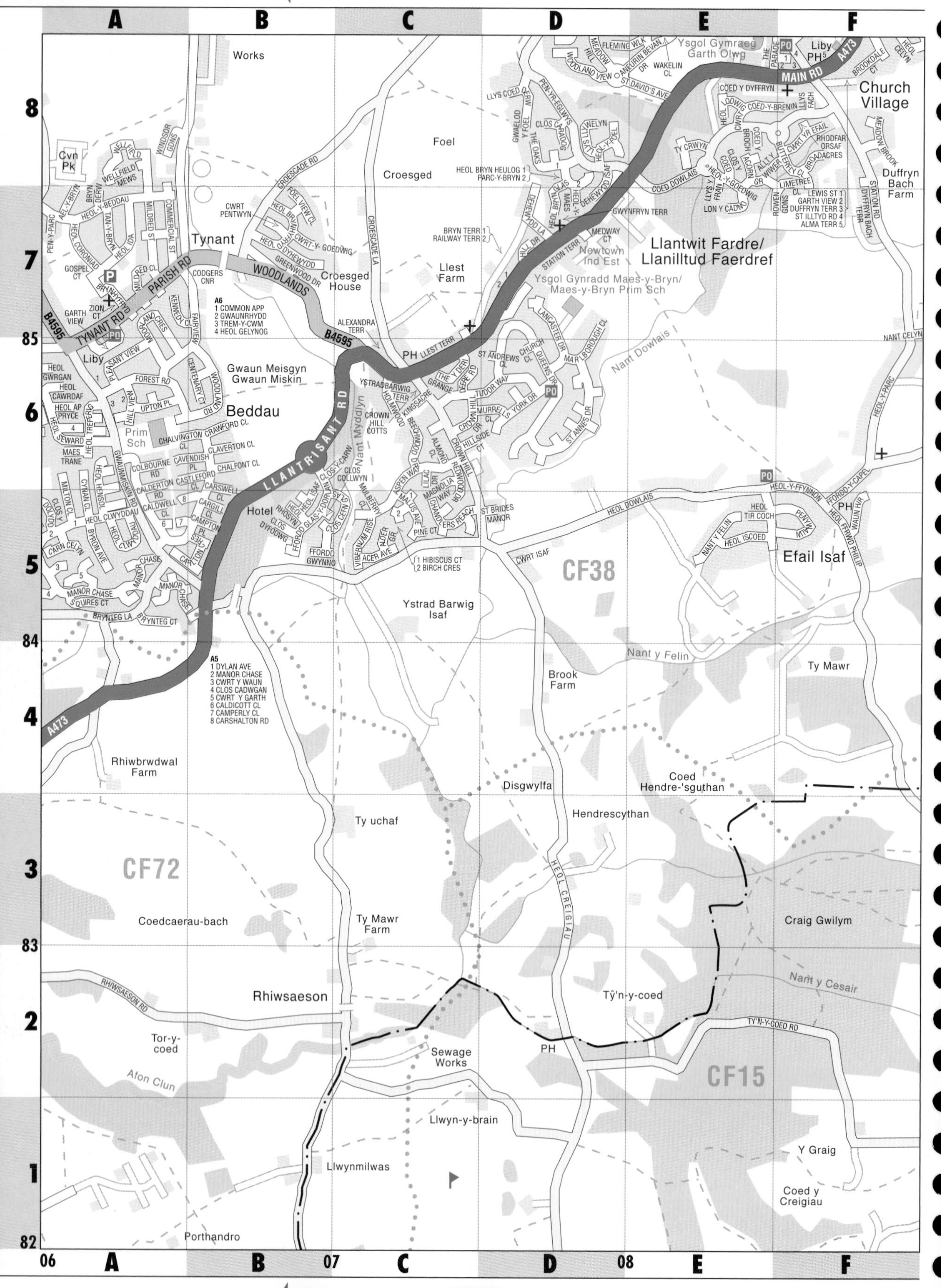

155
174

136
158

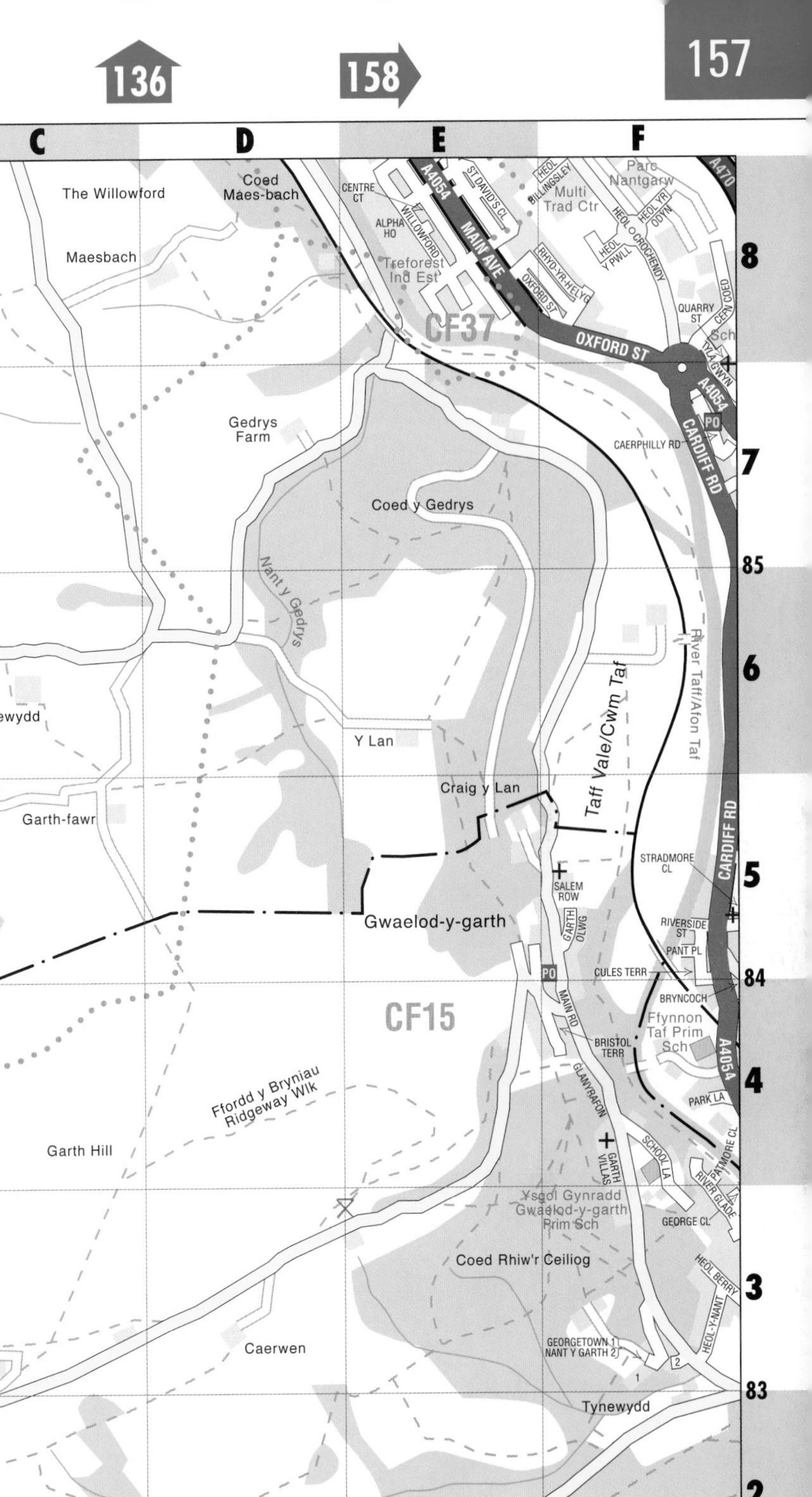

175
158

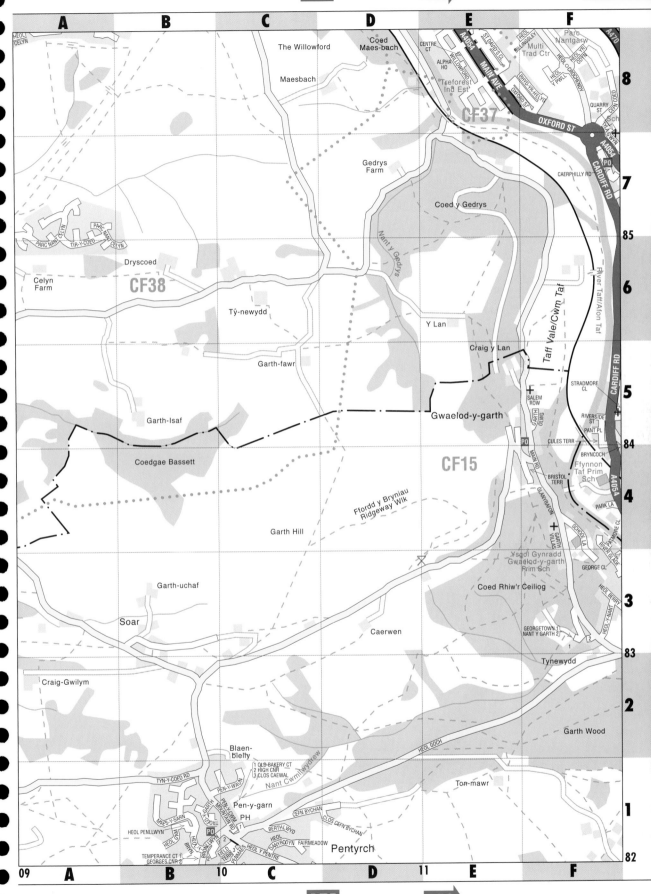

157 137

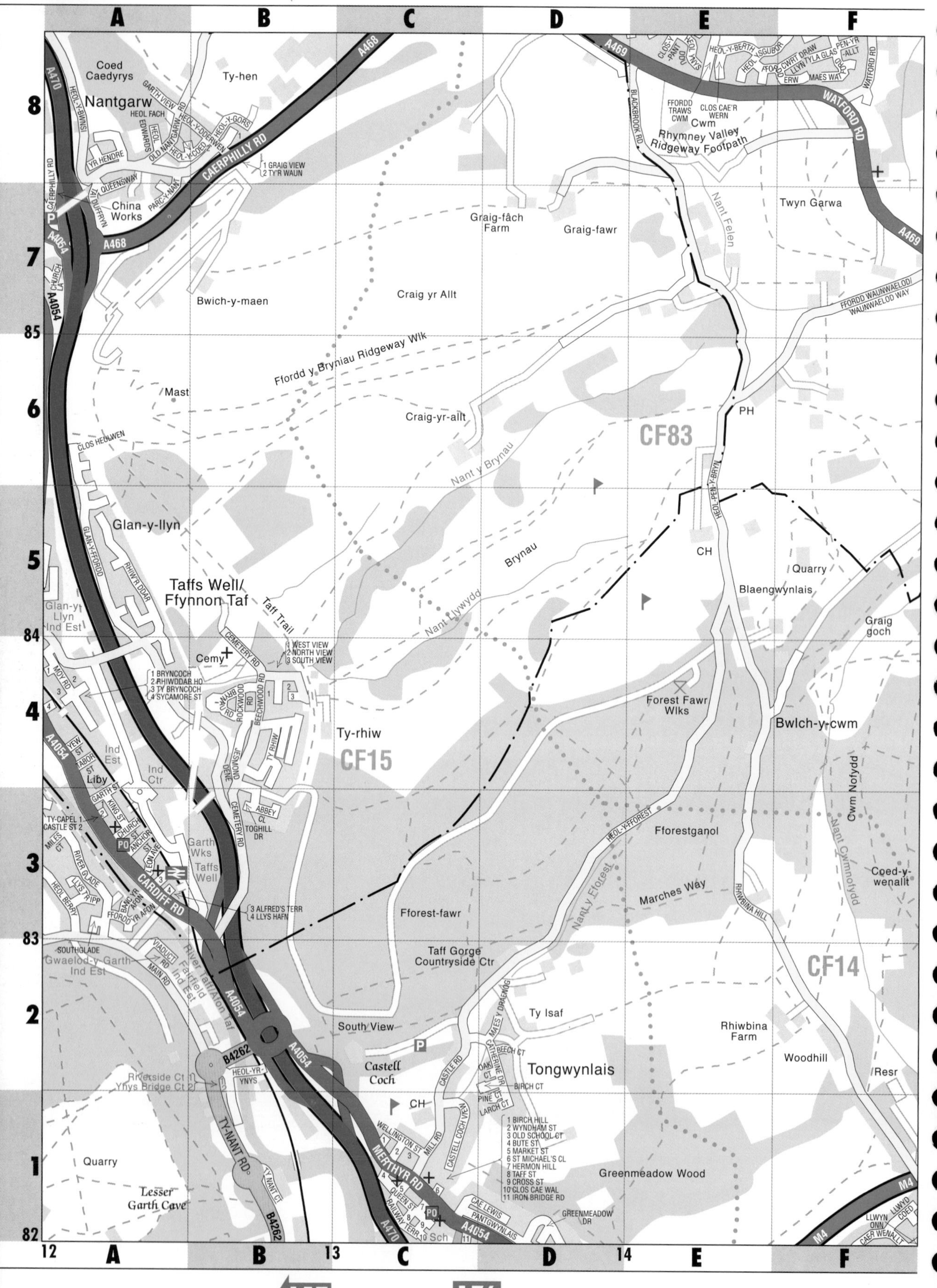

157 176

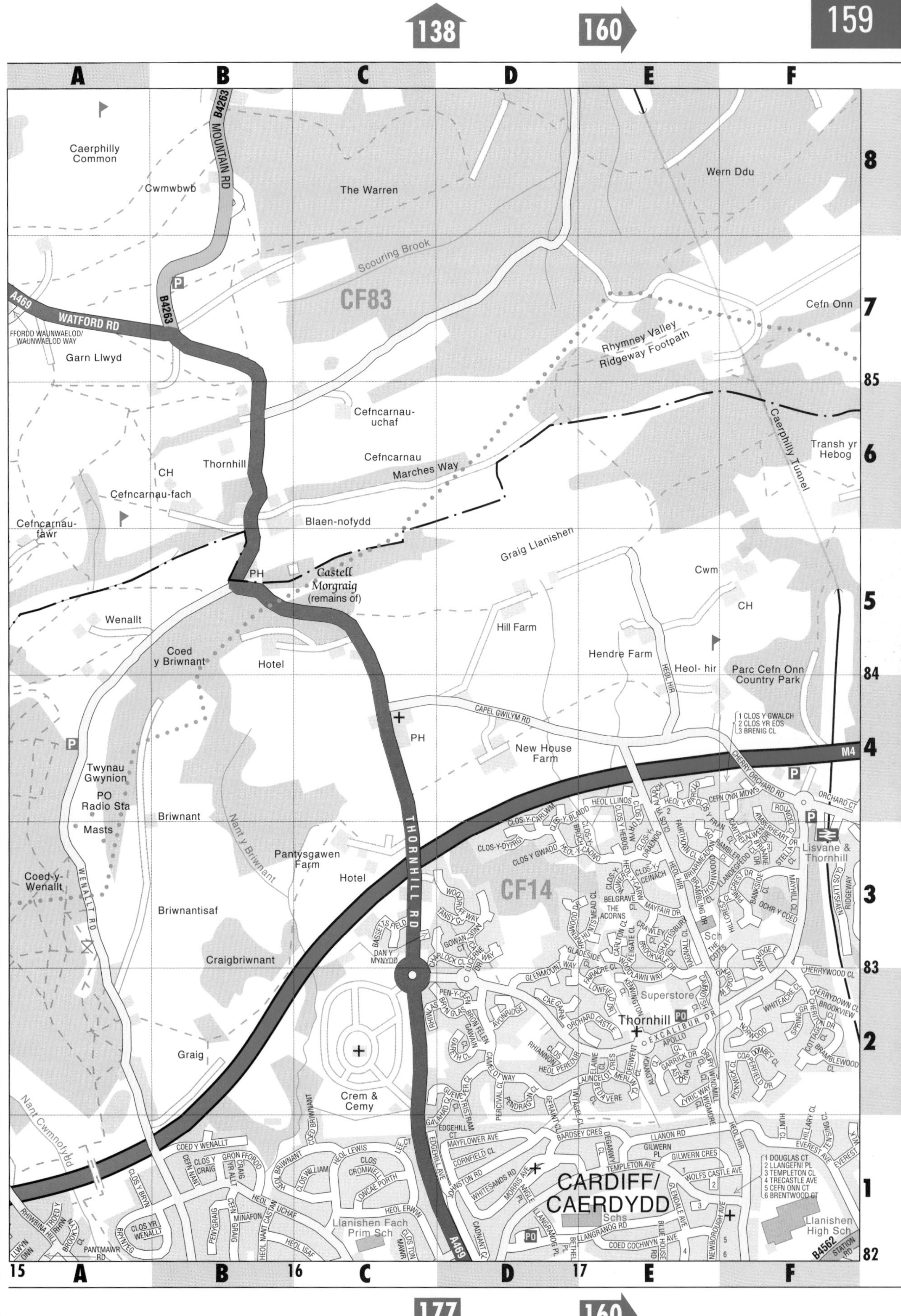

138
160
Caerphilly Common
Cwmwbwb
MOUNTAIN RD
B4263
The Warren
Wern Ddu
Scouring Brook
CF83
A469
WATFORD RD
FFORDD WAUNWAELOD/ WAUNWAELOD WAY
Garn Llwyd
Cefn Onn
Rhymney Valley Ridgeway Footpath
Cefncarnau-uchaf
Caerphilly Tunnel
Transh yr Hebog
Thornhill
CH
Cefncarnau
Marches Way
Cefncarnau-fach
Cefncarnau-fawr
Blaen-nofydd
Graig Llanishen
PH
Castell Morgraig (remains of)
Cwm
CH
Wenallt
Hill Farm
Hendre Farm
Coed y Briwnant
Hotel
Heol- hir
Parc Cefn Onn Country Park
CAPEL GWILYM RD
New House Farm
M4
Twynau Gwynion
PO Radio Sta
Masts
Briwnant
Nant y Briwnant
THORNHILL RD
Pantysgawen Farm
Hotel
Coed-y-Wenallt
WENALLT RD
Briwnantisaf
CF14
Craigbriwnant
Graig
Crem & Cemy
Nant Cwmnofydd
Lisvane & Thornhill
Superstore
Thornhill
Sch
CARDIFF/ CAERDYDD
Schs
Llanishen Fach Prim Sch
Llanishen High Sch
1 CLOS Y GWALCH
2 CLOS YR EOS
3 BRENIG CL
1 DOUGLAS CT
2 LLANGEFNI PL
3 TEMPLETON CL
4 TRECASTLE AVE
5 CEFN ONN CT
6 BRENTWOOD CT
CHERRY ORCHARD RD
ORCHARD CT
HEOL LLINOS
CLOS-Y-CARLWM
CLOS-Y-DYFRGI
CLOS Y GWADD
HEOL HIR
BELGRAVE CL
THE ACORNS
MAYFAIR DR
GLADESIDE
GLENMOUNT WAY
GOWAN CT
DAN Y MYNYDD
PEN-Y-CEFN
CAE GARN
ORCHARD CASTLE
EXCALIBUR DR
CAMELOT WAY
PENDRAGON CL
HEOL PEREDUR
LAUNCELOT CRES
MERLIN CL
GEDEHILL CT
EDGEHILL AVE
MAYFLOWER AVE
CORNFIELD CL
JOHNSTON RD
WHITESANDS RD
BARDSEY CRES
LLANON RD
GILWERN CRES
TEMPLETON AVE
WOLFS CASTLE AVE
GLENDALE AVE
NEWBOROUGH AVE
BLUE HOUSE RD
COED COCHWYN AVE
LLANGRANOG RD
CADNANT CL
COED Y WENALLT
HEOL LEWIS
HEOL BRIWNANT
HEOL ERWIN
HEOL ISAF
HEOL NANT CASTAN
MINAFON
PANTMAWR RD
RHIWBINA HILL
CLOS Y BRYN
CLOS YR WENALLT
HUNT CL
HILLARY CL
EVEREST AVE
STATION RD
B4562
PO
177
160
A B C D E F
8 7 85 6 5 84 4 3 83 2 1 82
15 16 17

159
139

A B C D E F

8
7
85
6
5
84
4
3
83
2
1
82

Crynant Farm
Coed Cefn-Onn
Rhymney Valley Ridgeway Footpath
Marches Way
Nant y Cwm
Ty'n-y-graig
Coed Coesau-whips
Nant Cwm-crynant
Coed Llwyn-celyn
Coed Coesau-whips Forest Walk
Llwyncelyn
Llwyncelyn
CF83
CF3
Pant Glas
Coed Gwineu
Coed y Graig
Pentwyn
Craig Llysfaen
Tai-mawr
The Mount
Coed y Coedcae
CEFN-PORTH RD
Springmeadow
Coed-bach
Brynhill Farm
Nant Fawr
RUDRY RD
PH
GRAIG RD
Cefn Porth
Fair Oak Farm
Pant Teg Farm
Nant-tyclraw-fach
The Hollies
Graig-llwyn
GRAIG-LLWYN RD
Wern Fawr
GRAIG LLWYN RD
CEFN MABLY RD
M4
Coed-y-llan
CHURCHILL CL
SABLE CL
JADE CL
THE COURT
BLOSSOM DR
LODGE CL
HOLLY GR
CARDINAL DR
Yellow-wells
Nant Ty-draw
CF14
Llan Farm
CORNFLOWER
CHERRY ORCHARD RD
MOUNT ST DENYS
THE PADDOCK
CHERRY ORCHARD RD
MILLBROOK PK
CHERRY TREE CL
Church House Farm
Ty-yn-y-Berllan
M4
RIDGEWAY
HEOL CEFN ON
HEOL ST DENYS
GRAIG VIEW
LLWYN Y PIA RD
CEFN MABLY RD
IVYDALE
MILLFIELD
HOLMESIDE
MILL PL
ROWAN WAY
Llysfaen Prim Sch
Liby
Malthouse Wood
THE BEECHES 1
THE LAURELS 2
COTSWOLD AVE
PO
CHURCH RD
RIDGEWAY
ROSEWOOD CL
LARCH GR
THE COPPINS
THE SPINNEY
PLAS Y DELYN
PH
Maes y Felin
MILLWOOD
LONG HOUSE CL
HEOL-Y-DELYN
CHURCH CL
Malthouse
THE OAKS
LISVANE HO
HILLCOT CL
CLOS COED-Y-DAFARN
Mill Farm
MAERDY LA
ST MELLONS RD
THE WOODLANDS
Lisvane/ Llys Faen
COEDYDAFARN
Nant Glandulas
CROES CADARN
PARKWALL RD
MILLRACE CL
CLOS MELIN DWR
MILL RD
OLD MILL RD
CRANFORD
BARNWOOD
ASHFORD
BARBROOK CL
CWRT CEFN
BUCKINGHAM CL
BALMORAL CL
Maerdy
CLOS NANT COSLECH 1
OAKLEAFE DR 2
AMBERGATE DR 3
AMBER CL 4
AMBLECOTE CL 5
PIPKIN CL 6
HUNTINGDON DR 7
FELSTED CL 8
CLOS ALYN 9
SINDERCOMBE CL 10
DUNGARVAN DR 11
CLOS NANT Y COR 12
AMBERWOOD CL 13
ALLT Y WENNOL 14
EVENWOOD CL 15
HEOL TY FFYNNON 16
B4562
MAES Y HEDYDD
CLOS NANT MWLAN
FALFIELD CL
MILLHEAD
GLEAT
GRAND
CHARTWELL DR
PORTLAND PL
TANGLEWOOD CL
LISVANE RD
MILL CL
WOODSIDE CT
MILLGATE
Prim Sch
Llangattock
CLOS NANT GLASWG
CLAVERTON WAY
LEACROFT PL
HEOL PONTPRENNAU
CLOS NANT Y CWM
CLOS CWM DU
HEOL GLANDULAIS
CWM CREUNANT
CLOS NANT DDU
CLOS CWM
CROESCADARN RD
NASEBY CL
CROFTA
WOOD CL
Corpus Christi RC High Sch
CF23
Bryngolau
TY-DRAW RD
CRAWBOURNE WAY
WISLEY PL
CHAMOMILE
BUTTERFIELD DR
CLOS DOL
HEULOG
MAES BRITH
CLOS Y GARN
CLOS Y FFYNNON
P
Llanishen
MARION CT
NORTH RISE
SOUTH RISE
B4562
STATION RD
THE GLADE
CARDIFF/ CAERDYDD
GWERN RHUDDI RD
ALDERBROOK
FOREST OAK CL
HAMPTON CRES W
HAMPTON CRES E
THE FAIRWAY
NASTURTIUM WAY
TARRAGON WAY
FELBRIGG CRES
GAULDEN GR
OAKFORD CL
OAKMEAD CL
AMBROOKE CL
ALMOND DR
THE MALTINGS
THE FARTHINGS
Sch
NEWLANDS CT
WEST RISE
RISE
BEVERLEY CL
BLACK OAK RD
SUTTON GR
PEPPERMINT DR
DARTINGTON DR
PENTWYN RD
BUPA H

18 A B 19 C D 20 E F

159
178

140
162

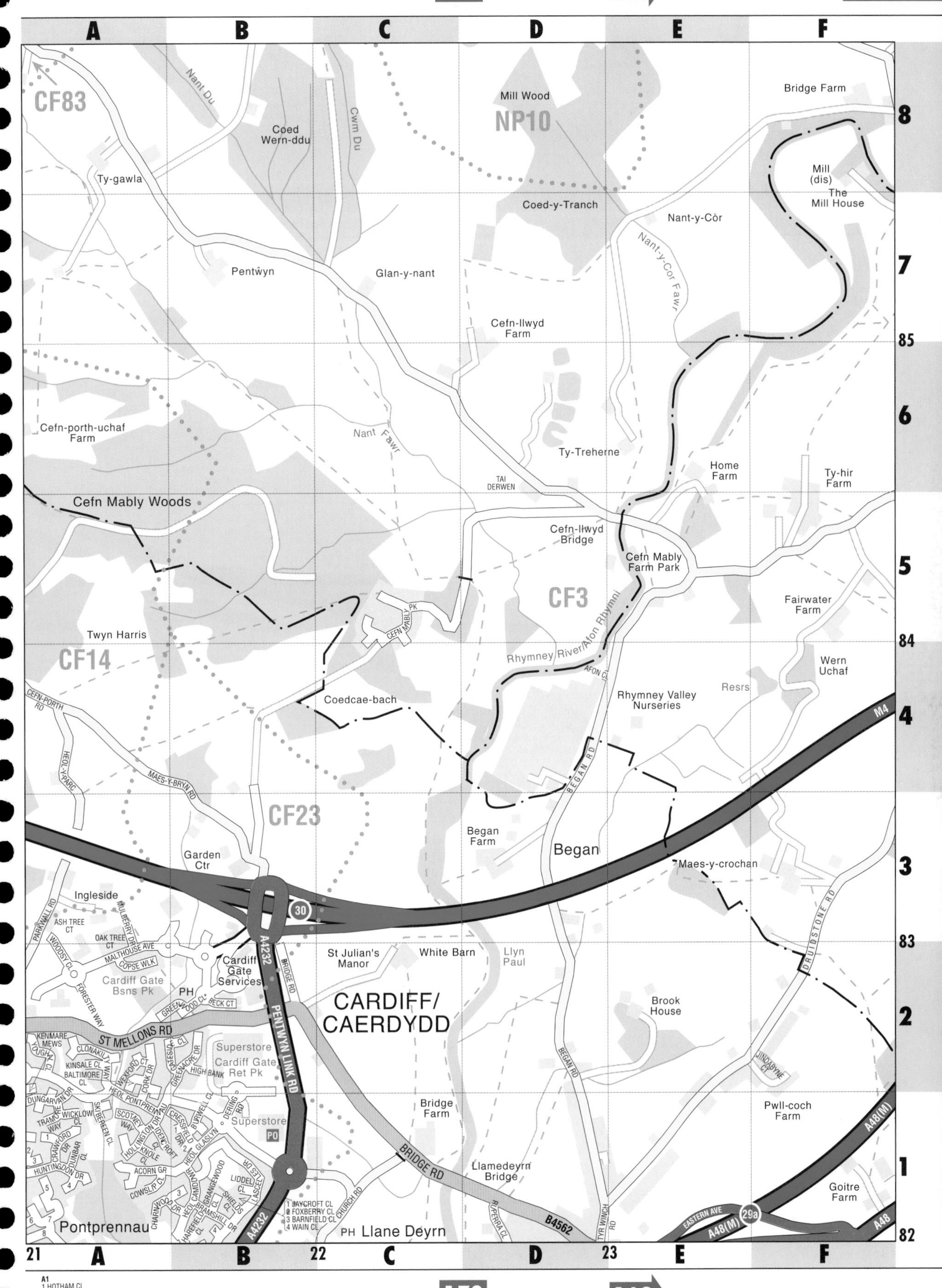

A1
1 HOTHAM CL
2 FELSTED CL
3 IRETON CL
4 LILBURNE CL
5 ENBOURNE DR
6 PIPKIN CL
7 BLACKBERRY WAY
8 CROESCADARN CL

179
162

161
141

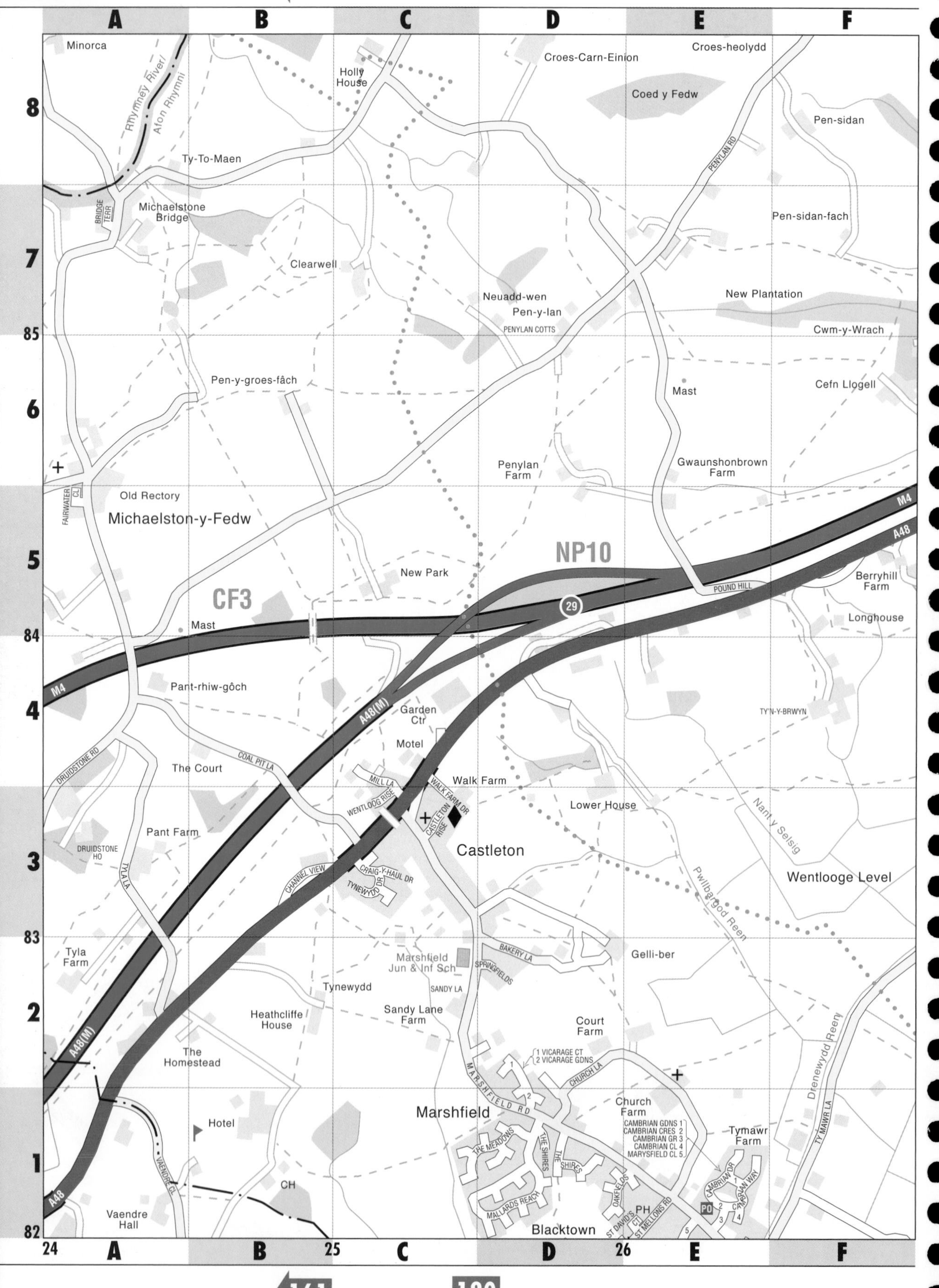

161
180

142
164

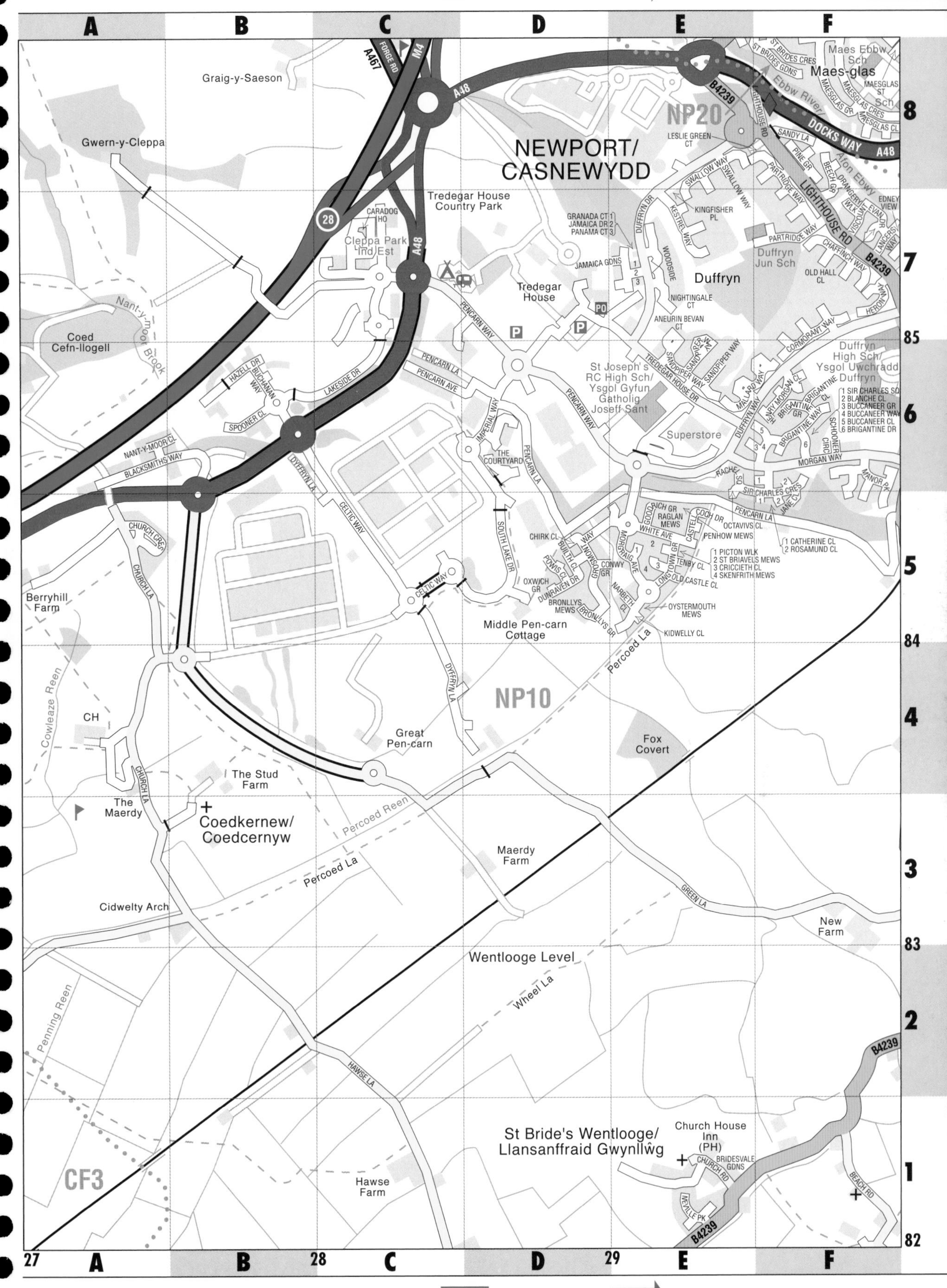

181
164

163
143

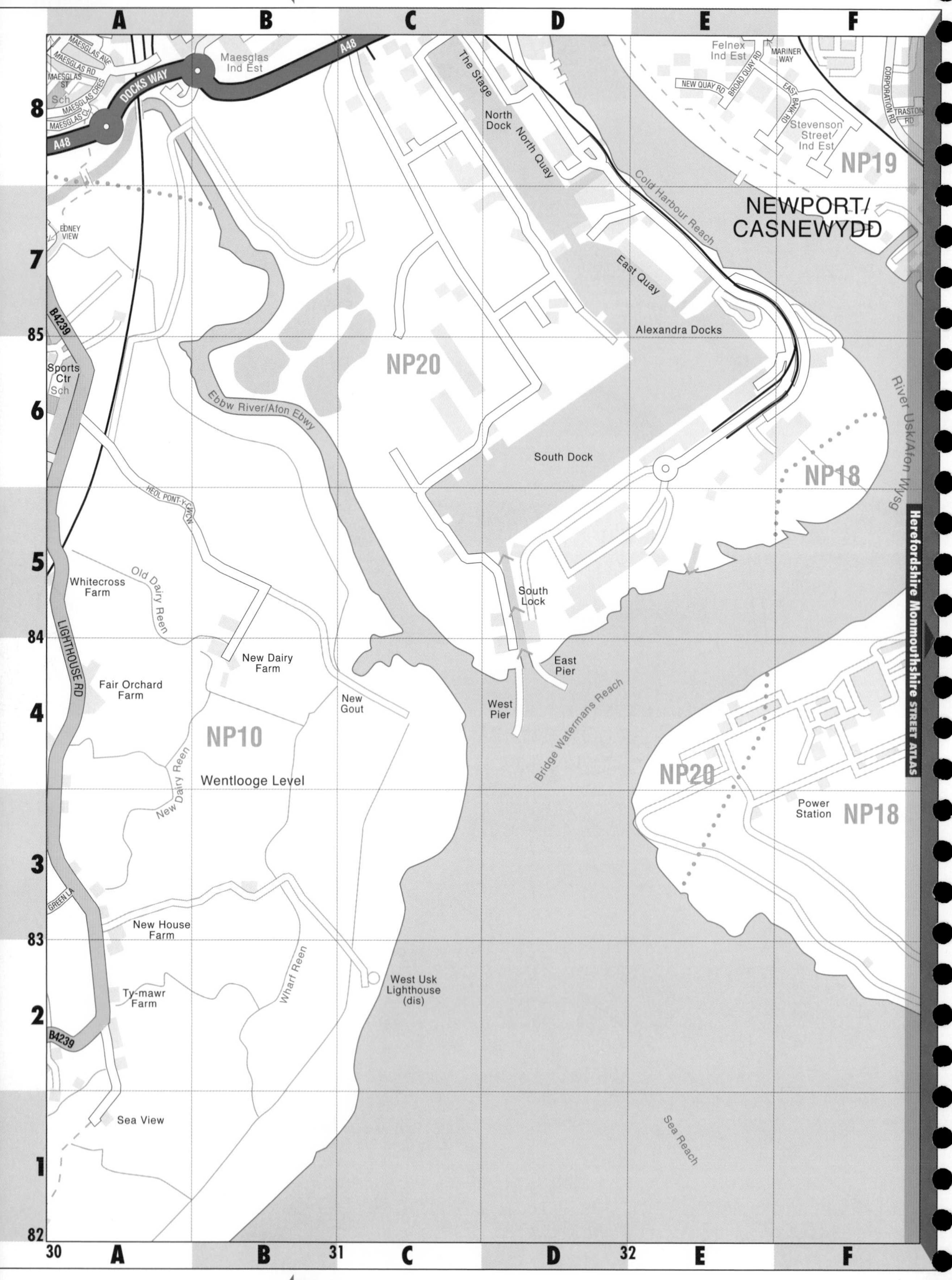
A
B
C
D
E
F
8
7
85
6
5
84
4
3
83
2
1
82
30
31
32
Maesglas Ind Est
DOCKS WAY
A48
MAESGLAS AVE
MAESGLAS RD
MAESGLAS ST
MAESGLAS CRES
MAESGLAS CL
Sch
EDNEY VIEW
B4239
Sports Ctr
Sch
The Stage
North Dock
North Quay
Felnex Ind Est
BROAD QUAY RD
MARINER WAY
NEW QUAY RD
EAST BANK RD
Stevenson Street Ind Est
CORPORATION RD
TRASTON RD
NP19
NEWPORT/
CASNEWYDD
Cold Harbour Reach
East Quay
Alexandra Docks
NP20
Ebbw River/Afon Ebwy
South Dock
River Usk/Afon Wysg
NP18
HEOL PONT-Y-CWCW
Whitecross Farm
Old Dairy Reen
LIGHTHOUSE RD
South Lock
New Dairy Farm
Fair Orchard Farm
East Pier
West Pier
New Gout
Bridge Watermans Reach
NP10
Wentlooge Level
New Dairy Reen
NP20
Power Station
NP18
GREEN LA
New House Farm
Wharf Reen
West Usk Lighthouse (dis)
Ty-mawr Farm
B4239
Sea View
Sea Reach
Herefordshire Monmouthshire STREET ATLAS

163

146 147 166

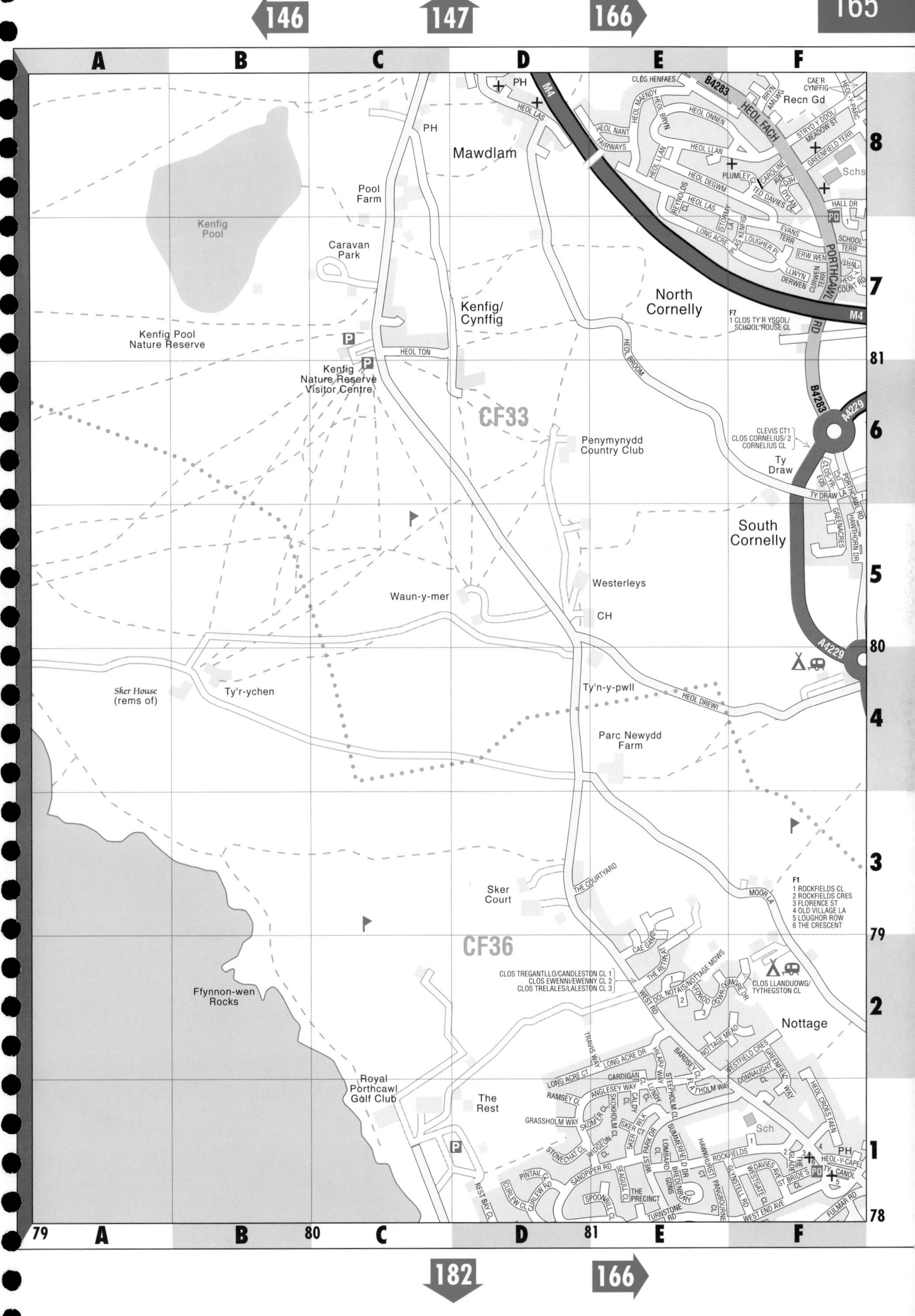

182 166

165
148

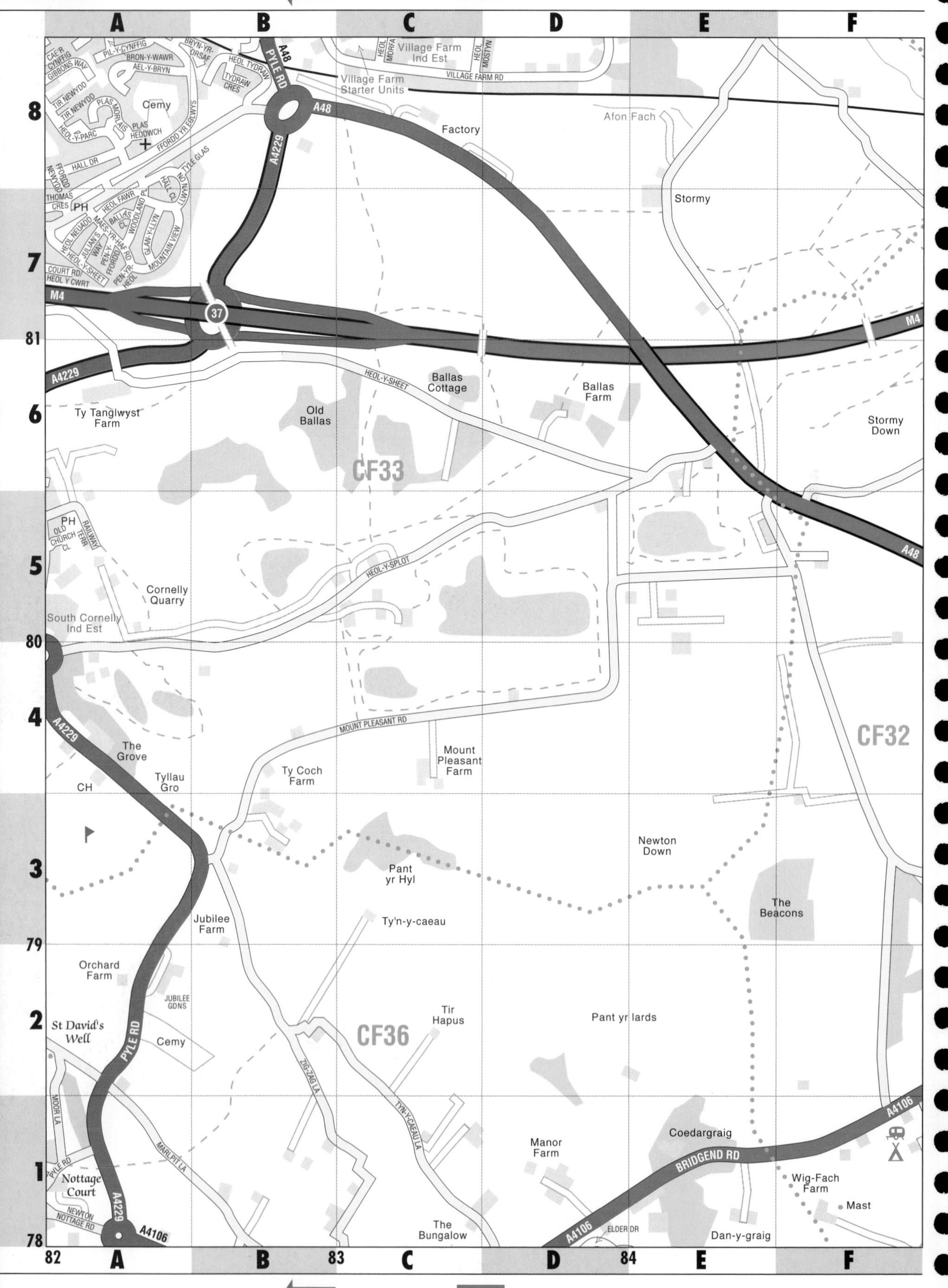

165
183

149
168

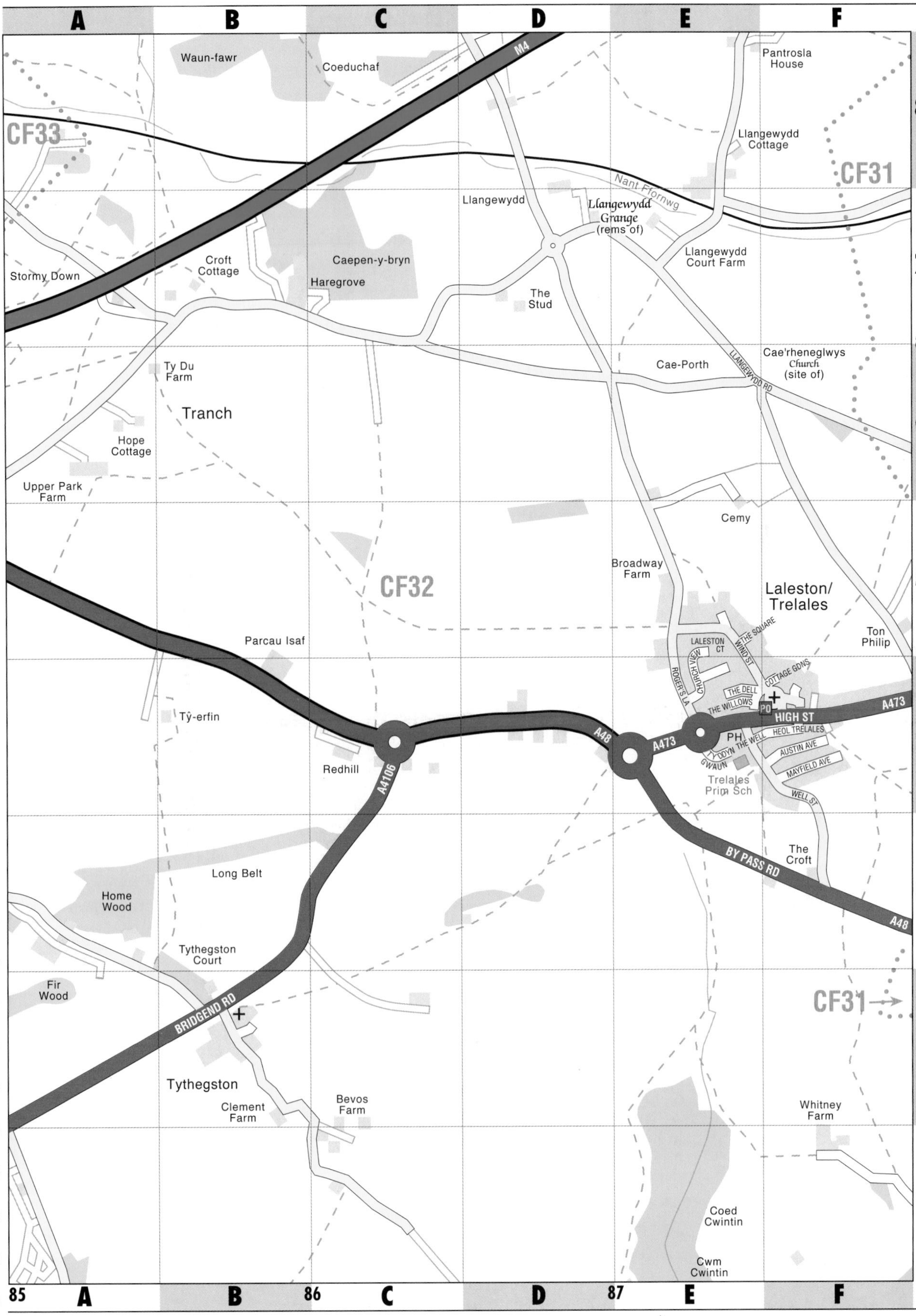

A B C D E F
8 7 81 6 5 80 4 3 79 2 1 78
85 86 87
M4
Waun-fawr
Coeduchaf
Pantrosla House
Llangewydd Cottage
CF33
CF31
Nant Ffornwg
Llangewydd
Llangewydd Grange (rems of)
Stormy Down
Croft Cottage
Caepen-y-bryn
Haregrove
Llangewydd Court Farm
The Stud
Ty Du Farm
Cae-Porth
LLANGEWYDD RD
Cae'rheneglwys Church (site of)
Tranch
Hope Cottage
Upper Park Farm
Cemy
Broadway Farm
CF32
Laleston/ Trelales
Ton Philip
Parcau Isaf
LALESTON CT
THE SQUARE
WIND ST
CHURCH VIEW
ROGER'S LA
COTTAGE GDNS
THE DELL
THE WILLOWS
PO
HIGH ST
A473
Tŷ-erfin
A48
A473
PH
TY ODYN
THE WELL
HEOL TRELALES
GWAUN
AUSTIN AVE
MAYFIELD AVE
Redhill
A4106
Trelales Prim Sch
WELL ST
BY PASS RD
The Croft
Long Belt
Home Wood
A48
Tythegston Court
Fir Wood
CF31
BRIDGEND RD
Tythegston
Clement Farm
Bevos Farm
Whitney Farm
Coed Cwintin
Cwm Cwintin

167
150

F5
1 GREYFRIARS CT
2 BROOK CT
3 BOULEVARD DE VILLENAVE O'ORON

F6
1 CAEFFATRI CL/ CLOS CAEFFATRI

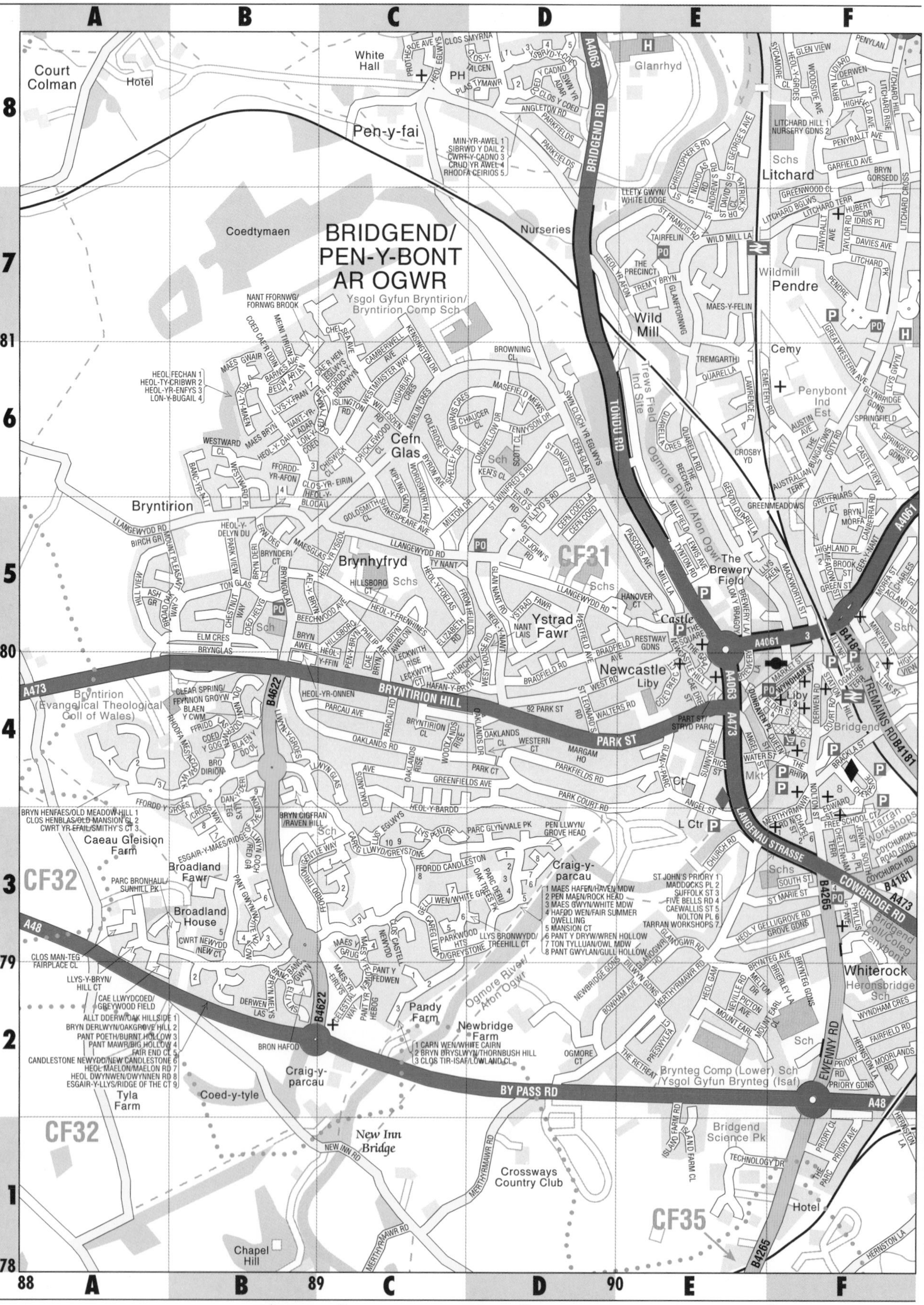

A B C D E F

8
7
81
6
5
80
4
3
79
2
1
78

BRIDGEND/
PEN-Y-BONT
AR OGWR

Court Colman
Hotel
White Hall
PH
Pen-y-fai
Glanrhyd
Coedtymaen
Nurseries
Litchard
Schs
Wildmill
Pendre
Wild Mill
Cemy
Penybont Ind Est
Ysgol Gyfun Bryntirion/ Bryntirion Comp Sch
Cefn Glas
Sch
Trews Field Ind Site
Ogmore River/Afon Ogwr
Bryntirion
Brynhyfryd
Schs
CF31
Ystrad Fawr
The Brewery Field
Castle
Newcastle
Liby
Bridgend
Mkt
L Ctr
Bryntirion (Evangelical Theological Coll of Wales)
Caeau Gleision Farm
Broadland Fawr
Broadland House
CF32
Craig-y-parcau
Pandy Farm
Newbridge Farm
Ogmore River/ Afon Ogwr
Tyla Farm
Coed-y-tyle
New Inn Bridge
Chapel Hill
Crossways Country Club
Bridgend Science Pk
CF35
Hotel
Whiterock
Heronsbridge Sch
Brynteg Comp (Lower) Sch/ Ysgol Gyfun Brynteg (Isaf)
Bridgend Coll/Coleg Penybont
Tarran Workshops
Sch

MIN-YR-AWEL 1
SIBRWD Y DAIL 2
CWRT-Y-CADNO 3
CRUD YR AWEL 4
RHODFA CEIRIOS 5

LITCHARD HILL 1
NURSERY GDNS 2

HEOL FECHAN 1
HEOL-TY-CRIBWR 2
HEOL-YR-ENFYS 3
LON-Y-BUGAIL 4

BRYN HENFAES/OLD MEADOW HILL 1
CLOS HENBLAS/OLD MANSION CL 2
CWRT YR EFAIL/SMITHY'S CT 3

1 MAES HAFEN/HAVEN MDW
2 PEN MAEN/ROCK HEAD
3 MAES GWYN/WHITE MDW
4 HAFOD WEN/FAIR SUMMER DWELLING
5 MANSION CT
6 PANT Y DRYW/WREN HOLLOW
7 TON TYLLUAN/OWL MDW
8 PANT GWYLAN/GULL HOLLOW

ST JOHN'S PRIORY 1
MADDOCKS PL 2
SUFFOLK ST 3
FIVE BELLS RD 4
CAEWALLIS ST 5
NOLTON PL 6
TARRAN WORKSHOPS 7

ALLT DDERW/OAK HILLSIDE 1
BRYN DERLWYN/OAKGROVE HILL 2
PANT POETH/BURNT HOLLOW 3
PANT MAWR/BIG HOLLOW 4
FAIR END CL 5
CANDLESTONE NEWYDD/NEW CANDLESTONE 6
HEOL MAELON/MAELON RD 7
HEOL DWYNWEN/DWYNNEN RD 8
ESGAIR-Y-LLYS/RIDGE OF THE CT 9

1 CARN WEN/WHITE CAIRN
2 BRYN DRYSLWYN/THORNBUSH HILL
3 CLOS TIR-ISAF/LOWLAND CL

88 A B 89 C D 90 E F

167
185

C3
1 MAES LLYSTEG/ FAIRCOURT MDW
2 TREM-Y-DYFFRYN/ VALLEY VIEW
3 CWRT BONT NEWYDD/ NEWBRIDGE CT
4 NANT Y WENNOL
5 MAES TRAWSCOED/ CROSSWOOD MDW

C3
6 MAES TAL COED/WOOD END MDW
7 TAI AFFRYN/HOUSES ON THE HILL
8 CLOS CASTELL COITY
9 LLYS WEN
10 LLYS COED

F4
1 LLYNFI ST
2 ODDFELLOWS' ST
3 ADARE ST
4 CROSS ST
5 CAROLINE ST/STRYD CAROLINE
6 The Rhiw Ctr
7 Nolton Arc
8 Brackla Street Ctr

151
170

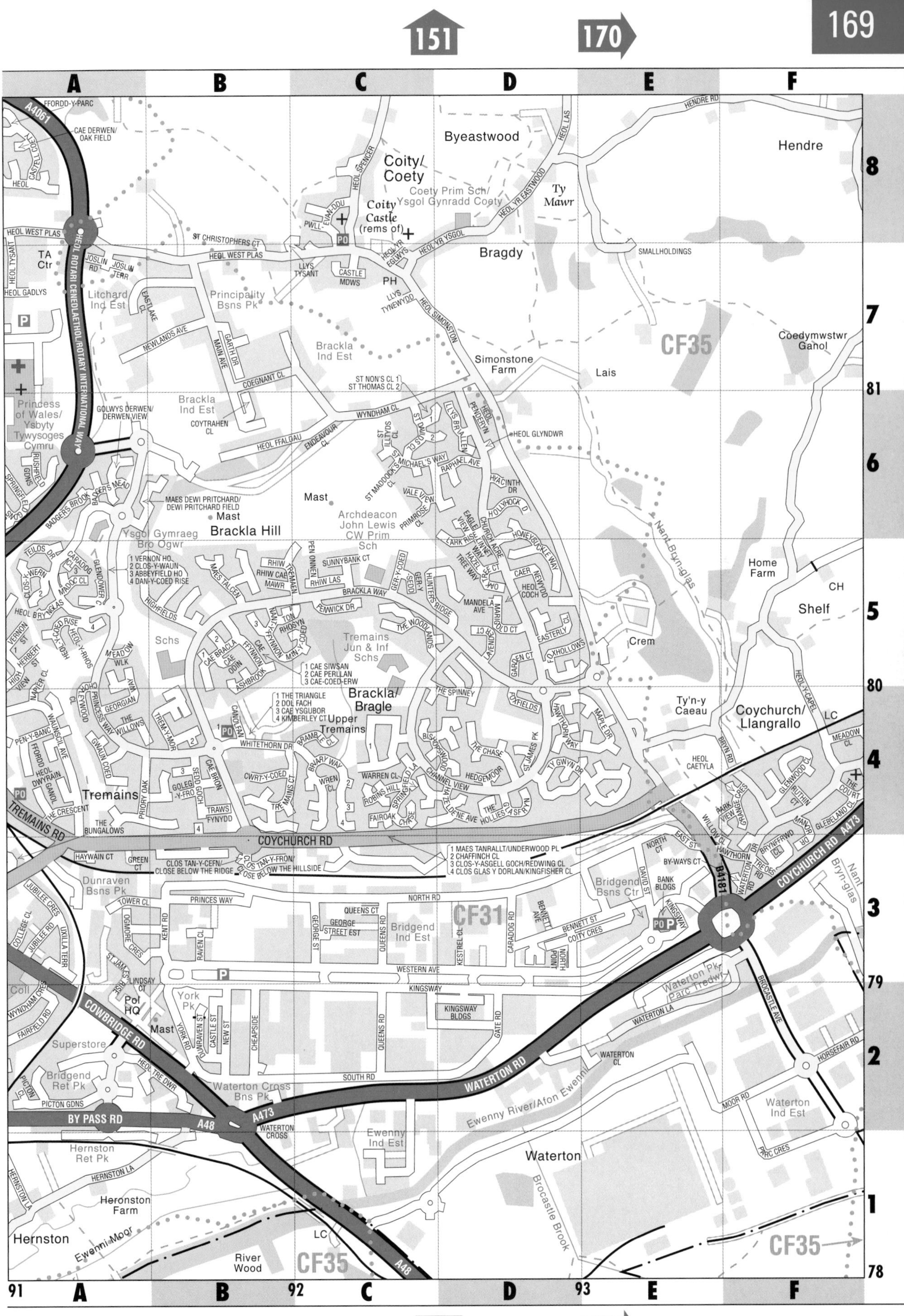

186
170

169
152

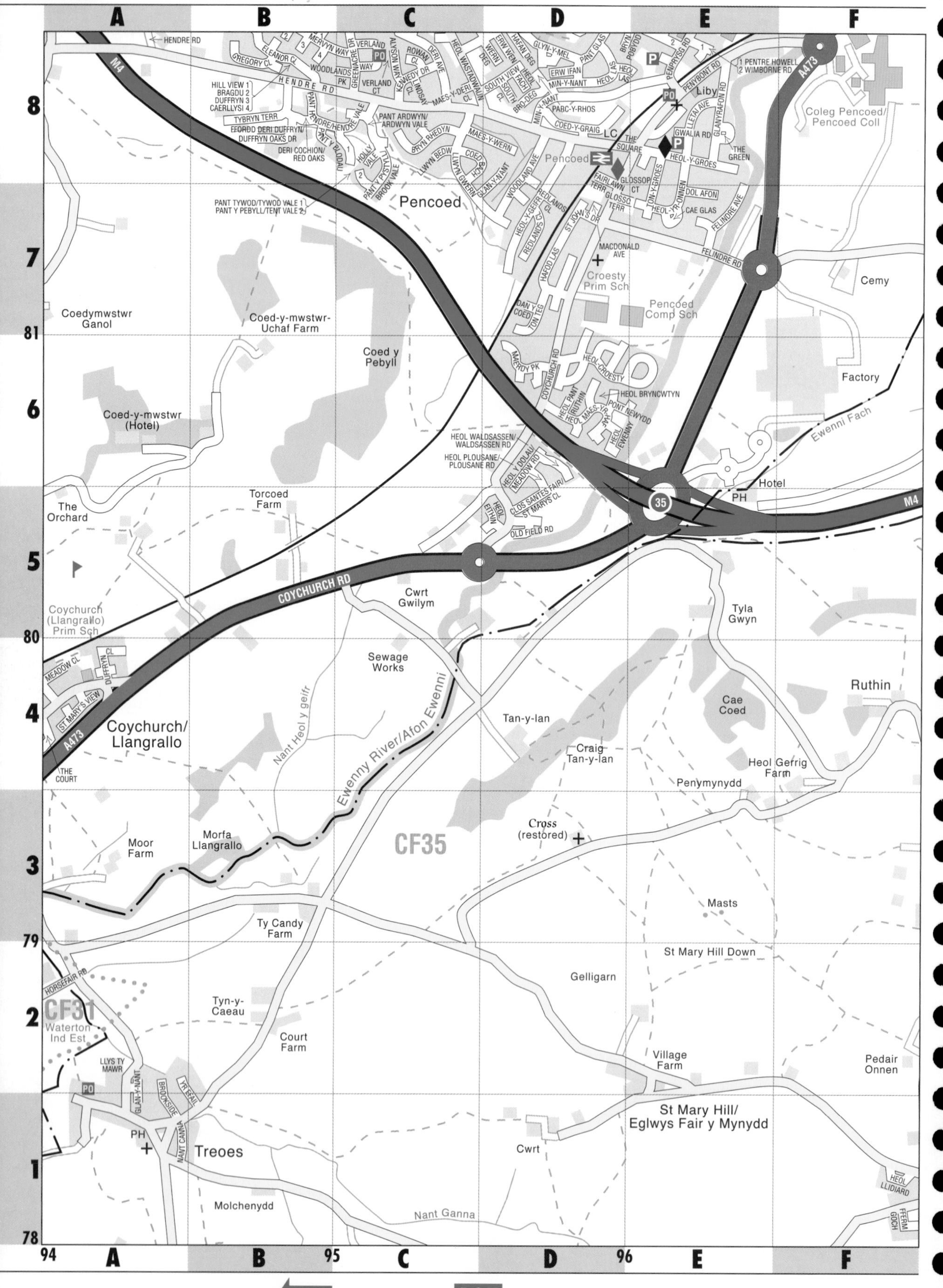

169
187

153
172

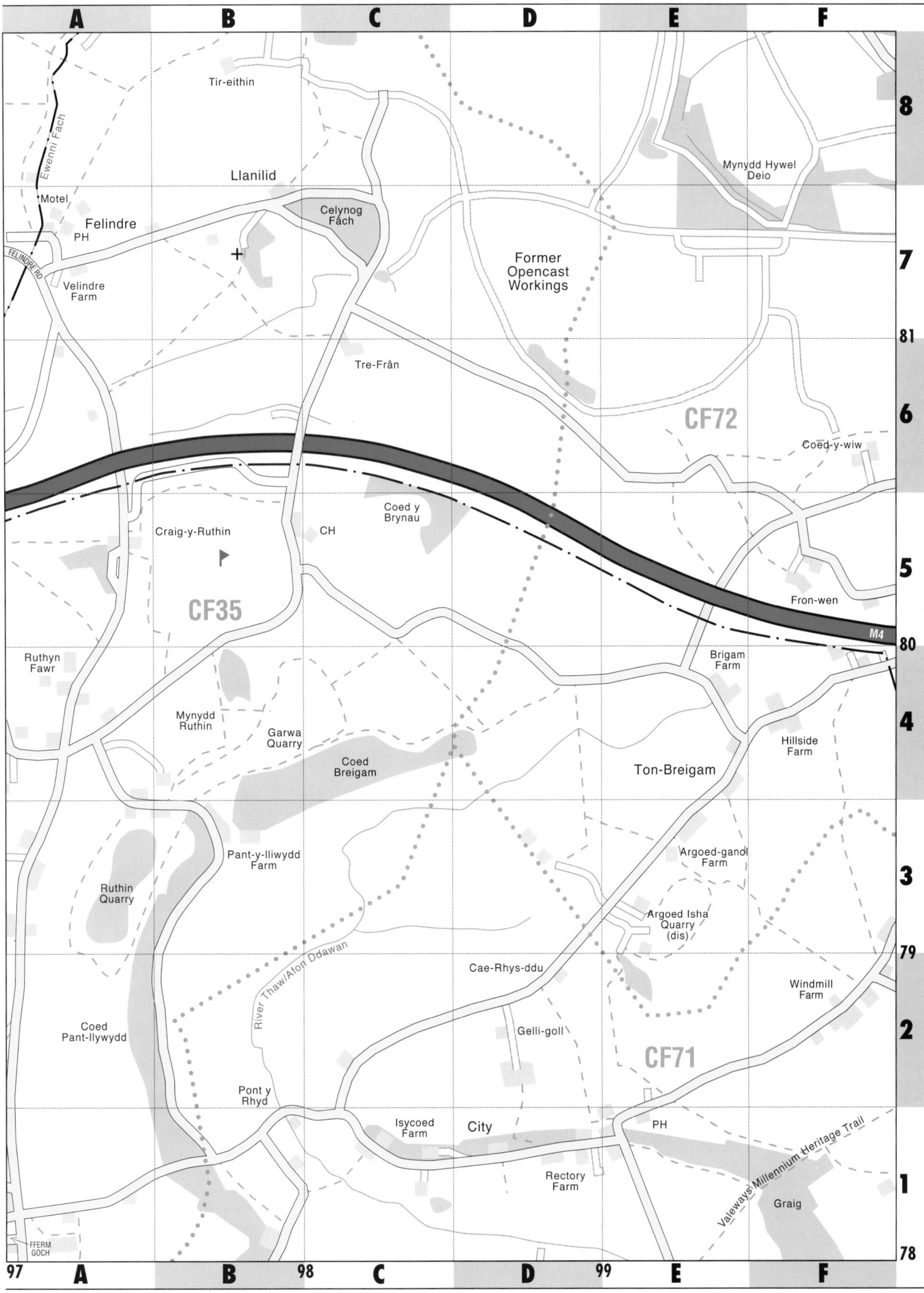

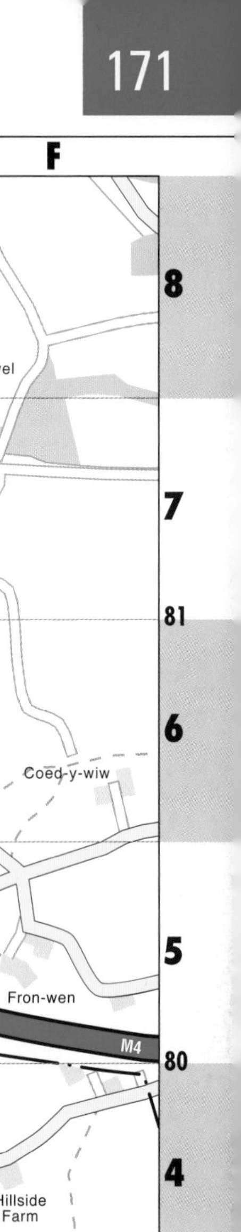

188
172

171
154

A B C D E F

Bryn Awel
Cwm Gran
Coed Trecastell
WOODLAND VILLA
WOODLAND TERR
PH
LC
GWAUN COTTS
LLANHARRY RD
TYLAGARW TERR
TYLE GARW
Ty'n-y-waun
Mast
Torgelli
Trecastell
Ty-du
Ty-draw
Tips (dis)
Nant Felin-fach
CLOS BRENIN
DANYBRYN
Brynsadler
CF72
Llechau Farm
1 CWRT LLECHAU
2 STATION TERR
3 PLAS-Y-ODYN
BRYN TERR
PADDOCKS CRES
Llwyna Farm
HIGH ST 1
TALYGARN DR 2
A4222
PH
LLANHARRY RD
FFORDD TRECASTELL
The Elms Farm
CASTELL-Y-MWNWS
M4
PO
THE PATCH
LLYS JOSEPH
Llanharry
TY ISAF
TYLACOCH
PENBRYN COCH
SGUBOR GOCH
HEOL YR ONNEN
HEOL YSGAWEN
APPLETREE CL
ALDER RD
BIRCH GR
TREM-Y-GARTH
HEOL GELYNNEN
STRYD SILURIAN
CLOS PUPREN
CARREG ARWYN
ADDISON AVE
AELFRYN
ELM RD
GELLI EST
CLOS GWERNEN
HELYGEN
FFORDD
CWRT YWEN
TALYGARN CL
SYCAMORE RD
THE POPLARS
Quarries (dis)
ST ANNES CT
Ysgol Gyfun Llanhari
MAPLE CL
BEECH RD
HAWTHORN RD
WILLOW RD
ASH GR
HOLLY RD
CLOS PINWYDDEN
Llanhari Prim Sch
ROWAN CT
OAK RD
HEOL PANT GWYN
STRYD Y BERLLAN
DROS COL
LINDEN CT
LAUREL DENE
DERI
LLYS
Tynewydd
M4
LLWYN GWYN 1
HAZELDENE 2
TREM-Y-FOREST
Degar Farm
Ty Dyffrwyth
FFOREST RD
Cemy
Forest Wood Quarry
Nant Rhydhalog
COWBRIDGE RD
Valeways Millennium Heritage Trail
COWBRIDGE RD
Rhydhalog
Fforest Fach
Fforest-fawr
Valeways Millennium Heritage Trail
Llansannor CW Prim Sch
Tynytranch Farm
Llwyn-nwydog
Tymaen
Crofta Farm
Mynydd y Fforest
Newforest House Farm
Morfa Ystradowen
Nant Dyfrgi
Bryn-y-fedwen
Coed Wern-fawr
CF71
A4222
Ash Hall
Wern Fawr
Halifax

8 7 81 6 5 80 4 3 79 2 1 78

00 A B 01 C D 02 E F

171
189

155
174

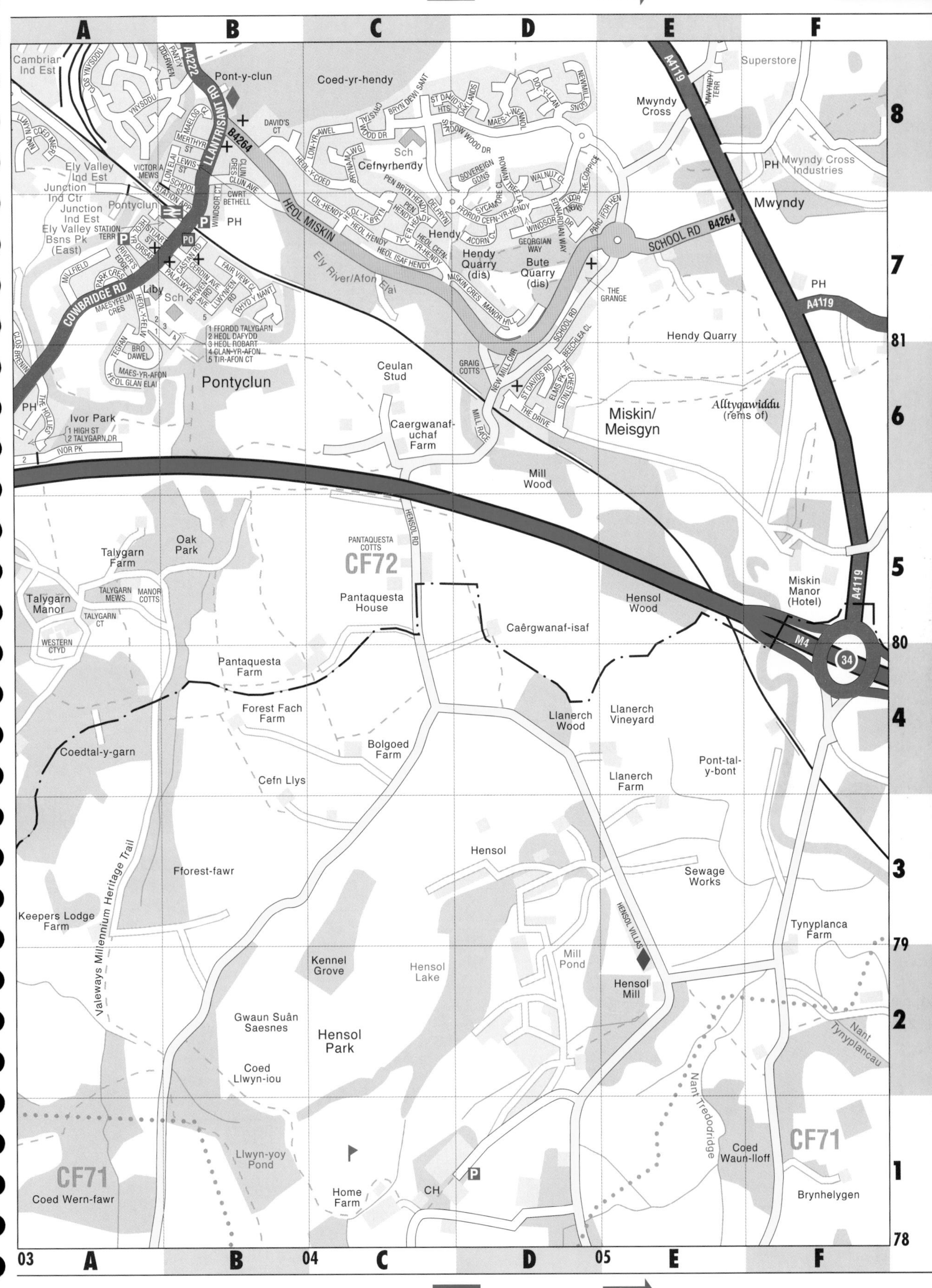

190
174

173 156

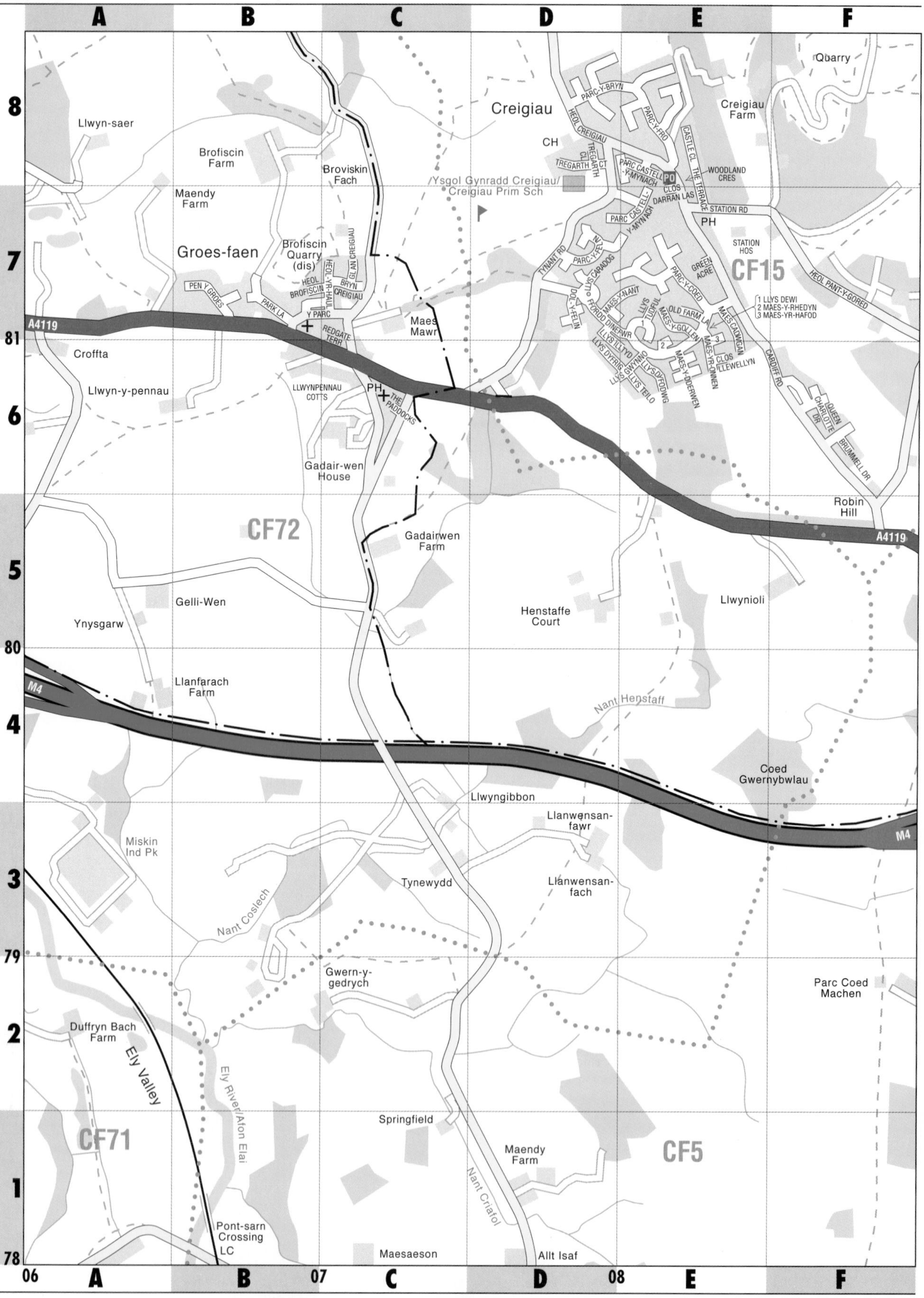

A B C D E F

8

Llwyn-saer

Brofiscin Farm

Broviskin Fach

Creigiau

Quarry

Creigiau Farm

CH

HEOL CREIGIAU

PARC-Y-BRYN

PARC-Y-FRO

TREGARTH CL

TREGARTH CT

PARC CASTELL-Y-MYNACH

PO

CLOS

DARRAN LAS

CASTLE CL

THE TERRACE

WOODLAND CRES

Ysgol Gynradd Creigiau/ Creigiau Prim Sch

Maendy Farm

STATION RD

PH

PARC CASTELL-Y-MYNACH

7

Groes-faen

Brofiscin Quarry (dis)

HEOL BROFISCIN

HEOL-YR-HAUL

GLAN CREIGIAU

BRYN CREIGIAU

PEN Y GROES

PARK LA

Y PARC

STATION HOS

CF15

TYNANT RD

PARC-Y-FELIN

LLYS CARADOG

GREEN ACRE

PARC-Y-COED

HEOL PANT-Y-GORED

1 LLYS DEWI

2 MAES-Y-RHEDYN

3 MAES-YR-HAFOD

DOL-Y-FELIN

FFORDD DINEFWR

MAES-Y-NANT

LLYS TUDFUL

OLD FARM LA

MAES-Y-GOLLEN

MAES CADWGAN

Maes Mawr

A4119

81

Croffta

REDGATE TERR

LLYS ILLTYD

LLYS DYFRIG

LLYS GWYNNO

LLYS TEILO

LLYS DYFODWG

MAES-Y-DDERWEN

MAES-YR-ONNEN

CLOS LLEWELLYN

CARDIFF RD

Llwyn-y-pennau

LLWYNPENNAU COTTS

PH

THE PADDOCKS

CHARLOTTE DR

QUEEN

BRUMMELL DR

6

Gadair-wen House

Robin Hill

CF72

Gadairwen Farm

A4119

5

Gelli-Wen

Ynysgarw

Henstaffe Court

Llwynioli

80

M4

Llanfarach Farm

Nant Henstaff

4

Coed Gwernybwlau

Llwyngibbon

Llanwensan-fawr

Miskin Ind Pk

M4

3

Tynewydd

Llanwensan-fach

Nant Coslech

79

Gwern-y-gedrych

Parc Coed Machen

2

Duffryn Bach Farm

Ely Valley

Ely River/Afon Elai

CF71

Springfield

Maendy Farm

CF5

1

Nant Criafol

Pont-sarn Crossing LC

Maesaeson

Allt Isaf

78

06 A B 07 C D 08 E F

173 191

157
176

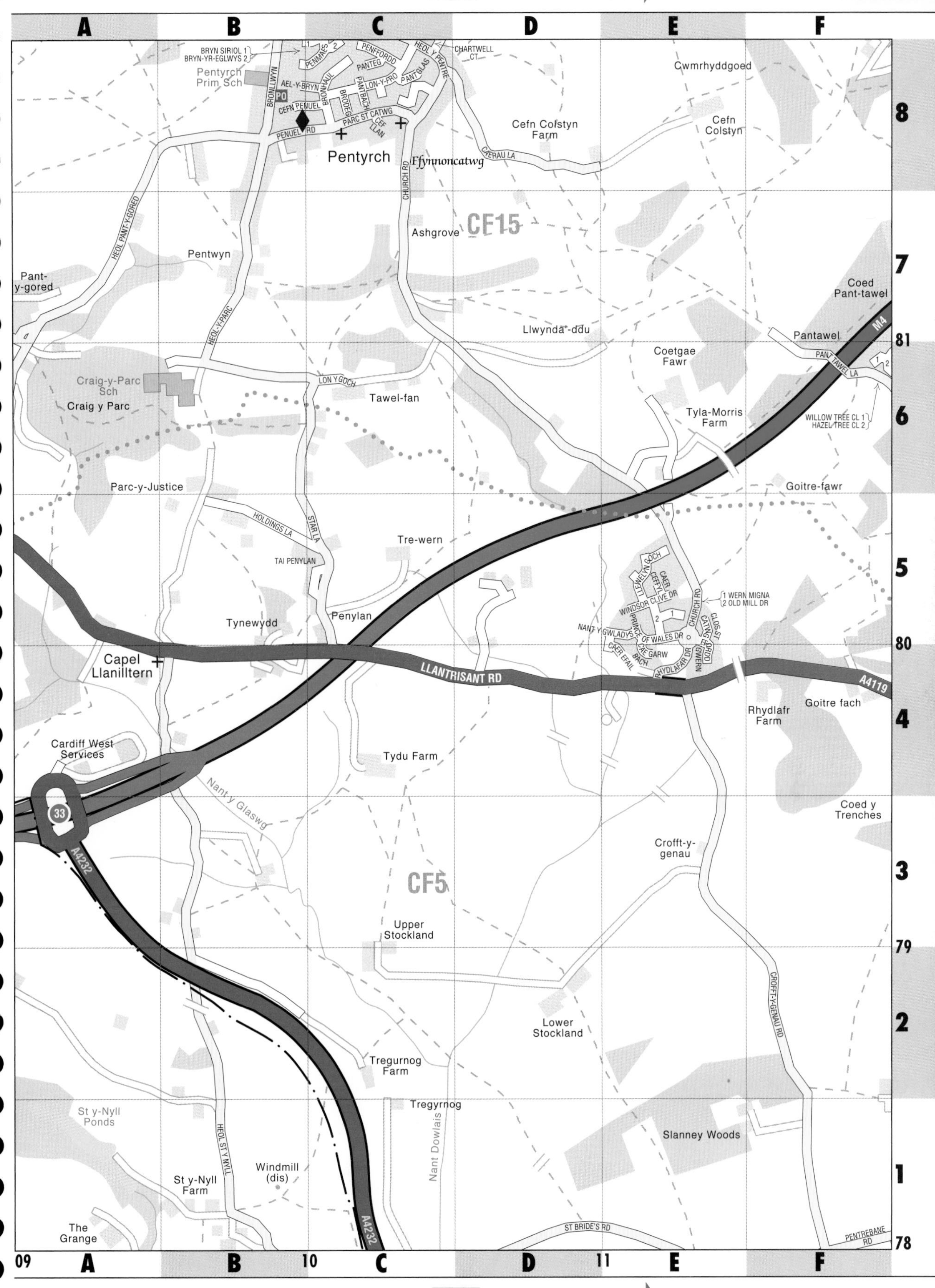

192
176

175 158

F6
1 BLANTHORN CT
2 AYLESBURY MANS
3 UNDERHILL MANS
4 ROCHESTER MANS
5 DORCHESTER MANS
6 EXETER MANS
7 YORK MANS
8 SUTHERLAND MANS
9 HANOVER CT

A B C D E F

8 81 7 6 5 80 4 3 79 2 1 78

Morganstown/ Treforgan
Tongwynlais Prim Sch
Pantmawr
Hotel
MERTHYR RD
NORTHERN AVE
Cemy
Coryton
Hotel & L Ctr
Hypermarket
Laboratories
Canal (dis)
Coryton Prim Sch
Hollybush Estate
Ind Est
Radyr Prim Sch
Radyr
Liby
Melingriffith/Melingruffydd Feeder
Forest Farm
Taff Trail
Forest Farm Nature Trail
Radyr
CF14
Whitchurch
Velindre
Wr Twr
CF15
River Taff/Afon Taf
Whitchurch/ Yr Eglwys Newydd
Burnt Mound
Radyr Farm
Radyr Comp Sch
Hailey Park
Llandaf
Maes-y-llech
Coed-y-Gof
CARDIFF/ CAERDYDD
Radyr Chain
Danescourt
Waterhall Plantation
Playing Field
CF5
Pentrebane
Ysgol Gyfun Gymraeg Plasmawr
Prim Sch
BBC Cymru Wales
High Sch

1 MAES-Y-BRYN
2 BRYNHYFRYD

1 PANTGWYNLAIS
2 PWLLHELYG

PANTMAWR CT 1
LISNAGARVEY CT 2
CEIRIOG DR 3

ODET CT 1
CORYTON CL 2

LARCH HO 1
SYCAMORE HO 2
POPLAR HO 3
CEDAR HO 4
ELM HO 6

B6
1 CLOS BRYNMELLYN
2 WINDSOR CT
3 NORFOLK CT
4 ARGYLL CT
5 YORK CT
6 SEFTON CT
7 OLD GARDEN CT

VELINDRE CT 1
TREDEGAR CT 2
BRYNHEULOG 3
CAMBOURNE AVE 4

POMMERGELLI RD 1
ROBERTS VILLAS 2
ALFREDA CT 3

1 Radyr Court Sh Prec
2 RESTWAY CT

CAMPION PL 1
BERRY PL 2
MEADOWBANK CT 3
CYPRESS PL 4
BRACKEN PL 5
SUNNYBROOK CT 6
KERRIGAN CL 7
CHERWELL CL 8

6 KENLEY CL
7 WOODFORD CL
8 FAIRWOOD CL

12 A B 13 C D 14 E F

175 193

E2
1 PRITCHARD CL
2 MARSHALL CL
3 DIGBY CL
4 CRANWELL CL
5 MANSTON CL

F3
1 LOUISE CT
2 FINNIMORE CT
3 MAPLEWOOD FLATS
4 MAPLEWOOD AVE
5 DURLSTON CL
6 CHAMBERLAIN RD

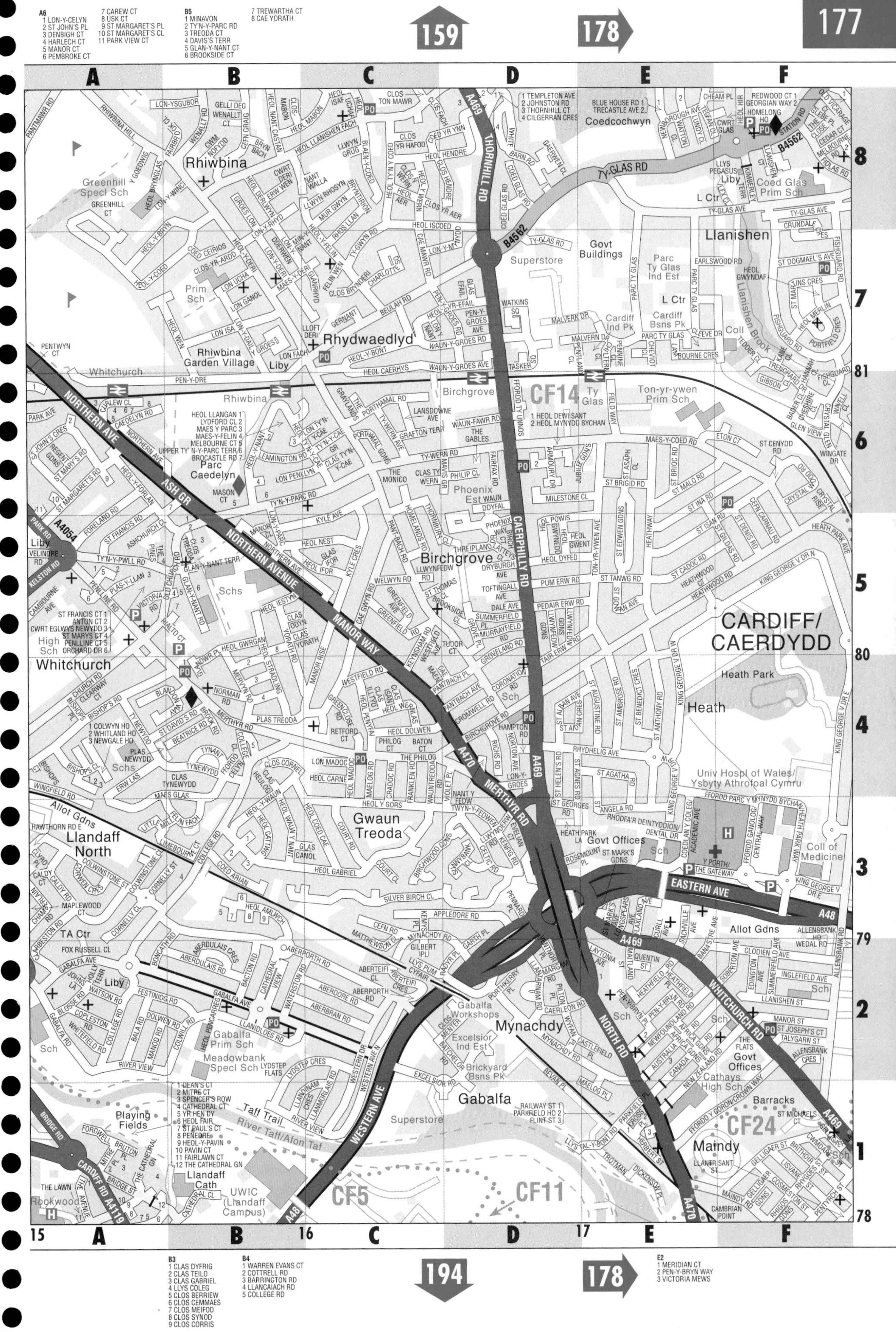
A6
1 LON-Y-CELYN
2 ST JOHN'S PL
3 DENBIGH CT
4 HARLECH CT
5 MANOR CT
6 PEMBROKE CT
7 CAREW CT
8 USK CT
9 ST MARGARET'S PL
10 ST MARGARET'S CL
11 PARK VIEW CT
B5
1 MINAVON
2 TY'N-Y-PARC RD
3 TREODA CT
4 DAVIS'S TERR
5 GLAN-Y-NANT CT
6 BROOKSIDE CT
7 TREWARTHA CT
8 CAE YORATH
159
178
A
B
C
D
E
F
8
7
81
6
5
80
4
3
79
2
1
78
15
16
17
Rhiwbina
Greenhill Specl Sch
Rhydwaedlyd
Rhiwbina Garden Village
Whitchurch
Coedcochwyn
Llanishen
Govt Buildings
Superstore
Parc Ty Glas Ind Est
Cardiff Ind Pk
Cardiff Bsns Pk
Ton-yr-ywen Prim Sch
Birchgrove
CF14
Ty Glas
Parc Caedelyn
Phoenix Est
CARDIFF/ CAERDYDD
Heath Park
Heath
Univ Hospl of Wales/ Ysbyty Athrofoal Cymru
Coll of Medicine
Gwaun Treoda
Llandaff North
Govt Offices
EASTERN AVE
A48
A469
A470
A4054
B4562
THORNHILL RD
CAERPHILLY RD
NORTHERN AVE
NORTHERN AVENUE
MANOR WAY
MERTHYR RD
NORTH RD
WHITCHURCH RD
WESTERN AVE
TY-GLAS RD
Allot Gdns
TA Ctr
Gabalfa Prim Sch
Meadowbank Specl Sch
Gabalfa Workshops
Excelsior Ind Est
Brickyard Bsns Pk
Mynachdy
Gabalfa
Cathays High Sch
Barracks
Maindy
CF24
CF11
CF5
Taff Trail
River Taff/Afon Taf
Playing Fields
Llandaff Cath
UWIC (Llandaff Campus)
Rookwood
Superstore
B3
1 CLAS DYFRIG
2 CLAS TEILO
3 CLAS GABRIEL
4 LLYS COLEG
5 CLOS BERRIEW
6 CLOS CEMMAES
7 CLOS MEIFOD
8 CLOS SYNOD
9 CLOS CORRIS
B4
1 WARREN EVANS CT
2 COTTRELL RD
3 BARRINGTON RD
4 LLANCAIACH RD
5 COLLEGE RD
194
178
E2
1 MERIDIAN CT
2 PEN-Y-BRYN WAY
3 VICTORIA MEWS

177 160

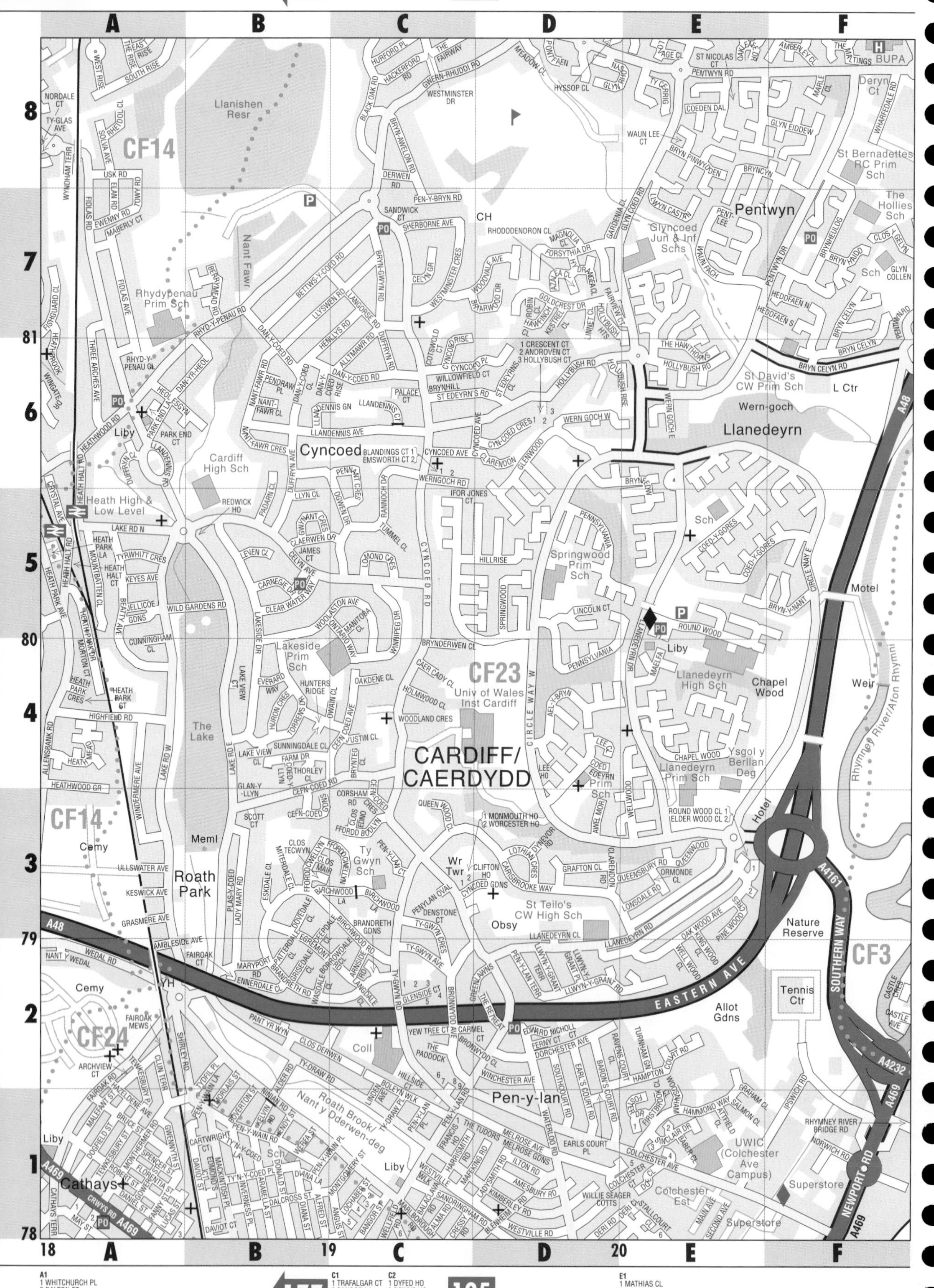

A1	C1	C2	E1
1 WHITCHURCH PL	1 TRAFALGAR CT	1 DYFED HO	1 MATHIAS CL
2 DALTON ST	2 BANGOR LA	2 POWYS HO	2 HUGON CL
3 WOODVILLE RD	3 BANGOR CT	3 CLWYD HO	3 SHARPE CL
	4 TULLOCH ST	4 GWENT HO	4 HOWARDIAN CL
	5 ESSICH ST	5 GWYNEDD HO	5 LADY MARGARET CT
	6 PEN-Y-LAN RD	6 MELROSE CT	6 WATERLOO CL
	7 PENYLAN CT	7 STONEWELL CT	
		8 REDWELL CT	
		9 OLDWELL CT	

177 195

C6
1 PETHERTON PL
2 BRENDON CL
3 BURNHAM CT
4 ST DYFRIG'S CT
5 CLEVEDON CT
D7
1 CHAPEL ROW LA
2 KENNETH TREASURE CT
D8
1 DRAWLINGS CL
2 EASTERN CL
3 ARCON HO
4 HEATHCLIFFE CL
5 SILVERSTONE CL
6 EURWG CRES
E7
1 ALDERWOOD CL
2 REDWOOD CL
3 SHEERWATER CL
4 BROADLANDS CT
5 BROADLANDS HO
6 MEADOWLARK CL
7 ASHFIELD CT
8 MALLARD CL
F6
1 CHESTER CL
2 CRAGSIDE CL
3 LINGHOLM CL
4 BROADWELL CL
161
5 PAVALAND CL
6 CASPIAN CL
7 CLOS PEN Y CLAWDD
8 CLOS-Y-BETWS
9 DRYBROOK CL
10 CLOS TREGARE
11 LANHYDROCK CL
180
12 CLOS PANTYCOSYN
13 CLOS GWERN-Y-MOR
14 HEOL MAES EIRWG
15 CLOS-Y-CULFOR
16 HEOL PWLLYPLACA
17 CLOS MAERUN
18 CLOS HAFODYRYNYS
F7
1 MALPAS CL
2 DUMMER CL
3 OAKMEADOW CT
4 ASHDOWN CL
5 PITMEDDEN CL
A B C D E F
8 7 6 5 4 3 2 1
81 80 79 78
21 22 23
CF23
CF3
CF24
EASTERN AVE
A48
29a
A4232
B4562
B4487
B4239
TYR WINCH RD
NEWPORT RD
WENTLOOG RD
WENTLOOG AVE
MARDY RD
Church Farm
Avenue Ind Pk
Hotel
Glan-yr-Afon Prim Sch
Rhymney River/Afon Rhymni
Sch
Llanrumney
Fishpond Wood
Llanrumney High Sch
Sports Field
Bryn-Hafod Prim Sch
Ysgol Bro Eirwg
Playing Fields
LCtr
Liby
Schs
St Illtyds RC High Sch
Cae Castell
Rumney High Sch
St John's Coll
St Mellons/ Llaneurwg
Willowbrook Laboratory Units
Bsns Pk
Bsns Ctr
Trowbridge
Green Meadows
Cardiff Tertiary Coll/ Coleg Glan Hafren
Rec Gd
Pil-du-Reen
Wentloog Corporate Ind Pk
Trowbridge Rd
Greenway Prim Sch
Rumney/ Rhymni
Alexandra Trad Est
Longcross Farm
Ind Pk
Caravan Pk
Pwll-Mawr
Spring Meadow Bsns Pk
Spring Meadow Trad Est
Ringside Bsns Ctr
East Point
The Laurels Bsns Pk
Capital Bsns Pk
Middle Newton Farm
Lamby Way Workshops
Lamby Ind Pk
Eastgate Bsns Pk
Rhosog Fach Reen
Ty-to-maen Farm
Newton
Sea Bank Farm
Maerdy Farm
CARDIFF/ CAERDYDD
Rumney Pottery
Senlan Ind Est
Rhymney River/ Afon Rhymni
1 BEAUFORT SQ
2 GLAN RHYMNI
3 CWRT BOSTON
4 CWRT COLES
1 WHITE OAKS DR
2 WILLIAM NICHOLLS DR
3 FFORDD BRYNHYFRYD
1 SANDPIPER CL
2 CORMORANT CL
3 OSPREY CL
1 POPPYFIELD CL
2 USKLEY CT
3 ELMFIELD CL
1 CANOPUS CL
2 BETHANIA ROW
3 ELLESMERE CT
1 CWRT PENSARN
2 CWRT YR ARDAL
CLOS GLAS LLWCH
1 MARCHWOOD CL
2 HOLMVIEW CT
THE OLD POLICE STA 1
HIGH CROFT WLK 2
HEOL CHUDLEIGH 1
FFORDD DANIEL LEWIS 2
1 LAUGHARNE RD
2 OSWESTRY CL
MORNINGTON CT 1
FARLINGTON CT 2
CHERITON CT 3
ROEHAMPTON CT 4
B3
1 TRELAWNEY AVE
2 TRELAWNEY CRES
3 THOMAS DAVIES CT
4 CASWELL RD
196
180

A6
1 THRUSH CL
2 STONECHAT CL
3 WINDHOVER CL
4 CLOS Y BERLLAN
5 CLOS-YR-GORNANT
6 CLOS HAFREN
7 CLOS CAS-BACH
8 CLOS DYFNAINT
9 CLOS GLANABER
10 CLOS GWLAD-YR-HAF
11 CLOS MAES-Y-MOR
12 LOCKE GR

179

162

A7
1 CARADOC CL
2 BASSALEG CL
3 BLAENAVON CL
4 BEDWAS CL
5 HORNBEAM CL
6 ASTER CL
7 WINDFLOWER CL
8 WHINCHAT CL
9 CHARTLEY CL
10 ABERNETHY CL
A8
1 LYTHAM GR
2 ST PIERRE CL
3 BIRKDALE CL
4 WENTWORTH CL
5 VAINDRE CL
6 VAINDRE DR
7 CWRT PENTRE BACH
8 FAIRHAVEN CL
9 FAIRVIEW CL
10 FENNEL CL
11 COMFREY CL
12 CHERVIL CL
13 EUGENE CL
14 CARAWAY CL
15 OREGANO CL

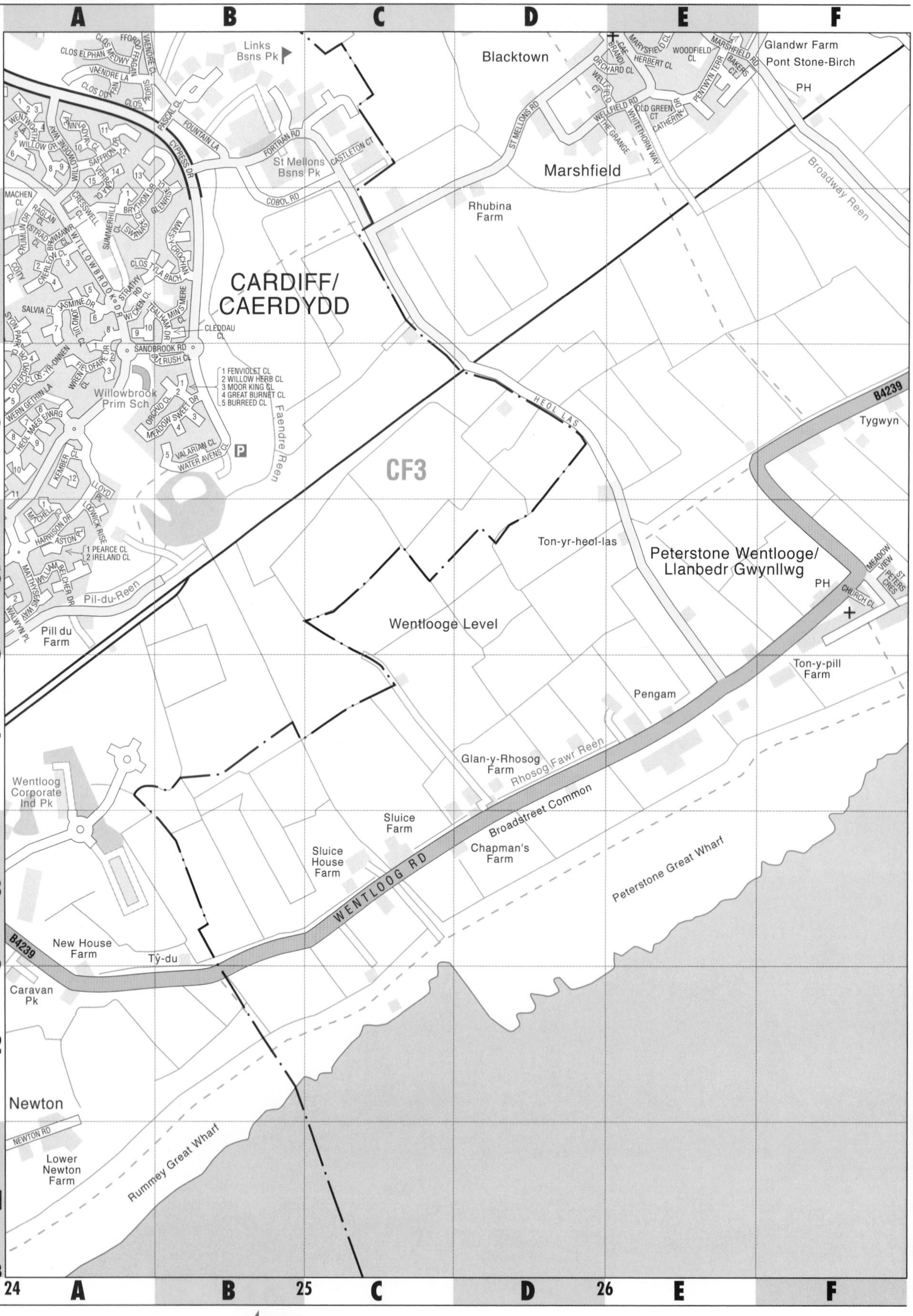

179

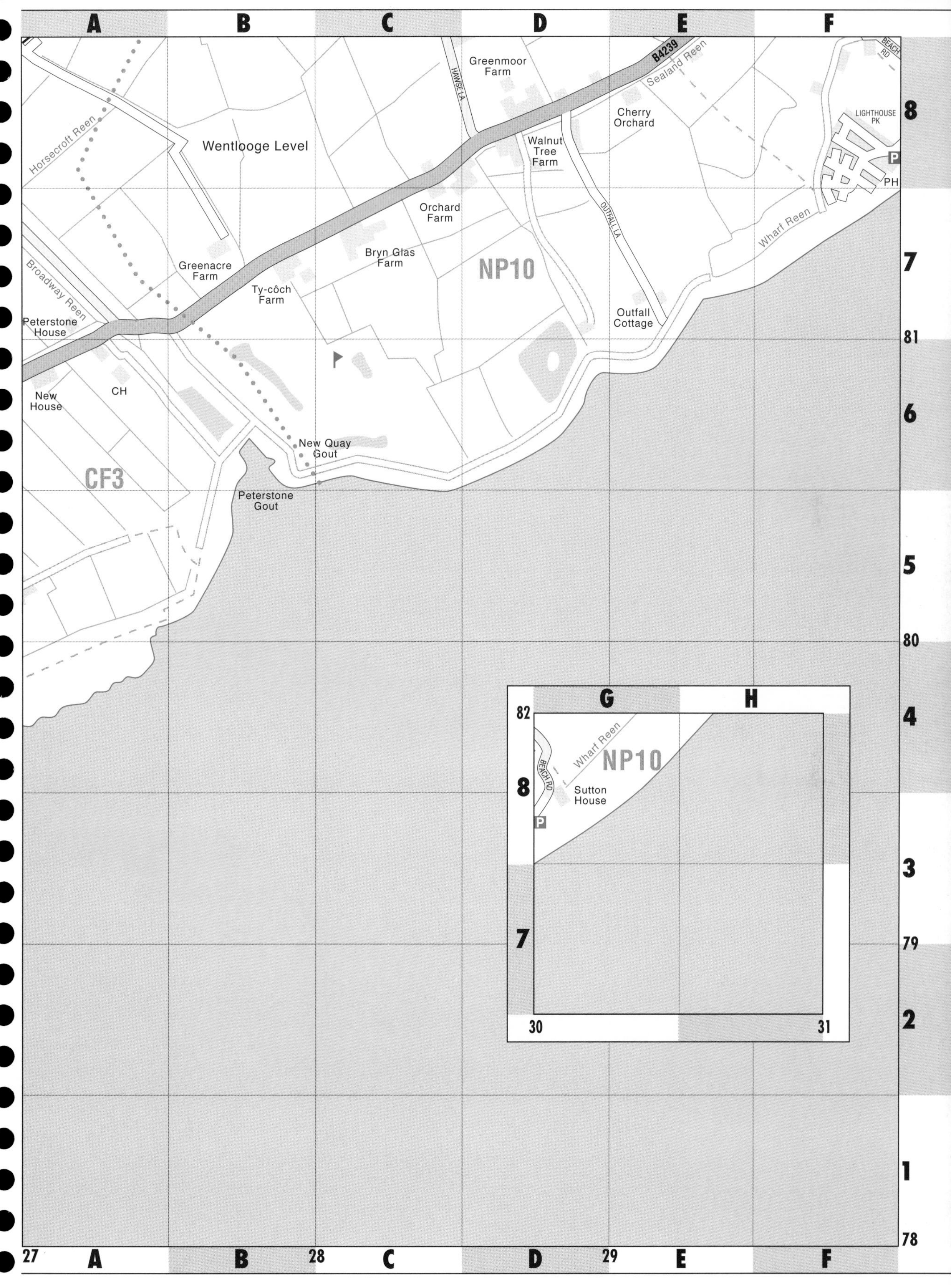
163
A
B
C
D
E
F
8
7
6
5
4
3
2
1
81
80
79
78
27
28
29
B4239
Greenmoor Farm
HAWSE LA
Sealand Reen
BEACH RD
LIGHTHOUSE PK
Cherry Orchard
Walnut Tree Farm
PH
Wentlooge Level
Horsecroft Reen
Orchard Farm
OUTFALL LA
Wharf Reen
Bryn Glas Farm
NP10
Greenacre Farm
Ty-côch Farm
Broadway Reen
Outfall Cottage
Peterstone House
New House
CH
New Quay Gout
CF3
Peterstone Gout
G
H
82
Wharf Reen
NP10
BEACH RD
Sutton House
30
31

165

F7
1 LLYSY ONNEN
2 LLYS Y GRUG/HEATHER CT
3 CLOS-YR-ORSAF/STATION CL
4 OLD STATION RD
5 NEW RD

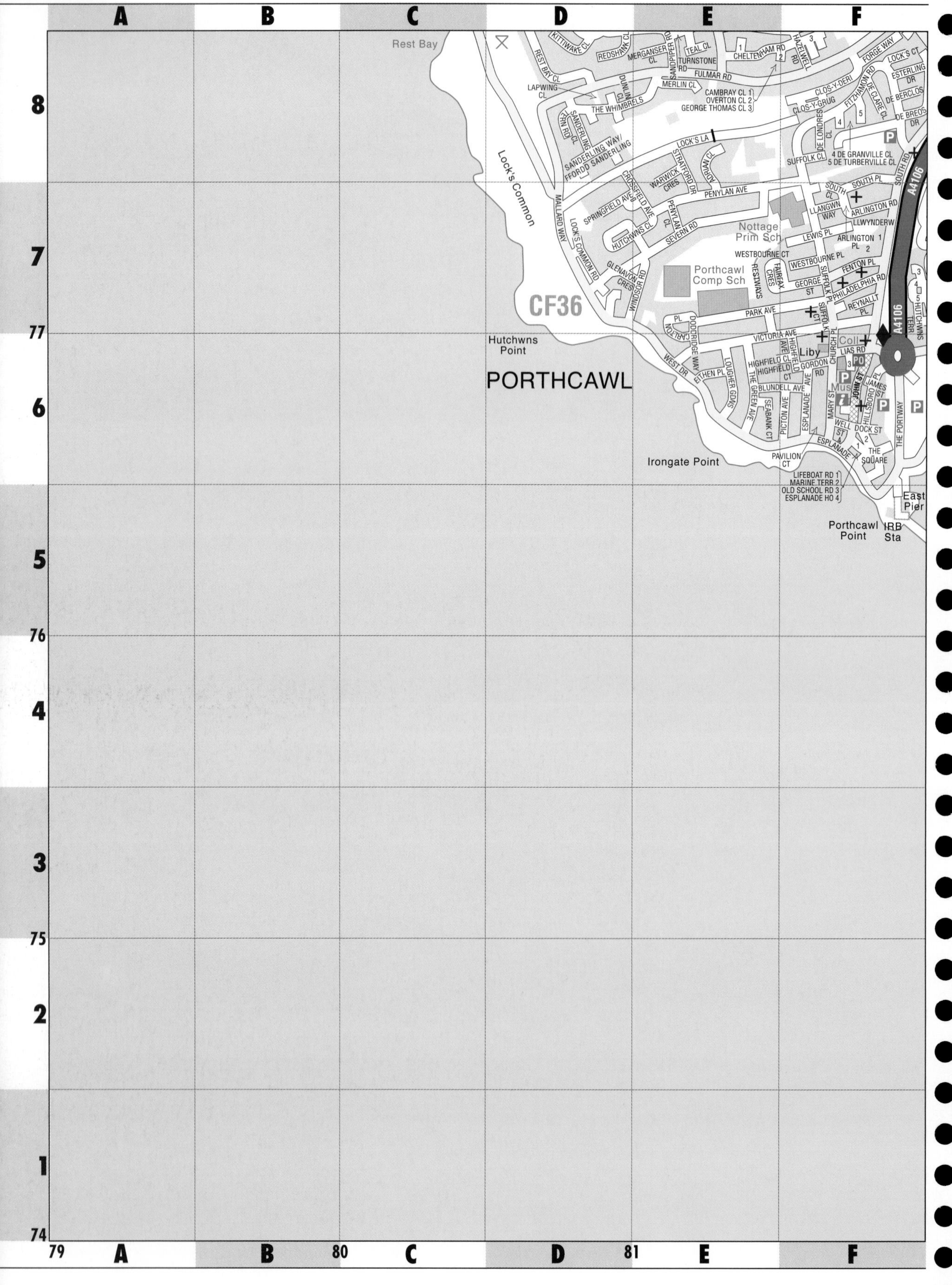

166
184

A4106 NEWTON NOTTAGE RD
The Wilderness
Prim Sch
Newton Prim Sch
Newton
CF36
Coney Beach Amusement Park
Sandy Bay
Rhych Point
Trecco Bay
Newton Point
Newton Burrows
Black Rocks
Y Graig
Wig Fach
Gorwelion
Caeaullaprau
CF32
Rifle Range (dis)
Schs
NEW RD
WOODLAND AVE
ST DAVID'S WAY
CHURCH ST
BEACH RD
BAY VIEW RD
RHYCH AVE
DANYGRAIG AVE
LIME TREE WAY
LABURNUM DR
BRIDGEND RD
A B C D E F
8 7 6 5 4 3 2 1
77 76 75 74
82 83 84

184

183
167

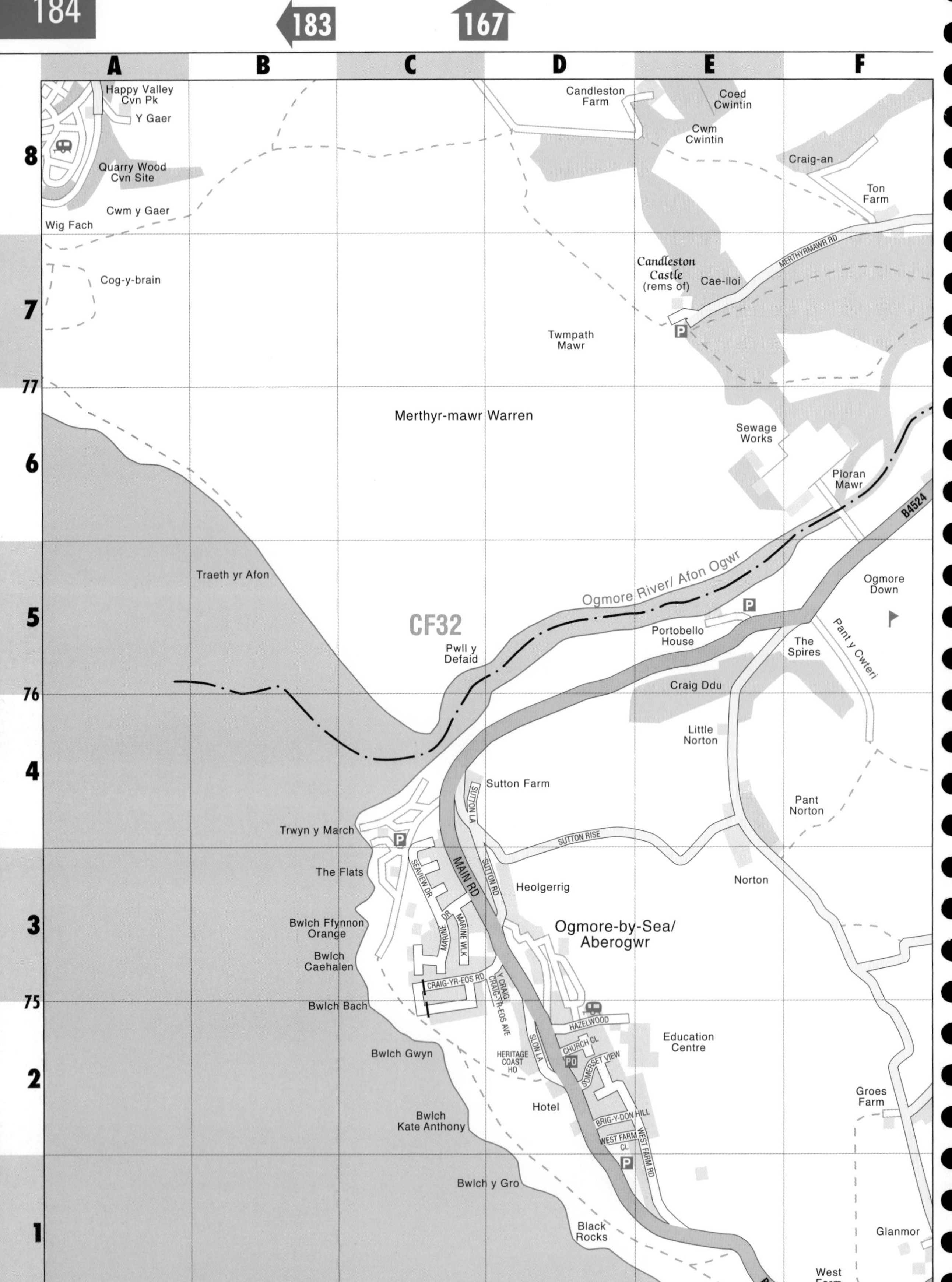
A
B
C
D
E
F
8
7
77
6
5
76
4
3
75
2
1
74
85
86
87
Happy Valley Cvn Pk
Y Gaer
Quarry Wood Cvn Site
Cwm y Gaer
Wig Fach
Cog-y-brain
Candleston Farm
Coed Cwintin
Cwm Cwintin
Craig-an
Ton Farm
MERTHYRMAWR RD
Candleston Castle (rems of)
Cae-lloi
Twmpath Mawr
Merthyr-mawr Warren
Sewage Works
Ploran Mawr
B4524
Traeth yr Afon
Ogmore River/ Afon Ogwr
Ogmore Down
CF32
Pwll y Defaid
Portobello House
The Spires
Pant y Cwteri
Craig Ddu
Little Norton
Sutton Farm
SUTTON LA
Pant Norton
Trwyn y March
SUTTON RISE
SEAVIEW DR
MAIN RD
SUTTON RD
Heolgerrig
Norton
The Flats
Bwlch Ffynnon Orange
MARINE DR
MARINE WLK
Ogmore-by-Sea/ Aberogwr
Bwlch Caehalen
CRAIG-YR-EOS RD
Y CRAIG
CRAIG-YR-EOS AVE
Bwlch Bach
HAZELWOOD
Education Centre
Bwlch Gwyn
SLON LA
CHURCH CL
HERITAGE COAST HQ
PO
SOMERSET VIEW
Groes Farm
Hotel
Bwlch Kate Anthony
BRIG-Y-DON HILL
WEST FARM CL
WEST FARM RD
Bwlch y Gro
Black Rocks
Glanmor
West Farm
B4524

183

168
186

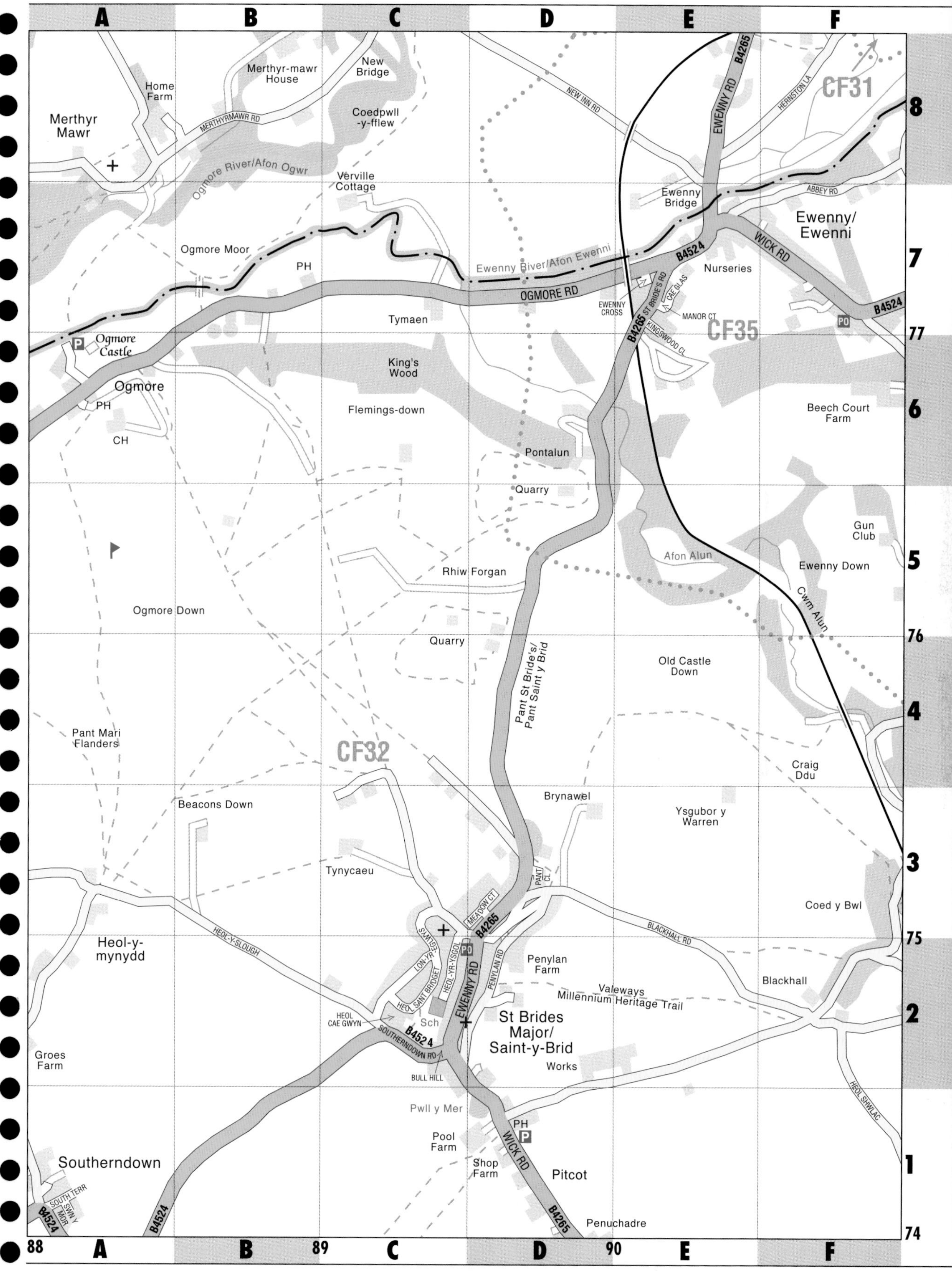

197
186

A B C D E F

8
7
77
6
5
76
4
3
75
2
1
74

91 A B 92 C D 93 E F

170
188

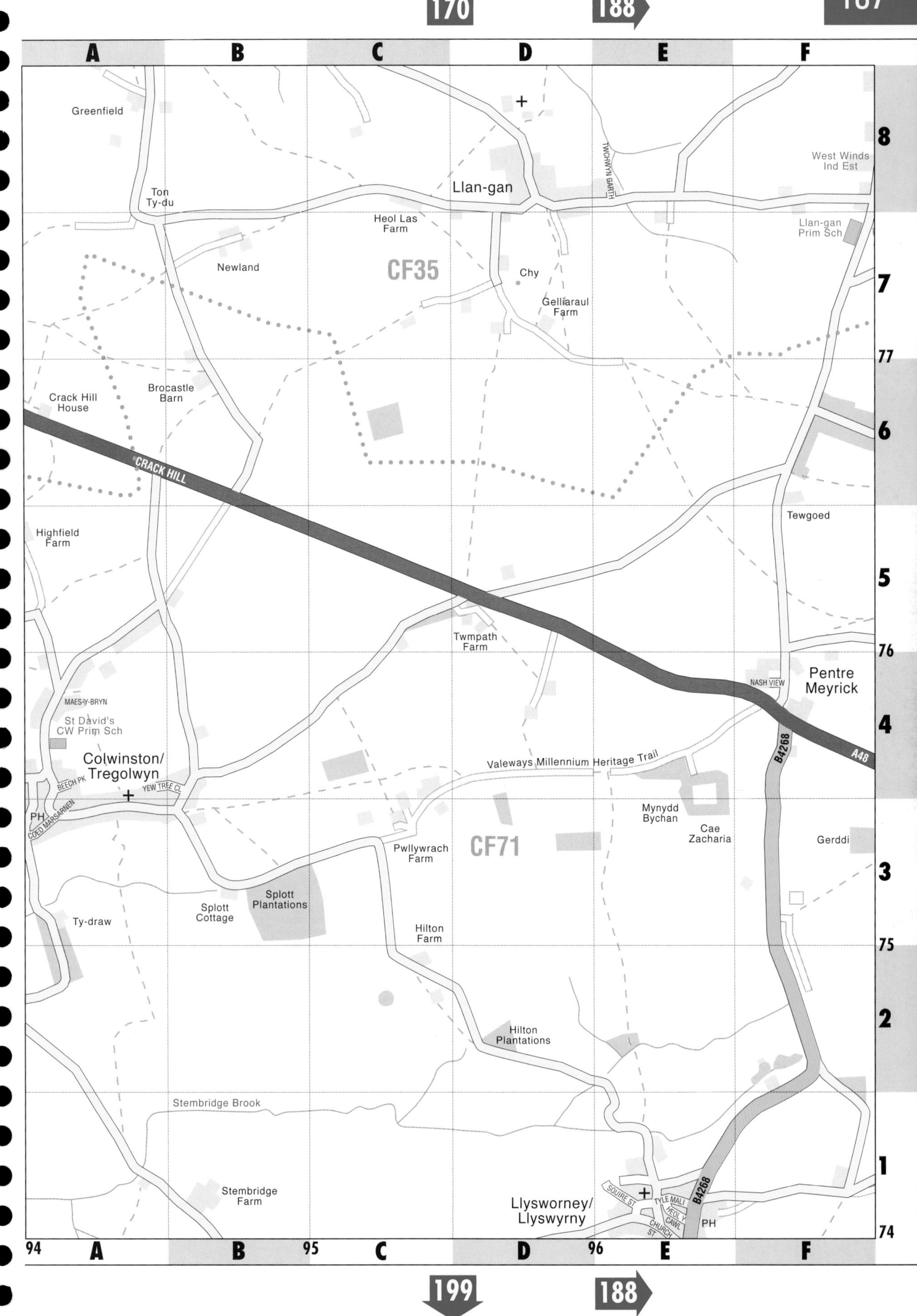

199
188

187
171

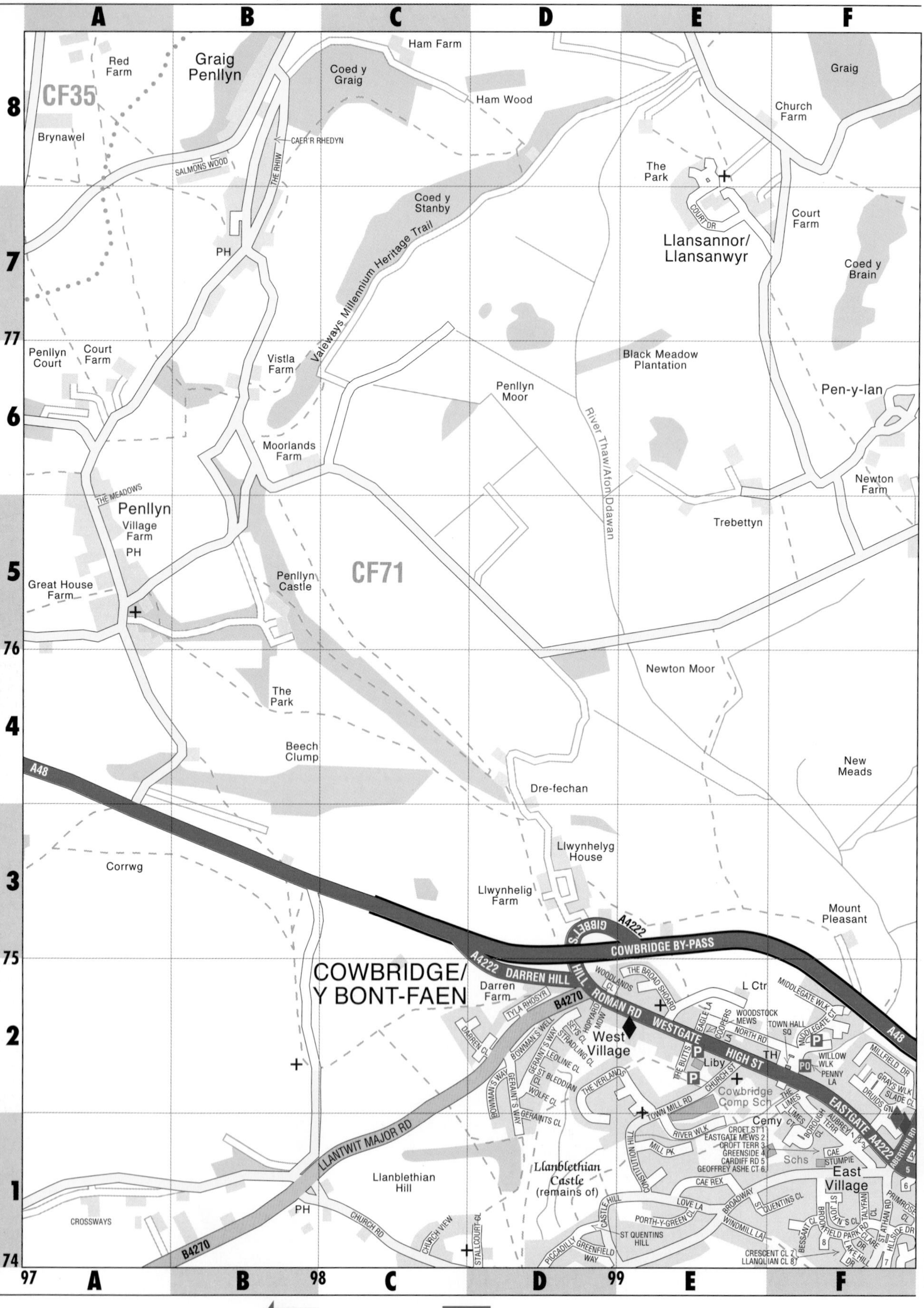

187
200

172
190

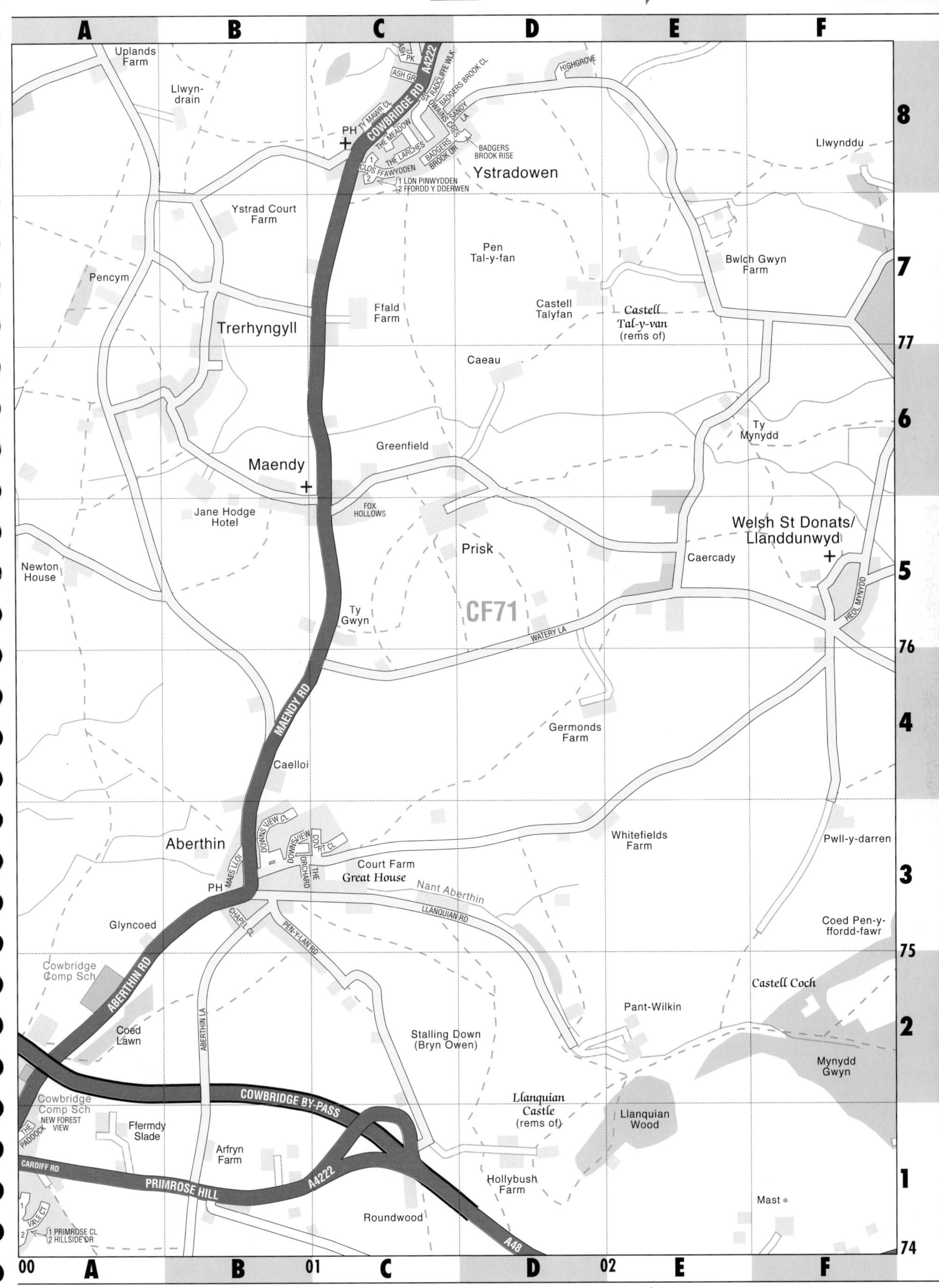
Uplands Farm
Llwyn-drain
Ystradowen
Ystrad Court Farm
Pencym
Trerhyngyll
Ffald Farm
Pen Tal-y-fan
Castell Talyfan
Castell Tal-y-van (rems of)
Caeau
Bwlch Gwyn Farm
Llwynddu
Greenfield
Maendy
Jane Hodge Hotel
Fox Hollows
Prisk
Ty Mynydd
Welsh St Donats/ Llanddunwyd
Caercady
Newton House
Ty Gwyn
CF71
Watery La
Heol Mynydd
Maendy Rd
Germonds Farm
Caelloi
Aberthin
Court Farm
Great House
Nant Aberthin
Llanquian Rd
Whitefields Farm
Pwll-y-darren
Glyncoed
Cowbridge Comp Sch
Aberthin Rd
Coed Lawn
Aberthin La
Stalling Down (Bryn Owen)
Pant-Wilkin
Castell Coch
Coed Pen-y-ffordd-fawr
Mynydd Gwyn
Cowbridge By-pass
Llanquian Castle (rems of)
Llanquian Wood
Ffermdy Slade
Arfryn Farm
Primrose Hill
A4222
Cardiff Rd
Hollybush Farm
Roundwood
Mast
A48
Cowbridge Rd
1 Lon Pinwydden
2 Ffordd y Derwen
Badgers Brook Rise
1 Primrose Cl
2 Hillside Dr
A B C D E F
8 7 77 6 5 76 4 3 75 2 1 74
00 01 02

201
190

189
173

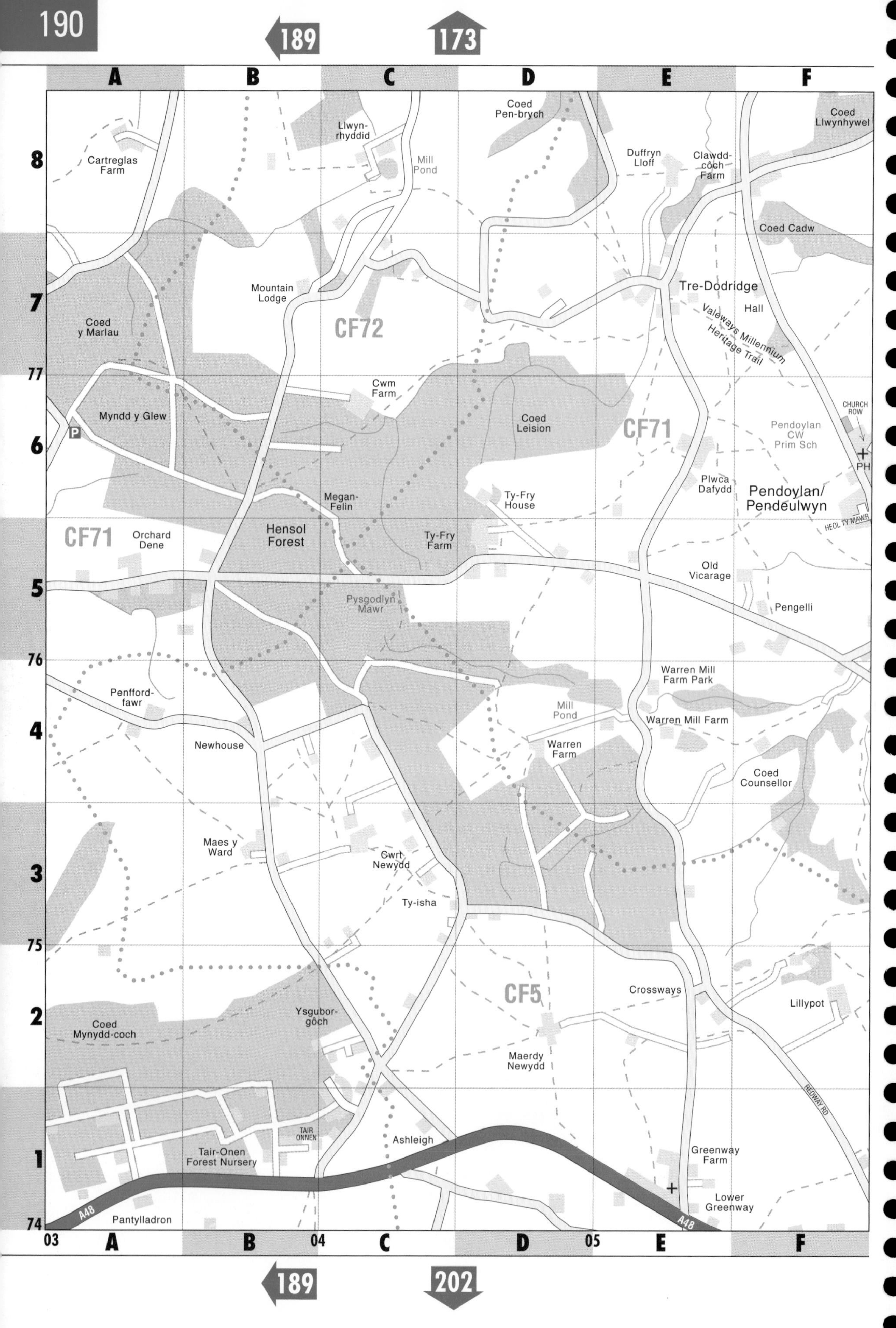

189
202

174
192

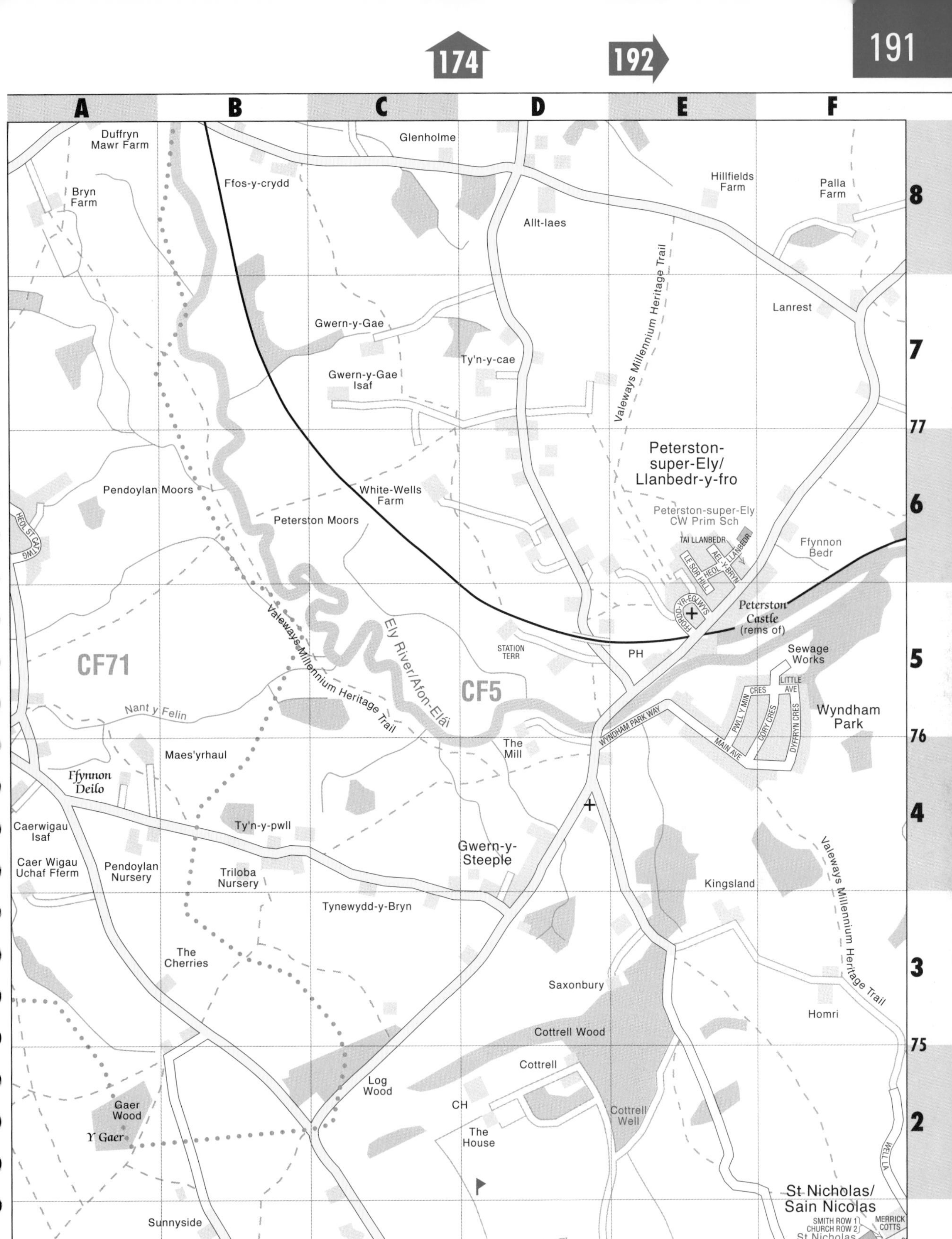
A
B
C
D
E
F
Duffryn Mawr Farm
Glenholme
Bryn Farm
Ffos-y-crydd
Hillfields Farm
Palla Farm
Allt-laes
Lanrest
Gwern-y-Gae
Valeways Millennium Heritage Trail
Ty'n-y-cae
Gwern-y-Gae Isaf
Peterston-super-Ely/ Llanbedr-y-fro
Pendoylan Moors
White-Wells Farm
Peterston Moors
Peterston-super-Ely CW Prim Sch
TAI LLANBEDR
Ffynnon Bedr
HEOL ST CATWG
Peterston Castle (rems of)
STATION TERR
PH
Sewage Works
CF71
CF5
Ely River/Afon-Elái
Nant y Felin
Wyndham Park
WYNDHAM PARK WAY
MAIN AVE
The Mill
Maes'yrhaul
Ffynnon Deilo
Caerwigau Isaf
Ty'n-y-pwll
Gwern-y-Steeple
Caer Wigau Uchaf Fferm
Pendoylan Nursery
Triloba Nursery
Kingsland
Tynewydd-y-Bryn
The Cherries
Saxonbury
Homri
Cottrell Wood
Cottrell
Log Wood
Gaer Wood
CH
Cottrell Well
Y Gaer
The House
St Nicholas/ Sain Nicolas
Sunnyside
SMITH ROW 1
CHURCH ROW 2
MERRICK COTTS
St Nicholas CW Prim Sch
Bonvilston/ Tresimwn
Sheep Court
Trehill
COTTERELL DR
MAES-Y-FFYNNON
VILLAGE FARM
RED LION COTTS
THE OLD FORGE
SYCAMORE CROSS
A48
A4226
REDWAY RD
BROOK LA
WELL LA
8
7
77
6
5
76
4
3
75
2
1
74
06
07
08

191
175

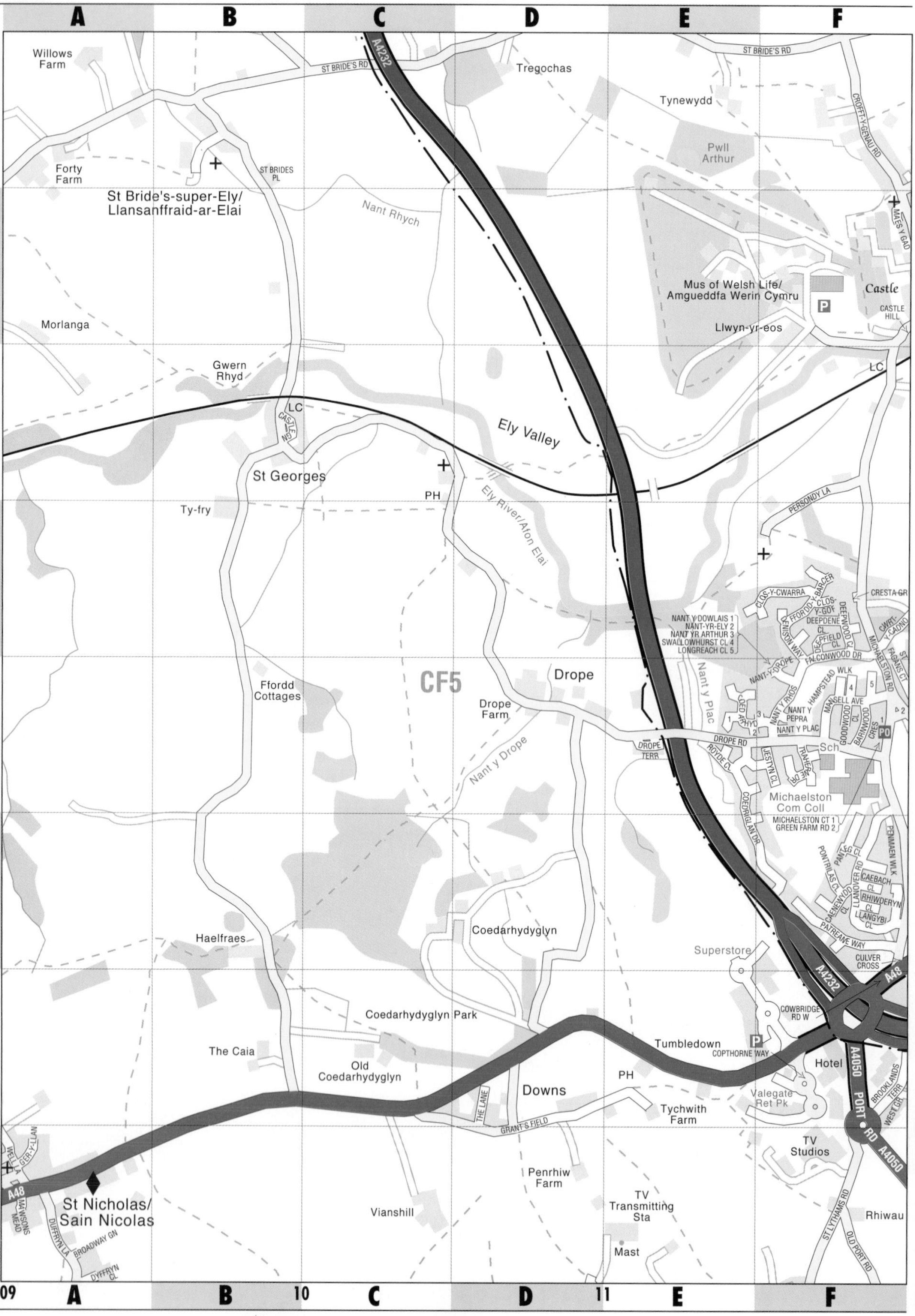

191
204

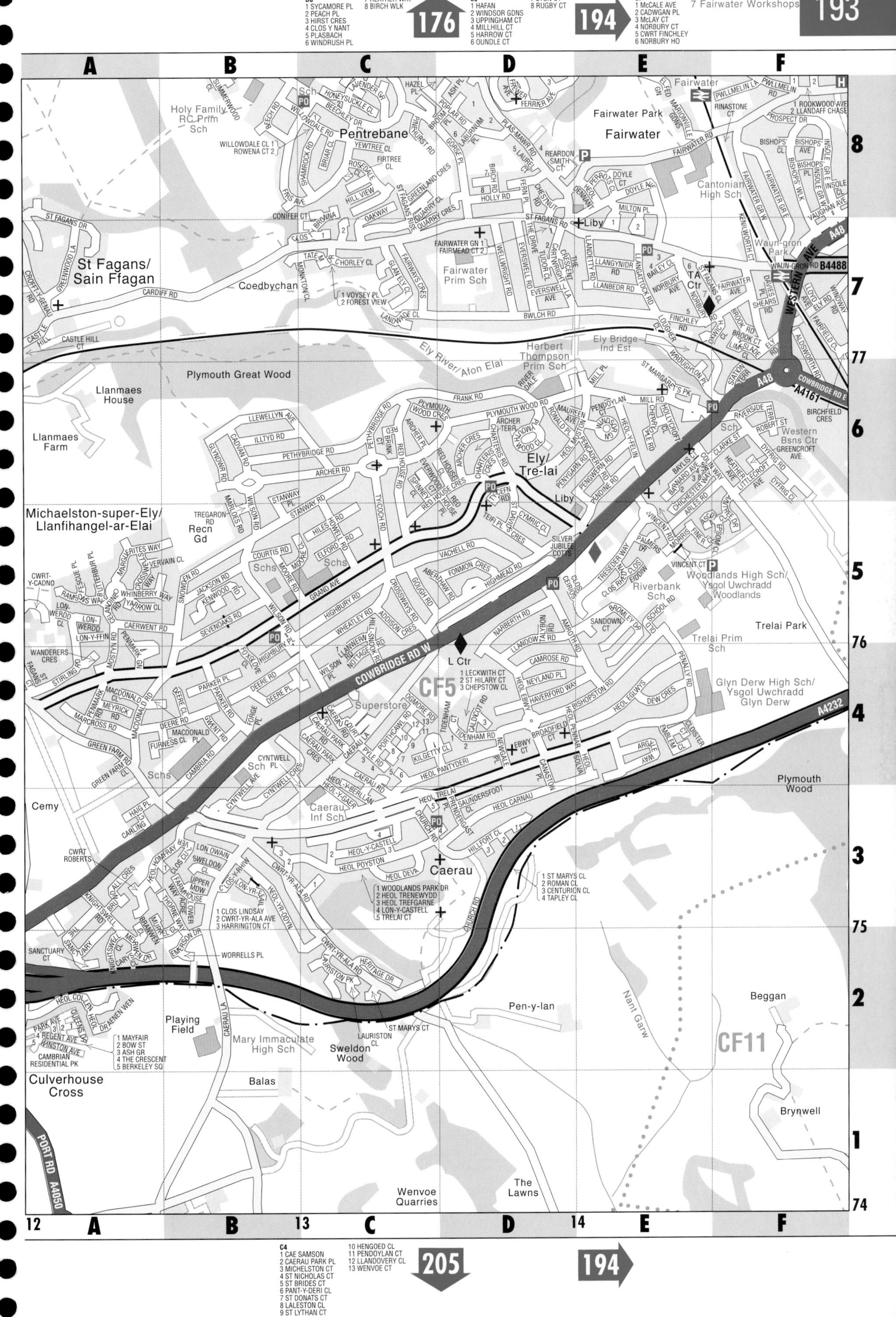

D8
1 SYCAMORE PL
2 PEACH PL
3 HIRST CRES
4 CLOS Y NANT
5 PLASBACH
6 WINDRUSH PL
7 HEATHER WAY
8 BIRCH WLK
176
E6
1 HAFAN
2 WINDSOR GDNS
3 UPPINGHAM CT
4 MILLHILL CT
5 HARROW CT
6 OUNDLE CT
7 ETON CT
8 RUGBY CT
194
E7
1 McCALE AVE
2 CADWGAN PL
3 McLAY CT
4 NORBURY CT
5 CWRT FINCHLEY
6 NORBURY HO
7 Fairwater Workshops
A
B
C
D
E
F
8
7
77
6
5
76
4
3
75
2
1
74
12
13
14
Holy Family RC Prim Sch
Pentrebane
Fairwater Park
Fairwater
Cantonian High Sch
St Fagans/ Sain Ffagan
Coedbychan
Fairwater Prim Sch
Waun-gron Park
WESTERN AVE
A48
B4488
Herbert Thompson Prim Sch
Ely Bridge Ind Est
Ely River/Afon Elai
Plymouth Great Wood
Llanmaes House
Llanmaes Farm
Ely/ Tre-lai
Western Bsns Ctr
Michaelston-super-Ely/ Llanfihangel-ar-Elai
Recn Gd
Woodlands High Sch/ Ysgol Uwchradd Woodlands
Riverbank Sch
Trelai Park
Trelai Prim Sch
COWBRIDGE RD W
COWBRIDGE RD E
A4161
L Ctr
CF5
Superstore
Glyn Derw High Sch/ Ysgol Uwchradd Glyn Derw
A4232
Plymouth Wood
Cemy
Caerau Inf Sch
Caerau
1 LECKWITH CT
2 ST HILARY CT
3 CHEPSTOW CL
1 WOODLANDS PARK DR
2 HEOL TRENEWYDD
3 HEOL TREFGARNE
4 LON-Y-CASTELL
5 TRELAI CT
1 CLOS LINDSAY
2 CWRT-YR-ALA AVE
3 HARRINGTON CT
1 ST MARYS CL
2 ROMAN CL
3 CENTURION CL
4 TAPLEY CL
Pen-y-lan
Beggan
Nant Garw
CF11
Playing Field
Mary Immaculate High Sch
Sweldon Wood
1 MAYFAIR
2 BOW ST
3 ASH GR
4 THE CRESCENT
5 BERKELEY SQ
CAMBRIAN RESIDENTIAL PK
Culverhouse Cross
Balas
Brynwell
PORT RD A4050
Wenvoe Quarries
The Lawns
C4
1 CAE SAMSON
2 CAERAU PARK PL
3 MICHELSTON CT
4 ST NICHOLAS CT
5 ST BRIDES CT
6 PANT-Y-DERI CL
7 ST DONATS CT
8 LALESTON CL
9 ST LYTHAN CT
10 HENGOED CL
11 PENDOYLAN CT
12 LLANDOVERY CL
13 WENVOE CT
205
194

B7
1 SLOCOMBE TRUST COTTS
2 WESTRA CT
3 PANTEG MEWS
4 LINDWAY CT
5 BAKERS CT
6 LORD PONTYPRIDD HO
7 VICTORIA CT
C6
1 THOMPSON CT
2 PARKSIDE CT
3 ROMILLY PL
4 OLD RECTORY
5 PARRY ST
6 CARDIGAN CT
7 CARMARTHEN CT
8 BRECON CT
9 THORNHILL ST
10 ANGLESEY ST
11 GLAMORGAN STREET MEWS
12 HARVEY ST
13 TINTERN CT
14 HAFOD CT
15 HAMILTON CT
D6
1 CWRT-Y-FARCHNAD
2 ALEXANDRA CT
3 SEVERN SQ
4 OLIVE CT
D7
1 WESTERN CT
2 CAERNARVON CT
3 FOREST CT
4 STONELEIGH CT
5 AQUILLA CT
6 ST JAMES MEWS
7 ST CATHERINES MEWS

193
177
232

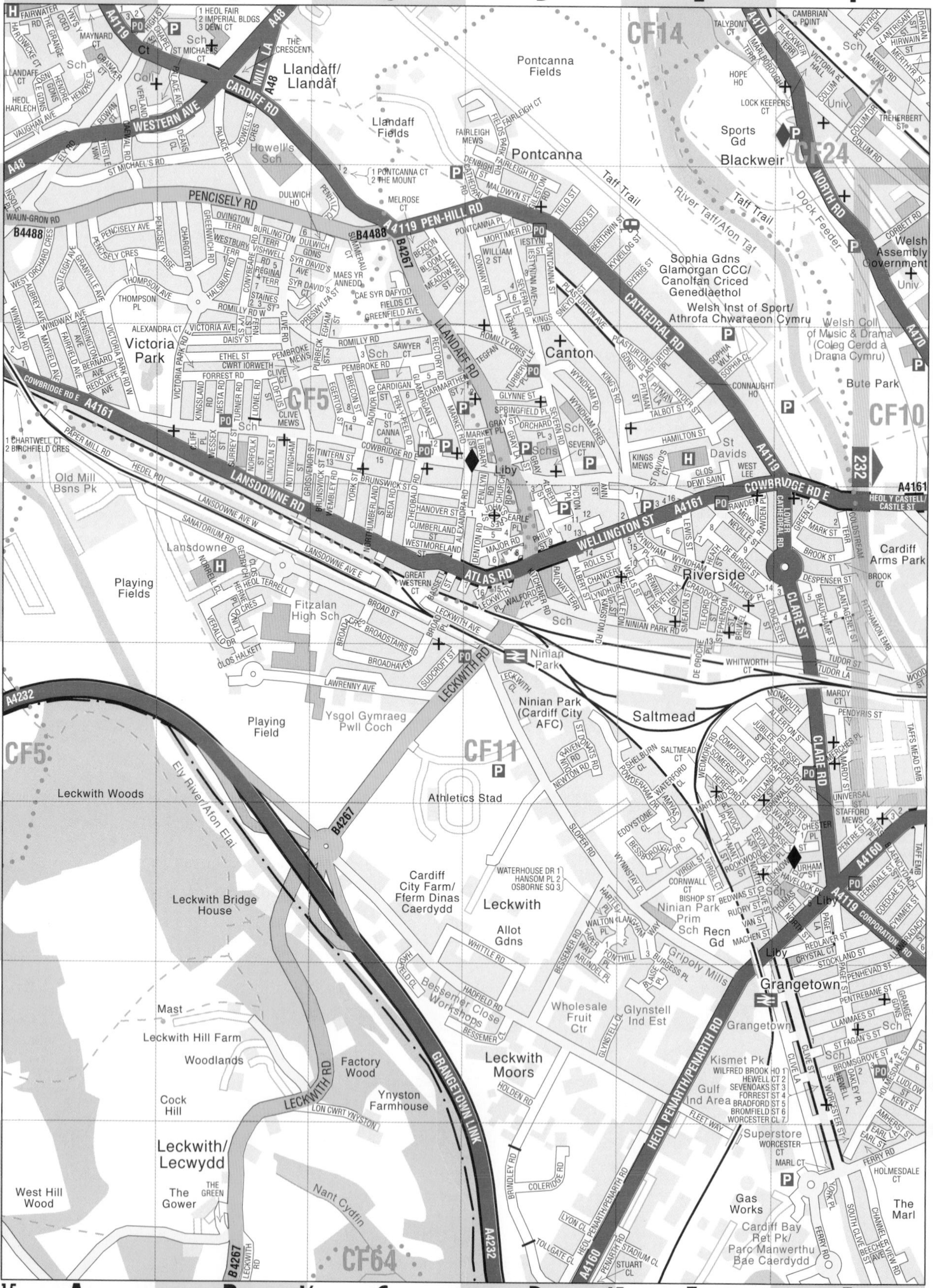

For full street detail of the highlighted area see pages 232.

193
206

D5
1 ETON PL
2 ST JOHN'S CT
3 DELTA ST
4 WELBY RD
5 WELBY LA
6 ATLAS PL
7 THURSTON ST
8 ANSTEE CT
9 COLBOURNE WLK
10 ALBERT WLK
11 GRAHAM WLK
12 PICTON WLK
13 MURRAY WLK
14 DUGDALE WLK
15 HARDING CT
16 FOUNDRY CL
E5
1 NORTH MORGAN ST
2 CANTON CT
3 WELLINGTON CT
4 WELLINGTON MEWS
5 GERRARD CT
6 SOUTH MORGAN PL
7 MANDEVILLE PL
8 MANDEVILLE ST
9 DE BURGH PL
10 BLACKSTONE ST
11 EDINBURGH CT
12 MANSFIELD ST
13 ELDON CT
14 NEVILLE PL
15 WELLS STREET LA
16 ST DAVIDS MANSION
F3
1 WARWICK PL
2 SKOMER CT
3 PENTRE PL
4 BLAENCLYDACH PL
5 FRANKLEN 5T
6 CLYDACH ST
F5
1 BELGRAVE CT
2 PARK VIEW CT
3 CLARE GDNS
4 CLARE PL
5 DESPENSER GDNS
6 DESPENSER PL

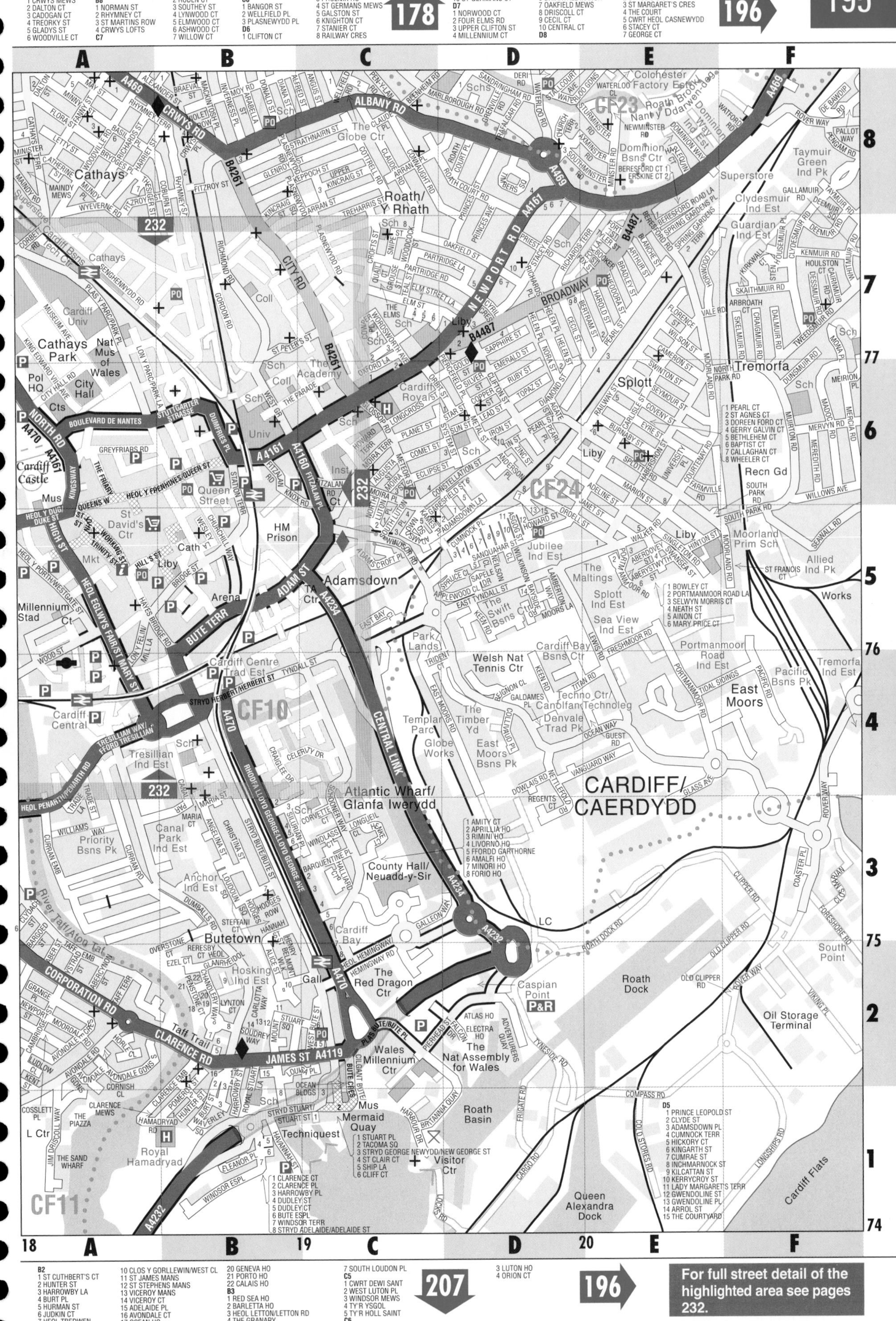
A8
1 CRWYS MEWS
2 DALTON CT
3 CADOGAN CT
4 TREORKY ST
5 GLADYS ST
6 WOODVILLE CT
7 THESIGER CT
B8
1 NORMAN ST
2 RHYMNEY CT
3 ST MARTINS ROW
4 CRWYS LOFTS
C7
1 WOODLAND PL
2 RODEN CT
3 SOUTHEY ST
4 LYNWOOD CT
5 ELMWOOD CT
6 ASHWOOD CT
7 WILLOW CT
8 OAK CT
C8
1 BANGOR ST
2 WELLFIELD PL
3 PLASNEWYDD PL
D6
1 CLIFTON CT
2 CLIFTON MEWS
3 PHOENIX HO
4 ST GERMANS MEWS
5 GALSTON ST
6 KNIGHTON CT
7 STANIER CT
8 RAILWAY CRES
178
9 SIDNEY AMES CT
10 ST GERMANS CT
D7
1 NORWOOD CT
2 FOUR ELMS RD
3 UPPER CLIFTON ST
4 MILLENNIUM CT
5 PARTRIDGE CT
6 BRIARTREE MANOR
7 OAKFIELD MEWS
8 DRISCOLL CT
9 CECIL CT
10 CENTRAL CT
D8
1 AGINCOURT RD
2 ST TELIO'S CT
3 ST MARGARET'S CRES
4 THE COURT
5 CWRT HEOL CASNEWYDD
6 STACEY CT
7 GEORGE CT
196
A
B
C
D
E
F
8
7
77
6
5
76
4
3
75
2
1
74
18
19
20
Cathays
Roath/
Y Rhath
CF23
Cathays Park
Cardiff Univ
Nat Mus of Wales
City Hall
Pol HQ
Cardiff Castle
Queen Street
St David's Ctr
HM Prison
Adamsdown
Splott
Tremorfa
CF24
CF10
Arena
Millennium Stad
Cardiff Central
Cardiff Centre Trad Est
Tresillian Ind Est
Atlantic Wharf/
Glanfa Iwerydd
County Hall/
Neuadd-y-Sir
Butetown
Cardiff Bay
The Red Dragon Ctr
Wales Millennium Ctr
The Nat Assembly for Wales
Mermaid Quay
Techniquest
Roath Basin
Roath Dock
Queen Alexandra Dock
Cardiff Flats
Oil Storage Terminal
CARDIFF/
CAERDYDD
East Moors
Ocean Park
Splott Ind Est
Sea View Ind Est
Welsh Nat Tennis Ctr
Jubilee Ind Est
Moorland Prim Sch
Allied Ind Pk
Pacific Bsns Pk
Tremorfa Ind Est
Portmanmoor Road Ind Est
Taymuir Green Ind Pk
Clydesmuir Ind Est
Guardian Ind Est
Dominion Bsns Ctr
Colchester Factory Est
Caspian Point
Royal Hamadryad
CF11
232
207
1 AMITY CT
2 APRILLIA HO
3 RIMINI HO
4 LIVORNO HO
5 FFORDD GARTHORNE
6 AMALFI HO
7 MINORI HO
8 FORIO HO
1 PEARL CT
2 ST AGNES CT
3 DOREEN FORD CT
4 GERRY GALVIN CT
5 BETHLEHEM CT
6 BAPTIST CT
7 CALLAGHAN CT
8 WHEELER CT
1 BOWLEY CT
2 PORTMANMOOR ROAD LA
3 SELWYN MORRIS CT
4 NEATH ST
5 AINON CT
6 MARY PRICE CT
1 STUART PL
2 TACOMA SQ
3 STRYD GEORGE NEWYDD/NEW GEORGE ST
4 ST CLAIR CT
5 SHIP LA
6 CLIFF CT
1 CLARENCE CT
2 CLARENCE PL
3 HARROWBY PL
4 DUDLEY ST
5 DUDLEY CT
6 BUTE ESPL
7 WINDSOR TERR
8 STRYD ADELAIDE/ADELAIDE ST
D5
1 PRINCE LEOPOLD ST
2 CLYDE ST
3 ADAMSDOWN PL
4 CUMNOCK TERR
5 HICKORY CT
6 KINGARTH ST
7 CUMRAE ST
8 INCHMARNOCK ST
9 KILCATTAN ST
10 KERRYCROY ST
11 LADY MARGARET'S TERR
12 GWENDOLINE ST
13 GWENDOLINE PL
14 ARROL ST
15 THE COURTYARD
B2
1 ST CUTHBERT'S CT
2 HUNTER ST
3 HARROWBY LA
4 BURT PL
5 HURMAN ST
6 JUDKIN CT
7 HEOL TREDWEN
8 FFORDD RADCLIFFE
9 TALIESIN CT
10 CLOS Y GORLLEWIN/WEST CL
11 ST JAMES MANS
12 ST STEPHENS MANS
13 VICEROY MANS
14 VICEROY CT
15 ADELAIDE PL
16 AVONDALE CT
17 OCEAN HO
18 CANNES HO
19 VIENNA HO
20 GENEVA HO
21 PORTO HO
22 CALAIS HO
B3
1 RED SEA HO
2 BARLETTA HO
3 HEOL LETTON/LETTON RD
4 THE GRANARY
5 SOUTH MEWS
6 MAES MAGRETIAN/MAGRETION PL
7 SOUTH LOUDON PL
C5
1 CWRT DEWI SANT
2 WEST LUTON PL
3 WINDSOR MEWS
4 TY'R YSGOL
5 TY'R HOLL SAINT
C6
1 FOUR ELMS CT
2 STEPHENSON CT
3 LUTON HO
4 ORION CT
207
196
For full street detail of the highlighted area see pages 232.

195
179

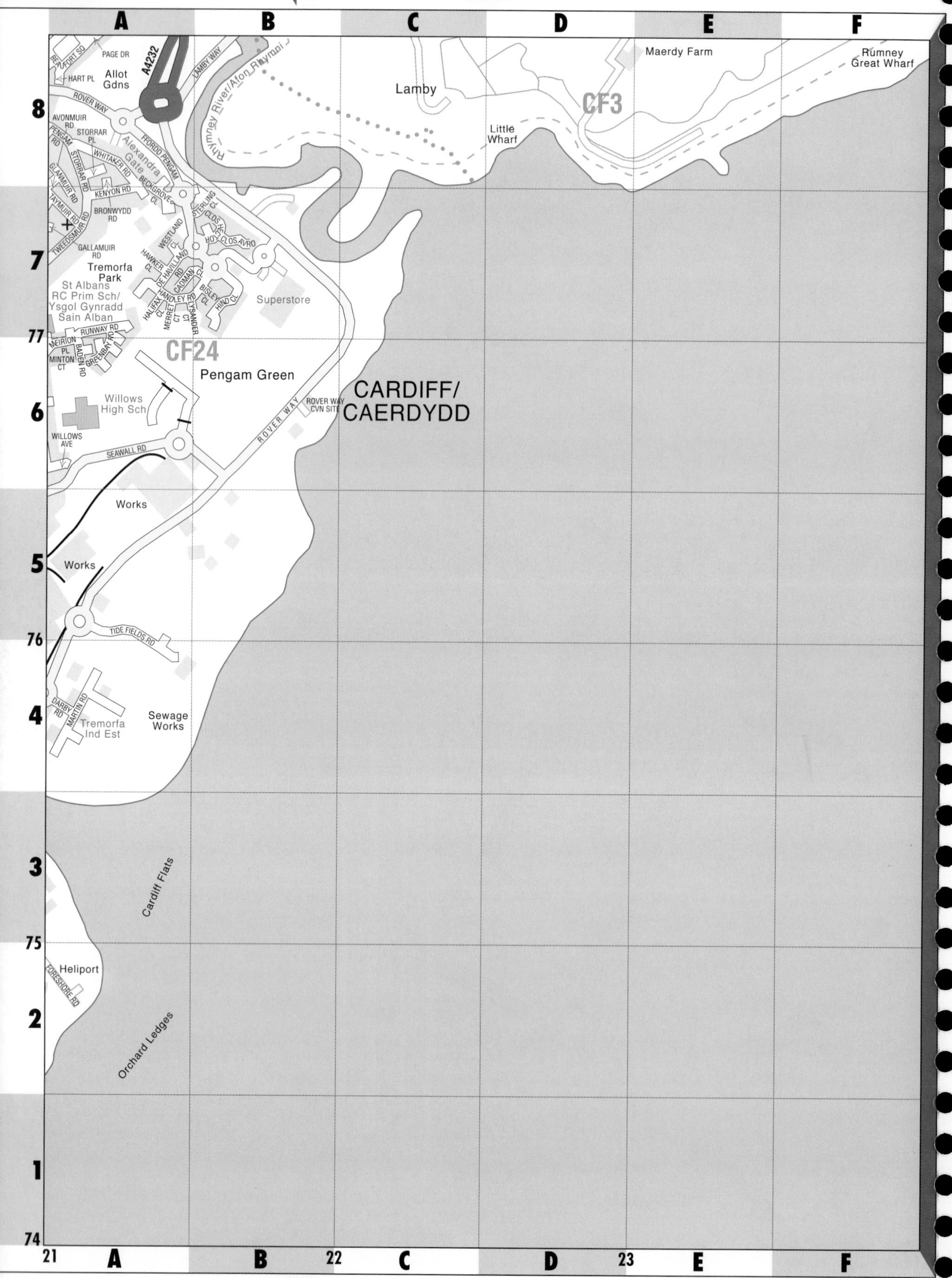

A
B
C
D
E
F
8
7
77
6
5
76
4
3
75
2
1
74
21
22
23
A4232
Allot Gdns
PAGE DR
HART PL
ROVER WAY
AVONMUIR RD
STORRAR PL
Alexandra Gate
FFORDD PENGAM
WHITAKER RD
KENYON RD
BRONWYDD RD
GALLAMUIR RD
TWEEDSMUIR RD
Tremorfa Park
St Albans RC Prim Sch/ Ysgol Gynradd Sain Alban
RUNWAY RD
MEIRION PL
MINTON CT
BADEN RD
GREENBAY RD
CF24
Pengam Green
Willows High Sch
WILLOWS AVE
SEAWALL RD
ROVER WAY
ROVER WAY CVN SITE
Superstore
WESTLAND CL
STERLING CL
CLOS AVRO
HIND CL
BISLEY CL
LYSANDER CT
CADMAN CL
HANDLEY RD
HALIFAX CL
MERRETT CT
HAWKER CL
DE HAVILLAND RD
Rhymney River/Afon Rhymni
Lamby
LAMBY WAY
Little Wharf
Maerdy Farm
CF3
Rumney Great Wharf
CARDIFF/ CAERDYDD
Works
Works
TIDE FIELDS RD
DARBY RD
MARTIN RD
Tremorfa Ind Est
Sewage Works
Cardiff Flats
Heliport
FORESHORE RD
Orchard Ledges

195

185
198

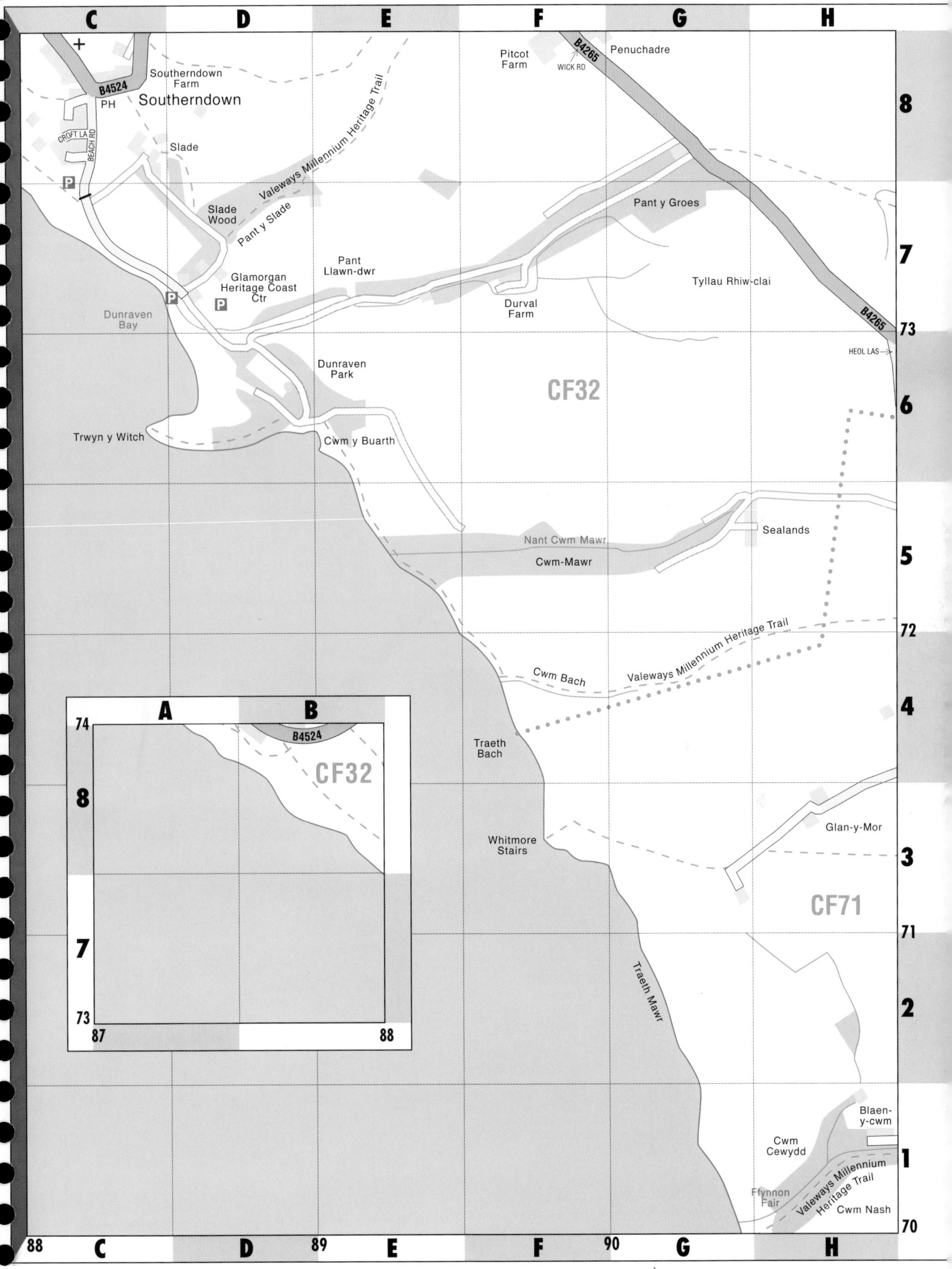

C
D
E
F
G
H
B4524
Southerndown Farm
Southerndown
PH
CROFT LA
BEACH RD
Slade
Pitcot Farm
B4265
WICK RD
Penuchadre
Valeways Millennium Heritage Trail
Slade Wood
Pant y Slade
Pant y Groes
Pant Llawn-dwr
Glamorgan Heritage Coast Ctr
Dunraven Bay
Durval Farm
Tyllau Rhiw-clai
B4265
HEOL LAS
Dunraven Park
CF32
Trwyn y Witch
Cwm y Buarth
Nant Cwm Mawr
Cwm-Mawr
Sealands
Valeways Millennium Heritage Trail
Cwm Bach
Traeth Bach
Whitmore Stairs
Glan-y-Mor
CF71
Traeth Mawr
Blaen-y-cwm
Cwm Cewydd
Ffynnon Fair
Valeways Millennium Heritage Trail
Cwm Nash
8
7
73
6
5
72
4
3
71
2
1
70
88
89
90
A
B
74
B4524
CF32
8
7
73
87
88

198

197 186

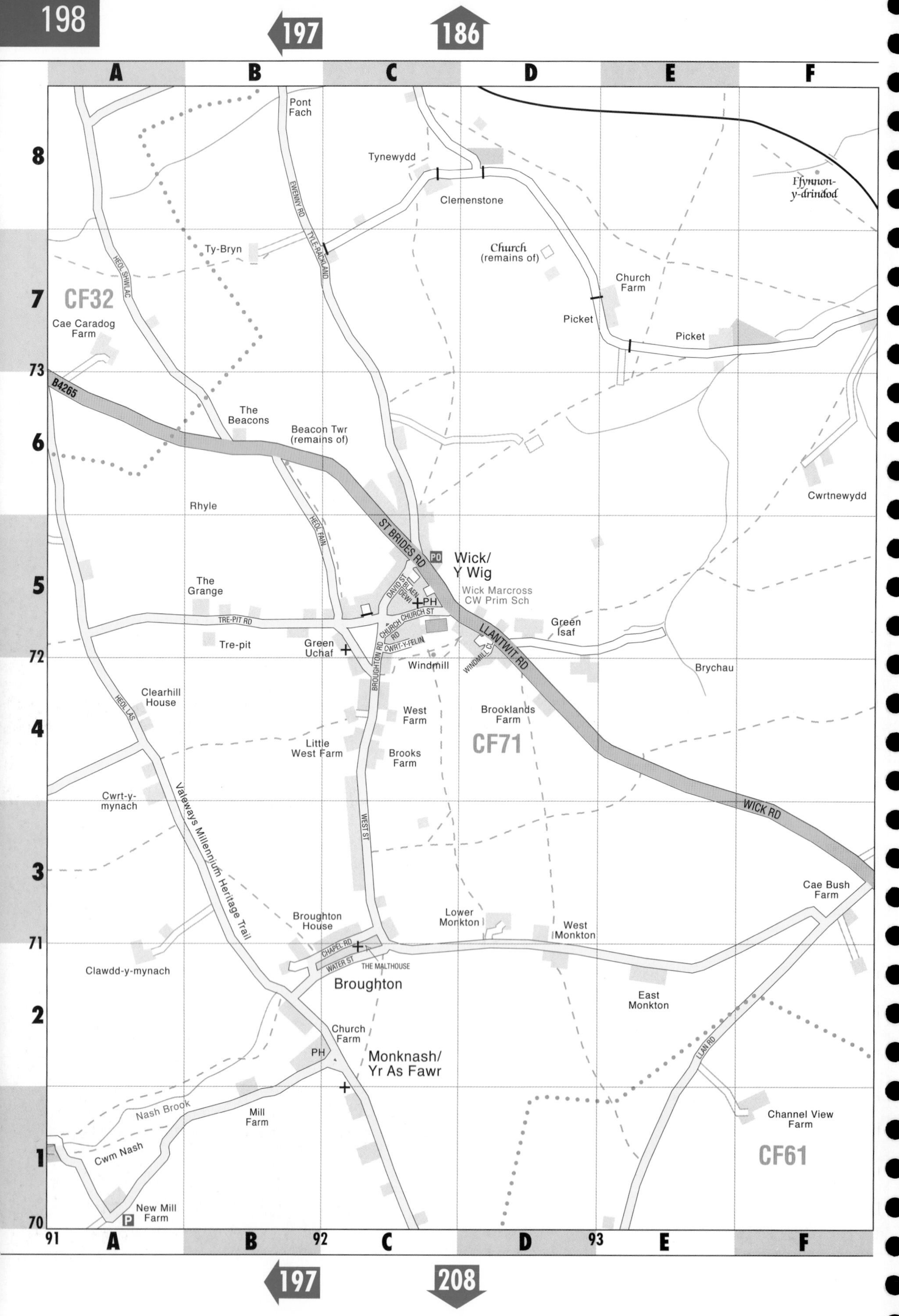

197 208

187
200

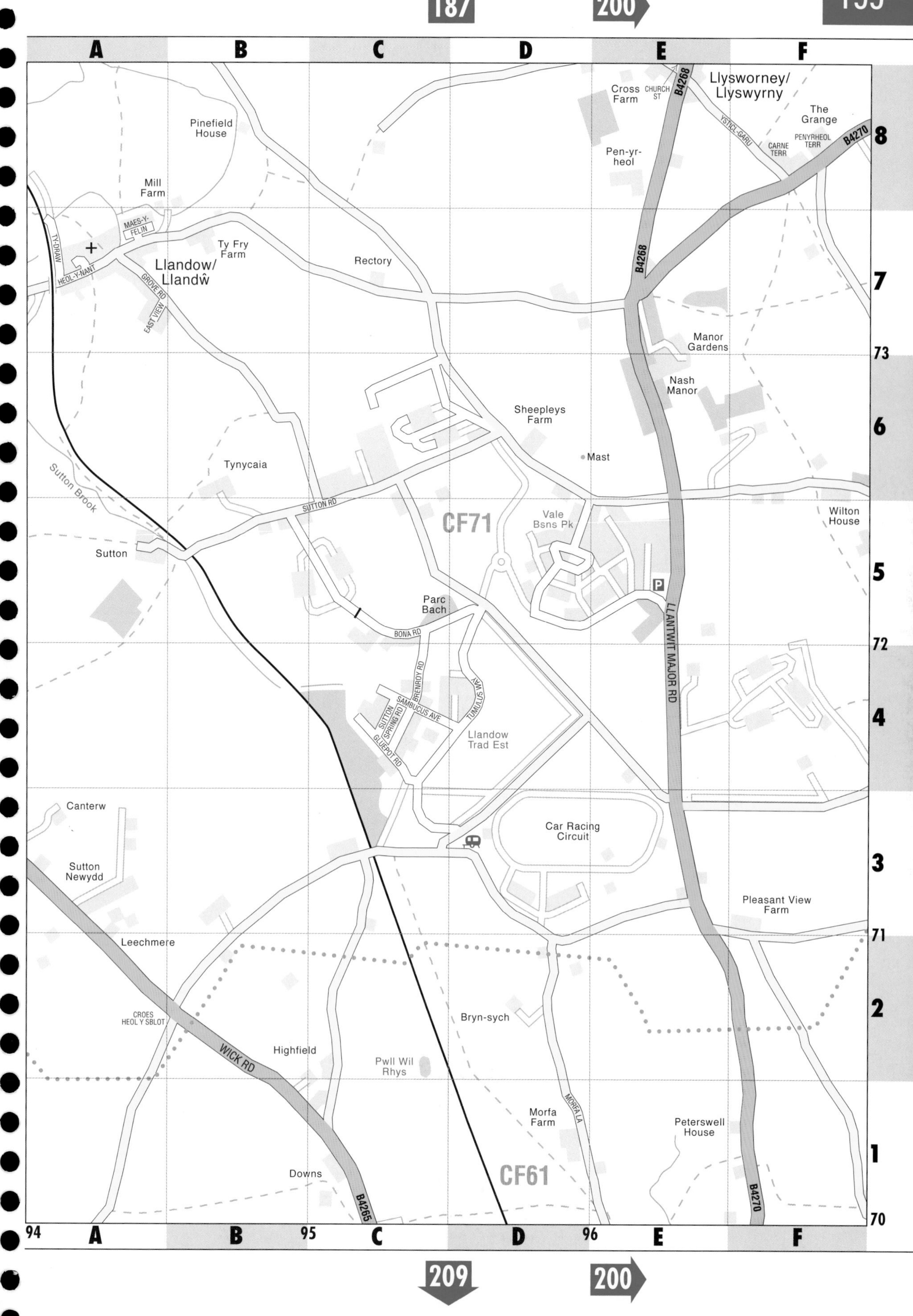

209
200

199
188

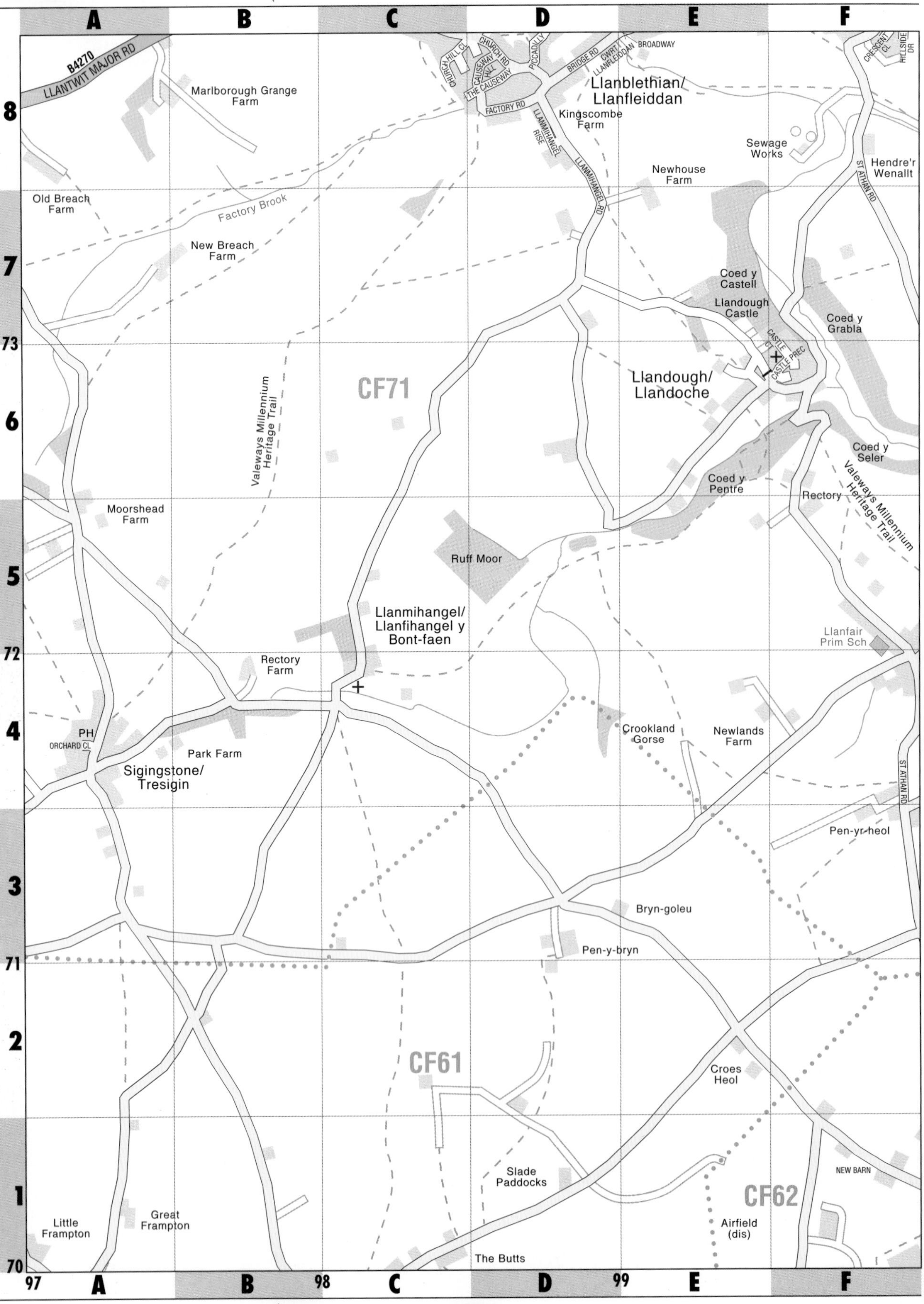

A B C D E F

8 7 73 6 5 72 4 3 71 2 1 70

B4270 LLANTWIT MAJOR RD
Marlborough Grange Farm
CHURCH HILL CL
CHURCH RD
THE CAUSEWAY
CAUSEWAY HILL
PICCADILLY
BRIDGE RD
CWRT LLANFLEIDDAN
BROADWAY
FACTORY RD
Llanblethian/ Llanfleiddan
Kingscombe Farm
LLANMIHANGEL RISE
LLANMIHANGEL RD
CRESCENT CL
HILLSIDE DR
Sewage Works
Hendre'r Wenallt
ST ATHAN RD
Newhouse Farm
Old Breach Farm
Factory Brook
New Breach Farm
Coed y Castell
Llandough Castle
Coed y Grabla
CASTLE CT
CASTLE PREC
Llandough/ Llandoche
CF71
Valeways Millennium Heritage Trail
Coed y Seler
Coed y Pentre
Rectory
Moorshead Farm
Ruff Moor
Llanmihangel/ Llanfihangel y Bont-faen
Llanfair Prim Sch
Rectory Farm
Crookland Gorse
Newlands Farm
PH
ORCHARD CL
Park Farm
Sigingstone/ Tresigin
ST ATHAN RD
Pen-yr-heol
Bryn-goleu
Pen-y-bryn
CF61
Croes Heol
Slade Paddocks
NEW BARN
CF62
Little Frampton
Great Frampton
Airfield (dis)
The Butts

97 A B 98 C D 99 E F

199
210

189
202

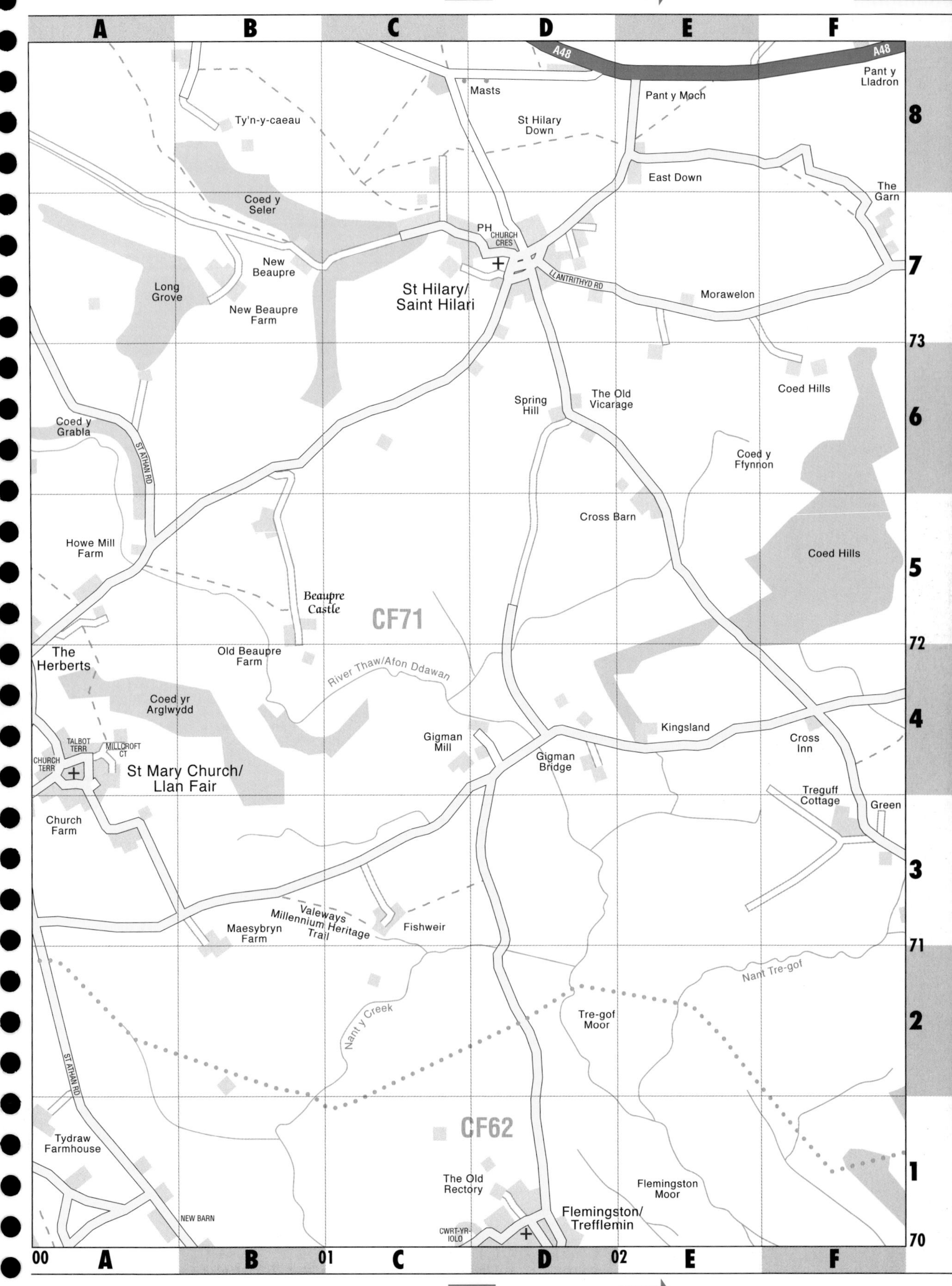

211
202

201
190

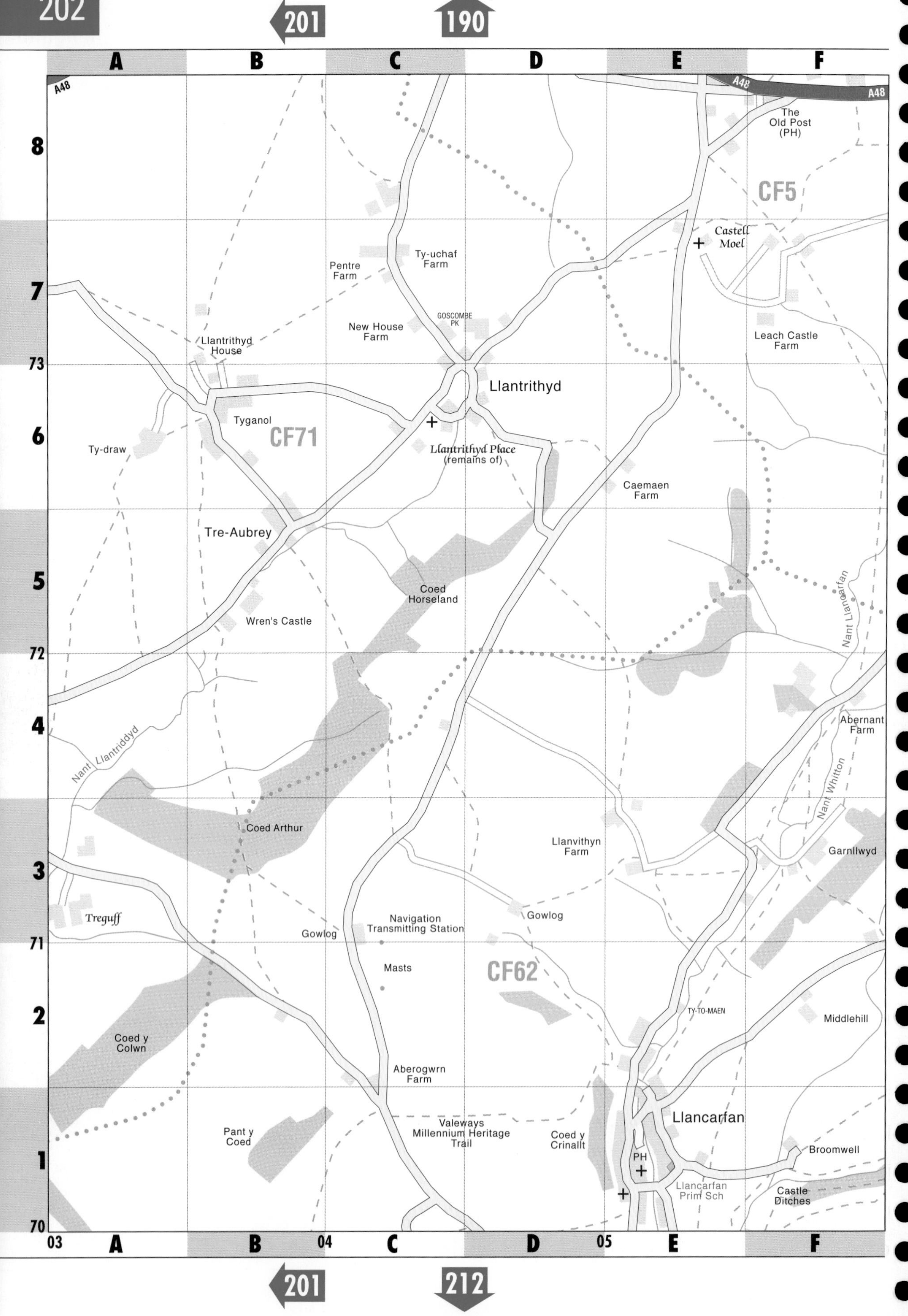

201
212

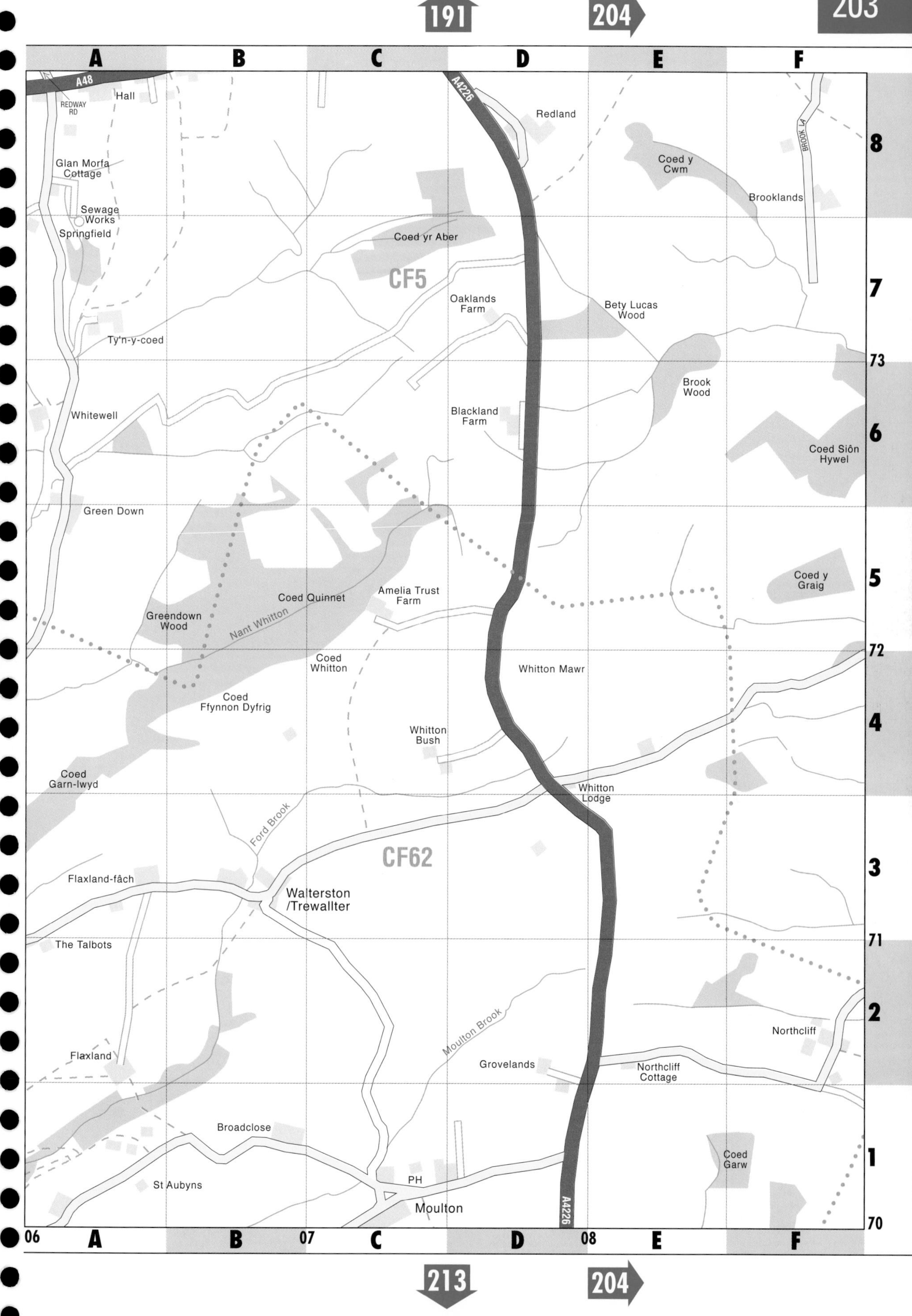
191
204
A
B
C
D
E
F
A48
REDWAY RD
Hall
A4226
Redland
BROOK LA
Coed y Cwm
Glan Morfa Cottage
Sewage Works
Springfield
Brooklands
Coed yr Aber
CF5
Oaklands Farm
Bety Lucas Wood
Ty'n-y-coed
Brook Wood
Whitewell
Blackland Farm
Coed Siôn Hywel
Green Down
Coed y Graig
Coed Quinnet
Amelia Trust Farm
Greendown Wood
Nant Whitton
Coed Whitton
Whitton Mawr
Coed Ffynnon Dyfrig
Whitton Bush
Coed Garn-lwyd
Whitton Lodge
Ford Brook
CF62
Flaxland-fâch
Walterston /Trewallter
The Talbots
Moulton Brook
Northcliff
Flaxland
Grovelands
Northcliff Cottage
Broadclose
Coed Garw
PH
St Aubyns
Moulton
8
7
73
6
5
72
4
3
71
2
1
70
06
07
08
213
204

203
192

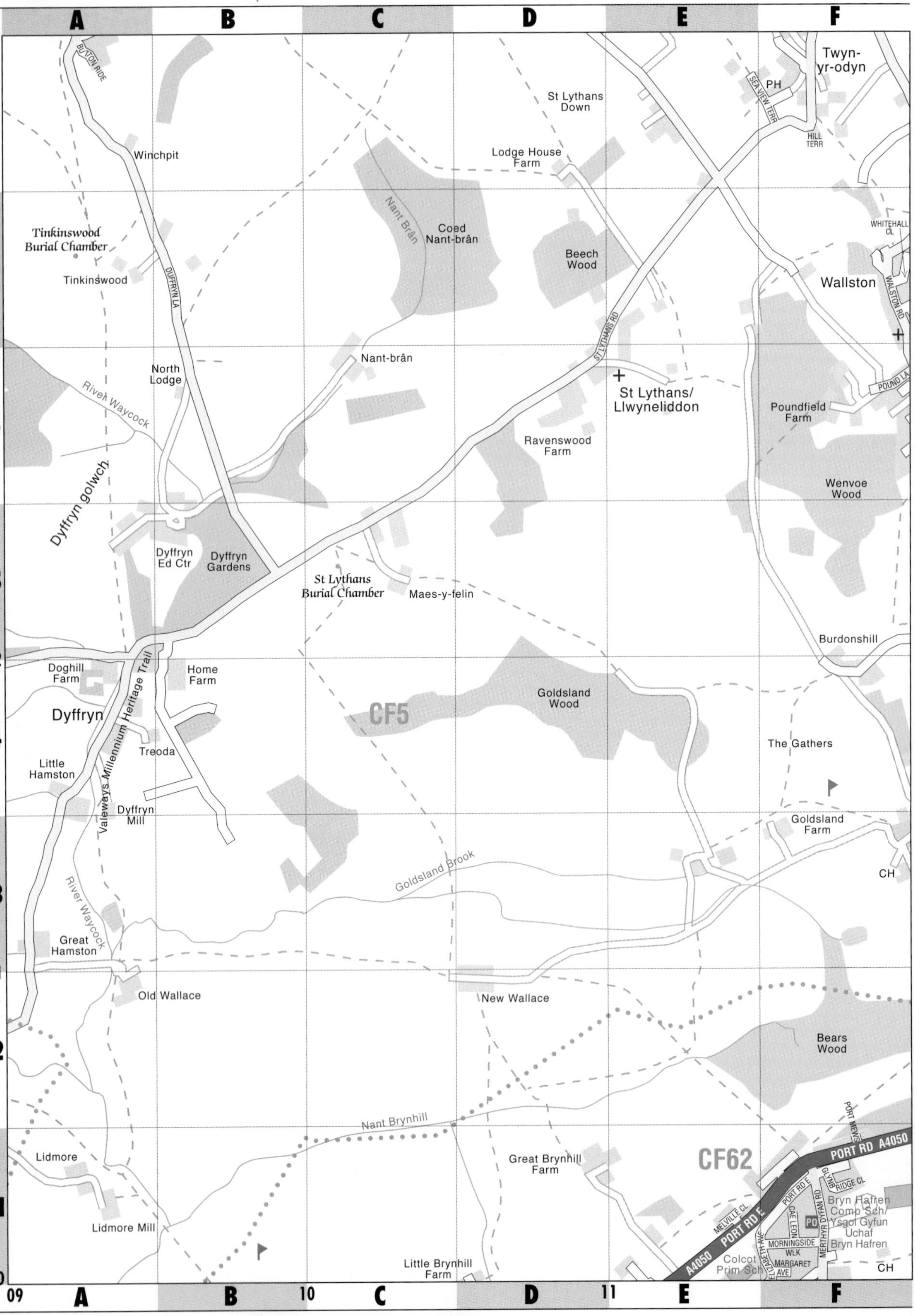

A B C D E F

8
7
73
6
5
72
4
3
71
2
1
70

BUTTON RIDE
Winchpit
St Lythans Down
Lodge House Farm
SEA VIEW TERR
PH
Twyn-yr-odyn
HILL TERR
Tinkinswood Burial Chamber
Tinkinswood
DUFFRYN LA
Nant Brân
Coed Nant-brân
Beech Wood
WHITEHALL CL
Wallston
WALSTON RD
ST LYTHANS RD
North Lodge
Nant-brân
River Waycock
St Lythans/ Llwyneliddon
POUND LA
Poundfield Farm
Ravenswood Farm
Dyffryn golwch
Wenvoe Wood
Dyffryn Ed Ctr
Dyffryn Gardens
St Lythans Burial Chamber
Maes-y-felin
Burdonshill
Doghill Farm
Home Farm
Goldsland Wood
Dyffryn
CF5
The Gathers
Valeways Millennium Heritage Trail
Treoda
Little Hamston
Dyffryn Mill
Goldsland Farm
Goldsland Brook
CH
River Waycock
Great Hamston
Old Wallace
New Wallace
Bears Wood
Nant Brynhill
PORT MEWS
Lidmore
Great Brynhill Farm
CF62
PORT RD A4050
GLYNE RIDGE CL
PORT RD E
Bryn Hafren Comp Sch/ Ysgol Gyfun Uchaf Bryn Hafren
MELVILLE CL
CAE LEON
MERTHYR DYFAN RD
PO
Lidmore Mill
MORNINGSIDE WLK
A4050 PORT RD E
ELIZABETH AVE
MARGARET AVE
Little Brynhill Farm
Colcot Prim Sch
CH

09 A B 10 C D 11 E F

203
214

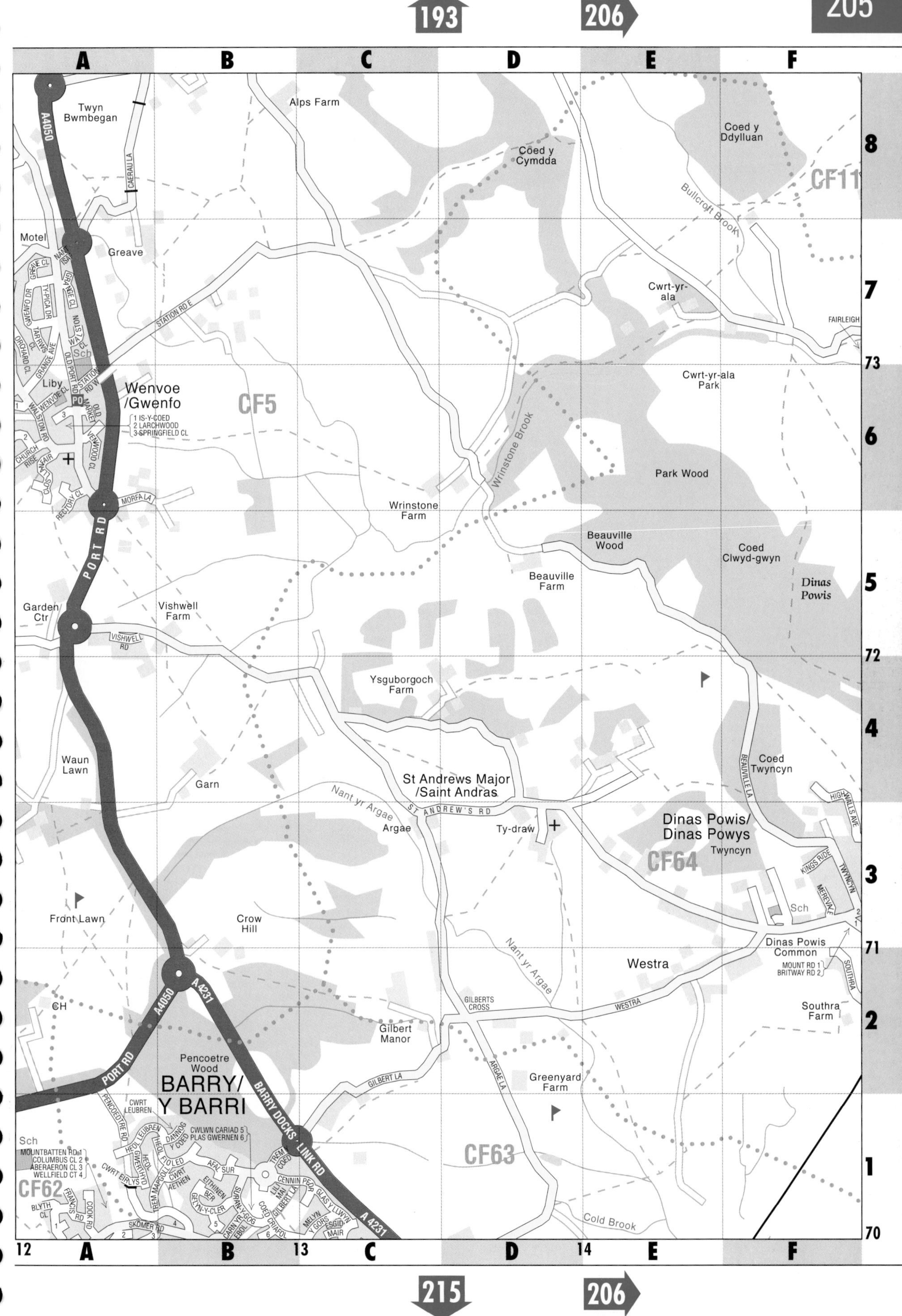
193
206
A B C D E F
8 7 73 6 5 72 4 3 71 2 1 70
12 13 14
Twyn Bwmbegan
Alps Farm
Coed y Cymdda
Coed y Ddylluan
CF11
Bullcroft Brook
Motel
Greave
Cwrt-yr-ala
FAIRLEIGH
STATION RD E
Wenvoe /Gwenfo
CF5
Cwrt-yr-ala Park
Liby
Sch
PO
1 IS-Y-COED
2 LARCHWOOD
3 SPRINGFIELD CL
Wrinstone Brook
Park Wood
MORFA LA
Wrinstone Farm
Beauville Wood
Coed Clwyd-gwyn
Beauville Farm
Dinas Powis
PORT RD
Garden Ctr
Vishwell Farm
VISHWELL RD
Ysguborgoch Farm
Waun Lawn
Garn
St Andrews Major /Saint Andras
Coed Twyncyn
BEAUVILLE LA
Nant yr Argae
ST ANDREW'S RD
Argae
Ty-draw
Dinas Powis/ Dinas Powys
Twyncyn
CF64
KINGS RIDE
Front Lawn
Crow Hill
Dinas Powis Common
MOUNT RD 1
BRITWAY RD 2
SOUTHRA
Westra
WESTRA
GILBERTS CROSS
CH
A4050
A4231
Gilbert Manor
Southra Farm
Pencoetre Wood
BARRY/ Y BARRI
GILBERT LA
ARGAE LA
Greenyard Farm
BARRY DOCKS LINK RD
CWLWN CARIAD 5
PLAS GWRNEN 6
Sch
MOUNTBATTEN RD 1
COLUMBUS CL 2
ABERAERON CL 3
WELLFIELD CT 4
CF62
CF63
Cold Brook
SKOMER RD
A 4231
215
206

205
194

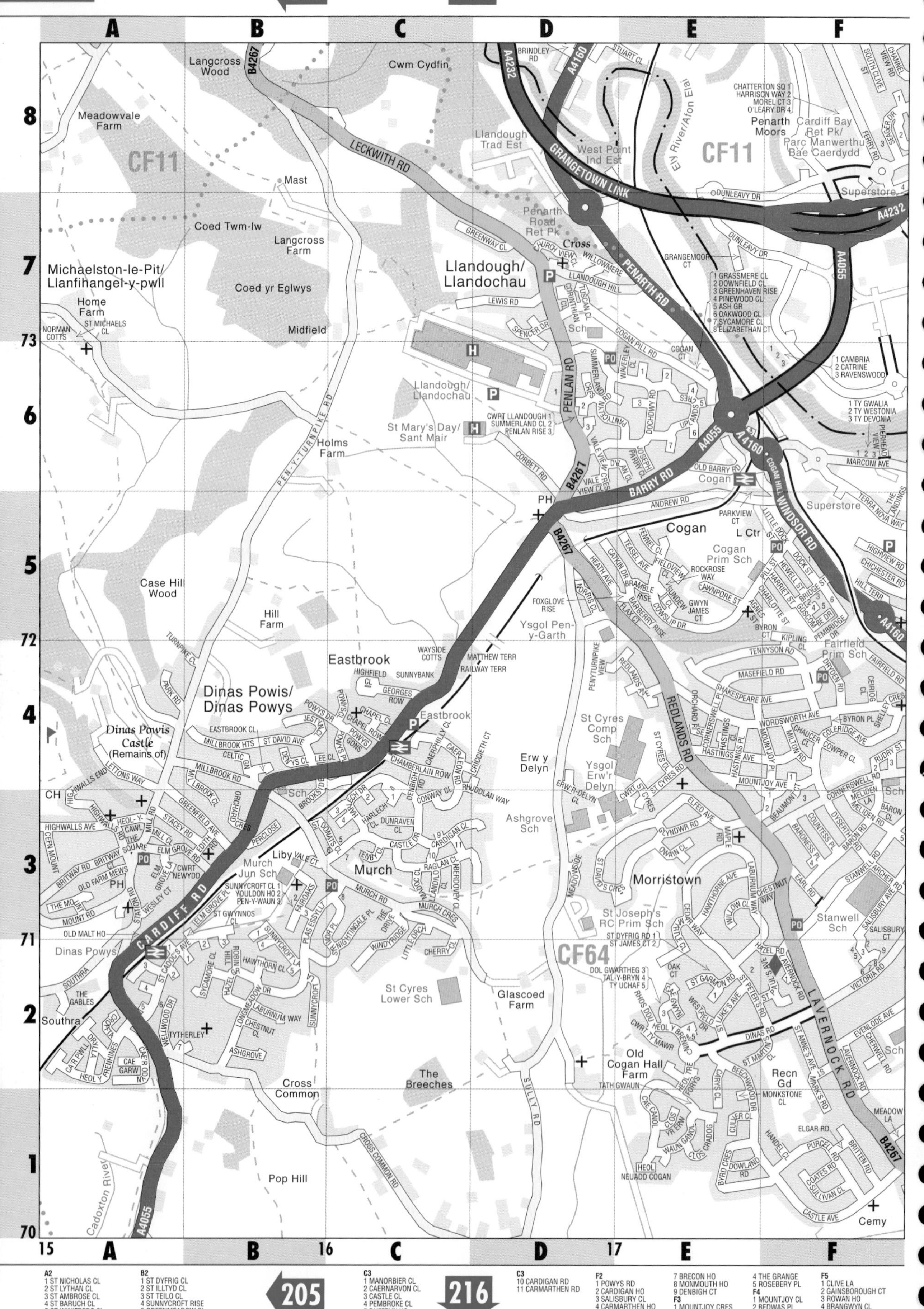

A2
1 ST NICHOLAS CL
2 ST LYTHAN CL
3 ST AMBROSE CL
4 ST BARUCH CL
5 ST WINIFREDS CL
6 ST PAULS CL
7 KINGS CT

B2
1 ST DYFRIG CL
2 ST ILLTYD CL
3 ST TEILO CL
4 SUNNYCROFT RISE
5 GREENMEADOW CL

205

C3
1 MANORBIER CL
2 CAERNARVON CL
3 CASTLE CL
4 PEMBROKE CL
5 DUFFRYN HO
6 CASTLE CT
7 THE PARADE
8 CAMM'S CNR
9 LLANDYFRIG CL

216

C3
10 CARDIGAN RD
11 CARMARTHEN RD

F2
1 POWYS RD
2 CARDIGAN HO
3 SALISBURY CL
4 CARMARTHEN HO
5 MERIONETH HO
6 RADNOR HO
7 BRECON HO
8 MONMOUTH HO
9 DENBIGH CT

F3
1 MOUNTJOY CRES
2 MOUNTJOY LA
3 CORNERSWELL LA
4 THE GRANGE
5 ROSEBERY PL

F4
1 MOUNTJOY CL
2 BEDWAS PL
3 MACHEN ST

F5
1 CLIVE LA
2 GAINSBOROUGH CT
3 ROWAN HO
4 BRANGWYN CL
5 ROMNEY WLK
6 GAINSBOROUGH RD

195

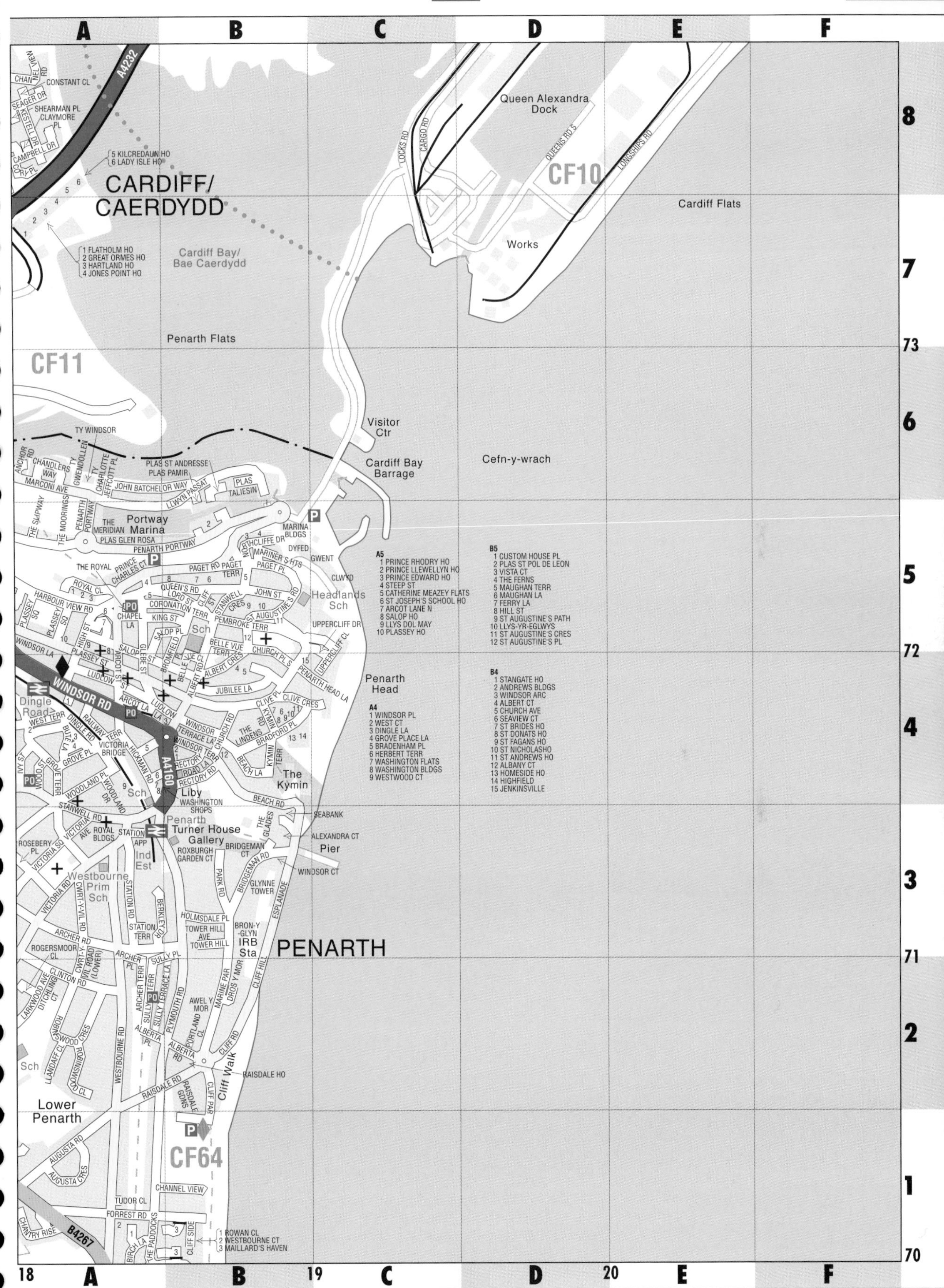

CARDIFF/ CAERDYDD
Cardiff Bay/ Bae Caerdydd
Penarth Flats
CF11
CF10
Queen Alexandra Dock
Works
Cardiff Flats
Visitor Ctr
Cardiff Bay Barrage
Cefn-y-wrach
Portway Marina
Headlands Sch
Penarth Head
The Kymin
Pier
Turner House Gallery
Westbourne Prim Sch
PENARTH
Lower Penarth
CF64
Cliff Walk
A5
1 PRINCE RHODRY HO
2 PRINCE LLEWELLYN HO
3 PRINCE EDWARD HO
4 STEEP ST
5 CATHERINE MEAZEY FLATS
6 ST JOSEPH'S SCHOOL HO
7 ARCOT LANE N
8 SALOP HO
9 LLYS DOL MAY
10 PLASSEY HO
B5
1 CUSTOM HOUSE PL
2 PLAS ST POL DE LEON
3 VISTA CT
4 THE FERNS
5 MAUGHAN TERR
6 MAUGHAN LA
7 FERRY LA
8 HILL ST
9 ST AUGUSTINE'S PATH
10 LLYS-YR-EGLWYS
11 ST AUGUSTINE'S CRES
12 ST AUGUSTINE'S PL
A4
1 WINDSOR PL
2 WEST CT
3 DINGLE LA
4 GROVE PLACE LA
5 BRADENHAM PL
6 HERBERT TERR
7 WASHINGTON FLATS
8 WASHINGTON BLDGS
9 WESTWOOD CT
B4
1 STANGATE HO
2 ANDREWS BLDGS
3 WINDSOR ARC
4 ALBERT CT
5 CHURCH AVE
6 SEAVIEW CT
7 ST BRIDES HO
8 ST DONATS HO
9 ST FAGANS HO
10 ST NICHOLASHO
11 ST ANDREWS HO
12 ALBANY CT
13 HOMESIDE HO
14 HIGHFIELD
15 JENKINSVILLE
1 FLATHOLM HO
2 GREAT ORMES HO
3 HARTLAND HO
4 JONES POINT HO
5 KILCREDAUN HO
6 LADY ISLE HO
1 ROWAN CL
2 WESTBOURNE CT
3 MAILLARD'S HAVEN
A B C D E F
8 7 73 6 5 72 4 3 71 2 1 70
18 19 20

217

198

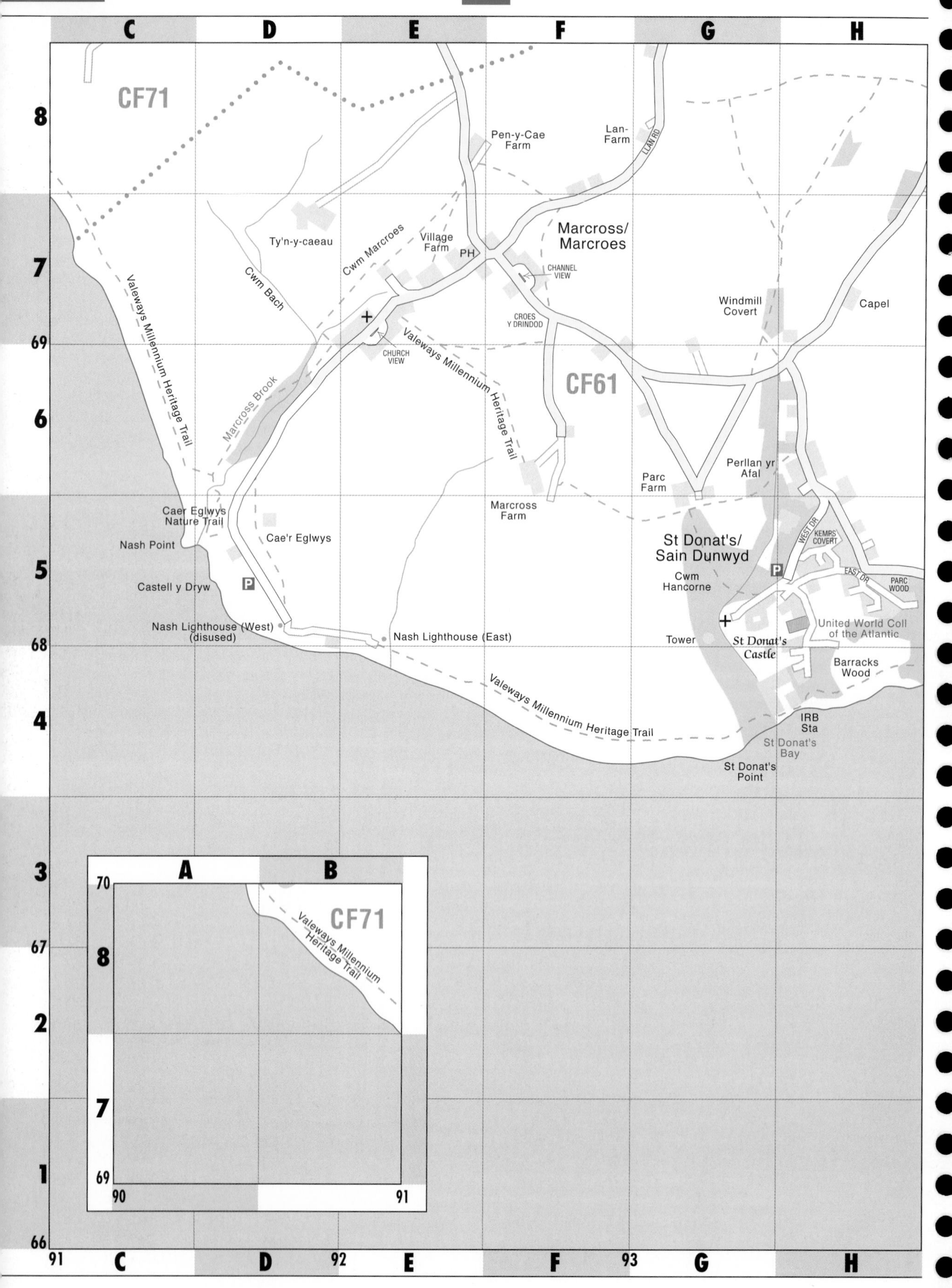
CF71
Pen-y-Cae Farm
Lan-Farm
LLAN RD
Ty'n-y-caeau
Cwm Marcroes
Village Farm
PH
Marcross/ Marcroes
CHANNEL VIEW
Cwm Bach
Valeways Millennium Heritage Trail
Windmill Covert
Capel
CROES Y DRINDOD
CHURCH VIEW
CF61
Marcross Brook
Parc Farm
Perllan yr Afal
Marcross Farm
Caer Eglwys Nature Trail
Cae'r Eglwys
Nash Point
St Donat's/ Sain Dunwyd
WEST DR
KEMPS COVERT
EAST DR
PARC WOOD
Cwm Hancorne
Castell y Dryw
United World Coll of the Atlantic
Nash Lighthouse (West) (disused)
Nash Lighthouse (East)
Tower
St Donat's Castle
Barracks Wood
IRB Sta
St Donat's Bay
St Donat's Point
CF71
Valeways Millennium Heritage Trail

199
210

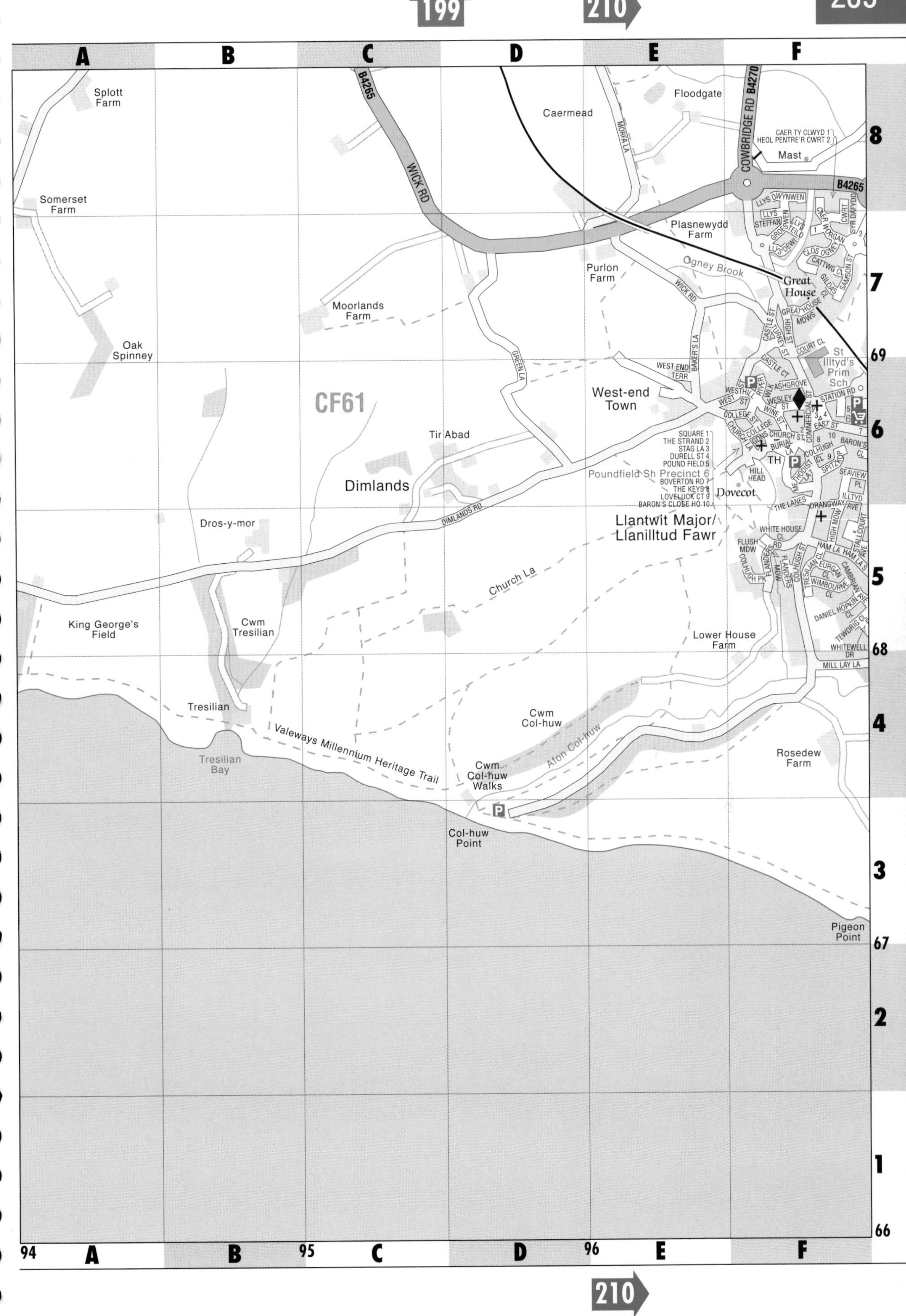
Splott Farm
Somerset Farm
Oak Spinney
Caermead
Floodgate
Plasnewydd Farm
Purlon Farm
Moorlands Farm
Great House
CF61
West-end Town
Tir Abad
Dimlands
Dros-y-mor
Llantwit Major/
Llanilltud Fawr
Church La
King George's Field
Cwm Tresilian
Lower House Farm
Tresilian
Tresilian Bay
Valeways Millennium Heritage Trail
Cwm Col-huw
Aton Col-huw
Cwm Col-huw Walks
Col-huw Point
Rosedew Farm
Pigeon Point
Dovecot
Poundfield Sh Precinct
WICK RD
B4265
B4270
COWBRIDGE RD
DIMLANDS RD
GREEN LA
MORFA LA
Mast
Ogney Brook
St Illtyd's Prim Sch
SQUARE 1
THE STRAND 2
STAG LA 3
DURELL ST 4
POUND FIELD 5
BOVERTON RD 7
THE KEYS 8
LOVELUCK CT 9
BARON'S CLOSE HO 10
CAER TY CLWYD 1
HEOL PENTRE'R CWRT 2
MILL LAY LA
WHITEWELL DR

210

209
200

A
B
C
D
E
F
8
7
69
6
5
68
4
3
67
2
1
66
97
98
99
Frampton Court Farm
Brook Farm
Blacksmith's Arms (PH)
Gadlys
Llanmaes
Great House Farm
Tremains Farm
Windmill (dis)
Airfield (dis)
Froglands Farm
Millands Farm
Old Brewery (PH)
MILLANDS CVN PK
Llantwit Major
Prim Sch
MOD St Athan
Liby
Llantwit Major/ Llanilltud Fawr
Boverton/ Trebefered
Sports Ctr
Ysgol Llanilltud Fawr
Cemy
Llanilltud Fawr Prim Sch
Hoddnant
ORCHARD LODGE
CF62
CF61
Airfield
Playing Field
B4265
Boverton Mill Farm
New Way Stair
Stout Bay
Stout Point
Hafod
Seawatch Ctr
Summerhouse Point
1 ANGLESEY CL
2 GEORGIAN CL
3 SEYS CT
4 CRAWSHAY CT
5 DE CLARE CT
6 CARMARTHEN CL
1 GWAUN ILLTUDS
2 WAUN GRON
FRAMPTON LA
LLANMAES RD
EAGLESWELL RD
BEDFORD RISE
GREY'S DR
NORDALE RD
VOSS PARK DR
BOVERTON RD
BOVERTON CT
LEIGH CL
GLANYMOR
HARDING CL
PERCY SMITH RD
COUNCIL HOS
GASKELL CL
ORCHARD CL
BOVERTON PARK DR
REDWOOD CL
TRE-BEFERAD
CASTLE CL
TENNYSON WAY
BYRON CT
WORDSWORTH CL
ILLTYD AVE
ST DONAT'S CT
TUDOR PL
STRADLING PL
FITZHAMON AVE
HAM LANE E
MANOR PK
ST DAVID'S AVE
HAM LANE S
CAMBRIAN AVE
RAGLANDE CT
MILL-LAY LA
WHITEWELL DR
HAM MANOR
HAM MEWS
MANOR SQ
ORCHARD DR
NUTWLK
BEECH AVE
HAM MANOR CVN PK
CLOS-YR-ONNEN
MANOR VIEW
LON-OD-NANT
HEOL-Y-FELIN
LLANTWIT RD
ROOK CL
EAGLE RD
WREN RD
PARTRIDGE RD
BULLFINCH RD
WAGTAIL RD
KINGFISHER SQ
CURLEW CRES
CHURCH MDW
BLACKBIRD RD
MAGPIE RD
STARLING RD
WOODPECKER SQ
BARON'S CL
SEAVIEW PL
STALLCOURT AVE
POUND FIELD
LE BOULIGUEN WAY
HEOL PENTRE'R CWRT
RECTORY CT
WEST ACRE
TYLE HOUSE CL
WINDMILL CL
WINDMILL LA
MAES ILLTUDS
REGENCY CL
WHITEWAYS
DYFRIG CT
TREVELYAN CT
GLAMORGAN CL
MONMOUTH WAY
FLINT AVE
BRECON ST
PEMBROKE PL
DENBIGH DR
RADNOR RD
CARDIGAN CRES
HEOL MERIONETH
CRAWSHAY DR
PICTON CT
FOUR ACRE
GRANGE GDNS
FAIRFIELD CL
FAIRFIELD RISE
ANDREWS CT
NICHOLL CT
BERRY CT
VACHELL CT
WINDSOR CL
CARNE CT
ALLEN CT
CAER MEAD CL
REES CT
BOVERTON BROOK
SHAKESPEARE DR
MILTON CL
P
PO

209

201
212

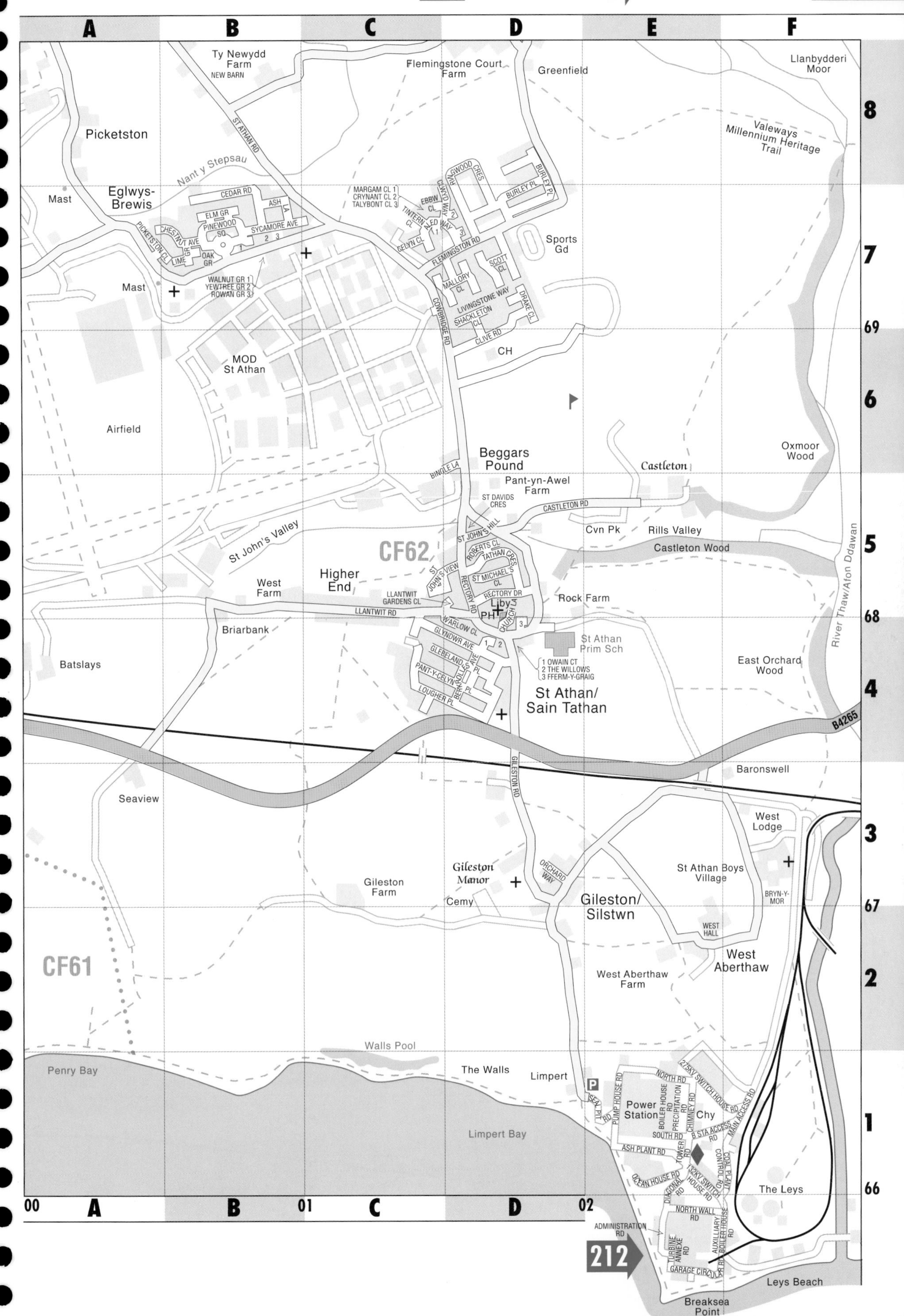
A
B
C
D
E
F
Ty Newydd Farm
NEW BARN
Flemingstone Court Farm
Greenfield
Llanbydderi Moor
Picketston
Valeways Millennium Heritage Trail
Nant y Stepsau
ST ATHAN RD
Mast
Eglwys-Brewis
CEDAR RD
ASH LA
ELM GR
PINEWOOD SQ
SYCAMORE AVE
CHESTNUT AVE
PICKETSTON CL
LIME GR
OAK GR
WALNUT GR 1
YEWTREE GR 2
ROWAN GR 3
MARGAM CL 1
CRYNANT CL 2
TALYBONT CL 3
EBBW CL
TINTERN CL
ALED WAY
CELYN CL
GWOOD CRES
BURLEY PL
FLEMINGSTON RD
SCOTT CL
MALLORY CL
LIVINGSTONE WAY
SHACKLETON CL
DRAKE CL
CLIVE RD
COWBRIDGE RD
Sports Gd
Mast
MOD St Athan
CH
Airfield
Beggars Pound
Pant-yn-Awel Farm
BINGLE LA
ST DAVIDS CRES
CASTLETON RD
Castleton
Oxmoor Wood
Cvn Pk
Rills Valley
Castleton Wood
St John's Valley
CF62
ST JOHN'S HILL
ROBERTS CL
TATHAN CRES
ST JOHN'S VIEW
ST MICHAEL'S CL
RECTORY RD
RECTORY DR
West Farm
Higher End
LLANTWIT GARDENS CL
LLANTWIT RD
Liby
PH
CHURCH LA
Rock Farm
River Thaw/Afon Ddawan
WARLOW CL
GLYNDWR AVE
Briarbank
St Athan Prim Sch
1 OWAIN CT
2 THE WILLOWS
3 FFERM-Y-GRAIG
GLEBELAND PL
BERKROLLES AVE
PANT-Y-CELYN PL
LOUGHER PL
Batslays
East Orchard Wood
St Athan/ Sain Tathan
B4265
GILESTON RD
Baronswell
Seaview
West Lodge
ORCHARD WAY
Gileston Manor
Gileston Farm
Cemy
St Athan Boys Village
BRYN-Y-MOR
Gileston/ Silstwn
WEST HALL
West Aberthaw
CF61
West Aberthaw Farm
Walls Pool
Penry Bay
The Walls
Limpert
P
Power Station
Chy
Limpert Bay
NORTH RD
275KV SWITCH HOUSE RD
MAIN ACCESS RD
PUMP HOUSE RD
BOILER HOUSE RD
PRECIPITATION RD
CHIMNEY RD
SOUTH RD
B STA ACCESS RD
ASH PLANT RD
TOWER RD
CONTROL RD
COAL PLANT RD
OCEAN HOUSE RD
DIAGONAL RD
132KV SWITCH HOUSE RD
NORTH WALL RD
The Leys
ADMINISTRATION RD
TURBINE ANNEXE RD
AUXILIARY BOILER HOUSE RD
GARAGE CIRCULAR RD
Leys Beach
Breaksea Point
8
7
69
6
5
68
4
3
67
2
1
66
00
01
02

212

211 202

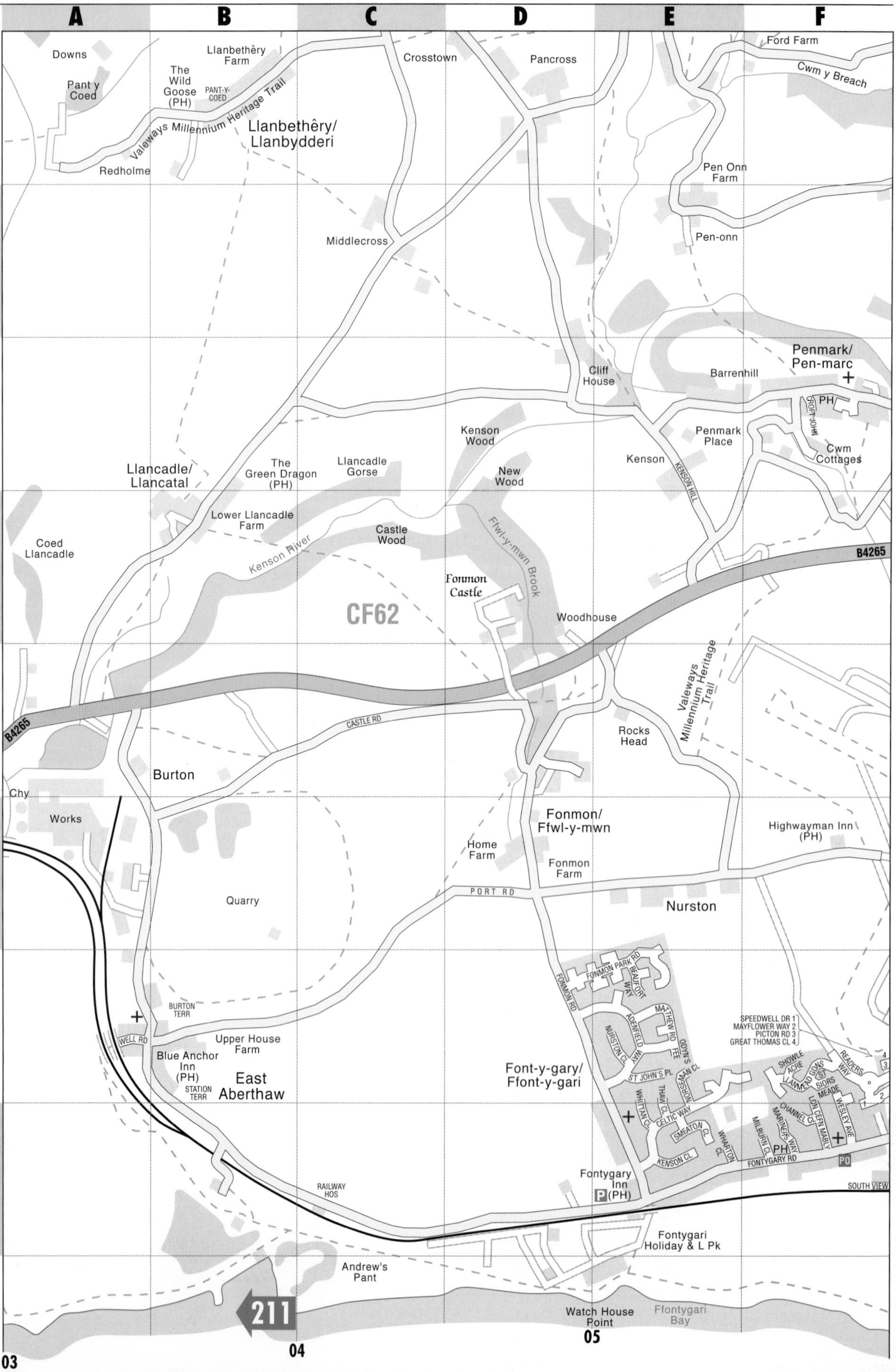

A B C D E F

8 7 69 6 5 68 4 3 67 2 1 66

Downs
Pant y Coed
The Wild Goose (PH)
Llanbethêry Farm
PANT-Y-COED
Valeways Millennium Heritage Trail
Llanbethêry/ Llanbydderi
Redholme
Crosstown
Pancross
Ford Farm
Cwm y Breach
Pen Onn Farm
Pen-onn
Middlecross
Penmark/ Pen-marc
Barrenhill
Cliff House
PH
CROFT JOHN
Penmark Place
Cwm Cottages
Kenson Wood
Kenson
KENSON HILL
New Wood
The Green Dragon (PH)
Llancadle Gorse
Llancadle/ Llancatal
Lower Llancadle Farm
Castle Wood
Coed Llancadle
Kenson River
Ffwl-y-mwn Brook
Fonmon Castle
B4265
CF62
Woodhouse
Valeways Millennium Heritage Trail
CASTLE RD
Rocks Head
Burton
Chy
Works
Fonmon/ Ffwl-y-mwn
Highwayman Inn (PH)
Home Farm
Fonmon Farm
PORT RD
Quarry
Nurston
FONMON RD
FONMON PARK RD
BEAUFORT WAY
MATHEW RD
ADENFIELD WAY
NURSTON CL
ODYN'S FEE
ST JOHN'S PL
SPEEDWELL DR 1
MAYFLOWER WAY 2
PICTON RD 3
GREAT THOMAS CL 4
BURTON TERR
WELL RD
Upper House Farm
Blue Anchor Inn (PH)
STATION TERR
East Aberthaw
Font-y-gary/ Ffont-y-gari
WHITTAN CL
THAW CL
CELTIC WAY
SMEATON CL
KENSON CL
WHARTON CL
SHOWLE ACRE
LLANMEAD GDNS
ST SIORS MEADE
READERS WAY
CHANNEL CL
LON CEFN MABLY
WESLEY AVE
MILBURN CL
MARINERS WAY
PH
FONTYGARY RD
PO
SOUTH VIEW
RAILWAY HOS
Fontygary Inn (PH)
P
Fontygari Holiday & L Pk
Andrew's Pant
Watch House Point
Ffontygari Bay

211

03 04 05

203
214

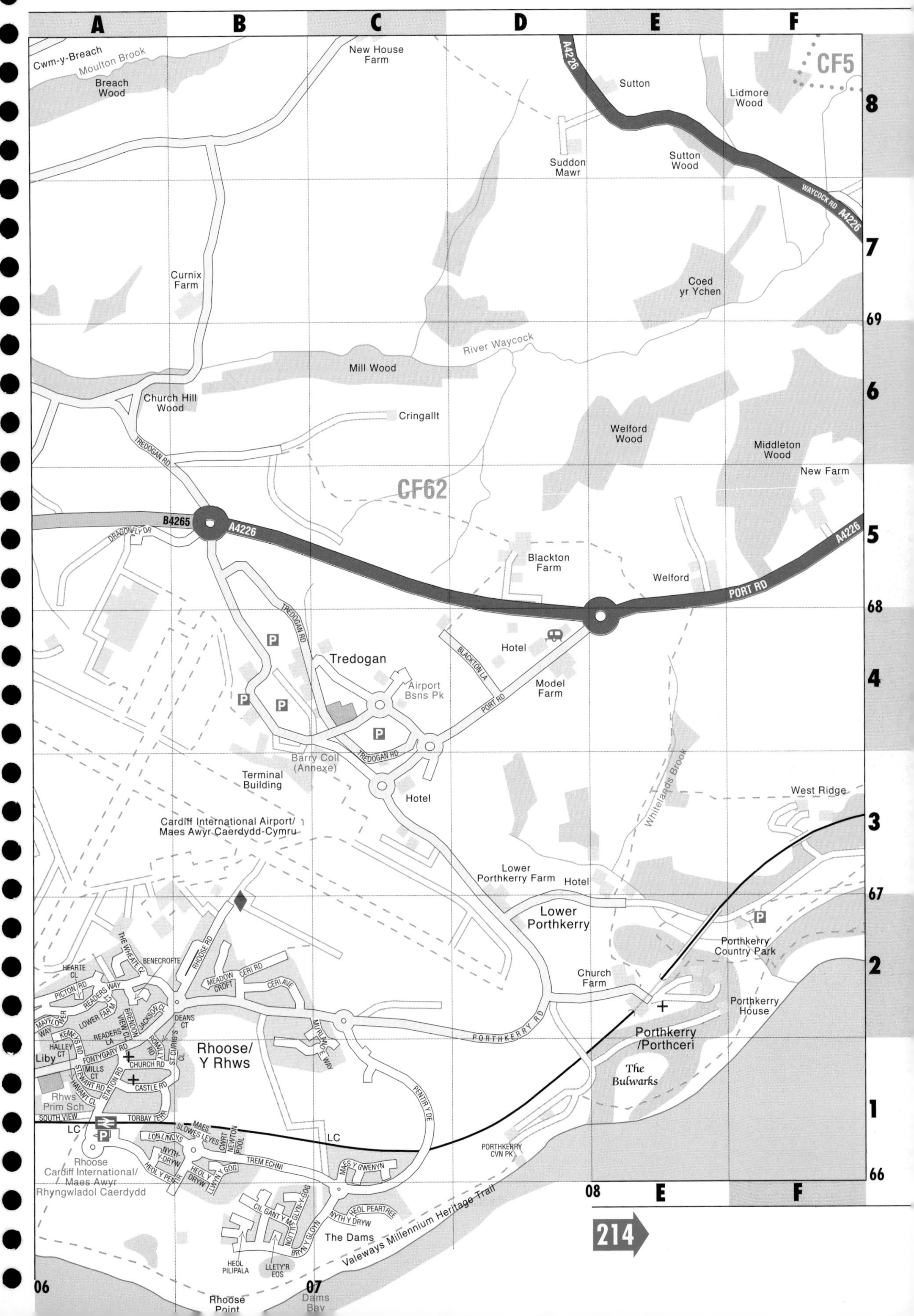
A
B
C
D
E
F
8
7
69
6
5
68
4
3
67
2
1
66
06
07
08
Cwm-y-Breach
Moulton Brook
Breach Wood
New House Farm
A4226
Sutton
CF5
Lidmore Wood
Suddon Mawr
Sutton Wood
WAYCOCK RD
Curnix Farm
Coed yr Ychen
River Waycock
Mill Wood
Church Hill Wood
Cringallt
TREDOGAN RD
Welford Wood
Middleton Wood
New Farm
CF62
B4265
DRAGONFLY DR
Blackton Farm
Welford
PORT RD
TREDOGAN RD
Tredogan
BLACKTON LA
Hotel
Model Farm
Airport Bsns Pk
Barry Coll (Annexe)
TREDOGAN RD
Terminal Building
Hotel
Whitelands Brook
West Ridge
Cardiff International Airport/ Maes Awyr Caerdydd-Cymru
Lower Porthkerry Farm
Hotel
Lower Porthkerry
Porthkerry Country Park
Church Farm
Porthkerry House
THE WHEATE CL
BENECROFTE
HEARTE CL
RHOOSE RD
MEADOW CROFT
CERI RD
CERI AVE
PICTON RD
READERS WAY
LOWER FARM CT
BRENDON VIEW CL
JACKSON CL
DEANS CT
MURLANDE WAY
PORTHKERRY RD
Porthkerry /Porthceri
The Bulwarks
MAYFLOWER WAY
KEMEYS RD
READERS LA
HALLEY CT
FONTYGARY RD
ROMILLY RD
ST CURIG'S CL
Rhoose/ Y Rhws
Liby
MILLS CT
CHURCH RD
STEWART RD
STATION RD
CASTLE RD
HAVANT CL
PENTIR Y DE
Rhws Prim Sch
SOUTH VIEW
TORBAY TERR
LC
LON LINDYS
SLOWES LEYES
MAES
CWRT NEWTON
POOL
LC
PORTHKERRY CVN PK
Rhoose Cardiff International/ Maes Awyr Rhyngwladol Caerdydd
NYTH-Y-DRYW
HEOL Y PENTIR
HEOL Y DRYW
LLWYN Y GOG
TREM ECHNI
MAES Y GWENYN
GLYN-Y-GOG
CIL GANT Y MEL
HEOL PEARTREE
NYTH Y DRYW
The Dams
Valeways Millennium Heritage Trail
HEOL PILIPALA
LLETY'R EOS
Rhoose Point
Dams Bay

213
204

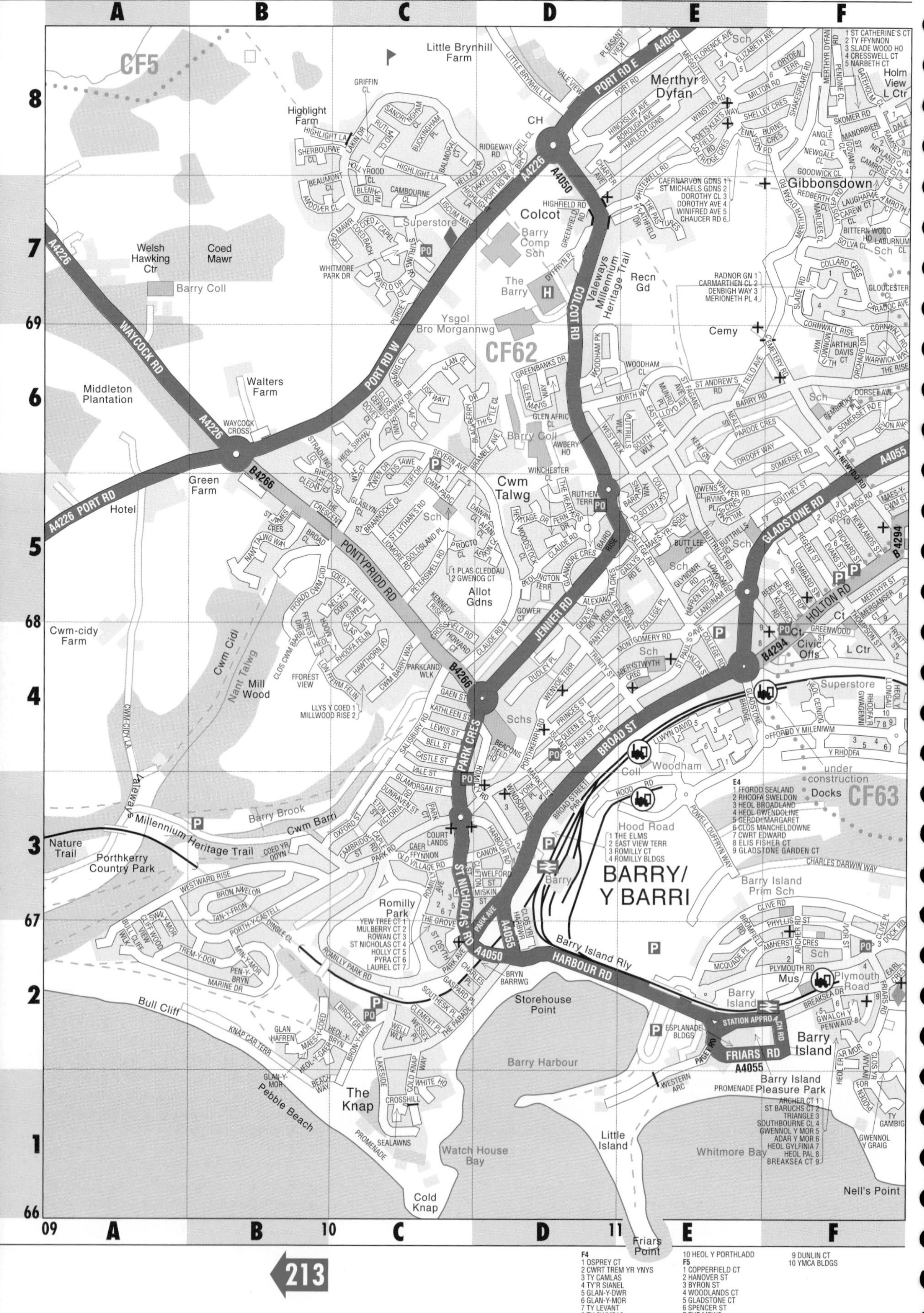
A
B
C
D
E
F
8
7
69
6
5
68
4
3
67
2
1
66
09
10
11
CF5
CF62
CF63
Little Brynhill Farm
Highlight Farm
Merthyr Dyfan
Gibbonsdown
Holm View L Ctr
Colcot
Barry Comp Sch
The Barry
Ysgol Bro Morgannwg
Recn Gd
Cemy
Welsh Hawking Ctr
Coed Mawr
Barry Coll
Middleton Plantation
Walters Farm
Waycock Cross
Green Farm
Hotel
Cwm Talwg
Allot Gdns
Cwm-cidy Farm
Cwm Cidi
Nant Talwg
Mill Wood
Valeways Millennium Heritage Trail
Nature Trail
Porthkerry Country Park
Barry Brook
Cwm Barri
Romilly Park
Bull Cliff
Pebble Beach
The Knap
Cold Knap
Watch House Bay
Storehouse Point
Barry Harbour
Little Island
Friars Point
Whitmore Bay
Barry Island Pleasure Park
Barry Island
Nell's Point
BARRY/
Y BARRI
Hood Road
Woodham
Docks
under construction
Barry Island Prim Sch
Plymouth Road
Mus
Superstore
Civic Offs
L Ctr
Schs
A4226
A4050
A4055
B4266
B4294
PORT RD E
PORT RD W
A4226 PORT RD
WAYCOCK RD
PONTYPRIDD RD
COLCOT RD
JENNER RD
BROAD ST
PARK CRES
ST NICHOLAS RD
HARBOUR RD
GLADSTONE RD
HOLTON RD
Barry Island Rly
CHARLES DARWIN WAY
FRIARS RD
STATION APPRO
E4
1 FFORDD SEALAND
2 RHODFA SWELDON
3 HEOL BROADLAND
4 HEOL GWENDOLINE
5 GERDDI MARGARET
6 CLOS MANCHELDOWNE
7 CWRT EDWARD
8 ELIS FISHER CT
9 GLADSTONE GARDEN CT
1 ST CATHERINE'S CT
2 TY FFYNNON
3 SLADE WOOD HO
4 CRESSWELL CT
5 NARBETH CT
CAERNARVON GDNS 1
ST MICHAELS GDNS 2
DOROTHY CL 3
DOROTHY AVE 4
WINIFRED AVE 5
CHAUCER RD 6
RADNOR GN 1
CARMARTHEN CL 2
DENBIGH WAY 3
MERIONETH PL 4
1 THE ELMS
2 EAST VIEW TERR
3 ROMILLY CT
4 ROMILLY BLDGS
YEW TREE CT 1
MULBERRY CT 2
ROWAN CT 3
ST NICHOLAS CT 4
HOLLY CT 5
PYRA CT 6
LAUREL CT 7
LLYS Y COED 1
MILLWOOD RISE 2
1 PLAS CLEDDAU
2 GWENOG CT
ARCHER CT 1
ST BARUCHS CT 2
TRIANGLE 3
SOUTHBOURNE CL 4
GWENNOL Y MOR 5
ADAR Y MOR 6
HEOL GYLFINIA 7
HEOL PAL 8
BREAKSEA CT 9
F4
1 OSPREY CT
2 CWRT TREM YR YNYS
3 TY CAMLAS
4 TY'R SIANEL
5 GLAN-Y-DWR
6 GLAN-Y-MOR
7 TY LEVANT
8 TY CWMPAS
9 TY CAPSTAN
10 HEOL Y PORTHLADD
F5
1 COPPERFIELD CT
2 HANOVER ST
3 BYRON ST
4 WOODLANDS CT
5 GLADSTONE CT
6 SPENCER ST
7 THE MEWS
8 BELVEDERE CRES
9 DUNLIN CT
10 YMCA BLDGS

213

215
205
216
A8
1 MOUNTBATTEN RD
2 BEATTY CL
3 CWRT PENCOEDTRE
4 BROUGHTON PL
5 GIBBONSDOWN CL
6 GWILYM PL
7 ISLWYN WAY
B7
1 PADDOCK PL
2 JENKIN ST
3 COWBRIDGE ST
4 NEW HOUSE CT
5 TY CERRIG
C8
1 FFORDD GWYNETH
2 PARC CLWYD
3 EASTBOURNE CT
4 HATHAWAY PL
5 STRATFORD GN
A
B
C
D
E
F
8
7
69
6
5
68
4
3
67
2
1
66
12
13
14
St Richard Gwyn RC High Sch
Biglis Farm
Pymbylu Moors
Playing Field
CF62
Channels Girt
1 CRWYS LA
2 AR Y NANT
3 HOLLAND WAY
1 LONGACRE CL
2 MEADOW VIEW
3 ST CADOC'S RISE
4 GREENWAY CT
5 SHIRLEY CL
6 PALMERSTOWN HO
A 4231
BARRY DOCKS LINK RD
Palmerston Prim Sch
1 RUNCORN CL
2 PHILADELPHIA CL
Palmerstown
Palmerston Workshops
Priority Workshops
Priority Ent Pk
Ty-Verlon Ind Est
Superstore
Cadoxton
Cadoxton River
CARDIFF RD
A4055
B4267
SULLY MOORS RD
Jenner Park
Pol HQ
GLADSTONE RD
Barry Dock
B4294
WESTON SQ
Cardiff Road Bsns Pk
1 LOWER HOLMES ST
2 LIDDICOAT CT
3 ST THOMAS' CT
4 ST AIDEN'S RISE
5 MENDIP VIEW
6 TY GWENFO
7 NORDALE RISE
8 CHURCHILL TERR
1 LENNOX GN
2 GRANGE CT
Works
CF63
CF64
Vale Ent Ctr
SOUTH RD
Liby
1 CAMBRIAN CT
2 BELVEDERE CRES
3 AVOCET CT
4 LOWER GUTHRIE ST
WIMBORNE RD
Windmill Ind Area
Windmill
HAYES RD
Barry Docks
DAVID DAVIES RD
FFORDD Y MILENIWM
WIMBORNE BLDGS
Hospice
Sully Bay
1 WAVERLEY CT
2 FRYATT ST
3 PHILIPPA FREETH CT
4 CAMBELL CT
5 CLOS PEIRIANT
6 CLOS TYNIAD GLO
7 HEOL CILFFRYDD
8 GLANFA DAFYDD
9 CEI DAFYDD
Coed-yr-Hayes
ATLANTIC WAY
Atlantic Trad Est
Hayes Point
Docks
Black Rocks
East Breakwater
CF62
LB Sta
Entrance Channel
Jackson's Bay
B6
1 BLACKWELL CL
2 LLANOVER ST
3 COURT NEWTON
4 COURT MEWS
5 DAVNIC CL
6 FORSTER ST
7 WESTON ST
8 RECTORY RD
9 COURTENAY RD
10 WESTERN CT
11 TENSING TERR
12 HUNT PL
13 HILLARY MEWS
14 CWRT MELIN Y RHOS
216

215 206

A B C D E F

8
Cadoxton River
A4055 CARDIFF RD A4055
CF63
GREEN LA
Downs Farm
Downs
Downs Wood
Cog Moors
Cogan Plantation
Cosmeston Lakes Country Park
7
Sully Brook
Cog Bridge
Visitor Ctr
Sully Moors
B4267
69
Cog Farm
Lower Cosmeston Farm
Cosmeston Medieval Village
6
ASHBY RD
Cog
Home Farm
CF64
COG RD
UPHILL CL
DONIFORD CL
SOUTH LODE
GLASTONBURY RD
BRIDGEWATER RD
CONYBEARE RD
SLADE CL
KETTERINGHAM CL
KINGSLEY CL
MEADOW VIEW CT
THE HALT
ROOKERY CL
ROOKERY WOOD
DESPENSER RD
BASSETT RD
CROFT GDNS
DANIELL CL
ECKLEY RD
STRADLING CL
DULVERTON DR
PORLOCK DR
1 WESTMINSTER DR
2 CANNINGTON CL
3 LYNTON CL
4 GRIMSON CL
SWANBRIDGE RD
LAVERNOCK RD
Ty-r-Orsaf
De Sully Grange
The Vineyard
5
B4267
CRAIG Y MOR CT
ELWORTHY CL
BREAN CL
ARLINGTON RD
Sully
ARLINGTON MEWS
HOLMS CT
DUNSTER DR
MINEHEAD AVE
LYNMOUTH DR
BURNHAM AVE
SOUTH RD
WIMBORNE CRES
WALSEA CT
WINSFORD RD
HIGHBRIDGE CL
SWANBRIDGE GR
ELM CL
68
BREAKSEA CL
WESTON AVE
PO
SMITHIES AVE
Sully Prim Sch
CLEVEDON AVE
OYSTER BEND
SOMERSET VIEW
ST MARY'S WELL BAY RD
4
Sports Gd
Swanbridge
BEACH RD
Sully Bay
St Mary's Well Bay
ISLAND VIEW CVN PK
THE SPINNEY CVN PK
PH
SWANBRIDGE FARM EST
St Hilary
Swanbridge Bay
Ball Bay
3
Sully Sound
67
West Point
CF64
Sully Island
Fort
East Point
2
1
66

15 A B 16 C D 17 E F

215

207

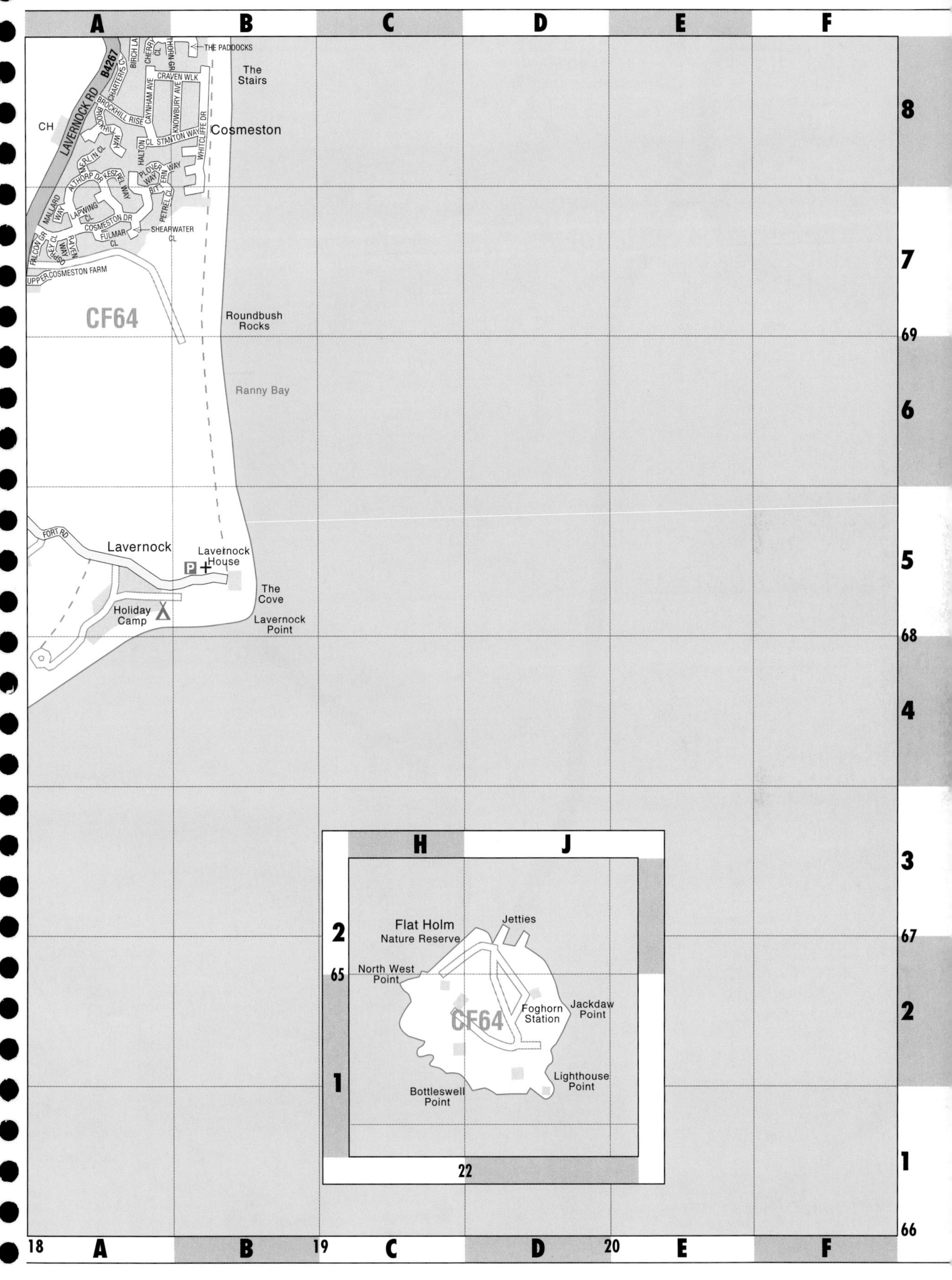
A
B
C
D
E
F
THE PADDOCKS
The Stairs
B4267
LAVERNOCK RD
BIRCH LA
CHERRY CL
THORN GR
CHARTERS CL
CRAVEN WLK
CAYNHAM AVE
KNOWBURY AVE
WHITCLIFFE DR
BROCKHILL RISE
BROCKHILL WAY
CH
Cosmeston
HALTON CL
STANTON WAY
MERLIN CL
ALTHORP DR
KESTREL WAY
PLOVER WAY
BITTERN WAY
PETREL CL
MALLARD WAY
LAPWING CL
COSMESTON DR
FULMAR CL
SHEARWATER CL
FALCON GR
OSPREY CL
RAVEN WAY
UPPER COSMESTON FARM
CF64
Roundbush Rocks
Ranny Bay
FORT RD
Lavernock
Lavernock House
The Cove
Holiday Camp
Lavernock Point
H
J
Flat Holm
Nature Reserve
Jetties
North West Point
CF64
Foghorn Station
Jackdaw Point
Lighthouse Point
Bottleswell Point
2
65
1
22
8
7
69
6
5
68
4
3
67
2
1
66
18
A
B
19
C
D
20
E
F

Scale: 1¾ inches to 1 mile

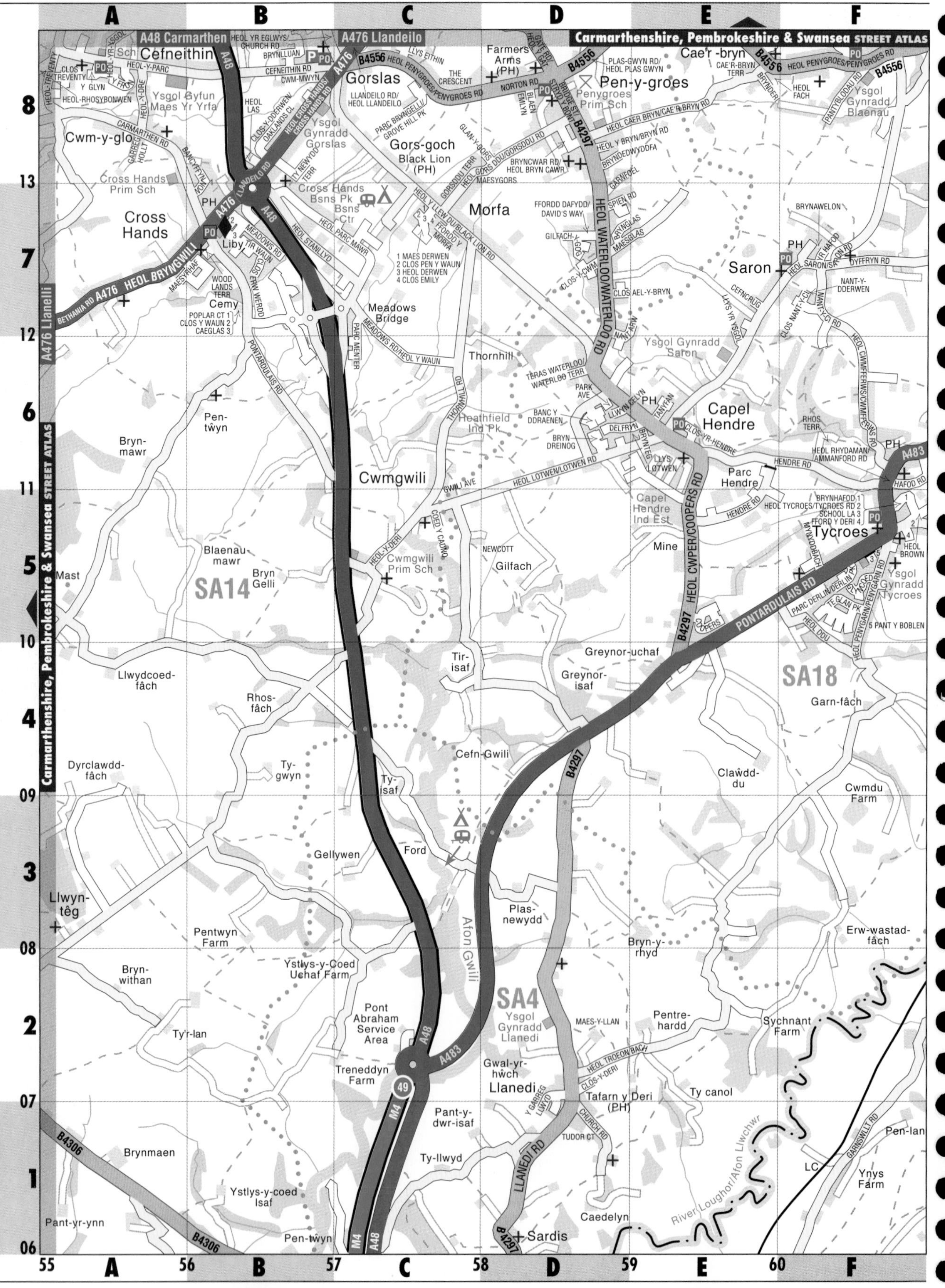

Scale: 1¾ inches to 1 mile
0 ¼ ½ mile
0 250m 500m 750m 1 km

B7
1 FFORDD FLORENCE/FLORENCE RD
2 BRYNDERWEN RD
3 HEOL NORMAN/NORMAN RD
4 STRYD HAROLD/HAROLD ST
5 FFORDD-YR-ORSAF/STATION RD
6 RHODFA BRYN-MAWR/BRYNMAWR AVE
7 Y GORSEDD
8 STRYD-YR-EGLWYS/CHURCH ST
9 LON BRYN-MAWR/BRYNMAWR LA
10 FFORDD TALBOT/TALBOT RD
11 LON TIR-Y-DAIL/TIR-Y-DAIL LA
12 FFORDD STEWART/STEWART DR
13 TERAS BRYNTEG/BRYN-TEG TERR
14 FFORDD IS-CENNEN/ISCENNEN RD
15 FFORDD Y FAENOR/MANOR RD
16 CROSS INN BLDGS
17 LLOYD ST
18 LON Y BEDYDD/BAPTIST LA
19 CARREGAMMAN
20 THE ARCADE

220

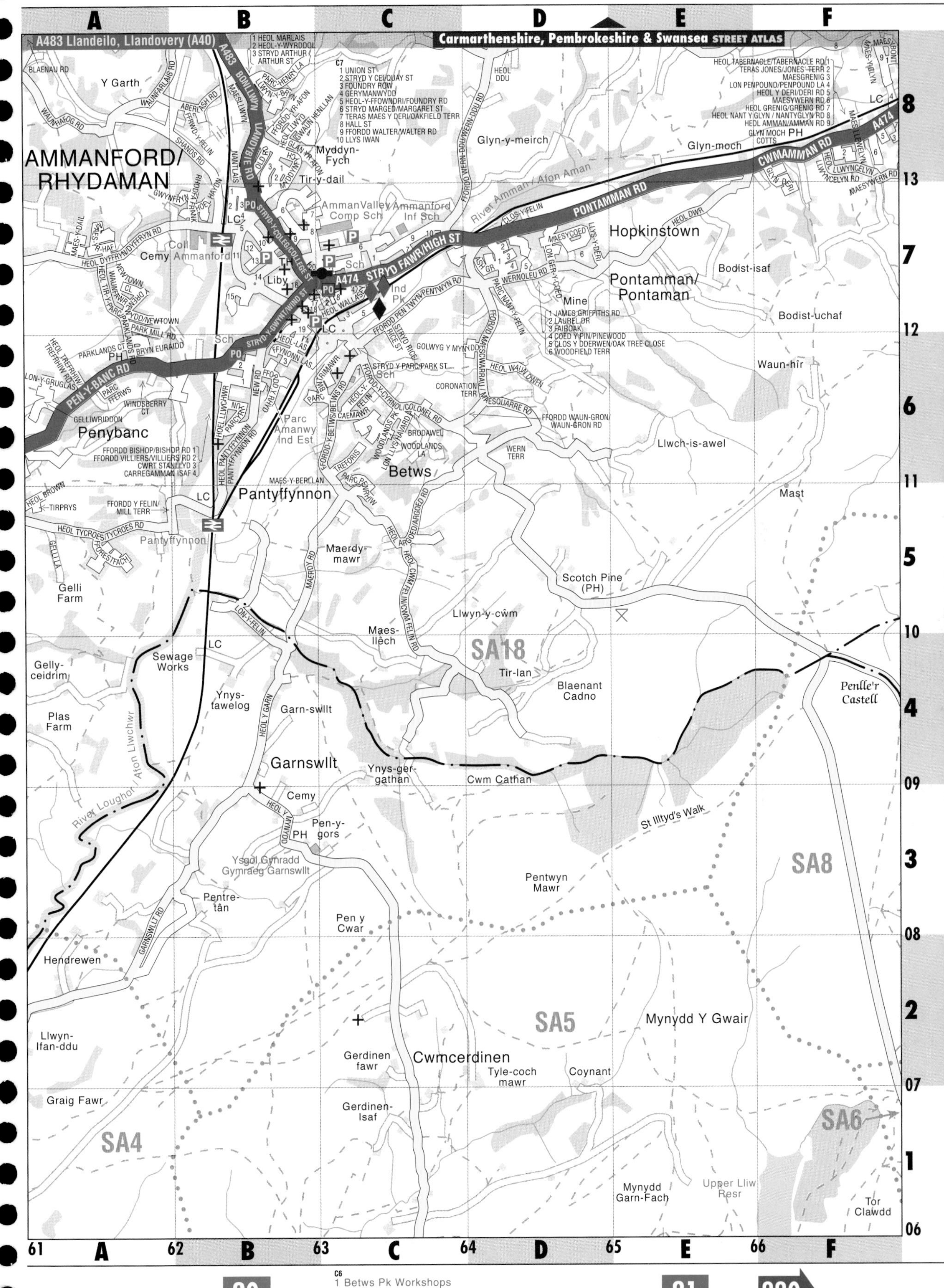

C6
1 Betws Pk Workshops

20 21 220

219

A8
1 Glanamman Workshops
2 HEOL TABERNACLE/TABERNACLE RD
3 HEOL TIR Y COED/TIRYCOED RD
4 STRYD FAWR/HIGH ST
5 HEOL BRYN-LLOI/BRYN-LLOI RD

B8
1 LON LLWYD
2 PARC GLAN YR AFON
3 CLOS FELEN
4 HEOL HENDRE/HENDRE RD
5 HEOL MAESDDERWEN/OAKFIELD RD
6 HEOL MAESGLAS/GREENFIELD RD
7 HEOL FICEROI/VICARAGE RD
8 CHURCH ROW
9 HEOL UCHAF YR ORSAF/UPPER STATION RD
10 LOWER STATION RD
11 TERAS YR ARCED/ARCADE TERR
12 PARC GLANFFRWD
13 MAES Y FRON
14 NEW CEIDRIM RD
15 HEOL YSGOL NEWYDD/NEW SCHOOL RD
16 HEOL Y CORONI/CORONATION RD
17 BISHOP RD

Scale: 1¾ inches to 1 mile
0 ¼ ½ mile
0 250m 500m 750m 1 km

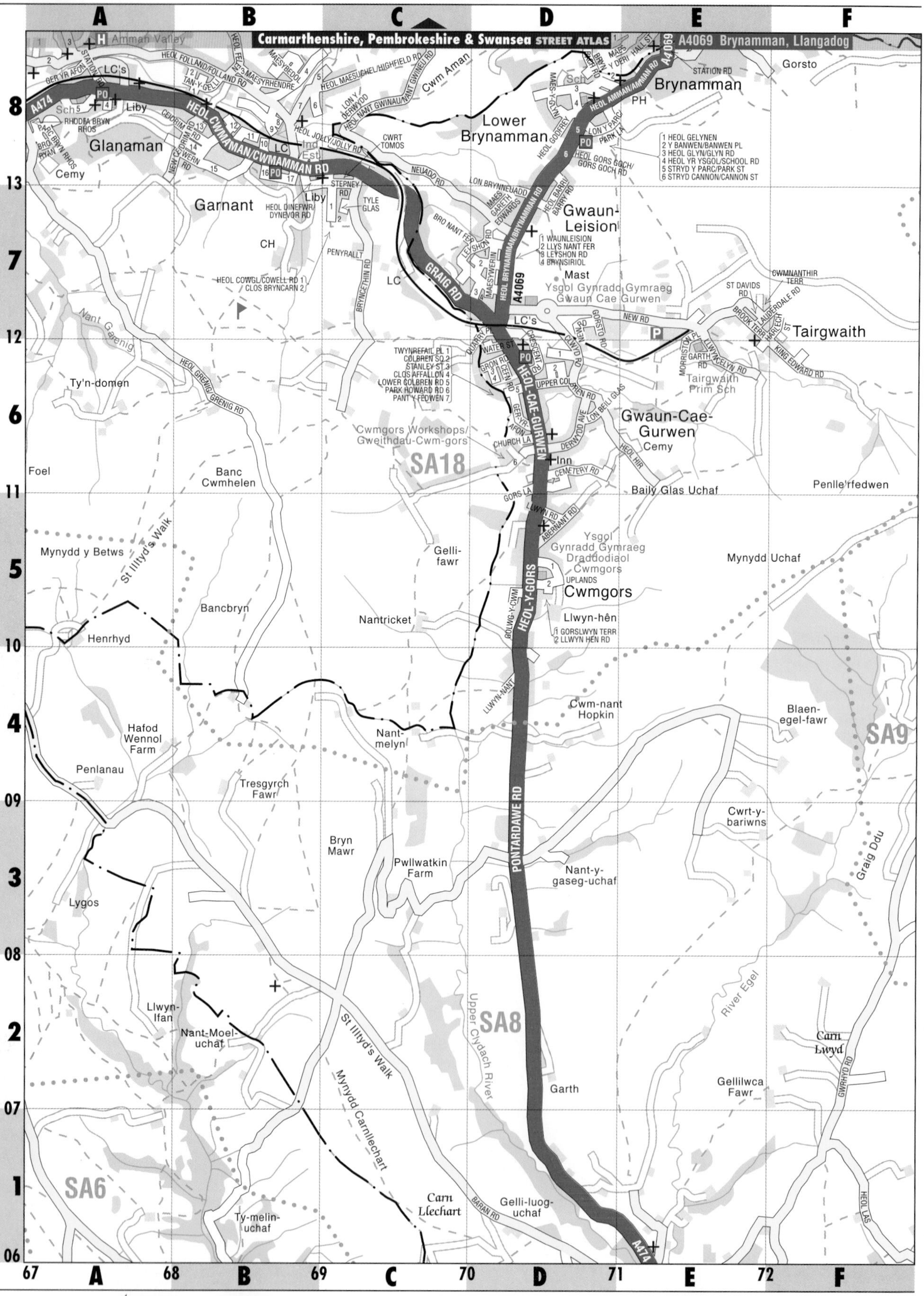

A4069 Brynamman, Llangadog

Glanaman
Garnant
Cwm Aman
Lower Brynamman
Brynamman
Gorsto
Gwaun-Leision
Tairgwaith
Gwaun-Cae-Gurwen
Cwmgors
Llwyn-hên
Cwm-nant Hopkin
Blaen-egel-fawr
Mynydd Uchaf
Penlle'rfedwen
Baily Glas Uchaf
Cwmgors Workshops/ Gweithdau-Cwm-gors
Ysgol Gynradd Gymraeg Gwaun Cae Gurwen
Ysgol Gynradd Gymraeg Draddodiaol Cwmgors
Tairgwaith Prim Sch
Ty'n-domen
Foel
Banc Cwmhelen
Mynydd y Betws
St Illtyd's Walk
Bancbryn
Henrhyd
Gelli-fawr
Nantricket
Nant-melyn
Hafod Wennol Farm
Penlanau
Tresgyrch Fawr
Bryn Mawr
Pwllwatkin Farm
Nant-y-gaseg-uchaf
Cwrt-y-bariwns
Graig Ddu
Lygos
Llwyn-Ifan
Nant-Moel-uchaf
Mynydd Carnllechart
Upper Clydach River
River Egel
Carn Lwyd
Gellilwca Fawr
Garth
Carn Llechart
Gelli-luog-uchaf
Ty-melin-uchaf
SA18
SA8
SA9
SA6
A474
A4069
HEOL CWMAMAN/CWMAMMAN RD
GRAIG RD
HEOL BRYNAMMAN/BRYNAMMAN RD
HEOL AMMAN/AMMAN RD
HEOL-CAE-GURWEN
HEOL-Y-GORS
PONTARDAWE RD
HEOL GRENIG/GRENIG RD
NEW RD
BARAN RD
GWRHYD RD
HEOL LAS

1 HEOL GELYNEN
2 Y BANWEN/BANWEN PL
3 HEOL GLYN/GLYN RD
4 HEOL YR YSGOL/SCHOOL RD
5 STRYD Y PARC/PARK ST
6 STRYD CANNON/CANNON ST

1 WAUNLEISION
2 LLYS NANT FER
3 LEYSHON RD
4 BRYNSIRIOL

TWYNREFAIL PL 1
COLBREN SQ 2
STANLEY ST 3
CLOS AFFALLON 4
LOWER COLBREN RD 5
PARK HOWARD RD 6
PANT Y FEDWEN 7

HEOL COWGL/COWELL RD 1
CLOS BRYNCARN 2

1 GORSLWYN TERR
2 LLWYN HEN RD

67 68 69 70 71 72
06 07 08 09 10 11 12 13
1 2 3 4 5 6 7 8

219
22
23

Scale: 1¾ inches to 1 mile

For full street detail of the highlighted area see pages 1 and 2.

222

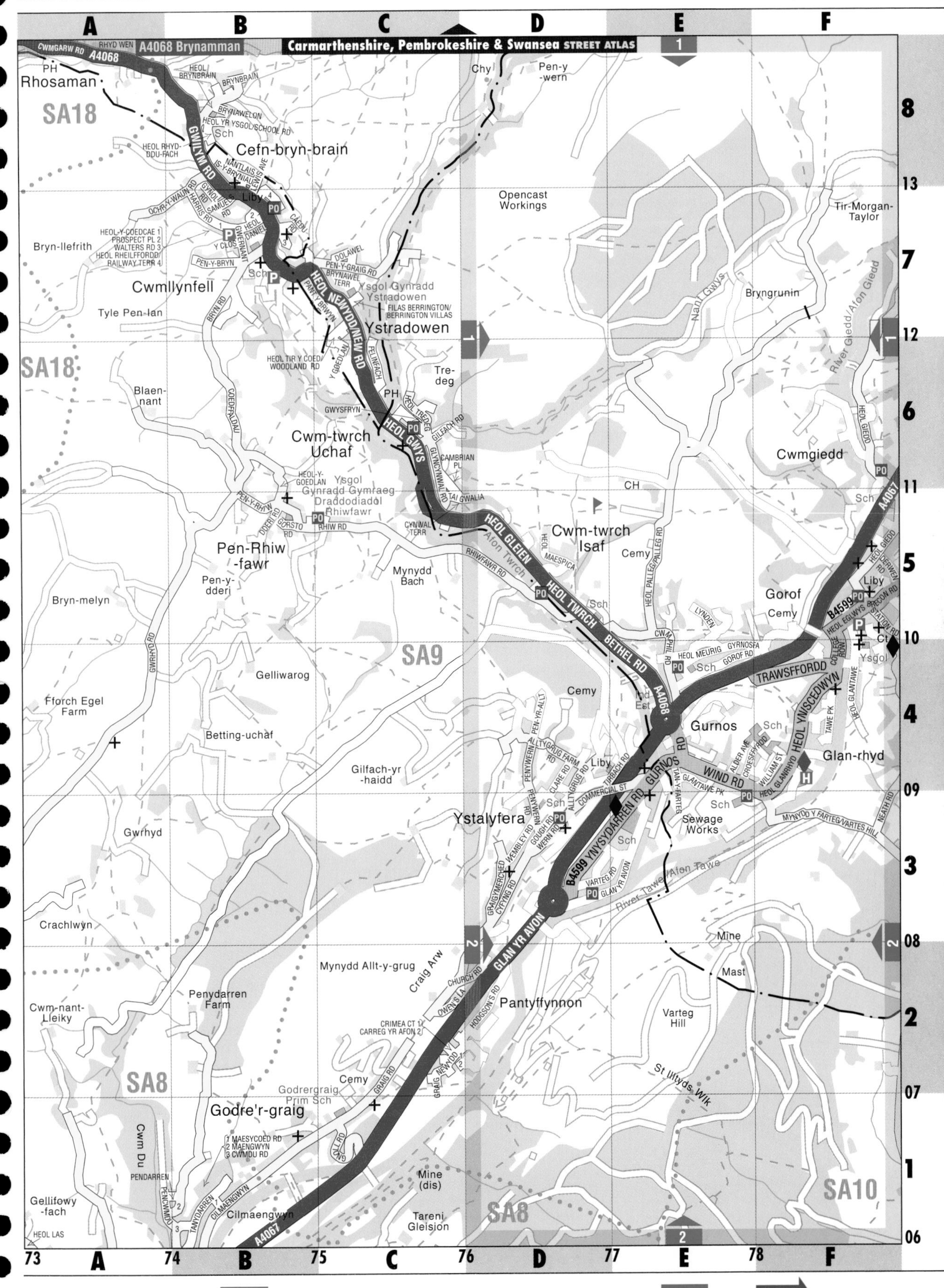

24
25
222

221

Scale: 1¾ inches to 1 mile

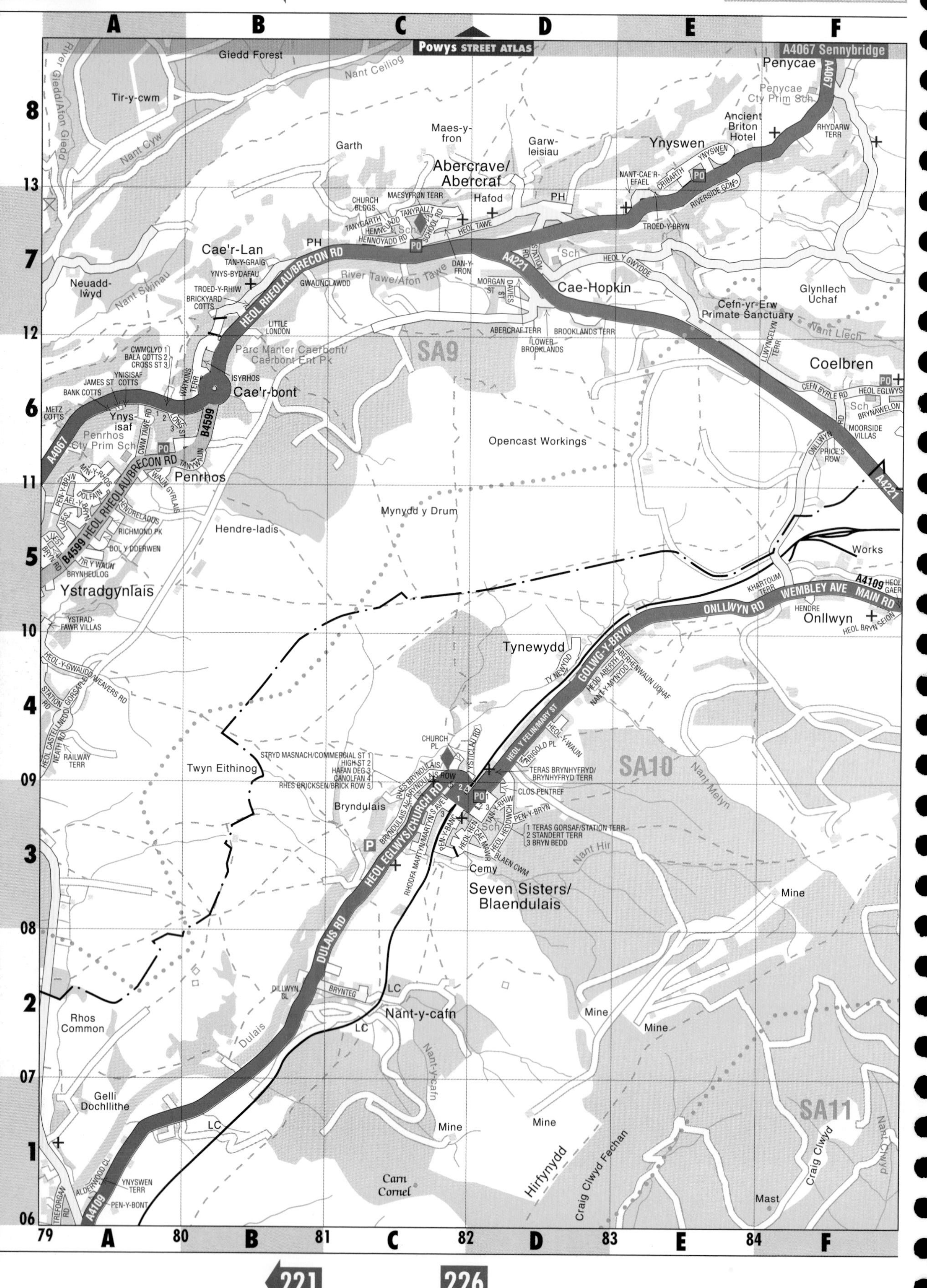

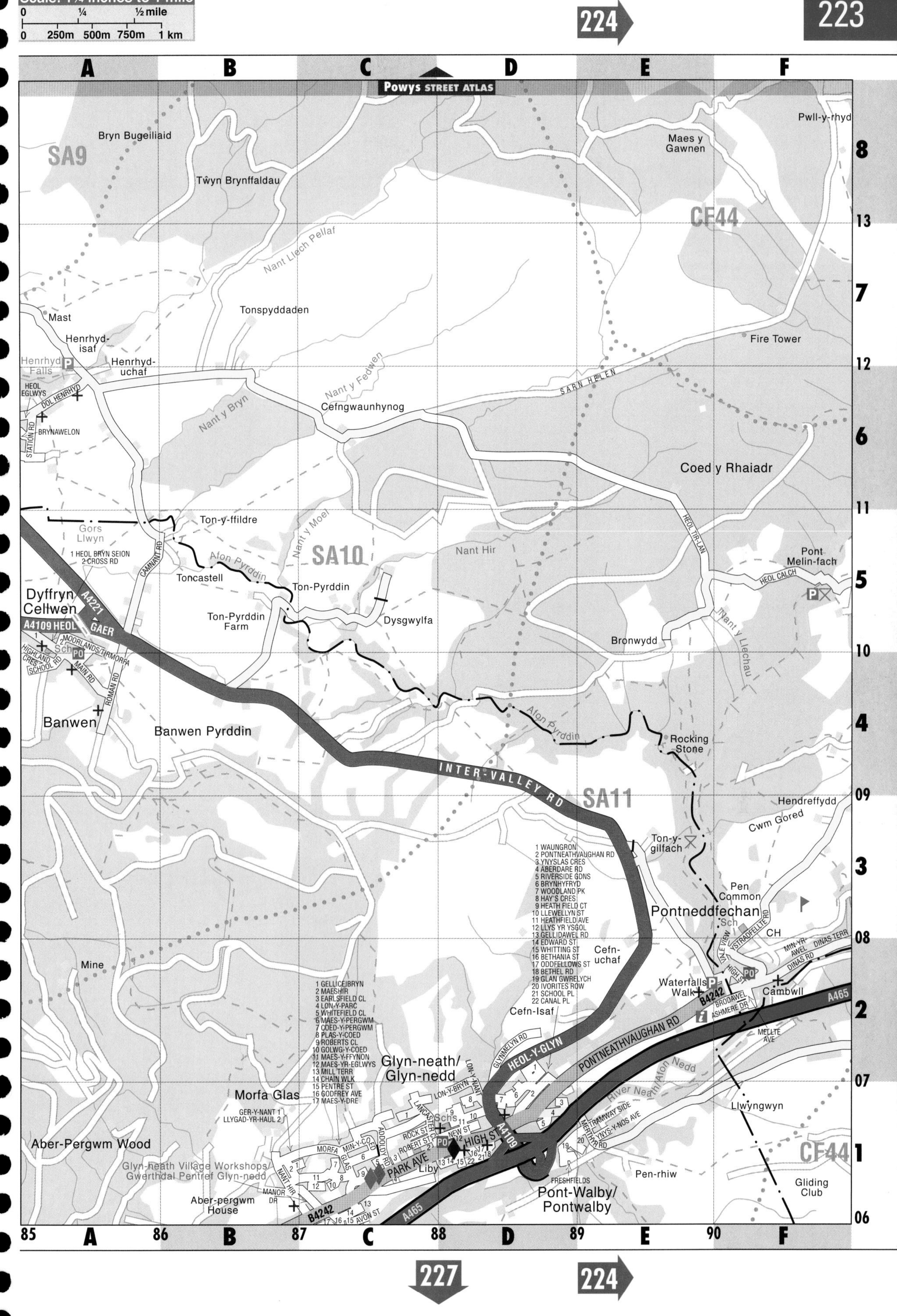

Scale: 1¾ inches to 1 mile
0 ¼ ½ mile
0 250m 500m 750m 1 km
224
Powys STREET ATLAS
Bryn Bugeiliaid
SA9
Twyn Brynffaldau
Maes y Gawnen
Pwll-y-rhyd
CF44
Nant Llech Pellaf
Tonspyddaden
Mast
Henrhyd-isaf
Henrhyd Falls
Henrhyd-uchaf
Fire Tower
Nant y Fedwen
SARN HELEN
Nant y Bryn
Cefngwaunhynog
Coed y Rhaiadr
Ton-y-ffildre
Gors Llwyn
Nant y Moel
SA10
Nant Hir
Pont Melin-fach
HEOL CALCH
Afon Pyrddin
Toncastell
Ton-Pyrddin
Dyffryn Cellwen
Ton-Pyrddin Farm
Dysgwylfa
Nant y Llechau
Bronwydd
Banwen
Banwen Pyrddin
Rocking Stone
INTER-VALLEY RD
SA11
Hendreffydd
Cwm Gored
Ton-y-gilfach
Pen Common
Pontneddfechan
Cefn-uchaf
Mine
Waterfalls Walk
Cambwll
Cefn-Isaf
PONTNEATHVAUGHAN RD
HEOL-Y-GLYN
Glyn-neath/ Glyn-nedd
River Neath/Afon Nedd
Morfa Glas
Llwyngwyn
Aber-Pergwm Wood
Glyn-neath Village Workshops/ Gwerthdal Pentref Glyn-nedd
PARK AVE
Liby
Pen-rhiw
Pont-Walby/ Pontwalby
Gliding Club
Aber-pergwm House
1 WAUNGRON
2 PONTNEATHVAUGHAN RD
3 YNYSLAS CRES
4 ABERDARE RD
5 RIVERSIDE GDNS
6 BRYNHYFRYD
7 WOODLAND PK
8 HAY'S CRES
9 HEATH FIELD CT
10 LLEWELLYN ST
11 HEATHFIELD AVE
12 LLYS YR YSGOL
13 GELLIDAWEL RD
14 EDWARD ST
15 WHITTING ST
16 BETHANIA ST
17 ODDFELLOWS ST
18 BETHEL RD
19 GLAN GWRELYCH
20 IVORITES ROW
21 SCHOOL PL
22 CANAL PL
1 GELLICEIBRYN
2 MAESHIR
3 EARLSFIELD CL
4 LON-Y-PARC
5 WHITEFIELD CL
6 MAES-Y-PERGWM
7 COED-Y-PERGWM
8 PLAS-Y-COED
9 ROBERTS CL
10 GOLWG-Y-COED
11 MAES-Y-FFYNON
12 MAES-YR-EGLWYS
13 MILL TERR
14 CHAIN WLK
15 PENTRE ST
16 GODFREY AVE
17 MAES-Y-DRE
1 HEOL BRYN SEION
2 CROSS RD
A B C D E F
85 86 87 88 89 90
8 13 7 12 6 11 5 10 4 09 3 08 2 07 1 06
227
224

Scale: 1¾ inches to 1 mile

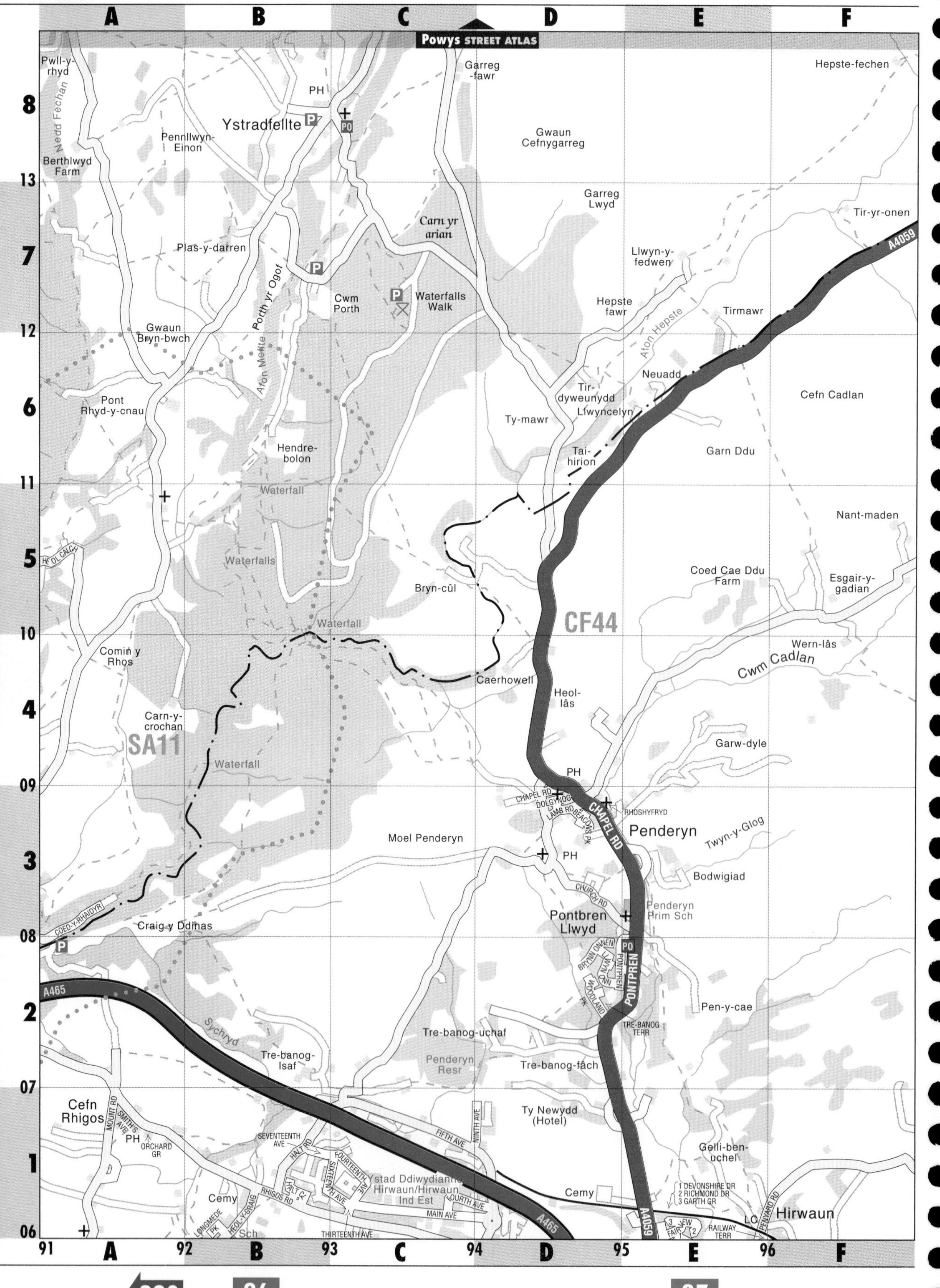

Scale: 1¾ inches to 1 mile
0 ¼ ½ mile
0 250m 500m 750m 1 km

3

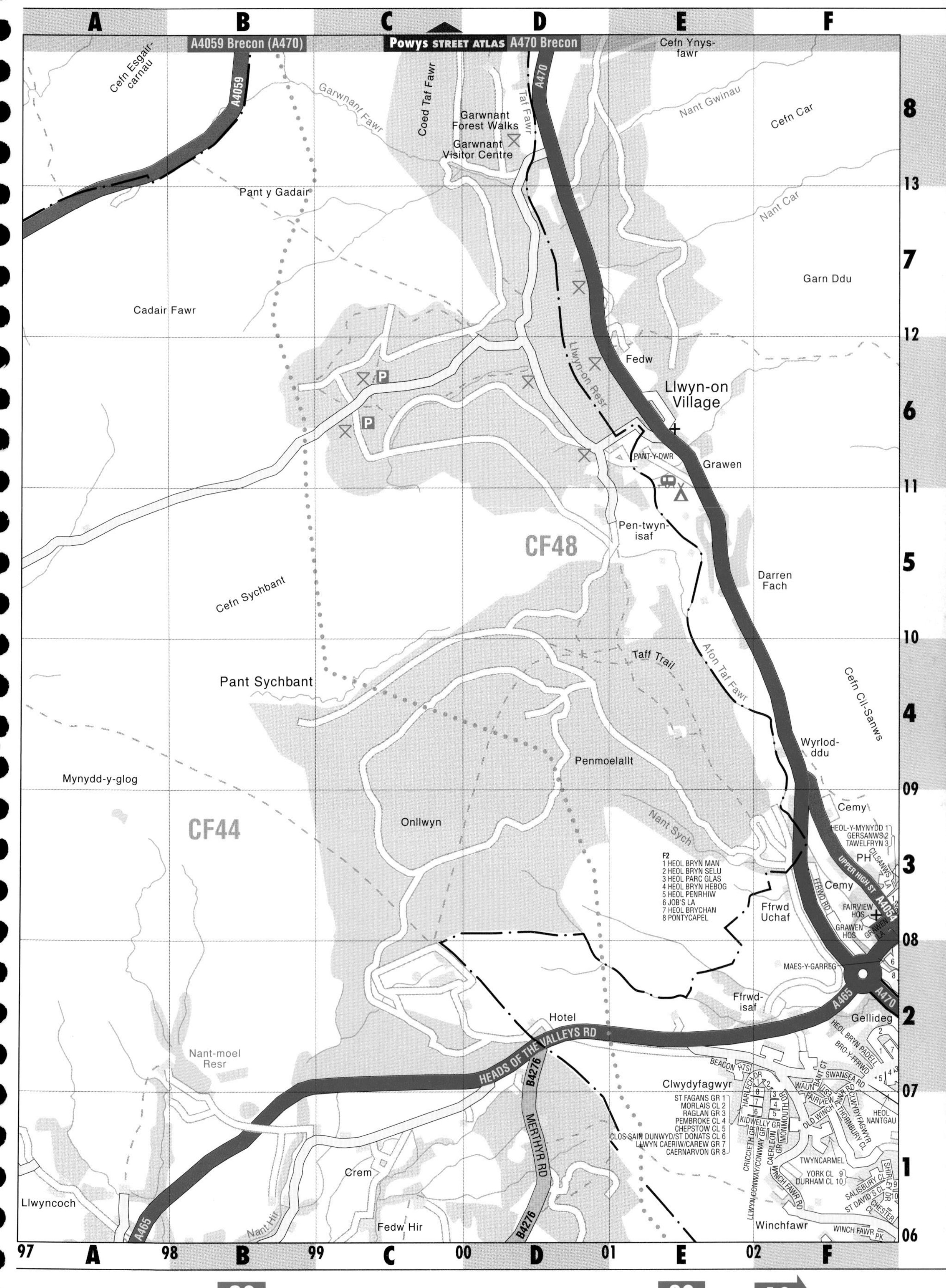

28 29 10

25
222

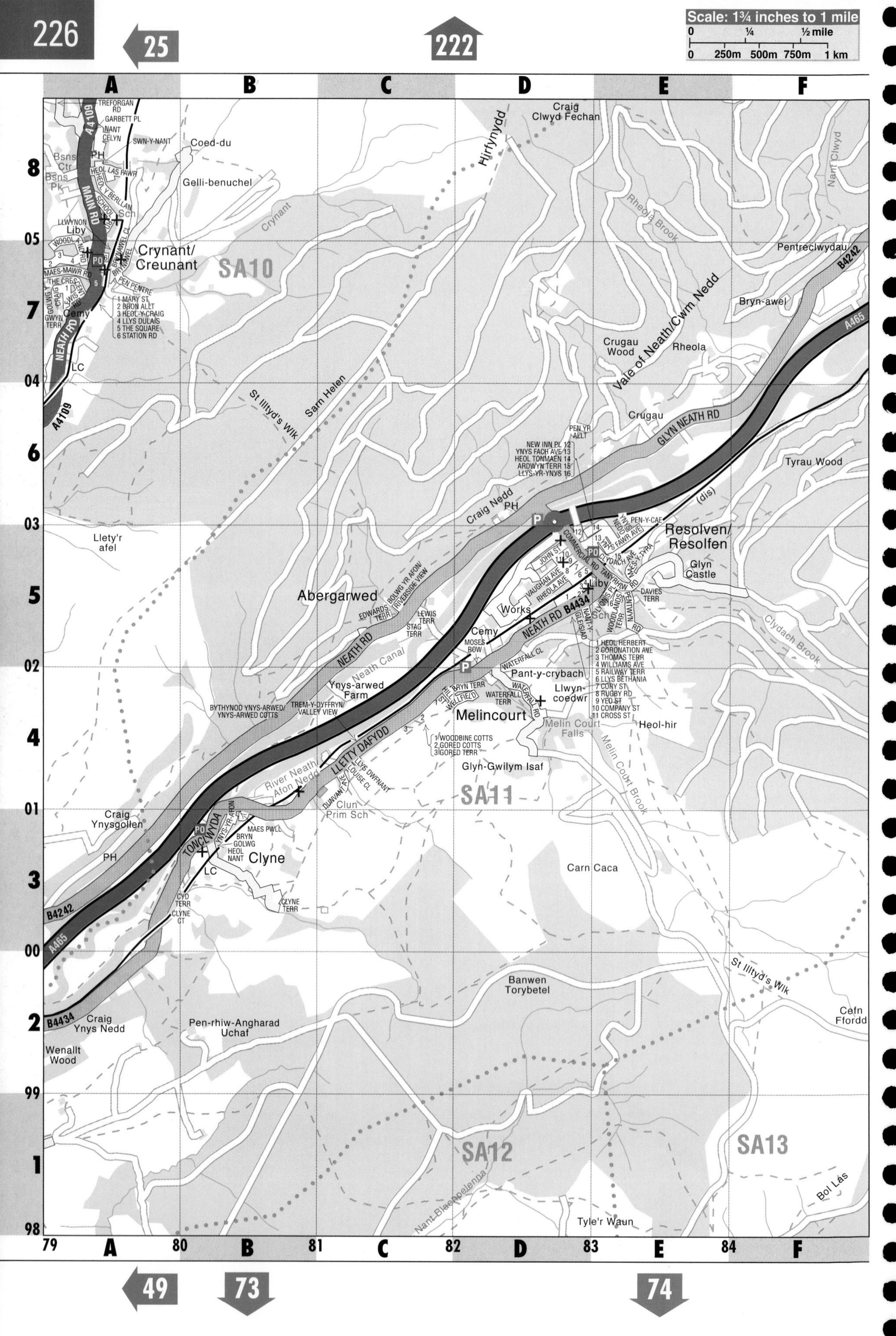

49
73
74

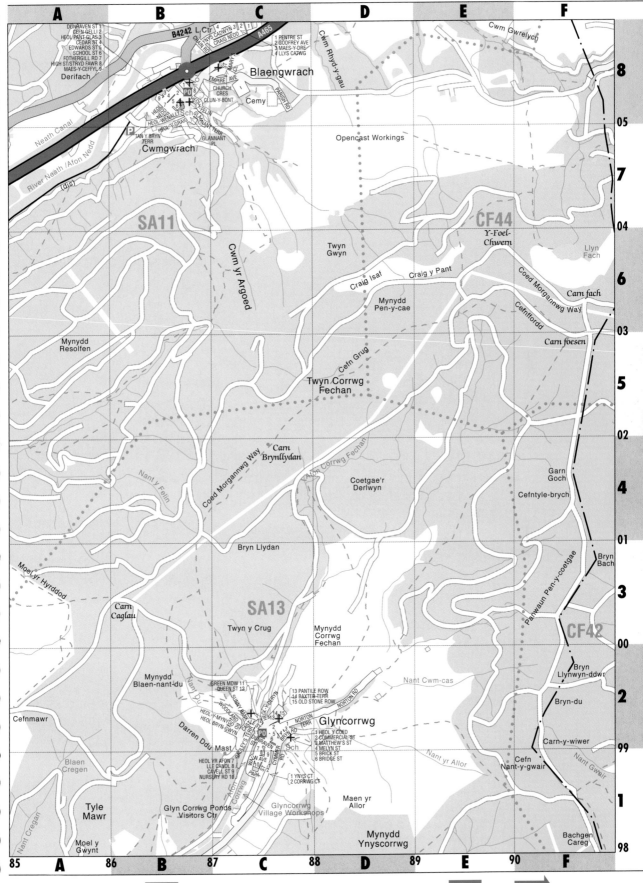

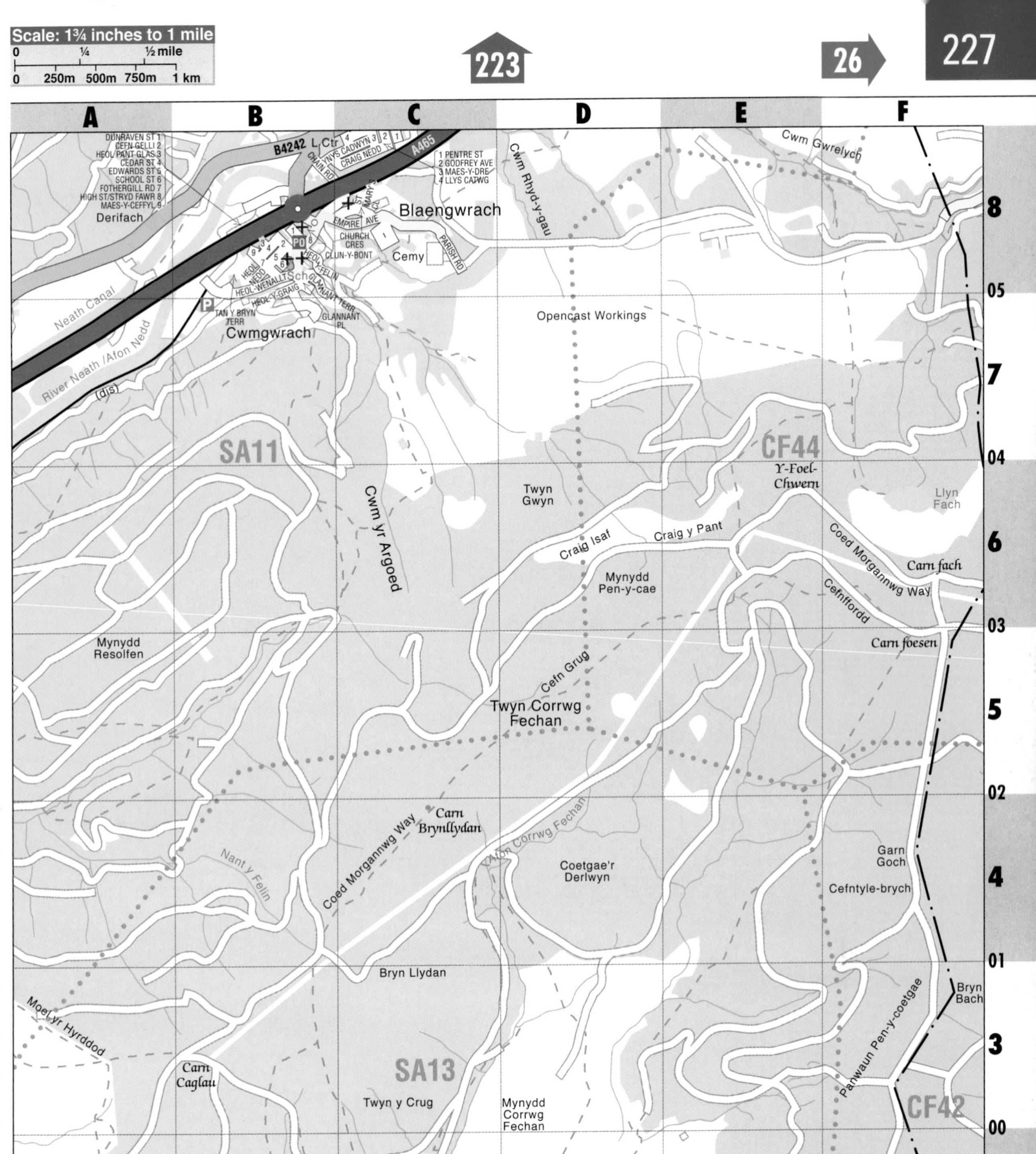
Scale: 1¾ inches to 1 mile
223
26
Blaengwrach
Derifach
Cwmgwrach
Cemy
Neath Canal
River Neath /Afon Nedd
Cwm Rhyd-y-gau
Cwm Gwrelych
Opencast Workings
SA11
CF44
Y-Foel-Chwern
Llyn Fach
Cwm yr Argoed
Twyn Gwyn
Craig Isaf
Craig y Pant
Mynydd Pen-y-cae
Coed Morgannwg Way
Carn fach
Cefnffordd
Carn foesen
Mynydd Resolfen
Cefn Grug
Twyn Corrwg Fechan
Carn Brynllydan
Nant y Felin
Afon Corrwg Fechan
Coetgae'r Derlwyn
Garn Goch
Cefntyle-brych
Bryn Llydan
Bryn Bach
Moel yr Hyrddod
Panwaun Pen-y-coetgae
Carn Caglau
SA13
Twyn y Crug
Mynydd Corrwg Fechan
CF42
Mynydd Blaen-nant-du
Nant Cwm-cas
Bryn Llynwyn-ddwr
Bryn-du
Cefnmawr
Glyncorrwg
Darren Ddu
Mast
Carn-y-wiwer
Nant yr Allor
Cefn Nant-y-gwair
Nant Gwair
Blaen Cregen
Tyle Mawr
Glyn Corrwg Ponds Visitors Ctr
Glyncorrwg Village Workshops
Maen yr Allor
Mynydd Ynyscorrwg
Moel y Gwynt
Nant Cregan
Bachgen Careg
75
76
50

Scale: 1¾ inches to 1 mile

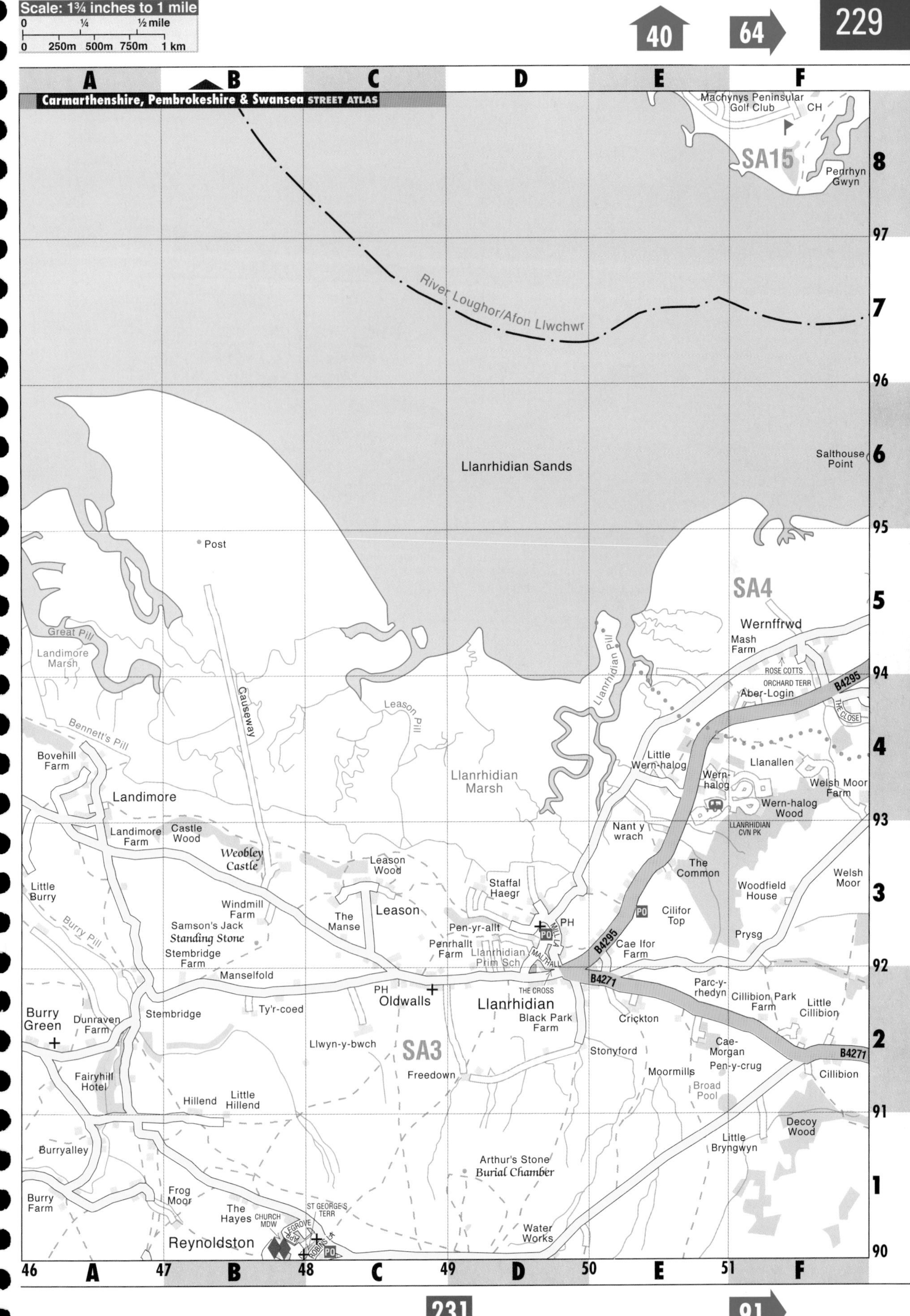
A B C D E F
Carmarthenshire, Pembrokeshire & Swansea STREET ATLAS
Machynys Peninsular Golf Club
CH
SA15
Penrhyn Gwyn
River Loughor/Afon Llwchwr
Llanrhidian Sands
Salthouse Point
Post
SA4
Wernffrwd
Mash Farm
Great Pill
Landimore Marsh
Causeway
Leason Pill
Llanrhidian Pill
ROSE COTTS
ORCHARD TERR
Aber-Login
B4295
THE CLOSE
Bennett's Pill
Bovehill Farm
Little Wern-halog
Llanallen
Llanrhidian Marsh
Wern-halog
Welsh Moor Farm
Landimore
Wern-halog Wood
Nant y wrach
LLANRHIDIAN CVN PK
Landimore Farm
Castle Wood
Weobley Castle
Leason Wood
The Common
Little Burry
Staffal Haegr
Welsh Moor
Woodfield House
Windmill Farm
Leason
Burry Pill
The Manse
Samson's Jack Standing Stone
Pen-yr-allt
PH
PO
Cilifor Top
Prysg
Stembridge Farm
Penrhallt Farm
Llanrhidian Prim Sch
MALTHALL
Cae Ifor Farm
Manselfold
THE CROSS
B4271
Parc-y-rhedyn
Cillibion Park Farm
Little Cillibion
Burry Green
Dunraven Farm
Stembridge
Ty'r-coed
PH
Oldwalls
Llanrhidian
Black Park Farm
Crickton
Llwyn-y-bwch
SA3
Stonyford
Cae-Morgan
Pen-y-crug
Fairyhill Hotel
Freedown
Moormills
Broad Pool
Cillibion
Hillend
Little Hillend
Decoy Wood
Burryalley
Little Bryngwyn
Arthur's Stone Burial Chamber
Frog Moor
Burry Farm
The Hayes
CHURCH MDW
ST GEORGE'S TERR
Water Works
Reynoldston
8 97 7 96 6 95 5 94 4 93 3 92 2 91 1 90
46 47 48 49 50 51

228

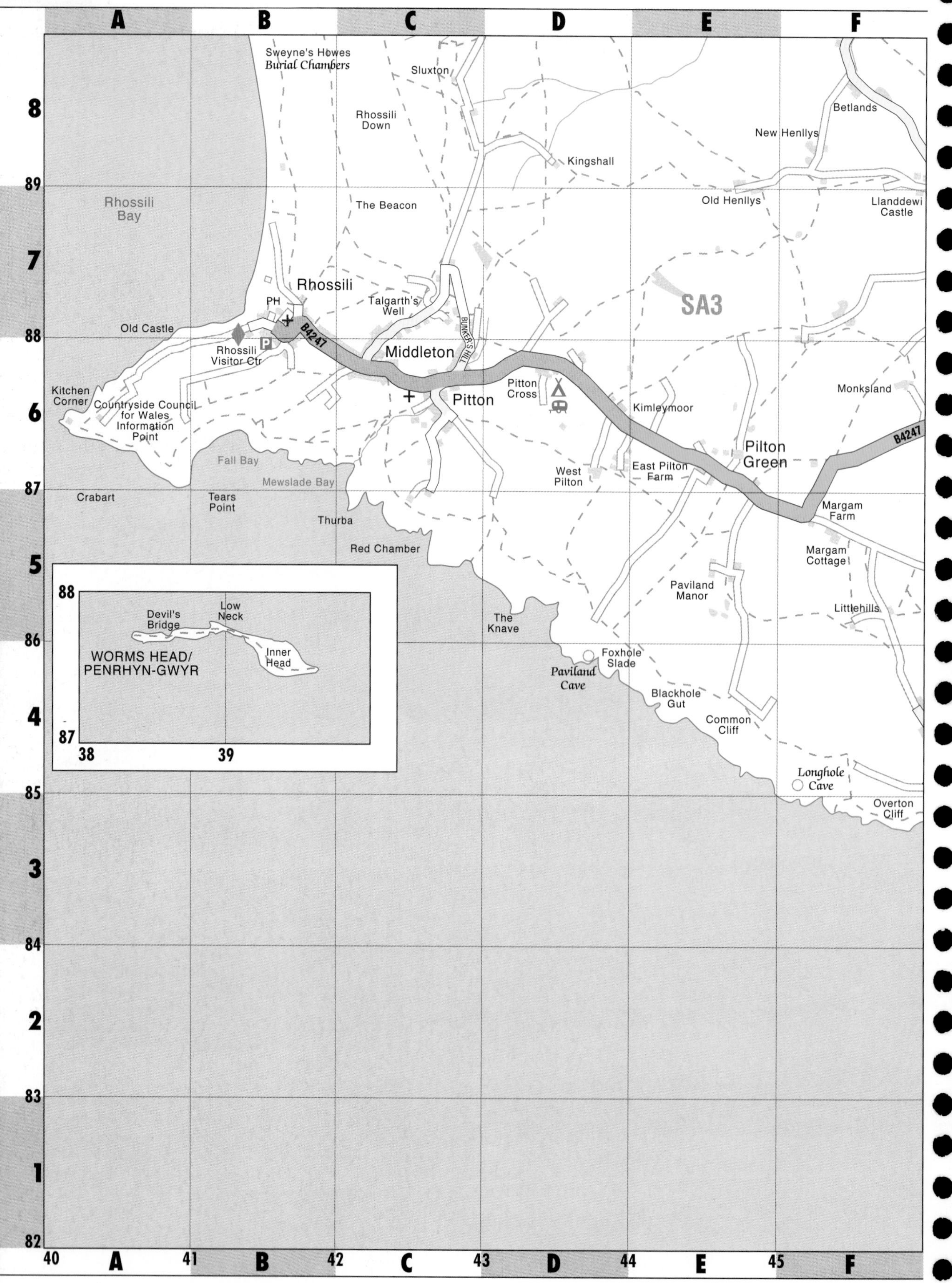

Scale: 1¾ inches to 1 mile
0 ¼ ½ mile
0 250m 500m 750m 1 km
A B C D E F
8 89 7 88 6 87 5 86 4 85 3 84 2 83 1 82
40 41 42 43 44 45
Sweyne's Howes
Burial Chambers
Sluxton
Rhossili
Down
Kingshall
Betlands
New Henllys
Old Henllys
Llanddewi
Castle
Rhossili
Bay
The Beacon
Rhossili
PH
Talgarth's
Well
SA3
Old Castle
B4247
Middleton
BUNKER'S HILL
Rhossili
Visitor Ctr
Kitchen
Corner
Countryside Council
for Wales
Information
Point
Pitton
Cross
Pitton
Kimleymoor
Monksland
Pilton
Green
Fall Bay
Mewslade Bay
West
Pilton
East Pilton
Farm
Crabart
Tears
Point
Thurba
Margam
Farm
Red Chamber
Margam
Cottage
Paviland
Manor
Littlehills
The
Knave
WORMS HEAD/
PENRHYN-GWYR
Devil's
Bridge
Low
Neck
Inner
Head
38 39
Foxhole
Slade
Paviland
Cave
Blackhole
Gut
Common
Cliff
Longhole
Cave
Overton
Cliff

229
120

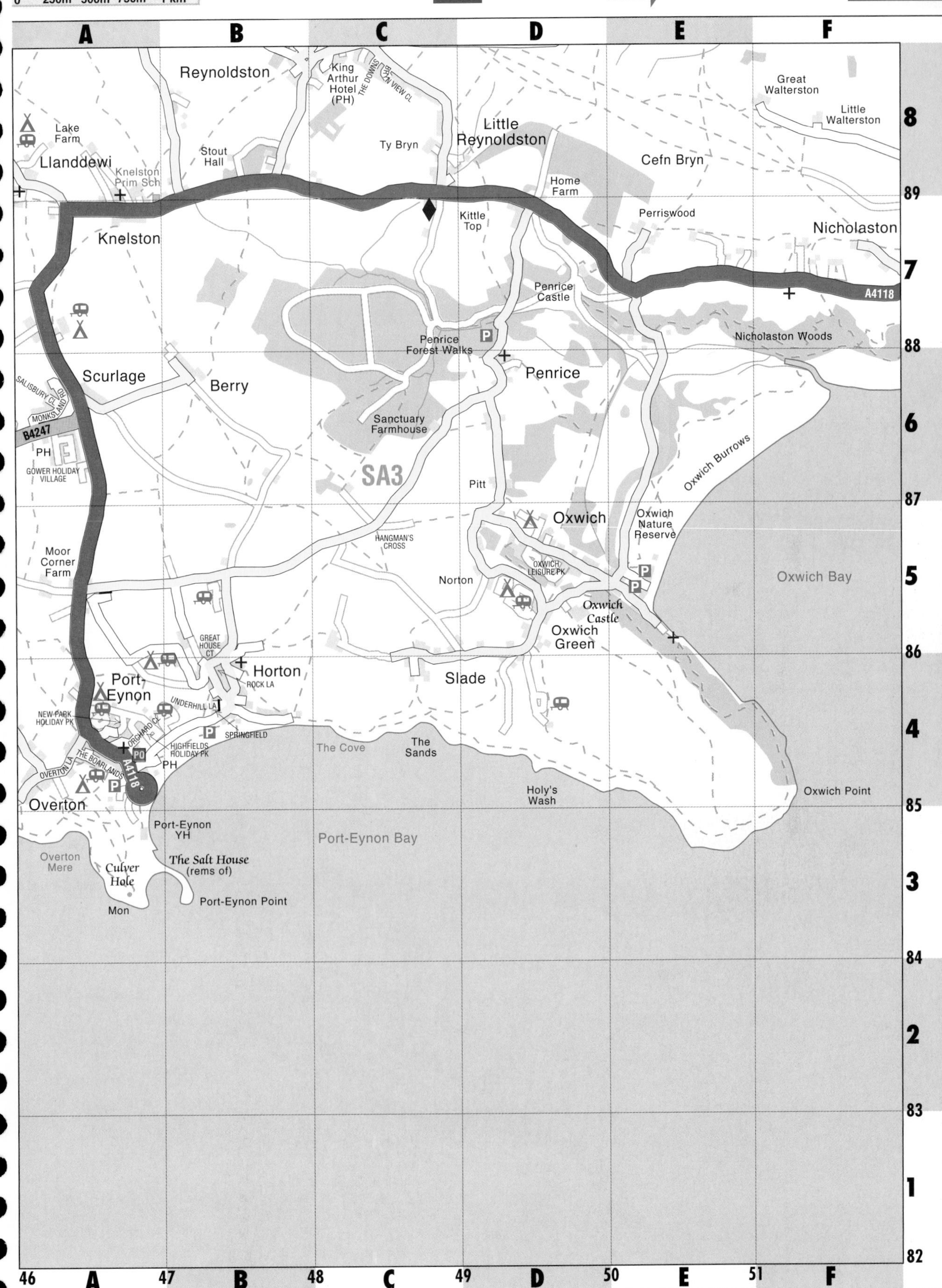
Scale: 1¾ inches to 1 mile
0 ¼ ½ mile
0 250m 500m 750m 1 km
A B C D E F
Reynoldston
King Arthur Hotel (PH)
THE DOWNS
BRYN VIEW CL
Great Walterston
Little Walterston
Lake Farm
Llanddewi
Knelston Prim Sch
Stout Hall
Ty Bryn
Little Reynoldston
Cefn Bryn
Home Farm
Kittle Top
Perriswood
Nicholaston
Knelston
Penrice Castle
A4118
Nicholaston Woods
Penrice Forest Walks
Scurlage
Berry
Penrice
SALISBURY CL
MONKSLAND RD
B4247
PH
GOWER HOLIDAY VILLAGE
Sanctuary Farmhouse
Oxwich Burrows
SA3
Pitt
Oxwich
Oxwich Nature Reserve
HANGMAN'S CROSS
Moor Corner Farm
OXWICH LEISURE PK
Norton
Oxwich Bay
Oxwich Castle
Oxwich Green
GREAT HOUSE CT
Horton
ROCK LA
Port-Eynon
Slade
UNDERHILL LA
NEW PARK HOLIDAY PK
ORCHARD CL
SPRINGFIELD
The Cove
The Sands
HIGHFIELDS HOLIDAY PK
PO
PH
THE BOARLANDS
OVERTON LA
A4118
Holy's Wash
Oxwich Point
Overton
Port-Eynon YH
Port-Eynon Bay
Overton Mere
Culver Hole
The Salt House (rems of)
Port-Eynon Point
Mon
8
89
7
88
6
87
5
86
4
85
3
84
2
83
1
82
46 A 47 B 48 C 49 D 50 E 51 F

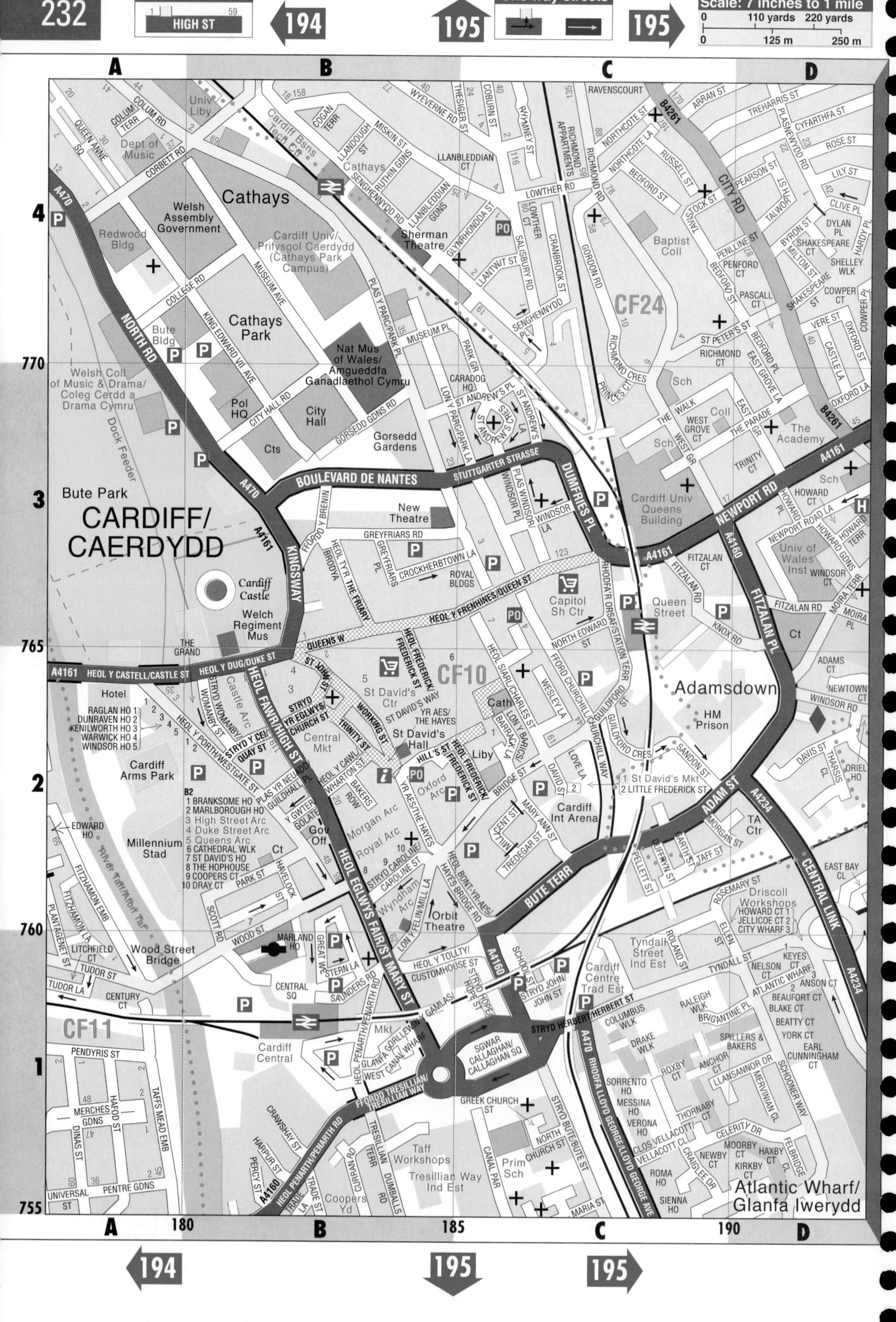
House numbers
HIGH ST
194
195
One-way streets
195
Scale: 7 inches to 1 mile
0
110 yards
220 yards
0
125 m
250 m
A
B
C
D
4
3
2
1
770
765
760
755
180
185
190
CARDIFF/
CAERDYDD
Cathays
Welsh Assembly Government
Redwood Bldg
Dept of Music
Univ Liby
Cardiff Bsns Tech Ctr
Cardiff Univ/
Prifysgol Caerdydd
(Cathays Park Campus)
Cathays Park
Bute Bldg
Welsh Coll of Music & Drama/
Coleg Cerdd a Drama Cymru
Pol HQ
City Hall
Cts
Nat Mus of Wales/
Amgueddfa Ganadlaethol Cymru
Gorsedd Gardens
Sherman Theatre
Baptist Coll
CF24
The Academy
Cardiff Univ Queens Building
Univ of Wales Inst
Bute Park
Cardiff Castle
Welch Regiment Mus
New Theatre
Capitol Sh Ctr
Queen Street
Adamsdown
HM Prison
CF10
St David's Ctr
St David's Hall
Central Mkt
Cath
Liby
Cardiff Arms Park
Millennium Stad
Cardiff Int Arena
Gov Off
Morgan Arc
Royal Arc
Oxford Arc
Wyndham Arc
Orbit Theatre
Wood Street Bridge
Cardiff Central
CF11
Tyndall Street Ind Est
Cardiff Centre Trad Est
Driscoll Workshops
TA Ctr
Taff Workshops
Tresillian Way Ind Est
Coopers Yd
Prim Sch
Atlantic Wharf/
Glanfa Iwerydd
NORTH RD
A470
BOULEVARD DE NANTES
STUTTGARTER STRASSE
DUMFRIES PL
KINGSWAY
A4161
HEOL Y CASTELL/CASTLE ST
HEOL Y DUG/DUKE ST
HEOL FAWR/HIGH ST
HEOL EGLWYS FAIR/ST MARY ST
HEOL Y FRENHINES/QUEEN ST
NEWPORT RD
CITY RD
B4261
FITZALAN PL
A4160
ADAM ST
A4234
CENTRAL LINK
BUTE TERR
STRYD HERBERT/HERBERT ST
RHODFA LLOYD GEORGE/LLOYD GEORGE AVE
HEOL PENARTH/PENARTH RD
FFORDD TRESILLIAN/TRESILLIAN WAY
SGWAR CALLAGHAN/CALLAGHAN SQ
STRYD BUTE/BUTE ST
River Taff/Afon Taf
Dock Feeder
B2
1 BRANKSOME HO
2 MARLBOROUGH HO
3 High Street Arc
4 Duke Street Arc
5 Queens Arc
6 CATHEDRAL WLK
7 ST DAVID'S HO
8 THE HOPHOUSE
9 COOPERS CT
10 DRAY CT
RAGLAN HO 1
DUNRAVEN HO 2
KENILWORTH HO 3
WARWICK HO 4
WINDSOR HO 5
1 St David's Mkt
2 LITTLE FREDERICK ST
HOWARD CT 1
JELLICOE CT 2
CITY WHARF 3
194
195
195

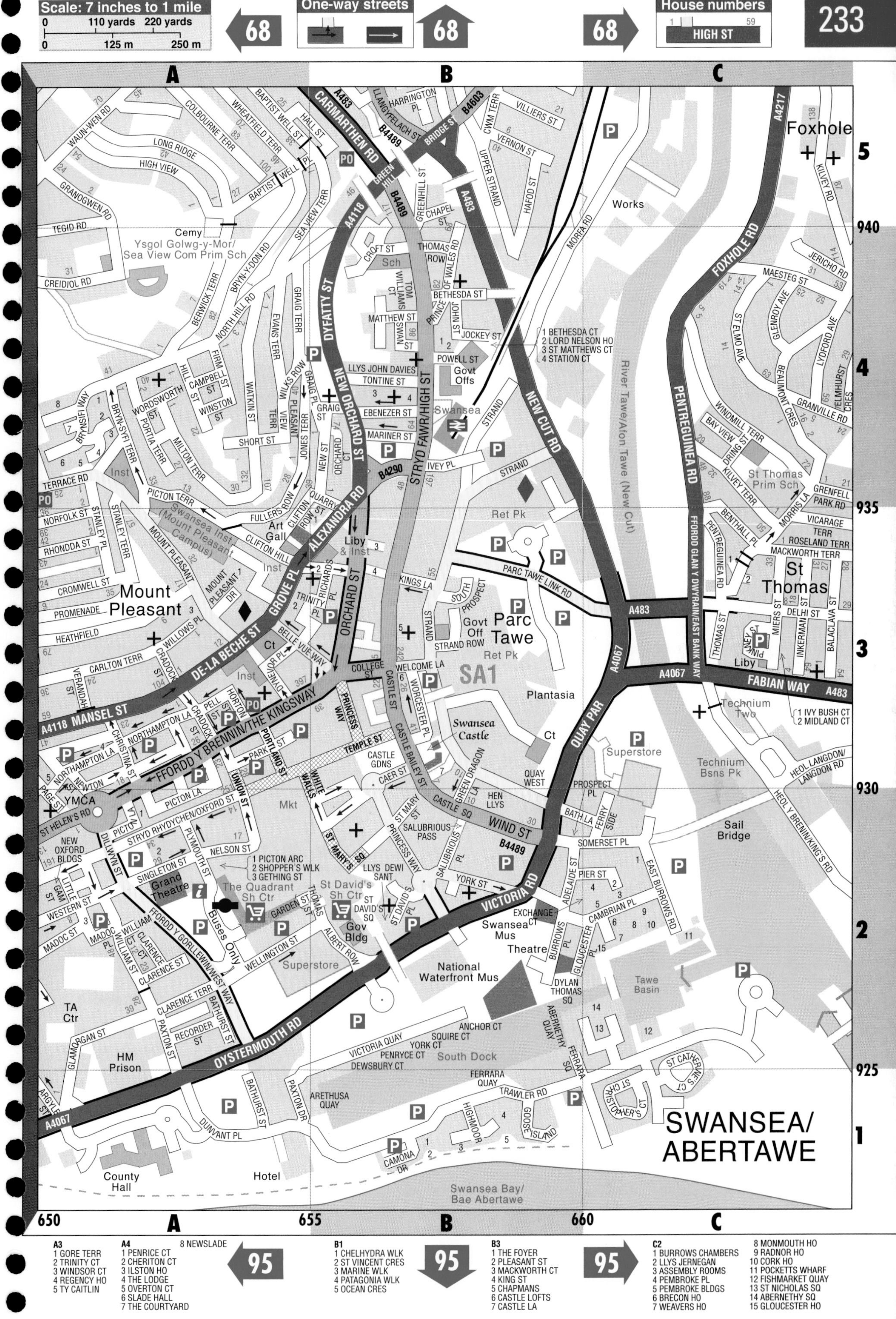

Scale: 7 inches to 1 mile
0 110 yards 220 yards
0 125 m 250 m
68
One-way streets
68
68
House numbers
1 59
HIGH ST
233
A
B
C
5
940
4
935
3
930
2
925
1
650
655
660
Foxhole
Works
Ysgol Golwg-y-Mor/
Sea View Com Prim Sch
Cemy
CARMARTHEN RD
NEW CUT RD
PENTREGUINEA RD
FFORDD GLAN Y DWYRAIN/EAST BANK WAY
FOXHOLE RD
River Tawe/Afon Tawe (New Cut)
DYFATTY ST
NEW ORCHARD ST
STRYD FAWR/HIGH ST
ALEXANDRA RD
ORCHARD ST
Swansea
Govt Offs
1 BETHESDA CT
2 LORD NELSON HO
3 ST MATTHEWS CT
4 STATION CT
St Thomas Prim Sch
St Thomas
Mount Pleasant
Swansea Inst (Mount Pleasant Campus)
Art Gall
Liby & Inst
Ret Pk
PARC TAWE LINK RD
Parc Tawe
Govt Off
SA1
Plantasia
FABIAN WAY
1 IVY BUSH CT
2 MIDLAND CT
Technium Two
Technium Bsns Pk
HEOL LANGDON/LANGDON RD
HEOL Y BRENIN/KING'S RD
DE-LA BECHE ST
MANSEL ST
FFORDD Y BRENNIN/THE KINGSWAY
Swansea Castle
Superstore
QUAY PAR
QUAY WEST
HEN LLYS
WIND ST
YMCA
Mkt
Sail Bridge
1 PICTON ARC
2 SHOPPER'S WLK
3 GETHING ST
The Quadrant Sh Ctr
St David's Sh Ctr
Grand Theatre
Busses Only
Gov Bldg
VICTORIA RD
Swansea Mus
Theatre
National Waterfront Mus
Tawe Basin
DYLAN THOMAS SQ
OYSTERMOUTH RD
TA Ctr
HM Prison
South Dock
VICTORIA QUAY
ARETHUSA QUAY
FERRARA QUAY
TRAWLER RD
SWANSEA/
ABERTAWE
County Hall
Hotel
Swansea Bay/
Bae Abertawe
A3
1 GORE TERR
2 TRINITY CT
3 WINDSOR CT
4 REGENCY HO
5 TY CAITLIN
A4
1 PENRICE CT
2 CHERITON CT
3 ILSTON HO
4 THE LODGE
5 OVERTON CT
6 SLADE HALL
7 THE COURTYARD
8 NEWSLADE
95
B1
1 CHELHYDRA WLK
2 ST VINCENT CRES
3 MARINE WLK
4 PATAGONIA WLK
5 OCEAN CRES
95
B3
1 THE FOYER
2 PLEASANT ST
3 MACKWORTH CT
4 KING ST
5 CHAPMANS
6 CASTLE LOFTS
7 CASTLE LA
95
C2
1 BURROWS CHAMBERS
2 LLYS JERNEGAN
3 ASSEMBLY ROOMS
4 PEMBROKE PL
5 PEMBROKE BLDGS
6 BRECON HO
7 WEAVERS HO
8 MONMOUTH HO
9 RADNOR HO
10 CORK HO
11 POCKETTS WHARF
12 FISHMARKET QUAY
13 ST NICHOLAS SQ
14 ABERNETHY SQ
15 GLOUCESTER HO

Index

Place name May be abbreviated on the map	Church Rd
Location number Present when a number indicates the place's position in a crowded area of mapping	6
Locality, town or village Shown when more than one place has the same name	Beckenham
Postcode district District for the indexed place	BR2
Page and grid square Page number and grid reference for the standard mapping	53 C6

Church Rd 6 Beckenham BR2..........53 C6

Cities, towns and villages are listed in **CAPITAL LETTERS**

Public and commercial buildings are highlighted in **magenta** **Places of interest** are highlighted in **blue** with a star★

Abbreviations used in the index

Acad	**Academy**
App	**Approach**
Arc	**Arcade**
Ave	**Avenue**
Bglw	**Bungalow**
Bldg	**Building**
Bsns, Bus	**Business**
Bvd	**Boulevard**
Cath	**Cathedral**
Cir	**Circus**
Cl	**Close**
Cnr	**Corner**
Coll	**College**
Com	**Community**
Comm	**Common**
Cott	**Cottage**
Cres	**Crescent**
Cswy	**Causeway**
Ct	**Court**
Ctr	**Centre**
Ctry	**Country**
Cty	**County**
Dr	**Drive**
Dro	**Drove**
Ed	**Education**
Emb	**Embankment**
Est	**Estate**
Ex	**Exhibition**
Gd	**Ground**
Gdn	**Garden**
Gn	**Green**
Gr	**Grove**
H	**Hall**
Ho	**House**
Hospl	**Hospital**
HQ	**Headquarters**
Hts	**Heights**
Ind	**Industrial**
Inst	**Institute**
Int	**International**
Intc	**Interchange**
Junc	**Junction**
L	**Leisure**
La	**Lane**
Liby	**Library**
Mdw	**Meadow**
Meml	**Memorial**
Mkt	**Market**
Mus	**Museum**
Orch	**Orchard**
Pal	**Palace**
Par	**Parade**
Pas	**Passage**
Pk	**Park**
Pl	**Place**
Prec	**Precinct**
Prom	**Promenade**
Rd	**Road**
Recn	**Recreation**
Ret	**Retail**
Sh	**Shopping**
Sq	**Square**
St	**Street**
Sta	**Station**
Terr	**Terrace**
TH	**Town Hall**
Univ	**University**
Wk, Wlk	**Walk**
Wr	**Water**
Yd	**Yard**

Translations Welsh – English

Aber	**Estuary, confluence**
Afon	**River**
Amgueddfa	**Museum**
Bro	**Area, district**
Bryn	**Hill**
Cae	**Field**
Caer	**Fort**
Canolfan	**Centre**
Capel	**Chapel**
Castell	**Castle**
Cilgant	**Crescent**
Clòs	**Close**
Coed	**Wood**
Coleg	**College**
Cwm	**Valley**
Cwrt	**Court**
Dinas	**City**
Dôl	**Meadow**
Eglwys	**Church**
Felin	**Mill**
Fferm	**Farm**
Ffordd	**Road, way**
Gelli	**Grove**
Gerddi	**Gardens**
Heol	**Road**
Isaf	**Lower**
Llan	**Church, parish**
Llyn	**Lake**
Llys	**Court**
Lôn	**Lane**
Maes	**Open area, field, square**
Môr	**Sea**
Mynydd	**Mountain**
Oriel	**Gallery**
Parc	**Park**
Parc busnes	**Business park**
Pen	**Top, end**
Pentref	**Village**
Plas	**Mansion, place**
Pont	**Bridge**
Prifysgol	**University**
Rhaeadr	**Waterfall**
Rhes	**Terrace, row**
Rhiw	**Hill, incline**
Rhodfa	**Avenue**
Sgwar	**Square**
Stryd	**Street**
Swyddfa post	**Post office**
Tref, Tre	**Town**
Tŷ	**House**
Uchaf	**Upper**
Ysbyty	**Hospital**
Ysgol	**School**
Ystad, stad	**Estate**
Ystad ddiwydiannol	**Industrial estate**
Ystrad	**Vale**

Translations English – Welsh

Avenue	**Rhodfa**
Bridge	**Pont**
Business Park	**Parc busnes**
Castle	**Castell**
Centre	**Canolfan**
Chapel	**Capel**
Church	**Eglwys**
City	**Dinas**
Close	**Clòs**
College	**Coleg**
Court	**Cwrt, Llys**
Crescent	**Cilgant**
District	**Bro**
Estate	**Ystad, stad**
Estuary	**Aber**
Farm	**Fferm**
Field	**Cae**
Fort	**Caer**
Gallery	**Oriel**
Gardens	**Gerddi**
Grove	**Gelli**
Hill	**Bryn, rhiw**
Hospital	**Ysbyty**
House	**Tŷ**
Industrial estate	**Ystad ddiwydiannol**
Lake	**Llyn**
Lane	**Lôn**
Lower	**Isaf**
Mansion	**Plas**
Meadow	**Dôl**
Mill	**Felin**
Mountain	**Mynydd**
Museum	**Amgueddfa**
Parish	**Llan, plwyf, eglwys**
Park	**Parc**
Place	**Plas, maes**
Post office	**Swyddfa post**
River	**Afon**
Road	**Heol**
School	**Ysgol**
Sea	**Môr**
Square	**Sgwâr, maes**
Street	**Stryd**
Terrace	**Rhes**
Top, end	**Pen**
Town	**Tref, tre**
University	**Prifysgol**
Upper	**Uchaf**
Vale	**Ystrad, glyn, dyffryn**
Valley	**Cwm**
Village	**Pentref**
Waterfall	**Rhaeadr**
Way	**Ffordd**
Wood	**Coed**

Index of towns, villages, streets, hospitals, industrial estates, railway stations, schools, shopping centres, universities and places of interest

92 Park St CF31 168 D4
132kv Switch House Rd CF62 211 E1
275kv Switch House Rd CF62 211 E1

A

Abbey Cl CF15 158 B3
Abbey Cotts NP44 117 B7
Abbey Ct CF38 135 E1
Abbeyfield Ho CF31 169 A5
Abbey Gn / Maes Yr Abaty 2 NP44 116 F8
Abbey Gr NP44 117 B6
Abbey Rd
  Ewenny / Ewenni CF35 185 F8
  Newport / Casnewydd NP19 144 D6
  Port Talbot SA13 125 C7
  Pyle / Y Pîl CF33 148 C2
Abbey Rd / Heol Abaty NP44 89 E2
Abbey Road Ind Est SA10 71 C7
Abbeyville Ave SA12 124 D8
Abbeyville Ave / Rhodfa Abbeyville 16 SA12 98 D1
Abbeyville Ct / Llys Abbeyville 11 SA12 98 D1
Abbeyville Ho 15 SA12 98 D1
Abbots Cl SA13 125 F3
Abbots Mews
  Margam SA13 125 F3
  Newport / Casnewydd NP20 143 B3
Abbot's Wlk SA10 71 C8
Aberaeron Cl CF62 215 A8
Aberafan Sh Ctr SA13 99 A1
ABERAMAN 53 B7
Aberaman Enterprise Pk CF44 53 E7
Aberaman Hos 5 CF44 53 D7
Aberaman Park Ind Est CF44 53 E6
Aberaman Terr CF44 53 D6
ABERAVON 124 F8
Aberavon Ct 12 SA12 98 F1
ABERAVON MOORS 98 E2
Aberavon Rd / Heol Aberavon SA12 98 E2
ABERAVON SANDS 124 C8
ABERBARGOD / ABERBARGOED 58 B4
ABERBARGOED / ABERBARGOD 58 B4
Aberbargoed & District Hospl CF81 58 B5
Aberbargoed Prim Sch CF81 58 A5
ABERBEEG / ABER-BIG 59 F8
Aberbeeg Rd NP13 36 B2
ABER-BIG / ABERBEEG 59 F8
Aberbran Rd CF14 177 C2
ABERCANAID 30 E4
Abercanaid Com Sch / Ysgol Gymunedol Abercanaid CF48 31 A4
Abercanaid Ind Est CF48 30 E6
Abercanaid Prim Sch CF48 30 F4
ABERCARN 87 C2
Abercarn Fach NP11 114 C8
Abercarn Prim Sch NP11 87 B4
Abercedy SA4 65 A4
Abercerdin Prim Sch CF39 132 B8
Abercerdin Rd CF39 132 B8
Aberclydach Pl SA6 46 D7
Aberconway Pl NP12 59 B1
ABERCRAF / ABERCRAVE 222 C8
ABERCRAVE / ABERCRAF 222 C8
Abercrave Cty Prim Sch SA9 222 C7
Abercrave Terr SA9 222 D7
ABERCREGAN 75 A6
Abercregan Rd SA13 74 F6
Aber Ct SA6 69 B7
ABERCWMBOI 53 E4
Abercwmboi-Isaf Rd CF45 54 B3
ABERCYNFFIG / ABERKENFIG 150 C4
ABERCYNON 82 D3
Abercynon Inf Sch CF45 82 E3
Abercynon North Sta CF45 82 E2
Abercynon Rd
  Abercynon CF45 82 C5
  Mountain Ash / Aberpennar CF45 82 A6
  Pontypridd CF37 109 D7
Abercynon South Sta CF45 82 E2
Abercynon St CF11 195 A2
ABERDÂR / ABERDARE 29 C2
ABERDARE / ABERDÂR 29 C2
Aberdare Boys' Sch CF44 28 D4
Aberdare Bsns Pk CF44 29 A3
Aberdare General Hospl CF44 29 B3
Aberdare Girls Comp Sch / Ysgol Gyfun Y Merched Aberdar CF44 29 B2
Aberdare Girls Lower Comp Sch CF44 28 F2
Aberdare Rd
  Abercynon CF45 82 D2
  Ferndale CF43 79 F8
  Glyn-neath / Glyn-nedd SA11 223 D1
  Merthyr Tydfil / Merthyr Tudful CF48 10 C1
  Mountain Ash / Aberpennar CF45 54 B3
Aberdare Sta CF44 29 A2
Aberdare Town CW Prim Sch / Ysgol Gynradd yr Eglwys Yng Nghymru Tref Aberdar CF44 29 B1
Aberdaron Rd CF3 179 E5
Aberdore Rd CF14 177 C2
Aberdovey Cl CF64 206 C3
Aberdovey St CF24 195 E5
ABERDULAIS 49 C4
Aberdulais Cres CF14 177 B2
Aberdulais Falls* SA10 49 C4
Aberdulais Rd CF14 177 B2
Aberdyberthi St SA1 68 D2
Aberfa Ho SA5 67 F3
ABERFAN 55 B5
Aberfan Cres CF48 55 C4
Aberfan Fawr CF48 55 C3
Aberfan Rd / Heol Abervan CF48 55 C7
Aberfawr Rd CF83 137 A7
Aber-Fawr Terr CF83 137 A7
Aberffrwd NP22 13 D5
Aber-Ffrwd Rd CF45 54 D4
Aberfields View CF32 104 F4
ABERGARW 151 A7
ABERGARWED 226 C5
Abergarw Rd CF32 150 F6
Abergarw Trad Est CF32 151 A6
Abergavenny Rd NP4 17 C8
Abergele Cl CF3 179 E6
Abergele Rd CF3 179 E5
Abergelly Rd SA5 67 C5
Abergorki Ind Est / Ystad Ddiwydiannol Abergorki CF42 78 C7
Abergwawr Pl CF44 53 B8
Abergwawr St CF44 53 C8
Abergwernffrwd Row SA12 73 C5
ABERGWYNFI 76 C5
Abergwynfi Inf Sch SA13 76 C5
Abergwynfi Jun Sch SA13 76 C5
Aber Halt CF83 137 F2
Aberhenwaun Uchaf SA10 222 E4
Aber Houses CF32 104 F4
ABERKENFIG / ABERCYNFFIG 150 C4
Aberlash Rd SA18 219 B8
Aberllechau Prim Sch CF39 107 D8
Aberllechau Rd CF39 107 D8
Aber Llwchwr SA14 42 B7
Abermorlais Terr / Teras Abermorlais 2 CF47 10 D1
ABERNANT 29 C3
Abernant Cres NP12 58 E7
Abernant Prim Sch CF44 29 C3
Abernant Rd
  Gwaun-Cae-Gurwen SA18 220 D5
  Markham NP12 58 D8
  Markham NP12 58 E7
Aber-Nant Rd CF44 29 B3
Abernethy Cl 10 CF3 180 A7
Abernethy Quay SA1 233 B2
Abernethy Sq 14 SA1 233 C2
ABEROGWR / OGMORE-BY-SEA 184 D3
ABERPENNAR / MOUNTAIN ASH 54 F3
Aberpennar St CF45 54 D2
Aberporth Rd CF14 177 B2
Aber Rd CF32 104 E3
Aber-Rhondda Rd CF39 107 E4
Aber St CF11 195 A2
ABERSYCHAN 37 E3
Abersychan Comp Sch NP4 37 F4
Abersychan Ind Est NP4 38 A3
Abertaf CF45 82 E3
Abertaf Prim Sch CF45 82 E3
ABERTAWE / SWANSEA 233 C1
Aberteifi Cl CF14 177 C2
Aberteifi Cres CF14 177 C2
Aberthaw Ave NP19 144 D4
Aberthaw Circ NP19 144 C5
Aberthaw Cl NP19 144 C5
Aberthaw Dr NP19 144 B4
Aberthaw Rd
  Cardiff / Caerdydd CF5 193 D5
  Newport / Casnewydd NP19 144 C4
ABERTHIN 189 B3
Aberthin La CF71 189 B2
Aberthin Rd CF71 189 A2
ABERTILLERY / ABERTYLERI 36 C5
Abertillery Comp Sch NP13 36 B6
Abertillery & District (Aberbeeg) Hospl NP13 59 F8
Abertillery & District Mus* NP13 36 B5
Abertillery Prim Sch NP13 36 B6
Abertillery Rd NP13 15 E3
Abertonllwyd St CF42 50 F2
ABERTRIDWR 137 B8
ABERTYLERI / ABERTILLERY 36 C5
ABERTYSSWG 33 C8
Abertysswg Prim Sch NP22 33 B8
Aberystwyth Cres CF62 214 E4
Aberystwyth St CF24 195 E5
Abingdon St CF63 215 B7
Acacia Ave
  Hengoed CF82 84 F3
  Merthyr Tydfil / Merthyr Tudful CF47 10 D4
  Newport / Casnewydd NP19 144 B5
  Porthcawl CF36 183 D7
  Port Talbot SA12 98 D2
Acacia Cl SA12 98 C2
Acacia Rd SA3 123 A8
Acacia Sq NP19 144 B5
Acacia St CF37 136 A5
Acacia Terr NP11 87 B4
Academic Ave / Coedlan Y Coleg CF14 177 E3
Academy The CF24 232 D3
Acer Ave CF38 156 C5
Acer Way NP10 141 E6
Acland Rd CF31 168 F5
Acorn Cl
  Abersychan NP4 37 F3
  Ebbw Vale / Glyn Ebwy NP23 7 C5
  Miskin / Meisgyn CF72 173 D7
  Rogerstone / Ty-du NP10 141 F7
Acorn Ct SA6 46 B1
Acorn Gr
  Cardiff / Caerdydd CF23 161 A1
  Llantwit Fadre / Llanilltud Faerdref CF38 156 E8
Acorn Pl / Lle Mesen SA12 98 D7
Acorns The
  Cardiff / Caerdydd CF14 159 E3
  Underwood NP18 145 E7
Acorn Villas / Tai Mesen NP23 14 E3
Acorn Wlk / Rhodfa Mes CF31 168 B4
Acre Cl NP11 60 C2
Adams Ave / Rhodfa Adams CF32 150 F4
Adamscroft Pl CF10 195 C5
Adams Ct CF24 232 D2
ADAMSDOWN 232 D2
Adamsdown La CF24 195 D5
Adamsdown Pl 3 CF24 195 D5
Adamsdown Prim Sch CF24 195 D6
Adamsdown Sq CF24 195 C5
Adams Sq NP23 14 E8
Adams St CF40 106 B7
Adam St
  Abertillery / Abertyleri NP13 36 C5
  Cardiff / Caerdydd CF24 232 C2
Adam Wlk SA10 71 C8
Adare St
  3 Bridgend / Pen-y-Bont ar Ogwr CF31 168 F4
  Evanstown CF39 132 B8
  Ogmore Vale CF32 104 E3
  Port Talbot SA12 124 E8
Adare Terr
  Tonypandy CF40 106 F5
Adare Terr *continued*
  Treorchy / Treorci CF42 78 C7
Adar Y Mor CF62 214 F2
Addison Ave CF72 172 A5
Addison Cres CF5 193 C5
Addison Pl SA12 124 E8
Addison Rd
  Neath / Castell-Nedd SA11 71 D4
  Port Talbot SA12 124 E8
Addison St NP12 85 D8
Addison Way CF83 139 C6
Addoldy Rd SA11 223 C1
Adelaide Ct NP12 85 C6
Adelaide Pl 15 CF10 195 B2
Adelaide St / Stryd Adelaide CF10 195 B1
Adelaide St
  Newport / Casnewydd NP20 143 C7
  Swansea / Abertawe SA1 233 B2
Adeline St
  Cardiff / Caerdydd CF24 195 E6
  Newport / Casnewydd NP20 143 C2
Adenfield Way CF62 212 E2
Adit Wlk / Llwybr Ceuffoadd NP44 89 C5
Administration Rd CF62 211 E1
Admirals Wlk SA2 94 C6
Adrian Boult Gn NP19 144 C4
Adrian Cl CF36 182 E8
Adrian Stephens Ho CF48 10 A3
Adventurers Quay CF10 195 D2
Aelfryn CF72 172 B5
Aelfryn Terr SA12 99 D6
Aelybryn CF37 109 A2
Ael-y-Bryn
  Beddau CF38 156 A7
  Bedwas CF83 138 F6
  Blaenavon NP4 17 D7
  Bridgend / Pen-y-Bont ar Ogwr CF31 168 B5
  Caerphilly / Caerffili CF83 137 F5
  Cardiff / Caerdydd CF23 178 D4
  Cwmdare CF44 28 D3
Ael Y Bryn CF82 85 A2
Ael-y-Bryn
  Maesteg CF34 75 A2
  North Cornelly CF33 166 A8
  Pen-clawdd SA4 64 F4
  Pentyrch CF15 175 C8
  Peterston-super-Ely / Llanbedr-y-fro CF5 191 E6
  Radyr CF15 176 B7
  Rhymney / Rhymni NP22 12 D6
  The Mumbles / Y Mwmbwls SA3 123 C3
  Trehafod CF37 108 C2
  Treherbert CF42 51 A1
  Trelewis CF46 83 D8
  Ystradgynlais SA9 222 A5
Aelybryn Cl SA15 40 E8
Aelybryn Dr SA15 40 E8
Ael-y-Bryn Rd SA5 67 E3
Aelybryn St CF81 32 D7
Ael-y-Bryn Terr NP11 86 F7
Ael-y-Coed CF62 214 C5
Ael-y-don SA3 122 F3
Ael-y-Fro SA8 23 D7
Aeron Cl CF62 214 D5
Aeron Ct CF81 58 A2
Aeron Pl
  Bargoed / Bargod CF81 58 A2
  Swansea / Abertawe SA1 69 B2
Aerons Ho 1 NP44 116 C8
Aeron Terr 4 CF47 30 F8
Afal Sur CF63 205 B1
Afan Cl CF62 214 D5
Afan Coll SA13 125 F3
Afandale SA12 98 C4
Afan Forest Park Visitor Ctr* SA13 74 A3
Afan Forest Pk* SA13 73 F1
Afan Rd SA13 74 D4
Afan St SA13 99 B1
Afan Terr
  Cwmavon / Cwmafan SA12 99 F6
  Cwmavon SA12 100 A7
Afan Valley Cl SA11 72 B5
Afan Valley Rd
  Cimla SA11 72 B5
  Cwmavon / Cwmafan SA12 99 E4
  Pontrhydyfen SA12, SA13 73 D2
Afan Way
  Aberavon SA12 124 F8
  Port Talbot SA12 98 D2
Afon Cl
  Michaelston-y-Fedw CF3 161 D4
  Pontypool / Pont-y-pwl NP4 63 A3
Afon Ct NP4 38 A3
Afon Fach CF33 148 A1
Afon Gdns NP18 118 A5
Afon-Llan Gdns SA5 67 D6
Afon Llwyd Terr / Teras Afon Llwyd 2 NP4 38 A1
Afon Lwyd Cl NP18 118 C3
Afon Mead NP10 141 D7
Afon Rd / Heol Afon SA14 42 C8
Afon St CF37 108 D2
Afon Taf High Sch CF48 31 C1
Afon Terr NP44 89 F5
Afon Villas SA12 100 A7
Afon-y-Felin SA10 49 C4
Afon-y-Felin Prim Sch CF33 147 F1
Africa Gdns CF14 177 E2
Agate St CF24 195 D6
Agent's Row CF44 29 C3
Agincourt Rd 1 CF23 195 D8
Agincourt St NP20 143 B7
Agnes St CF64 206 E5
Ailesbury St NP20 143 C7
Ainon Ct CF24 195 E5
Aintree Dr CF5 193 F5
Airport Bsns Pk CF62 213 C4
Aiwa Technology Pk NP11 87 A7
Alamein Rd SA1 68 E3
Alanbrooke Ave NP20 117 A4
Alan Cl 14 NP10 142 B4
Alandale Rd NP23 7 A4
Alaw Prim Sch CF40 107 B5
Alaw Rd CF40 107 B5
Alban Rd SA15 40 E6
Alban Terr SA13 74 F6
Albany Cl SA5 68 C4
Albany Ct 12 CF64 207 B4
Albany Hos NP4 38 A6
Albany Ind Est NP20 143 C7
Albany Prim Sch CF24 195 B8
Albany Rd
  Blackwood / Coed-Duon NP12 85 E6
  Cardiff / Caerdydd CF24 195 C8
  Pontycymer CF32 103 F3
Albany St
  Ferndale CF43 80 A6
  Mountain Ash / Aberpennar CF45 54 D1
  Newport / Casnewydd NP20 143 C7
Albany Trad Est NP20 143 C7
Alberta Pl CF64 207 A2
Alberta Rd CF64 207 B2
Alberta St CF48 55 D5
Albert Ave NP19 143 E6
Albert Cres CF64 207 B4
Albert Ct
  7 Newport / Casnewydd NP19 143 E5
  4 Penarth CF64 207 B4
Albert Cty Prim Sch CF64 207 B5
Albertina Rd NP11 59 F1
Alberto Rd SA6 69 A6
Albert Pl SA3 123 A5
Albert Rd
  Penarth CF64 207 B4
  Pontypridd CF37 135 B8
Albert Rd / Heol Albert NP4 37 D5
Albert Row SA1 233 B2
Albert St
  Aberdare / Aberdâr CF44 29 A1
  Barry / Y Barri CF63 215 D6
  Cardiff / Caerdydd CF11 194 D5
  Ferndale CF43 80 A7
  Llanelli SA15 40 C4
  Maesteg CF34 75 C1
  Mountain Ash / Aberpennar CF45 54 D1
  Newport / Casnewydd NP20 143 C3
  Treorchy / Treorci CF41 78 F5
Albert Terr
  Maesteg CF34 101 F3
  Newport / Casnewydd NP20 143 B4
Albert Wlk 10 CF11 194 D5
Albion Cl NP20 143 D2
Albion Ct
  Newport / Casnewydd NP20 143 D2
  Pontypridd CF37 109 F3
Albion Flats CF37 109 F5
Albion Ind Est CF37 109 F6
Albion Pl
  Pontypool / Pont-y-pwl NP4 62 A8
  Pyle / Y Pîl CF33 148 C1
Albion Rd NP4 62 B6
Albion Rd App SA12 98 C7
Albion Rd / Heol Albion SA12 98 D7

Albion St
Aberdare / Aberdâr CF44 53 B8
Ton Pentre CF41 79 A2
Albion Terr NP12 85 F6
Alcock Cl NP19 144 B3
Alden Dr SA2 67 D1
Aldenham Rd CF36 183 C7
Alder Ave SA9 2 D7
Alderbrook CF23 160 D1
Alderbrook Ct SA5 67 F6
Alder Cl NP4 63 B5
Alder Dr CF44 28 E2
Alder Gr
Ebbw Vale / Glyn Ebwy NP23 7 C5
Llantwit Fadre / Llanilltud Faerdref CF38 156 C5
Merthyr Tydfil / Merthyr Tudful CF47 10 D5
Newport / Casnewydd NP20 117 B2
Aldergrove Cl SA12 98 E4
Aldergrove Rd CF39 107 E5
Alderman Cl NP12 85 D7
Alderman Davies Prim Sch SA11 71 E7
Alderney St NP20 143 C7
Alder Rd
Cardiff / Caerdydd CF23 178 B2
Llanharry CF72 172 B5
Neath / Castell-Nedd SA11 72 A6
Alder Rise NP12 86 A4
Alders The
Blackwood / Coed Duon NP12 59 C1
Llanyrafon NP44 90 B1
Alder Terr SA13 75 D4
Alder Way
Gowerton / Tre-gwyr SA4 66 C6
The Mumbles / Y Mwmbwls SA3 122 F7
Alderwood Cl
1 Cardiff / Caerdydd CF3 179 E7
Crynant SA10 222 A1
Alderwood Rd SA3 123 A7
Aldsworth Rd CF5 193 F7
Aldwych Cl CF14 159 E2
Aldwyn Rd SA5 67 D2
Aled Way CF62 211 C7
Alexander Cres SA10 48 E2
Alexander Ct CF83 138 C3
Alexander Rd
Briton Ferry / Llansawel SA11 71 C3
Neath / Castell-Nedd SA10 48 E2
Alexander St
Abertysswg NP22 33 B8
Cardiff / Caerdydd CF24 195 B8
Alexandra Ave CF47 10 E3
Alexandra Cl CF47 10 E3
Alexandra Cres CF62 214 D5
Alexandra Ct
2 Cardiff / Caerdydd, Canton CF5 194 D6
Cardiff / Caerdydd CF5 194 B6
Newport / Casnewydd NP20 143 D2
Penarth CF64 207 B3
Ynysddu NP11 112 F6
Alexandra Gate CF24 196 A8
Alexandra Gdns CF44 29 B2
Alexandra La NP20 143 C1
Alexandra Pl
Abercanaid CF48 30 F4
Abercynon CF45 82 F3
Maesteg CF34 75 C2
Newbridge / Trecelyn NP11 86 F7
Rhymney / Rhymni NP22 12 E5
Tredegar NP22 13 E8
Alexandra Rd
Abertillery / Abertyleri NP13 36 C3
Cardiff / Caerdydd CF5 194 C5
Gorseinon SA4 43 A2
Hengoed CF82 85 A3
Maesteg CF34 75 B2
Merthyr Tydfil / Merthyr Tudful CF47 10 E3
Newport / Casnewydd NP20 143 C2
New Tredegar NP24 33 F2
Pontycymer CF32 103 F3
Pontypool / Pont-y-pwl NP4 62 E1
Pontypridd CF37 135 D8
Swansea / Abertawe SA1 233 B3
Ton Pentre CF41 79 A2
Ynysddu NP11 112 F6
Alexandra St
5 Aberavon SA12 99 A1
Blaina / Blaenau NP13 15 E4
Ebbw Vale / Glyn Ebwy NP23 14 D7
Alexandra Terr
Aberdare / Aberdâr CF44 29 B2

Alexandra Terr *continued*
Abertillery / Abertyleri NP13 36 C3
Cwmaman CF44 53 B4
Llantwit Fadre / Llanilltud Faerdref CF38 156 C6
20 Merthyr Tydfil / Merthyr Tudful CF47 30 E8
Mountain Ash / Aberpennar CF45 54 E3
Senghenydd CF83 110 F3
Swansea / Abertawe SA2 94 F6
Tredegar NP22 13 F6
Alexandra Trad Est CF3 179 D3
Alexandra Terr 8 NP23 8 C4
Alford Rd SA11 71 E7
Alfreda Ct CF14 176 F4
Alfreda Rd CF14 176 F4
Alfred Rd SA6 68 E6
Alfred St
Aberavon SA12 98 F1
Abertysswg NP22 33 C8
Bargoed / Bargod CF81 58 A2
Cardiff / Caerdydd CF24 178 B1
Ebbw Vale / Glyn Ebwy NP23 7 C1
Hendreforgan CF39 132 C5
Maesteg CF34 102 A3
Merthyr Tydfil / Merthyr Tudful CF47 10 F4
Neath / Castell-Nedd SA11 71 E7
2 Newport / Casnewydd NP19 143 D6
Tonypandy CF40 107 A2
Alfred's Terr CF15 158 A3
Alice Pl CF44 53 A3
Alice St
Cardiff / Caerdydd CF10 195 B2
Neath / Castell-Nedd SA11 71 D6
Newport / Casnewydd NP20 143 C1
Swansea / Abertawe SA5 68 A2
Alison Ct CF36 183 C7
Allan Durst Cl CF5 176 D3
Allaway Ct 1 SA1 68 C2
Allen Cl
Bettws NP20 116 C1
Cardiff / Caerdydd CF3 179 E8
Allen Ct CF61 210 B6
Allensbank Cres CF14 177 F2
Allensbank Ho CF14 177 F3
Allensbank Prim Sch CF14 177 F2
Allensbank Rd CF14 177 F3
Allen St CF45 54 D3
Allerton St CF11 194 F4
Alleyn Ho NP44 90 B4
Allgood Ave NP4 17 B6
Allied Ind Pk CF24 195 F5
Allister St 5 SA11 71 E7
Allotment Rd NP23 7 C3
Alloy Court Est SA8 23 F5
All Saints CIW Prim Sch CF23 178 D4
All Saints CW Prim Sch CF62 214 C5
All Saints Pl SA12 99 F5
All Saints RC Prim Sch NP23 14 B8
All Saints Way CF31 150 D1
ALLT 18 A1
Alltacham Dr SA8 23 E5
Allt Dderw / Oak Hillside CF31 168 B2
Allt-Iago Rd SA4 19 D4
Alltmawr Rd CF23 178 C6
ALLT-WEN 23 F3
Alltwen CF44 29 C3
Allt Wen CF14 176 F8
Alltwen Chwyth SA8 23 F3
Alltwen Hill SA8 23 F3
Alltwen Ind Est SA8 24 A5
Alltwen Prim Sch SA8 23 F4
Allt Y Dyffryn / Dyffryn Woods SA10 48 C3
Allt Y Felin / Woodmill SA10 48 C1
Allt-y-Graban Rd SA4 43 D8
Allt Y Grug SA10 70 C1
Alltygrug Farm Rd SA9 2 B7
Alltygrug Rd / Heol Alltygrug SA9 2 B7
ALLT-YR-YN 143 A6
Allt-yr-Yn Ave NP20 142 F5
Allt-yr-Yn Cl NP20 143 A6
Allt-yr-Yn Cres NP20 143 A7
Allt-yr-Yn Ct NP20 143 A7
Allt-yr-Yn Hts NP20 142 F6
Allt-yr-Yn Rd NP20 143 A6
Allt-yr-Yn View NP20 142 F6
Allt-yr-Yn Way NP20 143 A7
Allt-y-Waun SA8 23 D7
Allt Y Wennol CF23 160 F1
Alltywerin SA8 23 D6
Allt y Wiwer CF38 156 E8
Alma Cl 19 NP20 143 C3
Alma Hos CF34 102 B2
Alma Pl
Pontypool / Pont-y-pwl NP4 62 E1
Treorchy / Treorci CF41 78 F5
Alma Rd
Cardiff / Caerdydd CF23 178 C1

Alma Rd *continued*
Maesteg CF34 102 B2
Alma St
Aberdare / Aberdâr CF44 28 F4
Abertillery / Abertyleri NP13 36 B6
5 Blaenavon NP4 17 C7
Brynmawr NP23 8 C4
Dowlais CF48 11 A5
Machen CF83 140 A7
Merthyr Tydfil / Merthyr Tudful CF47 30 E8
Newport / Casnewydd NP20 143 C3
Treherbert CF42 50 E2
Alma Terr
Aberkenfig / Abercynffig CF32 150 C3
Brynmawr NP23 8 D5
Church Village CF38 156 F8
Dowlais CF48 11 A5
Maesteg CF34 102 B2
Ogmore Vale CF32 130 E8
Port Talbot SA13 125 D6
Almond Ave NP11 115 B2
Almond Cl CF38 156 C6
Almond Ct NP20 117 A3
Almond Dr
Cardiff / Caerdydd CF23 160 F1
Newport / Casnewydd NP20 117 B3
Almond Gr CF47 10 D4
Alpha Ho CF15 157 E8
Alpha Pl CF37 109 D2
Alpha Pl / Lle Alffa SA12 98 D7
Alpha St CF37 109 D2
Alphonso St CF48 11 B5
Als St SA15 40 E5
Althorp Dr CF64 217 A8
Alton Terr NP4 62 B7
Alun Rd SA1 68 B1
ALWAY 144 C5
Alway Cres NP19 144 D5
Alway Par NP19 144 D4
Alway Prim Sch NP19 144 C4
Alwen Dr
Barry / Y Barri CF62 214 C6
Cardiff / Caerdydd CF14 159 F3
Alwyn Cl NP10 142 A7
Alyson Way CF35 170 C8
Amalfi Ho CF10 195 C3
Aman Ct CF44 53 A3
Aman Pl CF44 53 A3
Aman St CF44 53 A3
Amanwy SA14 41 D5
Amber Cl
Cardiff / Caerdydd CF23 160 F1
Port Talbot SA12 98 B2
Ambergate Dr CF23 160 F1
Amberheart Dr CF14 159 F3
Amberley Cl CF23 178 F8
Amberley Dr SA3 123 A4
Amberton Pl 3 CF47 10 F4
Amberwood Cl CF23 160 F1
Amblecote Cl CF23 160 F1
Ambleside NP4 37 E5
Ambleside Ave CF23 178 A2
Ambleside Ct CF82 84 E8
Ambleside Pl SA3 123 A8
Ambrooke Cl CF23 160 F1
Ambrose Way NP4 63 A4
Ambryn Rd NP4 63 B4
Amelia Cl CF48 11 B7
Amelia Terr CF40 106 E7
Amelia Trust Farm* CF5 203 C5
America Pl CF39 107 F4
Amesbury Rd CF23 178 D1
Amethyst Rd CF5 176 D1
Amgueddfa Ganadlaethol Cymru / Nat Mus of Wales* CF10 232 B4
Amgueddfa Werin Cymru / Mus of Welsh Life* CF5 192 F7
Amherst Cres CF62 214 F2
Amherst St CF11 194 F2
Amity Ct CF10 195 C3
Ammanford Inf Sch SA18 219 C7
Ammanford Jun Sch SA18 219 C7
Ammanford Rd / Heol Rhydaman SA18 218 F6
AMMANFORD / RHYDAMAN 219 A8
Ammanford Sta SA18 219 B7
Amman Rd / Heol Amman
Brynamman SA18 220 E8
Glanaman SA18 219 F8
Amman Valley Comp Sch SA18 219 C7
Amman Valley Hospl SA18 220 A8
Amos Hill CF40 107 A3
Amos St SA15 40 C4
Amroth Ct
Barry / Y Barri CF62 214 F7
Swansea / Abertawe SA5 68 B7
Amroth Rd CF5 193 D5
Amroth Wlk / Rhodfa Amroth 14 NP44 89 C2
Amry Pl CF41 79 D3
Amyas Cl CF11 194 E3

Amy Johnson Cl NP19 144 B3
Anchor Bay Ct SA3 123 A6
Anchor Ct
Cardiff / Caerdydd CF10 232 C1
Swansea / Abertawe SA1 233 B2
Anchor Ind Est CF10 195 B3
Anchor Rd CF64 207 A6
Anchor St CF15 158 A3
Anderson Cl NP20 143 A3
Anderson La SA3 121 A5
Anderson Pl
Cardiff / Caerdydd CF24 195 D6
Newport / Casnewydd NP20 117 A4
Andover Cl CF62 214 B7
Andrew Cres SA6 46 B4
Andrew Rd CF64 206 E5
Andrews Bldgs 2 CF64 207 B4
Andrews Cl
Bargoed / Bargod CF81 58 A2
Merthyr Tydfil / Merthyr Tudful CF48 30 A8
Ton-du CF32 150 D5
Andrews Ct
Ebbw Vale / Glyn Ebwy NP23 7 B1
Llantwit Major / Llanilltud Fawr CF61 210 A6
Pontypridd CF37 135 C8
Andrew's Rd CF14 176 F2
Andrew St SA15 40 E6
Andrews Terr NP11 60 C4
Androven Ct CF23 178 D6
Aneddfan SA12 99 F6
Aneurin Ave
Newbridge / Trecelyn NP11 60 B3
Pengam NP12 85 B6
Aneurin Bevan Ave
Brynmenyn CF32 150 F6
Gelligaer CF82 84 C6
Aneurin Bevan Ct
Newport / Casnewydd NP10 163 E7
Pontypool / Pont-y-pwl NP4 62 C6
Aneurin Bevan Dr CF38 156 E8
Aneurin Bevan's Way CF34 102 D2
Aneurin Cl SA2 94 A6
Aneurin Cl / Rhiw Aneurin NP22 13 E7
Aneurin Cres CF47 30 F7
Aneurin Pl / Maes Aneurin NP23 8 C5
Aneurin Rd CF63 215 A6
Aneurin Terr NP22 12 E6
Aneurin Way SA2 94 A6
Angel Flats CF34 102 B3
Angelica Way CF14 159 D3
Angelina St CF10 195 B3
Angel La
Bargoed / Bargod CF81 58 A3
Blackwood / Coed-Duon NP12 58 B2
Angel Pl 8 SA11 71 E8
Angel Sq NP23 14 D6
Angel St
Aberavon SA12 98 F1
Bridgend / Pen-y-Bont ar Ogwr CF31 168 E4
7 Neath / Castell-Nedd SA11 71 E8
Angelton Gn CF31 150 D1
Angelton Rd CF31 168 D8
Angel Way / Ffordd Yr Angel CF33 147 E1
Angle Cl CF62 214 F8
Angle Pl CF14 159 D1
Anglesey Cl
Church Village CF38 136 A2
Llantwit Major / Llanilltud Fawr CF61 210 B7
Anglesey Ct NP18 117 F3
Anglesey St 10 CF5 194 C6
Anglesey Way CF36 165 E1
Angleton Rd CF31 168 D8
Anglia Cl CF31 150 F1
Angus St / Stryd Angus CF48 55 C5
Angus St
Cardiff / Caerdydd CF24 178 C1
7 Troedyrhiw CF48 31 B1
Anisa Mews 23 NP20 143 C4
Annes Ct NP23 7 C1
Annesley Rd NP19 143 E6
Annesley St SA15 40 C5
Anne St 7 NP4 17 C6
Ann's Cl CF47 30 E7
Ann St
Abercynon CF45 82 D2
Aberdare / Aberdâr CF44 28 F3
Cardiff / Caerdydd CF11 194 D5
Llanelli SA15 40 D4
Pontypridd CF37 109 F5
Ansari Ct CF72 155 A5
Anson Ct CF10 232 D1
Anson Gn NP19 144 E7
Anstee Ct 8 CF5 194 D5
Anthony Dr NP18 117 F4
Anthony Gr CF48 30 E4

Anthony Hill Ct / Cwrt Anthony Hill CF48 31 A4
Anton Ct CF14 177 A5
Antwerp Pl NP13 36 A6
Anwyll Cl NP18 118 A4
Apollo Cl CF14 159 E2
Apollo Way NP12 85 D7
Appledore Pl SA3 122 E6
Appledore Rd CF14 177 D3
Applegrove SA3 229 B1
Appletree Ave CF40 107 C4
Appletree Cl CF72 172 B5
Appletree Rd CF40 107 C4
Applewood Cl CF24 195 D5
Approach Rd SA5 68 C2
Aprilia Ho CF10 195 C3
Aqueduct Terr SA12 73 B1
Aquilla Ct 5 CF11 194 D7
Arabella St CF24 178 B1
Arael View NP13 35 F8
Aragon Ho NP20 143 A5
Aragon St NP20 143 C7
Arail St NP13 36 C3
Arail Street Flats NP13 36 C3
Aran Ct NP44 89 B5
Aran St SA6 68 F7
Arbroath Ct CF24 195 F7
Arbutus Cl CF47 10 D5
Arcade 1 SA15 40 D5
Arcade Terr / Teras Yr Arced 11 SA18 220 B8
Arcade The
20 Ammanford / Rhydaman SA18 219 B7
Cwmbran / Cwmbrân NP44 89 F3
Arcadia Way NP4 38 B2
Archbishop Mcgrath RC Sch CF32 150 E5
Archdeacon John Lewis CW Prim Sch CF31 169 C5
Archer Cres CF5 193 D6
Archer Ct CF62 214 F2
Archer Pl
Cardiff / Caerdydd CF5 193 C6
Penarth CF64 207 A3
Archer Rd
Barry / Y Barri CF62 214 F2
Cardiff / Caerdydd CF5 193 C6
Cwmbran / Cwmbrân NP44 89 B3
Penarth CF64 207 A3
Archer St
Troedyrhiw CF48 31 C2
Ynysybwl CF37 81 F1
Archer Terr
Cardiff / Caerdydd CF5 193 D6
Penarth CF64 207 A2
Arches Cl / Clos Y Bwau NP22 6 D2
Arches The 29 CF47 30 E8
Arch Hill NP11 114 C6
Archibald St NP19 143 E5
Archview Ct CF24 178 A2
Arcon Ho 3 CF3 179 D8
Arcot La CF64 207 A4
Arcot Lane N 7 CF64 207 A5
Arcot St CF64 207 A4
A R D Bsns Pk NP4 62 F4
Arden Way CF63 215 C7
Ardmore Ave 3 CF40 106 F4
Ardwyn CF14 176 F8
Ardwyn Pl CF32 104 E2
Ardwyn Terr
Resolven / Resolfen SA11 226 E5
Ton Pentre CF41 79 A2
Tonypandy CF40 106 E6
Ardwyn Vale / Pant Ardwyn CF35 170 C8
Arennig Rd SA5 68 B5
Arethuea Quay SA1 233 B1
Arethusa Ct SA2 93 C6
Arethusa Quay SA1 233 B1
Arfonfab Cres CF37 136 B4
Arfryn CF44 28 A6
Arfryn Ave SA15 40 E7
Arfryn Pl CF47 30 E8
Arfryn Prim Sch SA5 68 B5
Arfryn Rd SA2 94 E8
Arfryn Terr
Ebbw Vale / Glyn Ebwy NP23 7 D4
7 Merthyr Tydfil / Merthyr Tudful CF47 30 F8
Tylorstown CF43 80 B4
Argae La CF63, CF64 205 D2
ARGOED 58 E5
Argoed Ave CF72 154 A3
Argoed Prim Sch NP12 58 F5
Argoed Rd / Heol Argoed SA18 219 C5
Argoed Terr CF48 55 D5
Argoed Walk* SA13 73 F2
Argosy Way NP19 143 E4
Argyle St
Abercynon CF45 82 F3
Abertillery / Abertyleri NP13 36 B5
Merthyr Tydfil / Merthyr Tudful CF47 10 F1
Newport / Casnewydd NP20 143 C7
Porth CF39 107 E2
Swansea / Abertawe SA1 95 B6
Treorchy / Treorci CF41 78 F5

Argyle Terr CF40 ... 106 E8
Argyle Way CF5 ... 193 E4
Argyll Ave SA4 ... 43 B2
Argyll Ct 4 CF15 ... 176 B6
Arlan Gwilli SA4 ... 19 A4
Arles Rd CF5 ... 193 E5
Arlington Cl NP20 ... 117 A4
Arlington Cres CF3 ... 179 C6
Arlington Mews CF64 ... 216 B5
Arlington Pl CF36 ... 182 F7
Arlington Rd
Porthcawl CF36 ... 182 F7
Sully CF64 ... 216 B5
Armine Rd SA5 ... 67 E3
Armoury Dr CF14 ... 177 D6
Armoury Terr NP23 ... 14 D7
Armstrong Cl NP19 ... 144 B4
Arnant Villas CF32 ... 104 F5
Arne Cl NP19 ... 144 E5
Arnold Ave CF3 ... 179 C8
Arnold Cl NP20 ... 142 F2
Arnold Ct SA9 ... 2 B6
Arnold Pl NP22 ... 6 D1
Arnold St CF45 ... 54 E3
Arno Rd CF63 ... 215 C7
Arnott's Pl CF44 ... 28 F1
Arnside Rd CF23 ... 178 C2
Arosfa Ave CF36 ... 183 D8
Arosfa Ct NP22 ... 13 E6
Arran Cl
Pen-y-coedcae CF37 ... 135 B6
Risca / Rhisga NP11 ... 115 C1
Arran Pl CF24 ... 195 C8
Arran St CF24 ... 195 C8
Arrol St 14 CF24 ... 195 D5
Arthur Bliss Rd NP19 ... 144 C4
Arthur Cl NP20 ... 143 C2
Arthur Davis Ct CF62 ... 214 F6
Arthur St / Stryd Arthur
SA18 ... 219 B8
Arthur St
Aberavon SA12 ... 99 A1
Abertysswg NP22 ... 33 C8
Barry / Y Barri CF63 ... 215 D6
Blaengwynfi SA13 ... 76 B6
Caerleon / Caerllion
NP18 ... 118 C2
Cardiff / Caerdydd CF24 .. 195 E7
Cwmfelinfach NP11 ... 113 B4
Llanelli SA15 ... 40 D5
Mountain Ash / Aberpennar
CF45 ... 81 E8
Neath / Castell-Nedd
SA11 ... 71 E7
Newport / Casnewydd
NP20 ... 143 C2
Pentrebach CF48 ... 31 A3
Tonypandy CF40 ... 107 A2
Tredegar NP22 ... 13 F4
Ystrad CF41 ... 79 C3
Arthur Terr SA8 ... 23 E5
Arundel Cl NP44 ... 89 A3
Arundel Cl / Clos Arundel
3 NP44 ... 89 A3
Arundel Pl CF11 ... 194 D2
Arundel Rd NP19 ... 143 F5
Arvona Terr NP12 ... 85 B6
Arwelfa SA6 ... 45 D1
Ar-y-Nant CF63 ... 215 A7
Ascot Cl CF5 ... 193 F5
Ascot Dr SA12 ... 98 E7
Asgog St CF24 ... 195 D5
Ashbourne Ct CF44 ... 28 D2
Ashbrook CF31 ... 169 B5
Ashburnham Dr SA3 ... 93 E2
Ashburton Ave CF3 ... 179 C7
Ashby Rd CF64 ... 216 A6
Ashchurch Cl CF14 ... 177 A5
Ash Cres CF47 ... 10 D4
Ashcroft Cres CF5 ... 176 C1
Ash Ct
Blackwood / Coed-Duon
NP12 ... 85 F6
Pontllanfraith NP12 ... 86 A6
Ashdale Rd CF40 ... 107 A1
Ashdene Cl CF5 ... 176 D2
Ashdown Cl 4 CF3 ... 179 F7
Ashdown Ct CF37 ... 109 F4
Ashfield Cl CF39 ... 107 D4
Ashfield Ct 7 CF3 ... 179 E7
Ashfield Rd
Abertillery / Abertyleri
NP13 ... 36 B5
Newbridge / Trecelyn
NP11 ... 86 F7
Ashford CF14 ... 160 A2
Ashford Cl
Croesyceiliog NP44 ... 90 B5
Pontypridd CF37 ... 109 C5
Ashford Cl N NP44 ... 90 B5
Ashford Cl S NP44 ... 90 B4
Ash Gn NP44 ... 116 F8
Ash Gr
Ammanford / Rhydaman
SA18 ... 219 D7
Barry / Y Barri CF63 ... 215 C7
Bridgend / Pen-y-Bont ar Ogwr
CF31 ... 168 A5
Cardiff / Caerdydd CF14 .. 177 B6
Cardiff / Caerdydd,
Culverhouse Cross
CF5 ... 193 A2
Cimla SA11 ... 72 B5
Ebbw Vale / Glyn Ebwy
NP23 ... 14 E6
Gorseinon SA4 ... 43 A3
Llandough / Llandochau
CF64 ... 206 E6
Ash Gr *continued*
Llanharry CF72 ... 172 B5
Mountain Ash / Aberpennar
CF45 ... 81 E8
Pontyclun CF72 ... 172 F8
Pontypool / Pont-y-pwl
NP4 ... 38 D1
Porthcawl CF36 ... 183 E8
Swansea / Abertawe SA2 .. 93 D7
Trefechan CF48 ... 10 B6
Treorchy / Treorci CF41 ... 78 F5
Underwood NP18 ... 145 E6
Waunarlwydd SA5 ... 66 D4
Ystradowen CF71 ... 189 C8
Ashgrove
Aberdare / Aberdâr
CF44 ... 28 F3
Baglan SA12 ... 98 D7
Bedwas CF83 ... 138 F6
Bryn NP12 ... 85 E5
Dinas Powis / Dinas Powys
CF64 ... 206 B2
Hengoed CF82 ... 84 F2
Llantwit Major / Llanilltud
Fawr CF61 ... 209 F6
Pontypridd CF37 ... 109 D6
Treharris CF46 ... 82 F6
Ashgrove Cl NP4 ... 62 D1
Ashgrove Sch CF64 ... 206 D3
Ashgrove Terr CF46 ... 83 E3
Ashgrove Villas CF46 ... 56 A7
Ash La CF62 ... 211 B7
Ashlea Dr CF47 ... 10 F1
Ashleigh Cl SA2 ... 94 C3
Ashleigh Ct
Cwmbran / Cwmbrân
NP44 ... 89 A1
Tredegar NP22 ... 13 E8
Ashleigh Rd SA2 ... 94 C3
Ashleigh Terr SA10 ... 97 C8
Ashley Rd NP19 ... 144 B5
Ashlieigh Ct CF36 ... 183 C7
Ashman Cl CF83 ... 137 D1
Ashmere Dr SA11 ... 223 F2
Ashmount Bsns Parc
SA6 ... 46 B1
Ash Pk CF71 ... 189 C8
Ash Pl
Bargoed / Bargod CF81 ... 57 F2
Cardiff / Caerdydd CF5 ... 176 D1
Ash Plant Rd CF62 ... 211 E1
Ash Rd CF48 ... 31 B1
Ash Sq CF37 ... 136 A5
Ash St
Abercwmboi CF44 ... 53 E4
Cwm NP23 ... 35 A8
Gilfach Goch CF39 ... 132 B5
Swansea / Abertawe SA6 .. 69 A7
Ashton Ho 1 NP44 ... 89 D2
Ash Tree Cl CF15 ... 176 A6
Ash Tree Ct CF23 ... 161 A3
ASHVALE ... 6 C1
Ashvale NP22 ... 6 C1
Ashvale Ind Est NP22 ... 13 D8
Ash Villas 8 CF48 ... 31 C1
Ashville
Blackwood / Coed Duon
NP12 ... 59 A1
Tredegar NP22 ... 13 F5
Ashwell Cotts NP18 ... 144 C8
Ash Wlk CF72 ... 155 C2
Ashwood Cl NP12 ... 85 E5
Ashwood Ct 6 CF24 ... 195 C7
Ashwood Dr SA8 ... 24 B5
Aspen Ave NP12 ... 85 E5
Aspen Cl CF3 ... 179 E7
Aspen Way
Cimla SA11 ... 72 C6
Llantwit Fadre / Llanilltud
Faerdref CF38 ... 156 C6
Newport / Casnewydd
NP20 ... 117 A3
Asquith Ct SA1 ... 95 A6
Asquith St
Pontypool / Pont-y-pwl
NP4 ... 62 E3
Tir-Y-Berth CF82 ... 85 A6
Assembly Rooms 3
SA1 ... 233 C2
Aster Cl
6 Cardiff / Caerdydd
CF3 ... 180 A7
Risca / Rhisga NP11 ... 115 A2
Aster View SA12 ... 98 C3
Aston Cres NP20 ... 143 B8
Aston Pl CF3 ... 180 A5
Astoria Cl CF14 ... 159 E2
Athelstan Rd CF14 ... 176 F4
Athrofa Abertawe /
Swansea Inst (Townhill
Campus) SA2 ... 94 F8
Athrofa Chwaraeon Cymru /
Welsh Inst of Sport
CF11 ... 194 E7
Atlantic Cl SA7 ... 69 A5
Atlantic Cres CF63 ... 215 C3
Atlantic Haven SA3 ... 228 C2
Atlantic Pl CF63 ... 215 C7
Atlantic Trad Est CF63 ... 215 C3
Atlantic Way CF63 ... 215 B3
Atlantic Wharf CF10 ... 232 D1
ATLANTIC WHARF /
GLANFA IWERYDD ... 195 C3
Atlas Ho CF10 ... 195 D2
Atlas Pl 6 CF5 ... 194 D5
Atlas Rd CF5 ... 194 D5
Atlee Terr CF34 ... 75 A2
Attfield Cl CF23 ... 178 E1
Attlee Ave
Abertillery / Abertyleri
NP13 ... 36 A7
Port Talbot SA12 ... 124 E8
Attlee Cl
Ebbw Vale / Glyn Ebwy
NP23 ... 7 D6
Tredegar NP22 ... 13 D6
Attlee Ct CF83 ... 138 C3
Attlee Ho 3 CF47 ... 30 D8
Attlee Rd
Blackwood / Coed-Duon
NP12 ... 85 E7
Nantyglo NP23 ... 15 E7
Attlee St CF32 ... 150 F5
Attlee Way NP22 ... 13 D5
Aubrey Ave CF5 ... 194 A7
Aubrey Hames Cl
NP20 ... 143 A2
Aubrey Rd
Porth CF39 ... 107 F2
Tonypandy CF40 ... 107 A4
Aubrey Terr
Cowbridge / Y Bont-Faen
CF71 ... 188 F1
Cwm NP23 ... 35 B7
Auburn Ave / Rhodfa
Gwinau SA12 ... 98 B2
Auburn Rise CF44 ... 27 D8
Auckland Cl NP12 ... 86 A8
Auckland Rd NP20 ... 142 D3
Augusta Cres CF64 ... 207 A1
Augustan Cl NP18 ... 117 F3
Augustan Dr NP18 ... 117 F3
Augustan Way NP18 ... 117 F3
Augusta Pk NP23 ... 14 F2
Augusta Rd CF64 ... 207 A1
Augusta St
Cardiff / Caerdydd
CF24 ... 195 C6
Ebbw Vale / Glyn Ebwy
NP23 ... 14 E3
Treorchy / Treorci CF41 ... 79 A3
Augustus John Cl
NP19 ... 144 A8
Augustus St CF37 ... 81 F1
Austen Cl CF3 ... 179 D8
Austin Ave
Bridgend / Pen-y-Bont ar
Ogwr CF31 ... 168 F6
Laleston / Trelales
CF32 ... 167 F4
Porthcawl CF36 ... 183 C8
Austin Cl CF36 ... 183 D8
Austin Friars 6 NP20 ... 143 C5
Austin Rd NP4 ... 62 F1
Austin St CF45 ... 54 D3
Australian Terr CF31 ... 168 F6
Australia Rd CF14 ... 177 E2
Auxilliary Boiler House Rd
CF62 ... 211 E1
Avalon Ct
Newport / Casnewydd
NP19 ... 143 F7
Pontypool / Pont-y-pwl
NP4 ... 62 B6
Avalon Dr NP19 ... 143 F7
Avalon Terr NP22 ... 6 E1
Avenue Cilfig The SA15 .. 40 D6
Avenue Cl CF82 ... 84 F2
Avenue De Clichy CF47 ... 10 D1
Avenue Ind Pk CF23 ... 179 A8
Avenue The
Abersychan NP4 ... 37 E6
Bargoed / Bargod CF81 ... 58 A1
Bedwas CF83 ... 139 A6
Cardiff / Caerdydd CF5 ... 177 A1
Cardiff / Caerdydd, Rumney /
Rhymni CF3 ... 179 C2
Cardiff / Caerdydd, Whitchurch
CF14 ... 176 F4
Cwmavon / Cwmafan
SA12 ... 99 D6
Llanbradach CF83 ... 111 F1
Llanelli, Cwmcarnhywel
SA14 ... 41 C5
Llanelli SA15 ... 40 E2
Merthyr Tydfil / Merthyr Tudful
CF47 ... 10 E2
Mountain Ash / Aberpennar
CF45 ... 54 B5
Neath / Castell-Nedd
SA11 ... 71 D4
Pontycymer CF32 ... 103 E4
Pontypool / Pont-y-pwl, New
Inn NP4 ... 62 F5
Pontypool / Pont-y-pwl,
Sebastolpol NP4 ... 62 D1
Pontypridd CF37 ... 109 D2
Tonyrefail CF39 ... 133 D5
Treharris CF46 ... 82 F6
Tylorstown CF43 ... 107 C8
Wyllie NP12 ... 85 F1
Ystrad Mynach CF82 ... 85 A2
Averil Vivian Gr SA2 ... 94 E6
Avis Terr SA15 ... 40 E5
Avoca Pl CF11 ... 194 E3
Avocet Ct CF63 ... 215 A5
Avon Cl
Barry / Y Barri CF63 ... 215 C7
Bettws NP20 ... 116 E2
Bryn NP12 ... 85 D3
Avon Ct NP23 ... 7 C5
Avondale NP4 ... 17 C6
Avondale Cl NP44 ... 89 F6
Avondale Cres
Cardiff / Caerdydd
CF11 ... 195 A2
Avondale Cres *continued*
Cwmbran / Cwmbrân
NP44 ... 89 F7
Avondale Ct
Abercynon CF45 ... 82 C5
16 Cardiff / Caerdydd
CF10 ... 195 B2
Avondale Dr NP44 ... 89 F7
Avondale Gdns CF11 ... 195 A2
Avondale Gdns S CF11 .. 195 A2
Avondale Ind Est NP44 ... 89 F6
Avondale Rd
Cardiff / Caerdydd
CF11 ... 195 A2
Pontypool / Pont-y-pwl
NP4 ... 62 F1
Porth CF39 ... 108 A2
Ton Pentre CF41 ... 79 B2
Avondale Rd / Heol yr Glyn
NP44 ... 89 F6
Avondale Sq SA13 ... 75 C5
Avondale St CF45 ... 82 C5
Avondale Terr SA13 ... 75 C5
Avondale Way NP44 ... 89 F6
Avonmuir Rd CF24 ... 196 A8
Avon Pl NP44 ... 90 A3
Avon Rd NP4 ... 17 C5
Avonridge CF14 ... 159 D2
Avon St
Cymmer / Cymer SA13 ... 75 C5
Ferndale CF43 ... 79 F7
Glyn-neath / Glyn-nedd
SA11 ... 223 C1
Avon Terr CF39 ... 107 F7
Awbery Ho CF62 ... 214 D6
Awelfryn
Pen-y-coedcae CF37 ... 135 A3
Penywaun CF44 ... 28 B6
Awelfryn Cl NP23 ... 7 E4
Awelfryn Terr 7 CF47 ... 10 F4
Awel Mor CF23 ... 178 D3
Awel y Mor CF64 ... 207 B2
Axbridge Cres CF3 ... 179 D6
Axminster Rd CF23 ... 195 E8
Aylesbury Mans 2
CF14 ... 176 F6
Aylesbury Rd SA2 ... 94 F5
Aylward Ho 5 SA12 ... 98 F1
Aynho Pl 3 NP23 ... 14 D8
Ayron St CF43 ... 79 F5
Ayton Terr CF40 ... 106 E7
Azalea Cl CF23 ... 178 D7
Azalea Pk / Parc Asaleas
CF48 ... 11 C4
Aztec Bsns Ctr SA5 ... 67 D4

B

Baber Cl CF23 ... 178 E1
Bach Rd / Heol Bach 7
SA12 ... 98 B3
Back Dr SA10 ... 70 B7
Backhall St NP18 ... 118 C2
Back of Earl St NP22 ... 13 D7
Bacon Pl NP20 ... 117 A3
Bacton Rd CF14 ... 177 B2
Baden Powell Prim Sch
CF24 ... 195 F6
Baden Rd CF24 ... 196 A6
Baden Terr CF47 ... 10 F2
Bader Cl CF14 ... 177 F6
Badgers Brook CF31 ... 169 A6
Badgers Brook Cl
CF71 ... 189 C8
Badgers Brook Dr
CF71 ... 189 C8
Badgers Brook Rise
CF71 ... 189 D8
Badgers Mdw NP18 ... 117 F7
Badgers Mead CF31 ... 169 A6
Badgers Mede 5 NP44 ... 89 B3
Badgers Wood NP10 ... 141 F2
Badham Cl CF83 ... 137 D1
Badminton Gdns SA5 ... 67 E5
Badminton Gr NP23 ... 7 D3
Badminton Rd NP19 ... 143 F8
BAGLAN ... 98 E7
Baglan Hts SA12 ... 98 F7
Baglan Ind Pk SA12 ... 98 E2
BAGLAN MOORS ... 98 D4
Baglan Prim Sch SA12 ... 98 D6
Baglan St
Swansea / Abertawe
SA1 ... 96 A7
Treherbert CF42 ... 78 A8
Treorchy / Treorci CF41 ... 78 F5
Tylorstown CF43 ... 80 C1
Baglan Sta SA12 ... 98 D5
Baglan Way / Ffordd
Baglan SA12 ... 98 E3
Bagle Ct SA12 ... 98 E5
Bagley Ct NP44 ... 89 B5
Bagot St CF45 ... 82 B6
Baiden Ave CF33 ... 148 C2
Bailey Cl CF5 ... 193 E7
Bailey Cres NP4 ... 37 E6
Bailey St / Stryd Bailey
NP4 ... 37 E6
Bailey's Hos NP4 ... 61 F8
Bailey St
Aberavon SA12 ... 99 A1
Brynmawr NP23 ... 8 C4
Cwm NP23 ... 35 B8
Deri CF81 ... 33 B1
Mountain Ash / Aberpennar
CF45 ... 54 D2
Bailey St *continued*
Newport / Casnewydd
NP20 ... 143 B4
Treorchy / Treorci CF41 ... 79 A3
Wattstown CF39 ... 107 E8
Bailey's Terr / Rhes Bailey
NP4 ... 61 F8
Baillie Glas Ct 15 CF47 ... 30 E8
Baillie Smith Ave NP11 ... 60 B2
Baird Cl NP20 ... 116 F3
Baird Rise CF62 ... 214 D5
Bakers Ct
5 Cardiff / Caerdydd
CF5 ... 194 B7
Marshfield CF3 ... 180 E8
Baker's La CF61 ... 209 E7
Bakers Row CF10 ... 232 B2
Baker Street Ho 12 NP4 .. 17 C6
Bakers Way CF32 ... 150 F4
Bakers Wharf 9 CF37 ... 109 D2
Bakery La CF3 ... 162 D2
Bala Cl NP23 ... 7 A5
BALACLAVA ... 47 B5
Balaclava Ct CF40 ... 106 F3
Balaclava Rd
Cardiff / Caerdydd
CF23 ... 178 C1
Dowlais CF48 ... 11 A4
Glais SA7 ... 47 B5
Balaclava St SA1 ... 233 C3
Bala Cotts SA9 ... 222 A6
Bala Dr NP10 ... 142 B7
Bala Ho 2 NP44 ... 89 C2
Balance Mdws NP4 ... 37 C7
Balance Rd NP4 ... 37 E7
Bala Rd CF14 ... 177 A2
Baldwin Cl
Cardiff / Caerdydd
CF5 ... 176 D3
Newport / Casnewydd
NP20 ... 143 C2
Baldwin's Cres SA1 ... 96 E7
Baldwin St
Bargoed / Bargod CF81 ... 57 F4
Bryn SA13 ... 100 E5
Newport / Casnewydd
NP20 ... 143 C2
Balfe Rd NP19 ... 144 D4
Ballarat CF35 ... 152 E2
Ballards Ct SA10 ... 70 F8
Ballas Cl CF33 ... 166 A7
Ball La CF3 ... 179 A6
Ball Rd CF3 ... 179 B6
Balmond Terr NP4 ... 62 B8
Balmoral Cl
Cardiff / Caerdydd
CF14 ... 160 B2
Pen-y-coedcae CF37 ... 135 B6
Balmoral Ct CF62 ... 214 C8
Balmoral La 1 NP19 ... 144 A4
Balmoral Rd NP19 ... 144 A4
Baltic Terr NP44 ... 116 E7
Baltimore Cl CF23 ... 161 A2
Bamber Ho NP44 ... 90 B4
Bampton Rd CF3 ... 179 C7
Banalog Terr NP12 ... 34 C2
Banastre Ave CF14 ... 177 E2
Banc Bach SA4 ... 64 E4
Banc Gelli Las CF31 ... 168 B2
Banc Gwyn CF31 ... 168 B2
Banc-y-cwm SA4 ... 65 E5
Banc y Ddraenen
SA18 ... 218 D6
Bancyfelin / Millbank
SA10 ... 48 C1
Bancyffynnon SA14 ... 218 B7
Banc Yr Afon CF15 ... 158 A3
Banc-yr-Allt CF31 ... 168 B6
Banc-yr-Eithin SA4 ... 43 A3
BANESWELL ... 143 B4
Baneswell Ctyd 6
NP20 ... 143 B4
Baneswell Rd 6 NP20 ... 143 B5
Banfield Terr SA4 ... 42 E2
Bangor Ct 3 CF24 ... 178 C1
Bangor La 2 CF24 ... 178 C1
Bangor Rd NP23 ... 7 E4
Bangor St
Cardiff / Caerdydd
CF24 ... 178 C1
Maesteg CF34 ... 102 A6
Bangor Terr CF34 ... 102 A6
Bank Bldgs CF31 ... 169 E3
Bank Cotts SA9 ... 222 A6
Bankers Hill CF32 ... 149 D3
Bankes St 2 CF44 ... 29 A2
Bank La
3 Newport / Casnewydd
NP19 ... 143 E8
Tredegar NP22 ... 13 E7
Bank Rd SA14 ... 42 C8
Bankside NP19 ... 143 D4
Bank Side 1 SA11 ... 71 E8
Bankside Cl CF14 ... 159 F3
Bank St
Maesteg CF34 ... 102 B3
Newport / Casnewydd
NP19 ... 143 D8
Tonypandy CF40 ... 107 A3
Bank Terr CF48 ... 10 A4
Banna Bglws NP23 ... 8 C2
Bantock Cl NP19 ... 144 E5
Banwell Ct
Cwmbran / Cwmbrân
NP44 ... 89 B5

Banwell Ct *continued*
  Swansea / Abertawe SA6 68 F8
Banwell Pl CF3 179 C6
Banwell St SA6 68 F8
BANWEN 223 A4
Banwen La SA8 23 F4
Banwen Pl / Y Banwen SA18 220 D8
Banwy Rd SA6 45 D1
Baptist Ct CF24 195 E6
Baptist La / Lon Y Bedydd 18 SA18 219 B7
Baptist Pl
  Ebbw Vale / Glyn Ebwy NP23 7 D4
  Hirwaun CF44 27 E7
Baptist Row CF43 79 F8
Baptist Sq CF43 79 F8
Baptist Well Pl SA1 233 A5
Baptist Well St SA1 233 A5
Baran Rd
  Pontardawe SA8 220 D1
  Rhyd-y-fro SA8 23 B8
Barberry Rise CF64 206 E5
Barbirolli Gn NP19 144 D4
Barbrook Cl CF14 160 A2
Bardsey Ave SA5 67 E7
Bardsey Cl CF36 165 E2
Bardsey Cres CF14 159 E1
Bardsy Cl NP19 143 F7
BARGOD / BARGOED 57 A3
BARGOED / BARGOD 57 A3
Bargoed Cl CF46 83 B7
Bargoed St CF11 195 A3
Bargoed Sta CF81 58 A5
Bargoed Terr CF46 83 B7
Barker Ave NP13 36 A6
Barkley St NP22 33 C8
Barletta Ho 2 CF10 195 B3
Barleyfield Ind Est NP23 8 C3
Barley Field Rd NP23 8 C3
Barmouth Rd CF3 179 B3
Barnabas Cl SA5 66 F3
Barnard Ave CF5 193 E6
Barnardo St CF34 102 A6
Barnard St NP19 143 D6
BARNARDTOWN 143 E6
Barn Cl / Clos Y Sgubor NP4 38 B2
Barn Cotts SA11 71 C2
Barnes Ave CF31 168 B6
Barnes Cl NP23 7 A4
Barnets NP44 89 B3
Barnfield NP18 117 F5
Barnfield Cl CF23 161 B1
Barnfield Dr CF15 176 A8
Barnfield Pl NP44 89 C5
Barnfield Terr / Rhes Barnfield NP4 17 B6
Barnstaple Rd CF3 179 C6
Barnwood CF14 160 A2
Barnwood Cres CF5 192 F4
Baron Cl CF64 206 F3
Baroness Pl CF64 206 F3
Baron Rd CF64 206 F3
Baron's Cl
  Llantwit Major / Llanilltud Fawr CF61 209 F6
  Llantwit Major / Llanilltud Fawr CF61 210 A6
Baron's Close Ho CF61 209 F6
Baron's Court Rd CF23 178 D1
Barquentine Pl CF10 195 C3
BARRACK HILL 143 A7
Barrack Hill NP20 143 B7
Barrack La / Lon Y Barics CF10 232 C2
Barracks Row CF48 11 B5
Barrett St CF42 78 B4
Barrians Way CF62 214 E5
Barrie Gdns NP20 142 E2
Barrington Rd 3 CF14 177 B4
Barrington St / Stryd Barrington CF48 55 C5
Barry Cl CF82 84 E7
Barry Coll
  Barry / Y Barri CF62 214 A7
  Barry / Y Barri, Cwm Talwg CF62 214 D6
Barry Coll (Annexe) CF62 213 C4
Barry Coll Heritage Skills Training Ctr CF62 214 E4
Barry Comp Sch CF62 214 D7
BARRY DOCK 215 A6
Barry Docks Link Rd CF63 215 D8
Barry Docks Sta CF63 215 A4
Barry Ho SA12 98 A2
Barry Hospl The CF62 214 D7
BARRY ISLAND 214 F2
Barry Island Pleasure Pk* CF62 214 E2
Barry Island Prim Sch CF62 214 F3
Barry Island Rly* CF62 214 D2
Barry Island Sta CF62 214 E2
Barry Rd
  Barry / Y Barri CF62, CF63 214 E6
  Llandough / Llandochau CF64 206 E6
Barry Rd *continued*
  Pontypridd CF37 109 A1
Barry Rd / Heol Barri SA18 220 D7
Barry Sidings Countryside Pk* CF37 108 E2
Barry Sta CF62 214 D3
Barry View CF37 136 A6
Barry Wlk NP10 142 A6
BARRY / Y BARRI 214 E3
Barthropp St NP19 144 A3
Bartlett St CF83 138 B2
Bartley Terr SA6 68 E5
Basil Pl CF24 195 A8
BASSALEG 142 A2
Bassaleg Cl 2 CF3 180 A7
Bassaleg Rd NP20 142 E3
Bassaleg Sch NP10 142 A2
Bassett Ho 11 SA12 98 F1
Bassett Rd CF64 216 A5
Bassetts Field CF14 159 C3
Bassett St
  Abercynon CF45 82 E3
  Barry / Y Barri CF63 215 B5
  Cardiff / Caerdydd CF5 194 C5
  Pontypridd CF37 109 D2
Bastian Cl CF63 215 C7
Batchelor Rd
  Cardiff / Caerdydd CF14 177 D2
  2 Newport / Casnewydd NP19 143 F5
Bath Ave SA6 45 F1
Bath Gn / Maes Caerfaddon NP44 90 B2
Bath La
  Brynmawr NP23 8 A4
  Swansea / Abertawe SA1 233 B2
Bath Rd SA6 68 F8
Bath Row NP7 9 E7
Bath St
  Newport / Casnewydd NP19 143 D6
  Port Talbot SA13 99 B1
Bathurst St
  Swansea / Abertawe SA1 233 A1
  Swansea / Abertawe SA1 233 A2
Bath Villas SA6 68 F8
Baton Ct CF14 177 C4
Battenberg St CF45 82 C5
Batten Way CF37 109 F4
Baxter Terr SA13 227 C2
Baylis Ct CF5 193 E6
Bayliss Rd / Heol Bayliss CF32 150 F4
Baynton Cl CF5 176 E2
Bayside Rd CF24 195 D5
Bay St SA1 96 A7
Bayswater Ct SA3 94 C3
Bayswater Rd SA2 94 C8
Bay Tree Ave SA2 94 B6
Bay Tree Cl NP18 117 E2
Baytree Ct SA4 66 C4
Bay View
  Port Talbot SA13 99 C2
  Swansea / Abertawe SA1 233 C4
Bay View Cl SA10 70 F5
Bay View Cres SA1 95 A6
Bay View Gdns SA10 70 E5
Bay View Hts SA13 99 C2
Bay View Rd
  Llanelli SA14 41 A6
  Porthcawl CF36 183 D6
Bay View Terr SA1 95 A6
Baywood Ave SA3 123 A8
BBC Cymru Wales CF5 176 F1
Beach La CF64 207 B4
Beach Rd
  Llanelli SA15 40 A6
  Penarth CF64 207 B4
  Pen-clawdd SA4 64 E4
  Porthcawl CF36 183 D7
  Pyle / Y Pîl CF33 148 A1
  Southerndown CF32 197 C8
  St Bride's Wentloge / Llansanffraid Gwynllwg NP10 163 F1
  Swanbridge CF64 216 D4
Beach St
  Aberavon SA12 124 F8
  Swansea / Abertawe SA1 95 B5
Beachway CF62 214 B1
Beacon Hts CF48 225 E2
Beacon Rise / Rhiw Aberhonddu CF48 11 B7
Beacons Cl NP10 142 A7
Beaconsfield Ct SA2 94 B7
Beaconsfield Ho CF62 214 D4
Beaconsfield Rd SA10 48 F2
Beaconsfield Way SA2 94 B7
Beacons Pk CF44 224 D3
Beacon St CF11 194 C7
Beacons View
  Dowlais CF48 11 B5
  Neath / Castell-Nedd SA11 72 A5
Beacons View Rd SA6 45 D1
Beacon View NP23 8 D1
Beadon St CF45 54 D2
Beale Cl CF5 176 E2
Beatrice Rd
  Barry / Y Barri CF63 215 B6
  Cardiff / Caerdydd CF14 177 B4
Beatrice St SA13 76 C6
Beattie St SA5 68 B2
Beatty Ave CF23 178 A5
Beatty Cl 2 CF62 215 A8
Beatty Ct CF10 232 D1
Beatty Rd NP19 144 F7
Beatty St CF82 85 A6
Beauchamp St CF11 194 F5
BEAUFORT 7 D4
Beaufort Ave SA3 123 A3
Beaufort Cl
  Cwmbran / Cwmbrân NP44 89 C1
  The Mumbles / Y Mwmbwls SA3 123 A3
  Tredegar NP22 6 F1
Beaufort Ct
  Cardiff / Caerdydd CF10 232 D1
  Llantrisant CF72 155 E2
  Swansea / Abertawe, Caereithin SA5 67 E5
  Swansea / Abertawe SA6 68 F6
Beaufort Dr SA3 121 E7
Beaufort Gdns SA3 121 E7
BEAUFORT HILL 7 E3
Beaufort Hill
  Ebbw Vale / Glyn Ebwy NP23 7 E4
  Tredegar NP22 7 A1
Beaufort Hill Prim Sch NP23 7 F4
Beaufort Pl NP19 143 F8
Beaufort Rd
  Ebbw Vale / Glyn Ebwy NP23 7 D2
  Newport / Casnewydd NP19 144 A7
  Swansea / Abertawe SA6 68 F5
  Tredegar NP22 6 F1
Beaufort Rise NP23 7 D4
Beaufort Sq CF24 196 A8
Beaufort St NP23 8 C4
Beaufort Terr
  Ebbw Vale / Glyn Ebwy NP23 7 D3
  4 Newport / Casnewydd NP20 143 B4
Beaufort Way CF62 212 E2
Beaumaris Cl
  Bassaleg NP10 141 E3
  Church Village CF38 135 F2
Beaumaris Dr / Lon Biwmares NP44 90 B1
Beaumaris Ho 10 NP44 90 B2
Beaumaris Rd CF3 179 B3
Beaumaris Way NP12 58 E1
Beaumont Cl
  Barry / Y Barri CF62 214 C7
  Nantyglo NP23 15 D8
Beaumont Cres SA1 233 C4
Beaumont Ct CF64 206 F3
Beaupre Castle* CF71 201 B5
Beauville La CF64 205 F4
Beavers Wlk NP10 142 B4
Beckett St CF45 54 D4
Beckgrove Cl CF24 196 A7
Beck Ho SA2 94 F6
Beda Rd CF5 194 C5
Bedavere Cl CF14 159 E2
BEDDAU 156 B6
Beddick NP44 89 A3
Beddoe St CF44 53 C8
Beddoe Terr CF46 83 A5
Bedford Cl
  Cefn Cribwr CF32 149 A2
  Cwmbran / Cwmbrân NP44 89 A3
Bedford Cl / Clos Rhydwely 2 NP44 89 A3
Bedford Ho 3 SA6 68 F8
Bedford Pl CF24 232 D4
Bedford Rd
  Cefn Cribwr CF32 149 A3
  Newport / Casnewydd NP19 143 D5
Bedford Rise CF61 210 B6
Bedford St
  Aberdare / Aberdâr CF44 53 D7
  Cardiff / Caerdydd CF24 232 C4
  Swansea / Abertawe SA6 69 A8
Bedlington Terr CF62 214 D5
BEDLINOG 56 B7
Bedlinog Cty Prim Sch CF46 56 A7
Bedlinog Terr CF46 56 A7
Bedlwyn Rd NP24 33 E3
Bedw Arian CF31 168 B6
BEDWAS 138 D7
Bedwas Bsns Ctr CF83 138 D6
Bedwas Cl 4 CF3 180 A7
Bedwas High Sch CF83 138 E6
Bedwas House Ind Est CF83 138 C6
Bedwas Inf Sch CF83 138 D6
Bedwas Jun Sch CF83 138 E6
Bedwas Pl 2 CF64 206 F4
Bedwas Rd CF83 138 C4
Bedwas St CF11 194 E3
Bedw Cl CF39 107 F2
Bedwdellty Rd CF81, NP12 58 C5
BEDWELLTE / BEDWELLTY 58 D5
BEDWELLTY / BEDWELLTE 58 D5
Bedwellty Pits NP22 14 B1
Bedwellty Rd
  Aberbargoed / Aberbargod CF81 58 B5
  Bargoed / Bargod CF81 58 A5
  Blackwood / Coed-Duon NP12 85 C8
  New Tredegar NP24 33 F2
Bedw Farm Est CF39 107 F2
Bedwlwyn Cl CF82 84 F2
Bedwlwyn Rd CF82 84 F2
Bedwlwyn St CF82 84 F2
Bedw Rd
  Bedlinog CF46 56 A7
  Pontypridd CF37 109 F4
Bedw St
  Maesteg CF34 102 A8
  Porth CF39 107 F2
Beecham St NP19 144 D5
Beech Ave
  Bryn NP12 85 E4
  Llantwit Major / Llanilltud Fawr CF61 210 A4
Beech Cl
  Caerphilly / Caerffili CF83 137 D1
  Cwmbran / Cwmbrân NP44 89 D6
  Underwood NP18 145 E6
Beech Cres SA4 43 A4
Beechcroft
  Bryn NP12 85 E3
  Trelewis CF46 83 C7
Beechcroft Rd NP19 144 B6
Beech Ct
  Bargoed / Bargod CF81 57 E2
  Tongwynlais CF15 158 D2
Beechdale Rd NP19 144 A5
Beech Dr CF82 84 F3
Beech Emb CF82 84 F2
Beecher Ave CF11 194 F1
Beecher Terr NP11 114 C5
Beeches Cl The SA2 94 A8
Beeches Ind Est The CF72 155 A1
Beeches Rd NP4 38 B1
Beeches The
  Abercynon CF45 82 E3
  Bridgend / Pen-y-Bont ar Ogwr CF31 168 E6
  Cardiff / Caerdydd CF14 160 A3
  Pontypool / Pont-y-pwl NP4 38 A2
Beeches The / Y Fawydd 8 NP44 89 D2
Beechfield Ave
  Hengoed CF82 85 A3
  Newport / Casnewydd NP19 144 B6
Beechfield Cl NP23 7 D6
Beech Gr
  Blackwood / Coed Duon NP12 59 B1
  Ebbw Vale / Glyn Ebwy NP23 14 E2
  Merthyr Tydfil / Merthyr Tudful CF47 10 E4
  Newport / Casnewydd NP10 163 F8
  Porthcawl CF36 183 D8
Beechgrove
  Caerphilly / Caerffili CF83 138 C5
  Treharris CF46 82 F6
Beech Grove CF48 55 C8
Beech Ho CF14 176 E7
Beeching Way CF38 135 E2
Beechlea Cl CF72 173 D6
Beechleigh Cl NP44 88 F3
Beechley Dr CF5 193 C8
Beech Pk CF71 187 A4
Beech Rd
  Cardiff / Caerdydd CF5 193 B8
  Llanharry CF72 172 B5
  Pontypool / Pont-y-pwl NP4 62 D1
  Pont-y-rhyl CF32 129 F8
Beech St
  Ferndale CF43 79 F6
  Gilfach Goch CF39 132 B5
Beech Terr
  Abercarn NP11 87 A1
  Abercwmboi CF44 53 E4
Beechtree Cl SA6 45 D1
Beech Tree Cl CF15 176 A6
Beech Tree Cres NP13 15 F5
Beech Tree La SA2 94 C5
Beech Tree Terr / Ffordd Y Ffawydden NP4 61 F8
Beech Tree Way CF46 83 F3
BEECHWOOD 144 A6
Beechwood Ave
  Aberdare / Aberdâr CF44 28 E2
  Bridgend / Pen-y-Bont ar Ogwr CF31 168 C5
  Cwmfelinfach NP11 113 F4
  Neath / Castell-Nedd SA11 71 F7
  Trefechan CF48 10 B6
Beechwood Cl NP11 86 E6
Beechwood Cres NP19 144 A5
Beechwood Dr
  Llantwit Fadre / Llanilltud Faerdref CF38 156 C6
  Merthyr Tydfil / Merthyr Tudful CF48 29 F8
Beechwood Dr *continued*
  Penarth CF64 206 E2
Beech Wood Dr CF39 132 E5
Beechwood Gr CF35 152 D1
Beechwood Rd
  Margam SA13 125 F3
  Newport / Casnewydd NP19 144 A5
  Swansea / Abertawe SA2 94 F6
  Taffs Well / Ffynnon Taf CF15 158 B4
Beechwood St CF37 136 B5
Beechwood Wlk NP4 38 B2
BEGAN 161 D3
Began Rd CF3 161 D4
BEGGARS POUND 211 D6
Beidr Iorwg CF63 215 C8
Beignon Cl CF24 195 D4
Beili Glas SA4 42 E1
Beili Glas Rd NP12 85 B5
Belgrave Cl
  Cardiff / Caerdydd CF14 159 E3
  Gorseinon SA4 43 A1
Belgrave Ct
  1 Cardiff / Caerdydd CF11 194 F5
  15 Pontypool / Pont-y-pwl NP4 38 A1
  Swansea / Abertawe SA1 95 A6
Belgrave Gdns 2 SA1 95 A6
Belgrave La SA1 95 A6
Belgrave Rd SA4 43 A1
Belgrave St CF41 79 A2
Belgrave Terr CF37 109 E3
Belle View 2 CF40 107 A4
Belle View Ct 14 NP4 38 A1
Belle Vue
  Ebbw Vale / Glyn Ebwy NP23 14 D4
  Pen-clawdd SA4 64 F4
Belle Vue Cl
  Penarth CF64 207 B4
  Pontypool / Pont-y-pwl NP4 38 A1
Belle Vue Cres CF14 176 F3
Bellevue Gdns 6 NP44 89 E2
Belle Vue La NP20 143 B3
Bellevue Rd
  Cwmbran / Cwmbrân NP44 89 E2
  Llanelli SA14 41 E3
  The Mumbles / Y Mwmbwls SA3 122 F6
Belle Vue St CF44 28 F4
Bellevue Terr
  Merthyr Vale / Ynysowen CF48 55 D4
  2 Mountain Ash / Aberpennar CF45 81 F8
Belle Vue Terr
  Barry / Y Barri CF63 215 C7
  Penarth CF64 207 B5
  Pontypridd CF37 135 E6
Belle Vue Way SA1 233 A3
Bellin Cl NP18 118 A3
Bell La NP4 37 F3
Bell Pl CF44 53 D5
Bells Hill / Bryn Clychau CF48 55 D4
Bell St
  Aberdare / Aberdâr CF44 28 F4
  Barry / Y Barri CF62 214 C4
Bellvue Cl NP44 89 E2
Bell Vue Terr NP20 143 C2
Belmont CF35 153 B2
Belmont Cl CF34 102 B3
Belmont Hill NP18 144 D8
Belmont St CF63 215 A6
Belmont Terr
  Aberdare / Aberdâr CF44 53 C8
  Porth CF39 107 F2
Belmont Wlk CF10 195 B2
Below The Oak Trees / Dan-Y-Deri CF31 168 B4
Belvedere Cl
  Abertillery / Abertyleri NP11 59 F6
  Bishopston SA3 121 E7
Belvedere Cres 8 CF63 214 F5
Belvedere Rd SA15 40 C6
Belvedere Terr
  Newport / Casnewydd NP20 143 B7
  6 Risca / Rhisga NP11 114 F3
Belvoir Ct CF72 155 E2
Benbow Cl SA2 94 C6
Benbow Rd NP19 144 E7
Bendrick Dr SA3 120 F4
Bendrick Rd CF63 215 C4
Benecrofte CF62 213 A2
Benedict Cl SA10 71 B8
Benjamin Ct / Cwrt Benjamin NP22 13 A2
Ben Jonson Way NP20 142 E2
Bennett Ave CF31 169 D3
Bennett St
  Blaina / Blaenau NP13 15 E4
  Bridgend / Pen-y-Bont ar Ogwr CF31 169 D3
  Swansea / Abertawe SA1 68 D3
Benson Ave 7 NP10 142 B4
Benson Rd SA4 64 F4
Benson St SA4 64 F4
Benson Terr SA4 64 E4

Benson Way / Parc Landwr SA6 69 A6
Benthall Pl SA1 233 C3
Bentley Cl NP10 142 A7
Berea Cl / Clos Berea NP23 15 D7
Beresford Ct CF24 195 E7
Beresford Rd
Cardiff / Caerdydd CF24 195 E7
Newport / Casnewydd NP19 143 D5
Beresford Road La CF24 195 E7
Berkeley Cl SA7 47 A2
Berkeley Cres NP4 89 E8
Berkeley Ct NP44 89 B5
Berkeley Sq CF5 193 A2
Berkley Cl NP10 141 F3
Berkley Dr CF64 207 A3
Berkley Rd NP10 141 F3
Berkrolles Ave CF62 211 D4
Berllan Deg SA15 41 A6
Berllanllwyd St CF82 84 E8
Berllanlwyd Ave NP12 58 E7
Berma Cl SA3 123 C3
Bernard Ave CF5 194 A6
Bernard St
Abercarn NP11 114 C7
Swansea / Abertawe SA2 94 F6
Berrington Villas / Filas Berrington SA9 221 C7
BERRY 231 B6
Berry Ct CF61 210 B6
Berrylands SA12 124 D8
Berrymead Rd CF23 178 B7
Berry Pl CF5 176 D2
Berry Sq CF48 11 A4
Bertha Pl / Lle Bertha SA13 125 E4
Bertha Rd SA13 125 F3
Bertha St CF37 135 E5
Berthin NP44 89 B3
Berthin Rd NP4 39 D2
Berthlwyd CF15 157 C1
Berthon Rd NP4 39 E2
Berthwin St CF11 194 D7
Bertram St CF24 195 E7
Berwedd-dy Cotts CF37 109 E4
Berwick Rd SA14 41 F3
Berwick Terr SA1 233 A4
Berw Rd
Pontypridd CF37 109 D2
Swansea / Abertawe SA1 95 B8
Tonypandy CF40 106 E6
Berwyn Pl SA5 68 A4
Beryl Pl CF62 214 F5
Beryl Rd
Barry / Y Barri CF62 214 F5
Clydach SA6 46 F8
Bessant Cl CF71 188 F1
Bessborough Dr CF11 194 E3
Bessemer Cl
Cardiff / Caerdydd CF11 194 D2
Newport / Casnewydd NP20 116 F4
Bessemer Close Workshops CF11 194 C2
Bessemer Rd CF11 194 D3
Bethania CF45 82 E3
Bethania Chapel CF39 133 C2
Bethania Cl CF34 102 B2
Bethania Hill CF39 133 C2
Bethania Pl CF44 53 E8
Bethania Rd
Clydach SA6 46 D7
Cross Hands SA14 218 A7
Bethania Row
Cardiff / Caerdydd CF3 179 D6
Ogmore Vale CF32 104 E1
Bethania St / Stryd Bethania CF34 102 B2
Bethania St SA11 223 D1
Bethania Terr
1 Cwmavon / Cwmafan SA12 99 F6
Llanelli SA15 40 E2
Bethany Cl CF82 84 E1
Bethany Ct CF42 50 F2
Bethany La SA3 123 A7
Bethany Sq 4 SA13 99 B1
Bethcar St NP23 14 D7
Bethel Ave NP22 13 E6
Bethel Ct
Abersychan NP4 37 E6
Swansea / Abertawe SA5 68 C3
Trehafod CF37 108 C2
Bethel Ho CF44 53 A4
Bethel La
Cwmbran / Cwmbrân NP44 89 B6
Pen-clawdd SA4 64 E4
Bethel Pl
Cardiff / Caerdydd CF14 159 D1
Hirwaun CF44 27 D8
Bethel Rd
Glyn-neath / Glyn-nedd SA11 223 D1
Swansea / Abertawe SA7 69 E7
Ystradgynlais SA9 2 C8
Bethel St
10 Briton Ferry / Llansawel SA11 71 C1
Pontypridd CF37 135 B8
Bethesda Cl NP10 142 A6
Bethesda Ct SA1 233 B4
Bethesda Pl
3 Ebbw Vale / Glyn Ebwy NP23 14 D6
Rogerstone NP10 142 A6
Bethesda Rd SA8 24 B8
Bethesda St
Merthyr Tydfil / Merthyr Tudful CF47 10 D2
1 Merthyr Tydfil / Merthyr Tudful, Glebeland CF47 10 D1
Swansea / Abertawe SA1 233 B4
Trehafod CF37 108 C2
Bethlehem Ct CF24 195 E6
Bethlehem Hos NP23 8 C2
Bethlehem Rd / Heol Bethlehem SA10 70 F7
Bethlehem View CF72 153 F3
Bethuel St CF44 29 B1
Bettsland SA3 122 F8
BETTWS
Llangeinor 129 E2
Newport 116 E2
Bettws Cl NP20 116 F1
Bettws Ctr NP20 116 D2
Bettws High Sch NP20 116 F1
Bettws Hill NP20 116 D1
Bettws La NP20 116 F1
Bettws Rd SA5 68 A4
Bettws-y-Coed Rd CF23 178 B7
BETWS 219 C6
Betws Cty Prim Sch SA18 219 C6
Betws Ind Pk / Parc Ddiwydiannol Betws SA18 219 C7
Betws Pk Workshops 1 SA18 219 C6
Betws Prim Sch CF32 129 E2
Betws Rd CF32 129 E1
Betws Rd / Ffordd-y-Betws SA18 219 C6
Betwyns 8 NP44 89 B1
Beulah Pl 2 NP23 14 D8
Beulah Rd CF14 177 C7
Beulah St NP22 12 F3
Bevan Ave NP22 6 C1
Bevan Ave / Rhodfa Bevan SA10 48 E1
Bevan Cl CF83 138 F6
Bevan Cres
Blackwood / Coed-Duon NP12 85 D8
Ebbw Vale / Glyn Ebwy NP23 7 C3
Bevan Pl CF14 177 D2
Bevan Rise CF83 138 F6
Bevan's La NP4, NP44 89 D8
Bevans Row SA1 96 B7
Bevan St SA12 124 F8
Bevans Terr SA7 69 E5
Bevan's Terr SA12 73 A2
Bevan Way SA5 66 E3
Beverley Cl
Cardiff / Caerdydd CF14 160 A1
Swansea / Abertawe SA5 67 E4
Beverley Gdns SA5 67 E4
Beverley St
Barry / Y Barri CF63 215 B7
Port Talbot SA13 125 B8
Bevin Ave / Heol Bevin SA12 124 D8
Bevin Ho SA12 124 C8
Beynon St NP11 86 F6
Bible Coll of Wales The SA2 94 B3
Bicester Rd CF64 215 E6
Biddulph SA15 40 E2
Bideford Cl NP20 143 A1
Bideford Rd
Cardiff / Caerdydd CF3 179 C5
Newport / Casnewydd NP20 143 A1
Bigham's Row NP4 62 B4
Big Hollow / Pant Mawr CF31 168 B3
Big La NP23 7 F4
Big Pit National Mus of Mining★ NP4 16 F6
BIGYN 40 E4
Bigyn La SA15 40 D4
Bigyn Park Ct SA15 40 E4
Bigyn Park Terr / Teras Parc Bigyn SA15 40 E4
Bigyn Prim Sch SA15 40 E4
Bigyn Rd SA15 40 E4
Bill Harry Ct NP22 13 D8
Billingham Cres CF47 10 E3
Bilston St NP19 143 F4
Bilton Rd SA11 71 E7
Bingle La CF62 211 D6
Birch Cres
Cefn Hengoed CF82 84 F4
Llantwit Fadre / Llanilltud Faerdref CF38 156 C5
Birch Ct
Cardiff / Caerdydd CF14 177 D5
Tongwynlais CF15 158 D2
Birches The
Clydach SA6 46 F8
Cwmbran / Cwmbrân NP44 89 C5
Birchfield Cl CF38 136 A1
Birchfield Cres CF5 194 A6
Birchfield Rd
Pontardawe SA8 23 F6
The Mumbles / Y Mwmbwls SA3 122 F8
Birch Gr
Barry / Y Barri CF62 214 C2
Bridgend / Pen-y-Bont ar Ogwr CF31 168 A5
Brynmawr NP23 8 B5
Caerphilly / Caerffili CF83 138 C5
Church Village CF38 135 F1
Cwmbran / Cwmbrân NP44 116 A8
Llanharry CF72 172 B5
Merthyr Tydfil / Merthyr Tudful CF47 10 D5
Risca / Rhisga NP11 115 A2
Underwood NP18 145 F7
Waunarlwydd SA5 66 D4
BIRCHGROVE
Cardiff 177 D5
Neath 47 B2
Porth 107 F4
Birchgrove
Aberdare / Aberdâr CF44 28 E2
Bedwas CF83 138 F6
New Tredegar NP24 33 D3
Pontypridd CF37 135 C8
Rogerstone / Ty-du NP10 141 F6
Treharris CF46 82 F6
Birchgrove Cl NP20 117 B2
Birchgrove Comp Sch SA7 47 B2
Birchgrove Jun & Inf Schs SA7 47 A1
Birchgrove Prim Sch CF14 177 D4
Birchgrove Rd
Cardiff / Caerdydd CF14 177 D4
Glais SA7 47 A4
Swansea / Abertawe SA7 70 A8
Birchgrove St CF39 107 F4
Birchgrove Sta CF14 177 D6
Birch Hill
Newport / Casnewydd NP20 117 B3
Tongwynlais CF15 158 C1
Birch La CF64 207 A1
Birch La / Lon Bedw SA10 49 C5
Birch La / Lon Fedwen SA10 48 F2
Birchley CF37 135 D6
Birch Rd
Baglan SA12 98 D7
Cardiff / Caerdydd CF5 193 D8
Birch Tree Cl SA2 94 C6
Birch Trees NP10 142 B2
Birchway The CF48 10 A6
Birch Wlk
8 Cardiff / Caerdydd CF5 193 D8
Porthcawl CF36 183 D8
Birchwood Ave CF37 135 E5
Birchwood Cl
Baglan SA12 98 E5
Bryn-côch SA10 48 C5
Bryn NP12 85 E5
Birch Wood Dr CF39 132 E4
Birchwood Gdns
Bedwas CF83 138 D6
Cardiff / Caerdydd CF14 177 C3
Birchwood La CF23 178 C3
Birchwood Rd CF23 178 C3
Birkdale Cl
3 Cardiff / Caerdydd CF3 180 A8
The Mumbles / Y Mwmbwls SA3 93 F2
Birmingham Mount SA6 68 F6
Bishop Childs CW Prim Sch CF3 179 F7
Bishop Gore Sch / Ysgol Esgob Gore SA2 94 C6
Bishop Hannon Dr CF5 176 B1
Bishop Hedley High Sch CF47 10 E3
Bishop of Llandaff CW High Sch CF5 176 F1
Bishop Rd 17 SA18 220 B8
Bishop Rd / Ffordd Bishop SA18 219 B6
Bishops' Ave CF5 193 F8
Bishops Cl CF14 177 A4
Bishops' Cl CF5 193 F8
Bishops Ct CF14 177 A4
Bishops Gr CF47 10 E3
Bishop's Gr SA2 94 B5
Bishops Pl CF14 177 A4
Bishops' Pl CF5 193 F8
Bishop's Pl NP23 14 D8
Bishop's Rd CF14 177 A4
Bishop St
Abertillery / Abertyleri NP13 36 C5
Cardiff / Caerdydd CF11 194 E3
Newport / Casnewydd NP19 143 D6
Tonypandy CF40 107 A3
BISHOPSTON 121 F7
Bishopston Comp Sch SA3 122 A7
Bishopston Prim Sch SA3 121 F7
Bishopston Rd
Bishopston SA3 121 F6
Cardiff / Caerdydd CF5 193 E4
Bishops' Wlk CF5 193 F8
Bishop's Wlk SA6 45 F2
Bishopswood CF31 169 C4
Bishop's Wood Countryside Ctr★ SA3 122 D4
Bishop's Wood Nature Reserve★ SA3 122 C4
Bishop Vaughan RC Sch SA6 68 E8
BISHPOOL 144 D6
Bishpool Ave NP19 144 D6
Bishpool Cl NP19 144 D6
Bishpool Ct NP19 144 D6
Bishpool Gdns NP19 144 D6
Bishpool Gr NP19 144 D6
Bishpool La NP19 144 D6
Bishpool Pl NP19 144 E6
Bishpool Rise NP19 144 D6
Bishpool View NP19 144 D6
Bishpool Way NP19 144 D6
BISHTON 145 F3
Bishton Rd NP18 145 B5
Bishton St NP19 143 E5
Bishwell Rd SA4 66 D4
Bisley Cl CF24 196 B7
Bittern Ct SA10 48 E2
Bittern Way CF64 217 A8
Bittern Wood Ho CF62 214 F7
Bitterton Ho SA12 98 A2
Blackberry Dr CF62 214 C6
Blackberry Pl CF45 54 B6
Blackberry Way 7 CF23 161 A1
Blackbird Cl NP10 142 C3
Blackbird Rd CF62 210 D6
Blackbirds Cl NP44 117 A5
Blackbirds Way CF3 179 D8
Blackbrook CF46 83 A7
Blackbrook Rd CF83 158 E8
Blackett Ave NP20 117 A3
Blackfield Row CF32 149 F2
Blackhall Rd CF32 185 E3
Blackhill Rd SA4 43 A3
Blackhills La
Fairwood SA2 92 F3
Upper Killay SA2 93 B3
Black Lion Rd / Heol y Llew Du SA14 218 C7
BLACKMILL 130 E2
Blackmill Rd
Bryncethin CF32 151 B5
Lewistown CF32 130 E5
Blackmoor Pl CF5 179 C6
Black Oak Rd CF23 178 C8
BLACK PILL 94 B2
Black Rd CF37 135 B4
BLACKROCK 9 A6
Blacksmith Cl / Clos Y Gof NP12 59 C2
Blacksmiths Way NP10 163 A6
Blackstone St 10 CF11 194 E5
Blackthorn Ave CF47 10 D5
Blackthorn Gr NP18 117 E2
Blackthorn Pl SA2 67 B1
Blackton La CF62 213 D4
BLACKTOWN 162 D1
Blackvein Rd NP11 114 C3
Blackwater Cl NP20 116 D2
BLACKWEIR 194 E8
Blackweir Terr CF10 194 F8
Blackwell Cl 1 CF63 215 B6
BLACKWOOD / COED-DUON 85 D8
Blackwood Comp Sch NP12 85 D8
Blackwood Prim Sch NP12 85 D7
Blackwood Rd NP12 85 F4
Blaen-Afon Rd NP7, NP23 8 F3
Blaenant Ind Est NP23 8 D3
Blaenant St SA13 74 D4
BLAENAU / BLAINA 15 F4
BLAENAU GWENT 36 B6
Blaenau Gwent Rows NP13 36 A6
Blaenau Rd SA18 219 A8
BLAENAVON 17 E6
Blaenavon Cl 3 CF3 180 A7
Blaenavon Furnace Sta★ NP4 16 E7
Blaenavon Hospl NP4 17 B7
Blaenavon Ironworks★ NP4 17 B7
Blaenavon Terr SA12 73 C6
Blaenbaglan Prim Sch SA12 98 F6
Blaen-Blodau St NP11 86 F6
BLAENCAERAU 75 D2
Blaencaerau Est CF34 75 C2
Blaencaerau Jun Sch CF34 75 C2
Blaencaerau Rd CF34 75 C2
Blaencedi SA4 64 F3
Blaen Cefn SA1 69 D5
Blaen Cendl NP23 7 E4
BLAEN CLYDACH 106 C7
Blaenclydach Inf Sch CF40 106 D6
Blaenclydach Pl 4 CF11 194 F3
Blaenclydach St CF11 194 F3
Blaencoed Rd SA7 69 F7
BLAENCWM 50 C2
Blaen Cwm SA10 222 D3
Blaencwm Rd SA7 70 A7
Blaen-Cyffin Rd NP13 60 B6
Blaendare Farm La NP4 62 A4
Blaendare Rd NP4 62 C5
Blaen Dewi CF71 198 C5
Blaen Dowlais CF48 11 D4
Blaendulais Prim Sch SA10 222 D3
BLAENDULAIS / SEVEN SISTERS 222 D3
Blaen Emlyn SA14 218 D8
BLAENGARW 103 E6
Blaengarw Prim Sch CF32 103 E6
Blaengarw Rd CF32 103 D7
BLAENGWAWR 53 A8
Blaengwawr Cl CF44 53 B8
Blaengwawr Comp Sch / Ysgol Gyfun Blaen-Gwawr CF44 53 B8
Blaengwawr Prim Sch CF44 53 B8
BLAENGWRACH 227 C8
Blaengwrach Prim Sch SA11 227 B8
BLAENGWYNFI 76 C6
Blaenhonddan Prim Sch SA10 48 D3
Blaen Ifor CF83 137 E6
Blaenlau St 1 CF40 106 F4
BLAENLLECHAU 80 A7
Blaenllechau Inf Sch / Ysgol Fabanod Blaenllechchau CF43 79 F8
Blaenllechau Rd CF43 80 A7
Blaenllynfi Inf Sch CF34 75 B1
Blaenmorfa SA4 19 C3
Blaen-Nant Rd NP23 8 C2
Blaennantygroes Rd CF44 29 E1
Blaen Ogwr Ct CF32 104 F5
Blaenogwr Terr CF32 104 F6
BLAENRHONDDA 50 C4
Blaenrhondda Rd CF42 50 D3
Blaenrhondda Waterfalls Walk★ CF42 26 C1
Blaentillery Prim Sch / Ysgol Gynradd Blaentillery NP13 36 B8
Blaenwern
Cwmbran / Cwmbrân NP44 89 F6
Neath / Castell-Nedd SA10 48 E2
Blaen Wern
Cwmdare CF44 28 D3
Ebbw Vale / Glyn Ebwy NP23 14 B8
Blaen-y-Coed
Cardiff / Caerdydd CF14 177 C8
Radyr CF15 176 A6
BLAEN-Y-CWM 6 C3
Blaen-y-Cwm CF81 58 A5
Blaen Y Cwm CF31 168 B4
Blaen-y-cwm Prim Sch NP23 8 C3
Blaen-y-Cwm Rd
Abertillery / Abertyleri NP11 60 F6
Pontypool / Pont-y-pwl NP4 61 A4
Treherbert CF42 50 D3
Blaen-y-Cwm Terr CF42 50 E3
Blaen-y-Cwm View NP44 88 F1
Blaen Y Ddol CF31 168 B4
Blaen-y-Fro CF35 152 F1
Blaen-y-Maes Dr SA5 67 E6
Blaenymaes Prim Sch SA5 67 E7
Blaen-y-Morfa SA15 40 F2
Blaen-y-Pant Ave NP20 143 A8
Blaen-y-Pant Cres NP20 143 A8
Blaen-y-Pant Pl NP20 143 A8
Blagdon Cl CF3 179 B5
BLAINA / BLAENAU 15 F4
Blaina Cl CF3 179 F7
Blaina & District Hospl NP23 15 D8
Blaina Rd
Abertillery / Abertyleri NP13 35 E7
Brynmawr NP23 8 C3
Blair Way / Ffordd Blair SA12 98 F2
Blaise Pl CF11 194 E2
Blake Ct CF10 232 D1
Blake Rd NP19 144 B3
Blake St CF43 52 B1
Blanche Cl NP10 163 F6
Blanche St
Cardiff / Caerdydd CF24 195 E7
Dowlais CF48 11 C4

Blanche St continued
Pontypridd CF37 109 C2
Tonypandy CF40 107 A2
Blandings Ct CF23 178 C6
Blandon Way CF14 177 B4
Blandy Terr
Nant-y-Moel CF32 104 F6
Ogmore Vale CF32 104 E1
Pontycymer CF32 103 F3
Blanthorn Ct 1 CF14 176 F6
Blenheim Cl CF62 214 C7
Blenheim Ct NP44 89 C2
Blenheim Rd
Abertillery / Abertyleri NP13 36 C3
Cardiff / Caerdydd CF23 178 D1
Cwmbran / Cwmbrân NP44 89 C2
Newport / Casnewydd NP19 144 A5
Blenheim Rd / Heol Blenhein NP44 89 C2
Blenheim Sq / Sgwar Blenheim 12 NP44 89 C2
Bleriot Cl NP19 144 A3
Blethin Cl CF5 176 E3
Blewitt St NP20 143 B4
Blodwen Rd NP4 63 A4
Blodwen St SA12 98 F1
Blodwen Terr SA4 64 F4
Blodwen Way NP4 63 A4
Blodyn Y Gog CF63 215 C8
Bloomfield Cl NP19 144 D6
Bloomfield Rd NP12 85 D7
Bloom St CF11 194 C7
Blorenge Terr 1 NP4 17 D7
Blosse Rd CF14 177 A2
Blosse St CF34 102 A6
Blossom Cl NP18 145 B8
Blossom Dr CF14 160 A4
Bloss Terr CF39 107 F2
BLUE ANCHOR 65 A3
Blue Anchor Rd SA4 64 F3
Bluebell Ct NP44 88 F2
Bluebell Dr
Bryncae CF72 153 F2
Cardiff / Caerdydd CF3 179 D8
Bluebell Way
Rogerstone / Ty-du NP10 141 D7
Swansea / Abertawe SA5 68 A5
Blue House Rd CF14 159 E1
Blue Mountain / Mynydd Glas CF34 102 A7
Bluetts La NP4 37 E5
Blundell Ave CF36 182 F6
Blyth Cl CF62 205 A1
Blythe St NP13 36 B5
Board St CF81 12 F1
Boarlands The SA3 231 A4
Bodalaw CF48 11 B4
Boddington Terr NP18 118 C2
Bodnant Cl CF3 179 F6
Bodringallt Ct CF41 79 D3
Bodringallt Prim Sch CF41 79 D3
Bodringallt Terr CF41 79 C3
Bodwenarth Rd CF37 109 F4
Bogey Rd CF48 31 B8
Bog Rd SA7, SA10 69 E4
Bohun St SA5 68 C3
Boi Cl CF45 54 B3
Boiler House Rd CF62 211 E1
Boleyn Wlk CF23 178 C1
Bolgoed Rd SA4 19 E2
Bolt Cl NP20 143 D3
Bolton Rd NP20 143 A4
Bolton St NP20 143 B7
Bolts Row NP19 144 B5
Bolt St NP20 143 D3
Bolwg yr Afon / Riverside View SA11 226 C5
Bona Rd CF71 199 C5
Boncath Rd CF14 177 A2
Bond Ave SA15 40 E4
Bondfield Ho 4 SA12 98 F1
BONDFIELD PARK 137 F2
Bond St
Aberdare / Aberdâr CF44 29 A1
Newport / Casnewydd NP19 143 C6
Swansea / Abertawe SA1 95 B5
Bonllwyn SA18 219 B8
Bont Cl NP12 85 B7
Bontnewydd Terr CF46 83 C7
Bonville Terr SA1 95 A6
Bonvilston Rd CF37 109 D2
Bonvilston Terr 3 CF37 109 D2
BONVILSTON / TRESIMWN 191 B1
BON-Y-MAEN 69 C3
Bon-y-Maen Rd SA1 69 A3
Booker St CF24 195 E7
Boon Cl CF63 215 A7
Booth Ho SA12 98 A2
Boot La 6 NP4 17 C6
Boot The CF82 85 A1
Borage Cl CF23 160 E1
Border Rd SA12 98 C3
Borfa Pl NP12 85 C7
Borough Ave CF62 214 E8
Borough Cl CF71 188 F1
Borough Rd SA4 42 F2
Borough St SA12 124 F8
Borrowdale Cl CF23 178 C2
Borth Rd CF3 179 D5
Bosco La SA3 121 B3
Boswell Cl
Cardiff / Caerdydd CF3 179 B8
Newport / Casnewydd NP20 142 F2
Bosworth Dr NP20 143 A7
Bosworth Rd SA10 70 F7
Boulevard De Nantes CF10 232 B3
Boulevard De Villenave D'Oron CF31 168 F5
Boulevard De Villenave O'Oron 3 CF31 168 F5
Boulevard The NP23 14 E3
Boundary St NP23 8 B4
Boundary The NP12 85 D5
Bournville Rd NP13 15 E1
Bournville Terr NP22 13 D7
Boverton Brook CF61 210 C5
Boverton Ct CF61 210 C6
Boverton Park Dr CF61 210 C5
Boverton Pk CF61 210 C5
Boverton Rd
Llantwit Major / Llanilltud Fawr CF61 209 F6
Llantwit Major / Llanilltud Fawr CF61 210 B6
Boverton St CF23 178 B1
BOVERTON / TREBEFERED 210 C6
Bovil View CF83 140 A7
Bowden Rd SA11 71 E6
Bowen Cl NP4 17 C7
Bowen Ind Est NP12 58 C2
Bowen Pl 23 NP20 143 C3
Bowen St
Neath / Castell-Nedd SA11 71 D6
Swansea / Abertawe SA1 68 D2
Bowen Terr SA15 40 F3
Bower St CF33 148 C1
Bowham Ave CF31 168 E2
Bowleaze NP44 89 B3
Bowley Ct CF24 195 E5
Bowls Cl CF83 137 E5
Bowls La CF83 137 D7
Bowls Terr CF83 137 E5
Bowman's Way CF71 188 D2
Bowman's Well CF71 188 D2
Bow St CF5 193 A2
BOX 40 F6
Boxer Ind Est NP18 118 A4
Box Rd SA4 43 B7
Box Terr
Coytrahen CF32 150 C7
3 Llanelli SA15 40 F6
Boxtree Cl NP18 117 E2
Boyle Cl NP20 116 F2
Brace Ave NP13 35 F7
Brachdy Cl CF3 179 B2
Brachdy La CF3 179 B2
Brachdy Rd CF3 179 B2
Bracken Pl CF5 176 D1
Bracken Rd SA11 71 F8
Bracken Rd / Heol Rhedyn 7 SA13 125 E4
Bracken Rise CF44 29 D1
Bracken Way CF31 150 F1
BRACKLA / BRAGLE 169 C4
BRACKLA HILL 169 B6
Brackla Ind Est CF31 169 B6
Brackla Inf Sch / Ysgol Plant Bach Bracla CF31 169 B5
Brackla Jun Sch / Ysgol Plant Iau Bracla CF31 169 B5
Brackla St CF31 168 F4
Brackla Street Ctr 8 CF31 168 F4
Brackla Way CF31 169 C5
Bradenham Pl 5 CF64 207 A4
Brades The NP18 118 B3
Bradfield Ave CF31 168 D5
Bradfield Rd CF31 168 D4
Bradford Pl CF64 207 B4
Bradford St
Caerphilly / Caerffili CF83 138 A2
Cardiff / Caerdydd CF11 195 A2
1 Llanelli SA15 40 F6
Bradley Cl CF47 10 F2
Bradley Gdns CF47 10 F2
Bradley St
Abercynon CF45 82 D2
Cardiff / Caerdydd CF24 195 E7
Braeval St CF24 195 B8
Bragdu CF35 170 B8
BRAGDY 169 D7
BRAGLE / BRACKLA 169 C4
Brahms Ave SA12 98 B3
Braichycymer Rd CF32 103 E3
Brain Cl NP19 145 A6
Bramble Ave CF62 214 D6
Bramble Cl
Bridgend / Pen-y-Bont ar Ogwr CF31 169 C4
Cardiff / Caerdydd CF5 176 B1
Merthyr Tydfil / Merthyr Tudful CF47 10 C4
Bramble Rise CF64 206 E5
Brambles The CF72 155 E2
Bramblewood Cl
Baglan SA12 98 E5
Cardiff / Caerdydd CF14 159 F2
Bramblewood Ct NP12 85 B7
Brambling Dr CF14 159 E3
Bramley Cl NP18 145 C8
Bramley Dr SA3 122 F6
Bramshill Dr CF23 161 B1
Bran Cl SA7 69 C7
Brandon Cres SA1 69 D5
Brandreth Gdns CF23 178 C2
Brandreth Rd CF23 178 B2
Brandy Cove Cl SA3 123 B4
Brandy Cove Rd SA3 122 A5
Brangwyn Ave / Coedlan Brangwyn NP44 117 A8
Brangwyn Cl
4 Penarth CF64 206 F5
Swansea / Abertawe SA6 45 E2
Brangwyn Cres NP19 143 F7
Brangwyn Rd NP22 13 D5
Brankleys Hos NP4 17 E6
Branksome Ho 1 CF10 232 B2
Bransby Rd CF40 107 A4
Branwen Cl CF5 193 A2
Branwen Gdns SA1 68 B1
Braunton Ave CF3 179 C6
Braunton Cres CF3 179 B6
Brayford Pl CF3 179 C8
Brayley Rd SA6 45 F2
Breaksea Cl CF64 216 B4
Breaksea Ct CF62 214 F2
Breaksea Dr CF62 214 F2
Brean Cl CF64 216 C5
Brechfa Cl NP18 117 E7
Brecon Cl CF44 27 D8
Brecon Ct
Barry / Y Barri CF63 215 A6
Caerleon / Caerllion NP18 117 F3
8 Cardiff / Caerdydd CF5 194 C6
Brecon Ho
7 Penarth CF64 206 F2
Port Talbot SA12 124 D8
6 Swansea / Abertawe SA1 233 C2
Brecon Hts NP23 14 E2
Brecon Mountain Railway★ CF48 4 A4
Brecon Park Cotts NP7 9 C5
Brecon Pl CF44 53 D7
Brecon Rd
Hirwaun CF44 27 D7
Merthyr Tydfil / Merthyr Tudful CF47 10 B3
Merthyr Tydfil / Merthyr Tudful, Williamstown CF47 10 D2
Newport / Casnewydd NP19 143 F7
Pontardawe SA8 23 F6
Ystradgynlais SA9 1 F1
Brecon Rd / Heol Rheolau
Abercrave / Abercraf SA9 222 B7
Ystradgynlais SA9 222 A5
Brecon Road Inf Sch CF47 10 D2
Brecon St
3 Aberdare / Aberdâr CF44 53 D7
Cardiff / Caerdydd CF5 194 C6
Llantwit Major / Llanilltud Fawr CF61 210 B7
Brecon Terr
Deri CF81 57 B8
Tredegar NP22 5 F1
Brecon View CF44 27 F6
Brecon Way CF38 135 F2
Brecon Wlk NP44 89 F3
Bredenbury Gdns CF36 165 E1
Bredon Cl NP11 115 C1
Brendon Cl 2 CF3 179 C6
Brendon Ct CF83 138 C2
Brendon View Cl CF62 213 A2
Brenig Cl
Barry / Y Barri CF62 214 C6
Cardiff / Caerdydd CF14 159 F3
Brenig Rd SA5 68 A4
Brenroy Rd CF71 199 C4
Brentwood Ct CF14 159 F1
Brentwood Pl NP23 7 C1
Breon Rd CF64 215 E6
Bres Rd SA15 40 D5
Brettenham St SA15 40 C6
Brett Rd NP11 87 C3
Brewer St CF81 32 F8
Brewery Ct / Cwrt Bracty NP13 36 A1
Brewery Field The (Bridgend RUFC) CF31 168 E5
Brewery La CF48 10 A4
Brewery La / Lon Y Bragoy CF31 168 E5
Brewery Terr
Abertillery / Abertyleri NP13 35 F1
Ebbw Vale / Glyn Ebwy NP23 14 D6
Tylorstown CF43 107 C8
Brian Cres CF36 182 F7
Brianne Dr CF14 159 F3
Briar Cl
Cardiff / Caerdydd CF5 193 C8
Ebbw Vale / Glyn Ebwy NP23 7 C5
Briar Dene SA2 94 B6
Briarmead / Dol Fieri CF47 10 E2
Briarmeadow Dr CF14 159 E3
Briar Rd CF44 53 F7
Briar Rd / Heol Miaren SA12 98 C1
Briar's Ct SA5 67 F6
Briartree Manor 6 CF24 195 D7
Briar Way
Church Village CF38 136 A1
Hirwaun CF44 27 C8
Briarwood Cl SA10 48 D4
Briarwood Dr CF23 178 D7
Briarwood Gdns SA3 122 D5
Briary Way CF31 169 C4
Brickfield Cres CF47 30 E8
Brick Row CF34 102 C1
Brick Row / Rhes Bricksen SA10 222 C3
Brick St SA13 227 C2
Brickyard Bsns Pk CF14 177 D2
Brickyard Cotts
Abercrave / Abercraf SA9 222 B7
6 Neath / Castell-Nedd SA11 71 E8
Brickyard La NP20 142 D4
Brickyard Rd SA5 67 F3
Brickyard The CF36 183 C7
Bridesvale Gdns NP10 163 E1
Bridgefield St CF83 137 A8
Bridgeman Ct CF64 207 B3
Bridgeman Rd CF64 207 B3
Bridgend Bsns Ctr CF31 169 E3
Bridgend Coll / Coleg Penybont CF31 168 F3
Bridgend Ind Est CF31 169 C3
BRIDGEND / PEN-Y-BONT AR OGWR 168 C7
Bridgend PRU CF32 150 D4
Bridgend Rd
Aberkenfig / Abercynffig CF32 150 C4
Bryncae CF72 153 E2
Maesteg CF34 102 C2
Pen-y-fai CF32 150 D2
Pont Rhyd-y-cyff CF34 128 D6
Pontycymer CF32 103 E2
Porthcawl CF32, CF36 167 B2
Porthcawl, Newton CF36 183 D8
Bridgend Ret Pk CF31 169 A2
Bridgend Science Pk CF31 168 E1
Bridgend Sta CF31 168 F4
Bridge Rd
Aberdare / Aberdâr CF44 53 E8
Cardiff / Caerdydd CF5, CF14 176 F2
Cardiff / Caerdydd, Llane Deyrn CF3 161 C1
Llanblethian / Llanfleiddan CF71 200 D8
Upper Boat CF37 136 D2
Waunarlwydd SA5 66 E4
Bridge St / Stryd y Bont
Aberfan CF48 55 C5
Pen-y-groes SA14 218 D8
Bridge St
Abercarn NP11 87 A3
Abercarn NP11 87 B2
Aberdare / Aberdâr CF44 29 A3
Abertillery / Abertyleri NP13 36 A5
Abertillery / Abertyleri, Six Bells NP13 36 C2
Bargoed / Bargod CF81 58 A5
Barry / Y Barri CF63 215 B7
Blackwood / Coed-Duon NP12 85 F6
18 Blaenavon NP4 17 C6
Blaengarw CF32 103 E6
Cardiff / Caerdydd CF10 232 C2
Cardiff / Caerdydd, Llandaff / Llandaf CF5 177 A1
Clydach SA6 46 D7
Cwm-twrch Isaf SA9 1 B1
Ebbw Vale / Glyn Ebwy NP23 7 D1
Glais SA7 47 A6
Glyncorrwg SA13 227 C2
Llanelli SA15 40 D6
Llangennech SA14 42 C8
Maesteg CF34 102 B3
Neath / Castell-Nedd SA11 71 E8
Newbridge / Trecelyn NP11 87 A6
Newport / Casnewydd NP20 143 B5
Ogmore Vale CF32 130 E8
Penarth CF64 206 F5
Pontypool / Pont-y-pwl NP4 62 E3
Pontypridd CF37 109 C1
3 Pontypridd, Treforest CF37 135 E7
3 Port Talbot SA13 125 C8
Bridge St continued
Pyle / Y Pîl CF33 148 C2
Risca / Rhisga NP11 114 F2
Swansea / Abertawe SA1 233 B5
Tonypandy CF40 106 F5
Tredegar NP22 13 E6
Trehafod CF37 108 C3
Troedyrhiw CF48 31 C1
Ynysddu NP11 112 F6
Bridge Street Ind Est NP22 13 E6
Bridge Terr
Michaelston-y-Fedw CF3 162 A7
Newbridge / Trecelyn NP11 87 A6
2 Port Talbot SA13 125 C8
Bridgewater Rd CF64 216 B6
Bridgwater Rd CF3 179 D6
Bridle Mews SA3 123 C3
Brierley Cl NP11 115 C1
Brierley La CF83 168 F2
Brierly Pl NP11 114 B8
Briers Gate NP44 115 E8
Briery Ct NP23 14 D6
BRIERY HILL 14 C6
Briery Hill Prim Sch NP23 14 D6
Brigantine Cl NP10 163 F6
Brigantine Dr NP10 163 F6
Brigantine Gr NP10 163 F6
Brigantine Pl CF10 232 D1
Brigantine Way NP10 163 F6
Brigham Ct CF83 137 C4
Brighton Rd SA4 43 C2
Brights La 6 NP4 17 D6
Bright St NP11 114 C4
Brig-y-Don Hill CF32 184 D2
Brindley Rd CF11 194 D1
Brin Williams Ho 1 NP20 143 A4
Brisbane Ct NP12 85 C6
Bristol Ho NP4 62 A8
Bristol St
Aberkenfig / Abercynffig CF32 150 C4
Newport / Casnewydd NP19 143 E6
Bristol Terr
Bargoed / Bargod CF81 58 A5
New Tredegar NP24 58 A8
Taffs Well / Ffynnon Taf CF15 157 F4
Bristol View Cl NP44 89 A4
BRITANNIA 108 A2
Britannia Ctr for Enterprise NP12 58 B1
Britannia Quay CF10 195 C2
Britannia Rd SA6 68 E5
Britannia St CF39 108 A2
Britannia Terr NP12 58 B1
Britannia Villas NP12 58 B1
Britannia Wlk NP12 58 B2
BRITHDIR 58 A8
Brithdir St CF24 177 F1
Brithdir Sta NP24 58 A8
Brithwen Rd SA5 66 D3
Brithweunydd Rd CF40 107 A5
BRITISH 37 C4
British Legion Dr CF3 179 B4
British Rd NP4 37 C4
British School Cl NP4 37 E4
Briton Ferry Ind Est SA12 98 B8
BRITON FERRY / LLANSAWEL 71 B2
Briton Ferry Rd SA11 71 E6
Briton Ferry Specl Sch SA11 71 D3
Briton Ferry Sta SA11 71 C2
Briton Ferry Workshops Ind Est SA11 98 A8
Briton Ho 6 SA12 98 C3
Brittania Cl NP11 115 A1
Brittania Pl CF43 80 A5
Britten Cl NP19 144 D4
Britten Rd CF64 206 F1
Britway Ct CF64 206 A3
Britway Rd CF64 206 A3
Broadacre SA2 93 C7
Broadacres
Cardiff / Caerdydd CF11 194 C5
Llantwit Fadre / Llanilltud Faerdref CF38 156 F8
Broad Cl CF62 214 B5
Broadcommon Cl NP19 144 C3
Broadfield Cl CF40 107 A4
Broadfield Ct CF5 193 D4
Broadhaven CF11 194 C4
Broadhaven Cl SA5 68 A7
Broadlands Ct 4 CF3 179 E7
Broadlands Ho 5 CF3 179 E7
Broadlands Prim Sch / Ysgol Gynradd Tirllydan CF31 168 B3
Broadmead
Bryn NP12 85 D4
Swansea / Abertawe SA2 93 D7
Broadmead Cres SA3 122 B6
Broadmead Pk NP19 144 D3
Broadoak Ct SA4 42 E1
Broad Oak Way CF31 168 B5
Broadparks SA3 122 F8
Broad Pl CF11 194 C5

Broad Quay Rd NP19 164 E8
Broad Shoard The CF71 188 E2
Broad St
Abersychan NP4 37 F3
Barry / Y Barri CF62 214 D4
Blaenavon NP4 17 C6
Cardiff / Caerdydd CF11 194 C5
Dowlais CF48 11 A4
12 Merthyr Tydfil / Merthyr Tudful CF47 30 D8
Newport / Casnewydd NP20 143 D3
Pontypool / Pont-y-pwl NP4 62 E3
Port Talbot SA13 125 C8
Broadstairs Rd CF11 194 C5
Broad Street Par CF62 214 D3
Broad View CF32 150 C6
Broadview Cl SA3 123 B4
Broad View / Golygfan NP44 89 C5
Broadview La SA3 123 B4
Broadwalk NP18 118 B2
Broadwater Rd NP19 144 C1
Broadway
Caerleon / Caerllion NP18 118 B1
Cardiff / Caerdydd CF24 195 D7
Cowbridge / Y Bont-Faen CF71 188 E1
Llanblethian / Llanfleiddan CF71 200 E8
Pontypool / Pont-y-pwl NP4 62 B6
Pontypridd CF37 135 D8
Swansea / Abertawe SA2 94 D7
Broadway Ct SA2 94 D7
Broadway Gn CF5 192 A1
Broadweir Rd / Heol Broadweir 4 NP44 89 E2
Broadwell Cl 4 CF3 179 F6
Broadwell Ct NP18 118 B2
Broadwood Cl NP19 144 E5
Bro Athro CF3 179 D4
Brocastle Ave CF31 169 F2
Brocastle Rd CF14 177 B6
Brockhampton Rd CF3 179 F7
Brockhill Rise CF64 217 A8
Brockhill Way CF64 217 A8
Brock St CF63 215 B7
Brodawel
Ammanford / Rhydaman SA18 219 C6
Cimla SA11 72 B6
Maesteg CF34 102 B3
Merthyr Tydfil / Merthyr Tudful CF47 30 F7
Penywaun CF44 28 B6
Pontneddfechan SA11 223 F2
Bro Dawel
Dunvant SA2 93 D7
Pontyclun CF72 173 A6
Swansea / Abertawe SA6 45 C2
Bro Dedwydd SA2 93 D8
Brodeg CF15 175 C8
Bro Deg CF44 53 F8
Bro-Deg CF35 170 D8
Bro Dirion
Bridgend / Pen-y-Bont ar Ogwr CF31 168 B4
Dunvant SA2 93 D8
Brodorion Dr SA6 45 E3
Brohedydd CF43 52 A2
Brokesby Cl SA1 69 A3
Brokesby Rd SA1 69 A3
Brombil SA13 125 F4
Brombil Ct SA13 125 F4
Brombil Gdns SA13 125 F4
Brombil Paddocks SA13 125 F4
Brombil St SA13 125 D5
Bromfield Pl CF64 207 B5
Bromfield Rd CF62 214 E2
Bromfield St CF11 194 F2
Bromley Dr CF5 193 E5
Brompton Pl NP22 14 A3
Bromsgrove St CF11 194 F2
Bron Afon SA4 44 B5
Bron Afon Uchaf SA4 44 B5
Bron Allt SA10 226 A7
Bronallt Rd / Heol Bronallt SA4 19 A5
Bronallt Terr CF44 53 F4
Bro Nant Fer SA18 220 D7
Bronawelon NP11 60 B2
Bron Awelon CF62 214 B3
Broncynon Terr CF44 28 D3
Brondeg
Heolgerrig CF48 10 B1
Swansea / Abertawe SA5 68 B3
Bron Deg CF46 56 D1
Brondeg Cres SA5 68 B3
Brondeg La SA8 23 F3
Brondeg St CF43 80 B2
Brondeg Terr CF44 28 F1
Bron Felen CF14 159 D2
Bronhafod NP23 8 C5
Bron Hafod CF31 168 B2
Bronhall CF72 155 C2
Bronhaul CF15 175 C8
Bron Haul CF44 53 F8
Bronheulog Terr CF48 55 B8
Bronheulwen CF39 107 D4
Broniestyn Terr
Aberdare / Aberdâr CF44 28 F3
Broniestyn Terr *continued*
Hirwaun CF44 27 D8
Bron Las CF82 84 F6
Bronllan SA1 69 D5
Bronllwyn CF15 175 B8
Bronllwyn Rd CF41 79 B2
Bronllys CF44 28 B6
Bronllys Gr NP10 163 D5
Bronllys Mews NP10 163 D5
Bronllys Pl 3 NP44 90 A5
Bronmynnyd CF83 137 A6
Bron Rhiw CF83 139 F7
Bronrhiw Ave CF83 138 B1
Bronrhiw Fach CF83 138 B1
Bronte Cl CF3 179 C8
Bronte Cres CF3 179 C8
Bronte Gr NP20 142 E2
Bronte Ho 7 SA12 98 F1
Bronwydd
Blackwood / Coed Duon NP12 59 A2
Neath / Castell-Nedd SA7 70 C8
Bronwydd Ave CF23 178 C2
Bronwydd Cl CF23 178 D2
Bronwydd Rd CF24 196 A8
Bron-y-Bryn SA2 93 E8
Bron-y-De NP23 14 C7
Bron-y-Deri CF45 54 E3
Bron-y-Garth
Croesyceiliog NP44 90 B4
Pen-pedair-heol CF82 84 E7
Bron-y-Glyn CF64 207 B3
Bron-y-Mor CF62 214 C2
Bron Yr Allt SA9 2 A8
Bron-y-Waun CF34 102 D2
Bronywawr SA8 23 E5
Bron-y-Wawr CF33 148 A1
Brookbank Cl CF44 29 D1
Brook Ct
2 Bridgend / Pen-y-Bont ar Ogwr CF31 168 F5
Cardiff / Caerdydd, Fairwater CF5 193 F7
Cardiff / Caerdydd, Riverside CF11 194 F5
Brook Ct / Llys-y-Nant SA11 71 C4
Brookdale Ct CF38 156 F8
Brookdale St 17 SA11 71 E7
Brookfield
Neath Abbey SA10 71 B8
Neath / Castell-Nedd SA10 48 B1
Ynysybwl CF37 109 A6
Brookfield Ave
Barry / Y Barri CF63 215 C8
Rhymney / Rhymni NP22 13 A2
Brookfield Cl
Gorseinon SA4 42 F3
Newport / Casnewydd NP19 144 B3
Brookfield Dr CF3 179 E6
Brookfield La CF37 109 E3
Brookfield Park Rd CF71 188 F1
Brookfield Pl SA5 67 E6
Brookfield Prim Sch NP44 89 E3
Brookfield Rd
Maerdy CF43 79 C8
Maesteg CF34 102 D2
Pontllanfraith NP12 86 A4
Brookfield Terr CF48 31 C2
Brook La
Pontllanfraith NP12 86 A4
St Nicholas / Sain Nicolas CF5 203 F8
Brookland Ho 2 NP44 89 E5
Brookland Rd NP11 115 A1
Brooklands
Nelson CF46 83 D5
Tredegar NP22 6 C2
Brooklands Cl
Dunvant SA2 66 B1
Maesycwmmer CF82 85 B2
Merthyr Tydfil / Merthyr Tudful CF47 10 D3
Brooklands Cotts CF46 83 D5
Brooklands Terr
Abercarn NP11 114 C7
Abercrave / Abercraf SA9 222 D7
Cardiff / Caerdydd CF5 192 F2
Swansea / Abertawe SA1 95 B7
Brooklands The NP13 36 C6
Brookland Terr CF32 104 F5
Brookland Terr / Teras Brookland NP44 89 E6
Brookland View NP24 33 F3
Brooklea NP18 118 B4
Brooklyn Cl CF14 159 A1
Brooklyn Gdns
Baglan SA12 98 C4
The Mumbles / Y Mwmbwls SA3 123 A6
Brooklyn Terr
Abertillery / Abertyleri NP13 60 B6
The Mumbles / Y Mwmbwls SA3 122 F5
Brook Pl
Cwm NP23 35 A7
Treorchy / Treorci CF41 78 F5
Brook Rd
Cardiff / Caerdydd CF5 193 F7
Cardiff / Caerdydd, Whitchurch CF14 177 B4
Brook Row
Bryncethin CF32 151 A5
Fochriw CF81 32 C7
Brookside
Bettws NP20 116 E2
Church Village CF38 136 A1
Cwmbran / Cwmbrân NP44 89 C2
Dinas Powis / Dinas Powys CF64 206 B4
Gowerton / Tre-gwyr SA4 66 D3
Treoes CF35 170 A1
Brookside Cl
Baglan SA12 98 E5
Caerphilly / Caerffili CF83 137 D4
Cardiff / Caerdydd CF14 177 D5
Pontypridd CF37 109 F4
Brookside Cres CF83 138 C3
Brookside Ct 6 CF14 177 B5
Brookside Row NP13 36 B8
Brook St
Abercarn NP11 87 B4
Aberdare / Aberdâr CF44 53 C7
Abertridwr CF83 137 A8
Barry / Y Barri CF63 215 A5
Blaenrhondda CF42 50 D4
Bridgend / Pen-y-Bont ar Ogwr CF31 168 F5
Brynmawr NP23 8 B4
Cardiff / Caerdydd CF11 194 F5
Cwmbran / Cwmbrân NP44 89 E7
Ferndale CF43 79 F6
Maerdy CF43 52 B1
Mountain Ash / Aberpennar CF45 54 D2
Neath / Castell-Nedd SA10 70 F7
Pontypridd CF37 135 E6
Porth, Britannia CF39 108 A2
Porth CF39 107 E2
Port Talbot SA13 125 C7
Tonypandy CF40 107 A3
Treorchy / Treorci CF42 78 E6
Ystrad CF41 79 D2
Brook Terr
Church Village CF38 135 F1
Gwaun-Cae-Gurwen SA18 220 E7
Llanharan CF72 153 F3
Brookvale Dr CF14 159 E3
Brook Vale / Pant Y Pystyll CF35 170 C8
Brookvale Rd SA3 122 F7
Brookview Cl CF14 159 F2
Brookville Dr / Rhodfa Brookville Dr SA10 70 E7
Brookway CF38 136 A1
Brookway Cl SA12 98 E5
Broom Cl NP10 141 E6
Broome Path NP44 89 C2
Broomfield Cl CF38 136 A1
Broomfield St CF83 138 B2
Broomhill SA13 125 D8
Broom Pl CF5 193 D8
Bro Ryan SA18 220 A8
Brotalwg CF46 83 B7
BROUGHTON 198 C2
Broughton Ave SA5 67 E6
Broughton Pl 4 CF63 215 A8
Broughton Rd CF71 198 C4
Bro-Wen SA14 41 C5
Brown Ave SA15 40 F2
Brown Cl NP19 144 A3
Brownhills SA4 43 A3
Browning Cl
Bridgend / Pen-y-Bont ar Ogwr CF31 168 D6
Cardiff / Caerdydd CF3 179 B7
Newport / Casnewydd NP20 142 F2
Browns Dr SA3 121 A5
Brown St
Ferndale CF43 80 A6
Maesteg CF34 101 F5
Bro-y-Fan CF83 138 D5
Bro-y-Ffrwd CF48 225 F2
Bruce Knight Cl CF5 176 E2
Bruce Rd SA5 67 B4
Bruce St
Cardiff / Caerdydd CF24 178 A1
9 Mountain Ash / Aberpennar CF45 54 D3
Brummell Dr CF15 174 F6
Brunant Rd
Clydach NP7 9 E8
Gorseinon SA4 43 B3
Brundall Cres CF5 193 A3
Brunel Ave NP10 142 B6
Brunel Cl
Barry / Y Barri CF63 215 D8
Pen-pedair-heol CF82 84 E7
Tonna / Tonnau SA11 49 D3
Brunel Ct 5 SA1 95 B7
Brunel Rd / Heol Brunel NP44 89 A2
Brunel St
Cardiff / Caerdydd CF11 194 E5
Newport / Casnewydd NP20 143 D1
Brunel Way SA1 68 F3
Brunner Dr SA6 22 E1
Brunswick St
Cardiff / Caerdydd CF5 194 C6
11 Merthyr Tydfil / Merthyr Tudful CF47 10 D2
Swansea / Abertawe SA1 95 B6
Bruton Pl CF5 177 A1
Brwyna Ave SA12 98 F1
Brwynen Las SA10 48 C2
Bryanston Rd CF64 215 E6
Brychan 1 SA15 40 F4
Brychan Pl 7 CF47 10 D2
Brydges Pl CF24 195 A8
Brymbo Ave / Rhodfa Brymbo 2 SA13 125 D5
BRYN
Blackwood 85 D4
Hirwaun 26 C8
Llanelli 41 F6
Llanrhidian 91 B7
Maesteg 100 F5
Bryn Aber
Abertridwr CF83 137 A8
Senghenydd CF83 111 A1
Bryn Adar CF14 176 F8
Bryn Aeron SA2 66 C1
Bryn Aeron Ct SA2 66 C1
Brynafon Rd SA4 43 A3
Brynallt Terr SA15 40 F5
Brynamlwg
Abersychan NP4 37 F4
Clydach SA6 22 F1
Llanelli SA15 40 F6
Miskin / Meisgyn CF72 173 C8
9 Tonypandy CF40 106 E6
Bryn Amlwg
Hengoed CF82 84 F3
North Cornelly CF33 165 F8
Brynamlwg Rd SA4 43 A2
Bryn-Amlwg Rd SA5 67 E3
BRYNAMMAN 220 E8
Brynamman Rd / Heol Brynamman SA18 220 D7
Brynau Dr SA3 93 F2
Bryn Aur CF37 109 D6
Brynau Rd
Caerphilly / Caerffili CF83 138 B3
Taffs Well / Ffynnon Taf CF15 158 B4
Brynau Wood SA11 72 C6
Brynavon 10 NP4 17 C6
Brynavon Terr CF82 85 A3
BRYNAWEL 113 D3
Brynawel
Aberdare / Aberdâr CF44 28 F1
Brynmawr NP23 8 B5
Caerphilly / Caerffili CF83 137 D6
Crynant / Creunant SA10 226 A7
Pontardawe SA8 23 E5
Bryn Awel
Bedwas CF83 138 F6
Bettws CF32 129 E3
Bridgend / Pen-y-Bont ar Ogwr CF31 168 B5
Hengoed CF82 85 A4
Neath / Castell-Nedd SA11 71 F5
Pontypridd CF37 109 D6
Brynawel Cl SA10 226 A7
Brynawel Cres SA5 68 D5
Brynawelon
Ammanford / Rhydaman SA18 218 F7
Cefn-bryn-brain SA9 221 B8
Coelbren SA10 222 F6
Llanelli SA14 41 C6
Tonna / Tonnau SA11 49 E3
Winchestown NP23 8 B2
Bryn Awelon
Aberdare / Aberdâr CF44 53 F7
Bridgend / Pen-y-Bont ar Ogwr CF31 168 C5
Ebbw Vale / Glyn Ebwy, Beaufort Hill NP23 7 E3
Ebbw Vale / Glyn Ebwy NP23 7 D4
Pen-pedair-heol CF82 84 E7
Bryn-Awelon Rd CF23 178 C8
Brynawel Rd
Gorseinon SA4 43 A2
Ystradgynlais SA9 1 F1
Brynawel Terr
Abertillery / Abertyleri NP13 60 A7
Ystradowen SA9 221 C7
Bryn Bach
Cardiff / Caerdydd CF14 177 B8
Tircoed SA4 44 C5
Bryn Bach Countryside Ctr★ NP22 6 B1
Bryn Bach Pk★ NP22 6 B1
Bryn Bach Prim Sch NP22 6 C1
Bryn Bach Rd
Brynamman SA18 220 D8
Pontlliw SA4 20 B2
Bryn-Bach Rd SA4 44 A8
Brynbach St NP22 6 C1
Brynbala Way CF3 179 E5
Bryn Barrwg CF62 214 D2
Bryn Bedd SA10 222 D3
Bryn Bedw CF39 107 E1
Brynbedw Rd CF43 80 B3
Bryn-Bedw St CF32 103 E7
Bryn Bevan NP20 143 B8
Brynbrain SA9 221 B8
Bryn Brithdir NP11 59 C3
BRYNBRYDDAN 99 C6
Brynbryddan SA12 99 D5
BRYNCAE 153 E1
Bryncae Ind Est CF72 153 E2
Bryn Calch CF15 176 A8
Bryn Canol
Bedwas CF83 138 E6
Cefn Hengoed CF82 84 F5
Llanelli SA14 41 A6
Bryn Carno NP22 12 E6
Bryn Carwyn CF48 11 B4
Bryn Castell CF15 176 B7
Bryn Catwg SA10 48 F2
Bryncelyn
Blaina / Blaenau NP13 15 E6
Nelson CF46 83 D3
Swansea / Abertawe SA6 45 C1
Bryn Celyn
Cardiff / Caerdydd CF23 178 F7
Cwmfelin CF34 128 B8
Maesteg CF34 102 A1
Pontardawe SA8 23 D5
Swansea / Abertawe SA7 70 A6
Bryn Celynnog Comp Sch / Ysgol Gyfun Bryn Celynnog CF38 155 F7
Bryn Celyn Pl NP44 89 D5
Bryn Celyn Prim Sch CF23 178 F7
Bryncelyn Rd SA4 43 A2
Bryn Celyn Rd
Cardiff / Caerdydd CF23 178 F6
Cwmbran / Cwmbrân NP44 89 C5
Bryncerdin Rd SA3 122 E5
BRYNCETHIN 151 B5
Bryncethin Prim Sch / Ysgol Gynradd Bryncethin CF32 151 A4
Bryncethin Rd SA18 220 C7
Bryn Cigfran / Raven Hill CF31 168 B4
Bryn Cl
Bedwas CF83 138 F6
Gorseinon SA4 43 B3
Gowerton / Tre-gwyr SA4 66 D4
Bryn Clychau / Bells Hill CF48 55 D4
BRYN-CÔCH 48 D5
BRYN-COCH 151 A4
Bryncoch
Llanelli SA14 41 C6
Taffs Well / Ffynnon Taf CF15 158 A4
Bryn Coch NP23 7 D4
Bryn Coch / Bryn Farm NP23 8 A5
Bryncoch CW Sch SA10 48 C5
Bryncoch Rd CF32 150 E3
Bryncoed
Penywaun CF44 28 A6
Radyr CF15 176 A6
Bryn Coed SA13 75 E3
Bryncoed Terr
Abertridwr CF83 137 A8
Pen-pedair-heol CF82 84 E8
Bryn Cotts
Bryn SA13 100 F5
Pont-y-rhyl CF32 129 F7
Bryn Creigiau CF72 174 C7
Bryn Cres
Abertillery / Abertyleri NP13 60 A7
Markham NP12 58 E7
Bryn Crydd CF39 107 D1
Bryncwar Rd / Heol Bryn Cawr SA14 218 D8
Bryncyn CF23 178 E8
Bryncynon CF44 27 E8
Bryn-Dedwydd SA11 72 C5
Bryndedwyddfa SA14 218 D8
Brynderi SA18 218 E8
Bryn Deri
Bridgend / Pen-y-Bont ar Ogwr CF31 168 B5
Ebbw Vale / Glyn Ebwy NP23 14 C7
Bryn Deri Cl SA4 44 B2
Brynderi Ct CF31 168 B5
Bryn Deri Prim Sch CF15 176 B7
Bryn-Deri Terr NP11 86 F8
Bryn Derlwyn / Oakgrove Hill CF31 168 B2
Bryn Derw
Beddau CF38 156 A7
Blackwood / Coed-Duon NP12 85 D6
Brynderwen CF37 109 F5
Bryn Derwen
Caerphilly / Caerffili CF83 137 F6
Cwmdare CF44 28 C3
Pontardawe SA8 23 D5
Radyr CF15 176 A7
Swansea / Abertawe SA2 67 B1
Brynderwen Cl CF23 178 C4

Brynderwen Ct
Ferndale CF43 79 F7
1 Newport / Casnewydd NP19 143 E6
Brynderwen Gr NP19 143 E6
Brynderwen Rd
2 Ammanford / Rhydaman SA18 219 B7
Newport / Casnewydd NP19 143 E6
Pontypridd CF37 109 F5
Tonypandy CF40 106 F4
Bryn Derw Gdns SA6 45 E2
Bryn Dewi Sant CF72 173 C8
Bryndolau SA2 93 B8
Bryn-Dolwen CF83 138 E7
Bryn Dreinog SA14 218 D6
Bryn Dryslwyn / Thornbush Hill CF31 168 C2
Bryndulais Ave
Llanelli SA14 40 F7
Seven Sisters / Blaendulais SA10 222 C3
Bryndulais Row / Rhes Bryndulais SA10 222 C4
Bryndu Rd CF33 148 C3
Bryn Ebbw NP23 7 D2
Bryn Eglur Rd SA6 68 D7
Bryn Eglwys
Bryn SA13 100 F5
Croesyceiliog NP44 90 A5
Llanharan CF72 154 A3
Pontypridd CF37 109 A1
Tonypandy CF40 107 A2
Bryneglwys Ave CF36 183 D7
Bryn Eglwys Ct 7 NP23 14 D6
Bryneglwys Gdns CF36 183 D7
Bryneinon Rd SA4 43 A3
Bryn Eirw CF37 108 C2
Bryn Eithin
Cwmdare CF44 28 D3
Gowerton / Tre-gwyr SA4 66 B5
Bryneithin Rd SA4 43 A2
Bryneithin Terr SA6 45 F1
Bryneithyn SA9 1 C1
Bryn Elli SA14 41 A7
Bryn Euraidd SA18 219 A6
Brynfab Rd CF37 136 B5
Bryn Farm / Bryn Coch NP23 8 A5
Brynfa Terr SA4 64 E4
Brynfedw
Bedwas CF83 138 E6
Cardiff / Caerdydd CF23 178 E6
Brynfedwen Cl CF42 51 A1
Brynffordd SA1 67 E2
Brynffrwd Cl CF35 169 F3
Brynffynnon Rd SA4 43 A3
Bryn Ffynon CF39 107 D2
Brynffynon Cl CF44 29 A1
Brynfield Ct SA3 122 F4
Brynfield Rd SA3 122 E4
Bryn-Gaer SA14 41 A7
Bryn-Gaer Terr NP13 60 A7
Bryngarn Rd CF35 152 E3
Bryn-Garreg NP4 37 F5
Bryn Garw NP44 90 A5
Bryngarw Ctry Pk / Parc Gwledig★ CF32 150 E7
Bryngelli Cl CF44 27 C8
Bryngelli Dr SA5 68 C7
Bryngelli Est CF44 27 C7
Bryngelli Pk SA5 68 C7
Bryngelli Rd SA5 68 C7
Bryngelli Terr CF83 137 A8
Bryngerwn Ave CF46 83 B5
Bryngerwn Cotts CF46 83 B5
BRYNGLAS 143 B8
Brynglas
Bridgend / Pen-y-Bont ar Ogwr CF31 168 B4
Bryn-côch SA10 48 C3
Caerphilly / Caerffili CF83 137 E5
Cwmbran / Cwmbrân NP44 116 C8
Pen-y-groes SA14 218 D7
Pontlottyn CF81 32 E8
Bryn Glas
Aberdare / Aberdâr CF44 53 E8
Bedwas CF83 138 E7
Cardiff / Caerdydd CF14 159 D2
Cefn Cribwr CF32 149 C2
Ebbw Vale / Glyn Ebwy NP23 7 C3
Hengoed CF82 84 F2
Swansea / Abertawe SA6 45 C2
Brynglas Ave
Cwmavon / Cwmafan SA12 99 D5
Newport / Casnewydd NP20 143 C8
Pontllanfraith NP12 85 F4
Brynglas Cl NP20 117 B1
Brynglas Cres NP20 143 B8
Brynglas Ct NP20 117 B1
Brynglas Dr NP20 117 B1
Brynglas Prim Sch NP20 117 B1
Brynglas Rd NP20 143 B8
Bryn-Glas Rd SA5 67 E3
Brynglas St CF47 10 F3
Brynglas Terr CF34 75 C2
Bryn-Glas Terr CF33 148 B1
BRYN GOLAU 133 A5
Bryngolau
Bridgend / Pen-y-Bont ar Ogwr CF31 168 B5
Gorseinon SA4 43 A2
Llanelli SA14 41 A7
Rudry CF83 139 B3
Tonyrefail CF39 133 A5
Bryn Golau
Hengoed CF82 85 A4
Pontardawe SA8 23 F4
Bryngoleu CF48 55 C3
Bryn Goleu CF83 138 E7
Bryngoleu Cres CF43 79 F7
Bryn Goleu Rd SA5 67 F3
Bryngoleu St NP12 85 C7
Bryngoleu Terr
2 Pontllanfraith NP12 85 F4
Swansea / Abertawe SA2 94 D7
Bryngolwg CF44 53 F8
Bryn Golwg
Clyne SA11 226 B3
Radyr CF15 176 B7
Bryn Gomer NP44 90 A6
Bryn Gorof SA9 2 D8
Bryn Gors CF32 150 E6
Bryn Gorsedd CF31 168 F7
Bryngwastad Rd SA4 43 A2
Bryngwenith CF83 112 A5
Bryngwili Rd SA4 18 F3
BRYNGWYN 138 A1
Bryngwyn
Caerphilly / Caerffili CF83 137 F1
Neath / Castell-Nedd SA10 70 C6
Newbridge / Trecelyn NP11 86 E6
Bryngwyn Ave SA4 66 D8
Bryngwyn Bach SA14 41 A7
Bryn Gwyn Cl CF44 28 A6
Bryngwyn Comp Sch SA14 41 A8
Bryngwyn Cotts NP11 86 E6
Bryngwyn Pl NP4 62 B6
Bryngwyn Prim Sch NP13 36 C4
Bryngwyn Rd
Ebbw Vale / Glyn Ebwy NP23 7 D4
Llanelli SA14 41 B7
Newbridge / Trecelyn NP11 86 E6
Newport / Casnewydd NP20 143 A4
Pontypool / Pont-y-pwl NP4 62 B6
Bryn-Gwyn Rd
Abertillery / Abertyleri NP13 36 C3
Cardiff / Caerdydd CF23 178 C7
Bryngwyn St
Fleur-de-lis NP12 85 B5
Pontllanfraith NP12 85 B6
Porth CF39 107 E4
Bryn-Gwyn St CF83 138 D7
Bryngwynos St SA13 100 E5
Brynhafod
Bryn SA13 100 E5
Tycroes SA18 218 F5
Bryn-Hafod Prim Sch CF3 179 B5
Brynhafod Rd CF83 137 A7
Bryn Hafren Comp Sch / Ysgol Gyfun Uchaf Bryn Hafren CF62 204 F1
Bryn Haidd CF23 178 F7
Bryn Hawddgar SA6 46 E8
Bryn-Hedd CF39 132 D5
Bryn Hedydd
Bassaleg NP10 141 E3
Swansea / Abertawe SA6 45 C1
Bryn Helyg SA1 69 D5
Bryn Henfaes / Old Meadow Hill CF31 168 A4
Bryn Henllan
Brynna CF72 153 C3
Treherbert CF42 50 D4
Brynhenwysg CF37 108 F2
Bryn Heol CF83 138 E6
BRYNHEULOG 75 A2
Brynheulog
Blaina / Blaenau NP13 15 E5
Brynmenyn CF32 150 D6
Cardiff / Caerdydd CF14 176 F5
Cardiff / Caerdydd, Pentwyn CF23 178 F7
Llanelli SA14 40 F8
Mountain Ash / Aberpennar CF45 81 E8
Ystradgynlais SA9 222 A5
Bryn-Heulog NP13 60 A7
Bryn Heulog
Brynmenyn CF32 150 E6
Caerphilly / Caerffili CF83 137 E5
Heol-y-Cyw CF35 152 B6
Neath / Castell-Nedd SA10 48 C2
Pontypool / Pont-y-pwl NP4 62 D4
Treherbert CF42 51 A1
Brynheulog Ct CF32 150 D6
Brynheulog Pl 6 SA13 125 C8
Brynheulog Rd
Cymmer / Cymer SA13 75 C3
Newbridge / Trecelyn NP11 86 F7
Brynheulog St
Ebbw Vale / Glyn Ebwy NP23 14 C8
Merthyr Tydfil / Merthyr Tudful CF47 10 F3
Penybryn CF82 84 D5
5 Port Talbot SA13 125 C8
Brynheulog Terr
Aberdare / Aberdâr CF44 53 C6
2 Cwmavon / Cwmafan SA12 99 D5
Porth CF39 107 F4
Quakers Yard CF46 83 A5
Tonypandy CF40 106 C6
Tylorstown CF43 80 B5
Bryn Heulog Terr CF83 139 F7
Brynhill CF23 178 C6
Brynhill Cl CF62 214 D8
Brynhill Terr CF38 135 E2
Bryn Hir
Aberdare / Aberdâr CF44 53 F8
Pen-clawdd SA4 65 A2
Bryn Ho NP11 60 A1
Bryn-Howard Terr NP12 59 C2
Brynhyfrd NP22 13 A2
BRYNHYFRYD
Bridgend 168 C5
Neath 71 B3
Swansea 68 C4
Brynhyfryd
Abersychan NP4 37 F2
Abertillery / Abertyleri NP13 60 B7
Beddau CF38 156 A7
Bedwas CF83 138 D7
Bettws CF32 129 D3
Caerphilly / Caerffili CF83 137 F4
Croesyceiliog NP44 90 A5
Cwmaman CF44 52 F4
Glyn-neath / Glyn-nedd SA11 223 D1
Hendreforgan CF39 132 D5
Llangennech SA14 42 B6
Pontlottyn CF81 12 E1
Pontycymer CF32 103 F3
Radyr CF15 176 B7
Tircoed SA4 44 C5
Tonypandy CF40 106 E6
Tylorstown CF43 80 B3
Bryn Hyfryd CF32 150 F3
Brynhyfryd Ave
Nantyglo NP23 8 D1
Newport / Casnewydd NP20 143 B4
5 Tonypandy CF40 107 A4
Brynhyfryd Inf Sch SA5 68 D4
Brynhyfryd Jun Sch SA5 68 D4
Brynhyfryd Pl CF37 135 D7
Brynhyfryd Prim Sch SA11 71 B2
Brynhyfryd Rd
Briton Ferry / Llansawel SA11 71 B2
Gorseinon SA4 43 A3
Llanelli SA15 40 D6
Margam SA13 125 E3
Newport / Casnewydd NP20 143 A4
Brynhyfryd Sq 4 SA5 68 C4
Brynhyfryd St
Merthyr Tydfil / Merthyr Tudful CF47 10 F4
Pontllanfraith NP12 85 F4
Swansea / Abertawe SA5 68 C4
Tonypandy CF40 106 C7
Treorchy / Treorci CF42 78 B8
Brynhyfryd Terr
Cefn Coed / Cefn-coed-y-cymmer CF48 10 A4
Ferndale CF43 79 F6
Machen CF83 140 A7
Nantyglo NP23 8 C1
Pen-pedair-heol CF82 84 E8
1 Pontypridd CF37 109 B1
Bryn-Hyfryd Terr NP11 114 F2
Brynhyfryd Terr / Teras Brynhyfryd
Ebbw Vale / Glyn Ebwy NP23 14 F2
Seven Sisters / Blaendulais SA10 222 D4
Brynhyfryd Villas
New Tredegar NP24 33 F2
Troedyrhiw CF48 55 C8
Bryniago SA4 19 E4
Bryniau Rd CF48 10 F6
Bryn Ifor
Caerphilly / Caerffili CF83 137 D5
Mountain Ash / Aberpennar CF45 54 D2
Bryn Ilan CF37 135 F8
Bryn Isaf SA14 41 D4
BRYNITHEL 60 B7
Bryn-Ithel Terr NP13 60 A7
Bryn Ivor CF40 106 F8
Bryn Ivor St CF40 106 F8
Bryn Kendall NP23 7 E3
Bryn La NP12 85 D3
Bryn Llawen CF33 148 C2
Bryn Llewelyn SA8 23 F3
Bryn Llidiard CF31 168 F8
Bryn Lliw Cotts SA4 43 D6
Bryn-Lloi Rd / Heol Bryn-Lloi 5 SA18 220 A8
Brynlluan SA14 218 B8
Brynllwchwr Rd SA4 65 E8
Brynllys NP23 14 D6
Brynllywarch CF34 101 F1
Bryn Mair CF48 11 B4
Brynmair Cl CF44 53 B5
Brynmair Rd CF44 53 B5
Brynmair Terr 4 CF47 10 F4
BRYNMAWR 8 D4
Brynmawr CF32 129 D3
Brynmawr Ave / Rhodfa Bryn-Mawr 6 SA18 219 B7
Brynmawr Cl CF3 180 A7
Brynmawr La / Lon Bryn-Mawr 9 SA18 219 B7
Brynmawr Pl / Maes Brynmawr CF34 102 A3
Brynmawr Rd NP23 7 E1
Brynmawr Sch NP23 8 D6
Brynmead SA14 41 E6
Brynmead Cl SA2 94 C8
Brynmead Ct SA2 94 C8
Bryn Meadow Cl NP22 6 C1
Brynmelyn Ave SA15 40 E6
Bryn-Melyn St SA1 68 D2
Bryn Melys CF31 168 B2
BRYNMENYN 150 F6
Brynmenyn Bsns Ctr CF32 150 F5
Brynmenyn Ind Est CF32 150 F6
Brynmenyn Prim Sch / Ysgol Gynradd Brynmenyn CF32 150 E6
BRYNMILL 94 E5
Brynmill Ave SA2 94 F5
Brynmill Cres SA2 94 F5
Brynmill La SA2 94 E5
Brynmill Prim Sch SA2 94 F5
Brynmill Terr SA2 94 E5
Bryn Milwr NP44 116 C8
Bryn Moreia CF44 28 E6
Bryn Morfa
Bridgend / Pen-y-Bont ar Ogwr CF31 168 F5
Swansea / Abertawe SA1 69 D5
Brynmorgrug SA8 24 A5
Bryn Morlais SA14 41 F6
Brynmorlais St 6 CF47 10 F4
Brynmor Rd SA15 40 C4
Brynmynach Ave CF82 84 E1
BRYNNA 153 C3
Bryn Nant
Caerphilly / Caerffili CF83 137 D6
Fochriw CF81 32 D8
Brynna Rd
Brynna CF35 153 B2
Cwmavon / Cwmafan SA12 99 D5
Llanharan CF72 153 E3
BRYNNAU GWYNION 153 B2
Brynnau Prim Sch / Ysgol Gynradd Brynnau CF72 153 D3
Bryn Nedd SA11 71 F5
Brynnewydd Gdns SA2 94 C5
Brynogwy Terr CF32 104 F5
Bryn Olwg CF37 109 E2
Bryn-Onen Terr 5 CF47 10 F4
Bryn Onnen
Penderyn CF44 224 D2
Pontardawe SA8 23 E5
Pyle / Y Pîl CF33 148 D2
Brynonnen Ct NP44 115 F8
Bryn Owain CF83 137 E6
Bryn Parc SA6 68 F7
Bryn Pica NP22 6 F1
Bryn Pinwydden CF23 178 E8
Bryn Pl 6 SA15 40 C4
Bryn Pobydd CF35 170 D8
Bryn Prim Sch
Bryn SA13 100 E5
Llanelli SA14 41 E6
Pontllanfraith NP12 85 D3
Bryn Rd
Abercarn NP11 87 B3
Blackwood / Coed-Duon NP12 85 D6
Bridgend / Pen-y-Bont ar Ogwr CF35 169 F4
Brynmenyn CF32 150 D6
Bryn NP12 85 E3
Clydach SA6 46 D8
Cwmllynfell SA9 221 B7
Glyncorrwg SA13 227 C2
Llanelli SA15 40 C4
Loughor SA4 42 F1
Markham NP12 58 D7
Neath / Castell-Nedd SA11 71 E6
Ogmore Vale CF32 130 E8
Pontarddulais SA4 19 B4
Pontllanfraith NP12 85 C4
Pontllanfraith NP12 85 C5
Pontlliw SA4 44 A8
Swansea / Abertawe, Brynmill SA2 94 F5
Swansea / Abertawe SA5 67 E3
Bryn Rd *continued*
Waunarlwydd SA5 66 E3
Ystradgynlais SA9 222 A5
Bryn Rd / Heol y Bryn SA14 218 D8
Bryn-Rhedyn
Blackwood / Coed-Duon NP12 85 D6
Caerphilly / Caerffili CF83 138 D4
Bryn Rhedyn
Church Village CF38 135 F2
Cwmbran / Cwmbrân NP44 117 B8
Pencoed CF35 170 C8
Pontypridd CF37 109 D6
Tonyrefail CF39 133 B5
Treherbert CF42 51 B1
Bryn Rhodfa CF42 78 D7
Bryn Rhos
Llanelli SA14 41 C6
Penywaun CF44 28 A6
Bryn Rhos Cres SA4 44 B2
Bryn Rhosog SA4 65 E8
Bryn Rhosyn
Radyr CF15 176 A7
Swansea / Abertawe SA6 45 C2
Tredegar NP22 6 B2
BRYNSADLER 172 F6
Bryn Seion Ct CF41 79 B2
Bryn-Seion St CF48 11 A4
Bryn Seion St NP22 12 D5
Bryn-Serth Rd NP23 7 A3
Brynsierfel SA14 41 C5
Brynsifi Way SA1 233 A4
Brynsiriol
Cimla SA11 72 C5
Gwaun-Cae-Gurwen SA18 220 D7
Hirwaun CF44 27 E8
Llanelli SA14 40 F7
Ton-mawr SA12 73 B5
Bryn Siriol
Caerphilly / Caerffili CF83 137 D5
Cymmer / Cymer SA13 75 E3
Pen-pedair-heol CF82 84 F7
Pentyrch CF15 175 C8
Swansea / Abertawe SA5 67 E3
Bryn St
Merthyr Tydfil / Merthyr Tudful CF47 30 F8
Swansea / Abertawe SA5 68 C4
Bryn-Syfi Terr SA1 233 A4
Bryntaf
Aberfan CF48 55 C4
Cefn Coed / Cefn-coed-y-cymmer CF48 10 A4
Bryntawe Hall Cl SA6 46 C5
Bryntawel Terr CF40 106 C7
Bryntawe Rd SA6 46 B5
BRYNTEG 155 F5
Brynteg
Abersychan NP4 37 F3
Capel Hendre SA18 218 E6
Cardiff / Caerdydd CF14 159 A1
Clydach SA6 46 D7
Heol-y-Cyw CF35 152 B4
Maesteg CF34 101 F2
Seven Sisters / Blaendulais SA10 222 C2
Treharris CF46 83 B7
Bryn Teg
Bargoed / Bargod CF81 57 F2
Bedwas CF83 138 E7
Briton Ferry / Llansawel SA11 71 B3
Caerphilly / Caerffili CF83 137 E5
Hengoed CF82 85 A3
Swansea / Abertawe SA7 70 A7
Brynteg Ave
Bridgend / Pen-y-Bont ar Ogwr CF31 168 F3
Pontllanfraith NP12 85 F4
Pyle / Y Pîl CF33 148 A1
Brynteg Cl CF23 178 C4
Brynteg Comp (Lower) Sch / Ysgol Gyfun Brynteg (Isaf) CF31 168 E2
Bryn Teg Com Prim Sch SA14 41 C4
Brynteg Comp (Upper) Sch / Ysgol Gyfun Brynteg (Uchaf) CF31 168 F2
Bryn-Teg Cres NP22 12 F3
Brynteg Ct CF38 156 A5
Brynteg Gdns CF31 168 F2
Brynteg Ho NP13 36 B6
Brynteg La CF38 156 A5
Brynteg Pl NP4 39 E3
Brynteg Rd
Blaina / Blaenau NP13 15 E4
Gorseinon SA4 43 B3
Brynteg St SA13 100 E5
Brynteg Terr
Ebbw Vale / Glyn Ebwy NP23 14 C8
Ferndale CF43 80 A4
Fochriw CF81 32 C7
Merthyr Vale / Ynysowen CF48 55 D5
New Tredegar NP24 33 F2
Tonypandy CF40 107 B4
Bryn-teg Terr 9 CF47 10 E1
Bryn-Teg Terr / Teras Brynteg 13 SA18 219 B7

Bryn Terr
Abertillery / Abertyleri, Brynithel NP13 ... 60 A7
Abertillery / Abertyleri NP13 ... 36 B8
Abertillery / Abertyleri, Six Bells NP13 ... 36 C2
Blaenavon NP4 ... 17 D6
Cefn Cribwr CF32 ... 149 B2
Cwmdare CF44 ... 28 C4
Ebbw Vale / Glyn Ebwy NP23 ... 14 F3
Gorseinon SA4 ... 43 D1
Hengoed CF82 ... 85 A3
1 Llanelli SA15 ... 40 C3
Llanelli, Seaside SA15 ... 40 C4
Llangynwyd CF34 ... 129 A6
Llantwit Fadre / Llanilltud Faerdref CF38 ... 156 D7
Maesteg CF34 ... 75 B2
Melincourt SA11 ... 226 C4
Merthyr Tydfil / Merthyr Tudful CF47 ... 11 A1
Pontsticill CF48 ... 3 F3
Pontyclun CF72 ... 172 F6
Pontygwaith CF43 ... 80 B2
Pontypool / Pont-y-pwl NP4 ... 61 F8
Porth CF39 ... 107 F3
Swansea / Abertawe SA1 ... 68 D3
The Mumbles / Y Mwmbwls SA3 ... 123 B4
Tonypandy CF40 ... 106 D6
4 Tonypandy, Dinas CF40 ... 107 A4
Wattstown CF39 ... 107 D8
Ystrad CF41 ... 79 C3
Bryn The
Bedwas CF83 ... 138 F6
Bettws NP20 ... 116 E3
Rhigos CF44 ... 26 C7
Swansea / Abertawe SA2 ... 94 C5
BRYNTIRION ... 168 A5
Bryntirion
Bedwas CF83 ... 138 E7
Caerphilly / Caerffili CF83 ... 137 E5
Cardiff / Caerdydd CF14 ... 177 C8
Llanelli SA15 ... 40 E6
Mountain Ash / Aberpennar CF45 ... 82 B6
Bryn Tirion SA6 ... 46 E8
Bryntirion Cl CF31 ... 168 C4
Bryntirion Comp Sch / Ysgol Gyfun Bryntirion CF31 ... 168 C7
Bryntirion (Evangelical Theological Coll of Wales) CF31 ... 168 B4
Bryn Tirion / Fairhill NP44 ... 89 B2
Bryntirion Hill CF31 ... 168 C4
Bryntirion Inf Sch CF31 ... 168 B5
Bryntirion Jun Sch CF31 ... 168 C5
Bryntirion Rd
Merthyr Tydfil / Merthyr Tudful CF47 ... 10 E1
Pontarddulais SA4 ... 19 F1
Pontlliw SA4 ... 44 A8
Bryntirion St CF48 ... 11 A5
Bryntirion Terr SA15 ... 40 F6
Bryn-tywod SA4 ... 45 A3
Bryn Varteg SA13 ... 100 F5
Bryn Vernel SA4 ... 42 E1
Bryn View
Bryn NP12 ... 85 D3
Nantyglo NP23 ... 8 D1
Brynview Ave CF82 ... 84 E1
Bryn View Cl SA3 ... 231 C8
Bryn Villas NP13 ... 15 D5
Bryn-Welon Cl NP4 ... 17 E6
Brynwern NP4 ... 62 B6
Brynwern St CF48 ... 11 B5
Bryn Wyndham Terr CF42 ... 50 E3
Bryn-y-Don Rd SA1 ... 233 A4
Bryn-y-Fran Ave CF83 ... 138 F6
Bryn Y Glyon CF62 ... 213 B1
Bryn Y Gors SA6 ... 45 B2
Brynygroes Cotts SA9 ... 1 F2
Bryn-y-Grug SA9 ... 2 A7
Bryn-y-Gwynt NP23 ... 14 B8
Bryn-y-Mor
St Athan / Sain Tathan CF62 ... 211 F3
Three Crosses SA4 ... 65 D1
Bryn-y-mor Cres SA2 ... 95 A6
Brynymor Rd SA4 ... 42 E2
Bryn-y-Mor Rd
Gowerton / Tre-gwyr SA4 ... 65 F6
Gowerton / Tre-gwyr SA4 ... 66 A5
Swansea / Abertawe SA1 ... 95 A6
Bryn-y-Nant CF23 ... 178 F5
Bryn-y-Pwll CF81 ... 58 B4
Bryn-yr-eglwys
Hendreforgan CF39 ... 132 C5
Pentyrch CF15 ... 175 C8
Bryn-yr-Orsaf CF33 ... 166 A8
Bryn Yr Ysgol CF83 ... 137 D6
Bryony Cl 3 CF47 ... 30 F8
Brython Dr CF3 ... 180 A7
Brytwn Rd SA13 ... 75 A5
B Sta Access Rd CF62 ... 211 E1
Buarth-y-Capel CF37 ... 81 E2
Buarth Y Ddera / The Rickyard SA10 ... 48 D3
Buccaneer Cl NP10 ... 163 F6
Buccaneer Gr NP10 ... 163 F6
Buccaneer Way NP10 ... 163 F6
Buchanan Way NP10 ... 163 B6
Buchan Cl NP20 ... 142 F2
Buckingham Cl CF14 ... 160 B2
Buckingham Cres 8 NP19 ... 143 F6
Buckingham Pl
Barry / Y Barri CF62 ... 214 C8
Newport / Casnewydd NP19 ... 143 F6
Buckingham Rd SA1 ... 69 A2
Buckland Dr CF41 ... 79 E2
Buckland Ho 5 CF47 ... 30 D8
Buckley Cl
Cardiff / Caerdydd CF5 ... 176 D3
Tonypandy CF40 ... 106 F7
Buckley Rd CF40 ... 106 F7
Bude Haven Terr SA3 ... 123 A6
Bude Terr NP12 ... 85 B6
Builth Cl NP10 ... 163 D5
Bull Cliff Wlk CF62 ... 214 A2
Buller St NP4 ... 61 E8
Bullfinch Rd CF62 ... 210 E6
Bull Hill CF32 ... 185 C2
Bullin's La SA1 ... 95 A7
Bullring CF72 ... 155 D4
Bulmore Rd NP18 ... 118 E2
Bulrush Cl CF3 ... 180 B6
Bungalow Ave CF36 ... 183 A7
Bungalows The
Abersychan NP4 ... 37 C7
Abertillery / Abertyleri NP13 ... 36 C4
Blaina / Blaenau NP13 ... 15 E4
Bridgend / Pen-y-Bont ar Ogwr CF31 ... 168 F6
Bridgend / Pen-y-Bont ar Ogwr, Tremains CF31 ... 169 A3
Cwmfelinfach NP11 ... 113 E3
Evanstown CF39 ... 132 B8
Ogmore Vale CF32 ... 130 E8
Pont-y-rhyl CF32 ... 130 A6
Ystrad Mynach CF82 ... 84 F2
Bungalow The SA3 ... 228 C2
Bunker's Hill SA3 ... 230 C6
Bunyan Cl CF3 ... 179 D8
BUPA Hospl Cardiff CF23 ... 160 F1
Burberry Cl NP10 ... 141 D7
Burford St / Stryd Burford 4 NP4 ... 17 C6
Burgesse Cres CF72 ... 155 D2
Burgess Pl CF11 ... 194 E3
Burgley Ct SA5 ... 67 E5
Burial La CF61 ... 209 F6
Burke Ave SA12 ... 124 E7
Burleigh Rd 2 NP20 ... 143 A4
Burley Pl CF62 ... 211 D7
Burlington St CF63 ... 215 B5
Burlington Terr CF5 ... 194 B7
Burman St SA1 ... 95 B7
Burnaby St CF24 ... 195 E6
Burne Jones Cl CF5 ... 176 E2
Burnet Dr
Blackwood / Coed-Duon NP12 ... 85 D5
Pen-pedair-heol CF82 ... 84 E6
Burnfort Rd NP20 ... 142 F3
Burnham Ave
Cardiff / Caerdydd CF3 ... 179 C7
Sully CF64 ... 216 B5
Burnham Ct 3 CF3 ... 179 C6
Burnham Dr SA3 ... 122 E6
Burns Cl
Machen CF83 ... 139 C6
Newport / Casnewydd NP20 ... 142 E1
Burns Cres
Barry / Y Barri CF62 ... 214 F8
Bridgend / Pen-y-Bont ar Ogwr CF31 ... 168 C6
Burnside SA11 ... 71 E5
Burns La / Lon Burns 4 NP44 ... 89 D2
Burns Rd SA12 ... 124 E7
Burns St CF44 ... 53 A4
Burn's Way CF37 ... 135 B6
Burnt Hollow / Pant Poeth CF31 ... 168 B3
Burreed Cl CF3 ... 180 B6
Burrows Chambers 1 SA1 ... 233 C2
Burrows Cl SA3 ... 121 A5
Burrows La SA3 ... 228 C3
Burrows Pl SA1 ... 233 B2
Burrows Rd
Neath / Castell-Nedd, Pentreffynnon SA10 ... 70 E6
12 Neath / Castell-Nedd SA11 ... 71 E6
Swansea / Abertawe SA1 ... 95 B5
Burrows Rd / Heol Burrows SA12 ... 98 D6
Burrows The CF36 ... 183 E7
BURRY ... 228 F1
BURRY GREEN ... 229 A2
Burry Pl SA4 ... 64 F4
Burry Rd SA15 ... 40 E1
Burry St SA15 ... 40 C3
BURTON ... 212 B4
Burton Homes NP20 ... 143 B3
Burton Rd NP19 ... 143 F8
Burton Terr CF62 ... 212 B2
Burt Pl 4 CF10 ... 195 B2
Burt St CF10 ... 195 B1
Burwell Cl CF23 ... 161 B1
Bush Bach NP22 ... 6 C2
Bush La NP4 ... 62 B6
Bush Rd
Mountain Ash / Aberpennar CF45 ... 54 E1
Swansea / Abertawe SA6 ... 46 A1
Bush Row SA11 ... 71 D5
Bush Terr NP4 ... 61 C4
Bushy Pk NP4 ... 62 A7
Bute Cres / Cilgant Bute CF10 ... 195 C2
Bute Espl CF10 ... 195 B1
Bute La CF64 ... 207 A4
Bute Pl
Abertillery / Abertyleri NP13 ... 59 E6
Hirwaun CF44 ... 27 C8
Bute Pl / Plas Bute CF10 ... 195 C2
Bute St / Stryd Bute CF10 ... 232 C1
Bute St
Aberdare / Aberdâr CF44 ... 29 A1
Tongwynlais CF15 ... 158 C1
Treherbert CF42 ... 78 D7
Bute Terr
Aberdare / Aberdâr CF44 ... 29 B1
Cardiff / Caerdydd CF10 ... 232 C2
Hirwaun CF44 ... 27 C8
New Tredegar NP24 ... 58 A7
BUTETOWN ... 195 B3
BUTE TOWN ... 12 D7
Butleigh Ave CF5 ... 194 A7
Butleigh Terr NP22 ... 6 E1
Butler's Ct NP4 ... 37 E6
Butterbur Pl CF5 ... 193 A5
Buttercup Cl NP10 ... 141 D7
Buttercup Ct
Cwmbran / Cwmbrân NP44 ... 88 F1
The Mumbles / Y Mwmbwls SA3 ... 122 E6
Butterfield Dr CF23 ... 160 E1
Butterfly Cl CF38 ... 156 F8
Buttermere Way 3 NP19 ... 143 F8
Butterslade Gr SA6 ... 46 A4
Butterworth Cl NP19 ... 144 E5
Butt Lee Ct CF62 ... 214 E5
Button Ride CF5 ... 204 A8
Buttrills Cl CF62 ... 214 E5
Buttrills Rd CF62 ... 214 E5
Buttrills Wlk CF62 ... 214 E6
Buttry Terr NP12 ... 85 B5
Butts The CF71 ... 188 E2
Buxton Cl NP20 ... 142 F1
Buxton Ct CF83 ... 138 C3
Buzzard Way CF82 ... 84 E3
Bwlch Carnygelli CF46 ... 111 A7
Bwlch Cres SA11 ... 72 A4
Bwlch Rd
Cardiff / Caerdydd CF5 ... 193 D7
Loughor SA4 ... 42 E2
Neath / Castell-Nedd SA11 ... 72 A4
Bwlch-y-Clawdd Rd
Nant-y-Moel CF32 ... 104 F6
Treorchy / Treorci CF32, CF42 ... 77 F2
Bwlch-y-Garn Rd NP23 ... 7 E1
Bwlch Y Gwyn SA5 ... 20 E2
Bwllfa Cotts CF41 ... 79 A2
Bwllfa Dare Terr CF44 ... 28 A2
Bwllfa Rd
Cwmdare CF44 ... 28 B3
Ynystawe SA6 ... 46 C5
Bwl Rd CF46 ... 83 D4
Bwrw Rd SA4 ... 65 D8
Byass St SA13 ... 125 E3
BYEASTWOOD ... 169 D8
BYNEA ... 41 F3
Bynea Prim Sch / Ysgol Gynradd Bynea SA14 ... 41 F3
Bynea Sta SA14 ... 41 F3
Byng Morris Cl SA2 ... 94 B5
Byng St SA1 ... 68 D4
By Pass Rd
Bridgend / Pen-y-Bont ar Ogwr CF31, CF32 ... 168 D2
Laleston / Trelales CF32 ... 167 E3
Byrd Cres CF64 ... 206 E1
Byrde Cl NP19 ... 144 C5
Byron Ave
Beddau CF38 ... 156 A5
Bridgend / Pen-y-Bont ar Ogwr CF31 ... 168 C6
Byron Ct
Llantwit Major / Llanilltud Fawr CF61 ... 210 B5
Penarth CF64 ... 206 F5
Byron Ho SA12 ... 124 D7
Byron Pl
Blackwood / Coed Duon NP11 ... 59 D1
5 Cwmbran / Cwmbrân NP44 ... 89 D2
Penarth CF64 ... 206 F4
Byron Rd
Aberbargoed / Aberbargod CF81 ... 58 B3
Byron Rd *continued*
Newport / Casnewydd NP20 ... 142 F2
Byron St
3 Barry / Y Barri CF62 ... 214 F5
Cardiff / Caerdydd CF24 ... 232 D4
Cwmaman CF44 ... 53 A4
Byron Way SA2 ... 93 F8
Bythway Rd NP4 ... 38 B1
Bythynnod Y Llew Gwyn / White Lion Cotts NP22 ... 6 C2
Bythynod Ynys-Arwed / Ynys-arwed Cotts SA11 ... 226 B4
Bywater Row NP13 ... 36 B5
Byways NP44 ... 89 B3
By-Ways Ct CF35 ... 169 F3

C

Caban Cl NP10 ... 142 B7
Caban Isaac Rd SA4 ... 64 F3
Caddick's Row NP13 ... 15 E6
Cader Idris Cl NP11 ... 115 C2
Cadfan Rd SA1 ... 95 A8
Cadlan Bethel CF48 ... 10 C1
CADLE ... 67 D7
Cadle Cl SA5 ... 67 E6
Cadle Cres SA5 ... 67 D5
Cadle Dell Pl SA5 ... 67 E6
Cadle Mill SA5 ... 67 C7
Cadle Pl SA5 ... 67 E6
Cadle Prim Sch SA5 ... 67 D5
Cadle-Wood Rd SA5 ... 67 E6
Cadman Cl CF24 ... 196 A7
Cadnant Cl CF14 ... 159 D1
Cadnant Rd SA5 ... 68 A5
Cadoc Cres CF63 ... 215 D6
Cadoc Pl CF5 ... 176 E3
Cadoc Rd 5 NP44 ... 89 C6
Cadogan Cl CF41 ... 79 D3
Cadogan Ct 3 CF24 ... 195 A8
Cadogan St CF32 ... 104 F5
CADOXTON ... 215 B7
Cadoxton Com Prim Sch CF63 ... 215 B7
CADOXTON-JUXTA-NEATH / LLANGATWG ... 49 B3
Cadoxton Rd SA10 ... 71 D8
Cadoxton Sta CF63 ... 215 C6
Cadoxton Terr SA10 ... 49 A2
Cadrawd Rd SA1 ... 68 B1
Cadvan Rd CF5 ... 193 B6
Cadwaladr Cir 4 SA1 ... 95 B8
Cadwaladr St CF45 ... 54 C3
Cadwgan Pl 2 CF5 ... 193 E7
Cadwgan Rd
Craig-cefn-parc SA6 ... 22 B2
Treorchy / Treorci CF42 ... 78 E6
Cadwgan Terr CF37 ... 108 C2
Caeau Duon CF35 ... 152 E1
Cae Bach
Llangeinor CF32 ... 130 A3
Machen CF83 ... 139 E7
Caebach Cl CF5 ... 192 F3
Cae Banc SA2 ... 94 D7
Cae Bedw CF83 ... 137 F7
Cae Berllan / Orchard Pl 9 NP44 ... 89 D2
Cae Bracla CF31 ... 169 B5
Cae Brandi CF3 ... 180 E8
Cae-Bricks Rd SA5 ... 68 B2
Cae Bron CF31 ... 169 B4
Cae-Bryn CF83 ... 137 A7
Cae Bryn CF31 ... 168 C4
Cae-Bryn Ave SA2 ... 94 C5
Cae Bryn Hyfryd CF44 ... 27 C8
Cae Brynton Rd NP20 ... 143 A2
Cae Cadno CF38 ... 135 D1
Cae Calch CF83 ... 137 F6
Cae Canol
Baglan SA12 ... 98 E7
Hengoed CF82 ... 85 A3
Penarth CF64 ... 206 E1
Cae Caradog CF83 ... 137 D6
Cae Castell SA4 ... 65 D8
Cae Celyn NP11 ... 59 D1
Caecerrig Rd SA4 ... 19 D4
Cae Coed CF35 ... 152 B5
Cae-Coed-Erw CF31 ... 169 B5
Cae Collen NP12 ... 85 D6
Caeconna Rd SA5 ... 67 E5
Cae Cotton SA14 ... 40 F6
Cae Croes Heol CF83 ... 137 D1
Cae Crug SA6 ... 45 B1
Cae Crwn SA2 ... 93 E8
Caedegar Rd SA9 ... 1 F2
Cae Delyn Cl SA15 ... 40 B7
Caedelyn Rd CF14 ... 177 A6
Cae Derw SA10 ... 48 C2
Cae Derwen NP44 ... 89 D1
Cae Derwen / Oak Field CF31 ... 169 A8
Caederwen Rd SA11 ... 71 F5
CAE-DRAW ... 30 D8
Caedraw Prim Sch / Ysgol Gynradd Cae-draw CF47 ... 30 D8
Caedraw Rd CF47 ... 30 D8
Cae Dre St CF31 ... 168 E4
Cae Drwm / Drumfields SA10 ... 49 A2
Cae-Du-Bach 1 SA15 ... 40 E6
Cae Du Mawr CF83 ... 137 F6
Caedu Rd
Cwmllynfell SA9 ... 221 B7
Ogmore Vale CF32 ... 104 E1
Cae Eithin SA6 ... 45 B2
Cae Fardre CF38 ... 135 F1
Cae Felin Parc CF44 ... 27 E7
Cae Felin St NP13 ... 60 A6
Caeffatri Cl / Clos Caeffatri 1 CF31 ... 168 F6
Cae Ffynnon
Bridgend / Pen-y-Bont ar Ogwr CF31 ... 169 B5
Caerphilly / Caerffili CF83 ... 137 E6
Church Village CF38 ... 135 E2
Penybryn CF82 ... 84 D5
Cae Folland SA4 ... 64 E4
Cae Ganol CF36 ... 165 E2
Cae Gar SA14 ... 41 E5
Cae Garn CF35 ... 152 B6
Cae Garw
Cardiff / Caerdydd CF14 ... 159 D2
Dinas Powis / Dinas Powys CF64 ... 206 A2
Cae Garw Bach CF5 ... 175 E4
Cae Garw Cvn Site CF33 ... 148 A4
Caegarw Prim Sch CF45 ... 54 D3
Cae Gethin CF83 ... 137 F6
Caeglas
Cross Hands SA14 ... 218 B7
Cwmavon / Cwmafan SA12 ... 99 D4
Llanelli SA14 ... 40 F8
Cae Glas
Barry / Y Barri CF63 ... 215 B7
Caerphilly / Caerffili CF83 ... 137 E5
Ewenny / Ewenni CF35 ... 185 E7
Fochriw CF81 ... 32 C8
Gorseinon SA4 ... 43 C2
Nantyglo NP23 ... 15 D8
Pencoed CF35 ... 170 E7
Tonypandy CF40 ... 107 A2
Caeglas Ave CF3 ... 179 B3
Cae-glas Rd CF3 ... 179 C3
Cae Gorlan Ct NP11 ... 87 A3
Cae Gorlan St NP11 ... 87 B3
Cae Grawn SA4 ... 66 B5
Cae-groes Terr SA10 ... 48 F2
Caegwenith Cl SA11 ... 49 B1
Cae Gwyn CF64 ... 206 E2
Cae Gwyn Rd CF14 ... 177 C5
Cae-Gwyn Rd SA4 ... 19 D4
CAE-HOPKIN ... 222 D7
Caehopkin Cty Prim Sch SA9 ... 222 D7
Cae-is-Maen SA8 ... 23 C3
Caelbryn Terr CF32 ... 150 D6
Cae Leon CF62 ... 204 F1
Cae Lewis CF15 ... 158 C1
Cae Llwyd CF83 ... 138 B5
Cae Llwydcoed / Greywood Field CF31 ... 168 A2
Cae Llwyndu CF46 ... 83 E3
Cae Lynch SA10 ... 70 F6
Caemaen SA10 ... 48 B7
Cae Maen CF14 ... 177 D4
Cae Maen Llwyd CF82 ... 84 E5
Caemaen St CF45 ... 82 C5
Caemansel La SA4 ... 66 A3
Caemansel Rd SA4 ... 66 A4
Cae Mansel Rd SA4 ... 65 F3
Cae Marchog CF83 ... 137 F6
Cae Mari Dwn CF47 ... 10 E1
CAE-MAWR ... 45 E1
Caemawr SA18 ... 219 C6
Cae Mawr SA10 ... 222 D3
Caemawr Gdns CF39 ... 107 E3
Cae Mawr Ind Est / Ystad Ddiwydiannol Cae Mawr CF42 ... 78 E5
Caemawr Rd
Porth CF39 ... 107 E3
Swansea / Abertawe SA6 ... 68 E8
Cae Mawr Rd CF14 ... 177 C7
Caemawr Terr CF40 ... 107 A1
Cae Meillion CF83 ... 137 E2
Cae Melin NP4 ... 39 E3
Cae Melyn
Ebbw Vale / Glyn Ebwy NP23 ... 7 C2
Hengoed CF82 ... 85 A3
Swansea / Abertawe SA6 ... 45 C1
Cae Morfa Rd / Heol Cae Morfa SA12 ... 98 C2
Cae-Nan SA6 ... 46 B3
Caenant 1 CF37 ... 135 F6
Cae Nant Gledyr CF83 ... 137 D3
Cae Nant Goch CF83 ... 137 D1
Caenant Rd CF83 ... 138 A4
Caenant Terr SA10 ... 70 F7
Caenewydd Cl CF5 ... 192 F3
Cae Odin CF31 ... 169 B5
Caepalish Pl NP4 ... 62 A8
Cae Pandy CF83 ... 138 B5
Cae Pant CF83 ... 137 F6
CAE-PANT-TYWLL ... 10 D2
CAE PANT-Y-DUGOED ... 46 F7
Cae Penpant SA6 ... 45 B2
Cae Pentice CF32 ... 149 A2
Cae Pen-y-Graig CF83 ... 137 E7

Cae Pen Y Waun CF82 .... 85 A3
Cae Perllan CF31 .... 169 B5
Cae Perllan Rd NP20 .... 143 A3
Caepistyll St SA1 .... 68 D1
Cae-Pys Rd SA5 .... 68 C5
CAERACCA 11 B7
Caeracca Villas CF48 ..... 11 B6
CAERAU
Cardiff 193 D3
Maesteg 75 B1
Caerau Com Inf Sch
CF5 .... 193 C3
Caerau Court Rd CF5 ..... 193 C4
Caerau Cres NP20 .... 143 A4
Caerau Ct CF72 .... 155 F3
Caerau La
Cardiff / Caerdydd
CF5 .... 193 B2
Pentyrch CF15 .... 175 D8
Wenvoe / Gwenfo CF5 ... 205 A8
CAERAU PARK 142 F4
Caerau Park Cres CF5 ... 193 C4
Caerau Park Pl 2 CF5 .. 193 C4
Caerau Park Rd CF5 ..... 193 C4
Caerau Rd
Cardiff / Caerdydd
CF5 .... 193 C4
Maesteg CF34 .... 75 B1
Newport / Casnewydd
NP20 .... 143 A4
Cae'r Berllan CF35 ...... 152 F1
CAE'R-BONT 222 B6
Caerbont Ent Pk / Parc
Manter Caerbont
SA9 .... 222 B6
Caerbragdy CF83 .... 138 B3
CAE'R-BRYN 218 E8
Caerbryn NP11 .... 86 D5
Cae'r Bryn Rd / Heol Caer
Bryn SA14, SA18 .... 218 E8
Cae'r-Bryn Terr SA18 ... 218 E8
Caer Cady Cl CF23 ...... 178 C4
Caer Castell Pl CF3 ..... 179 D5
Caer Ceffyl CF5 .... 175 E5
Cae'r Cynffig CF33 ...... 166 A8
CAERDYDD /
CARDIFF 232 A3
Caer Efail CF5 .... 175 E5
Cae'r Efail CF35 .... 152 E1
Caer Eglwys Nature Trail*
CF61 .... 208 D5
CAER-EITHIN 67 F5
Cae Rex CF71 .... 188 E1
Cae'r Fferm CF83 .... 137 E3
CAERFFILI /
CAERPHILLY 138 D3
Caer Ffynnon CF62 ...... 214 C3
Cae'r Gelynnen CF46 ..... 83 E3
Cae'r Gerddi CF38 ...... 135 E1
Cae'r Graig CF15 .... 176 B7
Cae'rgwerlas CF39 ...... 133 A5
Caer Gymrig CF34 .... 102 D2
Caer-Gynydd Rd SA5 ..... 66 F3
Cae Rhedyn NP44 .... 90 B4
Cae Rhedyn / Fern Field
SA8 .... 24 C3
Caerhendy St CF47 .... 10 F4
Cae'r Hen Eglwys
CF31 .... 168 C6
Cae Rhos
Caerphilly / Caerffili
CF83 .... 138 B5
Llanelli SA14 .... 41 C6
Cae Rhys Ddu SA11 ...... 72 A5
CAE'R-LAN 222 B7
CAERLEON /
CAERLLION 118 C4
Caerleon Cl CF3 .... 180 A7
Caerleon Comp Sch
NP18 .... 118 A2
Caerleon Ct CF83 .... 137 C4
Caerleon Endowed Jun &
Inf Sch NP18 .... 118 B2
Caerleon Gr CF48 .... 225 F1
Caerleon (Lodge Hill) Inf
Sch NP18 .... 118 A3
Caerleon (Lodge Hill) Jun
Sch NP18 .... 117 F3
Caerleon Rd
Caerleon / Caerllion
NP18 .... 118 A5
Cardiff / Caerdydd
CF14 .... 177 D2
Dinas Powis / Dinas Powys
CF64 .... 206 C4
Newport / Casnewydd
NP19 .... 143 F8
Ponthir NP18, NP44 ..... 117 E7
Caerlicken La NP18 ..... 119 F5
CAERLLION /
CAERLEON 118 C4
Cae'r-llwyn Terr NP11 .. 112 F7
Caerllysi CF35 .... 170 B8
Caer Mead Cl CF61 ...... 210 B6
Caernarvon Cl 2
CF64 .... 206 C3
Caernarvon Cres / Cilgant
Caernarfon NP44 .... 90 A3
Caernarvon Ct
Caerphilly / Caerffili
CF83 .... 137 D4
2 Cardiff / Caerdydd
CF11 .... 194 D7
Caernarvon Dr NP10 .... 141 F3
Caernarvon Gdns
CF62 .... 214 E8
Caernarvon Gr CF48 ..... 225 F1
Caernarvon Pl NP12 ...... 58 D1
Caernarvon Rd NP10 .... 141 E3
Caernarvon Way
Cardiff / Caerdydd
CF3 .... 179 D5
Swansea / Abertawe SA1 .. 69 B4
Caer Newydd CF31 ...... 169 D5
Cae Robin NP7 .... 9 E6
Cae'r-Odyn NP13 .... 15 D5
Cae'r Odyn CF64 .... 206 A2
Cae Rowland St SA5 ..... 68 B3
Caerphilly Ave SA1 ...... 69 C4
Caerphilly Bsns Pk
CF83 .... 138 C2
CAERPHILLY /
CAERFFILI 138 D3
Caerphilly Castle*
CF83 .... 138 B3
Caerphilly Cl
Bassaleg NP10 .... 141 E3
Dinas Powis / Dinas Powys
CF64 .... 206 C4
Caerphilly & District
Miners Hospl CF83 ..... 137 F1
Caerphilly Rd
Bassaleg NP10 .... 141 E3
Cardiff / Caerdydd
CF14 .... 177 D5
Nantgarw CF15 .... 157 F7
Nantgarw CF15 .... 158 A7
Nantgarw CF15 .... 158 B8
Nelson CF46 .... 83 F3
Quakers Yard CF46 .... 83 B5
Senghenydd CF83 .... 110 F1
Tredomen CF46 .... 84 A3
Ystrad Mynach CF82 ..... 111 F8
Caerphilly Sta CF83 ..... 138 B2
Cae'r Rhedyn CF71 ...... 188 B8
Caersalem Terr / Teras
Caersalem 2 SA15 ..... 40 D3
Caer Salen Newydd
CF39 .... 107 E2
Caer St SA1 .... 233 B3
Caer Ty Clwyd CF61 ..... 209 F7
Caer Wenallt CF14 ...... 176 F8
Caerwent Rd
Cardiff / Caerdydd
CF5 .... 193 A5
Croesyceiliog NP44 ...... 90 A6
Caerwent Rd / Heol
Caerwent NP4 .... 38 D1
Cae'r Wern CF48 .... 30 D8
Caer Wetral CF33 .... 148 C2
Caer Worgan CF61 ...... 209 F7
Cae'r Ysgol SA10 .... 49 B4
Cae Samson 1 CF5 ..... 193 C4
Caesar Cres NP18 .... 118 A4
Cae Serth / Streepfield 7
NP44 .... 90 A6
Cae Sheldon NP11 .... 86 C5
Cae Siriol CF39 .... 107 E6
Cae Siwsan CF31 .... 169 B5
Cae Stumpie CF71 .... 188 F1
Cae Syr Dafydd CF11 .... 194 C7
Cae Talcen CF35 .... 152 F1
Cae Terr SA15 .... 40 F5
Cae Ty Mawr CF14 .... 176 E4
Cae Uwchllyn CF83 ...... 137 E1
Caewallis St CF31 .... 168 F3
Caewal Rd CF5 .... 194 A8
Cae Yorath 8 CF14 ..... 177 B5
Cae-yr-Ebol NP44 .... 89 E5
Cae Ysgubor
Bridgend / Pen-y-Bont ar
Ogwr CF31 .... 169 B4
Caerphilly / Caerffili
CF83 .... 137 E7
Cefn Hengoed CF82 .... 84 E5
Cafn Y Felin / Mill Race
SA10 .... 71 B8
Caiach Terr CF46 .... 83 D6
Cairn Ct CF43 .... 52 B1
Cairnmuir Rd CF24 ...... 195 F7
Cairo St CF40 .... 107 B5
Calais Ho 22 CF10 ...... 195 B2
Calcot Ho NP44 .... 90 B4
Calderton Rd CF38 ...... 156 A6
Caldey Pl SA5 .... 67 E7
Caldicot Cl
Blackwood / Coed-Duon
NP12 .... 58 D1
Swansea / Abertawe SA1 .. 69 C4
Caldicot Ct CF83 .... 137 D4
Caldicot Rd
Cardiff / Caerdydd
CF5 .... 193 D4
Swansea / Abertawe SA1 .. 69 C4
Caldicot St NP19 .... 143 F4
Caldicott Cl 6 CF38 .... 156 A5
Caldicot Way / Ffordd
Caldicott NP44 .... 89 F6
Caldwell Cl CF38 .... 156 A5
Caldy Cl
Barry / Y Barri CF62 .... 214 F8
Newport / Casnewydd
NP19 .... 143 F7
Porthcawl CF36 .... 165 E1
Caldy Ct CF14 .... 177 A3
Caldy Rd CF14 .... 177 A3
Caledfryn Way CF83 ..... 137 D5
Calfaria Chapel Ho
CF39 .... 107 D8
Calfaria Flats CF45 ...... 82 E3
Callaghan Ct CF24 ...... 195 E6
Callaghan Sq / Sgwar
Callaghan CF10 .... 232 C1
Calland St SA6 .... 68 E5
Calluna Cl / Clos Y Grug
CF48 .... 11 C4
Calvert Terr 4 SA1 ...... 95 B7
Cambell Ct CF63 .... 215 A4
Camberwell Ave CF31 ... 168 C6
Cambourne Ave CF14 ... 176 F5
Cambourne Cl CF62 ..... 214 C7
Cambray Cl CF36 .... 182 E8
Cambria CF11 .... 206 F6
Cambria Cl NP18 .... 118 C2
Cambrian Ave
Hendreforgan CF39 ..... 132 C5
Llantwit Major / Llanilltud
Fawr CF61 .... 210 A5
Cambrian Cl CF3 .... 162 E1
Cambrian Cres CF3 ..... 162 E1
Cambrian Ct
Barry / Y Barri CF63 .... 215 A5
Swansea / Abertawe SA6 .. 69 A7
Cambrian Dr CF3 .... 162 E1
Cambrian Gdns CF3 ..... 162 E1
Cambrian Gr CF3 .... 162 E1
Cambrian Ind Est
CF72 .... 173 A8
Cambrian Ind Pk / Parc
Ddiwydiannol Cambrian
CF40 .... 106 C6
Cambrian Pl
Cwm-twrch Uchaf SA9 .... 221 C6
5 Llanelli SA15 .... 40 C4
Pontarddulais SA4 .... 19 C4
1 Pontypridd CF37 ...... 135 E7
Port Talbot SA13 .... 125 C7
Swansea / Abertawe
SA1 .... 233 C2
Cambrian Point CF24 .... 177 F1
Cambrian Rd NP20 ...... 143 B5
Cambrian Residential Pk
CF5 .... 193 A2
Cambrian Ret Ctr 4
NP20 .... 143 B5
Cambrian St
Deri CF81 .... 57 B8
Llanelli SA15 .... 40 C4
12 Merthyr Tydfil / Merthyr
Tudful CF47 .... 10 D2
Rhymney / Rhymni NP22 ... 12 E5
Cambrian Terr
Merthyr Tydfil / Merthyr
Tudful CF47 .... 10 D3
Tonypandy CF40 .... 106 E7
Cambrian Way CF3 ...... 162 E1
Cambria Rd CF5 .... 193 B4
Cambria St NP4 .... 62 E2
Cambridge Cl SA3 ...... 123 A4
Cambridge Ct NP18 ..... 117 F3
Cambridge Gdns
Ebbw Vale / Glyn Ebwy
NP23 .... 7 D3
The Mumbles / Y Mwmbwls
SA3 .... 123 B4
Cambridge Rd
Newport / Casnewydd
NP19 .... 143 D5
The Mumbles / Y Mwmbwls
SA3 .... 123 A4
Cambridge St
Barry / Y Barri CF62 ..... 214 C3
Cardiff / Caerdydd CF11 .. 195 A2
Swansea / Abertawe SA2 .. 94 F7
Cam Ct NP44 .... 89 A5
Camellia Ave NP10 ...... 141 D7
Camellia Cl CF44 .... 28 D3
Camellia Dr SA6 .... 45 F3
Camelot Ct NP18 .... 118 C2
Camelot Pl 5 NP19 ..... 143 D6
Camelot Way CF14 ...... 159 D2
Cameron Pl SA4 .... 43 A2
Cameron St CF24 .... 195 E7
Camffrwd Way SA6 ...... 46 C1
Camm's Cnr 8 CF64 .... 206 C3
Camnant CF82 .... 111 E7
Camnant Rd SA10 .... 223 A5
Camona Dr SA1 .... 233 B1
Campanula Dr NP10 ..... 141 D7
Campbell Dr CF11 .... 207 A8
Campbell St
Llanelli SA15 .... 40 E2
Pontypool / Pont-y-pwl
NP4 .... 62 A7
Swansea / Abertawe
SA1 .... 233 A4
Campbell Terr
Mountain Ash / Aberpennar
CF45 .... 54 D3
Tonypandy CF40 .... 106 E7
Camperdown Rd NP19 .. 144 B3
Camperly Cl 7 CF38 .... 156 A5
Campion Cl
Cwmbran / Cwmbrân
NP44 .... 116 A8
Newport / Casnewydd
NP20 .... 143 A6
Campion Pl CF5 .... 176 D2
Campton Pl CF38 .... 156 B5
Camrose Ct CF62 .... 214 F8
Camrose Dr SA5 .... 66 E3
Camrose Rd CF5 .... 193 D4
Camrose Wlk 3 NP44 .... 89 C2
Canada Rd CF14 .... 177 E2
Canal Cl NP4 .... 62 E2
Canal Lock Cl CF48 ...... 55 C3
Canal Par
Cardiff / Caerdydd
CF10 .... 195 B3
Canal Par *continued*
Newport / Casnewydd
NP20 .... 143 D4
Canal Park Ind Est
CF10 .... 195 B3
Canal Pl SA11 .... 223 D1
Canal Rd
Abercwmboi CF44 .... 53 F6
Aberdare / Aberdâr CF44 .. 53 E8
Neath / Castell-Nedd
SA11 .... 71 D7
Canal Row CF48 .... 30 F4
Canal Side SA10 .... 49 C3
Canal St NP20 .... 143 B7
Canal Terr
Abercarn NP11 .... 87 A2
Newport / Casnewydd
NP20 .... 143 D3
Ystalyfera SA9 .... 2 B6
Canaston Ct SA5 .... 67 F7
Canaston Pl CF5 .... 193 D4
Canberra Cl
Blackwood / Coed-Duon
NP12 .... 85 F8
Cwmbran / Cwmbrân
NP44 .... 89 D2
Canberra Cres NP20 .... 142 E4
Canberra Rd CF31 ...... 168 F5
Candleston Cl / Clos
Tregantllo CF36 .... 165 E2
Candlestone Newydd /
New Candlestone
CF31 .... 168 B3
Candleston Pl SA1 .... 69 C3
Candwr Pk NP18 .... 117 F7
Candwr Rd NP18 .... 118 A6
Canford Cl NP4 .... 38 B2
Cannes Ho 18 CF10 ..... 195 B2
Canning St
Cwm NP23 .... 35 A8
Treorchy / Treorci CF41 .... 78 F3
Cannington Ave CF3 .... 179 C5
Cannington Cl CF64 ..... 216 B5
Cannisland Pk SA3 .... 92 D1
Cannon St / Stryd Cannon
SA18 .... 220 D8

Canolfan = centre

Canolfan
Bridgend / Pen-y-Bont ar
Ogwr CF31 .... 169 B4
Seven Sisters / Blaendulais
SA10 .... 222 C3
Canolfan Criced
Genedlaethol / Sophia
Gdns Glamorgan CCC
CF11 .... 194 E7
Canolfan Fenter
Tonypandy / Tonypandy
Ent Ctr CF40 .... 106 E7
Canolfan Mileniwm Cymru /
Wales Millennium Ctr
CF10 .... 195 C2
Canolfan Technoleg /
Techno Ctr CF24 .... 195 D4
Canonbie Cres / Cilgant
Canonbie CF48 .... 55 C3
Canon St
Aberdare / Aberdâr
CF44 .... 29 A2
Barry / Y Barri CF62 .... 214 D3
Newport / Casnewydd
NP19 .... 143 D6
Canopus Cl CF3 .... 179 D6
Canterbury Cl 9
NP20 .... 143 C6
Canterbury Rd
Ebbw Vale / Glyn Ebwy
NP23 .... 7 F3
Swansea / Abertawe SA2 .. 94 E5
CANTON 194 D6
Canton Ct 2 CF11 ...... 194 E5
Cantonian High Sch
CF5 .... 193 E8
Cantref Cl
Cardiff / Caerdydd
CF14 .... 159 F3
Rogerstone NP10 .... 142 B7
Cantref Ct SA5 .... 67 E5
Can-Yr-Aderyn SA6 ...... 45 D2
Can-Yr-Eos SA6 .... 45 E2
Capcoch Prim Sch / Ysgol
Gynradd Capcoch
CF44 .... 53 E5
CAPEL 41 A6
Capel Bldgs SA6 .... 46 E7
Capel Cres NP20 .... 143 C2
Capel Ct 16 NP4 .... 38 A1
Capel Edeyrn CF23 ..... 179 B8
Capel Ed La / Lon Capel
Ed NP4 .... 39 E7
Capel Farm CF39 .... 133 D5
Capel Gwilym Rd
CF14 .... 159 D4
CAPEL HENDRE 218 E6
Capel Hendre Ind Est
SA18 .... 218 E5
Capel Ifan CF39 .... 133 D5
Capel Isaf Rd SA15 ...... 41 A6
CAPEL LLANILLTERN 175 A4
Capel Newydd Ave NP4 ... 17 D5
Capel Newydd / Cross Rd
SA15 .... 40 D6
Capel-Newydd La SA15 .. 40 D6
Capel Newydd Rd 3
NP4 .... 17 D6
Capel Rd
Clydach SA6 .... 46 F8
Llanelli SA14 .... 41 A6
Capel Road Workshops
SA6 .... 46 F8
Capel St
Bargoed / Bargod CF81 ... 58 A4
Pontypool / Pont-y-pwl
NP4 .... 62 C6
Capel Terr SA15 .... 40 F6
Capital Bldgs SA9 .... 2 C7
Capital Bsns Pk CF3 .... 179 D2
Capital Valley Ind Pk
NP22 .... 12 E2
Capitol Sh Ctr CF10 ..... 232 C3
Caple Rd CF62 .... 214 C3
Capstan Ho SA1 .... 95 B5
Captains Hill CF46 .... 83 C7
Caradoc Ave CF63 ...... 215 A7
Caradoc Cl 1 CF3 ...... 180 A7
Caradoc Rd
Cwmbran / Cwmbrân
NP44 .... 89 E4
Mountain Ash / Aberpennar
CF45 .... 54 D2
Caradoc St
Abercarn NP11 .... 114 C7
Abersychan NP4 .... 37 F3
Merthyr Tydfil / Merthyr Tudful
CF47 .... 10 D2
Mountain Ash / Aberpennar
CF45 .... 54 D2
Caradoc Wlk 10 NP4 ..... 17 D7
Caradog Cl
Bridgend / Pen-y-Bont ar
Ogwr CF31 .... 169 A5
Caerleon / Caerllion
NP18 .... 118 A3
Caradog Ho
Cardiff / Caerdydd
CF10 .... 232 C3
Newport / Casnewydd
NP10 .... 163 C7
Caradog Pl SA1 .... 95 A8
Caradog Prim Sch CF44 .. 29 A1
Caradog Rd
Bridgend / Pen-y-Bont ar
Ogwr CF31 .... 169 D3
Tylorstown CF43 .... 80 B3
Caradog St SA13 .... 125 D7
Caraway Cl 14 CF3 ..... 180 A8
Cardiff Arms Park
CF10 .... 232 A2
Cardiff Bay Barrage Visitor
Ctr* CF10 .... 207 C6
Cardiff Bay Bsns Ctr
CF24 .... 195 D4
Cardiff Bay Ret Pk / Parc
Manwerthu Bae Caerdydd
Cardiff / Caerdydd
CF11 .... 194 F1
Cardiff / Caerdydd CF11 .. 206 F8
Cardiff Bay Sta CF10 .... 195 C2
Cardiff Bay Visitor Ctr*
CF10 .... 195 C1
Cardiff Bsns Pk CF14 .... 177 E7
Cardiff Bsns Tech Ctr
CF24 .... 232 B4
CARDIFF /
CAERDYDD 232 A3
Cardiff Castle* CF10 .... 232 B3
Cardiff Central Sta
CF10 .... 232 B1
Cardiff Centre Trad Est
CF10 .... 232 C1
Cardiff City Farm / Fferm
Dinas Caerdydd
CF11 .... 194 C3
Cardiff City Hall CF10 ... 232 B3
Cardiff County Hall
CF10 .... 195 C3
Cardiff Gate Bsns Pk
CF23 .... 161 A2
Cardiff Gate Ret Pk
CF23 .... 161 B2
Cardiff High Sch CF23 ... 178 B6
Cardiff Ind Pk CF14 ..... 177 E7
Cardiff International
Airport / Maes Awyr
Caerdydd-Cymru
CF62 .... 213 B3
Cardiff International Arena
CF10 .... 232 C2
Cardiff Pl CF42 .... 78 D6
Cardiff Rd
Abercynon CF45 .... 82 D1
Aberdare / Aberdâr CF44 .. 53 C7
Bargoed / Bargod CF81 ... 58 A3
Barry / Y Barri CF63 ..... 215 E6
Caerphilly / Caerffili
CF83 .... 138 B2
Cardiff / Caerdydd CF5 .. 194 B8
Cowbridge / Y Bont-Faen
CF71 .... 189 A1
Creigiau CF15 .... 174 F6
Dinas Powis / Dinas Powys
CF64 .... 206 A3
Edwardsville CF46 .... 82 E7
Glan-y-nant NP12 .... 85 A7
Hawthorn CF37 .... 136 B4
Llantrisant CF72 .... 155 D2
Merthyr Vale / Ynysowen
CF48 .... 55 D5
Mountain Ash / Aberpennar
CF45 .... 54 E2
Newport / Casnewydd
NP20 .... 143 B3
Pontypridd CF37 .... 135 F6

Cardiff Rd continued
Quakers Yard CF46 ... 83 B5
Quakers Yard CF46 ... 83 B6
St Fagans / Sain Ffagan CF5 ... 193 A7
Sully CF63, CF64 ... 216 A8
Taffs Well / Ffynnon Taf CF15 ... 157 F5
Treharris CF46 ... 83 A7
Trelewis CF46 ... 83 C7
Troedyrhiw CF48 ... 31 C1
Cardiff Road Bsns Pk CF63 ... 215 C6
Cardiff Royal Infmy West Wing CF24 ... 195 C6
Cardiff St
Abercanaid CF48 ... 30 F4
Aberdare / Aberdâr CF44 .. 29 A2
Ogmore Vale CF32 ... 104 E2
Treorchy / Treorci CF42 ... 78 D6
Cardiff Tertiary Coll / Coleg Glan Hafren CF3 ... 179 E4
Cardiff Tertiary College / Coleg Glan Hafren CF24 ... 232 C3
Cardiff Univ Bute Bldg CF10 ... 232 A4
Cardiff Univ (Dept of Music) CF10 ... 232 A4
Cardiff Univ / Prifysgol Caerdydd (Cathays Park Campus) CF10 ... 232 B4
Cardiff Univ Queens Building CF24 ... 232 C3
Cardiff Univ Redwood Bldg CF10 ... 232 A4
Cardigan Cl
Church Village CF38 ... 135 F1
Dinas Powis / Dinas Powys CF64 ... 206 C3
Porthcawl CF36 ... 165 E2
Cardigan Cl / Clos Aberteifi NP44 ... 89 F6
Cardigan Cres
Llantwit Major / Llanilltud Fawr CF61 ... 210 C6
Swansea / Abertawe SA1 .. 69 C5
Cardigan Cres / Cilgant Aberteifi 3 NP44 ... 89 F6
Cardigan Ct
Caerleon / Caerllion NP18 ... 117 F3
6 Cardiff / Caerdydd CF5 ... 194 C6
Cardigan Ho
2 Penarth CF64 ... 206 F2
Port Talbot SA12 ... 124 D8
Cardigan Pl 1 NP19 ... 143 F6
Cardigan Rd 10 CF64 ... 206 C3
Cardigan St CF5 ... 194 C6
Cardigan Terr CF32 ... 104 F6
Cardigan Way NP12 ... 58 D1
Cardinal Dr CF14 ... 160 A4
Cardinal Newman RC Comp Sch CF37 ... 136 B5
Cardonnel Rd SA10 ... 70 F6
Cardonnel Villas SA10 ... 70 F6
Careg Llwyd / Greystone CF31 ... 168 C3
Carew Cl CF62 ... 214 F7
Carew Ct 7 CF14 ... 177 A6
Carew Gr / Llwyn Caeriw CF48 ... 225 F1
Carew Pl SA1 ... 69 C5
Carey Rd NP19 ... 144 A5
Carey Wlk SA10 ... 71 C8
Carfax Path NP44 ... 89 B1
Cargill Cl CF38 ... 156 B5
Cargo Rd CF10 ... 207 C8
Carig Cres SA1 ... 68 B1
Carig Gdns SA1 ... 68 A1
Carisbrooke Rd NP19 ... 143 F5
Carisbrooke Way CF23 ... 178 D3
Carling Ct CF5 ... 193 A3
Carlin Rd NP23 ... 15 D8
Carlisle St
Cardiff / Caerdydd CF24 ... 195 E6
Newport / Casnewydd NP20 ... 143 D2
Carlos St 2 SA13 ... 99 B1
Carlotta Way CF10 ... 195 B2
Carlton Cl CF14 ... 159 E3
Carlton Cres CF38 ... 156 B5
Carlton Ct NP4 ... 62 A8
Carlton Dr NP11 ... 59 D3
Carlton Pl
Abercarn NP11 ... 114 C5
Porthcawl CF36 ... 182 E7
Carlton Rd
Clydach SA6 ... 22 E1
Newport / Casnewydd NP19 ... 143 E7
Carlton Terr
Abercarn NP11 ... 114 C5
Swansea / Abertawe SA1 ... 233 A3
Troedyrhiw CF48 ... 31 B1
Carlyle St
Abertillery / Abertyleri NP13 ... 36 A5
Briton Ferry / Llansawel SA11 ... 71 C3
Carlyon Rd NP11 ... 87 B8
Carmarthen Cl
Barry / Y Barri CF62 ... 214 F7

Carmarthen Cl continued
Llantwit Major / Llanilltud Fawr CF61 ... 210 B6
Carmarthen Ct
Caerphilly / Caerffili CF83 ... 137 D4
7 Cardiff / Caerdydd CF5 ... 194 C6
Carmarthen Dr CF38 ... 135 F2
Carmarthen Ho
4 Penarth CF64 ... 206 F2
Port Talbot SA12 ... 124 D8
Carmarthen Rd
Cross Hands SA14 ... 218 A8
11 Dinas Powis / Dinas Powys CF64 ... 206 C3
Fforest SA4 ... 18 F6
Swansea / Abertawe SA5 .. 67 E4
Carmarthenshire Coll / Coleg Sir Gâr / Ammanford Campus SA18 ... 219 B7
Carmarthen St CF5 ... 194 C6
Carmel Cl NP23 ... 7 C5
Carmel Ct CF24 ... 178 C1
Carmel Flats CF40 ... 107 A5
Carmel Rd
Pontlliw SA4 ... 43 F7
Swansea / Abertawe SA1 .. 69 D5
Carmel St
Abertillery / Abertyleri NP13 ... 36 B5
Tredegar NP22 ... 6 E1
Treherbert CF42 ... 78 A8
CARMELTOWN ... 7 C4
Carmen St CF34 ... 102 B8
Carn Celyn CF38 ... 156 A5
Carne Ct CF61 ... 210 B6
Carnegie Dr CF23 ... 178 B5
Carne St
Cwm NP23 ... 35 A8
Treorchy / Treorci CF41 ... 78 F5
Carne Terr CF71 ... 199 F8
CARNETOWN ... 82 D2
Carnetown Prim Sch CF45 ... 82 D2
Carnetown Prim Sch (Inf) CF45 ... 82 D1
CARNGLAS ... 94 B8
Carnglas Ave SA2 ... 94 C7
Carnglas Rd SA2 ... 94 C7
Carnhywel SA14 ... 41 C6
Carno Cl NP23 ... 7 C5
Carno Pl SA6 ... 68 D8
Carno St NP22 ... 12 D6
Carn Wen / White Cairn CF31 ... 168 C2
Carn Y Celyn Cl CF40 ... 106 F3
Carn-yr-Ebol CF63 ... 205 B1
Carn-y-Tyla Terr
Abertysswg NP22 ... 33 A8
Rhymney / Rhymni NP22 ... 13 A1
Caroline Way CF33 ... 165 F8
Caroline Rd NP4 ... 63 A4
Caroline St / Stryd Caroline
5 Bridgend / Pen-y-Bont ar Ogwr CF31 ... 168 F4
3 Briton Ferry / Llansawel SA11 ... 71 C1
Cardiff / Caerdydd CF10 .. 232 B2
Caroline St
Blaengwynfi SA13 ... 76 C6
Blaenrhondda CF42 ... 50 C5
3 Llanelli SA15 ... 40 C3
17 Newport / Casnewydd NP20 ... 143 C4
Tonypandy CF40 ... 107 A2
Caroline Terr SA13 ... 76 C6
Caroline Way NP4 ... 63 A4
Carpenter Cl NP18 ... 119 F1
Ca'r Pwll CF64 ... 206 A2
Carregamman 19 SA18 ... 219 B7
Carregamman Isaf SA18 ... 219 B6
Carreg Arwyn CF72 ... 172 A5
Carreg Cennen Gdns SA1 ... 69 B4
Carreg Erw
Birchgrove SA7 ... 46 F3
Pyle / Y Pîl SA13 ... 148 A5
Carreg Yr Afon SA9 ... 221 C2
Carrick Ave SA15 ... 40 D7
Carrog Rd SA5 ... 68 B5
Carshalton Rd 8 CF38 ... 156 A5
Carswell Cl CF38 ... 156 B6
Carter Pl CF5 ... 176 D1
Cartersford Pl SA3 ... 123 A8
Cartref
Neath / Castell-Nedd SA10 ... 70 F7
Penrhys CF43 ... 80 A2
Cartrefle Ho NP11 ... 60 A1
Cartwright Ct CF24 ... 178 B1
Cartwright Gn NP20 ... 117 A2
Cartwright La CF5 ... 193 D7
Caryl Terr SA6 ... 68 E6
Carys Cl
Cardiff / Caerdydd CF5 ... 193 A2
Penarth CF64 ... 206 E2
Cascade View CF44 ... 28 C3
Casllwchwr Prim Sch SA4 ... 42 D1
CASNEWYDD / NEWPORT ... 144 E4

Caspian Cl 6 CF3 ... 179 F6
Caspian Point CF10 ... 195 D2
Castan Rd CF72 ... 173 B7
Castellau Rd CF38, CF72 ... 155 E7
Castell Cl SA7 ... 69 C7
Castell Coch★ CF15 ... 158 C2
Castell Coch Dr NP10 ... 163 E5
Castell Coch View CF15 ... 158 C1
Castell Ddu Rd SA4 ... 19 B1
Castell Llwyd CF82 ... 111 F7
Castell Meredith CF83 ... 138 C5
Castell Morgraig CF83 .. 138 C5
Castell Morlais CF48 ... 3 F3
CASTELL-NEDD / NEATH ... 71 B6
Castell Tal-y-Van CF71 ... 189 E7
Castell y Fan CF83 ... 138 C5
Castell-y-Mwnws CF72 ... 172 E6
Castell-y-Mynach Rd CF38 ... 155 F7
Castle Acre SA3 ... 123 A6
Castle Arc CF10 ... 232 B2
Castle Ave
Cardiff / Caerdydd CF3 ... 178 F2
Penarth CF64 ... 206 F1
The Mumbles / Y Mwmbwls SA3 ... 123 A5
Castle Bailey St SA1 ... 233 B3
Castle Bldgs CF37 ... 135 E6
Castle Cl
Abercarn NP11 ... 114 C6
Creigiau CF15 ... 174 E8
3 Dinas Powis / Dinas Powys CF64 ... 206 C3
Llantwit Major / Llanilltud Fawr CF61 ... 210 C5
Rogerstone NP10 ... 142 B4
Castle Coch CF71 ... 189 F2
Castle Cotts CF82 ... 84 D6
Castle Court Sh Ctr / Cwrt Y Castell CF83 ... 138 B3
Castle Cres
Cardiff / Caerdydd CF3 ... 179 A2
The Mumbles / Y Mwmbwls SA3 ... 123 A5
Castle Ct
Church Village CF38 ... 135 F1
6 Dinas Powis / Dinas Powys CF64 ... 206 C3
Llandough / Llandoche CF71 ... 200 F6
Llantwit Major / Llanilltud Fawr CF61 ... 209 F6
Loughor SA4 ... 65 D8
Maesteg CF34 ... 102 A4
Swansea / Abertawe SA7 .. 69 B6
Castle Ct / Cwrt Y Castell NP44 ... 115 F8
Castle Dr
Cimla SA11 ... 72 B6
Dinas Powis / Dinas Powys CF64 ... 206 C3
Castlefield Pl CF14 ... 177 E2
Castle Fields NP22 ... 12 E4
Castleford Cl CF38 ... 156 B6
Castle Gdns SA1 ... 233 B3
Castle Gn CF5 ... 192 B6
Castle Graig SA6 ... 68 D5
Castle Graig Rd SA6 ... 68 D5
Castle Hill
Cowbridge / Y Bont-Faen CF71 ... 188 D1
Pen-pedair-heol CF82 ... 84 D6
St Fagans / Sain Ffagan CF5 ... 193 A7
Castle Hill Ct CF5 ... 193 A7
Castle Ivor St CF37 ... 109 A1
Castle La
Abercarn NP11 ... 114 C6
Caerleon / Caerllion NP18 ... 118 C2
Cardiff / Caerdydd CF24 ... 232 D4
7 Swansea / Abertawe SA1 ... 233 B3
Castleland St CF63 ... 215 A5
Castle Lofts 6 SA1 ... 233 B3
Castle Mdws CF35 ... 169 C7
Castle Mews NP18 ... 118 C1
CASTLE PARK ... 138 C2
Castle Park Cl NP20 ... 142 D3
Castle Park Rd NP20 ... 142 D3
Castle Prec CF71 ... 200 F6
Castle Quay / Cei'r Castell SA11 ... 71 E8
Castle Rd
East Aberthaw CF62 ... 212 C4
Rhoose / Y Rhws CF62 ... 213 A1
The Mumbles / Y Mwmbwls SA3 ... 123 A5
Tongwynlais CF15 ... 158 C2
Castle Rise CF3 ... 179 A2
Castle St / Heol Y Castell CF10 ... 232 A2
Castle St / Stryd Castell 14 SA11 ... 71 E8
Castle Sq
Merthyr Tydfil / Merthyr Tudful CF47 ... 10 C2
Swansea / Abertawe SA1 ... 233 B2

Castle Sq continued
The Mumbles / Y Mwmbwls SA3 ... 123 A5
Castle St
Aberavon SA12 ... 99 A1
Abertillery / Abertyleri NP13 ... 36 B4
Barry / Y Barri CF62 ... 214 C4
Blaenavon NP4 ... 17 C7
Bridgend / Pen-y-Bont ar Ogwr CF31 ... 169 B2
Caerleon / Caerllion NP18 ... 118 C2
Caerphilly / Caerffili CF83 ... 138 B3
Fleur-de-lis NP12 ... 85 B5
Glyncorrwg SA13 ... 227 C2
2 Llantrisant CF72 ... 155 D3
Llantwit Major / Llanilltud Fawr CF61 ... 209 F7
Loughor SA4 ... 42 D1
Maesteg CF34 ... 102 A4
Merthyr Tydfil / Merthyr Tudful CF47 ... 10 D1
Neath / Castell-Nedd SA10 ... 70 F7
Newport / Casnewydd NP20 ... 143 D2
Pentrebach CF48 ... 31 A4
5 Pontypridd CF37 ... 135 E7
Swansea / Abertawe SA1 ... 233 B3
Taffs Well / Ffynnon Taf CF15 ... 158 A3
The Mumbles / Y Mwmbwls SA3 ... 123 A5
Tredegar NP22 ... 13 E6
Treorchy / Treorci CF42 ... 78 C5
Castle Terr CF48 ... 31 B2
CASTLETON ... 162 D3
Castleton Ave CF42 ... 50 D3
Castleton Ct CF3 ... 180 C8
Castleton Rd CF62 ... 211 D5
Castleton Rise CF3 ... 162 C3
CASTLE-UPON-ALUN ... 186 A2
Castle View
Bridgend / Pen-y-Bont ar Ogwr CF31 ... 168 F6
Caerphilly / Caerffili CF83 ... 137 F6
Heolgerrig CF48 ... 10 B1
Tongwynlais CF15 ... 176 D8
Castle View / Golwg Y Castell 9 SA11 ... 71 E8
Castle Wood NP4 ... 37 D5
Castle Yd CF47 ... 10 D1
CASWELL ... 122 B4
Caswell Ave SA3 ... 122 E4
Caswell Bay Ct SA3 ... 122 C4
Caswell Bay Rd SA3 ... 122 A5
Caswell Cl CF44 ... 27 D7
Caswell Dr SA3 ... 122 D4
Caswell Rd
Bishopston SA3 ... 122 B4
4 Cardiff / Caerdydd CF3 ... 179 B3
The Mumbles / Y Mwmbwls SA3 ... 122 E4
Caswell St
Llanelli SA15 ... 40 E3
Swansea / Abertawe SA1 .. 95 B6
Caswell Way NP19 ... 144 A1
Catalpa Cl NP20 ... 117 B3
Cathan Cl SA5 ... 67 E6
Cathan Cres SA5 ... 67 E6
CATHAYS ... 232 B4
Cathays High Sch CF14 ... 177 E1
CATHAYS PARK ... 232 B4
Cathays Sta CF10 ... 232 B4
Cathays Terr CF24 ... 195 A8
Cath Cob Cl CF3 ... 179 E7
Cathedral Cl CF5 ... 177 B1
Cathedral Ct
Cardiff / Caerdydd CF5 ... 177 A1
9 Newport / Casnewydd NP20 ... 143 B4
Cathedral Gn The CF5 ... 177 A1
Cathedral Rd
Cardiff / Caerdydd CF11 ... 194 E7
Cardiff / Caerdydd, Pontcanna CF11 ... 194 D7
Cathedral Sch The CF5 ... 194 B8
Cathedral View CF14 ... 177 B2
Cathedral Way / Ffordd Y Gadeirlan SA12 ... 98 D3
Cathedral Wlk 6 CF10 ... 232 B2
Catherine Cl
Abercanaid CF48 ... 30 F4
Newport / Casnewydd NP10 ... 163 F5
Catherine Cres CF39 ... 107 E2
Catherine Dr
Marshfield CF3 ... 180 E8
Tongwynlais CF15 ... 158 D2
Catherine Meazey Flats 5 CF64 ... 207 A5
Catherine's Ct 16 CF47 ... 30 E8
Catherine St
6 Aberavon SA12 ... 98 E1
5 Aberdare / Aberdâr CF44 ... 29 A1
Cardiff / Caerdydd CF24 .. 195 A8
Llanelli SA15 ... 40 C3

Catherine St continued
7 Pontypridd CF37 ... 109 C1
Swansea / Abertawe SA1 .. 95 B6
Treorchy / Treorci CF41 ... 79 A5
Catholic Rd NP23 ... 8 C4
Catkin Dr CF64 ... 206 E5
Catrine CF11 ... 206 F6
CAT'S ASH ... 119 C2
Catsash Rd NP18 ... 118 F1
Cattle St SA11 ... 71 E8
Cattwg Cl CF61 ... 209 F7
Cattybrook Terr 2 SA12 ... 99 F6
Catwg Prim Sch SA10 ... 48 F2
Causeway Hill CF71 ... 200 D8
Causeway The
Llanblethian / Llanfleiddan CF71 ... 200 D8
Swansea / Abertawe SA2 .. 94 E7
Cavan Row CF34 ... 102 A4
Cavell Ho SA12 ... 98 F2
Cavell St SA13 ... 227 C1
Cavendish Cl CF14 ... 159 E2
Cavendish Pl CF38 ... 156 B6
Cave St SA5 ... 68 A2
Cawdor Pl SA15 ... 40 D6
Cawley Pl CF63 ... 215 B7
Cawnpore St CF64 ... 206 E5
Caxton Pl
Cardiff / Caerdydd CF23 ... 179 A8
5 Newport / Casnewydd NP20 ... 143 B5
Caynham Ave CF64 ... 217 A8
Cecil Ct 9 CF24 ... 195 D7
Cecil La 16 NP10 ... 142 B4
Cecil Rd
Gorseinon SA4 ... 43 C2
Gowerton / Tre-gwyr SA4 .. 66 C4
Cecil Sharp Rd NP19 ... 144 F5
Cecil St
Cardiff / Caerdydd CF24 ... 195 D7
Neath / Castell-Nedd SA11 ... 71 D6
Swansea / Abertawe SA5 .. 68 C3
Cedar Ave SA4 ... 43 A4
Cedar Cl
Aberdare / Aberdâr CF44 ... 28 E2
Bryn NP12 ... 85 D3
Ebbw Vale / Glyn Ebwy NP23 ... 7 C5
Gowerton / Tre-gwyr SA4 ... 66 D4
Merthyr Tydfil / Merthyr Tudful CF47 ... 31 A8
Cedar Cres
Church Village CF38 ... 136 A1
The Mumbles / Y Mwmbwls SA3 ... 122 F8
Cedar Ct
Cardiff / Caerdydd CF14 ... 177 F8
Coedkernew / Coedcernyw NP10 ... 163 B6
Swansea / Abertawe, Tircanol SA6 ... 46 D2
Cedar Gdns
Baglan SA12 ... 98 D5
Porthcawl CF36 ... 183 E8
Cedar Gr CF5 ... 176 C1
Cedar Ho CF14 ... 176 E6
Cedar La CF37 ... 136 B5
Cedar Rd
Abertillery / Abertyleri NP11 ... 59 F5
Neath / Castell-Nedd SA11 ... 71 F7
Newport / Casnewydd NP19 ... 143 D5
St Athan / Sain Tathan CF62 ... 211 B7
Cedar St SA11 ... 227 B8
Cedars The NP18 ... 145 F7
Cedar Way
Hendreforgan CF39 ... 132 E5
Merthyr Tydfil / Merthyr Tudful CF47 ... 10 D4
Penarth CF64 ... 206 E3
Ystrad Mynach CF82 ... 84 E1
Cedar Wlk NP44 ... 89 B5
Cedar Wood Cl NP10 ... 141 D7
Cedar Wood Dr
Hendreforgan CF39 ... 132 E5
Rogerstone / Ty-du NP10 ... 141 D7
Cedric Cl SA2 ... 94 B5
Cedric St SA15 ... 40 E5
CEFN ... 142 B5
Cefn Brith SA14 ... 41 B6
Cefn Bryn CF39 ... 107 D1
CEFN-BRYN-BRAIN ... 221 B8
Cefn Bychan CF15 ... 157 C1
Cefn Byrle Rd SA10 ... 222 F6
CEFNCAEAU ... 41 C4
Cefn Carfan Rd
Bryncethin CF32 ... 151 D6
Heol-y-Cyw CF35 ... 152 A6
Cefn Carnau Rd CF14 ... 177 F5
Cefn Celyn SA2 ... 66 B1
Cefn Cl
Croesyceiliog NP44 ... 90 B6
Pontypridd CF37 ... 109 C6
Rogerstone NP10 ... 142 B5

Cefn Coch CF15 176 A7
Cefn Coed
Bridgend / Pen-y-Bont ar Ogwr CF31 168 D5
Upper Boat CF15 157 F8
Cefn Coed Ave CF23 178 C4
Cefn Coed Colliery Mus★ SA10 25 E3
Cefn-Coed Cres CF23 178 C3
Cefn Coed Cres SA2 67 D1
Cefn-Coed Gdns CF23 178 B3
Cefn Coed Hospl SA2 67 C1
Cefn Coed La CF31 168 D5
Cefncoed Rd SA12 99 C5
Cefn-Coed Rd CF23 178 B4
CEFN-COED-Y-CYMMER 10 B5
Cefn Cres NP13 36 B6
CEFN-CRIB 60 E3
Cefn-Crib Rd
Newbridge / Trecelyn NP11 60 E3
Pontypool / Pont-y-pwl NP4 61 B4
CEFN CRIBWR 149 B2
Cefn Cribwr Prim Sch CF32 149 B2
CEFN CROSS 149 D2
Cefncrug SA18 218 E7
Cefn Ct
Blackwood / Coed-Duon NP12 85 E7
Newbridge / Trecelyn NP11 87 B8
Newport / Casnewydd NP20 143 A3
Rogerstone NP10 142 B5
Cefndon Terr
Cwmavon / Cwmafan SA12 99 D5
Hirwaun CF44 27 E8
Cefn Dr NP10 142 B5
Cefn-Draw SA4 65 D1
CEFNEITHIN 218 A8
Cefneithin Prim Sch SA14 218 A8
Cefneithin Rd SA14 218 B8
Cefnen Cas-Gwent / Chepstow Rise 1 NP44 90 A6
CEFN FFOREST 85 D8
Cefn-Fforest Ave
Blackwood / Coed-Duon NP12 85 C8
Pengam NP12 85 C7
Cefn Fforest Prim Sch NP12 85 C8
Cefn Ffynon SA13 125 F3
Cefn Gelli SA11 227 B8
CEFN GLAS 168 C6
Cefn Glas
Blackwood / Coed-Duon NP12 85 D6
Swansea / Abertawe SA2 94 B8
Tredegar NP22 13 D7
Ynysforgan SA6 46 A3
Cefn Glas Inf Sch CF31 168 D6
Cefn-Glas Rd CF31 168 D6
CEFN GOLAU 13 C5
Cefn Graig CF14 177 B8
Cefn Grwgan Rd SA13 125 E3
Cefn Helyg SA2 67 B1
CEFN HENGOED
Swansea 69 C3
Ystrad Mynach 84 E4
Cefn Hengoed Com Sch SA1 69 C4
Cefn Hengoed Rd SA1 69 D4
Cefn Ilan CF83 137 A6
Cefn Isaf CF48 10 A4
Cefn La
Pontypridd CF37 109 E5
Pontypridd, Glyncoch CF37 109 C5
Cefn Llan CF15 175 C8
Cefnllan Rd SA8 23 D6
Cefn Llwyn SA1 69 C5
Cefn Llwynau St CF82 84 C4
Cefn Mably Farm Park★ CF3 161 E5
Cefn Mably Pk CF3 161 C5
Cefn Mably Rd CF14 160 C3
Cefn Miaren SA11 72 A4
Cefn Milwr NP44 116 D8
Cefn Mount CF64 206 A3
Cefn Nant
Cardiff / Caerdydd CF14 159 B1
Pencoed CF35 152 C1
Cefn Onn Ct CF14 159 F1
Cefn Onn Mdws CF14 159 F4
Cefn Onn Prim Sch CF14 159 E1
CEFN PARC 70 E6
Cefn-Parc SA10 70 E6
Cefn Parc NP22 13 E5
CEFNPENNAR 54 A6
Cefnpennar Rd
Aberdare / Aberdâr CF44 53 F8
Mountain Ash / Aberpennar CF45 54 B7
Cefn-Pennar Rd CF45 54 B8
Cefn Penuel CF15 175 C8
Cefn-Porth Rd CF14 160 F6
Cefn Prim Sch CF37 109 C5
Cefn Rd
Blackwood / Coed-Duon NP12 85 E8
Cardiff / Caerdydd CF14 177 C3
Cefn Cribwr CF32 149 B2
Deri CF81 57 C8
Glais SA7 46 F6
Gwaun-Cae-Gurwen SA18 220 D6
Hengoed CF82 85 A3
Rogerstone NP10 142 A6
Swansea / Abertawe SA1 69 C3
Wattstown CF39 107 D8
CEFN RHIGOS 224 A1
Cefn Rhos NP22 13 D6
Cefn-Rhychdir Rd NP24 33 E4
Cefn Rise NP10 142 A6
Cefn-Saeson Cl SA11 72 A6
Cefn Saeson Comp Sch SA11 72 C5
Cefnsaeson Rd SA7 70 A8
Cefn Stylle Rd SA4 65 D4
Cefn Wlk NP10 142 B5
Cefn-y-Lon CF83 137 D6
Cefn-y-Maes SA5 67 E6
Cefn Y Mynydd NP24 33 D3
Cefn-yr-Allt SA10 49 C4
Cefn-yr-Erw Primate Sanctuary★ SA9 222 E7
Cei Dafydd CF63 215 A4
Ceidrim Rd SA18 220 B8
Cei'r Castell / Castle Quay SA11 71 E8
Ceiriog Cl
Barry / Y Barri CF63 215 A8
Penarth CF64 206 F4
Ceiriog Cres CF37 135 F6
Ceiriog Dr
Caerphilly / Caerffili CF83 138 A4
Cardiff / Caerdydd CF14 176 F8
Ceiriog Rd SA1 95 A8
Cei'r Morwr / Mariners Quay SA12 124 D7
Celandine Ct NP44 88 F2
Celandine Rd CF5 193 A5
Celerity Dr CF10 232 D1
Celestial Way CF31 168 C2
Celtic Bsns Pk 3 SA1 95 B7
Celtic Gn CF64 206 B4
Celtic Rd
Cardiff / Caerdydd CF14 177 D3
Maesteg CF34 102 D1
Celtic View CF31 150 F1
Celtic View / Golygfa Geltaido CF34 102 C1
Celtic Way
Bedwas CF83 138 E6
Newport / Casnewydd NP10 163 C5
Rhoose / Y Rhws CF62 212 E1
Celyn Ave
Caerphilly / Caerffili CF83 138 A4
Cardiff / Caerdydd CF23 178 B5
Celyn Cl CF62 211 C7
Celyn Ct 4 NP44 89 C6
Celynen Rd NP11 87 B4
Celyn Gr
Caerphilly / Caerffili CF83 138 A4
Cardiff / Caerdydd CF23 178 C7
Celyn Isaf CF39 133 C2
Cemaes Cres CF3 179 E5
Cemaes Rd NP11 59 D2
Cemetery La 14 NP20 143 B4
Cemetery Rd
Abercarn NP11 87 B3
Abercynon CF45 82 C4
Aberdare / Aberdâr CF44 28 E4
Abertillery / Abertyleri NP13 36 B1
Barry / Y Barri CF62 214 F6
Bridgend / Pen-y-Bont ar Ogwr CF31 168 E6
Ebbw Vale / Glyn Ebwy NP23 15 A1
Ebbw Vale / Glyn Ebwy, Pont-y-Gof NP23 7 D1
Ebbw Vale / Glyn Ebwy, Waun-lwyd NP23 14 F1
Gwaun-Cae-Gurwen SA18 220 D6
Maesteg CF34 102 C3
Ogmore Vale CF32 130 E7
Pontypridd CF37 135 F7
Porth CF39 107 D4
Swansea / Abertawe SA5 68 D6
Taffs Well / Ffynnon Taf CF15 158 B3
Taffs Well / Ffynnon Taf CF15 158 B4
Treorchy / Treorci CF42 78 D7
Cemetrey Rd 1 NP23 8 B4
Cenarth Dr CF44 29 E2
Cendl Cres NP23 7 C4
Cendl Terr NP23 35 B8
Cenfedd St NP19 143 D7
Cennin Pedr CF63 205 C1
Centenary Ct CF38 156 B6
Central Ave
Blackwood / Coed Duon NP12 59 A1
Blackwood / Coed-Duon NP12 85 C8
Central Ave *continued*
Newbridge / Trecelyn NP11 87 A6
Newport / Casnewydd NP19 144 D2
Pontypool / Pont-y-pwl NP4 39 B1
Central Ave / Rhodfa Canolog SA12 98 C5
Central Bldgs
Bedwas CF83 139 A6
Blackwood / Coed Duon NP12 59 B1
Central Bsns Pk / Parc Busnes Canolog SA7 46 C2
Central Ct 10 CF24 195 D7
Central Dr NP4 38 B1
Central Hos CF83 138 F6
Central Inf Sch SA13 125 C7
Central Jun Sch SA13 125 B8
Central Link CF10, CF24 232 D2
Central Rd SA13 125 D3
Central Sq
Cardiff / Caerdydd CF10 232 B1
5 Pontypridd CF37 109 D2
Central St
Caerphilly / Caerffili CF83 137 F6
Ystrad Mynach CF82 84 E1
Central Way
Barry / Y Barri CF64 215 E6
Cwmbran / Cwmbrân NP44 89 C5
Central Way / Ffordd Ganolog CF14 177 F3
Centre Ct CF15 157 E8
Centurion Cl CF5 193 D3
Centurion Gate NP18 118 C2
Century Ct CF11 232 A1
Century Pk SA6 69 A6
Cenydd Terr CF83 110 F4
Cerdin Ave CF72 173 B7
Cerdinen Terr 2 CF44 53 E8
Ceredig Ct / Cwrt Ceredig 6 NP44 90 B2
Ceredig St CF48 31 A4
Ceri Ave CF62 213 B2
Ceridwen St
Maerdy CF43 52 A1
Mountain Ash / Aberpennar CF45 54 D2
Ceridwen Terr 6 CF72 155 D3
Ceri Rd
Rhoose / Y Rhws CF62 213 B2
Swansea / Abertawe SA1 67 F1
Cerise Cl SA12 98 B3
Chaddesley Terr 1 SA1 95 B7
Chadwick Cl NP20 117 A2
Chaffinch Cl CF31 169 C4
Chaffinch Way NP10 163 F7
Chain Rd SA11 227 B8
Chain Wlk SA11 223 C1
Chalfont Cl CF38 156 B6
Chalice Ct SA12 98 D3
Challacombe Pl SA3 122 E6
Challis Row CF44 27 C8
Chalvington Cl CF38 156 B6
Chamberlain Rd
Cardiff / Caerdydd CF14 177 A3
Neath / Castell-Nedd SA11 71 D4
Chamberlain Row CF64 206 C4
Chamomile Cl CF23 160 E1
Chancery La
Cardiff / Caerdydd CF11 194 D5
7 Mountain Ash / Aberpennar CF45 54 D3
Chandlers Ct 7 CF37 109 D2
Chandlers Rd NP23 7 E4
Chandlers Reach
Llantwit Fadre / Llanilltud Faerdref CF38 156 C5
The Mumbles / Y Mwmbwls SA3 123 C4
Chandlers Way CF64 207 A6
Chandlery The CF40 106 F8
Chandlery Way CF10, CF11 195 B2
Channel Ave CF39 133 E8
Channel Cl CF62 212 F1
Channel Hts CF33 148 E1
Channel View
Bassaleg NP10 141 F3
Bridgend / Pen-y-Bont ar Ogwr CF31 169 D4
Bryn-côch SA10 48 D4
Castleton CF3 162 B3
Cwmbran / Cwmbrân NP44 89 C5
Marcross / Marcroes CF61 208 F7
Penarth CF64 207 B1
Pontypool / Pont-y-pwl NP4 62 D7
Risca / Rhisga NP11 115 B1
Swansea / Abertawe SA2 94 B5
The Mumbles / Y Mwmbwls SA3 123 B3
Channel View Ct NP11 115 B1
Channel View / Golwg Y Sianel SA12 124 D8
Channel View L Ctr★ CF11 195 A1
Channel View Rd CF11 194 F1
Chantal Ave CF31 150 D1
Chantry Ct SA5 67 E5
Chantry Rise CF64 207 A1
Chantry The CF5 176 E1
Chapel Banks CF48 10 C2
Chapel Cl
Abersychan NP4 37 E6
Aberthin CF71 189 B3
Baglan SA12 98 D3
Dinas Powis / Dinas Powys CF64 206 C4
29 Newport / Casnewydd NP20 143 C3
Pentrebach CF48 31 A4
Pontllanfraith NP12 86 A5
Chapel Farm Ind Est NP11 114 B7
Chapel Farm Terr NP11 114 B8
Chapel Hill CF72 153 F3
Chapel Hill Cl CF72 153 F3
Chapel La
Croesyceiliog NP44 90 A7
Penarth CF64 207 A5
Chapel Mead NP4 39 E7
Chapel Rd
Abertillery / Abertyleri NP13 36 C3
Blaina / Blaenau NP13 15 D5
Crofty SA4 64 B2
Llanharan CF72 154 A3
Monknash / Yr As Fawr CF71 198 C2
Morganstown / Treforgan CF15 176 B8
Nantyglo NP23 8 C2
New Tredegar NP24 33 B5
Penderyn CF44 224 D3
Pontypool / Pont-y-pwl NP4 61 F8
Three Crosses SA4 65 E1
Chapel Row
9 Aberdare / Aberdâr CF44 29 A2
5 Aberdare / Aberdâr CF44 53 E8
Cardiff / Caerdydd CF3 179 D7
Dinas Powis / Dinas Powys CF64 206 C4
Merthyr Tydfil / Merthyr Tudful CF47 10 C2
Chapel Row La 1 CF3 179 D7
Chapel Sq CF48 30 E5
Chapel St
Aberbargoed / Aberbargod CF81 58 A5
Abercanaid CF48 30 F4
Abercarn NP11 87 B4
Aberdare / Aberdâr CF44 53 C7
Abergwynfi SA13 76 C5
Abertillery / Abertyleri NP13 36 B5
Bedlinog CF46 56 A7
Blaencwm CF42 50 B2
Blaenrhondda CF42 50 D4
Bridgend / Pen-y-Bont ar Ogwr CF31 168 F3
Brynmawr NP23 8 B4
Brynmenyn CF32 150 F6
Cardiff / Caerdydd CF5 194 B8
Cwmbran / Cwmbrân NP44 89 E5
Deri CF81 57 B8
Gorseinon SA4 43 D2
Nant-y-Moel CF32 104 F6
New Tredegar NP24 33 E3
Pontlottyn CF81 12 F1
Pontycymer CF32 103 E3
Pontypridd CF37 135 F5
Pontypridd, Trallwn CF37 109 C1
Swansea / Abertawe SA1 233 B5
The Mumbles / Y Mwmbwls SA3 123 A5
Ton Pentre CF41 79 A3
8 Tonypandy CF40 106 E6
Tonypandy, Penygraig CF40 107 A3
Treorchy / Treorci CF42 78 D6
Troedyrhiw CF48 31 C1
Ystrad CF41 79 D3
Chapel Terr
Bryn SA13 100 E5
Hengoed CF82 84 F3
3 Port Talbot SA13 125 C6
Wattstown CF39 107 E8
Chapel View NP11 113 B4
Chapel Wood CF23 178 E4
Chapman Cl NP20 117 A3
Chapman Ct 10 NP20 142 F4
Chapmans 5 SA1 233 B3
Chapman St / Stryd Chapman SA15 40 B6
Chard Ave CF3 179 B5
Chargot Rd CF5 194 B7
Charles Ave CF35 152 D1
Charles Ct
Ebbw Vale / Glyn Ebwy NP23 7 B1
Gorseinon SA4 43 A1
Charles Darwin Way CF62 214 F3
Charles Pl CF62 214 D2
Charles Row CF34 102 A4
Charles St / Heol Siarl CF10 232 C2
Charles St
Abertillery / Abertyleri NP11 59 E6
Abertysswg NP22 33 C8
Blaenavon NP4 17 D6
Bridgend / Pen-y-Bont ar Ogwr CF31 168 F5
Caerphilly / Caerffili CF83 138 B3
Cwmbran / Cwmbrân NP44 89 E6
Llanelli SA15 40 F5
8 Neath / Castell-Nedd SA11 71 E7
Neath / Castell-Nedd, Skewen / Sciwen SA10 70 E7
Newport / Casnewydd NP20 143 C4
New Tredegar NP24 58 A8
Pontypool / Pont-y-pwl NP4 62 E3
Pontypridd CF37 109 A1
Porth CF39 107 F4
Tonypandy CF40 106 D6
Tonypandy, Trealaw CF40 107 B5
Tredegar NP22 6 D1
Treherbert CF42 78 A8
Tylorstown CF43 80 B3
Charles Terr SA15 40 C4
Charles Thomas Ho SA1 96 A7
CHARLESVILLE 37 F1
Charlesville Pl 15 SA11 71 E8
Charlock Cl CF14 159 D3
Charlotte Ct SA1 67 E2
Charlotte Dr NP20 143 C3
Charlotte Gdns CF48 11 B5
Charlotte Pl CF63 215 B6
Charlotte Sq CF14 177 C7
Charlotte St
Dowlais CF48 11 B4
13 Newport / Casnewydd NP20 143 C3
Penarth CF64 206 F5
Charlotte Wlk 12 NP20 143 C3
Charnwood Ct
Swansea / Abertawe SA1 69 D6
Upper Boat CF15 136 F1
Charnwood Dr CF23 161 A1
Charnwood Rd NP19 143 D8
Charston NP44 89 C3
Charter Ave CF62 214 D8
Charteris Cl CF64 217 A8
Charteris Cres CF5 193 D6
Charteris Rd CF5 193 D6
Chartist Ct NP11 115 B1
Chartist Dr NP10 142 A5
Chartist Rd CF72 155 D3
Chartist Twr 5 NP20 143 C5
Chartist Way
Blackwood / Coed-Duon NP12 85 D7
Tredegar NP22 6 E1
Chartley Cl 9 CF3 180 A7
Chartwell Ct
Cardiff / Caerdydd CF5 194 A6
Pentyrch CF15 175 C8
Chartwell Dr CF14 160 B2
Charwood Ho 4 NP44 89 C2
Chase The CF31 169 D4
Chase View CF47 10 E3
CHATHAM 140 B7
Chatham CF83 140 A7
Chatham Pl CF83 140 B7
Chatham St CF83 140 B7
Chatsworth Cl CF5 176 E1
Chatterton Sq CF11 206 F8
Chaucer Cl
Bridgend / Pen-y-Bont ar Ogwr CF31 168 C6
Cardiff / Caerdydd CF3 179 C8
Penarth CF64 206 F4
Chaucer Ct 4 NP19 143 F5
Chaucer Rd
Barry / Y Barri CF62 214 F8
Newport / Casnewydd NP19 143 F5
Chave Terr CF82 85 B2
Cheam Pl CF14 177 F8
Cheapside
Bridgend / Pen-y-Bont ar Ogwr CF31 168 F4
Bridgend / Pen-y-Bont ar Ogwr CF31 169 B2
Cheddar Cres CF3 179 B5
Chelhydra Wlk 1 SA1 233 B1
Chelmer Cl NP20 116 C1
Chelmer Wlk NP20 116 C1
Chelsea Ave CF31 168 C7
Chelston Pl NP20 143 B7
CHELTENHAM 9 C6
Cheltenham Rd CF36 182 E8
Cheltenham Terr CF31 168 F3
Chemical Rd SA6 46 A2
Chemical Row SA9 2 A4
Chepstow Cl
Blackwood / Coed-Duon NP12 58 D1
Cardiff / Caerdydd CF5 193 D4
Croesyceiliog NP44 90 A6
Merthyr Tydfil / Merthyr Tudful CF48 225 F1

Chepstow Ct CF83 137 D4
Chepstow Pl SA1 69 C4
Chepstow Rd
- Langstone NP18 145 B8
- Newport / Casnewydd NP19 144 C5
- Treorchy / Treorci CF42 78 C5

Chepstow Rise / Cefnen Cas-Gwent 1 NP44 90 A6
CHERITON 228 F4
Cheriton Ave CF82 84 F5
Cheriton Cres SA5 67 F5
Cheriton Ct
- Cardiff / Caerdydd CF3 179 A3
- 2 Swansea / Abertawe SA1 233 A4

Cheriton Dr CF14 159 F2
Cheriton Gr CF38 136 B1
Cheriton Path NP44 89 B2
Cherry Cl
- Cardiff / Caerdydd CF5 176 B1
- Dinas Powis / Dinas Powys CF64 206 C2
- Ebbw Vale / Glyn Ebwy NP23 7 D2
- Penarth CF64 217 A8

Cherry Ct CF44 28 D3
Cherrydale Rd CF5 193 E6
Cherrydown Cl CF14 159 F2
Cherry Dr CF44 28 D3
Cherry Gr
- Baglan SA12 98 E6
- Blackwood / Coed Duon NP11 59 D1
- Merthyr Tydfil / Merthyr Tudful CF47 10 E4
- Swansea / Abertawe SA2 94 B4

Cherry Orchard Rd CF14 159 F4
Cherry Tree Ave CF36 183 E8
Cherry Tree Cl
- Bedwas CF83 138 C7
- Caerleon / Caerllion NP18 118 B3
- Cardiff / Caerdydd CF14 160 B3
- Langstone NP18 145 B8
- Newport / Casnewydd NP20 117 B3
- Trefechan CF48 10 B6

Cherry Tree Cl / Clos y Coden Geirios NP44 90 B5
Cherry Tree Rd NP12 85 E3
Cherry Trees NP12 58 D7
Cherry Tree Way CF46 83 C8
Cherry Tree Wlk CF72 155 C2
Cherrywood Cl CF14 159 F2
Chervil Cl 12 CF3 180 A8
Cherwell Cl CF5 176 D1
Cherwell Rd CF64 206 F2
Cherwell Wlk NP20 116 C2
Cheshire Cl CF14 177 F6
Chesshyre St SA2 94 E5
Chester Cl
- 1 Cardiff / Caerdydd CF3 179 F6
- Merthyr Tydfil / Merthyr Tudful CF48 225 F1
- Pontypool / Pont-y-pwl NP4 63 B5

Chester Ct CF83 137 D4
Chesterfield St CF63 215 B7
Chesterholme NP20 143 A3
Chester Pl CF11 194 F3
Chester St CF11 194 F3
Chesterton Rd CF3 179 B7
Chestnut Ave
- Gorseinon SA4 43 A4
- St Athan / Sain Tathan CF62 211 B7
- The Mumbles / Y Mwmbwls SA3 122 E8

Chestnut Cl
- Aberdare / Aberdâr CF44 28 E2
- Dinas Powis / Dinas Powys CF64 206 B2
- Ebbw Vale / Glyn Ebwy NP23 7 C5
- Machen CF83 140 A7
- Neath / Castell-Nedd SA10 48 D2
- Pontypool / Pont-y-pwl NP4 63 B5

Chestnut Dr CF36 183 E8
Chestnut Gn NP44 89 B6
Chestnut Gr
- Bryn NP12 85 E3
- Caerleon / Caerllion NP18 117 E2
- Maesteg CF34 102 C3

Chestnut Rd
- Baglan SA12 98 E7
- Cardiff / Caerdydd CF5 193 D8
- Neath / Castell-Nedd SA11 72 A6

Chestnut St CF37 136 A5
Chestnuts The CF72 173 D6
Chestnut Tree Cl CF15 176 A6
Chestnut Way
- Bridgend / Pen-y-Bont ar Ogwr CF31 168 B5
- Merthyr Tydfil / Merthyr Tudful CF47 10 D5
- Penarth CF64 206 F3

Cheviot Cl
- Cardiff / Caerdydd CF14 177 E7
- Risca / Rhisga NP11 115 C2
- Swansea / Abertawe SA5 67 E3

Chevron St CF39 107 E4
Chichester Cl NP19 117 F1
Chichester Rd CF64 206 F5
Chichester Way CF5 193 E6
Chick La NP20 142 F3
Chilcote St CF63 215 B6
Chilcott Ave CF32 150 F5
Chiltern Cl
- Cardiff / Caerdydd CF14 177 E7
- Newport / Casnewydd NP19 144 C6
- Risca / Rhisga NP11 115 D1
- Swansea / Abertawe SA5 67 E3

Chimney Rd CF62 211 E1
Chirk Cl NP10 163 D5
Chirk Gdns SA1 69 C4
Chiswick Cl CF31 168 C6
Chopin Rd / Heol Chopin 4 SA12 98 B3
Chorley Cl CF5 193 C7
Chorleywood Cl CF31 169 A4
Chosen Ind Est SA12 98 B8
CHRISTCHURCH 144 C7
Christchurch CW Prim Sch SA1 95 B5
Christchurch Hill NP18 144 D7
Christchurch Rd
- Baglan SA12 98 D3
- Blackwood / Coed-Duon NP12 85 F8
- Newport / Casnewydd NP19 144 B6

Chris Thomas Ho 7 SA1 68 C2
Christina Cres NP10 142 C4
Christina St
- Cardiff / Caerdydd CF10 195 B3
- Swansea / Abertawe SA1 233 A3

Christopher Ct SA6 69 A6
Christopher Rd
- Maesteg CF34 102 C3
- Neath / Castell-Nedd SA10 70 E7
- Ynysforgan SA6 46 B4

Christopher Rise SA4 44 A5
Christopher St SA15 40 E4
Christopher Terr CF47 30 F7
Christ The King RC Prim Sch / Ysgol Gynradd RC Crist y Brenin CF14 160 A1
Chrome Ave / Rhodfa Crom SA12 98 B2
Chumleigh Cl CF3 179 A4
Church Acre CF31 169 D6
Church Ave
- Ebbw Vale / Glyn Ebwy NP23 7 F4
- Llwydcoed CF44 28 E6
- 5 Penarth CF64 207 B4
- Pontypool / Pont-y-pwl NP4 38 C1

Church Bldgs SA9 222 C7
Church Cl
- Bryn-côch SA10 48 D3
- Cardiff / Caerdydd CF14 160 C3
- Croesyceiliog NP44 90 A5
- Llantwit Fadre / Llanilltud Faerdref CF38 156 D6
- Ogmore-by-S / Aberogwr CF32 184 D2
- Peterstone Wentlooge / Llanbedr Gwynllwg CF3 180 F5
- Pontypool / Pont-y-pwl NP4 63 A2
- Rogerstone NP10 142 C4
- Swansea / Abertawe SA7 69 D8

Church Cotts SA5 45 B2
Church Cres
- Baglan SA12 98 E5
- Bassaleg NP10 142 A3
- Blaengwrach SA11 227 C8
- Coedkernew / Coedcernyw NP10 163 A5
- Ebbw Vale / Glyn Ebwy, Briery Hill NP23 14 D6
- Ebbw Vale / Glyn Ebwy, Carmeltown NP23 7 C4
- St Hilary / Saint Hilari CF71 201 D7

Church Ct NP19 144 A8
Church Farm Cl NP20 116 E1
Churchfield Cl CF82 84 F6
Churchfield Row CF41 79 A4
Churchfields CF63 215 B8
Church Gdns SA2 67 E2
Church Hill Cl CF71 200 C8
Churchill Cl
- Bridgend / Pen-y-Bont ar Ogwr CF31 168 D4
- Cardiff / Caerdydd CF14 160 A4

CHURCHILL PARK 138 A5
Churchill Terr CF63 215 C6
Churchill Way / Fford Churchill CF10 232 C2
Church La
- Bishopston SA3 121 F7
- Brynmawr NP23 8 C5
- Cardiff / Caerdydd CF3 179 D7

Church La *continued*
- Coedkernew / Coedcernyw NP10 163 A4
- Gwaun-Cae-Gurwen SA18 220 D6
- Llantwit Major / Llanilltud Fawr CF61 209 F6
- Marshfield CF3 162 D2
- Nantgarw CF15 158 A7
- Nelson CF46 83 E4
- Pen-clawdd SA4 64 F2
- Pontarddulais SA4 19 D3
- Pontypool / Pont-y-pwl, Mount Pleasant NP4 62 B8
- Pontypool / Pont-y-pwl, Panteg NP4 63 B2
- St Athan / Sain Tathan CF62 211 D4

Church La / Lon Yr Eglwys SA12 98 E5
Church Mdw
- Gelligaer CF82 84 D7
- Llantwit Major / Llanilltud Fawr CF61 210 D6
- Reynoldston SA3 229 B1

Churchmead NP10 142 B2
Church Mews NP4 62 C6
Church Park La SA3 123 B4
Church Pk SA3 123 B4
Church Pl
- Bargoed / Bargod CF81 58 A4
- Blaengarw CF32 103 E6
- Maesteg CF34 102 A3
- 10 Neath / Castell-Nedd SA11 71 E8
- Porthcawl CF36 182 F6
- Seven Sisters / Blaendulais SA10 222 C4

Church Pl S CF64 207 B5
Church Rd
- Abertillery / Abertyleri NP13 60 A8
- Abertridwr CF83 136 F7
- Barry / Y Barri CF63 215 B7
- Blaenavon NP4 17 C6
- Bridgend / Pen-y-Bont ar Ogwr CF31 168 E3
- Cardiff / Caerdydd, Caerau CF5 193 C3
- Cardiff / Caerdydd, Canton CF5 194 D5
- Cardiff / Caerdydd CF5 193 D3
- Cardiff / Caerdydd, Lisvane / Llys Faen CF14 160 C3
- Cardiff / Caerdydd, Llanedeyrn CF3 161 C1
- Cardiff / Caerdydd, Pentwyn CF23 179 A8
- Cardiff / Caerdydd, Rumney / Rhymni CF3 179 B3
- Cardiff / Caerdydd, Whitchurch CF14 177 A4
- Church Village CF38 135 F2
- Cwmbran / Cwmbrân NP44 89 D5
- Gelligaer CF82 84 C7
- Llanblethian / Llanfleiddan CF71 188 C1
- Llanedi SA4 218 D1
- Maesygwartha NP7 9 D8
- Neath / Castell-Nedd SA10 48 F2
- Newbridge / Trecelyn NP11 86 F7
- Newport / Casnewydd NP19 143 D6
- Penarth CF64 207 B4
- Penderyn CF44 224 D3
- Pentyrch CF15 175 C8
- Pontardawe, Cilybebyll SA8 24 D5
- Pontardawe SA8 24 A7
- Ponthir NP44 117 D8
- 1 Pontypridd CF37 109 E2
- Rhoose / Y Rhws CF62 213 A1
- Risca / Rhisga NP11 114 F3
- St Bride's Wentlooge / Llansanffraid Gwynllwg NP10 163 E1
- St Fagans / Sain Ffagan CF5 175 E5
- Swansea / Abertawe SA7 69 D8
- Ton Pentre CF41 79 A3
- Tonypandy CF40 107 A1
- Wick / Y Wig CF71 198 C5
- Ynysmeudwy SA8 23 F7
- Ystalyfera SA9 2 A4

Church Rd / Heol Eglwys SA10 222 C3
Church Rd / Heol Yr Eglwys
- Abersychan NP4 37 E4
- Baglan SA12 98 E5
- Gorslas SA14 218 B8

Church Rise CF5 205 A6
Church Road Terr 9 NP11 114 F3
Church Row
- Aberdare / Aberdâr CF44 28 E4
- Dowlais CF48 11 B4
- 8 Glanaman SA18 220 B8
- Pendoylan / Pendeulwyn CF71 190 F6
- St Nicholas / Sain Nicolas CF5 191 F1

Church St / Stryd-yr-Eglwys 8 SA18 219 B7
Church St / Stryd yr Eglwys CF10 232 B2
Church Sq SA12 99 E5
Church St
- 7 Aberavon SA12 99 A1
- Aberbargoed / Aberbargod CF81 58 B4
- 5 Aberdare / Aberdâr CF44 29 A2
- Aberkenfig / Abercynffig CF32 150 C4
- Abertillery / Abertyleri NP13 36 B5
- Bargoed / Bargod CF81 57 F4
- Bedwas CF83 138 E6
- Blaengarw CF32 103 E6
- Blaina / Blaenau NP13 15 E5
- Briton Ferry / Llansawel SA11 71 B1
- Brynna CF72 153 D3
- Caerleon / Caerllion NP18 118 B2
- Cowbridge / Y Bont-Faen CF71 188 E2
- Cymmer / Cymer SA13 75 D3
- Dowlais CF48 11 B4
- Ebbw Vale / Glyn Ebwy NP23 14 D6
- Ferndale CF43 79 F7
- Gowerton / Tre-gwyr SA4 66 B5
- Llanbradach CF83 111 F1
- Llandow / Llandw CF71 199 E8
- Llanelli SA15 40 D5
- Llantrisant CF72 155 D3
- Llantwit Major / Llanilltud Fawr CF61 209 F6
- Llysworney / Llyswyrny CF71 187 E1
- Machen CF83 140 A7
- Maerdy CF43 52 A1
- Maesteg, Brynheulog CF34 75 B2
- Maesteg CF34 102 A3
- Merthyr Tydfil / Merthyr Tudful, Pen-y-Darren CF47 10 F3
- Merthyr Tydfil / Merthyr Tudful, The Quar CF47 10 D2
- Merthyr Tydfil / Merthyr Tudful, Thomas Town CF47 10 E1
- Mountain Ash / Aberpennar CF45 81 F8
- Newport / Casnewydd NP20 143 D2
- Pontardawe SA8 23 E5
- Pontlottyn CF81 12 F1
- Pontycymer CF32 103 F3
- 6 Pontypridd CF37 109 C1
- Porthcawl CF36 183 D8
- Rhymney / Rhymni NP22 12 E5
- Rogerstone / Ty-du NP10 141 F6
- Taffs Well / Ffynnon Taf CF15 158 A3
- Ton Pentre CF41 79 A3
- Tonypandy CF40 106 E6
- Tonypandy, Llwynypia CF40 106 F8
- Tredegar NP22 13 E8
- Treherbert CF42 51 A1
- Treorchy / Treorci CF42 78 B5
- Troedyrhiw CF48 31 B1
- Wick / Y Wig CF71 198 C5
- Ynysybwl CF37 81 F1
- Ystrad Mynach CF82 84 E1

Church Terr
- Abercanaid CF48 30 F6
- Blaengarw CF32 103 E6
- Cardiff / Caerdydd CF23 195 D8
- Llanharan CF72 154 A3
- Nant-y-Moel CF32 104 E6
- New Tredegar NP24 33 E3
- 8 Pontypool / Pont-y-pwl NP4 38 A1
- Porth CF39 107 F6
- St Mary Church / Llan Fair CF71 201 A4
- Tonypandy CF40 107 A1
- Tylorstown CF43 80 C3

Church View
- Abercanaid CF48 30 F4
- Baglan SA12 98 E5
- 9 Blaenavon NP4 17 C6
- Brynna CF72 153 D3
- Ebbw Vale / Glyn Ebwy NP23 7 D3
- Laleston / Trelales CF32 167 E4
- Llanblethian / Llanfleiddan CF71 188 C1
- Marcross / Marcroes CF61 208 E7
- Pontllanfraith NP12 86 A6

Church View Cl
- Brynna CF72 153 D3
- Llandough / Llandochau CF64 206 D7

CHURCH VILLAGE 135 F1
Churchward Dr NP19 144 B4
Church Wlk CF39 108 A3
Churchwood Cl NP4 62 C7
Church Wood Rd NP44 89 D5
Cila Prim Sch SA2 93 D5
Cildaudy Rd CF32 150 B7
Cilfedw CF15 176 B7
CIL-FFRIW / CILFREW 49 B5
Cilffriw Prim Sch SA10 49 B4
CILFREW / CIL-FFRIW 49 B5
Cilfrow Ct SA1 68 C2
CILFYNYDD 109 E5
Cilfynydd Prim Sch CF37 109 F5
Cilfynydd Rd CF37 109 F5
Cilgant Aberteifi / Cardigan Cres 3 NP44 89 F6
Cilgant Bute / Bute Cres CF10 195 C2
Cilgant Caernarfon / Caernarvon Cres NP44 90 A3
Cilgant Canonbie / Canonbie Cres CF48 55 C3
Cilgant Gwyn / Gwyn Cres NP4 37 E7
Cil Gant Y Meillion CF62 213 B1
Cilgerran Cres CF14 177 D8
Cilgerran Ct NP44 90 B3
Cilgerran Pl SA1 69 C5
Cilgerran Way NP12 58 E1
Cilhaul CF46 83 B8
Cilhaul Terr CF45 54 D1
Cil-Hendy CF72 173 C7
Cilmaengwyn
- Godre'r-graig SA8 221 B1
- Pontardawe SA8 24 C8

Cilonen Rd SA4 65 D1
Cilparc CF36 183 A8
Cilsaig Rd SA14 41 B8
Cilsanws Ho CF48 10 A3
Cilsanws La CF48 225 F3
Cil-Sanws La CF48 10 A5
CILYBEBYLL 24 C6
Cil-y-Coed SA5 67 A3
Cil Yr Onnen SA14 42 B8
CIMLA 72 C6
Cimla Cl SA11 71 F6
Cimla Cres SA11 72 A6
Cimla Hospl SA11 72 A5
Cimla Rd SA11 71 F6
Cinema Bldgs 3 SA15 40 D3
Cinnabar Dr NP12 85 D5
Circle The
- Bryn NP12 85 E3
- Cwmbran / Cwmbrân NP44 89 D1
- Tredegar NP22 13 E6

Circle Way E CF23 178 F5
Circle Way W CF23 178 D4
Citadel Cl NP22 13 D7
Citrine Ave / Rhodfa Citrine 3 SA12 98 B2
Citrine Cl SA12 98 B2
CITY 171 D1
City Hall Rd CF10 232 B3
City Rd
- Bettws CF32 129 D1
- Cardiff / Caerdydd CF24 232 C4

City Wharf CF10 232 D1
Claerwen CF82 84 B6
Claerwen Cl CF44 29 E2
Claerwen Dr CF23 178 B5
Clairwain NP4 63 A3
Clan-yr-Afon CF72 173 B7
Clapham Terr NP4 17 B5
Clara St CF41 78 F3
Clarbeston Rd CF14 177 A3
Clare Ct SA4 42 E1
Clare Dr CF71 188 F1
Clare Drew Way NP44 90 A5
Clare Gdns 3 CF11 194 F5
Claremont NP20 117 B4
Claremont Ave CF3 179 B4
Claremont Cres CF3 179 B4
Claremont Dr CF46 83 C5
Claremont Rd NP11 87 B8
Clarence Ct
- Cardiff / Caerdydd CF10 195 B1
- Maesteg CF34 102 A3
- Swansea / Abertawe SA1 233 A2

Clarence Emb CF10 195 B2
Clarence Mews CF10 195 A1
Clarence Pl
- Cardiff / Caerdydd CF10 195 B1
- Newport / Casnewydd NP19 143 C5
- Pontypool / Pont-y-pwl NP4 62 D6
- Risca / Rhisga NP11 114 F2

Clarence Rd
- Cardiff / Caerdydd CF10 195 B2
- Pontypool / Pont-y-pwl NP4 62 D6

Clarence St
- Abertillery / Abertyleri NP13 36 C6
- Brynmawr NP23 8 C4
- Mountain Ash / Aberpennar CF45 54 D1
- Newport / Casnewydd NP20 143 D2
- Pontypool / Pont-y-pwl NP4 62 C6
- Swansea / Abertawe SA1 233 A2
- Ton Pentre CF41 79 A3

Clarence Terr
Aberdare / Aberdâr CF44 53 D6
Swansea / Abertawe SA1 233 A2
Clarendon CF23 178 D6
Clarendon Rd
Cardiff / Caerdydd CF23 178 D3
Swansea / Abertawe SA2 94 D7
Clare Pl 4 CF11 194 F5
Clare Rd
Cardiff / Caerdydd CF11 194 F4
Treorchy / Treorci CF42 78 C5
Ystalyfera SA9 2 B7
Clare St
Cardiff / Caerdydd CF11 194 F5
Merthyr Tydfil / Merthyr Tudful CF47 30 E7
Swansea / Abertawe SA5 68 C3
Clarice St 7 SA12 98 E1
Clarion Cl
Llansamlet SA6 46 B1
Swansea / Abertawe SA6 69 C8
Clarion Ct SA6 69 C8
Clark Ave NP44 89 E6
Clarke St CF5 193 F6
Clarke Way SA1 69 D6
Clark St CF42 78 D6
Clas Cwm CF37 109 D6
Clas Dyfrig 1 CF14 177 B3
CLASE 68 D8
Clasemont Rd
Swansea / Abertawe, Morriston / Treforys SA6 45 F2
Swansea / Abertawe SA6 45 D2
Clase Prim Sch SA6 68 D8
Clase Rd
Swansea / Abertawe SA6 46 A1
Swansea / Abertawe SA6 69 B8
Clas Gabriel 3 CF14 177 B3
Clas Gwernifor CF45 54 E2
Clas Heulog CF14 177 B4
Clas Illtyd CF14 177 C4
Clas Isan CF14 177 C4
Clas Odyn CF14 177 B5
Clas Teilo 2 CF14 177 B3
Clas-Ty-Gelli CF37 109 D6
Clas Tynewydd CF14 177 B4
Clas Ty'n-y-Cae CF14 177 C6
Clas Ty Wern CF14 177 C6
Clas-y-Bedw SA5 66 F3
Clas-y-Dderwen CF45 54 E3
Clas-y-Deri SA5 67 A3
Clas Yorath CF14 177 B5
Clas-yr-Onnen SA5 67 A3
Claude Pl CF24 195 C8
Claude Rd
Barry / Y Barri CF62 214 D5
Caerphilly / Caerffili CF83 138 A2
Cardiff / Caerdydd CF24 195 C8
Claude Rd W CF62 214 D4
Claverton Cl CF38 156 B6
Claverton Way CF23 160 E1
Claymore Pl CF11 207 A8
Clayton Cres CF37 109 C5
Clayton Rd SA4 19 A4
Clayton St
Newport / Casnewydd NP19 143 D6
Swansea / Abertawe SA1 68 D4
Clear Spring / Ffynnon Groyw CF31 168 B4
Clearwater Rd NP19 144 D1
Clear Water Way CF23 178 B5
Clearway Ct CF14 177 A4
Clearwell Ct NP10 141 E3
Cleddau Cl CF3 180 B7
Cledwen Cl CF62 214 B5
Cledwyn Gdns CF44 28 E4
Cledwyn Terr CF44 28 E4
Clees La SA9 2 A5
Cleeve Dr CF14 177 E7
Cleeves Terr NP4 37 F3
Cleighton Terr SA10 48 F2
Clement Atlee Dr NP19 144 D7
Clement Pl CF62 214 C2
Cleppa Park Ind Est NP10 163 C7
Clevedon Ave CF64 216 B4
Clevedon Ct
5 Cardiff / Caerdydd CF3 179 C6
Swansea / Abertawe SA2 94 F7
Clevedon Rd
Cardiff / Caerdydd CF3 179 C6
Newport / Casnewydd NP19 144 A6
Cleveland Ave SA3 123 C3
Cleveland Dr NP11 115 C1
Clevis Cres CF36 183 D8
Clevis Ct CF33 165 F6
Clevisfield Ave CF36 183 D8
Clevis Hill CF36 183 D8
Clevis La CF36 183 D8
Cleviston Gdns CF36 183 C8
Cleviston Pk SA14 42 A6
Clewer Court Mews 7 NP20 142 F4
Clewer Ct 6 NP20 142 F4
Cliff Ct CF10 195 C2
Cliff Hill CF64 207 B2
Clifflands Cl SA3 122 F4
Clifford St SA11 71 D6
Cliff Par CF64 207 B2
Cliff Pl CF5 194 B6
Cliff Rd
Blackwood / Coed-Duon NP12 85 F7
Penarth CF64 207 B2
Cliff Side CF64 207 B1
Cliff St
Mountain Ash / Aberpennar CF45 54 D2
Penarth CF64 207 B5
Cliff Terr CF37 135 D8
Cliff Wood View CF62 214 A2
Clifton Cres 6 CF44 53 D7
Clifton Ct
Aberdare / Aberdâr CF44 28 F2
1 Cardiff / Caerdydd CF24 195 D6
Swansea / Abertawe SA5 68 C6
Clifton Hill SA1 233 A3
Clifton Ho CF23 178 D3
Clifton Mews 2 CF24 195 D6
Clifton Pl NP20 143 B4
Clifton Rd NP20 143 B4
Clifton Row
Porth CF39 108 A2
Swansea / Abertawe SA1 233 A3
Clifton Sq NP4 62 E3
Clifton St
Aberdare / Aberdâr CF44 28 F1
Barry / Y Barri CF62 214 D3
Caerphilly / Caerffili CF83 138 B2
Cardiff / Caerdydd CF24 195 D6
Risca / Rhisga NP11 141 D8
Treorchy / Treorci CF42 78 D5
Clifton Terr
Aberavon SA12 99 B1
2 Llanelli SA15 40 F6
The Mumbles / Y Mwmbwls SA3 123 C4
Clifton Terr / Teras Clifton 3 NP4 17 C7
Clinton Rd CF64 207 A2
Clipper Cl NP19 117 F1
Clipper Rd CF10 195 F3
Clist Rd NP20 116 C2
Clist Wlk NP20 116 C2
Clive Cres CF64 207 B4
Clive Ct CF5 194 B6
Clive La
Cardiff / Caerdydd CF11 194 F2
1 Penarth CF64 206 F5
Clive Mews CF5 194 B6
Clive Pl
Aberdare / Aberdâr CF44 28 E4
Barry / Y Barri CF62 214 F2
Cardiff / Caerdydd CF24 232 D4
Penarth CF64 207 B4
Clive Rd
Barry / Y Barri CF62 214 F3
Cardiff / Caerdydd CF5 194 B6
St Athan / Sain Tathan CF62 211 D6
Clive St
Aberdare / Aberdâr CF44 28 E4
Caerphilly / Caerffili CF83 138 A2
Cardiff / Caerdydd CF11 194 F2
Senghenydd CF83 110 F2
Clive Terr CF37 81 F1
Cloda Ave SA10 48 C2
Clodien Ave CF14 177 F2
Cloister Ct CF5 193 E4
Cloisters The SA1 95 A6
Cloisters Wlk / Rhodfa'r Glwysti SA12 98 D3
Clomendy Rd NP44 89 E2
Clonakilty Way CF23 161 A2
Clordir Rd SA4 44 A7
Clos Aberteifi / Cardigan Cl NP44 89 F6
Clos Aderyn Du SA5 67 F3
Clos Ael-y-bryn SA14 218 D7
Clos Affalon SA18 220 D6
Clos Afon Llan SA4 66 C6
Clos Afon Llwyd NP4 62 C7
Clos Afon Tywi NP12 85 C6
Clos Alaw SA7 69 E6
Clos Allt-y-Gog SA4 19 C3
Clos Alun CF72 153 C3
Clos Alyn CF23 160 F1
Clos Andreas 3 SA15 40 E6
Clos Aneira SA5 67 D3
Clos Aneurin CF37 136 B4
Clos Ar Ddafen SA14 41 C5
Clos Arian / Silver Cl 15 SA12 98 B3
Clos Arthur Morris SA5 68 C3
Clos Arundel / Arundel Cl 3 NP44 89 A3
Clos Avro CF24 196 B7
Clos Banc Y Berllan SA4 19 D3
Clos Benallt Fawr SA4 19 A6
Clos Berea / Berea Cl NP23 15 D7
Clos Berriew 5 CF14 177 B3
Clos Bevan SA4 66 A5
Clos Blean Crymlyn SA7 69 F6
Clos Brenin CF72 173 A6
Clos Bron Iestyn CF37 109 A1
Clos Bronwydd NP23 7 D2
Clos Brynafon SA4 42 F3
Clos Bryn Brith NP22 12 E8
Clos Bryncarn SA18 220 C7
Clos Bryn Celyn CF82 84 E3
Clos Bryn Dafydd SA4 44 C2
Clos Brynderi CF14 177 C7
Clos Bryngwili SA4 18 F3
Clos Bryngwyn SA4 66 D8
Clos Bryn Isaf SA14 41 D4
Clos Brynlliw SA4 43 C7
Clos Brynmellyn 1 CF15 176 B6
Clos Burlais SA5 68 A2
Clos Bychan CF44 28 C3
Clos Cadno
Llansamlet SA7 46 D1
Swansea / Abertawe SA6 45 F5
Clos Cadwgan 4 CF38 156 A5
Clos Cae Dafydd SA4 66 A5
Clos Cae Fainc SA14 42 B7
Clos Caeffatri / Caeffatri Cl 1 CF31 168 F6
Clos Cae Mawr CF82 84 F7
Clos Cae Pwll CF46 83 D4
Clos Caer Elms SA15 40 B6
Clos-Cae-Rhos CF82 84 F6
Clos Caerloyn / Gloucester Cl NP44 90 B3
Clos Caersalem SA6 68 C7
Clos Cae'r Wern CF83 158 E8
Clos Caerwrangon / Worcester Cl 8 NP44 90 A3
Clos Cae Uchaf / Highfield Cl NP44 117 B8
Clos Caewal CF15 157 C1
Clos Cae Wal CF15 158 C1
Clos Calfaria SA5 67 E3
Clos Camlas
Pontypridd CF37 109 D2
10 Swansea / Abertawe SA6 69 A8
Clos Caradog CF38 156 D8
Clos Carolyn NP12 85 C6
Clos Cas-Bach 7 CF3 180 A6
Clos Castell Coity 8 CF31 168 C3
Clos Castell Newydd CF31 168 C3
Clos Cefn Bryn SA14 41 E4
Clos Cefn Bychan CF15 157 D1
Clos Cefn Glas CF38 156 C5
Clos Cefni CF62 214 C6
Clos Cefn-y-Maes SA14 41 C5
Clos Ceirios CF5 193 D5
Clos Ceirw NP12 85 C6
Clos Celyn
Bettws CF32 129 E3
Swansea / Abertawe SA7 69 D6
Clos Cemmaes 6 CF14 177 B3
Clos Cenawon SA6 46 A3
Clos Cerdinen SA4 44 C4
Clos Ceri SA6 46 E8
Clos Chappell CF3 179 F5
Clos Cilfwnwr SA4 44 B3
Clos Cilsaig SA14 41 C8
Clos Claerwen NP12 85 C6
Clos Clun Mil / Glynmil Cl CF47 10 F2
Clos Coed Arian SA12 98 D1
Clos Coed Bach NP12 85 D7
Clos Coed Cerdinen / Rowan Tree Cl SA10 48 D2
Clos Coed Duon NP12 85 D6
Clos Coed Hir CF14 176 F6
Clos Coedydafarn CF14 160 C2
Clos Coed-y-wennol / Swallow Tree Cl SA10 48 E2
Clos Collwyn CF38 156 B5
Clos Cornel CF14 177 B4
Clos Cornelius / Cornelius Cl CF33 165 F6
Clos Corris 9 CF14 177 B3
Clos Cradog CF64 206 E1
Clos Creyr CF38 135 D1
Clos Cromwell CF14 159 C1
Clos Crucywel SA6 46 A4
Clos Culver CF5 193 B3
Clos Cwm Barri CF62 214 B4
Clos Cwm Creunant CF23 160 F1
Clos Cwm Du CF23 160 F1
Clos Cwm Garw CF83 137 D3
Clos Cwm Y Glyn / Glendale Ct SA10 48 C3
Clos Cwningen SA7 47 B1
Clos Cwrt Y Carne SA4 43 A4
Clos Cydweli / Kidwelly Cl 1 NP44 90 A2
Clos Cynan SA2 93 F8
Clos Cyncoed CF83 137 D6
Clos Dalton / Dalton Cl SA12 124 D8
Clos Darran Las CF15 174 E7
Clos Ddu SA5 68 B7
Clos Ddyfan CF3 180 A8
Clos Delyth SA4 43 C2
Clos Dennithorne / Dennithorne Cl CF48 11 C4
Clos Derwen
Cardiff / Caerdydd CF23 178 B2
Swansea / Abertawe SA7 70 A6
Clos Dewi Medi SA15 40 E2
Clos Dewi Saint CF11 194 E6
Clos Dimbych-y-Pysgod / Tenby Cl 4 NP44 90 A3
Clos Dol Heulog CF23 160 F1
Clos Drybrook / Drybrook Cl NP44 89 F3
Clos Dwyerw CF83 137 E1
Clos Dyffrynlliw / Lliw Valley Cl SA4 66 C6
Clos Dyfnaint 8 CF3 180 A6
Clos Dyfodwg CF38 156 B5
Close Below the Hillside / Clos Tan-y-fron CF31 169 B3
Close Below the Ridge / Clos Tan-y-cefn CF31 169 B3
Clos Ebol SA6 45 F4
Clos Edith Mills / Edith Mills Cl SA11 71 C4
Clos Edno CF23 178 C3
Clos Eiddiw CF5 193 E5
Clos Eileen Chilcott SA7 69 E6
Clos Elphan CF3 180 A8
Clos Emily SA14 218 C7
Clos Enfys CF83 137 E1
Clos Erw Werdd SA14 218 B7
Close The
Aberdare / Aberdâr CF44 29 A1
Bargoed / Bargod CF81 58 A1
Cardiff / Caerdydd CF14 177 F8
Cefn Hengoed CF82 84 F4
Gorseinon SA4 43 A1
Llanrhidian SA4 229 F4
Oystermouth SA3 122 F6
Rhydyfelin CF37 136 A6
Sarn CF32 150 D4
Swansea / Abertawe SA5 45 C2
Close The / Y Clos 1 NP44 116 F8
Clos Ewenni / Ewenny Cl CF36 165 E2
Clos Fach CF14 177 C8
Clos Fairwater / Fairwater Cl NP44 89 B2
Clos Felen 3 SA18 220 B8
Clos Ffawydden CF71 189 C8
Clos Gathen SA15 40 D4
Clos Gedrych CF11 194 B5
Clos Gelli / Gelli Cl NP22 13 E7
Clos George Morgan SA6 45 E4
Clos Ger-y-Bryn SA4 44 C5
Clos Ger-y-Maes SA4 44 C5
Clos Glanaber 9 CF3 180 A6
Clos Glanlliw SA4 44 A6
Clos Glanllyn / Lakeside Cl
Brynmawr NP23 8 B3
Tredegar NP22 6 B1
Clos Glanmor SA15 40 C4
Clos Glan Nant CF83 138 A1
Clos Glan-yr-Afon SA2 94 C6
Clos Glanyrafon / Riverside Cl CF48 55 C5
Clos Glan-y-Wern SA7 69 E6
Clos Glas Llwch CF3 179 F5
Clos Glas Y Dorlan / Kingfisher Cl CF31 169 C4
Clos Glyndwr SA4 18 F5
Clos Golwg Y Coed / Wood View Cl 2 SA11 71 C1
Clos Golwg Y Parc / Park View Cl 1 SA11 71 C1
Clos Golwyg Yr Hafod / Hafod View Cl NP23 8 D4
Clos Gors Fawr SA4 43 C6
Clos Graddfa CF82 111 E7
Clos Granby SA15 40 E2
Clos Greig / Greig Cl 8 SA12 98 B3
Clos Gronw NP12 85 C6
Clos Guto CF83 138 D4
Clos Gwastir CF83 137 E1
Clos Gwaun Gledyr CF83 137 D3
Clos Gwendraeth NP12 85 C6
Clos Gwent CF38 155 F5
Clos Gwernen
Gowerton / Tre-gwyr SA4 66 C6
Llanharry CF72 172 D5
Clos Gwernydd CF83 137 D4
Clos Gwern-y-Mor 13 CF3 179 F6
Clos Gwlad-yr-Haf 10 CF3 180 A6
Clos Gwy CF23 160 F1
Clos Gwynedd CF38 155 F5
Clos Gwynle CF83 137 D1
Clos Hafodyrynys 18 CF3 179 F6
Clos Hafren 6 CF3 180 A6
Clos Halkett CF11 194 B4
Clos Harlech / Harlech Cl 2 NP44 90 A6
Clos Harvard Jones / Harvard Jones Cl SA11 71 C4
Clos Healy SA4 66 B6
Clos Hector CF24 196 B7
Clos Helyg SA4 66 B5
Clos Henblas / Old Mansion Cl CF31 168 A4
Clos Hendra SA6 22 B2
Clos Hendre CF14 177 D8
Clos Henfaes CF33 165 E8
Clos Hensol / Hensol Cl 7 NP44 90 A3
Clos Hereford CF72 155 D2
Clos Heulwen CF15 158 A6
Clos Hogarth / Hogarth Cl NP44 117 A8
Clos Islwyn SA2 93 E8
Clos Kern / Kern Cl SA12 98 B3
Clos Lancaster CF72 155 D2
Clos Leighton Davies SA4 66 B6
Clos Leland CF72 155 D2
Clos Lindsay CF5 193 A3
Clos Llanduowg / Tythegston Cl CF36 165 F2
Clos Llandyfan SA4 66 D8
Clos Llanfair CF5 205 A6
Clos Llanfihangel SA14 41 B6
Clos Llangefni CF38 155 F6
Clos Llarwydden SA4 44 C2
Clos Llawhaden CF62 215 A8
Clos Llewellyn CF15 174 E6
Clos Llwydlo / Ludlow Cl 3 NP44 90 B1
Clos Llwynallt SA8 23 E2
Clos Llwyn Y Pwll / Llwyn Y Pwll Cl NP23 8 D4
Clos Llyg SA7 70 B8
Clos Llyn Cwm SA6 69 A6
Clos Llysfaen CF14 159 F3
Clos Llyswen CF82 84 F7
Clos LLysweri / Liswerry Cl 2 NP44 90 B2
Clos Lorraine / Lorraine Cl 2 SA12 98 D1
Clos-Mabon CF14 177 B8
Clos Madlen SA5 67 D4
Clos Maedref CF15 176 D5
Clos Maerun 17 CF3 179 F6
Clos Maes Brag CF83 138 B3
Clos Maes Isaf SA14 42 C7
Clos Maes Mawr CF83 137 F6
Clos Maes-y-mor 11 CF3 180 A6
Clos Maes Yr Ysgol SA4 19 D3
Clos Mair CF23 178 B3
Clos Mancheldowne 6 CF62 214 E4
Clos Manmoel CF3 179 F6
Clos Man-Teg / Fairplace Ct CF31 168 A3
Clos Marian CF10 195 F3
Clos Marina SA4 66 B6
Clos Masons / Masons Cl CF33 148 D3
Clos Medwy CF3 180 A8
Clos Meifod 7 CF14 177 B3
Clos Melin Ddwr CF14 160 A2
Clos Melin Mynach SA4 66 C8
Clos Menter CF14 177 D2
Clos Milton / Milton Cl 7 NP44 89 D2
Clos Min Yr Afon SA4 42 F2
Clos Morfran / Cormorant Cl SA15 40 B6
Clos Morgan Gruffydd CF83 136 F7
Clos Morgannwg SA1 95 A8
Clos Morgan Owen SA4 66 A5
Clos Myddlyn CF38 155 F5
Clos Mynach CF82 84 F7
Clos Mynydd / Mountain Cl CF32 129 E3
Clos Nant Bran SA7 47 A2
Clos Nant Coslech CF23 160 E1
Clos Nant Ddu CF23 160 F1
Clos Nanteos CF23 179 B8
Clos Nant Glaswg CF23 160 E1
Clos Nant Mwlan CF23 160 F1
Clos Nant-y-Ci SA18 218 F7
Clos Nant Y Cor CF23 160 F1
Clos Nant Y Cwm CF23 160 F1
Clos Nantydd SA14 41 C4
Clos Nant Yr Aber CF83 137 F4
Clos Newydd CF14 176 F4
Clos Norfolk / Norfolk Cl 5 NP44 89 A3
Clos Ogney CF61 209 F7
Clos Olway / Olway Cl 1 NP44 90 B1
Clos Onnen SA13 148 A5
Clos Padrig CF3 180 A8
Clos Pandy CF83 138 D6
Clos Pant Glas CF83 138 F6
Clos Pantycosyn 12 CF3 179 F6
Clos Parc Radyr CF15 176 C4
Clos Peiriant CF63 215 A4

Clos Penbwl SA4 .... 44 C2
Clos Pendderi SA14 .... 41 F5
Clos Penderri SA4 .... 44 C2
Clos Pengelli SA4 .... 43 C7
Clos Penglyn CF35 ...... 152 E2
Clos Penllwyngwyn
SA14 .... 41 F6
Clos Pen Pant SA4 .... 19 D4
Clos Pentref SA10 .... 222 D3
Clos Pentyle SA8 .... 23 B2
Clos Pen y Banc SA6 ..... 68 C8
Clos Pen Y Clawdd 7
CF3 .... 179 F6
Clos Penyfai SA15 .... 40 B7
Clos Pen Y Waun
SA14 .... 218 C7
Clos Penywaun /
Penywaun Cl NP12 ..... 59 C2
Clos Pinwydden CF72 ... 172 D5
Clos Pisgah / Pisgah Cl
NP4 .... 37 E5
Clos Plas Isaf SA14 .... 42 C7
Clos Powys CF38 .... 155 F6
Clos Pupren CF72 .... 172 D5
Clos Redman / Redman Cl
CF33 .... 148 D2
Clos Rhandir SA4 .... 65 E8
Clos Rhedyn
Cardiff / Caerdydd
CF5 .... 193 E5
Cwmrhydyceirw SA6 ...... 46 A4
Clos Rhiannon CF14 ..... 159 D2
Clos Rhydwely / Bedford
Cl 2 NP44 .... 89 A3
Clos Rhymni SA6 .... 46 A4
Clos Sable / Sable Cl 7
SA12 .... 98 B2
Clos Sain Dunwyd / St
Donats Cl CF48 .... 225 F1
Clos Sain Ffraid / St
Brides Cl NP44 .... 90 A2
Clos St Catherine / St
Catherines Cl SA11 ..... 71 D5
Clos St Catwg CF5 ...... 175 E5
Clos St Cenydd SA3 ..... 228 C2
Clos Sandybrook /
Sandybrook Cl NP44 .... 89 C1
Clos San Pedr SA2 .... 67 E2
Clos Sant Antwn / St
Anthony's Cl NP4 .... 62 D2
Clos Sant Benedict / St
Benedict Cl NP4 .... 62 D2
Clos Sant Christopher / St
Christopher's Cl
CF83 .... 138 E6
Clos Sant Dunwyd / St
Donats Pl 7 NP44 ...... 90 B2
Clos Santes Fair / St
Marys Cl CF35 .... 170 D5
Clos Sant Lago / St James'
Cl CF48 .... 31 A5
Clos Sant Paul SA15 ...... 40 D4
Clos Sant Pedr 5 SA15 ... 40 D4
Clos Sant Pedr / St Peters
Cl NP44 .... 89 B2
Clos Sant Teilo SA5 ...... 45 B1
Clos Saron SA5 .... 67 F3
Clos Springfield CF72 ... 155 B2
Clos Synod 8 CF14 ..... 177 B3
Clos Taf CF5 .... 176 F2
Clos Tan-y-cefn / Close
Below the Ridge
NP12 .... 59 C2
CF31 .... 169 B3
Clos Tan-y-fron / Close
Below the Hillside
CF31 .... 169 B3
Clos Tawe CF62 .... 214 C6
Clos Tecwyn CF23 .... 178 B3
Clos Tirffordd SA4 .... 44 C2
Clos Tir-isaf / Lowland Cl
CF31 .... 168 C2
Clos Tir Twyn CF82 ..... 111 F7
Clos Tir-y-Pwll NP11 .... 87 B7
Clos Ton Mawr CF14 .... 159 C1
Clos Trafle SA4 .... 66 C6
Clos Trefeddyg CF83 .... 139 F6
Clos Trefin NP12 .... 85 F3
Clos Trefor / Trevor Cl
CF48 .... 11 B7
Clos Tregantllo /
Candleston Cl CF36 .... 165 E2
Clos Tregare 10 CF3 ..... 179 F6
Clos Tregwyr SA4 .... 66 C5
Clos Trelales / Laleston Cl
CF36 .... 165 E2
Clos Treoda CF14 .... 177 B5
Clos Treventy SA14 ..... 218 A8
Clos Tuar Mor / Seaward
Cl SA12 .... 98 C1
Clos Tudur / Tudor Cl
CF48 .... 55 D4
Clos Ty Bronna CF5 ..... 193 C7
Clos Ty Clyd CF14 ...... 176 E4
Clos Tygwyn
Clydach SA6 .... 46 E8
Gowerton / Tre-gwyr SA4 .. 66 B6
Clos Ty-Gwyn SA4 .... 18 F4
Clos Tyla Bach CF3 ..... 180 B7
Clos Ty Mawr SA4 .... 44 B2
Clos Ty-melin CF37 ..... 135 F6
Clos Tyniad Glo CF63 ... 215 A4
Clos Ty'r Ysgol / School
House Cl 1 CF33 ...... 165 F7
Clos Tyrywen CF83 ...... 138 D6
Clos Ty Tafol SA15 .... 40 D3
Clos Vellacott / Vellacott
Cl CF10 .... 232 C1
Clos Vernon Watkins
SA4 .... 43 A4
Clos Warren / Warren Cl
SA11 .... 71 D4
Clos Waun Ceffyl CF46 ... 83 D4
Clos Waun Fach CF83 ... 137 D1
Clos Waun Wen SA6 ..... 45 B1
Clos William CF14 ...... 159 C1
Clos William Price
CF37 .... 135 F8
Clos Wordsworth /
Wordsworth Cl 6
NP44 .... 89 D2
Clos-y-asgell Goch /
Redwing Cl CF31 ...... 169 C4
Clos Y Banc-yr-Eithin
SA4 .... 43 A3
Clos Y Berllan 4 CF3 ... 180 A6
Clos-y-Berllan SA14 ..... 41 F5
Clos y Berllan / Orchard Cl
CF48 .... 55 C6
Clos-y-Betws 8 CF3 .... 179 F6
Clos-y-Blaidd CF14 ..... 159 D4
Clos Y Bont Faen
Cwmrhydyceirw SA6 ...... 46 A5
Swansea / Abertawe SA6 .. 45 F4
Clos-y-Broch CF14 ..... 159 E3
Clos Y Bryn CF14 .... 159 A1
Clos Y Bwau / Arches Cl
NP22 .... 6 D2
Clos-y-Carlwm CF14 .... 159 D4
Clos-y-Carw CF38 ...... 156 B6
Clos-y-Cedr CF83 .... 138 A6
Clos-y-Ceinach CF14 ... 159 E3
Clos y Coden Geirios /
Cherry Tree Cl NP44 .... 90 B5
Clos y Coed
Llantwit Fadre / Llanilltud
Faerdref CF38 .... 156 E8
Pen-Y-Fai CF31 .... 168 D8
Clos Y Coedwr SA6 .... 46 D7
Clos Y Craig CF14 ...... 159 B1
Clos Y Crydd / Shoemaker
Cl NP23 .... 8 D4
Clos-y-Culfor 15 CF3 ... 179 F6
Clos-y-Cwarra CF5 ..... 192 F5
Clos-y-Cwm SA14 ...... 218 D7
Clos-y-Dderwen /
Oaklands Cl SA14 ...... 218 B8
Clos Y Dderwen / Oak
Tree Cl SA18 .... 219 D7
Clos-y-Deri SA4 .... 218 D2
Clos Y Deri SA14 .... 41 B8
Clos-y-Deri CF36 .... 182 F8
Clos y Dolydd CF38 ..... 156 A5
Clos-y-Draenog CF14 ... 159 E3
Clos Y Dryw CF14 ...... 159 E4
Clos-y-Dyfrgi CF14 ..... 159 D3
Clos-y-Felin SA18 ...... 219 D7
Clos Y Felin CF82 ...... 111 E7
Clos Y Ffynnon CF23 .... 160 F1
Clos Y Fran
Cardiff / Caerdydd
CF14 .... 159 E4
Glais SA7 .... 47 A6
Clos Y Fynwent SA4 ...... 19 D3
Clos Y Gamlas CF14 .... 176 E6
Clos Y Gelyn CF23 ...... 178 F7
Clos-y-Gof CF5 .... 192 F5
Clos Y Gof / Blacksmith Cl
NP12 .... 59 C2
Clos Y Gorllewin / West Cl
10 CF10 .... 195 B2
Clos Y Goron NP12 .... 85 D3
Clos-y-Grug CF36 ...... 182 F8
Clos Y Grug / Calluna Cl
CF48 .... 11 C4
Clos Y Gwadd CF14 ..... 159 D3
Clos Y Gwalch CF14 .... 159 E4
Clos-y-Gweydd SA4 ..... 66 A5
Clos y Gwyddfid CF15 ... 176 A8
Clos Y Hebog CF14 ..... 159 E4
Clos Y Lanfa / Pier Cl
SA12 .... 98 C1
Clos-y-Maerdy SA4 ..... 66 C8
Clos Y Mennol / Swallow
Cl CF33 .... 147 F1
Clos Y Morfa SA4 .... 42 F3
Clos Y Mynydd
Gorseinon SA4 .... 42 F2
Morganstown / Treforgan
CF15 .... 176 A7
Clos Y Nant
4 Cardiff / Caerdydd
CF5 .... 193 D8
Gorseinon SA4 .... 42 F2
Clos Ynysddu CF72 ..... 173 A8
Clos-y-pant CF83 ...... 158 E8
Clos Y Porthmon SA4 .... 66 C5
Clos-y-Priordy / Priory Ct
SA10 .... 48 C2
Clos Yr Ael SA1 .... 67 E2
Clos Yr Aer CF14 .... 177 C8
Clos Yr Alarch CF14 .... 159 E4
Clos Yr Allt SA1 .... 67 F2
Clos Yr Arad CF83 ..... 137 D1
Clos-Yr-Ardd CF14 ..... 177 B7
Clos Yr Aut / Hillside Cl
CF48 .... 55 C5
Clos Yr Eglwys SA1 ...... 67 F2
Clos-yr- Eirin CF31 .... 168 B6
Clos Yr Eos CF14 .... 159 E4
Clos-yr-Eos CF33 ...... 165 F6
Clos yr Erw CF64 .... 206 E1
Clos-yr-Gornant 5
CF3 .... 180 A6
Clos Yr Hafod CF14 .... 177 C8
Clos Yr Harbwr CF62 ... 214 D2
Clos-yr-Hendre SA18 ... 218 E6
Clos Yr Hesg SA7 .... 46 D1
Clos-y-Rhiw CF5 .... 193 B3
Clos-yr-Onnen CF3 ..... 180 A6
Clos Yr Onnen SA7 .... 46 D1
Clos-yr-Onnen CF61 .... 210 A5
Clos Yr Orsaf 9 SA6 ..... 69 A8
Clos-yr-Orsaf / Station Cl
3 CF36 .... 182 F7
Clos Yr Wenallt CF14 ... 159 B1
Clos Yr Wylan CF62 .... 214 F2
Clos Yr Ysgol
Llanelli SA15 .... 40 F5
Swansea / Abertawe SA7 .. 70 A7
Clos Yr Ysgol / School Cl
CF46 .... 83 E3
Clos Ysbyty
Caerphilly / Caerffili
CF83 .... 137 F1
Neath / Castell-Nedd
SA11 .... 72 A4
Clos Ysgallen SA7 .... 69 D6
Clos Y Sgubor / Barn Cl
NP4 .... 38 B2
Clos Ystum Taf CF14 ... 176 E4
Clos-y-Talcen CF31 .... 168 D8
Clos Y Tywod / Sandy Cl
12 SA12 .... 98 D1
Clos-y-Waun CF31 ..... 169 A5
Clos Y Waun SA14 ..... 218 B7
Clos Y Waun / Meadow Cl
CF39 .... 133 A3
Clos-y-Wern CF31 ..... 169 A5
Clos Y Wern CF14 ...... 177 C8
Clos-y-Wiwer
Cardiff / Caerdydd
CF14 .... 159 E3
Llantwit Major / Llanilltud
Fawr CF61 .... 210 A7
Cloth Hall La CF48 .... 10 A5
Clovelly Ave NP23 .... 14 E5
Clovelly Cres CF3 ...... 179 A5
Clovelly Pl SA3 .... 122 E6
Clover Ct NP44 .... 88 F1
Clover Gr CF5 .... 176 C1
Clover Rd CF47 .... 10 C4
Club La SA9 .... 1 F1
Club Rd NP4 .... 62 A6
Club Row
Abersychan NP4 .... 37 F2
Blaina / Blaenau NP13 .... 15 E5
Clydach NP7 .... 9 D6
Ystrad CF41 .... 79 D3
Club St CF44 .... 53 B8
Clun Ave CF72 .... 173 B8
Clun Cres CF72 .... 173 B8
CLUN-DU 45 F1
Clun Prim Sch SA11 .... 226 C4
Clun Terr CF24 .... 178 A2
Clun-y-Bont SA11 ...... 227 B8
Clwyd CF64 .... 207 C5
Clwyd Ave CF44 .... 29 E2
Clwyd Com Prim Sch
SA5 .... 68 A4
Clwyd Ho 3 CF23 ...... 178 C2
Clwyd Rd
Gwaun-Cae-Gurwen
SA18 .... 220 D6
Swansea / Abertawe SA5 .. 68 B4
Clwyd Way CF62 .... 211 D7
Clwyd -Wen SA4 .... 66 A5
Clwyd-y-Clap La NP4 .... 39 C4
Clwydyfagwyr CF48 .... 225 F1
CLYDACH
Brynmawr 9 E6
Swansea 46 D7
Clydach Ave
Ebbw Vale / Glyn Ebwy
NP23 .... 7 C5
Resolven / Resolfen
SA11 .... 226 E5
Clydach Cl
Bettws NP20 .... 116 E1
Pontypridd CF37 .... 109 D5
Clydach Cty Prim Sch
NP7 .... 9 D6
Clydach Hospl SA6 .... 46 D7
Clydach Inf Sch / Ysgol
Plant Bach Clydach
SA6 .... 46 D7
Clydach Jun Sch / Ysgol
Iau Clydach SA6 .... 46 D8
Clydach Rd
Craig-cefn-parc SA6 ...... 22 B2
Tonypandy CF40 .... 106 C7
Ynysforgan SA6 .... 46 A2
Ynystawe SA6 .... 46 C5
Ynysybwl CF37 .... 81 F2
Clydach St
Brynmawr NP23 .... 8 C5
Cardiff / Caerdydd CF11 .. 195 A3
Clydach Terr CF37 .... 81 F2
CLYDACH TERRACE 8 B7
CLYDACH VALE 106 B7
Clydach Vale Ctry Pk*
CF40 .... 105 F6
Clyde Cl NP12 .... 85 D4
Clydesmuir Ind Est
CF24 .... 195 F8
Clydesmuir Rd CF24 .... 195 F7
Clyde St
2 Cardiff / Caerdydd
CF24 .... 195 D5
Risca / Rhisga NP11 .... 115 A1
Clyffard Cres NP20 ..... 143 B4
Clyffes NP44 .... 89 B3
Clyn Cwm Gwyn SA2 ..... 93 F6
Clyndu St SA6 .... 68 F8
CLYNE 226 B3
Clyne Castle SA3 .... 94 A2
Clyne Cl SA3 .... 93 F1
Clyne Cres SA3 .... 93 F1
Clyne Ct
Clyne SA11 .... 226 A3
Swansea / Abertawe SA2 .. 94 B7
Clyne Dr SA2 .... 94 B1
Clyne Farm Activties Ctr*
SA3 .... 93 F2
Clyne Rd CF82 .... 84 F5
Clyne Terr SA11 .... 226 B3
Clyne Valley Cotts SA2 ... 93 E5
Clyne Valley Ctry Pk*
SA2 .... 94 A4
Clyne Valley La SA2 ...... 94 B2
Clyne Valley Rd SA2 ...... 93 E5
Clyne View SA2 .... 93 E6
Clyngwyn Rd
Treherbert CF42 .... 50 D3
Ystalyfera SA9 .... 2 B7
Clyngwyn Terr CF42 ...... 50 D3
Clynmaes Pl SA5 .... 67 E6
Clynmawr St NP13 .... 36 A5
Clyro Ct SA1 .... 69 C4
Clyro Pl CF14 .... 177 A3
Clytha Cres 3 NP20 .... 143 C3
CLYTHA PARK 143 A4
Clytha Park Rd NP20 ... 143 A5
Clytha Prim Sch NP20 ... 142 F4
Clytha Sq
Abercarn NP11 .... 87 C3
Newport / Casnewydd
NP20 .... 143 C3
CNAP-LLWYD 68 D5
Cnap Llwyd Rd SA6 ...... 68 D6
Coach Bach NP22 .... 6 D1
COALBROOK 43 B5
Coalbrook Rd SA4 .... 43 C5
COALBROOKVALE 15 D7
Coalbrook Valecourt
NP23 .... 15 C7
Coalbrookvale Terr
NP23 .... 15 C8
Coal Pit La CF3 .... 162 B4
Coal Plant Control Rd
CF62 .... 211 F1
Coaster Pl CF10 .... 195 F3
Coates Pl CF3 .... 179 D7
Coates Rd CF64 .... 206 F1
Cobblers Ct 1 SA15 ...... 40 D6
Cobden Pl
Abercarn NP11 .... 114 C4
4 Merthyr Tydfil / Merthyr
Tudful CF47 .... 30 E8
Cobden St
Abercarn NP11 .... 114 C4
Aberdare / Aberdâr CF44 .. 53 C6
Cobham Cl SA4 .... 43 A3
Cobham Dr SA11 .... 72 C5
Cobner Cl NP4 .... 38 C1
Cobol Rd CF3 .... 180 B7
Coburn St CF24 .... 195 B8
Coch-y-Cwm Rd SA1 ..... 69 C2
Coch-y-North Rd NP4 .... 61 E5
Cocker Ave NP44 .... 89 D1
COCKETT 67 E2
Cockett Rd SA2 .... 67 D2
Codgers Cnr CF38 ...... 156 B7
Coed Arhyd CF5 .... 192 E4
Coed Arian CF14 .... 177 B3
Coed Bach
Barry / Y Barri CF62 ..... 214 C7
Pencoed CF35 .... 170 C8
Coedbach Rd SA4 .... 19 C3
Coed Briwnant CF14 .... 159 C1
Coed Bychan Cres
CF72 .... 153 F3
COED CAE 41 A5
Coedcae
Ebbw Vale / Glyn Ebwy
NP23 .... 7 B4
Pontardawe SA8 .... 23 F6
Ystrad Mynach CF82 ..... 111 E8
Coed Cae
Caerphilly / Caerffili
CF83 .... 138 C4
Cwmbran / Cwmbrân
NP44 .... 89 C5
New Tredegar NP24 .... 33 E2
Coedcae Back CF48 ...... 11 D5
Coedcae Comp Sch
SA15 .... 40 F5
Coed-Cae-Ddu Rd
NP12 .... 85 F4
Coedcae Ganol / Middle
Coedcae 7 NP4 .... 17 D6
Coedcae Ind Est CF72 ... 154 F1
Coed Cae Jun Sch
NP13 .... 15 D7
Coedcae La CF72 .... 155 A1
Coedcae Pl NP4 .... 62 B6
Coedcae'r Cwrt 13 CF47 .. 30 E8
Coedcae Rd
Abertridwr CF83 .... 137 A7
Blaenavon NP4 .... 17 D7
Porth CF39 .... 108 A2
Trehafod CF37 .... 108 B3
Coed Cae Rd
Llanelli, Coed Cae SA15 .... 41 A5
Llanelli, Pen-y-Fan SA15 ... 40 F5
Coed Cae'r Odin CF31 ... 168 B6
Coedcae Row CF48 .... 11 D5
Coedcae St CF11 .... 194 F3
Coedcae Terr
Cwmaman CF44 .... 53 B3
Pontypool / Pont-y-pwl
NP4 .... 62 B6
Coed Cae Uchaf SA15 .... 40 F5
Coedcae Wlk NP12 .... 85 D7
Coed Camlas NP4 .... 62 F5
Coed Ceirios
Cardiff / Caerdydd
CF14 .... 177 B7
Llansamlet SA7 .... 46 D1
Coed Celynen Dr NP11 ... 87 B4
Coed Celyn Rd SA2 ...... 94 B4
COEDCERNYW /
COEDKERNEW 163 B3
Coed Cochwyn Ave
CF14 .... 159 E1
Coed Coesau-whips Forest
Walk* CF14 .... 160 D7
Coed Criafol CF63 ...... 205 B1
Coed Dowlais CF38 ..... 156 E8
COED-DUON /
BLACKWOOD 85 D8
Coed Duon Ct NP12 ...... 85 E7
Coed Duon View NP11 ... 86 D5
Coed Edeyrn CF23 ...... 178 D4
Coed Eithen St NP4 ...... 17 D5
COEDELY 154 E8
Coeden Dal CF23 .... 178 E8
COED EVA 116 B8
Coed Eva Jun & Inf Schs
NP44 .... 89 B1
Coedeva Mill NP44 ...... 116 C8
Coedfan SA2 .... 94 A6
Coed Fedwen SA7 .... 46 E3
Coedffaldau SA9 .... 221 B6
Coedffranc Inf Sch
SA10 .... 70 F7
Coedffranc Jun Sch
SA10 .... 70 F7
Coed Garw NP44 .... 90 A6
Coed Gelli Parc NP12 .... 58 E1
Coed Gethin CF83 ...... 137 E7
Coed Glas
Cwmbran / Cwmbrân
NP44 .... 89 D1
Penywaun CF44 .... 28 B6
Coed Glas Prim Sch
CF14 .... 177 F8
Coed Glas Rd CF14 ..... 177 D8
Coed Helyg CF31 .... 168 B5
COEDHIRWAUN 148 A5
Coed Hirwaun Prim Sch
SA13 .... 147 F6
Coed Isaf Rd CF37 ..... 135 A8
COEDKERNEW /
COEDCERNYW 163 B3
Coedlan SA9 .... 2 D8
Coed Lan SA4 .... 65 D1
Coedlan Brangwyn /
Brangwyn Ave NP44 .... 117 A8
Coedlan Y Coleg /
Academic Ave CF14 ... 177 E3
Coedlan-y-West End /
West End Ave NP4 ...... 37 F2
Coed Leddyn CF83 ...... 137 F6
Coed Lee NP44 .... 89 C1
Coed Lee Ct NP44 .... 89 C1
Coed Llydd NP4 .... 17 D6
Coed Main CF83 .... 138 D4
Coed Marsarnen CF71 ... 187 A3
Coed Mawr
Barry / Y Barri CF62 ..... 214 C7
Ystrad Mynach CF82 ..... 111 E7
Coed Mieri CF72 .... 173 A8
Coed Moelfa Rd NP11 .... 87 B3
Coed Mor SA2 .... 94 B5
Coed-Nant Clos SA1 ...... 68 D2
Coed Parc SA12 .... 99 D5
Coed Parc Ct CF31 ..... 168 E4
COED-PEN MAEN 109 E2
Coedpenmaen Prim Sch
CF37 .... 109 D2
Coedpenmaen Rd
Pontypridd CF37 .... 109 D1
Pontypridd CF37 .... 109 E2
Coed Pwll CF83 .... 138 C4
Coed Rd / Heol Y Coed
NP4 .... 17 D6
Coedriglan Dr CF5 ..... 192 E3
Coed-Saeson Cres SA2 ... 94 D7
Coed Terr
Abersychan NP4 .... 37 E4
4 Blaenavon NP4 .... 17 D6
Coed Tymaen CF31 ..... 168 C6
Coedwig Pl SA5 .... 68 A3
Coedybrain Ct CF83 .... 137 F8
Coed-y-Brain Prim Sch
CF83 .... 137 F8
Coed-y-Brain Rd CF83 .. 137 F8
Coed-y-Brenin /
Kingswood CF37 ...... 135 A8
Coed y Broch CF38 ..... 156 E8
Coed Y Bronallt SA4 ..... 19 A5
Coed Y Bryn NP12 .... 85 D6
Coed-y-Bwlch SA14 ...... 42 A2
Coed y Cadno
Cwmgwili SA14 .... 218 C5
Pen-Y-Fai CF31 .... 168 D8
COED-Y-CAERAU 119 E4
Coed-y-caerau La
NP18 .... 119 E4
Coed-y-Cando Rd NP4 ... 62 F5
Coed Y Capel CF62 ..... 214 C7
Coed-y-crwys SA4 .... 65 E1
COED Y CWM 109 C6
Coed Y Dryw / Wrenwood
SA10 .... 48 C1
Coed y Dyffryn CF38 ... 156 E8

Coed-y-Felln CF62 214 C5
Coed-y-Garn NP23 14 F2
Coed Y Gog CF31 168 B4
Coed-y-Gores CF23 178 E5
Coed-y-Graig
Pencoed CF35 170 D8
Ystrad Mynach CF82 111 E7
Coedygric Rd NP4 62 E3
Coedylan Comp Sch The CF37 109 F6
Coedylan Prim Sch CF37 109 C2
Coed-y-Lan Rd CF37 109 D5
Coed Y Llinos CF83 137 E3
Coed Y Llwyfen / Elmwood NP22 13 F5
Coed-y-Llyn
Cardiff / Caerdydd CF23 178 B4
Radyr CF15 176 A7
Coedymoeth Rd CF81 58 B6
Coed-y-Pandy CF83 138 D6
Coed-y-Pergwm SA11 223 C1
Coed-y-Pia CF83 112 A5
Coed-y-pica CF83 137 A6
Coed Y Pin / Pinewood SA18 219 D7
Coed Yr Eos CF83 137 E3
Coed Yr Esgob CF72 155 C4
Coed-yr-Esgob Prim Sch / Ysgol Gynradd Coed-yr-Esgob CF72 155 D4
Coed-yr-Haf CF82 84 D1
Coed-y-Rhaidyr SA11 224 A3
Coed Yr Odyn CF62 214 B3
Coed Yr Ynn CF14 177 D8
Coed Y Wenallt CF14 159 B1
Coed Y Wennol CF83 137 E2
Coegnant Cl CF31 169 B7
Coegnant Cotts CF34 102 A7
Coegnant Rd
Maesteg, Nantyffyllon CF34 102 A6
Maesteg, Spelter CF34 102 A7
COELBREN 222 F6
Coelbren Cty Prim Sch SA10 222 F6
COETY / COITY 169 C8
Coety Prim Sch / Ysgol Gynradd Coety CF35 169 D8
Coffins Row CF48 10 D1
COG 216 C6
COGAN 206 E5
Cogan Ct CF64 206 E6
Cogan Hill CF64 206 F6
Cogan Pill Rd CF64 206 E6
Cogan Prim Sch CF64 206 E5
Cogan Sta CF64 206 E6
Cogan Terr CF24 232 B4
Coggins Cl CF83 137 D1
Cog Rd CF64 216 B6
Coigne Terr CF63 215 B5
Coity Castle★ CF35 169 C8
Coity Cl CF3 180 A7
COITY / COETY 169 C8
Coity Cres CF31 169 E3
Coity Rd CF31 168 F6
Coity Terr NP4 17 A5
Colbourne Rd CF38 156 A6
Colbourne Terr SA1 233 A5
Colbourne Wlk 9 CF11 194 D5
Colbren Sq SA18 220 D6
Colchester Ave CF23 178 E1
Colchester Ct CF23 178 D1
Colchester Est CF23 178 E1
Colchester Factory Est CF23 195 E8
COLCOT 214 D7
Colcot Prim Sch CF62 204 E1
Colcot Rd CF62 214 D6
Cold Bath Rd NP18 118 B2
Coldbrook Cl CF63 215 D8
Coldbrook Rd E CF63 215 C8
Coldbrook Rd W CF63 215 B7
Cold Knap Way CF62 214 C1
COLDRA 144 F7
Coldra Est NP18 144 F7
Coldra Rd
Blaenrhondda CF42 50 D4
Newport / Casnewydd NP20 143 A3
Treherbert CF42 50 E3
Coldra The NP18 144 F7
Coldra Wood Dr NP18 144 E8
Cold Stores Rd CF10 195 E1
Cold Store The NP44 90 A1
Coldstream Cl NP44 90 A5
Coldstream St SA15 40 C6
Coldstream Terr CF11 194 F5
Cole Ct CF83 138 D4
Coleford Dr CF3 180 A6
Coleford Path NP44 89 C3

Coleg = college

Coleg Abertawe / Swansea Coll (Tycoch Campus) SA2 94 D7
Coleg Brifysgol Cymru / Univ Coll of Wales NP18 118 A3
Coleg Castell Nedd Port Talbot / Neath Port Talbot Coll SA10 71 D8
Coleg Cerdd a Drama Cymru / Welsh Coll of Music & Drama CF10 232 A3
Coleg Glan Hafren / Cardiff Tertiary Coll CF3 179 E4
Coleg Glan Hafren / Cardiff Tertiary College CF24 232 C3
Coleg Gwent (Crosskeys Campus) NP11 114 C4
Coleg Gwent Ebbw Vale Campus NP23 7 C2
Coleg Gwent (Newport Campus) NP19 144 C2
Coleg Gwent (Pontypool Campus) NP4 62 B5
Coleg Morgannwg
Cwmdare CF44 28 D4
Pontypridd CF37 135 F5
Coleg Morgannwg (Rhondda Campus) CF41 79 E1
Coleg Morgannwg (Rhydyfelin Campus) CF37 136 A5
Coleg Pencoed / Pencoed Coll CF35 170 F8
Coleg Penybont / Bridgend Coll CF31 168 F3
Coleg Sir Gâr / Carmarthenshire Coll Ammanford Campus SA18 219 B7
Colenso Terr
Rhymney / Rhymni NP22 12 E5
Tredegar NP22 13 F6
Coleridge Ave CF64 206 F4
Coleridge Cl CF31 168 C6
Coleridge Cres
Barry / Y Barri CF62 214 E8
Swansea / Abertawe SA2 93 F8
Coleridge Gdns CF83 139 C6
Coleridge Gn / Maes Coleridge 13 NP44 89 C2
Coleridge Rd
Cardiff / Caerdydd CF11 194 D1
Newport / Casnewydd NP19 144 A5
Coleshill Terr SA15 40 C5
Colhugh Cl CF61 209 F6
Colhugh Pk CF61 209 F5
Colhugh St CF61 209 F5
Colin Way CF5 193 E6
Collard Cres CF62 214 F7
Collections Ctr The (National Mus Wales)★ CF15 136 E1
College @ Aber Valley The CF83 136 F7
College Cl
Bridgend / Pen-y-Bont ar Ogwr CF31 169 A3
Cardiff / Caerdydd CF14 177 B4
Pontypridd CF37 135 F5
College Cres NP18 118 B3
College Fields Cl CF62 214 E5
College Gdns CF61 209 F6
College Glade NP18 118 A4
College Gn SA13 125 F3
College Hill SA15 40 E5
College Pl CF62 214 E5
College Rd
Barry / Y Barri CF62 214 E4
Barry / Y Barri, Cwm Talwg CF62 214 E5
Caerleon / Caerllion NP18 118 B3
Cardiff / Caerdydd, Cathays CF10 232 B4
Cardiff / Caerdydd CF14 177 A2
Cardiff / Caerdydd CF14 177 B3
5 Cardiff / Caerdydd CF14 177 B4
Cardiff / Caerdydd, Llandaff North CF14 177 B3
Ebbw Vale / Glyn Ebwy NP23 7 C3
Pontypool / Pont-y-pwl NP4 62 D7
College Row SA9 2 F8
College St / Stryd-y-Coleg SA18 219 B7
College Sq SA15 40 E5
College St
Aberdare / Aberdâr CF44 29 B2
Llantwit Major / Llanilltud Fawr CF61 209 F6
Swansea / Abertawe SA1 233 B3
College Terr 10 NP4 38 A1
College Way CF37 135 F5
Collenna Rd CF39 133 C6
Colliers Ave CF72 153 E2
Colliers Row NP24 33 D3
Colliers' Row NP23 7 D1
Collier St NP19 143 D6
Colliers Way / Ffordd Y Glowyr CF40 106 E7
Colliery Rd
Bedwas CF83 138 E7
Llanbradach CF83 111 F4
Colliery St CF37 108 D2
Collingwood Ave NP19 144 B4
Collingwood Cl 6 NP19 144 A4
Collingwood Cres 4 NP19 144 A4
Collingwood Rd 5 NP19 144 A4
Collins Cl
Newport / Casnewydd NP20 142 E2
Treherbert CF42 50 F1
Collins Row NP22 12 C7
Collins St SA11 71 C4
Collins Terr CF37 135 E6
Collivaud Pl CF24 195 D4
Collwyn Rd CF33 148 B1
Collwyn St CF39 154 D8
Colne St NP19 143 D5
Colonel Rd / Ffordd-y-Cyrnol SA18 219 C6
Colonel Road SA18 219 C6
Colston Ave NP19 144 A3
Colston Ct NP19 144 A3
Colston Pl NP19 144 A3
Colts Foot Cl NP20 143 A6
Coltshill Dr SA3 122 F5
Columbia Row 12 SA15 40 D5
Columbus Cl CF62 215 A8
Columbus Wlk CF10 232 C1
Colum Dr CF10 194 F8
Column St
Barry / Y Barri CF64 215 E6
Treorchy / Treorci CF42 78 D6
Colum Pl CF10 194 F8
Colum Rd CF10 194 F8
Colum Terr CF10 232 A4
Colwill Rd CF14 177 B2
Colwinstone Cl CF14 177 A3
Colwinstone St CF14 177 A3
COLWINSTON / TREGOLWYN 187 A4
Colwyn Ave SA1 69 C5
Colwyn Ho CF14 177 A4
Colwyn Rd
Cardiff / Caerdydd CF3 179 C3
Ton Pentre CF41 79 A2
Coly Row CF46 55 F8
Comet St CF24 195 C6
Comfrey Cl
11 Cardiff / Caerdydd CF3 180 A8
Newport / Casnewydd NP20 143 A6
Comin Inf Sch CF44 28 F3
Comin Jun Mix Sch CF44 28 F3
Commerce Pl CF44 53 C7
Commercial Bldgs
Blackwood / Coed Duon NP12 59 B2
Port Talbot SA13 125 B8
Commercial Cl NP4 37 E5
Commercial La NP11 115 A1
Commercial Pl
6 Cwmbran / Cwmbrân NP44 89 E5
Mountain Ash / Aberpennar CF45 82 B6
Pontycymer CF32 103 E3
Commercial Rd
Abercarn NP11 87 B1
Abersychan NP4 37 E5
Abertillery / Abertyleri NP13 60 A7
Barry / Y Barri CF63 215 A6
Cwmfelinfach NP11 113 A4
Machen CF83 139 F7
Machen, Chatham CF83 140 B6
Newbridge / Trecelyn NP11 60 A1
Newport / Casnewydd NP20 143 C3
Port Talbot SA13 125 C6
Resolven / Resolfen SA11 226 D5
Rhyd-y-fro SA8 23 C8
Commercial St Arc NP13 36 B5
Commercial St / Stryd Commercial NP44 89 E2
Commercial St / Stryd Masnach SA10 222 C3
Commercial St
Aberbargoed / Aberbargod CF81 58 B4
6 Aberdare / Aberdâr CF44 29 A2
Abergwynfi SA13 76 C5
Abertillery / Abertyleri NP13 36 B5
Bargoed / Bargod CF81 58 A1
Beddau CF38 156 A7
Bedlinog CF46 56 A7
10 Blaenavon NP4 17 C6
Cwmbran / Cwmbrân, Pontnewydd NP44 89 E5
Cwmfelinfach NP11 113 A6
Ebbw Vale / Glyn Ebwy NP23 14 D6
Ferndale CF43 80 A7
Gelligaer CF82 84 D7
Glyncorrwg SA13 227 C2
Llantrisant CF72 155 D3
Llantwit Major / Llanilltud Fawr CF61 209 F6
Maesteg CF34 102 A3
Mountain Ash / Aberpennar CF45 54 D3
Commercial St *continued*
Nant-y-Moel CF32 104 E6
3 Neath / Castell-Nedd SA11 71 E8
Nelson CF46 83 E3
Newport / Casnewydd NP20 143 C4
New Tredegar NP24 33 E3
Ogmore Vale CF32 104 E2
Pengam NP12 85 B7
Pontllanfraith NP12 85 F4
Pontypool / Pont-y-pwl, Griffithstown NP4 62 E3
Pontypool / Pont-y-pwl, Sowhill NP4 62 C6
Pyle / Y Pîl CF33 148 D2
Risca / Rhisga NP11 115 A1
Senghenydd CF83 110 F2
Tredegar NP22 13 E7
Ystalyfera SA9 2 B6
Ystradgynlais SA9 1 F1
Ystrad Mynach CF82 84 F1
Commercial Terr CF46 83 B6
Commerical St CF48 11 B4
Commin Cl NP12 58 D7
Commin Rd CF81 58 B6
Common App 1 CF38 156 A6
Common Rd CF37 109 D1
Commonwealth Rd NP23 7 D6
Company St SA11 226 D5
Compass Rd CF10 195 E1
Compass Row SA8 23 D5
Compass St SA5 68 C3
Compton Ave SA10 70 F7
Compton Cl NP10 142 B6
Compton Rd
Skewen / Sclwen SA10 71 A7
Tonypandy CF40 106 E5
Compton St CF11 194 E4
Concorde Dr CF39 133 E5
Conduit Pl SA13 125 D7
Conduit St SA13 125 D7
Coney Beach Amusement Pk★ CF36 183 A6
Conifer Cl NP18 117 E2
Conifer Ct CF5 193 B8
Conifers Cvn Site The CF83 138 D6
Coniston Cl 1 NP19 143 F8
Coniston Ho NP44 89 B3
Coniston Rise CF44 29 E1
Coniston Wlk SA2 94 D7
Connaught Cl CF36 165 F2
Connaught Ho CF11 194 E6
Connaught Rd CF24 195 C8
Connaught St SA13 125 C8
Consort St CF45 54 E1
Constable Dr NP19 144 A8
Constable Ho 3 SA12 98 D1
Constables Cl NP20 143 D2
Constance St NP19 143 D7
Constant Cl CF11 207 A8
Constantine Ct CF40 107 A3
Constantine St CF40 107 A3
Constant Rd SA13 125 D6
Constant Row NP11 115 A2
Constellation St CF24 195 D6
Constitution Hill
Cowbridge / Y Bont-Faen CF71 188 E1
Swansea / Abertawe SA1 95 B7
Convent St SA1 68 D1
Convil Rd CF32 103 E6
Conway Cl
Cwmbran / Cwmbrân NP44 89 E4
Dinas Powis / Dinas Powys CF64 206 C3
Pontypridd CF37 109 C5
Conway Cres CF38 135 F2
Conway Croft NP19 144 A4
Conway Ct
Blackwood / Coed-Duon NP12 58 D1
Caerphilly / Caerffili CF83 137 D4
Swansea / Abertawe SA5 68 A4
Conway Dr
Aberdare / Aberdâr CF44 29 E1
Barry / Y Barri CF62 214 C6
Conway Gr / Llwyn Conway CF48 225 F1
Conway Rd
Abertillery / Abertyleri NP11 59 F6
Cardiff / Caerdydd CF11 194 D7
Newport / Casnewydd NP19 143 F5
Pontypool / Pont-y-pwl NP4 62 B7
Swansea / Abertawe SA5 68 A4
Treorchy / Treorci CF42 78 D5
Conway Sac 2 NP19 144 A4
Conway Terr NP44 89 F5
Conwy Gr NP10 163 D5
Conybeare Rd
Cardiff / Caerdydd CF5 194 B7
Sully CF64 216 B5
Conybeare St CF45 54 D2
Cook Rd CF62 205 A1
Cook Rees Ave SA11 71 F6
Coolgreany Cl NP20 117 A1
Coolgreany Cres NP20 117 A1
Cools Cl NP23 35 B8
Coomassie St NP20 143 D1
Coombes Rd SA10 70 E7
Coombe-Tennant Ave SA10 70 D7
Co-operative Cotts CF42 78 C5
Co-Operative St CF41 78 F3
Co-operative Terr NP4 37 E5
Co operative Terr NP23 8 D1
Cooper Cl NP18 119 E1
Coopers SA18 218 E5
Coopers Ct 9 CF10 232 B2
Cooper's Hos NP4 37 F2
Coopers La CF71 188 E2
Coopers Pl CF83 137 D1
Coopers Rd / Heol Cwper SA18 218 E5
Coopers Terr CF82 111 F7
Coopers Way CF72 155 F3
Coopers Yd CF10 232 B1
Coplestone St CF45 54 D2
Copleston Rd CF14 177 A2
Copley Cl SA3 122 B7
Copley Lodge SA3 122 B7
Copley St CF45 54 D4
Copper Beech Cl NP18 117 E2
Copper Beeches CF82 84 E8
Copperfield Ct 1 CF62 214 F5
Copperfield Dr CF14 159 F2
Copper St CF24 195 D6
Copperworks Inf Sch SA15 40 D4
Copperworks Rd / Heol Copperwoks SA15 40 D3
Coppice The
Church Village CF38 136 A2
Miskin / Meisgyn CF72 173 D8
Coppins The
Cardiff / Caerdydd CF14 160 B3
Newport / Casnewydd NP20 117 B3
Copse The CF48 10 B7
Copse Wlk CF23 161 A2
Copthorne Way CF5 192 F2
Coral Ct / Cwrt Coral 4 SA12 98 B2
Cora St CF63 215 A5
Corban Ct NP13 36 B6
Corbett Cres CF83 138 B1
Corbett Gr CF83 137 E1
Corbett Rd
Cardiff / Caerdydd CF10 232 A4
Llandough / Llandochau CF64 206 D6
Corbetts La CF83 138 A6
Corbett St
Ogmore Vale CF32 104 E1
Treherbert CF42 51 A1
Corelli St NP19 143 D6
Coriander Cl NP20 143 A6
Corinthian Cl CF64 206 D7
Cork Dr CF23 161 A2
Cork Ho 10 SA1 233 C2
CORLANNAU 99 B2
Cormorant Cl CF3 179 F8
Cormorant Cl / Clos Morfran SA15 40 B6
Cormorant Way
Newport / Casnewydd NP10 163 F7
The Mumbles / Y Mwmbwls SA3 122 E6
Cornbrook Rd NP20 116 E2
Corneli Prim Sch / Ysgol Gynradd Corneli CF33 165 F8
Cornelius Cl / Clos Cornelius CF33 165 F6
Cornelly Cl CF14 177 A3
Cornelly St CF14 177 A3
Corner House St CF44 28 E7
Corner Mdw / Maes Y Cornel SA8 24 A3
Cornerswell La 3 CF64 206 F3
Cornerswell Pl CF64 206 E4
Cornerswell Rd CF64 206 F4
Cornfield Cl CF14 159 D1
Cornfield Rise CF83 138 D6
Cornflower Cl
Cardiff / Caerdydd CF14 160 A4
Rogerstone / Ty-du NP10 141 E6
Corn Glas CF63 215 C8
Cornish Cl CF11 195 A2
Cornish Pl SA15 40 E2
Corn St NP20 143 C5
CORNTOWN / CORNTWN 186 B7
Corntown Rd CF35 186 C7
CORNTWN / CORNTOWN 186 B7
Cornwall Ct CF11 194 E3
Cornwall Ho 4 SA12 98 C2
Cornwall Pl SA3 123 B5
Cornwall Rd
Barry / Y Barri CF62 214 F6
Newport / Casnewydd NP19 143 E7
Tonypandy CF40 107 A3
Cornwall Rise CF62 214 F6
Cornwall St CF11 194 F4
Cornwood Cl CF5 176 B1
Coronation Ave
Cymmer / Cymer SA13 75 D4

Coronation Ave *continued*
Resolven / Resolfen SA11 226 D5
Coronation Bldgs NP11 113 A4
Coronation Cres
Fochriw CF81 32 D6
Newbridge / Trecelyn NP11 87 B8
Coronation Ho SA12 124 D8
Coronation Pl NP11 114 C7
Coronation Pl / Maes y Coroni CF48 55 C5
Coronation Rd
Blackwood / Coed-Duon NP12 85 E6
Cardiff / Caerdydd CF14 177 D4
Evanstown CF39 132 B7
Llanelli SA15 40 E4
Pont Rhyd-y-cyff CF34 128 D6
Coronation Rd / Heol Y Coroni 16 SA18 220 B8
Coronation St
Aberkenfig / Abercynffig CF32 150 C4
Abertillery / Abertyleri NP13 36 C3
Barry / Y Barri CF63 215 A4
Bedwas CF83 139 A6
Blaina / Blaenau NP13 15 E4
Bryn SA13 100 E5
Ogmore Vale CF32 104 E4
Risca / Rhisga NP11 115 A1
Tonypandy CF40 107 A2
Tredegar NP22 13 E6
Coronation Terr
Abersychan NP4 37 F4
Ammanford / Rhydaman SA18 219 D6
Heolgerrig CF48 10 B1
Maesteg CF34 102 A5
Penarth CF64 207 B5
Pontypridd CF37 109 E3
Porth CF39 107 F5
Rhymney / Rhymni NP22 12 D5
Senghenydd CF83 110 F3
Coronet Way SA6 69 A7
Corporation Ave SA15 40 E7
Corporation Cl SA15 40 E6
Corporation Rd
Aberavon SA12 98 F1
Cardiff / Caerdydd CF11 195 A2
Loughor SA4 42 E1
Newport / Casnewydd NP19 143 E4
Newport / Casnewydd NP19 143 F1
Swansea / Abertawe SA5 67 C4
Corporation St CF47 10 F2
Corpus Christi RC High Sch CF23 160 D1
Corris 2 NP44 89 F6
Corrwg Ct SA13 227 C1
Corrymore Mans SA2 94 F6
Corsham Rd CF23 178 C3
Corvette Ct CF10 195 C3
Corwen Cres CF14 177 A3
Cory Cres CF5 191 F5
Cory Pk / Parc Cory NP44 117 B6
Cory Pl CF11 207 A8
Cory St
Resolven / Resolfen SA11 226 D5
Swansea / Abertawe SA2 94 D6
CORYTON 176 E7
Coryton Cl CF14 176 F7
Coryton Cres CF14 176 F7
Coryton Dr CF14 176 E7
Coryton Halt CF14 176 F6
Coryton Prim Sch CF14 176 E7
Coryton Rise CF14 176 E7
Cory Way CF63 215 A3
Cosheston Rd CF5 176 D1
COSMESTON 217 B8
Cosmeston Dr CF64 217 A7
Cosmeston Lakes Ctry Pk* CF64 216 F7
Cosmeston Lakes Ctry Pk Visitor Ctr* CF64 216 F7
Cosmeston Medieval Village* CF64 216 F6
Cosmeston St CF24 177 F1
Cosslett Pl CF11 195 A2
Cosy Pl 2 NP23 8 B4
Cot Farm Circ NP19 144 F6
Cot Farm Cl NP19 144 F6
Cot Farm Gdns NP19 144 F6
Cot Farm Wlk NP19 144 F6
Cot Hill NP18 145 A6
Cotman Cl NP19 144 A7
Cotswold Ave CF14 160 B3
Cotswold Cl
Newport / Casnewydd NP19 144 C6
Swansea / Abertawe SA5 67 E3
Cotswold Ct CF23 178 C6
Cotswold Rise CF63 215 B6
Cotswold Way
Newport / Casnewydd NP19 144 C6
Risca / Rhisga NP11 115 D2
Cottage Cl CF14 159 F2
Cottage Gdns CF32 167 F4
Cottage Homes CF44 53 F8
Cotterell Dr CF5 191 B1
Cotterells Hos NP4 17 D6
Cottesmore Way CF72 155 E2
Cotton Ct SA11 71 D5
Cottrell Rd
2 Cardiff / Caerdydd CF14 177 B4
Cardiff / Caerdydd, Roath / Y Rhath CF24 195 C8
Cottrell St / Stryd Cottrell CF48 55 C5
Cottrell Sq CF63 215 A8
Cotts The CF14 159 E3
Coulson Cl 27 NP20 143 C3
Council Hos
3 Cwmbran / Cwmbrân NP44 89 E2
Llantwit Major / Llanilltud Fawr CF61 210 C6
Council St
Ebbw Vale / Glyn Ebwy NP23 7 C1
Merthyr Tydfil / Merthyr Tudful CF47 10 F4
Coundley Cl NP12 85 B5
Cound Terr 4 SA13 125 C7
Countess Pl CF64 206 F3
Countisbury Ave
Cardiff / Caerdydd CF3 179 C6
Cardiff / Caerdydd CF3 179 C7
Countryside Council for Wales Information Point / Cyngor Cefn Gwlad Cymru* SA3 230 A6
Country View CF37 136 C4
County Hospl NP4 62 E4
Court Cl
Aberthin CF71 189 C3
Cardiff / Caerdydd CF14 177 C3
Llantwit Major / Llanilltud Fawr CF61 209 F7
COURT COLMAN 168 A8
Court Colman Flats CF32 104 E7
Court Colman St CF32 104 E7
Court Cres NP10 142 B2
Court Dr CF71 188 E7
Courtenay Cl CF3 179 D7
Courtenay Rd
9 Barry / Y Barri CF63 215 B6
Cardiff / Caerdydd CF24 195 E6
Llanelli SA15 40 C6
Courtenay St SA5 68 C2
Court Farm Cl NP44 117 A8
Court Farm Rd / Ffordd Ferm y Cwrt NP44 117 A8
Courtfield Cl NP10 141 E6
Court Gdns NP10 141 F6
Court House St CF37 135 C8
Courtis Rd CF5 193 B5
Court La SA8 23 E5
Courtland Bldgs 2 SA13 125 B8
Courtland Pl SA13 125 B8
Courtlands CF62 214 C3
Courtlands The 9 NP44 89 B3
Courtlands Way SA5 67 E5
Courtland Terr / Teras Tir Y Llys 8 CF47 10 E1
Court Mdw NP18 145 C8
Court Mews 4 CF63 215 B6
Court Newton 3 CF63 215 B6
Courtney St NP19 143 D6
Court Pl 3 CF40 106 E6
Court Rd
Barry / Y Barri, Barry Dock CF63 215 A5
Barry / Y Barri, Cadoxton CF63 215 B6
Bridgend / Pen-y-Bont ar Ogwr CF31 168 F4
Caerphilly / Caerffili CF83 137 F5
Caerphilly / Caerffili, Energlyn CF83 137 F4
Cardiff / Caerdydd CF11 194 F4
Cardiff / Caerdydd, Gwaun Treoda CF14 177 C3
Court Rd / Heol Cwrt NP44 90 A1
Court Rd / Heol Y Cwrt CF33 165 F7
Court Rd Ind Est NP44 90 A1
Court Rise 5 NP4 17 D7
Court Specl Sch The / Ysgol-y-Llys CF14 160 A1
Court St
Maesteg CF34 101 F3
2 Merthyr Tydfil / Merthyr Tudful CF47 30 E8
Tonypandy CF40 106 D6
Court Terr
Cefn Cribwr CF32 149 C3
12 Merthyr Tydfil / Merthyr Tudful CF47 30 E8
Court The
Bridgend / Pen-y-Bont ar Ogwr CF35 169 F4
Cardiff / Caerdydd, Lisvane / Llys Faen CF14 160 B4
4 Cardiff / Caerdydd, Roath / Y Rhath CF24 195 D8
Corntown / Corntwn CF35 186 C7
Court View NP18 145 C8
Court Wlk SA10 71 C8
Courtyard The
15 Cardiff / Caerdydd CF24 195 D5
Newport / Casnewydd NP10 163 D6
Porthcawl CF36 165 D3
7 Swansea / Abertawe SA1 233 A4
Courtyard Units SA10 70 D5
Courtybella Gdns NP20 143 D2
Courtybella Terr
Newport / Casnewydd NP20 143 B2
Newport / Casnewydd, Pillgwenlly NP20 143 D2
Cove Ho 5 SA12 98 D1
Coveny St CF24 195 E6
Coverack Rd NP19 143 E4
Cove Rd / Heol Cove SA12 98 D1
Covert Wlk NP44 89 B1
Cowbridge By-Pass CF71 188 E3
Cowbridge Comp Sch
Cowbridge / Y Bont-Faen, East Village CF71 189 A2
Cowbridge / Y Bont-Faen, West Village CF71 188 E2
Cowbridge Rd
Bridgend / Pen-y-Bont ar Ogwr CF31 169 A2
Pontyclun CF72 172 E4
St Athan / Sain Tathan CF62 211 D7
Talbot Green CF72 155 B1
Talbot Green CF72 155 B2
Cowbridge Rd E
Cardiff / Caerdydd, Canton CF5 194 C6
Cardiff / Caerdydd, Victoria Park CF5 194 A6
Cowbridge Rd W CF5 193 C4
Cowbridge Road CF61 209 F8
Cowbridge St 3 CF63 215 B7
COWBRIDGE / Y BONT-FAEN 188 C2
Cowell Prec 3 SA15 40 D5
Cowell Rd / Heol Cowgl SA18 220 C7
Cowell St SA15 40 D5
Cowper Cl
Newport / Casnewydd NP20 142 E2
Penarth CF64 206 F4
Swansea / Abertawe SA2 93 F7
Cowper Ct CF24 232 D4
Cowper Pl CF24 232 D4
Cowshed La NP10 142 A2
Cowslip Cl CF23 161 A1
Cowslip Dr CF64 206 E5
COYCHURCH / LLANGRALLO 169 F4
Coychurch (Llangrallo) Prim Sch CF35 170 A4
Coychurch Rd
Bridgend / Pen-y-Bont ar Ogwr CF31 169 B3
Coychurch / Llangrallo CF35 170 B5
Pencoed CF35 170 D6
Coychurch Rise CF63 215 A8
Coychurch Road Gdns CF31 168 F3
COYTRAHÊN 150 B8
Coytrahen Cl CF31 169 B6
Crabapple Cl CF47 10 D5
Crabtree Rd CF40 107 A5
Crabtree Wlk CF48 10 A6
Crack Hill CF35, CF71 187 A6
Craddock St CF11 194 E5
Cradock St
Llanelli SA15 40 D4
Swansea / Abertawe SA1 233 A3
Cradoc Rd CF14 177 C4
Cragside Cl 2 CF3 179 F6
CRAIG BERTHLWYD 83 B4
Craig Castell CF15 176 B7
CRAIG-CEFN-PARC 22 A2
Craig-cefn-parc Prim Sch SA6 22 B4
Craig Cres CF39 107 D2
Craigddu View / Trem Craigddu NP4 37 E7
Craig-fryn Terr CF32 104 E7
CRAIG GELLINUDD 24 B6
Craiglas Cres NP12 85 C8
Craiglee Dr CF10 232 C1
Craigmuir Rd CF24 195 F7
Craig Nedd SA11 227 C8
Craig Rd SA11 71 C1
Craig Rhymni NP24 33 D4
CRAIG TREBANOS 23 C3
Craig View Terr / Teras Trem Y Graig NP4 37 D6
Craigwen SA14 41 E4
Craig-y-Bwldan SA2 93 E8
Craig Y Darren CF44 28 C3
Craig-y-duke SA8 23 A1
Craig Y Fan Terr SA13 75 C5
Craig-y-Haul Dr CF3 162 C3
Craig-y-Hendre CF46 56 B7
Craig-y-Llyn Cres CF44 29 E2
Craig Y Mor Ct CF64 216 B5
Craig y nos Sch SA3 122 C7
Craig-y-Parc Sch CF15 175 B6
Craig Yr Allt CF14 159 B1
Craig-yr-Eos Rd CF32 184 C3
Craig-yr-Hesg Prim Sch CF37 109 D5
Cramic Way SA13 125 B8
Cranbourne Way CF23 160 E1
Cranbrook St CF24 232 C4
Crane St NP4 62 C6
Cranfield Ct SA5 67 E5
Cranford CF14 160 A2
Cranham Ho NP44 89 C2
Cranleigh Rise CF3 179 A4
Cranmer Ct
Cardiff / Caerdydd CF5 194 A8
Swansea / Abertawe SA5 67 E5
Cranwell Cl 4 CF5 176 E2
Craven Wlk CF64 217 B8
Crawford Cl CF38 156 B6
Crawford Dr CF23 161 A1
Crawford Gn SA12 98 D7
Crawford Rd / Heol Crawford SA12 98 C7
Crawford St NP19 143 D6
Crawford Trad Est NP19 143 D7
Crawley Cl CF14 159 E3
Crawshay Ct
Llantwit Major / Llanilltud Fawr CF61 210 B7
The Mumbles / Y Mwmbwls SA3 122 F3
Crawshay Dr CF61 210 B7
Crawshay Ho CF48 10 A3
Crawshay Rd CF40 107 A4
Crawshay St
Cardiff / Caerdydd CF10 232 B1
Hirwaun CF44 27 D8
Treorchy / Treorci CF41 79 A4
Ynysybwl CF37 109 A8
Crediton Rd CF3 179 C6
Creidiol Rd SA1 233 A4
CREIGIAU 174 D8
Creigiau Prim Sch / Ysgol Gynradd Creigiau CF15 174 D8
Cresawnt Dylan / Dylan Cres SA12 124 E7
Cresawnt Gordon / Gordon Cres 7 SA12 98 C2
Cresawnt Hafren / Severn Cres SA12 98 D1
Cresawnt Morrison / Morrison Cres 6 SA12 98 D1
Crescent Cl CF71 188 F1
Crescent Ct
Cardiff / Caerdydd CF23 178 D6
4 Newport / Casnewydd NP19 143 F6
Crescent Rd
Caerphilly / Caerffili CF83 138 A3
Gwaun-Cae-Gurwen SA18 220 D6
Newport / Casnewydd NP19 143 F6
Risca / Rhisga NP11 114 E3
Sarn CF32 150 E4
Crescent St CF48 55 D4
Crescent The
Aberkenfig / Abercynffig CF32 150 C4
Barry / Y Barri CF62 214 B5
Bedwas CF83 138 E6
Bridgend / Pen-y-Bont ar Ogwr CF31 169 A4
Caerphilly / Caerffili CF83 137 E4
Cardiff / Caerdydd CF5 193 D7
Cardiff / Caerdydd, Culverhouse Cross CF5 193 A2
Cardiff / Caerdydd, Llandaff / Llandaf CF5 194 B8
Crynant / Creunant SA10 226 A7
Cwmdare CF44 28 C4
Ebbw Vale / Glyn Ebwy NP23 14 D8
Gorslas SA14 218 C8
Machen CF83 139 F7
Maesycwmmer CF82 85 B1
Nantyglo NP23 15 D7
6 Porthcawl CF36 165 F1
Swansea / Abertawe SA5 67 F5
Tredegar NP22 6 C1
Crescent The / Y Cilgant NP44 89 D1
Cresselly Villas CF45 54 E3
Cressfield Dr CF23 161 B1
Cresswell Cl CF3 180 A7
Cresswell Ct CF62 214 F8
Cresswell Wlk NP44 89 C3
Cressy Rd CF23 178 C1
Crest Acre Cl SA3 122 E5
Cresta Gr CF5 192 F5
Creswell Rd
Neath / Castell-Nedd SA11 71 E7
Swansea / Abertawe SA6 68 D8
CREUNANT / CRYNANT 226 A7
Creunant Prim Sch SA10 226 A8
Cribarth SA9 222 E8
Cribbin-Ddu St CF37 109 A8
Cribb's Row 2 SA11 71 E8
Cribbwr Sq CF33 148 C1
Crib Yr Heliwr / Hunters Ridge SA11 49 B1
Crib Y Tywod / Sandy Ridge SA12 98 C1
Criccieth Cl
Blackwood / Coed-Duon NP12 58 D1
Newport / Casnewydd NP10 163 E5
Criccieth Ct CF64 206 C4
Criccieth Gr CF48 225 E1
Criccieth Pl SA1 69 C5
Criccieth Rd CF3 179 C3
Crichton St
Treherbert CF42 51 A1
Treorchy / Treorci CF42 78 C7
Crickhowell Pl SA1 69 C5
Crickhowell Rd CF3 179 F6
Crickhowell Wlk CF3 179 F7
Cricklewood Cl CF31 168 C6
Crimea Ct SA9 221 C2
Crimson Ave / Rhodfa Dugoch 6 SA12 98 B2
Crimson Cl SA12 98 B2
Crimson Ct 9 SA12 98 B2
CRINDAU 143 C7
Crindau Jun & Inf Sch NP20 143 C7
Crindau Rd NP20 143 B8
Cripps Ave NP22 13 D5
Crocketts Pl CF37 109 A2
Crockherbtown La CF10 232 B3
Crocus Cl NP10 141 E6
Croes Cadarn CF23 160 F2
Croescadarn Cl 8 CF23 161 A1
Croescadarn Rd CF23 160 F1
Croescade La CF38 156 C7
Croescade Rd CF38 156 B8
CROESERW 75 E3
Croeserw Ind Est SA13 75 D3
Croeserw Prim Sch SA13 75 D3
Croesffyrdd SA9 2 D7
Croes Heol Y Sblot CF71 199 A2
Croesllanfro Gdns NP10 142 A7
Croeso'r Swanwyn SA7 69 E6
Croeso Sq NP12 85 D7
CROESPENMAEN 59 E1
Croespenmaen Ind Est NP11 59 D1
Croesty Prim Sch CF35 170 D7
Croeswen NP44 116 F8
CROESYCEILIOG 90 B5
Croesyceiliog By-Pass NP44 90 B5
Croesyceiliog Jun Sch NP44 90 A5
Croesyceiliog North Road Inf Sch NP44 90 A5
Croesyceiliog Sch NP44 90 A4
Croes Y Drindod CF61 208 F7
CROES-Y-MWYALCH 117 A6
Croes-y-Pant La NP4 39 C5
Croffta CF64 206 A2
Crofft-y-Genau Rd CF5 175 F2
Crofta CF14 160 B1
Croft Ct NP23 8 A4
Croften Mede NP44 89 B1
Croftfield Cres SA3 122 E5
Croft Gdns CF64 216 A5
Croft Goch Gdns CF33 148 C2
Croft Goch Rd CF33 148 C2
Croft John CF62 212 F6
Croft La CF32 197 C8
Crofton Dr SA12 98 E6
Croft Rd SA11 71 E8
Crofts Cnr 4 NP44 89 B3
Crofts St CF24 195 C7
Croft St
Cowbridge / Y Bont-Faen CF71 188 F1
New Tredegar NP24 33 E4
Swansea / Abertawe SA1 233 B4
Croft Terr
Cowbridge / Y Bont-Faen CF71 188 F1
2 Swansea / Abertawe SA5 68 C4
Croft The
Bettws CF32 129 D3
Loughor SA4 42 D1
Neath Abbey SA10 71 B8
Sarn CF32 150 D3
CROFTY 64 B3
Crofty Ind Est SA4 64 B3
Crole St SA1 95 B7
Cromer St CF44 53 E4
Cromwell Ave SA10 48 E2
Cromwell Ct 7 NP19 144 A4
Cromwell Pl / Man Cromwell 10 NP44 89 E5
Cromwell Rd
Cardiff / Caerdydd CF14 177 D4

Cromwell Rd *continued*
- Neath / Castell-Nedd SA10 48 E2
- Newport / Casnewydd NP19 144 A4
- Risca / Rhisga NP11 114 E3

Cromwell Road Bglws NP11 114 D4
Cromwell St
- Abertillery / Abertyleri NP13 36 B5
- Merthyr Tydfil / Merthyr Tudful CF47 10 D2
- Swansea / Abertawe SA1 95 B7

Cronin Ave SA12 124 E7
Crook Hill (Lower) NP13 36 B7
Crosby Yd CF31 168 E6
Cross Acre SA3 122 E7
Cross Blanche St CF48 11 C5
Crossbrook St CF37 109 C1
Cross Brook St CF42 50 D5
Crosscombe Terr NP23 35 B7
Cross Common Rd CF64 206 C1
Crossfield Ave CF36 182 E7
Crossfield Rd CF62 214 C4
Crossfields NP11 59 D1
Cross Francis St CF48 11 A5
CROSS HANDS 218 A7
Cross Hands Bsns Pk SA14 218 B7
Cross Hands Prim Sch SA14 218 A8
Cross Hands Rd / Heol Cross Hands SA14 218 B8
Crosshill CF62 214 C1
Cross Houlson St CF48 11 B5
CROSS INN 155 F2
Cross Inn Bldgs 16 SA18 219 B7
Cross Inn Rd CF72 155 E3
Cross Ivor Terr CF48 11 A5
CROSSKEYS 114 C5
Cross King St CF48 11 A7
Cross La 18 NP20 143 C4
Cross Lake St CF43 79 F6
Cross Mardy St CF47 11 A1
Cross Margaret St CF47 10 C2
Cross Morgan St 5 CF47 10 D2
Cross Morlais St CF48 11 A5
Cross Mount Pleasant CF48 31 C1
Cross Pl CF14 177 E1
Cross Rd SA10 223 A5
Cross Rd / Capel Newydd SA15 40 D6
Crossroads CF15 136 F2
Cross Row CF40 106 F3
Cross St
- Abercynon CF45 82 C5
- 14 Aberdare / Aberdâr CF44 29 A1
- Aberfan CF48 55 C4
- Abersychan NP4 37 E6
- Abertillery / Abertyleri NP13 36 B4
- Abertridwr CF83 137 A7
- Bargoed / Bargod CF81 58 A4
- Bargoed / Bargod, Gilfach CF81 58 A2
- Barry / Y Barri CF63 215 A5
- Bedwas CF83 138 E6
- Blaenavon NP4 17 C6
- Blaengarw CF32 103 D7
- Blaina / Blaenau NP13 15 E5
- 4 Bridgend / Pen-y-Bont ar Ogwr CF31 168 F4
- Caerleon / Caerllion NP18 118 C2
- Deri CF81 57 B8
- Dowlais CF48 11 B5
- Ferndale CF43 79 F6
- Gorseinon SA4 43 C2
- Hirwaun CF44 27 D8
- Maesteg CF34 102 B3
- Mountain Ash / Aberpennar CF45 81 F8
- New Tredegar NP24 33 F2
- Pontarddulais SA4 19 D4
- Pontypridd, Cilfynydd CF37 109 F5
- 4 Pontypridd, Coed-Pen-Maen CF37 109 D2
- 4 Porth, Birchgrove CF39 107 F3
- Porth, Glynfach CF39 107 F2
- Porth, Ynyshir CF39 107 F7
- Port Talbot SA13 99 B1
- Resolven / Resolfen SA11 226 D5
- Rhymney / Rhymni NP22 12 E4
- Senghenydd CF83 110 F2
- Swansea / Abertawe SA5 68 C4
- Ton-du CF32 150 C5
- Tongwynlais CF15 158 C1
- Tonypandy, Blaen Clydach CF40 106 C7
- Tonypandy, Penygraig CF40 106 F4
- Trehafod CF37 108 D2
- Treharris CF46 83 B7
- Ystrad CF41 79 D2
- Ystradgynlais SA9 222 A6

Cross The SA3 229 D2
Cross Thomas St 5 CF47 30 E8
Cross Way NP22 6 D1
Cross Way / Ffordd Y Groes CF31 168 B3
Crossways
- Cowbridge / Y Bont-Faen CF71 188 A1
- Newbridge / Trecelyn NP11 87 B7

Crossways Rd CF5 193 C5
Crossways St
- Barry / Y Barri CF63 215 A5
- 2 Pontypridd CF37 109 D2

Crosswells Way CF5 193 A5
Crosswood Mdw / Maes Trawscoed 5 CF31 168 C3
Crosswood St CF42 78 E6
Crouch Cl NP20 116 D1
C Row NP4 17 A6
Crown Ave NP22 6 D2
Crown Ave NP22 6 E2
Crown Ave CF42 78 C8
Crownbridge Specl Day Sch NP4 62 E1
Crown Bsns Pk NP22 6 E3
Crown Cl
- Caerleon / Caerllion NP18 118 C2
- Cwmbran / Cwmbrân NP44 89 D6

Crown Cotts SA9 1 F2
Crown Est NP12 85 D3
Crown Hill CF38 156 C6
Crown Hill Cotts CF38 156 C6
Crown Hill Dr CF38 156 C6
Crown La NP12 85 D3
Crown Prec 13 SA15 40 D5
Crown Rd
- Llanyrafon NP44 90 B1
- Maesteg CF34 102 C3
- Pyle / Y Pîl CF33 148 E3

Crown Rise / Gelli Coron CF34 102 C3
Crown Rise / Tarddiad Goron 9 NP44 90 B1
Crown Row
- Aberdare / Aberdâr CF44 53 E7
- Maesteg CF34 102 B3

Crown St
- Abertillery / Abertyleri NP13 36 A6
- Newbridge / Trecelyn NP11 60 A1
- Newport / Casnewydd NP19 143 E6
- Port Talbot SA13 99 B1
- Swansea / Abertawe SA6 68 F8
- Swansea / Abertawe SA6 69 A8

Crown Terr CF42 78 C8
Crown Way / Ffordd Y Goron CF14 177 E1
Crown Wlk CF83 140 B7
Croyde Ave CF3 179 C6
Croydon Cl NP19 143 E8
Croydon Ct 8 NP19 143 E8
Crud-yr-Awel
- Gorseinon SA4 66 B8
- Neath / Castell-Nedd SA10 48 D2

Crud Yr Awel CF31 168 D8
CRUMLIN / CRYMLYN 60 B1
Crumlin Dr CF3 180 A7
Crumlin High Level Prim Sch NP11 60 A1
Crumlin Rd
- Newbridge / Trecelyn, Crumlin / Crymlyn NP11 60 A2
- Newbridge / Trecelyn NP11 60 B3
- Pontypool / Pont-y-pwl NP4 61 C4

Crumlin Sq NP11 60 A1
Crumlin St NP4 62 B6
Crundale Cres CF14 177 F8
Crwys La CF63 215 B8
Crwys Lofts 4 CF24 195 B8
Crwys Mews 1 CF24 195 A8
Crwys Pl CF24 195 B8
Crwys Prim Sch / Ysgol Gynradd y Crwys SA4 65 E1
Crwys Rd CF24 195 B8
Crwys Terr SA5 68 B6
Cryddan Rd SA11 71 E6
Crymlyn Bog Nature Reserve* SA1, SA7 69 E2
Crymlyn Bog Visitor Ctr* SA1 69 D1
CRYMLYN / CRUMLIN 60 B1
Crymlyn Gdns / Gerodi Crymlyn SA10 70 B6
Crymlyn Parc SA10 70 C6
Crymlyn Prim Sch / Ysgol Gynradd Crymlyn SA10 70 C1
Crymlyn Rd / Heol Crymlyn SA10 70 B6
Crymlyn St SA1 96 B7
Crymlyn Terr SA1 69 C2
Crynallt Farm Rd SA11 72 B5
Crynallt Inf Sch SA11 72 B5
Crynallt Jun Sch SA11 72 B5
Crynallt Rd SA11 72 B5
Crynant Bsns Ctr SA10 226 A8
Crynant Bsns Pk SA10 226 A8
Crynant Cl CF62 211 D7
CRYNANT / CREUNANT 226 A7
Crystal Ave CF23 178 A5
Crystal Ct CF11 194 F3
Crystal Glen CF14 177 F6
Crystal Rise CF14 177 F6
Crystal Wood Dr CF72 173 C8
Crystal Wood Rd CF14 177 F6
Cuckoofield Cl CF15 176 A8
Cuckoo St CF32 103 F1
Cudd Y Coed CF63 215 C8
Cules Terr CF15 157 F5
Culfor Rd SA4 65 E8
Culver Cl CF64 206 E1
Culver Cross CF5 192 F3
CULVERHOUSE CROSS 193 A1
Cumberland Rd 7 NP19 143 E8
Cumberland St CF5 194 C5
Cumnock Pl CF24 195 D5
Cumnock Terr 4 CF24 195 D5
Cumrae St 7 CF24 195 D5
Cunard Row 1 SA12 99 F5
Cunard Terr SA12 99 F5
Cunningham Cl
- Cardiff / Caerdydd CF23 178 A4
- Swansea / Abertawe SA2 94 C6

Cunningham Rd NP19 144 F7
Curie Cl NP20 117 A3
Curlew Cl
- Cardiff / Caerdydd CF14 177 A6
- Llanelli SA15 40 A6
- Neath / Castell-Nedd SA10 48 E2
- Newport / Casnewydd NP19 144 E1
- Porthcawl CF36 165 D1
- The Mumbles / Y Mwmbwls SA3 93 E1

Curlew Cres CF62 210 D6
Curlew Rd CF36 165 D1
Curll Ave CF14 177 E3
Curran Emb CF10 195 A3
Curran Rd CF10 195 A3
Curre St
- Aberdare / Aberdâr CF44 53 C8
- Cwm NP23 35 A8

Currie Ho SA12 98 F2
Curry Cl SA2 93 E8
Curtis St SA11 71 E5
Curwen Cl SA12 72 F3
Curwen Terr
- North Cornelly CF33 165 F7
- Pontrhydyfen SA12 72 F4

Curwood NP4 17 C6
Curzon St 9 NP23 8 C4
Custom House Pl 1 CF64 207 B5
Customhouse St / Heol Y Tollty CF10 232 B1
Cuthbertson St SA11 71 C4
Cuthbert St CF32 104 E2
Cutter Cl NP19 117 F1
Cwlwm Cariad CF63 205 B1
CWM
- Ebbw Vale 35 B7
- Pontrhydyfen 73 C1

Cwmaber Cty Inf Sch CF83 137 A8
Cwmaber Jun Sch CF83 137 A8
CWMAFAN / CWMAVON 99 C5
Cwmafan Ind Est SA12 99 D4
Cwmafan Inf Sch SA12 99 E5
Cwmafan Jun Sch SA12 99 E5
Cwm Alarch CF45 54 B3
Cwm Alarch Cl CF45 54 B3
Cwmalsie Cres NP12 86 A3
CWMAMAN 53 A4
Cwmaman Inf Sch CF44 53 A4
Cwmaman Rd CF44 53 C6
Cwmamman Rd SA18 219 F8
Cwmamman Rd / Heol Cwmaman SA18 220 B8
Cwm Arian SA6 46 A2
CWMAVON 17 F1
CWMAVON / CWMAFAN 99 C5
Cwmavon Rd
- Abersychan NP4 37 F7
- Blaenavon NP4 17 F4
- Cwmavon / Cwmafan SA12 99 C3

CWMBACH 29 F1
Cwmbach CW Prim Sch CF44 53 F7
Cwmbach Ind Est CF44 53 E7
Cwmbach Inf Sch / Ysgol Plant Bach Cwm-bach CF44 53 E8
Cwmbach Jun Sch CF44 29 E1
Cwmbach Rd
- Aberdare / Aberdâr CF44 29 C2
- Cwmbach CF44 53 E8
- Llanelli SA15 40 A8
- Neath / Castell-Nedd SA10 48 F3
- Swansea / Abertawe SA5 67 C3

Cwmbach Sta CF44 53 E7
Cwm Barry Way CF62 214 C4
Cwm Bath Rd SA6 45 F1
CWMBRAN / CWMBRÂN 89 D3
CWMBRÂN / CWMBRAN 89 D3
Cwmbran Dr / Ffordd Cwmbran NP44 89 E4
Cwmbran RC Jun & Inf Sch NP44 89 E2
Cwmbran Ret Pk NP44 89 D3
Cwmbran Sta NP44 89 F4
CWMBWRLA 68 C2
Cwmbwrla Prim Sch SA5 68 B2
Cwm Cadle SA5 67 E6
Cwm Cadno SA13 148 A6
CWMCARN 114 C8
Cwmcarn Cl CF3 179 F7
Cwmcarn Forest Dr NP11 114 E7
Cwmcarn Forest Drive & Visitor Ctr* NP11 114 D8
Cwmcarn High Sch NP11 114 B8
CWMCARNHYWEL 41 D5
Cwmcarn Prim Sch NP11 114 C7
CWMCELYN / CWM-CELYN 15 F6
CWM-CELYN / CWMCELYN 15 F6
Cwmcelyn Newydd NP13 15 F6
Cwm-Celyn Rd NP13 15 E6
CWMCERDINEN 219 C2
Cwm Chapel Rd SA1 69 B4
Cwm-Cidy La CF62 214 A4
Cwmclais Rd SA12 99 D5
Cwmclyd SA9 222 A6
Cwm Clyd SA5 67 A3
Cwmclydach Inf & Jun Schs CF40 106 B7
Cwm Clydach Nature Reserve* SA6 22 B3
Cwm Col-huw Walks* CF61 209 D4
Cwmcottage Rd NP13 36 C4
Cwm Crachen NP23 8 C2
Cwmcrachen Ind Est NP23 8 D3
Cwm Craig Bglws NP23 35 B6
Cwm Cwddy Dr NP10 141 E2
Cwm Cwddy Villas NP10 141 E3
Cwm Cynon Bsns Pk / Parc Busnes Cwm Cynon CF45 54 F1
Cwmdar Cty Prim Sch CF44 28 C3
CWMDARE 28 B3
Cwmdare Rd CF44 28 C4
Cwmdare St CF24 177 F1
Cwm Darran Pl CF81 33 B1
Cwm Ddu Ho CF48 10 A3
Cwmdonkin Dr SA2 95 A7
Cwmdonkin Terr SA2 94 F7
Cwmdows Terr NP11 86 E6
Cwm Draw Ct NP12 86 A3
Cwm Draw Ind Est NP23 14 E8
CWMDU 68 A2
Cwm Du Cl SA5 67 F3
Cwmdu Ind Est SA5 67 F2
CWM DULAIS 20 B4
Cwmdu Rd
- Godre'r-graig SA8 221 B1
- Maesteg CF34 102 D3
- Pontardawe SA8 24 C8
- Troedyrhiw CF48 31 B1

Cwmdu St CF34 102 B3
Cwm Dylan Cl NP10 141 E2
Cwm Eithin CF46 83 D3
Cwm Farm La NP13 36 C4
Cwm Farm La / Lon Fferm Y Cwm NP4 62 D5
Cwm Farm Rd NP13 36 C4
Cwm Farteg SA13 100 F4
Cwm Fedw CF83 140 A8
CWMFELIN
- Bedlinog 56 B6
- Maesteg 128 C8

Cwmfelin SA10 71 B8
Cwm Felin CF35 130 F2
CWMFELINFACH 113 B4
CWM-FELIN-FACH 46 A3
Cwmfelinfach Prim Sch NP11 113 A4
Cwmfelin Prim Sch CF34 128 C8
Cwmfelin Rd SA14 41 F3
Cwm Felin Rd / Heol Cwm Felin SA18 219 C5
Cwmfelin Way SA1 68 C2
Cwmfferws Rd / Heol Cwmfferws SA18 218 F6
Cwm Ffoes CF32 149 C2
CWM FFRWD-OER 61 F8
Cwmffrwdoer Prim Sch NP4 61 E8
CWM FIELDS 62 C5
Cwmgarw Rd SA18 221 A8
CWMGELLI 58 F1
Cwmgelli Cl SA5 68 D6
Cwmgelli Dr SA5 68 C6
Cwmgelli Rd SA6 68 C7
Cwmgelli Villas NP12 58 F1
CWMGIEDD 1 F3
Cwm Glas NP22 13 D8
Cwm Glas Inf Sch CF83 112 A3
Cwm Glas Prim Sch SA1 69 C4
Cwmglo Rd CF48 10 A1
CWMGORS 220 D5
Cwmgors Workshops / Gweithdau-Cwm-gors SA18 220 D6
Cwm Graig Bglws CF47 11 A5
CWMGWILI 218 C6
Cwmgwili Prim Sch SA14 218 C5
CWMGWRACH 227 B7
CWM GWYNN 94 E8
Cwm Gwynlais CF15 176 D8
Cwm Hir NP23 7 D3
Cwmhir Rd NP4 63 D7
CWM-HWNT 26 B8
Cwm Hyfryd CF39 133 A3
Cwm Ifor Prim Sch CF83 137 D5
Cwm Isaac CF44 26 C8
Cwm La NP10 142 B6
Cwm-Lai Prim Sch CF39 133 C2
Cwmlan Terr SA1 68 D4
Cwm Level Rd SA6 68 D5
CWMLLYNFELL 221 B7
Cwm-Mwyn SA14 218 B8
Cwm Nant SA11 72 A4
CWM NANT-GAM 8 F5
Cwmnanthir Terr SA18 220 E7
Cwm Nant-Llwyd Rd SA8 24 C5
Cwm Nant-yr-hwch CF44 28 C6
CWMNANTYRODYN 86 B4
Cwm Nedd Prim Sch SA11 223 D1
Cwmneol Pl CF44 53 A4
Cwmneol St CF44 53 A4
Cwm Nofydd CF14 177 B8
CWMPARC 78 C5
Cwm Parc CF62 214 C5
Cwmparc Forest Walk* CF42 78 D5
CWMPENNAR 54 C5
Cwmphil Rd SA9 1 C1
Cwm Prim Sch
- Cwm NP23 35 A8
- Swansea / Abertawe SA1 69 B4

Cwm Rd
- Aberbargoed / Aberbargod CF81 58 A5
- Argoed NP12 58 F4
- Ebbw Vale / Glyn Ebwy NP23 14 F2
- Swansea / Abertawe SA1 68 D1

Cwm Rhos View NP22 13 D6
CWMRHYDYCEIRW 45 F3
Cwmrhydyceirw Prim Sch SA6 45 F4
Cwmrhydyceirw Rd SA6 45 F3
Cwmsaerbren Flats CF42 50 F1
Cwmsaerbren St CF42 50 F1
Cwm Small Bsns Ctr NP23 35 B6
Cwm Sor Cl NP4 63 B4
CWMSYFIOG 34 A1
Cwmsyfiog Rd CF81 58 B7
CWM TALWG 214 D5
Cwmtawe Bsns Pk SA8 23 F5
Cwmtawe Coll SA8 23 E6
Cwmtawe Comp Sch / Ysgol Gyfun Cwmtawe SA8 23 E3
Cwm Tawe Rd SA9 222 A6
Cwm Terr
- Cwm NP23 35 B7
- 2 Llanelli SA15 40 C7
- Swansea / Abertawe SA1 233 B5

CWMTILLERY / CWMTYLERI 36 C8
Cwmtillery Ind Est / Ystad Ddiwydiannol Cwmtyleri NP13 36 B7
Cwmtorlais Rd NP11 86 E6
CWM-TWRCH ISAF 1 B1
CWM-TWRCH UCHAF 221 C6
CWMTYLERI / CWMTILLERY 36 C8
Cwm Y Dwr SA11 71 C1
CWM-Y-GLO 218 A8
Cwm-y-Nant NP11 141 A7
Cwm-y-Nant Fields NP44 89 D2
CWMYNYSCOY 62 C4
Cwmynyscoy Rd NP4 62 C4
Cwmynysmintan Rd CF44 28 D7
Cwmyrdderch Ct NP23 35 A8
Cwm-yr-Wch SA2 93 B8
Cwndonkin Cl SA2 95 A7
CWN-DWR 46 C6
Cwrdy Cl NP4 62 D2
Cwrdy La NP4 62 C2
Cwrdy Rd / Ffordd Cwrdy NP4 62 D2
Cwrdy Wlk NP4 62 D2
Cwrt Aethen CF63 205 B1
Cwrt Afon Lliedi SA15 40 B4
Cwrt Alexandre NP13 36 C4

Cwrt Alun Lewis CF44 .... 53 A3
Cwrt Andrew Buchan NP22 .... 12 E4
Cwrt Anghorfa CF33 .... 148 B2
Cwrt Anthony Hill / Anthony Hill Ct CF48 .... 31 A4
Cwrt Atifeddiaeth / Heritage Ct NP44 .... 117 B7
Cwrt Bala CF3 .... 179 E5
Cwrt Beaufort SA3 .... 123 A6
Cwrt Benjamin / Benjamin Ct NP22 .... 13 A2
Cwrt Bethel CF37 .... 109 F5
Cwrt Bethell CF72 .... 173 B8
Cwrt Bleddyn NP44 .... 89 D1
Cwrt Bont Newydd / Newbridge Ct 3 CF31 .... 168 C3
Cwrt Boston CF24 .... 179 A1
Cwrt Bracty / Brewery Ct NP13 .... 36 A1
Cwrt Briallen / Primrose Ct NP44 .... 88 F1
Cwrt Bryn Cynon CF45 .... 82 C5
Cwrt Bryn Isaf CF44 .... 26 C8
Cwrt Brynteg CF15 .... 176 C5
Cwrt Bryn Y Grug NP12 .... 85 D6
Cwrt Cambria SA15 .... 40 B4
Cwrt Cefn CF14 .... 160 B2
Cwrt Ceredig / Ceredig Ct 6 NP44 .... 90 B2
Cwrt Cilmeri SA6 .... 46 A2
Cwrt Clara Novello SA15 .... 40 B4
Cwrt-Coch St CF81 .... 58 B4
Cwrt Coed Parc CF34 .... 102 B2
Cwrt Coed Saeson SA7 .... 70 B8
Cwrt Coed-y-Brenin CF38 .... 156 E8
Cwrt Coles CF24 .... 179 A1
Cwrt Coral / Coral Ct 4 SA12 .... 98 B2
Cwrt Cwmderwen NP12 .... 59 B1
Cwrt Deri CF14 .... 177 B8
Cwrt Dewi Sant
1 Cardiff / Caerdydd CF24 .... 195 C5
Gorseinon SA4 .... 43 C2
Cwrt Dowlas NP44 .... 116 E8
Cwrt Draw Llyn CF83 .... 158 F8
Cwrt Dyfed CF63 .... 215 C8
Cwrt Edward 7 CF62 .... 214 E4
Cwrt Eglwys Newydd CF14 .... 177 A5
Cwrt Eirlys CF63 .... 205 A1
Cwrt Elusendy 4 SA15 .... 40 E5
Cwrt Emily SA7 .... 46 F1
Cwrt Faenor CF38 .... 155 F5
Cwrt Fforest CF45 .... 54 E2
Cwrt Finchley 5 CF5 .... 193 E7
Cwrt Glandwr / Waterside Ct 5 NP44 .... 89 E2
Cwrt Glanhowy NP12 .... 85 E8
Cwrt Glanrhyd CF44 .... 26 C8
Cwrt Glanwern 4 CF44 .... 53 E8
Cwrtglas NP44 .... 90 A4
Cwrt Glas CF14 .... 177 F8
Cwrt Glyndwr CF37 .... 135 D6
Cwrt Greig / Greig Ct 12 SA12 .... 98 B3
Cwrt Griffin CF83 .... 139 C2
Cwrt Gwalia CF32 .... 104 E2
Cwrt Gwaun Fach / Small Meadow Ct CF83 .... 138 B4
Cwrt Gwenllian CF63 .... 215 D6
Cwrt Gwt / Wye Ct NP44 .... 89 B4
Cwrt Gwyrrd / Greencourt 8 NP44 .... 90 A6
Cwrt Hendre NP12 .... 85 C7
Cwrt Heol Casnewydd 5 CF24 .... 195 D8
Cwrt Hocys SA7 .... 69 D6
Cwrt Hydd SA6 .... 45 F5
Cwrt Illtyd CF72 .... 155 E2
Cwrt Iorweth CF5 .... 194 B6
Cwrt Isaf
Birchgrove SA7 .... 47 B1
Llantwit Fadre / Llanilltud Faerdref CF38 .... 156 D5
Cwrt Ivor Sims SA6 .... 46 A2
Cwrt Lafant SA7 .... 69 E6
Cwrt Langstone / Langstone Ct NP44 .... 89 C1
Cwrt Leubren CF63 .... 205 A1
Cwrt Llandough CF64 .... 206 D6
Cwrt Llanfabon CF83 .... 137 F5
Cwrt Llanfleiddan CF71 .... 200 D8
Cwrt Llanwonno CF45 .... 54 D1
Cwrt Llechau CF72 .... 172 D6
Cwrt Lleision / Leyshon Ct SA10 .... 71 A7
Cwrt Llwyn Fedwen SA6 .... 46 A1
Cwrt Llwynog SA6 .... 45 F4
Cwrt Llynfi / Llynfi Ct CF34 .... 101 F1
Cwrt Llys Fynnon NP12 .... 86 B5
Cwrt Maescynon CF44 .... 27 E8
Cwrt Maes-y-Rhiw / Maes-y-Rhiw Ct 6 NP44 .... 89 A3
Cwrt Melin Y Rhos 14 CF63 .... 215 B6
Cwrt Merlyn SA6 .... 45 F5
Cwrt Mynwy / Monnow Ct NP44 .... 89 A4
Cwrt Myrddin SA15 .... 40 B4
Cwrt Naiad SA15 .... 40 B4
Cwrt Nant Y Felin CF83 .... 137 D1
Cwrt Neuadd Wen CF81 .... 58 C5
Cwrt Neville 2 SA15 .... 40 D4
Cwrt Newton Pool CF62 .... 213 B1
Cwrt Newydd CF64 .... 206 B3
Cwrt Newydd / New Ct CF31 .... 168 B3
Cwrt Noddfa CF44 .... 53 C6
Cwrt Olwyn Ddwr SA7 .... 47 A1
Cwrt Pandora SA15 .... 40 B4
Cwrt Pantycelyn NP12 .... 86 A5
Cwrt Penarth / Penarth Ct 5 NP44 .... 90 B1
Cwrt Pencoedtre 3 CF63 .... 215 A8
Cwrt Pensarn CF3 .... 179 E5
Cwrt Pentre Bach 7 CF3 .... 180 A8
Cwrt Pentwyn CF38 .... 156 B7
Cwrt Penylan / Penylan Ct NP44 .... 116 B8
Cwrt Pen Y Twyn / Head of the Hill Ct NP22 .... 6 D2
Cwrt Perry / Perry Ct NP44 .... 89 A4
Cwrt Rawlin Prim Sch CF83 .... 137 E1
Cwrt Rhian SA4 .... 43 C2
Cwrt Rhosyn SA7 .... 69 D6
Cwrt Rhyd NP23 .... 7 C4
Cwrt Roberts CF5 .... 193 A3
Cwrt Saffron / Saffrwn Ct NP44 .... 88 F1
Cwrt St Cyres CF64 .... 206 E4
Cwrt Saron CF40 .... 107 A2
CWRT SART 71 C4
Cwrt Sart SA11 .... 71 C3
Cwrt Sart Comp Sch SA11 .... 71 C3
Cwrt Snowden / Snowdon Ct NP44 .... 90 A5
Cwrt Stanllyd SA18 .... 219 B6
Cwrt Sycanor / Sycamore Ct NP44 .... 115 F8
Cwrt Syr Dafydd CF61 .... 209 F7
Cwrt Tabernacl CF82 .... 85 A3
Cwrt Tomos SA18 .... 220 C8
Cwrt Tre-aman CF44 .... 53 D6
Cwrt Treftadaeth / Heritage Ct NP4 .... 17 B7
Cwrt Trelyn NP12 .... 85 A6
Cwrt Trem y Bryn / Hillside Ct 2 NP44 .... 89 D5
Cwrt Trem Yr Ynys 2 CF63 .... 214 F4
Cwrt Twyn-Rhyd CF44 .... 26 C8
Cwrt Ty-Fferm CF83 .... 137 F8
Cwrt Ty Mawr
Caerphilly / Caerffili CF83 .... 138 D2
Penarth CF64 .... 206 E2
Cwrt-Ty-Mynydd CF15 .... 176 B6
Cwrt Tynewydd NP11 .... 86 F6
Cwrt Ty Y Felin / Mill House Ct 4 NP44 .... 116 C8
Cwrt-Ucha Terr 7 SA13 .... 125 C7
Cwrt Waddl 3 SA15 .... 40 D4
Cwrt Wern Fach / Wern Fach Ct NP44 .... 115 F8
Cwrt Y Babell NP11 .... 113 A3
Cwrt-y-Cadno
Cardiff / Caerdydd CF5 .... 192 F5
Llantwit Major / Llanilltud Fawr CF61 .... 210 A7
Pen-Y-Fai CF31 .... 168 D8
Cwrt Y Cadno SA7 .... 70 B8
Cwrt Y Carw SA13 .... 147 F6
Cwrt Y Castell SA4 .... 64 E4
Cwrt Y Castell / Castle Court Sh Ctr CF83 .... 138 B3
Cwrt Y Castell / Castle Ct NP44 .... 115 F8
Cwrt-y-Clafdy SA10 .... 70 F8
Cwrt-y-Clafdy Rd SA10 .... 70 F8
Cwrt Y Coed NP12 .... 85 D6
Cwrt-y-Coed CF31 .... 169 B4
Cwrt-y-Farchnad 1 CF5 .... 194 D6
Cwrt-y-Fedw SA7 .... 47 B1
Cwrt Y Fedwen
Cwmfelin CF34 .... 128 D8
Llansamlet SA7 .... 46 D1
Cwrt-y-Felin CF71 .... 198 C5
Cwrt Y Ffoundri CF37 .... 135 E7
Cwrt y Garth 5 CF38 .... 156 A5
Cwrt-y-Goedwig CF38 .... 156 B7
Cwrt Y Gollen / Hazel Tree Ct SA10 .... 48 C2
Cwrt Y Mwnws CF34 .... 102 A4
Cwrt Ynysmeurig CF45 .... 82 E2
Cwrt Yr Aeron SA6 .... 46 A4
Cwrt-yr-Ala Ave CF5 .... 193 B3
Cwrt-yr-Ala Jun Sch CF5 .... 193 B4
Cwrt-yr-Ala Rd CF5 .... 193 C2
Cwrt Yr Ardal CF3 .... 179 E5
Cwrt yr Efail CF38 .... 156 F8
Cwrt Yr Efail / Smithy's Ct CF31 .... 168 A4
Cwrt Yr Eos SA13 .... 148 A6
Cwrt Yr Gollen 14 NP23 .... 14 D6
Cwrt Yr Henbont / Old Bridge Ct NP12 .... 85 F3
Cwrt-yr-Iolo CF62 .... 201 C1
Cwrt Yr Ysgol 1 NP11 .... 114 F3
Cwrt-yr-Ysgol SA11 .... 49 C2
Cwrt-y-Vil Rd CF64 .... 207 A3
Cwrt-y-Vil Road (Lower) CF64 .... 207 A2
Cwrt y Waun
3 Beddau CF38 .... 156 A5
Blackwood / Coed-Duon NP12 .... 85 C7
Rhyd-y-fro SA8 .... 23 D7
Cwrt Ywen CF72 .... 172 D5
Cwt Cypreswydden CF32 .... 104 E1
Cwt Tegeirian / Orchid Ct NP44 .... 89 A1
Cyd Terr SA11 .... 226 A3
Cyfarthfa Gdns CF48 .... 10 B4
Cyfarthfa High (Lower) Sch CF47 .... 10 C3
Cyfarthfa High (Upper) Sch CF47 .... 10 F1
Cyfarthfa Ho CF48 .... 10 A3
Cyfarthfa Ind Est / Ystad Ddiwydiannol Cyfarthfa CF47 .... 10 C2
Cyfarthfa Jun Sch CF47 .... 10 C3
Cyfarthfa Mus & Art Gall★ CF47 .... 10 C3
Cyfarthfa Rd CF48, CF48 .... 10 C2
Cyfarthfa St CF24 .... 232 D4
Cyfyng Rd SA9 .... 2 A5
Cygnet Cl SA2 .... 93 E6
Cylla St CF82 .... 84 D5
CYMDDA 150 F3
Cymdda CF32 .... 150 E3
Cymer Afan Comp Sch SA13 .... 75 C4
Cymer Afan Prim Sch SA13 .... 75 B5
CYMER / CYMMER 75 C4
Cymer Rd CF34 .... 75 B2
CYMMER 107 E2
CYMMER / CYMER 75 C4
Cymmer Inf Sch CF39 .... 107 E2
Cymmer Jun Sch CF39 .... 107 E2
Cymmer Rd
Glyncorrwg SA13 .... 227 C1
Porth CF39 .... 107 D4
Cymmer St CF11 .... 194 F3
Cymric Cl
Cardiff / Caerdydd CF5 .... 193 D5
Hirwaun CF44 .... 27 F6
Cynan Cl
Barry / Y Barri CF63 .... 215 B8
Beddau CF38 .... 156 A5
Ebbw Vale / Glyn Ebwy NP23 .... 7 D5
CYNCOED 178 B6
Cyncoed CF37 .... 81 E3
Cyncoed Ave CF23 .... 178 D6
Cyncoed Cl SA2 .... 93 C8
Cyn-Coed Cres CF23 .... 178 D6
Cyncoed Gdns CF23 .... 178 C3
Cyncoed Pl CF23 .... 178 C6
Cyncoed Rd
Cardiff / Caerdydd CF23 .... 178 C5
Margam SA13 .... 125 E3
Cyncoed Rise CF23 .... 178 C6
Cynffig Comp Sch / Ysgol Gyfun Cynffig CF33 .... 148 D1
CYNFFIG / KENFIG 165 D7
Cyngor Cefn Gwlad Cymru / Countryside Council for Wales Information Point★ SA3 .... 230 A6
Cynllan Ave CF72 .... 153 F2
Cynllwyndu Rd CF43 .... 80 B3
Cynon Cl
1 Aberdare / Aberdâr CF44 .... 28 F4
Swansea / Abertawe SA6 .... 69 A7
Cynon St CF44 .... 53 D6
Cynon Terr
Abercynon CF45 .... 82 E2
Hirwaun CF44 .... 27 E7
Mountain Ash / Aberpennar CF45 .... 82 A7
Cynon Valley Mus★ CF44 .... 29 A3
Cynon View CF37 .... 109 F3
CYNONVILLE 74 B3
Cynore Rd / Ffordd Cynore SA5 .... 67 C6
Cyntwell Ave CF5 .... 193 B3
Cyntwell Cres CF5 .... 193 B4
Cyntwell Pl CF5 .... 193 B4
Cynulliad Cenedlaethol Cymru / Nat Assembly for Wales The CF10 .... 195 C2
Cynwal Terr SA9 .... 221 C5
Cypress Ave SA3 .... 122 F8
Cypress Cl
Caerleon / Caerllion NP18 .... 117 E2
Merthyr Tydfil / Merthyr Tudful CF47 .... 10 D5
Cypress Ct
Aberdare / Aberdâr CF44 .... 28 E2
Ogmore Vale CF32 .... 104 E1
Cypress Dr CF3 .... 180 B8
Cypress Gdns CF36 .... 183 E7
Cypress Pl CF5 .... 176 D2
Cypress St CF37 .... 136 A5
Cyrch-y-Gwas Rd CF37 .... 135 E7
Cyres St CF47 .... 10 F3
Cyril Cres CF24 .... 195 D7
Cyril Evans Way SA6 .... 45 E4
Cyril Pl NP13 .... 35 F6
Cyril St
Barry / Y Barri CF63 .... 215 B5
Newport / Casnewydd NP19 .... 143 D4
Cysgod-y-Fro SA8 .... 23 D7
Cysgod Y Llan SA15 .... 40 D6

D

DAFEN 41 B7
Dafen Inn Row SA14 .... 41 C7
Dafen Prim Sch SA14 .... 41 A7
Dafen Rd
Llanelli, Dafen SA14 .... 41 B7
Llanelli SA14 .... 41 A8
Dafen Row SA15 .... 40 E2
Daffodil Cl SA12 .... 98 C3
Daffodil Ct NP44 .... 88 F2
Daffodil La NP10 .... 141 D7
Dafolog Terr NP24 .... 33 F4
Dafydd Pl CF63 .... 215 A8
Dahlia Cl SA12 .... 98 C2
Daisy St CF5 .... 194 B6
Daisy View NP4 .... 62 D5
Dalcross St CF24 .... 178 B1
Dale Ave CF14 .... 177 D5
Dale Cl SA5 .... 67 B4
Dale Ct CF62 .... 214 F8
Dale Path NP44 .... 89 B2
Dale Rd NP19 .... 144 D6
Daleside CF32 .... 151 A5
Dale View
Cefn Cribwr CF32 .... 149 C2
Nantyglo NP23 .... 15 D8
Dalmuir Rd CF24 .... 195 F7
Dalrymple St 3 SA12 .... 99 A1
Dalton Cl 8 CF47 .... 30 F8
Dalton Cl / Clos Dalton SA12 .... 124 D8
Dalton Ct 2 CF24 .... 195 A8
Dalton Ho 8 SA12 .... 98 D1
Dalton Rd SA11 .... 71 E6
Dalton Rd / Heol Dalton SA12 .... 98 D1
Dalton St
2 Cardiff / Caerdydd, Cathays CF24 .... 178 A1
Cardiff / Caerdydd CF24 .... 195 A8
Dana Dr SA2 .... 94 C6
Dan Caerlan CF72 .... 155 E3
Dan Danino Way SA6 .... 45 E4
Danescourt Halt CF5 .... 176 E2
Danescourt Jun & Inf Sch CF5 .... 176 E2
Danescourt Way CF5 .... 176 E3
Dane St CF47 .... 10 D2
Dane Terr CF47 .... 10 D2
Daniel Hopkin Cl CF61 .... 209 F5
Daniel James Com Sch SA5 .... 68 C7
Daniell Cl CF64 .... 216 A5
Daniel Pl 11 NP20 .... 143 C3
Daniel St
Aberdare / Aberdâr CF44 .... 29 F1
Barry / Y Barri CF63 .... 215 B7
Cardiff / Caerdydd CF24 .... 178 A1
Dannog Y Coed CF63 .... 205 B1
Dantwyn Rd SA4 .... 19 E5
Danybanc SA15 .... 40 E8
Dan-y-bont SA12 .... 73 A1
Danybryn CF72 .... 172 F6
Dan Y Bryn
Bryn NP12 .... 85 E3
Evanstown CF39 .... 132 B7
Dan-y-Bryn
Maesteg CF34 .... 75 A1
Nant-y-Moel CF32 .... 104 F6
Tonna / Tonnau SA11 .... 49 D3
Dan-y-Bryn Ave CF15 .... 176 A6
Dan-y-bryn Bglws NP13 .... 15 E4
Dan-y-Bryn Cl CF15 .... 176 B6
Danybryn Rd SA4 .... 43 A1
Dan-y-Bryn Rd SA13 .... 125 C8
Danycoed
Caerphilly / Caerffili CF83 .... 138 B1
Clydach NP7 .... 9 D6
Tonypandy CF41 .... 79 E2
Dan-y-Coed
Aberkenfig / Abercynffig CF32 .... 150 C3
Blackmill CF35 .... 130 E1
Cefn Hengoed CF82 .... 84 F4
Cwmavon / Cwmafan SA12 .... 99 E5
Mountain Ash / Aberpennar CF45 .... 54 E3
Dan y Coed CF35 .... 170 D7
Dan-y-coed
Pontsticill CF48 .... 3 F3
Ton-mawr SA12 .... 73 B5
Dan-y-Coedcae Rd CF37 .... 135 B7
Dan-y-Coed Cl CF23 .... 178 B6
Dan-y-Coed Rd
Cardiff / Caerdydd CF23 .... 178 B6
Cardiff / Caerdydd CF23 .... 178 C6
Swansea / Abertawe SA7 .... 70 A8
Dan-y-Coed Rise
Bridgend / Pen-y-Bont ar Ogwr CF31 .... 169 A5
Cardiff / Caerdydd CF23 .... 178 B6
Danycoed Terr CF40 .... 106 D7
Dan-y-Craig Rd SA11 .... 71 E6
Dan Y Cribyn CF37 .... 109 A7
Danycwm SA14 .... 40 F8
Dan-y-Darren CF83 .... 112 A5
Dan-y-Deri CF83 .... 138 C7
Dan-Y-Deri / Below The Oak Trees CF31 .... 168 B4
Dan-y-Deri La CF48 .... 10 A4
Danyderi St CF44 .... 53 C6
Danyderi Terr CF48 .... 55 C5
Dan-y-Felin CF72 .... 155 D3
Danyffynon SA13 .... 99 C2
Dan-y-Fron SA9 .... 222 C7
Dan Y Fron CF39 .... 132 F4
Dan-y-Gaer Rd CF82 .... 84 C6
DAN-Y-GRAIG 96 A7
Danygraig
Aberavon SA12 .... 99 A2
Clydach SA6 .... 46 C8
Croesyceiliog NP44 .... 90 A7
Cwm-twrch Isaf SA9 .... 1 A2
Machen CF83 .... 139 B6
Ystrad CF41 .... 79 E3
Dan-y-Graig CF83 .... 137 A7
Dan Y Graig
Cardiff / Caerdydd CF14 .... 176 F8
Pontlottyn CF81 .... 33 A7
Risca / Rhisga NP11 .... 114 F2
Danygraig Ave CF36 .... 183 E8
Danygraig Bglws NP11 .... 114 E1
Danygraig Cl CF32 .... 130 E5
Danygraig Cres CF72 .... 155 C3
Danygraig Dr CF72 .... 155 C3
Dan y Graig Hts CF72 .... 155 C3
Danygraig Prim Sch SA1 .... 96 A7
Danygraig Rd
Llanharan CF72 .... 154 A3
Swansea / Abertawe SA1 .... 96 B7
Dan Y Graig Rd
Pontardawe SA8 .... 23 C2
Risca / Rhisga NP11 .... 114 F2
Dan-y-Graig Rd / Heol Dan-y-Graig SA10 .... 71 B8
Danygraig St CF37 .... 135 B7
Danygraig Terr CF72 .... 154 A3
Dan-y-graig Terr SA10 .... 49 A3
Dan-y-Lan CF32 .... 150 C3
Danylan Rd CF37 .... 109 A1
Dan Y Mynydd
Blaengarw CF32 .... 103 E6
Cardiff / Caerdydd CF14 .... 159 C3
Danyparc CF47 .... 10 E2
Dan-y-Parc SA6 .... 45 E1
Dan-y-Parc View / Trem Dan-y-Parc CF47 .... 10 F1
Danyrallt SA14 .... 40 F8
Dan Yr Allt SA4 .... 66 A5
Dan-yr-Allt Cl CF37 .... 136 B5
Dan Yr Ardd CF83 .... 137 E1
Dan-yr-eglwys CF32 .... 129 D2
Dan-Yr-Heol CF23 .... 178 B6
Dan Yr Heol CF32 .... 130 E4
Dan-yr-Heol CF44 .... 28 B6
Dan-y-Rhiw CF44 .... 53 A3
Dan-y-Rhiw Terr NP11 .... 87 A3
Dan-y-twyn CF46 .... 83 B5
Danywern Terr CF41 .... 79 D3
Daphne Cl SA10 .... 48 E2
Daphne Rd SA10 .... 48 E2
Darby Cres NP23 .... 14 B8
Darby Rd CF24 .... 196 A4
D'arcy Bsns Ctr SA10 .... 70 D5
Dare Ct CF44 .... 28 C3
Daren Cl CF34 .... 102 D2
Daren-Ddu Rd CF37 .... 109 C4
Daren-Felen Rd NP23 .... 8 C4
Darenfelin Jun & Inf Sch NP7 .... 9 B5
Darent Cl NP20 .... 116 C1
Darent Rd NP20 .... 116 C1
Darent Wlk NP20 .... 116 D1
Dare Rd CF44 .... 28 C3
Dare Valley Ctry Pk★ CF44 .... 28 B2
Dare Valley Visitor Ctr★ CF44 .... 28 C2
Dare Villas CF44 .... 28 F2
Darlington Ct NP19 .... 143 D8
Darran Cl SA10 .... 47 F1
Darran Park Prim Sch CF43 .... 79 F6
Darran Pk
Neath Abbey SA10 .... 47 F1
Pontypridd CF37 .... 109 D3
Darran Rd
Mountain Ash / Aberpennar CF45 .... 54 D2
Risca / Rhisga NP11 .... 114 E4
Darran St CF24 .... 194 F8
Darran Terr CF43 .... 79 F6
Darren Bglws CF32 .... 103 E6
Darren Cl
Caerphilly / Caerffili CF83 .... 138 D5
Cowbridge / Y Bont-Faen CF71 .... 188 D2

Darren Ct
Blackwood / Coed Duon NP12 . . . 59 B1
Pontypridd CF37 . . . 109 D5
Darren Dr NP11 . . . 87 A1
Darren Hill CF71 . . . 188 D2
DARRENLAS . . . 54 C2
Darren Las CF48 . . . 55 D2
Darrenlas Prim Sch CF45 . . . 54 D2
Darren Rd
Abertillery / Abertyleri NP13 . . . 36 C5
Briton Ferry / Llansawel SA11 . . . 71 C3
Ystalyfera SA9 . . . 2 B6
Darren View
Merthyr Tydfil / Merthyr Tudful CF47 . . . 10 F2
Pont Rhyd-y-cyff CF34 . . . 128 D7
Darren Wen SA12 . . . 98 F7
Dartford Dr SA1 . . . 69 A3
Dartford Pl SA1 . . . 69 A2
Dartford Rd SA1 . . . 69 A3
Dartington Dr CF23 . . . 160 E1
Dart Rd NP20 . . . 116 E1
Darwin Dr NP20 . . . 117 A2
Darwin Rd SA12 . . . 124 E7
David Cl NP20 . . . 143 C1
David Davies Rd CF63 . . . 215 B4
David Dower Cl CF45 . . . 82 E2
David Issac Cl SA1 . . . 68 D3
David Price St 11 CF44 . . . 29 A1
David's Ct CF72 . . . 173 B8
David St
Aberdare / Aberdâr CF44 . . . 28 E3
Barry / Y Barri CF63 . . . 215 C8
Blackwood / Coed-Duon NP12 . . . 85 F6
Blaengarw CF32 . . . 103 E7
Blaenrhondda CF42 . . . 50 D4
Cardiff / Caerdydd CF10 . . . 232 C2
Cwmdare CF44 . . . 28 C3
Ebbw Vale / Glyn Ebwy NP23 . . . 14 C8
16 Merthyr Tydfil / Merthyr Tudful, Cae-Pant-Tywll CF47 . . . 10 D2
Merthyr Tydfil / Merthyr Tudful, Ysgubor Newydd CF47 . . . 30 E7
Swansea / Abertawe SA5 . . 68 B2
Tonypandy, Blaen Clydach CF40 . . . 106 D7
Tonypandy, Williamstown CF40 . . . 107 A3
Treherbert CF42 . . . 50 F1
Treorchy / Treorci CF42 . . . 78 B4
Wick / Y Wig CF71 . . . 198 C5
David's Way / Ffordd Dafydd SA14 . . . 218 D7
David Williams Terr SA1 . . . 96 C7
David Wlk 9 NP10 . . . 142 B4
Davies Andrews Rd / Heol Davies Andrews SA11 . . . 49 B1
Davies Ave
Bridgend / Pen-y-Bont ar Ogwr CF31 . . . 168 F7
Porthcawl CF36 . . . 165 F1
Davies Cl CF40 . . . 107 C5
Davies Dr CF83 . . . 137 F5
Davies Pl
Cardiff / Caerdydd CF5 . . . 193 F7
Porth CF39 . . . 107 E6
Davies Rd
Neath / Castell-Nedd SA11 . . . 71 E7
Ynysmeudwy SA8 . . . 23 F6
Davies Row
Hirwaun CF44 . . . 27 D8
Swansea / Abertawe SA5 . . 68 D5
Davies Sq 3 SA15 . . . 40 E5
Davies St
Abercrave / Abercraf SA9 . . . 222 D7
Barry / Y Barri CF63 . . . 215 A6
Blackwood / Coed-Duon NP12 . . . 85 C7
5 Brynmawr NP23 . . . 8 C4
Dowlais CF48 . . . 11 B5
Porth CF39 . . . 107 E4
2 Swansea / Abertawe SA6 . . . 69 A8
Tonypandy CF40 . . . 106 D6
Ystrad Mynach CF82 . . . 84 F2
Davies Terr
Maesteg CF34 . . . 101 F6
14 Merthyr Tydfil / Merthyr Tudful CF47 . . . 30 E8
Daviot Ct CF24 . . . 178 B1
Daviot St CF24 . . . 178 B1
Davis Ave CF32 . . . 151 A6
Davis Cl NP4 . . . 62 C7
Davis Sq 14 NP20 . . . 143 C3
Davis St
Aberdare / Aberdâr CF44 . . . 53 C8
Cardiff / Caerdydd CF24 . . . 232 D2
Swansea / Abertawe SA6 . . 68 E5
Davis's Terr 4 CF14 . . . 177 B5
Davnic Cl 5 CF63 . . . 215 B6
Davy Cl NP20 . . . 117 A3
Davy Evans Ct NP13 . . . 36 B4
Dawan Cl CF62 . . . 214 D5
Dawkins Pl CF44 . . . 28 C5
Dawlish Cl SA3 . . . 122 E6
Dawson Cl NP19 . . . 144 F6
D C Griffiths Way SA11 . . . 71 D6
Dderi Rd SA9 . . . 221 B5
Ddol Rd SA2 . . . 93 B7
Dean Ct NP44 . . . 115 F8
Deanery Gdns 13 NP20 . . . 143 B4
Deans Cl CF5 . . . 194 B8
Deans Ct
Aberdare / Aberdâr CF44 . . . 29 A2
Rhoose / Y Rhws CF62 . . . 213 A2
Dean's Ct CF5 . . . 177 A1
Dean St
Aberdare / Aberdâr CF44 . . . 29 A2
Newport / Casnewydd NP19 . . . 143 E6
De-Barri St CF37 . . . 135 F4
De Bawdip Rd CF24 . . . 195 F8
De Berclos CF36 . . . 182 F8
De Braose Cl CF5 . . . 176 D3
De Breos Dr CF36 . . . 183 A8
De-Breos St SA2 . . . 94 F5
De Burgh Pl 9 CF11 . . . 194 E5
De Burgh St CF11 . . . 194 E5
De Clare Cl CF36 . . . 182 F8
De Clare Ct CF61 . . . 210 B6
De Clare Dr CF15 . . . 176 D5
De Croche Pl CF11 . . . 194 E5
Deeley Rd SA9 . . . 2 B6
Deemuir Rd CF24 . . . 195 F7
Deemuir Sq CF24 . . . 195 F7
Deepdale Cl CF23 . . . 178 B3
Deepdene Cl CF5 . . . 192 F5
Deepfield Cl CF5 . . . 192 F5
Dee Pl SA6 . . . 46 A4
Deepslade Cl SA3 . . . 121 A4
Deepwood Cl CF5 . . . 192 F5
Deerbrook NP44 . . . 89 B2
Deere Cl CF5 . . . 193 B4
Deere Pl CF5 . . . 193 B4
Deere Rd
Cardiff / Caerdydd CF5 . . . 193 B4
Llantwit Fadre / Llanilltud Faerdref CF38 . . . 156 C6
Deganwy Cl CF14 . . . 159 E1
De Granville Cl CF36 . . . 182 F8
De Havilland Rd CF24 . . . 196 A7
Dehewydd Isaf CF38 . . . 156 D8
Dehewydd La CF38 . . . 156 D7
Deighton Cl NP22 . . . 13 D8
Deighton Prim Sch NP22 . . . 13 D8
De-La-Beche Rd SA2 . . . 94 D6
Delabeche St / Ffordd Delabeche 12 SA15 . . . 40 D4
De-La Beche St SA1 . . . 233 A3
De La Beche Terr SA6 . . . 45 F1
Delfan
Swansea / Abertawe, Llangyfelach SA6 . . . 45 C2
Swansea / Abertawe, Trallwn SA7 . . . 69 F5
Delffordd SA8 . . . 24 B2
Delfryn
Capel Hendre SA18 . . . 218 D6
Llanelli SA14 . . . 41 D6
Llwydcoed CF44 . . . 28 F6
Miskin / Meisgyn CF72 . . . 173 C7
Del Guerra Ct CF39 . . . 133 B5
Delhi St SA1 . . . 233 C3
Delius Cl
Newport / Casnewydd NP19 . . . 144 C5
Rogerstone NP10 . . . 142 A6
Dell The
Baglan SA12 . . . 98 E5
Bryncethin CF32 . . . 151 A4
Cardiff / Caerdydd CF3 . . . 179 D8
Church Village CF38 . . . 135 F3
Cwmdare CF44 . . . 28 C2
Laleston / Trelales CF32 . . . 167 E4
Llanelli SA15 . . . 40 C8
Pontlliw SA4 . . . 43 F6
Swansea / Abertawe SA2 . . 93 E6
De Londres Cl CF36 . . . 182 F8
Delphinium Rd NP10 . . . 141 D7
Delta St 3 CF11 . . . 194 D5
Delwen Terr CF42 . . . 50 B2
Denbigh Cl
Blackwood / Coed-Duon NP12 . . . 58 E1
Church Village CF38 . . . 135 F2
Denbigh Cres SA6 . . . 46 B5
Denbigh Ct
Caerphilly / Caerffili CF83 . . . 137 C4
3 Cardiff / Caerdydd CF14 . . . 177 A6
9 Penarth CF64 . . . 206 F2
Denbigh Dr CF61 . . . 210 C6
Denbigh Rd
Dinas Powis / Dinas Powys CF64 . . . 206 C4
Newport / Casnewydd NP19 . . . 143 E8
Denbigh St CF11 . . . 194 D7
Denbigh Way CF62 . . . 214 F7
Denham Ave SA15 . . . 40 A7
Denison Way CF5 . . . 192 F5
Denleigh Cl CF81 . . . 57 F3
Dennis Pl CF32 . . . 151 B5
Dennithorne Cl / Clos Dennithorne CF48 . . . 11 C4
DENSCOMBE . . . 138 A2
Denstone Ct CF23 . . . 178 C3
Dental Dr / Rhodfa'r Deintyddion CF14 . . . 177 E3
Denton Ho NP44 . . . 90 B4
Denton Rd CF5 . . . 194 D5
Dents Cl NP19 . . . 144 D5
Dents Hill NP19 . . . 144 D5
Denvale Trad Pk CF24 . . . 195 D4
Denver Rd SA5 . . . 67 B5
Denys Cl CF64 . . . 206 B4
Depot Rd
Aberdare / Aberdâr CF44 . . . 28 F2
Cwmavon / Cwmafan SA12 . . . 99 E5
Derby Gr NP19 . . . 144 B2
DERI . . . 57 B8
Deri Ave CF35 . . . 170 C8
Deri Cl
Cardiff / Caerdydd CF23 . . . 178 E1
Pencoed CF35 . . . 152 C1
Deri Cochion / Red Oaks CF35 . . . 170 B8
Deri-Newydd CF81 . . . 33 B1
Dering Rd CF23 . . . 161 B1
Deri Prim Sch CF81 . . . 57 B8
Deri Rd CF23 . . . 178 D1
Deri Rd / Heol Y Deri SA18 . . . 219 F8
Deri Terr CF43 . . . 80 B2
Derlin Pk / Parc Derlin SA18 . . . 218 F5
Derllwyn Cl CF32 . . . 150 C6
Derllwyn Rd CF32 . . . 150 C6
Derlwyn
Dunvant SA2 . . . 93 D8
Neath / Castell-Nedd SA10 . . . 48 C1
Penywaun CF44 . . . 28 A6
Derlwyn St NP24 . . . 33 E3
DERWEN . . . 151 A1
Derwen Aur CF39 . . . 107 F5
Derwen Cl
Blackwood / Coed-Duon NP12 . . . 85 E8
Bridgend / Pen-y-Bont ar Ogwr CF31 . . . 168 F8
Tredomen CF82 . . . 84 D1
Waunarlwydd SA5 . . . 66 D4
Derwen Deg
Neath / Castell-Nedd SA10 . . . 48 C3
Pontardawe SA8 . . . 23 D6
Derwendeg Ave
Blackwood / Coed-Duon NP12 . . . 85 C8
Cefn Hengoed CF82 . . . 84 F4
Pontypridd CF37 . . . 109 D5
Derwendeg Prim Sch CF82 . . . 84 F5
Derwen Fawr SA10 . . . 49 C6
Derwen Fawr Rd SA2 . . . 94 B4
Derwen Las CF31 . . . 168 B2
Derwen Rd
Bridgend / Pen-y-Bont ar Ogwr CF31 . . . 168 F4
Cardiff / Caerdydd CF23 . . 178 C8
Pontardawe SA8 . . . 23 D2
Pontyclun CF72 . . . 173 B7
Ystrad CF41 . . . 79 C3
Ystradgynlais SA9 . . . 1 F1
Derwent Cl CF14 . . . 159 E2
Derwent Ct NP20 . . . 116 C1
Derwent Dr CF44 . . . 29 E1
Derwent St SA15 . . . 40 C6
Derwen View / Golwys Derwen CF31 . . . 169 A6
Derwlas SA4 . . . 44 B5
Derw Rd SA8 . . . 23 D3
Derwydd Ave SA18 . . . 220 D6
Derwydd Rd CF40 . . . 106 E5
Derwyn Las CF83 . . . 138 C7
Deryn Ct CF23 . . . 178 F8
Despenser Ave CF72 . . . 155 D2
Despenser Gdns 5 CF11 . . . 194 F5
Despenser Pl 6 CF11 . . . 194 F5
Despenser Rd CF64 . . . 216 A5
Despenser St CF11 . . . 194 F5
Dessmuir Rd CF24 . . . 195 F7
De Turberville Cl CF36 . . 182 F8
Devon Ave CF63 . . . 214 F6
Devon Ct NP18 . . . 118 A3
Devon Ho 5 SA12 . . . 98 B2
Devon Pl
Cardiff / Caerdydd CF11 . . . 194 F3
Newport / Casnewydd NP20 . . . 143 B5
The Mumbles / Y Mwmbwls SA3 . . . 123 B4
Devon Pl / Maes Dyfnaint NP4 . . . 37 E3
Devonshire Dr CF44 . . . 27 C8
Devonshire Pl SA13 . . . 125 C7
Devon St CF11 . . . 194 E3
Devon Terr SA1 . . . 95 A7
Devon View SA2 . . . 94 B7
Dewberry Gr NP10 . . . 141 D7
Dew Cres CF5 . . . 193 E4
Dewi Ct CF5 . . . 194 A8
De Winton St 7 CF40 . . . 106 E6
De Winton Terr
Llanbradach CF83 . . . 111 F1
Tonypandy CF40 . . . 106 E7
Dewi Pritchard Field / Maes Dewi Pritchard CF31 . . . 169 A6
Dewi Sant Hospl CF37 . . . 135 C8
Dewi St CF37 . . . 109 E3
Dewi Terr SA1 . . . 68 A1
Dew Rd / Heol Y Gwlith SA12 . . . 98 C2
Dewsbury Ct SA1 . . . 233 B2
Dewsland Park Rd NP20 . . . 143 B3
Dewstow St NP19 . . . 143 F4
Diagonal Rd CF62 . . . 211 E1
Diamond Cl CF83 . . . 137 F4
Diamond Jubilee Terr NP13 . . . 36 B5
Diamond St CF24 . . . 195 D6
Diana La CF24 . . . 178 B1
Diana St
Cardiff / Caerdydd CF24 . . . 178 B1
Troedyrhiw CF48 . . . 55 B8
Dibdin Cl NP19 . . . 144 F5
Dickens Ave CF3 . . . 179 B7
Dickens Ave / Rhodfa Dickens SA12 . . . 124 E7
Dickens Ct CF83 . . . 139 C6
Dickens Dr NP20 . . . 142 E2
Dickinson Cl SA12 . . . 98 E6
Dickslade SA3 . . . 123 C4
Digby Cl 3 CF5 . . . 176 E2
Digby Rd SA11 . . . 72 A8
Digby St CF63 . . . 215 A5
Dillington Terr CF45 . . . 81 F7
Dillwyn Cl SA10 . . . 222 B2
Dillwyn Ct
Pontlliw SA4 . . . 43 F6
Swansea / Abertawe SA2 . . 94 C6
Dillwyn Rd SA2 . . . 94 C6
Dillwyn St
Llanelli SA15 . . . 40 D4
Swansea / Abertawe SA1 . . . 233 A2
Dilwyn Ave CF82 . . . 84 F2
Dilwyn Cl SA4 . . . 43 F2
Dilwyn Gdns CF31 . . . 168 E2
Dilwyn Rd SA4 . . . 43 F2
Dilwyn St CF45 . . . 81 F8
Dilys St CF42 . . . 50 C2
Dimbath Ave CF35 . . . 131 A3
Dimbath La CF35 . . . 131 B5
DIMLANDS . . . 209 C6
Dimlands Rd CF61 . . . 209 D5
Dimpath Terr SA15 . . . 40 E7
Dinam Cl CF32 . . . 104 F6
Dinam Park Ave CF41 . . . 79 A3
Dinam Pk CF41 . . . 78 F3
Dinam Rd SA1 . . . 69 D1
Dinam St CF32 . . . 104 E6
DINAS . . . 107 B4
Dinas Baglan Rd SA12 . . . 98 F3
Dinas Ent Ctr CF39 . . . 107 E4
Dinas Isaf Cotts CF40 . . . 107 A1
Dinas Isaf Ind Est (East) CF40 . . . 107 B1
Dinas Isaf Ind Est (West) CF40 . . . 133 B8
Dinas Path NP44 . . . 89 B2
Dinas Pl CF11 . . . 194 F3
DINAS POWIS / DINAS POWYS . . . 206 B4
Dinas Powis Inf Sch CF64 . . . 206 B3
DINAS POWYS / DINAS POWIS . . . 206 B4
Dinas Powys Sta CF64 . . . 206 A2
Dinas Rd
Penarth CF64 . . . 206 F2
Pontneddfechan SA11 . . . 223 F2
Tonypandy CF40 . . . 107 A4
Dinas Rhondda Sta CF40 . . . 107 B4
Dinas St
Cardiff / Caerdydd CF11 . . . 232 A1
Swansea / Abertawe SA6 . . 68 E5
Dinas Terr SA11 . . . 223 F2
Dingle Cl CF62 . . . 214 B2
Dingle Dr CF40 . . . 106 E6
Dingle La
2 Cwmbran / Cwmbrân NP44 . . . 89 C6
3 Penarth CF64 . . . 207 A4
Dingle Nook / Pant Gilfach CF32 . . . 104 E4
Dingle Rd
Penarth CF64 . . . 207 A4
Pontypool / Pont-y-pwl NP4 . . . 62 D5
Dingle Road Sta CF64 . . . 207 A4
Dingle The NP23 . . . 14 D8
Discovery Ctr* SA15 . . . 40 B3
Discovery Pk NP20 . . . 143 B6
Distillery Road La CF37 . . . 108 F2
District St CF47 . . . 10 F3
Ditchling Ct CF64 . . . 207 A2
Division St NP13 . . . 36 B5
Dixon's Pl NP11 . . . 115 A2
Dixon St CF47 . . . 10 D1
Dobbins Rd CF63 . . . 215 D7
Dochdwy Rd CF64 . . . 206 E6
Dock Rd
Barry / Y Barri CF62 . . . 214 F2
Port Talbot SA13 . . . 125 A7
Dock Rd *continued*
Port Talbot SA13 . . . 125 A8
Dock St
Loughor SA4 . . . 65 C8
Penarth CF64 . . . 206 F5
Porthcawl CF36 . . . 182 F6
Docks Way NP20 . . . 164 A8
Dock View Rd CF63 . . . 215 A4
Dockwell Terr NP18 . . . 145 B4
Doddridge Way CF36 . . . 182 E6
Dodington Pl 2 CF37 . . . 109 E2
Doe Cl CF23 . . . 178 E1
Dogfield St CF24 . . . 178 A1
Dogo St CF11 . . . 194 D7
Dolafon SA14 . . . 41 E3
Dol Afon
Pencoed CF35 . . . 170 E7
Porth CF39 . . . 107 E4
DOLAU . . . 154 A2
Dolau Ct SA15 . . . 40 E2
Dolau Fach SA15 . . . 40 E3
Dolau Fawr SA15 . . . 40 E3
Dolau Ifan Ddu Terr CF35 . . . 130 F2
Dolau Prim Sch CF72 . . . 153 E2
Dolau Rd SA15 . . . 40 E3
Dolawel SA9 . . . 221 C7
Dol Beiriant / Machine Mdw 4 NP4 . . . 38 A1
Dolcoed CF44 . . . 28 E6
Dol Coed Pl SA11 . . . 49 C2
Dolcoed Terr SA11 . . . 49 C2
Dol Fach CF31 . . . 169 B4
Dolfain SA9 . . . 222 A5
Dol Fieri / Briarmead CF47 . . . 10 E2
Dol Fran CF83 . . . 138 D4
Dolgellau Ave CF38 . . . 135 F2
Dolgoch Cl CF3 . . . 179 D5
Dolgoy Cl SA3 . . . 123 A7
Dol Gwartheg CF64 . . . 206 E2
Dolgwilym St CF43 . . . 80 C1
Dolgynog CF44 . . . 224 D3
Dol Henrhyd SA10 . . . 223 A6
Dol Las SA12 . . . 98 E6
Dol Nant Dderwen CF31 . . . 168 B4
Dol Notais / Nottage Mdws CF36 . . . 165 E2
Dolphin Ct 30 NP20 . . . 143 C3
Dolphin Pl SA12 . . . 98 C3
Dolphin St NP20 . . . 143 D3
Dolwar Fach SA14 . . . 41 C5
Dol-Wen CF35 . . . 152 F1
Dolwen Rd CF14 . . . 177 A2
Dolwerdd SA14 . . . 40 F8
Dol Werdd SA10 . . . 48 C1
Dolwyddelan Cl NP12 . . . 58 E1
Dol-y-Coed SA2 . . . 93 B8
Dol Y Dderwen SA9 . . . 222 A5
Dol-y-Felin
Bedwas CF83 . . . 138 C7
Creigiau CF15 . . . 174 D7
Dol-y-Felin St CF83 . . . 138 B4
Dol-y-Garn Terr NP13 . . . 15 E6
Dol-y-Llan CF72 . . . 173 D8
Dol Y Pandy CF83 . . . 138 C7
Dol Y Paun CF83 . . . 137 E2
Dol yr Eos CF83 . . . 138 C4
Dombey Cl CF14 . . . 159 F2
Domen Ct 12 NP23 . . . 14 D6
Dominion Bsns Ctr CF24 . . . 195 E8
Dominion Way CF24 . . . 195 E8
Dominion Way Ind Est CF24 . . . 195 E8
Donald St
Abercanaid CF48 . . . 30 F4
Cardiff / Caerdydd CF24 . . 178 B1
Nelson CF46 . . . 83 E4
Don Cl NP20 . . . 116 D1
Doniford Cl CF64 . . . 216 B6
Donnen St / Stryd Donnen 5 SA13 . . . 125 D5
Donnington Rd CF64 . . . 215 E6
Dorallt Cl NP44 . . . 88 E1
Dorallt Way NP44 . . . 88 F1
Dorchester Ave CF23 . . . 178 D2
Dorchester Mans 5 CF14 . . . 176 F6
Doreen Ford Ct CF24 . . . 195 E7
Dorleigh Ct NP44 . . . 89 B5
Dorothy Ave CF62 . . . 214 E8
Dorothy Cl CF62 . . . 214 E8
Dorothy St
Pontypridd CF37 . . . 109 D2
Ton Pentre CF41 . . . 79 B3
Dorren Terr SA8 . . . 23 B3
Dorset Ave CF63 . . . 214 F6
Dorset Cl NP19 . . . 144 B2
Dorset Cres NP19 . . . 144 B2
Dorset Ho 3 SA12 . . . 98 C3
Dorset St CF11 . . . 194 F3
Dorstone Wlk / Tro Tref Y Cernyw NP44 . . . 90 A3
Dos Cotts NP20 . . . 143 B6
Dos Rd NP20 . . . 143 B7
Douglas Cl CF5 . . . 176 E2
Douglas Ct
Bishopston SA3 . . . 122 A5
Cardiff / Caerdydd CF14 . . 159 E1
Dovedale Cl CF23 . . . 178 B3
Dovedale St CF63 . . . 215 B6
Dove Rd SA5 . . . 67 E7
Dover St
Mountain Ash / Aberpennar CF45 . . . 54 D2
Ton Pentre CF41 . . . 79 B2

- Dovey Cl
  - Barry / Y Barri CF62 214 C6
  - Cardiff / Caerdydd CF3 179 D5
- DOWLAIS 11 B4
- Dowlais Inf Sch CF48 11 B4
- Dowlais Rd CF24 195 D4
- Dowlais St CF44 28 F2
- Dowlais Stables CF48 11 B4
- DOWLAIS TOP 11 C5
- Dowland Cl NP19 144 E5
- Dowland Rd CF64 206 E1
- Dowlands Way CF3 179 A2
- Downey Gr CF82 84 E6
- Downfield Cl CF64 206 E6
- Downing St
  - Llanelli SA15 40 C4
  - Newport / Casnewydd NP19 144 A3
- Down Leaze SA2 67 D1
- DOWNS 192 D2
- Downs Cl SA5 67 E3
- Down St SA6 46 E7
- Downs The SA3 231 C8
- Downs View CF71 189 B3
- Downs View Cl CF71 189 B3
- Downton Grange CF3 179 C2
- Downton Rd CF3 179 B2
- Downton Rise CF3 179 B2
- Doyle Ave CF5 193 E8
- Doyle Ct CF5 193 E8
- Dragon Auto Ctr SA7 69 B7
- Dragonfly Dr CF62 213 A5
- Drake Cl
  - Newport / Casnewydd NP19 144 E6
  - St Athan / Sain Tathan CF62 211 D7
- Drake Wlk CF10 232 C1
- Drangway CF61 209 F6
- Dranllwyn Cl CF83 139 F7
- Dranllwyn La CF83 139 F7
- Drawlings Cl 1 CF3 179 D8
- Dray Ct 10 CF10 232 B2
- Drayton Ct NP44 89 C3
- Dreflan SA9 1 F4
- Drenewydd Mus* NP22 12 C7
- Dring St SA1 233 C4
- Drinkwater Cl NP20 142 F2
- Drinkwater Gdns NP20 142 F2
- Drinkwater Rise NP20 142 F2
- Drinkwater View NP20 142 F2
- Driscoll Ct 8 CF24 195 D7
- Driscoll Workshops CF10 232 D2
- Drive The
  - Bargoed / Bargod CF81 58 A1
  - Cardiff / Caerdydd CF5 193 D7
  - Dinas Powis / Dinas Powys CF64 206 C3
  - Miskin / Meisgyn CF72 173 D6
  - Pontardawe SA8 23 C3
  - Southgate SA3 121 A4
- Drive The / Y Rhodfa SA10 71 B8
- DROPE 192 D4
- Drope Rd CF5 192 E4
- Drope Terr CF5 192 E4
- Dros Col CF72 172 B5
- Dros y Mor CF64 207 B2
- Dros-y-Morfa CF3 179 C2
- Drovers Mews 8 NP20 143 C3
- Drovers Way CF15 176 B5
- D Row NP4 17 A6
- Druce St SA15 40 C3
- Druids Cl
  - The Mumbles / Y Mwmbwls SA3 123 A6
  - Treorchy / Treorci CF42 78 D5
- Druids Gn CF71 188 F2
- Druidstone Ho CF3 162 A3
- Druidstone Rd CF3 161 F3
- Druidstone Way SA4 44 B2
- Drumau Cl SA10 70 F8
- Drumau Pk SA10 70 F8
- Drumau Rd
  - Birchgrove SA7 47 B1
  - Neath / Castell-Nedd SA7, SA10 70 D8
- Drumfields / Cae Drwm SA10 49 A2
- Drummau Rd / Heol Drummau SA11 71 A7
- Drum Tower View / Trem Twry Drwm CF83 137 D2
- Drury Cl CF14 159 E2
- Druslyn Rd SA3 122 F7
- Dr William Price Bsns Ctr CF37 135 E6
- Drybrook Cl 9 CF3 179 F6
- Drybrook Cl / Clos Drybrook NP44 89 F3
- Dryburgh Ave CF14 177 D5
- Dryden Cl CF3 179 B7
- Dryden Rd CF64 206 F4
- Dryden Terr CF62 214 F8
- Drylla CF64 206 A2
- Drysgol Rd CF15 176 B5
- Drysiog St NP23 14 D6
- Dryslwyn Cl SA4 44 B2
- Duckpool Rd NP19 143 E6
- Dudley Ct CF10 195 B1
- Dudley Pl CF62 214 D4
- Dudley St
  - Cardiff / Caerdydd CF10 195 B1
- Dudley St *continued*
  - 12 Neath / Castell-Nedd SA11 71 E7
  - Newport / Casnewydd NP19 143 E4
- DUFFRYN
  - Cymmer 74 D4
  - Newport 163 E7
- Duffryn CF35 170 B8
- Duffryn Afan Prim Sch SA13 74 C4
- Duffryn Ave CF23 178 B6
- Duffryn Bsns Pk / Parc Busnes Dyffryn CF82 111 F6
- Duffryn Cl
  - Bassaleg NP10 142 A3
  - Bridgend / Pen-y-Bont ar Ogwr CF35 170 A4
  - Cardiff / Caerdydd CF23 178 A6
  - Pen-pedair-heol CF82 84 D8
  - Tonyrefail CF39 133 B6
- Duffryn Cres CF72 153 E2
- Duffryn Dr NP10 163 E7
- Duffryn Fawr CF48 31 B4
- Duffryn High Sch / Ysgol Uwchradd Duffryn NP10 163 F6
- Duffryn Ho 5 CF64 206 C3
- Duffryn Jun Sch NP10 163 F7
- Duffryn La CF5 204 B7
- Duffrynmadog CF34 101 F5
- Duffryn Oaks Dr / Ffordd Deri Duffryn CF35 170 B8
- Duffryn Rd
  - Aberdare / Aberdâr CF44 53 F7
  - Abertillery / Abertyleri NP13 36 B6
  - Cardiff / Caerdydd CF23 178 C6
  - Cwmfelinfach NP11 113 D3
  - Gorseinon SA4 43 B1
- Duffryn St
  - Aberdare / Aberdâr CF44 53 C6
  - Cardiff / Caerdydd CF24 232 C2
  - Duffryn SA13 74 D4
  - Pontlottyn CF81 32 F8
  - Tir-Y-Berth CF82 85 A6
  - Ystrad Mynach CF82 84 E3
- Duffryn Terr
  - Church Village CF38 156 F8
  - Cwmfelinfach NP11 113 F3
  - New Tredegar NP24 33 E3
- Duffryn View NP22 12 F3
- Duffryn Way NP10 163 E6
- Duffynmadog CF34 101 F5
- Dugdale Wlk 14 CF11 194 D5
- Dukefield SA4 92 E8
- DUKEÌS MEADOW 6 C1
- Duke St / Heol Y Dug CF10 232 B2
- Duke St
  - Aberdare / Aberdâr CF44 29 A2
  - Abertillery / Abertyleri NP13 36 C4
  - 5 Blaenavon NP4 17 C6
  - Maesteg CF34 102 C2
  - Newport / Casnewydd NP20 143 D3
  - Pontypridd CF37 135 E7
  - Port Talbot SA13 125 D5
  - Swansea / Abertawe SA1 95 B6
  - Tredegar NP22 13 E6
- DUKESTOWN 6 D2
- Dukestown Rd NP22 6 E1
- Duke Street Arc 4 CF10 232 B2
- Dulais Cl SA10 49 C4
- Dulais Dr SA10 49 C4
- Dulais Fach Rd SA10, SA11 49 C3
- Dulais Gr SA2 94 A5
- Dulais Rd
  - Pontarddulais SA4 19 C4
  - Seven Sisters / Blaendulais SA10 222 C2
- Dulverton Ave CF3 179 D7
- Dulverton Dr CF64 216 B5
- Dulwich Gdns CF5 194 C7
- Dulwich Ho CF5 194 C7
- Dumballs Rd CF10 195 B3
- Dumbarton House Ct 4 SA1 95 A6
- Dumfries Pl
  - Brynmawr NP23 8 C5
  - Cardiff / Caerdydd CF10 232 C3
  - 16 Newport / Casnewydd NP20 143 C4
  - Ystradgynlais SA9 2 E7
- Dumfries St
  - Aberdare / Aberdâr CF44 29 A1
  - Treherbert CF42 50 F2
  - Treorchy / Treorci CF42 78 D7
- Dummer Cl 2 CF3 179 F7
- Dunbar Cl CF23 161 A1
- Duncan Cl CF3 179 D6
- Dungarvan Dr CF23 161 A1
- Dunkery Cl CF3 179 B5
- Dunleavy Dr CF11 206 E7
- Dunlin Cl CF36 182 D8
- Dunlin Ct 9 CF63 214 F5
- Dunnet Gdns NP4 63 B3
- Dunns Cl SA3 123 B5
- Dunns La SA3 123 B5
- Dunn Sq 20 NP20 143 C3
- Dunns The SA3 123 B5
- Dunraven Arc 10 CF40 106 E6
- Dunraven Bsns Pk CF31 169 A3
- Dunraven Cl
  - Dinas Powis / Dinas Powys CF64 206 C3
  - Pen-clawdd SA4 64 E4
- Dunraven Cres CF72 155 A2
- Dunraven Ct
  - Caerphilly / Caerffili CF83 137 C4
  - Treorchy / Treorci CF42 78 C7
- Dunraven Dr NP10 163 D5
- Dunraven Ho CF10 232 A2
- Dunraven Pl
  - Bridgend / Pen-y-Bont ar Ogwr CF31 168 E4
  - Evanstown CF39 132 B8
  - Ogmore Vale CF32 104 E3
- Dunraven Rd
  - Cardiff / Caerdydd CF11 194 D4
  - Llanyrafon NP44 90 B2
  - Swansea / Abertawe SA2 94 B7
- Dunraven St
  - Aberavon SA12 99 A1
  - Aberkenfig / Abercynffig CF32 150 C4
  - Barry / Y Barri CF62 214 C3
  - Blaengwrach SA11 227 B8
  - Bridgend / Pen-y-Bont ar Ogwr CF31 169 B2
  - Glyncorrwg SA13 227 C2
  - Tonypandy CF40 106 E5
  - Treherbert CF42 50 F1
- Dunraven Terr CF42 78 C7
- Dunsmuir Rd CF24 195 F6
- Dunstable Rd NP19 144 E5
- Dunster Cl SA3 122 E6
- Dunster Dr CF64 216 A5
- Dunster Rd CF3 179 D7
- Dunvant Ave SA11 226 C4
- DUNVANT / DYFNANT 93 B8
- Dunvant Pl SA1 233 A1
- Dunvant Prim Sch SA2 93 E8
- Dunvant Rd
  - Dunvant SA2 93 D8
  - Three Crosses SA2, SA4 66 A1
- Dunvant Sq SA2 93 C8
- Duport Cl SA12 98 C7
- Dupre Rd SA1 95 F8
- Durell St CF61 209 F6
- Durham Cl CF48 10 A1
- Durham La NP19 143 D7
- Durham Rd NP19 143 E7
- Durham Road Jun & Inf Sch NP19 143 D7
- Durham St CF11 194 F3
- Durleigh Cl CF3 179 C7
- Durlston Cl 5 CF14 176 F3
- Duxford Cl CF5 176 D2
- Dwr-y-Felin Comp (Lower) Sch SA10 71 A8
- Dwr-y-Felin Comp Sch
  - Neath Abbey SA10 48 A1
  - Neath / Castell-Nedd SA10 48 D1
- Dwr-y-Felin Comp (Upper) Sch SA10 71 D8
- Dwr-y-Felin Rd
  - Neath / Castell-Nedd SA10 48 C1
  - Neath / Castell-Nedd SA10 48 C3
- Dwyfor SA14 41 D5
- Dwyfor Rd SA13 75 D3
- Dwynnen Rd / Heol Dwynwen CF31 168 B3
- Dyfan Rd CF63 215 A7
- Dyfatty St SA1 233 B4
- Dyfed CF64 207 B5
- Dyfed Ave SA1 95 A8
- Dyfed Cl SA1 94 F8
- Dyfed Dr CF83 137 F5
- Dyfed Ho 1 CF23 178 C2
- Dyfed Rd SA11 71 F7
- DYFFRYN
  - Barry 204 A4
  - Maesteg 102 A8
- Dyffryn
  - Bryn-côch SA10 48 B4
  - Pen-pedair-heol CF82 84 D7
- Dyffryn-Aur Rd SA7 69 E6
- Dyffryn Ave CF37 136 A6
- Dyffryn Bach Terr CF38 156 F7
- DYFFRYN CELLWEN 223 A5
- Dyffryn Cl
  - St Nicholas / Sain Nicolas CF5 192 A1
  - Swansea / Abertawe SA6 69 A8
- Dyffryn Cres
  - Peterston-super-Ely / Llanbedr-y-fro CF5 191 F5
  - Rhydyfelin CF37 136 A6
- Dyffryn Gdns* CF5 204 B5
- Dyffryn Gdns CF37 136 A6
- Dyffryn La
  - Coedkernew / Coedcernyw NP10 163 C4
  - Newport / Casnewydd NP10 163 B6
- Dyffryn Lower Sch SA13 125 C7
- Dyffryn Pl
  - Barry / Y Barri CF62 214 D7
  - Cwm NP23 35 B6
  - Maesteg CF34 102 A8
- Dyffryn Rd
  - Bryn-côch SA10 48 C3
  - Ebbw Vale / Glyn Ebwy NP23 14 F3
  - Maesteg CF34 75 A1
  - Mountain Ash / Aberpennar CF45 54 D4
  - Pentrebach CF48 31 A4
  - Pontardawe SA8 23 F4
  - Pontypridd CF37 135 F5
  - Port Talbot SA13 125 D7
  - Rhydyfelin CF37 136 A5
  - Saron SA18 218 F7
- Dyffryn Rd / Heol Dyffryn SA18 219 A7
- Dyffryn Sch SA13 125 F3
- Dyffryn St
  - Aberbargoed / Aberbargod CF81 58 B4
  - Ferndale CF43 80 A5
  - Mountain Ash / Aberpennar CF45 54 D3
- Dyffryn Terr CF39 133 B5
- Dyffryn View SA10 48 C5
- Dyffryn Woods / Allt Y Dyffryn SA10 48 C3
- Dyfnallt Rd CF63 215 A8
- DYFNANT / DUNVANT 93 B8
- Dyfodwg St CF42 78 D6
- Dyfrig Cl CF5 193 F6
- Dyfrig Ct CF61 210 B7
- Dyfrig Rd CF5 193 F6
- Dyfrig St
  - Barry / Y Barri CF62 215 A2
  - Cardiff / Caerdydd CF11 194 E7
- Dyke St 18 CF47 30 E8
- Dylan SA14 41 D5
- Dylan Ave
  - 1 Beddau CF38 156 A5
  - Blackwood / Coed-Duon NP12 85 C7
- Dylan Cl
  - Llandough / Llandochau CF64 206 E6
  - Swansea / Abertawe SA2 93 F7
- Dylan Cres CF63 215 B8
- Dylan Cres / Cresawnt Dylan SA12 124 E7
- Dylan Dr CF83 138 A5
- Dylan Pl CF24 232 D4
- Dylan Rd SA2 93 F7
- Dylan's View SA2 94 F7
- Dylan Thomas Com Sch SA2 67 D2
- Dylan Thomas Sq SA1 233 B2
- Dylan Thomas Theatre* SA1 233 B2
- Dyllas Ct CF39 107 F2
- Dyllas Rd CF39 107 F2
- Dynea Cl CF37 136 B5
- Dynea Rd CF37 136 B5
- Dynevor Ave SA10 48 D1
- Dynevor Cl
  - Llanyrafon NP44 90 B3
  - Neath / Castell-Nedd SA10 70 F8
- Dynevor Pl SA1 233 A3
- Dynevor Pl / Man Dynefor SA10 70 D7
- Dynevor Rd
  - Cardiff / Caerdydd CF23 178 D3
  - Neath / Castell-Nedd SA10 70 F8
- Dynevor Rd / Heol Dinefwr SA18 220 B7
- Dynevor St
  - Fochriw CF81 32 C7
  - Merthyr Tydfil / Merthyr Tudful CF48 10 D1
- Dynevor Terr
  - Nelson CF46 83 E3
  - Pontardawe SA8 23 E5
- Dyrus Rd SA6 68 E5
- Dyserth Rd CF64 206 F3
- Dysgwylfa SA2 94 C6
- Dyson Cl SA6 22 D1

E

- Eagle La CF71 188 E2
- Eagle Mews SA13 125 B8
- Eagle Rd CF62 210 D6
- Eaglesbush Cl SA11 71 D4
- Eagles Pl SA5 67 E6
- Eagle St SA13 125 B8
- Eagleswell Prim Sch / Ysgol Gynradd Ffynnon-yr-Eryr CF61 210 B7
- Eagleswell Rd CF61 210 B6
- Eagle View CF31 169 D6
- Earl Cl NP4 37 E6
- Earl Cres CF62 214 F2
- Earl Cunningham Ct CF10 232 D1
- Earle Pl CF5 194 D5
- Earl La CF11 194 F1
- Earl Rd CF64 206 F3
- Earl Rd / Heol Iarll SA13 125 E5
- Earls Court Pl CF23 178 D1
- Earl's Court Rd CF23 178 D1
- Earlsfield Cl SA11 223 C1
- Earlsmede 7 NP44 89 B3
- Earl St
  - Abersychan NP4 37 E5
- Earl St *continued*
  - Abertillery / Abertyleri NP13 36 C4
  - Cardiff / Caerdydd CF11 194 F1
  - Swansea / Abertawe SA1 68 D1
  - Tredegar NP22 13 D7
- Earlswood Rd CF14 177 E7
- EAST ABERTHAW 212 B2
- East Ave
  - Aberdare / Aberdâr CF44 28 F2
  - Bedwas CF83 138 E6
  - Caerphilly / Caerffili CF83 137 F4
  - Cefn Cribwr CF32 149 B2
  - Pyle / Y Pîl CF33 148 C2
- East Ave / Rhodfa Dwyrain NP4 62 E1
- EAST BANK 16 C1
- East Bank NP13 36 B8
- East Bank Rd NP19 164 F8
- East Bank Way / Ffordd Glan Y Dwyrain SA1 233 C3
- East Bay Cl CF10 195 C5
- Eastbourne Ct 3 CF63 215 C8
- Eastbourne Gr SA2 94 C7
- Eastbourne Pl CF47 30 E7
- EASTBROOK 206 C4
- Eastbrook Cl CF64 206 B4
- Eastbrook Sta CF64 206 C4
- East Burrows Rd SA1 233 C2
- East Cliff SA3 121 B3
- East Crossways SA8 23 D6
- East Ct CF43 80 C4
- East Dock Rd
  - Newport / Casnewydd NP20 143 E3
  - Newport / Casnewydd, Pillgwenlly NP20 143 E2
- East Dr CF61 208 H5
- Easterfield Dr SA3 121 A4
- Easterly Cl CF31 169 D5
- Eastern Ave
  - Cardiff / Caerdydd CF23 178 E2
  - Cymmer / Cymer SA13 75 D4
- Eastern Bsns Pk The CF3 179 E8
- Eastern Cl 2 CF3 179 D8
- Eastern Prim Sch SA13 125 D6
- Eastern Prom CF36 183 A6
- Eastfield Cl
  - Caerleon / Caerllion NP18 118 A4
  - Swansea / Abertawe SA1 67 E2
- Eastfield Ct CF72 155 E2
- Eastfield Dr NP18 118 A4
- Eastfield Mews NP18 118 A4
- Eastfield Pl CF47 30 E6
- Eastfield Rd NP18 118 A4
- Eastfield Terr CF47 30 E7
- Eastfield View NP18 118 A4
- Eastfield Way NP18 118 A4
- Eastgate CF71 188 F1
- Eastgate Bsns Pk CF3 179 C1
- Eastgate Mews CF71 188 F1
- East Gr CF24 232 D3
- East Grove La CF24 232 D3
- East Grove Rd NP19 144 C5
- Eastlake Cl CF31 169 A7
- Eastland Cl SA3 122 E7
- Eastland Pl SA11 71 E6
- Eastlands Pk SA3 122 A7
- East Lynne Gdns NP18 118 C3
- East Market St NP20 143 D3
- Eastmoor Park Cres SA3 122 E7
- Eastmoor Rd NP19 144 C3
- EAST MOORS 195 F4
- East Moors Bsns Pk CF24 195 D4
- East Moors Rd CF24 195 D4
- East Pen-Twyn NP13 15 E4
- East Pen-Twyn Bglws NP13 15 E4
- East Pentwyn Rd NP13 15 E5
- East Point CF3 179 D2
- East Rd
  - Barry / Y Barri CF64 215 F6
  - Cefn Hengoed CF82 84 E5
  - Pontygwaith CF43 80 B2
  - Port Talbot SA13 125 D3
  - Tylorstown CF43 80 C4
- East Rd / Heol y Dwyrain NP44 116 F8
- East Rise CF14 178 A8
- East Roedin NP44 116 C8
- EAST SIDE 129 E1
- East St
  - Aberkenfig / Abercynffig CF32 150 C4
  - Barry / Y Barri CF62 214 D4
  - Bridgend / Pen-y-Bont ar Ogwr CF31 169 E3
  - Dowlais CF48 11 B4
  - Goytre SA13 125 F8
  - Llantwit Major / Llanilltud Fawr CF61 209 F6
  - Newport / Casnewydd NP20 143 B5
  - Pontypridd CF37 109 D2
  - Tonypandy CF40 106 D6
  - Tylorstown CF43 80 C4

East Tyndall St CF24 .... 195 D5
East Usk Rd NP19 ...... 143 C6
East View
Blaina / Blaenau NP13 .... 15 D5
Caerphilly / Caerffili CF83 .... 138 B2
Llandow / Llandw CF71 ... 199 A7
New Tredegar NP24 .... 34 A1
Pontypool / Pont-y-pwl, Griffithstown NP4 .... 62 E2
Pontypool / Pont-y-pwl, Sowhill NP4 .... 62 B6
Eastview Terr CF81 ...... 58 A3
East View Terr CF62 ..... 214 D3
EAST VILLAGE 188 F1
Eastville Rd
Abertillery / Abertyleri NP13 .... 36 C3
Ebbw Vale / Glyn Ebwy NP23 .... 14 F5
Eastway NP4 .... 39 B2
East Way Rd NP20 ...... 143 D1
East Wlk CF62 .... 214 E6
Eaton Cres SA1 .... 95 A6
Eaton Ct SA5 .... 68 D3
Eaton Rd SA5 .... 68 C3
Ebbw Cl CF62 .... 211 C7
Ebbw Ct NP11 .... 114 C4
Ebbw St NP11 .... 114 F2
Ebbw Terr NP11 .... 87 A3
Ebbw Vale Comp Sch NP23 .... 7 C2
EBBW VALE / GLYN EBWY 14 F8
Ebbw Vale Hospl NP23 ... 14 D7
Ebbw Vale Parkway Sta NP23 .... 14 E3
Ebbw Vale Row SA12 ..... 99 E5
Ebbw Vale Sh Ctr NP23 ... 14 D8
Ebbw View NP23 .... 7 D3
Ebbw View Terr NP11 .... 86 F6
Ebenezer Cl / Tai Ebenezer CF46 .... 83 D7
Ebenezer Ct NP22 .... 6 E1
Ebenezer Dr NP10 ...... 142 B4
Ebenezer Rd CF40 ...... 106 F5
Ebenezer St
2 Aberdare / Aberdâr CF44 .... 28 E4
Pontypridd CF37 .... 135 F6
Swansea / Abertawe SA1 .... 233 B4
Tredegar NP22 .... 6 E1
Ebenezer Terr
Blackmill CF35 .... 130 F3
14 Newport / Casnewydd NP20 .... 143 C4
Ebury Ho NP44 .... 90 B4
Ebwy Ct CF5 .... 193 D4
Eckley Rd CF64 .... 216 A5
Eclipse St CF24 .... 195 C6
Eddystone Cl CF11 ...... 194 E3
Eden Ave SA2 .... 94 F7
Edgar St CF47 .... 10 F4
Edgcort NP44 .... 89 B1
Edgehill
Bryn NP12 .... 85 D5
Llanyrafon NP44 .... 90 B1
Edgehill Ave CF14 ...... 159 C1
Edgehill Cl SA12 .... 98 E4
Edgehill Ct CF14 .... 159 D1
Edgemoor Cl SA2 .... 93 B5
Edgemoor Dr SA2 .... 93 B6
Edgeware Rd SA2 .... 94 E7
Edinburgh Cl 4 NP44 .... 89 A3
Edinburgh Ct 11 CF11 ... 194 E5
Edington Ave CF14 ...... 177 F2
Edison Cres SA6 .... 22 D1
Edison Ridge NP20 ...... 117 A3
Edith Mills Cl / Clos Edith Mills SA11 .... 71 C4
Edith Rd CF64 .... 206 B3
Edlogan Sq NP44 .... 90 A6
Edlogan Way / Ffordd Edlogan NP44 .... 90 A5
Edmond's Ct CF24 ...... 178 B1
EDMONDSTOWN 107 B1
Edmondstown Rd CF40 .... 107 C1
Edmonton Ct NP4 .... 62 C7
Edmund Pl
Barry / Y Barri CF63 ..... 215 D6
Newbridge / Trecelyn NP11 .... 86 C5
Edmunds Cl NP13 .... 15 D5
Edmund St
Pontlottyn CF81 .... 32 F8
Porth CF39 .... 108 A3
Tylorstown CF43 .... 80 C3
Edney View NP10 .... 163 F7
Edward Cl CF47 .... 10 F1
Edward Clarke Cl CF5 ... 176 E2
Edward German Cres NP19 .... 144 E5
Edward Ho CF11 .... 232 A2
Edwardian Way CF72 .... 173 D7
Edward Jarvis Ct 7 SA11 .... 71 E6
Edward Nicholl Ct CF23 .... 178 D2
Edwards Bldgs NP23 ...... 8 C1
Edwards Ct NP23 .... 7 C1
Edwards Row CF81 .... 57 B8
Edwards St
Blaengwrach SA11 ...... 227 B8
Edwards St *continued*
7 Mountain Ash / Aberpennar CF45 .... 54 E1
Tonypandy CF40 .... 106 F6
Edward St
Abercarn NP11 .... 114 C8
Abercynon CF45 .... 82 E2
Aberdare / Aberdâr CF44 .. 28 E4
Abertillery / Abertyleri NP13 .... 36 B5
Barry / Y Barri CF63 ..... 215 B7
Bridgend / Pen-y-Bont ar Ogwr CF31 .... 168 F3
Glyn-neath / Glyn-nedd SA11 .... 223 D1
Maerdy CF43 .... 52 A1
Neath / Castell-Nedd SA11 .... 71 E6
Pant CF48 .... 11 B7
Pengam NP12 .... 85 B6
Pontardawe SA8 .... 24 A5
Pontypool / Pont-y-pwl, Griffithstown NP4 .... 62 E3
Pontypool / Pont-y-pwl, Sowhill NP4 .... 62 B7
5 Porth CF39 .... 107 F3
Port Talbot SA13 .... 99 B1
5 Treharris CF46 .... 83 B6
Ystrad Mynach CF82 ..... 111 E7
Edward Stephens Terr CF48 .... 55 C8
Edwards Terr
Abergarwed SA11 .... 226 C5
Bedlinog CF46 .... 56 A7
Newbridge / Trecelyn NP11 .... 86 E6
Treharris CF46 .... 83 B5
Trelewis CF46 .... 83 C8
EDWARDSVILLE 82 F5
Edwardsville
Abercarn NP11 .... 114 B8
Treharris CF46 .... 82 F6
Edwardsville Prim Sch CF46 .... 82 F6
Edward Terr
Abertridwr CF83 .... 137 A8
Tredegar NP22 .... 13 F6
Edward Thomas Cl CF83 .... 139 B3
Edward Vii Ave NP20 .... 142 F4
Edward VII Cres NP20 ... 143 A5
Edward VII La NP20 ..... 143 A5
Edwin Ind Est NP20 ..... 143 C7
Edwin St NP20 .... 143 C7
EFAIL-FÇCH 72 F3
EFAIL ISAF 156 F5
EFI Ind Est CF47 .... 10 B3
Egerton St CF5 .... 194 C6
Egham St CF5 .... 194 C6
Eglwys Ave CF37 .... 136 A5
EGLWYS-BREWIS 211 A7
EGLWYS FAIR Y MYNYDD / ST MARY HILL 170 E1
Eglwys Fan NP22 .... 12 F3
Eglwysilan Rd
Abertridwr CF37, CF83 .... 136 D7
Pontypridd CF37 .... 110 B1
Rhydyfelin CF37 .... 136 E5
Eglwysilan Way CF83 .... 136 F7
Eglwys Newydd Prim Sch CF14 .... 177 B5
Eglwys Nunydd SA13 .... 147 C6
Eglwys Wen Prim Sch CF14 .... 177 A4
Egremont Rd CF23 ...... 178 B2
Egypt Ctr Mus* SA2 ..... 94 E5
Egypt St
Pontypridd CF37 .... 135 E8
Tonypandy CF40 .... 107 B5
Eiddil SA14 .... 41 D6
Eiddwen Rd SA5 .... 68 B4
Eider Cl CF3 .... 179 E8
Eifion Cl CF63 .... 215 A8
Eigen Cres SA1 .... 95 B8
Eighth Ave
Merthyr Tydfil / Merthyr Tudful CF47 .... 10 E5
Swansea / Abertawe SA6 .. 45 D1
Eileen Pl CF42 .... 50 E2
Eileen Rd SA7 .... 69 F7
Eileen Terr CF42 .... 50 E2
Einon Ct SA4 .... 43 D2
Eirw Rd CF39 .... 108 A2
Eisteddfa Rd CF40 .... 79 F2
Eisteddford Wlk NP19 ... 144 D6
Eithen Pl CF36 .... 182 E6
Eithinen Ber CF63 .... 205 B1
Elaine Cl CF14 .... 159 E2
Elaine Cres NP19 .... 143 F7
Elan Ave SA6 .... 45 D1
Elan Cl
Aberdare / Aberdâr CF44 .... 29 E2
Barry / Y Barri CF62 ..... 214 C6
Bettws NP20 .... 116 E1
Elan Rd CF14 .... 178 A7
Elan Wlk NP44 .... 89 C2
Elba Ave / Rhodfa Elba SA13 .... 125 D5
Elba Cres SA1 .... 97 A7
Elba St SA4 .... 66 C6
Elderberry Rd CF5 ...... 176 B1
Elder Cl NP18 .... 117 F2
Elder Dr CF36 .... 166 D1
Elder Rd / Heol Ysgawen SA12 .... 98 D7
Elder St CF31 .... 168 F4
Elder Wood Cl CF23 ..... 178 E3
Eldon Ct 13 CF11 .... 194 E5
Eleanor Cl CF35 .... 170 B8
Eleanor Pl CF10 .... 195 B1
Eleanor St
Tonypandy CF40 .... 106 E5
Treherbert CF42 .... 78 A8
Electra Ho CF10 .... 195 D2
Eleven St CF64 .... 215 E6
Eleventh Ave CF47 .... 10 F5
Elfed Ave
Penarth CF64 .... 206 E3
Port Talbot SA12 .... 124 D7
Elfed Gn CF5 .... 176 E1
Elfed Rd SA1 .... 95 B8
Elfed Way CF63 .... 215 B7
Elford Rd CF5 .... 193 C5
Elgam Ave NP4 .... 17 C7
Elgam Gn 4 NP4 .... 17 C7
Elgar Ave
Newport / Casnewydd NP19 .... 144 D5
Port Talbot SA12 .... 98 A2
Elgar Circ NP19 .... 144 D5
Elgar Cl
Blackwood / Coed-Duon NP12 .... 85 C7
Newport / Casnewydd NP19 .... 144 D5
Elgar Cres CF3 .... 179 D7
Elgar Rd CF64 .... 206 F1
Elgin St SA5 .... 68 B3
Elias Dr SA10 .... 48 D4
Elias Rd SA10 .... 48 C4
Elias St SA11 .... 71 E7
Elidyr Cres NP11 .... 86 F8
Elidyr Rd NP11 .... 86 F8
Elim St CF47 .... 10 F3
Elim Way NP12 .... 86 A5
Eliot Cl SA2 .... 93 F8
Elis Fisher Ct 8 CF62 ... 214 E4
Elizabethan Ct CF64 ..... 206 E6
Elizabeth Ave CF62 ...... 214 E8
Elizabeth Cl
Treorchy / Treorci CF41 .... 78 F4
Ynysforgan SA6 .... 46 B4
Elizabeth Rd CF31 ...... 168 C5
Elizabeth Row / Rhes Elizabeth NP4 .... 37 C3
Elizabeth St
Abercynon CF45 .... 82 D2
Aberdare / Aberdâr CF44 .. 29 A1
Llanelli SA15 .... 40 D5
Tonyrefail CF39 .... 133 B2
Treorchy / Treorci CF41 .... 78 F5
Elizabeth Way NP23 .... 7 C1
Elled Rd NP4 .... 62 A8
Ellen's Rd SA10 .... 70 D8
Ellen St CF10 .... 232 C2
Ellesmere Ct
Cardiff / Caerdydd CF3 .... 179 D6
Newbridge / Trecelyn NP11 .... 87 B8
Ellick St NP4 .... 17 C7
Elliot's Colliery Winding House Mus* NP24 ...... 33 F2
Elliot St NP24 .... 33 F2
ELLIOT'S TOWN 33 E2
Ellipse The / Yr Hirgylch NP4 .... 62 D1
Ellis CF72 .... 155 A5
Ellis Gr SA2 .... 93 B6
Ellwood Cl CF3 .... 179 F6
Elm Cl
Pontypool / Pont-y-pwl NP4 .... 38 B2
Sully CF64 .... 216 C4
Underwood NP18 .... 145 E6
Waunarlwydd SA5 .... 66 D4
Elm Cres
Bridgend / Pen-y-Bont ar Ogwr CF31 .... 168 B5
Penllergaer SA4 .... 44 C2
Elm Ct
Blackwood / Coed-Duon NP12 .... 85 F6
Gorseinon SA4 .... 43 A3
Newbridge / Trecelyn NP11 .... 60 C1
Elm Dr NP11 .... 115 C1
Elmfield Cl CF3 .... 179 E6
Elm Gr
Aberdare / Aberdâr CF44 .... 28 F2
Barry / Y Barri CF63 ..... 215 C8
Caerphilly / Caerffili CF83 .... 138 C5
Gorseinon SA4 .... 43 A3
Hirwaun CF44 .... 27 E8
Merthyr Tydfil / Merthyr Tudful CF47 .... 10 D3
Newport / Casnewydd NP20 .... 117 B2
Pontypool / Pont-y-pwl NP4 .... 62 E1
St Athan / Sain Tathan CF62 .... 211 B7
Elmgrove CF83 .... 138 F6
Elmgrove Cl CF37 .... 109 C5
Elm Grove La CF64 ...... 206 A3
Elm Grove Pl CF64 ...... 206 B3
Elmgrove Rd
Cardiff / Caerdydd CF14 .... 176 E4
The Mumbles / Y Mwmbwls SA3 .... 122 F8
Elm Grove Rd CF64 ...... 206 A3
Elm Ho CF14 .... 176 E6
Elmhurst Cl NP4 .... 38 B1
Elmhurst Cres SA1 ...... 233 C4
Elm Rd
Briton Ferry / Llansawel SA11 .... 71 B2
Llanharry CF72 .... 172 B5
Porthcawl CF36 .... 183 D8
Elm Rise CF32 .... 150 F4
Elms Pk CF72 .... 173 D6
Elm St
Aberbargoed / Aberbargod CF81 .... 58 B4
Abercwmboi CF44 .... 53 E4
Cardiff / Caerdydd CF24 .. 195 C7
Cwm NP23 .... 35 A8
Ferndale CF43 .... 79 F7
Gilfach Goch CF39 .... 132 B5
Rhydyfelin CF37 .... 136 B5
Troedyrhiw CF48 .... 31 B1
Elms The
Barry / Y Barri CF62 ..... 214 D3
Blackwood / Coed Duon NP12 .... 59 C2
Cardiff / Caerdydd CF24 .. 195 C7
Elm Street La CF24 ...... 195 C7
Elm Terr CF32 .... 104 E1
Elmwood / Coed Y Llwyfen NP22 .... 13 F5
Elmwood Ct 5 CF24 ..... 195 C7
Elmwood Dr SA11 .... 71 C2
Elm Wood Dr CF39 ...... 132 E4
Elmwood Gr / Ffordd Llwyfen NP22 .... 13 F5
Elmwood Path NP44 ...... 89 B2
Elmwood Rd SA12 .... 98 D6
Elmwood Terr NP22 .... 13 F5
Elphin Cres SA1 .... 67 E1
Elphin Gdns SA1 .... 68 A1
Elphin Rd SA1 .... 67 F1
Elworthy Cl CF64 .... 216 B5
Elwy Cres SA2 .... 67 F1
Elwy Gdns SA2 .... 67 F1
Elwyn Dr CF47 .... 30 F8
Elwyn St CF39 .... 154 D8
Ely Bridge Ind Est CF5 .. 193 E7
Ely Ind Est CF40 .... 107 A2
Ely Rd
Cardiff / Caerdydd CF5 .... 193 F7
Cardiff / Caerdydd, Llandaff / Llandaf CF5 .... 194 A8
Elysia St NP19 .... 143 D7
Ely St CF40 .... 106 E5
ELY / TRE-LAI 193 D6
Ely Valley Bsns Pk (East) CF72 .... 173 A7
Ely Valley Ind Est CF72 .... 173 A8
Ely Valley Rd
Coedely CF39 .... 133 D1
Coedely CF72 .... 154 F7
Talbot Green CF72 .... 155 C3
Ynysmaerdy CF72 .... 155 B5
Emanda Gdns CF35 ..... 153 B2
Emanuel Cl CF83 .... 137 D1
Emanuel Pl 5 SA11 .... 71 D6
Embankment Rd SA15 .... 40 E2
Emblem Cl CF5 .... 193 E4
Emerald St CF24 .... 195 D7
Emerson Dr CF5 .... 193 B2
Emlyn Ave NP23 .... 7 C2
Emlyn Cl CF39 .... 133 B3
Emlyn Dr CF83 .... 138 A4
Emlyn Gdns SA1 .... 68 B1
Emlyn Rd
Abersychan NP4 .... 37 E6
Cwm NP23 .... 35 B8
Swansea / Abertawe SA1 .. 68 B1
Emlyn Sq 20 NP20 .... 143 C4
Emlyn St 19 NP20 .... 143 C4
Emlyn Terr
Abersychan NP4 .... 37 D5
Merthyr Tydfil / Merthyr Tudful CF47 .... 10 C2
Swansea / Abertawe SA6 .. 68 E6
Tonypandy CF40 .... 106 B6
Emlyn Wlk 22 NP20 ...... 143 C4
Emmanuel Cl CF42 .... 50 F1
Emmanuel Gdns SA2 ..... 94 B3
Emma St / Stryd Emma 13 SA15 .... 40 D4
Empire Ave SA11 .... 227 C8
Empire Terr NP4 .... 37 E6
Emroch St SA13 .... 125 E8
Emsworth Ct CF23 ...... 178 C6
Ena Ave SA11 .... 71 F7
Enbourne Dr 5 CF23 .... 161 A1
Endeavour Cl
Bridgend / Pen-y-Bont ar Ogwr CF31 .... 169 C6
Port Talbot SA12 .... 98 A3
Endyngs NP44 .... 89 B1
ENERGLYN 137 F5
Energlyn Cl CF83 .... 137 F4
Energlyn Cres 1 CF83 .. 137 F5
Energlyn Terr CF83 ..... 137 E5
Enfield Cl SA6 .... 45 E4
Enfield Dr CF62 .... 214 C7
Enfield St SA12 .... 124 F8
Engine Row NP4 .... 17 B7
Enid Rd SA6 .... 46 F8
Enid St CF40 .... 107 B5
Ennerdale Cl CF23 ...... 178 B2
Ennerdale Ct 2 NP19 ... 143 F8
Enoch Morrell Cl CF48 ... 31 B1
Enterprise Park Ind Est NP20 .... 143 D3
Enterprise Way NP20 .... 143 D3
Enville Cl NP20 .... 142 E4
Enville Rd NP20 .... 142 E4
Eppynt Cl NP11 .... 115 C2
Eppynt Rd SA5 .... 68 A4
Epsom Cl CF5 .... 193 F5
Epstein Cl CF5 .... 176 D2
Erasmus Terr CF82 .... 85 B2
Eric Coates Cl NP19 .... 144 D4
Eric Coates Wlk NP19 ... 144 E4
Eridge Rd NP4 .... 37 F5
Ernald Pl SA2 .... 94 F6
Ernest St CF47 .... 30 E7
E Row NP4 .... 17 A6
Erris Ct CF37 .... 109 D3
Erskine Ct CF24 .... 195 E7
Erw Deg CF31 .... 168 B5
Erw Fach CF38 .... 135 D1
Erw Hir CF72 .... 155 E3
Erw Hydref SA9 .... 2 D8
Erw Ifan CF35 .... 170 D8
Erwlas SA14 .... 41 D3
Erw Las
Cardiff / Caerdydd CF14 .... 177 A4
Merthyr Tydfil / Merthyr Tudful CF48 .... 10 A2
Penywaun CF44 .... 28 C6
Erw Rd SA15 .... 40 C5
Erw'r-Delyn Cl CF64 .... 206 D4
Erw Wen
Cardiff / Caerdydd CF14 .... 177 B8
North Cornelly CF33 ..... 165 F7
Pencoed CF35 .... 170 D8
Erw Werdd SA7 .... 46 F4
Eschol Cl NP19 .... 144 B3
Eschol Court NP19 ...... 144 B3
Esgair-y-llys / Ridge of the Ct CF31 .... 168 B4
Esgair-y-Maes / Ridge of the Mdw CF31 .... 168 B3
Esgid Mair CF63 .... 205 C1
Eskdale Cl CF23 .... 178 B3
Espalone SA3 .... 122 C6
Esperanto Way NP19 .... 143 E1
Esplanade
Penarth CF64 .... 207 B3
Porthcawl CF36 .... 182 F6
Esplanade Ave CF36 ..... 182 F6
Esplanade Bldgs CF62 ... 214 E2
Esplanade Ho CF36 ...... 182 F6
Essex Ct NP18 .... 118 A3
Essex St NP19 .... 143 E4
Essex Terr SA6 .... 68 E6
Essich St 5 CF24 .... 178 C1
Estate Rd
Blaenavon NP4 .... 17 B7
Pontypool / Pont-y-pwl NP4 .... 62 A8
Esterling Dr CF36 .... 182 F8
Estuary Pk SA14 .... 42 C7
Estuary Rd NP19 .... 144 D1
Ethel St
Cardiff / Caerdydd CF5 .... 194 B6
Neath / Castell-Nedd SA11 .... 71 D6
Etna Terr CF39 .... 132 C7
Eton Ct
Cardiff / Caerdydd CF14 .... 177 F6
7 Cardiff / Caerdydd, Ely / Tre-lai CF5 .... 193 E6
Eton Pl 1 CF5 .... 194 D5
Eton Rd NP19 .... 143 D5
Eton St CF62 .... 214 C3
Eugene Cl 13 CF3 .... 180 A8
Eureka Pl NP23 .... 14 D7
Eurgan Cl CF61 .... 209 F5
Eurwg Cres 6 CF3 ...... 179 D8
Eustace Dr CF32 .... 150 F4
Evansfield Rd CF14 ..... 176 F3
Evan's Rd SA11 .... 71 D5
Evans Row CF48 .... 3 F3
Evans Sq CF37 .... 109 E3
Evans St
Barry / Y Barri CF62 ..... 214 F5
Newport / Casnewydd NP20 .... 143 C6
3 Port Talbot SA13 .... 99 C1
Pyle / Y Pîl CF33 .... 148 D3
Evans's Terr CF40 .... 106 C7
Evan St CF46 .... 83 B8
Evans Terr
Maesteg CF34 .... 102 B8
6 Merthyr Tydfil / Merthyr Tudful CF47 .... 30 F8
North Cornelly CF33 ..... 165 F7
Swansea / Abertawe SA1 .... 233 A4
Tonypandy CF40 .... 107 B5
Evans' Terr SA15 .... 40 F6
Evan's Terr NP22 .... 6 D2
EVANSTOWN 132 B8
Eva St
Mountain Ash / Aberpennar CF45 .... 54 D2
3 Neath / Castell-Nedd SA11 .... 71 E6
Evelian Ct CF14 .... 177 D3
Eveline Terr SA13 .... 125 B8
Evelyn Rd SA10 .... 70 E7
Evelyn St
Abertillery / Abertyleri NP13 .... 36 B5
Barry / Y Barri CF63 ..... 215 A5
Evenlode Ave CF64 ...... 206 F2

Evenlode Prim Sch
CF64 . . . 206 F2
Evenwood Cl CF23 . . . 160 F1
Everard St CF63 . . . 215 B6
Everard Way CF23 . . . 178 B4
Everest Ave CF14 . . . 159 F1
Everest Wlk CF14 . . . 159 F1
Evergreen NP20 . . . 143 A3
Evergreen Ct CF39 . . . 133 E6
Eversley Rd SA2 . . . 94 D6
Everswell Ave CF5 . . . 193 D7
Everswell Rd CF5 . . . 193 D7
Erwood Ct CF5 . . . 193 C6
Evesham Ct NP20 . . . 143 A7
Eve's Well Ct NP19 . . . 143 E5
Eveswell La 1 NP19 . . . 143 F5
Eveswell Park Rd
NP19 . . . 143 F5
Eveswell Prim Sch
NP19 . . . 143 F5
Eveswell St NP19 . . . 143 F5
Evtol Ind Est NP20 . . . 143 D2
Ewart Pl SA5 . . . 68 C4
Ewbank Cl CF63 . . . 215 C8
EWENNI / EWENNY . . . 185 F7
Ewenni Fach CF72 . . . 154 A3
Ewenny Cl CF63 . . . 215 A8
Ewenny Cl / Clos Ewenni
CF36 . . . 165 E2
Ewenny Cross CF35 . . . 185 E7
EWENNY / EWENNI . . . 185 F7
Ewenny Ind Est CF31 . . . 169 C1
Ewenny Pl SA6 . . . 68 D8
Ewenny Priory* CF35 . . . 186 A8
Ewenny Rd
Bridgend / Pen-y-Bont ar Ogwr CF31, CF35 . . . 168 F2
Cardiff / Caerdydd CF14 . . 178 A7
Maesteg CF34 . . . 102 B2
St Brides Major / Saint-y-Brid CF32 . . . 185 D2
Wick / Y Wig CF71 . . . 198 B8
Ewenny Road Sta
CF34 . . . 102 B2
Excalibur Dr CF14 . . . 159 E2
Excelsior Cl NP19 . . . 143 E4
Excelsior Ind Est CF14 . . 177 D2
Excelsior Rd CF14 . . . 177 C2
Excelsior St NP23 . . . 14 F2
Excelsior Terr CF43 . . . 79 C8
Exchange Ct
3 Risca / Rhisga NP11 . . . 114 F3
Swansea / Abertawe SA1 . . . 233 B2
Exchange Rd
Neath / Castell-Nedd SA11 . . . 71 D6
2 Risca / Rhisga NP11 . . 114 F3
Exchange Row SA14 . . . 41 C7
Exchange St CF34 . . . 101 F3
Exe Rd NP20 . . . 116 D2
Exeter Cl
Cwmbran / Cwmbrân NP44 . . . 89 A3
Heolgerrig CF48 . . . 10 A1
Exeter Mans 6 CF14 . . . 176 F6
Exeter Pl NP4 . . . 37 F3
Exeter Rd 6 NP19 . . . 143 E6
Exeter St NP19 . . . 143 E5
Exford Cres CF3 . . . 179 A5
Exhibition Row CF44 . . . 28 E7
Eynon St SA4 . . . 43 D2
Eyre St CF24 . . . 195 E6
Ezel Ct CF10 . . . 195 B2

F

Faber Way CF11 . . . 194 D3
Fabian Way SA1, SA10 . . . 96 C7
Factory La CF37 . . . 135 B8
Factory Rd
Bargoed / Bargod CF81 . . . 57 F5
Brynmawr NP23 . . . 8 C4
Clydach SA6 . . . 46 D7
Llanblethian / Llanfleiddan CF71 . . . 200 D8
Newport / Casnewydd NP20 . . . 143 B6
Factory Terr CF32 . . . 150 C3
FAENOR / VAYNOR . . . 3 D1
FAERDRE . . . 46 D8
FAGWR-ISAF . . . 22 B2
Fagwr Isaf SA6 . . . 22 B2
Fagwr Pl SA6 . . . 46 A1
Fagwr Rd SA6 . . . 22 B2
Fairacre Cl CF14 . . . 159 E2
Fairbrook Cl CF14 . . . 177 B8
Faircourt Mdw / Maes Llysteg 1 CF31 . . . 168 C3
Fair End Cl CF31 . . . 168 B3
Fairfax Cres CF36 . . . 182 E7
Fairfax Rd
Cardiff / Caerdydd CF14 . . . 177 D6
Newport / Casnewydd NP19 . . . 144 A4
FAIRFIELD . . . 37 E4
Fairfield
Aberavon SA12 . . . 98 F1
Penperlleni NP4 . . . 39 E6
Pontypool / Pont-y-pwl NP4 . . . 62 A7
Tredegar NP22 . . . 13 F8
Fairfield Ave
Cardiff / Caerdydd CF5 . . . 194 A6
Fairfield Ave continued
Maesteg CF34 . . . 102 A2
Fairfield Cl
Aberdare / Aberdâr CF44 . . . 29 D1
Blackwood / Coed-Duon NP12 . . . 85 E6
Caerleon / Caerllion NP18 . . . 117 F3
Cardiff / Caerdydd CF5 . . 193 F7
Hawthorn CF37 . . . 136 A4
Llantwit Major / Llanilltud Fawr CF61 . . . 210 A6
Fairfield Cres CF61 . . . 210 A6
Fairfield Ct SA7 . . . 69 D8
Fairfield Ind Est CF15 . . . 158 A2
Fairfield La CF37 . . . 136 A4
Fairfield Prim Sch
CF64 . . . 206 F4
Fairfield Rd
Bridgend / Pen-y-Bont ar Ogwr CF31 . . . 169 A2
Caerleon / Caerllion NP18 . . . 117 F3
Cymmer / Cymer SA13 . . . 75 D3
Penarth CF64 . . . 206 F4
Fairfield Rise CF61 . . . 210 A6
Fairfield Terr SA1 . . . 95 B7
Fairfield Way 13 SA11 . . . 71 E8
Fairford St CF63 . . . 215 B7
Fairhaven Cl 8 CF3 . . . 180 A8
Fairhaven Ct SA3 . . . 123 A3
Fairhill / Bryn Tirion
NP44 . . . 89 B2
Fairhill Dr
Baglan SA12 . . . 98 E4
Church Village CF38 . . . 136 B1
Fairhill Wlk NP44 . . . 89 B2
Fairland Cl CF72 . . . 155 E3
Fairlawn Ct CF5 . . . 177 A1
Fairlawns SA11 . . . 71 B3
Fairlawn Terr CF35 . . . 170 D8
Fairleigh CF64 . . . 205 F7
Fairleigh Ct CF11 . . . 194 D8
Fairleigh Mews CF11 . . . 194 D8
Fairleigh Rd CF11 . . . 194 D7
Fairmead Ct CF5 . . . 193 D7
Fairmeadow CF15 . . . 157 C1
Fairmeadows CF34 . . . 128 C8
Fairmound Pl CF38 . . . 136 B1
FAIROAK . . . 58 F4
Fairoak SA18 . . . 219 D7
Fairoak Ave NP19 . . . 143 E6
Fairoak Chase CF31 . . . 169 C4
Fair Oak Cl CF44 . . . 28 E2
Fairoak Ct
Cardiff / Caerdydd CF23 . . . 178 B2
4 Newport / Casnewydd NP19 . . . 143 E6
Fairoak Gr NP10 . . . 141 F2
Fairoak La NP44 . . . 90 B4
Fairoak Mews
Cardiff / Caerdydd CF24 . . . 178 A2
8 Newport / Casnewydd NP19 . . . 143 E6
Fairoak Rd CF24 . . . 178 A1
Fairoaks CF64 . . . 206 B3
Fairoak Terr NP19 . . . 143 E5
Fairplace Ct / Clos Man-Teg CF31 . . . 168 A3
Fair Summer Dwelling / Hafod Wen CF31 . . . 168 D3
Fairthorn Cl CF14 . . . 159 E3
Fairview
Beddau CF38 . . . 156 B7
Ebbw Vale / Glyn Ebwy NP23 . . . 14 C8
Hirwaun CF44 . . . 224 E1
Tonypandy CF40 . . . 107 B1
Fair View
Blackwood / Coed-Duon NP12 . . . 85 C7
Gilfach Goch CF39 . . . 106 C1
Tredegar NP22 . . . 6 C1
Treharris CF46 . . . 83 B5
Fairview Ave
Aberavon SA12 . . . 98 F1
Risca / Rhisga NP11 . . . 115 A2
Fairview Cl 9 CF3 . . . 180 A8
Fair View Cl
Pontyclun CF72 . . . 173 B7
Swansea / Abertawe SA7 . . 69 F6
Fairview Ct
Cardiff / Caerdydd CF23 . . . 178 E7
Pontypool / Pont-y-pwl NP4 . . . 62 A8
Fairview Est CF48 . . . 225 F1
Fair View / Golwg Deg
SA10 . . . 48 C1
Fairview Hos CF48 . . . 225 F3
Fairview Rd SA5 . . . 45 C2
Fairview / Tegfan
CF32 . . . 104 F6
Fairview Terr
Abercynon CF45 . . . 82 F3
Abersychan NP4 . . . 37 E5
Abertillery / Abertyleri NP13 . . . 36 B7
Merthyr Tydfil / Merthyr Tudful CF47 . . . 30 E8
Pontlottyn CF81 . . . 32 F8
Fair View Terr NP23 . . . 8 C1
FAIRWATER
Cardiff . . . 193 E8
Cwmbran . . . 89 A1
Fairwater Ave CF5 . . . 193 F7
Fairwater Cl CF3 . . . 162 A5
Fairwater Cl / Clos Fairwater NP44 . . . 89 B2
Fairwater Gn CF5 . . . 193 D7
Fairwater Gr E CF5 . . . 193 F8
Fairwater Gr W CF5 . . . 193 F8
Fairwater High Sch
NP44 . . . 89 A2
Fairwater Jun & Inf Sch / Ysgol Iau & Babanod Fairwater NP44 . . . 89 C2
Fairwater Prim Sch
CF5 . . . 193 D7
Fairwater Rd CF5 . . . 193 E8
Fairwater Square Shops
NP44 . . . 89 B1
Fairwater (Tyllgoed) Halt
CF5 . . . 193 E8
Fairwater Way / Ffordd Fairwater NP44 . . . 89 B1
Fairwater Workshops 7
CF5 . . . 193 E7
Fairway Cl NP10 . . . 142 A7
Fairway Ct CF37 . . . 136 C3
Fairway Dr
Caerphilly / Caerffili CF83 . . . 137 F6
Pontardawe SA8 . . . 23 D6
Fairway / Ffordd Deg
SA12 . . . 98 C2
Fairways
Bargoed / Bargod CF81 . . . 57 E5
North Cornelly CF33 . . . 165 E8
Fairways Cres CF5 . . . 193 C7
Fairways The NP12 . . . 85 E8
Fairways View CF72 . . . 155 A3
Fairway The
Cardiff / Caerdydd CF23 . . . 160 C1
Pontypool / Pont-y-pwl NP4 . . . 63 B4
FAIRWOOD . . . 92 D7
Fairwood Cl CF5 . . . 176 E1
Fairwood Dr SA12 . . . 98 E6
Fairwood Hospl / Ysbyty Fairwood SA2 . . . 93 A6
Fairwood La SA2 . . . 93 B5
Fairwood Rd
Cardiff / Caerdydd CF5 . . . 176 E1
Dunvant SA2 . . . 93 C8
The Mumbles / Y Mwmbwls SA3 . . . 123 A8
Fairwood Terr SA4 . . . 66 C6
Fairy Glen CF32 . . . 104 E4
Fairy Gr SA2 . . . 93 E7
Fairyland SA11 . . . 72 A8
Fairyland Rd SA11 . . . 49 B1
Falcon Chambers 4
SA15 . . . 40 D6
Falcon Dr
Cardiff / Caerdydd CF10 . . . 195 D2
Cimla SA11 . . . 72 B4
Falcon Gr CF64 . . . 217 A7
Falcon Pl SA5 . . . 67 E7
Falcon Rd CF63 . . . 215 D7
Falcon Terr
Cwmfelinfach NP11 . . . 113 E3
Cwm NP23 . . . 35 B7
Falconwood Dr CF5 . . . 192 F5
Falfield Cl CF14 . . . 160 A2
Fallowfield 10 NP44 . . . 89 B1
Fallowfield Dr NP19 . . . 144 C3
Fanheulog CF72 . . . 155 B2
Fan Heulog CF37 . . . 109 D6
Fanny St
Cardiff / Caerdydd, Cathays CF24 . . . 195 A8
Cardiff / Caerdydd CF24 . . 178 A1
Faraday Cl NP20 . . . 116 F2
Faraday Rd SA6 . . . 22 E1
Fardre Cres CF38 . . . 135 F1
Fardre Ct CF38 . . . 135 E1
Farlays NP44 . . . 89 A1
Farlington Ct CF3 . . . 179 A3
Farlow Wlk NP44 . . . 89 D2
Farm Cl
Abertridwr CF83 . . . 137 A7
Blackwood / Coed Duon NP12 . . . 59 A1
Farm Dr CF23 . . . 178 B4
Farm Dr / Rhodfa Fferm
SA12 . . . 98 C1
Farmers Rd SA10 . . . 48 C5
Farmfield Ave / Rhodfa Caer Fferm SA12 . . . 98 D2
Farm Fields Rd 9
NP23 . . . 14 D6
Farmhouse Way CF5 . . . 193 B3
Farm La
Cwmbran / Cwmbrân NP44 . . . 89 F4
Newport / Casnewydd NP19 . . . 143 E7
Farmleigh CF3 . . . 179 B3
Farm Rd
Aberdare / Aberdâr CF44 . . . 53 D6
Abersychan NP4 . . . 37 D5
Briton Ferry / Llansawel SA11 . . . 71 C3
Caerphilly / Caerffili CF83 . . . 138 C3
Cefn Cribwr CF32 . . . 149 E2
Ebbw Vale / Glyn Ebwy NP23 . . . 14 D5
Farm Rd continued
Heolgerrig CF48 . . . 10 A1
Nantyglo NP23 . . . 15 C8
Newbridge / Trecelyn NP11 . . . 60 B2
Pontardawe SA8 . . . 23 B1
Pontlottyn CF81 . . . 12 F1
Pontypool / Pont-y-pwl NP4 . . . 62 C5
Ton Pentre CF41 . . . 79 A2
Farm Terr
Heolgerrig CF48 . . . 10 B1
New Tredegar NP24 . . . 33 F4
Farm View NP12 . . . 58 B2
Farmville Rd CF24 . . . 195 E6
Farmwood Cl NP19 . . . 144 B5
Farnaby Cl NP19 . . . 144 E5
Farraday Dr CF82 . . . 84 E7
Farriers Gate NP10 . . . 142 B2
Farteg Row SA13 . . . 100 F5
Farthings The CF23 . . . 160 F1
Faulkner Rd NP20 . . . 143 B5
Faull St SA6 . . . 45 E1
Federation La CF32 . . . 103 F3
Feeder Bank NP22 . . . 6 D1
Feeder Row NP11 . . . 114 C7
Feering St NP19 . . . 143 E4
Felbridge Cl CF10 . . . 232 D1
Felbrigg Cres CF23 . . . 160 E1
FELINDRE
Pencoed . . . 171 A7
Pontarddulais . . . 20 F2
Felindre Ave CF35 . . . 170 E7
Felindre Rd CF35 . . . 170 E7
Felinfach SA9 . . . 221 C6
Felin Fach
Cardiff / Caerdydd CF14 . . . 177 B3
Swansea / Abertawe SA5 . . 67 C4
Felinfoel Jun Sch SA14 . . 41 A8
Felinfoel Rd SA15 . . . 40 E7
Felin Fran SA7 . . . 46 E2
Felin Lon Fferm CF62 . . . 214 C4
Felin Wen CF14 . . . 177 C7
Fell St CF46 . . . 83 B7
Felnex Ind Est NP19 . . . 164 E8
Felsted Cl 2 CF23 . . . 161 A1
Fenbrook Cl SA12 . . . 98 D5
Fendrod Bsns Pk SA6 . . . 69 A6
Fendrod Way SA7 . . . 69 C7
Fennel Cl
10 Cardiff / Caerdydd CF3 . . . 180 A8
Penarth CF64 . . . 206 E5
Fenner Brockway Cl
NP19 . . . 144 D7
Fenton Pl
Pontycymer CF32 . . . 103 F2
Porthcawl CF36 . . . 182 F7
Fenviolet Cl CF3 . . . 180 B6
Fenwick Dr CF31 . . . 169 C5
Fenwick St CF43 . . . 107 C8
Fermoy Ct SA5 . . . 67 F6
Fernbank NP44 . . . 89 B2
Fernbank Ho CF37 . . . 135 C8
Fernbrook Cl NP23 . . . 7 D6
Fern Cl NP11 . . . 59 D3
Fern Cres CF44 . . . 28 D2
Ferncroft Way NP4 . . . 38 B2
Fern Ct SA5 . . . 68 A5
FERNDALE . . . 79 F6
Ferndale Cl NP23 . . . 7 B5
Ferndale Com Sch
CF43 . . . 79 C8
Ferndale Ct CF43 . . . 79 F7
Ferndale Dr SA4 . . . 65 D8
Ferndale Ind Est / Ystad Ddiwydiannol Ferndale CF43 . . . 79 D8
Ferndale Inf Sch / Ysgol Plent Bach Ferndale CF43 . . . 79 F7
Ferndale Rd CF43 . . . 80 B2
Ferndale St CF11 . . . 194 F3
Fern Dr CF62 . . . 214 D5
Fernfield SA12 . . . 98 E4
Fern Field / Cae Rhedyn
SA8 . . . 24 C3
Fernfield Terr NP13 . . . 36 B5
FERNHILL . . . 54 A3
Fernhill CF45 . . . 54 A3
Fern Hill CF41 . . . 79 B2
Fernhill Cl
Merthyr Tydfil / Merthyr Tudful CF47 . . . 10 D5
The Mumbles / Y Mwmbwls SA2 . . . 94 B1
Troedyrhiw CF48 . . . 31 C1
Fernhill Rd SA4 . . . 43 A3
Fernhill Sta CF45 . . . 54 B4
Fernhill Terr
New Tredegar NP24 . . . 33 F3
Treharris CF46 . . . 83 A7
FERNLEA . . . 114 F3
Fernlea NP11 . . . 114 F3
Fern Pl CF5 . . . 193 D8
Fern Rise NP20 . . . 117 B3
Fernside NP19 . . . 144 B3
Fern St
Cardiff / Caerdydd CF5 . . . 194 B6
Hendreforgan CF39 . . . 132 C5
Ogmore Vale CF32 . . . 130 E8
Swansea / Abertawe SA5 . . 68 B2
Ferns The
4 Penarth CF64 . . . 207 B5
Quakers Yard CF46 . . . 83 C6
Fern Terr CF40 . . . 106 D6
Ferntree Dr CF3 . . . 179 E7
Ferny Ct CF23 . . . 178 D2
Ferrara Quay SA1 . . . 233 B1
Ferrara Sq SA1 . . . 233 B1
Ferrier Ave CF5 . . . 193 D8
Ferrier's Row CF34 . . . 102 B3
Ferryboat Cl SA6 . . . 69 A7
Ferry Cl SA11 . . . 71 C1
Ferry La 7 CF64 . . . 207 B5
Ferry Rd
Cardiff / Caerdydd CF11 . . . 206 F8
Loughor SA4 . . . 42 C1
Ferry Side SA1 . . . 233 C2
Fescue Pl CF5 . . . 193 A5
Festiniog Rd CF14 . . . 177 A2
Festival Cres NP4 . . . 63 B4
Festival Dr NP23 . . . 14 E4
Festival Pk Sh Ctr NP23 . . 14 F1
Fetty Pl NP44 . . . 89 D1
Ffaldau Ind Est CF32 . . . 103 E5
Ffaldau Prim Sch
CF32 . . . 103 F3
Ffaldau Terr CF43 . . . 79 D7
Ffald Rd CF33 . . . 148 B2
Ffald Road Sh Ctr
CF33 . . . 148 B1

Fferm = farm

Fferm Dinas Caerdydd / Cardiff City Farm CF11 . . . 194 C3
Fferm Goch CF35 . . . 170 F1
Fferm-y-Bryn CF82 . . . 84 E1
Fferm-y-Graig CF62 . . . 211 D4
Fferm Yr Orsaf / Station Farm NP44 . . . 89 F5
Fflorens Rd NP11 . . . 59 F1
FFONT-Y-GARI / FONT-Y-GARI . . . 212 D2
Fforchaman Rd CF44 . . . 53 B4
Fforch Cl CF42 . . . 78 D7
Fforch-Dwm Rd SA12 . . . 73 E6
Fforchneol Row CF44 . . . 53 B5
Fford Churchill / Churchill Way CF10 . . . 232 C2

Ffordd = road, way

Ffordd Abiah SA6 . . . 46 E8
Ffordd Afan SA12 . . . 99 D5
Ffordd Alltwen SA4 . . . 66 A5
Ffordd Aneurin Bevan
SA2 . . . 94 C8
Ffordd Baglan / Baglan Way SA12 . . . 98 E3
Ffordd Beck SA4 . . . 66 B6
Ffordd Bishop / Bishop Rd
SA18 . . . 219 B6
Ffordd Blair / Blair Way
SA12 . . . 98 F2
Ffordd Bodlyn CF23 . . . 178 C3
Ffordd Briallu SA7 . . . 69 D6
Ffordd Bryngwyn SA4 . . . 66 D8
Ffordd Brynheulog SA8 . . 23 D5
Ffordd Brynhyfryd
CF3 . . . 179 E8
Ffordd Butler SA4 . . . 66 B6
Ffordd Cae Duke SA4 . . . 66 A8
Ffordd Caldicot / Caldicot Way NP44 . . . 89 F6
Ffordd Candleston
CF31 . . . 168 C3
Ffordd Catraeth CF37 . . . 109 F3
Ffordd Cefn-yr-hendy
CF72 . . . 173 D7
Ffordd Celyn CF14 . . . 177 B4
Ffordd Croes Y De / South Cross Way 8 SA12 . . . 98 C2
Ffordd Cwellyn CF23 . . . 178 B3
Ffordd Cwell Yn CF23 . . . 178 C3
Ffordd Cwmbran / Cwmbran Dr NP44 . . . 89 E4
Ffordd Cwm Cldl CF62 . . 214 B5
Ffordd Cwm Tawe
Swansea / Abertawe SA6 . . . 68 F6
Ynysforgan SA6, SA7 . . . 46 D5
Ffordd Cwrdy / Cwrdy Rd
NP4 . . . 62 D2
Ffordd Cynghordy SA7 . . 69 D7
Ffordd Cynore / Cynore Rd
SA5 . . . 67 C6
Ffordd Dafydd / David's Way SA14 . . . 218 D7
Ffordd Daniel Lewis
CF3 . . . 179 F5
Ffordd Dawel SA7 . . . 69 E6
Ffordd Ddu CF33 . . . 148 B2
Ffordd Deg CF83 . . . 138 B1
Ffordd Deg / Fairway
SA12 . . . 98 C2
Ffordd Delabeche / Delabeche St 12 SA15 . . 40 D4
Ffordd Deri Duffryn / Duffryn Oaks Dr
CF35 . . . 170 B8
Ffordd Derwen SA13 . . . 148 A5
Ffordd Dewi SA6 . . . 45 B1
Ffordd Dillwyn-Llewellyn
SA4 . . . 44 C2
Ffordd Dinas SA12 . . . 99 D5
Ffordd Dinefwr CF15 . . . 174 D7

Ffordd Draenen Ddu SA3 122 E6
Ffordd Drindod / Trinity Rd NP44 89 D5
Ffordd Dryden SA2 93 E8
Ffordd Edlogan / Edlogan Way NP44 90 A5
Ffordd Eira SA4 43 C2
Ffordd Elin CF63 215 D7
Ffordd Ellen SA6 22 B2
Ffordd Emlyn SA9 2 B5
Ffordd Erw CF83 158 E8
Ffordd Eynon Evans CF83 137 D6
Ffordd Fairwater / Fairwater Way NP44 89 B1
Ffordd Ferm y Cwrt / Court Farm Rd NP44 117 A8
Ffordd Ffagan CF3 180 A8
Ffordd Florence / Florence Rd 1 SA18 219 B7
Ffordd Ganol CF31 169 A4
Ffordd Ganolog / Central Way CF14 177 F3
Ffordd Garthorne CF10 195 C3
Ffordd Gerdinan CF38 136 A1
Ffordd Ger-y-Llyn SA4 44 C4
Ffordd Glandwr SA9 2 B6
Ffordd Glanllyn / Lakeside way NP23 8 B3
Ffordd Glan y Dwyrain / East Bank Way SA1 233 C3
Ffordd Glas-y-Dorlan CF38 156 B5
Ffordd Gower Davies CF37 109 A7
Ffordd Greenforge / Greenforge Way NP44 89 C4
Ffordd Gwaun Hywel / Waun Hywel Rd 6 NP44 89 C6
Ffordd Gwely y Gaeau / Field View 5 NP44 90 A5
Ffordd Gwern CF5 175 E4
Ffordd Gwyn SA7 69 D7
Ffordd Gwyneth 1 CF63 215 C8
Ffordd Gwynno CF38 156 B5
Ffordd Haearn / Iron Way CF32 150 C5
Ffordd Helygen CF72 172 D5
Ffordd Henllys / Henllys Way
Cwmbran / Cwmbrân NP44 89 C2
Cwmbran / Cwmbrân NP44 115 F8
Ffordd Hollybush / Hollybush Way NP44 116 D8
Ffordd Is-Cennen / Iscennen Rd 14 SA18 219 B7
Ffordd Kilby SA4 66 A8
Ffordd Las
Abertridwr CF83 137 A8
Radyr CF15 176 A6
Ffordd Leyshon / Leyshon Way CF32 151 A5
Ffordd Llanbad CF39 132 D5
Ffordd Llanfrechfa / Llanfrechfa Way NP44 90 A2
Ffordd Llangors / Llangorse Rd 3 NP44 90 A2
Ffordd Llanyrafon / Llan-yr-Avon Way NP44 90 A3
Ffordd Llundain SA7 69 D7
Ffordd Llwyfen / Elmwood Gr NP22 13 F5
Ffordd Llyffant SA7 70 B8
Ffordd Maendy / Maendy Way NP44 89 C5
Ffordd Maescwarrau / Maesquarre Rd SA18 219 D6
Ffordd Mawdlam / Mawdlam Way CF33 147 E1
Ffordd May Drew / May Drew Way SA11 71 C4
Ffordd Melyn Mair SA7 69 D6
Ffordd Morgannwg CF14 176 E6
Ffordd Mr Llefarydd CF40 107 A4
Ffordd Newydd CF33 166 A8
Ffordd Ogwr / Ogmore Dr CF36 165 E2
Ffordd Oldbury / Oldbury Rd 9 NP44 89 E2
Ffordd Pace / Pace Rd NP44 89 B1
Ffordd Parc Y Mynydd Bychan / Heath Park Way CF14 177 F3
Ffordd Parc Ynysderw SA8 23 E4
Ffordd Pengam CF24 196 A8
Ffordd Penrhos CF83 137 D3
Ffordd Pen Twyn / Pentwyn Rd SA18 219 C7
Ffordd Penyland / Penylan Way NP44 116 B8
Ffordd Priordy CF32 150 D4
Ffordd Radcliffe 8 CF10 195 B2
Ffordd Rhaglan CF35 152 B6
Ffordd Sanderling / Sanderling Way CF36 182 D8
Ffordd Sant Awstin / St Augustine Rd NP4 62 D2
Ffordd Scott
Birchgrove SA7 46 F1
Swansea / Abertawe SA7 70 A8
Ffordd Sealand 1 CF62 214 E4
Ffordd Silkin SA8 23 E5
Ffordd Stewart / Stewart Dr 12 SA18 219 B7
Ffordd Sturmi / Sturmi Way CF33 148 C1
Ffordd Talbot / Talbot Rd 10 SA18 219 B7
Ffordd Talfan SA4 66 D8
Ffordd Taliesin
Pontypridd CF37 109 F4
Swansea / Abertawe SA2 93 F8
Ffordd Talygarn CF72 173 A7
Ffordd Tirion / Gentle Way CF31 168 B3
Ffordd Tirwaun CF44 53 D7
Ffordd Tollborth SA7 69 D7
Ffordd Ton Mawr / Ton-mawr Rd NP4 17 D6
Ffordd Traws Cwm CF83 137 E1
Ffordd Trecastell CF72 172 D6
Ffordd Treforgan CF15 176 A8
Ffordd Tresillian / Tresillian Way CF10 232 B1
Ffordd Tryweryn CF37 109 F3
Ffordd Ty Coch / Ty Coch Way NP44 116 E8
Ffordd Tyn-y-Coed SA6 47 A8
Ffordd Ty Unnos CF14 177 D6
Ffordd Tywosoges / Princess Dr SA10 48 C2
Ffordd Villiers / Villiers Rd SA18 219 B6
Ffordd Walter / Walter Rd 9 SA18 219 C7
Ffordd Waun-Gron / Waun-Gron Rd SA18 219 D6
Ffordd Waunwaelod / Waunwaelod Way CF83 158 F7
Ffordd Wellington / Wellington Rd NP4 37 E4
Ffordd Wern-Ddu / Wern-Ddu Rd SA18 219 D8
Ffordd Whitebrook / Whitebrook Way NP44 89 F2
Ffordd-y-Barcer CF5 192 F5
Ffordd Y Bedol CF37 109 D6
Ffordd-y-Berllan CF15 176 A7
Ffordd-y-Betws / Betws Rd SA18 219 C6
Ffordd Y Brain SA5 67 E5
Ffordd y Brenin CF10 232 B3
Ffordd Y Brennin / Kingsway The SA1 233 A3
Ffordd-y-Bryn
Birchgrove SA7 47 B1
Swansea / Abertawe SA7 70 B8
Ffordd-y-Capel CF38 156 F6
Ffordd Y Cefnor / Ocean Way SA12 98 C1
Ffordd-y-Cyrnol / Colonel Rd SA18 219 C6
Ffordd y Dderwen CF71 189 C8
Ffordd-y-Dderwyn CF31 168 C6
Ffordd y Deri SA18 218 F5
Ffordd-y-Derwen CF45 54 B6
Ffordd Y Dywysoges Margared / Princess Margaret Way The SA12 98 B1
Ffordd Y Faenor / Manor Rd 15 SA18 219 B7
Ffordd Y Felin / Mill Terr SA18 219 A5
Ffordd Y Ffawydden / Beech Tree Terr NP4 61 F8
Ffordd Y Frenhines CF34, SA13 126 E6
Ffordd Y Gadeirlan / Cathedral Way SA12 98 D3
Ffordd Y Gamlas SA4 66 B6
Ffordd Y Glowr SA4 19 D3
Ffordd Y Glowyr / Colliers Way CF40 106 E7
Ffordd Y Goedwig
Pyle / Y Pîl CF33 148 C3
Tircoed SA4 44 C4
Ffordd-y-Gollen CF38 135 F2
Ffordd Y Gorllewin / West Way SA1 233 A2
Ffordd Y Goron / Crown Way CF14 177 E1
Ffordd y Graig / Graig Rd NP44 89 A3
Ffordd Y Groes / Cross Way CF31 168 B3
FFORDD-Y-GYFRAITH 149 D5
Ffordd-y-Gyfraith CF32 149 E6
Ffordd y Mileniwm CF63 215 B4
Ffordd Y Morfa SA14 218 C7
Ffordd-y-Mynach SA10 71 A7
Ffordd Y Mynach CF33 148 B2
Ffordd-y-Mynydd
Birchgrove SA7 47 B1
Swansea / Abertawe SA7 70 B8
Ffordd-y-Parc
Bridgend / Pen-y-Bont ar Ogwr CF31 169 A8
Swansea / Abertawe SA6 45 E1
Ffordd-yr-Afon
Ammanford / Rhydaman SA18 219 B8
Bridgend / Pen-y-Bont ar Ogwr CF31 168 B6
Ffordd Yr Afon
Gorseinon SA4 43 C1
Taffs Well / Ffynnon Taf CF15 158 A3
Ffordd Yr Afon / River Way CF32 150 D6
Ffordd Yr Angel / Angel Way CF33 147 E1
Ffordd Yr Eglwys CF33 166 B8
Ffordd-yr-Eglwys CF5 191 E5
Ffordd Y Rhyd SA18 219 B6
Ffordd yr Iseldir / Lowlands Rd NP44 89 E6
Ffordd Yr Odyn SA4 19 D3
Ffordd Yr Odyn Galch / Limekiln Rd NP4 38 A3
Ffordd-yr-Orsaf / Station Rd 5 SA18 219 B7
Ffordd-yr-Ywen CF38 136 A2
Ffordd Ysgol SA12 98 D1
Ffordd Y Wagen / Railway Pl 8 SA15 40 C4
Ffordd Y Wiwer SA7 46 D1
Forddy-y-Graig / Graig Rd NP44 89 A5
Fford Y Dywysoges Margared / Princess Margaret Way The SA12 124 D8
FFOREST 19 A6
Fforest Bsns Ctr SA5 67 D4
Fforest Dr CF62 214 B4
FFOREST-FACH 67 C4
Fforestfach SA18 219 A5
Fforestfach Ret Pk SA5 67 C6
Fforest Glade NP19 143 F6
Fforest Hill SA10 49 C4
Fforest Rd
Llanharry CF72 172 C4
Mountain Ash / Aberpennar CF45 54 E3
Fforest Rd / Heol Fforest SA4 19 B5
Fforest View CF62 214 B4
Ffos Cl CF46 83 E4
Ffos Felen SA4 66 B5
Ffosmaen Rd NP23 8 D1
Ffos Y Cerridden CF46 83 D3
Ffos-y-Fran NP10 141 F2
Ffos y Fran Cl NP10 141 F2
Ffos-yr-Efail Terr SA4 19 C4
Ffos-yr-Hebog CF83 112 A5
Ffridd Las CF31 168 B4
Ffrwd Cres CF45 54 D3
Ffrwd Rd
Abersychan NP4 38 A4
Merthyr Tydfil / Merthyr Tudful CF48 225 F3
Ffrwd St CF44 53 C6
Ffrwd Terr
Hirwaun CF44 27 E7
Llanbradach CF83 111 F2
Ffrwd Vale SA10 48 D1
Ffrwdwyllt Cotts 4 SA13 125 C6
Ffrwd-Wyllt St SA13 125 C6
Ffrwd-y-Felin SA18 219 B8
FFWL-Y-MWN / FONMON 212 D3
Ffwrn Clai SA4 19 D3
Ffwrwm Rd CF83 139 F7
Ffynnonbwla Rd CF37 136 E4
Ffynnon Ct 3 NP23 8 B4
Ffynnon Dawel SA10 49 C3
Ffynnon Groyw / Clear Spring CF31 168 B4
Ffynnon-Las CF41 79 F2
Ffynnon Samlet SA7 69 D7
Ffynnon Taf Prim Sch CF15 157 F4
FFYNNON TAF / TAFFS WELL 158 B5
Ffynnon Tudful CF47 10 D2
Ffynnon Wen
Clydach SA6 46 C7
North Cornelly CF33 148 A1
Ffynnon-wen Terr NP12 58 B1
Ffynone Cl SA1 95 A7
Ffynone Dr SA1 95 A7
Ffynone House Sch SA1 95 A7
Ffynone Rd SA1 95 A7
Ffynnon Las SA18 219 B6
Ffynon Y Maen CF33 148 A2
Fiddlers Elbow CF46 83 A4
Fidlas Ave CF14 178 A7
Fidlas Rd CF14 178 A7
Field Cl
Pontllanfraith NP12 85 F4
Swansea / Abertawe SA6 46 A2
Fieldfare Dr CF3 180 A6
Fielding Cl CF3 179 B7
Fieldings 6 NP44 89 B1
Fields Ave NP44 89 D6
Fields Ct CF11 194 C7
Fields Park Ave NP20 142 F5
Fields Park Cres NP20 143 A5
Fields Park Ct NP20 143 A5
Fields Park Gdns NP20 142 F5
Fields Park La NP20 142 F5
Fields Park Rd
Cardiff / Caerdydd CF11 194 D8
Newport / Casnewydd NP20 142 F5
Field's Park Rd NP11 86 E7
Fields Park Terr NP11 114 B5
Fields Rd
Cwmbran / Cwmbrân NP44 116 F8
Newport / Casnewydd NP20 143 A5
Risca / Rhisga NP11 141 B8
Tredegar NP22 13 F5
Field St
Swansea / Abertawe SA1 68 D3
Tonypandy CF40 106 F4
Trelewis CF46 83 C7
Field Terr
New Tredegar NP24 33 E4
Pentyrch CF15 157 C1
Port Talbot SA13 125 D8
Fieldview Cl CF64 206 E5
Field View / Ffordd Gwely y Gaeau 5 NP44 90 A5
Field View Rd CF63 215 A7
Field Way CF14 177 E6
Fife St CF45 82 E3
Fifth Ave
Hirwaun CF44 224 C1
Merthyr Tydfil / Merthyr Tudful CF47 10 E5
Swansea / Abertawe SA6 45 D1
Filas Berrington / Berrington Villas SA9 221 C7
Filey Rd NP19 143 D7
Finchley Cl CF48 55 B8
Finchley Rd CF5 193 E7
Finnimore Ct 2 CF14 176 F3
Finsbury Terr SA2 94 F5
Firbank Ave NP19 144 A7
Firbank Cres NP19 144 A6
Firbanks Way CF72 155 A3
Firbank Terr NP11 113 A5
Firemans Ct 2 NP23 8 C4
Fir Grove St CF41 78 F5
Firm St SA1 233 A4
Firs Ave CF5 193 B8
Fir St CF43 79 F7
First Ave
Caerphilly / Caerffili CF83 137 F3
Merthyr Tydfil / Merthyr Tudful CF47 10 E5
Swansea / Abertawe SA6 68 C8
Firstbrook Cl CF23 178 E1
Firs The
Blaenavon NP4 17 E6
Newport / Casnewydd NP20 117 C2
Porthcawl CF36 183 E7
Firth Rd
Ebbw Vale / Glyn Ebwy NP23 14 B8
Llanelli SA15 40 E4
Firtree Cl
Caerleon / Caerllion NP18 117 E2
Cardiff / Caerdydd CF5 193 C8
Fir Tree Cl CF47 10 D5
Fir Tree Dr CF46 83 A6
Firwood Cl
Bryn-côch SA10 48 C5
Cardiff / Caerdydd CF14 176 F4
Fisher Cl NP19 144 F7
Fisher Hill Way CF15 176 D5
Fishguard Cl CF14 178 A7
Fishguard Rd CF14 177 F7
Fish La 4 CF37 109 C1
Fishmarket Quay 12 SA1 233 C2
Fishpond Rd CF3 179 B6
Fitzalan Ct CF24 232 C3
Fitzalan High Sch CF11 194 B5
Fitzalan Pl CF24 232 D3
Fitzalan Rd
Cardiff / Caerdydd CF24 232 C3
Cardiff / Caerdydd CF24 232 D3
Fitzhamon Ave CF61 210 A5
Fitzhamon Emb CF11 232 A2
Fitzhamon La CF11 232 A2
Fitzhamon Rd CF36 182 F8
Fitzroy Ave NP23 7 D2
Fitzroy Lodge NP12 85 C7
Fitzroy St
Brynmawr NP23 8 B5
Cardiff / Caerdydd CF24 195 A8
Cardiff / Caerdydd CF24 195 B8
Fitzwilliam Cl CF72 155 E2
Five Bells Rd CF31 168 F3
Five Hos
Ebbw Vale / Glyn Ebwy NP23 7 E4
Pontypool / Pont-y-pwl NP4 62 B4
FIVE LOCKS 89 C7
Five Locks Cl NP44 89 D7
Five Locks Rd NP44 89 D6
Five Oaks La NP44 90 A5
Flanders Mdw CF61 209 F5
Flanders Rd CF61 209 F5
Flatholm Ho CF11 207 A7
Flatholm Pl SA5 67 E7
Flatholm Way CF36 165 E1
Flats The CF14 177 F2
Flavius Cl NP18 117 F3
Flax Ct CF64 206 E5
Flaxland Ave CF14 177 E3
Fleet St SA1 95 B5
Fleet Way CF11 194 E2
Fleetwood Cl NP19 143 F4
Fleming Cl NP20 117 A2
Flemingston Rd CF62 211 D7
FLEMINGSTON / TREFFLEMIN 201 D1
Fleming Wlk CF38 156 D8
FLEUR-DE-LIS 85 B6
Fleur-De-Lys Ave NP12 85 E4
Fleur-de-Lys Prim Sch NP12 85 B5
Flindo Cres CF11 194 B5
Flint Ave CF61 210 B7
Flint Cl NP19 144 A7
Flint Ct NP18 118 A3
Flint Ho SA12 124 D8
Flint St CF14 177 E1
Floral Ave NP12 85 B7
Flora St CF24 195 A8
Florence Ave CF62 214 E8
Florence Cl NP13 36 C5
Florence Gr CF83 138 A2
Florence Pl NP4 62 E2
Florence Rd / Ffordd Florence 1 SA18 219 B7
Florence St
Cardiff / Caerdydd CF24 195 E7
Llanelli SA15 40 E3
1 Neath / Castell-Nedd SA11 71 E6
3 Porthcawl CF36 165 F1
Florentia St CF24 178 A1
Flush Mdw CF61 209 F5
FOCHRIW 32 C7
Fochriw Prim Sch CF81 32 D8
Fochriw Rd CF81 32 E8
Foel View Cl CF38 156 B7
Foley Ho NP44 90 B4
Folland Ct SA2 94 B1
Folland Rd / Heol Folland SA18 220 B8
Folly La
Penperlleni NP4 39 A3
Pontypool / Pont-y-pwl NP4 38 C1
Folly La / Lon Y Ffoledd NP4 38 D2
Folly Rd NP4 38 C1
Folly View NP4 62 D7
Fonmon Cres CF5 193 D5
FONMON / FFWL-Y-MWN 212 D3
Fonmon Park Rd CF62 212 E2
Fonmon Rd CF62 212 D2
Fonthill Pl CF11 194 E3
Fontigary Rd CF3 179 C3
FONT-Y-GARI / FFONT-Y-GARI 212 D2
Fontygari Holiday & L Pk CF62 212 E1
Fontygary Rd CF62 212 F1
Forbes St SA6 68 E5
Ford Farm La NP18 119 E1
Ford Rd
Fleur-de-lis NP12 85 A6
Pontypridd CF37 109 A1
Port Talbot SA13 99 B1
Upper Boat CF37 136 D2
Ford St NP20 143 B5
Fordwell CF5 177 A1
Foreland Rd CF14 177 A5
Foreshore Rd CF10 195 F3
Forest Ave CF82 84 F5
Forest Cl
Cwmbran / Cwmbrân NP44 116 B8
Newport / Casnewydd NP19 143 F6
Sarn CF32 150 E3
Forest Ct 3 CF11 194 D7
Forester Way CF23 161 A2
FOREST FARM 176 D6
Forest Farm Nature Trail★ CF14 176 D6
Forest Farm Rd
Cardiff / Caerdydd CF14 176 E5
Radyr CF14 176 D6
Forest Fawr Wlks★ CF83 158 E4
Forest Gr
Pontypridd CF37 135 E5
Treharris CF46 82 F6
Forest Hill NP12 85 E3
Forest Hills Dr CF72 155 A2
Forest Level CF45 54 E2
Forest Lodge La SA12 99 F4

Forest Oak Cl CF23 160 C1
Forest Rd
Beddau CF38 156 A6
Pontypridd CF37 135 E6
Treharris CF46 83 B7
Forest View
Abercarn NP11 114 D8
Blaengarw CF32 103 E6
Cardiff / Caerdydd CF5 193 C7
Cwmbran / Cwmbrân NP44 115 E8
Mountain Ash / Aberpennar CF45 54 A3
Neath / Castell-Nedd SA11 72 B4
Pontypridd CF37 109 C6
Pyle / Y Pîl CF33 148 A2
Talbot Green CF72 155 C2
Forest Wlk CF72 155 A2
Forge Cl NP18 118 B4
Forge Cres NP22 12 F2
Forge Fach SA6 46 D7
FORGE HAMMER 89 D4
Forge Hammer Ind Est NP44 89 D4
Forge Ind Est CF34 101 F4
Forge La
Bassaleg NP10 142 B2
Treorchy / Treorci CF41 79 A4
Forge Mews NP10 142 B3
Forge Pl
Aberdare / Aberdâr CF44 29 B3
Cardiff / Caerdydd CF5 193 B4
Forge Rd
Bassaleg NP10 142 C1
Crofty SA4 64 B2
Forge Side NP4 17 B6
Machen CF83 140 A7
Newport / Casnewydd NP10 163 C8
Port Talbot SA13 99 B1
Forge Row
Aberdare / Aberdâr CF44 53 D6
Maesygwartha NP7 9 E8
Pontypool / Pont-y-pwl NP4 61 F8
FORGE SIDE 17 A5
Forgeside / Ger-yr-Efail [7] NP44 89 E4
Forge Side Rd NP4 17 B5
Forge St CF41 79 A4
Forge Trip CF44 29 B3
Forge View CF44 53 C5
Forge Way CF36 182 F8
Forio Ho CF10 195 C2
Fornwg Brook / Nant Ffornwg CF31 168 B6
Forrest Rd
Cardiff / Caerdydd CF5 194 B6
Penarth CF64 207 A1
Forrest St CF11 194 F2
Forster Rd SA11 71 F7
Forster St [6] CF63 215 B6
Forsythia Cl
Merthyr Tydfil / Merthyr Tudful CF47 10 C5
Risca / Rhisga NP11 115 C1
Forsythia Dr CF23 178 D7
Fortlee NP20 142 E3
Fortran Rd CF3 180 B8
Fort Rd CF64 217 A5
Fort St CF24 195 E7
Fort View NP10 142 A3
Fosse Cl NP19 144 C2
Fosse Rd NP19 144 C2
Foster Dr CF23 178 E1
Fothergill Cres CF47 10 F2
Fothergill Rd SA11 227 B8
Fothergills Rd NP24 33 E3
Fothergill St
Aberdare / Aberdâr CF44 29 B3
Merthyr Tydfil / Merthyr Tudful CF47 10 F2
Pontypridd CF37 135 E7
Founders Row CF44 28 E5
Foundry Bridge NP13 36 B5
Foundry Cl [16] CF11 194 D5
Foundry Pl
[10] Merthyr Tydfil / Merthyr Tudful CF47 30 E8
Pontypridd CF37 109 D2
[6] Porth CF39 107 F3
Foundry Rd
Abersychan NP4 37 E3
Hirwaun CF44 27 D8
Neath / Castell-Nedd SA11 71 E5
Pontypridd CF37 109 A1
Swansea / Abertawe SA6 46 A1
Tonypandy CF40 106 F6
Foundry Rd / Heol-y-Ffowndri [5] SA18 219 C7
Foundry Row [3] SA18 219 C7
Foundry Row / Rhos Foundary SA10 70 E8
Foundry Terr CF45 54 D2
FOUNDRY TOWN 29 A1
Foundry View CF44 53 C5
Fountain Ct NP13 36 B7
Fountain La CF3 180 B8
Fountain Rd
Aberkenfig / Abercynffig CF32 150 B3
Fountain Rd *continued*
Pontypool / Pont-y-pwl NP4 62 E5
Fountain St
Ferndale CF43 80 A6
[3] Mountain Ash / Aberpennar CF45 54 D3
Trehafod CF37 108 D2
Fountain Terr CF32 129 D2
Four Acre CF61 210 A7
Fouracres Cl CF63 215 C7
Four Elms Ct [1] CF24 195 C6
Four Elms Rd [2] CF24 195 D7
Fourteen Locks Canal Ctr* NP10 142 B6
Fourteenth Ave CF44 224 C1
Fourth Ave
Hirwaun CF44 224 C1
Merthyr Tydfil / Merthyr Tudful CF47 10 E5
Swansea / Abertawe SA6 45 D1
Fowler's Pl CF34 102 A8
Fowler St NP4 62 A8
Fox Ave NP11 86 C5
Foxberry Cl CF23 161 B1
Foxfields CF31 169 D4
Foxglove Cl CF5 193 B4
Foxglove Rise CF64 206 E5
Fox Gr SA5 67 A4
Foxgrove SA4 66 B8
FOXHOLE 233 C5
Foxhole Dr SA3 121 A4
Foxhole Rd SA1 233 C4
Foxhollows CF31 169 D5
Fox Hollows CF71 189 C5
Fox La CF24 195 E7
Fox Russell Cl CF14 177 A2
Fox St
Cardiff / Caerdydd CF24 195 E7
Mountain Ash / Aberpennar CF45 54 D3
Treharris CF46 83 B7
Foxwood Cl NP10 141 F3
Foxwood Ct NP10 141 F3
Foyer The [1] SA1 233 B3
Frampton Ct SA4 42 F2
Frampton La CF61 210 A7
Frampton Rd SA4 43 A3
Francis Cl [22] NP20 143 C3
Francis Ct SA8 24 C3
Francis Dr NP20 143 C3
Francis Ho CF23 178 C1
Francis Morris Est [5] NP4 17 D6
Francis Rd
Barry / Y Barri CF62 205 A1
Swansea / Abertawe SA6 45 E1
Francis St
Bargoed / Bargod CF81 58 A4
Dowlais CF48 11 A5
Fleur-de-lis NP12 85 B6
Hawthorn CF37 136 A4
Neath / Castell-Nedd SA10 70 F7
[21] Newport / Casnewydd NP20 143 C3
Pontardawe SA8 23 E4
Risca / Rhisga NP11 115 A1
Swansea / Abertawe SA1 95 A5
Tonypandy CF40 106 B7
Tonyrefail CF39 133 B3
Francis Terr
Pant CF48 11 A7
Pontypridd CF37 109 E3
Franklen Rd CF14 177 C4
Franklen St [5] CF11 194 F3
Frank Rd CF5 193 D6
Frank St NP19 143 C6
Fransham St [2] SA15 40 E6
Fraternal Par [5] CF37 109 C1
Fred Edwards Cl NP19 144 F5
Frederick Ct [6] SA11 71 E6
Frederick Mews NP20 143 D3
Frederick Pl SA7 69 F7
FREDERICK PLACE 70 A6
Frederick St / Heol Frederic CF10 232 B3
Frederick St
[3] Aberdare / Aberdâr CF44 28 E4
Cardiff / Caerdydd CF10 232 C2
Ferndale CF43 79 F6
[2] Llanelli SA15 40 D5
Newport / Casnewydd NP20 143 D3
[1] Port Talbot SA12 124 F8
Swansea / Abertawe SA5 68 C3
Freehold Land Rd / Heol Rhydd-Dal NP4 38 A1
Freeman St SA5 68 C4
Free School Ct CF31 168 F3
Fremington Pl CF3 179 C5
Freshfields SA11 223 D1
Freshmoor Rd CF24 195 E5
Freshwater Rd NP19 144 D1
Frewer Ave CF5 176 D1
Friars Cl SA10 71 B8
Friars Ct NP20 143 B3
Friars Field NP20 143 B3
Friars Gdn / Gerddi'r Brodyr [8] NP44 90 B1
Friars Rd
Barry / Y Barri, Barry Island CF62 214 E2
Barry / Y Barri CF62 214 F2
Newport / Casnewydd NP20 143 B3
Friars St [1] NP20 143 C4
Friars The NP20 143 B3
Friary The CF10 232 B3
Frigate Rd CF10 195 D1
Frobisher Rd NP19 144 B3
Froglane SA3 228 E4
Frogmore Ave SA2 94 D6
Frome Wlk NP20 116 C2
Frondeg
Penperlleni NP4 39 E5
Tredegar NP22 13 D5
Frondeg Terr SA15 40 F6
Fronheulog CF37 109 A2
Fron Heulog CF31 168 D5
Fron Terr
Llanelli SA15 40 E3
[4] Pontypridd CF37 109 E2
Fron Wen NP12 85 C6
Fronwen Terr CF47 10 F3
Fron-Wen Terr CF32 104 E3
Frost Pl NP12 85 D7
Frost Rd NP23 7 E4
Fryatt St CF63 214 F4
Fullers Row SA1 233 A3
Fuller St SA8 23 E5
Full Moon Ind Est NP11 114 A3
Fulmar Cl
Cardiff / Caerdydd CF3 179 F8
Penarth CF64 217 A7
The Mumbles / Y Mwmbwls SA3 122 E7
Fulmar Rd CF36 182 E8
FURNACE 40 C7
Furnace Prim Sch SA15 40 B7
Furnace Rd CF43 80 C1
Furnace Row CF48 31 B2
Furnace St
Barry / Y Barri CF64 215 E6
Ebbw Vale / Glyn Ebwy NP23 7 D3
Furnace Terr SA11 71 C5
Furness Cl CF5 193 B4
Furze Cres SA6 45 D2
Furzeland Dr
Bryn-côch SA10 48 C4
Swansea / Abertawe SA2 94 B6
Fuschia Way NP10 141 E6
Fynnon Caeconna SA5 67 E6

G

GABALFA 177 D1
Gabalfa Ave CF14 177 A2
Gabalfa Prim Sch CF14 177 B2
Gabalfa Rd
Cardiff / Caerdydd CF14 177 A2
Swansea / Abertawe SA2 94 B5
Gabalfa Workshops CF14 177 D2
Gables The
Cardiff / Caerdydd CF14 177 D6
Dinas Powis / Dinas Powys CF64 206 A2
Three Crosses SA4 92 E8
Gadley's Terr SA13 227 C2
GADLYS
Aberdare 28 F2
Llantwit Major 210 C8
Gadlys Gdns [1] CF44 29 A2
Gadlys Rd CF44 28 F2
Gadlys Rd E CF62 214 E5
Gadlys Rd W CF62 214 D5
Gadlys St CF44 28 F2
Gadlys Terr CF44 28 F2
Gadlys Uchaf [3] CF44 28 F4
Gaen St
Abertillery / Abertyleri NP13 36 B6
Barry / Y Barri CF62 214 C4
GAER 142 E2
Gaer Inf Sch NP20 142 F3
Gaer Jun Sch NP20 142 F2
Gaer La NP20 143 A3
Gaer Park Ave NP20 142 E3
Gaer Park Dr NP20 142 E3
Gaer Park Hill NP20 142 E3
Gaer Park La NP20 142 E3
Gaer Park Par NP20 142 E2
Gaer Park Rd NP20 142 E3
Gaer Pl CF82 84 C6
Gaer Rd
Newport / Casnewydd, Glasllwch NP20 142 F3
Newport / Casnewydd NP20 142 F2
Gaer St NP20 143 A2
Gaer Vale NP20 142 F1
Gaerwen Cl CF14 177 D8
Gainsborough Cl
Cwmbran / Cwmbrân NP44 117 A8
Swansea / Abertawe SA2 94 E6
Gainsborough Ct [2] CF64 206 F5
Gainsborough Dr NP19 144 A8
Gainsborough Ho [1] SA12 98 D1
Gainsborough Rd
[6] Penarth CF64 206 F5
Tredegar NP22 13 C6
Galahad Cl CF14 159 D2
Galdames Pl CF24 195 D4
Gallagher Ret Pk CF83 138 B6
Gallamuir Rd CF24 195 F7
Galleon Way CF10 195 C3
Gallipoli Row SA13 125 D6
GALLOWSGREEN 17 F2
Galltcwm Terr SA13 100 F4
GALON UCHAF 10 E5
Galon Uchaf Rd CF47 10 E4
Galston St [5] CF24 195 D6
Gamlyn Terr CF44 27 F6
Gantre Cl NP23 7 C5
Gantref Way NP23 7 D3
Garage Circular Rd CF62 211 E1
Garbett Pl SA10 226 A8
Gardde SA14 41 E4
Gardd Jolyon NP12 85 C6
GARDEN CITY 14 D4
Garden City
Merthyr Tydfil / Merthyr Tudful CF47 10 F4
Rhymney / Rhymni NP22 12 F2
Garden Cl CF83 112 A2
Garden Cres SA4 66 D8
Garden Ct CF31 169 D5
Gardenia Cl CF23 178 D7
Garden St
Dowlais CF48 11 B4
Ebbw Vale / Glyn Ebwy NP23 14 D8
Llanbradach CF83 112 A2
Swansea / Abertawe SA1 233 A2
Gardens The
Ynysddu NP11 112 F6
Ystalyfera SA9 2 B6
Garden Suburbs NP11 114 C6
Gardner Cl CF37 109 D5
Gardners La SA11 71 D4
Garesfield St CF24 195 D6
Gareth Cl CF14 159 D2
Garfield Ave CF31 168 F8
Garfield Flats CF48 31 C1
Garfield St NP12 85 E6
Garfield Terr NP23 7 C1
GARNANT 220 B7
Garn Cross NP23 15 D8
GARNDIFFAITH 37 F6
Garn Dyrus Mount [3] NP4 17 D7
GARN FACH 8 D1
Garn Fach Inf Sch NP23 8 D1
Garnfoel SA14 218 D7
Garngoch Hospl SA4 66 F7
Garngoch Ind Est SA4 43 E1
Garngoch Terr SA4 66 D8
Garnlwyd Cl SA6 68 C7
GARNLYDAN 7 D5
Garnlydan Prim Sch NP23 7 D5
Garn Rd
Blaenavon NP4 16 F8
Maesteg CF34 102 B2
Nantyglo NP23 8 C1
Garn St NP11 87 B3
GARNSWLLT 219 B4
Garnswllt Rd SA4 218 F1
Garnteg Prim Sch NP4 37 F6
Garn Terr NP23 14 F3
Garnwen Rd CF34 101 F6
Garnwen Terr CF34 101 F6
GARN-YR-ERW 16 F8
Garon Terr CF32 104 E7
Garreg Hollt SA14 218 A8
Garreg Rd CF32 103 E3
Garreg Side CF32 103 E5
Garreg-Wen CF82 84 D8
Garrick Dr CF14 159 E2
Garrick Ho [3] SA12 98 B3
Garrod Ave SA2 66 C2
GARTH
Maesteg 102 D1
Newport 141 E2
Garth Ave
Maesteg CF34 102 D2
Pontypridd CF37 109 D5
Garth Cl
Bassaleg NP10 142 A3
Morganstown / Treforgan CF15 176 B8
Pontypool / Pont-y-pwl NP4 38 B2
Rudry CF83 139 B3
Garth Cotts CF47 10 E2
Garth Dan-y-Bryn NP23 7 D4
Garth Dr CF31 169 B7
Garth Est CF83 136 E7
Garth Gr CF44 224 E1
Garth La CF83 139 B3
Garth Lwyd CF83 138 D5
Garth Maelwg CF72 155 B2
Garth-mor Ct SA11 71 D4
Garth Newydd Ct [20] CF47 10 D2
Gartholwg CF34 128 D8
Garth Olwg CF15 157 F5
Garth Pl
Cardiff / Caerdydd CF14 177 D2
Rudry CF83 139 B3
Garth Prim Sch CF34 102 D1
Garth Rd
Cwmbran / Cwmbrân NP44 116 D8
Glais SA7 46 F6
Gwaun-Cae-Gurwen SA18 220 E6
Garth Rd *continued*
Tonypandy CF40 107 A5
Ynystawe SA6 46 D4
Garth St
Cardiff / Caerdydd CF24 232 C2
Coedely CF39 154 D8
[18] Merthyr Tydfil / Merthyr Tudful CF47 10 D2
Pontlottyn CF81 32 F8
Pyle / Y Pîl CF33 148 C2
Taffs Well / Ffynnon Taf CF15 158 A3
Garth Sta (Mid-Glamorgan) CF34 128 C8
Garth Terr
Bassaleg NP10 141 F2
Bedlinog CF46 56 A6
Merthyr Tydfil / Merthyr Tudful CF47 10 F2
Garth The
Abertridwr CF83 136 E7
Abertridwr CF83 136 F7
Garth View
Beddau CF38 156 A6
Bedwas CF83 138 D7
Church Village CF38 156 F8
Merthyr Tydfil / Merthyr Tudful CF47 10 F2
Nantgarw CF15 158 A8
Ynysforgan SA6 46 B4
Garth Villas
Merthyr Tydfil / Merthyr Tudful CF47 10 E2
Taffs Well / Ffynnon Taf CF15 157 F4
Garth Wen CF40 107 A5
Garth Wks CF15 158 B3
Garwellt CF44 28 A6
Garw Fechan Rd CF32 129 E8
Garw Fechan Woodland Park* CF32 103 D1
Garw Fechan (Woodland Park) Forest Walks* CF32 103 D1
Garwnant Forest Walks* CF48 225 D8
Garwnant Visitor Ctr* CF48 225 D8
Garw Row / Rhes Garw NP44 90 B5
Garw The / Y Graw NP44 90 B5
Garw Wood Dr / Lon Coed Garw [5] NP44 90 A6
Gaskell Cl CF61 210 C6
Gaskell St NP19 143 F3
Gaspard Pl CF62 214 C2
Gas Rd CF37 109 C1
Gasworks Rd CF44 53 D7
Gasworks Road Ind Est CF44 53 D7
Gasworks Terr CF32 150 D6
Gateholm Cl CF62 214 F8
Gate Rd CF31 169 D2
Gate Rd / Heol y Gat SA14 218 D8
Gateside Cl CF23 161 A2
Gateway The / Y Porth CF14 177 E3
Gathen Terr [11] SA15 40 D4
GATLAS 118 C6
Gaudi Wlk NP10 142 A6
Gaulden Gr CF23 160 E1
Gawain Cl CF14 159 D2
Gaynors NP44 89 B1
Geifr Rd SA13 125 E5
Geiriol Gdns SA1 67 E1
Geiriol Rd SA1 67 F1
Gelert St SA5 68 C5
GELLI 79 B2
Gelli Arael Rd CF39 132 B6
Gelliargwellt Rd CF82 84 D5
Gelliaur CF35 152 C1
Gelli Aur
Cwmdare CF44 28 C3
Neath / Castell-Nedd SA10 48 D2
Swansea / Abertawe SA5 68 D6
Gelli Ave NP11 115 A2
Gelliceibryn SA11 223 C1
Gelli Cl NP11 115 A2
Gelli Cl / Clos Gelli NP22 13 E7
Gelli Coron / Crown Rise CF34 102 C3
Gelli Cres NP11 115 A2
Gelli Crossing CF41 79 C3
Gelli Crug NP23 7 B5
Gelli-Crug Rd / Heol Gelli Crug NP13 36 B6
Gelli Dawel
Caerphilly / Caerffili CF83 137 F4
Neath / Castell-Nedd SA10 48 D2
Gellidawel Flats CF39 133 D5
Gellidawel Rd
Glyn-neath / Glyn-nedd SA11 223 D1
[3] Pontypridd CF37 135 F6
Rhydyfelin CF37 136 A6
GELLIDEG 10 A3
Gellideg SA8 23 D6

Gelli Deg
Caerphilly / Caerffili
CF83 . . . . 137 F5
Cardiff / Caerdydd CF14 . . 177 B8
Llanelli SA14 . . . . . . 41 A6
Gelli-deg CF48 . . . . . 10 A2
Gelli Deg
Neath / Castell-Nedd
SA10 . . . . 48 D2
Rhydyfelin CF37 . . . . . 136 C4
Swansea / Abertawe SA5 . . 67 C6
Gelli-Deg CF39 . . . . . 133 B3
Gellideg Cl CF82 . . . . . 85 C2
Gellideg Hts CF82 . . . . 85 C2
Gellideg Isaf Rise CF82 . . 85 B2
Gellideg La CF82 . . . . . 85 C2
Gellideg Rd CF37 . . . . 135 B8
Gelli-Deg St CF82 . . . . 85 B2
Gelliderw SA8 . . . . . . 23 D6
Gelli Est CF72 . . . . . 172 C5
Gellifach Cres SA6 . . . . 68 D7
Gellifaelog Old Rd
CF47 . . . . 11 A4
Gellifaelog Prim Sch
CF47 . . . . 11 A4
Gellifaelog Terr CF47 . . . 11 A4
Gelli Fawr Ct NP44 . . . 115 F8
Gellifawr Rd SA6 . . . . . 68 D7
Gellifedi Rd CF72 . . . . 153 D3
Gelli Fedi Rise CF72 . . . 153 D4
Gelli Fron CF41 . . . . . 79 A2
GELLIGAER 84 D6
Gelligaer Gdns CF24 . . . 177 F1
Gelligaer La CF24 . . . . 177 F1
Gelligaer Rd
Cefn Hengoed CF82 . . . . 84 F4
Gelligaer CF82 . . . . . . 84 B7
Trelewis CF46 . . . . . . 83 E6
Gelligaer St CF24 . . . . 177 F1
Gelligaled Rd CF41 . . . . 79 D3
Gelli Gdns SA7 . . . . . . 70 B8
Gelligeiros SA8 . . . . . . 24 B5
Gelliglas Rd SA6 . . . . . 68 D7
GELLIGROES 85 E2
Gelligroes Mill★ NP12 . . . . 85 F2
Gelli-Groes Rd NP12 . . . . 85 F3
Gelligron Ind Est CF39 . . 133 B5
Gelligron Rd SA8 . . . . . 23 D6
Gelligwyn Rd SA6 . . . . . 68 D7
Gelli-Gynore SA4 . . . . . 43 F2
Gellihaf Rd NP12 . . . . . 85 B5
Gelli Hirion Ind Est
CF37 . . . . 136 C4
Gelli Hos SA13 . . . . . . 75 E5
Gellihyll Rd SA4 . . . . . 43 F2
Gelli Ind Est / Ystad Ddiwydiannol Gelli
CF41 . . . . 79 C2
Gelli-Isaf CF44 . . . . . . 28 E5
Gelli La
Ammanford / Rhydaman
SA18 . . . . 219 A5
Pontllanfraith NP12 . . . . 85 F3
Gellinudd Hospl SA8 . . . . 24 B5
Gellionen Rd
Clydach SA6, SA8 . . . . . 22 F2
Pontardawe SA8 . . . . . 23 B5
Gelli-Onn SA15 . . . . . . 40 D6
Gellionnen Cl SA6 . . . . . 46 E8
Gelli Prim Sch / Ysgol Gynradd Gelli CF41 . . . . 79 B3
Gelli Rd
Gelli CF41 . . . . 79 B2
Llanelli SA14 . . . . . . 41 D6
Ton Pentre CF41 . . . . . 79 A3
Tonypandy CF40 . . . . . 106 E5
Tredegar NP22 . . . . . . 13 D7
Ynysybwl CF37 . . . . . . 82 A1
Gelli'r Felin CF83 . . . . 137 F4
Gelli'r Haidd CF39 . . . . 133 B3
Gelli Rhwy Rd NP4 . . . . 37 E6
Gelli-Ron CF82 . . . . . . 84 D8
Gelli'r Wynydd / Highland Gr NP44 . . . . . . 89 E6
Gelli Seren Cl CF39 . . . . 133 A3
Gelli St
Maesteg CF34 . . . . . . 102 A8
Swansea / Abertawe SA1 . . 96 B7
Gelli Terr
Abergwynfi SA13 . . . . . 76 C5
Senghenydd CF83 . . . . . 111 A1
Ton Pentre CF41 . . . . . 79 C2
Gelli Tudur / Tudor Gr
SA13 . . . . 125 F3
Gelli-Unig Pl NP11 . . . . 114 C6
Gelli-Unig Rd NP11 . . . . 114 C5
Gelli-Unig Terr NP11 . . . 114 C5
Gelliwastad Ct 2
CF37 . . . . 109 C1
Gelliwastad Gr CF37 . . . . 109 C1
Gelliwastad Rd CF37 . . . 109 C1
Gelliwen St CF82 . . . . . 84 D5
Gelli Wen / White Gr
CF31 . . . . 168 C3
Gelliwion Rd CF37 . . . . 134 F7
Gelliwion Woods CF37 . . 135 A8
Gelliwriddon SA18 . . . . 219 A6
Gellyfelen NP7 . . . . . . 9 B5
Gellyfowy Rd SA8 . . . . . 24 A7
Gelynis Terr CF15 . . . . 176 B8
Gelynis Terr N CF15 . . . 176 B8
Gelynog Ct CF38 . . . . . 155 F8
Gelynos Ave NP12 . . . . . 58 F5
Gelyn-y-Cler CF63 . . . . 205 B1
GENDROS 67 F3
Gendros Ave E SA5 . . . . . 68 A3
Gendros Ave W SA5 . . . . . 67 F4
Gendros Cl SA5 . . . . . . 68 A3
Gendros Cres SA5 . . . . . 68 A3
Gendros Dr SA5 . . . . . . 67 F3
Gendros Prim Sch SA5 . . . 67 F3
Geneva Ho 20 CF10 . . . . . 195 B2
Gentle Way / Ffordd Tirion
CF31 . . . . 168 B3
Genwen Rd SA14 . . . . . . 41 F4
Geoffrey Ashe Ct CF71 . . 188 F1
Geoffrey St 18 SA11 . . . . 71 E7
George Bank SA3 . . . . . 123 C4
George Cl CF15 . . . . . . 157 F3
George Ct 7 CF24 . . . . . 195 D8
George Daggar's Ave
NP13 . . . . 35 F7
George Lansbury Dr
NP19 . . . . 144 D7
George Manning Way
SA4 . . . . 66 B4
George Parry Ct 8
NP23 . . . . 14 D8
George St / Stryd Sior
NP4 . . . . 62 A8
Georges Cnr CF15 . . . . . 157 B1
Georges Row
Dinas Powis / Dinas Powys
CF64 . . . . 206 C4
Tonypandy CF40 . . . . . 107 B4
George's Row SA11 . . . . 71 B1
George St
Aberbargoed / Aberbargod
CF81 . . . . 58 B4
Abercarn NP11 . . . . . . 114 C8
Aberdare / Aberdâr CF44 . . 53 D7
Abertillery / Abertyleri
NP13 . . . . 36 B6
Argoed NP12 . . . . 58 F5
Barry / Y Barri CF63 . . . . 215 A5
Bedlinog CF46 . . . . . . 56 A7
Blackwood / Coed-Duon
NP12 . . . . 85 F7
8 Blaenavon NP4 . . . . . 17 C6
Bridgend / Pen-y-Bont ar Ogwr
CF31 . . . . 169 C3
Brynmawr NP23 . . . . . . 8 B4
Cwmbran / Cwmbrân
NP44 . . . . 89 E4
Cwmfelinfach NP11 . . . . 113 F4
Ferndale CF43 . . . . . . 80 A7
Llanelli SA15 . . . . . . 40 D3
Llantrisant CF72 . . . . . 155 D3
Maesteg CF34 . . . . . . 75 B2
Neath / Castell-Nedd
SA11 . . . . 71 E6
Newport / Casnewydd NP19,
NP20 . . . . 143 D4
New Tredegar NP24 . . . . 33 E3
Pontardawe SA8 . . . . . . 23 E5
Pontypool / Pont-y-pwl
NP4 . . . . 62 B7
Pontypool / Pont-y-pwl
NP4 . . . . 62 C7
Porthcawl CF36 . . . . . . 182 F7
Port Talbot SA13 . . . . . 125 C7
Swansea / Abertawe SA1 . . 95 B6
Tonypandy CF40 . . . . . 106 F3
Treherbert CF42 . . . . . . 78 A8
Ystrad Mynach CF82 . . . . 84 E2
George's Terr CF40 . . . . 106 D7
George Street Bridge
NP19 . . . . 143 E5
George Street Est
CF31 . . . . 169 C3
George Street Prim Sch
NP4 . . . . 62 B7
George Terr
1 Mountain Ash / Aberpennar CF45 . . . . . . 81 F8
Pentrebach CF48 . . . . . 31 B4
George Thomas Ave
CF32 . . . . 150 F6
George Thomas Cl
CF36 . . . . 182 F8
GEORGETOWN
Merthyr Tydfil 10 B2
Tredegar 13 F6
Georgetown CF15 . . . . . 157 F3
Georgetown Hill NP22 . . . 13 F6
Georgetown Prim Sch
NP22 . . . . 13 F5
Georgetown Villas
CF48 . . . . 10 C2
Georgian Cl
Llantwit Major / Llanilltud Fawr CF61 . . . . . . 210 B7
Porthcawl CF36 . . . . . . 183 A8
Georgian Way
Bridgend / Pen-y-Bont ar Ogwr CF31 . . . . . . 169 A4
Cardiff / Caerdydd CF14 . . 177 F8
Miskin / Meisgyn CF72 . . . 173 D7
Geotre Bellaf Rd SA2 . . . . 93 C7
Geraint Cl CF14 . . . . . . 159 D2
Geraint Ho SA13 . . . . . . 125 E3
Geraint Pl CF63 . . . . . . 215 A7
Geraints Cl CF71 . . . . . 188 D1
Geraint's Way CF71 . . . . 188 D2
Gerald St
5 Aberavon SA12 . . . . . 124 F8
Swansea / Abertawe SA1 . . 68 D2
Gerbera Dr NP10 . . . . . . 141 D7
Gerddi Alexander SA5 . . . 68 B3
Gerddi Brenhinol SA14 . . . 41 B6
Gerddi Lansdowne / Lansdowne Gdns
NP44 . . . . 117 A5
Gerddi Margaret 5
CF62 . . . . 214 E4
Gerddi Pinwydd / Pine Gdns NP4 . . . . 62 A6
Gerddi Quarella CF31 . . . 168 E5
Gerddi'r Brodyr / Friars Gdn 8 NP44 . . . . . . 90 B1
Gerddi Taf CF5 . . . . . . 176 E3
Gerddi Ty Celyn CF14 . . . 176 F7
Gerddi Ty Mawr NP12 . . . . 85 F2
Gernant CF14 . . . . 177 C7
Ger Nant CF82 . . . . 111 E7
Gernant La CF48 . . . . . . 29 F8
Gerodi Crymlyn / Crymlyn Gdns SA10 . . . . 70 B6
Gerrard Ct 5 CF11 . . . . . 194 E5
Gerretts Cl SA3 . . . . . . 122 A5
Gerry Galvin Ct CF24 . . . . 195 E6
Gersanws
Cefn Coed / Cefn-coed-y-cymmer CF48 . . . . 10 A5
Merthyr Tydfil / Merthyr Tudful
CF48 . . . . 225 F3
Gertrude St CF45 . . . . . . 82 E2
Ger Y Afon CF37 . . . . . . 109 D6
Ger-y-Bont CF44 . . . . . . 28 A6
Ger-y-Coed CF31 . . . . . . 169 C5
Ger-y-Felin NP12 . . . . . . 85 F2
Ger-y-Ffrwd SA7 . . . . . . 69 E5
Ger Y Llan SA15 . . . . . . 40 D4
Ger-y-Llan CF5 . . . . 192 A1
Ger-y-Llyn CF36 . . . . . . 183 A8
Ger-y-Maes SA14 . . . . . . 41 A7
Gerymanwydd 4
SA18 . . . . 219 C7
Ger Y Mor SA15 . . . . . . 40 C3
Ger y Nant SA7 . . . . . . 46 E3
Ger-y-nant
Bridgend / Pen-y-Bont ar Ogwr CF31 . . . . . . 168 F5
Glyn-neath / Glyn-nedd
SA11 . . . . 223 B1
Ger Y Nant SA14 . . . . . . 42 B8
Ger Y Pant SA4 . . . . 19 D4
Ger-y-Parc SA6 . . . . . . 45 E1
Ger-yr-afon
8 Aberdare / Aberdâr
CF44 . . . . 53 D7
Aberdulais SA10 . . . . . . 49 C4
Cwm-twrch Isaf SA9 . . . . . 1 A1
Ger Yr Afon SA18 . . . . . 220 A8
Ger-yr-Afon SA18 . . . . . 220 D6
Ger-yr-Efail / Forgeside
7 NP44 . . . . 89 E4
Ger-yr-Eglwys SA4 . . . . . 19 B4
Ger-y-Sedd CF31 . . . . . 169 C5
Gethin Cl SA5 . . . . 68 A3
Gething St SA1 . . . . . . 233 A2
Gething Terr NP4 . . . . . . 17 A6
Gethin Pl CF48 . . . . 30 F4
Gethin Rd
Tonypandy CF40 . . . . . 106 F3
Treorchy / Treorci CF42 . . . 78 E6
Gethin St
Abercanaid CF48 . . . . . . 30 F4
Briton Ferry / Llansawel
SA11 . . . . 71 B2
Gethin Terr CF39 . . . . . 108 B3
Gethin Woodland Park★
CF48 . . . . 30 D4
Giant's Grave Rd SA11 . . . 71 B2
Gibbet's Hill CF71 . . . . . 188 D3
Gibbons Cl NP19 . . . . . . 144 C4
GIBBONSDOWN 214 F7
Gibbonsdown Cl 5
CF63 . . . . 215 A8
Gibbonsdown Rise
CF63 . . . . 215 A7
Gibbons Villas NP23 . . . . . 7 E1
Gibbons Way CF33 . . . . . 166 A8
Gibbs Cl NP12 . . . . 85 D7
Gibbs Rd NP19 . . . . . . 144 B5
Gibson Cl CF14 . . . . . . 177 F6
Gielgud Ho SA12 . . . . . . 98 A2
Gifford Cl NP44 . . . . . . 89 D1
Gilar St 1 CF47 . . . . . . 30 E8
Gilbert Cl NP19 . . . . . . 144 D4
Gilbert Cres SA15 . . . . . 40 D6
Gilbert La
Barry / Y Barri CF63 . . . . 205 B1
Barry / Y Barri CF63 . . . . 205 C2
Gilbert La W CF63 . . . . . 215 B8
Gilbert Pl CF14 . . . . . . 177 C2
Gilbert Rd SA15 . . . . . . 40 D6
Gilbertscliffe SA3 . . . . . 122 F4
Gilberts Cross CF64 . . . . 205 D2
Gilbert St CF63 . . . . . . 215 A7
Gilboa NP11 . . . . 86 E6
Gilchrist Thomas Ct
NP4 . . . . 17 B7
Gilchrist Thomas Ind Est
NP4 . . . . 17 A7
Gilchrist Wlk 9 NP4 . . . . 17 D7
Gildas Cl CF61 . . . . . . 209 F7
Giles Ct CF44 . . . . 28 F3
Giles Rd NP4 . . . . 17 E6
Gileston Rd
Cardiff / Caerdydd
CF11 . . . . 194 D7
St Athan / Sain Tathan
CF62 . . . . 211 D3
GILESTON / SILSTWN 211 E3
Gileston Wlk 6 NP44 . . . . 89 C2
GILFACH 58 A1
Gilfach SA4 . . . . 44 A2
Gilfach Cotts CF34 . . . . . 127 F5
Gilfach-Cynon CF47 . . . . . 30 F8
Gilfach Fargoed Prim Sch
CF81 . . . . 58 A1
Gilfach Fargoed Sta
CF81 . . . . 58 A3
GILFACH GOCH 132 C7
Gilfach Goch Inf Sch
CF39 . . . . 106 C1
Gilfach Rd
Cwm-twrch Uchaf SA9 . . . 221 C6
Neath / Castell-Nedd
SA10 . . . . 48 E4
Tonypandy CF40 . . . . . 106 E6
Tonypandy, Penygraig
CF40 . . . . 106 F4
Tonyrefail CF39 . . . . . . 133 A5
Gilfach St CF81 . . . . . . 58 A3
Gilfach-y-Gog SA14 . . . . 218 D7
Gillian Rd CF5 . . . . 176 F1
Gilmour St CF40 . . . . . . 106 E6
Gilsea Bsns Pk SA6 . . . . . 69 A5
Gilwern Cres CF14 . . . . . 159 E1
Gilwern Farm Cl NP18 . . . 117 F7
Gilwern Pl
Cardiff / Caerdydd
CF14 . . . . 159 E1
Cwmbran / Cwmbrân
NP44 . . . . 89 D5
Glade Cl NP44 . . . . 116 A8
Gladeside Cl CF14 . . . . . 159 E3
Glades The CF64 . . . . . . 207 B3
Glade The
Aberdare / Aberdâr
CF44 . . . . 29 B2
Bryncethin CF32 . . . . . . 151 A4
Cardiff / Caerdydd CF14 . . 160 A1
Porthcawl CF36 . . . . . . 165 F1
The Mumbles / Y Mwmbwls
SA3 . . . . 122 F8
Wyllie NP12 . . . . 112 F8
Gladstone Bldgs NP13 . . . . 36 B8
Gladstone Bridge
CF62 . . . . 214 E4
Gladstone Ct 5 CF62 . . . . 214 F5
Gladstone Garden Ct 9
CF62 . . . . 214 E4
Gladstone Pl
Pontypool / Pont-y-pwl
NP4 . . . . 62 E1
Tredegar NP22 . . . . 13 F5
Gladstone Prim Sch
Barry / Y Barri CF62 . . . . 214 E5
Cardiff / Caerdydd CF24 . . 177 F1
Gladstone Rd
Barry / Y Barri CF62 . . . . 214 F5
Newbridge / Trecelyn
NP11 . . . . 60 B2
Gladstone St
Abercarn NP11 . . . . . . 114 B4
Aberdare / Aberdâr CF44 . . 53 D6
Abertillery / Abertyleri
NP13 . . . . 36 A5
Blaina / Blaenau NP13 . . . . 15 E4
10 Brynmawr NP23 . . . . . 8 C4
Maesteg CF34 . . . . 102 A3
15 Mountain Ash / Aberpennar
CF45 . . . . 54 E1
Gladstone Terr
Abersychan NP4 . . . . . . 37 E8
1 Blaenavon NP4 . . . . . 17 D6
Merthyr Tydfil / Merthyr Tudful
CF47 . . . . 30 E7
16 Mountain Ash / Aberpennar
CF45 . . . . 54 E1
Rhymney / Rhymni NP22 . . . 12 D5
Gladys St
Aberavon SA12 . . . . 98 F1
5 Cardiff / Caerdydd
CF24 . . . . 195 A8
Coedely CF39 . . . . 154 D8
GLAIS 47 B6
Glais Prim Sch SA7 . . . . . 47 A6
Glais Rd SA7 . . . . 23 D1
Glamorgan Centre for Art & Design Technology
CF37 . . . . 135 F7
Glamorgan Cl CF61 . . . . . 210 B7
Glamorgan Ct
4 Aberdare / Aberdâr
CF44 . . . . 53 D7
Pontypridd CF37 . . . . . . 135 D6
Glamorgan Heritage Coast Ctr★ CF32 . . . . . . 197 D7
Glamorgan St
Aberdare / Aberdâr
CF44 . . . . 53 D7
Barry / Y Barri CF62 . . . . 214 C3
Brynmawr NP23 . . . . . . 8 B4
Cardiff / Caerdydd CF5 . . 194 C6
Mountain Ash / Aberpennar
CF45 . . . . 81 F7
Swansea / Abertawe
SA1 . . . . 233 A2
Glamorgan Street Mews 11
CF5 . . . . 194 C6
Glamorgan Terr
Gilfach Goch CF39 . . . . . 132 C7
Tonypandy CF40 . . . . . 107 A1
Tonypandy, Llwynypia
CF40 . . . . 106 E7
Glamorgan Vale Ret Pk
CF72 . . . . 155 D1
Glanafan Comp (Lower) Sch SA13 . . . . 99 C1
Glan Afan Comp Sch
SA13 . . . . 125 B8
Glanafon Terr CF34 . . . . . 102 A8
GLANAMAN 220 A8
Glanaman Rd CF44 . . . . . 52 F4
Glanamman Workshops 1
SA18 . . . . 220 A8
Glanant St CF44 . . . . 27 D7
Glanavon Terr CF32 . . . . . 104 E7
Glanberis Terr CF32 . . . . 103 D7
Glanbran Rd SA7 . . . . . . 70 A8
Glanbrydan Ave SA2 . . . . . 94 F6
Glanbrynnar Row NP11 . . . 86 C5
Glan Creigiau CF72 . . . . 174 C7
Glancynon St CF45 . . . . . 54 E1
Glancynon Terr
Abercynon CF45 . . . . 82 E3
1 Aberdare / Aberdâr
CF44 . . . . 53 D7
Glandafen Rd SA15 . . . . . 40 F2
Glan-Ddu Rd NP12 . . . . . . 85 A6
Glan-Ddu Terr CF82 . . . . . 85 A6
Glandovery Terr NP22 . . . . 13 D7
Glandovey Gr CF3 . . . . . 179 E6
Glan Dulais SA2 . . . . 93 C7
GLANDWR 59 F7
Glandwr Cres SA1 . . . . . . 68 D4
Glandwr Ind Est NP13 . . . . 60 A7
GLANDWR / LANDORE 68 D4
Glandwr Pl CF14 . . . . . . 177 B4
Glandwr St
Abertillery / Abertyleri, Glandwr NP13 . . . . 59 F7
Abertillery / Abertyleri
NP13 . . . . 36 A5
Glandwr Terr CF40 . . . . . 106 E7
Glandyffryn Cl SA13 . . . . 125 D7
Glan Ebbw NP13 . . . . . . 15 D4
Glan Ebbw Terr
Abertillery / Abertyleri
NP13 . . . . 36 B5
Ebbw Vale / Glyn Ebwy
NP23 . . . . 14 E3
Glan Ely Cl CF5 . . . . . . 193 C7
Glanfa Dafydd CF63 . . . . . 215 A4
Glanfa Gorllewin Y Gamlas / West Canal Wharf
CF10 . . . . 232 B1
GLANFA IWERYDD / ATLANTIC WHARF 195 C3
Glanfelin CF37 . . . . 136 A4
Glanffornwg CF31 . . . . . 168 E7
Glan Ffrwd
Caerphilly / Caerffili
CF83 . . . . 137 E6
Porth CF39 . . . . 107 D1
Glanffrwd Ave NP23 . . . . . 7 C2
Glanffrwd Inf Sch / Ysgol Plant Bach Glanffrwd
CF37 . . . . 81 E2
Glanffrwd Rd SA4 . . . . . . 19 D6
Glanffrwd Terr
Ebbw Vale / Glyn Ebwy
NP23 . . . . 7 D2
Ynysybwl CF37 . . . . 81 F2
Glan Gwrelych SA11 . . . . . 223 D1
Glan Hafren
Baglan SA12 . . . . 98 D6
Barry / Y Barri CF62 . . . . 214 B2
Glanheulog NP23 . . . . . . 8 B5
Glanhowy Prim Sch
NP22 . . . . 6 E1
Glanhowy Rd NP12 . . . . . 112 F8
Glanhowy St / Stryd Glanhywl NP22 . . . . . . 6 D1
Glan Islwyn NP12 . . . . . . 85 E4
Glanlay St CF45 . . . . . . 81 F7
GLAN-LLIW 44 A6
Glan Llwyd SA4 . . . . 19 C6
Glanllyn Rd SA7 . . . . . . 47 A5
Glanlyn / Lakeside NP22 . . . 6 B1
Glanmor Cres
Newport / Casnewydd
NP19 . . . . 144 B5
Swansea / Abertawe SA2 . . 94 F7
Glanmor Ct
Newport / Casnewydd
NP19 . . . . 144 B5
Swansea / Abertawe SA2 . . 94 F7
Glanmore Cres CF62 . . . . 214 D5
Glanmorfa SA4 . . . . 66 B5
Glanmor La SA2 . . . . 94 F7
Glanmorlais CF48 . . . . . . 11 B7
Glanmor Mews SA2 . . . . . 94 E7
Glanmor Park Ave
NP19 . . . . 144 B5
Glanmor Park Rd SA2 . . . . 94 E7
Glanmor Pl 3 SA15 . . . . . 40 C4
Glanmor Rd
Llanelli SA15 . . . . 40 C3
Llanelli, Wern SA15 . . . . . 40 D4
Swansea / Abertawe SA2 . . 94 E7
Glanmor Terr
2 Llanelli SA15 . . . . . . 40 C4
Pen-clawdd SA4 . . . . 64 E4
Glanmuir Rd CF24 . . . . . 196 A8
Glannant Pl SA11 . . . . . . 227 B8
Glannant Rd
Evanstown CF39 . . . . . . 132 B7
Pontarddulais SA4 . . . . . 19 E5
Glan Nant Rd CF31 . . . . . 168 D5
Glannant Rise SA11 . . . . . 72 C6
Glan-nant Row CF32 . . . . 129 C2
Glannant St
8 Aberdare / Aberdâr
CF44 . . . . 29 A1
Cwmfelinfach NP11 . . . . . 113 A4
Tonypandy CF40 . . . . . . 106 F4
Glannant Terr
Blaengwrach SA11 . . . . . . 227 B8
Ystradgynlais SA9 . . . . . . 2 E7
Glannant Way SA11 . . . . . 72 B6
Glanogwr Ho CF31 . . . . . 168 E3

Glanogwr Rd CF31 ...... 168 E3
Glan-Pelenna SA12 ...... 72 F3
Glan Rd
Aberdare / Aberdâr CF44 .... 28 E2
Porthcawl CF36 .... 183 A7
GLAN-RHYD 2 F7
Glanrhyd CF14 .... 177 C7
Glan Rhyd
Caerphilly / Caerffili CF83 .... 137 F4
Cwmbran / Cwmbrân NP44 .... 116 A8
Glanrhyd Cl NP22 .... 6 D1
Glanrhyd Cty Prim Sch SA9 .... 2 D6
Glanrhyd Hospl CF31 .... 150 E1
Glan-Rhyd Rd SA8 .... 23 D5
Glanrhyd Rd / Heol Glanrhyd SA9 .... 2 E7
Glanrhyd St CF44 .... 52 E4
Glanrhyd Terr SA4 .... 66 C8
Glan Rhymni CF24 ...... 179 A1
Glanselsig St CF42 .... 50 B2
Glanshon Ct NP11 .... 60 C1
Glansychan Hos NP4 ..... 37 F4
Glansychan La NP4 ...... 37 F4
Glantaff Rd CF48 .... 31 B1
Glantaf Inf Sch CF37 .... 135 F6
Glantawe Pk SA9 .... 2 D7
Glantawe St
[2] Swansea / Abertawe SA6 .... 46 A1
Swansea / Abertawe SA6 .. 69 A8
Glantorvaen Rd NP4 ..... 62 C6
Glantwrch SA9 .... 2 C7
Glanville Terr CF43 ...... 79 C8
Glanwern Ave NP19 ..... 144 C6
Glanwern Cl NP19 .... 144 C6
Glanwern Dr NP18 ...... 144 C5
Glanwern Gr NP19 ...... 144 C6
Glanwern Ho NP18 .... 62 B6
Glanwern Rise NP19 .... 144 C6
Glanwern Terr NP4 ...... 62 B5
Glan-y-Dwr [5] CF63 ..... 214 F4
Glan-y-Ffordd CF15 ..... 158 A5
Glan y Gorllewin / West Bk [12] NP44 .... 90 B2
Glan-y-Gors SA14 ...... 218 D8
Glan Y Lli SA4 .... 65 A4
GLAN-Y-LLYN 158 A5
Glan-y-llyn
Cardiff / Caerdydd CF23 .... 178 B3
North Cornelly CF33 ..... 166 A7
Tonypandy CF40 .... 106 C6
Glan-y-Llyn Ind Est CF15 .... 158 A5
Glanymor CF61 .... 210 C6
Glan-y-Mor
[6] Barry / Y Barri, Barry Dock CF63 .... 214 F4
Barry / Y Barri CF62 ...... 214 B2
Glan-y-Mor Ave / Rhodfa Glan-y-Mor [4] SA13 ... 125 E4
Glanymor La SA4 .... 42 E1
Glanymor Park Dr SA4 ... 42 D1
Glan-y-Mor Prim Sch SA12 .... 98 D1
Glanymor Rd SA4 .... 42 E1
Glan-y-Mor Rd CF3 ..... 179 E5
Glanymor St SA11 .... 71 B3
GLAN-Y-NANT 85 A7
Glan-y-Nant
Fochriw CF81 .... 32 D7
Pencoed CF35 .... 170 D7
Glan Y Nant CF37 .... 136 C4
Glan-y-nant
Rhymney / Rhymni NP22 .... 12 E6
Ton-du CF32 .... 150 D5
Treoes CF35 .... 170 A2
Glan-y-Nant Cl NP44 ..... 89 D1
Glan-y-nant Ct [5] CF14 .... 177 B5
Glan-y-Nant Rd CF14 ... 177 B5
Glan-y-Nant Terr CF14 .... 177 B5
Glanynys Ho CF44 .... 29 B2
Glan-y-Parc CF31 .... 168 E4
Glanyrafon
Ebbw Vale / Glyn Ebwy NP23 .... 7 D3
Taffs Well / Ffynnon Taf CF15 .... 157 F4
Glan-yr-Afon CF48 .... 55 C3
Glan yr Afon SA18 .... 219 B8
Glan-yr-Afon CF34 ...... 128 C8
Glan Yr Afon
Gorseinon SA4 .... 43 C1
Llanelli SA15 .... 40 F8
Machen CF83 .... 140 A6
Glan-yr-afon
Rhymney / Rhymni NP22 .... 12 D5
Treorchy / Treorci CF42 .... 78 C7
Glanyrafon Cl
Penllergaer SA4 .... 44 B2
Tredegar NP22 .... 6 E1
Glan-Yr-Afon Ct CF34 .... 75 A1
Glan-yr-Afon Gdns SA2 .. 94 C6
Glan-yr-Afon Prim Sch / Ysgol Gynradd Glan-yr-Afon CF3 .... 179 B7
Glanyrafon Rd
Pencoed CF35 .... 170 E8
Pontarddulais SA4 .... 19 D4
Glan Yr Afon Rd
Pyle / Y Pîl CF33 .... 148 C4
Swansea / Abertawe SA2 .. 94 C7
Glanyrafon Terr NP13 .... 15 E2
Glan-yr-avon NP24 ...... 33 E3
Glan Yr Avon
Pantyffynnon SA9 .... 2 A5
Ystalyfera SA9 .... 2 C5
Glan-yr-Ely CF72 .... 155 A5
Glan-yr-Ysgol SA9 .... 2 B6
Glanystruth NP13 .... 15 F5
Glan-y-Wern Rd SA7 ..... 69 E7
Glasbrook Pl SA5 .... 67 E5
Glasbrook Terr CF45 ..... 82 A7
Glasbury Rd SA6 .... 68 D7
Glas Canol CF14 .... 177 B3
Glascoed La NP4 .... 63 E6
Glascoed Rd NP4 .... 63 B4
Glas Efail CF14 .... 177 D7
Glasfryn
Blackwood / Coed-Duon NP12 .... 85 D6
Bridgend / Pen-y-Bont ar Ogwr CF31 .... 169 D4
Cwmdare CF44 .... 28 D3
Llanelli SA14 .... 41 A7
Glas Fryn CF82 .... 84 E7
Glasfryn Cl SA2 .... 67 E2
Glasfryn Rd SA4 .... 19 C3
Glasfryn Sq CF33 .... 148 B1
Glasfryn Terr SA4 .... 66 F7
Glasfryn Terr / Rhodfa Glasfryn SA15 .... 40 E7
Glasier Rd CF47 .... 30 F8
Glas Ifor CF14 .... 177 C5
Glaslawr Tynewydd / Tynewydd Gn NP44 ..... 89 E6
GLASLLWCH 142 D3
Glasllwch Cres NP10, NP20 .... 142 C4
Glasllwch Cty Prim Sch NP20 .... 142 D4
Glasllwch La NP20 ...... 142 D3
Glasllwch View NP20 .... 142 C3
Glaslyn Cl CF62 .... 214 C5
Glaslyn Ct NP44 .... 90 A6
Glaslyn Dr CF44 .... 29 E2
Glaslyn Pl SA6 .... 45 D1
Glass Ave CF24 .... 195 E4
Glass Works Cotts NP20 .... 143 C8
Glastonbury Cl [4] NP20 .... 143 C6
Glastonbury Rd CF64 .... 216 B5
Glastonbury Terr CF3 ... 179 B6
Glas Y Llwyn CF63 ...... 205 C1
Glas-y-Pant CF14 .... 176 F7
GLEBELAND 10 D1
Glebeland Cl CF35 ...... 169 F4
Glebeland Pl CF62 ...... 211 D4
Glebeland St
[5] Merthyr Tydfil / Merthyr Tudful CF47 .... 10 D1
Neath / Castell-Nedd SA10 .... 48 F2
Glebe Pl CF14 .... 177 F8
Glebe Rd SA4 .... 42 F1
Glebe St
Barry / Y Barri CF63 ..... 215 A7
Bedwas CF83 .... 138 E6
Bedwas, Trethomas CF83 .... 139 A6
Newport / Casnewydd NP19 .... 143 E5
Penarth CF64 .... 207 A4
Glebe The SA3 .... 122 A7
Glen Afric Cl CF62 ...... 214 D6
Glenalla Rd SA15 .... 40 E5
Glenavon Cres CF36 ..... 182 D7
Glenavon St / Stryd Glenafon [12] SA12 .... 124 F8
Glenavon St SA13 .... 75 B5
Glenavon Terr CF39 ..... 132 C7
GLENBOI 54 A3
Glenboi CF45 .... 54 B3
Glenboi Prim Sch CF45 ... 54 B3
Glenbrook CF45 .... 54 B3
Glenbrook Dr CF63 ...... 215 D8
Glen Cl CF45 .... 54 B3
Glen Coed CF82 .... 85 A1
Glencoe St CF63 .... 215 A6
Glencourt NP4 .... 62 E1
Glendale SA10 .... 48 C3
Glendale Ave CF14 ...... 159 E1
Glendale Ct / Clos Cwm Y Glyn SA10 .... 48 C3
Glendale Gdns NP12 ..... 85 A5
Glendower Cl CF31 ...... 169 A5
Glendower Ct CF14 ...... 176 F5
Glendower St CF48 .... 11 A5
Glenfield Cl SA2 .... 94 A7
Glengariff Ct NP4 .... 62 E2
Glen Garw CF32 .... 103 E6
Glengower Cl SA3 .... 123 A5
Glen Mavis Way CF62 ... 214 D6
Glenmount Way CF14 ... 159 D2
Glen Rd
Neath / Castell-Nedd SA11 .... 72 A8
The Mumbles / Y Mwmbwls SA3 .... 122 F6
Glenrhondda Ct CF42 .... 50 F2
Glenrise Cl CF3 .... 180 B7
Glenroy Ave SA1 .... 233 C4
Glenroy St CF24 .... 195 C8
Glenside NP44 .... 89 D6
Glenside Ct CF24 .... 178 C1
Glenside Rd SA5 .... 67 E6
Glen The
Langstone NP18 .... 119 D1
Sarn CF32 .... 150 F4
Glen-Usk View NP18 .... 118 A4
Glenview
Newbridge / Trecelyn NP11 .... 60 A1
Pen-y-fai CF31 .... 150 C1
Glen View
Bridgend / Pen-y-Bont ar Ogwr CF31 .... 168 F8
Cardiff / Caerdydd CF14 .. 177 F6
Cwmbran / Cwmbrân NP44 .... 89 D4
Glynllan CF35 .... 131 A3
Hollybush NP12 .... 34 C2
Maesycwmmer CF82 ...... 85 A1
Ystrad Mynach CF82 ...... 84 E2
Glen View Bglws NP23 ..... 8 B2
Glen View Ct NP11 .... 86 D5
Glen View Rd NP4 .... 38 B2
Glen View Rise NP11 ..... 86 D5
Glen View St CF40 ...... 106 D7
Glenview Terr
Llanbradach CF83 .... 112 A2
Ynysddu NP11 .... 112 F6
Glen View Terr
Aberavon SA12 .... 99 B1
Fochriw CF81 .... 32 C6
Glenview Villas [4] CF46 .. 83 B6
Glenville Rd SA3 .... 123 A6
Glenwood CF23 .... 178 D6
Glenwood Cl
Barry / Y Barri CF63 ..... 215 D8
Bridgend / Pen-y-Bont ar Ogwr CF35 .... 169 F4
Glevering St SA15 .... 40 E5
Globe Ctr The CF24 ..... 195 C8
Globe Hill NP23 .... 14 D6
Globe Row SA14 .... 41 B8
Globe St [1] SA6 .... 69 A8
Globe Works CF24 ...... 195 D4
Glog Ct CF43 .... 80 B3
Glossop Ct CF35 .... 170 E7
Glossop Rd CF24 .... 195 C6
Glossop Terr CF35 ...... 170 D7
Gloster Pl [1] NP19 .... 143 D6
Gloster's Par NP4 .... 63 B3
Gloster St [3] NP19 ...... 143 D6
Gloucester Bldgs CF32 .. 103 F2
Gloucester Cl CF62 ..... 214 F6
Gloucester Cl / Clos Caerloyn NP44 .... 90 B3
Gloucester Ct NP18 ..... 118 A3
Gloucester Ho
[5] Port Talbot SA12 .... 98 C3
[15] Swansea / Abertawe SA1 .... 233 C2
Gloucester Pl
Swansea / Abertawe SA1 .... 233 C2
The Mumbles / Y Mwmbwls SA3 .... 123 B4
Gloucester St
Aberdare / Aberdâr CF44 .... 29 A2
Cardiff / Caerdydd CF11 .. 194 F5
Gloucester Terr CF45 .... 82 C5
Gluepot Rd CF71 .... 199 C4
Glynbargoed Cl CF46 ..... 83 C7
Glyn Bargoed Rd CF46 ... 83 C7
Glyn Bedw CF83 .... 112 A4
Glynbridge Cl CF62 ..... 204 F1
Glynbridge Gdns CF31 ... 168 F6
GLYNCOCH 109 C5
Glyncoch Terr CF37 ..... 109 E5
GLYNCOED 7 D2
Glyncoed SA18 .... 218 F5
Glyn Coed CF43 .... 79 B8
Glyncoed Comp Sch / Ysgol Gyfun Glyncoed NP23 .... 7 C3
Glyncoed Jun & Inf Schs CF23 .... 178 E7
Glyncoed Prim Sch / Ysgol Gynradd Glyncoed NP23 .... 7 D3
Glyn Coed Rd CF23 ...... 178 E7
Glyncoed Terr
Llanelli SA15 .... 41 A5
Merthyr Tydfil / Merthyr Tudful CF47 .... 30 E7
Glyncoli Cl CF42 .... 78 D7
Glyncoli Rd CF42 .... 78 D6
Glyn Collen
Cardiff / Caerdydd CF23 .... 179 A7
Llanbradach CF83 .... 112 A4
Glyncollen Cres SA6 ..... 46 A3
Glyncollen Dr SA6 .... 46 B3
Glyncollen Prim Sch SA6 .... 46 A4
Glyncornel Cl CF40 ...... 106 E8
GLYNCORRWG 227 D2
Glyn Corrwg Ponds Visitors Ctr★ SA13 ..... 227 B1
Glyncorrwg Prim Sch SA13 .... 227 C2
Glyncorrwg Village Workshops SA13 .... 227 C1
Glyn Cres SA3 .... 94 C2
Glyncrug Cotts NP13 ..... 36 B5
Glyncynwal Rd SA9 ..... 221 C6
Glyn Deri SA18 .... 219 F8
Glynderw CF83 .... 138 A4
Glyn Derw CF81 .... 33 B1
Glyn Derwen CF83 ...... 112 A3
Glynderwen Cl SA2 ...... 94 B3
Glynderwen Cres SA2 .... 94 B3
Glynderwen Rd SA14 ..... 41 D4
Glyn Derw High Sch / Ysgol Uwchradd Glyn Derw CF5 .... 193 E4
Glyndwr Ave CF62 .... 211 D4
Glyn-Dwr Ave CF37 ..... 135 F6
Glyndwr Ct CF41 .... 79 A4
Glyndwr Ho
Baglan SA12 .... 98 C7
Cwmbran / Cwmbrân NP44 .... 89 F3
[7] Merthyr Tydfil / Merthyr Tudful CF47 .... 30 D8
Glyndwr Pl SA1 .... 95 A8
Glyndwr Rd
Barry / Y Barri CF62 ..... 214 E5
Cardiff / Caerdydd CF5 ... 193 B6
Cwmbran / Cwmbrân NP44 .... 89 F3
Ebbw Vale / Glyn Ebwy NP23 .... 7 B5
Penarth CF64 .... 206 E3
Glyndwr St
Merthyr Vale / Ynysowen CF48 .... 55 D5
Port Talbot SA13 .... 99 B1
Glyndyrus Cl CF48 .... 30 E5
GLYN EBWY / EBBW VALE 14 F8
Glyn Eiddew
Cardiff / Caerdydd CF23 .... 178 F8
Llanbradach CF83 .... 112 A4
GLYNFACH 107 F2
Glynfach Rd CF39 .... 107 F2
Glyn Gaer Prim Sch CF82 .... 84 D6
Glyn-Gaer Rd CF82 ...... 84 E7
Glyngwyn St CF45 .... 54 E1
Glynhafod Jun Sch CF44 .... 52 F4
Glynhafod St CF44 .... 52 E4
Glyn Hirnant SA6 .... 46 A3
Glynhir Rd SA4 .... 19 D5
Glyn Jones Ct CF48 ...... 11 A4
Glynleiros Gdns SA10 ..... 71 D8
GLYNLLAN 131 A3
Glynllan CF35 .... 131 A3
Glyn-Llwchwr Rd SA4 .... 19 C4
Glyn Llwyfen CF83 ...... 112 A4
Glynmarch St CF81 .... 57 B8
Glyn-Meirch Rd SA8 ..... 23 C3
Glynmelyn Rd SA11 ..... 223 D2
Glynmil Cl / Clos Clun Mil CF47 .... 10 F2
Glynmil Cvn Site CF48 .... 30 F6
Glyn Milwr NP13 .... 15 F5
Glyn Moch Cotts SA18 ... 219 F8
Glyn-Mynach St CF37 ... 109 A8
GLYN-NEATH / GLYN-NEDD 223 C2
Glyn Neath Rd SA11 ..... 226 E6
Glyn-neath Village Workshops / Gwerthdal Pentref Glyn-nedd SA11 .... 223 C1
GLYN-NEDD / GLYN-NEATH 223 C2
Glynne St CF11 .... 194 D6
Glynne Tower CF64 ..... 207 B3
Glynn Terr CF47 .... 10 E2
Glynn Vivian Art Gall SA1 .... 233 A3
GLYNOGWR 131 D3
Glyn Rd / Heol Glyn SA18 .... 220 D8
Glynrhondda St
Cardiff / Caerdydd CF24 .... 232 C4
Treorchy / Treorci CF42 .... 78 C7
Glyn Rhosyn
Cardiff / Caerdydd CF23 .... 178 E8
Gorseinon SA4 .... 43 B1
Glyn Rhymni CF3 .... 179 C2
Glyn Simon Cl CF5 ...... 176 E2
Glyn St
Aberavon SA12 .... 124 F8
Abertysswg NP22 .... 33 B8
Ogmore Vale CF32 .... 104 E1
Porth CF39 .... 108 A2
Swansea / Abertawe SA1 .. 68 D2
Ynysybwl CF37 .... 109 A8
Glynstell Cl CF11 .... 194 D2
Glynstell Ind Est CF11 ... 194 E2
Glynstell Rd CF36 .... 165 F1
Glynsyfi NP24 .... 33 F2
Glyntaf Ct [5] CF48 .... 31 B1
GLYNTAFF 135 F7
Glyntaff Cl CF37 .... 136 A6
Glyntaff Rd CF37 .... 135 F8
Glyn Teg CF32 .... 129 D1
Glynteg Rd SA4 .... 19 D5
Glyn Terr
Fochriw CF81 .... 32 C7
Tonypandy CF40 .... 106 C7
Tredegar NP22 .... 13 F4
Glyntirion NP44 .... 89 D1
Glyn View CF39 .... 133 E6
Glyn-y-Coed Rd SA11 .... 71 F7
Glyn-y-Gog CF62 .... 213 B1
Glyn-y-Mel CF35 .... 152 D1
Gnoll Ave SA11 .... 71 F7
Gnoll Bank SA11 .... 72 A8
Gnoll Cres SA11 .... 71 F7
Gnoll Dr SA11 .... 71 F7
Gnoll Gardens★ SA11 .... 72 A8
Gnoll Park Rd SA11 ...... 71 F8
Gnoll Prim Sch / Ysgol Gynradd Y Gnoll SA11 ... 71 F7
Gnoll Rd SA9 .... 221 C1
Gnoll View SA11 .... 72 A7
Goat Mill Rd
Dowlais CF48, CF47 .... 11 A3
Merthyr Tydfil / Merthyr Tudful CF47 .... 11 A1
Gobaith Terr CF44 .... 28 C3
Godfrey Ave SA11 .... 227 C8
Godfrey Rd
Cwmbran / Cwmbrân NP44 .... 89 D5
Newport / Casnewydd NP20 .... 143 B5
Godra Bryn CF32 .... 129 D2
GODREAMAN 53 C5
Godreaman St CF44 ...... 53 C5
Godrer Coed CF82 .... 84 F7
Godre'r Coed SA10 .... 48 E2
Godre'r Coed SA6 .... 45 D2
Godre'r Coed Rd CF48 .... 10 A4
Godre'r Fro SA8 .... 23 D7
GODRE'R-GRAIG 221 B1
Godrergraig Prim Sch SA9 .... 221 C1
Godwin Cl CF15 .... 176 D4
GOETRE 39 F8
Goetre Bellaf Rd SA2 ..... 93 C7
Goetre Fach Rd SA2 ...... 93 E7
Goetre Fawr Rd SA2 ..... 93 D7
Goetre Inf & Jun Schs CF47 .... 10 C4
Goitre Coed Isaf CF45 .... 82 F4
Goitre-Coed Rd CF46 .... 83 A5
Goitre La CF47 .... 10 D5
Golate / Y Gwter CF10 .... 232 B2
Goldcliff Ct NP44 .... 89 F3
Goldcliff Ho NP44 .... 89 F3
Goldcrest Dr CF23 ...... 178 D7
Goldcroft Comm NP18 .. 118 B2
Goldcroft Ct NP18 ...... 118 B2
Golden Ave / Rhodfa Aur SA12 .... 98 B2
Golden Cl SA3 .... 122 F7
Golden Gr NP11 .... 86 F6
Golden Mile View NP20 .... 142 C2
Golden Terr CF34 .... 102 B3
Goldsland Pl CF62 ...... 214 C5
Goldsmith Cl
Bridgend / Pen-y-Bont ar Ogwr CF31 .... 168 C5
Cardiff / Caerdydd CF3 ... 179 B7
Newport / Casnewydd NP20 .... 142 E2
Gold St CF24 .... 195 D6
GOLD TOPS 143 B5
Gold Tops NP20 .... 143 B5
Goleg-y-Fro CF31 ...... 169 B4
Golf Rd NP23 .... 8 B2
Golf Rd / Heol Golff
Pontypool / Pont-y-pwl NP4 .... 63 B4
Port Talbot SA12 .... 98 D1
Golf View NP23 .... 8 C2
Golwg Deg / Fair View SA10 .... 48 C1
Golwg Hafren SA2 .... 94 C4
Golwg Y Bont NP12 ...... 85 C6
Golwg-y-Bryn SA10 ..... 222 D4
Golwg Y Castell / Castle View [9] SA11 .... 71 E8
Golwg Y Coed CF83 ..... 137 D5
Golwg-y-coed SA11 ..... 223 C1
Golwg y Craig SA10 ..... 226 A7
Golwg-y-Cwm SA18 .... 220 D5
Golwg-y-Gamlas SA10 ... 48 E1
Golwg Y Garn SA4 .... 43 F2
Golwg Y Lon SA6 .... 22 D1
Golwg Y Mor SA4 .... 64 F4
Gol Wg-y-mor SA12 .... 124 C8
Golwg Y Mor / Ocean View SA10 .... 97 C8
Golwg Y Mynydd
Craig-cefn-parc SA6 ...... 22 B1
Godre'r-graig SA9 .... 2 A3
Golwg-y-Mynydd
Neath / Castell-Nedd SA10 .... 48 C2
Rhymney / Rhymni NP22 ... 12 E5
Tredegar NP22 .... 6 C3
Golwg-yr-Afon
Aberdulais SA10 .... 49 C4
Llangennech SA14 .... 42 B7
Golwg Yr Afon / River View SA4 .... 19 A5
Golwg yr Eglwys CF83 ... 138 D6
Golwg Y Rhodfa / Promenade View SA12 .... 98 C1
Golwg-yr-Ysgol / School View NP23 .... 8 B2
Golwg Y Sianel / Channel View SA12 .... 124 D8
Golwg Y Twr SA4 .... 19 D3
Golwg Y Waun SA7 ...... 46 E2
Golwyg Y Mynydd SA18 .... 219 D6
Golwys Derwen / Derwen View CF31 .... 169 A6
Golygafa'r Eglwys CF37 .... 109 B1

Golygfa Geltaido / Celtic View CF34 102 C1
Golygfan / Broad View NP44 89 C5
Golygfa'r Goedwig / Woodland View 4 NP44 90 A5
Golygfa'r Rheilffordd / Railway View NP22 13 E8
Golygfor SA15 40 F4
GOLYNOS 37 D5
Gomer Gdns SA1 68 A1
Gomer Rd SA1 67 F1
Gonhill SA3 122 E8
Goodrich Ave CF83 138 C2
Goodrich Cres NP20 143 B7
Goodrich Ct 1 NP44 90 B2
Goodrich Gr NP10 163 E5
Goodrich La NP20 143 B7
Goodrich St CF83 138 B2
Goodwick Cl CF62 214 F8
Goodwick Rd CF3 179 C3
Goodwin St CF34 102 B3
Goodwood Cl CF5 192 F4
Goole Rd SA5 67 D5
Goose Island SA1 233 B1
Goossens Cl NP19 144 F6
Goppa Rd SA4 19 E3
Gordings NP44 89 B3
Gordon Ave NP11 60 B3
Gordon Cl NP12 85 D6
Gordon Cres / Cresawnt Gordon 7 SA12 98 C2
Gordon Rd
Abersychan NP4 37 E4
Blackwood / Coed-Duon NP12 85 E6
Cardiff / Caerdydd CF24 232 C4
Llanelli SA14 41 B7
Porthcawl CF36 182 F6
Gordon Rd / Heol Gordon 6 SA12 98 C2
Gordon Rowley Way SA6 45 E4
Gordon St
Aberdare / Aberdâr CF44 53 B5
Newport / Casnewydd NP19 143 E5
Treorchy / Treorci CF41 78 F3
Gordon Thomas Cl 4 SA1 68 C2
Gordon Villas CF44 29 B2
Gored Cotts SA11 226 C4
Gored Terr SA11 226 C4
Gore St NP19 143 D7
Gore Terr 1 SA1 233 A3
Goring Rd / Heol Goring SA15 40 D6
GOROF 1 E1
Gorof Rd SA9 2 D8
Goronwy Rd SA2 67 E1
Gorsafle SA9 222 A4
Gorsaf Y Glowr SA4 19 D3
Gors Ave SA1 68 B1
Gors Ddu Rd / Heol Gors Ddu SA14 218 D8
Gorsddu Terr SA14 218 C8
Gorsedd SA15 40 F4
Gorsedd Cl NP23 7 D5
Gorsedd Gardens Rd CF10 232 B3
Gorsedd St CF45 54 D2
Gorsedd Terr CF47 10 E2
GORSEINON 43 C3
Gorseinon Bsns Pk SA4 43 C1
Gorseinon Coll
Gorseinon SA4 43 A1
Loughor SA4 42 F1
Gorseinon Cty Jun Sch SA4 43 B2
GORSEINON GARDEN VILLAGE 66 D8
Gorseinon Hospl SA4 43 A3
Gorseinon Inf Sch SA4 43 C2
Gorseinon Rd SA4 43 E1
Gorseinon Sh Pk SA4 43 C2
Gorse La SA1 95 A5
Gorse Pl CF5 193 D8
Gorse Terr NP24 33 F3
Gors-Fach SA14 41 C6
GORS-GOCH 218 C8
Gors Goch Rd / Heol Gors Goch SA18 220 D8
Gors La SA18 220 D6
GORSLAS 218 C8
Gorslas CF33 147 F1
Gorslas Com Prim Sch / Ysgol Gynradd Gorslas SA14 218 B8
Gorslwyn Terr SA18 220 D5
Gors Prim Sch SA1 67 E1
Gors Rd SA4 44 A3
Gorsto Rd
Gwaun-Cae-Gurwen SA18 220 D7
Pen-Rhiw-fawr SA9 221 B5
Gorwydd Rd SA4 66 C4
Gorwyl Flats CF32 104 E2
Gorwyl Rd CF32 104 E2
Goscombe Dr CF64 206 F5
Goscombe Pk CF71 202 C7
Goshen Cl NP22 12 E4
Goshen Pk SA10 70 F8
Goshen St NP22 12 E4
Gospel Ct CF38 156 A7
Gospel Hall Terr CF44 28 F3
Gough Ave SA9 2 D7
Gough Rd
Cardiff / Caerdydd CF5 193 C5
Ystalyfera SA9 2 B6
Gould Cl CF3 179 E8
Govilion Pl NP44 89 D5
Gowan Ct CF14 159 D3
Gower Cres SA12 98 C7
Gower Ct CF62 214 D5
Gower Davies Ct CF37 109 A7
Gower Gn / Maes Gwr 4 NP44 90 A6
Gower Heritage Ctr★ SA3 120 E7
Gower Holiday Village SA3 231 A6
Gower Pl SA3 123 A5
Gower Rd
Aberdare / Aberdâr CF44 29 E1
Swansea / Abertawe, Penyrheol SA2 94 C7
Swansea / Abertawe SA2 93 D5
Gower Rise SA4 66 C4
Gower's Bldgs SA11 71 B1
Gower St
Briton Ferry / Llansawel SA11 71 C3
Cardiff / Caerdydd CF24 178 A1
Port Talbot SA13 125 C7
Gower Terr SA4 64 F4
Gowerton Rd
Pen-clawdd SA4 65 A4
Three Crosses SA4 65 E1
Gowerton Sch SA4 66 C4
Gowerton Sta SA4 66 C5
GOWERTON / TRE-GWYR 66 B4
Gower View SA15 40 E8
Gower View Rd SA4 43 A4
Goya Cl NP19 144 A7
Goya Pl SA12 124 D8
GOYTRE 125 F7
Goytre Cl SA13 125 F8
Goytre Cres SA13 125 E8
Goytre Fawr Prim Sch NP4 39 E5
Goytre Ho SA13 125 F8
Goytre Rd SA13 125 F8
Grace Pope Ct NP13 60 B6
Graddfa Ind Est / Ystad Ddiwydiannol Graddfa CF83 111 F2
Graddfa Villas CF83 111 F3
Gradon Cl CF63 215 C6
Grafog St SA1 96 B7
Grafton Cl CF23 178 D3
Grafton Dr CF72 155 E2
Grafton La NP19 143 D5
Grafton Rd NP19 143 C5
Grafton Terr CF14 177 C6
Graham Ave CF31 150 D2
Graham Bell Cl NP20 116 F4
Graham Berry Ct SA5 68 A5
Graham Cl CF23 178 E2
Graham Ct CF83 138 C3
Graham St
7 Merthyr Tydfil / Merthyr Tudful CF47 10 D1
Newport / Casnewydd NP20 143 B4
Swansea / Abertawe SA1 68 D2
Graham's Yd NP22 6 E1
Graham Terr / Teras Graham SA10 70 F7
Graham Way 8 CF47 10 D1
Graham Wlk 11 CF11 194 D5
GRAIG 135 C7
Graig Ave
Abercwmboi CF44 53 E5
Llanelli SA15 40 E4
3 Margam SA13 125 E4
Pontypridd CF37 135 B7
Graig Cl
Abercanaid CF48 30 E4
Bassaleg NP10 142 A3
Graig Cotts CF72 173 D6
Graig Cres CF44 53 E5
Graig Ddu CF43 79 B8
Graig Ddu Pl CF40 107 C4
Graigddu Rd CF40 107 B4
Graig Ebbw NP23 7 B4
Graig Fach CF37 135 F7
GRAIGFELEN 46 C8
Graigfelen Prim Sch SA6 46 C8
Graig Gellinudd SA8 24 B5
Graig Hir CF15 176 B7
Graig Inf Sch SA6 68 F8
Graig Isaf CF44 28 F1
Graiglas CF32 130 A2
Graig Llanguicke SA8 23 F7
Graig Llwyn Rd CF14 160 D4
Graig-Llwyn Rd CF14 160 E4
Graiglwyd CF44 28 C4
Graig Lwyd CF15 176 B7
Graiglwyd Rd SA2 94 E8
Graiglwyd Sq SA1 94 F8
Graig Newydd SA9 221 C2
Graigola Rd SA7 47 B6
Graig Parc
Neath Abbey SA10 71 B8
Neath / Castell-Nedd SA10 48 B1
Graig Park Ave NP20 117 B1
Graig Park Circ NP20 117 A1
Graig Park Hill NP20 117 B1
Graig Park La NP20 117 B1
Graig Park Par NP20 117 B1
Graig Park Rd NP20 117 B1
Graig Park Villas NP20 117 A1
GRAIG PENLLYN 188 B8
Graig Pl
Aberdare / Aberdâr CF44 28 F1
Swansea / Abertawe SA1 233 B4
Graig Rd
Abercanaid CF48 30 E4
Abergwynfi SA13 76 B6
Abertillery / Abertyleri NP13 36 C2
Cardiff / Caerdydd CF14 160 A5
Glais SA7 47 A6
Glanaman SA18 220 C7
Godre'r-graig SA9 221 C2
Hengoed CF82 84 F2
Neath / Castell-Nedd SA10 70 D7
Newbridge / Trecelyn NP11 87 A6
Pontardawe SA8 24 A5
Porth CF39 107 E7
Swansea / Abertawe SA6 68 F7
Trebanos / Trebannws SA8 23 C3
Graig Rd / Ffordd y Graig NP44 89 A3
Graig Rd / Ffordy-y-Graig NP44 89 A5
Graig St
Aberdare / Aberdâr CF44 28 F1
4 Mountain Ash / Aberpennar CF45 54 D3
Pontygwaith CF43 80 B1
Pontypridd CF37 135 C8
Swansea / Abertawe SA1 233 B4
Graig Terr
Abercwmboi CF44 53 E5
Abergwynfi SA13 76 B5
Bargoed / Bargod CF81 57 F5
Bedlinog CF46 56 A7
Blackmill CF35 130 F2
Cwm NP23 35 B6
Dowlais CF48 11 A5
Ferndale CF43 80 A5
Glais SA7 47 A6
Pontypridd CF37 135 C8
Senghenydd CF83 110 F4
Swansea / Abertawe SA1 233 A4
Graig The
Bridgend / Pen-y-Bont ar Ogwr CF31 168 E4
Cefn Cribwr CF32 149 C2
GRAIG TREWYDDFA 68 F7
Graig Twrch SA9 1 A1
Graig View
Abertillery / Abertyleri NP13 60 A7
Cardiff / Caerdydd CF14 160 B3
Cwmbran / Cwmbrân NP44 89 B6
Cwmfelinfach NP11 113 A5
Machen CF83 140 B7
Nantgarw CF15 158 B8
Risca / Rhisga NP11 114 F1
GRAIGWEN 109 B1
Graig Wen
Maerdy CF43 79 B8
Morganstown / Treforgan CF15 176 B8
Graigwen Cres CF83 137 B7
Graig-Wen Hos NP11 87 C3
Graigwen Parc CF37 109 A3
Graigwen Pl CF37 109 B1
Graigwen Rd
Pontypridd CF37 109 B2
Porth CF39 107 E2
Graig Wood Cl NP20 117 B1
Graig-y-Bedw NP24 33 F3
Graig-y-Coed SA4 64 D4
Graig Y Darren SA9 2 A3
Graig-y-Ddelw CF42 50 D3
Graig-y-Dderi SA7 47 A6
Graigymerched SA9 2 A5
Graig Y Mynydd CF39 133 A3
Graig y Nos NP22 6 F1
Graig Y Pal SA7 47 A5
Graig-yr-Eos Terr CF40 107 A3
Graig-y-Rhacca Prim Sch / Ysgol Gynradd Graig-y-Rhacca CF83 139 C6
Graig-yr-Helfa Rd CF37 135 E8
Graigyrhesg Pl CF37 109 D3
Graigyrhesg Rd CF37 109 D3
Graig Yr Wylan CF83 137 E2
Graig Ysguthan CF83 112 A5
Graig-y-Wion Prim Sch CF37 135 C8
Grampian Way SA5 67 E3
Granada Ct NP10 163 E7
Granary The 4 CF10 195 B3
Grand Ave CF5 193 C5
Grandison St / Stryd Grandison SA11 71 C2
Grandison St 2 SA1 68 D1
Grand The CF10 232 B2
Grand Theatre★ SA1 233 A2
Grand View Terr CF40 107 A3
Grange Ave CF5 205 A6
Grange Cl
Caerphilly / Caerffili CF83 137 F3
Wenvoe / Gwenfo CF5 205 A7
Grange Cres
Bridgend / Pen-y-Bont ar Ogwr CF35 169 F4
The Mumbles / Y Mwmbwls SA3 123 A7
Grange Ct
Barry / Y Barri CF63 215 D6
3 Newport / Casnewydd NP20 143 A4
Grange Gdns
Cardiff / Caerdydd CF11 194 F2
Llantwit Major / Llanilltud Fawr CF61 210 A6
Grange Hill NP12 85 C6
Grange Ind Site NP44 89 F2
Grange La
6 Cwmbran / Cwmbrân NP44 89 E4
The Mumbles / Y Mwmbwls SA3 123 A8
Grangemoor Ct CF11 206 E7
Grange Path / Llwybr y Plasty 7 NP44 90 B1
Grange Pl CF11 195 A2
Grange Prim Sch SA3 123 A7
Grange Rd
Cwmbran / Cwmbrân, Northville NP44 89 F3
The Mumbles / Y Mwmbwls SA3 123 A7
Grange Rd / Helo Y Plas NP44 89 F2
Grange St SA13 125 C8
Grange Terr CF40 106 E7
Grange The
Caerphilly / Caerffili CF83 137 F3
Cardiff / Caerdydd CF5 194 A8
Llantwit Fadre / Llanilltud Faerdref CF38 156 C6
Marshfield CF3 180 D8
Miskin / Meisgyn CF72 173 D7
4 Penarth CF64 206 F3
GRANGETOWN 194 F2
Grangetown Link CF11 206 D8
Grange Town Prim Sch CF11 194 F2
Grangetown Sta CF11 194 E2
Grangewood Cl CF23 161 B1
Granogwen Rd SA1 233 A5
Granston Sq NP44 89 B2
Grantham Cl CF5 176 E2
Grant's Cl CF15 176 C8
Grant's Field CF5 192 D2
Grant St SA15 40 E4
Granville Ave CF5 194 A7
Granville Cl NP10 142 C4
Granville La NP20 143 D4
Granville Rd SA1 233 C4
Granville St
Abertillery / Abertyleri NP13 36 A6
Newport / Casnewydd NP20 143 D4
Granville Terr
Llanelli SA14 41 C6
Mountain Ash / Aberpennar CF45 54 D4
Grasmere Ave CF23 178 A3
Grasmere Dr CF44 29 E1
Grassholm Gdns SA5 67 E7
Grassholm Way CF36 165 D1
Grassmere Cl CF64 206 E6
Grawen CF47 10 C2
Grawen Hos CF48 225 F3
Grawen La CF48 225 F3
Grawen St CF39 107 E4
Grawen Terr CF47 10 D2
Gray La CF11 194 D6
Graylands The CF14 177 C6
Grays Gdns CF83 139 C6
Gray's Pl CF48 55 D4
Gray St
Abertillery / Abertyleri NP13 36 B5
Cardiff / Caerdydd CF11 194 D6
Grays Wlk CF71 188 F2
Great Burnet Cl CF3 180 B6
Great House Ct SA3 231 B5
Great House Mdws CF61 209 F7
Great Oaks Pk NP10 141 F7
Great Ormes Ho CF11 207 A7
Great St CF37 108 D2
Great Thomas Cl CF62 212 F2
Great War Memorial★ CF47 10 E2
Great Western Ave CF31 168 F6
Great Western Cres SA15 40 D3
Great Western Ct CF5 194 C5
Great Western La CF10 232 B1
Great Western Terr
Cwmavon / Cwmafan SA12 99 F6
1 Llanelli SA15 40 D3
Greave Cl CF5 205 A7
Greek Church St CF10 232 C1
Green Acre
Creigiau CF15 174 E7
Cwmbran / Cwmbrân NP44 89 D1
Greenacre Dr
Bedwas CF83 138 D6
Cardiff / Caerdydd CF23 161 B2
Glais SA7 47 A5
Pencoed CF35 170 C8
Green Acre Dr CF40 106 E5
Greenacre Gdns CF83 138 F6
Greenacres
Barry / Y Barri CF63 215 D7
Pen-clawdd SA4 64 D4
Port Talbot SA13 126 A1
South Cornelly CF33 165 F5
Green Ave The CF36 182 E6
Green Bank Rd SA3 122 F7
Greenbanks Dr CF62 214 D6
Greenbay Rd CF24 196 A6
Green Circ CF33 148 A1
Green Cl SA2 94 A1
Green Close Rd CF14 177 C4
Greencourt / Cwrt Gwyrrd 8 NP44 90 A6
Greencroft Ave CF5 193 F6
Green Ct
Bridgend / Pen-y-Bont ar Ogwr CF31 169 A3
Pyle / Y Pîl CF33 148 D1
Green Dragon La SA1 233 B2
Greene Cl NP19 144 F5
Green Farm Cl CF5 193 A4
Green Farm Rd CF5 193 A4
Greenfield
Caerleon / Caerllion NP18 117 F3
Newbridge / Trecelyn NP11 87 A7
New Tredegar NP24 33 D4
Greenfield Ave
Cardiff / Caerdydd, Birchgrove CF14 177 C5
Cardiff / Caerdydd, Canton CF11 194 C7
Dinas Powis / Dinas Powys CF64 206 B3
2 Margam SA13 125 E4
Newbridge / Trecelyn NP11 87 A7
Pontypridd CF37 109 C5
Greenfield Cl
Cwmbran / Cwmbrân NP44 89 D6
Swansea / Abertawe SA7 69 F7
Greenfield Cotts NP22 6 D2
Greenfield Cres
Ebbw Vale / Glyn Ebwy NP23 7 C4
Swansea / Abertawe SA7 69 F7
Greenfield Ct CF48 31 A4
Greenfield Gdns CF48 31 A4
Greenfield Pl
Abertridwr CF83 136 E7
Blaenavon NP4 17 D6
Loughor SA4 65 F8
Greenfield Rd
Barry / Y Barri CF62 214 D7
Cardiff / Caerdydd CF14 177 C5
Rogerstone NP10 142 B4
Greenfield Rd / Heol Maesglas 6 SA18 220 B8
Greenfields SA4 18 F4
Greenfields Ave CF31 168 C4
Greenfield Specl Sch CF48 31 A4
Greenfield St
Bargoed / Bargod CF81 58 A4
Maesteg CF34 102 B3
Pontlottyn CF81 32 F8
Tonypandy CF40 107 A3
Greenfields Terr SA2 94 C7
Greenfield Stores NP10 142 C4
Greenfield Terr
Abercynon CF45 82 E4
Aberdare / Aberdâr CF44 53 F7
Abersychan NP4 37 E7
Argoed NP12 58 F4
Blaengarw CF32 103 E7
Bryncethin CF32 151 E6
Ebbw Vale / Glyn Ebwy NP23 14 E6
Llansamlet SA7 69 D8
Maesteg CF34 75 B1
Merthyr Tydfil / Merthyr Tudful CF47 11 A4
Mountain Ash / Aberpennar CF45 54 B6
North Cornelly CF33 165 F8
Ogmore Vale CF32 104 E1
Pentrebach CF48 31 A4
Pont Rhyd-y-cyff CF34 128 E6
Swansea / Abertawe, Landore / Glandwr SA1 68 D4
Tredegar NP22 13 F6
Treorchy / Treorci CF42 78 A4
Troedyrhiw CF48 31 C2
Ynysddu NP11 112 F6
Greenfield Way
Cowbridge / Y Bont-Faen CF71 188 D1
Porthcawl CF36 165 F2
Greenforge Way / Ffordd Greenforge NP44 89 C4
Greenhaven Rise CF64 206 E6

Green Hedges SA10 . . . . . 48 C7
Green Hill
Pontycymer CF32 . . . . 103 E3
Swansea / Abertawe
SA1 . . . . 233 B5
Ton Pentre CF41 . . . . 79 B3
Greenhill Ct CF14 . . . . 177 A8
Greenhill Dr CF44 . . . . 53 C7
Greenhill Ho CF44 . . . . 53 C7
Greenhill Pl CF82 . . . . 84 C6
Greenhill Prim Sch
CF82 . . . . 84 C7
Greenhill Rd NP4 . . . . 62 E2
Greenhill Rd / Heol
Greenhill NP44 . . . . 89 D4
Greenhill Specl Sch
CF14 . . . . 177 A8
Greenhill St SA1 . . . . 233 B5
Green La
Barry / Y Barri CF63 . . . . . 215 C8
Llantwit Major / Llanilltud
Fawr CF61 . . . . 209 D6
St Bride's Wentlooge /
Llansanffraid Gwynllwg
NP10 . . . . 163 E3
Sully CF64 . . . . 216 B8
Greenland Cres CF5 . . . . . 193 C8
Greenland Rd
Brynmawr NP23 . . . . 8 C4
Pontypool / Pont-y-pwl
NP4 . . . . 62 C8
Greenlands
Blackwood / Coed Duon
NP11 . . . . 59 D1
Newbridge / Trecelyn
NP11 . . . . 87 A7
Greenlands Rd CF72 . . . . 155 E3
Greenlawn Jun Sch /
Ysgol Iau Greenlawn
NP4 . . . . 63 B4
Greenlawns CF23 . . . . 178 D2
Green Lawns CF62 . . . . . . 215 A7
Green Mdw
Glyncorrwg SA13 . . . . 227 C2
Tredegar NP22 . . . . 6 F1
Green Mdws CF3 . . . . 179 E5
GREENMEADOW 89 A2
Greenmeadow
Bettws CF32 . . . . 129 C2
Cefn Cribwr CF32 . . . . 149 B2
Machen CF83 . . . . 139 D5
Greenmeadow Ave
NP19 . . . . 144 C3
Greenmeadow Bglws
NP12 . . . . 85 A7
Greenmeadow Cl
Cwmbran / Cwmbrân
NP44 . . . . 89 D2
5 Dinas Powis / Dinas Powys
CF64 . . . . 206 B2
Pontypridd CF37 . . . . 109 D5
Greenmeadow Community
Farm* NP44 . . . . 89 B4
Greenmeadow Cres
NP4 . . . . 39 E3
Greenmeadow Ct
CF72 . . . . 155 E2
Greenmeadow Dr
Risca / Rhisga NP11 . . . . . 114 D4
Tongwynlais CF15 . . . . 176 D8
Greenmeadow Ho
NP44 . . . . 89 D2
Greenmeadow Prim Sch /
Ysgol Gynradd Maes-glas
NP44 . . . . 89 A3
Greenmeadow Rd
Cwmfelinfach NP11 . . . . . . 113 C3
Newport / Casnewydd
NP19 . . . . 144 C3
Greenmeadows CF31 . . . . 168 F5
Greenmeadow Terr
Abertillery / Abertyleri
NP13 . . . . 36 B7
Tonypandy CF40 . . . . 107 A2
Green Meadow Terr
CF32 . . . . 130 B4
Greenmeadow Way / Helo
Greenmeadow NP44 . . . . 89 C3
Greenock Rd CF3 . . . . 179 D6
Green Park St SA12 . . . . . . 125 A8
Green Pk CF72 . . . . 154 F1
Green Pk CF72 . . . . 155 C2
Green Pl CF15 . . . . 176 B5
Green Row CF83 . . . . 139 F6
Greenside CF71 . . . . 188 F1
Green St
7 Aberavon SA12 . . . . 124 F8
Bridgend / Pen-y-Bont ar Ogwr
CF31 . . . . 168 F5
Cardiff / Caerdydd CF11 . . 194 F5
Ebbw Vale / Glyn Ebwy
NP23 . . . . 14 F1
Neath / Castell-Nedd
SA11 . . . . 71 E8
Swansea / Abertawe SA6 . . 69 A8
Greensway NP22 . . . . 33 C8
Green The
Abertysswg NP22 . . . . 33 C8
Bryn NP12 . . . . 85 D4
Leckwith / Lecwydd
CF11 . . . . 194 B1
Neath / Castell-Nedd
SA11 . . . . 71 D7
Pencoed CF35 . . . . 170 E8
Radyr CF15 . . . . 176 C5
Sarn CF32 . . . . 150 E3
Trefechan CF48 . . . . 10 B6
Green Villas NP13 . . . . 36 B6
Greenway CF83 . . . . 138 C6
Green Way NP4 . . . . 37 E5
Greenway Ave CF3 . . . . . . 179 C3
Greenway Cl
Llandough / Llandochau
CF64 . . . . 206 D7
Pontypool / Pont-y-pwl
NP4 . . . . 62 D2
Greenway Ct CF63 . . . . . . 215 D8
Greenway Dr NP4 . . . . 62 D2
Greenway Prim Sch
CF3 . . . . 179 C4
Greenway Rd
Cardiff / Caerdydd
CF3 . . . . 179 D5
Neath / Castell-Nedd
SA11 . . . . 71 E7
Greenways
Aberdare / Aberdâr
CF44 . . . . 29 D3
Ebbw Vale / Glyn Ebwy
NP23 . . . . 14 B8
Porthcawl CF36 . . . . 183 B8
Waunarlwydd SA5 . . . . 66 D3
Greenway St SA15 . . . . 40 C6
Greenways The CF34 . . . . 102 A2
Greenway The SA10 . . . . . . 70 C3
Greenway Wlk NP4 . . . . 62 D3
Greenway Workshops
CF83 . . . . 138 D6
Greenwich Rd
Cardiff / Caerdydd
CF5 . . . . 194 B7
Newport / Casnewydd
NP20 . . . . 143 B1
Green Willows NP44 . . . . 116 F8
Greenwood NP18 . . . . 144 A8
Greenwood Ave
Cwmbran / Cwmbrân
NP44 . . . . 89 C5
Maesteg CF34 . . . . 102 A1
Tredegar NP22 . . . . 6 C1
Greenwood Cl
Bridgend / Pen-y-Bont ar
Ogwr CF31 . . . . 168 F7
Cardiff / Caerdydd CF23 . . 161 B2
Merthyr Tydfil / Merthyr Tudful
CF47 . . . . 30 F7
Swansea / Abertawe SA2 . . 94 C6
Greenwood Ct
Caerphilly / Caerffili
CF83 . . . . 138 C3
New Tredegar NP24 . . . . . . 33 D3
Greenwood Dr
Beddau CF38 . . . . 156 B7
Cimla SA11 . . . . 72 C5
Cwmbran / Cwmbrân
NP44 . . . . 115 E8
Hirwaun CF44 . . . . 27 F7
Greenwood La CF5 . . . . . . 193 A7
Greenwood Pl SA5 . . . . 67 D6
Greenwood Rd
Abersychan NP4 . . . . 37 F5
Blackwood / Coed-Duon
NP12 . . . . 85 D8
Cardiff / Caerdydd CF5 . . . 176 F2
Neath / Castell-Nedd
SA11 . . . . 71 D4
Greenwood Rd / Heol
Greenwood SA12 . . . . 98 D7
Greenwood St CF63 . . . . . 214 F4
Gregory Cl CF35 . . . . 170 B8
Greig Cl / Clos Greig 8
SA12 . . . . 98 B3
Greig Ct / Cwrt Greig 12
SA12 . . . . 98 B3
Grenadier Dr NP18 . . . . . . 145 C8
Grenfell Ave SA4 . . . . 43 A3
Grenfell Park Rd SA1 . . . . . 95 F7
Grenfell Town SA1 . . . . 68 F3
Grenig Rd / Heol Grenig
SA18 . . . . 220 B6
Grenville Rd CF23 . . . . 195 D8
Gresford Cl CF3 . . . . 179 D6
Gresham Pl CF46 . . . . 83 A6
Grey Cres CF82 . . . . 85 A6
Greyfriars Ct
1 Bridgend / Pen-y-Bont ar
Ogwr CF31 . . . . 168 F5
Porthcawl CF36 . . . . 183 D8
Greyfriars Pl CF10 . . . . . . 232 B3
Greyfriars Rd CF10 . . . . . . 232 B3
Grey's Dr CF61 . . . . 210 B6
Grey's Pl CF44 . . . . 28 F7
Greys Rd NP4 . . . . 62 C5
Grey St SA1 . . . . 68 D3
Greys Terr SA7 . . . . 47 B1
Greystone / Careg Llwyd
CF31 . . . . 168 C3
Grey Waters NP44 . . . . 90 A3
Greywood Field / Cae
Llwydcoed CF31 . . . . 168 A2
Griffin Ave NP4 . . . . 17 D6
Griffin Cl CF62 . . . . 214 C8
Griffin Ct NP4 . . . . 62 B7
Griffin Park Ct CF36 . . . . . 183 A7
Griffin Pk CF42 . . . . 78 F5
Griffin St
Abertillery / Abertyleri
NP13 . . . . 36 C3
3 Newport / Casnewydd
NP20 . . . . 143 C5
Griffin The NP10 . . . . 142 A2
Griffith John St SA1 . . . . . . 68 D1
Griffiths Ct NP4 . . . . 17 A6
Griffiths Gdns NP22 . . . . . . 6 C1
Griffiths Sq NP22 . . . . 6 C1
Griffiths St CF82 . . . . 84 E2
Griffith St
1 Aberdare / Aberdâr
CF44 . . . . 29 A1
Maerdy CF43 . . . . 52 A2
Treorchy / Treorci CF41 . . . . 78 F4
Griffiths Terr CF34 . . . . 75 A2
Griffith's Terr CF48 . . . . . . 31 B3
GRIFFITHSTOWN 62 D3
Griffithstown Inf Sch
NP4 . . . . 62 E3
Griffithstown Jun Sch
NP4 . . . . 62 E2
Griffithstown Railway
Mus* NP4 . . . . 62 F2
Griffiths Way NP4 . . . . 37 E5
Griffith Terr CF48 . . . . 55 C4
Grimson Cl CF64 . . . . 216 B5
Grindle Wlk NP10 . . . . 142 A6
Gripoly Mills CF11 . . . . . . 194 E3
Grisedale Cl CF23 . . . . 178 B2
Groes Cl NP10 . . . . 142 A7
GROES-FAEN 174 B7
Groes-Faen Terr CF81 . . . . 57 D5
Groes Lon CF14 . . . . 177 B8
Groes Prim Sch SA13 . . . . 125 F3
Groes Rd
Rogerstone NP10 . . . . 142 A6
Rogerstone NP10 . . . . 142 A7
Groeswen CF61 . . . . 209 F7
Groeswen Dr CF83 . . . . . . 137 D4
Groeswen Hospl SA13 . . . 125 E5
Groes-wen La / Lon
Groeswen 4 SA13 . . . . . 125 D5
Groeswen Rd
Caerphilly / Caerffili CF15,
CF83 . . . . 137 C3
Caerphilly / Caerffili
CF83 . . . . 137 D4
Gron Ffordd CF14 . . . . 159 B1
Grongaer Terr CF37 . . . . . 135 C8
Gron Rd SA18 . . . . 220 D6
Grosmont Cl NP12 . . . . 58 E1
Grosmont Pl / Maes y
Grysmwnt NP44 . . . . 90 A6
Grosmont Rd NP4 . . . . 63 B5
Grosmont Way NP10 . . . . 163 D5
Grosvenor Pl NP4 . . . . 62 E1
Grosvenor Rd
Abertillery / Abertyleri
NP13 . . . . 36 B6
Swansea / Abertawe SA2 . . 94 D7
Grosvenor St CF5 . . . . 194 B6
Grosvenor Terr CF34 . . . . . 75 A1
Grouse St CF24 . . . . 195 C7
Grove Cl NP4 . . . . 37 F1
Grove Cres NP4 . . . . 38 B1
Grove Est
Bedwas CF83 . . . . 139 A7
Pontypool / Pont-y-pwl
NP4 . . . . 38 A1
Grove Farm Rd SA4 . . . . . . 43 C7
Grovefield Ho 9 CF40 . . . 106 F4
Grovefield Terr 8
CF40 . . . . 106 F4
Grove Head / Pen Llwyn
CF31 . . . . 168 D3
Grove Hill Pk / Parc
Bryngelli SA14 . . . . 218 C8
Grove House Ct CF43 . . . . . 80 C1
Grove La
Neath / Castell-Nedd
SA10 . . . . 70 E7
1 Newport / Casnewydd
NP20 . . . . 143 C3
Penrhiwtyn SA11 . . . . 71 C5
Groveland Rd CF14 . . . . . . 177 D5
Grovenor Rd NP10 . . . . . . 141 F3
Grove Park Ave NP44 . . . . . 89 E6
Grove Park Dr NP20 . . . . . 117 B1
Grove Pk
Cwmbran / Cwmbrân
NP44 . . . . 89 E6
Merthyr Tydfil / Merthyr Tudful
CF47 . . . . 10 D3
Grove Pl
Cardiff / Caerdydd
CF14 . . . . 177 D5
Cwmbran / Cwmbrân
NP44 . . . . 89 E6
Penarth CF64 . . . . 207 A4
Pontypool / Pont-y-pwl
NP4 . . . . 62 E2
Port Talbot SA13 . . . . 125 B8
Swansea / Abertawe
SA1 . . . . 233 A3
Grove Place La 4
CF64 . . . . 207 A4
Grove Rd
Bridgend / Pen-y-Bont ar
Ogwr CF31 . . . . 168 F3
Clydach SA6 . . . . 22 D1
Llandow / Llandw CF71 . . . 199 A7
Pontardawe SA8 . . . . 23 F5
Pontypool / Pont-y-pwl
NP4 . . . . 62 A8
Risca / Rhisga NP11 . . . . . 114 F3
Grove Rd / Heol Y Gelli
CF31 . . . . 168 F3
Grovers Cl CF37 . . . . 109 D6
Grovers Field CF45 . . . . . . 109 D8
Grover St CF37 . . . . 135 B8
Groves Ave SA3 . . . . 122 F4
GROVESEND 43 B6
Groveside Rd NP12 . . . . . . 86 A8
Groveside Villas 9
NP4 . . . . 38 A1
Groves Rd
Neath / Castell-Nedd
SA11 . . . . 71 F5
Newport / Casnewydd
NP20 . . . . 142 D4
Grove St
Gorseinon SA4 . . . . 43 B3
Llanbradach CF83 . . . . 111 F1
Maesteg CF34 . . . . 102 A6
Newbridge / Trecelyn
NP11 . . . . 86 F6
Grove Terr
Abercwmboi CF44 . . . . 53 E5
Bedlinog CF46 . . . . 56 A7
Llanharan CF72 . . . . 153 F3
Penarth CF64 . . . . 207 A4
11 Pontypool / Pont-y-pwl
NP4 . . . . 38 A1
Senghenydd CF83 . . . . 110 E2
Ynysybwl CF37 . . . . 109 A8
Grove The
Aberdare / Aberdâr
CF44 . . . . 29 A1
Barry / Y Barri CF62 . . . . . 214 C2
Bryn NP12 . . . . 85 E4
Cardiff / Caerdydd CF3 . . . 179 C3
Fochriw CF81 . . . . 32 D7
Merthyr Tydfil / Merthyr Tudful
CF47 . . . . 10 D2
Pontypridd CF37 . . . . 109 D6
Swansea / Abertawe SA2 . . 94 F6
The Mumbles / Y Mwmbwls
SA3 . . . . 123 A5
Grove The / Y Gelli
CF48 . . . . 55 C6
Grove Way CF3 . . . . 179 C3
Grove Wlk NP11 . . . . 59 D1
Gruffyd Dr CF83 . . . . 138 A5
Grwyne Pl NP12 . . . . 58 F4
Grwyne Terr NP12 . . . . 58 F4
Guardian Ind Est CF24 . . . 195 F7
Guenever Cl CF14 . . . . 159 D2
Guest Cotts CF48 . . . . 11 B5
Guest Rd CF24 . . . . 195 E4
Guest St CF81 . . . . 32 C7
Guildford Cres CF10 . . . . . 232 C2
Guildford St CF10 . . . . 232 C2
Guildhall Pl / Plas yr
Neuadd CF10 . . . . 232 B2
Guildhall Rd N SA1 . . . . 95 A5
Guildhall Rd S SA1 . . . . 95 A5
Gulf Ind Area CF11 . . . . . . 194 E2
Gull Hollow / Pant Gwylan
CF31 . . . . 168 D3
Gulliver's Cl SA3 . . . . 123 B8
GURNOS
Merthyr Tydfil 10 D4
Ystalfera 2 D7
Gurnos Cty Prim Sch
SA9 . . . . 2 D8
Gurnos Est NP23 . . . . 8 A5
Gurnos Rd
Gowerton / Tre-gwyr
SA4 . . . . 66 B5
Merthyr Tydfil / Merthyr Tudful
CF47 . . . . 10 C4
Ystradgynlais SA9 . . . . 2 C7
Guthrie St CF63 . . . . 215 A5
Guy's Rd CF63 . . . . 215 B6
Gwaelod Y Foel CF38 . . . . 156 D8
GWAELOD-Y-GARTH 157 E5
Gwaelodygarth CF47 . . . . . 10 E3
Gwaelodygarth Cl CF47 . . 10 D3
Gwaelod-y-Garth Ind Est
CF15 . . . . 158 A2
Gwaelodygarth Rd
CF47 . . . . 10 D3
Gwaelod-y-Garth Rd
CF37 . . . . 136 C2
Gwaelodywaun Villas
CF81 . . . . 58 B3
Gwalch Y Penwaig
CF62 . . . . 214 F2
Gwalia Cl
Bridgend / Pen-y-Bont ar
Ogwr CF31 . . . . 150 F1
Gorseinon SA4 . . . . 43 D2
Gwalia Cres SA4 . . . . 43 D2
Gwalia Ct
Clydach SA6 . . . . 46 D7
Swansea / Abertawe SA1 . . 95 B5
Gwalia Gr CF37 . . . . 135 F6
Gwalia Rd CF35 . . . . 170 E8
Gwalia Terr
Aberdare / Aberdâr
CF44 . . . . 53 C8
Blaina / Blaenau NP13 . . . . 15 E6
Gorseinon SA4 . . . . 43 D2
Gwan-y-garw CF32 . . . . . 103 F3
Gwar-y-Caeau SA13 . . . . . 125 C8
Gwastad Farm NP13 . . . . . . 16 B1
Gwaun Afan SA12 . . . . 99 F5
Gwaun-Bant CF32 . . . . . . 103 E4
Gwaun Bedw CF39 . . . . . . 107 E2
GWAUN-CAE-
GURWEN 220 E6
Gwauncelyn Inf Sch
CF38 . . . . 135 F1
Gwauncelyn Jun Sch
CF38 . . . . 135 F1
Gwaun Cl CF14 . . . . 176 E4
Gwaunclawdd SA9 . . . . 222 B7
Gwaun Coed CF31 . . . . . . 169 A4
Gwaun Cotts CF72 . . . . . . 172 A8
Gwaun Delyn Cl NP23 . . . . 15 D7
Gwaunfarren Cl CF47 . . . . 10 F4
Gwaunfarren Gdns
CF47 . . . . 10 E3
Gwaunfarren Gr CF47 . . . . 10 E3
Gwaunfarren Prim Sch
CF47 . . . . 10 E3
Gwaunfarren Rd CF47 . . . . 10 E3
Gwaunfelin Wlk 8 NP4 . . 17 D7
Gwaun-Fro CF82 . . . . 84 D7
Gwaun Helyg NP23 . . . . 14 B8
Gwaun Helyg Rd NP23 . . . . . 7 B1
Gwaun Henllan SA18 . . . . . 219 B8
Gwaun-Hyfryd CF83 . . . . . 138 D4
Gwaun Illtuds CF61 . . . . . 210 A7
GWAUN-LEISION 220 D7
Gwaun Llwyfen CF46 . . . . . 83 E3
Gwaunmeisgyn Prim Sch
CF38 . . . . 156 A6
Gwaunmiskin Rd CF38 . . . 156 A6
Gwaun Newydd CF83 . . . . 138 D4
Gwaun Rd CF37 . . . . 135 F6
Gwaunrhydd 2 CF38 . . . . 156 A6
Gwaun-Ruperra Cl
CF72 . . . . 155 D4
Gwaunruperra Rd
CF72 . . . . 155 D4
GWAUN TREODA 177 C3
Gwaun Y Cwrt CF83 . . . . . . 137 D1
Gwaun-y-groes CF72 . . . . 155 F2
Gwawr St CF44 . . . . 53 B8
Gwbert Cl CF3 . . . . 179 E5
Gweithdau-cwm-gors /
Cwmgors Workshops
SA18 . . . . 220 D6
Gwelfor
Cefn Cribwr CF32 . . . . 149 A2
Dunvant SA2 . . . . 93 E8
Llanelli SA14 . . . . 41 E4
Gwel Y Llyn / Lake View
NP44 . . . . 117 A6
Gwenalt Ind Est NP4 . . . . . 61 E8
Gwendoline Pl 13
CF24 . . . . 195 D5
Gwendoline Rd NP11 . . . . 114 F1
Gwendoline St
4 Aberavon SA12 . . . . 99 A1
Blaengarw CF32 . . . . 103 E6
12 Cardiff / Caerdydd
CF24 . . . . 195 D5
Merthyr Tydfil / Merthyr Tudful
CF47 . . . . 10 E3
Nant-y-Moel CF32 . . . . 104 F5
Treherbert CF42 . . . . 50 E2
Gwendoline Terr
Abercynon CF45 . . . . 82 E3
Cwmfelin CF34 . . . . 128 B8
Gwendraeth Pl SA1 . . . . 69 B2
Gwenfo CW Prim Sch
CF5 . . . . 205 A6
Gwenfo Dr CF5 . . . . 205 A7
GWENFO / WENVOE 205 A6
Gwenfron Terr CF40 . . . . . 107 B2
Gwenlais Rd SA4 . . . . 43 E7
Gwenllian St CF63 . . . . . . 215 D6
Gwenllian Terr CF37 . . . . . 135 F4
Gwennol Y Graig CF62 . . . 214 F1
Gwennol Y Mor CF62 . . . . . 214 F2
Gwennyth St CF24 . . . . . . 178 A1
Gwenog Ct CF62 . . . . 214 C5
Gwent CF64 . . . . 207 C5
Gwent Ct
Ebbw Vale / Glyn Ebwy
NP23 . . . . 14 E3
Fleur-de-lis NP12 . . . . 85 A6
Gwent Gdns SA1 . . . . 67 F1
Gwent Gr SA2 . . . . 94 A6
Gwent Ho
4 Cardiff / Caerdydd
CF23 . . . . 178 C2
Port Talbot SA12 . . . . 124 D8
Gwent Rd
Cardiff / Caerdydd
CF5 . . . . 193 B4
Swansea / Abertawe SA1 . . 68 A1
Upper Boat CF37 . . . . 136 D1
Gwent Sh Ctr NP22 . . . . . . 13 E7
Gwent Sq NP44 . . . . 89 E3
Gwent St NP4 . . . . 62 B6
Gwent Terr
Blaina / Blaenau NP13 . . . . 15 E6
Nantyglo NP23 . . . . 8 D1
Porth CF39 . . . . 107 E4
Gwent Way NP22 . . . . 13 D8
Gwerna Cres CF82 . . . . 85 A1
Gwernant SA9 . . . . 221 B7
Gwern Ave CF83 . . . . 110 F2
Gwern-Berthi Rd NP13 . . . . 36 B7
Gwern Einon Rd SA2 . . . . . 94 B3
Gwern Fadog Rd SA6 . . . . . 46 A3
Gwern Heulog CF39 . . . . . 133 D2
Gwernifor St CF45 . . . . 54 D1
Gwern Las NP13 . . . . 36 B6
Gwernllwynchwyth Rd
Birchgrove SA7 . . . . 46 F1
Swansea / Abertawe SA7 . . 69 F8
Gwernllwyn Cl CF48 . . . . . . 11 A4
Gwernllwyn Jun Sch
CF48 . . . . 11 C4
Gwernllwyn Terr CF43 . . . . 80 B4
Gwernllwyn Uchaf CF48 . . . 11 B5
Gwernllyn Rd CF48 . . . . 11 B4
Gwernos SA6 . . . . 46 A2
Gwern Rhuddi Rd
CF23 . . . . 160 D1
Gwern-Rhuddi Rd
CF23 . . . . 178 C8
Gwern-y-Milwr CF83 . . . . . 110 F2
Gwern Y Sant NP12 . . . . . . 85 B7

GWERN-Y-STEEPLE 191 D4
Gwerthdal Pentref Glyn-nedd / Glyn-neath Village Workshops SA11 223 C1
Gwerthonor La
Bargoed / Bargod CF81 58 A1
Gilfach CF81 85 A8
Gwerthonor Pl CF81 58 A1
Gwerthonor Rd
Bargoed / Bargod CF81 58 A1
Gilfach CF81 85 A8
GWEUNYDD MARGAM / MARGAM MOORS 146 E6
Gwili Ave SA14 218 C6
Gwili Terr SA1 68 B1
Gwilym Pl 6 CF63 215 A8
Gwilym Rd SA9 221 B8
Gwilym St CF37 135 F4
Gwilym Terr CF47 30 E7
Gwlad Du Gwyrdd CF39 132 B5
Gwlad-y-Gan SA6 45 D1
Gwladys Pl NP18 118 A3
Gwladys St
Merthyr Tydfil / Merthyr Tudful CF47 10 F3
Pant CF48 11 B7
Penywaun CF44 28 B6
GWRHAY 59 A4
Gwrhyd Rd
Pen-Rhiw-fawr SA9 221 A4
Pontardawe SA8, SA9 220 F2
Rhyd-y-fro SA8 23 D8
Gwyddon Ct NP11 87 B2
Gwyddon Rd NP11 87 C3
Gwydr Cres SA2 94 F6
Gwydr Mews SA2 94 F6
Gwydr Pl SA4 42 D1
Gwydr Sq SA2 94 F6
Gwylfa SA14 41 D6
Gwylfa Rd SA1 67 F1
Gwylym St SA5 68 A2
Gwynant Cres CF23 178 B5
Gwyn Cres / Cilgant Gwyn NP4 37 E7
Gwyn Ct 3 SA12 125 A8
Gwyn Dr CF83 138 A4
Gwyndy Rd SA1 69 A2
Gwynedd Ave
Cymmer / Cymer SA13 75 D3
Swansea / Abertawe SA1 67 F1
Gwynedd Gdns SA1 68 A1
Gwynedd Ho 5 CF23 178 C2
Gwynfan Pl CF47 30 E7
Gwynfe Rd SA4 42 E3
Gwynfi St
Blaengwynfi SA13 76 B6
Swansea / Abertawe SA5 68 C5
Gwynfi Terr CF72 154 A3
Gwynfor Rd SA2 67 E1
Gwynfryn SA18 219 B7
Gwynfryn Rd SA4 19 C3
Gwynfryn Terr CF38 156 D7
Gwyn James Ct CF64 206 E5
Gwynllyw 3 NP44 89 C6
Gwynnes Cl CF47 10 E2
Gwynne Terr SA1 96 A8
Gwyn's Pl SA8 23 F3
Gwyn St
Pontardawe SA8 23 E3
Pontypridd CF37 135 E5
Gwyn Terr
2 Aberavon SA12 125 A8
Crynant / Creunant SA10 226 A7
Gwyrddgoed SA8 23 E6
Gwyrosydd Prim Sch SA5 68 C5
Gwysfa Rd SA6 46 B5
Gwysfryn SA9 221 C6
Gyfeillon Rd CF37 108 E2
Gynol Rd SA9 221 B7
Gynor Ave CF39 107 E5
Gynor Pl CF39 107 E6
Gypsy La
Caerphilly / Caerffili CF15 137 C2
Pontypool / Pont-y-pwl NP4 37 E1
Gyrnosfa SA9 2 D8

H

Habershon St CF24 195 E6
Hackerford Rd CF23 178 C8
Haden St NP4 62 B6
Hadfield Cl CF11 194 C2
Hadfield Rd CF11 194 D2
Hadland Terr SA3 123 A6
Hadrian Cl NP18 118 A3
Hadrian's Cl CF82 84 C7
Hael La SA3 121 B4
Hafan
1 Cardiff / Caerdydd CF5 193 E6
4 Llanelli SA15 40 D4
Hafandeg CF44 28 F6
Hafan Deg
Aberkenfig / Abercynffig CF32 150 C3
Cwmfelin CF34 128 C8
Pencoed CF35 170 D8
Hafan Deg *continued*
Seven Sisters / Blaendulais SA10 222 C3
Hafan Elim CF47 10 F3
Hafan Glyd SA6 46 E8
Hafan Heulog CF37 109 D7
Hafan-Werdd CF83 138 D5
Hafan-y-Bryn CF31 168 C4
Hafan Y Don SA2 93 E8
Hafan-y-Morfa SA15 40 F2
Hafnant SA1 69 D5
HAFOD 68 E2
Hafod CF72 155 A5
Hafodarthen NP13 60 B7
Hafodarthen Rd NP13 60 B7
Hafod Bryan SA14 41 C4
Hafod Cl
Fleur-de-lis NP12 85 A6
Ponthir NP18 117 F6
Hafod Cotts CF48 11 B6
Hafod Court Rd NP44 89 A5
Hafod Ct 14 CF5 194 C6
Hafod Decaf CF33 148 B2
Hafod-fan Rd NP13 36 C3
Hafod-fan Terr NP13 36 C3
Hafod Gdns NP18 117 F6
Hafod Goch CF82 85 A3
Hafod La
Ebbw Vale / Glyn Ebwy NP23 14 E2
Trehafod CF37 108 D3
Hafod Las CF35 170 D7
Hafod Pk SA1 68 D2
Hafod Prim Sch
Swansea / Abertawe SA1 68 D2
Trehafod CF37 108 C2
Hafod Rd
Ponthir NP18 117 F6
Tycroes SA18 218 F6
Hafod St
Cardiff / Caerdydd CF11 232 A1
Pentrebach CF48 31 B3
Swansea / Abertawe SA1 233 B5
Hafod The CF48 11 B6
Hafod Tudor Terr NP11 113 E3
Hafod View Cl / Clos Golwyg Yr Hafod NP23 8 D4
Hafod Wen
Cwmdare CF44 28 C3
Tonyrefail CF39 133 D6
Hafod Wen / Fair Summer Dwelling CF31 168 D3
Hafod-y-Bryn NP11 115 B1
Hafod-y-Mynydd NP22 12 F3
HAFODYRYNYS 60 D3
Hafod-yr-Ynys Rd NP11 60 C2
Hafon Mews NP18 117 F6
Haford St SA13 125 C8
Hafren Ct CF11 194 D7
Hafren Rd CF62 214 E5
Hafren Rd / Heol Hafren NP44 89 A4
Haig Pl
Cardiff / Caerdydd CF5 193 A3
Swansea / Abertawe SA5 67 F4
Hailey Ct CF14 176 F3
Haines Cl CF83 137 E1
Haisbro' Ave NP19 143 E8
Haldane Ct CF83 138 D3
Haldane Pl NP20 117 A2
Haldens The NP44 89 B1
Half Acre Ct / Llys Hanner Erw CF83 138 B5
HALF WAY 41 B6
Halfway Prim Sch SA14 41 A6
Halifax Cl CF24 196 A7
Halifax Terr CF42 50 E3
Hallam Ho SA12 98 A2
Hallbank SA3 123 B4
Hallbank Terr SA3 123 B4
Hall Cl CF33 166 A8
Hall Dr CF33 166 A8
Halle Cl NP19 145 A5
Halley Ct CF62 213 A1
Halliard Ct CF10 195 C3
Hall La SA4 64 D4
Hall St Ind Est NP23 14 E3
Halls Rd NP11 86 E6
Hall's Rd NP11 114 C5
Hall's Road Terr NP11 114 C5
Hall St
Aberdare / Aberdâr CF44 29 A2
8 Ammanford / Rhydaman SA18 219 C7
Blackwood / Coed-Duon NP12 85 F7
Brynamman SA18 220 E8
Ebbw Vale / Glyn Ebwy NP23 14 E2
Llanelli SA15 40 D6
Swansea / Abertawe SA1 233 A5
Halsbury Rd CF5 194 B7
Halstead St NP19 143 E4
Halswell St CF45 82 B6
Halt Cl CF44 224 B1
Halton Cl CF64 217 A8
Halt Rd CF44 224 B1
Halt The CF64 216 A5
Hamadryad Rd CF10 195 A1
Haman Pl CF82 84 C6
Hamilton Ct 15 CF5 194 C6
Hamilton St
Cardiff / Caerdydd CF11 194 E6
Mountain Ash / Aberpennar CF45 54 C3
Newport / Casnewydd NP19 143 F3
Pentrebach CF48 31 A4
Swansea / Abertawe SA1 68 D4
Hamilton Terr CF34 75 C2
Ham La CF61 209 F5
Ham Lane E CF61 210 A5
Ham Lane S CF61 210 A5
Ham La S CF61 209 F5
Ham Manor CF61 210 A5
Ham Manor Cvn Pk CF61 210 A4
Ham Mews CF61 210 A4
Hammond Dr NP19 143 F4
Hammond Way CF23 178 E1
Hampden Ct NP19 144 A3
Hampden Rd NP19 144 A3
Hampshire Ave NP19 144 B2
Hampshire Cl NP19 144 B2
Hampshire Cres NP19 144 B2
Hampstead Wlk CF5 192 F4
Hampton Court Rd CF23 178 E2
Hampton Cres E CF23 160 D1
Hampton Cres W CF23 160 C1
Hampton Pl 26 CF47 30 E8
Hampton Rd CF14 177 D4
Hampton St CF47 30 E8
Hanbury Cl
Caerleon / Caerllion NP18 118 C1
Cardiff / Caerdydd CF14 176 E5
Cwmbran / Cwmbrân NP44 89 E4
Hanbury Gdns NP4 62 A8
Hanbury Rd
Bargoed / Bargod CF81 58 A4
Pontypool / Pont-y-pwl NP4 62 C6
Hanbury Rd / Heol Hanbury NP4 62 A8
Hanbury Sq CF81 58 A4
Hanbury St NP12 85 A7
Handel Ave / Rhodfa Handel SA12 98 B3
Handel Cl
Newport / Casnewydd NP19 145 A5
Penarth CF64 206 F1
Hand Farm Rd NP4 62 F5
Handley Rd CF24 196 A7
Handsworth St NP19 143 F4
Hanfield Pk NP44 90 A4
Hangman's Cross SA3 231 C5
Hankey Pl CF47 30 E7
Hankey Terr CF47 30 E7
Hanley Path 8 NP44 89 C2
Hannah Cl CF14 177 F6
Hannah St
Barry / Y Barri CF63 215 A6
Cardiff / Caerdydd CF10 195 B3
Porth CF39 107 F3
Hannants The SA10 71 C8
Hanover Cl SA3 123 A6
Hanover Ct
Barry / Y Barri CF63 215 D7
Bridgend / Pen-y-Bont ar Ogwr CF31 168 E5
9 Cardiff / Caerdydd CF14 176 F6
Swansea / Abertawe SA2 94 D7
Hanover La SA1 95 A7
HANOVER SQUARE 69 B3
Hanover St
2 Barry / Y Barri CF62 214 F5
Cardiff / Caerdydd CF5 194 C5
Merthyr Tydfil / Merthyr Tudful CF47 10 D2
Swansea / Abertawe SA1 95 B7
Hansom Pl CF11 194 E3
Happy Valley Cvn Pk CF32 184 A8
Harbour Dr CF10 195 C1
Harbour Rd
Barry / Y Barri, Barry Island CF62 214 D2
Barry / Y Barri CF62 214 D3
Harbour View Rd
Penarth CF64 207 A5
Swansea / Abertawe SA1 96 A8
Harbour Winds Ct SA3 123 A4
Harcombe Rd CF40 107 A8
Harcourt Pl NP22 12 D5
Harcourt Rd
Brynmawr NP23 8 B5
Mountain Ash / Aberpennar CF45 54 C3
Harcourt St
Ebbw Vale / Glyn Ebwy NP23 7 D1
Swansea / Abertawe SA1 95 B7
Harcourt Terr
Abertillery / Abertyleri NP13 36 A6
Mountain Ash / Aberpennar CF45 81 F8
New Tredegar NP24 34 A1
Tredegar NP22 13 E6
HARDDFAN 42 A6
Harddfan SA14 41 F6
Harding Ave NP20 117 A3
Harding Cl
Gorseinon SA4 66 A8
Llantwit Major / Llanilltud Fawr CF61 210 C6
Harding Ct 15 CF11 194 D5
Hardingsdown La SA3 228 E2
Hardwicke Ct CF5 194 A8
Hardy Cl
Barry / Y Barri CF62 215 A8
Newport / Casnewydd NP20 142 E1
Hardy Ct 18 NP4 38 A1
Hardy Pl CF24 232 D4
Harebell Cl SA6 46 B4
Harefield Cl CF23 161 B1
Harford Cl CF14 176 E5
Harford Ct SA2 94 C5
Harford Gdns NP22 13 F8
Harford Sq NP23 7 E1
Harford St NP22 13 F8
Hargreaves Dr NP20 117 A3
Harlech Cl
Blackwood / Coed-Duon NP12 58 D1
Dinas Powis / Dinas Powys CF64 206 C3
Swansea / Abertawe SA2 94 B7
Harlech Cl / Clos Harlech
2 NP44 90 A6
Harlech Cres SA2 94 B7
Harlech Ct
Caerphilly / Caerffili CF83 137 D4
4 Cardiff / Caerdydd CF14 177 A6
Harlech Dr
Bassaleg NP10 141 E3
Dinas Powis / Dinas Powys CF64 206 C3
Merthyr Tydfil / Merthyr Tudful CF48 225 E1
Harlech Gdns CF62 214 E8
Harlech Ho CF15 176 C6
Harlech Pl CF44 28 F1
Harlech Rd CF3 179 C3
Harlech Ret Pk NP20 143 A1
Harlech St SA18 220 E7
Harlequin Ct
Cardiff / Caerdydd CF24 195 E8
Newport / Casnewydd NP20 143 B6
Harlequin Dr NP20 143 B6
Harlequin Rd SA12 98 F1
Harlequin Rdbt 3 NP20 143 C6
Harle St / Stryd Harle SA11 71 F8
Harleyford Rd SA4 19 A4
Harlington Rd SA5 68 A2
Harold St / Stryd Harold
4 SA18 219 B7
Harold St
Bryncae CF72 153 F2
Cardiff / Caerdydd CF24 195 E7
7 Cwmbran / Cwmbrân NP44 89 E5
Harold Wlk 6 NP10 142 B4
Harper's Rd / Heol Harper NP4 37 F5
Harpur St CF10 232 B1
Harries Ave SA15 40 C6
Harries La SA15 40 C6
Harries St SA1 95 B8
Harriet St
Aberdare / Aberdâr CF44 28 E4
Cardiff / Caerdydd CF24 195 A8
Penarth CF64 206 F5
Harriet Town 2 CF48 31 B1
Harrington Ct CF5 193 B3
Harrington Pl
3 Swansea / Abertawe SA1 68 D1
Swansea / Abertawe SA1 233 B5
Harrington St SA1 68 D1
Harris Ave CF3 179 D4
Harrismith Rd CF23 178 C1
Harrison Dr CF3 180 A5
Harrison St CF47 10 F4
Harrison Way CF11 206 F8
Harris Rd SA9 221 B7
Harris St
Hirwaun CF44 27 D7
Swansea / Abertawe SA6 68 F8
Harris Terr CF45 81 F7
Harris View CF45 81 F7
Harrogate Rd 2 NP19 143 E8
Harrowby La 3 CF10 195 B2
Harrowby Pl CF10 195 B1
Harrowby St CF10 195 B1
Harrow Cl NP18 117 F4
Harrow Ct 5 CF5 193 E6
Harrow Rd NP19 143 D5
Harry St SA6 45 E1
Hartfield Cl SA2 94 A7
Hart Gdns 16 NP20 143 C3
Hartland Ho CF11 207 A7
Hartland Rd CF3 179 A5
Hartley Pl CF11 194 E3
Hart Pl CF24 196 A8
Hartridge Farm Rd NP18, NP19 144 E4
Hartridge High Sch NP18 144 E4
Hartshorn Ct CF83 138 D3
Hartshorn Ho CF34 102 A3
Hartshorn Terr CF34 75 A2
Harvard Jones Cl / Clos Harvard Jones SA11 71 C4
Harvey Cl NP20 117 A2
Harvey Cres SA12 124 E8
Harvey St
Barry / Y Barri CF63 215 C6
12 Cardiff / Caerdydd CF5 194 C6
Maesteg CF34 102 B3
Hassocks Lea 4 NP44 89 B1
Hastings Ave CF64 206 E4
Hastings Cl CF64 206 E4
Hastings Cres CF3 179 D8
Hastings Pl CF64 206 E4
Hatfield Ct SA5 67 E5
Hathaway Ho SA12 98 F2
Hathaway Pl 4 CF63 215 C8
Hathaway St NP19 143 F4
Hatherleigh NP19 144 B6
Hatherleigh Dr SA3 122 E5
Hatherleigh Rd CF3 179 A3
Hatter St 4 NP23 8 B4
Haul Bryn CF32 104 F6
Haul Fron CF40 107 A2
Haulfryn
Brynmenyn CF32 150 E6
Bryn SA14 41 F6
Clydach NP7 9 D6
Penywaun CF44 28 B6
Pontardawe SA8 23 E5
Haul Fryn
Birchgrove SA7 47 A2
Cardiff / Caerdydd CF14 176 F8
Haulfryn / Sunneyhill CF33 148 E3
Haulfryn / Sunnybank SA10 48 C1
Haulwen CF44 28 D3
Haulwen Rd
Pen-pedair-heol CF82 84 E8
Swansea / Abertawe SA2 67 D1
Havannah St CF10 195 B1
Havant Cl CF62 213 A1
Havard Rd
Abertridwr CF83 136 F7
Llanelli SA14 41 A6
Havard's Row NP22 12 F3
Havelock Pl CF11 194 F3
Havelock St
Cardiff / Caerdydd CF10 232 B2
Llanelli SA15 40 E2
8 Newport / Casnewydd NP20 143 B4
Haven Cl CF48 31 B1
Haven Mdw / Maes Hafen CF31 168 D3
Haven The
Hirwaun CF44 27 D7
Penperlleni NP4 39 E6
Havenwood Dr CF14 159 D3
Haverford Way CF5 193 D4
Havergal Cl SA3 122 D4
Hawarden Bldgs SA1 68 D3
Hawarden Gn / Maes Hawarden 13 NP44 90 B2
Hawarden Pl 6 CF48 31 B1
Hawarden Rd NP19 144 A5
Hawfinch Cl CF23 178 D7
Hawke Cl NP19 144 E7
Hawker Cl CF24 196 A7
Hawkes Ridge NP44 88 F2
Hawkhurst Ct CF36 165 E1
Hawkins Cres NP19 144 E6
Hawks Moor Cl NP10 142 B6
Hawkstone Cl SA3 122 E7
Hawksworth Gr NP19 144 B4
Hawkwood Cl CF5 176 B1
Hawse La NP10 163 C2
HAWTHORN 136 B3
Hawthorn Ave
Gorseinon SA4 43 A2
Hengoed CF82 84 F3
Merthyr Tydfil / Merthyr Tudful CF47 10 D4
Neath / Castell-Nedd SA11 71 F6
Newport / Casnewydd NP19 144 B4
Hawthorn Ave / Rhodfa Ddraenen Wen SA12 98 D6
Hawthorn Cl
Cwmavon / Cwmafan SA12 99 E4
Dinas Powis / Dinas Powys CF64 206 B2
Underwood NP18 145 E6
Hawthorn Cres CF37 136 B4
Hawthorn Ct 1 NP44 90 A5
Hawthorn Dr
Bridgend / Pen-y-Bont ar Ogwr CF35 169 F3
Bryn NP12 85 E3
South Cornelly CF33 165 F5
Hawthorne Ave
Penarth CF64 206 E3
Swansea / Abertawe SA2 94 F7
Hawthorne Fosse NP19 144 B4
Hawthorne Gdns NP18 118 C3
Hawthorne Glade NP13 15 F5
Hawthorne Rd CF46 83 F2
Hawthorne Sq 3 NP19 144 A4

Hawthorne Terr 12 CF44 29 A1
Hawthorn High Sch / Ysgol Uwchradd Hawthorn CF37 136 B3
Hawthorn Hill CF48 10 B7
Hawthorn Inf Sch CF14 176 F3
Hawthorn Jun Sch CF14 176 F3
Hawthorn Pk CF72 153 D3
Hawthorn Pl
Abercarn NP11 114 C6
Porthcawl CF36 183 D8
Hawthorn Prim Sch CF37 136 B4
Hawthorn Rd
Barry / Y Barri CF62 214 C4
Ebbw Vale / Glyn Ebwy NP23 7 D4
Hawthorn CF37 136 B4
Llanharry CF72 172 C5
Pontypool / Pont-y-pwl NP4 62 D1
Hawthorn Rd E CF14 176 F3
Hawthorn Rd W CF14 176 F3
Hawthorn Rise CF44 28 D3
Hawthorns The
Caerleon / Caerllion NP18 118 B3
Cardiff / Caerdydd CF23 178 E6
Cwmbran / Cwmbrân NP44 89 B6
Pant CF48 11 A7
Hawthorn Terr CF45 81 F8
Hawthorn Villas SA9 1 F1
Hawthorn Way CF31 169 D4
Hawtin Pk Ind Est NP12 85 C4
Haxby Ct CF10 232 D1
Haydn Terr CF47 10 F4
Hayes Bridge Rd / Heol Bont-yr-Aes CF10 232 C2
Hayes La CF64 215 D4
Hayes Rd CF64 215 E4
Hayes The / Yr Aes CF10 232 B2
Hayling Cl NP19 143 F7
Haynes Ct NP20 143 D2
Hay's Cres SA11 223 D1
Hayswayn 1 NP44 89 B1
Haywain Ct CF31 169 A3
Hazel Cl
Pontypool / Pont-y-pwl NP4 63 B5
Porthcawl CF36 183 D8
Hazel Ct
Ebbw Vale / Glyn Ebwy NP23 7 C5
Swansea / Abertawe SA2 94 B6
Tonyrefail CF39 133 D6
Hazeldene CF72 172 B5
Hazeldene Ave
Bridgend / Pen-y-Bont ar Ogwr CF31 169 D4
Cardiff / Caerdydd CF24 178 A1
Hazel Dr CF44 28 D2
Hazel Gr
Bedwas CF83 138 F6
Caerphilly / Caerffili CF83 138 C5
Dinas Powis / Dinas Powys CF64 206 B2
Hendreforgan CF39 132 E5
Hazelhurst Ct CF14 176 F3
Hazelhurst Rd CF14 176 F3
Hazell Dr NP10 163 B6
Hazel Mead CF32 150 E6
Hazelmere Rd SA2 94 D7
Hazel Pl CF5 176 D1
Hazel Rd
Penarth CF64 206 F2
Swansea / Abertawe SA2 94 E7
Underwood NP18 145 F7
Hazel Terr
Mountain Ash / Aberpennar CF45 81 F8
Troedyrhiw CF48 31 B2
Hazel Tree Cl CF15 176 A6
Hazeltree Copse SA4 64 B2
Hazel Tree Ct / Cwrt Y Gollen SA10 48 C2
Hazel Tree Ho SA12 98 E6
Hazel Tree Way CF31 169 D5
Hazelwell Rd CF36 182 F8
Hazel Wlk NP18 117 F2
Hazel Wlk / Rhoofa Helys 6 NP44 90 A6
Hazelwood CF32 184 D2
Hazelwood Dr CF3 179 E7
Hazelwood Rd
Neath / Castell-Nedd SA11 71 F8
Newbridge / Trecelyn NP11 87 B8
Hazelwood Row 3 SA12 99 F5
Hazelwood Terr 2 SA12 99 F5
Hazledene Cl CF63 215 A7
Hazlitt Cl
Cardiff / Caerdydd CF3 179 C8
Newport / Casnewydd NP20 142 E1
Headland Cl SA3 122 A5
Headland Rd
Bishopston SA3 122 A5
Swansea / Abertawe SA1 95 F8
Headlands Sch CF64 207 B5
Head of the Hill Ct / Cwrt Pen Y Twyn NP22 6 D2
Heads Of The Valleys Ind Est NP22 12 D4
Heads Of The Valleys Rd
Aberdare / Aberdâr CF44 28 A7
Brynmawr NP23 8 D5
Clydach NP7 9 D6
Dowlais CF48 11 E6
Ebbw Vale / Glyn Ebwy NP23 7 C4
Merthyr Tydfil / Merthyr Tudful CF47, CF48 10 E5
Rhymney / Rhymni NP22 12 C7
Hearte Cl CF62 213 A2
Hearts Of Oak Cotts CF34 102 A7
Heaselands Pl SA2 93 D7
HEATH 177 E4
Heath Ave CF64 206 D5
Heathbrook CF23 178 A6
Heath Cl
Aberdare / Aberdâr CF44 29 D1
Newport / Casnewydd NP19 144 C2
The Mumbles / Y Mwmbwls SA3 122 F6
Heathcliffe Cl 4 CF3 179 D8
Heathcote Cl 7 NP23 8 B4
Heath Cres CF37 109 B1
Heath Ct SA3 122 F6
Heather Ave CF5 193 F6
Heather Cl
Sarn CF32 150 E3
Tonypandy CF40 106 F6
Tredegar NP22 6 F1
Heather Cres SA2 94 B6
Heather Ct NP44 88 F1
Heather Ct / Llys Y Grug 2 CF36 182 F7
Heather Rd
Merthyr Tydfil / Merthyr Tudful CF47 10 C5
Newport / Casnewydd NP19 143 F7
Heatherslade Cl
Southgate SA3 121 A3
The Mumbles / Y Mwmbwls SA3 123 B4
Heatherslade Rd SA3 121 A4
Heathers The CF62 214 D5
Heatherview Rd CF37 109 E2
Heather Way
7 Cardiff / Caerdydd CF5 193 D8
Porth CF39 108 A3
Heathfield
Gorseinon SA4 43 A1
Swansea / Abertawe SA1 233 A3
Tredegar NP22 14 A3
Heathfield Ave SA11 223 D1
Heathfield Cl NP23 7 D5
Heathfield Cres CF72 153 E2
Heath Field Ct SA11 223 D1
Heathfield Dr CF62 214 E7
Heathfield Ind Pk SA14 218 C6
Heathfield Pl CF14 177 E2
Heathfield Rd
Cardiff / Caerdydd CF14 177 E2
Pontardawe SA8 23 F6
Heathfield Villas 4 CF37 135 E7
Heathfield Wlk CF81 58 A5
Heath Halt Ct CF23 178 A5
Heath Halt Rd CF14, CF23 178 A5
Heath High Level Sta CF23 178 A5
Heathlands CF82 84 E2
Heathlands The CF39 132 C6
Heath Low Level Sta CF23 178 A5
Heath Mead CF14 178 A4
Heathmont SA12 99 A2
Heath Park Ave CF14 178 A5
Heath Park Cres CF14 178 A4
Heath Park Ct CF14 178 A4
Heath Park Dr CF14 178 A5
Heath Park La
Cardiff / Caerdydd, Cyncoed CF23 178 A5
Cardiff / Caerdydd, Heath CF14 177 D3
Heath Park Way / Ffordd Parc Y Mynydd Bychan CF14 177 F3
Heath Rd NP12 85 D4
Heath St CF11 194 E5
Heath Terr
4 Pontypridd CF37 109 B1
Porth CF39 107 F7
Heathway CF14 177 E5
Heathwood Ct CF14 177 E5
Heathwood Gr CF14 178 A4
Heathwood Rd
Cardiff / Caerdydd CF14 177 E5
The Mumbles / Y Mwmbwls SA3 123 A8
Hebbles La CF63 215 B7
Hebron Cl SA6 46 D7
Hebron Rd SA6 46 D7
Hebron Villas CF45 82 C6
Hector Ave NP11 60 B3
Hedd Aberth SA10 222 D4
Heddfaen N CF23 178 F7
Heddfaen S CF23 178 F7
Heddfan NP23 8 C5
Heddwch Cl CF48 11 A6
Hedel Rd CF11 194 A6
Hedgemoor CF31 169 D4
Hedley Terr SA15 40 D6
Heilbronn Way SA12 99 A1
Helen Pl CF24 195 D7
Helen's Rd SA11 71 D5
Helen St CF24 195 D7
Helford Sq NP20 116 D2
Helig Fan CF33 148 B1
Helios Dr / Rhodfa Helios SA12 98 C5
Hellas Dr CF62 214 C8
Helol Y Plas / Grange Rd NP44 89 F2
Helpstone Terr NP4 62 A7
Helwick Cl SA3 123 A5
Hemingway Rd / Heol Hemingway CF10 195 C2
Henderson Rd NP23 8 A4
HENDRE 169 F8
Hendre
Caerphilly / Caerffili CF83 137 F6
Dunvant SA2 93 D8
Dyffryn Cellwen SA10 222 F5
Ebbw Vale / Glyn Ebwy NP23 7 E1
Hendre Ave CF32 104 E4
Hendrecafn Rd CF40 106 F4
Hendre Cl
Cardiff / Caerdydd CF5 194 A8
Llangennech SA14 42 A7
Hendre Cres SA14 42 B7
Hendre Ct NP44 115 F8
Hendredenny Dr CF83 137 D4
HENDREDENNY PARK 137 C4
Hendredenny Park Prim Sch / Ysgol Gynradd Parc Hendredenni CF83 137 D4
Hendrefadog St CF43 80 C4
Hendre Farm Ct NP19 144 F6
Hendre Farm Dr NP19 144 F5
Hendre Farm Gdns NP19 144 E5
Hendrefoilan Ave SA2 94 B7
Hendrefoilan Cl SA2 94 A7
Hendrefoilan Ct SA2 94 B8
Hendrefoilan Dr SA2 94 A7
Hendrefoilan Prim Sch SA2 93 F7
Hendre-Foilan Rd SA2 94 B8
Hendrefoilan Student Village SA2 94 A8
HENDREFORGAN 132 C6
Hendreforgan Cres CF39 132 C5
Hendreforgan Prim Sch / Ysgol Gynradd Hendreforgan CF39 132 C5
Hendre Gdns CF5 194 A8
Hendregwilym CF40 106 F3
Hendre Inf Sch CF83 137 E4
Hendre Isaf SA14 41 D4
Hendre Jun Sch CF83 137 E4
Hendreladus SA9 222 A5
Hendremawr Cl SA2 94 C8
Hendre Owain SA2 94 C8
Hendre Owen Rd SA13 74 D4
Hendre Pk SA14 42 A7
Hendre Rd
Abertridwr CF83 136 E7
Cardiff / Caerdydd CF3 179 E5
Llangennech SA14 42 B7
Pencoed CF35 170 B8
Tycroes SA18 218 F6
Hendre Rd / Heol Hendre
4 Glanaman SA18 220 B8
Llanelli SA14 41 D4
Hendre Selaig CF42 50 D3
Hendre Terr 3 CF40 107 A4
Hendre The NP19 144 E5
Hendre Vale / Pant Hendre CF35 170 B8
Hendrewen Rd CF42 50 C2
HENDY 19 A5
Hendy Cl SA2 94 B4
Hendy Cty Prim Mixed Sch SA4 19 A4
Hendy Ind Est SA4 19 A4
Hendy Rd SA4 64 F4
Hendy St CF23 178 B1
Heneage Dr SA2 94 B1
Henfaes Rd SA11 49 C2
Henfaes Terr SA11 49 C2
Hen Felin
Pontardawe SA8 24 B5
Ystradgynlais SA9 2 C7
Henfron CF83 137 E6
HENGOED 85 A3
Hengoed Ave CF82 85 A4
Hengoed Cl 10 CF5 193 C4
Hengoed Cres CF82 84 F4
Hengoed Hall Cl CF82 84 F3
Hengoed Hall Dr CF82 84 F4
Hengoed Hall Gdns CF82 84 F4
Hengoed Parc CF82 85 A3
Hengoed Prim Sch CF82 84 F3
Hengoed Rd
Hengoed CF82 84 F3
Pen-pedair-heol CF82 84 E6
Hengoed Sta CF82 85 A2
Hen Heol / Old Rd
Neath / Castell-Nedd SA10 70 F7
Skewen / Sciwen SA10 71 A7
Henke Ct CF10 195 C3
HENLLYS 115 F7
Henllys CF39 133 E8
Hen Llys SA1 233 B2
Henllys CW Prim Sch NP44 88 F1
Henllys La NP44 115 F7
Henllys Rd CF23 178 C7
Henllys Village Rd NP44 115 F8
Henllys Way / Ffordd Henllys
Cwmbran / Cwmbrân NP44 89 C2
Cwmbran / Cwmbrân NP44 115 F8
Henneuadd SA9 222 C7
Hennoyadd Rd SA9 222 C7
Hen Orsaf Yr Heddlu 7 SA6 68 F8
Hen Parc Ave SA2 93 B5
Hen Parc La SA2 93 C4
Henrhyd Falls* SA10 223 A6
Henrietta St SA1 95 B6
Henry Morgan Cl NP10 163 F6
Henry Richard St CF48 55 C8
Henry St
Aberdare / Aberdâr CF44 53 C8
Bargoed / Bargod CF81 57 F4
Barry / Y Barri CF63 215 D6
Cardiff / Caerdydd CF10 195 B3
Mountain Ash / Aberpennar CF45 54 D3
16 Neath / Castell-Nedd SA11 71 E7
Pontypridd CF37 109 A2
Henry Wood Cl NP19 144 C4
Henry Wood Wlk NP19 144 C4
Henshaw St SA12 124 F8
Hensol Cl NP10 142 B6
Hensol Cl / Clos Hensol 7 NP44 90 A3
Hensol Rd CF72 173 C5
Hensol Villas CF72 173 E3
Henson St NP19 143 F4
Henwaun Bglws NP13 15 E3
Henwaun St NP13 15 E3
Henwysg Cl CF37 109 A2
Heol Aaron SA9 2 D8
Heol Abaty Abbey Rd NP44 89 E2
Heol Abaty / Abbey Rd NP44 89 E2
Heol Aberavon / Aberavon Rd SA12 98 E2
Heol Abervan / Abervan Rd CF48 55 C7
Heol Abram SA9 2 D8
Heol Adam CF82 84 B8
Heol Adare CF32 150 D5
Heolaelfryn CF32 130 E4
Heol-Ael-y-Bryn NP23 7 C3
Heol Aer CF14 177 C8
Heol Afon / Afon Rd SA14 42 C8
Heol Albert / Albert Rd NP4 37 D5
Heol Albion / Albion Rd SA12 98 D7
Heol Alfred CF43 79 B8
Heol Alltygrug / Alltygrug Rd SA9 2 B7
Heol Amlwch CF14 177 B3
Heol Amman / Amman Rd
Brynamman SA18 220 E8
Glanaman SA18 219 F8
Heol Aneurin
Caerphilly / Caerffili CF83 137 E6
Tonyrefail CF39 133 D5
Heol Aneurin Bevan NP22 12 E5
Heol Ap Gethin NP23 15 E7
Heol Ap Pryce CF38 156 A6
Heol Aradur CF5 176 D3
Heol Arfryn CF32 129 E2
Heol Argoed / Argoed Rd SA18 219 C5
Heol Arthur Fear NP13 15 E5
Heol Aur SA14 41 C8
Heol Awstin SA5 67 E5
Heol Bach / Bach Rd 7 SA12 98 B3
Heol Barcud SA7 70 B8
Heol Barri CF83 137 F5
Heol Barri / Barry Rd SA18 220 D7
Heol Bayliss / Bayliss Rd CF32 150 F4
Heol Bedw CF39 107 E2
Heol Bedwas SA7 47 A1
Heol Berllan CF83 138 B5
Heol Berry CF15 158 A3
Heol Bethlehem / Bethlehem Rd SA7 70 F7
Heol Beulah CF83 137 F8
Heol Beuno NP4 63 A5
Heol Bevin / Bevin Ave SA12 124 D8
Heol Billingsley CF15 157 F8
Heol Blakemore CF14 176 F5
Heol Blenhein / Blenheim Rd NP44 89 C2
Heol Bont-yr-Aes / Hayes Bridge Rd CF10 232 C2
Heol Bonymaen CF48 11 A6
Heol Booker CF14 176 F5
Heol Bradford CF32 129 E2
Heol Briallu SA6 45 F2
Heol Brithdir SA7 70 B8
Heol Briwnant CF14 159 B1
Heol Broadland 3 CF62 214 E4
Heol Broadweir / Broadweir Rd 4 NP44 89 E2
Heol Broch SA7 70 B8
Heol Brofiscin CF72 174 B7
Heol Bronallt / Bronallt Rd SA4 19 A5
Heol Broom CF33 165 E7
Heol Bro Wen CF83 138 B5
Heol Brown SA18 219 A5
Heol Brunel / Brunel Rd NP44 89 A2
Heol Brychan
Bargoed / Bargod CF81 57 E3
7 Merthyr Tydfil / Merthyr Tudful CF48 225 F2
Heol Bryn CF33 165 E8
Heol Brynamman / Brynamman Rd SA18 220 D7
Heol Brynbrain SA9 221 B8
Heol Bryn Cawr / Bryncwar Rd SA14 218 D8
Heol Bryncelyn SA14 41 C8
Heol Bryncwils CF32 150 E3
Heol Bryncwtyn CF35 170 D6
Heol Bryncyn SA7 47 A1
Heol Bryn Fab CF46 83 D3
Heol Brynglas
Bridgend / Pen-y-Bont ar Ogwr CF31 169 A5
Cardiff / Caerdydd CF14 177 A8
Gorseinon SA4 66 B8
Heol Bryn Glas CF38 156 D7
Heol Bryngwili SA14 218 A7
Heol Bryngwyddyl CF48 10 A3
Heol Bryn-gwyn SA13 227 C2
Heol Bryn Gwyn CF44 28 A6
Heol Bryn Hebog 4 CF48 225 F2
Heol Bryn Heulog CF38 156 D8
Heol Brynhyfryd CF38 156 B7
Heol Bryn-Lloi / Bryn-Lloi Rd 5 SA18 220 A8
Heol Bryn Man 1 CF48 225 F2
Heol Brynmor John CF38 135 E1
Heol Brynna SA11 72 C5
Heol Brynnau CF44 28 C3
Heol Bryn Padell CF48 225 F2
Heol Bryn Seion SA10 222 F5
Heol Bryn Selu 2 CF48 225 F2
Heol Brynteg
Tonyrefail CF39 133 B4
Ystrad Mynach CF82 111 E8
Heol Brython SA2 93 B8
Heol Buckley SA15 40 E8
Heol Buddug / Victoria St NP44 89 E2
Heol Burrows / Burrows Rd SA12 98 D6
Heol Cadifor SA5 68 B6
Heol Cadnawes SA6 45 F4
Heol Cadrawd CF34 128 D6
Heol Cae Bach CF83 138 B5
Heol Cae Celynnen CF83 138 B5
Heol Cae Copyn SA4 42 E1
Heol Cae-Defaid CF34 102 C3
Heol Cae-Derwen CF81 57 E3
Heol Cae Fan Heulog CF83 138 B5
Heol Caeglas CF32 150 D5
Heol Cae Glas CF32 150 F3
Heol Cae-Glas SA7 69 F6
Heol-cae-globe SA4 65 F8
Heol-Cae-Gurwen SA18 220 D6
Heol Cae Gwyn
Caerphilly / Caerffili CF83 137 E1
St Brides Major / Saint-y-Brid CF32 185 C2
Heol Cae Maen CF83 138 B5
Heol Cae Morfa / Cae Morfa Rd SA12 98 C2
Heolcae'r-Bont
Margam Moors / Gweunydd Margam SA13 146 E12
Port Talbot SA13 147 A8
Heol Caer Bryn / Cae'r Bryn Rd SA14, SA18 218 E8
Heol Cae Rhosyn SA7 47 A1
Heol Caerhys CF14 177 C7
Heol Caerlan CF38 155 F6
Heol Caerllion SA6 46 B5

- Heol Caerwent / Caerwent Rd NP4 38 D1
- Heol Caetyla CF35 169 F4
- Heol Cae Tynewydd SA4 42 F1
- Heol Calch SA11 223 F5
- Heol Calfin SA5 67 E4
- Heol Cambrensis CF33 148 A2
- Heol Camddwr CF23 161 B1
- Heol Camlan SA7 47 A1
- Heol Camlas SA12 99 E6
- Heol Canola CF32 150 F4
- Heol Capel CF39 133 C6
- Heol Caradoc
  - Bargoed / Bargod CF81 57 E3
  - Penywaun CF44 28 C6
- Heol Caredig SA11 49 D3
- Heol Carnau CF5 193 D3
- Heol Carne CF14 177 C4
- Heol Carodog SA13 125 D7
- Heol Casnewydd / Newport Rd NP44 117 A6
- Heol Castell CF32 149 A2
- Heol Castell Coety CF31 169 A8
- Heol Castellnedd / Neath Rd SA9 2 F6
- Heol Cattwg
  - Cardiff / Caerdydd CF14 177 B3
  - Gelligaer CF82 84 D6
- Heol Catwg SA10 48 D2
- Heol Cawrdaf CF38 156 A6
- Heol Cefni SA6 68 E8
- Heol Cefn On CF14 160 A3
- Heol Cefn Ydfa
  - Coytrahen CF32 150 B8
  - Maesteg CF34 101 F1
- Heol Cefn-yr-Hendy CF72 173 C7
- Heol Ceiniog CF63 214 F4
- Heol Ceiriog CF39 80 D1
- Heol Celyn
  - Church Village CF38 156 F8
  - Cimla SA11 72 B6
  - Hengoed CF82 85 A3
- Heol Celynen CF37 109 D6
- Heol Celynnen CF72 172 D5
- Heol Cerdin CF34 128 D8
- Heol Ceri SA5 66 D3
- Heol Ceulanydd CF34 75 A2
- Heol Chappell CF14 176 F5
- Heol Chopin / Chopin Rd 4 SA12 98 B3
- Heol Chudleigh CF3 179 F5
- Heol Cilffrydd CF63 215 A4
- Heol Cleddau SA5 66 D3
- Heol Cledwyn SA7 47 A1
- Heol Clwyddau CF38 156 A5
- Heol Clyd CF83 137 D5
- Heol Coch CF31 169 D5
- Heol Coedcae CF81 57 E3
- Heol Coed Cae CF14 177 C3
- Heol Coed Cae Ganol / Middle Coedcae Rd NP4 17 D6
- Heol Coed Leyshon CF32 150 B8
- Heol Coflorna CF46 83 C6
- Heol Collen CF5 193 A2
- Heol Copperworks / Copperworks Rd SA15 40 D3
- Heol Coroniad CF38 156 A7
- Heol Corswigen CF63 215 B8
- Heol Cove / Cove Rd SA12 98 D1
- Heol Cowgl / Cowell Rd SA18 220 C7
- Heol Crawford / Crawford Rd SA12 98 C7
- Heol Creigiau CF38, CF15 156 D3
- Heol Crochendy CF15, CF37 136 E1
- Heol-Croeserw SA13 75 D4
- Heol Croes Faen CF36 165 F1
- Heol-Croesty CF35 170 D6
- Heol Croes Y De / Southcross Rd 9 SA12 98 C2
- Heol Cronfa CF37 109 F4
- Heol Cropin SA14 41 C8
- Heol Cross Hands / Cross Hands Rd SA14 218 B8
- Heol-Crwys SA12 99 E6
- Heol Crwys SA4 43 B4
- Heol Crymlyn / Crymlyn Rd SA7, SA10 70 B6
- Heol Cwarrel Clark CF83 137 E7
- Heol Cwmaman / Cwmamman Rd SA18 220 B8
- Heol Cwm Felin / Cwm Felin Rd SA18 219 C5
- Heol Cwmfferws / Cwmfferws Rd SA18 218 F6
- Heol Cwm Ifor CF83 137 D6
- Heol Cwm Mawr SA12 99 D6
- Heol Cwper / Coopers Rd SA18 218 E5
- Heol Cwrdy CF32 150 E4
- Heol Cwrt / Court Rd NP44 90 A1
- Heol Cydweli / Kidwelly Rd 11 NP44 90 B2
- Heol Cynan
  - Gorseinon SA4 43 B4
  - Pont Rhyd-y-cyff CF34 128 D6
- Heol Cynllan CF72 154 A2
- Heol Cynwyd CF34 128 D6
- Heol Dafydd CF72 173 A7
- Heol Dalton / Dalton Rd SA12 98 D1
- Heol Dalycopa SA7 69 E6
- Heol Daniel
  - Cwmllynfell SA9 221 B7
  - Llanelli SA14, SA15 40 F8
- Heol Dan-y-Graig / Dan-y-Graig Rd SA10 71 B8
- Heol Danyrodyn CF15 157 C1
- Heol Davies Andrews / Davies Andrews Rd SA11 49 B1
- Heol Dderwen
  - Church Village CF38 136 A2
  - Llanelli SA15 40 F4
- Heol Ddeusant CF38 155 F6
- Heol Ddu
  - Ammanford / Rhydaman SA18 219 D8
  - Beddau CF72 134 C1
  - Swansea / Abertawe SA5 68 B7
  - Tycroes SA18 218 F5
- Heolddu Ave CF81 57 E4
- Heolddu Comp Sch / Ysgol Gyfun Heolddu CF81 57 E4
- Heolddu Cres CF81 57 F4
- Heolddu Dr CF81 57 E4
- Heolddu Gn CF81 57 F4
- Heolddu Gr CF81 57 F4
- Heolddu Rd
  - Bargoed / Bargod CF81 57 F4
  - Gelligroes NP12 85 F2
- Heol Deg CF38 136 A1
- Heol Degwm CF33 165 E8
- Heol Deiniol NP4 63 A5
- Heol Dennant CF5 193 E8
- Heol Deri CF39 133 B4
- Heol Derlwyn CF14 177 B8
- Heol Derw
  - Brynmawr NP23 8 A5
  - Hengoed CF82 84 F3
- Heol Derwen
  - Cimla SA11 72 B5
  - Cross Hands SA14 218 C7
  - Pontypool / Pont-y-pwl NP4 63 A5
- Heol Deva CF5 193 C3
- Heol Dewi
  - Brynna CF72 153 C3
  - Hengoed CF82 85 A2
- Heol Dewi Sant
  - Barry / Y Barri CF62 214 E5
  - Bettws CF32 129 D3
  - Cardiff / Caerdydd CF14 177 D6
  - Penllergaer SA4 44 A2
- Heol Dewi Sant / St David's Rd 3 SA12 124 E8
- Heol Dinbych SA15 40 F4
- Heol Dinefwr / Dynevor Rd SA18 220 B7
- Heol Dolfain SA6 46 A4
- Heol Dolwen CF14 177 C4
- Heol Don CF14 176 F4
- Heol Don Ct CF14 176 F4
- Heol Dowlais CF38 156 E5
- Heol Draenen Wen CF5 193 A2
- Heol Drenewydd / Newtown Rd NP4 39 F6
- Heol Drewi CF33, CF36 165 E4
- Heol Drummau / Drummau Rd SA11 71 A7
- Heol Dulais SA7 47 A1
- Heol Dwr SA18 219 E7
- Heol Dwy Loc / Two Locks Rd NP44 89 D1
- Heol Dwynwen / Dwynnen Rd CF31 168 B3
- Heol Dwyrain CF31 169 A4
- Heol Dyddwr SA11 49 D3
- Heol Dyfan SA6 45 F3
- Heol Dyfed
  - Beddau CF38 155 F5
  - Cardiff / Caerdydd CF14 177 D5
  - Gorseinon SA4 43 B4
  - Maesteg CF34 102 D2
  - Penrhys CF43 80 A2
  - Penywaun CF44 28 C6
- Heol Dyffryn / Dyffryn Rd SA18 219 A7
- Heol Dyfodwg CF72 155 D4
- Heol Dyhewydd CF38 156 B7
- Heol Dylan
  - Gorseinon SA4 43 B4
  - North Cornelly CF33 165 F8
- Heol Dynys SA5 67 E5
- Heol Dywyll SA6 46 C7
- Heol Ebwy CF5 193 D4
- Heol Edward Lewis CF82 84 C6
- Heol Edwards CF15 158 A8
- Heol Eglwys
  - Cardiff / Caerdydd CF5 193 E4
  - Coelbren SA10 222 F6
  - Pen-y-fai CF31 150 C1
- Heol Eglwys *continued*
  - Ystradgynlais SA9 1 F1
- Heol Eglwys / Church Rd SA10 222 C3
- Heol Eglwys Fair / St Mary St CF10 232 B2
- Heol Eifion SA4 43 C2
- Heol Eifion Wyn SA7 69 E6
- Heol Eirlys SA6 45 F2
- Heol Eithin CF35 170 D5
- Heol Eithrim SA6 46 D8
- Heol Elan NP23 7 B5
- Heol Elfed
  - Gorseinon SA4 43 B4
  - Llanelli SA14 41 C5
  - Maesteg CF34 102 D2
  - Swansea / Abertawe SA7 69 E6
- Heol Elli SA15 40 F5
- Heol Emrys SA5 68 A5
- Heol Erwin CF14 159 C1
- Heol Erw-y-Rhos CF83 138 B5
- Heol Eryr Mor CF62 214 F2
- Heol Esgyn
  - Cardiff / Caerdydd CF23 178 A6
  - Neath / Castell-Nedd SA10 48 B1
  - Rhigos CF44 26 C8
- Heol Evan Wynne CF81 12 F1
- Heol Ewenny CF35 170 D6
- Heol Fach
  - Ammanford / Rhydaman SA18 218 E8
  - Bargoed / Bargod CF81 57 F2
  - Caerphilly / Caerffili CF83 137 E4
  - Nantgarw CF15 158 A8
  - North Cornelly CF33 165 F8
  - Pencoed CF35 170 D8
  - Sarn CF32 150 F4
  - Swansea / Abertawe, Llangyfelach SA5 45 B3
  - Swansea / Abertawe, Waun-Gron SA5 68 C6
- Heol Faen CF34 102 D2
- Heol Faenor CF38 155 F5
- Heol Fain
  - Sarn CF32 150 E3
  - Wick / Y Wig CF71 198 B5
- Heol Fair CF5 177 A1
- Heol-Fair CF36 183 A7
- Heol Fargoed CF81 57 F2
- Heol Fawr
  - Caerphilly / Caerffili CF83 137 D6
  - Nelson CF46 83 F2
  - North Cornelly CF33 166 A7
  - Tredomen CF46 84 A1
  - Tredomen CF46 84 B1
- Heol Fawr / High St CF10 232 B2
- Heol Fechan CF31 168 B6
- Heol Fedw SA6 45 F3
- Heol Felen SA18 220 B8
- Heol Felyn Fach CF32 150 C5
- Heol Fer CF83 137 E6
- Heol Ffaldau CF31 169 B6
- Heol Ffion SA4 43 C2
- Heol Fforest / Fforest Rd SA4 19 B5
- Heol Ffranc SA10 70 C6
- Heol Ffrwd Philip CF38 156 F5
- Heol Ffynnon
  - Llanelli SA15 40 F4
  - Loughor SA4 42 E1
- Heol Ffynnon Wen CF14 176 F8
- Heol Ficeroi / Vicarage Rd 7 SA18 220 B8
- Heol Fiola / Viola Rd SA12 98 C2
- Heol Fioled CF63 205 B1
- Heol Folland / Folland Rd SA18 220 B8
- Heol Frank SA5 68 B5
- Heol Frederic / Frederick St CF10 232 B3
- Heol Gabriel CF14 177 C3
- Heol Gadlys CF31 169 A7
- Heol Gaer SA10 223 A5
- Heol Gam
  - Bridgend / Pen-y-Bont ar Ogwr CF31 168 E2
  - Pentyrch CF15 157 B1
- Heol Ganol
  - Brynmawr NP23 8 B4
  - Caerphilly / Caerffili CF83 137 F3
  - Nant-y-Moel CF32 104 F6
  - Sarn CF32 150 E4
- Heol Gelli Crug / Gelli-Crug Rd NP13 36 B6
- Heol Gelli Lenor CF34 101 F1
- Heol Gellilodra CF32 130 A3
- Heol Gelynen
  - Brynamman SA18 220 D8
  - Penywaun CF44 28 A6
- Heol Gelynog 4 CF38 156 A6
- HEOLGERRIG 10 A1
- Heolgerrig
  - Abertillery / Abertyleri NP13 36 B5
  - Heolgerrig CF48 10 A1
- Heol Gerrig
  - Merthyr Tydfil / Merthyr Tudful CF48 29 F8
- Heol Gerrig *continued*
  - Swansea / Abertawe SA5 68 C6
- Heolgerrig Prim Sch CF48 30 A8
- Heol Ger-y-Felin CF61 210 A7
- Heol Gethin CF82 85 A4
- Heol Giedd
  - Cwmgiedd SA9 1 F3
  - Ystradgynlais SA9 1 F2
- Heol Glandulais CF23 160 F1
- Heol Glan Elai CF72 173 A6
- Heol Glanllechau SA8 23 E3
- Heol Glannant
  - Bettws CF32 129 D3
  - Tonypandy CF40 107 B1
- Heol Glan-Nant SA6 46 A4
- Heol Glanrheidol CF10, CF11 195 B2
- Heol Glanrhyd / Glanrhyd Rd SA9 2 E7
- Heol Glantawe SA9 2 F8
- Heol Glan-yr-Afon NP11 113 C3
- Heol Glaslyn CF23 161 B1
- Heol Glasnant SA2 93 F7
- Heol Gledyr CF83 138 A2
- Heol Gleien SA9 1 A2
- Heol Glyn CF83 137 F5
- Heol Glyncoch CF39 132 D5
- Heol Glyndernwen SA8 23 E3
- Heol Glynderwen SA10 48 C1
- Heol Glyn Derwen SA10 48 C1
- Heol Glyndwr CF31 169 D6
- Heol Glyn-Dyfal SA5 20 F4
- Heol Glyn / Glyn Rd SA18 220 D8
- Heol Goch CF15 157 E2
- Heol Godfrey SA18 220 D8
- Heol Goedog CF32 149 B2
- Heol Goffa SA15 40 E7
- Heol Golff / Golf Rd
  - Pontypool / Pont-y-pwl NP4 63 B4
  - Port Talbot SA12 98 D1
- Heol Gordon / Gordon Rd 6 SA12 98 C2
- Heol Goring / Goring Rd SA15 40 D6
- Heol Goronwy CF39 80 D1
- Heol Gorsaf / Station Rd NP23 14 F2
- Heol Gors Ddu / Gors Ddu Rd SA14 218 D8
- Heol Gors Goch / Gors Goch Rd SA18 220 D8
- Heol Graig-Felen SA6 46 D8
- Heol Graig Wen CF83 137 E6
- Heol Greenhill / Greenhill Rd NP44 89 D4
- Heol Greenmeadow / Greenmeadow Way NP44 89 C3
- Heol Greenwood / Greenwood Rd SA12 98 D7
- Heol Grenig / Grenig Rd SA18 220 B6
- Heol Groeswen CF37 136 D3
- Heol Gron SA9 2 D8
- Heol Gruffydd SA5 67 F5
- Heol Grug SA6 45 E2
- Heol Gwalia SA14 41 C5
- Heol Gwanwyn SA7 69 F7
- Heol Gwaun Rhos CF83 138 B5
- Heol Gwell SA5 68 D5
- Heol Gwenallt SA4 43 B4
- Heol Gwendoline 4 CF62 214 E4
- Heol Gwent CF14 177 D5
- Heol Gwernen
  - Cwmrhydyceirw SA6 46 A3
  - Swansea / Abertawe SA6 45 F3
- Heol Gwerthyd CF63 205 A1
- Heol Gwili
  - Gorseinon SA4 43 B4
  - Llanelli SA14 41 D5
  - Swansea / Abertawe SA7 69 E6
- Heol Gwilym CF5 176 D1
- Heol Gwlad yr Haf / Somerset Rd NP44 89 F4
- Heol Gwrangfryn CF44 26 C8
- Heol Gwrgan
  - Beddau CF38 155 F6
  - Cardiff / Caerdydd CF14 177 B5
- Heol Gwyndaf CF14 177 F7
- Heol Gwynedd CF14 177 D5
- Heol Gwyn Lliw NP23 7 F3
- Heol Gwynno CF72 155 D4
- Heol Gwyr SA15 40 F4
- Heol Gwyrosydd SA5 68 B5
- Heol Gwys SA9 221 C6
- Heol Gylfinir CF62 214 F2
- Heol Hafdy SA7 69 F7
- Heol Hafren / Hafren Rd NP44 89 A4
- Heol Hanbury / Hanbury Rd NP4 62 A8
- Heol Harlech CF5 194 A8
- Heol Harper / Harper's Rd NP4 37 F5
- Heol Harri Lewis CF46 83 D3
- Heol Haulfryn CF39 133 B4
- Heol Haydn SA18 219 B7
- Heol Heddwch
  - Neath / Castell-Nedd SA10 48 A1
- Heol Heddwch *continued*
  - Seven Sisters / Blaendulais SA10 222 D3
- Heol Helig NP23 8 A4
- Heol Hemingway / Hemingway Rd CF10 195 C2
- Heol Hen
  - Llanelli SA14 41 C4
  - Seven Sisters / Blaendulais SA10 222 C3
- Heol Hendre
  - Bryn-côch SA10 48 C5
  - Cardiff / Caerdydd CF14 177 D8
- Heol Hendre / Hendre Rd
  - 4 Glanaman SA18 220 B8
  - Llanelli SA14 41 D4
- Heol Hendy CF72 173 C7
- Heol Hensol CF38 156 A6
- Heol Herbert SA11 226 D5
- Heol Hermas SA5 68 B6
- Heol Heulog CF39 132 B7
- Heol Hir
  - Cardiff / Caerdydd CF14 159 E3
  - Cardiff / Caerdydd CF14 159 F1
  - Gwaun-Cae-Gurwen SA18 220 E6
- Heol Homfray CF5 193 A3
- Heol Hopcyn John CF35 151 B2
- Heol Horeb CF39 107 E2
- Heol Iago CF81 32 D7
- Heol Iarll / Earl Rd SA13 125 E5
- Heol Ida CF38 156 A7
- Heol Iestyn CF14 177 B5
- Heol Ifor CF14 177 C5
- Heol Illtyd
  - Llantrisant CF72 155 D4
  - Neath / Castell-Nedd SA10 48 D1
- Heol Innes SA15 40 E8
- Heol Ioan CF43 80 A2
- Heol Isaf
  - Beddau CF38 156 B5
  - Brynmawr NP23 8 B4
  - Cardiff / Caerdydd CF14 159 C1
  - Cimla SA11 72 C5
  - 4 Cwmavon / Cwmafan SA12 99 D5
  - Nelson CF46 83 F3
  - Pontypool / Pont-y-pwl NP4 63 A5
  - Radyr CF15 176 C5
  - Tonyrefail CF39 133 C2
  - Trelewis CF46 83 C8
- Heol Isaf Hendy CF72 173 C7
- Heol Iscoed
  - Cardiff / Caerdydd CF14 177 C8
  - Efail Isaf CF38 156 E5
  - Swansea / Abertawe SA5 67 C6
- Heol Iscoed / Iscoed Rd SA4 19 A4
- Heol Islwyn
  - Gorseinon SA4 43 B4
  - Nelson CF46 83 D3
  - Swansea / Abertawe SA5 67 C6
  - Tonyrefail CF39 133 C6
- Heol Is Ty Gwyn / Lower Ty Gwyn Rd NP4 37 E7
- Heol-Jiwbili SA12 99 E5
- Heol Johnson CF72 155 C2
- Heol Jolly / Jolly Rd SA18 220 C8
- Heol Keir Hardie CF44 28 B5
- Heol Klockner NP22 12 D3
- HEOL-LAETHOG 151 E6
- Heol Laethog CF32 151 E5
- Heol Langdon / Langdon Rd
  - Swansea / Abertawe SA1 95 F7
  - Swansea / Abertawe SA1 96 A6
- Heol Langland / Langland Rd SA15 40 E3
- Heol-Las
  - Ammanford / Rhydaman SA18 219 B6
  - Birchgrove SA7 46 F2
- Heol Las
  - Caerphilly / Caerffili CF83 137 E7
  - Coity / Coety CF35 151 E1
  - Cross Hands SA14 218 B8
  - Llantrisant CF72 155 C4
  - Marshfield CF3 180 D6
  - Mawdlam CF33 165 D8
  - North Cornelly CF33 165 E8
  - Pencoed CF35 170 D8
  - Tredomen CF46 111 B8
  - Wick / Y Wig CF71 198 A4
  - Ynysmeudwy SA8 24 A8
- Heol-Las Cl SA7 46 F1
- Heol Las Fawr SA10 226 A8
- Heol Leigh Isaf / Lower Leigh Rd NP4 38 A1
- Heol Letton / Letton Rd 3 CF10 195 B3
- Heol Leubren CF62 205 A1
- Heol Lewis
  - Caerphilly / Caerffili CF83 138 D5
  - Cardiff / Caerdydd CF14 159 C1
- Heol Llan
  - Coity / Coety CF35 151 F3
  - North Cornelly CF33 165 E8

- Heol Llanbedr CF5 191 E6
- Heol Llandeilo / Llandeilo Rd SA14 218 C8
- Heol Llangan CF14 177 B6
- Heol Llangeinor CF32 130 A3
- Heol Llanishen Fach CF14 177 C8
- Heol Llansantffraid CF32 150 E4
- Heol Llantarnam / Llantarnam Cl NP44 89 F2
- Heol Llantarnam / Llantarnam Rd NP44 89 F1
- Heol Llechau CF39 80 D1
- Heol Llidiard CF35 170 F1
- Heol Llinos CF14 159 E4
- Heol Llwyd SA18 219 B8
- Heol Llwyn Bedw SA4 18 F4
- Heol Llwyn Brain CF48 10 A3
- Heol Llwyn Celyn SA10 48 D2
- Heol Llwyncelyn / Llwyncelyn Rd SA18 219 F8
- Heol Llwyn Deri CF48 10 A3
- Heol Llwyn Drysi CF48 10 A3
- Heol Llwyndyrus CF34 128 C6
- Heol Llwyn Gollen CF48 10 A3
- Heol Llwynhendy / Llwynhendy Rd SA14 41 D4
- Heol Llwynon SA10 48 D2
- Heol Llwyn Onnen CF48 10 A3
- Heol Llwynyffynnon CF32 130 A3
- Heol Llyswen CF46 83 E4
- Heol Llywelyn / Llywelyn NP44 89 E3
- Heol Lodwig CF38 156 E8
- Heol Longford / Longford Rd
  - Neath Abbey SA10 71 B8
  - Neath / Castell-Nedd SA10 48 B2
- Heol Lotwen / Lotwen Rd SA18 218 D6
- Heol Lucy / Lucy Rd SA10 70 D7
- Heol Mabon
  - Cardiff / Caerdydd CF14 177 C8
  - Cwmavon / Cwmafan SA12 99 E6
  - Nelson CF46 83 D3
- Heol Madoc
  - Cardiff / Caerdydd CF14 177 C4
  - Pontypool / Pont-y-pwl NP4 63 A5
- Heol Maelon / Maelon Rd CF31 168 B3
- Heol Maendy
  - North Cornelly CF33 165 E8
  - Sarn CF32 150 F3
- Heol Maerdy CF83 138 D4
- Heol Maesbryn SA4 42 F1
- Heol Maesdderwen / Oakfield Rd 5 SA18 220 B8
- Heol Maes Eglwys SA6 45 E4
- Heol Maes Eirwg 14 CF3 179 F6
- Heol Maes Eiwrg CF3 180 A6
- Heol Maesglas / Greenfield Rd 6 SA18 220 B8
- Heol Maes / Maes Rd SA14 42 C8
- Heol Maespica SA9 1 B2
- Heol Maesuchel / Highfield Rd SA18 220 C8
- Heol Maes Y Cerrig SA4 42 E1
- Heol Maes-y-Dre SA9 1 F1
- Heol Maes-y-Gelynen SA6 45 F2
- Heol Maes-yr-Haf CF35 170 D6
- Heol Mair
  - Bridgend / Pen-y-Bont ar Ogwr CF31 150 F1
  - Penrhys CF43 80 A2
- Heol Mansel / Mansel St 15 SA15 40 D4
- Heol Marchog / Knights Rd SA13 125 E3
- Heol Margam / Margam Rd SA13 125 E4
- Heol Marlais SA18 219 B8
- Heol Marlborough / Marlborough Rd NP44 89 A3
- Heol Masarnen / Maple Rd NP4 62 D2
- Heol Mathew CF14 176 F5
- Heol Mayberry / Mayberry Rd SA12 98 D7
- Heol Merioneth CF61 210 C6
- Heol Merlin CF14 177 F7
- Heol Meurig SA9 2 D8
- Heol Miaren
  - Barry / Y Barri CF63 215 C8
  - Swansea / Abertawe SA6 45 F2
- Heol Miaren / Briar Rd SA12 98 C1
- Heol Milborough / Milborough Rd SA9 2 B7
- Heol Miles CF72 155 B2
- Heol Miskin CF72 173 B7
- Heol Moor CF62 214 B4
- Heol Mora / Moorland Rd SA12 124 D8
- Heol Morfa
  - Llanelli SA15 40 F3
  - North Cornelly CF33 166 C8
  - Pyle / Y Pîl CF33 148 C1
- Heol Morfa / Moorland Rd 3 SA12 98 E1
- Heol Morien CF46 83 D3
- Heol Morlais SA4 18 F3
- Heol Morlais / Morlais Rd SA14 42 B7
- Heol Mostyn CF33 148 C1
- Heol Moy / Moy Rd CF48 55 B5
- Heol Muston CF5 193 D6
- Heol Mwrwg SA14 42 B8
- Heol Mwyrdy CF38 155 F6
- Heol Myddfai SA5 20 F2
- Heol Mynydd
  - Church Village CF38 136 A1
  - Cowbridge / Y Bont-Faen CF71 189 F5
  - Pontypridd CF37 110 A4
- Heol Mynydd Bychan CF14 177 D6
- Heol Nant
  - Church Village CF38 135 F1
  - Clyne SA11 226 B3
  - Cwmdare CF44 28 C4
  - North Cornelly CF33 165 E8
  - Pontypridd CF37 109 F4
- Heol Nant Bran SA7 47 A2
- Heol Nant Caiach CF46 83 C6
- Heol Nant Castan CF14 177 B8
- Heol Nantgau CF48 10 A2
- Heol Nant Gelli SA5 68 D5
- Heol Nant Gwinau / Nant Gwineu Rd SA18 220 C8
- Heol Nant-y-Felin SA15 40 E7
- Heol Nant Y Glyn / Nant Y Glyn Rd SA18 219 F8
- Heol Nedd SA11 227 B8
- Heol Nest CF14 177 C5
- Heol Neuadd CF33 166 A7
- Heol Neuadd Cogan CF64 206 E1
- Heol Neuadd Domos CF34 128 C8
- Heol Newydd
  - Cardiff / Caerdydd CF3 179 D4
  - Cefn Cribwr CF32 149 B2
  - Cwmbran / Cwmbrân NP44 89 C6
  - Swansea / Abertawe SA5 67 F5
- Heol Newydd / New Rd
  - Abersychan NP4 37 E7
  - Neath / Castell-Nedd SA10 70 C1
  - Ystradowen SA9 221 C7
- Heol Norman / Norman Rd 3 SA18 219 B7
- Heol Oakfield / Oakfield Rd NP44 89 F1
- Heol Onen NP23 8 A4
- Heol Onnen CF33 165 E8
- Heol Orchwy CF42 78 D7
- Heol Padarn NP4 63 A5
- Heol Pal CF62 214 F2
- Heol Palleg / Palleg Rd SA9 1 C2
- Heol Pandy CF32 129 F2
- Heol Pantglas SA10 48 C5
- Heol Pant Glas SA11 227 B8
- Heol Pant-Glas / Pantglas Rd CF48 55 C6
- Heol Pant Gwyn CF72 172 C5
- Heol Pant Ruthin CF35 170 D6
- Heol Pantycelyn
  - Barry / Y Barri CF62 214 D4
  - Cardiff / Caerdydd CF14 176 F7
- Heol Pantyderi CF5 193 D4
- Heol Pant Y Dwr SA4 42 F2
- Heol Pantyffynnon / Pantyffynnon Rd SA18 219 B6
- Heol Pant-y-Gored CF15 175 A7
- Heol Pant-y-Lliw SA4 44 A6
- Heol Pant-yr-awel CF32 130 D4
- Heol Pant y Rhyn CF14 176 F7
- Heol Parc Glas 3 CF48 225 F2
- Heol Parc Maen CF48 10 A2
- Heol Parc Mawr SA14 218 C7
- Heol Parc-y-Lan CF48 10 A3
- Heol Pardoe CF15 136 F1
- Heol Parry / Parry Rd SA12 98 B3
- Heol Peartree CF62 213 C1
- Heol Pellau / Pellau Rd SA13 125 E5
- Heol Penallta CF82 84 D6
- Heol Penar SA5 68 B6
- Heol Penarth / Penarth Rd CF11 194 E2
- Heol Pencarreg
  - Bargoed / Bargod CF81 57 E3
  - Cardiff / Caerdydd CF14 177 B2
- Heol Pencastell CF33 148 D2
- Heol Pencerdd CF34 102 D2
- Heol Pencoed Isaf / Pen Coed Isaf Rd SA14 42 B4
- Heol Pendarren CF44 26 C8
- Heol Penderyn
  - Bridgend / Pen-y-Bont ar Ogwr CF31 169 D6
  - Neath / Castell-Nedd SA10 48 A1
- Heol Pendyrus CF43 80 B3
- Heol Penfelyn SA6 45 F5
- Heol Penhydd SA13 100 E5
- Heol Penlan
  - Cardiff / Caerdydd CF14 176 F5
  - Neath Abbey SA10 71 A8
  - Neath / Castell-Nedd SA10 48 A1
- Heol Penllwyn CF15 157 B1
- Heol Penmaen 3 CF72 155 D3
- Heol-Pen-Nant CF44 29 C4
- Heol Pen-Nant SA6 46 A4
- Heol Pennar CF5 193 D4
- Heol Penprys SA14 41 E6
- Heol Penrhiw
  - 5 Merthyr Tydfil / Merthyr Tudful CF48 225 F2
  - Mountain Ash / Aberpennar CF45 54 B5
- Heol Penrhiwiau SA8 23 E3
- Heol Pen-Rhiw'r-Eglwys NP12 58 F6
- Heol Pen-Rhiw'r Eglwys NP12 58 E6
- Heol Pen-Tir-Garw SA5 67 F6
- Heol Pentre CF34 101 F1
- Heol Pentre Bach SA4 42 F2
- Heol Pentre Felen SA6 45 C1
- Heol Pentre'r Cwrt CF61 210 A7
- Heol Pentre'r Felin CF61 210 B7
- Heol Pentwyn
  - Cardiff / Caerdydd CF14 176 F7
  - Neath / Castell-Nedd SA10 70 C6
  - Tonyrefail CF39 133 B4
- Heol Pentwyn / Pentwyn Rd NP4 37 F2
- Heol Pentyla
  - Sarn CF32 150 D3
  - Swansea / Abertawe SA7 69 F6
- Heol Pen-y-Beili SA4 42 E1
- Heol-Pen-y-Bryn CF83 158 E5
- Heol Pen-y-Bryn CF43 80 A2
- Heol-Pen-y-Cae NP23 7 C2
- Heol Pen Y Cae SA4 42 F2
- Heol Pen-y-Coed SA11 72 B5
- Heol Penyfai CF14 177 C4
- Heol Pen-y-Foel CF37 109 D6
- Heol Penygarn / Penygarn Rd SA18 218 F5
- Heol Penygroes / Penygroes Rd
  - Ammanford / Rhydaman SA18 218 F8
  - Gorslas SA14 218 C8
- Heol Penylan / Penylan Rd NP4 37 E7
- Heol Pen-y-Parc
  - Llantrisant CF72 155 D3
  - Pontypridd CF37 109 D7
- Heol Pen-y-Scallen SA4 42 E1
- Heol Peredur CF14 159 D2
- Heol Persondy
  - Aberkenfig / Abercynffig CF32 150 D4
  - Bettws CF32 129 D2
  - Sarn CF32 150 D3
- Heol Philip SA9 1 D1
- Heol Phillip SA8 23 E3
- Heol Pibydd Y Dorlan / Sandpiper Rd SA15 40 B6
- Heol Pilipala CF62 213 B1
- Heol Pit-y-Ceiliogod
  - Blackwood / Coed-Duon NP12 58 D1
  - Blackwood / Coed-Duon NP12 58 E2
- Heol Plas Gwyn / Plas-Gwyn Rd SA14 218 D8
- Heol Plas Isaf SA14 42 B7
- Heol Plousane / Plousane Rd CF35 170 D6
- Heol Pont George CF33 148 B2
- Heol Pontprennau CF23 161 A1
- Heol Pont-y-Cwcw NP10 164 A5
- Heol Pont Y Seison CF46 84 C2
- Heol Porth Mawr / Porth Mawr Rd NP44 89 E4
- Heol Powis CF14 177 D5
- Heol Poyston CF5 193 C3
- Heol Pwllypant CF83 138 A6
- Heol Pwllyplaca 16 CF3 179 F6
- Heol Pymmer CF39 133 B4
- Heol Rees CF82 85 A2
- Heol Rhayader CF14 176 E4
- Heol Rhedyn / Bracken Rd 7 SA13 125 E4
- Heol Rheilffordd / Railway Terr SA9 221 B7
- Heol Rheolau / Brecon Rd
  - Abercrave / Abercraf SA9 222 B7
  - Ystradgynlais SA9 222 A5
- Heol Rhos CF83 137 D3
- Heol Rhos Las CF48 10 A3
- Heol-Rhosybonwen SA14 218 A8
- Heol Rhosyn
  - Beddau CF38 156 B5
  - Swansea / Abertawe SA6 45 F2
- Heol Rhuddos SA7 70 A7
- Heol Rhyd SA6 22 B3
- Heol Rhydaman / Ammanford Rd SA18 218 F6
- Heol Rhydd-Dal / Freehold Land Rd NP4 38 A1
- Heol Rhyd-Ddu-Fach SA9 221 B8
- Heol Rhyd-y-Bedd CF48 11 A6
- Heol Rhys CF44 53 F8
- Heol Richard Price CF32 129 E3
- Heol Robart CF72 173 B7
- Heol Roberts / Roberts Rd SA1 95 F5
- Heol Romney / Romney Rd 14 SA12 98 D1
- Heol Rotari Cenedlaethol / Rotary International Way CF31 169 A7
- Heol Ruth / Ruth Rd NP4 63 A5
- Heol Saffrwm SA6 45 F2
- Heol St Cattwg CF71 191 A6
- Heol St Denys CF14 160 A3
- Heol St Y Nyll CF5 175 B1
- Heol Salem CF38 135 F1
- Heol Sandown / Sandown Rd 17 SA12 98 D1
- Heol Sant Bridget CF32 185 C2
- Heol Santes Catherine / St Catherine's Rd SA12 98 E5
- Heol Sant Luc / St Luke's Rd NP22 6 D2
- Heol Sant Paul / St Paul's Rd SA12 124 E8
- Heol Sants Fair / St Mary's Rd 2 NP44 90 A5
- Heol Saron / Saron Rd SA18 218 F7
- Heol Scwrfa CF48 10 A3
- Heol Seddon CF5 176 D2
- Heol Seion SA14 42 B7
- Heol Serth CF83 137 D5
- Heol Seward CF38 155 F6
- Heol Shakespeare / Shakespeare Rd NP44 89 C2
- Heol Shon CF32 149 A2
- Heol Shwlac CF32 198 A7
- Heol Siarl / Charles St CF10 232 C2
- Heol Siloam NP23 7 E4
- Heol Siloh SA15 40 C4
- Heol Silyn CF44 28 C6
- Heol Simonston CF35 169 D7
- Heol Sirhwi CF62 214 C6
- Heol S O Davies CF48 10 C1
- Heol Solva CF5 193 E4
- Heol Southdown / Southdown Rd SA12 98 C2
- Heol Southville / Southville Rd SA12 98 C2
- Heol Spencer CF32, CF35 151 B3
- Heol Stallcourt / Stallcourt Rd 6 SA13 125 E4
- Heol Stanllyd SA14 218 B7
- Heol Sticil-y-Beddau 7 CF72 155 D3
- Heol Stradling CF14 177 B4
- Heol Strauss / Strauss Rd SA12 98 A2
- Heol Syr Lewis CF15 176 B8
- Heol Syr William SA13 75 D3
- Heol Tabernacle / Tabernacle Rd 2 SA18 220 A8
- Heol Tabor SA12 99 E6
- Heol Tai Mawr CF48 10 A3
- Heol Taliesin SA12 99 F6
- Heol Tasker CF46 83 D3
- Heol Tawe SA9 222 D7
- Heol Tegfryn CF33 148 B2
- Heol Teifionydd CF43 80 A2
- Heol Teilo NP4 63 A5
- Heol Terrell CF11 194 B5
- Heol-Tewdwr SA13 75 D4
- Heol Tewgoed SA12 99 E6
- Heol Tirbach CF83 137 D6
- Heol Tir Coch CF38 156 E5
- Heol Tircoed SA4 44 B5
- Heol Tir Du
  - Cwmrhydyceirw SA6 46 A3
  - Swansea / Abertawe SA6 45 F3
- Heol Tir Gibbon CF83 137 E5
- Heol Tir Gwaidd CF43 80 B3
- Heol Tir-Lan SA11 223 E5
- Heol Tir Morfa / Tir Morfa Rd SA12 98 B1
- Heol Tir Ton NP11 113 B3
- Heol Tir Y Coed / Tirycoed Rd 3 SA18 220 A8
- Heol Tir Y Coed / Woodland Rd SA9 221 C7
- Heol Tir-y-Llan CF81 58 B4
- Heol Tir-y-Parc / Parklands Rd SA18 219 A7
- Heol Ton
  - North Cornelly CF33 165 C7
  - Sarn CF32 150 F3
  - Tonyrefail CF39 133 B4
- Heol Tonmaen SA11 226 E5
- Heol Ton / Ton Rd
  - Cwmbran / Cwmbrân NP44 89 B2
  - Cwmbran / Cwmbrân NP44 89 C1
- Heol Trane CF39 133 B4
- Heol Trecastell CF83 138 A2
- Heol Tredeg SA9 221 C6
- Heol Tredwen 7 CF10 195 B2
- Heol Tre Dwr CF31 169 B2
- Heol Treferig CF38 156 A6
- Heol Treffynnon SA6 46 B5
- Heol Trefgarne CF5 193 C3
- Heol Trefor SA5 68 B6
- Heol Tre Forys CF64 206 E2
- Heol Trefrhiw / Trefrhiw Rd SA18 219 A6
- Heol Tregoning SA15 40 F2
- Heol Treharne
  - Abergwynfi SA13 76 A6
  - Coytrahen CF32 150 B7
- Heol Trelai CF5 193 C3
- Heol Trelales CF32 167 F4
- Heol Trelyn Rd NP12 85 D4
- Heol Trenewydd CF5 193 C3
- Heol Treth CF33 148 C1
- Heol-Treventy SA14 218 A8
- Heol Trewilliam CF40 107 B1
- Heol Troeon Bach SA4 218 D2
- Heol Troserch / Troserch Rd SA14 18 B2
- Heol Trostre CF3 179 F6
- Heol Trubshaw SA15 40 E8
- Heol Trussel / Trussel Rd 1 NP44 89 E4
- Heol Tudor / Tudor St SA9 2 E7
- Heol Twrch SA9 1 B1
- Heol Twyn Du CF48 10 A3
- Heol Ty Aberaman CF44 53 D6
- Heol Ty Bocs / Ty Box Rd NP44 89 D5
- Heol-Ty-Cribwr CF31 168 B6
- Heol Tycroes / Tycroes Rd
  - Ammanford / Rhydaman SA18 219 A5
  - Tycroes SA18 218 F5
- Heol Ty Crwn CF83 138 B5
- Heol Tyddewi / St David's Rd NP44 89 F3
- Heol Tyddyn CF83 137 D1
- Heol Tydraw CF33 166 B8
- Heol Ty Ffynnon CF23 160 F1
- Heol Ty Fry / Ty-fry Rd SA13 125 E4
- Heol Ty Gwyn SA10 48 C4
- Heol Ty-Gwyn CF83 112 A3
- Heol Ty Gwyn CF34 101 F4
- Heol Ty Gwyn Ind Est CF34 101 F4
- Heol Ty Gwyn / Ty-Gwyn Rd NP4 37 E7
- Heol Ty Gwyn / Ty Gwyn Rd NP44 89 B3
- Heol Tyle-Du CF42 78 D7
- Heol Tylluan SA7 70 B8
- Heol Tyllwyd CF39 133 D6
- Heol-Ty-Maen CF31 168 B6
- Heol Ty Maen CF37 136 D2
- Heol Ty Mawr CF71 190 F6
- Heol Ty Merchant CF83 138 B5
- Heol Ty Nant CF32 130 B4
- Heol Tynewydd NP12 58 E4
- Heol Tynton CF32 130 A3
- Heol Ty'n-y-Cae CF14 177 C6
- Heol Ty'n Y Coed CF14 177 C8
- Heol Tynygarn CF31 150 D2
- Heol Ty'n-y-Garn CF31 150 D2
- Heol Tyn-y-Waun CF34 128 D6
- Heol Ty'r Brodya CF10 232 B3
- Heol Tysant CF31 169 A7
- Heol Tywith CF34 102 A6
- Heol Uchaf
  - Cardiff / Caerdydd CF14 159 B1
  - Cimla SA11 72 C5
  - Hengoed CF82 84 F3
  - Nelson CF46 83 F3
  - Penywaun CF44 28 A6
- Heol-Uchaf NP22 12 E6
- Heol Uchaf Yr Orsaf / Upper Station Rd 9 SA18 220 B8
- Heol Uchel CF44 27 D7
- Heol Undeb
  - Beddau CF38 155 F6
  - Cwmavon / Cwmafan SA12 99 F5
- Heol Urban CF5 176 E2

- Heol Valentine SA6 46 D8
- Heol Varteg / Varteg Rd NP4 37 E8
- Heol Verdi / Verdi Rd SA12 98 B2
- Heol Waen NP23 7 B4
- Heol Wagner / Wagner Rd [10] SA12 98 B3
- Heol Waldsassen / Waldsassen Rd CF35 170 D6
- Heol Wallasey / Wallasey Rd SA18 219 C7
- Heol Wastadwaun CF35 170 C8
- Heol Waterloo / Waterloo Rd
  - Abersychan NP4 37 F4
  - Pen-y-groes SA14, SA18 218 D7
- Heol Waun
  - Abersychan NP4 37 E4
  - Tonyrefail CF39 133 A4
- Heol Waun Dwfn SA18 219 D6
- Heol Waun Fawr CF83 137 E1
- Heol Waun Waelod CF83 137 F1
- Heol Waun Wen SA6 45 B1
- Heol Waun Y Nant CF14 177 B3
- Heol Wen CF14 177 B7
- Heol-wenallt SA11 227 B8
- Heol Wernlas CF14 177 C4
- Heol Wern / Wern Rd SA10 70 E7
- Heol Westfa SA14 40 F8
- Heol West Plas CF31, CF35 169 B7
- Heol Wil Hopcyn CF34 128 D6
- Heol Will George SA5 66 E3
- Heol William Trigg CF32 103 E6
- Heol Windsor / Windsor Rd NP44 89 B2
- Heol Winifred / Winifred Rd SA10 70 E7
- Heol Wyllt SA4 19 E4
- Heol Y Barcud CF14 159 E4
- Heol-y-Bardd CF31 168 C3
- Heol Y Barna SA4 20 A3
- Heol-y-Beddau CF38 156 A7
- Heol y Beddau CF83 138 A2
- Heol Y Bedw-Hirion NP12 58 D4
- Heol-y-Beiliau [5] CF72 155 D3
- Heol-y-Berllan CF5 193 C3
- Heol Y Berllan
  - Crynant / Creunant SA10 226 A8
  - Pyle / Y Pîl CF33 148 B2
- Heol-y-Berth CF83 158 E8
- Heol-y-Blodau CF31 168 B5
- Heol-y-Bont
  - Cardiff / Caerdydd CF14 177 C7
  - Ton-du CF32 150 E4
- Heol Y Brenin CF64 206 E2
- Heol y Brenin / King's Rd SA1 233 C2
- Heol Y Bronwen SA12 98 E1
- Heol-y-Bryn
  - Barry / Y Barri CF62 214 C2
  - Cardiff / Caerdydd CF14 177 A7
  - Fochriw CF81 32 D8
  - Hendreforgan CF39 132 D5
  - Miskin / Meisgyn CF72 173 C7
  - Pentyrch CF15 157 B1
  - Pont Rhyd-y-cyff CF34 128 D6
  - Rhigos CF44 26 C8
  - Rhydyfelin CF37 136 B6
  - Sarn CF32 150 F3
- Heol y Bryn / Bryn Rd SA14 218 D8
- Heol Y Bryn / Hillside Ave NP4 17 D7
- Heol-y-Bryniau CF48 11 A7
- Heol Y Bwlch SA12 99 C5
- Heol-y-Bwlch SA14 42 A2
- Heol-y-Bwnsy CF15 136 F2
- Heol-y-Cadno CF14 159 E3
- Heol-y-Cae
  - Cefn Coed / Cefn-coed-y-cymmer CF48 10 B4
  - Clydach SA6 46 D7
  - Pontarddulais SA4 19 E5
- Heol Y Caeau-Meinion NP12 58 D4
- Heol-y-Capel
  - Bridgend / Pen-y-Bont ar Ogwr CF35 169 F4
  - Porthcawl CF36 165 F1
- Heol y Carnau CF83 138 B5
- Heol-y-Carw CF14 159 E3
- Heol-y-Castell
  - Cardiff / Caerdydd CF5 193 C3
  - Duffryn SA13 74 D4
  - Pant CF48 11 A7
- Heol Y Castell / Castle St CF10 232 A2
- Heol-y-Cawl
  - Corntown / Corntwn CF35 186 C7
  - Dinas Powis / Dinas Powys CF64 206 A3
- Heol y Cawl CF71 187 E1
- Heol y Cawl / Wharton St CF10 232 B2
- Heol y Cefn NP12 58 C2
- Heol Y Celyn SA7 46 D1
- Heol-y-Celyn Prim Sch / Ysgol Heol-y-Celyn CF37 136 A5
- Heol y Clun CF38 155 F6
- Heol Y Cnap SA5 68 D5
- Heol y Coed CF38 155 F6
- Heol-y-Coed CF14 177 A7
- Heol y Coed SA13 227 C2
- Heol-y-Coed
  - Llantwit Major / Llanilltud Fawr CF61 210 A5
  - Miskin / Meisgyn CF72 173 C8
  - Nantgarw CF15 158 B8
  - Pontarddulais SA4 19 E5
  - Wyllie NP12 85 F1
- Heol-y-Coedcae SA9 221 B7
- Heol Y Coed / Coed Rd NP4 17 D6
- Heol-y-Coed Rise CF31 169 A5
- Heol Y Coroni / Coronation Rd [16] SA18 220 B8
- Heol-y-Craig SA10 226 A7
- Heol-y-Cwm CF83 137 F1
- Heol Y Cwm CF15 176 A7
- Heol Y Cwmdu SA5 67 F2
- Heol Y Cwrt / Court Rd CF33 165 F7
- HEOL-Y-CYW 152 A5
- Heol Y Cyw SA7 70 B8
- Heolcyw Prim Sch / Ysgol Gynradd Heolycyw CF35 152 B5
- Heol-y- Dail CF31 168 B6
- Heol Y Dderwen NP12 85 C7
- Heol-y-Dderwen CF15 158 B8
- Heol-y-Ddol CF83 138 B5
- Heol-y-De CF44 26 C8
- Heol-Y-Deiliaid
  - Margam SA13 125 F1
  - Port Talbot SA13 126 A1
- Heol Y Delyn CF14 160 A2
- Heol-y-Delyn CF14 160 B3
- Heol-y-Delyn Du CF31 168 B5
- Heol-y-Deri
  - Cardiff / Caerdydd CF14 177 B7
  - Cwmgwili SA14 218 C5
  - Cwmrhydyceirw SA6 46 A3
  - Pontypridd CF37 109 A2
  - Swansea / Abertawe SA6 45 F3
- Heol Y Deri / Deri Rd SA18 219 F8
- Heol Y Derw CF39 132 B7
- Heol-y-Deryn SA13 227 C2
- Heol y De / South Rd NP44 116 F8
- Heol Y Dolau / Meadow Rd CF35 170 D6
- Heol-y-Dre SA14 218 A8
- Heol-y-Dreflan CF83 138 B5
- Heol Y Drudwen SA6 45 F5
- Heol Y Dryw CF62 213 B1
- Heol Y Dug / Duke St CF10 232 B2
- Heol y Dwyrain / East Rd NP44 116 F8
- Heol-y-Fagwr SA6 22 F1
- Heol-y-Fedw SA13 75 D4
- Heol-y-Fedwen
  - Church Village CF38 136 A2
  - Nant-y-Moel CF32 104 F6
- Heol-y-Felin
  - Abergwynfi SA13 75 F6
  - Ammanford / Rhydaman SA18 219 C6
- Heol Y Felin CF32 129 E1
- Heol-y-Felin
  - Blaengwrach SA11 227 B8
  - Caerphilly / Caerffili CF83 137 F3
  - Cardiff / Caerdydd, Ely / Trelai CF5 193 E6
  - Cardiff / Caerdydd, Rhydwaedlyd CF14 177 C7
- Heol Y Felin
  - Cefn Hengoed CF82 84 E5
  - Fforest SA4 18 F5
- Heol-y-Felin
  - Heol-y-Cyw CF35 152 B6
  - Llantwit Major / Llanilltud Fawr CF61 210 A5
  - Neath / Castell-Nedd SA10 48 D2
  - Penllergaer SA4 44 B2
  - Pontyclun CF72 173 A7
- Heol Y Felin / Mary St SA10 222 D4
- Heol-y-Fferm CF32 150 E5
- Heolyffin SA8 23 B1
- Heol-y-Ffin CF31 168 C4
- Heol-y-Fforest CF14, CF15, CF83 158 E3
- Heol-y-Ffowndri / Foundry Rd [5] SA18 219 C7
- Heol-y-Ffynnon CF38 156 F6
- Heol Y Ffynon SA11 72 C5
- Heol-y-Ffynon CF43 80 A2
- Heol-y-Foel
  - Cwmavon / Cwmafan SA12 99 D5
- Heol-y-Foel *continued*
  - Llantwit Fadre / Llanilltud Faerdref CF38 156 D8
- Heol-y-Foelas CF31 168 C5
- Heol-y-Forlan CF14 177 A6
- Heol Y Fran SA6 45 F5
- Heol-y-Frenhines CF31 168 C5
- Heol y Frenhines CF64 206 A2
- Heol Y Frenhines / Queen St CF10 232 C3
- Heol-y-Fro
  - Church Village CF38 135 E1
  - Llantwit Major / Llanilltud Fawr CF61 210 A7
- Heol-y-Gadarn SA13 74 E4
- Heol-y-Gaer
  - Barry / Y Barri CF62 214 B2
  - Cardiff / Caerdydd CF5 193 C3
- Heol Y Gamlas CF15, CF37 136 E1
- Heol Y Garn SA18 219 B4
- Heol Y Garreg Wen SA3 122 E6
- Heol y Garth CF83 139 B3
- Heol y Gat / Gate Rd SA14 218 D8
- Heol-y-Geifr
  - Pencoed CF35 170 D7
  - Swansea / Abertawe SA5 45 B2
- Heol-y-Gelli
  - Aberdare / Aberdâr CF44 53 B5
  - Penllergaer SA4 43 F2
- Heol Y Gelli / Grove Rd CF31 168 F3
- Heol-y-Gerddi CF35 152 D1
- Heol-y-Glo
  - Pyle / Y Pîl CF33 148 C5
  - Tonna / Tonnau SA11 49 E3
- Heol-y-Glyn
  - Cymmer / Cymer SA13 75 C7
  - Glyn-neath / Glyn-nedd SA11 223 D1
- Heol Y Glyn
  - Tonyrefail CF39 133 C5
  - Treharris CF46 83 C6
- Heol-y-Goedlan SA9 221 B6
- Heol-y-Goedwig
  - Llantwit Fadre / Llanilltud Faerdref CF38 156 E8
  - Porthcawl CF36 183 A8
- Heol-y-Gog SA4 66 B5
- Heol-y-Gogledd CF83 137 E6
- Heol Y Gogledd / North Rd
  - Croesyceiliog NP44 90 A5
  - Pontypool / Pont-y-pwl NP4 62 B6
- Heol-y-Gors CF83 138 B5
- Heol Y Gors CF14 177 C3
- Heol-y-Gors
  - Gwaun-Cae-Gurwen SA18 220 D5
  - Nantgarw CF15 158 B8
  - Pyle / Y Pîl SA13 147 C6
  - Swansea / Abertawe SA1, SA5 68 A2
- Heol-y-Graig
  - Blaengwrach SA11 227 B8
  - Clydach SA6 46 D7
  - Cwmavon / Cwmafan SA12 99 F7
- Heol Y Graig SA14 41 E4
- Heol-y-Graig
  - Llantrisant CF72 155 D3
  - Penrhys CF43 80 A3
  - Porthcawl CF36 183 D8
  - Rhigos CF44 26 C8
  - Tonna / Tonnau SA11 49 D3
  - Ystrad Mynach CF82 111 E8
- Heol-y-Groes
  - Bridgend / Pen-y-Bont ar Ogwr CF31 150 F1
  - Pencoed CF35 170 E8
- Heol-Y-Grug CF39 132 D5
- Heol Y Gwartheg SA4 66 C5
- Heol-y-Gwaudd / Weaver Rd SA9 222 A4
- Heol Y Gwlith / Dew Rd SA12 98 C2
- Heol-y-Gwrgan SA13 125 E3
- Heol Y Gwydde SA9 222 E7
- Heol y Gyfraith CF72 155 C2
- Heol-y-Llan SA4 65 E8
- Heol y Llew Du / Black Lion Rd SA14 218 C7
- Heol Y Llew / Lion St [2] NP4 17 C6
- Heol Y Llongau CF63 214 F4
- Heol-y-Llwynan SA8 23 B1
- Heol-y-Llwyni CF34 102 C2
- Heol-y-Llyfrall CF32 150 C4
- Heol-y-Maes
  - Llantwit Fadre / Llanilltud Faerdref CF38 156 D7
  - Pontarddulais SA4 19 D4
- Heol Y Moch
  - Maesteg CF34 101 C3
  - Port Talbot CF34 127 B8
- Heol Y Mwyn Ct [8] NP23 14 D6
- Heol-y-Mynach CF37 81 E3
- Heol-y-Mynydd CF44 28 F1
- Heol Y Mynydd
  - Ammanford / Rhydaman SA18 219 B3
  - Bargoed / Bargod CF81 57 E3
- Heol-y-Mynydd
  - Bargoed / Bargod CF81 57 E3
  - Bryn SA14 41 F6
  - Cefn Coed / Cefn-coed-y-cymmer CF48 10 A5
  - Glyncorrwg SA13 227 C2
- Heol Y Mynydd SA4 43 D3
- Heol-Y-Mynydd
  - Hendreforgan CF39 132 D5
  - Sarn CF32 150 F3
  - Ystrad CF41 79 C3
- Heol-y-Nant
  - Baglan SA12 98 E4
  - Barry / Y Barri CF63 215 A7
  - Blaengwynfi SA13 76 B6
  - Bridgend / Pen-y-Bont ar Ogwr CF31 168 D5
  - Caerphilly / Caerffili CF83 137 F3
  - Cardiff / Caerdydd CF14 177 B6
  - Clydach SA6 46 E8
- Heol Y Nant
  - Gorseinon SA4 42 F3
  - Heol-y-Cyw CF35 152 B5
- Heol-y-Nant
  - Llandow / Llandw CF71 199 A7
  - Maesteg CF34 102 D2
  - Neath / Castell-Nedd SA10 48 D2
  - Rhos SA8 24 B3
  - Sarn CF32 150 F4
  - Taffs Well / Ffynnon Taf CF15 157 F3
- Heol Y Nantlais SA4 43 B4
- Heol Ynysawdre CF32 150 E4
- Heol Ynyscedwyn / Yniscedwyn Rd SA9 2 E8
- Heol Ynys Ddu CF83 137 E1
- Heol Ynysydarren / Ynysydarren Rd SA9 2 B6
- Heol Ynysygored / Ynysygored Rd CF48 55 C6
- Heol-y-Parc
  - Aberdare / Aberdâr CF44 29 C3
  - Caerphilly / Caerffili CF83 138 A3
  - Cardiff / Caerdydd CF14 161 A4
  - Cefneithin SA14 218 A8
  - Cwmavon / Cwmafan SA12 99 D5
  - Efail Isaf CF38 156 F6
  - Evanstown CF39 132 B7
- Heol Y Parc
  - Hendy SA4 18 F4
  - Llangennech SA14 42 C7
- Heol-y-Parc
  - North Cornelly CF33 165 F8
  - Pentyrch CF15 175 B7
- Heol Y Parc SA8 23 F3
- Heol-y-Parc
  - Pontlliw SA4 44 A7
  - Trehafod CF37 108 B3
- Heol-y-Pavin CF5 177 A1
- Heol Y Pentir CF62 213 A1
- Heol Y Pentre CF15 157 C1
- Heol Y Pia CF83 137 E3
- Heol-y-Plas SA4 18 F6
- Heol Y Plas / Manor Rd NP4 37 F4
- Heol-y-Plwyf CF37 81 F2
- Heol Y Porthladd [10] CF63 214 F4
- Heol Y Porth / Westgate St CF10 232 B2
- Heol Y Pwca NP44 89 C6
- Heol Y Pwll CF15 157 F8
- Heol-Yr-Afael SA13 74 E4
- Heol Yr Afon
  - Bridgend / Pen-y-Bont ar Ogwr CF31 168 E7
  - Glyncorrwg SA13 227 C2
- Heol-yr-Afon CF32 150 D5
- Heol Yr Drsaf / Station Rd SA14 42 A4
- Heol Yr Eastwood CF35 169 D8
- Heol-Yr-Efail CF14 177 D7
- Heol Yr Eglwys
  - Bryncethin CF32 151 A5
  - Coity / Coety CF35 169 C7
- Heol Yr Eglwys / Church Rd
  - Abersychan NP4 37 E4
  - Baglan SA12 98 E5
  - Gorslas SA14 218 B8
- Heol Yr Eithen SA6 46 A3
- Heol-yr-Enfys CF31 168 B6
- Heol-yr-Eos SA4 43 F2
- Heol Yr Eryr
  - Cwmrhydyceirw SA6 46 A5
  - Swansea / Abertawe SA6 45 F5
- Heol yr Glyn / Avondale Rd NP44 89 F6
- Heol-yr-Haul CF72 174 C7
- Heol-yr-Rhedyn SA6 45 E2
- Heol-y-Rhos CF31 169 A5
- Heol Y Rhosog CF3 179 D2
- Heol-yr-Odyn CF5 193 B3
- Heol Yr Odyn CF15 157 F8
- Heol-yr-Onen CF83 137 F3
- Heol-yr-Onnen CF31 168 B4
- Heol yr Onnen CF72 172 D5
- Heol-yr-Onnen CF35 170 E7
- Heol yr Orsaf CF72 173 A7
- Heol-yr-Orsaf CF33 148 D3
- Heol yr Orsaf / Station Rd
  - Cwmbran / Cwmbrân NP44 89 F5
  - Llanelli SA15 40 D4
- Heol-yr-Orsedd SA13 125 D6
- Heol Yr Wylan SA6 45 F5
- Heol-yr-Ynys CF15 158 B2
- Heol-yr-Ysbyty CF83 137 E1
- Heol yr Ysgol
  - Bedwas CF83 139 A6
  - Bridgend / Pen-y-Bont ar Ogwr CF31 168 C5
- Heol-yr-Ysgol SA14 218 A8
- Heol Yr Ysgol CF35 169 D8
- Heol-yr-Ysgol
  - Ebbw Vale / Glyn Ebwy NP23 14 B7
  - Pont Rhyd-y-cyff CF34 128 D6
  - St Brides Major / Saint-y-Brid CF32 185 C2
  - Ton-du CF32 150 D5
- Heol Y Ysgol / School Rd
  - Brynamman SA18 220 D8
  - Cefn-bryn-brain SA9 221 B8
  - Neath / Castell-Nedd SA10 70 C1
- Heol-y-Sarn CF72 155 D5
- Heol Ysgawen
  - Llanharry CF72 172 D6
  - Swansea / Abertawe SA2 94 C8
- Heol Ysgawen / Elder Rd SA12 98 D7
- Heol Ysgol Newydd CF81 58 A5
- Heol Ysgol Newydd / New School Rd [15] SA18 220 B8
- Heol Ysgubor CF83 158 E8
- Heol Ysgyfarnog SA7 70 B8
- Heol-y-Sheet
  - North Cornelly CF33 166 A7
  - North Cornelly CF33 166 C6
- Heol-y-Slough CF32 185 B2
- Heol-y-Splot CF33 166 C5
- Heol Y Stepsau CF35 186 A4
- Heol Y Tollty / Customhouse St CF10 232 B1
- Heol-y-Twyn
  - Cwmdare CF44 28 C4
  - Pontlliw SA4 43 F7
  - Rhymney / Rhymni NP22 12 E6
- Heol Y Twyn CF39 80 D1
- Heol-y-Tyla SA13 74 E4
- Heol-y-Waun
  - Cardiff / Caerdydd CF14 177 B3
  - Gelligaer CF82 84 C6
  - Penrhys CF43 80 A3
  - Pontarddulais SA4 19 D5
- Heol Y Waun SA4 43 F7
- Heol-y-Waun
  - Pontlottyn CF81 33 A8
  - Seven Sisters / Blaendulais SA10 222 D4
- Heol Y Waunfach SA14 41 C8
- Heol y Waun / Meadows Rd SA14 218 C6
- Heol-y-Wern CF83 138 B5
- Heol Y Wern CF14 177 C8
- Heol-y-Wern
  - Loughor SA4 65 E8
  - Neath / Castell-Nedd SA10 48 D1
  - Nelson CF46 83 F4
- Heol-y-Wyrddol SA18 219 B8
- Herbert Ave NP11 141 C8
- Herbert Cl CF3 180 E8
- Herbert Dr [4] CF83 137 F5
- Herbert March Cl CF5 176 D3
- Herbert Rd
  - Neath / Castell-Nedd SA11 71 D5
  - Newport / Casnewydd NP19 143 D6
- Herbert St / Stryd Herbert CF10 232 C1
- Herbert's Cl NP4 37 E6
- Herbert's Rd NP4 37 E6
- Herbert St
  - Abercynon CF45 82 E2
  - Aberdare / Aberdâr CF44 29 A1
  - Barry / Y Barri CF63 215 A7
  - Blaengarw CF32 103 E7
  - Bridgend / Pen-y-Bont ar Ogwr CF31 169 A5
  - Cardiff / Caerdydd CF14 177 E1
  - Newbridge / Trecelyn NP11 60 D2
  - [2] Newport / Casnewydd NP20 143 C3
  - New Tredegar NP24 34 A1
  - Pontardawe SA8 23 E4
  - Treherbert CF42 51 B1
  - Treorchy / Treorci CF42 78 D6
- Herbert Terr
  - Newbridge / Trecelyn NP11 60 D2
  - [6] Penarth CF64 207 A4
- Herbert Thomas Way SA7 46 E2
- Herbert Thompson Prim Sch CF5 193 D6
- Herbert Wlk NP20 143 C3
- Hereford Ct NP18 118 A3
- Hereford Rd NP23 7 E3
- Hereford St
  - Cardiff / Caerdydd CF11 194 E4

Hereford St *continued*
Newport / Casnewydd NP19 143 D6
Heritage Coast Ho CF32 184 D2
Heritage Ct CF47 10 E3
Heritage Ct / Cwrt Atifeddiaeth NP44 117 B7
Heritage Ct / Cwrt Treftadaeth NP4 17 B7
Heritage Dr
Barry / Y Barri CF62 214 D5
Cardiff / Caerdydd CF5 193 C2
Heritage Pk CF3 179 F8
Hermon Cl CF48 11 A4
Hermon Flats CF43 80 B1
Hermon Hill CF15 158 C1
Hermon Rd CF34 102 A8
Hermon St CF42 78 E6
Herne Pl CF11 194 B5
Herne St SA11 71 B1
HERNSTON 169 A1
Hernston La CF31 168 F1
Hernston Ret Pk CF31 169 A1
Heron Ave / Rhodfa'r Creyr SA15 40 B5
Heron Rd CF3 179 C3
Heronsbridge Sch CF31 168 F2
Herons View NP12 85 A7
Herons Way
Caerphilly / Caerffili CF83 137 E1
Neath / Castell-Nedd SA10 48 E2
Heron Way
Newport / Casnewydd NP10 163 F7
Swansea / Abertawe SA6 69 B8
Herrick Pl CF83 139 D7
Hertford Pl NP19 143 F6
Heulwen Cl CF48 11 A6
Hewell Ct CF11 194 F2
Hewell St
Cardiff / Caerdydd CF11 194 F2
Penarth CF64 206 F5
Hewson St SA1 95 B8
Hibbert Rd SA11 71 F8
Hibiscus Ct CF38 156 C5
Hickman Rd CF64 207 A4
Hickman St CF48 31 A4
Hickory Ct [5] CF24 195 D5
Hick St SA15 40 D4
High Bank CF23 161 B2
High Banks NP19 143 E8
Highbridge Cl CF64 216 C4
Highbury Cl SA5 68 B2
Highbury Cres CF31 168 C6
Highbury Ct SA11 71 F6
Highbury Dr NP12 85 E6
Highbury Pl CF5 193 B4
Highbury Rd CF5 193 C5
High Cl
Llanyrafon NP44 90 B1
Nelson CF46 83 E3
Highcliffe Ct SA3 122 F4
High Cnr CF15 157 C1
Highcroft Rd NP20 143 A6
High Croft Wlk CF3 179 B4
HIGH CROSS 142 B4
High Cross Cl NP10 142 C4
High Cross Dr NP10 142 C4
High Cross La NP10 142 C4
High Cross Prim Sch NP10 142 C5
Highcross Rd NP10 142 C5
Highdale Cl CF72 155 E2
HIGHER END 211 C5
Higher La SA3 123 A4
Highfield
Ferndale CF43 79 D8
Gorseinon SA4 66 A8
[14] Penarth CF64 207 B4
Penperlleni NP4 39 E7
Highfield Ave
Bridgend / Pen-y-Bont ar Ogwr CF31 168 F8
Porthcawl CF36 182 F6
Highfield Cl
Caerleon / Caerllion NP18 117 F4
Church Village CF38 136 A1
Dinas Powis / Dinas Powys CF64 206 C4
Neath / Castell-Nedd SA10 48 E2
Pontypool / Pont-y-pwl NP4 37 F1
Porthcawl CF36 182 F6
Risca / Rhisga NP11 114 F2
Sarn CF32 150 E3
Tredegar NP22 6 C2
Highfield Cl / Clos Cae Ucha f NP44 117 B8
Highfield Cres
Aberbargoed / Aberbargod CF81 58 B6
Bryn NP12 85 E3
Highfield Ct
Bassaleg NP10 141 F3
Newbridge / Trecelyn, Cwm-dows NP11 86 F6
Porthcawl CF36 182 F6
Highfield Gdns NP10 141 F3
Highfield Ind Est / Ystad Ddiwydiannol Highfeld CF43 79 E8
Highfield La NP10 141 F3
Highfield Pl CF32 150 E3
Highfield Rd
Barry / Y Barri CF62 214 D7
Bassaleg NP10 142 A3
Briton Ferry / Llansawel SA11 71 B2
Bryn NP12 85 E3
Caerleon / Caerllion NP18 117 F4
Cardiff / Caerdydd CF14, CF23 178 A4
Newport / Casnewydd NP20 142 E3
Highfield Rd / Heol Maesuchel SA18 220 C8
Highfields
Bridgend / Pen-y-Bont ar Ogwr CF31 169 B5
Cardiff / Caerdydd CF5 176 F2
Highfields Holiday Pk SA3 231 A4
Highfields Way NP12 85 D5
Highfield Terr
Llanelli SA15 40 E4
[2] Pontypridd CF37 109 B1
Highfield Way NP18 117 F4
Highgrove CF71 189 D8
Highland Ave CF32 151 A6
Highland Cl
Merthyr Tydfil / Merthyr Tudful CF47 30 E8
Neath / Castell-Nedd SA10 70 F8
Sarn CF32 150 E3
Highland Cres
Dyffryn Cellwen SA10 223 A5
Pontllanfraith NP12 86 B4
Highland Ct CF32 151 A6
Highland Gdns SA10 48 A1
Highland Gr / Gelli'r Wynydd NP44 89 E6
Highland Pl
Aberdare / Aberdâr CF44 28 F1
Bridgend / Pen-y-Bont ar Ogwr CF31 168 F5
Ogmore Vale CF32 104 E1
Highlands
Cardiff / Caerdydd CF3 179 A2
Tonyrefail CF39 133 D6
Highlands Cl CF39 133 C6
Highlands Cres NP23 7 E4
Highlands Rd NP23 7 E4
Highlands The SA10 70 F8
Highland Terr
Blackwood / Coed-Duon NP12 85 E7
Pontarddulais SA4 19 E3
Highland View CF47 30 E8
Highlight La
Barry / Y Barri CF62 214 C7
Barry / Y Barri CF62 214 C8
High Mdw
Abercarn NP11 87 B4
Llantwit Major / Llanilltud Fawr CF61 209 F5
Highmead NP12 85 D4
Highmead Ave
Llanelli SA15 40 E8
The Mumbles / Y Mwmbwls SA3 122 E6
Highmead Cl SA3 122 E5
HIGH MEADOWS 87 B5
Highmead Rd CF5 193 D5
Highmoor SA1 233 B1
Highpool Cl SA3 122 E5
Highpool La SA3 122 E5
High Row CF45 54 C5
High St / Heol Fawr CF10 232 B2
High St / Prif Ffordd SA15 40 C4
High St / Stryd Fawr
Abersychan NP4 37 F3
Ammanford / Rhydaman SA18 219 C7
Blaengwrach SA11 227 B8
[4] Glanaman SA18 220 A8
Neath / Castell-Nedd, Pentreffynnon SA10 70 F7
Swansea / Abertawe SA1 233 B4
High St
Abercanaid CF48 30 F4
Abercarn, Llanfach NP11 87 B2
Abercarn, Pontywaun NP11 114 C5
Aberdare / Aberdâr CF44 29 A2
Abergwynfi SA13 76 C5
Abersychan, Garndiffaith NP4 37 E6
Abertillery / Abertyleri, Llanhilleth / Llanhiledd NP13 60 B6
Abertillery / Abertyleri, Rhiw Park / Rhiw Parc NP13 36 B5
Abertillery / Abertyleri, Six Bells NP13 36 C3
Abertridwr CF83 137 A8
Allt-wen SA8 23 F3
Argoed NP12 58 F5
Bargoed / Bargod CF81 58 A4
Barry / Y Barri CF62 214 D4
Bedlinog CF46 56 A7
Blackwood / Coed-Duon NP12 58 F1
High St *continued*
Blackwood / Coed-Duon NP12 85 E7
Blaenavon NP4 17 C6
Blaina / Blaenau NP13 15 D5
Caerleon / Caerllion NP18 118 B2
Cardiff / Caerdydd CF5 194 A8
Cefn Coed / Cefn-coed-y-cymmer CF48 10 A4
Clydach SA6 46 E7
Cowbridge / Y Bont-Faen CF71 188 E2
Cwmavon / Cwmafan SA12 99 D5
Cwmfelinfach NP11 113 A5
Dowlais CF48 11 C4
Ebbw Vale / Glyn Ebwy NP23 14 D6
Ferndale CF43 79 F6
Fleur-de-lis NP12 85 B6
Gilfach Goch CF39 132 C7
Glyn-neath / Glyn-nedd SA11 223 D1
Gorseinon SA4 43 C2
Grovesend SA4 43 C6
Heol-y-Cyw CF35 152 B5
Hirwaun CF44 27 D8
Laleston / Trelales CF32 167 F4
Llanbradach CF83 111 F1
[1] Llantrisant CF72 155 D3
Llantwit Major / Llanilltud Fawr CF61 209 F7
Maesteg CF34 102 A5
Merthyr Tydfil / Merthyr Tudful, Cae-Draw CF47 30 D8
Merthyr Tydfil / Merthyr Tudful, Pen-y-Darren CF47 10 E2
Merthyr Tydfil / Merthyr Tudful, Pen-y-Darren CF47 10 F3
Merthyr Tydfil / Merthyr Tudful, Twynyrodyn CF47 10 D1
Mountain Ash / Aberpennar CF45 54 D3
Neath / Castell-Nedd, Ty'n-y-Caeau SA11 71 E8
Nelson CF46 83 D4
Newbridge / Trecelyn, Cwm-dows NP11 86 F6
Newbridge / Trecelyn, Pentwyn-mawr NP11 86 C5
Newport / Casnewydd NP20 143 C5
New Tredegar NP24 33 C5
Ogmore Vale CF32 104 E1
Penarth CF64 207 A5
Pengam NP12 85 B8
Pontardawe SA8 23 E5
Pontarddulais SA4 19 C5
Pontlottyn CF81 12 F1
Pontneddfechan SA11 223 F2
Pontyclun CF72 172 F6
Pontycymer CF32 103 F3
Pontypool / Pont-y-pwl, Griffithstown NP4 62 E3
Pontypool / Pont-y-pwl, Sowhill NP4 62 B6
Pontypool / Pont-y-pwl, Sowhill NP4 62 C6
Pontypridd CF37 135 C8
Porth CF39 107 E2
Port Talbot SA13 99 B1
Pyle / Y Pîl CF32, CF33 148 E2
Rhymney / Rhymni NP22 12 E4
Senghenydd CF83 110 F2
Seven Sisters / Blaendulais SA10 222 C3
Tonypandy CF40 106 B6
Tonyrefail CF39 133 C5
Trelewis CF46 83 C7
Treorchy / Treorci CF42 78 E6
Ynysddu NP11 112 F6
Ynysybwl CF37 81 F1
High Street Arc [3] CF10 232 B2
High Street Prim Sch CF62 214 E4
Hightree Rise NP12 86 A8
High Trees
Risca / Rhisga NP11 115 B2
Trefechan CF48 10 B7
High View
Bridgend / Pen-y-Bont ar Ogwr CF31 168 F5
Swansea / Abertawe SA1 233 A5
High View Gdns SA2 94 B2
Highview Rd CF64 206 F5
High View Way CF37 109 D5
Highwalls Ave CF64 206 A3
Highwalls End CF64 206 A3
Highwalls Rd CF64 206 A3
Highway The
Croesyceiliog NP44 90 B5
Cwmbran / Cwmbrân NP44 116 F8
Pontypool / Pont-y-pwl NP4 63 A4
Hilary Ct NP11 87 B8
Hilary Rd NP11 87 B8
Hilary Way CF36 165 E2
Hilda St
Barry / Y Barri CF62 214 E4
Pontypridd CF37 135 E5
Hiles Rd CF5 193 C5
Hileys Row NP7 9 E7
Hilland Dr SA3 122 B6
Hilla Rd NP20 143 A4
Hillary Cl CF14 159 F1
Hillary Ho SA11 72 B5
Hillary Mews [13] CF63 215 B6
Hillary Rise
Abercarn NP11 114 C6
Barry / Y Barri CF63 215 B6
Hillbrook Cl
Aberdare / Aberdâr CF44 53 B7
Waunarlwydd SA5 66 D3
Hillcot Cl CF14 160 A2
Hill Cres NP23 8 B4
Hillcrest
Abersychan NP4 37 E6
Brynna CF72 153 E3
Caerleon / Caerllion NP18 117 F4
Merthyr Tydfil / Merthyr Tudful CF47 10 F4
Pen-y-fai CF31 150 D1
Pontypool / Pont-y-pwl NP4 63 B4
Hill Crest
Brynmawr NP23 8 B4
The Mumbles / Y Mwmbwls SA3 123 B4
Hillcrest Ave CF44 53 B7
Hillcrest Cl CF14 159 F3
Hillcrest Dr CF39 107 F2
Hillcrest Rd NP4 62 F5
Hillcrest View CF43 79 C8
Hill Crest View NP13 36 B7
Hillcroft Cres SA13 75 D3
Hill Ct / Llys-y-bryn CF31 168 A3
Hill Dr CF38 156 D7
Hill Flats NP4 62 B6
Hillfort Cl CF5 193 D3
Hillgrove SA3 122 E4
Hill Head CF61 209 F6
Hill Ho [10] CF45 54 E1
Hill House Hospl SA2 94 D8
Hill Rd
Abertysswg NP22 33 C8
Neath Abbey SA10 71 A8
Pontlottyn CF81 12 E1
Hillrise
Abersychan NP4 37 F5
Cardiff / Caerdydd CF23 178 D5
Hillrise Pk SA6 46 C7
Hill St / Stryd Y Bryn NP4 62 A8
Hillsboro CF31 168 C5
Hillsboro Ct CF31 168 C5
Hillsboro Pl CF36 182 F6
Hillside
Caerphilly / Caerffili CF83 138 B1
Cwmdare CF44 28 D3
Fochriw CF81 32 D8
Llanelli SA15 40 C7
Loughor SA4 42 E1
Mountain Ash / Aberpennar CF45 81 E8
Neath / Castell-Nedd SA11 71 F6
Newbridge / Trecelyn NP11 60 A1
Pant-yr-awel CF32 130 D4
Pen-y-fai CF31 150 D1
Risca / Rhisga NP11 115 A1
Hillside Ave
Abertridwr CF83 136 E7
Llanharan CF72 154 A3
Markham NP12 58 D8
Hillside Ave / Heol Y Bryn NP4 17 D7
Hillside Cl CF63 215 C6
Hillside Cl / Clos Yr Aut CF48 55 C5
Hillside Cres
Rogerstone NP10 142 B4
Swansea / Abertawe SA2 95 A7
Hillside Ct
Cardiff / Caerdydd CF24 178 C1
Llantwit Fadre / Llanilltud Faerdref CF38 156 C6
Hillside Ct / Cwrt Trem y Bryn [2] NP44 89 D5
Hillside Dr
Cowbridge / Y Bont-Faen CF71 188 F1
Cowbridge / Y Bont-Faen CF71 200 F8
Hillside Dr / Lon Y Bryn NP4 62 C4
Hillside Gdns CF81 57 F2
Hillside Gn CF31 150 D1
Hillside Pk CF81 57 F2
Hillside Prim Sch / Ysgol Gynradd Hillside NP4 17 D7
Hill Side Rd NP4 62 D3
Hill Side St CF41 78 F5
Hillside Terr
Abertillery / Abertyleri NP13 60 C6
Bedwas CF83 138 E6
Blackwood / Coed-Duon NP12 85 E7
Deri CF81 33 A2
Ebbw Vale / Glyn Ebwy NP23 14 F2
Pant-yr-awel CF32 130 D4
Pontypridd CF37 109 C2
Ton Pentre CF41 79 B2
Hillside Terr *continued*
Tonypandy CF40 106 E7
Tredomen CF82 84 D1
Wattstown CF39 107 D8
Hillside View
Bargoed / Bargod CF81 57 F2
Pontypridd CF37 109 B2
Hill-Snook Rd CF5 193 C4
Hill's St CF10 232 B2
Hill St
Abercarn NP11 87 B4
Abercynon CF45 82 D1
Aberdare / Aberdâr CF44 53 C7
Abertillery / Abertyleri NP13 36 B4
Bargoed / Bargod CF81 57 F5
Barry / Y Barri CF63 215 B5
Blaenavon NP4 17 C6
[5] Briton Ferry / Llansawel SA11 71 C1
Brynmawr NP23 8 B4
Cwmbran / Cwmbrân NP44 89 E1
Deri CF81 57 C8
Ebbw Vale / Glyn Ebwy NP23 14 E6
Gowerton / Tre-gwyr SA4 66 B5
Hendreforgan CF39 132 C5
Maerdy CF43 52 A1
Maesteg CF34 102 A6
Melincourt SA11 226 C4
Nant-y-Moel CF32 104 F5
Newbridge / Trecelyn NP11 86 F6
Newport / Casnewydd NP20 143 C4
Ogmore Vale CF32 104 E2
[8] Penarth CF64 207 B5
Pontypool / Pont-y-pwl NP4 62 E3
Rhymney / Rhymni NP22 12 F3
Risca / Rhisga NP11 115 A1
Swansea / Abertawe SA1 233 A4
The Mumbles / Y Mwmbwls SA3 123 C4
Tonypandy CF40 106 F4
Treherbert CF42 50 F2
Troedyrhiw CF48 31 B1
Ystrad Mynach CF82 84 E2
Hill Terr
Aberavon SA12 99 B1
Penarth CF64 206 F5
Wenvoe / Gwenfo CF5 204 F8
HILLTOP 14 C8
Hilltop NP23 14 C8
Hill Top CF44 28 F5
Hilltop Ave CF37 109 F3
Hilltop Cl
Baglan SA12 98 F6
Treharris CF46 83 A6
Hilltop Cres
Newbridge / Trecelyn NP11 87 A7
Pontypridd CF37 109 E1
Hilltop Gn NP44 89 C5
Hill Top Rd NP44 89 D2
Hilltop Sh Ctr NP23 14 C8
Hillview NP20 142 F3
Hill View
Beddau CF38 156 A6
Bridgend / Pen-y-Bont ar Ogwr CF31 168 A5
Bryn NP12 85 E4
Cardiff / Caerdydd CF5 193 C8
Cwmfelinfach NP11 113 B4
Hengoed CF82 85 A2
Maesycwmmer CF82 85 B1
Pencoed CF35 170 B8
Pontycymer CF32 103 E4
Pyle / Y Pîl CF33 148 C2
Swansea / Abertawe SA10 97 B8
Tredegar NP22 13 F5
Hillview Cres NP19 144 B3
Hill View Cres SA6 68 D8
Hill View Ct SA13 76 B6
Hill View La NP12 59 A1
Hillview Terr
Merthyr Vale / Ynysowen CF48 55 D3
[4] Port Talbot SA13 125 C8
Hilton Pl CF14 176 F3
Hinchsliff Ave CF62 214 D8
Hind Cl CF24 196 B7
Hinter Path NP44 89 B1
Hinton St CF24 195 E5
Hirst Cres CF5 176 D1
Hirwain Pl CF43 80 C4
Hirwain St CF24 194 F8
HIRWAUN 27 C8
Hirwaun Ind Est / Ystad Ddiwydiannol Hirwaun CF44 224 C1
Hirwaun Prim Sch CF44 27 D7
Hirwaun Rd
Aberdare / Aberdâr CF44 28 F3
Penywaun CF44 28 B5
Hirwaun Terr CF47 10 E3
Hillside Dr CF71 188 F1
Hobart Cl NP20 142 E4
Hoddinotts Hos CF41 79 A5
Hodges Cres NP12 58 B2

- Hodges Row CF10 . . . 195 B3
- Hodges Sq CF10 . . . 195 B3
- Hodges St CF47 . . . 10 F4
- Hodges Terr NP44 . . . 89 D3
- Hodgson's Rd SA9 . . . 2 A4
- HOEL-LAS . . . 46 F2
- Hoel Llwchwr SA18 . . . 219 B6
- Hogarth Cl NP19 . . . 143 F7
- Hogarth Cl / Clos Hogarth NP44 . . . 117 A8
- Hogarth Ho SA12 . . . 124 D8
- Hogarth Pl SA12 . . . 124 D8
- Holbein Rd NP19 . . . 144 A7
- Holborn Terr CF40 . . . 106 F5
- Holbrook Cl CF42 . . . 78 D7
- Holden Rd CF11 . . . 194 D2
- Holdings La CF5 . . . 175 B5
- Holford St
  - Aberdare / Aberdâr CF44 . . . 53 C8
  - Cefn Coed / Cefn-coed-y-cymmer CF48 . . . 10 A4
- Holford Terr CF44 . . . 28 C3
- Holgate Cl CF15 . . . 176 D4
- Holland Cl NP10 . . . 142 A7
- Holland St
  - Ebbw Vale / Glyn Ebwy NP23 . . . 14 D7
  - Port Talbot SA13 . . . 125 C8
- Holland Way CF63 . . . 215 A7
- Hollett Rd SA5 . . . 68 C4
- Hollies Specl Sch The CF23 . . . 178 F7
- Hollies The
  - Blackwood / Coed Duon NP11 . . . 59 D1
  - Bridgend / Pen-y-Bont ar Ogwr CF31 . . . 169 D4
  - Heolgerrig CF48 . . . 10 B1
  - Pontyclun CF72 . . . 173 A6
  - Quakers Yard CF46 . . . 83 C5
- Hollington Dr CF23 . . . 161 A1
- Hollins The SA11 . . . 72 A5
- HOLLYBUSH
  - Cwmbran . . . 116 C8
  - Markham . . . 34 C3
- Hollybush Ave NP20 . . . 117 A2
- Hollybush Cl
  - Church Village CF38 . . . 136 A1
  - Cwmbran / Cwmbrân NP44 . . . 89 D1
  - Newport / Casnewydd NP20 . . . 117 A2
- Hollybush Ct CF23 . . . 178 D6
- Hollybush Dr SA2 . . . 94 B8
- HOLLYBUSH ESTATE . . . 176 E6
- Hollybush Gr CF39 . . . 108 A3
- Hollybush Hts CF23 . . . 178 D7
- Hollybush Prim Sch NP44 . . . 89 C1
- Hollybush Rd CF23 . . . 178 D6
- Hollybush Rise CF23 . . . 178 D6
- Hollybush Terr
  - Church Village CF38 . . . 136 A1
  - Pontypool / Pont-y-pwl NP4 . . . 62 A8
- Hollybush View NP44 . . . 116 D8
- Hollybush Villas CF38 . . . 135 F1
- Hollybush Way / Ffordd Hollybush NP44 . . . 116 D8
- Hollybush Wlk NP10 . . . 141 F3
- Holly Cl NP23 . . . 7 C5
- Hollycroft Cl CF5 . . . 193 E6
- Holly Ct CF62 . . . 214 C3
- Holly Dr CF44 . . . 28 C3
- Holly Gr CF14 . . . 160 A4
- Hollyhock Cl NP10 . . . 141 E6
- Hollyhock Dr CF31 . . . 169 D6
- Hollylodge Cl NP44 . . . 90 B6
- Holly Lodge Gdns NP44 . . . 90 B6
- Holly Lodge Gn NP44 . . . 90 B6
- Holly Lodge Rd NP44 . . . 90 A6
- Holly Pl NP12 . . . 85 E7
- Holly Rd
  - Cardiff / Caerdydd CF5 . . . 193 D8
  - Llanharry CF72 . . . 172 C5
  - Neath / Castell-Nedd SA11 . . . 72 A5
  - Risca / Rhisga NP11 . . . 115 B2
- Hollyrood Cl CF62 . . . 214 C8
- Holly Row CF45 . . . 81 E8
- Holly St
  - Gilfach Goch CF39 . . . 132 B5
  - Pontardawe SA8 . . . 23 E5
  - Rhydyfelin CF37 . . . 136 B5
- Holly Terr
  - Cardiff / Caerdydd CF14 . . . 177 A2
  - Newbridge / Trecelyn NP11 . . . 86 F6
  - Troedyrhiw CF48 . . . 31 B2
- Holly Vale CF35 . . . 170 C8
- Holly Way CF47 . . . 10 D4
- Holly Wlk CF36 . . . 183 E8
- Holmdale [10] NP44 . . . 89 B3
- Holmesdale Ct CF11 . . . 194 F1
- Holmesdale St CF11 . . . 194 F2
- Holmeside CF14 . . . 160 A3
- Holmes St CF63 . . . 215 B6
- Holms Ct CF64 . . . 216 A5
- Holmsdale Pl CF64 . . . 207 B3
- Holmsview Cl CF3 . . . 179 C4
- Holmview Ct CF3 . . . 179 C5
- Holmwood CF38 . . . 156 C6
- Holmwood Cl CF23 . . . 178 C4
- Holst Cl NP19 . . . 145 A6
- Holton Prim Sch CF63 . . . 215 A5
- Holton Rd
  - Barry / Y Barri, Barry Dock CF63 . . . 215 A5
  - Barry / Y Barri CF62, CF63 . . . 214 F5
- Holts Field SA3 . . . 122 C5
- Holy Family RC Prim Sch CF5 . . . 193 B8
- Holyhead Ct CF83 . . . 137 C4
- Holyoake Terr
  - Abersychan NP4 . . . 37 F2
  - Pontypool / Pont-y-pwl NP4 . . . 62 A8
- Holyrood Terr CF40 . . . 106 E8
- Holywell Rd CF38 . . . 136 A2
- Home Farm Cl NP18 . . . 117 F2
- Home Farm Cres NP18 . . . 117 F2
- Home Farm Gn NP18 . . . 117 F2
- Home Farm Way SA4 . . . 44 C2
- Homegower Ho SA1 . . . 95 B6
- Homeland Pl NP12 . . . 85 F6
- Homelands Rd CF14 . . . 177 C5
- Home Leigh NP11 . . . 86 F7
- Homelong Ho CF14 . . . 177 F8
- Home Of The Oak Tree / Trederwen CF33 . . . 148 D3
- Homerton St CF45 . . . 82 B6
- Homeside Ho [13] CF64 . . . 207 B4
- Homevalley Ho [4] NP20 . . . 142 F4
- Homfray St CF34 . . . 102 A6
- Honeyfield Rd NP23 . . . 7 B4
- Honeysuckel Cl NP10 . . . 142 B3
- Honeysuckle Cl
  - Cardiff / Caerdydd CF5 . . . 193 C8
  - Ebbw Vale / Glyn Ebwy NP23 . . . 7 C5
  - Merthyr Tydfil / Merthyr Tudful CF47 . . . 10 C5
- Honeysuckle Dr SA6 . . . 45 D2
- Honeysuckle La SA4 . . . 43 B3
- Honeysuckle Way CF31 . . . 169 D5
- Hong Kong Terr CF32 . . . 151 A4
- Honiton Rd CF3 . . . 179 C7
- Hood Rd
  - Barry / Y Barri CF62 . . . 214 E3
  - Newport / Casnewydd NP19 . . . 144 F7
- Hood Road Sta* CF62 . . . 214 E3
- Hookland Rd CF36 . . . 183 C8
- Hoo St / Stryd Hoo SA11 . . . 71 C2
- Hoo St SA1 . . . 96 B7
- Hope Ave CF32 . . . 150 C4
- Hopefield NP20 . . . 143 B7
- Hopefield Ct NP20 . . . 143 B7
- Hope Ho CF10 . . . 194 E8
- Hope St / Stryd Hope CF10 . . . 232 C1
- Hope St NP13 . . . 15 E5
- Hophouse The [8] CF10 . . . 232 B2
- Hopkins Cl CF48 . . . 30 F4
- Hopkins St SA5 . . . 68 C4
- Hopkin St
  - Aberavon SA12 . . . 98 F1
  - Pontardawe SA8 . . . 23 E5
  - Treherbert CF42 . . . 78 A8
- Hopkins Terr SA13 . . . 74 F6
- HOPKINSTOWN
  - Ammanford . . . 219 E7
  - Pontypridd . . . 108 F2
- Hopkinstown Rd CF37 . . . 109 A1
- Hopkins Wlk NP19 . . . 144 F5
- Hopyard Mdw CF71 . . . 188 D2
- Horace Terr CF83 . . . 137 F8
- Horeb Cl CF47 . . . 10 F3
- Horeb Ct NP11 . . . 59 F5
- Horeb Rd SA6 . . . 45 F1
- Horeb St
  - Merthyr Tydfil / Merthyr Tudful CF48 . . . 29 F8
  - Treorchy / Treorci CF42 . . . 78 D6
- Horeb Terr CF44 . . . 28 E7
- Horizon Pk SA6 . . . 69 A6
- Horle Cl CF11 . . . 195 A2
- Hornbeam Cl
  - Caerleon / Caerllion NP18 . . . 117 E2
  - [5] Cardiff / Caerdydd CF3 . . . 180 A7
  - Cimla SA11 . . . 72 C5
  - Merthyr Tydfil / Merthyr Tudful CF47 . . . 10 C6
- Hornbeam Wlk NP10 . . . 141 F3
- Hornchurch Cl CF5 . . . 176 E1
- Horner St CF82 . . . 85 A6
- Horrocks Cl NP20 . . . 117 A4
- Horsefair Rd CF31 . . . 169 F2
- HORTON . . . 231 B4
- Horton St SA1 . . . 233 A3
- Horton Way CF64 . . . 215 E6
- Horwood Cl CF24 . . . 195 F7
- Hosea Row SA1 . . . 68 D4
- Hosking Ind Est CF10 . . . 195 B2
- Hoskins St NP20 . . . 143 C6
- Hospital Flats CF44 . . . 29 B2
- Hospital Rd
  - Gorseinon SA4 . . . 66 F8
  - Nantyglo NP23 . . . 15 D8
  - Penllergaer SA4 . . . 43 E1
  - Pen-pedair-heol CF82 . . . 84 D8
- Hospital Rd *continued*
  - Pontypool / Pont-y-pwl NP4 . . . 62 B8
  - Pontypridd CF37 . . . 109 E1
  - Port Talbot SA12 . . . 124 E8
- Hotham Cl [1] CF23 . . . 161 A1
- Houlson St CF48 . . . 11 B5
- Houlston Ct CF24 . . . 195 F7
- Houses on the Hill / Tai Arfryn [7] CF31 . . . 168 C3
- Housman Cl CF3 . . . 179 C8
- Hove Ave NP19 . . . 144 A6
- Howard Cl NP19 . . . 144 E6
- Howard Ct
  - Barry / Y Barri CF62 . . . 214 C4
  - Cardiff / Caerdydd, Atlantic Wharf / Glanfa Iwerydd CF10 . . . 232 D1
  - Cardiff / Caerdydd CF10 . . . 232 D3
- Howard Dr CF83 . . . 138 A5
- Howard Gdns CF24 . . . 232 D3
- Howardian Cl [4] CF23 . . . 178 E1
- Howard Pl CF24 . . . 232 D3
- Howard St
  - Cardiff / Caerdydd CF24 . . . 195 D5
  - Tonypandy CF40 . . . 106 A6
  - Treorchy / Treorci CF42 . . . 78 D6
- Howards Way
  - Ebbw Vale / Glyn Ebwy NP23 . . . 14 E3
  - Gorseinon SA4 . . . 43 C3
- Howard Terr CF24 . . . 232 D3
- Howe Circ NP19 . . . 144 F7
- Howell Cl CF48 . . . 10 C1
- Howell Griffiths Ct NP13 . . . 36 A6
- Howell Rd CF5 . . . 193 C5
- Howell's Cres CF5 . . . 194 B8
- Howells Rd SA2 . . . 93 C8
- Howells Row
  - Aberdare / Aberdâr CF44 . . . 53 C5
  - Cwmdare CF44 . . . 28 C3
- Howell's Sch CF5 . . . 194 B8
- Howell St
  - Nant-y-Moel CF32 . . . 104 E7
  - Pontypridd CF37 . . . 109 F5
- Howel Rd SA11 . . . 71 C4
- Howy Rd NP23 . . . 7 B5
- Hubert Dr CF31 . . . 168 F7
- Hubert Rd NP19 . . . 143 E7
- Hubert Rise
  - [11] Rogerstone NP10 . . . 142 B4
  - Rogerstone NP10 . . . 142 B5
- Hughes Ave NP23 . . . 7 C1
- Hughes St
  - [4] Mountain Ash / Aberpennar CF45 . . . 54 E1
  - Tonypandy CF40 . . . 106 F4
- Hughs Cl CF5 . . . 176 E3
- Hugon Cl [2] CF23 . . . 178 E1
- Humber Cl NP20 . . . 116 E1
- Humber Rd NP20 . . . 116 E1
- Humphrey St SA1 . . . 95 B7
- Humphreys Terr CF34 . . . 102 A8
- Hunt Cl CF14 . . . 159 F1
- Hunter Cl NP10 . . . 142 A6
- Hunters Ridge
  - Bridgend / Pen-y-Bont ar Ogwr CF31 . . . 169 C5
  - Cardiff / Caerdydd CF23 . . . 178 B4
- Hunters Ridge / Crib Yr Heliwr SA11 . . . 49 B1
- Hunter St
  - Barry / Y Barri CF63 . . . 215 C6
  - Briton Ferry / Llansawel SA11 . . . 71 C1
  - Cardiff / Caerdydd CF10 . . . 195 B1
  - [2] Cardiff / Caerdydd CF10 . . . 195 B2
- Huntingdon Cl NP44 . . . 89 A3
- Huntingdon Dr CF23 . . . 161 A1
- Huntingdon Way SA2 . . . 94 B8
- Huntington Cl SA3 . . . 123 B8
- Huntington Ct SA3 . . . 123 B8
- Hunt Pl [12] CF63 . . . 215 B6
- Huntsmans Cove SA3 . . . 122 E7
- Huntsmead Cl CF14 . . . 159 E3
- Hurford Cres CF37 . . . 109 B1
- Hurford Pl CF23 . . . 178 C8
- Hurford St CF37 . . . 135 A8
- Hurman St [5] CF10 . . . 195 B2
- Huron Cres CF23 . . . 178 B4
- Hurst Gr CF44 . . . 29 B3
- Hutchwns Cl CF36 . . . 182 D7
- Hutchwns Terr CF36 . . . 182 F7
- Huxley Gn NP20 . . . 117 A2
- Hyacinth Dr CF31 . . . 169 D6
- Hyde St NP13 . . . 60 C6
- Hydrangea Cl
  - Cardiff / Caerdydd CF23 . . . 178 D7
  - Rogerstone NP10 . . . 142 B3
- Hyland Pl CF44 . . . 27 E8
- Hylton Terr CF46 . . . 56 A7
- Hynam Pl NP4 . . . 37 F5
- Hyssop Cl CF23 . . . 178 D8
- Hywel Cres CF63 . . . 215 A6
- Hywel Dda Inf Sch CF5 . . . 193 B4
- Hywel Dda Jun Sch CF5 . . . 193 B4
- Hywel Ho [9] CF47 . . . 30 D8

I

- Ian's Wlk SA6 . . . 46 B4
- Idencroft Cl CF23 . . . 161 A1
- Idris Davies Pl NP22 . . . 12 F2
- Idris Pl CF31 . . . 168 F7
- Idris Terr SA6 . . . 68 E6
- Idwal Pl SA5 . . . 68 B5
- Idwal St SA11 . . . 72 A8
- Iestyn Dr CF35 . . . 152 D1
- Iestynian Ave CF11 . . . 194 D7
- Iestyn St
  - Aberdare / Aberdâr CF44 . . . 28 E4
  - Cardiff / Caerdydd CF11 . . . 194 D7
- Ifor Hael Rd NP10 . . . 141 F6
- Ifor Jones Ct CF23 . . . 178 C5
- Ifor St CF45 . . . 54 D2
- Ifor Terr CF35 . . . 130 E3
- Ifton Pl NP19 . . . 144 A3
- Ifton St NP19 . . . 144 A3
- Ilan Ave CF37 . . . 135 F6
- Ilan Rd CF83 . . . 137 A7
- Ilchester Rd CF3 . . . 179 C6
- Ilex Cl CF14 . . . 177 F8
- Ilfracombe Cres CF3 . . . 179 C5
- Illtyd Ave
  - Llantwit Major / Llanilltud Fawr CF61 . . . 209 F6
  - Llantwit Major / Llanilltud Fawr CF61 . . . 210 A5
- Illtyd Rd CF5 . . . 193 B6
- Illtyd St
  - Neath / Castell-Nedd SA11 . . . 72 A8
  - Pontypridd CF37 . . . 135 B7
  - Treorchy / Treorci CF42 . . . 78 D6
- Ilminster Cl CF63 . . . 215 B6
- Ilminster St CF63 . . . 215 B6
- ILSTON . . . 92 B2
- Ilston SA15 . . . 40 F4
- Ilston Ho [3] SA1 . . . 233 A4
- Ilston Way SA3 . . . 123 A7
- Ilton Rd CF23 . . . 178 D1
- Imperial Bldgs
  - Cardiff / Caerdydd CF5 . . . 194 A8
  - Glan-y-nant NP12 . . . 85 A8
- Imperial Ct CF45 . . . 82 E2
- Imperial Ctr SA7 . . . 69 B7
- Imperial Way NP10 . . . 163 D6
- Inchmarnock St [8] CF24 . . . 195 D5
- Incline Bridge CF47 . . . 30 F8
- Incline La NP44 . . . 88 F1
- Incline Rd
  - Aberdare / Aberdâr CF44 . . . 29 F1
  - Abersychan NP4 . . . 37 F4
- Incline Row SA13 . . . 125 D6
- Incline Side CF48 . . . 31 B8
- INCLINE TOP . . . 10 F2
- Incline Top CF45 . . . 82 F4
- Industrial Terr [3] CF48 . . . 31 C1
- Inglefield Ave CF14 . . . 177 F2
- Ingles [12] NP44 . . . 89 B1
- Ingram Ho [1] CF37 . . . 109 D2
- Inkerman Row NP13 . . . 15 D5
- Inkerman Row / Rhes Inkerman SA13 . . . 125 D6
- Inkerman St
  - Llanelli SA15 . . . 40 D5
  - Swansea / Abertawe SA1 . . . 233 C3
- Inkerman Terr NP22 . . . 13 D5
- Innovation Ctr The NP23 . . . 14 E3
- Insole Cl CF5 . . . 193 F8
- Insole Gdns CF5 . . . 194 A8
- Insole Gr E CF5 . . . 193 F8
- Insole Gr W CF5 . . . 193 F8
- Insole Pl CF5 . . . 194 A7
- Insole Terr CF72 . . . 155 D3
- Institute Blgs NP11 . . . 60 A1
- Institute Pl CF40 . . . 106 E7
- Institute Rd CF40 . . . 106 E7
- Institute St CF43 . . . 52 A1
- Institution Terr NP23 . . . 14 D6
- Instow Pl CF3 . . . 179 D6
- Intermediate Rd NP23 . . . 8 C5
- Inter-Valley Rd SA10, SA11 . . . 223 D4
- Inverleith Terr CF40 . . . 106 E7
- Inverness Pl CF24 . . . 178 B1
- Investiture Pl CF39 . . . 133 D6
- Iolo Pl CF63 . . . 215 B7
- Iorwerth St SA5 . . . 68 C2
- Ipswich Rd CF23 . . . 178 F1
- Ireland Cl CF3 . . . 180 A5
- Irene St CF45 . . . 81 E8
- Ireton Cl [3] CF23 . . . 161 A1
- Irfon St CF43 . . . 79 F6
- Iris Cl SA12 . . . 98 C3
- Iris Rd NP10 . . . 141 D6
- Iron Bridge Rd CF15 . . . 176 C8
- Iron Row NP22 . . . 13 E6
- Iron St
  - Cardiff / Caerdydd CF24 . . . 195 D6
  - Tredegar NP22 . . . 13 E6
- Iron Way / Ffordd Haearn CF32 . . . 150 C5
- Ironworks Rd CF44 . . . 27 D8
- Irvine Ct SA3 . . . 123 B4
- Irving Ho [1] SA12 . . . 98 B3
- Irving Pl CF62 . . . 214 E5
- Isaac's Pl SA12 . . . 124 F8
- Isaf Rd NP11 . . . 115 B1
- Isca Cl NP44 . . . 89 F4
- Isca Ct NP18 . . . 118 B3
- Isca Mews NP18 . . . 118 C2
- Isca Rd NP18 . . . 118 C1
- Iscennen Rd / Ffordd Is-Cennen [14] SA18 . . . 219 B7
- Iscoed SA15 . . . 40 B6
- Iscoed Rd / Heol Iscoed SA4 . . . 19 A4
- Is-Fryn NP22 . . . 12 E6
- Isfryn Ind Est CF35 . . . 130 F2
- Island Farm Cl CF31 . . . 168 E1
- Island Farm Rd CF31 . . . 168 E1
- Island Mews SA13 . . . 99 B1
- Island Pl SA15 . . . 40 D5
- Island Rd CF62 . . . 214 D4
- Island View Cvn Pk CF64 . . . 216 D4
- Islawen Mdws CF35 . . . 152 E1
- Islington Rd CF31 . . . 168 C6
- Islwyn SA14 . . . 41 E5
- Islwyn Cl
  - Ebbw Vale / Glyn Ebwy NP23 . . . 14 C8
  - Pengam NP12 . . . 85 B7
  - Ynysddu NP11 . . . 112 F6
- Islwyn Ct NP11 . . . 115 B1
- Islwyn Dr CF83 . . . 138 A4
- Islwyn Meml Chapel* NP11 . . . 113 B3
- Islwyn Rd
  - Cwmfelinfach NP11 . . . 113 F3
  - Swansea / Abertawe SA1 . . . 95 B8
- Islwyn St
  - Abercarn NP11 . . . 87 A3
  - Cwmfelinfach NP11 . . . 113 B4
- Islwyn Terr
  - Pontllanfraith NP12 . . . 86 A4
  - Porth CF39 . . . 107 D4
  - Tredegar NP22 . . . 13 E6
- Islwyn Way [7] CF63 . . . 215 A8
- Islwyn Workshops NP11 . . . 141 A8
- Is y Bryniau SA9 . . . 221 B8
- Is Y Coed CF43 . . . 79 C8
- Is-Y-Coed CF5 . . . 205 A6
- Isyrhos SA9 . . . 222 B6
- Itchen Cl NP20 . . . 116 D3
- Itchen Rd NP20 . . . 116 D3
- Itton St NP23 . . . 35 A7
- Ivey Pl SA1 . . . 233 B4
- Ivorites Row SA11 . . . 223 D1
- Ivor John Wlk NP18 . . . 118 A4
- Ivor Pk CF72 . . . 173 A6
- Ivor St
  - Abercarn NP11 . . . 114 C7
  - Barry / Y Barri CF62 . . . 214 F2
  - Blaenavon NP4 . . . 17 C6
  - Dowlais CF48 . . . 11 B4
  - Fleur-de-lis NP12 . . . 85 A6
  - Fleur-de-lis NP12 . . . 85 B6
  - Maesteg CF34 . . . 102 A2
  - Newport / Casnewydd NP20 . . . 143 C4
  - Pontycymer CF32 . . . 103 F3
  - Trehafod CF37 . . . 108 D2
  - Ystrad CF41 . . . 79 D3
- Ivor Terr CF48 . . . 11 A5
- Ivy Ave SA11 . . . 72 A8
- Ivy Bush Ct SA1 . . . 233 C3
- Ivy Cl
  - Ebbw Vale / Glyn Ebwy NP23 . . . 7 A4
  - Merthyr Tydfil / Merthyr Tudful CF47 . . . 10 E3
- Ivy Cottage Ct NP12 . . . 86 A8
- Ivydale CF14 . . . 160 A3
- Ivy Dene Cl NP4 . . . 38 B1
- Ivy Rd NP20 . . . 143 A4
- Ivy Row NP24 . . . 58 A8
- Ivy St
  - Cardiff / Caerdydd CF5 . . . 194 B6
  - Penarth CF64 . . . 207 A4
- Ivy Terr CF37 . . . 109 A2

J

- Jackson Cl CF62 . . . 213 A2
- Jackson Ct [2] NP19 . . . 143 E6
- Jackson Pl [3] NP19 . . . 143 E6
- Jackson Rd CF5 . . . 193 B5
- Jack-y-Ddu Rd SA11 . . . 71 B2
- Jade Cl CF14 . . . 160 A4
- Jamaica Dr NP10 . . . 163 E7
- Jamaica Gdns NP10 . . . 163 E7
- James Cl
  - Fleur-de-lis NP12 . . . 85 A6
  - Sarn CF32 . . . 150 F4
- James Ct
  - Cardiff / Caerdydd CF23 . . . 178 B5
  - Swansea / Abertawe SA1 . . . 69 D6
- James Griffiths Rd SA18 . . . 219 D7
- James Pl CF37 . . . 135 E7
- James' Rd CF32 . . . 103 E6
- James St / Stryd James NP22 . . . 13 F5
- James's Row NP23 . . . 7 C4
- James St
  - Aberbargoed / Aberbargod CF81 . . . 58 B4
  - Aberdare / Aberdâr CF44 . . . 53 C6

James St *continued*
Abertillery / Abertyleri NP13 . . . . 36 B5
Barry / Y Barri CF63 . . . . 215 D6
Bedwas CF83 . . . . 139 A7
Blaenavon NP4 . . . . 17 C6
Cardiff / Caerdydd CF10 . . 195 B2
Cwmdare CF44 . . . . 28 C3
Cwmsyfiog NP24 . . . . 34 A1
Ebbw Vale / Glyn Ebwy NP23 . . . . 14 D8
Gorof SA9 . . . . 2 F8
3 Llanbradach CF83 . . . . 111 F1
Llanelli SA15 . . . . 40 E6
Maerdy CF43 . . . . 52 A2
Markham NP12 . . . . 58 D7
23 Merthyr Tydfil / Merthyr Tudful CF47 . . . . 30 E8
5 Mountain Ash / Aberpennar CF45 . . . . 54 E1
Newport / Casnewydd NP20 . . . . 143 D2
New Tredegar NP24 . . . . 33 E3
Penrhos SA9 . . . . 222 A6
Pontardawe SA8 . . . . 23 D5
Pontarddulais SA4 . . . . 19 D3
Pontypool / Pont-y-pwl NP4 . . . . 62 D7
Pontypridd CF37 . . . . 135 E7
Porthcawl CF36 . . . . 182 F6
1 Port Talbot SA13 . . . . 125 C8
Tonypandy CF40 . . . . 107 A4
Treorchy / Treorci CF42 . . . . 78 E6
James Terr
Clydach NP7 . . . . 9 C6
Hengoed CF82 . . . . 85 A3
Llantrisant CF72 . . . . 155 E2
Porth CF39 . . . . 107 E5
Tonypandy CF40 . . . . 106 F3
Jamesville NP11 . . . . 114 B8
Jane Austen Cl NP20 . . . . 142 E1
Jane Cl NP10 . . . . 163 F5
Janet St
Cardiff / Caerdydd CF24 . . . . 195 E5
Pontypridd CF37 . . . . 135 F5
Japonica Cl NP20 . . . . 117 B3
Japonica Dr / Rhodfa Clesin CF48 . . . . 11 C4
Jasmin Cl SA12 . . . . 98 C3
Jasmine Cl
Merthyr Tydfil / Merthyr Tudful CF47 . . . . 10 C5
Rogerstone / Ty-du NP10 . . . . 141 D7
Swansea / Abertawe SA2 . . 94 B7
Jasmine Dr CF3 . . . . 180 A7
Jasper Cl CF5 . . . . 176 E2
Jaycroft Cl CF23 . . . . 161 B1
Jays Field SA11 . . . . 72 B4
Jeans Cl NP20 . . . . 117 A3
Jeddo Cl NP20 . . . . 143 C2
Jeddo St NP20 . . . . 143 C2
Jeffcott Pl CF64 . . . . 207 A6
Jeffreys Ct SA5 . . . . 68 B5
Jeffrey St
Mountain Ash / Aberpennar CF45 . . . . 54 D3
Newport / Casnewydd NP19 . . . . 143 E5
Jellicoe Cl NP19 . . . . 144 F7
Jellicoe Ct CF10 . . . . 232 D1
Jellicoe Gdns CF23 . . . . 178 A5
Jenkin Houses CF48 . . . . 30 F4
Jenkins Pl 21 CF47 . . . . 30 E8
Jenkins Rd
Neath / Castell-Nedd SA11 . . . . 71 F5
Skewen / Sclwen SA10 . . . . 71 A7
Jenkins Row
Deri CF81 . . . . 57 B8
Rhymney / Rhymni NP22 . . . 12 F3
Jenkins St
Abercynon CF45 . . . . 82 F3
Newport / Casnewydd NP19 . . . . 143 F3
Pontypridd CF37 . . . . 109 A1
Jenkin St
Abercwmboi CF44 . . . . 53 F4
4 Aberdare / Aberdâr CF44 . . . . 29 A1
2 Barry / Y Barri CF63 . . 215 B7
Bridgend / Pen-y-Bont ar Ogwr CF31 . . . . 168 F3
Maesycwmmer CF82 . . . . 85 B2
Porth CF39 . . . . 107 F3
Jenkins Terr
Abergwynfi SA13 . . . . 76 C5
Cwmfelin CF34 . . . . 128 C8
Port Talbot SA13 . . . . 125 D7
Jenkinsville 15 CF64 . . . . 207 B4
Jenkins Way CF3 . . . . 179 F5
Jenner Park Prim Sch CF63 . . . . 215 A6
Jenner Rd CF62 . . . . 214 D5
Jenner St CF63 . . . . 215 C6
Jenner Wlk CF38 . . . . 135 E1
Jericho Rd SA1 . . . . 233 C4
Jerries La CF83 . . . . 138 D7
JERSEY MARINE 70 C1
Jersey Quay SA12 . . . . 124 D7
Jersey Rd
Blaengwynfi SA13 . . . . 76 C6
Swansea / Abertawe SA1 . . 69 B4
Jersey Row SA12 . . . . 99 E5
Jersey St
Port Talbot SA13 . . . . 99 C1
Swansea / Abertawe SA1 . . 68 D1
Jersey Terr
Briton Ferry / Llansawel SA11 . . . . 71 B1
Cwmavon / Cwmafan SA12 . . . . 99 E5
Swansea / Abertawe SA1 . . 96 A7
Jerusalem Cl NP4 . . . . 63 B3
Jerusalem La NP4 . . . . 63 B4
Jerusalem St NP22 . . . . 12 F3
Jervis Wlk NP19 . . . . 144 E6
Jesmond Dene CF15 . . . . 158 B4
Jessop Cl NP10 . . . . 142 B6
Jessop Ct SA6 . . . . 45 E4
Jessop Rd NP10 . . . . 142 B6
Jestyn Cl
Cardiff / Caerdydd CF5 . . . . 192 F4
Dinas Powis / Dinas Powys CF64 . . . . 206 B4
Jestyn St CF39 . . . . 107 E4
Jevan Cl CF5 . . . . 176 D3
Jewell La NP20 . . . . 143 B8
Jewel St CF63 . . . . 215 B5
Jim Driscoll Way CF11 . . . . 195 A1
Jim Harvard Ct 5 SA6 . . . 69 A8
Jindabyne Ct CF3 . . . . 161 F2
Job's La CF48 . . . . 10 A4
Jockey St SA1 . . . . 233 B4
John Baker Cl NP44 . . . . 116 F8
John Batchelor Way CF64 . . . . 207 A6
John Bull Cl NP19 . . . . 144 E6
John Field Wlk NP19 . . . . 144 E4
John Frost Sq 2 NP20 . . . . 143 C4
John Ireland Cl NP19 . . . . 144 D5
John Morgan Cl CF5 . . . . 176 E3
John Penry Cres SA5 . . . . 68 B6
John Pl CF37 . . . . 135 E6
John St / Stryd John CF10 . . . . 232 C1
John's Cotts CF32 . . . . 150 F4
John's Dr CF35 . . . . 170 D7
Johns La CF14 . . . . 177 A2
Johnson Pk CF44 . . . . 27 E7
John St
Aberavon SA12 . . . . 99 A1
Abercarn NP11 . . . . 114 C8
Abercwmboi CF44 . . . . 53 F4
7 Aberdare / Aberdâr CF44 . . . . 29 A1
Bargoed / Bargod CF81 . . . 57 F3
Barry / Y Barri CF63 . . . . 215 D6
Cefn Cribwr CF32 . . . . 149 C2
Ebbw Vale / Glyn Ebwy NP23 . . . . 7 C1
Hirwaun CF44 . . . . 27 E8
Llanelli SA15 . . . . 40 D5
Maesteg CF34 . . . . 101 F5
Markham NP12 . . . . 58 E7
Merthyr Tydfil / Merthyr Tudful CF47 . . . . 10 D1
Mountain Ash / Aberpennar CF45 . . . . 54 F2
Nant-y-Moel CF32 . . . . 104 F5
Newport / Casnewydd NP20 . . . . 143 D3
Penarth CF64 . . . . 207 B5
Pontypool / Pont-y-pwl NP4 . . . . 62 C6
Pontypridd CF37 . . . . 135 E6
Porth, Birchgrove CF39 . . . 107 F3
Porthcawl CF36 . . . . 182 F6
Porth, Ynyshir CF39 . . . . 107 F6
Resolven / Resolfen SA11 . . . . 226 D5
Swansea / Abertawe, Cockett SA2 . . . . 67 D2
Swansea / Abertawe SA1 . . . . 233 B4
The Mumbles / Y Mwmbwls SA3 . . . . 123 A4
Treharris CF46 . . . . 83 B6
Treherbert CF42 . . . . 51 A1
Treorchy / Treorci CF41 . . . . 78 F5
Ynysddu NP11 . . . . 112 F5
John's Terr SA12 . . . . 73 C5
Johnston Cl NP10 . . . . 142 A7
Johnston Rd CF14 . . . . 159 D1
John's Villas CF32 . . . . 151 A5
Joiners Rd SA4 . . . . 65 D1
Jolly Rd / Heol Jolly SA18 . . . . 220 C8
Jonathans Terr CF37 . . . . 109 F5
Jones Pl 3 CF37 . . . . 109 E2
Jones Point Ho CF11 . . . . 207 A7
Jones St
Dowlais CF48 . . . . 11 B5
3 Mountain Ash / Aberpennar CF45 . . . . 54 E1
Newport / Casnewydd NP20 . . . . 143 B4
New Tredegar NP24 . . . . 33 F3
Pontardawe SA8 . . . . 23 E5
Pontypridd CF37 . . . . 109 F6
Tonypandy CF40 . . . . 106 C6
Treherbert CF42 . . . . 78 B8
Jones Terr
Merthyr Tydfil / Merthyr Tudful, Heolgerrig CF48 . . 29 F8
Merthyr Tydfil / Merthyr Tudful, Thomas Town CF47 . . . . 10 F1
Swansea / Abertawe SA1 . . . . 233 A4
Jones' Terr / Teras Jones SA18 . . . . 219 F8
Jonquil Cl CF3 . . . . 180 A7
Joseph Davies' Cl 6 SA1 . . . . 68 C2
Joseph Parry Cl CF64 . . . . 206 E6
Joseph Parry Ct 8 CF47 . . . . 30 D8
Joseph Parry's Cottage Mus★ CF48 . . . . 10 C2
Joseph Row CF33 . . . . 148 D3
Joseph St SA13 . . . . 99 B2
Joslin Rd CF35 . . . . 169 A7
Joslin Terr CF35 . . . . 169 A7
Jowett Ave CF47 . . . . 30 F8
Joyce Cl NP20 . . . . 142 E2
Joyce Ho SA12 . . . . 98 F2
Jubilee Cres
Bridgend / Pen-y-Bont ar Ogwr CF31 . . . . 169 A3
Neath / Castell-Nedd SA10 . . . . 70 F8
Sarn CF32 . . . . 150 E4
Jubilee Ct
Pontygwaith CF43 . . . . 80 B2
Swansea / Abertawe SA5 . . 67 C4
Jubilee Gdns
Barry / Y Barri CF63 . . . . 215 D8
Cardiff / Caerdydd CF14 . . 177 E6
Porthcawl CF36 . . . . 166 A2
Jubilee Ind Est CF24 . . . . 195 D5
Jubilee La
Gorseinon SA4 . . . . 66 A8
Penarth CF64 . . . . 207 B4
Jubilee Pl NP4 . . . . 37 F5
Jubilee Rd
Aberdare / Aberdâr CF44 . . . . 53 C6
Abertillery / Abertyleri NP13 . . . . 36 C3
Bridgend / Pen-y-Bont ar Ogwr CF31 . . . . 169 A3
New Tredegar NP24 . . . . 34 A2
Jubilee St
Bryncae CF72 . . . . 153 F2
Cardiff / Caerdydd CF11 . . 194 E4
Jubilee Terr NP4 . . . . 62 A8
Judkin Ct 6 CF10 . . . . 195 B2
Jule Rd NP44 . . . . 89 B1
Julian's Cl CF82 . . . . 84 C7
Julian's Way CF33 . . . . 166 A7
Julian Terr SA12 . . . . 98 F1
Julius Cl NP18 . . . . 117 F3
Junction 47 Ret Pk SA4 . . 43 E2
Junction Ind Ctr CF72 . . . 173 A7
Junction Ind Est CF72 . . . 173 A7
Junction Rd NP19 . . . . 143 D6
Junction Terr CF15 . . . . 176 C5
Juniper Cl
Porthcawl CF36 . . . . 183 E7
Swansea / Abertawe SA2 . . 94 B8
Juniper Cres NP44 . . . . 116 A7
Justin Cl CF23 . . . . 178 C4

K

Kames Pl CF24 . . . . 195 C5
Kane Cl CF14 . . . . 177 F7
Kathleen St CF62 . . . . 214 C4
Katie St CF32 . . . . 103 E7
Kays & Kears Ind Est NP4 . . . . 17 A7
Kean Ho 6 SA12 . . . . 98 B3
Kear Ct NP20 . . . . 143 C4
Kear's Row NP4 . . . . 17 F1
Keats Cl
Bridgend / Pen-y-Bont ar Ogwr CF31 . . . . 168 D6
Cwmbran / Cwmbrân NP44 . . . . 89 D2
Newport / Casnewydd NP20 . . . . 142 E2
Keats Gr SA2 . . . . 93 F7
Keats Way CF62 . . . . 214 E8
Keble Ct CF83 . . . . 139 D7
Keene Ave NP10 . . . . 142 C3
Keene St NP19 . . . . 143 F4
Keen Rd
Cardiff / Caerdydd CF24 . . . . 195 D4
Cardiff / Caerdydd CF24 . . . . 195 D5
Keen's Pl CF32 . . . . 150 F4
Keepers Cl SA4 . . . . 44 C2
Keir Hardie Cl NP23 . . . . 7 D6
Keir Hardie Rd CF34 . . . . 101 F1
Keir Hardie Terr NP11 . . . 60 A3
Keir Hardy Rd SA12 . . . . 98 D7
Keith St CF43 . . . . 80 B4
Keller Ho 1 SA12 . . . . 98 F1
Kelly Rd NP19 . . . . 144 A7
Kelston Cl CF14 . . . . 176 F5
Kelston Pl CF14 . . . . 176 F5
Kelston Rd CF14 . . . . 176 F5
Kelvedon St NP19 . . . . 143 E4
Kelvin Cl NP20 . . . . 117 A2
Kelvin Rd
Cardiff / Caerdydd CF24 . . . . 178 B1
Clydach SA6 . . . . 22 D1
Kember Cl CF3 . . . . 180 A6
Kemble Ho SA12 . . . . 98 A2
Kemble St SA2 . . . . 94 F5
Kemeys Fawr Cl NP4 . . . . 62 D1
Kemeys Fawr Inf Sch NP4 . . . . 62 D1
Kemeys Rd CF62 . . . . 213 A2
Kemp Ho 2 SA12 . . . . 98 B3
Kemps Covert CF61 . . . . 208 H5
Kemsley Ho 4 CF47 . . . . 30 D8
Kemys Pl CF14 . . . . 177 C3
Kemys St NP4 . . . . 62 E2
Kemys Way SA6 . . . . 69 B7
Kemys Wlk NP44 . . . . 89 D1
Kendal Cl CF44 . . . . 29 D1
Kendle Dr SA2 . . . . 94 C8
KENDON 59 E2
Kendon Ct CF44 . . . . 27 D8
Kendon Rd NP11 . . . . 59 F2
Kendrick Rd CF62 . . . . 214 F5
KENFIG / CYNFFIG 165 D7
KENFIG HILL / MYNYDDCYNFFIG 148 E3
Kenfig Ind Est SA13 . . . . 147 B4
Kenfig Nature Reserve Visitor Ctr★ CF33 . . . . 165 C6
Kenfig Pl
Llanyrafon NP44 . . . . 90 A3
Swansea / Abertawe SA1 . . 69 A2
Kenfig Pool Nature Reserve★ CF33 . . . . 165 A7
Kenfig Rd CF14 . . . . 177 D3
Kenilworth Ct
Baglan SA12 . . . . 98 E5
Cardiff / Caerdydd CF5 . . . 193 F7
Kenilworth Ho CF10 . . . . 232 A2
Kenilworth Pl
Cwmbran / Cwmbrân NP44 . . . . 89 C1
The Mumbles / Y Mwmbwls SA3 . . . . 123 A8
Kenilworth Rd
Barry / Y Barri CF63 . . . . 215 B6
3 Newport / Casnewydd NP19 . . . . 144 A5
Kenley Cl CF5 . . . . 176 E1
Kenmare Mews CF23 . . . . 161 A2
Kenmuir Rd CF24 . . . . 195 F7
Kennard Cres NP4 . . . . 17 B6
Kennard Ct NP4 . . . . 17 B6
Kennard Pl NP4 . . . . 17 B7
Kennard St CF41 . . . . 78 F2
Kennard Terr NP11 . . . . 59 F1
Kennedy Cl CF38 . . . . 156 A7
Kennedy Dr CF35 . . . . 170 C8
Kennedy Rise CF62 . . . . 214 C5
Kennel Row SA11 . . . . 71 B1
Kennerleigh Rd CF3 . . . . 179 A4
Kenneth Treasure Ct 2 CF3 . . . . 179 D7
Kennington Cl
Cardiff / Caerdydd CF14 . . . . 159 E2
Swansea / Abertawe SA2 . . 93 D6
Kenry St
Evanstown CF39 . . . . 132 B8
Tonypandy CF40 . . . . 106 E5
Treorchy / Treorci CF42 . . . 78 B8
Kensington Ave CF5 . . . . 194 A6
Kensington Dr
Bridgend / Pen-y-Bont ar Ogwr CF31 . . . . 168 C6
Porth CF39 . . . . 108 A2
Kensington Gdns 6 NP19 . . . . 143 F6
Kensington Gr NP19 . . . . 143 F5
Kensington Pl NP19 . . . . 143 F5
Kenson Cl CF62 . . . . 212 E1
Kenson Hill CF62 . . . . 212 E6
Kent Cl NP10 . . . . 142 A7
Kent Ct NP18 . . . . 118 A3
Kent Gn CF62 . . . . 214 E6
Kent Rd CF31 . . . . 169 B3
Kent St CF11 . . . . 194 F2
Kenway Ave SA11 . . . . 71 F6
Kenwood Rd CF5 . . . . 193 B5
Kenyon Rd CF24 . . . . 196 A7
Keppoch St CF24 . . . . 195 C8
Kern Cl / Clos Kern SA12 . . . . 98 B3
Kerrigan Cl CF5 . . . . 176 D1
Kerrycroy St 10 CF24 . . . . 195 D5
Kerslake Terr CF40 . . . . 106 F3
Kestell Dr CF11 . . . . 207 A8
Kestrel Cl
Bridgend / Pen-y-Bont ar Ogwr CF31 . . . . 169 D3
Cardiff / Caerdydd CF23 . . . . 178 D7
Neath / Castell-Nedd SA10 . . . . 48 E2
Kestrel View CF82 . . . . 84 F3
Kestrel Way
Newport / Casnewydd NP10 . . . . 163 E7
Penarth CF64 . . . . 217 A8
Penllergaer SA4 . . . . 43 F1
Keswick Ave CF23 . . . . 178 A3
Keteringham Cl CF64 . . . . 216 A5
Kevin Ryan Ct CF48 . . . . 10 C1
Kewstoke Ave CF3 . . . . 179 B5
Kewstoke Cl CF3 . . . . 179 B5
Kewstoke Pl CF3 . . . . 179 B5
Keyes Ave CF23 . . . . 178 A5
Keyes Ct CF10 . . . . 232 D1
Keynsham Ave NP20 . . . . 143 C3
Keynsham Rd CF14 . . . . 177 C5
Keys The CF61 . . . . 209 F6
Keyston Rd CF5 . . . . 176 E1
Khartoum Terr SA10 . . . . 222 F5
Kidwelly Cl
Blackwood / Coed-Duon NP12 . . . . 58 E2
Newport / Casnewydd NP10 . . . . 163 E5
Kidwelly Cl / Clos Cydweli 1 NP44 . . . . 90 A2
Kidwelly Ct CF83 . . . . 137 D4
Kidwelly Gr CF48 . . . . 225 F1
Kidwelly Rd / Heol Cydweli 11 NP44 . . . . 90 B2
Kier Hardie Cres NP19 . . . . 144 D7
Kier Hardie Dr NP19 . . . . 144 D7
Kier Hardy SA12 . . . . 98 D7
Kilcattan St 9 CF24 . . . . 195 D5
Kilcredaun Ho CF11 . . . . 207 A8
Kildare St SA5 . . . . 68 C3
Kilfield Rd SA3 . . . . 122 B5
Kilgetty Cl CF5 . . . . 193 C4
Killan Rd SA2 . . . . 93 B8
KILLAY 93 E7
Kiln St CF44 . . . . 53 C8
Kilvey Rd SA1 . . . . 233 C5
Kilvey Terr SA1 . . . . 233 C4
Kimberley Cl SA2 . . . . 94 D7
Kimberley Ct CF31 . . . . 169 B4
Kimberley Pl CF48 . . . . 31 C2
Kimberley Rd
Abertillery / Abertyleri NP13 . . . . 36 C3
Cardiff / Caerdydd CF23 . . . . 178 D1
Swansea / Abertawe SA2 . . 94 D7
Kimberley Terr
Cardiff / Caerdydd CF14 . . . . 177 F8
Tredegar NP22 . . . . 13 F6
Kimberley Way CF39 . . . . 107 F2
Kincoed Rd NP12 . . . . 59 B1
Kincraig St CF24 . . . . 195 B8
Kingarth St 6 CF24 . . . . 195 D5
King Charles Rd NP11 . . . . 86 D5
Kingcraft St CF45 . . . . 54 D2
Kingdon-Owen Rd SA11 . . . . 71 F5
King Edward Ave CF83 . . 138 B2
King Edward Rd
Brynmawr NP23 . . . . 8 C5
Gwaun-Cae-Gurwen SA18 . . . . 220 F6
King Edward's Rd SA1 . . . . 95 A6
King Edward St CF32 . . . . 103 E5
King Edward Terr NP22 . . 12 E5
King Edward VII Ave CF10 . . . . 232 B4
King Edward Villas 8 CF47 . . . . 10 D2
Kingfisher Cl CF3 . . . . 179 F7
Kingfisher Cl / Clos Glas Y Dorlan CF31 . . . . 169 C4
Kingfisher Ct SA15 . . . . 41 A5
Kingfisher Pl NP10 . . . . 163 E7
Kingfisher Sq CF62 . . . . 210 D6
King George Ave SA15 . . . 40 E5
King George Ct SA2 . . . . 94 B3
King George V Dr E
Cardiff / Caerdydd CF14 . . . . 177 F3
Cardiff / Caerdydd CF14 . . 177 F4
King George V Dr N CF14 . . . . 177 F5
King George V Dr W CF14 . . . . 177 E4
King La 12 NP20 . . . . 143 C4
Kingleys The CF34 . . . . 102 A8
Kingrosia Pk SA6 . . . . 47 A8
Kingsacre CF38 . . . . 156 C6
Kings Acre NP20 . . . . 142 F5
Kings Ave NP22 . . . . 12 E5
King's Ave CF15 . . . . 176 C5
Kingsbridge Bsns Pk SA4 . . . . 66 C8
Kingsbury Ct CF44 . . . . 28 E6
Kingsbury Pl
Cwmaman CF44 . . . . 53 A4
Llwydcoed CF44 . . . . 28 E6
Kings Cl CF83 . . . . 137 A7
Kings Ct 7 CF64 . . . . 206 A2
Kingsdale Ct NP20 . . . . 143 A3
Kingsfield NP23 . . . . 7 E1
King's Head Rd SA5 . . . . 67 F3
King's Hill
Hengoed CF82 . . . . 85 A3
Porthcawl CF36 . . . . 183 A7
Kingshill Ct 9 NP20 . . . . 143 C4
Kings La SA1 . . . . 233 B3
Kingsland Cres CF63 . . . . 215 A4
Kingsland Rd
Cardiff / Caerdydd, Canton CF5 . . . . 194 B6
Cardiff / Caerdydd, Whitchurch / Yr Eglwys Newydd CF14 . . . . 176 F4
Kingsland Terr CF37 . . . . 135 E7
Kingsland Wlk NP44 . . . . 89 C2
Kingslea 9 NP44 . . . . 89 B1
Kingsley Cl CF64 . . . . 216 B5
Kingsley Pl CF83 . . . . 110 F2
Kingsley Terr
Aberfan CF48 . . . . 55 C4
Merthyr Tydfil / Merthyr Tudful CF47 . . . . 10 F1
Kings Mews CF11 . . . . 194 E6
Kingsmill Terr 3 NP20 . . . . 143 B4
Kings Monkton Sch CF24 . . . . 232 C3
King's Par NP20 . . . . 143 D2
Kings Rd
Cardiff / Caerdydd CF11 . . . . 194 D7

Kings Rd *continued*
The Mumbles / Y Mwmbwls SA3 123 A4
King's Rd
Cardiff / Caerdydd CF11 194 D6
Radyr CF15 176 C5
Kings Ride CF64 205 F3
King's Road / Heol Y Brenin SA1 233 C2
King St
Abercynon CF45 82 F3
Aberdare / Aberdâr CF44 53 C8
Abertillery / Abertyleri NP13 36 B5
Abertridwr CF83 137 A7
Blaenavon NP4 17 C7
Brynmawr NP23 8 B4
Cwmdare CF44 28 C3
Cwmfelinfach NP11 113 A4
Cwm NP23 35 B6
Ebbw Vale / Glyn Ebwy NP23 7 F4
Ferndale CF43 80 A5
Mountain Ash / Aberpennar CF45 81 E8
Nantyglo NP23 8 C1
Neath / Castell-Nedd SA11 71 E7
Newport / Casnewydd NP20 143 C4
Pant CF48 11 A6
Penarth CF64 207 B5
Pontlottyn CF81 12 F1
Pontypool / Pont-y-pwl NP4 62 B7
Pontypridd CF37 135 E6
Port Talbot SA13 99 C1
4 Swansea / Abertawe SA1 233 B3
Taffs Well / Ffynnon Taf CF15 158 A3
Ton Pentre CF41 79 B2
Tredegar NP22 6 F1
Kings Terr CF34 101 F6
Kingston Rd
Cardiff / Caerdydd CF11 194 D5
3 Newport / Casnewydd NP19 143 E5
Swansea / Abertawe SA2 94 D7
Kingsvale 10 NP20 143 C4
Kingsway
Bridgend / Pen-y-Bont ar Ogwr CF31 169 C2
Cardiff / Caerdydd CF10 232 B3
Newport / Casnewydd NP20 143 C5
Swansea / Abertawe SA5 67 C4
Kingsway Bldgs CF31 169 D2
Kingsway Ctr 5 NP20 143 C4
Kingsway The / Ffordd Y Brenin SA1 233 A3
Kingswood Cl
Ewenny / Ewenni CF35 185 E7
Hengoed CF82 85 A3
Kingswood / Coed-y-Brenin CF37 135 A8
King Wood Cl CF23 178 E2
Kinley St SA1 95 F7
Kinnock Ct NP44 90 A6
Kinsale Cl CF23 161 A2
Kipling Cl
Cardiff / Caerdydd CF3 179 B7
Penarth CF64 206 F5
Kipling Gdns CF31 168 C5
Kipling Hill NP20 142 E2
Kirby Daniel Ct 26 NP20 143 C3
Kirby La NP20 143 C3
Kirkby Ct CF10 232 D1
Kirkhouse St CF37 135 B8
Kirkwall Ct CF24 195 F7
Kirton Cl CF5 176 E1
Kismet Pk CF11 194 E2
Kitchener Prim Sch CF11 194 D5
Kitchener Rd CF11 194 D5
Kitchener St NP4 61 F8
Kittiwake Cl CF36 182 D8
KITTLE 121 E7
Kittle Gn SA3 121 E7
Kittle Hill La SA3 121 E7
Kitty Hawk Dr NP19 144 B3
Knap Car Terr CF62 214 B2
KNELSTON 231 A7
Knelston Pl SA5 67 F7
Knelston Prim Sch SA3 231 A8
Knight Cl 25 NP20 143 C3
Knighton Ct
Caerleon / Caerllion NP18 118 B2
6 Cardiff / Caerdydd CF24 195 D6
Knights Rd / Heol Marchog SA13 125 E3
Knight St
Aberavon SA12 99 A1
8 Mountain Ash / Aberpennar CF45 54 D3
Knights Terr CF45 82 F3
Knightswell Cl CF5 193 A2
Knightswell Rd CF5 193 A3
Knights Wlk / Llwybr Y Marchog CF83 137 D2
Knole Cl CF23 161 A1
Knoll Ave SA2 94 E6
Knoll Terr CF40 106 D7
Knowbury Ave CF64 217 B8
Knox Rd CF24 232 C3
Knox St SA13 125 E3
Knoyle Dr SA5 68 C7
Knoyle St SA5 68 C7
Kyfts La SA3 228 E3
Kyle Ave CF14 177 C5
Kyle Cres CF14 177 C5
Kymin Rd CF64 207 B4
Kymin Terr CF64 207 B4
Kyveilog St CF11 194 D7

L

Laburnam Ave NP22 6 D1
Laburnham Bush La NP19 144 C3
Laburnham Pl SA2 94 B6
Laburnum Ave
Baglan SA12 98 E7
Newport / Casnewydd NP19 144 B4
Laburnum Cl
Barry / Y Barri CF62 214 F7
Ebbw Vale / Glyn Ebwy NP23 7 C5
Merthyr Tydfil / Merthyr Tudful CF47 10 D4
Rogerstone / Ty-du NP10 141 E7
Laburnum Ct CF37 136 B5
Laburnum Dr
Cwmbran / Cwmbrân NP44 116 A8
Cwmdare CF44 28 D3
Pontypool / Pont-y-pwl NP4 63 B5
Porthcawl CF36 183 E8
Laburnum Gr NP12 85 E3
Laburnum La CF48 10 B6
Laburnum Pl CF5 193 D8
Laburnum Terr
Abercarn NP11 87 C4
Rhydyfelin CF37 136 B5
Troedyrhiw CF48 31 B2
Laburnum Way
Dinas Powis / Dinas Powys CF64 206 B2
Penarth CF64 206 E3
Ladies Row NP22 6 F1
Lady Aberdare Flats CF45 54 D4
Ladybench NP44 89 B1
Lady Charlotte La 1 SA13 125 D5
Ladyhill Gn NP19 144 C4
Ladyhill Rd NP19 144 D5
Lady Housty Ave SA3 122 E5
Lady Isle Ho CF11 207 A8
Lady Jane St 4 SA12 124 F8
Lady Margaret Ct 5 CF23 178 E1
Lady Margaret's Terr 11 CF24 195 D5
Lady Margaret Villas SA2 94 E7
Lady Mary Rd CF23 178 B3
Ladysmith Pl CF48 31 C2
Ladysmith Rd
Blackwood / Coed-Duon NP12 85 E6
Cardiff / Caerdydd CF23 178 D1
Ladysmith Terr NP22 13 F6
Lady Tyler Terr NP22 12 F3
Ladywell NP44 89 E5
Laing St CF33 148 C1
Lake Ct SA12 124 E7
Lakefield Cl 1 SA15 40 D4
Lakefield Pl SA15 40 C4
Lakefield Prim Sch SA15 40 C4
Lakefield Rd SA15 40 C4
Lake Hill Dr CF71 188 F1
Lake Rd
Brynmawr NP23 8 C4
Newport / Casnewydd NP19 144 C1
Port Talbot SA12 124 F7
Lake Rd E CF23 178 B4
Lake Rd N CF23 178 A5
Lake Rd W CF23 178 A4
Lakeside
Barry / Y Barri CF62 214 C1
Cwmdare CF44 28 C2
Lakeside Cl NP44 117 A6
Lakeside Cl / Clos Glanllyn
Brynmawr NP23 8 B3
Tredegar NP22 6 B1
Lakeside Dr
Cardiff / Caerdydd CF23 178 B5
Newport / Casnewydd NP10 163 C6
Lakeside Farm Pk* CF35 132 A5
Lakeside Gdns CF48 10 B4
Lakeside / Glanlyn NP22 6 B1
Lakeside Prim Sch CF23 178 B4
Lakeside Ret Pk NP23 8 B3
Lakeside Tech Pk SA7 69 B6
Lakeside Way / Ffordd Glanllyn NP23 8 B3
Lake St CF43 79 F6
Lakeview Cl CF36 183 A8
Lake View Cl
Cardiff / Caerdydd CF23 178 B4
Llanelli SA15 40 C7
Lake View Ct CF23 178 B4
Lake View / Gwel Y Llyn NP44 117 A6
Lakeview Terr SA15 40 C7
Lakin Dr CF62 214 C8
Laleston Cl
Barry / Y Barri CF63 215 A8
8 Cardiff / Caerdydd CF5 193 C4
Laleston Cl / Clos Trelales CF36 165 E2
Laleston Ct CF32 167 E5
LALESTON / TRELALES 167 F5
Lamb Cl NP20 142 E1
Lambert Cl NP20 143 B7
Lamberton Way CF24 195 D5
Lambert St NP20 143 B7
Lambert Terr CF44 28 F2
Lamb La
Ponthir NP18 117 E7
Swansea / Abertawe SA2 93 E8
Lambourne Cres
Bettws NP20 116 D2
Cardiff / Caerdydd CF14 177 E7
Lambourne Dr SA3 122 F6
Lambourne Ho NP20 116 D2
Lambourne Way NP20 116 D2
Lambourne Wlk NP20 116 D1
Lamb Rd CF44 224 D3
Lamb's Sq NP23 7 C4
Lambs Well Cl SA3 123 B4
Lamby Ind Pk CF3 179 C1
Lamby Way CF3 179 B1
Lamby Way Workshops CF3 179 C2
Lan Ave 1 SA6 68 F8
Lancaster Cl SA11 223 C1
Lancaster Ct SA5 67 D5
Lancaster Dr CF38 156 D7
Lancaster Rd NP4 63 A2
Lancaster St
Abertillery / Abertyleri NP13 36 B3
Blaina / Blaenau NP13 15 E3
Merthyr Tydfil / Merthyr Tudful CF47 10 D2
Lancaster Terr 10 CF47 10 D2
Lancaster Villas 9 CF47 10 D2
Lancers Way NP10 163 F7
Lan Cl CF37 109 B2
Lan Coed SA1 69 D5
Landeg St SA6 68 E5
Lan Deri SA1 69 C5
LANDIMORE 229 A4
Landings The CF64 206 F5
Landor Ave SA2 93 F7
Landor Dr SA4 42 D1
Landore Ave / Rhodfa Landore 8 SA13 125 E4
LANDORE / GLANDWR 68 D4
Landraw Rd CF37 109 A1
Landsdowne Ct SA5 67 D3
Landseer Cl NP19 144 A7
Landwade Cl CF5 193 C7
Lanelay Cl CF72 155 A2
Lanelay Cres CF37 109 B1
Lanelay Ind Est CF72 155 A1
Lanelay Pk CF72 155 B2
Lanelay Rd CF72 155 B2
Lanelay Terr CF37 135 B8
Lanes The CF61 209 F6
Lane The CF5 192 D2
Langcliffe Pk SA3 123 C3
Langdale Cl CF23 178 C2
Langdon Rd / Heol Langdon
Swansea / Abertawe SA1 95 F7
Swansea / Abertawe SA1 96 A6
Langenau Strasse CF31 168 E3
Langer Way SA6 22 E1
Langham Way CF11 194 E3
LANGLAND 122 F4
Langland Bay Rd SA3 122 F3
Langland Cl
Hirwaun CF44 27 D7
The Mumbles / Y Mwmbwls SA3 123 A4
Langland Court Rd SA3 122 F4
Langland Mews SA15 40 E3
Langland Rd
Cardiff / Caerdydd CF3 179 C3
The Mumbles / Y Mwmbwls SA3 123 A4
Langland Rd / Heol Langland SA15 40 E3
Langlands Rd CF63 215 D7
Langland Terr SA2 94 E5
Langland Villas SA3 123 A4
Langland Way NP19 144 A1
Langport Ave CF3 179 D6
LANGSTONE 119 D1
Langstone Bsns Vill NP18 145 A8
Langstone Cotts NP18 145 A8
Langstone Court Rd NP18 145 C8
Langstone Ct / Cwrt Langstone NP44 89 C1
Langstone La NP18 145 B6
Langstone Prim Sch NP18 119 E2
Langstone Rise NP18 119 F2
Lanhydrock Cl 11 CF3 179 F6
Lan Manor SA6 68 E8
Lan Park Rd CF37 109 C2
Lansbury Ave CF82 84 F4
Lansbury Ave / Rhodfa Lansbury SA13 125 E5
Lansbury Cl
Caerphilly / Caerffili CF83 137 F5
Maesteg CF34 101 F1
Lansbury Cres CF34 101 F1
LANSBURY PARK 138 C3
Lansbury Rd
Brynmawr NP23 8 A4
Merthyr Tydfil / Merthyr Tudful CF48 10 A3
Lansbury Terr NP23 7 F4
Lansdale Dr CF38 136 A1
Lansdown SA3 122 F4
Lansdown Ct SA11 71 D4
Lansdowne NP4 62 E1
Lansdowne Ave CF14 177 C6
Lansdowne Ave E CF11 194 C5
Lansdowne Ave W CF11 194 B5
Lansdowne Gdns / Gerddi Lansdowne NP44 117 A5
Lansdowne Hospl CF11 194 B5
Lansdowne Prim Sch CF5 194 B6
Lansdowne Rd
Caerleon / Caerllion NP18 118 B2
Cardiff / Caerdydd CF5 194 B5
Ebbw Vale / Glyn Ebwy NP23 7 D5
Newport / Casnewydd NP20 142 F2
Lan St SA6 45 F1
Lanwern Rd CF37 135 B8
Lanwood Rd CF37 109 C2
Lan-y-Parc CF46 83 E4
Lapwing Cl
Penarth CF64 217 A7
Porthcawl CF36 182 D8
Lapwing Rd SA15 40 B5
Larch Cl
Cimla SA11 72 C5
Merthyr Tydfil / Merthyr Tudful CF47 10 D5
Pontypool / Pont-y-pwl NP4 63 A4
Porthcawl CF36 183 E7
Larch Ct
Newport / Casnewydd NP20 117 A3
Tongwynlais CF15 158 D1
Larch Dr CF72 155 F3
Larches The CF71 189 C8
Larch Gr
Caerphilly / Caerffili CF83 138 C5
Cardiff / Caerdydd CF14 160 B3
Newport / Casnewydd NP20 117 B3
Underwood NP18 145 E6
Larch Ho CF14 176 E6
Larchwood CF5 205 A6
Larch Wood CF39 132 E5
Larkfield Ave CF44 29 D1
Larkfield Cl NP18 117 F4
Larkhill SA12 98 F7
Lark Pl SA5 67 E7
Lark Rise CF31 169 D5
Larkspur Cl SA10 48 E2
Larkspur Dr SA3 122 E7
Larkwood Ave CF64 207 A2
Lascelles Dr CF23 161 B1
Lasgarn La NP4 38 B3
Lasgarn Pl NP4 38 A3
Lasgarn View NP4 37 F7
Latch Sq 15 NP20 143 C3
Latimer Ct SA5 67 E5
Latteys Cl CF14 177 D5
Lauderdale Rd SA18 220 E7
Laugharne Ave CF3 179 C3
Laugharne Ct
Barry / Y Barri CF62 214 F7
Swansea / Abertawe SA2 94 A6
Laugharne Rd CF3 179 C3
Launcelot Cres CF14 159 E2
Laundry Rd CF37 109 B1
Laural Wlk NP44 89 B6
Laura St
Barry / Y Barri CF63 215 D6
Pontypridd CF37 135 D8
Laureate Cl CF3 179 B7
Laurel Ave
Baglan SA12 98 E6
Hawthorn CF37 136 B4
Laurel Cl
Cwmdare CF44 28 D3
Sarn CF32 150 F4
Laurel Cres NP20 117 B2
Laurel Ct
Barry / Y Barri CF62 214 C3
Bedwas CF83 138 E7
Laurel Ct *continued*
Cardiff / Caerdydd CF5 193 D8
Laureldene CF72 172 B5
Laurel Dr
Ammanford / Rhydaman SA18 219 D7
Bassaleg NP10 142 B3
Bryn NP12 85 E3
Penperlleni NP4 39 E7
Waunarlwydd SA5 66 D4
Laurel Gn NP44 89 B6
Laurel Pl SA2 94 B6
Laurel Rd NP10 142 A3
Laurels Bsns Pk The CF3 179 D2
Laurels The
Blaina / Blaenau NP13 15 E5
Cardiff / Caerdydd CF14 160 A3
Lauriston Cl CF5 193 C2
Lauriston Pk CF5 193 C2
Lavender Ct CF31 169 D5
Lavender Gr CF5 193 C8
Lavender Rd CF47 10 B5
Lavender Way NP10 141 D7
LAVERNOCK 217 A5
Lavernock Rd CF64 216 E5
Lavery Cl NP19 144 A7
Lawns Ind Est The NP22 12 E3
Lawn Terr
Newbridge / Trecelyn NP11 60 A2
Pontypridd CF37 135 E7
Rhymney / Rhymni NP22 12 E4
Lawn The CF5 177 A1
Lawrence Ave
Abertillery / Abertyleri NP13 35 F7
Markham NP12 58 D7
Penywaun CF44 28 A6
Lawrence Cl CF31 168 E6
LAWRENCE HILL 144 C6
Lawrence Hill NP19 144 B5
Lawrence Hill Ave NP19 144 B5
Lawrence St CF83 138 B3
Lawrence Terr
2 Llanelli SA15 40 E5
New Tredegar NP24 33 B5
Lawrenny Ave CF11 194 C4
Law St CF32 149 D4
Laybourne Cl NP44 89 E5
Laytonia Ave CF14 177 E2
Leach Rd NP20 116 D3
Lea Cl NP20 116 D2
Leacroft Pl CF23 160 E1
Lea Ct NP12 86 A3
Leadon Ct NP44 89 A4
Lead St CF24 195 D6
Leamington Rd CF14 177 B6
LEASON 229 C3
Leas The NP44 89 C5
Le-Breos SA3 93 F1
Le-Breos Ave SA2 94 E6
LECKWITH 194 D3
Leckwith Ave CF11 194 C5
Leckwith Cl CF11 194 D4
Leckwith Ct
Bridgend / Pen-y-Bont ar Ogwr CF31 168 C4
Cardiff / Caerdydd CF5 193 D4
LECKWITH / LECWYDD 194 B1
LECKWITH MOORS 194 D2
Leckwith Pl CF11 194 D5
Leckwith Rd
Cardiff / Caerdydd CF11 194 C4
Cardiff / Caerdydd, Leckwith / Leckwydd CF11 194 C2
Leckwith / Lecwydd CF11 194 B1
Llandough / Llandochau CF64 206 C8
Leckwith Rise CF31 168 C4
LECWYDD / LECKWITH 194 B1
Ledbrooke Cl NP44 89 C1
Ledbury Dr NP20 143 C6
Lee Cl
Cardiff / Caerdydd CF23 178 D4
Dinas Powis / Dinas Powys CF64 206 B4
Lee Ct CF14 159 C1
Lee Ho CF23 178 D4
Lee Rd CF63 215 A6
Lee St
Pontypridd CF37 109 B1
Swansea / Abertawe SA1 95 F7
Lee Way NP19 144 C1
Leeway Ct NP19 144 D1
Leeway Ind Est NP19 144 C1
Legion's Way CF82 84 B7
Leicester Dr NP44 89 A3
Leicester Rd NP19 143 E6
Leicester Sq CF82 84 E7
Leigh Cl CF61 210 C6
Leigh Rd NP4 62 B8
Leigh Terr CF46 83 A5
Leighton Ct NP44 89 C2
Leighton Rees Cl CF37 81 F2
Leiros Parc Dr SA10 48 E2
Lennard St NP19 143 E4
Lennox Gn CF63 215 D6
Leoline Cl CF71 188 D2
Leonard St
Fleur-de-lis NP12 85 B6

Leonard St continued
Neath / Castell-Nedd SA11 71 F8
Leon Ave CF15 158 A3
Le Pouliguen Way CF61 210 A6
Leslie Green Ct NP10 163 E8
Leslie St 14 SA12 98 F1
Leslie Terr
Porth CF39 108 A3
13 Rogerstone NP10 142 B4
Le Sor Hill CF5 191 E6
Letchworth Rd NP23 7 C1
Lethbridge Terr NP4 37 F3
Letterston Rd CF3 179 D5
Letton Rd / Heol Letton 3 CF10 195 B3
Lettons Way CF64 206 A4
Letty St CF24 195 A8
Level The NP23 14 D7
Leven Cl CF23 178 B5
Lewis Ave
Bridgend / Pen-y-Bont ar Ogwr CF31 168 E5
Cwmllynfell SA9 221 B8
Lewis Cl
Abersychan NP4 37 E6
Newbridge / Trecelyn NP11 60 B2
Newport / Casnewydd NP20 143 C3
Lewis Cres
Bargoed / Bargod CF81 58 A1
Gilfach CF81 85 A8
Llanelli SA14 41 D5
Lewis Dr CF83 138 A4
Lewis Girls' Comp Sch / Ysgol Gyfun Lewis I Ferched CF82 84 F1
Lewis Lewis Ave NP12 85 E8
Lewis Pl
Porthcawl CF36 182 F7
Porth CF39 107 E2
Lewis Rd
Cardiff / Caerdydd CF24 195 E5
Crynant / Creunant SA10 226 A7
Llandough / Llandochau CF64 206 D7
Maesteg CF34 102 B3
Neath / Castell-Nedd SA11 71 F6
Lewis Sch Pengam CF81 85 A8
Lewis Sq CF48 30 E5
Lewis St
Aberbargoed / Aberbargod CF81 58 B6
Aberdare / Aberdâr CF44 53 C7
Abersychan NP4 37 F4
Barry / Y Barri CF62 214 C4
Bedlinog CF46 56 B7
Blackwood / Coed-Duon NP12 85 E7
Cardiff / Caerdydd CF11 194 E5
Church Village CF38 156 F8
Machen CF83 140 A7
Mountain Ash / Aberpennar CF45 54 D4
Newbridge / Trecelyn NP11 60 B2
Pontrhydyfen SA12 73 A1
Pontyclun CF72 173 B8
Pontypridd CF37 135 C8
Pontypridd, Treforest CF37 135 E7
Swansea / Abertawe, St Thomas SA1 95 F7
Swansea / Abertawe, Sketty SA2 94 C6
Tonypandy CF40 107 A3
Trehafod CF37 108 C2
Treorchy / Treorci CF41 78 F4
Ystrad Mynach CF82 84 E1
Lewis's Terr CF48 10 B1
Lewis Terr
Abergarwed SA11 226 C5
6 Llanbradach CF83 111 F1
Merthyr Tydfil / Merthyr Tudful CF47 10 F3
Pontypool / Pont-y-pwl NP4 62 B8
Pontypridd CF37 109 D2
Porth CF39 108 B3
Wattstown CF39 107 D8
LEWISTOWN 130 E5
Lewis View NP10 142 B5
Lewis Wood NP4 37 F1
Leydene Cl NP11 114 F3
Leyshan Wlk SA3 122 E8
Leyshon Ct / Cwrt Lleision SA10 71 A7
Leyshon Rd
Gwaun-Cae-Gurwen SA18 220 D7
Ynysmeudwy SA8 23 F6
Leyshon St CF37 135 B7
Leyshon Terr CF39 108 A2
Leyshon Way / Ffordd Leyshon CF32 151 A5
Lias Rd CF36 182 F6
Lias St CF31 168 F4
Libanus Prim Sch NP12 85 E5
Libanus Rd
Ebbw Vale / Glyn Ebwy NP23 7 D1
Gorseinon SA4 43 C1
Libanus Rd continued
Pontllanfraith NP12 85 F5
Libanus St CF48 11 A5
Libby Way SA3 123 C3
Libeneth Rd NP19 144 B4
Library Cl
Rhydyfelin CF37 136 A5
Treorchy / Treorci CF41 79 A4
Library La
5 Merthyr Tydfil / Merthyr Tudful CF47 10 E1
5 Port Talbot SA13 125 C6
Library Rd
Maesteg CF34 75 B1
Pontypridd CF37 109 C1
6 Tonypandy CF40 106 F4
Library St CF5 194 D6
Liddel Cl CF23 161 B1
Liddicoat Ct CF63 215 C6
Lidmore Rd CF62 214 C5
Lifeboat Rd CF36 182 F6
Lighthouse Pk NP10 181 F8
Lighthouse Rd NP10 164 A4
Lilac Cl
Cardiff / Caerdydd CF5 176 C1
The Mumbles / Y Mwmbwls SA3 122 F8
Lilac Dr CF38 156 C6
Lilac Gr
Baglan SA12 98 E7
Rogerstone / Ty-du NP10 141 D7
Lilburne Cl 4 CF23 161 A1
Lilburne Dr NP19 143 F4
Lilian Gr NP23 7 D2
Lilian Rd NP12 85 E6
Lilian St SA12 98 F1
Lili Mai CF63 205 B1
Lilleshall St NP19 143 E4
Lilliput La SA3 123 B8
Lily St CF24 232 D4
Lily Way NP10 141 E6
Limebourne Ct CF14 177 B3
Lime Cl
Newport / Casnewydd NP20 143 C2
Radyr CF15 176 C4
Lime Cres NP19 144 B4
Lime Ct NP11 87 B8
Lime Gr
Bryn NP12 85 E3
Cardiff / Caerdydd CF5 176 B1
Cimla SA11 72 A5
Merthyr Tydfil / Merthyr Tudful CF47 10 D4
St Athan / Sain Tathan CF62 211 B7
Swansea / Abertawe SA2 93 D7
Underwood NP18 145 F7
Lime Kiln La SA3 122 B6
Limekiln Rd SA3 123 A5
Limekiln Rd / Ffordd Yr Odyn Galch NP4 38 A3
Limes Ct CF71 188 F2
LIMESLADE 123 C3
Limeslade Cl
Cardiff / Caerdydd CF5 193 F7
Hirwaun CF44 27 D7
Limeslade Ct SA3 123 C3
Limeslade Dr SA3 123 C3
Lime St
Ferndale CF43 79 F6
Gorseinon SA4 43 C2
Rhydyfelin CF37 136 A5
Limes The CF71 188 F2
Limestone Rd NP23 8 C2
Limestone Rd E NP23 8 C3
Limetree Cl CF38 156 F8
Lime Tree Gr 6 SA6 69 A8
Lime Tree Way CF36 183 E8
Limewood Cl CF3 179 E7
Lincoln Cl NP19 143 F6
Lincoln Ct
Caerleon / Caerllion NP18 118 A3
Cardiff / Caerdydd CF23 178 D5
Lincoln St
Cardiff / Caerdydd CF5 194 B6
Porth CF39 107 E2
Lincoln Terr 23 CF47 30 E8
Lindbergh Cl NP19 144 A3
Linde Ind Pk / Parc Ddwyidiannol Linde CF48 31 B4
Linden Ave
Cardiff / Caerdydd CF23 178 C1
The Mumbles / Y Mwmbwls SA3 123 A8
Linden Cl SA10 48 C4
Linden Cres CF44 28 D2
Linden Ct
Llanharry CF72 172 B5
Newbridge / Trecelyn NP11 87 C8
Linden Gr
Caerphilly / Caerffili CF83 138 C5
Cardiff / Caerdydd CF3 179 B4
Linden Lea Dr NP12 85 D6
Linden Rd NP19 144 A5
Lindens The CF64 207 B4
Linden Way
Porthcawl CF36 183 E8
Linden Way continued
Trefechan CF48 10 B7
Lindsay Cl CF35 170 C8
Lindsay Ct CF31 169 A3
Lindsay Gdns NP22 6 D1
Lindway Ct 4 CF5 194 B7
Lingfield Ave SA12 98 D2
Lingfield Ave / Rhodfa Lingfield SA12 98 E1
Lingholm Cl 3 CF3 179 F6
Link Rd NP4 63 A4
Links Bsns Pk CF3 180 B8
Links Ct SA3 122 E3
Linkside SA3 122 E4
Linkside Dr SA3 121 A6
Links The NP4 38 C1
Link The SA2 94 A5
Linley Cl NP19 145 A6
Linnet Cl CF23 178 D7
Linnet Way CF31 169 D5
Linton Ct NP4 38 A3
Linton St NP20 143 D2
Lion Ct 1 NP4 17 C6
Lionel Rd CF5 194 B6
Lionel Terr CF37 135 F5
Lion St / Heol Y Llew 2 NP4 17 C6
Lion St SA1 68 C2
Lion Way SA7 69 B7
LISBON 68 C5
Lisbon Ct CF82 84 E1
Lisburn Rd CF82 84 E1
Lisburn Rise CF44 27 D8
Liscombe St NP19 144 A4
Liscum Way CF62 214 C7
Lisnagarvey Ct CF14 176 F8
Lister Ave 6 SA12 98 F1
Lister Cl CF38 135 D1
Lister Gn NP20 117 A2
Lisvane Ho CF14 160 B2
LISVANE / LLYS FAEN 160 B2
Lisvane Rd CF14 160 B2
Lisvane St CF24 177 F1
Lisvane & Thornhill / Llys-faen Sta CF14 159 F3
LISWERRY 144 C3
Liswerry Cl / Clos LLysweri 2 NP44 90 B2
Liswerry Dr / Rhodfa Llysweri NP44 90 B2
Liswerry Park Dr NP19 144 C4
Liswerry Rd NP19 144 C4
LITCHARD 168 F8
Litchard Bglws CF31 168 F7
Litchard Cross CF31 168 F7
Litchard Hill
Bridgend / Pen-y-Bont ar Ogwr CF31 150 F1
Bridgend / Pen-y-Bont ar Ogwr CF31 168 F8
Litchard Ind Est CF31 169 A7
Litchard Inf Sch / Ysgol y habanod Litchard CF31 168 F8
Litchard Jun Sch CF31 168 F8
Litchard Pk CF31 168 F7
Litchard Rise CF31 168 F8
Litchard Terr CF31 168 F7
Litchfield Ct CF11 232 A1
Little Ave CF5 191 F5
Little Brynhill La CF62 214 D8
Littlecroft Ave CF5 193 F6
Littledene NP44 89 B3
Little Dock St CF64 206 F5
Little Frederick St CF10 232 C2
Little Gam St SA1 233 A2
Little La NP23 7 F4
Little London SA9 222 B7
LITTLE MILL 39 E2
Little Mill CF14 177 A3
Little Moors Hill CF63 215 C6
Little Oaks View NP10 142 A6
Little Orch CF64 206 C3
Little Orchard CF5 176 F1
LITTLE REYNOLDSTON 231 D8
Little Row CF44 29 B4
Little Station Rd CF33 148 E3
Littleton St CF11 194 E5
Little Wind St 9 CF44 29 A1
Little Woods CF45 82 D2
Livale Cl NP20 116 E2
Livale Ct NP20 116 E2
Livale Rd NP20 116 E2
Livale Wlk NP20 116 E2
Liverpool St 5 NP19 143 E6
Livingstone Pl NP19 143 E5
Livingstone Way CF62 211 D7
Livorno Ho CF10 195 C3
Llanarth Cl CF83 140 B6
Llanarth Rd
Newbridge / Trecelyn NP11 86 F8
Pontllanfraith NP12 86 A4
Llanarth Sq NP11 115 A1
Llanarth St
Cwmfelinfach NP11 113 E3
Machen CF83 140 B7
3 Newport / Casnewydd NP20 143 C4
Llanarth Villas NP11 113 D3
Llanbad CF72 153 D3
LLANBEDER 119 E2
LLANBEDR GWYNLLWG / PETERSTONE WENTLOOGE 180 E5
Llanbedr Rd CF5 193 E7
LLANBEDR-Y-FRO / PETERSTON-SUPER-ELY 191 E6
Llanberis Cl
Bassaleg NP10 141 E3
Church Village CF38 135 E2
LLANBETHÊRY / LLANBYDDERI 212 B8
Llanbleddian Ct CF24 232 C4
Llanbleddian Gdns CF24 232 B4
LLANBLETHIAN / LLANFLEIDDAN 200 E8
LLANBRADACH 111 F1
Llanbradach St
Cardiff / Caerdydd CF11 194 F3
3 Pontypridd CF37 109 B1
Llanbradach Sta CF83 111 F1
Llanbryn Gdns CF72 153 E3
LLANBYDDERI / LLANBETHÊRY 212 B8
LLANCADLE / LLANCATAL 212 B6
Llancaeach Jun Sch CF46 83 E3
Llancaiach Ct CF46 83 E5
Llancaiach-fawr* CF46 83 E6
Llancaiach Rd 4 CF14 177 B4
Llancaiach View CF46 83 E5
LLANCARFAN 202 E1
Llancarfan Prim Sch CF62 202 E1
LLANCATAL / LLANCADLE 212 B6
Llancayo Pk CF81 57 F5
Llancayo St CF81 57 F5
Llandafal Ct NP23 35 B6
Llandafen Rd SA14 41 B5
Llandaff Cath* CF5 177 B1
Llandaff Chase CF5 176 F1
Llandaff City CW Prim Sch CF5 194 A8
Llandaff Cl CF64 207 A2
Llandaff Ct CF5 194 A8
Llandaff Gn 5 NP44 89 E4
LLANDAFF / LLANDÂF 194 B8
LLANDAFF NORTH 177 A3
Llandaff Rd
Cardiff / Caerdydd CF5 194 C6
Ebbw Vale / Glyn Ebwy NP23 7 E3
Llandaff Sq CF3 179 D7
Llandaff St NP20 143 A3
Llandaff Way CF39 133 E8
LLANDÂF / LLANDAFF 194 B8
Llandaf Sta CF14 176 F4
LLANDARCY 70 D3
LLANDDEWI 231 A8
Llanddewi Ct CF44 53 C7
Llanddewi St CF44 53 C7
LLANDDUNWYD / WELSH ST DONATS 189 F5
Llandegefedd Way NP4 63 A3
Llandegfedd Cl
Cardiff / Caerdydd CF14 159 F3
Rogerstone NP10 142 B7
Llandegfedd Reservoir* NP4 63 F3
Llandegveth Cl NP44 90 B6
Llandeilo Rd
Cross Hands SA14 218 B8
Glanaman SA18 220 C8
Llandeilo Rd / Heol Llandeilo SA14 218 C8
Llandennis Ave CF23 178 C6
Llandennis Ct CF23 178 C6
Llandennis Gn CF23 178 B6
Llandennis Rd CF23 178 A6
Llandenny Wlk NP44 89 E3
Llanderfel Ct NP44 89 A5
Llandetty Rd CF5 193 E7
Llandilo Cl CF64 206 C3
Llandinam Cres CF14 177 B1
Llandinam Rd CF62 214 E5
LLANDOCHAU / LLANDOUGH 206 D7
LLANDOCHE / LLANDOUGH 200 E6
Llandogo Rd CF3 179 F7
Llandough Hill CF64 206 D7
Llandough Hospl / Ysbyty Llandochau CF64 206 C6
LLANDOUGH / LLANDOCHAU 206 D7
LLANDOUGH / LLANDOCHE 200 E6
Llandough Prim Sch / Ysgol Gynradd Llandochau CF64 206 D7
Llandough St CF24 232 B4
Llandough Trad Est CF11 206 D8
Llandovery Cl 12 CF5 193 C4
Llandovery Villas NP13 15 E2
Llandowlais St / Strydd Llandowlais NP44 89 E1
LLANDOW / LLANDW 199 B7
Llandow Rd CF5 193 D5
Llandow Trad Est CF71 199 D4
Llandraw Ct CF37 109 A1
Llandraw Woods CF37 135 A8
Llandudno Rd CF3 179 C4
LLANDW / LLANDOW 199 B7
Llandybie Rd SA18 219 B8
Llandyfrig Cl 9 CF64 206 C3
LLANEDEYRN 178 E6
LLANE DEYRN 161 C1
Llanedeyrn Cl CF23 178 D3
Llanedeyrn Dr CF23 178 E4
Llanedeyrn High Sch CF23 178 E4
Llanedeyrn Prim Sch CF23 178 E4
Llanedeyrn Rd CF23 178 E3
LLANEDI 218 D2
Llanedi Rd
Llanedi SA4 218 D1
Pontarddulais SA4 19 A7
LLANELLI 41 B5
Llanelli Ent Workshops SA15 40 F3
Llanelli Gate Ind Pk SA14 41 C8
Llanelli Sta SA15 40 D3
Llanelli Workshops SA14 41 A3
LLANELLY HILL 9 C4
LLANERCH 40 E7
Llanerch Cl NP4 62 A7
Llanerch Cotts SA15 40 E7
Llanerch Cres SA4 43 B3
Llanerch Goed CF38 135 D1
Llanerch La NP11 59 F4
Llanerch Path / Llwybr Llannerch NP44 89 B2
Llanerch Rd
Abertillery / Abertyleri NP11 59 F5
Dunvant SA2 93 D8
Swansea / Abertawe SA1 69 B2
Llanerch Terr SA15 40 E7
Llanerch Vineyard* CF72 173 E4
LLANEURWG / ST MELLONS 179 E7
Llanewrwg Way CF3 179 E7
LLANFABON 110 D8
Llanfabon Ct CF37 109 F4
Llanfabon Dr CF83 138 F7
Llanfabon Drive Shops CF83 138 F7
Llanfabon Inf Sch / Ysgol Plant Bach Llanfabon CF46 83 E3
Llanfabon Rd CF46 83 D2
LLANFACH 87 C3
Llan-Fach Rd NP11 87 B3
Llanfaes SA9 2 F8
Llanfair Gdns SA3 123 A6
Llanfair Hill CF44 79 A2
Llanfair Prim Sch CF71 200 F5
Llanfair Rd
Cardiff / Caerdydd CF11 194 C7
Pontypridd CF37 135 B8
Tonypandy CF40 107 A4
LLAN FAIR / ST MARY CHURCH 201 A4
Llanfedw Cl CF83 138 E5
LLANFIHANGEL-AR-ELAI / MICHAELSTON-SUPER-ELY 193 A5
LLANFIHANGEL Y BONT-FAEN / LLANMIHANGEL 200 C5
LLANFLEIDDAN / LLANBLETHIAN 200 E8
Llanfoist Cres 4 NP4 17 D7
Llanfoist St CF41 79 A3
LLANFRECHFA 117 D7
Llanfrechfa Grange Hospl NP44 90 C2
Llanfrechfa Way / Ffordd Llanfrechfa NP44 90 A2
LLAN-GAN 187 D8
Llan-gan Prim Sch CF35 187 F7
Llangattock Ct NP44 90 B5
Llangattock Rd CF5 193 E7
Llangattwg Cl NP23 7 E4
LLANGATWG / CADOXTON-JUXTA-NEATH 49 B3
Llangatwg Comp Sch SA10 49 B3
Llangefni Pl CF14 159 E1
LLANGEINOR 130 B3
Llangeinor Rd CF32 150 F6
Llangeinor Terr CF32 130 E5
LLANGENNECH 42 B8
Llangennech Jun & Inf Schs SA14 18 C1
Llangennech Sta SA14 42 C7
LLANGENNITH 228 D2
Llangewydd Jun Sch / Ysgol Iau Llangewydd CF31 168 C5
Llangewydd Rd
Bridgend / Pen-y-Bont ar Ogwr CF31 168 C5
Laleston / Trelales CF32 167 E6

Llangiwg Prim Sch SA8 .. 23 F6
Llangorse Cotts NP13 .... 36 B8
Llangorse Dr NP10 ...... 142 B7
Llangorse Path / Llwybr Llan-Gors 4 NP44 ..... 90 A2
Llangorse Rd
Aberdare / Aberdâr CF44 .... 29 E1
Cardiff / Caerdydd CF23 .. 178 C7
Swansea / Abertawe SA5 .. 68 B5
Llangorse Rd / Ffordd Llangors 3 NP44 .... 90 A2
LLANGRALLO / COYCHURCH 169 F4
Llangranog Pl CF14 ..... 159 D1
Llangranog Rd CF14 ..... 159 E1
Llangwm SA5 .... 67 F6
Llangwm Pl CF3 .... 179 C4
Llangwn Way CF36 ...... 182 F7
Llangybi Cl CF5 .... 192 F3
LLANGYFELACH 45 A2
Llangyfelach Prim Sch SA5 .... 45 B2
Llangyfelach Rd SA5 ..... 68 C5
Llangyfelach St SA1 ..... 68 D1
Llangynidr Rd
Cardiff / Caerdydd CF5 ...... 193 E7
Ebbw Vale / Glyn Ebwy NP23 .... 7 D6
LLANGYNWYD 128 B6
Llangynwyd Prim Sch CF34 .... 128 D6
LLANHARAN 154 A3
Llanharan Ho CF72 ...... 154 B3
Llanharan Prim Sch CF72 ..... 154 A3
Llanhari Prim Sch CF72 ...... 172 A5
Llanharran Terr CF32 ... 104 F5
LLANHARRY 172 A5
Llanharry Rd
Bryncae CF72 .... 172 A8
Llanharry CF72 .... 172 C6
LLANHENNOCK 118 E6
LLANHILEDD / LLANHILLETH 60 B6
LLANHILEDD / ST ILLTYD 60 B8
Llanhilleth Ind Est NP13 .... 60 C5
LLANHILLETH / LLANHILEDD 60 B6
Llanidloes Rd CF14 ...... 177 B2
LLANIHANGEL-Y-PWLL / MICHAELSLON-LE-PIT 206 A7
LLANILID 171 B8
LLANILLTUD FAERDREF / LLANTWIT FADRE 156 E7
Llanilltud Faerdref Prim Sch / Ysgol Gynradd Llanilltud Faerdref CF38 .... 135 F1
LLANILLTUD FAWR / LLANTWIT MAJOR 210 A6
Llanilltud Fawr Prim Sch CF61 .... 210 A5
Llanina Gr CF3 .... 179 E5
LLANISHEN 177 F7
Llanishen Ct CF14 .... 177 F8
Llanishen Fach Prim Sch CF14 .... 159 C1
Llanishen High Sch CF14 .... 159 F1
Llanishen St CF14 .... 177 F2
Llanishen Sta CF14 ...... 160 A1
Llanllienwen Cl
Swansea / Abertawe SA6 ...... 45 F4
Ynysforgan SA6 .... 46 A4
Llanllienwen Rd
Swansea / Abertawe SA6 ...... 45 F3
Ynysforgan SA6 .... 46 A3
LLANMADOC 228 E4
Llanmadoc Camping Site SA3 ...... 228 C4
LLANMAES 210 C8
Llanmaes Rd CF61 ...... 210 A7
Llanmaes St CF11 ...... 194 F2
Llanmartin Prim Sch NP18 .... 145 E6
Llanmead Gdns CF62 .... 212 F2
LLANMIHANGEL / LLANFIHANGEL Y BONT-FAEN 200 C5
Llanmihangel Rd CF71 .. 200 D7
Llanmihangel Rise CF71 ...... 200 D8
LLANMORLAIS 64 C2
Llanmorlais Prim Sch SA4 ...... 64 B1
Llanmorlais Rd CF14 .... 177 C1
Llannant Rd SA4 .... 42 F5
Llanofer Rd SA13 .... 75 D3
Llanon 1 NP44 ...... 89 F6
Llanon Rd CF14 ...... 159 E1
Llanover Ave NP12 ...... 85 E4
Llanover Cl
Blaenavon NP4 ...... 17 E6
Newport / Casnewydd NP20 ...... 117 A1
Llanover Rd
Blaenavon NP4 ...... 17 D6
Llanover Rd *continued*
Cardiff / Caerdydd CF5 ... 192 F3
Cwmavon NP4 ...... 17 F1
Pontypridd CF37 .... 109 D2
Llanover Road Est NP4 ... 17 E6
Llanover St
Abercarn NP11 .... 87 A3
2 Barry / Y Barri CF63 .. 215 B6
Pontypridd CF37 .... 109 D1
Llanquian Castle CF71 .. 189 D1
Llanquian Cl CF71 ...... 188 F1
Llanquian Rd CF71 ...... 189 C3
Llan Rd
Llangynwyd CF34 ...... 128 B6
Marcross / Marcroes CF61 .... 198 E2
Pont Rhyd-y-cyff CF34 ... 128 C6
LLANRHIDIAN 229 D2
Llanrhidian Cvn Pk SA3 ...... 229 F3
Llanrhidian Prim Sch SA3 ...... 229 D2
Llanrhyd 8 CF48 ...... 31 B1
LLANRUMNEY 179 B6
Llanrumney Ave CF3 .... 179 B5
Llanrumney High Sch CF3 .... 179 A6
LLANSAMLET 69 D8
Llansamlet Ind Est
Swansea / Abertawe SA6 ...... 68 F5
Swansea / Abertawe SA7 .. 69 B7
Llansamlet Sta SA7 ...... 69 F8
LLANSANFFRAID-AR-ELAI / ST BRIDE'S-SUPER-ELY 192 B7
LLANSANFFRAID GWYNLLWG / ST BRIDE'S WENTLOOGE 163 D1
Llansannor CW Prim Sch CF71 ...... 172 A3
Llansannor Dr CF10 ..... 232 D1
LLANSANNOR / LLANSANWYR 188 E7
LLANSANWYR / LLANSANNOR 188 E7
Llansawel 7 SA11 ...... 71 C1
LLANSAWEL / BRITON FERRY 71 B2
Llansawel Cres SA11 .... 71 B3
Llansawel Prim Sch SA11 ...... 71 B1
Llanstephan Rd CF3 ..... 179 C3
LLANTARNAM 117 A7
Llantarnam Cl / Heol Llantarnam NP44 ..... 89 F2
Llantarnam Dr CF15 ..... 176 B5
Llantarnam Gdns NP44 ...... 117 B7
Llantarnam Ind Pk NP44 ...... 116 F7
Llantarnam Park Way NP44 ...... 117 A6
Llantarnam Rd CF14 .... 177 D2
Llantarnam Rd / Heol Llantarnam NP44 ..... 89 F1
Llantarnam Sch NP44 ... 117 A7
Llanthewy Cl NP44 ..... 90 B6
Llanthewy Rd NP20 ..... 143 A4
LLANTRISANT 155 C4
Llantrisant Bsns Pk CF72 ..... 155 C6
Llantrisant Hos 8 CF72 ..... 155 D3
Llantrisant Ind Est CF72 ..... 155 B6
Llantrisant Rd
Beddau CF38 ...... 155 F7
Cardiff / Caerdydd CF5 ... 176 D3
Llantrisant CF72 ...... 155 F3
Llantwit Fadre / Llanilltud Faerdref CF38 ...... 156 B6
Pentyrch CF5, CF15 ..... 175 C4
Pen-y-coedcae CF37 ..... 135 B5
Pontyclun CF72 .... 173 B8
Tonyrefail CF39 ...... 133 D6
Llantrisant Rise CF5 .... 176 F2
Llantrisant St CF24 ..... 194 F8
Llantrisant Welsh Prim Sch / Ysgol Gymraeg Llantrisant CF72 ...... 155 D3
LLANTRITHYD 202 D6
Llantrithyd Rd CF71 .... 201 D7
LLANTWIT 72 A8
LLANTWIT FADRE / LLANILLTUD FAERDREF 156 E7
Llantwit Gardens Cl CF62 ...... 211 D5
LLANTWIT MAJOR / LLANILLTUD FAWR 210 A6
Llantwit Major Rd
Cowbridge / Y Bont-Faen CF71 ..... 188 C1
Llanblethian / Llanfleiddan CF71 ..... 200 A8
Llandow / Llandw CF71 ... 199 E4
Llantwit Major Sch / Ysgol Llanilltud Fawr CF61 ... 210 A5
Llantwit Major Sta CF61 ..... 210 A6
Llantwit Rd
Boverton / Trebefered CF62 ..... 210 D5
Neath / Castell-Nedd SA11 ..... 72 A8
Pontypridd CF37 ..... 135 E5
Llantwit Rd *continued*
St Athan / Sain Tathan CF62 ..... 211 C5
Wick / Y Wig CF71 ..... 198 D5
Llantwit St
Barry / Y Barri CF63 ..... 215 A5
Cardiff / Caerdydd CF24 .. 232 C4
Llanvair Rd NP19 ...... 143 D6
LLANVIHANGEL PONTYMOEL 63 A6
LLANWERN 145 B5
Llanwern Hill Circular Wlk* NP18 ...... 145 C4
Llanwern Rd
Cardiff / Caerdydd CF5 ...... 193 C5
Newport / Casnewydd NP19 ...... 144 E7
Llanwern St NP19 ..... 143 E5
Llanwonno Cl CF37 .... 109 A2
Llanwonno Rd
Cwmaman CF44 ..... 53 A3
Mountain Ash / Aberpennar CF45 ..... 54 D1
Pontypridd CF37 ..... 109 A2
Porth CF39 ..... 107 F5
Tylorstown CF43 ..... 80 C2
LLANYRAFON 90 C2
Llanyrafon Prim Sch / Llanyrafon Ysgol Gynradd NP44 ..... 90 A2
Llanyrafon Ysgol Gynradd / Llanyrafon Prim Sch NP44 ..... 90 A2
Llan-yr-Avon Sq 2 NP44 ..... 90 A2
Llan-yr-Avon Way / Ffordd Llanyrafon NP44 ..... 90 A3
Llan-yr-newydd SA4 ..... 64 F3
Lle Alffa / Alpha Pl SA12 ..... 98 D7
Lle Bertha / Bertha Pl SA13 ..... 125 E4
Lle Canol SA13 ..... 227 C1
LLECHRYD 12 D7
Lle Hyfryd CF44 ..... 28 E6
Lle Mesen / Acorn Pl SA12 ..... 98 D7
Llest Terr CF38 ..... 156 C6
Lletai Ave CF35 ..... 170 E8
LLETTY BRONGU 129 A5
Lletty Dafydd SA11 ..... 226 C4
Llettyharri SA13 ..... 99 C2
Llety Gwyn / White Lodge CF31 ..... 168 E7
LLETYHARRI 99 C2
Llety'r Bugail CF34 ..... 128 C7
Llety'r Eos CF62 ..... 213 B1
Llewellin St 4 NP19 .... 144 A5
Llewellyn Ave
Cardiff / Caerdydd CF5 ..... 193 B6
Neath / Castell-Nedd SA10 ..... 48 D1
Llewellyn Cl SA13 ..... 125 D7
Llewellyn Ct CF41 ..... 79 A4
Llewellyn Dr
Caerphilly / Caerffili CF83 ..... 138 A4
Pen-y-fai CF31 ..... 150 D1
Llewellyn Gr 3 NP20 .... 117 A3
Llewellyn Pl CF41 ..... 79 A4
Llewellyn Rd SA4 ..... 43 F2
Llewellyn St / Stryd Llewelyn 14 SA15 ..... 40 D4
Llewellyn's Rd SA13 ..... 125 B7
Llewellyn's Row NP7 ..... 9 D5
Llewellyn St
Aberavon SA12 ..... 99 A1
Aberdare / Aberdâr CF44 .. 28 E4
Barry / Y Barri CF63 ..... 215 A6
Blaencwm CF42 ..... 50 C2
Dowlais CF48 ..... 11 A5
Glyn-neath / Glyn-nedd SA11 ..... 223 D1
Hendreforgan CF39 ..... 132 C5
Merthyr Tydfil / Merthyr Tudful CF47 ..... 10 D2
Neath / Castell-Nedd SA11 ..... 71 E6
Pontygwaith CF43 ..... 80 B1
Tonypandy CF40 ..... 106 E4
Treorchy / Treorci CF41 .... 79 A4
Llewellyn Terr
Tonypandy CF40 ..... 106 E7
Ynysybwl CF37 ..... 81 F1
Llewellyn Wlk
Cwmbran / Cwmbrân NP44 ..... 89 E3
4 Newport / Casnewydd NP20 ..... 117 A3
Llewelyn Ave NP11 ..... 59 D2
Llewelyn Circ SA1 ..... 95 B8
Llewelyn Ct CF44 ..... 28 D4
Llewelyn Goch CF5 ..... 175 E5
Llewelyn Park Dr SA6 .... 68 E7
Llewelyn St
Bargoed / Bargod CF81 ... 58 A1
Nant-y-Moel CF32 ..... 104 E7
Pontypridd CF37 ..... 109 A2
Swansea / Abertawe SA2 .. 94 C6
Lle Wenham / Wenham Pl SA11 ..... 71 F7
Llewitna Terr SA5 ..... 67 B6
Lliedi Cres SA15 ..... 40 E6
Lliswerry High Sch NP19 ..... 144 C1
Lliswerry Inf Sch NP19 .. 144 B3
Lliswerry Jun Sch NP19 ..... 144 B3
Lliw Valley Cl / Clos Dyffrynlliw SA4 ..... 66 C6
Ll Maendy / Maendy Pl NP44 ..... 89 C6
Lloft Deri CF14 ..... 177 C7
Lloyd Ave
Barry / Y Barri CF62 ..... 214 E6
Cardiff / Caerdydd CF5 ... 193 F7
Newbridge / Trecelyn NP11 ..... 60 B3
Lloyd George Ave / Rhodfa Lloyd George CF10 .... 195 B3
Lloyd Pl CF3 ..... 180 A6
Lloyd Rd SA5 ..... 68 C5
Lloyd St / Stryd Lloyd SA15 ..... 40 C5
Lloyds Ct CF47 ..... 10 F3
Lloyd St
17 Ammanford / Rhydaman SA18 ..... 219 B7
Maesteg CF34 ..... 75 B1
Newport / Casnewydd NP19 ..... 144 A3
Pontardawe SA8 ..... 23 B2
Ton Pentre CF41 ..... 79 B3
Lloyds Terr CF47 ..... 10 F3
Lloyd's Terr SA13 ..... 75 C4
Lluest SA9 ..... 222 A5
Llwncelyn Cl CF48 ..... 10 C1
Llwybr Caerwrangon / Worcester Path 3 NP44 ..... 90 A3
Llwybr Ceuffoadd / Adit Wlk NP44 ..... 89 C5
Llwybr Llan-Gors / Llangorse Path 4 NP44 ..... 90 A2
Llwybr Llannerch / Llanerch Path NP44 .... 89 B2
Llwybr Llyswen / Llyswen Wlk 2 NP44 ..... 90 B1
Llwybr Marston / Marston Path 11 NP44 ..... 89 C2
Llwybr Picton / Picton Wlk NP44 ..... 89 B2
Llwybr Steynton / Steynton Path 15 NP44 ..... 89 C2
Llwybr Stowe / Stowe Path 4 NP44 ..... 90 B2
Llwybr Ty Coch / Ty-Coch La NP44 ..... 116 F6
Llwybr Y Marchog / Knights Wlk CF83 ..... 137 D2
Llwybr y Plasty / Grange Path 7 NP44 ..... 90 B1
Llwydarth Cotts CF34 ... 102 B1
Llwydarth Rd
Cwmfelin CF34 ..... 128 B8
Maesteg CF34 ..... 102 C1
LLWYDCOED 28 F6
Llwyd Coed CF14 ..... 158 F1
Llwydcoed Prim Sch / Ysgol Gynradd Llwydcoed CF44 ..... 28 E6
Llwydcoed Rd CF44 ..... 28 E6
Llwyd Y Berth CF83 ..... 137 E2
Llwyfen CF47 ..... 10 D2
Llwyfen St CF47 ..... 10 D2
Llwyn Afanc SA6 ..... 45 F5
Llwyn Arian SA13 ..... 148 A5
Llwyn Arosfa SA2 ..... 94 C7
Llwyn-Bach Terr NP12 ... 34 C2
Llwyn Bedw
Mountain Ash / Aberpennar CF45 ..... 54 B6
Pencoed CF35 ..... 170 C8
Swansea / Abertawe SA5 .. 67 D4
Llwyn Berry CF48 ..... 10 C1
Llwynbrain Terr CF72 ... 154 A3
LLWYNBRWYDRAU 70 A7
Llwyn Brwydrau SA7 ..... 70 A6
Llwyn Bryn Melyn CF15 ..... 176 A6
Llwyn Caeriw / Carew Gr CF48 ..... 225 F1
Llwyn Carw SA6 ..... 45 F5
Llwyn Castan CF23 ..... 178 E7
LLWYNCELYN
Cardiff 160 E7
Porth 108 B3
Llwyncelyn
Bettws CF32 ..... 129 E3
Llanelli SA15 ..... 40 E4
Llwyn Celyn
Capel Hendre SA18 ..... 218 D6
Cwmbran / Cwmbrân NP44 ..... 89 D1
Ebbw Vale / Glyn Ebwy NP23 ..... 14 B8
Swansea / Abertawe SA5 .. 67 D4
Llwyncelyn Ave SA4 ..... 19 D4
Llwyncelyn Cl CF48 ..... 30 C8
Llwyncelyn Ct CF39 ..... 108 A3
Llwyncelyn Ind Est CF39 ..... 108 A3
Llwyncelyn Inf Sch / Ysgol Babanod Llwyncelyn CF39 ..... 108 A3
Llwyncelyn Pk CF39 ..... 108 A3
Llwyncelyn Rd
Gwaun-Cae-Gurwen SA18 ..... 220 E6
Porth CF39 ..... 108 A3
Llwyncelyn Rd / Heol Llwyncelyn SA18 ..... 219 F8
Llwyncelyn Terr
Abertillery / Abertyleri NP13 ..... 59 E6
Coelbren SA10 ..... 222 F6
Nelson CF46 ..... 83 D3
Llwyncethin Rd SA5 ..... 68 A3
Llwyn Cl SA15 ..... 40 F5
Llwyn Coch / Red Gr CF31 ..... 168 B3
Llwyn Coed NP12 ..... 85 D6
Llwyn Conway / Conway Gr CF48 ..... 225 F1
Llwyncrwn Prim Sch CF38 ..... 155 F6
Llwyncrwn Rd CF38 ..... 155 F6
Llwyn-Crwn Rd SA7 ..... 69 D7
Llwyncyfarthwch SA15 ... 41 A5
Llwyn David CF62 ..... 214 E4
Llwynderi CF44 ..... 28 B6
Llwyn Deri Cl NP10 ..... 141 E2
Llwynderi Rd NP20 ..... 143 A4
Llwynderw
Gorseinon SA4 ..... 43 B1
Porthcawl CF36 ..... 182 F7
Three Crosses SA4 ..... 65 E1
Llwyn Derw
Pontardawe SA8 ..... 23 E4
Swansea / Abertawe SA5 .. 67 D4
4 Tonypandy CF40 ..... 106 E6
Llwynderw Ave CF34 ..... 102 C3
Llwynderw Cl SA2 ..... 94 B1
Llwynderw Dr SA3 ..... 123 B8
Llwyn Derwen CF33 ..... 165 F7
Llwynderw Rd CF14 ..... 177 D3
Llwyn Dic Penderyn CF48 ..... 10 C1
Llwyn Drysgol CF15 ..... 176 A6
Llwyn Eithin
Caerphilly / Caerffili CF83 ..... 138 D5
Swansea / Abertawe SA5 .. 67 D4
Llwyneryr Hospl SA6 ..... 45 E2
Llwynfedw Gdns CF14 ... 177 D5
Llwynfedw Rd CF14 ..... 177 C5
Llwynfen Rd CF72 ..... 173 B7
Llwyn Glas CF31 ..... 168 C4
Llwyn Grug CF14 ..... 177 C8
Llwyn Gwern CF35 ..... 170 C8
Llwyn Gwyn CF72 ..... 172 B5
Llwyn Helig CF33 ..... 148 E1
Llwyn Helyg
Swansea / Abertawe SA5 ..... 67 D5
Tredegar NP22 ..... 6 C2
Llwyn Helyg / Willow Gr SA12 ..... 98 E6
LLWYNHENDY 41 E4
Llwynhendy Rd / Heol Llwynhendy SA14 ..... 41 D4
Llwyn Hen Rd SA18 ..... 220 D5
Llwynifan SA14 ..... 18 B2
Llwynmadoc St CF37 ..... 109 B1
Llwyn Mallt CF15 ..... 176 D8
Llwyn Mawr Cl SA2 ..... 94 B8
Llwynmawr La SA4 ..... 65 E5
Llwyn Mawr La SA2 ..... 67 B1
Llwyn Mawr Rd
Swansea / Abertawe SA2 ..... 67 B1
Swansea / Abertawe, Ty-coch SA2 ..... 94 C8
Llwyn Melin NP7 ..... 9 D6
Llwyn-Nant SA18 ..... 220 D4
Llwynon
Clydach SA6 ..... 22 E1
Crynant / Creunant SA10 ..... 226 A7
Risca / Rhisga NP11 ..... 115 A2
Llwyn On
Caerleon / Caerllion NP18 ..... 118 A6
North Cornelly CF33 ..... 166 A8
Swansea / Abertawe SA5 .. 67 D4
Llwyn-On Cl CF83 ..... 137 F4
Llwyn on Cres NP12 ..... 59 B1
Llwyn-on La NP12 ..... 59 B1
Llwyn Onn
Cardiff / Caerdydd CF14 ..... 159 A1
Croesyceiliog NP44 ..... 90 B4
Penderyn CF44 ..... 224 D2
Pen-pedair-heol CF82 ..... 84 E7
Pontyclun CF72 ..... 173 A8
Llwyn-On Rd
Abertillery / Abertyleri NP13 ..... 36 C3
Blackwood / Coed Duon NP12 ..... 59 B1
Llwyn-On St CF83 ..... 137 F4
LLWYN-ON VILLAGE 225 E6
Llwyn Passat CF64 ..... 207 B6
Llwynpennau Cotts CF72 ..... 174 C6
Llwyn Rd SA18 ..... 220 D5
Llwyn Rhedyn SA2 ..... 94 B8
Llwyn Rhosyn CF14 ..... 177 C8
LLWYN-TÊG 218 A3
Llwyn Teg SA5 ..... 67 C6
Llwynwhilwg Terr 3 SA14 ..... 40 F4
Llwyn Y Bioden SA6 ..... 45 F5
Llwyn-y-Bryn
Ammanford / Rhydaman SA18 ..... 219 B8
Neath / Castell-Nedd SA10 ..... 70 C6

Llwyn-y-Gelynen CF48 ... 30 C8
Llwyn Y Gog
Cwmrhydyceirw SA6 ... 46 A5
Rhoose / Y Rhws CF62 ... 213 B1
Swansea / Abertawe SA6 .. 45 F5
Llwyn Y Golomen SA6 ... 46 A5
Llwyn Y Graig SA4 ... 43 F1
Llwyn-y-Grant Pl
CF23 ... 178 D2
Llwyn-y-Grant Rd
CF23 ... 178 D2
Llwyn-y-Grant Terr
CF23 ... 178 D2
Llwyn Y Groes CF31 ... 168 B4
Llwyn-Y-Mor SA3 ... 122 E4
LLWYNYPIA ... 106 E8
Llwynypia Hospl CF40 ... 79 F1
Llwynypia Prim Sch
CF40 ... 106 E7
Llwynypia Rd CF40 ... 106 E7
Llwyn Y Pia Rd CF14 ... 160 B3
Llwynypia Sta CF40 ... 106 F8
Llwynypia Terr CF40 ... 106 E8
Llwyn Y Pwll Cl / Clos
Llwyn Y Pwll NP23 ... 8 D4
Llwyn-yr-Eos CF48 ... 30 F4
Llwyn Yr Eos SA14 ... 41 B6
Llwyn-yr-Eos
Nelson CF46 ... 83 E4
Swansea / Abertawe SA6 .. 45 E2
Llwyn Yr Eos Gr CF47 ... 10 F1
Llwyn Yr Hebog SA6 ... 46 A5
Llwyn Yr Iar SA6 ... 46 A5
Llwyn Yr Ynys SA14 ... 41 C4
Llygad-yr-Haul
Glyn-neath / Glyn-nedd
SA11 ... 223 B1
Neath / Castell-Nedd
SA10 ... 48 D2
Llyn Berwyn Cl NP10 ... 142 B6
Llyn Celyn Cl NP10 ... 142 B7
Llyn Cl CF23 ... 178 B5
Llyn Cres CF43 ... 79 F6
Llyn Cwm Llwydrhew
NP13 ... 36 C2
Llynfa Rd SA4 ... 65 A4
Llynfi Ct CF34 ... 101 F1
Llynfi Ct / Cwrt Llynfi
CF34 ... 101 F1
Llynfi Ent Ctr CF34 ... 101 E4
Llynfi La
Bridgend / Pen-y-Bont ar
Ogwr CF31 ... 168 F4
Maesteg CF34 ... 102 A3
Llynfi Rd CF34 ... 102 A3
Llynfi St
1 Bridgend / Pen-y-Bont ar
Ogwr CF31 ... 168 F4
Ton-du CF32 ... 150 C5
Llynfi View CF34 ... 102 B8
Llyn Pandy CF83 ... 138 D6
Llyn Tircoed SA4 ... 44 C5

Llys = court

Llys Aaron SA4 ... 19 C4
Llys Abbeyville /
Abbeyville Ct 11 SA12 ... 98 D1
Llys Ael-y-Bryn SA7 ... 46 F2
Llys Ael Y Bryn SA4 ... 44 A2
Llys Alaw CF40 ... 107 B5
Llys Alys SA15 ... 40 E5
Llys Andrew SA10 ... 70 F6
Llys Aneirin SA4 ... 66 D8
Llys Baldwin SA4 ... 66 B6
Llys Bartlett 7 SA11 ... 71 E7
Llys Bethania SA11 ... 226 D5
Llys Bethel SA14 ... 41 C5
Llys Briallen CF31 ... 169 D6
Llys Bronallt SA4 ... 19 A4
Llys Bronwydd / Treehill
Ct CF31 ... 168 D3
Llys Bryn Felin CF39 ... 133 C5
Llys Brynteg SA4 ... 43 B3
Llys Caeglas 15 SA15 ... 40 D5
Llys Caer Felin SA5 ... 67 C4
Llys Cambria CF83 ... 137 F8
Llys Caradog
Creigiau CF15 ... 174 D7
Llanelli SA14 ... 41 D5
Llys Castell SA13 ... 148 A6
Llys Catwg
Glyn-neath SA11 ... 227 C8
Talbot Green CF72 ... 155 C2
Llys Celyn CF38 ... 136 A1
Llys Cennech SA14 ... 18 C1
Llys Cilsaig SA14 ... 41 B8
Llys Coed
10 Bridgend / Pen-y-Bont ar
Ogwr CF31 ... 168 C3
Pontypridd CF37 ... 109 D6
Llys Coed Derw CF38 ... 156 D8
Llys Coleg 4 CF14 ... 177 B3
Llys Corrwg CF37 ... 136 C5
Llys Cyncoed NP12 ... 59 B1
Llys Cynffig CF33 ... 148 B2
Llys Cynon CF44 ... 27 F7
Llys Deri CF72 ... 172 B5
Llys Derwen
Llantrisant CF72 ... 155 D2
Pontypridd CF37 ... 109 D6
Llys Dewi
Creigiau CF15 ... 174 E7
Llantwit Major / Llanilltud
Fawr CF61 ... 209 F7
Llys Dewi Sant
Gorseinon SA4 ... 43 C2
Llys Dewi Sant *continued*
Swansea / Abertawe
SA1 ... 233 B2
Llys Dol SA6 ... 46 A2
Llys Dol May 9 CF64 ... 207 A5
Llys Dulais SA10 ... 226 A7
Llys Dur SA6 ... 46 A2
Llys Dwfnant SA11 ... 226 C4
Llys Dwrgi SA7 ... 70 B8
Llys Dwynwen CF61 ... 209 F8
Llys Dyfodwg
Creigiau CF15 ... 174 E6
Talbot Green CF72 ... 155 C2
Llys Dyfrig CF15 ... 174 D6
Llys Ebwy NP23 ... 14 D7
Llys Eglwys CF31 ... 168 C3
Llys Eithin SA14 ... 128 C8
Llys Elba SA4 ... 66 B6
Llys Fach CF38 ... 156 F8
Llys Faen CF31 ... 168 F5
LLYS FAENLISVANE ... 160 B2
LLYS FAEN /
LISVANE ... 160 B2
Llys-faen / Lisvane &
Thornhill Sta CF14 ... 159 F3
Llysfaen Prim Sch
CF14 ... 160 B3
Llys Felin SA10 ... 49 C4
Llys Felin Newydd SA7 ... 69 C6
Llys Fran SA15 ... 40 E7
Llys Fredrick Jones SA9 ... 2 C7
Llys Garth CF38 ... 135 D1
Llys Ger Y Llan SA4 ... 19 D3
Llys Glanrafon SA8 ... 23 E4
Llys Glanrhondda CF41 ... 78 F5
Llys Glan Y Mor 2
SA15 ... 40 C3
Llys Glowr CF37 ... 82 A1
Llys Groeswen SA13 ... 125 D6
Llys Gwalia SA4 ... 43 D2
Llys Gwenci SA7 ... 70 B8
Llys Gwent CF63 ... 215 C8
Llys Gwernen
Cwmrhydyceirw SA6 ... 46 A2
Swansea / Abertawe SA6 .. 45 F2
Llys Gwernifor CF45 ... 54 D2
Llys Gwilym
Trebanos / Trebannws SA6,
SA8 ... 23 B1
Ynysybwl CF37 ... 109 A8
Llysgwyn SA6 ... 45 C2
Llys Gwyn
Bridgend / Pen-y-Bont ar
Ogwr CF31 ... 168 F6
Maesteg CF34 ... 102 A2
Llys Gwynfaen SA4 ... 42 F2
Llys Gwynfryn SA10 ... 48 C5
Llys Gwynno CF15 ... 174 E6
Llysgwyn Terr SA4 ... 19 D5
Llys Gwyrdd NP44 ... 116 A7
Llys Hafn CF15 ... 158 A3
Llys Hanner Erw / Half
Acre Ct CF83 ... 138 B5
Llys Hebog SA7 ... 70 B8
Llys Hebron CF41 ... 79 A3
Llys Hendre SA14 ... 42 B7
Llys Illtyd
Creigiau CF15 ... 174 D7
Talbot Green CF72 ... 155 C2
Llys Iris SA10 ... 48 C1
Llys Iwan 10 SA18 ... 219 C7
Llys Jernegan 2 SA1 ... 233 C2
Llys John Davies SA1 ... 233 B4
Llys Joseph CF72 ... 172 B6
Llys Joseph Parry NP22 .. 12 D5
Llys-Le-Breos SA3 ... 93 F1
Llys Llwyfen SA7 ... 46 D1
Llys Llywelyn CF38 ... 156 D8
Llys Lotwen SA18 ... 218 E6
Llys Mabon NP22 ... 12 D5
Llys Maelwg CF72 ... 155 C2
Llys Maendy CF41 ... 79 A3
Llys Marl / Marl Ct
NP44 ... 89 B5
Llys Moreia SA5 ... 68 C6
Llys Morfa SA13 ... 75 D3
Llys Nant Fer SA18 ... 220 D7
Llys Nant Glas CF45 ... 82 A7
Llys Nant Pandy CF83 ... 138 A4
Llys Nant Y Clais / Nant Y
Clais Ct SA12 ... 99 C5
Llys Nant Yr Aber
CF83 ... 137 F4
Llys Nazareth CF41 ... 78 F5
Llys Nedd SA10 ... 48 D2
Llysnewydd 4 SA15 ... 40 C3
Llys Onnen
Ebbw Vale / Glyn Ebwy
NP23 ... 14 B8
1 Porthcawl CF36 ... 182 F7
Llys Pabi / Poppy Ct 9
SA11 ... 71 E6
Llys Pat Chown / Pat
Chown Ct SA8 ... 23 E4
Llys Pegasus CF14 ... 177 F8
Llys Penallt 4 SA15 ... 40 F6
Llys Pendderi SA14 ... 41 F5
Llys Penpant SA6 ... 45 C2
Llys Pentre
Bridgend / Pen-y-Bont ar
Ogwr CF31 ... 168 C3
Swansea / Abertawe SA5 .. 68 D4
Llys Perl SA6 ... 46 F8
Llys Pum Cyfair CF14 ... 177 C2
Llys Royston / Royston Ct
SA10 ... 48 C1
Llys Sant Teilo SA5 ... 45 B2
Llys Seion CF34 ... 75 B1
Llys Siloh CF41 ... 78 F5
Llys Soar CF42 ... 50 E2
Llys Steffan CF61 ... 209 F7
Llys Sycamorwydden /
Sycamore Ct SA12 ... 98 D7
Llys Tal-y-Bont Rd
CF14 ... 177 E1
Llys Tawel SA9 ... 1 F1
Llys Teg CF31 ... 168 B3
Llys-Teg SA2 ... 93 D8
Llys Teilo
Creigiau CF15 ... 174 E6
Llantwit Major / Llanilltud
Fawr CF61 ... 209 F7
Talbot Green CF72 ... 155 C2
Llys Trerobart CF37 ... 109 A7
Llys Tripp CF15 ... 158 A3
Llys Tudful CF15 ... 174 E7
Llys Ty Gwyn 6 CF37 ... 109 E2
Llys Tylcha Fawr CF39 ... 133 C5
Llys Ty Mawr CF35 ... 170 A2
Llys Tynewydd CF35 ... 169 C7
Llys Tysant CF35 ... 169 C7
Llys-uchaf
Birchgrove SA7 ... 47 B1
Swansea / Abertawe SA7 .. 70 B8
Llys Warner SA15 ... 40 E7
Llyswen
Machen CF83 ... 139 F7
Pen-pedair-heol CF82 ... 84 F7
Penywaun CF44 ... 28 B6
Llys Wen 9 CF31 ... 168 C3
Llys Wenallt SA11 ... 49 E3
Llyswen Rd CF23 ... 178 B7
Llyswen Wlk / Llwybr
Llyswen 2 NP44 ... 90 B1
Llys Wern SA10 ... 48 C2
LLYSWORNEY /
LLYSWYRNY ... 187 D1
LLYSWYRNY /
LLYSWORNEY ... 187 D1
Llys Y Brenin SA4 ... 66 B8
Llys-y-Bryn SA7 ... 70 B8
Llys-y-Bryn / Hill Ct
CF31 ... 168 A3
Llys-y-Capel NP13 ... 15 E5
Llys-y-Celyn CF83 ... 138 C5
Llys Y Coed CF62 ... 214 C4
Llys-y-Coed
Birchgrove SA7 ... 47 B1
Loughor SA4 ... 42 D1
Neath / Castell-Nedd
SA10 ... 71 D8
Llys Y Coed CF82 ... 111 E7
Llys Y Dderwen SA14 ... 42 B7
Llys Y Ddraenog SA13 ... 148 A5
Llys-y-Deri SA18 ... 219 D7
Llys Y Drindod SA15 ... 40 E3
Llys Y Farchnad SA4 ... 66 C5
Llys-y-Fedwen CF83 ... 138 C4
Llys Y Felin
Hendy SA4 ... 19 A6
Llangennech SA14 ... 18 B1
Llys-y-Felin SA5 ... 68 C3
Llys-y-Fran CF31 ... 168 B6
Llys y Fran CF38 ... 156 E8
Llys Y Gof SA15 ... 40 C4
Llys-y-graig SA10 ... 70 F8
Llys Y Grug / Heather Ct
2 CF36 ... 182 F7
Llys Y Morwr SA15 ... 40 D4
Llys-y-Nant SA7 ... 47 A6
Llys-y-Nant / Brook Ct
SA11 ... 71 C4
Llys Ynyscedwyn SA9 ... 2 D8
Llys Y Parc CF81 ... 58 A2
Llys Y Pobydd SA15 ... 40 E5
Llys Yr Ardd SA6 ... 46 A2
Llys Yr Efail
Blaina / Blaenau NP13 ... 15 D5
Tonyrefail CF39 ... 133 C5
Llys-yr-Eglwys 10
CF64 ... 207 B5
Llys Yr Hen Felin 5
SA15 ... 40 D6
Llys Yr Onnen SA14 ... 41 A8
Llys Yr Orsaf 7 SA15 ... 40 C4
Llys-yr-Ynys SA11 ... 226 E5
Llys Yr Ysgol
Glyn-neath / Glyn-nedd
SA11 ... 223 D1
Saron SA18 ... 218 E6
Llys yr Ysgol / School Ct
SA11 ... 71 D5
Llys-y-Waun SA7 ... 47 B1
Llythrid Ave SA2 ... 94 E6
Llywelyn Ho NP44 ... 89 F2
Llywelyn Rd / Heol
Llywelyn NP44 ... 89 E3
Llywelyn St CF32 ... 104 E2
Load Of Hay Rd NP11 ... 59 F2
Lochaber St CF24 ... 178 C1
Lock Ct CF37 ... 109 D1
Locke Gr 12 CF3 ... 180 A6
Locke St NP20 ... 143 B5
Lock Keepers Ct CF10 ... 194 F8
Lock's Common Rd
CF36 ... 182 D7
Lock's Ct CF36 ... 182 F8
Lock's La CF36 ... 182 E8
Locks Rd CF10 ... 207 C8
Lock St CF45 ... 82 F3
Lock-up La / Lon Y Gell
NP4 ... 37 F3
Lodden Cl NP20 ... 116 E2
Lodge Ave NP18 ... 118 A3
Lodge Cl CF14 ... 160 A4
Lodge Cl The SA2 ... 94 A7
Lodge Ct SA11 ... 71 C2
Lodge Dr SA12 ... 98 D6
Lodge Hill
Caerleon / Caerllion
NP18 ... 117 F3
Llanwern NP18 ... 145 B5
Lodge Rd
Abersychan NP4 ... 37 E3
Caerleon / Caerllion
NP18 ... 117 F2
Caerleon / Caerllion
NP18 ... 118 A3
Lodge The 4 SA1 ... 233 A4
Lodge View NP4 ... 37 F1
Lodge Wood NP4 ... 62 E5
Lodwick Rise CF3 ... 180 A5
Loftus St CF5 ... 194 B6
Login Rd SA5 ... 67 A3
Lombard Cl CF36 ... 165 E1
Lombard St
Barry / Y Barri CF62 ... 214 F5
3 Neath / Castell-Nedd
SA11 ... 71 D6
Lombardy Villas SA10 ... 48 E1
Lomond Cres CF23 ... 178 C5
Lon Aber SA15 ... 40 F4
Lon Alfa SA2 ... 93 F8
Lon Bedw / Birch La
SA10 ... 49 C5
Lon Bedwen SA2 ... 94 D8
Lon Beili Glas SA18 ... 220 D6
Lon Biwmares / Beaumaris
Dr NP44 ... 90 B1
Lon Brydwen SA4 ... 43 B1
Lon Brynawel SA7 ... 69 F6
Lon Bryngwyn SA2 ... 94 E8
Lon Bryn-Mawr /
Brynmawr La 9
SA18 ... 219 B7
Lon Brynneuadd SA18 ... 220 D7
Lon Brynteg SA10 ... 48 C1
Lon Burns / Burns La 4
NP44 ... 89 D2
Lon Cadog SA2 ... 94 E7
Lon Cae Banc SA2 ... 94 D7
Loncae Porth CF14 ... 159 C1
Lon Camlad SA6 ... 68 E8
Lon Capel Ed / Capel Ed
La NP4 ... 39 E7
Lon Caron SA2 ... 94 E7
Lon Carreg Bica SA7 ... 70 B8
Lon Catwg SA8 ... 24 B5
Lon Cedwyn SA2 ... 94 E7
Lon Cefn Mably CF62 ... 212 F1
Lon Ceiriog SA14 ... 41 D5
Lon Claerwen SA6 ... 68 E8
Lon Coed Bran SA2 ... 94 E8
Lon Coed Garw / Garw
Wood Dr 5 NP44 ... 90 A6
Lon Coed Parc SA2 ... 94 E8
Lon Cothi SA2 ... 67 E1
Lon Cwmgwyn SA2 ... 94 E8
Lon Cwrt Ynyston
CF11 ... 194 C2
Lon Cynfor SA2 ... 94 E7
Lon Cynlais SA2 ... 94 D7
Lon Dan-y-Coed SA2 ... 94 E8
Londeg SA8 ... 23 D6
Lon Derw SA2 ... 94 D8
London Cl SA12 ... 99 D4
London Rd SA11 ... 71 E7
London Row SA12 ... 99 D4
London St
Mountain Ash / Aberpennar
CF45 ... 54 D3
Newport / Casnewydd
NP19 ... 143 E6
London Terr SA12 ... 99 D4
Lon Draenen SA2 ... 94 C7
Lon Draenog SA6 ... 45 F5
Lon Einon SA4 ... 43 F2
Lon Eithrym SA6 ... 46 D8
Lon Elai CF72 ... 173 B8
Lon Enfys SA7 ... 69 D6
Lone Rd SA6 ... 22 D1
Lone The SA6 ... 22 C2
Lon Fach
Caerphilly / Caerffili
CF83 ... 137 F2
Cardiff / Caerdydd CF14 .. 177 B7
Lon Fawr CF83 ... 137 F2
Lon Fedwen / Birch La
SA10 ... 48 F2
Lon Fferm Felin CF62 ... 214 C4
Lon Fferm Y Cwm / Cwm
Farm La NP4 ... 62 D5
Long Acre
Bishopston SA3 ... 122 B6
Cwmbran / Cwmbrân
NP44 ... 89 B1
North Cornelly CF33 ... 165 E7
Longacre Cl
Barry / Y Barri CF63 ... 215 D8
Llantrisant CF72 ... 155 E2
Long Acre Ct
Bishopston SA3 ... 122 B6
Porthcawl CF36 ... 165 D2
Long Acre Dr CF36 ... 165 E2
Long Acre Gdns SA3 ... 93 F1
Lon Gaer SA4 ... 43 F2
Lon Ganol CF14 ... 177 B7
Longbridge NP18 ... 117 F6
Longbridge Ct 11
NP11 ... 114 F3
Longcross St CF24 ... 195 C6
Longditch Rd NP19 ... 144 E1
Lon Gellideg NP11 ... 59 C4
Lon Ger-y-Coed
Ammanford / Rhydaman
SA18 ... 219 D7
Swansea / Abertawe SA2 .. 94 E8
Longfellow Dr CF31 ... 168 D6
Longfellow Gdns CF83 ... 139 D7
Longfield Ct CF44 ... 27 D7
Longford Cres SA1 ... 96 A7
Longford La SA10 ... 48 A1
Longford Rd / Heol
Longford
Neath Abbey SA10 ... 71 B8
Neath / Castell-Nedd
SA10 ... 48 B2
Long Hollow / Pant Hir 2
NP44 ... 89 E4
Long House Barn Est
NP4 ... 39 E7
Long House Cl CF14 ... 160 A2
Longhouse Gr NP44 ... 115 F8
Longlands Cl CF33 ... 148 B2
Longleat Cl CF14 ... 160 B2
Lon Glynfelin SA10 ... 48 B1
Long Meadow CF33 ... 147 E1
Long Meadow Ct
NP19 ... 144 C3
Longmeadow Dr CF64 ... 206 B2
Long Meadow Dr
CF62 ... 215 A7
Longmede Pk CF44 ... 224 B1
Long Oaks Ave SA2 ... 94 E6
Long Oaks Ct SA2 ... 94 E7
Long Oaks Mews SA2 ... 94 E7
Longreach Cl CF5 ... 192 F4
Long Ridge SA1 ... 233 A5
Lon Groeswen / Groes-
wen La 4 SA13 ... 125 D5
Long Row
Ferndale CF43 ... 79 F8
Llanelli SA15 ... 40 E6
New Tredegar NP24 ... 33 F2
Pontypridd CF37 ... 135 E6
Long Shepherds Dr
SA3 ... 122 D4
Longships Rd CF10 ... 207 E8
Longspears Ave CF14 ... 177 E3
Long St SA9 ... 222 A6
Longtown Gr NP10 ... 163 E5
Longueil Cl CF10 ... 195 C3
Long View Rd SA6 ... 45 D1
Long Vue Rd SA12 ... 98 C2
Lon Gwendraeth SA6 ... 68 E8
Lon Gwesyn SA7 ... 47 A1
Longwood Dr CF14 ... 176 C7
Lon Gwynfryn SA2 ... 94 E7
Lon Hafren
Caerphilly / Caerffili
CF83 ... 137 F1
Swansea / Abertawe SA6 .. 68 E8
Lon Heddwch
Craig-cefn-parc SA6 ... 22 B2
Swansea / Abertawe SA7 .. 69 E6
Lon Helyg NP44 ... 90 B4
Lon Helygen CF37 ... 109 D6
Lon Heulog
Brynmenyn CF32 ... 150 D6
Hawthorn CF37 ... 136 A4
Lon Hir SA8 ... 23 F4
Lon Illtyd SA2 ... 94 E7
Lon Iorwg SA2 ... 94 C7
Lon Irfon SA2 ... 67 E1
Lon Isa CF14 ... 177 B7
Lon Isaf CF83 ... 137 F2
Lon Ithon SA6 ... 68 E8
Lon Killan SA2 ... 93 C8
LON-LAS ... 70 B7
Lon Las CF44 ... 28 D6
Lonlas Ave SA10 ... 70 C7
Lonlas Bsns Pk SA10 ... 70 D7
Lonlas Village Workshops
SA10 ... 70 D8
Lonlas Villas SA10 ... 70 C7
Lon Lindys CF62 ... 213 A1
Lon Llwyd 1 SA18 ... 220 B8
Lon Llys Havard SA18 ... 219 C6
Lon Madoc CF14 ... 177 C4
Lon Mafon SA2 ... 94 D7
Lon Masarn SA2 ... 94 C8
Lon Mefus SA2 ... 94 D8
Lon Menai SA7 ... 47 A1
Lon Nant NP44 ... 89 F5
Lon Nedd SA6 ... 68 F8
Lon-Od-Nant CF61 ... 210 A5
Lon Ogwen SA7 ... 47 A1
Lon Olchfa SA2 ... 94 A6
Lon Owain CF5 ... 193 B3
Lon Parc Henri / Parc
Henry La SA18 ... 219 B8
Lon Penfro SA6 ... 46 A4
Lon Penllyn CF14 ... 177 B6
Lon Pennant NP12 ... 58 E1
Lon Penpound / Penpound
La SA18 ... 219 F8
Lon Pentre / Pentre La
NP44 ... 116 E5
Lon Pen-y-Coed SA2 ... 67 D1
Lon Pen Y-coed SA2 ... 94 E8
Lon Pinwydden CF71 ... 189 C8
Lon Robin Goch CF83 ... 137 E3
Lon Sawdde SA6 ... 68 E8
Lonsdale Rd CF23 ... 178 E3
Lon Sutcliffe La SA4 ... 66 B5
Lon Tanyrallt SA8 ... 23 E3
Lon Tanywen / Tanywern
La SA9 ... 2 B7

Lon Teify SA2 67 E1
Lon Tir-y-Dail / Tir-y-Dail La 1 SA18 219 B7
Lon Towy SA2 67 D1
Lon Ty'n-y-Cae CF14 177 C6
Lon Tyr Haul SA7 69 F6
Lon Ucha CF14 177 B7
Lon Uchaf CF83 137 F2
Lon-Werdd CF5 193 A5
Lon-Werdd Cl CF5 193 A5
Lon Y Barics / Barrack La CF10 232 C2
Lon-y-Barri CF83 137 F5
Lon Y Bedydd / Baptist La 18 SA18 219 B7
Lon y Berllan / Orchard La NP44 89 F4
Lon Y Bracty / Malthouse Rd
Caerleon / Caerllion NP18 118 A5
Ponthir NP18, NP44 117 D6
Lon Y Bragoy / Brewery La CF31 168 E5
Lon-y-Bryn SA11 223 D1
Lon Y Bryn / Hillside Dr NP4 62 C4
Lon-y-Bugail CF31 168 B6
Lon-y-Byrnnau CF44 28 C3
Lon Y Cadno CF38 156 E7
Lon-y-Cariadon CF33 148 A1
Lon-y-Castell CF5 193 C3
Lon-y-Celyn
Cardiff / Caerdydd CF14 176 F6
Nelson CF46 83 D4
Lon-y-Coed
Bridgend / Pen-y-Bont ar Ogwr CF31 168 B6
Pontardawe SA8 23 D6
Lon-y-Dail CF14 177 B7
Lon-y-Dderwen CF14 177 B7
Lon Y Dderwen SA15 40 E8
Lon-y-Dderwen CF46 83 D4
Lon-y-Ddraenen CF83 137 F2
Lon-y-Deri
Caerphilly / Caerffili CF83 137 F2
Cardiff / Caerdydd CF14 177 B7
Lon Y Derwydd SA18 220 C8
Lon-y-Felin
Garnswllt SA18 219 B5
Mountain Ash / Aberpennar CF45 54 B5
Lon Y Felin / Mill La CF10 232 B2
Lon-y-Ffin CF5 193 A5
Lon Y Ffoledd / Folly La NP4 38 D2
Lon Y Fran CF83 137 E3
Lon-y-Fro CF15 175 C8
Lon-y-Garwa CF83 137 F1
Lon Y Gell / Lock-up La NP4 37 F3
Lon Y Goch CF15 175 C6
Lon-y-Gors CF83 137 E2
Lon-y-Groes CF14 177 D4
Lon-y-Gruglas SA18 219 A6
Lon-y-Llwyn CF46 83 D4
Lon-y-Llyn CF83 137 F2
Lon Y Maes SA14 41 B6
Lon-y-Mynydd CF14 177 D7
Lon Y Nant CF14 177 C7
Lon-y-Nant SA11 223 D1
Lon y Neuado Wen / White Hall La 10 NP44 90 B1
Lon-y-Parc
Cardiff / Caerdydd CF14 177 B5
Glyn-neath / Glyn-nedd SA11 223 C1
Maesteg CF34 75 A2
Ton Pentre CF41 79 A3
Lon Y Parc / Park La
Brynamman SA18 220 D8
Cardiff / Caerdydd CF10 232 C3
Lon-yr-Afon CF83 112 A2
Lon-yr-Awel CF72 173 C8
Lon-yr-Efail CF5 193 B3
Lon-yr-Eglwys CF32 185 C2
Lon Yr Eglwys / Church La SA12 98 E5
Lon-y-Rhedyn CF83 137 F2
Lon-y-Rhyd CF14 177 B8
Lon yr Odyn CF83 138 C4
Lon Yr Ysgol CF83 138 D6
Lon-Yr-Ysgol SA14 41 A7
Lon Yr Ysgol SA14 42 C7
Lon-yr-Ysgol SA8 24 B3
Lon-Ysgubor CF14 177 B8
Lon Y Tresglen CF83 137 E3
Lon-y-Twyn CF83 138 B2
Lon-y-Waun CF83 137 E2
Lon-y-Wern
Caerphilly / Caerffili CF83 137 F2
Pontardawe SA8 23 F3
Lon-y-Winci CF14 177 B8
Lord Nelson Ho SA1 233 B4
Lord Pontypridd Ho 6 CF5 194 B7
Lord St
Aberdare / Aberdâr CF44 53 C8
Lord St *continued*
4 Newport / Casnewydd NP19 143 D6
Penarth CF64 207 B5
Lorraine Cl / Clos Lorraine 2 SA12 98 D1
Lothian Cres CF23 178 D3
Lotwen Rd / Heol Lotwen SA18 218 D6
Loudoun Sq CF10 195 B3
Lougher Cl CF5 193 E7
Lougher Gdns CF36 182 E6
Lougher Pl
North Cornelly CF33 165 F7
St Athan / Sain Tathan CF62 211 C4
LOUGHOR 42 E2
Loughor Castle* SA4 65 D8
Loughor Comm SA4 43 B2
Loughor Rd SA4 66 B8
Loughor Row 5 CF36 165 F1
Louisa Pl CF10 195 B2
Louise Cl SA11 226 C4
Louise Ct 1 CF14 176 F3
Louvain Terr NP23 14 E8
Lovage Cl CF23 178 E8
Love La
Cardiff / Caerdydd CF10 232 C2
Llanblethian / Llanfleiddan CF71 188 E1
Loveluck Ct CF61 209 F6
Lowdon Terr CF62 214 E5
Lower Acre CF5 193 B3
Lower Adare St CF32 103 F4
Lower Alma Pl CF41 79 A4
Lower Alma Terr CF37 135 D8
Lower Bailey St
4 Brynmawr NP23 8 C4
Wattstown CF39 107 E8
Lower Banwell St 6 SA6 68 F8
Lower Bridge St NP4 62 C6
Lower Brooklands SA9 222 D7
LOWER BRYNAMMAN 220 D8
Lower Brynhyfryd Terr CF83 110 F2
Lower Castle St NP13 36 B4
Lower Cathedral Rd CF11 194 F5
Lower Church St CF32 103 F3
LOWER COEDCAE 15 D8
Lower Colbren Rd SA18 220 D6
Lower Coronation St NP22 13 E6
Lower Court Terr NP13 60 B6
Lower Cross Rd SA15 40 F5
Lower Cross St
Hirwaun CF44 27 D8
New Tredegar NP24 33 D3
Lowerdale Dr CF72 155 E2
Lower Dell The 1 SA15 40 C7
Lower Dock St NP20 143 D4
Lower Dunraven St CF40 106 F5
Lower Edward St 15 CF47 10 D2
Lower Farm Ct CF62 213 A2
Lower Forest Level CF45 54 E2
Lower Francis St CF83 136 F7
Lower Garn Terr NP4 16 F8
Lower Glantorvaen Terr NP4 17 B6
Lower Glyn-gwyn St CF83 139 A6
Lower Guthrie St CF63 215 A5
Lower Gwastad Terr NP13 36 B8
Lower Harper's Rd NP4 37 F5
Lower High St CF47 30 E8
Lower Hill St 15 NP4 17 C6
Lower Holmes St CF63 215 C6
Lower James St NP12 58 F4
Lower Lancaster St NP13 36 B3
Lower Leigh Rd / Heol Leigh Isaf NP4 38 A1
Lower Llansantffraid Rd CF32 150 D4
Lower Morel St CF63 215 A5
Lower Mount Pleasant 9 CF48 31 C1
Lower New Hos SA9 1 A1
LOWER NEW INN 63 A3
LOWER OCHRWYTH 141 B7
Lower Ochrwyth NP11 141 A7
Lower Pantteg SA9 2 A4
Lower Park Gdns NP4 62 C7
Lower Park Terr NP4 62 C6
LOWER PENARTH 207 A1
LOWER PORTHKERRY 213 D2
Lower Pyke St CF63 215 A5
LOWER RACE 62 A5
Lower Rd NP24 34 A1
Lower Rhymney Prim Sch NP22 12 F3
Lower Row
Dowlais CF48 11 B5
Rhymney / Rhymni NP22 12 C7
Lower Royal La NP13 36 A6
Lower Royal Lane Terr NP13 36 A6
Lower Salisbury St NP22 13 E6
LOWER SKETTY 94 B3
Lower Sq NP23 7 C4
Lower St CF44 53 D7
Lower Stanley Terr NP24 33 F2
Lower Station Rd 10 SA18 220 B8
Lower Station St 2 CF44 53 D7
Lower Stoney Rd NP4 37 F5
Lower Taff View CF37 109 E3
Lower Ten Hos NP13 15 E6
Lower Terr
Treorchy / Treorci CF42 78 C5
Tylorstown CF43 80 C2
Lower Thomas St CF47 10 E1
Lower Trostre Rd SA15 40 F3
Lower Ty Gwyn Rd / Heol Is Ty Gwyn NP4 37 E7
Lower Union St CF48 11 B4
Lower Vaynor Rd CF48 10 A5
Lower Waun St NP4 17 C7
Lower Wern Rd SA9 2 B6
Lower West End 1 SA13 125 C6
Lower Woodland St 11 NP4 17 D7
Lower Wyndham Terr NP11 115 B1
Lowfield Dr CF14 159 E2
Lowland Cl / Clos Tir-isaf CF31 168 C2
Lowland Dr CF38 136 A1
LOWLANDS 89 D6
Lowlands Cres NP44 89 E6
Lowlands Ct NP44 89 E6
Lowlands Rd / Ffordd yr Iseldir NP44 89 E6
Lowndes Cl NP10 141 F3
Low Row CF45 54 C5
Lowther Ct CF24 232 C4
Lowther Rd CF24 232 C4
Lucania Bldgs 1 SA13 125 C7
Lucas Cl CF63 215 C8
Lucas Rd SA7 47 A5
Lucas St
Cardiff / Caerdydd CF24 178 A1
Newport / Casnewydd NP20 143 B6
Lucerne Dr CF14 159 D3
Lucknow St CF11 194 E3
Lucy Rd / Heol Lucy SA10 70 D7
Ludlow Cl
Cardiff / Caerdydd CF11 195 A2
Newport / Casnewydd NP19 143 F4
Ludlow Cl / Clos Llwydlo 3 NP44 90 B1
Ludlow La CF64 207 B4
Ludlow St
Caerphilly / Caerffili CF83 138 A2
Cardiff / Caerdydd CF11 194 F2
Penarth CF64 207 A4
Lulworth Rd NP18 118 C1
Lundy Cl
Cardiff / Caerdydd CF14 177 E8
Porthcawl CF36 165 E1
Lundy Dr
Newport / Casnewydd NP19 143 F7
The Mumbles / Y Mwmbwls SA3 122 F7
LUNNON 120 F8
Lunnon Cl SA3 120 F8
Lupin Cl
Merthyr Tydfil / Merthyr Tudful CF47 10 C5
Port Talbot SA12 98 C3
Lupin Gr NP10 141 E6
Luther La CF47 10 F1
Luther St CF47 30 F8
Luton Ho 3 CF24 195 C6
Luton St CF42 78 D6
Luton Terr 4 SA15 40 C7
Lydbrook Ct 2 SA1 68 C2
Lydford Ave SA1 233 C4
Lydford Cl CF14 177 B6
Lydstep Cres CF14 177 B2
Lydstep Flats CF14 177 B2
Lydstep Rd CF62 214 F7
Lydwood Cl CF83 140 A7
Lye Ind Est SA4 19 D7
Lyle St CF45 54 C3
Lynch Blosse Cl CF5 176 E2
Lyncroft NP44 89 B3
Lyncroft Cl CF3 179 D8
Lynden SA9 1 D1
Lyndhurst Ave NP20 143 A2
Lyndhurst St
Cardiff / Caerdydd CF11 194 D5
Mountain Ash / Aberpennar CF45 54 D4
Lyndon Way 10 NP10 142 B4
Lyne Rd
Newport / Casnewydd NP20 143 C7
Lyne Rd *continued*
Risca / Rhisga NP11 115 A1
Lynmouth Cres CF3 179 A3
Lynmouth Dr CF64 216 A4
Lynn St SA5 68 B2
Lyn Pac Trad Est NP44 89 E5
Lynsdale Rd SA5 68 C4
Lynton Cl
Cardiff / Caerdydd CF3 179 B4
Sully CF64 216 B5
Lynton Ct
Cardiff / Caerdydd CF10 195 B2
The Mumbles / Y Mwmbwls SA3 122 E6
Lynton Pl CF3 179 B4
Lynton Terr CF3 179 A4
Lynwood Ct
4 Cardiff / Caerdydd CF24 195 C7
Radyr CF15 176 B5
Lyon Cl CF11 194 D1
Lyon's Pl SA11 226 E5
Lyric Ct SA8 23 E4
Lyric Way CF14 159 E2
Lysander Ct CF24 196 A7
Lystep Ho 3 NP44 89 D2
Lytham Gr 1 CF3 180 A8

M

Maberly Ct CF14 178 A7
Mabon Cl SA4 42 F3
McArthur Glen Designer Village CF32 150 F2
MacAulay Ave CF3 179 B7
MacAulay Gdns NP20 142 E1
McCale Ave 1 CF5 193 E7
MacDonald Ave CF35 170 D7
MacDonald Cl CF5 193 A4
MacDonald Pl CF5 193 A4
MacDonald Rd CF5 193 A4
McDonnell Rd CF81 57 F4
Mace La CF42 78 B8
MacGregor Row CF34 102 A4
MACHEN 140 A7
Machen Cl
Cardiff / Caerdydd CF3 180 A7
Risca / Rhisga NP11 115 B1
Machen Pl CF11 194 E5
Machen Prim Sch / Ysgol Gynradd Machen CF83 139 F7
Machen St
Cardiff / Caerdydd CF11 194 E3
3 Penarth CF64 206 F4
Risca / Rhisga NP11 114 F2
Machine Mdw / Dol Beiriant 4 NP4 38 A1
MACHYNYS 40 D1
Machynys Rd SA15 40 E1
McIntyre Ct NP4 62 E2
Mackintosh Pl CF24 178 B1
Mackintosh Rd CF37 109 D1
Mackintosh St / Stryd Mackintosh CF48 55 C5
Mackintosh Terr CF46 83 D6
Mackworth Ct 3 SA1 233 B3
Mackworth Dr SA11 72 C5
Mackworth Rd CF36 183 A7
Mackworth St CF31 168 F5
Mackworth Terr SA1 233 C3
McLaren Cotts NP22 33 D8
McLay Ct 3 CF5 193 E7
McQuade Pl CF62 214 E2
McRitchie Pl SA5 67 F3
Maddocks Pl CF31 168 F3
Maddox St CF40 106 D6
MADE Enterprise Ctr CF48 31 A3
Madeline St
Pontygwaith CF43 80 B1
Treorchy / Treorci CF41 78 F5
Madison Dr CF44 27 D7
Madison Gdns 12 NP11 114 F3
Madoc Cl
Bridgend / Pen-y-Bont ar Ogwr CF31 169 A5
Dinas Powis / Dinas Powys CF64 206 C3
Madoc Pl SA1 233 A2
Madoc Rd CF24 195 F6
Madoc St
Pontypridd CF37 135 C8
Swansea / Abertawe SA1 233 A2
Madog Cl CF43 80 B4
Maelfa CF23 178 E4
Maelgwyn Terr CF44 28 F2
Maelog Cl CF72 173 B8
Maelog Pl CF14 177 E1
Maelog Rd CF14 177 C4
Maelon Rd / Heol Maelon CF31 168 B3
MAENDY 189 B6
Maendy Cres CF48 10 A2
Maendy Pl CF44 29 A2
Maendy Pl / Ll Maendy NP44 89 C6
Maendy Prim Sch NP44 89 E4
Maendy Rd CF71 189 B4
Maendy Sq NP44 89 C5
Maendy Way / Ffordd Maendy NP44 89 C5
Maendy Wood Rise NP44 89 C5
Maen Ganol CF46 56 D1
Maen Gilfach CF46 56 D1
Maengwyn SA8 221 B1
Maen Moel 11 NP23 14 D6
Maenol Glasfryn SA14 42 B7
MAERDY 52 B1
Maerdy Cl NP20 142 F1
Maerdy Ct CF43 52 A1
Maerdy Inf Sch CF43 52 A1
Maerdy Jun Sch CF43 79 B8
Maerdy La CF14 160 C2
Maerdy Pk CF35 170 D6
Maerdy Rd
Aberdare / Aberdâr CF44 52 E7
Ammanford / Rhydaman SA18 219 B5
Maerdy CF43 52 B1
Maerdy Rd Flats CF43 52 B1
Maerdy Road Ind Est / Ystad Ddiwydiannol Maerdy Road CF43 79 D8
Maerdy View NP22 13 A1
Maes Alarch / Swanfield SA9 2 C7
Maes Aneurin / Aneurin Pl NP23 8 C5
Maes-Ar-Ddafen Rd SA14 41 C4
Maes Awyr Caerdydd-Cymru / Cardiff International Airport CF62 213 B3
Maes Awyr Rhyngwladol Caerdydd / Rhoose Cardiff International Sta CF62 213 A1
Maes Bedw CF39 107 E2
Maes Briallu
Caerphilly / Caerffili CF83 138 D4
Swansea / Abertawe SA7 69 F7
Maes Brith Y Garn CF23 160 F1
Maes Bryn CF31 168 B6
Maes Brynmawr / Brynmawr Pl CF34 102 A3
Maes Brynna CF44 28 C4
Maes Cadwgan CF15 174 E7
Maes Caerfaddon / Bath Gn NP44 90 B2
Maescanner Rd SA14 41 B7
Maes-Cefn-Mabley CF72 155 D4
Maes Coleridge / Coleridge Gn 13 NP44 89 C2
Maes Collen SA6 45 F3
Maes Conwy SA14 41 B6
Maescynog SA9 1 F1
Maescynon CF44 27 E8
Maes Dafydd SA4 66 B8
Maesderi SA4 18 F4
Maes-Deri SA1 69 D5
Maes Derwen SA14 218 C7
Maesderwen Cres NP4 62 D5
Maesderwen Rd NP4 62 E5
Maes Dewi Pritchard / Dewi Pritchard Field CF31 169 A6
Maes Dyfnaint / Devon Pl NP4 37 E3
Maes Ebbw Sch NP20 163 F8
Maes Ganol CF37 136 C4
Maes Gareth Edwards SA18 220 D7
MAES-GLAS 163 F8
Maesglas
Bettws CF32 129 E2
Bridgend / Pen-y-Bont ar Ogwr CF31 168 C5
Cwmavon / Cwmafan SA12 99 D5
Pen-y-groes SA14 218 D7
Pyle / Y Pîl CF33 148 C2
Maes Glas
Barry / Y Barri CF62 214 C5
Caerphilly / Caerffili CF83 138 C2
Cardiff / Caerdydd CF14 177 B4
Cefn Cribwr CF32 149 B2
Ebbw Vale / Glyn Ebwy NP23 7 B4
Gorseinon SA4 43 B1
Pontypridd CF37 109 D6
Ton-du CF32 150 E5
Tredegar NP22 13 E8
Maesglas Ave NP20 143 A1
Maesglas Cl NP20 164 A8
Maesglas Cres NP20 163 F8
Maesglas Gr NP20 163 F8
Maesglas Ind Est NP20 143 B1
Maesglas Park Prim Sch NP20 164 A8
Maesglas Rd
Newport / Casnewydd NP20 142 F1
Newport / Casnewydd NP20 164 A8
Swansea / Abertawe SA5 68 B3
Maesglas St NP20 164 A8
Maes Golau SA15 40 F8
Maesgrenig SA18 219 F8
Maes Gwair CF31 168 B6

Maes Gwr / Gower Gn 4 NP44 90 A6
Maesgwyn
Cwmbran / Cwmbrân NP44 89 D6
Cwmdare CF44 28 C4
Maesteg CF34 102 C2
Newbridge / Trecelyn NP11 86 C5
Maes Gwyn CF83 138 B2
Maes-Gwyn SA12 73 B5
Maes Gwyn SA10 49 B3
Maesgwyn Dr SA4 19 C4
Maesgwyn Hospl / Ysbyty Maesgwyn CF32 151 A6
Maesgwynne CF48 10 B3
Maesgwynne Ind Est CF48 10 B3
Maesgwyn Rd SA4 19 C4
Maesgwyn Specl Sch CF44 28 D4
Maes-Gwyn St SA12 124 E8
Maes Gwyn / White Mdw CF31 168 D3
Maes Hafen / Haven Mdw CF31 168 D3
Maeshafod NP13 15 E3
Maes Hawarden / Hawarden Gn 13 NP44 90 B2
Maeshir SA11 223 C1
Maes Hir CF83 137 F5
Maes Hyfryd CF44 53 F7
Maes Illtuds CF61 210 A7
Maeslan SA8 24 B3
Maes Lan CF33 148 D2
Maes-Lan SA7 69 F6
Maesllan CF34 128 B6
Maes Llewelyn SA18 219 F8
Maes Lliedi SA15 40 F8
Maes Lloi CF71 189 B3
Maesllwyn SA18 219 B8
Maes Llwynonn SA10 48 E1
Maes Llysteg / Faircourt Mdw 1 CF31 168 C3
Maes Maddock SA4 43 B1
Maes Maelwg CF38 155 F6
Maes Magretian / Magretion Pl 6 CF10 195 B3
Maesmarchog Prim Sch SA10 223 A5
Maes Margam / Margam Pl SA15 40 E4
Maes-Mawr Rd SA10 226 A7
Maes Meillion SA7 69 F7
Maes Meisgyn / Miskin Gn 2 NP44 90 A3
Maesmelyn CF44 28 C3
Maesmelyn St 6 SA13 125 D5
Maes Morrison SA4 19 D3
Maes Pencoed / Pencoed PL 4 NP44 89 F6
Maes Penrhyn SA14 41 B6
Maes Prospect / Prospect Pl NP4 37 F1
Maes Pwll SA11 226 B3
Maesquarre Rd / Ffordd Maescwarrau SA18 219 D6
Maes Rd / Heol Maes SA14 42 C8
Maes Rhedyn SA12 98 D6
Maes Rhodri / Rhodri Pl 5 NP44 90 B2
Maes Rhosyn SA8 24 B3
Maes-rhydwen Flats 1 CF44 28 E4
Maesruddud La NP12 58 F2
Maes Sant Teilo SA5 45 B2
Maes Sarn CF72 155 D4
Maes Slowes Leyes CF62 213 B1
Maes St SA1 95 F7
Maes Stanley / Stanley Pl SA10 48 F2
Maes Sycamorwydden / Sycamore Pl NP44 89 B6
Maestaf St CF48 31 A4
Maes Talcen CF31 169 B5
Maes Tal Coed / Wood End Mdw 6 CF31 168 C3
Maes Tanrallt / Underwood Pl CF31 169 C4
MAESTEG 102 B1
Maes Teg
Newbridge / Trecelyn NP11 86 C5
Pontarddulais SA4 19 D5
Maesteg Bsns Ctr CF34 101 E4
Maesteg Com Hospl CF34 101 E4
Maesteg Comp Lower Sch CF34 102 C3
Maesteg Comp (Upper) Sch CF34 128 D5
Maesteg Cres CF38 136 A1
Maesteg Eweny Road Sta CF34 102 B2
Maesteg Gdns CF38 136 A1
Maesteg Gr CF38 136 A1
Maesteg Rd
Bryn CF34, SA13 101 B4
Bryn SA13 100 F5
Cwmfelin CF34 128 C7
Cymmer / Cymer SA13 75 C4
Cymmer / Cymer SA13 75 C5
Ton-du CF32 150 C5
Maesteg Row CF34 102 B2
Maesteg St SA1 233 C4
Maesteg Sta CF34 102 A3
Maesteg Terr CF36 183 A7
Maestir SA15 40 F7
Maes Trane CF38 156 A6
Maes Trawscoed / Crosswood Mdw 5 CF31 168 C3
Maestref SA15 40 F8
Maes Trisant CF72 155 C2
Maes Ty-canol SA12 98 E6
Maes Ty Cwrdd / Meadow Ct SA14 41 D4
Maes Ty Gwyn SA14 18 C1
Maes Uchaf CF37 136 C4
Maes Watford CF83 158 F8
Maeswerdd SA15 40 F8
Maesybedol SA18 220 B8
Maes-y-Bedw CF46 55 F8
Maes-y-berllan SA18 219 C6
Maes-y-Bettws SA12 100 A8
Maesybont SA18 219 F8
Maes Y Briallu CF15 176 A7
Maes Y Bryn CF23 179 B8
Maes-y-Bryn
Colwinston / Tregolwyn CF71 187 A4
Radyr CF15 176 B7
Swansea / Abertawe SA6 45 F2
Tonyrefail CF39 133 C6
Maes-y-Bryn Prim Sch / Ysgol Gynradd Maes-y-Bryn CF38 156 D7
Maes-y-Bryn Rd CF14, CF23 161 B4
Maes-y-Ceffyl SA11 227 B8
Maes-y-Celyn NP4 62 D4
Maes Y Celyn SA4 65 D1
Maes-y-Cnyw Terr NP13 60 C6
MAESYCOED 135 A8
Maesycoed SA18 219 D7
Maes-y-Coed CF62 214 B2
Maes Y Coed NP12 85 D6
Maes-y-coed
Cwmdare CF44 28 C3
Gorseinon SA4 66 B8
Llanelli SA15 40 B6
Swansea / Abertawe SA6 45 F2
Trelewis CF46 83 D6
Maes-y-Coed Prim Sch / Ysgol Grynradd Maes-y-Coed CF37 135 B8
Maesycoed Rd
Godre'r-graig SA8 221 B1
Pontypridd CF37 109 B1
Maes-y-Coed Rd CF14 177 E6
Maes-y-Coed Terr CF82 84 D1
Maes Y Cored CF14 176 E6
Maes Y Cornel / Corner Mdw SA8 24 A3
Maes y Coroni / Coronation St CF48 55 C5
Maes-y-Crochan CF3 180 B7
Maes Y Crofft CF15 176 A7
Maesycwm SA9 1 F1
MAESYCWMMER 85 B1
Maesycwmmer Prim Sch CF82 85 B2
Maes-y-Cwm St CF63 215 A5
Maes-y-Cwrt Terr 5 SA13 125 C7
Maes-y-Dail SA18 219 A7
Maes-y-darren SA9 2 C6
Maesydderwen
Llangennech SA14 18 D1
Ystradgynlais SA9 2 E7
Maes-y-Dderwen
Creigiau CF15 174 E6
Maesteg CF34 102 A6
Pen-pedair-heol CF82 84 D7
Swansea / Abertawe, Llangyfelach SA6 45 B2
Swansea / Abertawe, Llwynbrwydrau SA7 70 A6
Maes Y Dderwen Gdns SA9 2 E7
Maes-y-Deri CF44 53 D6
Maes Y Deri SA18 220 E8
Maes-y-Deri
Cardiff / Caerdydd CF14 177 B7
Cilfrew / Cil-ffriw SA10 49 C6
Gowerton / Tre-gwyr SA4 66 A5
Maes Y Deri SA7 46 D1
Maes-y-Deri CF37 109 A2
Maes-y-Deri Cl CF35 170 C8
Maes Y Draenog CF15 158 D2
MAES-Y-DRE 29 A3
Maes-y-Dre SA11 227 C8
Maes Y Drudwen CF83 137 E2
Maes Y Fedwen
Bridgend / Pen-y-Bont ar Ogwr CF31 168 C2
Swansea / Abertawe SA6 45 F3
Maes-y-Felin
Bridgend / Pen-y-Bont ar Ogwr CF31 168 E7
Caerphilly / Caerffili CF83 138 B3
Cardiff / Caerdydd CF14 177 B6
Llandow / Llandw CF71 199 A7
Rhydyfelin CF37 136 B4
Rhydyfelin CF37 136 C4
Maes Y Felin SA5 67 D5
Maesyfelin Cres CF72 173 A7
Maes-y-Ffynnon
Bonvilston / Tresimwn CF5 191 B1
Dowlais CF48 11 B4
Maes-y-Ffynnon Cl 10 SA11 71 E6
Maes-y-Ffynon SA11 223 C1
Maesyffynnon Gr CF44 53 B8
Maesyffynnon La CF44 53 A8
Maesyffynnon Terr CF40 107 A5
Maes-y-Fioled CF15 176 A7
Maes Y Fron 13 SA18 220 B8
Maesyfron Terr SA9 222 C7
Maes Y Gad CF5 192 F7
Maes-y-Garn Rd NP12 59 B1
Maes-y-Garreg
Cefn Coed / Cefn-coed-y-cymmer CF48 10 A4
Ebbw Vale / Glyn Ebwy NP23 7 A4
Merthyr Tydfil / Merthyr Tudful CF48 225 F2
Maes-y-Glyn
Brynamman SA18 220 D8
Glanaman SA18 219 F8
Maes-y-Gollen CF15 174 E7
Maes Y Gollen SA2 94 B6
Maes Y Gorof SA9 2 E8
Maesygors SA14 218 C8
Maes Y Gors SA15 40 D4
Maes-y-Graig St CF81 58 A2
Maes Y Gruffydd Rd SA2 94 C8
Maes Y Grug
Bridgend / Pen-y-Bont ar Ogwr CF31 168 C3
Church Village CF38 135 E1
Maes y Grysmwnt / Grosmont Pl NP44 90 A6
MAESYGWARTHA 9 D8
Maes Y Gwenyn CF62 213 C1
Maes Y Gwernen Cl SA6 45 E4
Maes Y Gwernen Dr SA6 45 E4
Maes-y-Gwernen Rd SA6 45 F4
Maes Y Hedydd CF23 160 F2
Maes-y-Ilan SA4 218 D2
Maes-y-Meillion SA10 48 C2
Maes Y Mynnydd SA10 48 A1
Maes-y-Nant CF15 174 D7
Maes Y Pandy CF83 138 C7
Maes Y Parc CF14 177 B6
Maes-y-Parc SA12 99 E5
Maes Y Parc SA5 67 D5
Maes-y-Pergwm SA11 223 C1
Maes Yr Abaty / Abbey Gn 2 NP44 116 F8
Maes-yr-Afon CF83 138 D5
Maes Yr Afon SA11 71 F8
Maes-yr-Afon CF72 173 A6
Maes Yr Annedd CF5 194 B7
Maes-Yr-Awel CF34 75 A2
Maes Yr Awel
Radyr CF15 176 B6
Rhydyfelin CF37 136 C4
Swansea / Abertawe SA7 69 F7
Maes-yr-Efail
Dunvant SA2 93 D8
Gorseinon SA4 43 B1
Maes Yr Efail SA14 42 B7
Maes-yr-Eglwys SA11 223 C1
Maes-yr-eirlys CF31 168 C2
Maes-yr-Eithin SA7 47 B1
Maesyrhaf
Cross Hands SA14 218 B7
Llanelli SA15 40 F7
Maes-yr-Haf SA18 219 A7
Maes Yr Haf
Cardiff / Caerdydd CF14 176 F8
Llwydcoed CF44 28 F6
Maes-yr-Haf CF47 10 F1
Maes-yr Haf SA4 64 E4
Maes-yr-haf
Rhymney / Rhymni NP22 12 F2
Swansea / Abertawe SA7 69 F6
Maes-yr-Hafod CF15 174 E7
Maes Yr Hafod SA10 48 E1
Maesyrhaf Pl SA4 43 A1
Maes-yr-Haf Rd
4 Neath / Castell-Nedd SA11 71 E8
North Cornelly CF33 166 A7
Maes-yr-Haul CF32 150 E6
Maes yr Haul Cotts CF72 155 E2
Maes-y-Rhedyn CF15 174 E6
Maes Y Rhedyn CF43 79 B8
Maes-y-Rhedyn
Neath / Castell-Nedd SA10 48 C2
Talbot Green CF72 155 B2
Maes-yr-Helyg CF44 28 E6
Maesyrhendre SA18 220 B8
Maes-y-Rhiw Ct NP44 89 A3
Maes-y-Rhiw Ct / Cwrt Maes-y-Rhiw 6 NP44 89 A3
Maes Yr Odyn CF15 176 A7
Maes-yr-Onen CF46 83 D4
Maes-yr-Onnen
Creigiau CF15 174 E6
Cwmrhydyceirw SA6 46 A3
Maes Yr Orchis CF15 176 A7
Maes-Yr-Ysgol
Barry / Y Barri CF62 214 E5
Pyle / Y Pîl CF33 148 D1
Maes Yr Ysgol / Ysgol Pl NP44 89 C6
Maes-y-Sarn CF15 157 B1
Maes Y Siglen CF83 137 E3
Maes-y-Tyra SA11 226 E5
Maes-y-Wawr SA7 46 E3
Maes Y Wennol CF23 160 F2
Maes-y-Wennol CF72 173 D8
Maesywerin SA18 220 D7
Maes-y-Wern CF35 170 D8
Maesywern Rd SA18 219 F8
Mafeking Rd CF23 178 D1
Mafeking Terr NP22 13 F6
Mafon Rd CF46 83 D3
Magazine St CF34 102 A8
Magellan Cl CF62 215 A8
Magna Porta Gdns NP44 117 B6
Magnolia Cl
Cardiff / Caerdydd CF23 178 D7
Merthyr Tydfil / Merthyr Tudful CF47 10 D5
Newport / Casnewydd NP20 117 B3
Porth CF39 108 A3
Magnolia Dr NP12 85 E5
Magnolia Way CF38 156 C6
Magor Rd NP18 145 F8
Magor St NP19 143 F3
Magpie Rd CF62 210 D6
Magretion Pl / Maes Magretian 6 CF10 195 B3
Maiden St CF34 128 C8
Maillard's Haven CF64 207 B1
Main Access Rd CF62 211 F1
Main Ave
Bridgend / Pen-y-Bont ar Ogwr CF31 169 B7
Cardiff / Caerdydd CF23 178 E1
Hirwaun CF44 224 C1
Peterston-super-Ely / Llanbedr-y-fro CF5 191 E4
Upper Boat CF15, CF37 136 D1
MAINDEE 143 F5
Maindee Par NP19 143 E6
Maindee Prim Sch NP19 143 D5
Maindee Rd NP11 113 A5
Maindee Terr NP44 89 D5
MAINDY 177 E1
Maindy Cres CF41 78 F4
Maindy Croft CF41 78 F4
Maindy Ct CF38 135 E1
Maindy Gr CF41 78 F3
Maindy Mews CF24 195 A8
Maindy Rd
Cardiff / Caerdydd CF24 194 F8
Pen-y-coedcae CF37 135 B6
Treorchy / Treorci CF41 78 F3
Main Rd
Aberdulais SA10 49 C4
Bryn-côch SA10 48 C4
Church Village CF38 156 F8
Cilfrew / Cil-ffriw SA10 49 C5
Clydach NP7 9 C6
Crynant / Creunant SA10 226 A8
Dyffryn Cellwen SA10 223 A4
Llantrisant CF72 155 F3
Maesycwmmer CF82 85 A2
Mountain Ash / Aberpennar CF45 82 B6
Neath / Castell-Nedd SA10 48 E1
Ogmore-by-S / Aberogwr CF32 184 C3
Pontrhydyfen SA12 73 A1
Taffs Well / Ffynnon Taf CF15 157 F4
Tonna / Tonnau SA10 49 A3
Main St
Barry / Y Barri CF63 215 B7
Crumlin / Crymlyn NP11 60 A1
Newbridge / Trecelyn NP11 86 F6
Mainwaring Terr SA1 68 D2
Maitland Pl CF11 194 E4
Maitland St CF14 177 E2
Major Cl NP44 88 F2
Major Rd CF5 194 D5
Major St SA5 68 C2
Malcolm Sargent Cl NP19 144 D4
Maldwyn St CF11 194 D7
Malefant St CF24 178 A1
Maliphant St SA1 68 D1
Mallard Cl 8 CF3 179 E7
Mallards Reach CF3 162 D1
Mallard Way
Newport / Casnewydd NP10 163 F6
Penarth CF64 217 A7
Porthcawl CF36 182 D7
Swansea / Abertawe, Tircanol SA7 46 B2
Mallory Cl CF62 211 D7
Mall The NP44 89 E3
Malmesbury Cl 7 NP20 143 C6
Malmsmead Rd CF3 179 C7
MALPAS 117 B2
Malpas C in W Jun & Inf Schs NP20 117 B2
Malpas Cl 1 CF3 179 F7
Malpas Court Prim Sch NP20 116 F3
Malpas La NP20 143 B8
Malpas Park Prim Sch NP20 117 A3
Malpas Rd NP20 117 A3
Malpas St 7 NP44 89 E2
Malthall SA3 229 D3
Malthouse Ave CF23 161 A2
Malthouse La NP4 62 B7
Malthouse Rd / Lon Y Bracty
Caerleon / Caerllion NP18 118 A5
Ponthir NP18, NP44 117 D6
Malthouse The CF71 198 C2
Maltings The CF23 160 F1
Maltings The CF24 195 E5
Malus Ave CF38 156 C5
Malvern Cl
Newport / Casnewydd NP19 144 A8
Risca / Rhisga NP11 115 D1
Malvern Dr CF14 177 D7
Malvern Rd NP19 143 D5
Malvern Terr
Risca / Rhisga NP11 115 A1
Swansea / Abertawe SA2 94 F5
MAMHILAD 39 B3
Mamhilad Park Est NP4 39 B2
Manchester Ho NP13 59 F8
Manchester Pl CF44 27 D7
Manchester St NP19 143 D6
Man Cromwell / Cromwell Pl 10 NP44 89 E5
Mandeg CF46 83 D6
Mandela Ave CF31 169 D5
Manderville Rd NP12 85 C6
Mandeville Pl 7 CF11 194 E5
Mandeville St 8 CF11 194 E5
Mandinam Pk SA2 94 A7
Man Dynefor / Dynevor Pl SA10 70 D7
Manest St NP22 12 E4
Mangoed CF44 28 A6
Manitoba Cl CF23 178 C5
Manley Cl CF39 133 C5
Manley Rd NP20 143 A4
MAN-MOEL 34 F4
Manmoel Ct NP12 59 C1
Manmoel Rd NP11 59 C2
Man-Moel Rd
Ebbw Vale / Glyn Ebwy NP22, NP23 14 C5
Hollybush NP12, NP23 34 F6
Mannesmann Cl SA7 69 C7
Manod Rd CF14 177 A2
Manorbier Cl
Blackwood / Coed-Duon NP12 58 D1
Church Village CF38 135 F2
1 Dinas Powis / Dinas Powys CF64 206 C3
Manorbier Cres CF3 179 C4
Manorbier Ct CF62 214 F8
Manorbier Dr / Rhodfa Maenorbyr NP44 90 A3
Manor Chase 2 CF38 156 A5
Manor Cl
Cardiff / Caerdydd CF14 177 B5
Risca / Rhisga NP11 115 B1
Manor Cotts CF72 173 A5
Manor Court Flats NP11 115 B2
Manor Ct
5 Cardiff / Caerdydd CF14 177 A6
Church Village CF38 135 E1
Ewenny / Ewenni CF35 185 E7
Swansea / Abertawe SA5 68 C3
Treharris CF46 82 E6
Manor Dr
Bridgend / Pen-y-Bont ar Ogwr CF35 169 F4
Glyn-neath / Glyn-nedd SA11 223 B1
Manor Gate 6 NP44 89 B3
Manor Gr CF36 183 D8
Manor Hill CF72 173 D7
Manor Pk
Brynna CF35 153 B2
Llantwit Major / Llanilltud Fawr CF61 210 A5
Newbridge / Trecelyn NP11 87 A8
Newport / Casnewydd NP10 163 F6
Manor Rd
Pontllanfraith NP12 85 F3
Risca / Rhisga NP11 115 B1
Swansea / Abertawe SA5 68 C3
Manor Rd / Ffordd Y Faenor 15 SA18 219 B7
Manor Rd / Heol Y Plas NP4 37 F4
Manor Rise CF14 177 C4
Manor Sq CF61 210 A4
Manor St
Cardiff / Caerdydd CF14 177 F2
Port Talbot SA13 125 C8

Manor The / Y Faenor NP44 117 A5
Manor View CF61 210 A4
Manor Way
Abersychan NP4 37 F4
Briton Ferry / Llansawel SA11 71 D3
Cardiff / Caerdydd CF14 177 C5
Risca / Rhisga NP11 115 C1
Man St Kitts / St Kitts Pl 5 SA12 98 C2
Mansel Ct SA4 66 B5
Mansel Dr SA3 122 C6
MANSELFIELD 122 C6
Manselfield Rd SA3 122 C6
Mansell Ave CF5 192 F4
Mansel Rd SA1 69 B4
Mansel St / Heol Mansel 15 SA15 40 D4
Mansel St / Stryd Mansel SA11 71 C2
Mansel St
Gowerton / Tre-gwyr SA4 66 B5
Newport / Casnewydd NP19 144 A5
Port Talbot SA13 125 B8
Swansea / Abertawe SA1 233 A3
MANSELTON 68 B3
Manselton Prim Sch SA5 68 C3
Manselton Rd SA5 68 B3
Mansfield St 12 CF11 194 E5
Mansfield Terr CF47 11 A1
Mansion Ct CF31 168 D3
Manston Cl 5 CF5 176 E2
Man Webb / Webb Pl SA12 124 E7
Man Y Coed / Timber Pl 3 SA12 98 C2
Maple Ave
Baglan SA12 98 E7
Risca / Rhisga NP11 115 B2
Tredegar NP22 6 D1
Maple Cl
Barry / Y Barri CF62 215 A7
Bryn NP12 85 D3
Cimla SA11 72 C6
Gorseinon SA4 43 A3
Llanharry CF72 172 B5
Merthyr Tydfil / Merthyr Tudful CF47 10 D4
Underwood NP18 145 E6
Maple Cres
Pontypool / Pont-y-pwl NP4 62 D1
Swansea / Abertawe SA2 94 E7
Trefechan CF48 10 B6
Maple Ct CF39 133 D5
Maple Dr
Aberdare / Aberdâr CF44 28 D2
Bridgend / Pen-y-Bont ar Ogwr CF31 169 E4
Waunarlwydd SA5 66 D4
Maple Gdns NP11 141 C8
Maple Gr SA2 94 E6
Maple Rd
Cardiff / Caerdydd CF5 176 B1
Penarth CF64 206 E3
Maple Rd / Heol Masarnen NP4 62 D2
Maple Rd S NP4 62 D1
Maple St CF37 136 A5
Maple Terr
Abercarn NP11 87 B3
Abercwmboi CF44 53 F4
Maesteg CF34 102 A2
Mapletree Cl SA6 45 D1
Maple Tree Cl CF15 176 A6
Maple Way NP23 7 C5
Maple Wlk CF36 183 E8
Maplewood Ave 4 CF14 176 F3
Maplewood Cl SA10 48 C4
Maplewood Ct CF14 177 A3
Maplewood Flats 3 CF14 176 F3
Marayat Wlk NP20 142 E1
MARBLE HALL 40 E5
Marblehall Rd SA15 40 E5
March Hywel
Cilfrew / Cil-ffriw SA10 49 C5
Rhos SA8 24 C3
Marchwood Cl CF3 179 C5
Marconi Ave CF64 206 F6
Marconi Cl NP20 116 F2
MARCROES / MARCROSS 208 F7
MARCROSS / MARCROES 208 F7
Marcross Rd CF5 193 A4
Mardy CF72 155 A5
Mardy Cl
Caerphilly / Caerffili CF83 138 C3
Merthyr Tydfil / Merthyr Tudful CF47 30 F7
Mardy Cres CF83 138 C3
Mardy Ct CF11 194 F4
Mardy Rd CF3 179 C2
Mardy St
Cardiff / Caerdydd CF11 194 F4
Merthyr Tydfil / Merthyr Tudful CF47 11 A1
Mardy Terr CF47 30 E7
Mardy Trad Est SA4 66 C8
MARGAM 125 E4
Margam Ave SA6 69 A8
Margam Cl CF62 211 C7
Margam Country Park* SA13 126 E1
Margam Ho CF31 168 D4
MARGAM MOORS / GWEUNYDD MARGAM 146 E6
Margam Pl / Maes Margam SA15 40 E4
Margam Rd
Cardiff / Caerdydd CF14 177 D2
Port Talbot SA13 126 A2
Margam Rd / Heol Margam SA13 125 E4
Margam Row CF33 148 D3
Margam St
Cymmer / Cymer SA13 75 B5
Maesteg CF34 102 B8
Margaret Ave
Barry / Y Barri CF62 204 F1
Newport / Casnewydd NP19 143 D7
Margaret St / Stryd Marged 6 SA18 219 C7
Margaret's Cl SA11 71 B1
Margaret St
Abercwmboi CF44 53 F4
Abercynon CF45 82 E2
Aberdare / Aberdâr, Aberaman CF44 53 D6
Aberdare / Aberdâr, Trecynon CF44 28 E3
Bargoed / Bargod CF81 58 A1
Bryn-côch SA10 48 C4
Merthyr Tydfil / Merthyr Tudful CF47 10 C2
Pontypridd CF37 108 F2
Port Talbot SA13 99 C1
Swansea / Abertawe SA1 96 A7
Trehafod CF37 108 D2
Treherbert CF42 50 E2
Treorchy / Treorci CF41 78 F5
Tylorstown CF43, CF39 107 C8
Margaret Terr SA13 76 C5
Marged St SA15 40 D3
Marguerites Way CF5 193 A5
Maria Ct CF10 195 B3
Marian St
Blaengarw CF32 103 E7
Tonypandy CF40 106 A7
Marianwen St NP12 85 C8
Maria St CF10 195 B3
Marigold Cl
Merthyr Tydfil / Merthyr Tudful CF47 10 C5
Rogerstone / Ty-du NP10 141 D6
Marigold Ct CF31 169 D5
Marigold Pl SA10 222 D4
Marina Bldgs CF64 207 B5
Marina Ct 6 NP19 143 E8
Marine Cl SA12 98 C1
Marine Dr
Barry / Y Barri CF62 214 B2
Ogmore-by-S / Aberogwr CF32 184 C3
Marine Dr / Rhodfa Mar SA12 98 C1
Marine Par CF64 207 B2
Mariner's Hts CF64 207 B5
Mariners Point SA12 124 E6
Mariners Quay / Cei'r Morwr SA12 124 D7
Mariner St SA1 233 B4
Mariners The SA15 40 C3
Mariners Way CF62 212 F1
Mariner Way NP19 164 E8
Marine St
Cwm NP23 35 B6
Llanelli SA15 40 C3
Marine Terr CF36 182 F6
Marine Wlk
Ogmore-by-S / Aberogwr CF32 184 C3
3 Swansea / Abertawe SA1 233 B1
Marion Ct CF14 160 A1
Marion Jones Ct NP12 85 F1
Marion Pl NP20 143 C2
Marion St
Cardiff / Caerdydd CF24 195 E6
Newport / Casnewydd NP20 143 C2
Marionville Gdns CF5 193 E8
Maritime Ct CF83 138 C6
Maritime Ind Est CF37 135 B7
Maritime Rd SA13 125 B7
Maritime St CF37 135 B8
Maritime Terr CF37 135 B8
Maritime Workshops CF37 135 B7
Marjorie St CF40 107 B4
Market Arc 1 NP20 143 C5
Market Mews 4 SA6 68 F8
Market Pl
Abercarn NP11 87 B2
Cardiff / Caerdydd CF5 194 D6
Market Pl The NP12 85 E7
Market Rd
Cardiff / Caerdydd CF5 194 C6
Nantyglo NP23 8 C2
Market Sq
Brynmawr NP23 8 C4
Ebbw Vale / Glyn Ebwy NP23 14 D8
6 Merthyr Tydfil / Merthyr Tudful CF47 10 D1
Pontypool / Pont-y-pwl NP4 62 C6
Market St
7 Aberdare / Aberdâr CF44 29 A2
Abertillery / Abertyleri NP13 36 B5
Barry / Y Barri CF62 214 D3
Blaenavon NP4 17 C6
Bridgend / Pen-y-Bont ar Ogwr CF31 168 F4
Caerphilly / Caerffili CF83 138 B2
Dowlais CF48 11 B4
Ebbw Vale / Glyn Ebwy NP23 14 D8
Llanelli SA15 40 D5
2 Newport / Casnewydd NP20 143 C5
Pontypool / Pont-y-pwl NP4 62 C6
Pontypridd CF37 109 C1
8 Swansea / Abertawe SA6 69 A8
Tongwynlais CF15 158 C1
Tredegar NP22 13 E6
MARKHAM 58 D6
Markham Cres NP12 59 B2
Markham Prim Sch NP12 58 D7
Markham Terr NP12 58 D8
Mark St CF11 194 F5
Marland Ho CF10 232 B1
Marlas Cl CF33 148 B1
Marlas Rd CF33 148 A1
Marlborough Cl
Barry / Y Barri CF63 215 C7
Llantwit Fadre / Llanilltud Faerdref CF38 156 D6
Marlborough Ho 2 CF10 232 B2
Marlborough Inf Sch CF23 195 D8
Marlborough Jun Sch CF23 195 D8
Marlborough Rd
Abertillery / Abertyleri NP13 36 C3
Cardiff / Caerdydd CF23 195 D8
Gorseinon SA4 66 B8
Newport / Casnewydd NP19 143 D5
Swansea / Abertawe SA2 94 F6
Marlborough Rd / Heol Marlborough NP44 89 A3
Marlborough Terr CF10 194 E8
Marl Ct CF11 194 F1
Marl Ct / Llys Marl NP44 89 B5
Marle Cl CF23 178 F8
Marloes Cl CF62 214 F7
Marloes Ct SA5 67 F6
Marloes Path 2 NP44 89 B3
Marloes Rd CF5 193 B5
Marlow Cl NP10 142 B6
Marlowe Gdns NP20 142 E1
Marlowe Ho 9 SA12 98 B3
Marlpit La CF36 166 A1
Marne St NP11 114 B8
Marquis Cl CF62 215 A2
Marsden St 5 SA1 68 C2
Marshall Cl 2 CF5 176 E2
Marshall Cres CF47 10 F5
MARSHES 143 C6
MARSHFIELD 162 C1
Marshfield Ave CF33 148 B1
Marshfield Ct
Pontllanfraith NP12 85 F2
Tonyrefail CF39 133 D5
Marshfield Jun & Inf Sch CF3 162 C2
Marshfield Rd
Abertillery / Abertyleri NP11 59 F5
Maerdy CF43 79 C8
Marshfield CF3 162 D1
Neath / Castell-Nedd SA11 71 D6
Marshfield St NP19 144 A3
Marsh St
Aberavon SA12 98 F1
Llanelli SA15 40 D4
Marston Ct NP20 143 A7
Marston Path / Llwybr Marston 11 NP44 89 C2
Mars Wesley / Wesley Pl CF48 55 D4
Martell St SA5 67 E3
Martin Cl CF48 10 A1
Martin Cres CF39 133 C5
Martindale Cl NP22 6 D1
Martindale Rd NP4 62 E2
Martin Rd
Cardiff / Caerdydd CF24 196 A4
Martin Rd *continued*
Llanelli SA15 40 E4
Martins Cl CF45 82 E2
Martin's Field NP11 86 E6
Martin's La CF45 82 E2
Martins Row CF81 32 C8
Martin St
Clydach SA6 46 D7
Swansea / Abertawe SA6 68 F8
Martin's Terr CF45 82 E2
Martin Terr NP4 17 A6
Martyn's Ave / Rhodfa Martyn SA10 222 C3
Marwyn Gdns CF81 57 F2
Mary Ann St CF10 232 C2
Mary Immaculate High Sch CF5 193 B2
Maryland Rd NP11 115 A1
Maryport Rd CF23 178 B2
Mary Price Ct CF24 195 E5
Mary St / Heol Y Felin SA10 222 D4
Marysfield Cl CF3 162 E1
Mary St
Abercwmboi CF44 53 F4
6 Aberdare / Aberdâr CF44 29 A1
Bedlinog CF46 56 A7
Bedwas CF83 139 A6
14 Blaenavon NP4 17 C6
Blaengwynfi SA13 76 C6
Cardiff / Caerdydd CF14 176 F2
Crynant / Creunant SA10 226 A7
Dowlais CF48 11 A4
Merthyr Tydfil / Merthyr Tudful CF47 30 E8
Mountain Ash / Aberpennar CF45 54 E2
15 Neath / Castell-Nedd SA11 71 E7
Pontypridd CF37 109 F5
Porthcawl CF36 182 F6
Porth CF39 107 F4
Treharris CF46 83 B6
Treherbert CF42 51 A1
Mary Twill La SA3 122 E4
Masefield Mews CF31 168 D6
Masefield Rd CF64 206 F4
Masefield Vale NP20 142 F2
Masefield Way
Rhydyfelin CF37 136 B6
Swansea / Abertawe SA2 94 E6
Mason Ct CF14 177 B6
Masonic St 13 CF47 30 D8
Masons Cl / Clos Masons CF33 148 D3
Mason St CF44 53 C7
Matexa St CF41 78 F3
Mathews Terr CF37 135 A4
Mathew Wlk CF5 176 E2
Mathias Cl 1 CF23 178 E1
Matthew Rd CF62 212 E2
Matthewson Cl CF14 177 C2
Matthews' St SA13 227 C2
Matthew St SA1 233 B4
Matthew Terr
Dinas Powis / Dinas Powys CF64 206 C4
Pontypool / Pont-y-pwl NP4 61 F8
Matthysens Way CF3 180 A5
Mattie Collins Way The CF42 78 D5
Maugham Cl NP20 142 F1
Maughan La 6 CF64 207 B5
Maughan Terr 5 CF64 207 B5
Maureen Ave CF5 193 E6
Mavis Gr CF14 177 D6
MAWDLAM 165 D8
Mawdlam Way / Ffordd Mawdlam CF33 147 E1
Mawsons Mead CF5 192 A1
Maxime Ct SA2 94 D6
Maximin Rd SA13 125 E3
Maxton Ct CF83 138 C3
Maxwell Rd CF3 179 C4
Maxwell St CF43 79 F6
Maxworthy Rd 1 NP4 17 C7
MAYALS 93 F1
Mayals Ave SA2 94 A1
Mayals Gn SA3 93 F1
Mayals Prim Sch SA3 123 A8
Mayals Rd SA2 94 A1
Mayberry Rd / Heol Mayberry SA12 98 D7
Maybury Ho 11 NP44 89 B3
May Drew Way / Ffordd May Drew SA11 71 C4
Mayfair CF5 193 A2
Mayfair Dr CF14 159 E3
Mayfield Ave
Cardiff / Caerdydd CF5 194 A6
Laleston / Trelales CF32 167 F4
Porthcawl CF36 183 D7
Mayfield Pl CF72 155 E2
Mayfield Rd CF37 109 B2
Mayfield St 2 SA13 125 C7
Mayfield Terr
Ebbw Vale / Glyn Ebwy NP23 7 D4
Swansea / Abertawe SA5 68 B3
Mayflower Ave CF14 159 D1
Mayflower Cl SA2 94 B6
Mayflower Way CF62 213 A2
MAYHILL 68 A1
Mayhill Cl CF14 159 F3
Mayhill Gdns SA1 68 B1
Mayhill Rd SA1 68 B1
Maynard Ct CF5 194 A8
Maynes 3 NP44 89 B1
May's Ct 11 SA11 71 E7
May St
Cardiff / Caerdydd CF24 195 A8
8 Newport / Casnewydd NP19 143 E5
Maytree Ave SA3 122 F7
Maytree Cl
Loughor SA4 42 F2
Swansea / Abertawe SA6 68 D8
Maywood CF72 153 D3
Mead La NP44 89 E4
Meadow Ave CF33 148 C1
Meadow Bank NP4 39 E6
Meadowbank Cl CF44 29 D1
Meadowbank Ct CF5 176 D2
Meadowbank Specl Sch CF14 177 B2
Meadow Brook CF38 156 F8
Meadowbrook Ave NP44 89 D6
Meadow Cl
Bridgend / Pen-y-Bont ar Ogwr CF35 170 A4
Cardiff / Caerdydd CF23 178 D8
Hirwaun CF44 27 F7
Llanharan CF72 153 F3
Mountain Ash / Aberpennar CF45 54 B3
Neath / Castell-Nedd SA11 71 E5
Pengam NP12 85 B6
Pontypool / Pont-y-pwl NP4 89 E8
Risca / Rhisga NP11 114 D3
Meadow Cl / Clos Y Waun CF39 133 A3
Meadow Cres
Caerphilly / Caerffili CF83 138 B2
Church Village CF38 136 A1
Risca / Rhisga NP11 141 C8
Tredegar NP22 6 D2
Meadowcroft SA3 121 A5
Meadow Croft CF62 213 B2
Meadowcroft Cl SA5 66 E4
Meadow Ct CF32 185 D3
Meadow Ct / Maes Ty Cwrdd SA14 41 D4
Meadow Dr SA4 42 F2
Meadowgate NP12 85 D2
Meadowgate Cl CF14 176 F7
Meadowhall Ct CF83 111 A1
Meadow Hill CF38 156 D8
Meadow La
Croesyceiliog NP44 90 B5
Gilfach Goch CF39 132 B6
Hirwaun CF44 27 C8
Penarth CF64 206 F1
Porthcawl CF36 183 B8
Meadowlands Dr NP10 141 D7
Meadowlane Prim Sch CF3 179 F5
Meadowlark Cl 6 CF3 179 E7
Meadow Rd
Neath / Castell-Nedd SA11 71 D5
Pontllanfraith NP12 86 A4
Meadow Rd / Heol Y Dolau CF35 170 D6
Meadow Rise
Brynna CF72 153 E4
Sarn CF32 150 F4
Swansea / Abertawe, Cockett SA1 67 E2
Swansea / Abertawe, Lower Sketty SA2 94 C4
Meadow Row SA13 100 F5
Meadow St / Stryd Y Ddol CF33 165 F8
Meadowside CF64 206 D3
Meadow Side NP44 88 F3
Meadows Rd
Cross Hands SA14 218 B7
Newport / Casnewydd NP19 144 D1
Meadows Rd / Heol y Waun SA14 218 C6
Meadow St
Aberkenfig / Abercynffig CF32 150 C4
Abertillery / Abertyleri NP13 60 B6
Bridgend / Pen-y-Bont ar Ogwr CF31 168 F5
Cardiff / Caerdydd CF11 194 C7
Cwmavon / Cwmafan SA12 99 F6
Gilfach Goch CF39 132 B6
Maesteg CF34 102 A3
Ogmore Vale CF32 104 E1
Pontycymer CF32 103 E3
Pontypridd CF37 135 E5
Swansea / Abertawe SA1 67 F2
Meadows The
Cimla SA11 72 C6
Corntown / Corntwn CF35 186 B7
Marshfield CF3 162 D1
Penllyn CF71 188 A5

Meadows The *continued*
Porthcawl CF36 183 C7
Risca / Rhisga NP11 114 D4
Meadows The / Y Waun SA10 70 E7
Meadow Sweet Dr CF3 180 B6
Meadow Terr NP24 33 F4
Meadow The CF71 189 C8
Meadow Vale CF63 215 C8
Meadow View
Barry / Y Barri CF63 215 D8
Bedwas CF83 138 C7
Blackmill CF35 130 E2
Dunvant SA2 93 C8
Peterstone Wentlooge / Llanbedr Gwynllwg CF3 180 F5
Swansea / Abertawe SA7 70 A6
Meadow View Ct CF64 216 A5
Meadow Way
Caerphilly / Caerffili CF83 137 D1
Penperlleni NP4 39 E7
Meadow Wlk
Blackwood / Coed Duon NP11 59 D1
Bridgend / Pen-y-Bont ar Ogwr CF31 169 A5
Ton Pentre CF41 79 B3
Meads Cl NP19 144 C2
Mead The SA2 93 D8
Meadvale Rd CF3 179 D6
Mechanic's Sq NP22 6 E1
Medart Pl NP11 114 D4
Medart St NP11 114 D4
Medlock Cl NP20 116 E2
Medlock Cres NP20 116 E3
Medlock Wlk NP20 116 E2
Medway Cl NP20 116 D3
Medway Ct
Bettws NP20 116 D3
Llantwit Fadre / Llanilltud Faerdref CF38 156 D7
Medway Rd NP20 116 C2
Medway Workshops SA4 43 F1
Megan Cl SA4 43 C3
Megan St SA5 68 A2
Meggitt Rd CF62 214 E8
Meini Tirion CF31 168 B6
Meirion Cl CF63 215 B8
Meirion Pl CF24 196 A6
Meirion St CF44 28 F4
Meirwen Dr CF5 193 A2
MEISGYN / MISKIN 173 E6
Melbourne Ct
Blackwood / Coed-Duon NP12 85 C6
Cardiff / Caerdydd CF14 177 B6
Cwmbran / Cwmbrân NP44 89 D2
Melbourne Rd
Abertillery / Abertyleri NP13 36 B5
Cardiff / Caerdydd CF14 177 F8
Melbourne Terr CF72 153 D3
Melbourne Way NP20 142 D3
Melcorn Dr SA3 122 E5
Melfort Gdns NP20 142 F3
Melfort Rd NP20 142 F3
Meliden La CF64 206 F3
Meliden Rd CF64 206 F3
Melin Caiach CF46 83 C6
MELINCOURT 226 D4
Melin Court Falls★ SA11 226 D4
MELINCRYDDAN 71 D6
Melin Dwr NP10 140 C3
Melingriffith Dr CF14 176 E5
Melin Gwlan CF83 137 F4
Melin Inf Sch SA11 71 D5
Melin Jun Sch SA11 71 D5
Melin Pl NP11 59 D2
Melin St NP11 113 B4
Mellon St NP20 143 C4
Mellte Ave SA11 223 F2
Mellte Villas CF44 28 E6
Melrose Ave CF23 178 D1
Melrose Cl
Cardiff / Caerdydd CF3 179 F8
Swansea / Abertawe SA6 69 B7
Melrose Ct
Cardiff / Caerdydd, Canton CF11 194 C7
6 Cardiff / Caerdydd, Pen-y-lan CF23 178 C2
Melrose Gdns CF23 178 D1
Melrose St CF63 215 B6
Melton Dr CF31 168 E2
Melville Ave CF3 179 F8
Melville Cl CF62 204 E1
Melville Terr CF83 138 B4
Melyn Bach Ave NP4 39 E3
Melyn Cl SA11 71 C5
Melyn St SA13 227 C2
Melyn Y Gors CF63 205 C1
Menai Ave SA13 75 C3
Menai Cl CF38 135 E2
Menai Way CF3 179 D6
Mendalgief Rd NP20 143 C2
Mendip Cl
Newport / Casnewydd NP19 144 D6
Risca / Rhisga NP11 115 D1
Swansea / Abertawe SA5 67 D3
Mendip Rd CF3 179 A5
Mendip View CF63 215 C6
Menelaus Sq CF48 11 B4
Meon Cl NP20 116 F2
Merchant's Hill NP4 62 B8
Merchant's Hill Cl NP4 62 A8
Merchant St
15 Aberdare / Aberdâr CF44 29 A1
Pontlottyn CF81 12 F1
Merches Gdns CF11 232 A1
Merches Pl CF11 194 F4
Mercia Rd CF24 195 F6
Mercies The CF36 183 B7
Meredith Cl NP20 142 F2
Meredith Rd CF24 195 F6
Meredith Terr NP11 86 F6
Mere Path NP44 89 B3
Merevale CF64 205 F3
Merfield Cl CF32 150 E4
Merfield Ho CF32 150 E4
Merganser Cl CF36 182 E8
Merganser Ct CF63 214 F5
Meridian Ct 1 CF14 177 E2
Meridian The CF64 207 A5
Merioneth Ho 5 CF64 206 F2
Merioneth Pl CF62 214 F7
Merion St CF40 107 A3
Merios Cl CF72 153 E2
Merlin Cl
Cardiff / Caerdydd CF14 159 E2
Penarth CF64 217 A8
8 Pontypridd CF37 109 B1
Porthcawl CF36 182 E8
Merlin Cres
Bridgend / Pen-y-Bont ar Ogwr CF31 168 C6
Newport / Casnewydd NP19 143 F7
Swansea / Abertawe SA1 94 F8
Merlin Pl CF63 215 A7
Merret Ct CF24 196 A7
Merrick Cotts CF5 191 F1
Merriots Pl NP19 143 E5
Mersey Cl NP12 85 D3
Mersey Wlk NP20 116 C1
MERTHYR DYFAN 214 E8
Merthyr Dyfan Rd
Barry / Y Barri CF62 204 F1
Barry / Y Barri, Gibbonsdown CF62 214 F7
MERTHYR MAWR 185 A8
Merthyrmawr Rd
Bridgend / Pen-y-Bont ar Ogwr CF31 168 E2
Bridgend / Pen-y-Bont ar Ogwr CF32 168 D1
Merthyrmawr Rd N CF31 168 F3
Merthyr Rd
Abercanaid CF48 30 F5
Cardiff / Caerdydd, Gwaun Treoda CF14 177 D3
Cardiff / Caerdydd, Whitchurch CF14 177 B4
Hirwaun CF44 27 D7
Llwydcoed CF44 28 E7
Merthyr Tydfil / Merthyr Tudful, Pen-y-Darren CF47 10 F4
Merthyr Tydfil / Merthyr Tudful, Tre-Gibbon CF44 29 A8
Pont-Walby / Pontwalby SA11 223 E1
Pontypridd CF37 109 D2
Tongwynlais CF15 158 C1
Tredegar, Llechryd NP22 5 F1
Troedyrhiw CF48 31 C2
Merthyr St
Barry / Y Barri CF63 214 F5
Cardiff / Caerdydd CF24 194 F8
Pontyclun CF72 173 B8
MERTHYR TUDFUL / MERTHYR TYDFIL 11 A3
Merthyr Tydfil Coll CF48 10 D1
Merthyr Tydfil Ind Pk / Parc Diwydiannol Merthyr Tydfil CF48 31 B3
MERTHYR TYDFIL / MERTHYR TUDFUL 11 A3
Merthyr Tydfil Sta CF47 10 E1
Merthyr Vale Sta CF48 55 D3
MERTHYR VALE / YNYSOWEN 55 D4
Mervinian Cl CF10 232 D1
Mervyn Rd
Cardiff / Caerdydd, Tremorfa CF24 195 F6
Cardiff / Caerdydd, Whitchurch CF14 177 B4
Mervyn St / Stryd Merfyn CF48 55 C5
Mervyn St CF37 135 F5
Mervyn Terr
Cwmavon / Cwmafan SA12 99 C5
Pontypool / Pont-y-pwl NP4 62 B7
Mervyn Way CF35 170 B8
Mescoed Rd NP10 142 B8
Messina Ho CF10 232 C1
Metal St CF24 195 D6
Metcalfe St CF34 102 B8
Meteor St CF24 195 C6
Methodist La CF61 209 F6
Methuen Rd NP19 143 E5
Metro Mon Ind Est NP44 89 F7
Metz Cotts SA9 222 A6
Mewslade Ave SA5 67 E6
Mews The
Abercarn NP11 114 C7
7 Barry / Y Barri CF63 214 F5
Llantrisant CF72 155 D3
9 Neath / Castell-Nedd SA11 71 E7
Newport / Casnewydd NP20 143 A5
Meyler St CF39 133 B2
Meyrick Rd CF5 193 A4
Meyricks NP44 116 B8
Meyricks Row CF40 107 A1
Meyrick Villas CF47 10 D3
Michael's Field SA3 123 C3
MICHAELSLON-LE-PIT / LLANIHANGEL-Y-PWLL 206 A7
Michael's Rd CF42 50 B2
Michaelston Cl CF63 215 B8
Michaelston Com Coll CF5 192 F4
Michaelston Ct CF5 192 F4
Michaelstone Ct SA12 99 D4
Michaelston Rd CF5 192 F5
MICHAELSTON-SUPER-ELY / LLANFIHANGEL-AR-ELAI 193 A5
MICHAELSTON-Y-FEDW 162 A5
Michael Way NP4 62 B7
Michelston Ct 3 CF5 193 C4
Michna St SA12 98 F1
MIDDLE COEDCAE 17 D6
Middle Coedcae / Coedcae Ganol 7 NP4 17 D6
Middle Coedcae Rd / Heol Coed Cae Ganol NP4 17 D6
Middlecroft La SA3 121 F7
Middlegate Ct CF71 188 F2
Middlegate Wlk CF71 188 F2
Middle Rd SA5 67 F4
Middle Row
Ferndale CF43 79 F8
Mountain Ash / Aberpennar CF45 54 C5
Rhymney / Rhymni NP22 12 C7
Middle St
Pontypridd CF37 109 D2
4 Tonypandy CF40 106 F4
Middle Terr CF43 80 C2
MIDDLETON 230 C6
Middleton St
Blaengwynfi SA13 76 C6
Briton Ferry / Llansawel SA11 71 C2
Swansea / Abertawe SA1 95 F7
Midfield NP4 39 E6
Midland Ct SA1 233 C3
Midland Pl SA7 69 D7
Midland Rd SA7 69 D7
Midland Terr SA9 2 D8
Midway NP4 39 B2
Miers St SA1 233 C3
Mikado St CF40 106 F4
Milborough Ct SA9 2 B7
Milborough Rd / Heol Milborough SA9 2 B7
Milbourne Cl CF47 30 F7
Milbourne St
Mountain Ash / Aberpennar CF45 82 B6
Tonypandy CF40 107 A4
Milbourne Terr CF47 30 F7
Milburn Cl CF62 212 F1
Mildred Cl CF38 156 A7
Mildred St CF38 156 A7
Mile End Cl SA5 67 F3
Mile End Row SA11 71 D5
Miles Ct CF15 158 A3
Miles La SA3 122 C6
Miles Rd SA5 68 C4
Miles St
Llanelli SA15 40 C7
Maerdy CF43 52 A1
Merthyr Tydfil / Merthyr Tudful CF47 10 C2
Milestone Ct CF14 177 D6
Milford Cl CF38 135 F2
Milford Ho 2 NP44 89 D2
Milford Way SA5 67 F6
Milfraen Ave NP23 8 D1
Milland Rd SA11 71 D7
Milland Road Ind Est SA11 71 D6
Millands Cl SA3 122 D5
Millands Cvn Pk CF61 210 D7
Millbank / Bancyfelin SA10 48 C1
Millbank Prim Sch CF5 193 F6
Mill Brook SA12 98 E5
Millbrook Cl CF64 206 B4
Millbrook Ct NP4 39 E3
Millbrook Dr SA6 46 C2
Millbrook Hts CF64 206 B4
Millbrook Jun & Inf Schs NP20 116 F2
Millbrook Pk CF14 160 A3
Millbrook Pl NP4 39 E2
Millbrook Rd
Dinas Powis / Dinas Powys CF64 206 B4
Pontllanfraith NP12 86 A4
Millbrook St SA6 68 D5
Millbrook Trad Est SA1 68 D4
Millbrook Yd SA1 68 E4
Mill Cl
Caerphilly / Caerffili CF83 137 F4
Cardiff / Caerdydd CF14 160 A1
Dinas Powis / Dinas Powys CF64 206 A3
Millcroft Ct CF71 201 A4
Millennium Coastal Park★ SA14, SA15 41 B1
Millennium Ct 4 CF24 195 D7
Millennium Stad★ CF10 232 A2
Miller Cl NP18 119 F1
Millers Ave CF32 150 F5
Miller's Ct SA5 67 F6
Millers Ride / Rhodfa'r Melinydd 6 NP44 90 A3
Millers Row CF46 83 A5
Millfield
Bridgend / Pen-y-Bont ar Ogwr CF31 168 E5
Cardiff / Caerdydd CF14 160 A3
Pontyclun CF72 173 A7
Quakers Yard CF46 83 C6
Millfield Cl
Cardiff / Caerdydd CF3 179 E6
Swansea / Abertawe SA2 94 B5
Millfield Dr CF71 188 F2
Millgate CF14 160 A1
Mill Gdns (Cvn Pk) SA3 94 B2
Mill Heath NP20 116 E3
Millheath Dr CF14 160 A2
Millhill Ct 4 CF5 193 E6
Mill House Ct / Cwrt Ty Y Felin 4 NP44 116 C8
Millicent St CF10 232 C2
Mill La
Bridgend / Pen-y-Bont ar Ogwr CF31 168 E5
Cardiff / Caerdydd, Llandaff / Llandaf CF5 194 B8
Cardiff / Caerdydd, Llane Deyrn CF3 179 C8
Castleton CF3 162 C4
Llanelli SA15 40 D6
Llanrhidian SA3 229 D3
Llanyrafon NP44 90 B2
The Mumbles / Y Mwmbwls SA3 94 B2
Ystrad Mynach CF82 111 E6
Mill La / Lon Y Felin CF10 232 B2
Mill Lay La CF61 209 F4
Mill-Lay La CF61 210 A4
Mill Par NP20 143 D1
Mill Pk CF71 188 E1
Mill Pl
Cardiff / Caerdydd, Ely / Tre-lai CF5 193 E6
Cardiff / Caerdydd, Lisvane / Llys Faen CF14 160 B3
Mountain Ash / Aberpennar CF45 54 C4
Mill Race CF72 173 D6
Mill Race / Cafn Y Felin SA10 71 B8
Millrace Cl CF14 160 A2
Mill Rd
Caerphilly / Caerffili CF83 138 A3
Cardiff / Caerdydd, Ely / Tre-lai CF5 193 E6
Cardiff / Caerdydd, Lisvane / Llys Faen CF14 160 A2
Deri CF81 57 B8
Dinas Powis / Dinas Powys CF64 206 A3
Mountain Ash / Aberpennar CF45 54 C4
Neath / Castell-Nedd SA10 48 D2
Pontllanfraith NP12 86 A3
Pontypool / Pont-y-pwl NP4 62 B8
Pyle / Y Pîl CF33 148 A1
Tongwynlais CF15 158 C1
Ynysybwl CF37 81 E3
Mill Row SA8 23 F4
Mills Ct CF62 213 A1
Mill's Ho 2 SA12 98 B2
Mill St
Aberdare / Aberdâr CF44 28 E4
Aberdare / Aberdâr CF44 28 F4
Blaina / Blaenau NP13 15 E4
Caerleon / Caerllion NP18 118 C2
Cwmfelin CF34 128 C8
Cwmfelinfach NP11 113 A4
Gorseinon SA4 43 C2
Gowerton / Tre-gwyr SA4 66 B5
Newport / Casnewydd NP20 143 B5
Pen-clawdd SA4 64 F4
Pontypridd CF37 109 B1
8 Pontypridd CF37 109 C1
Risca / Rhisga NP11 115 B1
Tonyrefail CF39 133 B4
Treharris CF46 83 C6
Ystrad CF41 79 D2
Mill Stream Way SA6 46 C2
Mill Terr
Cwm NP23 35 A7
Glyn-neath / Glyn-nedd SA11 223 C1
Risca / Rhisga NP11 115 B1
Mill Terr / Ffordd Y Felin SA18 219 A5
Mill View CF34 102 D1
Millwood CF14 160 A3
Millwood Ct 3 SA1 68 C2
Millwood Gdns SA2 93 F6
Millwood Rise CF62 214 C4
Millwood St SA5 68 C3
Milman St NP20 143 C1
Milner St NP19 143 F3
Milton Cl
Aberbargoed / Aberbargod CF81 58 B4
Beddau CF38 156 A5
Ebbw Vale / Glyn Ebwy NP23 14 B8
Llantwit Major / Llanilltud Fawr CF61 210 B5
Milton Cl / Clos Milton 7 NP44 89 D2
Milton Ct NP19 144 F6
Milton Dr CF31 168 C5
Milton Hill NP18 145 B5
Milton Inf Sch NP19 144 F6
Milton Jun Sch NP19 144 F6
Milton Pl
Cardiff / Caerdydd CF5 193 E8
Machen CF83 139 C7
8 Merthyr Tydfil / Merthyr Tudful CF47 30 E8
Milton Rd
Barry / Y Barri CF62 214 E8
Newport / Casnewydd NP19 144 A5
Penarth CF64 206 F4
Milton St
Cardiff / Caerdydd CF24 232 D4
Cwmaman CF44 53 A4
Milton Terr
7 Merthyr Tydfil / Merthyr Tudful CF47 30 E8
New Tredegar NP24 33 F1
Swansea / Abertawe SA1 233 A4
Milverton Rd CF3 179 C7
Milward Rd CF63 215 B6
Minafon CF14 159 B1
Minavon 1 CF14 177 B5
Mincing La SA15 40 D5
Minehead Ave CF64 216 A5
Minehead Rd CF3 179 C6
Miners Row CF44 28 E6
Minerva St CF31 168 F5
Minffrwd Cl CF35 152 E1
Minffrwd Rd
Pencoed CF35 152 E1
Pencoed, Pen-prysg CF35 152 F2
Mining School Hill NP11 60 A1
Minister St CF24 195 A8
Minny St CF24 195 A8
Minories 14 NP44 89 B1
Minori Ho CF10 195 C2
Minsmere Cl CF3 180 B7
Minster Cl
Barry / Y Barri CF63 215 B8
Swansea / Abertawe SA6 69 B7
Minster Ct SA6 69 B7
Minster Rd CF23 195 E8
Minton Ct CF24 196 A6
Min-y-Coed CF31 169 C5
Min Y Coed SA11 72 B6
Min-y-Coed
Glyn-neath / Glyn-nedd SA11 223 C1
Pyle / Y Pîl SA13 148 A6
Radyr CF15 176 B7
Ton-mawr SA12 73 B5
Min-y-Don SA13 125 E3
Minyffordd SA9 2 B6
Min-y-Mor CF62 214 B2
Min Y Mor SA15 40 C5
Min-y-Nant
Cardiff / Caerdydd CF14 177 B7
Pencoed CF35 170 D8
Minyrafon SA9 2 B5
Min yr Afon CF83 140 A7
Minyrafon Rd SA6 22 D1
Min-yr-Allt SA10 48 E2
Min-yr-awel
Pen-Y-Fai CF31 168 D8
Pontneddfechan SA11 223 F2
Min-y-Rhos SA9 222 A6
Mirador Cres SA2 95 A6
MISKIN 54 E1
Miskin Cres CF72 173 D7
Miskin Gn / Maes Meisgyn 2 NP44 90 A3
Miskin Ho 1 NP44 90 A3
Miskin Ind Pk CF72 174 A3
MISKIN / MEISGYN 173 E6
Miskin Prim Sch CF45 54 D1
Miskin Rd
Mountain Ash / Aberpennar CF45 54 E2
Tonypandy CF40 106 F5
Miskin St
Barry / Y Barri CF62 214 D3
Cardiff / Caerdydd CF24 232 B4
Treherbert CF42 50 E2
Miskin Terr CF45 54 E2

Mission Rd CF34 102 C1
Misty Hills Cl SA4 65 C1
Mitchell Cl
Cardiff / Caerdydd CF3 180 A5
Llanyrafon NP44 90 B1
Mitchell Cres CF47 10 F5
Mitchell Ct 2 CF40 106 E6
Mitchell Terr
5 Pontypool / Pont-y-pwl NP4 38 A1
Pontypridd CF37 135 D8
Miterdale Cl CF23 178 B3
Mithras Way NP18 118 A4
Mitre Ct CF5 177 A1
Mitre Pl CF5 177 A1
Mitre St NP13 36 B5
Mixen Cl SA3 122 F5
Model Cotts CF47 10 F2
Moel Fryn CF83 137 D6
Moel Gilau CF32, CF34 129 D5
Moira Pl CF24 232 D3
Moira St CF24 195 C6
Moira Terr
Cardiff / Caerdydd CF24 232 D3
Ogmore Vale CF32 104 E2
Mole Cl NP20 116 C2
Molescombe 5 NP44 89 B1
Mona Cl
Cwmbran / Cwmbrân NP44 89 F5
Swansea / Abertawe SA6 69 A6
Mona Pl
Cardiff / Caerdydd CF24 195 F7
Maerdy CF43 52 A2
Monastery Bsns Ctr SA10 71 B8
Monastery Rd SA10 71 B7
Monet Cres NP19 144 A7
Monger St 1 SA1 68 D1
Monica St CF34 102 B2
Monico The CF14 177 C6
MONKNASH / YR AS FAWR 198 C2
Monks Cl SA10 71 C8
Monk's Cl CF33 148 B2
Monksland Rd SA3 231 A6
Monk St CF44 29 A1
Monkstone Cl CF64 206 E1
Monkstone Rise CF3 179 C5
Monkton Cl CF5 193 C7
Monmouth Cl
Church Village CF38 135 F2
Pontypool / Pont-y-pwl NP4 63 A2
Monmouth Ct
Caerphilly / Caerffili CF83 137 D4
Newport / Casnewydd NP20 142 F3
Monmouth Dr
Merthyr Tydfil / Merthyr Tudful CF48 225 F1
Newport / Casnewydd NP19 144 A8
Monmouth Ho
Cardiff / Caerdydd CF23 178 C3
Cwmbran / Cwmbrân NP44 89 E3
8 Penarth CF64 206 F2
8 Swansea / Abertawe SA1 233 C2
Monmouth Pl SA6 46 A5
Monmouth St
Cardiff / Caerdydd CF11 194 F4
Mountain Ash / Aberpennar CF45 81 F7
Monmouth View CF83 112 A1
Monmouth Way
Barry / Y Barri CF62 214 F6
Llantwit Major / Llanilltud Fawr CF61 210 B7
Monmouth Wlk
Cwmbran / Cwmbrân NP44 89 E3
Markham NP12 58 D7
Monnow Ct NP44 89 A4
Monnow Ct / Cwrt Mynwy NP44 89 A4
Monnow Inf Sch NP20 116 D2
Monnow Jun Sch NP20 116 D2
Monnow Way NP20 116 E2
Monnow Wlk NP20 116 D2
Mons Cl NP20 143 A6
Montague St NP13 36 B6
Montana Pk CF44 27 E7
Montana Pl SA1 68 D3
Montclaire Ave NP12 85 E6
Monterey St SA5 68 C3
Montgomery Rd
Barry / Y Barri CF62 214 E4
Newport / Casnewydd NP20 117 A4
Montgomery St CF24 178 C1
Monthermer Rd CF24 178 A1
Monton Terr SA1 96 A7
Montpellier Terr SA1 95 B7
Montreal Cl NP20 142 D3
Montresor Ct NP44 117 B7
Monumental Terr CF48 10 A4
Moorby Ct CF10 232 D1
Moordale Rd CF11 195 A2
Moore Cl CF5 193 C5
Moore Cres NP19 145 A6
Moore Rd CF5 193 B5
Moore's Row CF81 32 D7
MOORE TOWN 70 E8
Moorings The
Newport / Casnewydd NP19 143 F8
Penarth CF64 207 A5
Pontypool / Pont-y-pwl NP4 62 E5
Moor King Cl CF3 180 B6
Moor La
Llangennith SA3 228 C2
Porthcawl CF36 165 F3
Moorland Ave
Newport / Casnewydd NP19 144 C3
The Mumbles / Y Mwmbwls SA3 122 E6
Moorland Cl CF44 27 F7
Moorland Cres CF38 156 A7
Moorland Gdns NP19 144 C3
Moorland Hts CF37 135 E8
Moorland Pk NP19 144 C3
Moorland Prim Sch CF24 195 E5
Moorland Rd
Bargoed / Bargod CF81 57 E4
Cardiff / Caerdydd CF24 195 F5
Cardiff / Caerdydd, Tremorfa CF24 195 E6
Ebbw Vale / Glyn Ebwy NP23 14 C7
Neath / Castell-Nedd SA11 71 F5
Moorland Rd / Heol Mora SA12 124 D8
Moorland Rd / Heol Morfa 3 SA12 98 E1
Moorlands Rd CF31 168 F2
Moorlands / Tirmorfa SA10 223 A5
Moor Rd
Baglan SA12 98 D3
Bridgend / Pen-y-Bont ar Ogwr CF31 169 F2
Moorside Rd SA3 122 F7
Moorside Villas SA10 222 F6
Moors La CF24 195 D5
Moor View
Bishton NP18 145 F3
Ebbw Vale / Glyn Ebwy, Rassau NP23 7 A4
Ebbw Vale / Glyn Ebwy, Willowtown NP23 14 C8
Moorview Cl SA5 67 F4
Moorview Rd SA5 67 F4
Morawel SA1 69 D5
Mor-Awel SA14 41 C5
Morden La NP19 143 E7
Morden Rd NP19 143 E6
Morel Ct CF11 206 F8
Morel St CF63 215 A5
MORFA
Cross Hands 218 D7
Llanelli 40 F2
Morfa Ave SA13 125 E5
MORFA BANK 125 B4
Morfa CP Jun Mix Sch SA15 40 F3
Morfa Cres CF3 179 E5
Morfa Glas SA11 223 C1
Morfa Ind Est SA1 68 E3
Morfa Inf Sch SA15 40 E2
Morfa La
Llantwit Major / Llanilltud Fawr CF61 199 D1
Wenvoe / Gwenfo CF5 205 A6
Morfa Rd
Margam SA13 125 E3
Swansea / Abertawe SA1 233 B4
Morfa St CF31 168 F5
Morfydd St SA6 68 F8
Morgan Arc CF10 232 B2
Morgan Cl SA4 43 F2
Morgan Ct
Swansea / Abertawe SA1 95 A5
Tonypandy CF40 79 F1
Morgan Jones Flats CF83 138 A3
Morgan Jones Sq 4 CF48 31 C1
Morgannwg Ho SA12 124 D8
Morgannwg St CF37 108 D2
Morgan Rise 7 NP4 17 D7
Morgan Row CF44 53 F8
Morgan's Pl CF32 151 A5
Morgan's Rd SA11 71 C5
Morgan St
Abercrave / Abercraf SA9 222 D7
Aberdare / Aberdâr CF44 28 F2
Abertillery / Abertyleri NP13 36 B6
Barry / Y Barri CF63 215 B5
Blaenavon NP4 17 C6
Caerphilly / Caerffili CF83 138 A4
Cardiff / Caerdydd CF24 232 C2
Dowlais CF48 11 A4
Llanbradach CF83 111 F2
4 Merthyr Tydfil / Merthyr Tudful CF47 10 D2
Morgan St *continued*
9 Mountain Ash / Aberpennar CF45 54 E1
Newport / Casnewydd NP19 143 D6
New Tredegar NP24 33 E3
Pontardawe SA8 23 C2
Pontypridd CF37 109 C2
Porth CF39 107 F3
Swansea / Abertawe SA1 68 D2
Tredegar NP22 13 E6
Morgan's Terr
Briton Ferry / Llansawel SA11 71 C3
Pontrhydyfen SA12 73 A2
MORGANSTOWN / TREFORGAN 176 A8
Morgan Terr
Porth CF39 107 F2
Tredegar NP22 13 D5
Treorchy / Treorci CF42 78 B4
Morgan Way NP10 163 F6
Morgraig Ave NP10 163 E5
Moriah Hill NP11 115 A2
Moriah Pl
Llwydcoed CF44 28 E6
Pyle / Y Pîl CF33 148 D2
Moriah Rd SA5 68 C6
Moriah St
Bedlinog CF46 56 A7
17 Merthyr Tydfil / Merthyr Tudful CF47 10 D2
Rhymney / Rhymni NP22 12 F2
Morien Cres CF37 135 F6
Morlais Bldgs 1 CF47 10 E1
Morlais Cl CF48 225 F2
Morlais Ct
Caerphilly / Caerffili CF83 137 D4
11 Merthyr Tydfil / Merthyr Tudful CF47 30 D8
Morlais Heritage Trail* CF48 10 E8
Morlais Rd
Margam SA13 125 E4
Swansea / Abertawe SA5 68 B5
Morlais Rd / Heol Morlais SA14 42 B7
Morlais St
Barry / Y Barri CF63 215 C6
Cardiff / Caerdydd CF23 178 B1
Dowlais CF48 11 A5
Pentrebach CF48 31 A4
Morley Cl NP19 144 E5
Morley Rd NP13 36 A6
Morningside Wlk CF62 204 F1
Mornington Ct CF3 179 A3
MORNINGTON MEADOWS 138 D4
Morrell St 22 CF47 30 E8
Morris Ave
Cardiff / Caerdydd CF14 159 D1
Mountain Ash / Aberpennar CF45 81 F7
Morris Finer Cl CF5 193 E5
Morris La SA1 233 C3
Morrison Cres / Cresawnt Morrison 6 SA12 98 D1
Morrison Ct SA12 98 D1
Morrison Ho 7 SA12 98 D1
Morrison Rd SA12 98 D1
Morrison St NP12 85 E7
Morris Rise 6 NP4 17 D7
Morris St
Cwmaman CF44 53 A4
Maesteg CF34 102 A3
Newport / Casnewydd NP19 143 E4
7 Swansea / Abertawe SA6 69 A8
3 Treherbert CF42 51 A1
Morris Terr
Ferndale CF43 79 E7
Swansea / Abertawe SA5 67 B6
Morriston Coll SA6 68 F8
Morriston Comp Sch SA6 45 F4
Morriston Hospl / Ysbyty Treforys SA6 45 E5
Morriston North Ind Est
Llansamlet SA6 46 B1
Swansea / Abertawe SA6 69 C8
Morriston Pl SA18 220 E6
Morriston Prim Sch / Ysgol Gynradd Treforys SA6 69 A8
Morriston South Ind Est SA6 69 A7
MORRISTON / TREFORYS 45 E1
MORRISTOWN 206 E3
Morrisville NP11 113 D3
Morse Row CF32 150 F4
Mortimer Rd CF11 194 D7
Morton Ct CF14 178 A4
Morton's Farm NP23 8 A4
Morton Terr CF40 106 A7
Morton Way NP20 142 F1
Moseley Terr NP44 89 E7
Moses Row SA11 226 D5
Moss Pl CF44 29 B4
Moss Rd NP44 89 B3
Moss Row CF44 29 B4
Mostyn Cl CF72 153 D3
Mostyn Mews CF72 153 D3
Mostyn Rd CF5 193 A4
Mostyn St CF44 53 F4
Mostyn Thomas Cl NP13 15 D5
MOULTON 203 C1
Mound Rd CF37 135 B8
MOUNTAIN AIR 14 B8
MOUNTAIN ASH / ABERPENNAR 54 F3
Mountain Ash Comp Sch / Ysgol Gyfun Aberpennar CF45 54 C4
Mountain Ash General Hospl CF45 54 D4
Mountain Ash Rd CF45 82 D2
Mountain Ash Sta CF45 54 D3
Mountain Cl / Clos Mynydd CF32 129 E3
MOUNTAIN HARE 11 A1
Mountain La NP4 62 D3
Mountain Rd
Aberavon SA12 99 A2
Bedwas CF83 138 D8
Caerphilly / Caerffili CF83 159 B8
Craig-cefn-parc SA6 22 C1
Cwmaman CF44 53 A4
Cwmbran / Cwmbrân NP44 89 B7
Llanbradach CF83 112 D1
Pentyrch CF15 157 C1
Pontypool / Pont-y-pwl NP4 62 B1
Risca / Rhisga NP11 115 C2
Rogerstone NP10 142 A8
Tonypandy CF40 107 A2
Mountain Row CF43 79 F8
Mountain Stream / Nant-y-Mynydd SA10 48 C1
Mountain View
Abertridwr CF83 137 B7
Briton Ferry / Llansawel SA11 71 B3
5 Brynmawr NP23 8 B4
Hendreforgan CF39 132 E4
Machen CF83 139 F7
Markham NP12 58 D7
North Cornelly CF33 166 A7
Pontypool / Pont-y-pwl NP4 61 F8
4 Pontypridd CF37 135 F6
Pwllypant CF83 138 A6
Tonypandy CF40 106 F8
Treherbert CF42 50 E2
Mountain View / Mynydd Golwg CF32 130 E5
Mountain View Rd NP4 61 F8
Mountain Way CF46 83 F2
Mountbatten NP22 12 F3
Mountbatten Cl
Cardiff / Caerdydd CF23 178 A5
Newport / Casnewydd NP19 144 F7
Mountbatten Ct SA5 67 E5
Mountbatten Rd CF62 205 A1
Mount Bax NP19 144 C5
Mount Cres SA6 45 D2
Mount Earl CF31 168 E2
Mount Earl Cl CF31 168 E2
Mountford Cl NP10 142 A7
Mount Hill St CF44 53 C7
Mountjoy Ave CF64 206 F4
Mountjoy Cl 1 CF64 206 F4
Mountjoy Cres 1 CF64 206 F3
Mountjoy La 2 CF64 206 F3
Mountjoy Pl
4 Newport / Casnewydd NP20 143 C3
Penarth CF64 206 F4
Mountjoy Rd 5 NP20 143 C3
Mountjoy St 6 NP20 143 C3
Mount Libanus St CF42 51 A1
MOUNT PLEASANT
Llanelli 40 D7
Neath 71 E5
Newport 233 A3
Pontypool 62 A8
Porth 107 D5
Treharris 55 E2
Mount Pleasant
Abercarn NP11 87 A3
Aberkenfig / Abercynffig CF32 150 C3
Abersychan NP4 37 F4
Bargoed / Bargod CF81 57 F5
Barry / Y Barri CF63 215 B6
Bedlinog CF46 56 A7
Blaengarw CF32 103 E7
Blaina / Blaenau NP13 15 D5
Bridgend / Pen-y-Bont ar Ogwr CF31 168 B5
Cwmfelinfach NP11 113 A6
Fleur-de-lis NP12 85 B6
Gowerton / Tre-gwyr SA4 66 B4
Heolgerrig CF48 10 A1
Llanelly Hill NP7 9 C5
Maesycwmmer CF82 85 B2
Merthyr Vale / Ynysowen CF48 55 D2
5 Newport / Casnewydd NP20 117 A3
Pen-pedair-heol CF82 84 E8
Pen-y-fai CF31 150 C1
Pontardawe SA8 23 E5
Pontycymer CF32 103 E3
Swansea / Abertawe SA1 233 A3
Tonna / Tonnau SA11 49 C2
Mount Pleasant *continued*
Trehafod CF37 108 C2
Mount Pleasant Ave CF3 179 C6
Mount Pleasant Bldgs 2 SA15 40 D6
Mount Pleasant Cl 1 NP44 89 D5
Mount Pleasant Cotts
Abertillery / Abertyleri NP13 36 B5
Llangeinor CF32 130 B5
1 Mountain Ash / Aberpennar CF45 54 E1
Mount Pleasant Ct
Neath / Castell-Nedd SA10 70 E7
Pontypool / Pont-y-pwl NP4 62 C6
Mount Pleasant Dr SA1 233 A3
Mount Pleasant Est NP13 60 B7
Mount Pleasant La CF3 179 C6
Mount Pleasant Pl 6 CF45 54 E1
Mount Pleasant Prim Sch
Merthyr Vale / Ynysowen CF48 55 D2
Rogerstone NP10 142 A6
Mount Pleasant Rd
Cwmbran / Cwmbrân NP44 89 D5
Ebbw Vale / Glyn Ebwy NP23 7 C1
Pontypool / Pont-y-pwl NP4 62 A8
Porthcawl CF33 166 C4
Porth CF39 107 E4
Risca / Rhisga NP11 115 A2
Mount Pleasant Row NP13 36 B7
Mount Pleasant Sq NP23 7 C1
Mount Pleasant St
Aberbargoed / Aberbargod CF81 58 A5
Aberdare / Aberdâr CF44 28 F3
Dowlais CF48 11 A5
Mount Pleasant Terr
Abercarn NP11 114 C5
Mountain Ash / Aberpennar CF45 54 E1
Mount Rd
Dinas Powis / Dinas Powys CF64 206 A3
Pontypool / Pont-y-pwl NP4 38 D1
Rhigos CF44 224 A1
Risca / Rhisga NP11 115 A2
Mount St Denys CF14 160 B4
Mountside NP11 115 D1
Mount St
Aberdare / Aberdâr CF44 53 C7
Ebbw Vale / Glyn Ebwy NP23 14 D6
Gowerton / Tre-gwyr SA4 66 B5
1 Merthyr Tydfil / Merthyr Tudful CF47 10 D2
Pontlottyn CF81 12 F1
Swansea / Abertawe SA6 45 E1
Tredegar NP22 13 E7
Mount Stuart Prim Sch CF10 195 B1
Mount Stuart Sq CF10 195 B2
Mount Terr 3 CF47 10 D2
Mount The
Cardiff / Caerdydd CF5 194 C7
Dinas Powis / Dinas Powys CF64 206 A3
Gowerton / Tre-gwyr SA4 66 B5
Mount View
Merthyr Tydfil / Merthyr Tudful CF47 11 A1
Merthyr Vale / Ynysowen CF48 55 D2
Mount View Terr 2 SA12 99 A1
Moxon Rd NP20 117 A1
Moxon St CF63 215 C6
Moyle Gr NP18 117 F6
Moy Rd
Cardiff / Caerdydd CF24 195 B8
Taffs Well / Ffynnon Taf CF15 158 A4
Moy Rd / Heol Moy CF48 55 B5
Moy Road Ind Est CF15 158 A4
Mozart Ct SA12 98 B3
Mozart Dr / Rhodfa Mozart SA12 98 B3
Mozart Mews 13 SA12 98 B3
Muirfield Dr SA3 93 F1
Muirton Rd CF24 195 F6
Mulberry Ave SA3 122 F8
Mulberry Cl
Llantwit Fadre / Llanilltud Faerdref CF38 156 C5
Rogerstone / Ty-du NP10 141 E7
Mulberry Ct CF62 214 C3
Mulberry Dr CF23 161 A3
Mulcaster Ave NP19 144 C2
Mulgrave Way SA2 94 A1

Mullins Ave CF3 179 D5
Multi Trad Ctr CF15 157 F8
Mumbles Bay Ct SA2 94 B1
Mumbles Pier★ SA3 123 E3
Mumbles Rd
Swansea / Abertawe SA2 94 D3
The Mumbles / Y Mwmbwls, Thistleboon SA3 123 C4
The Mumbles / Y Mwmbwls, West Cross SA3 123 A7
Mundy Pl CF24 195 A8
Munnings Dr NP19 144 A7
Munro Pl CF62 214 E6
MURCH 206 C3
Murch Cres CF64 206 C3
Murch Jun Sch CF64 206 B3
Murch Rd CF64 206 C3
Mur Gwyn CF14 177 C8
Muriel Terr
Bedlinog CF46 56 B7
Dowlais CF48 11 C5
Murlande Way CF62 213 C2
Murrayfield Cl SA5 67 D3
Murrayfield Rd CF14 177 D5
Murray St SA15 40 D5
Murray Wlk 13 CF11 194 D5
Murrel Cl CF5 193 A3
Murrells Cl CF38 156 D6
MURTON 122 B6
Murton La SA3 122 D5
Museum Ave CF10 232 B4
Museum Ct NP4 62 E2
Museum Pl CF10 232 B4
Museum St NP18 118 B2
Mus of Welsh Life / Amgueddfa Werin Cymru★ CF5 192 F7
Musselwhite Ct NP12 86 A4
MWYNDY 173 F7
Mwyndy Cross Industries CF72 173 F8
Mwyndy Terr CF72 173 E8
Mydam La SA4 43 A2
Myddynfych SA18 219 B8
Mydriam Pl NP22 6 E1
Mylo-Griffiths Cl CF5 176 E3
MYNACHDY 177 D2
Mynachdy Rd
Cardiff / Caerdydd CF14 177 D2
Cardiff / Caerdydd, Gwaun Treoda CF14 177 C3
Ynysybwl CF37 81 D3
Mynachlog Nedd Jun Sch / Ysgol Gymraeg Mynachlog Nedd SA10 71 A7
MYNYDD-BACH 68 B8
Mynyddbach SA18 218 F5
MYNYDD-BACH-Y-GLO 67 A4
Mynydd Ct NP4 62 C4
Mynydd Cynffig Inf Sch CF33 148 D2
Mynydd Cynffig Jun Sch CF33 148 C2
MYNYDDCYNFFIG / KENFIG HILL 148 E3
Mynydd Garnllwyd Rd SA6 68 D8
Mynydd Gelli Wastad Rd
Clydach SA6 46 B6
Swansea / Abertawe SA6 45 E5
Mynydd Glas / Blue Mountain CF34 102 A7
Mynydd Golwg / Mountain View CF32 130 E5
MYNYDDISLWYN 113 D8
Mynydd Islwyn Cl NP12 85 D4
Mynydd Maen Rd NP44 89 C6
Mynydd Newydd Rd SA5 68 A7
Mynydd View / Trem y Mynydd NP4 62 C4
Mynydd Y Farteg / Vartes Hill SA9 2 F6
Mynydd-yr-Eos CF40 107 A4
Mynydd Y Seren CF39 133 A3
Myra Hess Cl NP19 144 F6
Myrddin Gdns SA1 69 B3
Myrddin Rd SA1 69 B3
Myrtle Cl
Penarth CF64 206 E3
Rogerstone NP10 142 B3
Myrtle Cotts NP18 118 C2
Myrtle Dr NP10 142 B3
Myrtle Gr
Barry / Y Barri CF63 215 C7
Hengoed CF82 84 F3
Newport / Casnewydd NP19 144 B5
Swansea / Abertawe SA2 94 E7
Myrtle Hill
Pen-clawdd SA4 64 E3
Pontarddulais SA4 19 C5
Myrtle Rd
Gorseinon SA4 66 D8
Neath / Castell-Nedd SA11 72 A6
Myrtle Row CF42 78 F6
Myrtle Terr
Llanelli SA15 40 E5
The Mumbles / Y Mwmbwls SA3 123 B4
Mysydd Rd SA1 68 D4
Mysydd Terr SA1 68 D3

N

Nailsea Ct CF64 216 C5
Nant Arw SA18 218 D6
Nant Cadle SA5 67 E6
Nant-cae'r-efael SA9 222 E8
Nant Canna CF35 170 A1
Nantcarn Rd NP11 114 C8
Nant Celyn
Crynant / Creunant SA10 226 A8
Hirwaun CF44 27 C8
Llantwit Fadre / Llanilltud Faerdref CF38 156 F7
Rhymney / Rhymni NP22 12 F3
Nant Celyn Cl NP44 89 C6
Nant Coch Dr NP20 142 E4
Nant Coch Rise NP20 142 E4
Nant Ddu CF83 138 A2
Nant-Ddu Terr CF46 82 F6
Nant Dyfed CF72 155 F5
Nant Eirin CF39 133 A4
Nant-Fawr Cl CF23 178 B6
Nant-Fawr Cres CF23 178 B6
Nant-Fawr Rd CF23 178 B6
Nant Ffornwg / Fornwg Brook CF31 168 B6
NANTGARW 158 A8
Nantgarw China Works★ CF15 158 A7
Nantgarw Inf Sch CF15 157 F8
Nantgarw Rd CF83 137 E2
Nant-gau NP12 59 B2
Nant Glas SA4 44 C5
Nant Gwineu Rd / Heol Nant Gwinau SA18 220 C8
Nantgwyddon Cl CF41 79 C2
Nantgwyn CF44 28 C4
Nant Gwyn
Porth CF39 107 D1
Trelewis CF46 83 D6
Nantgwyn St CF40 106 F4
Nant Hir SA11 223 B1
Nanthir Lodge CF32 103 E6
Nanthir Rd CF32 103 E6
Nant Isaf CF5 205 A7
Nantlais
Ammanford / Rhydaman SA18 219 B8
Cefn-bryn-brain SA9 221 B8
Corntown / Corntwn CF35 186 B7
Nant Lais CF31 168 D5
Nant Melyn NP23 7 B4
Nant Melyn Terr CF39 133 D2
Nant Morlais CF48 11 B6
Nantong Way SA1 68 F4
Nant Row 16 CF44 29 A1
Nant Talwg Way CF62 214 B5
Nant Twyn Yr Harris CF82 111 E7
Nant Walla CF14 177 C8
Nantwen SA14 41 F4
Nantyboda SA13 100 E4
Nantybryn SA14 41 A7
NANT-Y-BWCH 6 B1
NANT-Y-CAFN 222 C2
Nant-y-Ci Rd SA18 218 F7
Nant Y Clais Ct / Llys Nant Y Clais SA12 99 C5
Nant Y Coed CF37 108 F2
Nant-y-coed
Tonyrefail CF39 133 A3
3 Troedyrhiw CF48 31 B1
Nant-y-croft NP23 6 F4
Nant-y-Cwm NP13 60 C6
Nant-y-Dall Ave CF37 136 A4
Nant-y-Dderwen SA18 218 F7
Nantydd Terr SA14 41 C5
Nant Y Derwen / Oak Stream CF34 102 A7
Nant Y Dowlais CF5 192 E4
Nant-y-Drope CF5 192 F4
Nant-y-Dwrgi CF72 154 A3
Nant-y-Fedw CF45 82 C5
Nant Y Fedw CF14 177 D4
Nant-y-Fedw Rd SA13 75 D3
Nant y Felin
Efail Isaf CF38 156 E5
Machen NP10 140 C3
Nantyffin N SA7 69 D7
Nantyffin Rd
Pontarddulais SA4 19 D3
Swansea / Abertawe SA7 69 C7
Nantyffin S SA7 69 C6
Nant-y-Ffyddlon CF82 84 D7
NANTYFFYLLON 102 A6
Nantyffyllon Prim Sch CF34 101 F5
Nantyffyllon Terr CF34 101 F6
Nant-y-Ffynnon CF31 169 B5
Nant Y Garn NP11 114 E4
Nant Y Garth CF15 157 F3
Nant-y-Gleisiad SA11 226 D5
NANTYGLO 8 D2
Nantyglo Comp Sch NP23 8 B2
Nantyglo Cvn Site NP23 8 C3
Nant-y-glo Round Towers★ NP23 8 B1
Nant Y Glyn Rd / Heol Nant Y Glyn SA18 219 F8
Nant-y-Gro
Llanelli SA14 41 C6
Llangennech SA14 18 B1
Nantygwenith Ct CF48 10 C1
Nantygwenith St CF48 10 C2
Nant Y Gwladys CF5 175 E5
Nant-y-Gwyddon Rd CF40, CF41 79 D2
Nant Y Hwyad CF83 137 E3
Nant-y-Milwr Cl NP44 115 F7
NANT-Y-MOEL 104 E6
Nantymoel Prim Sch CF32 104 F5
Nant-y-Moel Row CF32 104 E7
Nant-y-Moor Cl NP10 163 A6
Nant-y-Mynydd
Pontypridd CF37 109 D7
Seven Sisters / Blaendulais SA10 222 E4
Nant-y-Mynydd / Mountain Stream SA10 48 C1
Nant y Parc Prim Sch CF83 110 E3
Nant Y Pepra CF5 192 F4
Nant Y Plac CF5 192 F4
Nant-yr-Adar
Bridgend / Pen-y-Bont ar Ogwr CF31 168 B6
Llantwit Major / Llanilltud Fawr CF61 210 A5
Nant Yr Arthur CF5 192 F4
Nantyrcrynwydd CF34 101 F3
Nant-yr-Ely CF5 192 E4
Nant Y Rhos CF5 192 F4
Nant-y-Rhos NP12 85 F3
Nantyrychain Terr CF32 103 F2
Nant Y Wedal CF14 178 A2
Nant Y Wennol 4 CF31 168 C3
Nant Y Wiwer SA13 148 A5
Napier Cl CF31 169 A4
Napier St
Machen CF83 140 A7
Mountain Ash / Aberpennar CF45 54 D2
Narberth Cres NP44 90 B3
Narberth Ct CF83 137 C4
Narberth Rd CF5 193 D5
Narbeth Cl NP10 163 E5
Narbeth Ct CF62 214 F7
Narcissus Gr NP10 141 E6
Naseby Cl CF23 160 F1
Nash Cl NP10 142 B6
Nash Dr NP19 144 B2
Nash Gr NP19 144 B3
Nash Rd NP19 144 B2
Nash St CF45 82 D2
Nash View CF71 187 F4
Nasturtium Way CF23 160 D1
Nat Assembly for Wales The / Cynulliad Cenedlaethol Cymru CF10 195 C2
Nathan Ho NP22 12 E4
Nathan St SA15 40 C3
National Bldgs 13 NP20 143 C4
National Waterfront Mus★ SA1 233 B2
National Wetland Centre Wales★ SA14 41 C2
Nat Mus of Wales / Amgueddfa Ganadlaethol Cymru★ CF10 232 B4
Navigation Cl CF46 83 C7
Navigation Rd NP11 114 F3
Navigation St
Bedwas CF83 139 A7
1 Mountain Ash / Aberpennar CF45 54 D3
Navigation Terr CF34 75 A1
Navigation Villas 2 CF45 54 E1
Navigation Yd CF45 54 E3
Neale St CF62 214 E6
NEATH ABBEY 71 A8
Neath Abbey★ SA10 71 B7
Neath Abbey Bsns Pk SA10 71 A7
Neath Abbey Inf Sch SA10 71 B8
Neath Abbey Rd SA10 71 C8
Neath Archives Access Point★ SA11 71 E8
NEATH / CASTELL-NEDD 71 C6
Neath Ct NP44 89 A4
Neath Mus & Art Gallery★ SA11 71 E8
Neath Port Talbot Coll SA10 48 D1
Neath Port Talbot Coll / Coleg Castell Nedd Port Talbot SA10 71 D8
Neath Port Talbot Hospl / Ysbyty Castell Nedd Port Talbot SA12 98 E1
Neath Rd
Abergarwed SA11 226 C5
Briton Ferry / Llansawel SA11 71 C1
Bryn-côch SA10 48 C6
Bryn SA12, SA13 100 E6
Crynant / Creunant SA10 226 A7
Maesteg CF34 101 E4
Resolven / Resolfen SA11 226 D5
Neath Rd *continued*
Swansea / Abertawe, Plasmarl SA1, SA6 68 E5
Swansea / Abertawe SA6 69 A7
Swansea / Abertawe, Tircanol SA6 46 A2
Tonna / Tonnau SA11 49 B1
Neath Rd / Heol Castellnedd SA9 2 F6
Neath St CF24 195 E5
Neath Sta SA11 71 E7
Neath Villas NP4 37 E3
Nebo Est CF41 79 C3
Neerings NP44 89 A1
Neilson Cl CF24 195 D5
NELSON 83 E4
Nelson Ct CF10 232 D1
Nelson Dr NP19 144 E6
Nelson Rd CF62 215 A8
Nelson St
Aberdare / Aberdâr CF44 53 B5
Ebbw Vale / Glyn Ebwy NP23 7 D4
Swansea / Abertawe SA1 233 A2
Nelson Terr
Llanelli SA15 40 C4
New Tredegar NP24 33 F1
Neol St CF44 53 B4
Nesta Rd CF5 194 B6
Neston Rd NP19 144 D6
Nethercourt NP44 89 B3
Nettlefold Rd CF24 195 D4
Neuadda Cl NP10 141 F2
Neuadd Rd SA18 220 C8
Neuadd St NP13 36 A6
Neuaddwen St CF81 58 B5
Nevern Wlk 3 NP44 90 B2
Neville Pk NP10 163 E1
Neville Pl 14 CF11 194 E5
Neville Rd
Bridgend / Pen-y-Bont ar Ogwr CF31 168 E2
Porthcawl CF36 183 A7
Neville St
Abersychan NP4 37 E6
Cardiff / Caerdydd CF11 194 E5
Neville Terr CF44 28 F2
Nevills Cl SA4 66 C6
Nevill St SA15 40 C4
Nevill Terr 2 NP4 17 D7
Nevin Cres CF3 179 C4
Newall St NP13 36 B5
New Barn
St Mary Church / Llan Fair CF62 200 F1
St Mary Church / Llan Fair CF62 201 B1
Newbarn Path 6 NP44 90 B1
New Blandy Terr CF39 106 C1
Newborough Ave CF14 177 E8
Newbridge Comp Sch NP11 87 A6
Newbridge Ct 8 CF37 109 D2
Newbridge Ct / Cwrt Bont Newydd 3 CF31 168 C3
Newbridge Gdns CF31 168 E3
Newbridge Rd
Llantrisant CF72 155 E4
Pontllanfraith NP12 86 A4
Port Talbot SA12 124 E8
Newbridge Road Ind Est NP12 86 B5
NEWBRIDGE / TRECELYN 87 B7
New Bryngwyn Rd NP11 86 E6
New Bryngwyn St NP12 85 B6
New Bryn Terr CF39 107 D8
Newby Ct CF10 232 C1
New Candlestone / Candlestone Newydd CF31 168 B3
NEWCASTLE 168 E4
Newcastle Hill CF31 168 E4
New Castle St 2 CF47 10 E1
New Ceidrim Rd 14 SA18 220 B8
New Century St CF40 107 B5
New Chapel Ct NP44 89 D1
New Chapel St CF42 78 D6
NEWCHURCH 7 E1
Newchurch Ct NP44 89 C3
Newchurch Rd NP23 7 D2
New Church St CF48 10 A5
Newcott SA18 218 D5
New Cross Bldgs 1 SA6 46 A1
New Ct / Cwrt Newydd CF31 168 B3
New Cut Rd SA1 233 B4
New Cwm Terr NP23 35 B7
New Dock Rd SA15 40 D3
New Dock St SA15 40 D2
Newell Rd SA10 70 E8
Newent Rd CF3 179 F6
New Forest View CF71 189 A1
Newfoundland Rd CF14 177 E2
Newfoundland Way NP12 85 D6
Newgale Cl
Barry / Y Barri CF62 214 F8
Swansea / Abertawe SA5 67 F7
Newgale Ho
Cardiff / Caerdydd CF14 177 A4
Cwmbran / Cwmbrân NP44 89 F3
Newgale Pl CF5 193 D4
Newgale Row NP44 89 F3
New George St / Stryd George Newydd CF10 195 C1
New Gladstone St NP13 15 E5
New Henry St 4 SA11 71 D6
New High St NP13 36 C2
New Hos
Pant CF48 11 B6
Pontypool / Pont-y-pwl NP4 61 C4
10 Pontypridd CF37 109 D2
New House Ct 4 CF63 215 B7
NEW INN 63 A4
New Inn Inf Sch / Ysgol Babanod New Inn NP4 63 B4
New Inn Pl SA11 226 D5
New Inn Rd CF31, CF32 168 C1
New James St 2 NP4 17 D6
New King St CF41 79 B2
Newlands SA12 98 E5
Newlands Ave CF31 169 B7
Newlands Cl CF33 148 C2
Newlands Ct
Cardiff / Caerdydd CF14 160 A1
13 Pontypool / Pont-y-pwl NP4 38 A1
Newlands Rd CF3 179 F3
Newlands St CF62 214 F5
Newlyn Rd NP11 87 B7
Newman Cl NP19 144 F5
Newman Rd NP4 38 B1
Newmarket Wlk 10 CF47 10 D1
New Mill Cnr CF72 173 D6
Newmill Gdns CF72 173 D8
New Mill Rd SA2 94 A6
Newminster Rd CF23 195 E8
Newnham Cres SA2 94 E7
Newnham Pl NP44 89 E3
New Orchard St SA1 233 B4
New Oxford Bldgs SA1 233 A2
New Park Cres 2 CF37 135 E7
Newpark District Sh Ctr / Parc Manwerthu Parcnewydd CF72 155 C2
New Park Holiday Pk SA3 231 A4
New Park Rd NP11 114 D3
New Park Terr CF37 135 E6
New Pastures NP20 143 A2
Newport Arc 3 NP20 143 B5
NEWPORT / CASNEWYDD 143 F2
Newport Castle★ NP20 143 C6
Newport Ctr(L Ctr) NP20 143 C4
Newport Mkt NP20 143 C5
Newport Mus & Art Gal★ NP20 143 C4
Newport Rd
Abercarn NP11 114 B8
Bedwas CF83 138 E6
Cardiff / Caerdydd, Roath / Y Rhath CF24 195 D7
Cardiff / Caerdydd, Rumney / Rhymni CF3 179 C5
Croesyceiliog NP44 90 B6
Hollybush NP22, NP12 34 C4
Machen CF83 139 C6
Pontllanfraith NP12 85 F3
Pontypool / Pont-y-pwl NP4 63 A2
Risca / Rhisga NP11 141 C8
Newport Rd / Heol Casnewydd NP44 117 A6
Newport Retail Pk NP19 144 D2
Newport RFC (Rodney Parade) NP19 143 D5
Newport Road La CF24 232 D3
Newport St CF11 195 A2
Newport Sta NP20 143 B5
Newport Stadium NP19 144 B2
Newport War Meml★ NP19 143 D6
New Quarr Rd SA5 68 C5
New Quay Rd NP19 164 E8
New Queen St 3 NP4 17 C6
New Rank NP7 9 C5
New Rd
Aberbargoed / Aberbargod CF81 58 A6
Abersychan NP4 37 D5
Ammanford / Rhydaman SA18 219 B6
Argoed NP12 58 F4
Birchgrove SA7 46 F1
Bryncae CF72 153 C1
Caerleon / Caerllion NP18 118 C1
Cardiff / Caerdydd CF3 179 B2

New Rd *continued*
Cefn Cribwr CF32 149 E5
Cilfrew / Cil-ffriw SA10 49 C5
Crofty SA4 64 B3
Cwmfelinfach NP11 113 B4
Deri CF81 57 C8
Dowlais CF48 11 A4
Grovesend SA4 43 C6
Gwaun-Cae-Gurwen SA18 220 E7
Hengoed CF82, NP12 85 A3
Llanelli, Mount Pleasant SA15 40 C6
Llanelli, Penceiliogi SA14 41 B6
Mountain Ash / Aberpennar, Caegarw CF45 54 D3
Mountain Ash / Aberpennar CF45 82 C6
Nantyglo NP23 8 C2
Neath Abbey SA10 71 B8
Neath / Castell-Nedd SA10 70 F7
Pontardawe SA8 24 A7
Pontarddulais SA4 19 B4
Pontypool / Pont-y-pwl NP4 62 F3
5 Porthcawl CF36 182 F7
Porthcawl, Newton CF36 183 B7
Pyle / Y Pîl CF33 148 C3
Rhos SA8 24 B4
Skewen / Sclwen SA10 71 A7
Swansea / Abertawe SA2 67 D1
Swansea / Abertawe, Tre-boeth SA5 68 C6
Ton-du CF32 150 B5
Trebanos / Trebannws SA8 23 B2
Ynysybwl CF37 109 A7
New Rd / Heol Newydd
Abersychan NP4 37 E7
Neath / Castell-Nedd SA10 70 C1
Ystradowen SA9 221 C7
New Row
Cwmbran / Cwmbrân NP44 88 E1
Machen CF83 139 F6
New Ruperra St NP20 143 C3
New Scales Hos CF44 28 E6
New School Rd / Heol Ysgol Newydd 15 SA18 220 B8
Newslade 8 SA1 233 A4
New St
Aberavon SA12 99 A1
Abercynon CF45 82 D2
Aberdare / Aberdâr CF44 53 C6
Aberkenfig / Abercynffig CF32 150 C4
Bridgend / Pen-y-Bont ar Ogwr CF31 169 B2
Caerphilly / Caerffili CF83 137 F6
Cwmbran / Cwmbrân NP44 89 E5
Ferndale CF43 80 A5
Glyn-neath / Glyn-nedd SA11 223 D1
Llanelli SA15 40 E2
Neath / Castell-Nedd SA11 71 E8
Newport / Casnewydd NP20 143 D2
Pontycymer CF32 103 F2
Swansea / Abertawe SA1 233 B4
Tonna / Tonnau SA11 49 D3
Treherbert CF42 50 E3
Ystalyfera SA9 2 A4
New Terr NP4 62 A8
New Theatre★ CF10 232 B3
NEWTON
Cardiff 179 F1
Porthcawl 183 C7
The Mumbles 122 E5
Newton Ave SA12 98 F1
Newton Cl CF82 84 E7
Newton Nottage Rd
Porthcawl CF36 183 B8
Porthcawl, Newton CF36 183 C8
Newton Prim Sch
Porthcawl CF36 183 A7
The Mumbles / Y Mwmbwls SA3 122 E5
Newton Rd
Cardiff / Caerdydd, Newton CF3 179 F2
Cardiff / Caerdydd, Saltmead CF11 194 D4
Clydach SA6 22 D1
Oystermouth SA3 122 F5
The Mumbles / Y Mwmbwls SA3 123 A5
Newton St
Abercanaid CF48 30 F3
Barry / Y Barri CF63 215 B6
Swansea / Abertawe SA1 233 A2
Newton Terr 9 CF47 30 E8
Newton Way NP20 116 F2
Newton Wynd NP44 89 B1
NEWTOWN
Crosskeys 114 B3

NEWTOWN *continued*
Ebbw Vale 7 E1
Mountain Ash 54 F2
Penerlleni 39 F7
Newtown SA5 68 C3
Newtown Cl SA18 219 A7
Newtown Ct CF24 232 D2
Newtown Ind Est
Abercarn NP11 114 B4
Llantwit Fadre / Llanilltud Faerdref CF38 156 D7
Newtown Prim Sch CF45 54 E2
Newtown Rd / Heol Drenewydd NP4 39 F6
Newtown / Y Drenewydd SA18 219 A7
NEW TREDEGAR 33 F3
New Tynybedw St CF42 78 E6
New Villas
Cwmaman CF44 53 A3
The Mumbles / Y Mwmbwls SA3 123 B4
New Well La SA3 122 F5
New William St 17 NP4 17 C6
Newydd Ct CF15 176 C8
New Zealand Rd CF14 177 E2
New Zealand St SA15 40 C6
Neyland Cl CF38 135 F2
Neyland Ct CF62 214 F8
Neyland Dr SA5 67 F7
Neyland Path NP44 89 B2
Neyland Pl CF5 193 D4
Niagara St CF37 135 D8
Nibloe Terr 1 CF47 10 F4
Nicander Par SA1 95 B8
Nicander Pl SA1 95 B8
Nicholas Cl CF15 176 D5
Nicholas Ct
Gorseinon SA4 43 C3
Treorchy / Treorci CF41 78 F3
Nicholas Rd SA7 47 A6
Nicholas St NP4 62 C6
NICHOLASTON 231 F7
Nicholl Ct
Llantwit Major / Llanilltud Fawr CF61 210 B6
The Mumbles / Y Mwmbwls SA3 123 C3
Nicholls Ave CF36 183 A7
Nicholls Rd CF32 150 C8
Nicholl St SA1 95 B6
Nicholson Webb Cl CF5 176 D3
Nidd Cl NP20 116 C1
Nidd Wlk NP20 116 C1
Nidum Cl SA10 71 C8
Nightingale Ct
Llanelli SA15 41 A5
Newport / Casnewydd NP10 163 E7
Nightingale Gdns CF38 135 D1
Nightingale Ho
2 Aberavon SA12 98 F1
3 Cwmbran / Cwmbrân NP44 89 D5
Nightingale Pk SA11 72 A5
Nightingale Pl CF64 206 C3
Nightingale's Bush CF37 135 E8
Nightingale St CF48 30 F4
Nightingale Terr NP4 62 A8
Nile Rd CF40 107 B5
Nile St CF37 135 D8
Nine Mile Point Ct NP11 113 B4
Nine Mile Point Ind Est NP11 113 C3
Nine Mile Point Rd NP11 113 E3
Ninian Park (Cardiff City AFC) CF11 194 D4
Ninian Park Prim Sch CF11 194 E3
Ninian Park Rd CF11 194 E5
Ninian Park Sta CF11 194 D4
Ninian Rd CF23 178 B1
Ninian St
Treherbert CF42 51 A1
Treorchy / Treorci CF42 78 D7
Ninth Ave
Hirwaun CF44 224 D1
Merthyr Tydfil / Merthyr Tudful CF47 10 E5
Swansea / Abertawe SA6 45 D2
Nith St 13 CF44 29 A1
Nixon Terr SA6 46 A1
Nixonville CF48 55 C4
Nobel Ave SA12 98 F1
Nobel Square Ind Est NP23 8 D4
Noddfa Flats CF39 106 C1
Noel Terr / Teras Noel CF48 55 C4
Nolton Arc 7 CF31 168 F4
Nolton Ct SA5 67 F6
Nolton Pl
Bridgend / Pen-y-Bont ar Ogwr CF31 168 F3
Cwmbran / Cwmbrân NP44 89 C1
Nolton St CF31 168 F4
Nora St CF24 195 D6
Norbury Ave CF5 193 E7
Norbury Ct 4 CF5 193 E7

Norbury Ho
6 Cardiff / Caerdydd CF5 193 E7
10 Cwmbran / Cwmbrân NP44 89 C2
Norbury Rd CF5 193 E7
Nordale Ct CF14 178 A8
Nordale Rd CF61 210 B6
Nordale Rise CF63 215 C6
Norfolk Cl NP44 89 A3
Norfolk Cl / Clos Norfolk 5 NP44 89 A3
Norfolk Ct 3 CF15 176 B6
Norfolk Ho 2 SA12 98 C3
Norfolk Rd NP19 143 F6
Norfolk St
Cardiff / Caerdydd CF5 194 B6
Swansea / Abertawe SA1 95 B7
Norman Cotts CF64 206 A7
Normands Ho 2 NP44 116 C8
Normandy Rd SA1 68 E3
Norman Rd CF14 177 B4
Norman Rd / Heol Norman 3 SA18 219 B7
Norman St
Aberavon SA12 99 A1
Abertillery / Abertyleri NP13 36 B6
Caerleon / Caerllion NP18 118 B2
1 Cardiff / Caerdydd CF24 195 B8
Norman Terr
Merthyr Tydfil / Merthyr Tudful CF47 10 D2
Pentrebach CF48 31 B3
Norrell Cl CF11 194 B5
Norris Cl CF64 206 D5
Norseman Cl CF62 212 E2
Northam Ave CF3 179 A5
Northampton La SA1 233 A3
North Ave
Aberdare / Aberdâr CF44 28 F2
Maesycwmmer CF82 85 B2
Pyle / Y Pîl CF33 148 C2
Tredegar NP22 6 C1
North Ave / Rhodfa'r Gogledd SA14 41 A3
North Bank Rd SA13 124 F8
North Blackvein Ind Est NP11 114 A4
North Church St CF10 232 C1
Northcliffe Dr CF64 207 B5
North Clive St CF11 194 E3
NORTH CORNELLY 165 E7
Northcote La CF24 232 C4
Northcote St CF24 232 C4
Northcote Terr CF63 215 C6
North Cottage Dr SA4 43 B1
North Ct CF31 169 E3
North Edward St CF10 232 C3
Northern Ave
Cardiff / Caerdydd CF14 177 A6
Cardiff / Caerdydd CF14 177 B5
Northeron SA3 122 F8
Northfield Cl NP18 117 F4
Northfield Rd NP18 118 A4
North Hill Rd SA1 233 A4
North Hills La SA3 120 C6
Northlands CF3 179 B2
Northlands Pk SA3 122 A7
North Lodge Cl SA4 44 B3
North Luton Pl CF24 195 C5
North Mead CF32 150 E3
North Morgan St 1 CF11 194 E5
North Park Rd CF24 195 E6
North Point CF31 169 D3
North Rd
Abercarn NP11 114 C6
Abersychan NP4 37 F3
Bargoed / Bargod CF81 57 F4
Barry / Y Barri CF64 215 E6
Bridgend / Pen-y-Bont ar Ogwr CF31 169 C3
Cardiff / Caerdydd, Cathays CF10 232 A4
Cefn Hengoed CF82 84 E5
Cowbridge / Y Bont-Faen CF71 188 E2
Ferndale CF43 79 F7
Gileston / Silstwn CF62 211 E1
Loughor SA4 42 F1
Newbridge / Trecelyn NP11 87 A7
Ogmore Vale CF32 104 E2
Porth CF39 107 F3
North Rd / Heol Y Gogledd
Croesyceiliog NP44 90 A5
Pontypool / Pont-y-pwl NP4 62 B6
North Rise CF14 160 A1
North St
Abercynon CF45 82 E3
Blaenavon NP4 17 B7
Cardiff / Caerdydd CF11 194 F3
Dowlais CF48 11 A4
Ebbw Vale / Glyn Ebwy NP23 7 E4
Maesteg CF34 75 B2
Merthyr Tydfil / Merthyr Tudful, Pen-y-Darren CF47 10 F4
Newport / Casnewydd NP20 143 B4
Pontypridd CF37 109 D2

North St *continued*
Port Talbot SA13 125 D7
North Terr
Llanelli SA14 41 B7
Maerdy CF43 52 A2
Tonypandy CF40 106 C6
Northumberland Rd 2 NP19 143 F6
Northumberland St CF5 194 C5
North Vale View CF32 104 E7
North View CF15 158 B4
North View Terr
Aberdare / Aberdâr CF44 53 C5
Caerphilly / Caerffili CF83 138 B2
NORTHVILLE 89 F4
North Wall Rd CF62 211 E1
Northway
Bishopston SA3 122 B7
Pontypool / Pont-y-pwl NP4 39 B2
Northway Ct SA3 122 A7
Northways CF36 183 A7
North Wlk
Barry / Y Barri CF62 214 E6
Cwmbran / Cwmbrân NP44 89 E4
NORTON 123 A6
Norton Ave
Cardiff / Caerdydd CF14 177 D4
The Mumbles / Y Mwmbwls SA3 123 A6
Norton Dr SA3 121 A6
Norton La SA3 121 B7
Norton Rd
Glyncorrwg SA13 227 D2
Pen-y-groes SA14 218 D8
The Mumbles / Y Mwmbwls SA3 123 A6
Norton Terr SA13 227 C2
Norwich Rd CF23 178 F1
Norwood CF14 159 F2
Norwood Cres CF63 215 C7
Norwood Ct 1 CF24 195 D7
NOTTAGE 165 F2
Nottage Mdws / Dol Notais CF36 165 E2
Nottage Mead CF36 165 E2
Nottage Mews SA3 122 E4
Nottage Prim Sch CF36 182 F7
Nottage Rd
Cardiff / Caerdydd CF5 193 C4
The Mumbles / Y Mwmbwls SA3 122 E4
Nottingham St CF5 194 B6
Notts Gdns SA2 94 F7
Novello Ho SA12 98 A2
Novello Wlk NP19 144 E4
Nuns Cres CF37 109 B2
Nurseries The NP18 145 D8
Nursery Cres NP22 13 A2
Nursery Gdns CF31 168 F8
Nursery Rd SA13 227 C1
Nursery Rise CF83 138 C7
Nursery Terr NP22 13 E8
Nurses Cnr SA4 64 F4
NURSTON 212 E3
Nurston Cl CF62 212 E2
Nut Wlk CF61 210 A4
Nydfa Rd NP12 85 A7
Nythbran Terr CF39 108 B3
Nythfa SA4 44 C5
Nyth-y-Drydw CF62 213 A1
Nyth Y Dryw CF62 213 C1

O

Oakbrook Dr CF44 27 F8
Oak Cl CF72 155 C2
Oak Ct
Blackwood / Coed-Duon NP12 85 F6
8 Cardiff / Caerdydd CF24 195 C7
Penarth CF64 206 E2
12 Pontypool / Pont-y-pwl NP4 38 A1
Tongwynlais CF15 158 D2
OAKDALE 59 C1
Oakdale Cl NP18 117 F2
Oakdale Comp Sch NP12 86 A8
Oakdale Hospl NP12 59 A1
Oakdale Inf Sch NP12 59 B2
Oakdale Path 5 NP44 89 C2
Oakdale Pl NP4 62 A8
Oakdale Rd CF40 107 A1
Oakdale Terr
Blackwood / Coed Duon NP12 86 A8
Tonypandy CF40 107 A2
Oakdene SA2 93 D7
Oakdene Cl
Baglan SA12 98 E5
Cardiff / Caerdydd CF23 178 C4
Oak Dr SA5 66 D4
Oakengates CF36 183 D8
OAKFIELD 116 F8
Oakfield
Caerleon / Caerllion NP18 117 F3
Pontllanfraith NP12 86 B4

Oak Field / Cae Derwen CF31 169 A8
Oakfield Cres CF38 136 B1
Oakfield Gdns
Machen CF83 140 B6
Newport / Casnewydd NP20 143 A4
Oakfield Mews 7 CF24 195 D7
Oakfield Prim Sch
Cardiff / Caerdydd CF3 179 E7
Cwmbran / Cwmbrân NP44 116 F8
Oak Field Prim Sch / Ysgol Gwaun-y-Nant CF62 214 F7
Oakfield Rd
Barry / Y Barri CF62 214 D7
Newport / Casnewydd NP20 143 A4
Pontardawe SA8 23 E5
Tredegar NP22 13 F5
Oakfield Rd / Heol Maesdderwen 5 SA18 220 B8
Oakfield Rd / Heol Oakfield NP44 89 F1
Oakfields CF3 162 D1
Oakfield St / Stryd Cae Derw CF48 55 C6
Oakfield St
Cardiff / Caerdydd CF24 195 D7
Llanbradach CF83 112 A3
Pontarddulais SA4 19 C4
Ystrad Mynach CF82 84 F1
Oakfield Terr
Ebbw Vale / Glyn Ebwy NP23 14 E6
Nant-y-Moel CF32 104 F5
Tonypandy CF40 106 F8
Oakfield Terr / Teras Maes Y Deri 7 SA18 219 C7
Oakford Cl CF23 160 E1
Oakford Pl SA5 67 D6
Oak Gr
Cimla SA11 72 B5
St Athan / Sain Tathan CF62 211 B7
Oakgrove Hill / Bryn Derlwyn CF31 168 B2
Oak Hill Pk SA10 70 E8
Oak Hillside / Allt Dderw CF31 168 B2
Oak Ho CF14 176 E7
Oak La CF83 140 B6
Oakland Cl
Glais SA7 47 A5
Hirwaun CF44 27 F7
Oakland Cres CF37 109 F4
Oakland Dr SA10 48 C3
Oakland Gdns CF81 57 F3
Oakland Rd SA3 123 A4
Oaklands
Bargoed / Bargod CF81 57 F2
Merthyr Vale / Ynysowen CF48 55 D3
Miskin / Meisgyn CF72 173 D8
Ponthir NP18 117 E6
Port Talbot SA13 99 C2
The Mumbles / Y Mwmbwls SA3 122 F6
Oaklands Ave CF31 168 C4
Oaklands Bsns Pk / Parc Masnachol Bsns CF43 80 A5
Oaklands Cl
Bridgend / Pen-y-Bont ar Ogwr CF31 168 D4
Cardiff / Caerdydd CF3 179 E7
Oaklands Cl / Clos-y-Dderwen SA14 218 B8
Oaklands Ct SA2 94 A1
Oaklands Dr
Bridgend / Pen-y-Bont ar Ogwr CF31 168 D4
Ton Pentre CF41 79 B3
Oaklands Ho NP11 60 A1
Oaklands Park Dr NP10 141 E3
Oaklands Prim Sch CF44 53 D6
Oaklands Rd
Bridgend / Pen-y-Bont ar Ogwr CF31 168 C4
Newport / Casnewydd NP19 143 F5
Pontlliw SA4 44 A6
Pontypool / Pont-y-pwl NP4 89 D8
Oaklands Rise CF31 168 C4
Oakland St
Bedlinog CF46 56 B6
Mountain Ash / Aberpennar CF45 54 E1
Oaklands Terr SA1 95 B7
Oaklands View NP44 89 A3
Oakland Terr
Cwmbran / Cwmbrân NP44 116 E8
Ferndale CF43 80 A5
Newbridge / Trecelyn NP11 60 A1
Pontypridd CF37 109 F4
Rhymney / Rhymni NP22 12 E5
Treharris CF46 83 B7
Oakleafe Dr CF23 178 E8
Oak Leaf Terr NP13 60 A6
Oakleigh Ct NP44 115 F8

Oakleigh House Sch SA2 94 F7
Oakleigh Rd SA4 42 F2
Oakley Pl CF11 194 F2
Oakley St NP19 143 F3
Oakley Terr CF40 107 A1
Oakmead Cl CF23 160 F1
Oakmeadow Ct 3 CF3 179 F7
Oakmeadow Dr CF3 179 F6
Oakmead Rd CF72 154 A4
Oak Pl CF81 57 E2
Oak Rd
Llanharry CF72 172 B5
Merthyr Tydfil / Merthyr Tudful CF47 10 D3
Rogerstone / Ty-du NP10 141 F6
Oakridge CF14 159 F2
Oak Ridge
Blackmill CF35 130 E2
Swansea / Abertawe SA2 94 A6
Oakridge E CF14 159 F3
Oakridge W CF14 159 F2
Oak St / Stryd Y Dderwen
8 NP44 89 E2
Oaks Cl NP20 143 A2
Oaks Ct NP4 37 F3
Oaks End Cl CF82 84 E7
Oaksford NP44 89 A2
Oaks Rd NP4 37 F2
Oak St
Abercarn NP11 87 B4
Aberdare / Aberdâr CF44 29 A1
Aberkenfig / Abercynffig CF32 150 C4
Abertillery / Abertyleri NP13 36 A5
Blackwood / Coed-Duon NP12 85 E7
Cwm NP23 35 A7
Ferndale CF43 79 F7
Gorseinon SA4 66 D8
Hendreforgan CF39 132 C5
Newport / Casnewydd NP19 143 E8
Rhydyfelin CF37 136 B5
Ton Pentre CF41 79 A2
Tonypandy CF40 106 B7
Treherbert CF42 78 A8
Treorchy / Treorci CF42 78 E6
Oaks The
Aberdare / Aberdâr CF44 28 D2
Blackwood / Coed Duon NP12 59 C1
Cardiff / Caerdydd CF14 160 B2
Llantwit Fadre / Llanilltud Faerdref CF38 156 D8
Machen CF83 140 B6
Neath / Castell-Nedd SA11 72 B4
Quakers Yard CF46 83 C5
Underwood NP18 145 E7
Oaks The / Y Dderwen NP44 90 B5
Oak Stream / Nant Y Derwen CF34 102 A7
Oak Terr
Abercarn NP11 114 C5
Abercwmboi CF44 53 E4
Coytrahen CF32 150 C8
Fleur-de-lis NP12 85 B6
5 Llanbradach CF83 111 F1
Mountain Ash / Aberpennar CF45 81 F8
Ogmore Vale CF32 104 E1
Oak Tree Ave SA2 94 C6
Oak Tree Cl
Fleur-de-lis NP12 85 B6
Pontypool / Pont-y-pwl NP4 63 A5
Radyr CF15 176 A6
The Mumbles / Y Mwmbwls SA3 122 E6
Oak Tree Cl / Clos Y Dderwen SA18 219 D7
Oaktree Ct NP44 89 E1
Oak Tree Ct
Bridgend / Pen-y-Bont ar Ogwr CF31 169 D5
Cardiff / Caerdydd CF23 161 A3
Newbridge / Trecelyn NP11 60 C1
Newport / Casnewydd NP19 144 B5
Oak Tree Dr
Cefn Hengoed CF82 84 E5
Porthcawl CF36 183 E7
Rogerstone / Ty-du NP10 141 E7
Oak Tree Pk / Parc Deri CF31 168 D3
Oak View
Blaenavon NP4 17 E6
Cilfrew / Cil-ffriw SA10 49 C6
Oakview Ct NP4 17 E6
Oakway CF5 193 C8
Oak Way
Penllergaer SA4 44 C2
Sarn CF32 150 F4
Oakwood CF34 102 C1
Oakwood Ave
Pontrhydyfen SA12 73 A1
Swansea / Abertawe SA6 45 D1
Oak Wood Ave CF23 178 E3
Oakwood Cl
Blackwood / Coed Duon NP11 59 D4
Oakwood Cl *continued*
Clydach SA8 23 A1
Llandough / Llandochau CF64 206 E6
Oakwood Ct CF44 28 D2
Oakwood Dr
Clydach SA8 23 A1
Gowerton / Tre-gwyr SA4 66 D4
Maesteg CF34 102 C2
Tonyrefail CF39 133 B3
Oakwood Ho SA12 100 A8
Oakwood La SA13 125 B8
Oakwood Pl 1 SA12 99 C1
Oakwood Rd
Neath / Castell-Nedd SA11 71 F8
Port Talbot SA13 125 B8
Swansea / Abertawe SA2 94 F6
Oakwood Rise SA8 23 A1
Oakwood St
Pontypridd CF37 135 E5
Port Talbot SA13 125 B8
Oban St CF63 215 B6
Ocean Bldgs CF10 195 C2
Ocean Cres 5 SA1 233 B1
Ocean Ho 17 CF10 195 B2
Ocean House Rd CF62 211 E1
Ocean St CF42 78 B4
Ocean View Cl SA2 94 B3
Ocean View / Golwg Y Mor SA10 97 C8
Ocean Way CF24 195 E4
Ocean Way / Ffordd Y Cefnor SA12 98 C1
Ochr Y Coed CF14 159 F3
Ochr-y-Waun Rd SA9 221 B7
Octavivs Cl NP10 163 E5
Oddfellows St SA11 223 D1
Oddfellows' St
2 Bridgend / Pen-y-Bont ar Ogwr CF31 168 F4
Ystradgynlais SA9 1 F2
Odessa St CF48 11 A5
Odet Ct CF14 176 E7
Odette Ho 3 SA12 98 F1
O'donnell Rd CF63 215 A7
Odo St SA1 68 D2
Odyn's Fee CF62 212 E2
Office St CF39 107 F3
Offway NP44 116 C8
Ogilvie Terr CF81 33 A2
OGMORE 185 A6
OGMORE-BY-SEA / ABEROGWR 184 D3
Ogmore Castle* CF32 185 A6
Ogmore Comp Sch / Ysgol Gyfun Ogwr CF32 151 A6
Ogmore Cres
Bettws NP20 116 C1
Bridgend / Pen-y-Bont ar Ogwr CF31 169 A3
Ogmore Ct
Bridgend / Pen-y-Bont ar Ogwr CF31 168 D2
Caerphilly / Caerffili CF83 137 D4
Ogmore Vale CF32 104 E2
Ogmore Dr / Ffordd Ogwr CF36 165 E2
Ogmore Pl
Barry / Y Barri CF63 215 A8
8 Llanyrafon NP44 90 B2
Swansea / Abertawe SA1 69 A2
Ogmore Rd
Cardiff / Caerdydd CF5 193 C4
Ewenny / Ewenni CF32, CF35 185 D7
Ogmore Terr
Bridgend / Pen-y-Bont ar Ogwr CF31 168 F4
Bryncethin CF32 151 A5
Nant-y-Moel CF32 104 F6
OGMORE VALE 104 D1
Ogmore Vale Prim Sch CF32 104 E2
Ogwen Dr CF23 178 C5
Ogwen Ho NP44 89 C2
Ogwr Ent Ctr CF32 150 C5
Ogwy St CF32 104 F5
Okehampton Ave CF3 179 C8
OLCHFA 94 A7
Olchfa Cl SA2 94 A6
Olchfa La SA2 94 A7
Olchfa Sch SA2 94 A6
Old Abergavenny Rd NP4 39 B5
Old Bakery Ct CF15 157 C1
Old Barn 4 NP19 143 F8
Old Barn Way NP13 36 C4
Old Barry Rd CF64 206 E6
Old Blaen-Afon Rd
7 Brynmawr NP23 8 C4
Brynmawr NP23 8 D4
Old Blaina Rd NP13 35 F6
Old Brewery La NP22 12 D4
Oldbridge Ct NP44 89 A5
Old Bridge Ct / Cwrt Yr Henbont NP12 85 F3
Old Brithweunydd Rd CF40 107 A5
Oldbury Bsns Ctr NP44 89 E2
Oldbury Rd / Ffordd Oldbury 9 NP44 89 E2
Old Cardiff Rd NP20 142 F1
Old Castle Cl NP10 163 E5
Oldcastle Jun & Inf Schs CF31 168 F3
Old Castle Rd SA15 40 C5
Old Chapel Rd CF48 10 A4
Old Chepstow Rd NP18 145 D8
Old Church Cl CF33 166 A5
Old Church La CF82, NP12 85 B3
Old Church Rd CF14 177 B5
Old Church St CF48 10 A4
Old Clipper Rd CF10 195 F2
OLD CWMBRAN 89 D3
Old Danyderi CF48 55 C5
Old Duke Rd NP22 6 E2
Old Estate Yd NP4 62 E5
Old Farm Ct SA7 69 F6
Old Farm La CF15 174 E7
Old Farm Mews CF64 206 A3
Old Field Rd
Cardiff / Caerdydd CF15 176 E8
Pencoed CF35 170 D5
Old Forge The CF5 191 B1
OLD FURNACE 61 F5
Old Furnace SA10 48 C5
Old Furnace Ho SA11 71 C5
Old Furnace Rd CF83 137 E4
Old Garden Ct 7 CF15 176 B6
Old Green Ct CF3 180 E8
Old Green Intc NP20 143 C5
Old Hall Cl NP10 163 F7
Old Hill
Cardiff / Caerdydd CF3 179 D6
Newport / Casnewydd NP18 144 C8
Old Hill Cres NP18 144 D7
Old James St 11 NP4 17 C6
Old Kittle Rd SA3 121 F7
Old La NP4 37 F4
Old Langstone Court Rd NP18 145 B8
Old Library Flats CF34 102 A5
Old Llangfelach Rd SA4 44 B3
Old Llanharan Rd CF72 153 C1
Old Lodge SA15 40 D4
Old Malt Ho CF64 206 A3
Old Mansion Cl / Clos Henblas CF31 168 A4
Old Market CF5 205 A6
Old Market Pl SA12 99 D5
Old Market St 12 SA11 71 E8
Old Meadow Hill / Bryn Henfaes CF31 168 A4
Old Mill Bsns Pk CF11 194 A6
Old Mill Dr CF5 175 E5
Old Mill La CF47 10 D1
Oldmill Rd CF63 215 C7
Old Mill Rd CF14 160 A2
Old Nantgarw Rd CF15 137 B1
Old Newport Rd CF3 179 F8
Old Pant Rd NP11 87 B7
Old Parish Rd
Blackmill CF35 130 F2
Hengoed CF82 85 A3
Ynysybwl CF37 109 A7
Old Parish Road Ind Est CF37 109 A7
Old Park Rd SA13 147 D7
Old Park Terr CF37 135 E7
Old Pen-Rhys Rd CF41 79 E2
Old Police Sta The CF3 179 B4
Old Police Station & Mus* CF36 182 F6
Old Port Rd CF5 205 A6
Old Queen St NP4 17 C6
Old Rd
Abersychan NP4 37 F3
Ammanford / Rhydaman SA18 219 B8
Baglan SA12 98 C7
Llanelli SA15 40 D6
Neath / Castell-Nedd, Cwrt Sart SA11 71 D4
Pontardawe SA8 24 A7
Old Rd / Hen Heol SA10 70 F7
Old Rd / Hen Hoel SA10 71 A7
Old Rectory 4 CF5 194 C6
Old Road Prim Sch SA15 40 D6
Old Roman Rd NP18 119 D2
Old Row NP44 88 E1
Old School Cl CF48 10 C2
Old School Ct
Abercarn NP11 114 C5
Tongwynlais CF15 158 C1
Old School Grange CF82 84 F2
Old School Pl NP4 61 F8
Old School Rd
Cardiff / Caerdydd CF5 193 E5
Porthcawl CF36 182 F6
Old St CF40 106 D6
Old Stables CF32 104 F5
Old Station Rd 4 CF36 182 F7
Old Station Yd
Bedwas CF83 138 D7
2 Treharris CF46 83 B6
Old Stone Row SA13 227 C2
OLD TREOWEN 86 F7
Old Vicarage Cl
Cardiff / Caerdydd CF14 177 F8
Glan-y-nant NP12 85 A7
Old Village La 4 CF36 165 F1
Old Village Rd CF62 214 C3
OLDWALLS 229 C2
OLDWAY 122 B6
Oldway SA3 122 A6
Oldwell Ct 9 CF23 178 C2
Old Wern Rd SA9 2 B6
Old William St 13 NP4 17 C6
Old Winch Fawr Rd CF48 225 F1
Old Ynysybwl Rd CF37 81 E2
O'Leary Dr CF11 206 F8
Oliphant Circ NP20 116 F3
Olive Branch Cres SA11 71 B3
Olive Ct 4 CF11 194 D6
Olive Rd SA3 122 F8
Oliver Jones Cres NP22 13 D7
Oliver Rd NP19 144 A3
Oliver St CF37 109 A1
Oliver Terr CF37 135 E6
Olive St
Aberavon SA12 99 A1
Llanelli SA15 40 F3
Olive Terr CF39 107 D1
Ollivant Cl CF5 176 D3
Olway Cl / Clos Olway 1 NP44 90 B1
Ombersley La NP20 142 F4
Ombersley Rd NP20 142 F4
ONLLWYN 222 F5
Onllwyn Rd
Coelbren SA10 222 F6
Dyffryn Cellwen SA10 222 E5
Onslow Terr CF32 150 D6
Ontario Way CF23 178 C5
Open Hearth Cl NP4 62 E2
Orange Gr CF5 176 C1
Orangery Wlk NP10 163 F7
Orbit St CF24 195 C6
Orbit Theatre* CF10 232 B2
Orchard Castle CF14 159 E2
Orchard Cl
Bassaleg NP10 141 F3
Gorseinon SA4 43 B3
Llanblethian / Llanfleiddan CF71 200 A4
Llantwit Major / Llanilltud Fawr CF61 210 D5
Marshfield CF3 180 D8
Pencoed CF35 152 E1
Pontypool / Pont-y-pwl NP4 38 B1
Port-Eynon SA3 231 A4
Porth CF39 108 A3
Wenvoe / Gwenfo CF5 205 A7
Orchard Cl / Close y Berllan CF48 55 C6
Orchard Cres CF64 206 B3
Orchard Ct
Cardiff / Caerdydd CF14 159 F4
Newport / Casnewydd NP19 143 D7
Pontllanfraith NP12 86 B4
Swansea / Abertawe SA1 233 B4
Orchard Dr
Barry / Y Barri CF62 214 F6
Cardiff / Caerdydd CF14 177 A5
Llantwit Major / Llanilltud Fawr CF61 210 A4
Pontypridd CF37 109 C5
Porthcawl CF36 183 E8
Three Crosses SA4 65 D1
Orchard Farm Est NP4 38 C1
Orchard Gdns NP19 143 E8
Orchard Gr
Morganstown / Treforgan CF15 176 B8
Penllergaer SA4 44 A2
Rhigos CF44 224 A1
Orchard La
Blackwood / Coed-Duon NP12 58 B2
Newport / Casnewydd NP19 143 E7
Orchard La / Lon y Berllan NP44 89 F4
Orchard Lodge CF61 210 C5
Orchard Mews NP19 143 D7
Orchard Park Cl CF3 179 E7
Orchard Pk CF3 179 E7
Orchard Pl CF11 194 D6
Orchard Pl / Cae Berllan 9 NP44 89 D2
Orchard Rd NP18 118 A4
Orchard Rise CF64 206 E4
Orchard St
Brynmawr NP23 8 B4
Neath / Castell-Nedd SA11 71 E7
Newport / Casnewydd NP19 143 D7
New Tredegar NP24 33 E4
Pontardawe SA8 23 E5
Swansea / Abertawe SA1 233 B3
Orchard Terr SA4 229 F4
Orchard The
Aberthin CF71 189 B3
Ponthir NP18 117 F6
The Mumbles / Y Mwmbwls SA3 122 F5
Orchard Way CF62 211 D3
Orchid Cl
Cardiff / Caerdydd CF3 180 B6
Port Talbot SA12 98 C2
Tir-Y-Berth CF82 84 F6
Orchid Ct SA3 122 E6
Orchid Ct / Cwt Tegeirian NP44 89 A1
Ordell St CF24 195 D5
Oregano Cl 15 CF3 180 A8
Oriel Ho CF24 232 D2
Oriel Rd 2 NP19 143 E5
Oriel Rheifordd Railway Gallery* CF10 195 C2
Orion Ct 4 CF24 195 C6
Orion Suite The NP20 143 D3
Ormes Rd SA10 70 E8
Ormonde Cl CF23 178 E3
Ormond St SA11 71 C3
Ormsby Terr SA1 96 A7
Orpheus Rd SA6 46 B4
Osborne Cl
Bridgend / Pen-y-Bont ar Ogwr CF31 150 F1
6 Newport / Casnewydd NP19 143 E5
Osborne Pl
Brynmenyn CF32 150 E6
Llanmorlais SA4 64 B2
Osborne Rd
Abertillery / Abertyleri NP11 59 F5
Brynmawr NP23 8 A4
Pontypool / Pont-y-pwl NP4 62 B7
Pontypool / Pont-y-pwl NP4 62 B8
Osborne Sq CF11 194 E3
Osborne St SA11 71 E7
Osborne Terr
Nant-y-Moel CF32 104 F6
Swansea / Abertawe SA2 94 F5
Oscar Chess Ho 5 SA1 95 A6
Osprey Bsns Ctr SA1 68 D4
Osprey Cl
Cardiff / Caerdydd CF3 179 F8
Neath / Castell-Nedd SA10 48 E2
Penarth CF64 217 A7
The Mumbles / Y Mwmbwls SA3 122 E7
Osprey Ct 1 CF63 214 F4
Osprey Dr SA11 72 B5
Osterley St / Stryd Osterley SA11 71 C2
Osterley St SA1 96 A7
Oswald Rd
Newport / Casnewydd NP20 143 C1
Newport / Casnewydd NP20 143 C2
Oswestry Cl CF3 179 C3
Other St CF37 81 F2
Othery Pl CF3 179 C8
Otter Cl NP20 116 C2
Oundle Ct 6 CF5 193 E6
Our Lady's RC Prim Sch CF45 54 E2
Outfall La NP10 181 E7
Oval The CF47 10 F1
Overdale Wlk NP11 59 D1
Overdene NP12 85 F3
Overland Cl SA3 123 A4
Overland Rd SA3 123 A4
Overstone Ct CF10 195 B2
OVERTON 231 A4
Overton Cl CF36 182 F8
Overton Ct 5 SA1 233 A4
Overton La SA3 231 A4
Overton St CF48 11 A5
Ovington Terr CF5 194 B7
Owain Cl
Cardiff / Caerdydd CF23 178 C4
Penarth CF64 206 E3
Owain Ct CF62 211 D4
Owen Cl NP18 118 A4
Owendale Terr NP4 37 F2
Owens Cl CF62 214 E5
Owen's La SA9 221 C2
Owen's Pl SA12 98 C1
Owen St
Hawthorn CF37 136 A4
Pontypridd CF37 135 F4
Owl Mdw / Ton Tylluan CF31 168 D3
Owls Lodge La SA3 93 F1
Oxford Arc CF10 232 B2
Oxford Bldgs CF45 54 D2
Oxford Cl NP18 117 F4
Oxford Ct CF32 104 E2
Oxford La CF24 195 C6
Oxford Pl NP13 60 C6
Oxford St
Aberdare / Aberdâr CF44 28 F2
Abertillery / Abertyleri NP13 36 B6
Barry / Y Barri CF62 214 C3
Cardiff / Caerdydd CF24 232 D4
Gelligaer CF82 84 D7
Maerdy CF43 52 B1

- Oxford St *continued*
  - Mountain Ash / Aberpennar CF45 54 D3
  - Newport / Casnewydd NP19 143 E5
  - Pontycymer CF32 103 E3
  - Pontypool / Pont-y-pwl NP4 62 E2
  - Pontypridd CF37 135 E6
  - Upper Boat CF15 157 F8
- Oxford Street / Stryd Rhydychen SA1 233 A2
- Oxford Terr NP4 17 A5
- Oxtens NP44 116 B8
- OXWICH 231 D5
- Oxwich Castle★ SA3 231 D5
- Oxwich Cl
  - Cardiff / Caerdydd CF5 193 F7
  - Cefn Hengoed CF82 84 F5
- Oxwich Ct SA6 69 A7
- Oxwich Gr NP10 163 D5
- OXWICH GREEN 231 D5
- Oxwich Leisure Pk SA3 231 D5
- Oxwich Nature Reserve★ SA3 231 E5
- Oxwich Rd NP19 144 A1
- Oyster Bend CF64 216 B4
- OYSTERMOUTH 123 A5
- Oystermouth Castle★ SA3 123 A5
- Oystermouth Ct SA3 123 A6
- Oystermouth Mews NP10 163 E5
- Oystermouth Prim Sch SA3 123 A5
- Oystermouth Rd SA1 233 A1
- Ozanam Ct SA5 67 F6

P

- Pace Cl CF5 176 D2
- Pace Rd / Ffordd Pace NP44 89 B1
- Pacific Bsns Pk CF24 195 F4
- Pacific Rd CF24 195 F4
- Packers Rd CF39 107 E4
- Padarn Cl CF23 178 B5
- Padarn Pl 9 NP44 89 E5
- Paddock Cl NP44 89 D5
- Paddock Pl 1 CF63 215 B7
- Paddock Rise 4 NP44 90 B1
- Paddocks Cres CF72 172 F6
- Paddock St SA15 40 D4
- Paddocks The
  - Aberdare / Aberdâr CF44 53 C8
  - Blackwood / Coed-Duon NP12 58 E1
  - Caerleon / Caerllion NP18 117 F3
  - Church Village CF38 135 D1
  - Groes-faen CF72 174 C6
  - Langstone NP18 145 D8
  - Llanyrafon NP44 90 B1
  - Penarth CF64 217 A8
  - Tonyrefail CF39 133 D6
- Paddocks The / Y Dolydd SA11 49 B2
- Paddock The
  - Cardiff / Caerdydd, Lisvane / Llys Faen CF14 160 A3
  - Cardiff / Caerdydd, Pen-y-lan CF23 178 C2
  - Cowbridge / Y Bont-Faen CF71 189 A1
  - Heol-y-Cyw CF35 152 A5
  - The Mumbles / Y Mwmbwls SA3 123 A8
- Padfield Court Bsns Pk CF39 132 F4
- Padley's Cl CF34 102 D2
- Page Dr CF24 179 A1
- Page La SA1 95 B6
- Page's Ho NP13 15 E6
- Page St SA1 95 B7
- Paget La CF11 194 F3
- Paget Pl CF64 207 B5
- Paget Rd
  - Barry / Y Barri CF62 214 E2
  - Penarth CF64 207 B5
- Paget St
  - Cardiff / Caerdydd CF11 194 F2
  - Ynysybwl CF37 81 F1
- Paget Terr CF64 207 B5
- Painter's Row CF42 78 B8
- Palace Ave
  - Cardiff / Caerdydd CF5 194 B8
  - Llanelli SA15 40 E5
- Palace Ct CF23 178 C6
- Palace Rd CF5 194 B8
- Palace Row NP13 16 B1
- Palalwyf Ave CF72 173 B7
- Pale Rd SA10 70 F6
- Palleg Rd / Heol Palleg SA9 1 C2
- Pallot Way CF24 195 F8
- Palm Cl NP4 63 B5
- Palmer Pl NP12 85 D7
- Palmers Dr CF5 193 E5
- Palmer St CF63 215 D7
- Palmerston Prim Sch CF63 215 D7
- Palmerston Rd CF63 215 D6
- Palmerston Workshops CF63 215 D7
- PALMERSTOWN 215 D7
- Palmerstown Ho CF63 215 D8
- Palmers Vale Bsns Ctr CF63 215 D7
- Palm Rd CF47 10 D5
- Palm Sq NP19 144 A4
- Palmyra Ct SA3 123 A6
- Palmyra Pl 11 NP20 143 C4
- Pamela St CF45 54 C2
- Panama Ct NP10 163 E7
- Pandy NP44 89 C3
- Pandy Bglws CF32 129 F2
- Pandy Cl CF47 10 B3
- Pandy Cres CF33 148 A1
- Pandy Inf Sch CF32 150 D4
- Pandy La CF83 140 A7
- Pandy-Mawr Rd
  - Bedwas CF83 138 C8
  - Llanbradach CF83 112 B1
- Pandy Pk CF32 150 D4
- Pandy Rd
  - Aberkenfig / Abercynffig CF32 150 C4
  - Bedwas CF83 138 C7
  - Blackwood / Coed Duon NP11 59 D2
- Pandy The CF44 27 D8
- Pandy View
  - Abercarn NP11 114 C5
  - Neath / Castell-Nedd SA11 72 A4
  - Trelewis CF46 83 D6
- Pangbourne Cl CF36 165 E1
- PANT 11 B6
- Pantanas CF46 83 B6
- Pantaquesta Cotts CF72 173 C5
- Pant Ardwyn / Ardwyn Vale CF35 170 C8
- Pantbach CF15 175 C8
- Pant Bach CF33 148 A2
- Pantbach Ave CF14 177 D4
- Pantbach Pl CF14 177 D4
- Pant-Bach Rd CF14 177 C5
- Pant Bryn Isaf SA14 41 E5
- PANTCADIFOR 11 B7
- Pant Celydd SA13 125 E4
- PANTCERDDINEN 11 A7
- Pant Cl
  - Pant CF48 11 A7
  - St Brides Major / Saint-y-Brid CF32 185 D3
- Pant Cotts CF48 11 A7
- Pantddu Rd NP13 59 F8
- Pant-Du Rd CF37 110 A6
- PANTEG 63 C2
- Panteg
  - Ebbw Vale / Glyn Ebwy NP23 7 D2
  - Pentyrch CF15 175 C8
- Panteg Cl CF5 192 F3
- Panteg Ind Est NP4 62 E3
- Panteg Mews 3 CF5 194 B7
- Panteg Terr NP11 86 F6
- Panteg Way NP4 62 F4
- Pant Farm Cl NP11 87 A6
- Pant Gilfach / Dingle Nook CF32 104 E4
- Pantglas
  - Gorseinon SA4 43 B1
  - Pentyrch CF15 175 C8
- Pant-glas NP4 37 D3
- Pant Glas
  - Cardiff / Caerdydd CF23 179 A7
  - Llanbradach CF83 112 A3
  - Pencoed CF35 170 D8
- Pant Glas Ct NP10 141 F2
- Pantglas Fawr CF48 55 C6
- Pant Glas Ind Est CF83 138 F5
- Pantglas La NP44 116 E6
- Pantglas Rd / Heol Pant-Glas CF48 55 C6
- Pantglas View CF83 138 F6
- Pant Gwylan / Gull Hollow CF31 168 D3
- Pantgwyn SA2 94 C6
- Pant Gwyn Cl NP44 115 F8
- Pantgwynlais CF15 158 D1
- Pant Gwyn / White Hollow CF31 168 B3
- Pant Hendre / Hendre Vale CF35 170 B8
- Pant Hirgoed CF35 152 C1
- Pant Hir / Long Hollow 2 NP44 89 E4
- Pant Hirwaun CF32, CF35 151 F4
- Pant Howel Ddu SA11 71 E2
- Pant Howell Ddu SA11 71 D3
- Pantiago Rd SA4 19 D4
- Pantile Row SA13 227 C2
- Pant Ind Est CF48 10 F6
- Pant La NP20 143 B8
- Pant Lasau Rd SA5, SA6 45 C4
- Pant Llygodfa CF83 137 D1
- PANTMAWR 176 F8
- Pant Mawr / Big Hollow CF31 168 B3
- Pantmawr Ct CF14 176 F8
- Pantmawr Rd CF14 176 F7
- Pant Morfa CF36 183 B8
- Pant Pl CF15 157 F5
- Pant Poeth / Burnt Hollow CF31 168 B3
- Pant Rd
  - Newbridge / Trecelyn NP11 87 A6
  - Newport / Casnewydd NP20 143 B8
  - Pant CF48 11 B6
- PANTSIDE 87 B7
- Pantside Prim Sch NP11 87 B7
- Pant St
  - Aberbargoed / Aberbargod CF81 58 B5
  - Pontycymer CF32 103 F2
  - Swansea / Abertawe SA1 96 B7
- Pant Sta CF48 10 F8
- Pant Tawel La CF15 175 F6
- Pantteg SA9 2 A4
- Pant-Teg SA15 40 F8
- Pant Terr CF48 11 A5
- Pant Tywod / Tywod Vale CF35 170 C8
- Pant View
  - Nantyglo NP23 15 E7
  - Newbridge / Trecelyn NP11 87 A7
- Pantybland Cvn Site SA7 46 B1
- Pant-y-Blawd Rd
  - Llansamlet SA7 69 D8
  - Llansamlet, Tircanol SA6, SA7 46 B1
  - Swansea / Abertawe SA6 69 A8
- Pant Y Blodau CF35 170 B8
- Pant-y-Blodau SA6 45 B2
- Pantyblodau Rd SA18 218 F8
- Pant y Boblen SA18 218 F5
- Pant-y-Brad CF39 133 E4
- Pant Y Brwyn SA9 221 C7
- Pantycefn Rd NP12 58 D7
- Pantycelyn SA4 43 B1
- Pant Y Celyn SA14 41 C5
- Pantycelyn Dr 3 CF83 137 F5
- Pantycelynen CF48 10 B1
- Pant-y-Celyn Pl CF62 211 D4
- Pantycelyn Rd CF64 206 D6
- Pant-y-Celyn Rd SA1 94 F8
- Pantycelyn St CF82 84 E2
- Pant-y-Cerdin CF44 53 E8
- Pant-y-Coed CF62 212 B8
- Pant y Dderwen CF72 155 B1
- Pant Y Deri SA4 43 F7
- Pant-y-Deri Cl 6 CF5 193 C4
- Pant Y Dryw / Wren Hollow CF31 168 D3
- Pant-y-Dwr
  - Merthyr Tydfil / Merthyr Tudful CF48 225 E6
  - Three Crosses SA4 65 D1
  - Tredegar NP22 6 C2
- Pant-y-Fedwen CF44 53 C5
- Pant Y Fedwen
  - Bridgend / Pen-y-Bont ar Ogwr CF31 168 C2
  - Gwaun-Cae-Gurwen SA18 220 D6
- Pant-y-Felin Rd SA4 19 D6
- Pant-y-Fforest NP23 7 E1
- PANTYFFYNNON 219 B5
- Pant-y-Ffynnon CF35 152 F1
- Pantyffynnon Rd / Heol Pantyffynnon SA18 219 B6
- Pantyffynnon Sta SA18 219 B5
- Pantyffynnon Terr SA9 2 A4
- Pantyffynnon Rd SA9 2 F8
- Pantyffyn Rd CF47 10 F1
- Pantyfid Rd CF81 58 B6
- PANTYGASSEG 61 C4
- Pantygasseg Rd NP4 61 D5
- Pant-y-Glan NP23 7 F4
- Pant-y-Gog CF32 103 F2
- PANTYGRAIG-WEN 109 A2
- Pantygraigwen Rd CF37 109 A2
- Pantygwydr Rd SA2 94 F6
- Pant-y-Mynydd NP23 7 F4
- Pant Y Pebyll / Tent Vale CF35 170 C8
- Pant-y-Pistyll SA8 23 C3
- PANT-Y-PWDYN 36 C4
- Pant-y-Pwdyn Rd NP13 36 C4
- PANT-Y-PYLLAU 151 D1
- Pant Y Pystyll / Brook Vale CF35 170 C8
- Pant-yr-Arian La SA12 98 F5
- PANT-YR-AWEL 130 E4
- Pant-yr-Eos
  - Aberdare / Aberdâr CF44 29 C4
  - Cwmbran / Cwmbrân NP44 89 E4
- Pant-y-Resk Rd NP11 86 F4
- Pant Yr Hebog CF31 168 C2
- Pant Y Rhedyn SA13 148 A5
- Pant Yr Helyg SA5 67 B6
- Pantyrheol SA11 71 C4
- Pant-y-Rheol Cl NP44 115 F7
- Pant-yr-Odyn SA2 67 C1
- Pant yr Wyn CF23 178 B2
- Pant-y-Sais SA10 70 C1
- Pant-Y-Seren CF39 133 B2
- Pantysgallog CF48 11 A7
- Pantysgallog Prim Sch CF48 11 A6
- Pantysgallog Terr CF48 11 B6
- Pan Y Lan Ct NP19 144 A5
- Paper Mill Rd CF11 194 A6
- Parade CF37 109 D2
- Parade The
  - Barry / Y Barri CF62 214 C2
  - Cardiff / Caerdydd, Adamsdown CF24 232 D3
  - Cardiff / Caerdydd, Llandaff North CF14 176 F4
  - Cwmbran / Cwmbrân NP44 89 E3
  - 7 Dinas Powis / Dinas Powys CF64 206 C3
  - Ferndale CF43 79 E7
  - Llantwit Fadre / Llanilltud Faerdref CF38 156 E8
  - Merthyr Tydfil / Merthyr Tudful CF47 10 E1
  - Neath / Castell-Nedd SA11 71 E8
  - Porth CF39 107 F3
  - Treorchy / Treorci CF41 78 F3
- Paradise Cotts SA14 41 D4
- Paradise View SA1 95 A8
- Parc Afon CF40 107 C4
- Parc Amanwy Ind Est SA18 219 B6
- Parc Andrew SA10 70 F6
- Parc Asaleas / Azalea Pk CF48 11 C4
- Parcau Ave CF31 168 C4
- Parcau Rd CF31 168 C4
- Parc Ave
  - Caerphilly / Caerffili CF83 138 C5
  - Cwmbran / Cwmbrân NP44 89 D6
  - Swansea / Abertawe SA6 68 F6
  - Swansea / Abertawe SA6 68 F7
- Parc Bedford Country Park★ CF32 149 A3
- Parc Berwig SA14 41 F2
- Parc Bevan NP11 59 C2
- Parc Bronhaul / Sunhill Pk CF31 168 A3
- Parc Bryn
  - Bryn NP12 85 D3
  - Neath / Castell-Nedd SA10 70 E5
- Parc Bryn Derwen CF72 153 F1
- Parc Bryngelli / Grove Hill Pk SA14 218 C8
- Parc Brynmawr SA15 40 E8
- Parc Bryn Rhos SA18 220 A8
- Parc Bsns Fictoria NP23 14 E4
- Parc Busnes Canolog / Central Bsns Pk SA7 46 C2
- Parc Busnes Coed Cedwyn / Woodlands Bsns Pk SA9 2 D7
- Parc Busnes Cwm Cynon / Cwm Cynon Bsns Pk CF45 54 F1
- Parc Busnes Dyffryn / Duffryn Bsns Pk CF82 111 F6
- Parc Busnes Glan yr Afon / Riverside Bsns Pk SA7 46 B1
- Parc Busnes y Triongl / Triangle Bsns Pk CF48 30 F5
- Parc Bwtrimawr SA18 219 C6
- Parc Bychan NP23 7 E1
- Parc Castell-y-Mynach CF15 174 E8
- Parc Cefn Onn Ctry Pk★ CF14 159 F5
- Parc Clwyd 2 CF63 215 C8
- Parc Cory / Cory Pk NP44 117 B6
- Parc Cotts
  - Bridgend / Pen-y-Bont ar Ogwr CF35 151 B2
  - Senghenydd CF83 110 F2
- Parc Cres CF31 169 F1
- Parc Cwm Darran★ CF81 32 F3
- Parc Cwm Darran Visitor Ctr★ CF81 32 E3
- Parc Cymunedol Penallta / Penallta Community Pk★ CF82 84 C3
- Parc Ddiwydiannol Betws / Betws Ind Pk SA18 219 C7
- Parc Ddiwydiannol Cambrian / Cambrian Ind Pk CF40 106 C6
- Parc Ddwyidiannol Linde / Linde Ind Pk CF48 31 B4
- Parc Deri / Oak Tree Pk CF31 168 D3
- Parc Derlin / Derlin Pk SA18 218 F5
- Parc Derllwyn CF32 150 C6
- Parc Derwen CF82 84 F5
- Parc Diwydiannol Merthyr Tydfil / Merthyr Tydfil Ind Pk CF48 31 B3
- Parc Eirin CF39 132 F4
- Parc Fferws SA18 219 A6
- Parc Gellifaelog CF40 106 E5
- Parc Gitto SA14 41 D4
- Parc Glanffrwd 12 SA18 220 B8
- Parc Glan Yr Afon 2 SA18 220 B8
- Parc Glas
  - Cwmdare CF44 28 D3
  - Neath / Castell-Nedd SA10 70 F6
- Parc Glyn / Vale Pk CF31 168 D3
- Parc Gwledig / Bryngarw Ctry Pk★ CF32 150 E7
- Parc Gwledig Cwm Sirhywi / Sirhowy Valley Ctry Pk★ NP11 113 F2
- Parc Hafod CF14 176 F6
- Parc Hendy Cres SA4 64 F3
- Parc-Henry La / Lon Parc Henri SA18 219 B8
- PARC HOWARD 40 D7
- Parc Howard Art Gall★ SA15 40 D7
- Parc Howard Ave SA15 40 D7
- Parc Howard Mus★ SA15 40 D7
- Parc Ifor Hen CF72 173 E7
- Parc Landwr / Benson Way SA6 69 A6
- Parc Le Breos Burial Chamber★ SA3 120 D8
- Parclewis Prim Sch CF37 135 E8
- Parc Manter Caerbont / Caerbont Ent Pk SA9 222 B6
- Parc Manwerthu Bae Caerdydd / Cardiff Bay Ret Pk
  - Cardiff / Caerdydd CF11 194 F1
  - Cardiff / Caerdydd CF11 206 F8
- Parc Manwerthu Parcnewydd / Newpark District Sh Ctr CF72 155 C2
- Parc Manwerthu Tonysgyboriau / Talbot Green Ret Pk CF72 155 C2
- Parc Masnachol Bsns / Oaklands Bsns Pk CF43 80 A5
- Parc Mawr Cl SA4 44 B2
- Parc Menter SA14 218 C7
- Parc Menter Ynyscedwyn / Ynyscedwyn Ent Pk SA9 2 E8
- Parc Morlais SA14 18 C1
- Parc Nant Celyn CF38 157 A6
- Parc Nantgarw CF15, CF37 136 E1
- Parc Nant-y-felin SA18 219 D7
- Parc Newydd
  - Briton Ferry / Llansawel SA11 71 B3
  - Talbot Green CF72 155 C2
- Parc Onen SA10 70 E6
- Parc Penrhiw SA18 219 C5
- Parc Penscynnor SA10 49 B4
- Parc Plas NP12 85 D6
- Parc Pontypandy CF83 138 C5
- Parc Prim Sch CF42 78 C5
- Parc Rd SA6 68 F6
- Parc Rhosyn / Rose Pk CF34 102 C1
- Parc Richard SA14 41 E4
- Parc St Catwg CF15 175 C8
- Parc St Joseff / St Josephs Pk SA12 98 E2
- Parc Sandringham / Sandringham Pk SA6, SA7 46 C1
- PARC TAWE 233 B3
- Parc Tawe Link Rd SA1 233 B3
- Parc Terr
  - Senghenydd CF83 110 E2
  - Swansea / Abertawe SA6 68 F7
- Parc The CF31 168 F1
- Parc Tir-y-coed / Woodlands Pk SA18 219 C6
- Parc Tredomen / Tredomen Pk CF82 84 D2
- Parc Tredwr / Waterton Pk CF31 169 E2
- Parc Trostre SA14 41 A4
- Parc Ty Glas CF14 177 E7
- Parc Ty Glas Ind Est CF14 177 E7
- Parc-Tyn-y-Waun CF34 128 D6
- Parc Wenallt CF46 83 B7
- Parc Wern SA10 70 F6
- Parc Wern Rd SA2 94 E7
- Parc Wood CF61 208 H5
- Parc-y-Berllan CF36 183 A7
- Parc-y-Bont CF32 150 F6
- Parc-y-Brain Rd
  - Bettws NP20 116 C1
  - Rogerstone NP10 142 B8
- Parc-y-Bryn
  - Creigiau CF15 174 D8
  - Goytre SA13 125 E8
  - Llantwit Fadre / Llanilltud Faerdref CF38 156 D8
- Parc-y-Coed CF15 174 E7
- Parc-y-Delyn SA6 45 B1
- Parc-y-Deri SA10 70 E6
- Parc-y-Duc Terr SA6 68 F7
- Parc-y-Felin CF15 174 D7
- Parc-y-Felin St CF83 138 B4
- Parc-y-Fro CF15 174 E8
- Parc-y-Nant CF15 158 A7

Parc-yr-Helig Rd
Birchgrove SA7 47 B1
Swansea / Abertawe SA7 70 B8
Parc-y-Rhos CF35 170 D8
Parcyrhun SA18 219 B6
Pardoe Cres CF62 214 E6
Pardoe-Thomas Cl 17 NP20 143 C3
Parfitt Cl CF43 80 B4
Parfitt Pl NP12 85 D7
Parfitt St NP19 144 B3
Parfitt Terr
Cwmbran / Cwmbrân NP44 89 D5
2 Merthyr Tydfil / Merthyr Tudful CF47 30 F8
Parish Rd
Beddau CF38 156 A7
Blaengwrach SA11 227 C8
Park Ave
Barry / Y Barri CF62 214 C2
Barry / Y Barri CF62 214 D3
Bedwas CF83 138 E6
Capel Hendre SA18 218 D6
Cardiff / Caerdydd CF14 176 F6
Cardiff / Caerdydd, Culverhouse Cross CF5 193 A2
Glyn-neath / Glyn-nedd SA11 223 C1
Neath / Castell-Nedd SA10 70 C7
Newport / Casnewydd NP20 142 E1
Ogmore Vale CF32 104 E1
Porthcawl CF36 182 E7
Rogerstone / Ty-du NP10 141 F6
The Mumbles / Y Mwmbwls SA3 123 B4
Park Cl
Cwmbran / Cwmbrân NP44 115 F8
Gorseinon SA4 43 B2
Newport / Casnewydd NP20 142 E1
Pontarddulais SA4 19 C3
Pontypridd CF37 135 D6
Swansea / Abertawe, Bon-y-maen SA1 69 B3
Swansea / Abertawe, Cae-mawr SA6 45 E1
Treherbert CF42 50 F1
Park Court Rd CF31 168 D4
Park Cres
Bargoed / Bargod CF81 57 F3
Barry / Y Barri CF62 214 C4
Brynmawr NP23 8 B4
Cardiff / Caerdydd CF14 176 F6
Clydach NP7 9 E7
Llanelli SA15 40 C5
Merthyr Tydfil / Merthyr Tudful CF47 10 E1
Neath / Castell-Nedd SA10 70 C7
Newport / Casnewydd NP20 142 E1
Pontyclun CF72 173 A7
Pontypool / Pont-y-pwl NP4 62 D7
Porth CF39 107 E3
Treharris CF46 83 B7
Treorchy / Treorci CF42 78 D5
Park Ct
Abercarn NP11 114 B8
Barry / Y Barri CF62 214 C3
Bridgend / Pen-y-Bont ar Ogwr CF31 168 D4
Parkdale View CF72 155 E2
Park Dr
Bargoed / Bargod CF81 57 F3
Neath / Castell-Nedd SA10 70 C7
Newport / Casnewydd NP20 142 F1
Swansea / Abertawe SA2 94 F7
Park End NP18 145 C8
Park End Ct CF23 178 A6
Park End La CF23 178 A6
Parker Pl CF5 193 B4
Parker Rd CF5 193 B4
Parke's La NP4 62 A6
Park Eynon 6 SA15 40 D5
Park Field SA11 49 D3
Parkfield Ho CF14 177 E1
Parkfield Pl
Cardiff / Caerdydd CF14 177 E1
Newport / Casnewydd NP20 143 A5
Parkfield Rd CF44 29 D1
Parkfields CF31 168 D8
Parkfields Rd CF31 168 D4
Park Gdns
Blaenavon NP4 17 C6
Newport / Casnewydd NP20 142 E1
Pontypool / Pont-y-pwl NP4 62 C7
Park Gr
Aberdare / Aberdâr CF44 28 F3
Cardiff / Caerdydd CF10 232 C4
Park Hill
Mountain Ash / Aberpennar, Darrenlas CF45 54 D3
11 Mountain Ash / Aberpennar, Miskin CF45 54 E1
Park Hill *continued*
Tredegar NP22 13 D5
Parkhill Cres NP23 7 E3
Parkhill Rd SA5 68 C5
Parkhill Terr SA5 68 C5
Park Ho 8 SA13 125 C7
Park House Flats NP4 62 C7
Park Howard Rd SA18 220 D6
Park La
Aberdare / Aberdâr CF44 28 E4
Abergwynfi SA13 76 C5
Blaengwynfi SA13 76 B6
Caerphilly / Caerffili CF83 138 A2
Cardiff / Caerdydd CF14 176 F6
Groes-faen CF72 174 B7
Llangennech SA14 42 C8
Taffs Well / Ffynnon Taf CF15 157 F4
Tonyrefail CF39 133 B4
Tredomen CF82 84 D1
Treharris CF46 83 A6
Park La / Lon Y Parc
Brynamman SA18 220 D8
Cardiff / Caerdydd CF10 232 C3
Parkland Cres CF39 133 C5
Parkland Prim Sch SA2 94 B6
Parkland Rd CF39 133 C5
Parklands
Blackwood / Coed-Duon NP12 85 E8
Corntown / Corntwn CF35 186 B7
Penperlleni NP4 39 F7
Park Lands CF24 195 C5
Parklands Cl
Cwmbran / Cwmbrân NP44 89 E6
Rogerstone NP10 142 C3
Parklands Ct
Ammanford / Rhydaman SA18 219 A6
Swansea / Abertawe SA2 94 B6
Parklands Rd / Heol Tir-y-Parc SA18 219 A7
Parklands View SA2 94 B5
Parkland Wlk CF62 214 C4
Park Lane Specl Sch CF44 28 E3
Parklawn Cl NP44 89 E6
PARKMILL 120 F7
Park Mill Rd SA18 219 A7
Park Pl
Abercarn NP11 114 C5
Abertillery / Abertyleri NP13 36 B5
Bargoed / Bargod CF81 58 A2
Bargoed / Bargod CF81 58 A3
Ebbw Vale / Glyn Ebwy NP23 14 F2
Maerdy CF43 52 A2
Merthyr Tydfil / Merthyr Tudful CF47 10 E2
Newbridge / Trecelyn NP11 86 F7
Pontypridd CF37 109 F6
Risca / Rhisga NP11 115 A1
Swansea / Abertawe SA2 94 E5
Tonypandy CF40 106 E6
Tredegar NP22 13 F5
Treherbert CF42 50 F2
Troedyrhiw CF48 55 C8
Park Pl / Plas Y Parc
Cardiff / Caerdydd CF10 232 B4
Sarn CF32 150 F4
Park Prim Sch CF81 57 F3
Park Prospect CF37 109 B2
Park Rd
Abercynon CF45 82 E3
Aberdare / Aberdâr CF44 53 C7
Aberkenfig / Abercynffig CF32 150 C3
Bargoed / Bargod CF81 57 F4
Barry / Y Barri CF62 214 C3
Cardiff / Caerdydd CF14 176 F6
Clydach SA6 46 E8
Dinas Powis / Dinas Powys CF64 206 A4
Ebbw Vale / Glyn Ebwy, Garden City NP23 14 D4
Ebbw Vale / Glyn Ebwy, Victoria NP23 14 E3
Ferndale CF43 80 A5
Gorseinon SA4 43 B2
Gowerton / Tre-gwyr SA4 66 C4
Hengoed CF82 85 A2
Maerdy CF43 52 A2
Maesycwmmer CF82 85 A1
Newbridge / Trecelyn NP11 86 F7
Penarth CF64 207 B3
Pen-clawdd SA4 64 E4
Pontypool / Pont-y-pwl NP4 62 C7
Radyr CF15 176 B6
Risca / Rhisga NP11 115 A1
Southgate SA3 121 A5
Tonypandy CF40 107 A4
Treorchy / Treorci CF42 78 B4
Ynystawe SA6 46 C4
Park Road Ind Est NP11 115 A1
Park Row
Cwmavon / Cwmafan SA12 99 E6
Tredegar NP22 13 E6
Park Row Gdns CF47 10 D3
Park St / Stryd Parc CF31 168 E4
Park St / Stryd Y Parc
Ammanford / Rhydaman SA18 219 C6
Brynamman SA18 220 D8
Skewen / Sclwen SA10 71 A7
Parkside NP44 89 D2
Parkside Ct
2 Cardiff / Caerdydd CF5 194 C6
19 Pontypool / Pont-y-pwl NP4 38 A1
Park Side La CF37 109 C1
Park Slip Nature Park★ CF32 149 F5
Park Sq NP20 143 C4
Park St
Abercarn, Crosskeys NP11 114 B5
Abercarn, Cwmcarn NP11 114 C8
Abercynon CF45 82 D1
Blaenavon NP4 17 C6
Bridgend / Pen-y-Bont ar Ogwr CF31 168 D4
Cardiff / Caerdydd CF10 232 B2
Glyncorrwg SA13 227 C1
Llanelli SA15 40 D5
Maesteg CF34 102 B2
Mountain Ash / Aberpennar CF45 81 E8
Nant-y-Moel CF32 104 F5
Neath / Castell-Nedd SA11 71 F8
Pontycymer CF32 103 F4
Pontypool / Pont-y-pwl NP4 62 E2
Pontypridd CF37 135 E7
Porth CF39 107 D4
Port Talbot SA13 125 C7
Pyle / Y Pîl CF33 148 C2
Swansea / Abertawe SA1 233 A3
The Mumbles / Y Mwmbwls SA3 123 B5
Tonna / Tonnau SA11 49 D3
Tonypandy CF40 106 B6
Tylorstown CF43 80 B4
Parkstone Ave CF3 179 E8
Park Terr
Blackwood / Coed-Duon NP12 85 F6
Llanharan CF72 153 F3
Merthyr Tydfil / Merthyr Tudful CF47 10 D2
Pentrebach CF48 31 A4
Pontarddulais SA4 19 D2
7 Pontypool / Pont-y-pwl NP4 38 A1
Swansea / Abertawe SA1 68 C1
Ton-du CF32 150 B5
Trelewis CF46 83 D6
Treorchy / Treorci CF42 78 B5
Park The
Blaenavon NP4 17 C7
Swansea / Abertawe SA2 94 A7
Treharris CF46 83 B7
Park View
Abercarn NP11 114 B5
Abercynon CF45 82 E4
Abertillery / Abertyleri NP13 36 A5
Bargoed / Bargod CF81 57 E3
Bassaleg NP10 142 B3
Bridgend / Pen-y-Bont ar Ogwr, Brynhyfryd CF31 168 B5
Bridgend / Pen-y-Bont ar Ogwr, Coychurch / Llangrallo CF35 169 F4
Bryncae CF72 154 A2
Brynmawr NP23 8 B4
Cwmaman CF44 53 A3
Cwmbran / Cwmbrân NP44 89 E6
Cwmfelin CF34 128 C8
Ebbw Vale / Glyn Ebwy NP23 7 D4
2 Llanbradach CF83 111 F1
Llantrisant CF72 155 D3
Loughor SA4 65 D8
Maesteg CF34 102 C1
Nantyglo NP13 15 E7
Pontypool / Pont-y-pwl NP4 62 D5
Port Talbot SA13 125 C7
Swansea / Abertawe SA1 95 A5
Ton Pentre CF41 79 A3
Tredegar NP22 13 D6
Tylorstown CF43 80 C3
Wattstown CF39 107 E8
Park View Bglws
Blackwood / Coed-Duon NP12 85 F7
Blackwood / Coed Duon NP12 86 A7
Park View Cl / Clos Golwg Y Parc 1 SA11 71 C1
Parkview Ct CF64 206 E5
Park View Ct
2 Cardiff / Caerdydd CF11 194 F5
11 Cardiff / Caerdydd, Whitchurch CF14 177 A6
Park View Gdns NP10 142 B3
Park View St NP23 14 F2
Park View Terr
Abercwmboi CF44 53 E5
Aberdare / Aberdâr CF44 29 B3
Merthyr Tydfil / Merthyr Tudful CF48 29 F8
Pontypool / Pont-y-pwl NP4 61 F8
Swansea / Abertawe SA2 94 D6
Parkview Terr / Trem Y Parc SA15 40 C5
Park View / Trem-y-parc
1 NP4 38 A1
Parkville NP22 13 E5
Parkwall Rd CF14, CF23 161 A3
Parkway
Blackwood / Coed Duon NP11 59 D5
Cardiff / Caerdydd CF3 179 D2
Park Way SA2 94 B6
Parkwood SA4 66 C4
Parkwood Cl NP18 117 E3
Parkwood Dr NP10 141 E2
Parkwood Hts CF31 168 C3
Park Y Brain La NP4 39 D7
Parracombe Cl CF3 179 C7
Parracombe Cres CF3 179 C7
Parr Ave SA11 71 F8
Parret Cl NP20 116 F2
Parret Rd NP20 116 F2
Parret Wlk NP20 116 F2
Parrish Pl CF83 110 F2
Parrot Row NP13 15 D7
Parry Bldgs NP11 86 F6
Parry Cl SA10 71 B8
Parry Dr NP19 144 C5
Parry Jones Cl NP13 15 D5
Parry Rd SA6 45 E1
Parry Rd / Heol Parry SA12 98 B3
Parrys Dr CF45 82 C5
Parry St
5 Cardiff / Caerdydd CF5 194 C6
Pontygwaith CF43 80 B2
Ton Pentre CF41 79 A3
Treorchy / Treorci CF41 78 F3
Parry Terr NP11 59 F1
Parsons La SA11 49 C2
Parson's Row NP13 15 D5
Partridge Ave CF40 106 F8
Partridge Ct 5 CF24 195 D7
Partridge La CF24 195 D7
Partridge Rd
Abertillery / Abertyleri NP13 60 A6
Cardiff / Caerdydd CF24 195 C7
St Athan / Sain Tathan CF62 210 E6
Tonypandy CF40 79 F1
Partridge Row NP23 7 C4
Partridge Sq CF40 106 F8
Partridge St CF41 79 A3
Partridge Way NP10 163 F7
Part St NP13 15 E3
Pascal Cl CF3 180 B8
Pascall Ct CF24 232 D4
Pascoes Ave CF31 168 E5
Pasteur Gr CF38 135 D1
Pastoral Way SA2 94 B8
Pastures The
Barry / Y Barri CF62 214 E7
Llanyrafon NP44 90 B3
Patagonia Wlk 4 SA1 233 B1
Pat Chown Ct / Llys Pat Chown SA8 23 E4
Patch The CF72 172 B6
Patchway Cres CF3 179 A4
Patmore Cl CF15 157 F4
Patreane Way CF5 192 F3
Patricia Cl 27 CF47 30 E8
Patterdale Cl CF23 178 B2
Patti Cl NP19 144 F6
Patti Ho 8 SA12 98 F1
Pavaland Cl 5 CF3 179 F6
Pavia Ct CF37 109 C1
Paviland Pl SA5 67 F5
Pavilion Ct CF36 182 F6
Pavilion Est NP4 62 A8
Pavilion Ind Est CF45 54 D2
Pavillion Bldgs CF40 106 C6
Pavin Ct CF5 177 A1
Paxton Cl CF82 84 E7
Paxton Dr SA1 233 A1
Paxton St SA1 233 A2
Paxton Wlk NP10 142 A7
Payne St 1 SA11 71 D6
Peacehaven NP22 14 A3
Peacehaven Ct NP22 14 A3
Peach Pl 2 CF5 193 D8
Pearce Cl CF3 180 A5
Pearce Ct CF63 215 A8
Pearce's Ct CF48 10 A5
Pearl Ct CF24 195 E7
Pearl Pl CF24 195 D6
Pearl St
Cardiff / Caerdydd, Splott CF24 195 D6
Cardiff / Caerdydd, Tremorfa CF24 195 E7
Clydach SA6 46 F8
Pearson Cres CF37 109 D5
Pearson St CF24 232 D4
Pear Tree Cl NP18 117 E2
Pear Tree La NP19 144 B3
Pease La CF47 30 E7
Peckham Cl CF5 176 D3
Pedair Erw Rd CF14 177 D5
Pedrog Terr SA1 68 B1
Pegler St SA5 68 C3
Pelican St SA9 1 F2
Pellau Rd / Heol Pellau SA13 125 E5
Pellett St CF10 232 C2
Pell St SA1 233 A3
PEMBERTON 41 B5
Pemberton Pk SA14 41 C6
Pemberton Rd SA14 41 C5
Pemberton St SA15 40 D4
Pembrey Gdns NP12 86 A4
Pembrey Path NP44 89 C3
Pembrey Rd SA15 40 C6
Pembridge Dr CF64 206 F5
Pembroke Bldgs 5 SA1 233 C2
Pembroke Cl
Blackwood / Coed-Duon NP12 58 D1
Church Village CF38 135 F2
4 Dinas Powis / Dinas Powys CF64 206 C3
Merthyr Tydfil / Merthyr Tudful CF48 225 F1
Ystrad CF41 79 D3
Pembroke Cres CF72 155 A5
Pembroke Ct
Caerphilly / Caerffili CF83 137 D4
6 Cardiff / Caerdydd CF14 177 A6
Pembroke Gr NP19 144 A2
Pembroke Ho SA12 124 D8
Pembroke Mews CF5 194 B6
Pembroke Pl
Barry / Y Barri CF63 214 F6
Llantwit Major / Llanilltud Fawr CF61 210 B6
Llanyrafon NP44 90 B3
Merthyr Tydfil / Merthyr Tudful CF47 10 F3
4 Swansea / Abertawe SA1 233 C2
Pembroke Rd CF5 194 C6
Pembroke St
Aberdare / Aberdâr CF44 29 A2
Swansea / Abertawe SA5 68 B3
Tredegar NP22 6 C1
Troedyrhiw CF48 31 C2
Pembroke Terr
10 Aberavon SA12 124 F8
Cwmavon NP4 17 E1
Nant-y-Moel CF32 104 F6
Penarth CF64 207 B5
Pembrook St CF39 133 B2
PENALLT 40 F6
Penallt
Dunvant SA2 93 E8
Llanelly Hill NP7 9 D5
Penallta Community Pk / Parc Cymunedol Penallta★ CF82 84 C3
Penallta Ind Est CF82 84 D5
Penallta Rd CF82 84 E3
Penallta Villas CF82 84 E3
Penallt Rd SA15 40 F6
Penallt Terr SA15 40 F6
Penally Rd CF5 193 E4
PENARTH 207 C3
Penarth Ct / Cwrt Penarth 5 NP44 90 B1
Penarth Head La CF64 207 B4
Penarth Portway CF64 207 B5
Penarth Rd CF11 206 E7
Penarth Rd / Heol Penarth CF11 194 E2
Penarth Road Ret Pk CF11 206 D7
Penarth Sta CF64 207 A3
Penbedw NP44 90 B4
Penbryn Coch CF72 172 C6
Pen Bryn Hendy CF72 173 C7
Penbryn Rd SA10 70 F7
Penbryn Terr SA2 94 F5
Pencader Rd CF5 193 E6
Pen-Cae-Crwn Rd SA4 43 A3
PENCAERAU 71 E4
Pencaerfenni Ct SA4 64 B3
Pencaerfenni La SA4 64 B3
Pencaerfenni Pk SA4 64 B3
Pencae Terr SA15 40 F5
Pencai Terr CF42 78 D5
Pencarn Ave NP10 163 C6
Pencarn La NP10 163 E5
Pencarn Way NP10 163 D6
Pen-Cefn-Arda Rd SA4 43 B4
PENCEILIOGI 41 D6
Pencerrig St
Llanbradach CF83 111 F1
Pontypridd CF37 109 B1
Pencisely Ave CF5 194 A7
Pencisely Cres CF5 194 A7
Pencisely Rd CF5 194 B7
Pencisely Rise CF5 194 B7
PEN-CLAWDD 64 E3
Penclawdd CF83 138 D5
Penclawdd Prim Sch SA4 64 E4
Penclawdd Rd SA4 65 C5
PENCOED 170 C7
Pencoed
Dunvant SA2 93 E8
Tredegar NP22 13 D6

Pencoed Ave
Blackwood / Coed-Duon NP12 85 C8
Pontypridd CF37 109 E1
Pencoed Coll / Coleg Pencoed CF35 170 F8
Pencoed Comp Sch CF35 170 E7
Pencoed Inf Sch CF35 152 E1
Pen Coed Isaf Rd / Heol Pencoed Isaf SA14 42 B4
Pencoed Jun Sch CF35 152 E1
Pencoed Pl / Maes Pencoed 4 NP44 89 F6
Pencoed Sta CF35 170 D8
Pencoedtre Rd
Barry / Y Barri, Cadoxton CF63 215 B8
Barry / Y Barri CF62, CF63 205 A1
Pencwmdu SA8 221 A1
Pendarren SA8 221 B1
Pen Darren CF39 107 C1
Pendarren St
Aberdare / Aberdâr CF44 28 F1
Pen-pedair-heol CF82 84 E8
Pendarvis St SA12 98 E1
Pendarvis Terr 6 SA12 124 F8
Pendderi Rd SA14 41 F5
Pen-Deri Cl NP12 59 C1
Penderri Rd SA14 42 A4
Penderry Rd SA5 68 B4
PENDERYN 224 E3
Penderyn Ave / Rhodfa Penderyn SA13 125 E5
Penderyn Pl CF44 53 B8
Penderyn Prim Sch CF44 224 E3
Penderyn Rd
Cymmer / Cymer SA13 75 D3
Hirwaun CF44 27 C8
PENDEULWYN / PENDOYLAN 190 F6
Pen Dinas CF40 107 B4
Pendinas Ave NP11 59 D2
Pendine Cl CF62 214 F8
Pendine Rd CF5 193 E6
Pendine Wlk NP44 89 B2
Pendoylan Cl CF63 215 B8
Pendoylan Ct
11 Cardiff / Caerdydd, Caerau CF5 193 C4
Cardiff / Caerdydd, Ely / Trelai CF5 193 E6
Pendoylan CW Prim Sch CF71 190 F6
PENDOYLAN / PENDEULWYN 190 F6
Pendoylan Wlk NP44 89 C1
Pendragon Cl CF14 159 D2
Pendraw Pl CF23 178 B6
PENDRE 168 F7
Pendre CF31 168 F7
Pendre Cres CF72 153 F3
Pendrill St SA11 71 D6
Pendwyallt Rd CF14 176 E7
Pendyris St CF11 232 A1
Pendyrus Ct CF43 80 C4
Penedre CF5 177 A1
Penffordd CF15 175 C8
PENFILIA 68 C5
Penfilia Rd SA5 68 C4
Penfilia Terr 3 SA5 68 C4
Penford Ct CF24 232 C4
PENGAM 85 B7
PENGAM GREEN 196 B6
Pengam Prim Sch NP12 85 B7
Pengam Rd
Blackwood / Coed-Duon NP12 58 B2
Cardiff / Caerdydd CF24 195 F8
Pengam NP12 85 B8
Pen-pedair-heol CF82, NP12 84 F8
Ystrad Mynach CF82 84 F2
Pengam St NP12 85 A7
Pengam Sta NP12 85 A8
PENGARNDDU 11 C6
Pengelli Prim Sch SA4 43 C6
Pengeulan Prim Sch CF45 54 E1
Pengorof Ct SA9 1 E1
Pengors Rd SA5 45 B2
Pengry Rd SA4 42 F1
Pen Gurnos CF47 10 C5
Pen Gwern CF35 152 D1
Pengwern Rd
Cardiff / Caerdydd CF5 193 E6
Swansea / Abertawe SA6 68 C8
Pen Hendy CF72 173 C7
Penheol Ely Rd CF37 109 F2
Penheolferthyr CF47 11 A1
Pen Heol-Shenkyn NP12 58 D5
Penhevad St CF11 194 F2
Penhill Cl CF5 194 C7
Pen-Hill Rd CF11 194 C7
Penhow Mews NP10 163 E5
Penhydd Ho SA12 100 A8
Penhydd Rd SA13 75 D3
Pen-Hydd St SA12 73 A1
Penhydd-waelod Cotts SA13 100 C4
PEN-IARD / PENYARD 10 F2
PENIEL GREEN 69 F8
Peniel Green Rd SA7 70 A8
Peniel Rd SA5 68 D5
Pen Isa Coed SA1 95 F7
Penkin Cl NP19 144 D4
Penkin Hill NP19 144 D4
PEN-LAN 68 A5
Penlan SA14 42 A6
Penlan Cres SA2 94 F7
Penlan Fach SA5 68 C4
Penlan Gr SA5 68 B5
Penlan Rd
Llandough / Llandochau CF64 206 D6
Loughor SA4 42 F1
Neath / Castell-Nedd SA10 70 D8
Swansea / Abertawe SA5 68 C6
Penlan Rise CF64 206 D6
Penlan St CF48 31 B4
Penlan Terr SA5 68 C6
Penlan View CF48 30 C8
Penlas NP23 14 B8
Pen Lasgan CF3 179 F6
PENLLERGAER 44 A2
Penllergaer Bsns Pk SA4 44 D3
Penllergaer Forest Walks* SA4 44 D4
Penllergaer Prim Sch SA4 44 B3
Pen Llew Ct CF44 28 D3
Penlline Ct CF14 177 A5
Penlline Rd CF14 177 A5
Penlline St CF24 232 C4
PENLLWYN 85 E4
Pen-Llwyn Ave NP12 85 F4
Pen Llwyn / Grove Head CF31 168 D3
Penllwyngwent Ind Est CF32 104 E3
Penllwyngwent Starter Units CF32 104 E2
Penllwyngwyn Farm Dr SA14 41 F6
Penllwyngwyn Rd SA14 42 A6
Penllwyn La
Machen CF83 139 D7
Pontllanfraith NP12 85 F4
Pen-Llwyn-March Rd SA5 68 A3
Penllwyn Prim Sch NP12 85 E4
Penllwynrhodyn Rd SA14 41 E4
Penllwyn St NP11 113 A4
Penllwyn Terr 1 NP12 85 F4
Penllwyn Wlk CF83 139 C7
PENLLYN 188 A5
Penllyn SA12 99 E5
Penllyn Ave
Cwmbran / Cwmbrân NP44 89 E6
Newport / Casnewydd NP20 142 F4
Penllyn La NP20 142 F4
Penllyn Rd CF5 194 D5
Pen Locks CF46 83 A5
Penmachno SA6 45 D1
PENMAEN
Blackwood 86 A8
Southgate 120 B6
Penmaen Ave NP12 59 B2
Penmaen Burrows Burial Chamber* SA3 120 C5
Penmaen Cl CF82 84 F5
Penmaen Cnr NP12 59 A1
Penmaen Est NP12 86 A8
Penmaen Ind Est NP12 85 F5
Penmaen Rd NP12 86 A5
Pen Maen / Rock Head CF31 168 D3
Penmaen Small Bsns Ctr NP12 86 A5
Penmaen Terr SA1 95 B7
Penmaen Villas NP12 86 A8
Penmaen Wlk CF5 192 F3
Penmaes CF15 175 C8
Penmaesglas Terr 2 CF40 106 F4
Penmaes Rd NP44 88 F3
Penmain St CF39 107 E4
PEN-MARC / PENMARK 212 F6
Penmark Gn CF5 193 A4
PENMARK / PEN-MARC 212 F6
Penmark Rd CF5 193 A4
Penmark Row CF44 27 C8
Penmynydd SA4 43 B1
Pen-Mynydd NP4 17 D7
Penmynydd Rd SA5 68 B5
Pennant Cres CF23 178 C6
Pennant St NP23 14 D8
Pennar Cl NP11 86 E6
PENNARD 121 C6
Pennard Dr SA3 121 A6
Pennard Pl CF14 177 D3
Pennard Prim Sch SA3 121 A5
Pennard Rd
Bishopston SA3 121 E7
Southgate SA3 121 B5
Pennard St SA5 68 C3
Pennar La NP11 86 D6
Pennar St NP11 86 F6
Pennine Cl
Cardiff / Caerdydd CF14 177 E7
Risca / Rhisga NP11 115 D1
Swansea / Abertawe SA5 67 E3
Penn St CF46 83 B7
Pennsylvania CF23 178 D5
Penny Cres NP20 116 F3
Pennyfields 8 NP44 89 B3
Penny La CF71 188 F2
Pennyroyal Cl CF3 180 A8
Pen Onnen CF31 169 C5
Pen Parcau CF32 129 D3
PEN-PEDAIR-HEOL 84 D8
Pen Pentre SA10 226 A7
PENPERLLENI 39 F6
Penpisgah Rd CF40 106 F4
Penplas Rd
Swansea / Abertawe, Cadle SA5 67 E7
Swansea / Abertawe SA5 67 F8
Penpound La / Lon Penpound SA18 219 F8
PEN-PRYSG 152 F2
Penprysg Rd CF35 152 E1
Penprys Rd SA14 41 E7
Pen-Pych Cl CF42 50 D3
Penpych Com Prim Sch CF42 50 D3
PENRHIW 115 A3
Pen-Rhiw Ave NP12 59 B1
Pen-Rhiw Bengi La NP12 59 B2
PENRHIWCEIBER 82 A8
Penrhiwceiber Rd CF45 54 E1
Penrhiwceiber Sta CF45 82 A8
Penrhiwceibr Prim Sch CF45 81 F8
Pen-rhiw Est NP13 60 A8
PEN-RHIW-FAWR 221 B5
Penrhiwfer Ct CF39 133 B5
Penrhiwfer Inf Sch CF40 133 A8
Penrhiw-Fer Rd
Tonypandy CF40 107 A1
Tonyrefail CF40 133 B7
Penrhiwgarreg NP13 36 C4
Pen-Rhiw-Garreg Rd NP13 36 C5
Penrhiw Goch SA12 98 C8
Penrhiwgwynt Rd CF39 107 F3
Penrhiw La CF83 140 A8
Penrhiw Rd
Pontypridd CF37 135 B7
Risca / Rhisga NP11 115 A2
Swansea / Abertawe SA6 45 D2
Ton Pentre CF41 79 A2
Penrhiw St SA13 100 E5
Pen-Rhiw Terr
Abercarn NP11 87 C3
Blackwood / Coed Duon NP12 59 A2
PENRHIWTYN 71 C5
Penrhiwtyn Dr / Rhodfa Penrhiwtyn SA11 71 C4
Penrhiwtyn St SA11 71 C4
PENRHOS 222 B6
Penrhos
Gorseinon SA4 43 A1
Radyr CF15 176 A7
Penrhos Cres CF3 179 C4
Penrhos Cty Prim Sch SA9 222 A6
Penrhos Dr NP18 118 C3
Penrhos Pl SA5 67 F4
Penrhyn Ave SA5 68 B4
Penrhyn Cl CF3 179 E5
Penrhyn Ct SA6 46 A3
Penrhyn St SA13 125 D6
Penrhyn Terr NP24 33 F3
PENRHYS 80 B2
Penrhys Ave CF43 80 B2
Penrhys Prim Sch CF43 80 A2
Penrhys Rd
Pontygwaith CF43 80 B2
Ystrad CF41 79 F2
Penrhys Sp Ctr CF43 80 A2
Penrhys Uchaf CF43 80 B2
PENRICE 231 D6
Penrice Ct SA6 69 A6
Penrice Ct 1 SA1 233 A4
Penrice Forest Wlks* SA3 231 C7
Penrice Gn 9 NP44 90 B2
Penrice St SA6 45 F1
Penryce Ct SA1 233 B2
Penry Pl SA15 40 E5
Penry St CF48 10 D1
Pensalem Rd SA5 68 B5
Pensarn Rd CF3 179 E5
Pensarn Way NP44 115 F8
Penscynor SA10 49 B3
Penscynor La SA10 49 B3
Penshannel
Neath Abbey SA10 47 F1
Neath / Castell-Nedd SA10 70 F8
Pensidan View NP10 141 F2
Penstone Ct CF10 195 B2
Pentewan Cl SA6 46 A4
Pentip CW Prim Sch SA15 40 C6
Pentir Y De CF62 213 C1
Pentland Cl
Cardiff / Caerdydd CF14 177 D7
Risca / Rhisga NP11 115 D1
Swansea / Abertawe SA5 67 D4
Pent-Lee CF23 178 E7
Pentonville NP20 143 B5
PENTRAPEOD 59 D7
PENTRE 68 D2
Pentre CF72 155 A5
Pentre Afan SA12 98 C3
PENTREBACH
Merthyr Tydfil 31 B4
Pontypridd 135 E8
Pentre Bach SA5 67 F3
Pentrebach Ind Est CF48 31 A5
Pentrebach Rd
Merthyr Tydfil / Merthyr Tudful CF48 30 F6
Pontypridd CF37 135 E8
Pentrebach Sta CF48 30 F4
Pentre Banadl SA2 93 E7
PENTREBANE 193 C8
Pentrebane Prim Sch CF5 193 C8
Pentrebane Rd CF5 176 B1
Pentrebane St
Caerphilly / Caerffili CF83 138 A2
Cardiff / Caerdydd CF11 194 F2
Pentrebeili Pl CF32 130 E5
Pentrebeili Terr CF32 130 E5
PENTRE-CHWYTH 69 A2
Pentrechwyth Prim Sch / Ysgol Gynradd Pentrechwyth SA1 69 A3
Pentrechwyth Rd SA1 68 F2
Pentre-Chwyth Rd SA1 69 A3
Pentre Cl NP44 116 B8
Pentre Ct CF41 79 A4
Pentre Doc Y Gogledd SA15 40 B4
Pentre-Dwr Rd SA7 69 E5
Pentre Fedwen SA11 72 B5
PENTREFFYNNON 70 F6
Pentre Gdns CF11 232 A1
Pentregethin Rd SA5 67 E5
Pentreguinea Rd SA1 233 C4
Pentrehafod Sch / Ysgol Pentrehafod SA1 68 D3
Pentre Howell CF35 170 E8
Pentre La NP4 39 C4
Pentre La / Lon Pentre NP44 116 E5
Pentremalwed Rd SA6 68 F7
Pentre Mawr Rd SA1 68 D2
PENTRE MEYRICK 187 F4
PENTREPIOD / PENTRE-PIOD 37 E1
PENTRE-PIOD / PENTREPOID 37 E1
Pentrepiod Rd NP4 37 F1
Pentre Pl
3 Cardiff / Caerdydd CF11 194 F3
Pyle / Y Pîl CF33 148 C2
PENTRE-POETH
Llanelli 40 D8
Newport 141 F2
Pentre-Poeth Cl NP10 141 E2
Pentrepoeth Cty Prim Sch NP10 141 F3
Pentrepoeth Jun & Inf Schs SA6 46 A1
Pentrepoeth Rd
Llanelli SA15 40 D8
Swansea / Abertawe SA6 45 F2
Pentre-Poeth Rd NP10 141 E2
Pentrepoeth School Rd SA6 46 A1
Pentre Prim Sch CF41 78 F5
Pentre Rd
Maerdy CF43 52 A1
Pontarddulais SA4 19 C2
Treorchy / Treorci CF41 78 F5
Pentre St
Cardiff / Caerdydd CF11 194 F3
Glyn-neath SA11 227 C8
Pentre Tai Rd NP10 141 E5
Pentre-Treharne Hill SA1 68 D4
Pentre-Treharne Rd SA1 68 D3
Pentre Wern SA13 125 D5
PENT-TWYN 37 E3
PENTWYN
Cardiff 178 E7
Rhymney 32 D5
PEN-TWYN 59 E6
Pentwyn
Bryn-côch SA10 48 B4
Caerphilly / Caerffili CF83 137 E6
Ebbw Vale / Glyn Ebwy NP23 14 C7
Heolgerrig CF48 10 A1
Neath / Castell-Nedd SA11 71 E5
Radyr CF15 176 A6
Three Crosses SA4 65 E1
Pentwyn Ave
Blackwood / Coed-Duon NP12 85 E8
Mountain Ash / Aberpennar CF45 82 A6
Pentwyn Baglan Rd SA12 98 E5
PENTWYN BERTHLWYD 83 C5
Pentwyn Ct
Blackwood / Coed-Duon NP12 85 E8
Cardiff / Caerdydd CF14 177 A7
Penywaun CF44 28 A6
Pentwyn Deintyr CF46 83 A4
Pentwyn Dr
Baglan SA12 98 E5
Cardiff / Caerdydd CF23 178 F7
Pentwyngwyn Rd CF83 139 B4
Pentwyn Hts NP4 37 F3
Pentwyn Isaf
Blaina / Blaenau NP13 15 E4
Caerphilly / Caerffili CF83 137 F6
Pentwyn Isaf Rise CF83 137 F6
Pentwyn La NP4 37 F3
Pen-Twyn La NP20 116 E3
Pentwyn Link Rd CF3, CF23 161 B2
Pentwynmawr Prim Sch NP11 86 D5
Pentwyn Prim Sch NP4 37 E3
Pentwyn Rd
Abertillery / Abertyleri NP11 59 F5
Blackwood / Coed-Duon NP12 85 E7
Cardiff / Caerdydd CF23 178 E8
Cynonville SA13 74 B3
Pencoed CF35 152 E1
Quakers Yard CF46 83 C4
Resolven / Resolfen SA11 226 E5
Ystalyfera SA9 2 B7
Pen-Twyn Rd CF41, CF42 78 E4
Pentwyn Rd / Ffordd Pen Twyn SA18 219 C7
Pentwyn Rd / Heol Pentwyn NP4 37 F2
Pentwyn Terr
Abersychan NP4 37 F3
Abertillery / Abertyleri NP11 59 F6
Marshfield CF3 180 E8
Pentwyn Villas CF47 10 D3
Pentyla
Maesteg CF34 101 F4
Neath / Castell-Nedd SA10 70 F7
Pentyla-Baglan Rd SA12 99 A2
Pentyla Gdns CF32 150 E3
Pentyla Rd SA2 94 E8
Pen Tyntyla CF43 80 A2
PENTYRCH 175 C8
Pentyrch Prim Sch CF15 175 B8
Pentyrch St CF24 177 F1
Penuel Cl SA4 43 A1
Penuel La CF37 109 C1
Penuel Rd CF15 175 B8
Penuel St 1 CF47 30 F8
PENYARD / PEN-IARD 10 F2
Penyard Rd
Hirwaun CF44 224 E1
Merthyr Tydfil / Merthyr Tudful CF47 10 E2
Neath Abbey SA10 71 B8
PENYBANC 219 A6
Pen-y-Banc
Bridgend / Pen-y-Bont ar Ogwr CF31 169 A4
Cwmavon SA12 100 A7
Porth CF39 107 D1
Seven Sisters / Blaendulais SA10 222 C3
Penybanc La SA4 43 A4
Pen-y-Banc Rd SA18 219 A6
Pen-y-Bigyn SA15 40 E4
PEN-Y-BONT 36 C7
Pen-y-Bont
Crynant SA10 222 A1
Pen-pedair-heol CF82 84 D8
Tredegar NP22 6 C2
PEN-Y-BONT AR OGWR / BRIDGEND 168 C7
Penybont Ind Est CF31 168 F6
Penybont Prim Sch CF31 168 F5
Penybont Rd
Pencoed CF35 170 E8
Pencoed, Pen-prysg CF35 152 F1
Pen-y-Bont Rd NP13 36 B7
PENYBRYN 84 C5
PEN-Y-BRYN 148 D6
Penybryn
Llanelli SA14 41 E6
Merthyr Tydfil / Merthyr Tudful CF47 10 F4
Pontycymer CF32 103 E3
Pen-y-Bryn
Barry / Y Barri CF62 214 B2
Bridgend / Pen-y-Bont ar Ogwr CF31 168 C5
Caerphilly / Caerffili CF83 137 E6
Cwmllynfell SA9 221 B7
Cymmer / Cymer SA13 75 C3
Maesteg CF34 102 B8

Pen-y-Bryn *continued*
Neath / Castell-Nedd, Mount Pleasant SA11 ... 71 F5
Neath / Castell-Nedd, Pen-yr-Heol SA10 ... 70 E6
Pontypool / Pont-y-pwl NP4 ... 62 D7
Pontypridd CF37 ... 109 D5
Seven Sisters / Blaendulais SA10 ... 222 D3
Tonna / Tonnau SA11 ... 49 D3
Ystradgynlais SA9 ... 222 A5
Penybryn Ave
Blackwood / Coed-Duon NP12 ... 58 C1
Blackwood / Coed-Duon NP12 ... 85 C8
Pen-y-Bryn Cl
Bettws NP20 ... 116 E2
Penllergaer SA4 ... 44 B2
Pen-y-Bryn Ct NP11 ... 59 D2
Pen-y-Bryn Pl CF14 ... 177 E2
Penybryn Rd
Gorseinon SA4 ... 43 B2
Mountain Ash / Aberpennar CF45 ... 81 F7
Pen-Y-Bryn Rd
Brynmenyn CF32 ... 150 E6
Cardiff / Caerdydd, Cyncoed CF23 ... 178 C7
Cardiff / Caerdydd, Mynachdy CF14 ... 177 E2
Pen-y-bryn Residential Cvn Site SA14 ... 41 E2
Pen-y-Bryn Senior Specl Sch SA6 ... 68 D7
Penybryn St
Aberdare / Aberdâr CF44 ... 28 F2
Hendreforgan CF39 ... 132 C5
Penybryn Terr
Brynmenyn CF32 ... 150 E6
Mountain Ash / Aberpennar CF45 ... 81 F8
Penybryn CF82 ... 84 D5
Pen-y-bryn Terr
Bryn NP12 ... 85 D3
Ebbw Vale / Glyn Ebwy NP23 ... 14 D6
Penybryn View CF47 ... 10 F2
Pen-Y-Bryn View CF32 ... 150 F4
Penybryn Villas 8 CF47 ... 10 F4
Pen-y-Bryn Way 2 CF14 ... 177 E2
Pen-y-Byrn Prim Sch CF3 ... 179 D7
PENYCAE ... 222 F8
PEN-Y-CAE
Bridgend ... 150 F1
Port Talbot ... 125 D8
Pen-y-cae
Bridgend / Pen-y-Bont ar Ogwr CF32 ... 150 E2
Caerphilly / Caerffili CF83 ... 138 D5
Resolven / Resolfen SA11 ... 226 E6
Ystrad Mynach CF82 ... 111 E8
Pen-y-caeau Ct NP11 ... 60 C1
Pen-y-Cae Cl NP11 ... 59 D1
Penycae Cty Prim Sch SA9 ... 222 F8
Pen-y-Cae La SA4 ... 42 E2
Pen-y-Cae Rd SA13 ... 125 C8
Pen-y-Cefn CF14 ... 159 D2
PEN-Y-COEDCAE ... 135 A4
Penycoedcae Rd CF37, CF38 ... 134 F2
Pen-y-Craig CF82 ... 84 E7
Pen-y-Crug NP23 ... 7 B5
Pen-y-Cwarel Rd NP12 ... 112 F8
Pen-y-cwm
Pentyrch CF15 ... 157 C1
Rhymney / Rhymni NP22 ... 13 A1
Pen Y Cwm SA2 ... 67 D2
Pen-y-cwm Specl Sch NP23 ... 7 F4
PEN-Y-DARREN ... 10 F3
Pen-y-Darren Cl CF37 ... 109 C2
Penydarren Dr CF14 ... 176 E5
Penydarren Gdns CF47 ... 10 E2
Penydarren Pk CF47 ... 10 E2
Penydarren Rd CF47 ... 10 E2
PENYDRE ... 22 F1
Pen-y-Dre
Caerphilly / Caerffili CF83 ... 137 E7
Cardiff / Caerdydd CF14 ... 177 B6
Ebbw Vale / Glyn Ebwy NP23 ... 7 C3
Gowerton / Tre-gwyr SA4 ... 66 B4
Merthyr Tydfil / Merthyr Tudful CF47 ... 10 C5
Neath / Castell-Nedd SA11 ... 71 F8
Pen Y Dre CF39 ... 133 D8
Pen-y-Dre NP22 ... 12 E6
Pen y Dre High Sch CF47 ... 10 D6
Penydre Rd SA6 ... 22 F1
PEN-Y-FAI ... 168 C8
Penyfai CW Prim Sch CF31 ... 150 C1
Penyfai La SA15 ... 40 B8
Penyfai Rd CF32 ... 150 C2
PEN-Y-FAN ... 40 F4
Pen-y-Fan SA7 ... 69 F6
Pen-y-Fan Cl NP11 ... 59 F6
Penyfan Cvn & L Pk NP13 ... 59 B7
Pen-y-fan Ind Est NP11 ... 59 D4
Pen-y-fan Pond Ctry Pk* NP11, NP13 ... 59 D6
Penyfan Rd SA15 ... 40 F4
Penyfan View CF47 ... 10 C5
Pen-y-Fan Way NP12 ... 59 C1
Penyffordd CF83 ... 137 F4
Pen-y-Ffordd CF33 ... 166 A7
Pen-y-Fon St SA15 ... 40 E3
Pen-y-Fro
Cwmdare CF44 ... 28 C3
Dunvant SA2 ... 66 B1
Pencoed CF35 ... 152 C1
Pen-y-Fro Cl SA2 ... 66 B1
Pen Y Fro Prim Sch SA2 ... 93 B8
Pen-y-Gaer Cotts SA14 ... 41 A8
Penygaer Prim Sch SA14 ... 40 F7
Penygaer Rd SA14, SA15 ... 40 F6
PENYGARN ... 62 D7
Pen-y-garn
Pontsticill CF48 ... 3 F2
Swansea / Abertawe SA1 ... 69 A3
Penygarnddu Ind Est CF48 ... 11 D6
Penygarn Inf Sch NP4 ... 62 D8
Penygarn Jun Sch NP4 ... 62 D8
Penygarn Rd
Cardiff / Caerdydd CF5 ... 193 D6
Pontypool / Pont-y-pwl NP4 ... 62 D8
Penygarn Rd / Heol Penygarn SA18 ... 218 F5
Penygarn Terr CF34 ... 102 B2
Penygarreg Rd CF39 ... 133 C2
Penygawsi Prim Sch / Ysgol Gynradd Penygawsi CF72 ... 155 D2
PENYGRAIG ... 106 E3
Penygraig CF14 ... 159 B1
Penygraig Ind Est CF40 ... 106 F4
Penygraig Inf Sch CF40 ... 106 F4
Penygraig Jun Sch CF40 ... 106 F4
Penygraig Rd
Llanelli SA14 ... 41 E4
Tonypandy CF40 ... 106 F3
Pen-y-Graig Rd
Pontardawe SA8 ... 23 F3
Swansea / Abertawe SA1 ... 95 B8
Ystradowen SA9 ... 221 C7
Penygraig Terr CF37 ... 81 F1
Pen-y-Graig Terr NP13 ... 60 A7
Pen-y-Graig Terr / Rhes Pen-y-Graig NP4 ... 62 D5
PENYGRAIGWEN ... 109 B3
PEN-Y-GROES ... 218 D8
Pen-y-Groes
Blackwood / Coed Duon NP11 ... 59 C2
Caerphilly / Caerffili CF83 ... 137 E6
Pen y Groes CF72 ... 174 B7
Pen-y-Groes Ave CF14 ... 177 D7
Pen y Groes Gr NP10 ... 141 E2
Penygroes Prim Sch SA14 ... 218 D8
Pen-y-Groes Rd CF14 ... 177 D7
Penygroes Rd / Heol Penygroes
Ammanford / Rhydaman SA18 ... 218 F8
Gorslas SA14 ... 218 C8
Pen-y-Heol SA10 ... 70 D4
PEN-Y-LAN
Cardiff ... 178 D1
Cowbridge ... 188 F6
Penylan CF31 ... 168 F8
Pen-y-Lan
Ebbw Vale / Glyn Ebwy NP23 ... 7 D3
Pen-clawdd SA4 ... 64 F3
Penylan Ave CF36 ... 182 E7
Penylan Cl
Bassaleg NP10 ... 142 A3
Pontypool / Pont-y-pwl NP4 ... 63 B4
Porthcawl CF36 ... 182 E7
Penylan Cotts NP10 ... 162 D7
Penylan Ct 7 CF24 ... 178 C1
Pen-y-lan Ct CF23 ... 178 C3
Penylan Ct / Cwrt Penylan NP44 ... 116 B8
Penylan Oval CF23 ... 178 C3
Pen-y-Lan Pl CF23 ... 178 C1
Penylan Rd
Argoed NP12 ... 58 F6
Michaelston-y-Fedw NP10 ... 162 E7
Newport / Casnewydd NP19 ... 144 A5
Pencoed CF35 ... 152 E1
Pontypridd CF37 ... 135 B8
St Brides Major / Saint-y-Brid CF32 ... 185 D2
Pen-y-Lan Rd
Aberthin CF71 ... 189 B3
Cardiff / Caerdydd CF24 ... 195 C8
Penylan Rd / Heol Penylan NP4 ... 37 E7
Pen-y-Lan Terr
Cardiff / Caerdydd CF23 ... 178 D2
Newbridge / Trecelyn NP11 ... 86 F7
Penylan Way / Ffordd Penyland NP44 ... 116 B8
Pen-y-Llan La NP4 ... 63 B8
Pen Y Maes SA6 ... 45 C2
Pen-y-Mead NP12 ... 85 D4
Pen-y-Morfa SA15 ... 40 E3
Pen Y Morfa SA4 ... 65 A4
Pen-y-Mor Rd SA5 ... 68 C5
Pen Y Mynydd CF32 ... 129 D3
Pen-y-Mynydd
Cymmer / Cymer SA13 ... 75 D3
Pontypridd CF37 ... 109 D6
Penyparc NP44 ... 89 D6
Pen-y-Parc CF38 ... 156 A7
Pen Y Parc NP23 ... 14 B8
Pen-y-Peel Rd CF5 ... 194 C6
Pen Y Pwll SA4 ... 19 D3
Pen-yr-Alley Ave SA10 ... 70 E6
Penyrallt SA18 ... 220 C7
Pen-yr-Allt CF83 ... 158 F8
Pen yr Allt SA11 ... 226 D6
Pen-yr-Allt SA9 ... 2 B8
Penyrallt Ave CF31 ... 168 F8
Pen Yr Alltwen SA8 ... 24 A3
Penyralltwen Pk SA8 ... 24 A3
Pen-yr-Eglwys CF38 ... 135 D1
PEN-YR-ENGLYN ... 78 B8
Penyrenglyn Com Prim Sch CF42 ... 78 A8
Pen-yr-Grug SA9 ... 2 A8
PENYRHEOL
Caerphilly ... 137 E5
Gorseinon ... 43 B4
Pontypool ... 62 C2
Swansea ... 94 B7
PEN-YR-HEOL
Bridgend ... 151 C2
Neath ... 70 F6
Pen-yr-Heol
Neath / Castell-Nedd SA10 ... 70 E5
North Cornelly CF33 ... 166 A7
Pen-y-fai CF31 ... 150 C1
Penywaun CF44 ... 28 B6
Penyrheol Com Sch SA4 ... 43 B3
Pen Yr Heol Dr SA15 ... 40 E8
Pen-yr-Heol Dr SA2 ... 94 B7
Penyrheol Prim Sch SA4 ... 43 B3
Penyrheol Rd
Gorseinon SA4 ... 43 A4
Pontypool / Pont-y-pwl NP4 ... 62 C3
Pen-yr-Heol Rd
Abertillery / Abertyleri NP11 ... 60 F5
Pontypool / Pont-y-pwl NP4 ... 61 A4
Penyrheol Terr CF71 ... 199 F8
Pen-y-Rhiw
Pen-Rhiw-fawr SA9 ... 221 B5
Ystrad CF41 ... 79 D3
Pen-Yr-Yrfa SA6 ... 45 D1
Pen-Yr-Ysgol CF34 ... 102 A2
Pen Yr Ysgol CF37 ... 135 D7
Pen-y-Turnpike Rd CF64 ... 206 B6
Penyturnpike View CF64 ... 206 D4
Penywain La NP4 ... 62 B6
Pen-y-Wain La CF24 ... 178 B1
Pen-y-Wain Pl CF24 ... 178 B1
Penywain Rd NP4 ... 62 A7
Pen-y-Wain Rd CF24 ... 178 B1
Penywain St NP4 ... 62 B7
Penywain Terr NP4 ... 62 B7
Penywarc Rd SA15 ... 40 F5
PENYWAUN ... 28 A5
Penywaun CF38 ... 156 F5
Pen-y-Waun
Dinas Powis / Dinas Powys CF64 ... 206 B3
Pentyrch CF15 ... 157 C1
Pen-y-Waun Cl NP44 ... 89 D2
Penywaun Cl / Clos Penywaun NP12 ... 59 C2
Pen-y-Waun Cotts NP12 ... 58 D6
Penywaun Prim Sch CF44 ... 28 B6
Pen-y-Waun Rd
Abertillery / Abertyleri NP11 ... 59 F5
Cwmbran / Cwmbrân NP44 ... 89 D2
Pen-y-Werlod Rd NP12 ... 58 D8
Pen-y-werlod Terr NP12 ... 58 D8
PEN-Y-WERN ... 11 B5
Penywern
Llanelli SA15 ... 40 A7
Ystalyfera SA9 ... 2 A7
Pen-y-Wern SA13 ... 75 E3
Penywern Rd
Neath / Castell-Nedd SA10 ... 48 E2
Ystalyfera SA9 ... 2 A6
Pen-y-Wern Rd SA6 ... 46 E8
Pen-y-Wern Terr SA1 ... 68 D4
Penywrlod CF82 ... 84 C7
Peppermint Dr CF23 ... 160 D1
Pepys Cres CF3 ... 179 B6
Pepys Gr NP20 ... 142 E2
Percival Cl CF14 ... 159 D2
Perclose CF64 ... 206 B3
Percy Rd SA13 ... 74 B3
Percy Smith Rd CF61 ... 210 C6
Percy St CF10 ... 232 B1
Pergoed La NP4 ... 63 F7
Pergwm St CF40 ... 107 B5
Peris Rd SA5 ... 68 A5
Perrots Cl CF5 ... 193 E8
Perrott Pl CF46 ... 83 B6
Perrott St CF46 ... 83 B6
Perry Ct / Cwrt Perry NP44 ... 89 A4
PERSONDY ... 87 C4
Persondy La CF5 ... 192 F6
Persondy Terr NP11 ... 87 C3
PERTHCELYN ... 81 E8
Perthcelyn Com Prim Sch CF45 ... 81 F7
Perth Ct NP12 ... 85 C6
Perthlwyd CF44 ... 28 A6
Perthy Cl NP44 ... 116 B8
Perthygleision CF48 ... 55 C3
Peter Cash Ho SA1 ... 95 A5
Peter Lea Prim Sch CF5 ... 176 D1
Peter St SA1 ... 68 C1
PETERSTONE WENTLOOGE / LLANBEDR GWYNLLWG ... 180 E5
Peterston-super-Ely CW Prim Sch CF5 ... 191 E6
PETERSTON-SUPER-ELY / LLANBEDR-Y-FRO ... 191 E6
Peterswell Rd CF62 ... 214 C5
Peter Terr SA1 ... 68 C1
Petherton Mews CF5 ... 176 F1
Petherton Pl 1 CF3 ... 179 C6
Pethybridge Rd CF5 ... 193 C6
Petrel Cl CF64 ... 217 A7
Pettingale Rd NP44 ... 90 B5
Petunia Wlk NP10 ... 141 D7
Pheasant Rd SA8 ... 23 B2
Phelps Ho 11 SA12 ... 98 B3
Philadelphia Cl CF63 ... 215 D7
Philadelphia Ct 4 SA6 ... 69 A8
Philadelphia La SA1 ... 68 D2
Philadelphia Rd CF36 ... 182 F7
Philip Ave CF31 ... 168 C5
Philip Cl CF14 ... 177 D6
Philippa Freeth Ct CF63 ... 215 A4
Philip St
Abertillery / Abertyleri NP11 ... 59 F6
Cardiff / Caerdydd CF11 ... 194 D5
Philips Terr 25 CF47 ... 30 E8
Phillip Ct 9 NP19 ... 143 E5
Phillip Row CF44 ... 53 F8
Phillips Cl NP23 ... 7 B5
Phillip's Gn 3 NP10 ... 142 B4
Phillips Par SA1 ... 95 B6
Phillips St
Blaenavon NP4 ... 17 C7
New Tredegar NP24 ... 33 F2
Phillip St
Aberdare / Aberdâr CF44 ... 29 A3
Mountain Ash / Aberpennar CF45 ... 54 D3
Newport / Casnewydd NP19 ... 143 E5
Pontypridd CF37 ... 135 B7
Risca / Rhisga NP11 ... 114 F2
Swansea / Abertawe SA5 ... 68 C2
Phillips Terr
Senghenydd CF83 ... 110 F3
Trehafod CF37 ... 108 C3
PHILLIP'S TOWN ... 33 F4
Phillipstown Prim Sch NP24 ... 33 E4
Phillip's Wlk NP22 ... 12 E5
Philog Ct CF14 ... 177 C4
Philog The CF14 ... 177 C4
Philsay Ho 3 NP44 ... 116 C8
Phoenix Ave / Rhodfa Phoenix 3 SA13 ... 125 D5
Phoenix Bsns Pk SA7 ... 69 B7
Phoenix Ctr SA7 ... 69 C7
Phoenix Est CF14 ... 177 D6
Phoenix Ho 3 CF24 ... 195 D6
Phoenix Ind Est CF48, CF47 ... 11 A3
Phoenix Way
Cardiff / Caerdydd CF14 ... 177 D5
Penllergaer SA4 ... 43 F1
Swansea / Abertawe SA7 ... 69 B6
Phyllis Ave CF31 ... 168 F3
Phyllis St
Barry / Y Barri CF62 ... 214 F3
Swansea / Abertawe SA5 ... 68 A2
Troedyrhiw CF48 ... 31 C2
Piazza The CF11 ... 195 A1
Piccadilly CF71 ... 200 D8
Piccadilly Sq CF83 ... 138 B3
Picket Mead Rd SA3 ... 122 E5
PICKETSTON ... 211 A8
Picketston Cl CF62 ... 211 A7
Pickwick Cl CF14 ... 159 F2
Picton Arc SA1 ... 233 A2
Picton Ave
Bridgend / Pen-y-Bont ar Ogwr CF31 ... 168 E2
Picton Ave *continued*
Porthcawl CF36 ... 182 F6
Picton Cl CF31 ... 169 A2
Picton Ct CF61 ... 210 A7
Picton Gdns CF31 ... 169 A2
Picton La SA1 ... 233 A2
Picton Pl
Cardiff / Caerdydd CF11 ... 194 D5
Maesteg CF34 ... 102 A6
Picton Rd
Abersychan NP4 ... 37 E4
Neath / Castell-Nedd SA10 ... 70 F7
Rhoose / Y Rhws CF62 ... 213 A2
Tredegar NP22 ... 6 E1
Picton St
Maesteg CF34 ... 102 A6
Pontlottyn CF81 ... 32 F8
Pontypool / Pont-y-pwl NP4 ... 62 E3
Pyle / Y Pîl CF33 ... 148 D3
Picton Terr
Llanharan CF72 ... 154 A3
Swansea / Abertawe SA1 ... 233 A4
Picton Wlk
12 Cardiff / Caerdydd CF11 ... 194 D5
Newport / Casnewydd NP10 ... 163 E5
Picton Wlk / Llwybr Picton NP44 ... 89 B2
Picwic Gn NP44 ... 89 B2
Piercefield Pl CF24 ... 195 D6
Pier Cl / Clos Y Lanfa SA12 ... 98 C1
Pierhead St CF10 ... 195 C2
Pierhead View CF64 ... 206 F6
Pier St SA1 ... 233 C2
Pier Way SA12 ... 98 C1
Pilgrim Cl CF15 ... 176 B5
Pilgrims Cl SA10 ... 71 C8
PILLGWENLLY ... 143 D2
Pillgwenlly Prim Sch NP20 ... 143 C2
Pillmawr Circ NP20 ... 117 B2
Pillmawr Rd
Caerleon / Caerllion NP18 ... 118 A3
Newport / Casnewydd NP18, NP20 ... 117 D2
Pill St CF64 ... 206 F5
Pill Terr SA11 ... 71 B2
Pil Prim Sch CF33 ... 148 B2
PILTON GREEN ... 230 E6
Pilton Pl CF14 ... 177 D2
Pilton Vale NP20 ... 117 B3
Pil-y-Cynffig CF33 ... 166 A8
Pineacre Cl SA2 ... 94 C6
Pine Cl
Merthyr Tydfil / Merthyr Tudful CF47 ... 10 D5
Porthcawl CF36 ... 183 D7
Risca / Rhisga NP11 ... 115 A2
Pine Cres SA6 ... 45 E2
Pinecrest Dr CF14 ... 159 F3
Pinecroft Ave CF44 ... 29 D1
Pine Ct
Llantwit Fadre / Llanilltud Faerdref CF38 ... 156 C5
Talbot Green CF72 ... 155 A3
Tongwynlais CF15 ... 158 D1
Pine Gdns / Gerddi Pinwydd NP4 ... 62 A6
Pine Gr
Cimla SA11 ... 72 B5
Newport / Casnewydd NP10 ... 163 F8
Ystrad Mynach CF82 ... 84 E1
Pinehurst Rd CF5 ... 193 C8
Pine St CF43 ... 79 F7
Pines The
Abertillery / Abertyleri NP13 ... 36 C6
Cardiff / Caerdydd CF14 ... 177 A5
Cilfrew / Cil-ffriw SA10 ... 49 B4
Hirwaun CF44 ... 27 F7
Pine Tree Cl CF15 ... 176 A7
Pinetree Ct SA2 ... 94 C6
Pine Tree Ho SA12 ... 98 E6
Pine Tree Rd NP4 ... 63 B4
Pine Tree Way CF46 ... 83 F2
Pine Valley SA12 ... 99 C5
Pine Walk Dr CF39 ... 108 A2
Pineway SA5 ... 68 C6
Pinewood Ave CF37 ... 136 C5
Pinewood Cl
Llandough / Llandochau CF64 ... 206 E6
Newport / Casnewydd NP20 ... 117 B2
Swansea / Abertawe SA6 ... 45 D1
Pinewood / Coed Y Pin SA18 ... 219 D7
Pine Wood Cres CF23 ... 178 E3
Pinewood Ct
Bryn NP12 ... 85 E5
Llanelli SA14 ... 41 D6
Pinewood Dr CF40 ... 107 A5
Pinewood Hill CF72 ... 155 A2
Pinewood Rd SA2 ... 94 E6
Pinewood Sq CF62 ... 211 B7
Pinewood Terr SA12 ... 98 D6
Pinewood View CF37 ... 109 C6

Pinkney St SA1 .... 233 C3
Pinnell Pl 18 NP20 ...... 143 C3
Pintail Cl CF36 .... 165 D1
Pioden For CF62 .... 214 F1
Pioneer Terr NP11 ...... 113 A4
Piper Cl
Cardiff / Caerdydd
CF5 .... 176 D2
Newport / Casnewydd
NP19 .... 144 A8
Pipkin Cl 6 CF23 .... 161 A1
Pisgah Cl / Clos Pisgah
NP4 .... 37 E5
Pisgah Rd NP4 .... 37 E5
Pisgah St CF33 .... 148 C2
PITCOT 185 D1
Pitman La CF11 .... 194 E6
Pitman St CF11 .... 194 E6
Pitmedden Cl 5 CF3 .... 179 F7
Pit Pl 3 CF44 .... 53 E8
Pit Row CF44 .... 53 B4
Pit St CF34 .... 102 C1
PITTON 230 C6
Pittsburgh Ct SA5 .... 67 F7
Plane Gr CF47 .... 10 D5
Plane St CF37 .... 136 A5
Plane Tree Cl NP18 ..... 117 F2
Planet St CF24 .... 195 C6
Plantagenet St CF11 .... 232 A2
Plantasia* SA1 .... 233 B3
Plantation Cl CF47 ...... 10 E3
Plantation Dr / / Rhodfa'r Blanhigfa NP44 .... 90 B4
Plantation Gdns CF45 .... 82 E3
Plantation Rd CF45 ...... 82 E3
Plantation Row NP23 ..... 14 D6
Plantation Sq 1 CF48 .... 31 B1
Plantation Terr
Fochriw CF81 .... 32 C7
Rhymney / Rhymni NP22 ... 12 F2
Plasbach 5 CF5 .... 193 D8
Plas Bryn Gomer NP44 ... 90 A6
Plas Bute / Bute Pl
CF10 .... 195 C2
Plas Cadwgan SA4 .... 44 C2
Plas-Cadwgan Rd SA6 ... 46 C5
Plas Cae Llwyd 7
CF83 .... 111 F1
Plas Cleddau CF62 ...... 214 C5
Plas Craig NP44 .... 89 F4
Plas Croeso SA4 .... 43 B1
Plas Cwm Parc CF83 .... 110 E2
Plas Cwrt
Cwmbran / Cwmbrân
NP44 .... 116 F8
Fleur-de-lis NP12 .... 85 B6
Plas Dafydd CF44 .... 28 E3
Plas Derwen
Croesyceiliog NP44 .... 90 A4
Troedyrhiw CF48 .... 31 B2
Plasdraw Ave CF44 .... 29 B2
Plasdraw Pl CF44 .... 29 B2
Plasdraw Rd CF44 .... 29 B2
Plas Ebbw NP44 .... 89 F4
Plas Essyllt CF64 .... 206 B3
Plas Glen Rosa CF64 .... 207 A5
Plas Grug CF83 .... 137 F1
Plas Gwernen CF63 ..... 205 B1
Plas Gwernfadog Dr
SA6 .... 46 A5
Plasgwyn SA4 .... 19 D4
Plas-Gwyn Rd / Heol Plas Gwyn SA14 .... 218 D8
Plasgwyn Terr NP12 ...... 85 B6
Plas Heddwch CF33 ..... 166 A8
Plas Horab CF42 .... 50 F2
Plas Hos SA4 .... 43 C6
Plas Islwyn NP44 .... 89 E4
Plas Kenfig CF33 .... 165 F7
PLASMARL 68 E5
Plasmarl CF44 .... 28 D6
Plasmarl Ind Est SA6 ...... 68 F6
Plasmarl Prim Sch / Ysgol Gynradd Plasmarl
SA6 .... 68 E5
Plasmarl Terr SA6 .... 68 E5
Plas-Mawr Rd CF5 ...... 193 D8
Plasmawr Welsh Comp Sch / Ysgol Gyfun Gymraeg Plasmawr CF5 .... 176 C1
Plas Melin CF14 .... 176 F4
Plas Melyn SA5 .... 67 F6
Plas Morlais CF33 .... 166 A8
Plas Nant CF83 .... 137 A7
Plas Newydd
Cardiff / Caerdydd
CF14 .... 177 A4
Dunvant SA2 .... 93 B8
13 Ebbw Vale / Glyn Ebwy
NP23 .... 14 D6
Grovesend SA4 .... 43 C6
Plasnewydd Pl 3
CF24 .... 195 C8
Plasnewydd Prim Sch / Ysgol Gynradd Plasnewydd CF34 ...... 102 A3
Plasnewydd Rd
Cardiff / Caerdydd
CF24 .... 195 B8
Cardiff / Caerdydd
CF24 .... 232 D4
Plasnewydd Sq CF24 .... 195 C8
Plasnewydd St CF34 ..... 102 A3
Plas Pamir CF64 .... 207 B6
Plas Phillips CF83 .... 137 F3
Plas Rd
Fleur-de-lis NP12 .... 85 B6
Grovesend SA4 .... 43 C6
Rhos SA8 .... 24 C4
Plas St Andresse CF64 .. 207 B6
Plas St Pol De Leon 2
CF64 .... 207 B5
Plassey Ho 10 CF64 ..... 207 A5
Plassey Sq CF64 .... 207 A5
Plassey St CF64 .... 207 A4
Plas Taliesin CF64 ...... 207 B6
Plas Terr NP12 .... 85 B6
Plas Thomas CF83 ...... 137 F3
Plas Treoda CF14 .... 177 B4
Plas Trosnant 11 NP44 ... 89 E5
Plasturton Ave CF11 .... 194 D7
Plasturton Gdns CF11 ... 194 E6
Plasturton Pl CF11 ...... 194 E6
Plasturtwyn CF83 .... 112 A3
Plas Twyn NP44 .... 89 F5
Plas Ty-Coch NP44 ..... 116 F8
Plas Tymawr CF31 ...... 168 D8
Plas View NP12 .... 85 E6
Plas Windsor / Windsor Pl
CF10 .... 232 C3
Plas Y Biswail CF3 ...... 179 F6
PLAS-Y-COED 61 E7
Plasycoed SA9 .... 1 F2
Plas-y-Coed
Cardiff / Caerdydd
CF23 .... 178 B3
Glyn-neath / Glyn-nedd
SA11 .... 223 C1
Plas Y Coed Ave SA6 ..... 68 F8
Plasycoed Rd NP4 .... 61 E7
Plas Y Coed Rd SA6 ...... 68 F8
Plas Y Delyn CF14 .... 160 B3
Plas-y-Fedwen CF37 .... 109 D6
Plasyfelin Prim Sch
CF83 .... 138 A4
Plas-y-Fforest
Fforest SA4 .... 18 F6
Penllergaer SA4 .... 44 C2
Plas-y-Llan CF14 .... 177 A5
Plas-Y-Mynach CF15 .... 176 C4
Plas-y-Odyn CF72 ...... 172 D6
Plas Y Parc / Park Pl
Cardiff / Caerdydd
CF10 .... 232 B4
Sarn CF32 .... 150 F4
Plas Yr Eglwys 6
CF37 .... 109 D2
Plas yr Neuadd / Guildhall Pl CF10 .... 232 B2
Plas Y Wen NP23 .... 14 B8
Players Ave SA6 .... 46 D8
Players Ind Est SA6 .... 46 D6
Playford Cres NP19 ..... 144 F5
Plaza Ct 4 NP12 .... 85 F4
Pleasant Cl
Gorseinon SA4 .... 42 F3
Pontllanfraith NP12 .... 86 A6
Pleasant Ct NP4 .... 38 A3
Pleasant Gr CF44 .... 29 F1
Pleasant Hill
Cilfrew / Cil-ffriw SA10 .... 49 C5
Ferndale CF43 .... 80 A6
Pleasant Hts / Trum Hyfryd CF39 .... 107 E5
Pleasant Pl CF83 .... 137 E5
Pleasant Rd
Gorseinon SA4 .... 43 E2
Tonypandy CF40 .... 106 F3
Pleasant Row
5 Llanelli SA15 .... 40 E5
Swansea / Abertawe SA5 .. 68 C3
Pleasant St
Swansea / Abertawe, Clun-Du SA6 .... 45 F1
2 Swansea / Abertawe, Mount Pleasant SA1 .... 233 B3
Treorchy / Treorci CF41 .... 78 F4
Pleasant Terr
Tonypandy CF40 .... 106 B7
Ystrad CF41 .... 79 D3
Pleasant View
Aberfan CF48 .... 55 C3
Aberkenfig / Abercynffig
CF32 .... 150 C3
Abersychan NP4 .... 37 F4
Barry / Y Barri CF62 ..... 214 D8
Beddau CF38 .... 156 A6
Bedlinog CF46 .... 56 B8
Blackwood / Coed Duon
NP11 .... 59 D2
Blackwood / Coed-Duon
NP12 .... 85 E8
Brynmawr NP23 .... 8 B5
Brynmenyn CF32 .... 150 F6
Cefn Cribwr CF32 .... 149 B2
Cymmer / Cymer SA13 .... 75 C5
Ebbw Vale / Glyn Ebwy
NP23 .... 14 D8
Fochriw CF81 .... 32 D7
Llanelli SA15 .... 40 F8
Maesteg CF34 .... 75 B1
Maesycwmmer CF82 .... 85 A1
New Tredegar NP24 .... 33 E2
Pontygwaith, Stanleytown
CF43 .... 80 B2
Pontypool / Pont-y-pwl
NP4 .... 61 F8
Pontypridd CF37 .... 109 D2
Tonypandy CF40 .... 133 A8
Trehafod CF37 .... 108 C2
Treharris CF46 .... 83 A6
Treorchy / Treorci CF41 .... 79 A4
10 Troedyrhiw CF48 ...... 31 C1
Pleasant View *continued*
Wattstown CF39 .... 107 D8
Ynysybwl CF37 .... 81 E4
Pleasant View Pk CF44 ... 28 C5
Pleasantview St CF47 .... 10 C2
Pleasant View St CF44 ... 53 C6
Pleasant View Terr
Swansea / Abertawe, Mount Pleasant SA1 .... 233 A4
1 Swansea / Abertawe, Penfilia SA5 .... 68 C4
Plough Cnr NP12 .... 86 A4
Plough Rd
Penperlleni NP4 .... 39 F5
Swansea / Abertawe SA1 .. 68 D3
Plousane Rd / Heol Plousane CF35 .... 170 D6
Plover Cl
Newport / Casnewydd
NP19 .... 144 E1
Swansea / Abertawe SA5 .. 68 C7
Plover Way CF64 .... 217 A8
Plumley Cl CF33 .... 165 F8
Plunch La SA3 .... 123 C3
Plymouth Dr CF15 .... 176 C5
Plymouth Gdns CF48 ..... 31 A4
Plymouth Rd
Barry / Y Barri CF62 ..... 214 F2
Penarth CF64 .... 207 B2
Pontypridd CF37 .... 109 A1
Plymouth Road Sta*
CF62 .... 214 F2
Plymouth St
Merthyr Tydfil / Merthyr Tudful CF47 .... 30 E7
Swansea / Abertawe
SA1 .... 233 A2
Plymouth Terr CF47 ...... 30 E7
Plymouth Wood Cl
CF5 .... 193 D6
Plymouth Wood Cres
CF5 .... 193 C6
Plymouth Wood Rd
CF5 .... 193 D6
Plym Wlk NP20 .... 116 E2
Plynlimon Ave NP11 ...... 59 E2
Plynlimon Cl NP11 .... 59 E2
Pobbles Cl SA3 .... 121 A4
Pochin Cres NP22 .... 14 A4
Pochin Hos NP22 .... 34 C6
Pocketts Wharf 11
SA1 .... 233 C2
Poets Cl CF37 .... 136 A6
Poets Field Rd CF62 ..... 214 E8
Poets Way CF72 .... 153 E2
Police Row NP22 .... 6 D2
Pollard Cl NP18 .... 117 E2
Polo Ground Ind Est
NP4 .... 62 F4
Pomeroy St CF10 .... 195 B1
Pommergelli Rd CF14 .... 176 F4
Pond Mawr CF34 .... 102 D1
Pond Pl CF44 .... 53 F8
Pond Rd NP23 .... 8 B3
Pond Row
Abercanaid CF48 .... 30 E5
Abercarn NP11 .... 114 C7
Pontalun Cl CF63 .... 215 A8
PONTAMAN / PONTAMMAN 219 E7
PONTAMMAN / PONTAMAN 219 E7
Pontamman Rd SA18 .... 219 D7
Pont Ap Hywell NP4 ...... 62 C7
PONTARDAWE 23 D4
Pontardawe Ind Est
SA8 .... 23 F5
Pontardawe Rd
Birchgrove SA6 .... 47 A8
Pontardawe SA8 .... 220 D3
PONTARDDULAIS 19 E5
Pontarddulais Prim Sch
SA4 .... 19 D3
Pontarddulais Road Ret Pk
SA5 .... 67 D6
Pontardulais Comp Sch
SA4 .... 19 D5
Pontardulais Ind Est
SA4 .... 19 C6
Pontardulais Junction
SA4 .... 19 B5
Pontardulais Rd
Cross Hands SA14 .... 218 B6
Gorseinon SA4 .... 43 C3
Llangennech SA14 .... 18 E2
Penllergar SA4 .... 44 B3
Swansea / Abertawe SA5 .. 67 C6
Tycroes SA18 .... 218 E5
Pontardulais Workshops
SA4 .... 19 C6
Pont Aur SA9 .... 2 E7
PONTBREN LLWYD 224 D3
PONTCANNA 194 D8
Pontcanna Ct CF5 .... 194 C7
Pontcanna Pl CF11 ...... 194 D7
Pontcanna St CF11 ...... 194 D7
PONTCYNON 82 C4
Pontcynon Ind Est
CF45 .... 82 D5
Pontcynon Terr CF45 ..... 82 D4
Pontfaen CF23 .... 178 D8
Pont Faen Rd NP19 ..... 144 C3
Pontgam Terr NP11 ..... 112 F8
Pont George Rd CF33 ... 148 B3
PONTHIR 117 E6
Ponthir Prim Sch
NP18 .... 117 E7
Ponthir Rd NP18 .... 118 B4
PONTLLANFRAITH 85 C4
Pontllanfraith Comp Sch
NP12 .... 85 F4
Pontllanfraith Prim Sch
NP12 .... 86 A5
PONTLLIW 44 A7
Pontlliw Prim Sch SA4 ... 44 A7
PONTLOTTYN 12 E1
Pontlottyn Cty Prim Sch / Ysgol Gynradd Pontlottyn
CF81 .... 32 F8
Pontlottyn Rd CF81 ...... 32 D8
Pontlottyn Sta CF81 ...... 12 F1
Pontmorlais CF47 .... 10 D1
Pontmorlais W CF47 ..... 10 D2
Pontneathvaughan Rd
SA11 .... 223 E2
PONTNEDDFECHAN 223 E3
PONTNEWYDD 89 E5
Pont Newydd CF35 ...... 170 D6
Pontnewydd Prim Sch
NP44 .... 89 D5
Pontnewydd Wlk / Rhodfa Pontnewydd 3 NP44 ... 89 E4
PONTNEWYNYDD 62 A8
Pontnewynydd Ind Est
NP4 .... 62 A8
Pontnewynydd Prim Sch
NP4 .... 38 A2
Pontnewynydd Small Bsns Ctr NP4 .... 61 F8
Pont-Pentre Cvn Pk
CF37 .... 136 C3
Pontpren CF44 .... 224 E2
PONTPRENNAU 161 A1
Pontrhondda Ave CF40 ... 79 E1
Pontrhondda Prim Sch
CF40 .... 79 F1
Pontrhondda Rd CF40 .... 79 F1
PONT RHYD-Y-CYFF 128 C7
PONTRHYDYFEN 73 B1
Pontrhydyfen Prim Sch
SA12 .... 73 A1
PONTRHYDYRUN 89 F6
Pontrhydyrun Ho NP44 ... 90 A7
Pontrhydyrun Rd NP44 ... 89 F7
Pontrilas Cl CF5 .... 192 F3
Pontsarn Cl CF48 .... 10 D7
Pontsarn Flats CF48 ...... 10 D7
Pontshonnorton Rd
CF37 .... 109 E3
PONT-SIÔN-NORTON 109 F3
Pont St SA13 .... 125 C8
PONTSTICILL 3 F4
Pontsticill Sta* CF48 ...... 4 A5
PONTWALBY / PONT-WALBY 223 D1
PONT-WALBY / PONTWALBY 223 D1
Pontybrenin Prim Sch / Ysgol Gynradd Y Sir Pontybrenin SA4 .... 43 B1
Pontycapel Rd CF48 ...... 10 A4
PONTYCLUN 173 B6
Pontyclun Prim Sch / Ysgol Gynradd Pontyclun
CF72 .... 173 B7
Pontyclun Sta CF72 ..... 173 B7
Pont-y-Cob Rd SA4 ...... 65 F6
PONTYCYMER 103 E3
PONT-Y-FELIN 63 A2
Pont-y-Felin Ave NP4 .... 62 F2
Pontyfelin Ind Est NP4 ... 63 A3
Pont-y-Felin La NP4 ..... 63 A2
Pont-y-Felin Rd NP4 ..... 63 A2
Pont-y-glasdwr 4 SA1 .. 68 D1
PONT-Y-GOF 7 D1
Pontygof NP23 .... 8 D5
Pont-y-Gof NP23 .... 7 D1
Pontygof Prim Sch NP23 .. 7 D1
PONTYGWAITH 80 C1
Pontygwaith Prim Sch
CF43 .... 80 B1
Pontygwindy Ind Est
CF83 .... 138 A6
Pontygwindy Rd CF83 ... 138 A5
Pontymason Cl NP10 ..... 141 E7
Pontymason Ct NP10 ..... 141 E7
Pontymason La NP1 ..... 141 E8
Pontymason Rise
NP10 .... 141 E7
PONTYMISTER 114 F1
Pontymister Ind Est
NP11 .... 141 A8
PONTYMOEL 62 D5
Pontymoile Prim Sch / Ysgol Gynradd Pont-y-moel NP4 .... 62 D5
Pontypandy La CF83 .... 138 A5
Pontypool & Blaenavon Rly* NP4 .... 16 E8
Pontypool & New Inn Sta
NP4 .... 63 A5
Pontypool North Ind Est
NP4 .... 62 A8
PONTYPOOL / PONT-Y-PWL 62 E6
PONTYPRIDD 135 C7
Pontypridd & District Cottage Hospl CF37 .... 109 E1
Pontypridd Mus*
CF37 .... 109 C1
Pontypridd Rd
Barry / Y Barri CF62 ..... 214 C5
Porth CF39 .... 107 F3
Pontypridd St CF63 ..... 215 B6
Pontypridd Sta CF37 .... 135 C8
PONT-Y-PWL / PONTYPOOL 62 E6
PONT-Y-RHYL 129 F8
Pont-y-Shoot SA6 .... 68 D5
PONTYWAUN 114 C6
Pool La NP19 .... 143 E7
Poplar Ave
Pontypool / Pont-y-pwl
NP4 .... 63 B5
Porthcawl CF36 .... 183 A7
Poplar Cl
Cardiff / Caerdydd
CF5 .... 176 C1
Swansea / Abertawe SA2 .. 94 B8
Poplar Cres CF36 .... 183 A7
Poplar Ct
Barry / Y Barri CF62 ..... 215 A7
Cross Hands SA14 .... 218 B7
Poplar Ho CF14 .... 176 E6
Poplar Mews
Porthcawl CF36 .... 183 A7
5 Troedyrhiw CF48 .... 31 C1
Poplar Pl CF48 .... 10 B7
Poplar Rd
Caerphilly / Caerffili
CF83 .... 138 C2
Cardiff / Caerdydd CF5 ... 193 D8
Croesyceiliog NP44 .... 90 A4
Newport / Casnewydd
NP19 .... 144 B5
Porthcawl CF36 .... 183 A7
Rhydyfelin CF37 .... 136 A5
Tredegar NP22 .... 13 F5
Poplars Ave SA11 .... 72 A6
Poplars Ct NP18 .... 117 F3
Poplar St CF48 .... 31 C1
Poplars The
Llanharry CF72 .... 172 C5
2 Mountain Ash / Aberpennar
CF45 .... 54 D3
Risca / Rhisga NP11 ..... 114 D3
Poplars / Y Poplys
SA12 .... 98 E1
Poplar Terr
Pentrebach CF48 .... 31 A4
Pontypool / Pont-y-pwl
NP4 .... 62 A8
Poplar Way CF47 .... 10 D5
Poppy Cl SA12 .... 98 C3
Poppy Ct / Llys Pabi 9
SA11 .... 71 E6
Poppyfield Cl CF3 .... 179 E6
Poppy Pl NP10 .... 141 D7
Porcher Ave CF37 .... 109 D5
Porlock Dr CF64 .... 216 B5
Porlock Rd CF3 .... 179 D7
Porset Cl CF83 .... 138 C3
Porset Dr CF83 .... 138 C2
Porset Row CF83 .... 138 D5
Portal Ho 1 CF47 .... 30 D8
Porters Rd NP23 .... 8 C2
PORT-EYNON 231 A4
Portfield Cres CF14 ..... 177 F7
PORTH 107 E3
Porthamal Gdns CF14 ... 177 C6
Porthamal Rd CF14 ..... 177 C6
PORTHCAWL 182 D6
Porthcawl Coll CF36 .... 182 F6
Porthcawl Comp Sch
CF36 .... 182 E7
Porthcawl Prim Sch
CF36 .... 183 B8
Porthcawl Rd
Cardiff / Caerdydd
CF5 .... 193 C4
South Cornelly CF33 ..... 165 F6
PORTHCERI / PORTHKERRY 213 E1
Porth Cty Comp Sch
CF39 .... 107 D4
Porth Inf Sch CF39 ...... 107 F4
Porth Jun Sch CF39 ..... 107 F3
Porthkerry Country Pk*
CF62 .... 213 F2
Porthkerry Country Pk Nature Trail* CF62 ..... 214 A3
Porthkerry Cvn Pk
CF62 .... 213 D1
Porthkerry Pl CF14 ...... 177 D2
PORTHKERRY / PORTHCERI 213 E1
Porthkerry Rd
Barry / Y Barri CF62 ..... 214 D4
Rhoose / Y Rhws CF62 ... 213 D2
Porth Mawr Rd / Heol Porth Mawr NP44 ...... 89 E4
Porth Pl 1 CF39 .... 107 F3
Porth Rhufeinig / Roman Gate CF82 .... 84 D7
Porth St CF39 .... 107 F3
Porth Sta CF39 .... 107 F3
Porth-y-Castell CF62 .... 214 B2
Porth Y Gar SA14 .... 42 B1
Porth-y-Green Cl
CF71 .... 188 E1
Porth Y Waun SA4 .... 66 A6
Portia Terr SA1 .... 233 A4
Portland Cl CF64 .... 207 B2
Portland Pl
Blackwood / Coed-Duon
NP12 .... 85 D6
Cardiff / Caerdydd CF14 .. 160 B2
Portland St
Abertillery / Abertyleri
NP13 .... 36 B6
Newport / Casnewydd
NP20 .... 143 D2

Portland St *continued*
Swansea / Abertawe
SA1 233 A3
Port Madoc Rd CF3 179 E5
Portmanmoor Rd
Cardiff / Caerdydd
CF24 195 E5
Cardiff / Caerdydd, East Moors
CF24 195 E4
Portmanmoor Road Ind Est
CF24 195 E4
Portmanmoor Road La
CF24 195 E5
PORT MEAD 67 D6
Portmead Ave SA5 67 E7
Portmead Pl SA5 67 E7
Portmead Prim Sch
SA5 67 F5
Port Mews CF62 204 F1
Porto Ho 21 CF10 195 B2
Port Rd
Barry / Y Barri CF5, CF62,
CF63 205 A2
Barry / Y Barri, Merthyr Dyfan
CF62 214 E8
Cardiff / Caerdydd CF5 192 F2
East Aberthaw CF62 212 D3
Newport / Casnewydd
NP20 143 B1
Rhoose / Y Rhws CF62 213 F5
Wenvoe / Gwenfo CF5 205 A5
Port Rd E CF62 214 D8
Port Rd W
Barry / Y Barri CF62 214 C6
Barry / Y Barri, Colcot
CF62 214 D7
Portreeve Cl CF72 155 D2
Portskewett St NP19 143 F3
PORT TALBOT 124 C7
Port Talbot Ind Est
SA13 125 A8
Port Talbot Parkway Sta
SA13 125 B8
Port Talbot Pl SA5 67 E5
Port Talbot Workshops 4
SA12 124 E8
Port Talbot Wrkshps 5
SA12 98 E1
PORT TENNANT 96 C8
Port Tennant Rd SA1 96 A7
Port Terr CF34 102 A3
Portway SA3 122 A7
Portway The CF36 182 F6
Postern 7 NP44 89 B1
Post Office La 4 CF47 10 D1
Post Office Row 6
CF40 106 E6
Potters Field CF44 28 E4
Potters Gn CF32 150 E4
Potter St NP20 143 D2
Pottery Pl SA15 40 D5
Pottery Rd
Cefn Hengoed CF82 84 E5
Newport / Casnewydd
NP20 143 D2
Pottery St / Stryd Y Crochendy 7 SA15 40 D5
Pottery Terr NP20 143 C2
POUNDFFALD 65 D2
Pound Field CF61 210 A6
Poundfield Sh Precinct
CF61 209 F6
Pound Hill NP10 162 E5
Pound La CF5 204 F6
Pound Rd or Trafalgar Rd
NP23 8 C5
Powderham Dr CF11 194 E4
Powell Dr CF72 153 E2
Powell Duffryn Way
CF62 214 E3
Powell's Pl NP20 143 D4
Powell St
Abertillery / Abertyleri
NP13 36 B5
Bedlinog CF46 56 A7
Swansea / Abertawe
SA1 233 B4
Tir-Y-Berth CF82 85 A6
Powell's Terr NP24 33 E4
Power St NP20 143 B7
Powis Cl
Blackwood / Coed-Duon
NP12 58 D1
Newport / Casnewydd
NP10 163 D5
Powis View CF63 215 C7
Powys Ave SA1 95 A8
Powys Cl CF64 206 C4
Powys Dr CF64 206 B4
Powys Gdns
Dinas Powis / Dinas Powys
CF64 206 C4
Swansea / Abertawe SA1 94 F8
Powys Ho 2 CF23 178 C2
Powys Pl
Dinas Powis / Dinas Powys
CF64 206 C4
Pontypridd CF37 135 F6
Powys Rd
1 Penarth CF64 206 F2
Upper Boat CF37 136 D1
Precinct The
Bridgend / Pen-y-Bont ar
Ogwr CF31 168 E7
Church Village CF38 136 A1
Porthcawl CF36 165 E1
Precipitation Rd CF62 211 E1
Premier Blg CF83 138 F6
Prendergast Pl CF5 193 D3
Prendergast St SA15 40 E4
Presceli Cl NP11 115 C2
Prescelli Rd SA5 68 A5
Prescelly Rd SA13 75 D3
Prescoch La NP4 62 D4
Prestatyn Rd CF3 179 D5
Presteign Ave CF38 135 F2
Presteigne Wlk NP44 89 C1
Preston Ave NP20 142 F4
Preston St NP13 36 B6
Preswylfa Ct CF31 168 E2
Preswylfa Ho SA15 40 E2
Preswylfa Row 5 SA15 40 D3
Preswylfa St CF5 194 B7
Pretoria Rd
Abertillery / Abertyleri
NP13 36 C3
Tonyrefail CF39 133 D5
Pretoria St CF32 103 E6
Pretoria Terr NP22 13 F6
Prettyman Dr SA10 70 D3
Price Ave CF63 215 B7
Price Cl
Newport / Casnewydd
NP20 143 C2
Pontypool / Pont-y-pwl
NP4 38 C1
Prices Ct NP11 87 B2
Price's Pl CF44 28 F2
Price's Row SA10 222 F6
Price St
2 Aberdare / Aberdâr
CF44 29 A1
Cefn Coed / Cefn-coed-y-cymmer CF48 10 A4
Rhymney / Rhymni NP22 12 E5
Treorchy / Treorci CF41 78 F5
PRICE TOWN 104 F4
Prichard St CF39 133 C5
Priestley Cl NP20 142 F1
Priest Rd CF24 195 D7
Prif Ffordd / High St
SA15 40 C4

Prifysgol = university

Prifysgol Caerdydd / Cardiff Univ (Cathays Park Campus) CF10 232 B4
Prifysgol Cymru Abertawe / Univ of Wales Swansea
SA2 94 D4
Prifysgol Morgannwg / Univ of Glamorgan
CF37 135 E6
Primitive Pl NP23 7 D4
Primrose Bank SA10 48 B5
Primrose Cl
Bridgend / Pen-y-Bont ar
Ogwr CF31 169 C6
Cardiff / Caerdydd CF3 179 B2
Cowbridge / Y Bont-Faen
CF71 189 A1
Nelson CF46 83 E4
Pant CF48 11 A6
Primrose Ct
Swansea / Abertawe
SA5 68 A5
Tonyrefail CF39 133 D6
Primrose Ct / Cwrt Briallen NP44 88 F1
Primrose Hill
4 Aberdare / Aberdâr
CF44 28 E4
Cowbridge / Y Bont-Faen
CF71 189 B1
Merthyr Tydfil / Merthyr Tudful
CF47 30 F8
Swansea / Abertawe SA1 95 B7
Primrose La
Ebbw Vale / Glyn Ebwy
NP23 7 A4
Pontardawe SA8 23 D5
Rhos SA8 24 B2
Primrose Rd SA11 71 D4
Primrose Row SA8 23 D5
Primrose St
Swansea / Abertawe
SA1 95 B7
Tonypandy CF40 106 E5
Primrose Terr
Aberdare / Aberdâr
CF44 53 C8
Porth CF39 108 A3
Primrose Way NP10 141 D7
Prince Andrew Rd NP11 59 F5
Prince Charles Ct
CF64 207 A5
Prince Charles Hospl / Ysbyty Twysog Siarl
CF47 10 C5
Prince Edward Cres
NP23 14 D4
Prince Edward Ho 3
CF64 207 A5
Prince Leopold St 1
CF24 195 D5
Prince Llewellyn Ho 2
CF64 207 A5
Prince of Wales Dr
CF5 175 E5
Prince Of Wales Dr / Rhodfa Tywysog Cymru
SA11 71 E8
Prince of Wales Ind Est
NP11 87 A2
Prince Of Wales Rd
SA1 233 B4
Prince Philip Ave NP23 7 D5
Prince Philip Hospl The
SA14 41 B7
Prince Rd CF33 148 D3
Prince Rhodry Ho 1
CF64 207 A5
Princes Ave
Caerphilly / Caerffili
CF83 138 B1
Cardiff / Caerdydd
CF24 195 D7
Princes Ct
Cardiff / Caerdydd
CF24 232 C3
Ebbw Vale / Glyn Ebwy
NP23 7 E1
Princes Rise CF83 138 B1
Princess Cres NP13 59 E6
Princess Ct
Llanelli SA15 40 C5
Tredegar NP22 13 E8
Princess Dr / Ffordd Tywysoges SA10 48 C2
Princess Louise Rd
CF40 106 F8
Princess Margaret Way The / Ffordd Y Dywysoges Margared
SA12 98 B1
Princess Margaret Way The / Fford Y Dywysoges Margared The SA12 124 D8
Princess of Wales Ct
SA1 69 C5
Princess of Wales Hospl / Ysbyty Tywysoges Cymru
CF31 169 A6
Princess St
Abertillery / Abertyleri
NP13 36 B4
Ferndale CF43 79 F8
Gorseinon SA4 43 B2
Llanelli SA15 40 C5
Maesteg CF34 102 B2
Pontypridd CF37 135 E7
Ton Pentre CF41 79 C3
Princes St
Barry / Y Barri CF62 214 D4
Cardiff / Caerdydd
CF24 195 D8
Prince's St
2 Treherbert CF42 51 A1
Treorchy / Treorci CF42 78 E6
Princess Way
Bridgend / Pen-y-Bont ar
Ogwr CF31 169 A4
Swansea / Abertawe
SA1 233 B2
Prince St
Blaenavon NP4 17 C6
Cwmfelinfach NP11 113 F4
Margam SA13 125 D5
Nantyglo NP23 8 C1
Newport / Casnewydd
NP19 143 D6
Pontypool / Pont-y-pwl
NP4 62 B7
Princes Way CF31 169 B3
Prince's Wlk NP4 63 B4
Principality Bsns Pk
CF31 169 B7
Priority Bsns Pk CF10 195 A3
Priority Ent Pk CF63 215 E7
Priority Workshops
CF63 215 E7
Priors Cres SA2 93 B8
Priorsgate NP12 59 C2
Prior St SA13 99 B1
Priors Town SA3 228 C2
Priors Way SA2 93 B8
Priory Ave CF31 168 F1
Priory Cl
Bridgend / Pen-y-Bont ar
Ogwr CF31 168 F1
Caerleon / Caerllion
NP18 117 E3
Pontypridd CF37 109 B3
Priory Cres NP18 145 B8
Priory Ct NP11 114 B8
Priory Ct / Clos-y-Priordy
SA10 48 C2
Priory Dr NP18 145 A8
Priory Gdns
Barry / Y Barri CF63 215 B8
Bridgend / Pen-y-Bont ar Ogwr
CF31 168 F2
Langstone NP18 119 B1
Priory Gr NP18 145 B8
Priory Oak CF31 169 A4
Priory Rd CF31 168 F2
Priory St NP11 115 A1
Priory Terr CF34 101 F3
Priory View NP18 145 B8
Priory Way NP18 145 B8
Priscilla Terr CF46 83 C8
PRISK 189 D5
Pritchard Cl 1 CF5 176 E2
Pritchard St CF46 83 B8
Pritchard Terr
Fleur-de-lis NP12 85 B4
New Tredegar NP24 33 E4
Probert Pl 4 NP19 143 E5
Proctor Cl CF62 214 C5
Promenade
Barry / Y Barri, Barry Island
CF62 214 E1
Promenade *continued*
Barry / Y Barri, The Knap
CF62 214 C1
Swansea / Abertawe
SA1 233 A3
Promenade D'orvault The
NP22 13 E6
Promenade Terr SA3 123 B4
Promenade The
Abersychan NP4 37 E3
Pen-clawdd SA4 64 C4
Swansea / Abertawe SA2 94 E4
The Mumbles / Y Mwmbwls
SA3 123 B8
Promenade View / Golwg Y Rhodfa SA12 98 C1
Prospect Dr CF5 193 F8
Prospect Pl
Abertysswg NP22 33 B8
Cwmaman CF44 53 A4
Cwmbran / Cwmbrân
NP44 89 E2
Cwmllynfell SA9 221 B7
Llanelli SA15 40 D6
Ogmore Vale CF32 104 E1
Pont Rhyd-y-cyff CF34 128 D6
Pontycymer CF32 103 E4
Pontypool / Pont-y-pwl
NP4 63 A4
Swansea / Abertawe,
Penyrheol SA2 94 C7
Swansea / Abertawe
SA1 233 B2
Tredegar NP22 13 F6
Treorchy / Treorci CF42 78 E6
Tylorstown CF43 80 C4
Ystalyfera SA9 2 B6
Prospect Pl / Maes Prospect NP4 37 F1
Prospect St NP20 143 B7
Prospect Terr SA3 122 F6
Prosser La 3 NP20 142 F4
Prosser St
8 Mountain Ash / Aberpennar CF45 54 E1
1 Treharris CF46 83 B6
Prosser's Terr SA13 75 A6
Protheroe Ave CF31 168 C8
Protheroe St
Ferndale CF43 80 A5
Maesteg CF34 75 B2
Providence La SA3 122 A7
Provident Cotts CF82 85 B2
Pryce St
Llanelli SA15 40 C6
Mountain Ash / Aberpennar
CF45 54 D3
Treorchy / Treorci CF41 79 A3
Pryderi Footpath SA1 95 B8
Prydwen Rd SA5 67 B4
Pugh Bldgs 14 SA15 40 D5
Pugsley Gdns CF32 150 F4
Pugsley St NP20 143 C6
Pum Erw Rd CF14 177 D5
Pump House Rd CF62 211 E1
Pump St 7 NP20 143 B5
Punch House Flats
NP22 13 E6
Purbeck St CF5 194 C6
Purcell Ave / Rhodfa Purcell SA12 98 A3
Purcell Rd
Cardiff / Caerdydd
CF3 179 D7
Penarth CF64 206 F1
Purcell Sq NP19 144 C5
Purdey Cl CF62 214 C7
Purple Cl SA12 98 B3
Pwllcarn Terr CF32 103 E8
Pwlldu La SA3 121 F4
Pwll-Evan-Ddu CF35 169 C8
Pwllfa Pl CF44 52 F3
Pwllfa Rd CF44 53 A4
Pwllglas Rd NP12 85 C7
PWLLGWAUN 109 A1
Pwllgwaun Rd CF37 109 B1
Pwllheli Ct CF3 179 C4
Pwllhelyg CF15 176 D8
PWLL- MAWR 179 D2
Pwll Mawr Ave CF3 179 C3
Pwllmelin La CF5 193 F8
Pwllmelin Rd CF5 176 E1
Pwll Melyn CF35 152 C1
Pwll St SA1 68 D4
Pwll-y-Domen Rd SA5 68 B3
Pwllygath St CF33 148 D2
Pwll-y-Glaw SA12 100 A7
Pwll y Min Cres CF5 191 E5
PWLLYPANT 138 A6
Pwll Yr Allt CF82 84 F7
Pwll-yr-Hwyaid SA5 67 E6
Pwll-y-Waun CF36 183 B8
Pye Cnr NP10 142 C3
Pyke St CF63 215 A5
PYLE 122 A5
Pyle Cross CF33 148 B1
Pyle Ct SA3 122 A5
Pyle Ent Ctr CF33 148 D1
Pyle Inn Way CF33 148 B2
Pyle Rd
Bishopston SA3 122 A5
Cardiff / Caerdydd CF5 193 C4
Porthcawl CF36 166 A2
Pyle / Y Pîl CF33 148 B2
Pyle Sta CF33 148 A1
PYLE / Y PÎL 148 A2
Pyntws Terr 2 SA15 40 F4
Pyra Ct CF62 214 C3
Pytchley Cl CF72 155 E2

Q

Quadrangle The
Pyle / Y Pîl CF33 148 A1
Sarn CF32 150 E4
Quadrant Sh Ctr The
SA1 233 A2
Quadrant The SA2 94 E6
Quail Ct CF24 195 C7
Quakers View CF46 82 F6
QUAKERS YARD 83 B5
Quakers Yard Sta CF46 82 F6
Quantock Cl NP11 115 C1
Quantock Dr NP19 144 C6
Quarella CF31 168 E6
Quarella Cres CF31 168 E6
Quarella Rd CF31 168 E6
Quarella St CF63 215 B6
Quar Rd SA11 71 E6
Quarr Dr SA6 46 D7
Quarr Rd
Clydach SA6 46 D7
Pontardawe SA8 23 E5
Quarry Cl CF5 193 C8
Quarry Cotts 11 CF45 54 D3
Quarry Cres CF5 193 C7
Quarry Dale CF3 179 B2
Quarry Hill Cl CF37 109 A1
Quarry Pl SA18 220 D7
Quarry Rd
10 Mountain Ash / Aberpennar CF45 54 D3
Pontypridd CF37 109 A1
Swansea / Abertawe SA5 68 D5
Tonna / Tonnau SA11 49 C2
Quarry Row
Blaina / Blaenau NP13 15 F6
Merthyr Tydfil / Merthyr Tudful
CF47 10 D2
Quarry St
Nantgarw CF15 157 F8
Swansea / Abertawe
SA1 233 B4
Tylorstown CF43 80 B4
Quarry Wood Cvn Site
CF32 184 A8
Quay Par SA1 233 C3
Quay Rd SA11 71 E8
Quay Row CF48 30 E5
Quay St / Stryd Y Cei
2 Ammanford / Rhydaman
SA18 219 C7
Cardiff / Caerdydd CF10 232 B2
Quay W SA1 233 B3
Quebec Cl NP20 142 D3
Queen Anne Sq CF10 232 A4
Queen Charlotte Dr
CF15 174 F6
Queen Mary's Wlk / Rhodfa'r Frenhines Mary
SA15 40 E4
Queen St / Heol Y Frenhines CF10 232 C3
Queens Arc 5 CF10 232 B2
Queen's Ave
Gorseinon SA4 43 B1
Porthcawl CF36 183 B7
Queen's Ave / Rhodfa Frenhines CF32 150 E4
Queensbury Rd CF23 178 E3
Queen's Chambers 1
NP20 143 B5
Queen's Cl NP20 143 B6
Queen's Cres NP22 12 E5
Queen's Croft NP20 143 B6
Queens Ct CF31 169 C3
Queens Dr
Cardiff / Caerdydd
CF5 193 A2
Llantwit Fadre / Llanilltud Faerdref CF38 156 D6
Queen's Hill NP20 143 B6
Queen's Hill Cres
NP20 143 B6
Queens Lofts SA15 40 C5
Queen Sq
6 Brynmawr NP23 8 B4
Tredegar NP22 13 E6
Queens Rd
Bridgend / Pen-y-Bont ar
Ogwr CF31 169 C2
Bridgend / Pen-y-Bont ar Ogwr
CF31 169 C3
Cymmer / Cymer SA13 75 D3
Newbridge / Trecelyn
NP11 87 A7
Swansea / Abertawe SA2 94 D6
Queen's Rd
Cwmsyfiog NP24 34 A2
Merthyr Tydfil / Merthyr Tudful
CF47 10 E1
Neath / Castell-Nedd
SA10 70 F7
New Tredegar NP24 33 F2
Penarth CF64 207 B5
The Mumbles / Y Mwmbwls
SA3 123 A5
Queens Rd S CF10 207 D8
Queen's Sq NP23 14 D8
Queen St
Aberdare / Aberdâr
CF44 53 C7

Queen St *continued*
Abertillery / Abertyleri NP13 36 B4
Barry / Y Barri CF62 214 D4
Blaengarw CF32 103 E7
Blaina / Blaenau NP13 15 E5
Bridgend / Pen-y-Bont ar Ogwr CF31 168 F4
Brynmawr NP23 8 C5
Brynmenyn CF32 150 E6
Cwmdare CF44 28 C3
Ebbw Vale / Glyn Ebwy NP23 14 E2
Glyncorrwg SA13 227 C2
Maesteg CF34 102 A3
Nantyglo NP23 15 D8
Neath / Castell-Nedd SA11 71 E7
Newport / Casnewydd NP20 143 C3
Pant CF48 11 B6
Pontlottyn CF81 12 E1
Pontrhydyfen SA12 73 A1
Pontypool / Pont-y-pwl, Griffithstown NP4 62 E3
Pontypool / Pont-y-pwl, Sowhill NP4 62 B7
Pontypridd CF37 135 E6
Tongwynlais CF15 158 C1
Ton Pentre CF41 78 F3
Ton Pentre CF41 79 A3
Treorchy / Treorci CF41 78 F5
Queen's Terr CF48 55 B8
Queen Street Back Rd 3 SA11 71 E7
Queen Street Prim Sch NP13 36 C4
Queen Street Sta CF10 232 C3
Queens Villas NP23 7 D2
Queens W CF10 232 B3
Queensway
Ebbw Vale / Glyn Ebwy NP23 7 D5
Nantgarw CF15 158 A7
Newport / Casnewydd NP20 143 B5
Swansea / Abertawe SA5 67 D4
Queens Way CF63 215 A3
Queen's Way
Llanwern NP18, NP26 145 D1
Newport / Casnewydd NP19 144 E2
Queensway Bsns Ctr SA5 67 D4
Queensway Mdws NP19 144 D2
Queensway Meadows Ind Est NP19 144 D1
Queen Victoria Meml Almshouses 11 NP20 143 B4
Queen Victoria Rd SA15 40 C4
Queen Victoria St NP22 13 D6
Queenwood CF23 178 E3
Queen Wood Cl CF23 178 C3
Quentin St CF14 177 E2
Quilter Cl NP19 144 D4

R

Raby St / Stryd Raby SA15 40 C6
Rachel Cl CF5 176 D3
Rachel Sq NP10 163 E6
Rachel St 3 CF44 29 A1
Radcliffe Wlk CF71 189 C8
Radford Terr NP23 7 D4
Radnor Dr
Church Village CF38 135 F2
Swansea / Abertawe SA6 46 B4
Radnor Gn CF62 214 F7
Radnor Ho
6 Penarth CF64 206 F2
Port Talbot SA12 124 D8
9 Swansea / Abertawe SA1 233 C2
Radnor Prim Sch CF5 194 C6
Radnor Rd
Cardiff / Caerdydd CF5 194 C6
Llantwit Major / Llanilltud Fawr CF61 210 C6
Newport / Casnewydd NP19 143 F6
Radnor Way
Cwmbran / Cwmbrân NP44 89 E3
Porth CF39 133 D8
RADYR 176 B6
Radyr Ave SA3 93 F2
Radyr Comp Sch CF15 176 D4
Radyr Court Cl CF5 176 F2
Radyr Court Rd
Cardiff / Caerdydd CF5 176 E3
Cardiff / Caerdydd CF5 176 F2
Radyr Court Rise CF5 176 F2
Radyr Court Sh Prec CF5 176 E3
Radyr Farm Rd CF15 176 C4
Radyr Pl CF14 177 D2
Radyr Rd CF14 176 F3
Radyr Sta CF15 176 C5
Raglan Cl
Abersychan NP4 37 E4
Blackwood / Coed-Duon NP12 58 D1
Cardiff / Caerdydd CF3 180 A7
Dinas Powis / Dinas Powys CF64 206 C3
Raglan Ct
Caerphilly / Caerffili CF83 137 D4
Croesyceiliog NP44 89 F6
Newport / Casnewydd NP20 143 C2
Raglande Ct CF61 210 A5
Raglan Gr CF48 225 F1
Raglan Ho CF10 232 A2
Raglan Mews NP10 163 E5
Raglan Rd
Hengoed CF82 85 A3
Swansea / Abertawe SA2 94 C7
Raglan St NP11 114 E3
Raglan Terr NP23 7 D3
Ragnall Cl CF14 159 E3
Railmill La SA12 99 F5
Railway Cotts SA6 45 F3
Railway Cres 8 CF24 195 D6
Railway Heritage Mus* CF62 214 F2
Railway Hos
East Aberthaw CF62 212 C1
Hollybush NP12 34 D3
Tredegar NP22 34 B8
Railway Pl / Ffordd Y Wagen 8 SA15 40 C4
Railway Row CF32 129 C2
Railway St
Aberdare / Aberdâr CF44 28 F3
Abertillery / Abertyleri NP13 60 B6
Cardiff / Caerdydd, Maindy CF14 177 E1
Cardiff / Caerdydd, Splott CF24 195 E6
Newport / Casnewydd NP20 143 B5
Risca / Rhisga NP11 114 F2
Trelewis CF46 83 C7
Railway Terr
Abercarn NP11 87 A3
Abertillery / Abertyleri NP13 59 F8
Bargoed / Bargod CF81 58 A2
Blaenavon NP4 17 B6
Blaengarw CF32 103 D7
Blaina / Blaenau NP13 15 D5
Briton Ferry / Llansawel SA11 71 C1
Bryncethin CF32 151 E6
Caerphilly / Caerffili CF83 138 B2
Cardiff / Caerdydd CF11 194 D5
Cymmer / Cymer SA13 75 B5
Dinas Powis / Dinas Powys CF64 206 C4
Fochriw CF81 32 C8
Gorseinon SA4 43 C1
Hirwaun CF44 224 E1
Hollybush NP12 34 D3
Llantwit Fadre / Llanilltud Faerdref CF38 156 D7
Maesteg CF34 75 B1
Merthyr Tydfil / Merthyr Tudful CF47 30 E7
Mountain Ash / Aberpennar CF45 82 A8
New Tredegar NP24 33 D3
Ogmore Vale CF32 104 E1
Penarth CF64 207 A4
Pontycymer CF32 103 E4
Pontypool / Pont-y-pwl NP4 89 E8
Porth CF39 107 E6
Resolven / Resolfen SA11 226 D5
South Cornelly CF33 166 A5
Swansea / Abertawe SA5 67 E3
Talbot Green CF72 155 B1
Tongwynlais CF15 158 C1
Ton-mawr SA12 73 D5
Ton Pentre CF41 79 B3
Tonypandy, Blaen Clydach CF40 106 C6
Tonypandy, Penygraig CF40 106 F4
Tredegar NP22 6 A6
Treharris CF46 83 C7
Treorchy / Treorci CF42 78 B4
Ystradgynlais SA9 222 A4
Railway Terr / Heol Rheilffordd SA9 221 B7
Railway Terr / Rhes Yr Orsaf 9 SA15 40 C4
Railway View
Ebbw Vale / Glyn Ebwy, Beaufort NP23 7 D4
Ebbw Vale / Glyn Ebwy, Briery Hill NP23 14 D6
Fleur-de-lis NP12 85 B4
Tonypandy, Llwynypia CF40 79 F1
Tonypandy, Williamstown CF40 107 A2
Railway View / Golygfa'r Rheilffordd NP22 13 E8
Rainbow Bsns Ctr SA7 69 B6
Raisdale Gdns CF64 207 B2
Raisdale Ho CF64 207 B2
Raisdale Rd CF64 207 A2
Raldan Cl CF63 215 B8
Raleigh Cl SA2 94 C6
Raleigh Wlk CF10 232 C1
RALLT 91 A8
Ralph St
Llanelli SA15 40 D5
Pontypridd CF37 109 D2
Ralph Terr SA15 40 C4
Ramah St CF42 78 C7
Rambler Cl CF14 159 F3
Ramping Rd NP11 114 C8
Ramsay Rd SA6 22 E1
Ramsden Rd SA6 46 C7
Ramsden St NP22 12 F3
Ramsey Cl CF36 165 D1
Ramsey Dr SA6 45 D1
Ramsey Pl SA5 67 E7
Ramsey Rd CF62 214 F8
Ramsey Wlk
Cwmbran / Cwmbrân NP44 89 C5
Newport / Casnewydd NP19 143 F7
Ramson Cl CF82 84 E6
Ramsons Way CF5 193 A5
Rankine Cl NP20 116 F2
Ranks The NP11 87 B2
Rannoch Dr CF23 178 C5
Rannoch Ho 1 NP44 89 C2
Raphael Ave CF31 169 D6
Raphael Cl NP19 144 A7
Raphael Ho 4 SA12 98 D1
RASSAU 7 B4
Rassau Ind Est NP23 7 A6
Rassau Rd NP23 7 B4
Rathbone Terr CF34 75 A2
Raven Cl CF31 169 B3
RAVEN HILL 67 E4
Raven Hill / Bryn Cigfran CF31 168 B4
Ravenhill Rd SA5 67 F4
Ravenhill St CF41 79 B2
Raven Ind Est SA18 220 B8
Ravensbrook CF15 176 B8
Ravenscourt
Cardiff / Caerdydd CF24 232 C4
Cwmbran / Cwmbrân NP44 89 B3
Ravens Court Cl CF23 178 E2
Ravens Ct SA11 72 B5
Ravensfield SA4 66 D3
Ravenshoe Rd CF63 215 D7
Ravens Wlk SA3 122 F6
Ravenswood CF11 206 F6
Ravenswood Cl SA10 48 E2
Ravenswood Ct NP11 114 E3
Raven Way CF64 217 A7
Rawden Mews CF11 194 E5
Rawden Pl CF11 194 E5
Rawlinson Terr / Teras Rawlinson Isaf NP22 13 F5
Raymond Terr CF37 135 F6
Readers La CF62 213 A2
Readers Way CF62 213 A2
Reardon Smith Ct CF5 193 D8
Rechabite Hall CF48 55 D4
Recorder St SA1 233 A2
Rectory Cl
Caerphilly / Caerffili CF83 138 A1
Dowlais CF48 11 B5
Loughor SA4 42 F1
Sarn CF32 150 E3
Wenvoe / Gwenfo CF5 205 A6
Rectory Ct CF61 210 B8
Rectory Dr CF62 211 D5
Rectory Gdns CF83 140 A7
Rectory Rd
8 Barry / Y Barri CF63 215 B6
Bedwas CF83 138 E7
Caerphilly / Caerffili CF83 138 A2
Cardiff / Caerdydd CF5 194 C6
Gelligaer CF82 84 C7
Neath / Castell-Nedd SA11 71 E7
Newbridge / Trecelyn NP11 60 C2
Penarth CF64 207 B4
St Athan / Sain Tathan CF62 211 D5
Rectory Road La CF64 207 B4
Redberth Cl CF62 214 F7
Redbrink Cres CF62 215 A2
Red Brink Ct CF5 193 C6
Redbrook Ave CF83 139 A6
Redbrook Ct CF83 138 A1
Redbrook Ho NP44 89 F3
Redbrook Rd NP20 142 E4
Redbrook Way NP44 89 F3
Redcliffe SA3 122 B4
Redcliffe Ave CF5 194 A6
Red Dragon Ctr The CF10 195 C2
Rede Rd NP44 89 B1
Redfield St CF41 79 D2
Redgate Terr CF72 174 C7
Red Gr / Llwyn Coch CF31 168 B3
Redhill Cl CF44 27 C8
Red House Cl CF5 193 D6
Red House Cres CF5 193 D6
Red House Pl CF5 193 D6
Red House Rd CF5 193 C6
Redlands Ave CF64 206 E4
Redlands Cl CF35 170 D7
Redlands Rd CF64 206 E4
Redland St NP20 143 B7
Redlands The NP19 144 C4
Redlaver St CF11 194 F3
Red Lion Cotts CF5 191 B1
Red Lion Flats NP4 37 F3
Redman Cl / Clos Redman CF33 148 D2
Red Oaks / Deri Cochion CF35 170 B8
Red Roofs Cl CF35 153 B2
Redrose Hill CF41 79 B3
Red Sea Ho 1 CF10 195 B3
Redshank Cl CF36 182 D8
Redvers St NP19 143 F4
Redway Rd CF5 190 F1
Redwell Ct 8 CF23 178 C2
Redwick Ct NP44 89 F2
Redwick Ho
Cardiff / Caerdydd CF23 178 B5
Cwmbran / Cwmbrân NP44 89 F2
Redwing Cl / Clos-y-asgell Goch CF31 169 C4
Redwood Cl
Bryn-côch SA10 48 C5
Caerleon / Caerllion NP18 117 E2
2 Cardiff / Caerdydd CF3 179 E7
Llantwit Major / Llanilltud Fawr CF61 210 C5
Redwood Ct
Cardiff / Caerdydd CF14 177 F8
Cwmdare CF44 28 D3
Swansea / Abertawe SA5 68 A5
Redwood Dr
Cwmdare CF44 28 D3
Llantwit Fadre / Llanilltud Faerdref CF38 156 C6
Redwood Meml Hospl NP22 12 E4
Redwood Pl 5 NP23 14 D6
Redwood Rd SA3 122 F7
Reece's Terr NP11 114 D8
Reene Ct NP19 144 A3
Rees Cl NP20 117 A3
Rees Ct CF61 210 B6
Rees Pl
14 Neath / Castell-Nedd SA11 71 E7
Treorchy / Treorci CF41 78 F5
Rees Row / Rhes Rees CF32 150 F4
Rees St
Aberavon SA12 98 F1
Dowlais CF48 11 B5
Ebbw Vale / Glyn Ebwy NP23 14 D8
Merthyr Tydfil / Merthyr Tudful CF47 30 E8
Ton Pentre CF41 79 B2
Tonypandy CF40 107 B1
Treorchy / Treorci CF42 78 E6
Rees Terr
Llanbradach CF83 111 F2
Pontypridd CF37 135 E6
Reevesland Ind Est NP19 144 A1
Reform St CF81 32 F8
Regalia Terr SA15 40 E5
Regency Cl CF61 210 A7
Regency Ho 4 SA1 233 A3
Regent Ave CF5 193 A2
Regent Gdns CF14 177 A6
Regent St E SA11 71 C1
Regent St W SA11 71 B1
Regents Ct CF24 195 D3
Regent St
Aberdare / Aberdâr CF44 53 C7
Abertillery / Abertyleri NP13 60 C6
Barry / Y Barri CF62 214 F5
Dowlais CF48 11 A5
Ferndale CF43 79 F6
Treorchy / Treorci CF42 78 E6
Reginald St
Port Talbot SA13 99 C1
Swansea / Abertawe SA1 96 A7
Reginald Terr 2 NP10 142 B4
Regina Terr CF5 194 B7
Reigate Cl CF14 159 E3
Reigit La SA3 122 C6
Relf Rd CF3 179 C4
Rembrandt Ct SA2 94 E6
Rembrandt Ho 2 SA12 98 E1
Rembrandt Pl 1 SA12 98 E1
Rembrandt Way NP19 143 F7
Rennie St CF11 194 E5
Renoir Ho 10 SA12 98 D1
Renoir Rd NP19 144 A7
Reresby Ct CF10 195 B2
Reservoir Cl NP10 142 B4
Reservoir Rd NP23 7 C5
RESOLFEN / RESOLVEN 226 E5
RESOLVEN / RESOLFEN 226 E5
Rest Bay Cl CF36 182 D8
Restway Ct CF5 176 E3
Restway Gdns CF31 168 E5
Restways CF36 182 E7
Restways Cl CF5 176 D2
Retford Ct CF14 177 C4
Retreat The
Bridgend / Pen-y-Bont ar Ogwr CF31 168 E2
Cardiff / Caerdydd CF23 178 D2
Porthcawl CF36 165 E2
Sarn CF32 150 E4
Reynallt Pl CF36 182 F7
Reynolds Cl
Newport / Casnewydd NP19 143 F7
North Cornelly CF33 165 E8
REYNOLDSTON 229 B1
Rhanallt St / Stryd Rhanallt 7 SA13 125 D5
Rhandir SA14 41 E4
Rhandir Terr SA14 18 B1
Rheidol Ave SA6 68 C8
Rheidol Cl
Aberdare / Aberdâr CF44 29 E1
Cardiff / Caerdydd CF14 178 A8
Treorchy / Treorci CF42 78 B8
Rheidol Ct SA6 68 C8
Rheidol Dr CF62 214 C5
Rheola Ave SA11 226 D5
Rheola Ind Est CF39 107 E4
Rheola St CF45 82 A7
Rheolau Terr CF37 108 C2
Rhes Bailey / Bailey's Terr NP4 61 F8
Rhes Barnfield / Barnfield Terr NP4 17 B6
Rhes Bricksen / Brick Row SA10 222 C3
Rhes Bryndulais / Bryndulais Row SA10 222 C4
Rhes Elizabeth / Elizabeth Row NP4 37 C3
Rhes Garw / Garw Row NP44 90 B5
Rhes Gwaith Tyn SA15 40 F2
Rhes Inkerman / Inkerman Row SA13 125 D6
Rhes Pen-y-Graig / Pen-y-Graig Terr NP4 62 D5
Rhes Rees / Rees Row CF32 150 F4
Rhestr Fawr SA9 1 F2
Rhes y Parot NP13 15 D7
Rhes-yr-Afon / River Row NP4 38 A1
Rhes Yr Orsaf / Railway Terr 9 SA15 40 C4
Rhianfa Gdns SA1 95 A7
Rhianfa La SA1 95 A7
RHIGOS 26 C8
Rhigos Gdns CF24 177 F1
Rhigos Prim Sch CF44 26 C8
Rhigos Rd
Blaenrhondda CF42 50 E5
Hirwaun CF44 27 C8
Rhigos CF44 27 A8
Rhigos CF44 224 B1
Treherbert CF44 26 D4
RHISGA / RISCA 115 B2
RHIW 59 F1
Rhiw Aberhonddu / Brecon Rise CF48 11 B7
Rhiwamoth St CF81 58 B5
Rhiw Aneurin / Aneurin Cl NP22 13 E7
RHIWBINA 177 B8
Rhiwbina Hill
Cardiff / Caerdydd CF14 159 A1
Tongwynlais CF15, CF83 158 E3
Rhiwbina Prim Sch / Ysgol Gynradd Rhiwbeina CF14 177 B7
Rhiwbina Sta CF14 177 B6
Rhiw Cae Mawr CF31 169 B5
Rhiw Ceris CF44 53 E8
Rhiw Ctr The 6 CF31 168 F4
Rhiwddar Ho CF15 158 A4
RHIWDERIN 141 E4
Rhiwderyn
Birchgrove SA7 47 B8
Swansea / Abertawe SA7 70 B8
Rhiwderyn Cl CF5 192 F3
Rhiw Fach CF83 137 E5
Rhiw Farm Cres NP11 59 F2
Rhiwfawr Rd SA9 1 A1
Rhiw Felin CF37 136 A6
Rhiwfer CF46 83 D3
Rhiwgarn CF39 107 D1
Rhiwgarn Inf Sch CF39 133 D8
Rhiwglyn Rd CF32 130 F7
Rhiwlas
Cardiff / Caerdydd CF14 159 C2
Dunvant SA2 93 E8
Neath / Castell-Nedd SA10 48 B2
Rhiw Las CF31 169 C5
Rhiw Llech View SA13 75 E3
Rhiw Melin NP44 89 B6
Rhiw Nant CF44 29 C3
RHIW PARC / RHIW PARK 36 C5
Rhiw Parc Terr NP13 36 B5
Rhiw Park Rd NP13 36 B5
RHIW PARK / RHIW PARC 36 C5
Rhiw Rd SA9 221 C5

Rhiw'r Ddar CF15 158 A5
Rhiwr Derwen CF72 153 F2
Rhiwr Rd NP7 9 D6
Rhiwsaeson Rd CF72 156 A2
Rhiw Syr Dafydd Hill
Blackwood / Coed-Duon NP12 58 F2
Blackwood / Coed Duon NP12 59 A2
Rhiw Syr Dafydd Prim Sch NP12 59 B2
Rhiw The
Bridgend / Pen-y-Bont ar Ogwr CF31 168 F4
Graig Penllyn CF71 188 B8
Rhiw Tremaen CF31 169 B5
Rhiw Wen NP23 7 C2
Rhodes Ave SA12 98 F1
Rhodfa Abbeyville / Abbeyville Ave 16 SA12 98 D1
Rhodfa Adams / Adams Ave CF32 150 F4
Rhodfa Amroth / Amroth Wlk 14 NP44 89 C2
Rhodfa Arian / Silver Ave SA12 98 B2
Rhodfa Aur / Golden Ave SA12 98 B2
Rhodfa Bevan / Bevan Ave SA10 48 E1
Rhodfa Brookville / Brookville Dr SA10 70 E7
Rhodfa Brymbo / Brymbo Ave 2 SA13 125 D5
Rhodfa Bryn-Mawr / Brynmawr Ave 6 SA18 219 B7
Rhodfa Bryn Rhos SA18 220 A8
Rhodfa Caer Fferm / Farmfield Ave SA12 98 D2
Rhodfa Canolog / Central Ave SA12 98 C5
Rhodfa Ceirios CF31 168 D8
Rhodfa Citrine / Citrine Ave 3 SA12 98 B2
Rhodfa Clesin / Japonica Dr CF48 11 C4
Rhodfa Coed Cerdinen / Rowan Tree Ave SA12 98 E4
Rhodfa Crom / Chrome Ave SA12 98 B2
Rhodfa Ddraenen Wen / Hawthorn Ave SA12 98 D6
Rhodfa Dickens / Dickens Ave SA12 124 E7
Rhodfa Dugoch / Crimson Ave 6 SA12 98 B2
Rhodfa Elba / Elba Ave SA13 125 D5
Rhodfa Fadog
Cwmrhydyceirw SA6 46 A4
Swansea / Abertawe SA6 45 F4
Rhodfa Felin CF62 214 C4
Rhodfa Fferm / Farm Dr SA12 98 C1
Rhodfa Frank SA18 219 B7
Rhodfa Frenhines / Queen's Ave CF32 150 E4
Rhodfa Ganol CF81 32 D7
Rhodfa Glan-y-Mor / Glan-y-Mor Ave 4 SA13 125 E4
Rhodfa Glascoed NP12 85 D6
Rhodfa Glasfryn / Glasfryn Terr SA15 40 E7
Rhodfa Gorllewin / Western Ave SA12 98 C2
Rhodfa Gwifir / Wyvern Ave 2 SA12 98 C2
Rhodfa Gwinau / Auburn Ave SA12 98 B2
Rhodfa Handel / Handel Ave SA12 98 B3
Rhodfa Helios / Helios Dr SA12 98 C5
Rhodfa Heulwen SA15 40 E7
Rhodfa Landore / Landore Ave 8 SA13 125 E4
Rhodfa Lansbury / Lansbury Ave SA13 125 E5
Rhodfa Lingfield / Lingfield Ave SA12 98 E1
Rhodfa Lloyd George / Lloyd George Ave CF10 195 B3
Rhodfa Llwyneithin SA15 40 D7
Rhodfa Llysweri / Liswerry Dr NP44 90 B2
Rhodfa Maenorbyr / Manorbier Dr NP44 90 A3
Rhodfa Marics CF72 155 B4
Rhodfa Mar / Marine Dr SA12 98 C1
Rhodfa Martyn / Martyn's Ave SA10 222 C3
Rhodfa Mes / Acorn Wlk CF31 168 B4
Rhodfa Mozart / Mozart Dr SA12 98 B3
Rhodfa Newydd CF44 53 E8
Rhodfa Parc Vivian / Vivian Park Dr SA12 98 D2
Rhodfa Penderyn / Penderyn Ave SA13 125 E5
Rhodfa Penrhiwtyn / Penrhiwtyn Dr SA11 71 C4
Rhodfa Phoenix / Phoenix Ave 8 SA13 125 D5
Rhodfa Pontnewydd / Pontnewydd Wlk 3 NP44 89 E4
Rhodfa Purcell / Purcell Ave SA12 98 A3
Rhodfa'r Blanhigfa / Plantation Dr NP44 90 B4
Rhodfa'r Brain SA5 67 E5
Rhodfa'r Coed CF34 128 C8
Rhodfa'r Creyr / Heron Ave SA15 40 B5
Rhodfa'r Deintyddion / Dental Dr CF14 177 E3
Rhodfa'r De / South Ave SA14 41 A3
Rhodfa'r Dryw
Cwmrhydyceirw SA6 46 A5
Swansea / Abertawe SA6 45 F5
Rhodfar Dwyrain / East Ave NP4 62 E1
Rhodfa'r Eos
Cwmrhydyceirw SA6 46 A5
Swansea / Abertawe SA6 45 F5
Rhodfa'r Frenhines Mary / Queen Mary's Wlk SA15 40 E4
Rhodfa'r Glwysti / Cloisters Wlk SA12 98 D3
Rhodfa'r Gogledd / North Ave SA14 41 A3
Rhodfa'r Gwagenni CF63 214 F4
Rhodfa'r Melinydd / Millers Ride 6 NP44 90 A3
Rhodfar Orsaf CF38 156 F8
Rhodfa'r Orsaf / Station Terr CF10 232 C3
Rhodfar Pant CF48 11 A7
Rhodfa'r Wennol SA6 46 A5
Rhodfa'r Wiwer / Squirrel Wlk SA4 19 A5
Rhodfa Sabl / Sable Ave 8 SA12 98 B2
Rhodfa St Helier / St Helier Dr SA12 98 B3
Rhodfa Samson / Samson's Ave NP4 37 E7
Rhodfa Sirius / Sirius Dr SA12 98 C5
Rhodfa Sweldon 2 CF62 214 E4
Rhodfa Terr CF48 31 C2
Rhodfa Toronto / Toronto Ave 9 SA13 125 E4
Rhodfa Tuar Mor / Seaward Ave SA12 98 C1
Rhodfa Tywysog Cymru / Prince Of Wales Dr SA11 71 E8
Rhodfa Wheatley / Wheatley Ave 2 SA12 124 E8
Rhodfa Wilden / Wilden Ave 3 SA13 125 D5
Rhodfa Ysgarlad / Scarlet Ave SA12 98 A2
Rhododendron Cl CF23 178 D7
Rhodri Pl / Maes Rhodri 5 NP44 90 B2
Rhondda Cl NP23 7 B4
Rhondda Fechan Farm CF43 79 F7
Rhondda Heritage Park & Visitor Ctr* CF37 108 C3
Rhondda Rd
Ferndale CF43 79 F7
Pontypridd CF37 109 B1
Rhondda Specl Sch CF40 107 C4
Rhondda St SA1 95 B7
Rhondda Terr
Ferndale CF43 79 F6
Tonypandy CF40 106 F8
Rhonos Rd NP7 9 D7
Rhoofa Helys / Hazel Wlk 6 NP44 90 A6
Rhoose Cardiff International Sta / Maes Awyr Rhyngwladol Caerdydd CF62 213 A1
Rhoose Rd CF62 213 B2
RHOOSE / Y RHWS 213 B1
RHOS 24 B3
RHOSAMAN 221 A8
Rhos Ave CF82 84 E8
Rhos Cotts SA10 2 F3
Rhos Ddu CF64 206 E2
Rhos Dyfed CF44 53 B7
Rhos Foundary / Foundry Row SA10 70 E8
Rhos Helyg
Caerphilly / Caerffili CF83 138 D4
Cwmfelin CF34 128 C8
Rhoshyfryd CF44 224 D3
Rhosili Rd CF82 84 F5
Rhoslan NP22 6 F1
Rhos Llan CF14 177 C8
Rhos Mdw SA8 24 B4
Rhos Nathan Wyn CF44 53 B8
Rhosnewydd Terr NP12 85 E6
Rhos Prim Sch / Ysgol Gymradd Y Rhos SA8 24 B3
Rhos Rd SA5 67 F4
RHOSSILI 230 B7
Rhossili Visitor Ctr* SA3 230 B6
Rhossilli Cl CF44 27 D7
Rhossily Ave CF3 179 C4
Rhossily Rd CF3 179 C4
Rhos St CF83 138 A5
Rhos Terr SA18 218 F6
Rhos-y-Bettws CF82 84 D7
Rhos Y Dderwen NP12 85 D6
Rhos-y-Fedwyn Prim Sch NP23 7 B4
Rhosyn Gwyn NP24 33 F2
Rhuddlan Cl NP10 141 E3
Rhuddlan Ct CF83 137 D4
Rhuddlan Way CF64 206 C4
Rhws Prim Sch CF62 213 A1
Rhych Ave CF36 183 B6
RHYDAMAN / AMMANFORD 219 A8
Rhydarw Terr SA9 222 F8
Rhyd Clydach NP23 8 D5
RHYDDING 48 E3
Rhyddings Park Rd SA2 94 F6
Rhyddings Terr SA2 94 F6
Rhyddwen Pl SA6 22 B1
Rhyddwen Rd
Craig-cefn-parc SA6 22 B1
Swansea / Abertawe SA6 21 F1
Rhydfach CF48 31 B3
Rhydhelig Ave CF14 177 E4
Rhyd-Hir SA10 48 A1
Rhydlafar Dr CF5 175 E4
Rhydri Prim Sch CF83 139 C3
Rhyd Terr NP22 14 A4
Rhyd The NP22 14 A4
RHYDWAEDLYD 177 C7
Rhydwen SA9 2 E6
Rhyd Wen SA18 221 A8
RHYD-Y-BEDD 11 A6
Rhyd-y-Cae NP23 7 B4
RHYD-Y-CAR 30 D7
Rhydycar Bsns Pk CF48 30 D8
Rhyd-y-Coed SA7 70 A8
Rhyd-y-Defaid Dr SA2 94 B5
RHYDYFELIN 136 C5
Rhyd-y-Felin SA7 69 F5
Rhyd Y Fenni SA4 64 B3
RHYD-Y-FRO 23 D8
Rhyd-y-fro Prim Sch SA8 23 D8
Rhyd-y-Glyn SA7 69 F6
Rhyd-y-Gwern Cl CF83 138 E5
Rhyd Y Gwern Isaf CF83 140 A7
Rhyd-y-Nant CF35 152 C1
Rhyd y Nant CF72 173 B7
Rhydynos St NP4 17 C6
RHYD-Y-PANDY 21 F1
Rhyd-y-Pandy Rd SA6 45 E7
Rhyd-y-Penau Cl CF14 178 A7
Rhydypenau Prim Sch CF14 178 A7
Rhyd-y-Penau Rd CF23 178 B7
Rhyd-y-Pennau SA10 48 C2
Rhyd Y Polon SA4 43 B1
Rhydyrafon SA15 40 F7
Rhyd-yr-Helyg
Swansea / Abertawe SA2 94 C5
Upper Boat CF15 157 F8
Rhygoes St CF24 177 F1
Rhyl Rd CF3 179 C4
Rhymney Cl
Bryn NP12 85 D4
Ebbw Vale / Glyn Ebwy NP23 7 C4
Rhymney Comp Sch NP22 33 A8
Rhymney Ct
2 Cardiff / Caerdydd CF24 195 B8
Cwmbran / Cwmbrân NP44 89 A5
RHYMNEY / RHYMNI 12 F4
Rhymney River Bridge Rd CF23 179 A1
Rhymney Row NP22 6 A6
Rhymney St CF24 232 C4
Rhymney Sta NP22 12 E3
Rhymney Terr
Caerphilly / Caerffili CF83 138 A2
Cardiff / Caerdydd CF24 195 A8
RHYMNI / RHYMNEY 12 F4
RHYMNI / RUMNEY 179 B3
Rhyslyn Walk* SA13 73 C1
Rhys Rd NP12 85 C6
Rhys St
Tonypandy CF40 106 F5
Tylorstown CF43 107 C8
Rhyswg Rd NP11 87 B2
Rialto Ct CF14 177 B5
Ribble Sq NP20 116 E2
Ribble Wlk NP20 116 E2
Rice St / Stryd Rice SA18 219 C6
Rice St
Bridgend / Pen-y-Bont ar Ogwr CF31 168 E4
Llanelli SA15 40 E4
Port Talbot SA13 125 C7
Rice Street SA18 219 C6
Richard Burton Ho 1 SA12 98 B2
Richard Lewis Cl CF5 176 E2
Richardson Rd SA1 95 B6
Richardson St
Pontardawe SA8 23 C3
Swansea / Abertawe SA1 95 B6
Richards Pl CF24 195 D7
Richard's Pl SA1 233 B3
Richards Row CF44 53 F7
Richards St CF24 195 A8
Richard St
Abercwmboi CF44 53 E4
Barry / Y Barri CF62 214 F5
10 Llanelli SA15 40 D5
Maerdy CF43 79 B8
Pontycymer CF32 103 F3
Pontypridd CF37 109 F5
Swansea / Abertawe SA5 68 C2
Richards Terr
Cardiff / Caerdydd CF24 195 D7
Tonypandy CF40 106 E6
Trelewis CF46 83 C7
Richard's Terr CF44 53 F7
Richley Cl SA12 98 E5
Richmond Appartments CF24 232 C4
Richmond Cl
Cwmbran / Cwmbrân NP44 89 E5
8 Llanbradach CF83 111 F1
Richmond Cres CF24 232 C4
Richmond Ct
Cardiff / Caerdydd CF24 232 C4
Swansea / Abertawe SA1 95 A7
Tredegar NP22 13 F5
Richmond Dr CF44 224 E1
Richmond Mews 1 SA1 95 A6
Richmond Pk
Loughor SA4 42 F1
Ystradgynlais SA9 222 A5
Richmond Pl
Cwmbran / Cwmbrân NP44 89 E5
Port Talbot SA13 125 D6
Richmond Rd
Abertillery / Abertyleri NP13 36 C3
Cardiff / Caerdydd CF24 232 C4
Cwmbran / Cwmbrân NP44 89 E5
Loughor SA4 42 F1
Mountain Ash / Aberpennar CF45 54 D4
Newport / Casnewydd NP19 143 E7
Pontypool / Pont-y-pwl NP4 62 E1
Swansea / Abertawe SA2 95 A7
Richmond St
1 Cwmbran / Cwmbrân NP44 89 E5
13 Neath / Castell-Nedd SA11 71 E7
Richmond Terr
Aberdare / Aberdâr CF44 29 B3
Llanelli SA15 40 C4
Swansea / Abertawe SA2 94 F7
Tredegar NP22 13 F5
Richmond Villas SA1 95 A7
Richmond Way SA5 67 E5
Richs Rd CF14 177 D4
Rickards St
Pontypridd CF37 135 C8
Porth CF39 107 F2
Rickards Terr CF37 135 C8
Rickyard The / Buarth Y Ddera SA10 48 D3
Ridge Acre SA2 94 C4
Ridge of the Ct / Esgair-y-llys CF31 168 B4
Ridge of the Mdw / Esgair-y-Maes CF31 168 B3
Ridge The SA2 94 C4
RIDGEWAY 142 E5
Ridgeway
Cardiff / Caerdydd CF14 159 F3
Machen CF83 139 B6
Newport / Casnewydd NP20 142 E4
Pontypool / Pont-y-pwl NP4 38 D1
Swansea / Abertawe SA2 93 D6
Ridgeway Ave NP20 142 E5
Ridgeway Cl
Newport / Casnewydd NP20 142 F5
Pontypridd CF37 109 B2
Ridgeway Cres NP20 142 E4
Ridgeway Ct NP20 142 E5
Ridgeway Dr NP20 142 F4
Ridgeway Gdns NP20 142 F5
Ridgeway Gr NP20 142 E5
Ridgeway Hill NP20 142 F5
Ridgeway Park Rd NP20 142 E5
Ridgeway Pl CF38 136 A1
Ridgeway Rd
Barry / Y Barri CF62 214 D8
Cardiff / Caerdydd CF3 179 A4
Ridgeway Reach NP20 142 F5
Ridgeway Rise NP20 142 F5
Ridgeway The CF3 179 A4
Ridgeway View NP20 142 F5
Ridgeway Villas NP20 142 F5
Ridgeway Wlk NP20 142 F5
Ridgewood Gdns SA11 72 C5
Ridgewood Pk SA15 41 A5
Ridings The
Aberdare / Aberdâr CF44 28 D2
Church Village CF38 136 A1
Ridley Way SA3 122 A6
Rifle Gn 2 NP4 17 C7
RIFLE GREEN 17 D8
Rifleman's Row SA1 68 F2
Rifleman St 4 NP11 114 F3
Rifle St NP4 17 C7
Rimini Ho CF10 195 C3
Rinastone Ct CF5 193 F8
RINGLAND 144 E6
Ringland Circ NP19 144 E5
Ringland Ctr NP19 144 F6
Ringland Prim Sch NP19 144 E5
Ringland Way NP18, NP19 145 A6
Ringside Bsns Ctr CF3 179 D2
Ringwood Ave NP19 144 D6
Ringwood Cres CF62 211 D8
Ringwood Hill NP19 144 C5
Ringwood Pl NP19 144 D5
Rink The CF47 10 E2
Risca Cl CF3 179 F7
Risca Com Sch NP11 115 D1
Risca Day Hospl NP11 114 F3
Risca Rd
Abercarn NP11 114 C4
Newport / Casnewydd NP20 142 E4
Rogerstone / Ty-du NP10 141 E7
RISCA / RHISGA 115 B2
Risca Town Prim Sch NP11 114 F1
Rise The
Barry / Y Barri CF63 214 F6
Cardiff / Caerdydd CF14 160 A1
Church Village CF38 135 F2
Cwmbran / Cwmbrân NP44 89 C5
Cwmdare CF44 28 C3
Hawthorn CF37 136 C3
Nantyglo NP23 15 D7
Pant CF48 11 B7
Pengam NP12 85 B7
Porth CF39 107 E5
Ton Pentre CF41 79 B2
Rising Sun Cl NP12 59 A2
Rising Sun Ind Est NP13 15 D6
Ritson St SA11 71 C1
Riverbank Sch CF5 193 E5
River Ct CF45 82 E2
River Dale CF5 193 D6
River Glade CF15 158 A3
Rivermead Way NP10 141 D7
River Rd
Cwm NP23 35 A7
Pontlottyn CF81 12 F1
River Row
Abercanaid CF48 30 F4
Abercynon CF45 82 E3
Blackwood / Coed Duon NP12 59 A1
Blaina / Blaenau NP13 15 E4
River Row / Rhes-yr-Afon NP4 38 A1
Riversdale CF5 176 F2
Riversdale Rd SA3 122 F6
River's Edge CF72 173 A7
RIVERSIDE 194 E5
Riverside
Aberkenfig / Abercynffig CF32 150 D3
Blaina / Blaenau NP13 15 E5
Ebbw Vale / Glyn Ebwy NP23 7 C4
Hirwaun CF44 27 F7
Llanmorlais SA4 64 B2
Newport / Casnewydd NP19 143 C6
Pontypool / Pont-y-pwl NP4 62 C7
Tonna / Tonnau SA10 49 C3
Riverside Bsns Pk / Parc Busnes Glan yr Afon SA7 46 B1
Riverside Cl CF39 107 F6
Riverside Cl / Clos Glanyrafon CF48 55 C5
Riverside Ct
Blackwood / Coed-Duon NP12 85 F7
Pontypool / Pont-y-pwl NP4 62 C7
Senghenydd CF83 110 F2
Riverside Ct CF15 158 B2
Riverside Cvn Pk SA6 46 B3
Riverside Dr
Blaenavon NP4 17 C5
Neath / Castell-Nedd SA11 71 E8
Riverside Flats CF32 130 E8
Riverside Gdns
Abercrave / Abercraf SA9 222 E8
Glyn-neath / Glyn-nedd SA11 223 D1
Riverside Ho SA12 99 E4
Riverside Ind Est CF37 136 D1

Riverside Ind Pk SA14 .... 42 C8
Riverside Park CF83 .... 138 C7
Riverside Pk CF47 .... 10 C2
Riverside Pl CF63 .... 215 D6
Riverside Rd SA12 ...... 124 F7
Riverside St CF15 .... 157 F5
Riverside Terr
Cardiff / Caerdydd
CF5 .... 193 F6
Machen CF83 .... 139 F6
Newbridge / Trecelyn
NP11 .... 87 A6
Riverside View / Bolwg yr
Afon SA11 .... 226 C5
Riversmead NP44 .... 90 A2
River St
Maesteg CF34 .... 102 B3
Ogmore Vale CF32 .... 104 E1
Pontypridd CF37 .... 135 E7
Ystrad CF41 .... 79 D3
River Terr
Glan-y-nant NP12 .... 85 A7
Hendy SA4 .... 19 A4
7 Porth CF39 .... 107 F3
Treorchy / Treorci CF42 .... 78 C6
River View
Cardiff / Caerdydd
CF14 .... 177 A2
Cardiff / Caerdydd, Gabalfa
CF14 .... 177 C1
Tonypandy CF40 .... 106 E6
River View Ct CF5 .... 176 F2
River View / Golwg Yr
Afon SA4 .... 19 A5
River Way / Ffordd Yr
Afon CF32 .... 150 D6
River Wlk
Cowbridge / Y Bont-Faen
CF71 .... 188 E1
Llantwit Major / Llanilltud
Fawr CF61 .... 209 F6
9 Merthyr Tydfil / Merthyr
Tudful CF47 .... 10 D1
Road No 1 SA12 .... 98 B4
Roam Rd CF72 .... 155 D3
Roath Court Pl CF24 .... 195 D8
Roath Court Rd CF24 .... 195 D8
Roath Ct 5 NP44 .... 90 A3
Roath Dock Rd CF10 ..... 195 E3
ROATH PARK 178 B3
Roath Park Prim Sch
CF24 .... 178 B1
ROATH / Y RHATH 195 C8
Robbin's La 15 NP20 .... 143 C4
Robert Cl NP20 .... 143 C2
Robert Davies Ct SA4 .... 19 C4
Robert Owen Gdns SA1 ... 96 B8
Roberts Ave CF47 .... 10 F5
Roberts Cl
Glyn-neath / Glyn-nedd
SA11 .... 223 C1
Rogerstone NP10 .... 142 A7
St Athan / Sain Tathan
CF62 .... 211 D5
Roberts La 3 CF47 .... 10 D1
Robertson Ho 5 SA12 .... 98 B3
Robertson Way NP20 .... 117 A4
Roberts Rd / Heol Roberts
SA1 .... 95 F5
Robert's Row NP13 .... 16 B1
Robert St
Barry / Y Barri CF63 ..... 215 B5
Bryncae CF72 .... 153 F2
Cardiff / Caerdydd, Cathays
CF24 .... 178 A1
Cardiff / Caerdydd, Ely / Tre-
lai CF5 .... 193 F6
Glyn-neath / Glyn-nedd
SA11 .... 223 C1
Swansea / Abertawe SA5 .. 68 C3
Treorchy / Treorci CF41 .... 78 F4
Ynysybwl CF37 .... 109 A8
Roberts Terr NP22 .... 13 F6
ROBERTSTOWN 29 A4
Robertstown Ind Est
CF44 .... 29 A2
Roberts Villas CF14 ..... 176 F4
Robin Cl CF23 .... 178 D7
Robin Hill CF64 .... 206 B2
Robin Hood La NP18 .... 119 E2
Robin Rd SA5 .... 67 E7
Robins Hill CF31 .... 169 C4
Robins La
Barry / Y Barri CF63 ..... 215 B7
Reynoldston SA3 .... 229 C1
Robinson St SA15 .... 40 D5
Robinswood Cl CF64 .... 207 A2
Robinswood Cres
CF64 .... 207 A2
Rochdale Terr 6 NP4 .... 38 A1
Roche Cres CF5 .... 176 C1
Rochester Mans 4
CF14 .... 176 F6
Rochester Rd NP19 ..... 143 F5
Roch St NP13 .... 36 C6
ROCK 58 F2
Rock Chwyth Rd SA8 ..... 23 F3
Rock Cotts CF37 .... 109 A2
Rock Dr CF41 .... 79 A2
Rockfield Ho NP4 .... 62 B8
Rockfields CF36 .... 165 E1
Rockfields Cl 1 CF36 ... 165 F1
Rockfields Cres 2
CF36 .... 165 F1
Rockfield St NP19 ...... 143 D7
Rockfield Terr SA11 ...... 71 D5
Rock Head / Pen Maen
CF31 .... 168 D3
Rockhill SA3 .... 123 B4
Rockhill Rd NP4 .... 62 D5
Rock Hos CF46 .... 83 A5
Rockingham Terr / Teras
Rockingham SA11 ...... 71 C2
Rockingstone Terr
CF37 .... 135 E8
Rock La
Cefn Coed / Cefn-coed-y-
cymmer CF48 .... 10 A4
Horton SA3 .... 231 B4
Rockland Terr SA1 .... 68 C1
Rockleigh Ave CF81 ...... 58 B5
Rockrose Way CF64 ..... 206 E5
Rock St
Aberkenfig / Abercynffig
CF32 .... 150 C4
Glyn-neath / Glyn-nedd
SA11 .... 223 C1
Mountain Ash / Aberpennar
CF45 .... 54 D2
Rock Terr
Swansea / Abertawe
SA6 .... 45 F1
Ynysybwl CF37 .... 81 E2
Rock View CF46 .... 82 F6
Rock Villa Cl NP4 .... 37 E7
Rock Villas NP12 .... 59 A3
Rockwood Rd CF15 ..... 158 B4
Rocky Rd CF47 .... 10 F5
Roden Ct 2 CF24 .... 195 C7
Roderick Hill Ct NP22 ..... 6 C2
Roderick Pl 2 NP23 ...... 14 D6
Rodericks Terr CF46 ..... 83 B6
Roding Cl NP20 .... 116 D1
Rodney Rd NP19 .... 143 C5
Rodney St SA1 .... 95 B5
Roehampton Ct CF3 ..... 179 A3
Rofton Bglws SA12 .... 99 E6
Rogart Terr CF37 .... 109 D4
Roger Beck Way SA2 ..... 94 E6
Roger's La CF32 .... 167 E4
Rogersmoor Cl CF64 .... 207 A2
Roger St SA5 .... 68 B7
Rogerstone Cl CF3 ...... 179 F7
ROGERSTONE / TY-
DU 141 F6
Roland Ave SA15 .... 40 C7
Roland Dr CF83 .... 137 E1
Roland St CF10 .... 232 C1
Rolls Ave CF82 .... 84 E7
Rolls Cl NP44 .... 89 A2
Rolls St CF11 .... 194 D5
Rolls Wlk NP10 .... 142 A6
Roma Ho CF10 .... 232 C1
Roman Amphitheatre
Caerllion★ NP18 .... 118 B1
Roman Baths Mus★
NP18 .... 118 C2
Roman Bridge Cl SA3 .... 94 B2
Roman Cl CF5 .... 193 D3
Roman Ct SA3 .... 94 B2
Roman Fortress
Caerllion★
NP18 .... 118 B1
Roman Gate / Porth
Rhufeinig CF82 .... 84 D7
Roman Gates NP18 ...... 118 C2
Roman Legionary Mus★
NP18 .... 118 B2
Roman Rd SA10 .... 223 A4
Roman Reach NP18 ..... 117 F2
Roman Ridge CF82 .... 84 B7
Roman Way
Caerleon / Caerllion
NP18 .... 117 F3
Neath / Castell-Nedd
SA10 .... 71 D8
Romilly Ave CF62 .... 214 C3
Romilly Bldgs
Barry / Y Barri, Barry Dock
CF63 .... 215 B4
Barry / Y Barri CF62 ..... 214 D3
Romilly Cres CF11 ...... 194 D6
Romilly Ct CF62 .... 214 D3
Romilly Inf & Jun Schs
CF62 .... 214 D4
Romilly Park Rd CF62 ... 214 C2
Romilly Pl 3 CF5 .... 194 C6
Romilly Rd
Barry / Y Barri CF62 ..... 214 D3
Cardiff / Caerdydd CF5 ... 194 C6
Rhoose / Y Rhws CF62 .... 213 A1
Romilly Rd W CF5 .... 194 B7
Romney Cl NP19 .... 144 B7
Romney Ho SA12 .... 124 D8
Romney Rd SA12 .... 124 D8
Romney Rd / Heol Romney
14 SA12 .... 98 D1
Romney Wlk 5 CF64 .... 206 F5
Romsley Ct 9 NP44 ...... 89 C2
Ronald Pl CF5 .... 193 D6
Ronald Rd NP19 .... 143 E6
Rook Cl CF62 .... 210 D5
Rookery Cl CF64 .... 216 A5
Rookery Wood CF64 .... 216 A5
Rookwood Ave CF5 ..... 176 F1
Rookwood Cl
Cardiff / Caerdydd
CF5 .... 176 F1
Merthyr Tydfil / Merthyr Tudful
CF47 .... 10 D3
Neath / Castell-Nedd
SA11 .... 71 F7
Rookwood Hospl CF5 ... 177 A1
Rookwood St CF11 ...... 194 E3
Roper Cl CF5 .... 176 D2
Roperwright Cl SA4 ...... 66 B5
Ropewalk Rd SA15 .... 40 F2
Ropewalk The SA11 ...... 71 E7
Rope Wlk Terr SA11 ...... 71 E7
Rosamund Cl NP10 ..... 163 F5
Roseberry Terr SA6 ...... 66 E5
Rosebery Pl CF64 .... 207 A3
Rosebery St
Abertillery / Abertyleri
NP13 .... 36 A5
Pontypool / Pont-y-pwl
NP4 .... 62 E3
Rose Cotts
Abersychan NP4 .... 37 F8
Llanrhidian SA4 .... 229 F5
5 Pontypridd CF37 ..... 109 B1
Rosecroft Dr NP18 ...... 145 C8
Rose Ct
Cwmbran / Cwmbrân
NP44 .... 88 F2
Newbridge / Trecelyn
NP11 .... 87 B8
Rosedale Cl CF5 .... 193 C8
Rosedale Terr CF40 ..... 106 E8
Rose Farm Bglws NP22 ..... 6 B1
Rosegarden The NP20 ... 142 F5
Rose Gdns NP44 .... 90 B4
Roseheyworth Bsns Pk
NP13 .... 35 E8
Rose Heyworth Est
NP13 .... 36 A7
Roseheyworth Millennium
Prim Sch / Ysgol
Gynradd Y Mileniwm
Roseheyworth NP13 ..... 35 F7
Rose Heyworth Rd
NP13 .... 15 E1
Rose Hill SA1 .... 95 A7
Rosehill Terr
Gilfach Goch CF39 ...... 106 C1
Swansea / Abertawe SA1 .. 95 B7
Roseland Rd SA5 .... 66 F4
Roseland Terr SA1 .... 95 F7
Rosemary Cl SA2 .... 67 B1
Rosemary Ct SA6 .... 45 F1
Rosemary La NP4 .... 62 C6
Rosemary St CF10 ...... 232 C2
Rosemead NP44 .... 88 F3
Rosemont Ave NP11 ..... 115 A2
Rosemount Pl CF14 ..... 177 D3
Rosendale Ct 5 NP19 ... 143 F5
Rose Pk / Parc Rhosyn
CF34 .... 102 C1
Rose Row CF44 .... 53 F7
Rose St
Cardiff / Caerdydd
CF24 .... 232 D4
Newport / Casnewydd
NP20 .... 143 B6
Rose Terr
Bettws CF32 .... 129 D2
Bryncae CF72 .... 153 F2
Pontypool / Pont-y-pwl
NP4 .... 61 F8
Rosewarne Cl SA5 .... 66 F3
Rose Wlk NP10 .... 141 D7
Rosewood Ave SA12 ...... 98 E6
Rosewood Cl
Bryn-côch SA10 .... 48 C4
Cardiff / Caerdydd CF14 .. 160 A3
Rosewood Way SA5 ...... 67 F5
Ross Cl CF37 .... 135 B6
Rosser's Field SA3 ...... 123 C3
Rosser St
Ferndale CF43 .... 80 A5
Neath / Castell-Nedd
SA11 .... 71 F8
Pontypool / Pont-y-pwl
NP4 .... 62 A7
Pontypridd CF37 .... 135 B8
Rosser Terr SA10 .... 49 C4
Rosset Cl CF3 .... 179 E6
Rossetti Cl CF5 .... 176 E3
Ross Ho NP44 .... 89 F2
Ross La NP20 .... 143 B7
Rosslyn Rd NP19 .... 143 F5
Ross Rise CF42 .... 51 A1
Ross St NP20 .... 143 B8
Rotary International Way /
Heol Rotari Cenedlaethol
CF31 .... 169 A7
Rother Cl NP20 .... 116 D3
Rotherslade Rd SA3 ..... 122 F4
Rothesay Rd NP19 ..... 143 F5
Rougemont Sch NP20 ... 116 F4
Roundabout Ct CF83 .... 138 B6
Roundel Cl CF14 .... 159 F4
Roundhouse Cl NP23 ...... 8 C1
Round Wood CF23 ...... 178 E5
Round Wood Cl CF23 .... 178 E3
Routs View NP18 .... 145 B5
Rover Way
Cardiff / Caerdydd
CF24 .... 196 A8
Cardiff / Caerdydd, Pengam
Green CF24 .... 196 B6
Rover Way Cvn Site
CF24 .... 196 B6
Rowan Ave SA2 .... 94 B8
Rowan Cl
Clydach SA6 .... 46 E8
Gorseinon SA4 .... 43 A4
Mountain Ash / Aberpennar
CF45 .... 54 E3
Nelson CF46 .... 83 E4
Penarth CF64 .... 207 A1
Rowan Cl continued
Pencoed CF35 .... 170 C8
Pen-y-coedcae CF37 ..... 135 B6
Swansea / Abertawe SA2 .. 93 D5
Rowan Cres NP4 .... 62 D2
Rowan Ct
Aberdare / Aberdâr
CF44 .... 28 D2
Barry / Y Barri CF62 ..... 214 C3
Cardiff / Caerdydd CF5 ... 194 A8
Llanharry CF72 .... 172 B5
Rowan Dr CF36 .... 183 E8
Rowan Gr CF62 .... 211 B7
Rowan Ho 3 CF64 ...... 206 F5
Rowan Pl NP22 .... 12 E5
Rowan Rd NP11 .... 115 B2
Rowan Rise CF48 .... 10 B6
Rowan's La CF32 .... 151 A5
Rowan Tree Ave / Rhodfa
Coed Cerdinen SA12 .... 98 E4
Rowan Tree Cl / Clos Coed
Cerdinen SA10 .... 48 D2
Rowan Tree La CF72 .... 173 D8
Rowan Way
Cardiff / Caerdydd
CF14 .... 160 B3
Ebbw Vale / Glyn Ebwy
NP23 .... 7 C5
Merthyr Tydfil / Merthyr Tudful
CF47 .... 10 D4
Newport / Casnewydd
NP20 .... 117 B3
Rowena Ct CF5 .... 193 C8
Rowen Gdns CF38 ...... 156 E7
Rowland Ho SA11 .... 72 B5
Rowlands Cotts SA13 .... 100 F5
Rowland Terr CF32 ...... 104 F6
Rowley Terr CF43 .... 52 B1
Rowling St CF40 .... 107 A3
Row The NP10 .... 140 C3
Roxburgh Garden Ct
CF64 .... 207 B3
Roxby Ct CF10 .... 232 C1
Royal Arc CF10 .... 232 B2
Royal Bldgs
Cardiff / Caerdydd
CF10 .... 232 C3
Penarth CF64 .... 207 A3
Royal Cl
Abercarn NP11 .... 87 A3
Penarth CF64 .... 207 A5
Royal Cotts CF43 .... 52 B1
Royal Cres
Merthyr Tydfil / Merthyr
Tudful CF47 .... 10 E3
Newbridge / Trecelyn
NP11 .... 59 F1
Royal Glamorgan Hospl /
Ysbyty Frenhinol
Morgannwg CF72 ...... 155 B5
Royal Gwent Hospl
NP20 .... 143 B3
Royal Hamadryad Hospl
CF10 .... 195 B1
Royal La NP13 .... 36 A6
Royal Mint CF72 .... 155 B6
Royal Oak CF83 .... 140 B6
Royal Oak Cl CF83 ...... 140 B6
Royal Oak Dr NP18 ..... 144 E7
Royal Oak Gn NP44 ...... 90 B4
Royal Oak Hill NP18 .... 144 E7
Royal Oak Ho NP11 ...... 60 C4
Royal Oak Rd SA2 .... 94 B3
Royal Stuart La CF10 .... 195 B2
Royal Terr CF40 .... 107 A5
Royal The CF64 .... 207 A5
Royce Cl CF82 .... 84 E7
Royce Wlk NP10 .... 142 A6
Royde Cl CF5 .... 192 E4
Royston Cres NP19 ..... 144 B4
Royston Ct / Llys Royston
SA10 .... 48 C1
Rubens Cl NP19 .... 143 F7
Ruby St CF24 .... 195 D6
RUDRY 139 C2
Rudry Cl CF83 .... 138 E5
Rudry Common Walk★
CF83 .... 139 A1
Rudry Rd
Caerphilly / Caerffili
CF83 .... 138 D5
Cardiff / Caerdydd
CF14 .... 160 D5
Rudry St
Cardiff / Caerdydd
CF11 .... 194 E3
Newport / Casnewydd
NP19 .... 143 C6
Penarth CF64 .... 206 F4
Rufus Lewis Ave SA4 ..... 43 A3
Rugby Ave SA11 .... 71 E7
Rugby Ct 8 CF5 .... 193 E6
Rugby Rd
Newport / Casnewydd
NP19 .... 143 D5
Resolven / Resolfen
SA11 .... 226 D5
Ruggles Terr SA6 .... 45 D1
Rumney High Sch CF3 .. 179 C5
Rumney Inf Sch CF3 .... 179 B3
Rumney Jun Sch CF3 ... 179 B3
Rumney Pottery★ CF3 ... 179 A2
RUMNEY / RHYMNI 179 B3
Rumney Wlk / Tro Rhymni
NP44 .... 90 B3
Runcorn Cl
Barry / Y Barri CF63 ..... 215 D7
Cardiff / Caerdydd CF3 ... 179 D8
Runnymede SA2 .... 94 E7
Runway Rd CF24 .... 196 A7
Ruperra Cl
Bassaleg NP10 .... 142 B3
Cardiff / Caerdydd CF3 ... 179 D8
Ruperra Ct CF37 .... 109 C2
Ruperra La NP20 .... 143 C3
Ruperra St
Llantrisant CF72 .... 155 D4
Newport / Casnewydd
NP20 .... 143 D3
New Tredegar NP24 ...... 33 E3
Rupert Brooke Dr
NP20 .... 142 F2
Rural Way SA2 .... 94 B8
Rushbrook 1 NP44 .... 89 B3
Rushbrook Cl CF14 ..... 176 E4
Rush Dr NP11 .... 59 D5
Rushfield Gdns CF31 .... 169 A6
Rushmere Rd NP12 ...... 85 E3
Rushwind Cl SA3 .... 122 E6
Rushwind Mews SA3 .... 122 E6
Ruskin Ave
Port Talbot SA12 .... 124 E8
Rogerstone NP10 .... 142 A7
Ruskin Cl
Cardiff / Caerdydd
CF3 .... 179 B7
Cwmbran / Cwmbrân
NP44 .... 89 A2
Ruskin Rise NP20 ...... 142 E2
Ruskin St SA11 .... 71 B3
Russell Cl
Bassaleg NP10 .... 141 F3
Ebbw Vale / Glyn Ebwy
NP23 .... 7 A4
Pontypool / Pont-y-pwl
NP4 .... 63 B4
Russell Dr NP20 .... 117 A2
Russell Drive Gdns
NP20 .... 117 A2
Russell St
Cardiff / Caerdydd
CF24 .... 232 C4
4 Cwmbran / Cwmbrân
NP44 .... 89 E5
Dowlais CF48 .... 11 A4
Llanelli SA15 .... 40 D3
New Tredegar NP24 ...... 34 A1
Swansea / Abertawe SA1 .. 95 B6
Russell Terr 17 CF47 ..... 30 E8
Russet Cl
Langstone NP18 .... 145 C8
Port Talbot SA12 .... 98 B3
Rustic Cl SA2 .... 94 B8
Ruthen Terr CF62 ...... 214 D5
Rutherford Hill NP20 .... 117 A2
RUTHIN 170 F4
Ruthin Ct CF35 .... 169 F4
Ruthin Gdns CF24 ...... 232 B4
Ruthin Way CF38 ...... 136 A2
Ruth Rd / Heol Ruth
NP4 .... 63 A5
Ruth St CF81 .... 57 F3
Rutland Cl CF62 .... 214 C8
Rutland Pl 10 NP20 ..... 143 C3
Rutland St CF11 .... 194 E4
Ryan Cl SA4 .... 43 F2
Ryans Cl SA10 .... 71 C8
Ryder St CF11 .... 194 E6
Ryw Blodyn SA7 .... 69 D6

S

Sable Ave / Rhodfa Sabl 8
SA12 .... 98 B2
Sable Cl CF14 .... 160 A4
Sable Cl / Clos Sable 7
SA12 .... 98 B2
Sachville Ave CF14 ..... 177 E3
Saddler St SA1 .... 68 D4
Saffron Dr CF3 .... 180 A8
Saffrwn Ct / Cwrt Saffron
NP44 .... 88 F1
SAIN DUNWYD / ST
DONAT'S 208 G5
SAIN FFAGAN / ST
FAGANS 193 A7
SAIN NICOLAS / ST
NICHOLAS 191 F1
St Aarons Dr CF72 ...... 153 F4
St Agatha Rd CF14 ..... 177 E4
St Agnes Ct CF24 ...... 195 E7
St Agnes Rd CF14 ...... 177 D4
St Aidan Cres CF14 ..... 177 D4
St Aiden Dr SA2 .... 93 D6
St Aiden's Rise CF63 .... 215 C6
St Alban Ave CF14 ..... 177 D4
St Alban's RC High Sch
NP4 .... 62 C6
St Alban's RC Prim Sch
NP4 .... 62 B7
St Albans RC Prim Sch /
Ysgol Gynradd Sain Alban
CF24 .... 195 F7
St Alban's Rd
Swansea / Abertawe
SA2 .... 94 F5
Treherbert CF42 .... 50 D3
St Alban's Terr
6 Port Talbot SA13 ..... 125 C6
Treherbert CF42 .... 50 E3
St Aloysius Prim Sch
CF47 .... 10 D4
St Ambrose Cl 3
CF64 .... 206 A2
St Ambrose Rd CF14 .... 177 E4

SAINT ANDRAS / ST ANDREWS MAJOR 205 D4
St Andrews Cl
Cwmbran / Cwmbrân NP44 89 F7
Llantwit Fadre / Llanilltud Faerdref CF38 156 D6
The Mumbles / Y Mwmbwls SA3 93 E1
St Andrew's Cl NP23 7 F4
St Andrew's Cl CF37 135 B6
St Andrew's Cres CF10 232 C3
St Andrews Ct 5 CF40 106 E6
St Andrews Dr NP12 85 E5
St Andrews Ho 11 CF64 207 B4
St Andrew's Inf Sch NP19 143 F3
St Andrew's Jun Sch NP19 143 F3
St Andrew's La CF10 232 C3
St Andrews Major CW Prim Sch CF5 205 F3
ST ANDREWS MAJOR / SAINT ANDRAS 205 D4
St Andrew's Pl CF10 232 C3
St Andrew's Rd
Barry / Y Barri CF62 214 E6
Bridgend / Pen-y-Bont ar Ogwr CF31 168 E7
Dinas Powis / Dinas Powys CF64 205 D3
St Angela Rd CF14 177 E3
St Anne's Ave CF64 206 F2
St Anne's Cl
Cwmbran / Cwmbrân NP44 89 E5
Newbridge / Trecelyn NP11 86 D5
Rogerstone NP10 142 B4
The Mumbles / Y Mwmbwls SA3 123 A3
St Anne's Cres
Bargoed / Bargod CF81 58 A2
Newport / Casnewydd NP19 143 E7
Porthcawl CF36 183 C7
St Annes Ct CF72 172 F5
St Anne's CW Inf Sch CF24 195 C7
St Annes Dr CF38 156 D6
St Anne's Dr SA11 49 C2
St Annes Gdns CF83 137 A7
St Anne's Gdns CF82 85 B2
St Annes Rd NP12 85 C7
St Anne's Terr SA11 49 C2
St Ann's Ct CF62 215 A8
St Ann St CF81 57 F2
St Anthony Rd CF14 177 E4
St Anthony's Cl / Clos Sant Antwn NP4 62 D2
St Arvans Cres CF3 179 F7
St Arvans Rd NP44 89 F3
St Arvan's Terr NP13 15 E5
St Asaph Cl CF14 177 E6
St Asaph Dr SA12 98 C2
St Asaphs Ct SA12 98 C2
St Asaph's Way CF83 138 A1
St Athan Prim Sch CF62 211 D4
St Athan Rd CF62, CF71 200 F4
ST ATHAN / SAIN TATHAN 211 D4
SAIN TATHAN / ST ATHAN 211 D4
St Athan's Ct CF83 137 F2
St Augustine Rd CF14 177 E4
St Augustine Rd / Ffordd Sant Awstin NP4 62 D2
St Augustine's Cres 11 CF64 207 B5
St Augustine's Path 9 CF64 207 B5
St Augustine's Pl 12 CF64 207 B5
St Augustine's Rd CF64 207 B5
St Baruch Cl 4 CF64 206 A2
St Baruchs Ct CF62 214 F2
St Basil's Cres NP10 142 A3
St Basil's Stores NP10 142 A3
St Benedict Cl / Clos Sant Benedict NP4 62 D2
St Benedict Cres CF14 177 E4
St Benedict Ct NP10 142 A2
St Bernadettes RC Prim Sch CF23 178 F8
St Bleddian Cl
Bryn NP12 85 E4
Cowbridge / Y Bont-Faen CF71 188 D2
St Brannocks Cl CF62 214 C5
St Briavels Mews NP10 163 E5
St Brides Cl SA4 19 D4
St Bride's Cl CF36 165 F1
St Brides Cl / Clos Sain Ffraid NP44 90 A2
St Brides Cres NP20 163 F8
St Brides Ct 5 CF5 193 C4
St Brides CW Prim Sch / Ysgol Gynradd Saint-y-Brid CF32 185 C2
St Brides Gdns NP20 163 F8
St Brides Ho 7 CF64 207 B4
ST BRIDES MAJOR / SAINT-Y-BRID 185 D2
St Brides Manor CF38 156 D5
St Brides Pl CF5 192 B8
St Brides Rd CF71 198 C5
St Bride's Rd
Aberkenfig / Abercynffig CF32 150 C4
Ewenny / Ewenni CF35 185 E7
St Fagans / Sain Ffagan CF5 175 D1
ST BRIDE'S-SUPER-ELY / LLANSANFFRAID-AR-ELAI 192 B7
St Bride's Way CF63 215 A8
ST BRIDE'S WENTLOOGE / LLANSANFFRAID GWYNLLWG 163 D1
St Brigid Rd CF14 177 E6
St Brioc Rd CF14 177 E6
St Cadoc Rd CF14 177 E5
St Cadoc's Ave CF64 206 A2
St Cadoc's Cl NP18 118 A3
St Cadoc's Hospl NP18 118 A2
St Cadoc's Prim Sch CF3 179 B7
St Cadoc's Rd NP4 38 D1
St Cadoc's Rise CF63 215 D8
St Canna Cl CF5 194 C6
St Catherine's Cl CF83 138 D6
St Catherines Cl / Clos St Catherine SA11 71 D5
St Catherines Ct CF83 138 B3
St Catherine's Ct
Abercarn NP11 114 B4
Barry / Y Barri CF62 214 F8
Swansea / Abertawe SA1 233 C1
St Catherines Mews 7 CF11 194 D7
St Catherine's Rd / Heol Santes Catherine SA12 98 E5
St Cattwg's Ave CF82 84 C6
St Catwg Wlk SA2 94 A2
St Cecilia Ct NP20 143 A5
St Cenydd Cl
Bryn NP12 85 E5
Caerphilly / Caerffili CF83 137 E4
St Cenydd Comp Sch / Ysgol Gyfun Sant Cenydd CF83 137 D4
St Cenydd Rd
Caerphilly / Caerffili CF83 137 E3
Cardiff / Caerdydd CF14 177 F6
Swansea / Abertawe SA5 67 F6
St Christopher Dr SA2 93 D6
St Christopher's Cl / Clos Sant Christopher CF83 138 E6
St Christophers Ct CF35 169 B8
St Christopher's Ct SA1 233 C1
St Christopher's Dr CF83 137 F2
St Christopher's Rd
Bridgend / Pen-y-Bont ar Ogwr CF31 168 E8
Porthcawl CF36 183 C7
St Clair Ct CF10 195 C2
St Clares NP22 12 F2
St Clare's Sch CF36 183 D8
St Clears Cl CF83 138 A2
St Clears Pl SA5 68 B7
St Curig's Cl CF62 213 A1
St Cuthbert's Ct 1 CF10 195 B2
St Cuthberts RC Prim Sch / Ysgol Gynradd Sant Cuthbert CF10 195 C3
St Cynidr Cl NP23 14 C8
St Cynons Ct CF40 106 F8
St Cynwyd's Ave CF34 102 A1
St Cyres Cl CF64 206 E4
St Cyres Comp Sch CF64 206 E4
St Cyres Lower Sch CF64 206 C2
St Cyres Rd CF64 206 E4
St David Ave CF64 206 B4
St David Dr SA2 93 D6
St David Lewis RC Prim Sch NP20 116 F2
St David's Ave NP12 85 F7
St David's Ave CF38 156 E8
St David's Ave CF61 210 A5
St Davids Cl
Bridgend / Pen-y-Bont ar Ogwr CF31 169 C6
Bryn NP12 85 E5
Penllergaer SA4 44 B2
Porth CF39 133 D8
Rhymney / Rhymni NP22 12 E4
St David's Cl
Bridgend / Pen-y-Bont ar Ogwr CF31 168 E7
Ebbw Vale / Glyn Ebwy NP23 14 C8
Hendy SA4 19 B4
Llanelli SA15 40 C3
Loughor SA4 42 F1
Merthyr Tydfil / Merthyr Tudful CF48 225 F1
Pen-pedair-heol CF82 84 E7
Pontypool / Pont-y-pwl NP4 62 C7
Treorchy / Treorci CF41 78 F3
St David's Cl *continued*
Upper Boat CF15 157 E8
St Davids Cres
Cardiff / Caerdydd CF5 193 D5
Newport / Casnewydd NP20 142 F1
St Athan / Sain Tathan CF62 211 D5
St David's Cres CF64 206 D3
St David's Ct
Cardiff / Caerdydd CF11 194 E6
Marshfield CF3 162 E1
St David's Ctr CF10 232 B2
St David's CW Prim Sch
Cardiff / Caerdydd CF23 178 F6
Colwinston / Tregolwyn CF71 187 A4
St David's Dr CF83 139 C6
St David's Est SA6 69 B8
St David's Hall★ CF10 232 B2
St David's Ho 7 CF10 232 B2
St Davids Hospl CF11 194 E6
St David's Hts CF72 173 C8
St Davids Ind Est NP12 85 B8
St Davids Mansion 16 CF11 194 E5
St David's Metropolitan Cathedral Church CF10 232 C2
St Davids Mews CF33 148 D2
St David's Mkt CF10 232 C2
St Davids Pk
New Tredegar NP24 33 E2
Pyle / Y Pîl SA13 147 C6
St David's Pl
Llantrisant CF72 155 E4
Maesteg CF34 102 A1
12 Mountain Ash / Aberpennar CF45 54 D3
Swansea / Abertawe SA1 233 B2
St David's RC Coll CF23 178 C2
St David's RC Jun & Inf Sch NP20 142 E1
St Davids RC Jun & Inf Sch Cwmbran NP44 89 F5
St Davids RC Prim Sch SA3 123 A6
St Davids Rd
Gwaun-Cae-Gurwen SA18 220 E7
Miskin / Meisgyn CF72 173 D6
St David's Rd
Bridgend / Pen-y-Bont ar Ogwr CF31 168 D6
Cardiff / Caerdydd CF14 177 B4
Maesycwmmer CF82 85 B2
Pengam NP12 85 B7
Swansea / Abertawe SA6 69 B8
Ystalyfera SA9 2 C6
St David's Rd / Heol Dewi Sant 3 SA12 124 E8
St David's Rd / Heol Tyddewi NP44 89 F3
St David's Sh Ctr SA1 233 B2
St David's Sq SA1 233 B2
St David's St SA11 71 E7
St David St
Pontycymer CF32 103 E4
Ton Pentre CF41 79 A3
St David's Way
Caerphilly / Caerffili CF83 137 F1
Cardiff / Caerdydd CF10 232 B2
Porthcawl CF36 183 B8
St Deinols Cl NP12 85 B6
St Denis Rd CF14 177 F5
ST DIALS 89 C2
St Dials Ct 2 NP44 89 E2
St Dials Rd
Cwmbran / Cwmbrân, Greenmeadow NP44 89 B3
Cwmbran / Cwmbrân, Old Cwmbran NP44 89 D3
St Dogmael's Ave CF14 177 F7
St Dominics Retreat NP4 62 B6
St Donat's Ave SA2 94 B7
St Donat's Castle★ CF61 208 G5
St Donats Cl CF64 206 C3
St Donats Cl / Clos Sain Dunwyd CF48 225 F1
St Donats Ct 7 CF5 193 C4
St Donat's Ct
Caerphilly / Caerffili CF83 137 F2
Llantwit Major / Llanilltud Fawr CF61 210 A5
St Donats Ho 8 CF64 207 B4
St Donats Pl / Clos Sant Dunwyd 7 NP44 90 B2
St Donats Rd CF11 194 D4
ST DONAT'S / SAIN DUNWYD 208 G5
St Dyfrig Cl 1 CF64 206 B2
St Dyfrig Rd CF64 206 E2
St Dyfrig's Ct 4 CF3 179 C6
St Edeyrns Cl CF23 178 D6
St Edeyrn's Rd CF23 178 C6
St Edward St NP20 143 B4
St Edwen Gdns CF14 177 E5
St Elli Sh Ctr SA15 40 D5
St Elmo Ave SA1 233 C4
St Fagans Ave CF62 214 E6
St Fagans Cl CF5 193 E7
St Fagans Ct CF5 192 F4
St Fagan's CW Prim Sch CF5 192 F4
St Fagans Dr CF5 193 A7
St Fagans Gr CF48 225 F2
St Fagans Ho 9 CF64 207 B4
St Fagan's Ho CF83 138 A2
St Fagans Rd CF5 193 D7
St Fagans Rise CF5 193 C8
ST FAGANS / SAIN FFAGAN 193 A7
St Fagans St CF83 138 A2
St Fagan's St CF11 194 F2
St Francis Ct
Cardiff / Caerdydd, East Moors CF24 195 F5
Cardiff / Caerdydd, Whitchurch CF14 177 A5
St Francis RC Prim Sch
Abersychan NP4 37 F4
Cardiff / Caerdydd CF5 193 B5
St Francis Rd
Bridgend / Pen-y-Bont ar Ogwr CF31 168 E7
Cardiff / Caerdydd CF14 177 A5
St Gabriel & St Raphael RC Prim Sch CF40 106 F5
St Gabriel's RC Prim Sch NP19 144 E6
St Garmon Rd CF64 206 E2
St George SA15 41 A4
ST GEORGES 192 B6
St George's Ave CF31 168 E8
St George's Cres NP19 143 F7
St George's Ct NP22 13 E7
St Georges Rd CF14 177 D3
St George's Terr SA3 229 C1
St Germans Ct 10 CF24 195 D6
St Germans Mews 4 CF24 195 D6
St Gildas Rd CF14 177 F5
St Govan's Cl CF62 214 F8
St Govans Pl SA5 66 D3
St Gowan Ave CF14 177 E5
St Gwladys Ave CF81 57 F5
St Gwladys Bargoed Sch CF81 57 F5
St Gwladys Ct CF81 57 F4
St Gwynnos Cl CF64 206 B3
St Helen's Ave SA1 95 A5
St Helen's Cres SA1 95 A5
St Helen's Ct CF83 137 F2
St Helens Prim Sch SA1 95 B6
St Helens RC Inf Sch CF63 215 A5
St Helens RC Jun Sch / Ysgol Iau Sant Helen CF62 214 F6
St Helen's RC Prim Sch CF83 138 D4
St Helen's Rd
Cardiff / Caerdydd CF14 177 D4
Swansea / Abertawe SA1 95 B6
St Helens Rugby & Cricket Gd SA2 94 F5
St Helier Dr / Rhodfa St Helier SA12 98 B3
SAINT HILARI / ST HILARY 201 C7
St Hilary Ct CF5 193 D4
St Hilary Dr SA2 93 D7
ST HILARY / SAINT HILARI 201 C7
St Hilda's Rd NP4 62 E2
St Ilan Sch CF83 138 A4
St Ilan's Way CF83 138 A1
St Illtyd Cl 2 CF64 206 B2
ST ILLTYD / LLANHILEDD 60 B8
St Illtyd Rd CF38 135 E1
St Illtyds Cl CF31 169 C6
St Illtyd's Cl SA12 98 E5
St Illtyd's Cres SA1 96 A7
St Illtyd's Dr SA12 98 E5
St Illtyd's Prim Sch
Dowlais CF48 11 A4
Llantwit Major / Llanilltud Fawr CF61 209 F6
St Illtyd's Prim Sch / Ysgol Gynradd St Illtyd's NP13 60 B6
St Illtyds RC High Sch CF3 179 D5
St Illtyd's RC Prim Sch SA1 69 A3
St Illtyd's Rd CF31 168 D5
St Ina Rd CF14 177 E6
St Isan Rd CF14 177 E5
St James Cl
Caerphilly / Caerffili CF83 138 E5
Maesycwmmer CF82 85 B1
Tredegar NP22 14 A4
St James' Cl / Clos Sant Lago CF48 31 A5
St James Cres CF62 214 B5
St James' Cres CF33 148 B2
St James Ct
Penarth CF64 206 E2
3 Swansea / Abertawe SA1 95 A6
St James' Field NP4 62 C6
St James Gdns SA1 95 A7
St James Mans 11 CF10 195 B2
St James Mews
6 Cardiff / Caerdydd CF11 194 D7
Llanharan CF72 153 F3
St James Pk
Bridgend / Pen-y-Bont ar Ogwr CF31 169 D4
Tredegar NP22 14 A5
St James Prim Sch CF83 138 D4
St James' Rise CF31 169 A3
St James's Cres SA1 95 A6
St James Way NP22 13 F7
St John Baptist CW High Sch CF44 28 E2
St John Lloyd RC Comp Sch / Ysgol Gyfun Gatholig Sant Ioan Llwyd SA14 41 B6
St John Lloyd RC Prim Sch CF3 179 E5
St Johns Cl NP4 62 A7
St John's Cl
Cefn Coed / Cefn-coed-y-cymmer CF48 10 A5
Cowbridge / Y Bont-Faen CF71 188 F1
Maesteg CF34 102 D2
St John's Coll CF3 179 E8
St John's Cres
Cardiff / Caerdydd, Canton CF5 194 D5
Cardiff / Caerdydd, Coryton CF14 177 A6
St John's Cres NP4 62 A7
St John's Cres NP10 141 F6
St Johns Ct SA6 46 B1
St John's Ct
2 Cardiff / Caerdydd CF11 194 D5
Rogerstone / Ty-du NP10 141 F6
St Johns Dr
Bryn NP12 85 E5
Treorchy / Treorci CF41 78 F4
St John's Dr
Pencoed CF35 170 D7
Porthcawl CF36 183 C7
St John's Gdns 24 CF47 30 E8
St John's Gr CF47 10 F3
St John's Hill CF62 211 D5
St John's Ho SA1 68 D2
St John's La CF46 83 D3
St John's Pl
2 Cardiff / Caerdydd CF14 177 A6
Rhoose / Y Rhws CF62 212 E2
St John's Priory CF31 168 F3
St Johns Rd NP19 143 F5
St John's Rd
Bridgend / Pen-y-Bont ar Ogwr CF31 168 D5
Clydach SA6 46 E7
Swansea / Abertawe SA5 68 B3
Tonyrefail CF39 133 C5
St John's Sch CF36 183 D8
St John's St CF39 107 F2
St John St
2 Aberdare / Aberdâr CF44 28 F4
Cardiff / Caerdydd CF10 232 B2
Ogmore Vale CF32 130 E8
St John's Terr SA10 71 A7
St John's Terr / Teras St Ioan SA10 71 A7
St John's View CF62 211 C5
St Joseph Pl NP44 117 B6
St Joseph's Cathdral Inf Sch SA1 68 D1
St Joseph's Cathedral Jun Sch SA1 68 D1
St Joseph's Ct CF14 177 F2
St Joseph's Ct SA15 40 E5
St Joseph's Jun Sch SA12 98 F2
St Josephs Park / Parc St Joseff SA12 98 E2
St Joseph's Private Hospl NP20 117 B4
St Joseph's RC Comp Sch SA12 98 F2
St Joseph s RC High Sch / Ysgol Gyfun Gatholig Joseff NP10 163 E6
St Joseph's RC Inf Sch SA12 99 A1
St Joseph's RC Prim Sch
Cardiff / Caerdydd CF14 177 E2
Clydach SA6 47 A7
Neath / Castell-Nedd SA11 71 F6
Newport / Casnewydd NP19 143 E6
Penarth CF64 206 D3
St Joseph's RC Sch NP22 6 C1
St Joseph's School Ho 6 CF64 207 A5
St Joseph's Terr CF44 53 A3
St Judes Cl SA5 68 C7
St Julian Cl CF63 215 C7

St Julian Hts CF82 85 A4
ST JULIANS 143 F8
St Julian's Ave NP19 143 E7
St Julian's Comp Sch NP19 143 E8
St Julians Ct NP19 143 E7
St Julian's Ct CF83 137 F1
St Julian's Inf Sch NP19 144 A7
St Julian's Jun Sch NP19 144 A7
St Julians Lo 5 NP19 143 E8
St Julian's Rd NP19 143 E7
St Julian St NP20 143 B4
St Julius Cres CF72 153 F3
St Katherines Ct SA1 69 D6
St Kitts Pl / Man St Kitts 5 SA12 98 C2
St Lawrence Ct SA5 68 B7
St Leger Cres SA1 95 F7
St Leonards SA3 122 F3
St Leonard's Rd CF31 168 D4
St Luke's Ave
Hawthorn CF37 136 A4
Penarth CF64 206 E2
St Luke's Cl
Llanharan CF72 153 F4
Pant CF48 11 A6
St Lukes Ct SA1 69 D6
St Luke's Rd
Pontypool / Pont-y-pwl NP4 38 A1
Porth CF39 108 A3
St Luke's Rd / Heol Sant Luc NP22 6 D2
St Lythan Cl 2 CF64 206 A2
St Lythan Ct 9 CF5 193 C4
St Lythans Burial Chamber* CF5 204 C5
St Lythans Rd CF5 204 D7
St Lythan's Rd CF62 214 C5
St Maddock's Cl CF31 169 C6
St Madoc Cl NP12 85 E5
St Maelog Cl NP12 85 E5
St Malo Rd CF14 177 E6
St Margaret's Ave
Blackwood / Coed-Duon NP12 85 C7
Neath / Castell-Nedd SA10 97 C8
St Margarets Cl CF83 138 F6
St Margaret's Cl 10 CF14 177 A6
St Margaret's Cres 3 CF23 195 D8
St Margarets Cwrt 17 CF44 29 A1
St Margaret's Dr SA15 40 B7
St Margaret's Pk CF5 193 E6
St Margaret's Pl 9 CF14 177 A6
St Margaret's RC Prim Sch CF44 28 F1
St Margaret's Rd
Caerphilly / Caerffili CF83 137 F2
Cardiff / Caerdydd CF14 177 A6
St Marie St CF31 168 F3
St Mark's Ave CF14 177 E3
St Mark's Cl CF72 153 F4
St Mark's Cres NP20 143 B5
St Mark's Gdns CF14 177 E3
St Mark's Rd CF64 206 F2
St Mark's Villas CF37 109 A1
St Martin Comp Sch CF83 138 B1
ST MARTINS 138 A1
St Martin's Cl CF64 206 F2
St Martins Cres
Cardiff / Caerdydd CF14 177 F7
Tredegar NP22 6 C1
St Martin's Cres CF83 138 A1
St Martins Ct NP20 142 F3
St Martin's Rd CF83 138 A1
St Martins Row 3 CF24 195 B8
ST MARY CHURCH / LLAN FAIR 201 A4
ST MARY HILL / EGLWYS FAIR Y MYNYDD 170 E1
St Mary Pl 6 SA12 99 A1
St Mary St / Heol Eglwys Fair CF10 232 B2
St Mary's Ave CF63 215 A5
St Mary's Brynmawr CW Sch NP23 8 C5
St Marys Cl CF5 193 D3
St Mary's Cl
Blaengwrach SA11 227 C8
Briton Ferry / Llansawel SA11 71 B1
Merthyr Tydfil / Merthyr Tudful CF47 10 D3
Pontypool / Pont-y-pwl NP4 62 D3
St Mary's Cl CF42 51 A2
St Marys Cl / Clos Santes Fair CF35 170 D5
St Mary's Cres CF34 102 D1
St Marys Ct
Cardiff / Caerdydd CF5 193 C2
Cardiff / Caerdydd CF14 177 A5
10 Risca / Rhisga NP11 114 F3
St Mary's Ct
7 Newport / Casnewydd NP20 143 B4
Porthcawl CF36 183 C8
St Mary's Day Hospl / Ysbyty Sant Mair CF64 206 C6
St Mary's RC Prim Sch
Bridgend / Pen-y-Bont ar Ogwr CF31 168 E5
Brynmawr NP23 8 C4
Cardiff / Caerdydd CF11 194 D6
Llanelli SA14 41 B6
Newport / Casnewydd NP20 143 B6
St Mary's RC Prim Sch / Ysgol Gynradd Gatholig Y Santes-Fair CF47 30 D8
St Mary's Rd
Bryn NP12 85 E4
Cardiff / Caerdydd CF14 177 A6
Ynysmeudwy SA8 24 B8
St Mary's Rd / Heol Santes Fair 2 NP44 90 A5
St Marys & St Patricks RC Prim Sch CF34 102 B3
St Mary's Sq SA1 233 B2
St Mary's St CF83 138 D6
St Mary St
Aberavon SA12 99 A1
Bargoed / Bargod CF81 58 A2
Newport / Casnewydd NP20 143 B4
Pontypool / Pont-y-pwl NP4 62 D3
Risca / Rhisga NP11 114 F3
Swansea / Abertawe SA1 233 B2
Trelewis CF46 83 C7
St Mary's View CF35 170 A4
St Mary's Well Bay Rd CF64 216 E4
St Mary the Virgin CW Prim Sch CF10 232 C1
St Matthews Ct SA1 233 B4
St Matthew's Rd NP4 62 D5
St Mellons Bsns Pk CF3 180 B8
St Mellons Ct CF83 137 F2
St Mellons CW Prim Sch CF3 179 D7
St Mellons Enterprise Workshops CF3 179 F7
ST MELLONS / LLANEURWG 179 E7
St Mellons Rd
Cardiff / Caerdydd CF14 160 E2
Marshfield CF3 180 D8
St Michael Gr NP44 117 B7
St Michael's Ave
Pontarddulais SA4 19 B4
Pontypridd CF37 135 D7
St Michaels Cl
Beddau CF38 155 F6
Colwinston / Tregolwyn CF71 186 F3
Dinas Powis / Dinas Powys CF64 206 A7
St Michael's Cl
St Athan / Sain Tathan CF62 211 D5
Tongwynlais CF15 158 C1
St Michael's Coll CF5 194 A8
St Michaels Ct
Cardiff / Caerdydd, Llandaff / Llandaf CF5 194 B8
Cardiff / Caerdydd, Maindy CF24 177 F1
Newport / Casnewydd NP20 143 D2
St Michaels Gdns CF62 214 E8
St Michaels Mews NP20 143 D2
St Michaels RC Prim Sch NP20 143 C2
St Michael's RC Prim Sch CF37 135 E6
St Michael's Rd
Cardiff / Caerdydd CF5 194 A7
Maesteg CF34 102 A3
Porthcawl CF36 183 C8
St Michael's Sch SA14 41 E6
St Michael St NP20 143 D2
St Michael's Way CF31 169 C6
St Monica's CW Prim Sch CF24 194 F8
St Nicholas Cl
1 Dinas Powis / Dinas Powys CF64 206 A2
Waunarlwydd SA5 66 E3
St Nicholas Ct
Barry / Y Barri CF62 214 C3
Caerphilly / Caerffili CF83 137 F2
4 Cardiff / Caerdydd CF5 193 C4
Swansea / Abertawe SA2 93 F6
St Nicholas CW Prim Sch CF5 191 F1
St Nicholas Ho 10 CF64 207 B4
St Nicholas Rd CF31 168 E8
St Nicholas' Rd CF62 214 C3
ST NICHOLAS / SAIN NICOLAS 191 F1
St Nicholas Sq 13 SA1 233 C2
St Nicolas Ct CF23 178 E8
St Non's Cl CF31 169 C6
St Oswalds Cl NP4 62 E1
St Oswald's Rd CF63 215 C7
St Osyth Ct CF62 214 C2
St Owains Cres CF71 189 C8
St Patrick's Dr CF31 168 E7
St Patrick's RC Prim Sch CF11 194 F3
St Patrick's RC Prim Sch / Ysgol Gynradd Gatholig Padrig Sant NP19 144 A4
St Paul's Ave
Barry / Y Barri CF62 214 E4
Penarth CF64 206 F2
St Pauls Cl 6 CF64 206 A2
St Paul's Ct CF5 177 A1
St Paul's CW Prim Sch CF11 194 F2
St Paul's Rd / Heol Sant Paul SA12 124 E8
St Paul's Terr SA4 66 D8
St Peters Ave CF72 153 F2
St Peter's Ave SA5 67 D3
St Peters Cl
Abercwmboi CF44 53 E4
Llanharan CF72 153 F4
St Peter's Cl NP11 87 B7
St Peters Cl / Clos Sant Pedr NP44 89 B2
St Peters Cres CF3 180 F5
St Peter's Cl CF41 78 F5
St Peter's CW Prim Sch NP4 17 C6
St Peters Dr NP12 85 E5
St Peter's RC Prim Sch CF24 195 C7
St Peter's Rd
Penarth CF64 206 E2
The Mumbles / Y Mwmbwls SA3 122 E5
St Peter's St CF24 232 C4
St Peters Terr 1 SA15 40 C4
St Peter's Terr SA2 67 E2
St Philips NP19 143 F4
St Phillip Evans RC Prim Sch CF23 178 E5
St Pierre Cl 2 CF3 180 A8
St Quentins Cl CF71 188 E1
St Quentins Hill CF71 188 D1
St Rhidian Cl NP12 85 E5
St Rhidian Dr SA2 93 D7
St Rhidian Rd SA5 67 F6
St Richard Gwyn RC High Sch CF63 215 D8
St Robert's RC Prim Sch / Ysgol Gynradd Catholig Sant Roberts CF32 150 C3
St Sannan Rd NP12 85 D4
St Siors Meade CF62 212 F2
St Stephen's Ave CF41 78 F5
St Stephens Dr CF35 152 C1
St Stephens Mans 12 CF10 195 B2
St Stephen's Rd NP20 143 D2
St Tanwg Rd CF14 177 E5
St Teilo Ave CF62 214 E6
St Teilo Cl 3 CF64 206 B2
St Teilo's Cl
Bryn NP12 85 E5
Ebbw Vale / Glyn Ebwy NP23 14 C8
St Teilo's Ct SA1 121 F6
St Teilo's CW High Sch CF23 178 D3
St TeilO's Rd CF31 168 D5
St Teilo St SA4 19 C4
St Teilo's Way CF83 137 F1
St Telio's Ct 2 CF23 195 D8
St Theodore's Way CF32 150 F5
St Therese's RC Sch SA12 98 C1
ST THOMAS 233 C3
St Thomas Cl
Bridgend / Pen-y-Bont ar Ogwr CF31 169 C6
Cardiff / Caerdydd CF14 177 C5
St Thomas Ct NP4 37 E5
St Thomas' Ct CF63 215 C6
St Thomas Prim Sch SA1 233 C4
St Tudor's View NP12 85 E6
St Tydfil's Ave CF47 10 E1
St Tydfil's Ct 10 CF47 30 D8
St Tydfils Hospl / Ysbyty'r Santes Tudful CF47 10 E1
St Tydfil Square Sh Ctr 11 CF47 10 D1
St Vincent Cres 2 SA1 233 B1
St Vincent Rd NP19 143 C5
St Vincents Ct NP19 143 D5
St Winifreds Cl 5 CF64 206 A2
St Winifred's Rd CF31 168 D6
ST WOOLOS 143 C3
St Woolos' Cath NP20 143 B4
St Woolos Ct 10 NP20 143 B4
St Woolos Gn 4 NP44 89 E4
St Woolos Hospl (General) NP20 143 B3
St Woolos Pl NP20 143 B4
St Woolos Prim Sch NP20 143 B4
St Woolos Rd NP20 143 B4
SAINT-Y-BRID / ST BRIDES MAJOR 185 D2
Salem Cotts NP22 13 E8
Salem La CF38 135 F1
Salem Rd
Cwmavon / Cwmafan SA12 99 F6
Llanelli SA15 40 F8
Pwll-y-Glaw SA12 100 A7
Swansea / Abertawe SA6 68 D5
Salem Row CF15 157 F5
Salem Terr CF40 106 F8
Salisbury Ave CF64 206 F3
Salisbury Cl
Merthyr Tydfil / Merthyr Tudful CF48 225 F1
2 Newport / Casnewydd NP20 143 C6
3 Penarth CF64 206 F2
Scurlage SA3 231 A6
Salisbury Ct
Cwmbran / Cwmbrân NP44 89 C3
Penarth CF64 206 F3
Salisbury Rd
Abercynon CF45 82 D2
Barry / Y Barri CF62 214 C4
Cardiff / Caerdydd CF24 232 C4
Maesteg CF34 101 F3
Salisbury St NP11 114 C4
Salisbury Terr
Cwmavon NP4 17 E1
New Tredegar NP24 34 A1
Salmon Cl CF23 178 E1
Salmons Wood CF71 188 B8
Salop Ho 8 CF64 207 A5
Salop Pl CF64 207 B5
Salop St
Caerphilly / Caerffili CF83 138 B2
Penarth CF64 207 A4
Salthouse Cl SA4 64 A3
SALTMEAD 194 E4
Saltmead Ct CF11 194 E4
Saltoun St SA13 125 E3
Salubrious Pass SA1 233 B2
Salubrious Pl SA1 233 B2
Salvia Cl CF3 180 A7
Salway Ave NP12 58 B2
Sambucus Ave CF71 199 C4
Samlet Rd SA7 69 C8
Samlet Sh Ctr SA7 69 C8
Samson's Ave / Rhodfa Samson NP4 37 E7
Samson St CF61 209 F7
Samuel Cres SA5 68 A3
Samuels Rd SA9 221 B7
Sanatorium Rd CF11 194 B5
Sanctuary Ct CF5 193 A2
Sanctuary The CF5 193 A2
Sandbrook Rd CF3 180 B6
Sanderling Cl CF36 182 D8
Sanderling Dr CF3 179 F8
Sanderling Way / Ffordd Sanderling CF36 182 D8
SANDFIELDS 98 A1
Sandfields Comp Sch SA12 98 C3
Sandfields Prim Sch SA12 98 F1
Sandfields Rd
Aberavon SA12 98 F1
Aberkenfig / Abercynffig CF32 150 D4
Sand La 9 SA11 71 C1
Sandon St CF24 232 C2
Sandown Ct CF5 193 E5
Sandown Ho 9 SA12 98 D1
Sandown Rd SA12 124 E8
Sandown Rd / Heol Sandown 17 SA12 98 D1
Sandpiper Cl CF3 179 F8
Sandpiper Ct SA12 98 C1
Sandpiper Rd CF36 165 D1
Sandpiper Rd / Heol Pibydd Y Dorlan SA15 40 B6
Sandpiper Way NP10 163 E6
Sandringham Cl
Barry / Y Barri CF62 214 C8
Gorseinon SA4 66 B8
Sandringham Pk SA7 46 C1
Sandringham Pk / Parc Sandringham SA6, SA7 46 C1
Sandringham Rd CF23 178 C1
Sand St 14 CF47 10 D2
Sand Wharf The CF11 195 A1
Sandwick Ct CF23 178 C7
SANDY 40 B6
Sandybank Rd CF41 79 C3
Sandybrook Cl / Clos Sandybrook NP44 89 C1
Sandy Cl / Clos Y Tywod 12 SA12 98 D1
Sandy La
Marshfield CF3 162 C2
Newport / Casnewydd NP10 163 F8
Porthcawl CF36 183 A7
Southgate SA3 121 A6
Ystradowen CF71 189 D8
SANDY LANE 121 A6
Sandymeers CF36 183 A7
Sandy Rd SA15 40 A6
Sandy Ridge / Crib Y Tywod SA12 98 C1
Sandy Water Park* SA15 40 A5
Sannan St CF81 58 B5
Sanquahar St CF24 195 D5
Sansom St NP11 114 F3
Sapele Dr CF24 195 D5
Sapphire St CF24 195 D7
Sarah St CF48 55 D5
SARDIS 218 D1
Sardis Cl SA5 66 E3
Sardis Rd
Pontypridd CF37 135 C8
Pontypridd, Maesycoed CF37 135 B8
Sarlou Cl SA3 123 C3
Sarlou Ct SA2 94 F6
SARN 150 F4
Sarnfan Baglan Rd SA12 98 E4
Sarn Helen SA10, CF44 223 E6
Sarn Hill CF32 150 E3
Sarn Pl 7 NP11 114 F3
Sarn Sta CF32 150 D3
SARON 218 E7
Saron Cl SA4 42 F3
Saron Cotts 4 SA12 99 C1
Saron Pl 6 NP23 14 D6
Saron Rd
Bynea SA14 41 F4
Penperlleni NP4 39 C8
Saron Rd / Heol Saron SA18 218 F7
Saron St CF37 135 E7
Saundersfoot Cl CF5 193 D3
Saunders Rd CF10 232 B1
Saunders Way SA2 94 B5
Saville Rd CF32 104 E3
Sawel Ct SA4 19 A4
Sawel Terr SA4 19 A4
Sawtells Terr NP4 61 F8
Sawyer Ct CF5 194 C6
Saxons Hos NP4 37 F4
Saxon St CF47 10 D2
Scales Row CF44 53 D8
Scarborough Rd
1 Newport / Casnewydd NP19 143 E8
5 Pontypridd CF37 109 E2
Scard St 5 NP20 143 B4
Scarlet Ave / Rhodfa Ysgarlad SA12 98 A2
Sch of Nursing & Midwifery Studies NP18 118 A2
School Ave NP23 8 D1
School Cl NP4 62 B6
School Cl / Clos Yr Ysgol CF46 83 E3
School Cres NP4 62 E1
School Ct
1 Cwmbran / Cwmbrân NP44 89 E2
Llanbradach CF83 112 A3
School Ct / Llys yr Ysgol SA11 71 D5
School House Terr / Clos Ty'r Ysgol 1 CF33 165 F7
School La
Abersychan NP4 37 F4
Ebbw Vale / Glyn Ebwy NP23 7 B4
Hawthorn CF37 136 B4
Newport / Casnewydd NP20 143 C4
Penperlleni NP4 39 E6
Pontardawe SA8 23 E5
Pontypool / Pont-y-pwl NP4 62 B7
Taffs Well / Ffynnon Taf CF15 157 F4
Tycroes SA18 218 F5
School Pl SA11 223 D1
School Rd
Abercrave / Abercraf SA9 222 C7
Crynant / Creunant SA10 226 A8
Cymmer / Cymer SA13 75 C5
Dyffryn Cellwen SA10 223 A4
Ebbw Vale / Glyn Ebwy NP23 7 B4
Glais SA7 47 A5
Llanelli SA15 40 F2
Maesteg CF34 102 A2
Miskin / Meisgyn CF72 173 D7
Neath / Castell-Nedd SA11 71 D5
Ogmore Vale CF32 104 E1
Pyle / Y Pîl CF33 148 D3
Tonna / Tonnau SA11 49 C2
Troedyrhiw CF48 31 C1
Ystalyfera SA9 2 B6
Ystradgynlais SA9 2 D8
School Rd / Heol Yr Ysgol
Brynamman SA18 220 D8
Cefn-bryn-brain SA9 221 B8
Neath / Castell-Nedd SA10 70 C1
School Row CF44 53 F8
School St
Aberbargoed / Aberbargod CF81 58 A5
Abercwmboi CF44 53 E5
Blaencwm CF42 50 B2
Blaengwrach SA11 227 B8
Brithdir NP24 34 A1
Caerphilly / Caerffili CF83 137 F8
Cardiff / Caerdydd CF10 232 C1
Deri CF81 57 B8

School St continued
Ferndale CF43 79 F8
Fleur-de-lis NP12 85 B5
Llanbradach CF83 111 F1
Llantrisant CF72 155 D3
Maerdy CF43 52 A1
New Tredegar NP24 33 F2
Pontlottyn CF81 12 F1
Pontrhydyfen SA12 73 A1
Pontyclun CF72 173 B8
Pontygwaith CF43 80 B1
Porth, Birchgrove CF39 107 F2
Porth, Cymmer CF39 107 F4
Senghenydd CF83 110 F3
Tir-Phil NP24 33 D3
Ton Pentre CF41 79 A3
Tonypandy CF40 107 A2
Tonyrefail CF39 133 C5
Wattstown CF39 107 D8
School Terr
Blaengarw CF32 103 E5
Cwmavon / Cwmafan SA12 99 E5
Cwm NP23 35 A8
Llanharan CF72 153 F3
North Cornelly CF33 165 F7
Pontycymer CF32 103 F3
Pontypool / Pont-y-pwl NP4 61 F8
Rogerstone / Ty-du NP10 141 F5
Tonypandy CF40 106 E7
School View
Nelson CF46 83 F4
Pontypool / Pont-y-pwl NP4 62 D5
School View / Golwg-yr-Ysgol NP23 8 B2
School Villas CF43 80 C2
Schooner Circ NP10 163 F6
Schooner Way CF10 232 D1
SCLWEN / SKEWEN 70 D7
Scotch St SA13 76 C5
Scotney Way CF23 161 A1
Scott Cl
Bridgend / Pen-y-Bont ar Ogwr CF31 168 D6
Newport / Casnewydd NP20 142 E1
St Athan / Sain Tathan CF62 211 D7
Scott Ct CF23 178 B3
Scott Rd CF10 232 B2
Scott St CF42 50 E2
Scott Wlk NP10 142 A6
SCURLAGE 231 A6
Scutari Row SA13 125 C6
Scwd-yr-Afon SA10 49 C4
SCWRFA 6 E1
Scwrfa Rd NP22 6 E1
Seabank Ct CF36 182 E6
Sea Breeze SA12 98 C1
Seabrook Pl 1 SA12 124 E8
Seaforth Cl SA12 98 B3
Seager Dr CF11 206 F8
Seagull Cl CF36 165 E1
Sealands Dr SA3 123 C3
Sealawns CF62 214 C1
Seal Pit Rd CF62 211 E1
SEASIDE 40 C3
Seaside Cres 4 SA15 40 C4
Seaton's Pl CF37 109 B1
Seaton St CF37 109 B1
Sea View
Cefn Cribwr CF32 148 F2
Pen-clawdd SA4 64 E4
Sea View Com Prim Sch / Ysgol Golwg-y-Mor SA1 233 A4
Seaview Ct 6 CF64 207 B4
Seaview Dr CF32 184 C3
Seaview Ind Est CF24 195 E5
Seaview Pl
Llantwit Major / Llanilltud Fawr CF61 209 F6
Llantwit Major / Llanilltud Fawr CF61 210 A6
Seaview Terr SA1 69 C2
Sea View Terr
Aberavon SA12 99 A2
Barry / Y Barri CF63 215 C7
Swansea / Abertawe SA1 233 B5
Wenvoe / Gwenfo CF5 204 F8
Seawall Rd CF24 196 A6
Seaward Ave / Rhodfa Tuar Mor SA12 98 C1
Seaward Cl / Clos Tuar Mor SA12 98 C1
Seawatch Ctr★ CF61 210 E1
Seaway Par SA12 98 C4
Seaway Parade Ind Est SA12 98 C5
SEBASTOPOL 62 E1
Sebastopol St SA1 95 F7
Second Ave
Caerphilly / Caerffili CF83 137 F3
Cardiff / Caerdydd CF23 178 E1
Merthyr Tydfil / Merthyr Tudful CF47 10 E5
Swansea / Abertawe SA6 68 C8
Sedd Goch CF31 169 B4
Sedgemoor Ct NP20 143 A6
Sedgemoor Rd CF3 179 C7
Sefton Ct 6 CF15 176 B6
Selby Cl NP44 90 B2
Selina Rd CF45 82 C5
Selwyn Morris Ct CF24 195 E5
Senghennydd Pl CF24 232 C4
Senghennydd Rd CF24 232 B4
SENGHENYDD 110 E2
Senghenydd St CF42 78 D6
Senlan Ind Est CF23 179 A1
Senni Cl CF62 214 C6
Senny Pl SA6 46 A5
Sepia Cl SA12 98 B2
Serecold Ave SA10 70 D6
Seren Twyn / Twyn Star NP22 6 D1
Serpentine Rd NP20 143 B5
Sevenoaks Rd CF5 193 B5
Sevenoaks St CF11 194 F2
SEVEN SISTERS / BLAENDULAIS 222 D3
Seven Stiles Ave NP19 144 D2
Seventeenth Ave CF44 224 B1
Seventh Ave CF47 10 E5
Severn Ave CF62 214 C6
Severn Cl NP11 115 B1
Severn Cres / Cresawnt Hafren SA12 98 D1
Severn Ct CF11 194 D6
Severn Gr CF11 194 D7
Severn Inf Sch CF11 194 D6
Severn Jun Sch CF11 194 D6
Severn Rd
Bryn NP12 85 D4
Cardiff / Caerdydd CF11 194 D6
Porthcawl CF36 182 E7
Swansea / Abertawe SA6 68 D8
Upper Boat CF37 136 C2
Severn Sq 3 CF11 194 D6
Severn Terr 12 NP20 143 B4
Severn View
Abersychan NP4 37 F6
Cwmbran / Cwmbrân NP44 89 A6
Severn View Terr NP4 37 F3
Sevins NP44 89 C1
Seward St CF47 10 F3
Seymour Ave CF72 154 A4
Seymour St
Aberdare / Aberdâr CF44 29 A2
Cardiff / Caerdydd CF24 195 E6
Mountain Ash / Aberpennar CF45 54 D3
Seys Cl CF71 188 D2
Seys Ct CF61 210 B7
Sgubor Goch CF72 172 D5
Sgwar Blenheim / Blenheim Sq 12 NP44 89 C2
Sgwar Callaghan / Callaghan Sq CF10 232 C1
Sgwd Gwladus Waterfalls Wlk★ SA11 223 E2
Sgwer Yr Orsaf / Station Sq CF48 55 D4
Shackleton Cl CF62 211 D7
Shadow Wood Dr CF72 173 C8
Shady Rd CF41 79 B2
Shaftesbury Cl CF14 159 E3
Shaftesbury St NP20 143 C6
Shaftesbury Wlk 5 NP20 143 C6
Shakespeare Ave
Bridgend / Pen-y-Bont ar Ogwr CF31 168 C5
Penarth CF64 206 E4
Shakespeare Cres
Ebbw Vale / Glyn Ebwy NP23 14 C8
Newport / Casnewydd NP20 142 E2
Shakespeare Ct CF24 232 D4
Shakespeare Dr CF61 210 B5
Shakespeare Rd
Barry / Y Barri CF62 214 F8
Cwmbran / Cwmbrân NP44 89 C2
Shakespeare Rd / Heol Shakespeare NP44 89 C2
Shakespeare Rise CF37 136 A6
Shakespeare St CF24 232 D4
Shamrock Rd CF5 193 C8
Shands Rd SA18 219 B8
Shannon Cl NP12 85 D4
Shannon Rd NP20 116 F2
Sharpe Cl 3 CF23 178 E1
Sharpsburgh Pl SA1 68 D3
Shaw Cl
Cardiff / Caerdydd CF3 179 B7
Ebbw Vale / Glyn Ebwy NP23 14 A8
Shaw Gr NP20 142 E2
Shawley Ct 7 NP44 89 C2
Shaw St SA4 66 B5
Sheaf La NP19 143 D6
Shea Gdns 24 NP20 143 C3
Shearman Pl CF11 207 A8
Shears Rd CF5 193 F7
Shearwater Cl
Penarth CF64 217 A7
The Mumbles / Y Mwmbwls SA3 122 F6
Sheen Ct CF82 84 F2
Sheerwater Cl 3 CF3 179 E7
Sheffield Ho NP12 85 A6
Shelburn Cl CF11 194 E4
Shelley Cl
Aberbargoed / Aberbargod CF81 58 B4
Blackwood / Coed Duon NP11 59 D1
Shelley Cres
Barry / Y Barri CF62 214 E8
Penarth CF64 206 F4
Shelley Ct CF83 139 C7
Shelley Dr CF31 168 C6
Shelley Gn NP44 89 C2
Shelley Rd NP19 143 F5
Shelley Wlk
Cardiff / Caerdydd CF24 232 D4
Rhydyfelin CF37 136 A6
Shelone Rd SA11 71 B2
Shelone Terr SA11 71 C3
Shepherd Dr NP18 119 E1
Shepherds Cl NP22 6 E1
Shepherd's Hill Cvn Site NP4 62 B5
Shepherd's Rd SA6 68 E6
Shepherd's Terr SA4 43 A3
Sheppard St CF37 109 B1
Sherborne Ave CF23 178 C7
Sherborne Wlk SA2 94 A1
Sherbourne Cl CF62 214 B8
Sherbourne Ct NP4 62 E1
Sherbourne Rd NP4 62 E1
Sheridan Cl
Cardiff / Caerdydd CF3 179 B7
Newport / Casnewydd NP20 142 E2
Sherman Theatre★ CF24 232 B4
Sherringham Dr SA3 122 F5
Sherwood Ct CF5 176 D1
Sherwood St CF40 79 F1
Shetland Cl NP19 143 F7
Shetland Wlk NP19 143 F7
Shields Cl CF23 161 B1
Shiloh La CF47 10 E1
Shingrig Rd CF46 83 E4
Ship La CF10 195 C2
Shirdale Cl CF82 85 B2
Shire Ct CF46 83 C6
Shires The CF3 162 D1
Shirley Cl CF63 215 D7
Shirley Dr CF48 10 A1
Shirley Rd CF23 178 A2
Shoemaker Cl / Clos Y Crydd NP23 8 D4
Shoemakers' Row CF34 102 B3
Shop Hos CF44 28 F5
Shopper's Wlk SA1 233 A2
Shopping Ctr CF44 28 A6
Shop Rd NP4 17 F1
Shop Row
Blaina / Blaenau NP13 15 D5
Tredegar NP22 13 E6
Tredegar, Trefil NP22 6 A6
Shop Terr NP7 9 E7
Short St
Briton Ferry / Llansawel SA11 71 C3
Clydach SA6 22 D1
Swansea / Abertawe SA1 233 A4
Showle Acre CF62 212 F2
Shrewsbury Ave CF39 133 D8
Shrewsbury Cl 8 NP20 143 C6
SHWT 129 B2
Sibrwd Y Dail CF31 168 D8
Sickert Cl NP19 144 A6
Sid Griffiths Ct NP4 37 E5
Siding Terr SA10 70 D7
Sidney Ames Ct 9 CF24 195 D6
Sidney St NP20 143 B4
Siemens Way SA7 69 A5
Sienna Ho CF10 232 C1
Sierra Pines CF45 54 A3
SIGINGSTONE / TRESIGIN 200 A4
Siloam Ct CF41 79 A2
Siloam Hill CF83 139 F7
Siloh Chapel CF34 102 A5
Siloh Cres SA1 68 D4
Siloh Rd SA1 68 D4
SILSTWN / GILESTON 211 E3
Silure Way NP18 145 B8
Silurian Pl CF10 195 B3
Silurian Way CF33 148 D2
Silver Ave / Rhodfa Arian SA12 98 B2
Silver Birch Cl
Caerleon / Caerllion NP18 117 E2
Cardiff / Caerdydd CF14 177 C3
Silver Cl SA3 122 F7
Silver Cl / Clos Arian 15 SA12 98 B3
Silver Ct 14 SA12 98 B3
Silver Fir Sq NP10 142 B3
Silverhill Cl CF37 109 F4
Silverhurst SA3 123 B3
Silver Jubilee Cotts CF5 193 D5
Silver St
Abercarn NP11 114 C6
Cardiff / Caerdydd CF24 195 D6
Silverstone Cl 5 CF3 179 D8
Silverton Dr CF72 155 E2
Simon Terr CF40 107 B2
Simpson Cl 2 NP20 117 A3
Simpson's Way CF33 148 B2
Sims Sq NP19 144 D5
Sinclair Dr CF23 178 E1
Sindercombe Cl CF23 160 F1
Singleton Botanical Gdns★ SA2 94 D6
Singleton Hospl SA2 94 D4
Singleton Rd CF24 195 E5
Singleton St SA1 233 A2
Sinnatts The SA10 71 C8
Sion Pl CF44 53 E8
Sion St CF37 109 C2
Sion Terr CF44 53 E8
Sir Alfred Owen Way CF83 138 A6
Sir Charles Cres NP10 163 F5
Sir Charles Sq NP10 163 F6
Sirhowy Ct
Cwmbran / Cwmbrân NP44 89 B4
Tredegar NP22 6 F1
Sirhowy Hill Ind Est NP22 13 F7
Sirhowy Inf Sch NP22 6 F1
SIRHOWY / SIRHWYI 6 F1
Sirhowy Valley Ctry Pk / Parc Gwledig Cwm Sirhwyi★ NP11 113 F2
Sirhowy View NP12 86 A3
SIRHYWI / SIRHOWY 6 F1
Sirius Dr / Rhodfa Sirius SA12 98 C5
Sir Ivor Pl CF64 206 C2
Sir Ivor Rd NP12 85 F4
Sir Stafford Cl CF83 138 C5
Sitwell Way SA12 124 E7
SIX BELLS 36 C3
Six Bells Est CF48 10 B1
Six Bells Rd NP13 36 B2
Six Mills Ave SA4 43 C1
Six Pit Junction Sta★ SA7 69 C6
Sixteenth Ave CF44 224 B1
Sixth Ave CF47 10 E5
Skaithmuir Rd CF24 195 F7
Skelmuir Rd CF24 195 F7
Skenfrith Cl NP12 58 E1
Skenfrith Mews NP10 163 E5
Sker Ct CF36 165 E1
Sker Wlk CF36 165 E1
SKETTY 94 D6
Sketty Ave SA2 94 D7
Sketty Ct SA2 94 D6
Sketty La SA2 94 D4
Sketty Park Cl SA2 94 C6
Sketty Park Dr SA2 94 B6
Sketty Park Rd SA2 94 C6
Sketty Prim Sch / Ysgol Gynradd Sgeti SA2 94 C8
Sketty Rd SA2 94 E6
SKEWEN / SCLWEN 70 D7
Skewen Sta SA10 70 E7
Skibereen Cl CF23 161 A1
Skillion Bsns Ctr NP19 143 F1
Skinner La 4 NP20 143 C5
Skinner St
Newport / Casnewydd NP20 143 C5
Swansea / Abertawe SA1 68 C1
Skokholm Cl CF36 165 E1
Skomer Cl CF36 165 E1
Skomer Ct 2 CF11 194 F3
Skomer Pl SA5 67 D7
Skomer Rd CF62, CF63 215 A8
SLADE 231 D4
Slade Cl
Cowbridge / Y Bont-Faen CF71 188 F2
Sully CF64 216 B5
Slade Gdns SA3 122 F6
Slade Hall 6 SA1 233 A4
Slade Rd
Barry / Y Barri CF62 214 F7
The Mumbles / Y Mwmbwls SA3 122 F5
Slade St NP19 143 F3
Slade Wood Ho CF62 214 F8
Slate St
Swansea / Abertawe SA6 68 F8
Swansea / Abertawe SA6 69 A8
Slipway The CF64 207 A5
Slocombe Trust Cotts 1 CF5 194 B7
Slon La CF32 184 D2
Sloper Rd CF11 194 D3
Sluvad Rd NP4 63 C3
Smallbrook Cl NP44 89 F3
Smallholdings CF35 169 E7
Small Meadow Ct / Cwrt Gwaun Fach CF83 138 B4
Smallwood Rd SA12 98 E5
Smeaton Cl CF62 212 E1
Smeaton St CF11 194 E5
Smithfield Rd SA8 23 E5
Smithies Ave CF64 216 B4
Smith Rd NP13 36 A6
Smith Row
St Nicholas / Sain Nicolas CF5 191 F1
Tonypandy CF40 133 B8
Smith's Ave CF44 224 A1
Smiths Ct CF48 11 D5
Smith's Rd SA7 47 A2
Smith St
Maesteg CF34 101 F3
Ton Pentre CF41 79 B2
Smiths Terr NP12 86 A6
Smithy's Ct / Cwrt Yr Efail CF31 168 A4
Smyrna Cotts SA13 125 D6
Smyrna St SA6 68 E5
Snail Creep Terr / Teras Llsyg Falwen NP4 37 F8
SNATCHWOOD 37 F2
Snatchwood Ct NP4 37 F1
Snatchwood Rd NP4 37 F2
Snatchwood Terr NP4 37 F2
Sneyd St CF11 194 D7
Snipe St CF24 195 C7
Snowden Ct CF83 138 C3
Snowden Rd CF5 193 B5
Snowdon Cl NP11 115 B2
Snowdon Ct / Cwrt Snowden NP44 90 A5
Snowdon Dr SA5 67 D3
Snowdrop La NP10 141 D7
Snow Terr SA9 2 E6
Soane Cl NP10 142 A7
SOAR 157 B3
Soar Cl
Croesyceiliog NP44 90 B6
Loughor SA4 42 F1
Soar Ct CF72 155 D3
Soarel Cl CF3 179 F5
Soar Rd SA14 41 E4
Soar Terr SA6 46 A1
Soberton Ave CF14 177 F2
Sofrydd Prim Sch NP11 60 B2
Sofrydd Rd NP11 60 B2
Soho St
Newport / Casnewydd NP19 143 E5
Newport / Casnewydd NP19 143 F5
Solent Cl NP12 85 D4
Solent Rd CF63 215 C8
Solva Ave CF14 178 A8
Solva Cl CF62 214 F7
Solva Rd SA6 68 C8
Somerset Cl CF48 10 A5
Somerset Ct CF3 179 C7
Somerset Ho 4 SA12 98 C3
Somerset Ind Est NP44 89 F5
Somerset La
Cefn Coed / Cefn-coed-y-cymmer CF48 10 A5
Port Talbot SA13 125 D6
Somerset Pl
Cwmavon / Cwmafan SA12 99 E5
7 Merthyr Tydfil / Merthyr Tudful CF47 10 E1
Swansea / Abertawe SA1 233 C2
Somerset Rd
Barry / Y Barri CF62 214 F6
Newport / Casnewydd NP19 143 E7
The Mumbles / Y Mwmbwls SA3 123 A4
Somerset Rd E CF63 214 F6
Somerset Rd / Heol Gwlad yr Haf NP44 89 F4
Somerset St
Abertillery / Abertyleri NP13 36 B4
1 Brynmawr NP23 8 C4
Cardiff / Caerdydd CF11 194 E4
Port Talbot SA13 125 D6
Somerset Terr NP23 7 D4
Somerset View
Ogmore-by-S / Aberogwr CF32 184 D2
Sully CF64 216 B4
SOMERTON 144 B4
Somerton Cres NP19 144 B5
Somerton Ct NP19 144 B3
Somerton La NP19 144 A4
Somerton Pk NP19 144 A4
Somerton Pl NP19 144 B5
Somerton Prim Sch NP19 144 B5
Somerton Rd NP19 144 A3
Somerville Ct SA2 94 E7
Sophia Cl CF11 194 E6
Sophia Gdns Glamorgan CCC / Canolfan Criced Genedlaethol CF11 194 E7
Sophia Wlk CF11 194 E6
Sor Brook Picnic Site★ NP44 90 E8
Sorrel Dr
Newport / Casnewydd NP20 143 A6
Pen-pedair-heol CF82 84 E6
Sorrento Ho CF10 232 C1
Soudrey Way CF10 195 B2
Southall Ave SA10 70 E6
Southall St CF72 153 D3
South Ave
Aberdare / Aberdâr CF44 28 F2
Cymmer / Cymer SA13 75 D3
Pontypool / Pont-y-pwl, NP4 62 D1
South Ave / Rhodfa'r De SA14 41 A3
South Bank NP23 7 F4

South Blackvein Ind Est NP11 114 B4
Southbourne Cl CF62 214 F2
South Cl
Bishopston SA3 122 A6
Llanyrafon NP44 90 B1
Pencoed CF35 170 D8
Porthcawl CF36 182 F7
South Clive St CF11 194 F1
SOUTH CORNELLY 165 F5
South Cornelly Ind Est CF33 166 A5
Southcourt Rd CF23 178 D1
Southcross Rd / Heol Croes Y De 9 SA12 98 C2
South Cross Way / Ffordd Croes Y De 8 SA12 98 C2
South Ct NP4 62 A8
Southdown Ct 7 SA12 98 C3
Southdown Rd / Heol Southdown SA12 98 C2
Southdown View SA12 98 C3
South Dr CF72 155 E3
Southend
The Mumbles / Y Mwmbwls SA3 123 C4
Tredegar NP22 14 A4
Southend Terr CF81 32 F8
SOUTHERNDOWN 197 D8
Southerndown Ave SA3 93 F1
Southerndown Rd CF32 185 C2
Southern St CF83 138 B2
Southern Way CF23 178 F2
Southesk Pl CF62 214 C2
Southey St
Barry / Y Barri CF62 214 F5
3 Cardiff / Caerdydd CF24 195 C7
SOUTHGATE 121 A5
Southgate Ave CF72 155 E3
Southgate Rd SA3 121 A4
Southgate St SA11 71 E6
Southglade CF15 158 A3
South Griffin Terr NP13 15 E2
South Lake Dr NP10 163 D5
Southlands NP13 15 E5
Southlands Dr SA3 122 F6
South Loudoun Pl 7 CF10 195 B3
South Luton Pl CF24 195 C5
South Market St NP20 143 D3
South Mews 5 CF10 195 B3
Southminster Rd CF23 195 E8
South Morgan Pl 6 CF11 194 E5
South Pandy Rd CF83 138 A5
South Par
Maesteg CF34 102 B3
3 Port Talbot SA13 99 B1
South Park Rd CF24 195 F5
South Pl
Bridgend / Pen-y-Bont ar Ogwr CF31 168 F3
Porthcawl CF36 182 F7
South Point CF10 195 F2
South Pontypool Ind Pk NP4 62 F4
South Prospect SA1 233 B3
Southra CF64 206 A2
South Rd
Bridgend / Pen-y-Bont ar Ogwr CF31 169 C2
Gileston / Silstwn CF62 211 E1
Penybryn CF82 84 D5
Porthcawl CF36 182 F8
Sully CF64 216 B5
South Rd / Heol y De NP44 116 F8
South Rise CF14 178 A8
South St
Abercynon CF45 82 D2
Bargoed / Bargod CF81 57 F4
Bridgend / Pen-y-Bont ar Ogwr CF31 168 F3
Dowlais CF48 11 B4
Ebbw Vale / Glyn Ebwy NP23 7 E4
Pontypool / Pont-y-pwl NP4 62 E1
Pontypridd CF37 109 D1
Porth CF39 107 E6
Port Talbot SA13 125 C7
South Terr
Cefn Coed / Cefn-coed-y-cymmer CF48 10 A4
Southerndown CF32 185 A1
South View
Bryncae CF72 153 E2
Gorseinon SA4 43 D2
Merthyr Vale / Ynysowen CF48 55 D2
Pencoed CF35 170 D8
Pontypool / Pont-y-pwl NP4 62 B7
Pyle / Y Pîl CF33 148 D1
Rhoose / Y Rhws CF62 213 A1
Taffs Well / Ffynnon Taf CF15 158 B4
Troedyrhiw CF48 31 C2
South View Dr CF3 179 C5
South View Rd NP12 85 E8
Southview Terr 10 NP4 17 C6
South View Terr NP24 33 E4
South View / Trem Y De CF32 103 F4
SOUTHVILLE 89 F2
Southville Rd 8 NP20 142 F4
Southville Rd / Heol Southville SA12 98 C2
South Wales Baptist Coll CF24 232 C4
South Wales Fire Service HQ CF72 155 A2
Southward La SA3 122 F4
Southway NP4 39 B1
South Wlk
Barry / Y Barri CF62 214 E6
Cwmbran / Cwmbrân NP44 89 E3
Sovereign Arc 4 NP20 143 C4
Sovereign Gdns CF72 173 D8
SOWHILL 62 B6
Spartan Cl NP18 145 C8
Speedwell Dr CF62 212 F2
Speke St NP19 143 E5
SPELTER 102 B8
Spelter Ind Est CF34 102 A7
Spencer David Way CF3 179 F5
Spencer Dr CF64 206 D7
Spencer La CF37 136 A4
Spencer Pl CF37 136 A4
Spencer Rd NP20 143 A4
Spencer's Row CF5 177 A1
Spencer St
6 Barry / Y Barri CF62 214 F5
Cardiff / Caerdydd CF24 178 A1
Cwmaman CF44 53 A4
Ebbw Vale / Glyn Ebwy NP23 14 D6
Swansea / Abertawe SA5 68 C4
Spencer Terr SA9 2 D8
Spien Rd SA14 218 D7
Spillers & Bakers CF10 232 D1
Spinney Cl CF5 193 C6
Spinney Cvn Pk The CF64 216 D4
Spinney The
Bridgend / Pen-y-Bont ar Ogwr CF31 169 D4
Bryn NP12 85 D3
Cardiff / Caerdydd CF14 160 B2
Newport / Casnewydd NP20 117 B2
Swansea / Abertawe SA2 94 A6
Spion Kop CF32 104 E2
Spionkop Rd SA6 46 C6
Spires Wlk CF63 215 B8
Spitzkop CF61 209 F6
SPLOTT 195 E6
Splott Ind Est CF24 195 E5
Splott Rd CF24 195 E6
Spoonbill Cl CF36 165 E1
Spooner Cl NP10 163 B6
Spowart Ave SA15 40 C6
Spring Bank NP13 36 A6
Springbourne Cl SA4 66 D3
SPRINGFIELD 86 B4
Springfield
Horton SA3 231 B4
Maesycwmmer CF82 85 A1
Porth CF39 107 F7
Springfield Ave
Porthcawl CF36 182 D7
Upper Killay SA2 93 B5
Springfield Cl
Aberdare / Aberdâr CF44 53 F8
Bassaleg NP10 141 D3
Bridgend / Pen-y-Bont ar Ogwr CF31 168 F6
Croesyceiliog NP44 90 A6
Gowerton / Tre-gwyr SA4 66 B5
Wenvoe / Gwenfo CF5 205 A6
Springfield Ct
Church Village CF38 135 E1
Pontllanfraith NP12 86 A3
Springfield Dr
Abercynon CF45 82 F3
Newport / Casnewydd NP19 144 D6
Springfield Gdns
Bridgend / Pen-y-Bont ar Ogwr CF31 169 A6
Hirwaun CF44 27 F8
Morganstown / Treforgan CF15 176 B8
Springfield La
Bassaleg NP10 141 D3
Bridgend / Pen-y-Bont ar Ogwr CF31 169 C4
Springfield Pl CF11 194 D6
Springfield Rd
Bassaleg NP10 141 D3
Maerdy CF43 52 A2
Neath / Castell-Nedd SA10 70 F7
Pontypool / Pont-y-pwl NP4 62 D1
Risca / Rhisga NP11 141 B8
Springfield Rise CF63 215 A7
Springfields
Blackwood / Coed Duon NP11 59 D1
Llanelli SA15 40 F2
Marshfield CF3 162 D2
Springfield St SA6 45 F1
Springfield Terr
Abertillery / Abertyleri NP13 60 B6
Hollybush NP12 34 C2
8 Neath / Castell-Nedd SA11 71 E6
Nelson CF46 83 F3
Pontllanfraith NP11 86 C5
Pontypool / Pont-y-pwl, New Inn NP4 63 A3
Pontypool / Pont-y-pwl, Plas-Y-Coed NP4 61 E7
2 Pontypridd CF37 135 F6
Springfield Terr / Teras Maes-y-Gwanwyn SA12 99 A1
Spring Gardens Pl CF24 195 E7
Spring Gardens Terr CF24 195 E7
Spring Gdns
Gorseinon SA4 43 D1
Newport / Casnewydd NP20 143 C2
Spring Gdns N SA10 70 F7
Spring Gdns S SA10 70 F7
Spring Gr
Cardiff / Caerdydd CF14 159 F2
Cwmbran / Cwmbrân NP44 89 A3
Springhurst Cl CF14 176 F7
Spring La
Croesyceiliog NP44 90 A5
Newport / Casnewydd NP20 143 A4
Spring Meadow Bsns Pk CF3 179 C2
Spring Meadow Rd CF3 179 D2
Spring Meadow Trad Est CF3 179 D2
Spring St
Barry / Y Barri CF63 215 D6
Dowlais CF48 11 A5
Newport / Casnewydd NP20 143 B7
Spring Terr SA1 95 B6
Spring Terr / Teras Y Ffynnon NP4 62 D2
Springvale NP44 89 C4
Springvale Ind Est NP44 89 C4
Springvale Way NP44 89 D4
Springwood CF23 178 D5
Springwood Prim Sch CF23 178 D5
Spruce Cl CF24 195 D5
Spruce Tree Gr CF47 10 D4
Spruce Way SA4 44 C2
Spytty La NP19 144 A2
Spytty Rd NP19 144 C2
Square
Llantwit Major / Llanilltud Fawr CF61 209 F6
Pontlottyn CF81 12 F1
Square The
Abertridwr CF83 136 F7
Beddau CF38 155 F7
Bedwas CF83 138 E6
Bridgend / Pen-y-Bont ar Ogwr CF31 168 E5
Bryncethin CF32 151 A5
Crynant / Creunant SA10 226 A7
Cwmbran / Cwmbrân NP44 89 A6
Dinas Powis / Dinas Powys CF64 206 A3
Glan-y-nant NP12 85 A8
Laleston / Trelales CF32 167 E5
Llanharan CF72 154 A3
11 Neath / Castell-Nedd SA11 71 E8
Nelson CF46 83 E4
New Tredegar NP24 33 D3
Pencoed CF35 170 D8
Pen-pedair-heol CF82 84 F7
Porthcawl CF36 182 F6
2 Porth CF39 107 F3
Tonyrefail CF39 133 B2
Treharris CF46 83 B7
Squire Ct SA1 233 B2
Squire Dr CF32 150 F5
Squires Cl NP10 142 B6
Squires Ct CF38 156 A5
Squires Gate NP10 142 A6
Squires Row CF40 107 B5
Squire St CF71 187 E1
Squirrel Wlk / Rhodfa'r Wiwer SA4 19 A5
Stable La NP22 13 E5
Stable Row NP4 17 C7
Stables Ct CF48 11 B4
Stacey Ct 6 CF24 195 D8
Stacey Prim Sch CF24 195 D7
Stacey Rd
Cardiff / Caerdydd CF24 195 D7
Dinas Powis / Dinas Powys CF64 206 A3
Stack Sq 6 NP4 17 C7
Stadium Cl CF11 194 E1
Stadwen Rd SA7 69 E7
Stafford Comm SA4 66 D7
Stafford Mews CF11 194 F4
Stafford Rd
Cardiff / Caerdydd CF11 194 F4
Newport / Casnewydd NP19 143 E7
Pontypool / Pont-y-pwl NP4 62 E4
Stafford St SA15 40 D3
Stag La CF61 209 F6
Stag St CF44 28 E4
Stag Terr SA11 226 C5
Staines St CF5 194 B7
Stair St 8 SA12 98 E1
Stallcourt Ave
Cardiff / Caerdydd CF23 195 D8
Llantwit Major / Llanilltud Fawr CF61 210 A6
Stallcourt Cl
Cardiff / Caerdydd CF23 178 E1
Llanblethian / Llanfleiddan CF71 188 D1
Margam SA13 125 E4
Stallcourt Rd / Heol Stallcourt 6 SA13 125 E4
Stamford Ct NP20 143 A6
Standard Signs Est NP19 143 D7
Standard St CF83 139 A6
Standard Terr CF39 107 F7
Standard View CF39 107 F7
Standard Villas CF83 139 A6
Standert Terr SA10 222 D3
Stanfield Cl CF48 30 F4
Stanfield St NP23 35 B6
Stanford Rd NP19 144 D5
Stangate Ho 1 CF64 207 B4
Stanier Ct 7 CF24 195 D6
Stanley Ct
Abertillery / Abertyleri NP13 60 B6
2 Newport / Casnewydd NP20 143 B5
Treorchy / Treorci CF42 78 B5
Stanley Dr 2 CF83 137 F5
Stanley Pl
8 Cwmbran / Cwmbrân NP44 89 E5
Swansea / Abertawe SA1 233 A3
Stanley Pl / Maes Stanley SA10 48 F2
Stanley Rd
Abersychan NP4 37 E6
4 Llanelli SA15 40 D3
Neath / Castell-Nedd SA10 70 F7
Newport / Casnewydd NP20 143 B5
Ton Pentre CF41 79 A2
Stanley Sq CF43 80 C2
Stanley St
Blackwood / Coed-Duon NP12 85 E7
Cwmfelinfach NP11 113 A4
Gwaun-Cae-Gurwen SA18 220 D6
Llanelli SA15 40 D2
Senghenydd CF83 110 F2
The Mumbles / Y Mwmbwls SA3 123 A5
Stanley Terr SA1 233 A3
STANLEYTOWN 80 C2
Stanton Way CF64 217 B8
Stanway Pl CF5 193 B6
Stanway Rd CF5 193 C5
Stanwell Cres CF64 207 B5
Stanwell Rd
Penarth CF64 206 F3
Penarth CF64 207 A3
Stanwell Sch CF64 206 F3
Stapleton Pl 2 SA6 68 F8
Starbuck St CF83 139 B3
Star La
Pentyrch CF15 175 C5
Pontypool / Pont-y-pwl NP4 62 B8
Starling Rd CF62 210 D6
Star Rd NP4 39 F6
Star St
Cardiff / Caerdydd CF24 195 D6
Cwmbran / Cwmbrân NP44 89 E2
Tredegar NP22 6 D2
Star Trad Est NP18 118 A5
Star Villas NP18 118 A5
Station App
Bassaleg NP10 142 B3
Ebbw Vale / Glyn Ebwy NP23 7 D1
Penarth CF64 207 A3
Pontyclun CF72 173 B7
Ton-du CF32 150 C5
Station Approach Ind Est CF64 207 A3
Station Approach Rd CF62 214 F2
Station Ave NP11 112 F6
Station Bldgs 3 NP12 85 F4
Station Cl CF44 27 E8
Station Cl / Clos-yr-Orsaf 3 CF36 182 F7
Station Ct SA1 233 B4
Station Farm / Fferm Yr Orsaf NP44 89 F5
Station Hill
Abertillery / Abertyleri NP13 36 B5
Bridgend / Pen-y-Bont ar Ogwr CF31 168 F4
Maesteg CF34 102 A3
Station Hos CF15 174 E7
Station Pl
Aberdare / Aberdâr CF44 28 D4
Risca / Rhisga NP11 114 F2
Station Rd
Abercrave / Abercraf SA9 222 D7
Abercynon CF45 82 E2
Abergwynfi SA13 76 C5
Abertysswg NP22 33 C8
Bargoed / Bargod CF81 58 A5
Blaina / Blaenau NP13 15 D5
Briton Ferry / Llansawel SA11 71 C3
Brynamman SA18 220 E8
11 Brynmawr NP23 8 C4
Caerleon / Caerllion NP18 118 B3
Cardiff / Caerdydd CF14 159 F1
Cardiff / Caerdydd, Landaff North CF14 176 F3
Cefn Coed / Cefn-coed-y-cymmer CF48 10 A4
Clydach NP7 9 E7
Coelbren SA10 223 A6
Creigiau CF15 174 E7
Crynant / Creunant SA10 226 A7
Cymmer / Cymer SA13 75 C5
Dinas Powis / Dinas Powys CF64 206 A3
Dowlais CF48 11 B5
6 Ebbw Vale / Glyn Ebwy NP23 14 D8
Ebbw Vale / Glyn Ebwy, Waun-lwyd NP23 14 F3
Ferndale CF43 80 A7
Glais SA7 47 A6
Glanaman SA18 220 A8
Glan-rhyd SA9 2 F8
Glan-y-nant NP12 85 A8
Gowerton / Tre-gwyr SA4 66 C5
Grovesend SA4 43 D6
Hirwaun CF44 27 D8
Llanbradach CF83 111 F1
Llangennech SA14 42 C8
Llanmorlais SA4 64 C2
Llantwit Fadre / Llanilltud Faerdref CF38 156 F7
Llantwit Major / Llanilltud Fawr CF61 209 F6
Llanwern NP18 145 B4
Loughor SA4 65 C8
Maerdy CF43 52 A1
Nant-y-Moel CF32 104 E7
Neath / Castell-Nedd SA10 70 E7
Newbridge / Trecelyn NP11 60 A1
New Tredegar NP24 34 A1
Penarth CF64 207 A3
Pen-clawdd SA4 64 F4
Pontarddulais SA4 19 B5
Ponthir NP18 117 F6
Pont Rhyd-y-cyff CF34 128 E6
Pontrhydyfen SA12 73 B1
Pontypool / Pont-y-pwl NP4 62 E2
Porth CF39 107 F6
Port Talbot SA13 99 B1
Pyle / Y Pîl CF33 148 D3
Radyr CF15 176 C5
Rhoose / Y Rhws CF62 213 A1
Risca / Rhisga NP11 114 F1
Swansea / Abertawe, Cockett SA5 67 E3
Swansea / Abertawe, Landore / Glandwr SA1 68 D4
Swansea / Abertawe, Trallwn SA7 69 E7
Tonna / Tonnau SA10 49 C3
Tonypandy CF40 107 A5
Tonyrefail CF39 133 B5
Tredegar NP22 6 C2
Treorchy / Treorci CF42 78 D5
Tylorstown CF43 80 C1
Ystradgynlais SA9 1 F1
Ystrad Mynach CF82 84 E2
Station Rd E CF5 205 B7
Station Rd / Ffordd-yr-Orsaf 5 SA18 219 B7
Station Rd / Heol Gorsaf NP23 14 F2
Station Rd / Heol Yr Drsaf SA14 42 A4
Station Rd / Heol yr Orsaf
Cwmbran / Cwmbrân NP44 89 F5
Llanelli SA15 40 D4
Station Rd W CF5 205 A6
Station Row
New Tredegar NP24 33 E3
Pont-y-rhyl CF32 129 F7
Station Sq 1 SA11 71 E7
Station Sq / Sgwar Yr Orsaf CF48 55 D4
Station St
8 Aberdare / Aberdâr CF44 29 A2
Abersychan NP4 37 F3
Barry / Y Barri CF63 215 A4

Station St *continued*
Blaengarw CF32 103 E6
Machen CF83 140 A7
Maesteg CF34 102 A2
Newbridge / Trecelyn NP11 86 C5
8 Newport / Casnewydd NP20 143 B5
Pontlottyn CF81 12 F1
3 Porth CF39 107 F3
Tonypandy CF40 106 F4
Treherbert CF42 50 F1
Station Terr
Aberdare / Aberdâr CF44 53 B5
Bargoed / Bargod CF81 58 A8
Bedlinog CF46 56 A7
Bryn SA13 100 F4
Caerphilly / Caerffili, Denscombe CF83 138 B2
Caerphilly / Caerffili, Penyrheol CF83 137 E4
Cardiff / Caerdydd CF5 193 F6
3 Cwmbran / Cwmbrân NP44 89 E5
Cwm NP23 35 B7
Dowlais CF48 11 C5
East Aberthaw CF62 212 B2
Fochriw CF81 32 C7
Llanharry CF72 172 D6
Llantwit Fadre / Llanilltud Faerdref CF38 156 D7
Maerdy CF43 52 A1
Maesteg CF34 102 A6
Merthyr Vale / Ynysowen CF48 55 D3
Mountain Ash / Aberpennar CF45 81 F8
Nelson CF46 83 E4
Penarth CF64 207 A3
Pen-clawdd SA4 64 F4
Peterston-super-Ely / Llanbedr-y-fro CF5 191 D5
Pontyclun CF72 173 A7
2 Port Talbot SA12 124 F8
Senghenydd CF83 110 E2
Tonypandy CF40 106 E8
Tredegar NP22 6 B2
Treherbert CF42 50 F1
Station Terr / Rhodfa'r Orsaf CF10 232 C3
Station Terr / Teras Gorsaf SA10 222 D3
Statue of Howel Gwyn★ SA12 71 E7
Stebonheath Prim Sch / Ysgol Gynradd Stebonheath SA15 40 F5
Stebonheath Terr SA15 40 F5
Steel Wave★ NP20 143 C5
Steel Works Rd NP23 14 E6
Steepfield / Cae Serth 7 NP44 90 A6
Steepholm Cl CF36 165 E1
Steep St 4 CF64 207 A5
Steer Cres NP19 144 A7
Steffani Ct CF10 195 B3
Stella Cl CF14 159 F3
Stella Maris Cl CF15 176 B5
STELVIO 142 F3
Stelvio Park Ave NP20 142 F3
Stelvio Park Cl NP20 142 F3
Stelvio Park Cres NP20 142 F3
Stelvio Park Ct NP20 142 F3
Stelvio Park Dr NP20 142 F3
Stelvio Park Gdns NP20 142 F3
Stelvio Pk Gr NP20 142 F3
Stelvio Pk Rise NP20 142 F3
Stelvio Pk View NP20 142 F3
Stembridge Ave SA5 67 E5
Stenhousemuir Pl CF24 195 F7
Stephenson Ct 2 CF24 195 C6
Stephenson Rd SA2 93 F6
Stephenson St
Cardiff / Caerdydd CF11 194 E5
Newport / Casnewydd NP19 143 E1
Stephen's Terr CF45 82 F3
Stephen Wlk 8 NP10 142 B4
Stepney La SA2 67 D1
Stepney Mews SA5 68 B2
Stepney Pl SA15 40 D5
Stepney Prec 4 SA15 40 D5
Stepney Rd
Glanaman SA18 220 C8
Swansea / Abertawe SA2 67 D1
Waunarlwydd SA5 66 E3
Stepney St
3 Llanelli SA15 40 D5
Swansea / Abertawe SA5 68 B2
Stepping Stones The NP4 39 E7
Sterling Cl CF24 196 B7
Sterndale Bennett Rd NP19 144 F5
Sterry Rd SA4 66 B5
Stevelee NP44 89 C1
Stevenson Cl NP10 142 A6
Stevenson Ct NP10 142 A6
Stevenson Street Ind Est NP19 164 F8
Stewart Dr / Ffordd Stewart 12 SA18 219 B7
Stewart Hall SA2 94 D6
Stewart Rd CF62 213 A1
Stewart St
Cwm NP23 35 B6
Llanelli SA15 40 C6
Steynton Path / Llwybr Steynton 15 NP44 89 C2
Stiels NP44 116 B8
Stirling Rd
Barry / Y Barri CF62 214 C7
Cardiff / Caerdydd CF5 193 A4
Stockholm Cnr Ho 2 SA11 71 E6
Stockland St
Caerphilly / Caerffili CF83 138 A2
Cardiff / Caerdydd CF11 194 F3
Stockton Cl NP19 117 E1
Stockton Rd NP19 143 D8
Stocktonville NP22 13 D8
Stockton Way NP22 13 E8
Stockwood Cl NP18 119 B1
Stockwood View NP18 145 B8
Stokes Cotts NP18 117 F6
Stokes Ct NP18 117 F6
Stokes Dr NP18 118 A6
Stonebridge Rd NP23 7 A4
Stonechat Cl
2 Cardiff / Caerdydd CF3 180 A6
Porthcawl CF36 165 D1
Stoneleigh Ct 4 CF11 194 D7
Stonerwood View NP11 87 B8
Stone's Hos NP13 15 D6
Stones Mus★ SA13 126 C1
Stonewell Ct 7 CF23 178 C2
Stony La CF35 186 A6
Stony Rd NP4 37 F5
Stormy La
Nant-y-Moel CF32 104 F5
North Cornelly CF33 165 E7
Storrar Pl CF24 196 A8
Storrar Rd CF24 196 A8
Stour Ct NP44 89 A4
Stowe Path / Llwybr Stowe 4 NP44 90 B2
Stow Hill
Newport / Casnewydd NP20 143 B4
Pontypridd CF37 135 D7
STOW PARK 143 A3
Stow Park Ave NP20 143 A3
Stow Park Circ NP20 143 A3
Stow Park Cres NP20 143 A4
Stow Park Dr NP20 143 A3
Stow Park Gdns NP20 143 A3
Stradey Ct 3 SA15 40 C7
Stradey Park Ave SA15 40 C6
Stradey Rd SA15 40 C7
Stradling Cl
Barry / Y Barri CF62 214 B6
Cowbridge / Y Bont-Faen CF71 188 D2
Sarn CF32 150 F4
Sully CF64 216 B5
Stradling Pl CF61 210 A5
Stradmore Cl CF15 157 F5
Strand
Ferndale CF43 79 F6
Swansea / Abertawe SA1 233 B3
Swansea / Abertawe SA1 233 B4
Strand Row SA1 233 B3
Strand St CF45 54 F2
Strand The
Blaengarw CF32 103 E7
Llantwit Major / Llanilltud Fawr CF61 209 F6
Stratford Dr CF36 182 E8
Stratford Gn 5 CF63 215 C8
Stratford Ho NP20 142 E3
Strathnairn St CF24 195 B8
Strathview NP11 86 C5
Strathy Rd CF3 180 A7
Stratton Way SA10 71 C8
Strauss Rd / Heol Strauss SA12 98 A2
Strawberry Pl SA6 45 F1
Stream St CF45 54 D2
Street No 17 SA12 98 B4
Street No 19 SA12 98 B5
Street No 21 SA12 98 B5
Stryd Adelaide / Adelaide St CF10 195 B1
Stryd Angus / Angus St CF48 55 C5
Stryd Arthur / Arthur St SA18 219 B8
Stryd Bailey / Bailey St NP4 37 E6
Stryd Barrington / Barrington St CF48 55 C5
Stryd Bethania / Bethania St CF34 102 B2
Stryd Burford / Burford St 4 NP4 17 C6
Stryd Bute / Bute St CF10 232 C1
Stryd Cae Derw / Oakfield St CF48 55 C6
Stryd Cannon / Cannon St SA18 220 D8
Stryd Caroline / Caroline St
5 Bridgend / Pen-y-Bont ar Ogwr CF31 168 F4
Stryd Caroline / Caroline St *continued*
3 Briton Ferry / Llansawel SA11 71 C1
Cardiff / Caerdydd CF10 232 B2
Stryd Castell / Castle St 14 SA11 71 E8
Stryd Chapman / Chapman St SA15 40 B6
Stryd Commercial / Commercial St NP44 89 E2
Stryd Cottrell / Cottrell St CF48 55 C5
Strydd Llandowlais / Llandowlais St NP44 89 E1
Stryd Donnen / Donnen St 5 SA13 125 D5
Stryd Emma / Emma St 13 SA15 40 D4
Stryd Fawr / High St
Abersychan NP4 37 F3
Ammanford / Rhydaman SA18 219 C7
Blaengwrach SA11 227 B8
4 Glanaman SA18 220 A8
Neath / Castell-Nedd, Pentreffynnon SA10 70 F7
Swansea / Abertawe SA1 233 B4
Stryd George Newydd / New George St CF10 195 C1
Stryd Glanhywl / Glanhowy St NP22 6 D1
Stryd Glenafon / Glenavon St 12 SA12 124 F8
Stryd Grandison / Grandison St SA11 71 C2
Stryd Harle / Harle St SA11 71 F8
Stryd Harold / Harold St 4 SA18 219 B7
Stryd Herbert / Herbert St CF10 232 C1
Stryd Hoo / Hoo St SA11 71 C2
Stryd Hope / Hope St CF10 232 C1
Stryd Hywel Harris CF82 111 E7
Stryd James / James St NP22 13 F5
Stryd John / John St CF10 232 C1
Stryd Llewellyn / Llewellyn St 14 SA15 40 D4
Stryd Lloyd / Lloyd St SA15 40 C5
Stryd Mackintosh / Mackintosh St CF48 55 C5
Stryd Mansel / Mansel St SA11 71 C2
Stryd Marged / Margaret St 6 SA18 219 C7
Stryd Masnach / Commercial St SA10 222 C3
Stryd Merfyn / Mervyn St CF48 55 C5
Stryd Osterley / Osterley St SA11 71 C2
Stryd Parc / Park St CF31 168 E4
Stryd Raby / Raby St SA15 40 C6
Stryd Rhanallt / Rhanallt St 7 SA13 125 D5
Stryd Rhydychen / Oxford St SA1 233 A2
Stryd Rice / Rice St SA18 219 C6
Stryd Silurian CF72 172 D5
Stryd Sior / George St NP4 62 A8
Stryd Stuart / Stuart St CF10 195 B1
Stryd Ton-Bach / Ton-Bach St NP4 17 D6
Stryd Tydraw / Ty-Draw St 1 SA13 125 B8
Stryd Vernon / Vernon St SA11 71 C2
Stryd Wesley / Wesley St NP44 89 D2
Stryd Wingfield / Wingfield St CF48 55 C5
Stryd Womanby / Womanby St CF10 232 B2
Stryd Wyndham / Wyndham St CF31 168 F4
Stryd y Berllan CF72 172 B5
Stryd y Bont / Bridge St
Aberfan CF48 55 C5
Pen-y-groes SA14 218 D8
Stryd Y Bryn / Hill St NP4 62 A8
Stryd Y Cei / Quay St
2 Ammanford / Rhydaman SA18 219 C7
Cardiff / Caerdydd CF10 232 B2
Stryd Y Coed / Wood St SA13 125 D6
Stryd-y-Coleg / College St SA18 219 B7
Stryd Y Crochendy / Pottery St 7 SA15 40 D5
Stryd Y Dderwen / Oak st 8 NP44 89 E2
Stryd Y Ddol / Meadow St CF33 165 F8
Stryd-y-Gwynt / Wind St SA18 219 B7
Stryd Y Parc / Park St
Ammanford / Rhydaman SA18 219 C6
Brynamman SA18 220 D8
Skewen / Sclwen SA10 71 A7
Stryd-yr-Eglwys / Church St 8 SA18 219 B7
Stryd yr Eglwys / Church St CF10 232 B2
Stryd Yr Undeb / Union St NP4 37 F3
Stuart Cl
Cardiff / Caerdydd CF11 194 D1
Port Talbot SA12 98 B3
Stuart Crystal Factory & Shop★ CF81 58 B2
Stuart Pl CF10 195 C1
Stuart St / Stryd Stuart CF10 195 B1
Stuart St
Aberdare / Aberdâr CF44 29 A1
Merthyr Tydfil / Merthyr Tudful CF47 10 D2
Pontlottyn CF81 12 F1
Pontyclun CF72 173 B7
Treherbert CF42 50 F2
Treorchy / Treorci CF42 78 D7
Stuart Terr CF72 155 B2
Sturminster Rd CF23 195 E8
Sturmi Way / Ffordd Sturmi CF33 148 C1
Stuttgarter Strasse CF10 232 C3
Subway Rd CF63 215 A4
Sudbury Wlk 1 NP20 143 C6
Sudcroft St CF11 194 C4
Suffolk Cl CF36 182 F8
Suffolk Ct CF36 182 F7
Suffolk Ho 1 SA12 98 C3
Suffolk Pl
Ogmore Vale CF32 104 E1
Porthcawl CF36 182 F7
Suffolk St CF31 168 F3
Sullivan Circ NP19 144 D4
Sullivan Cl
Cardiff / Caerdydd CF3 179 D7
Penarth CF64 206 F1
SULLY 216 B5
Sully Moors Rd CF64 215 F6
Sully Pl CF64 207 B3
Sully Prim Sch CF64 216 A4
Sully Rd CF64 206 D1
Sully Terr CF64 207 A2
Sully Terrace La CF64 207 A2
Sully View CF63 215 E7
Summerau Ct CF5 194 C7
Summercliffe Chalet Pk SA3 122 D4
Summerdale Cl CF38 135 F1
Summerfield Ave CF14 177 F2
Summerfield Ct CF40 107 A5
Summerfield Dr
Llantrisant CF72 155 E2
Porthcawl CF36 165 E1
Summerfield Hall La CF82, NP12 85 B3
Summerfield La CF83 139 C6
Summerfield Pl
Cardiff / Caerdydd CF14 177 D5
2 Merthyr Tydfil / Merthyr Tudful CF47 10 F4
2 Neath / Castell-Nedd SA11 71 E7
Summerfield Rd NP23 7 B5
Summerfield Terr NP12 85 B5
SUMMERHILL 143 F6
Summerhill CF47 10 F1
Summerhill Ave NP19 143 E6
Summerhill Cl CF3 180 A7
Summerhill Ho 9 NP19 143 E6
Summerhill Pl CF47 10 F1
Summerland Cl CF64 206 D6
Summerland Cres CF64 206 D6
Summerland La SA3 122 E5
Summerland Pk SA2 93 B5
Summer Pl SA7 69 F7
Summer's Hos NP13 36 B7
Summerwood Cl CF5 193 B8
Sumner Cl CF5 176 E2
Sunbean Cl NP19 143 E4
Sundew Cl
Cardiff / Caerdydd CF5 176 D2
Penarth CF64 206 E5
Sunhill Pk / Parc Bronhaul CF31 168 A3
Sunlea Cres NP4 62 F6
Sunneyhill / Haulfryn CF33 148 E3
Sunningdale CF83 137 E2
Sunningdale Ave SA3 93 F1
Sunningdale Cl CF23 178 B4
Sunningdale Ct NP19 144 D6
Sunningdale Dr SA4 43 B4
Sunningdale Rd SA12 98 E5
Sunninghill Terr SA15 40 E6
Sunnybank
Abertridwr CF83 137 B7
Bassaleg NP10 141 F2
Sunnybank *continued*
Brynmawr NP23 8 B5
Cwmbran / Cwmbrân NP44 115 F8
Dinas Powis / Dinas Powys CF64 206 C4
Merthyr Tydfil / Merthyr Tudful CF47 10 D2
New Tredegar NP24 33 E3
Pyle / Y Pîl CF33 148 B2
Sunny Bank
Glyncorrwg SA13 227 C2
4 Llantrisant CF72 155 D3
Ogmore Vale CF32 104 E2
Porth CF39 107 E5
Tonypandy, Blaen Clydach CF40 106 D7
Tonypandy, Williamstown CF40 107 A2
Treharris CF46 83 A5
Sunnybank Cl
Cardiff / Caerdydd CF14 177 D3
The Mumbles / Y Mwmbwls SA3 122 F8
Sunnybank Ct
Bridgend / Pen-y-Bont ar Ogwr CF31 169 C5
Brynmawr NP23 8 B5
Pontypool / Pont-y-pwl NP4 62 E3
Sunnybank / Haulfryn SA10 48 C1
Sunnybank Pl SA12 124 D8
Sunnybank Rd
Blackwood / Coed-Duon NP12 85 E8
Pontypool / Pont-y-pwl NP4 62 D3
Port Talbot SA12 124 D8
Sunnybank St CF44 53 B8
Sunnybank Terr
Abertillery / Abertyleri NP13 59 F7
Treorchy / Treorci CF42 78 C5
Sunny Bank Terr CF83 139 F7
Sunnybank Way NP4 62 D2
Sunnybrook Ct CF5 176 D1
Sunny Cres SA13 75 D3
Sunny Crest NP11 87 A7
Sunnycroft Cl CF64 206 B3
Sunnycroft La CF64 206 B2
Sunnycroft Rd SA12 98 D5
Sunnycroft Rise 4 CF64 206 B2
Sunny Hill
Llanelli SA15 40 D6
Maerdy CF43 52 A1
Rhymney / Rhymni NP22 13 A2
Sunnyland Cres SA10 70 F8
Sunnymead Cl SA1 67 E2
Sunny Mount SA12 98 D5
Sunny Rd
Llanelli SA15 40 D6
Port Talbot SA12 124 D8
Sunnyside
Llanelly Hill NP7 9 C4
Ogmore Vale CF32 130 E8
Sunny Side CF37 109 B2
Sunnyside Rd CF31 168 E4
Sunnyside Terr SA13 75 C6
Sunnyview
Argoed NP12 58 F4
Pontlottyn CF81 32 F8
Tredegar NP22 13 D7
Sun St CF24 195 D6
Suran-y-Gog CF63 205 B1
Surgery Rd NP13 15 E6
Surgery Road Bglws NP13 15 E6
Surrey Pl NP19 143 E7
Surrey St CF5 194 B6
Susannah Pl CF46 83 A6
Sussex Cl NP19 144 A2
Sussex St CF11 194 F4
Sutherland Cres NP19 144 A7
Sutherland Mans 8 CF14 176 F6
Sutton Gr CF23 160 D1
Sutton La CF32 184 C4
Sutton Rd
Llandow / Llandw CF71 199 C5
Newport / Casnewydd NP19 143 D8
Ogmore-by-S / Aberogwr CF32 184 D3
Sutton Rise CF32 184 D4
Sutton Spring Rd CF71 199 C4
Swallow Cl / Clos Y Mennol CF33 147 F1
Swallowhurst Cl CF5 192 F4
Swallow Tree Cl / Clos Coed-y-wennol SA10 48 E2
Swallow Way NP10 163 E8
Swanage Cl CF3 180 A7
SWANBRIDGE 216 D4
Swanbridge Farm Est CF64 216 D3
Swanbridge Gr CF64 216 C4
Swanbridge Rd CF64 216 C5
Swan Cres NP23 7 E4
Swan Ct SA2 93 E6

Swanfield / Maes Alarch SA9 2 C7
Swanfield Pl 3 SA15 40 D6
Swan Gdns SA1 95 B6
Swan La SA9 2 C7
Swan Rd SA12 98 C7
SWANSEA / ABERTAWE 233 C1
Swansea Castle★ SA1 233 B3
Swansea Coll / Coleg Abertawe (Tycoch Campus) SA2 94 D7
Swansea Ent Pk SA7 69 B7
Swansea Inst SA1 233 B3
Swansea Inst / Athrofa Abertawe (Townhill Campus) SA2 94 F8
Swansea Inst (Dynevor Ctr) SA1 233 A3
Swansea Inst (Mount Pleasant Campus) SA1 233 A3
Swansea Mus★ SA1 233 B2
Swansea Rd
Gorseinon SA4 66 E7
Hirwaun CF44 27 E8
Llanelli, Box SA15 40 F6
Llanelli, Marble Hall SA15 40 E6
Merthyr Tydfil / Merthyr Tudful, Gellideg CF48 10 A2
Merthyr Tydfil / Merthyr Tudful, Georgetown CF48, CF47 10 C2
Penllergaer SA4 44 B2
Pontardawe SA8 23 C2
Pontlliw SA4 44 A4
Swansea / Abertawe, Cadle SA5 67 C7
Swansea / Abertawe, Llangyfelach SA5 45 B2
Waunarlwydd SA5 66 E4
Swansea St CF24 195 E5
Swansea Sta SA1 233 B4
Swansea Vale Rly★ SA7 69 B5
Swansea West Ind Pk SA5 67 C4
Swan Sq NP4 37 F3
Swan St
Baglan SA12 98 C7
Llantrisant CF72 155 D3
Merthyr Tydfil / Merthyr Tudful CF47 30 D8
Swansea / Abertawe SA1 233 B4
Swan Terr 7 CF40 106 F4
Swan Wlk SA15 40 B5
Sward Cl NP10 142 A7
Sway Rd SA6 46 A1
Sweet Briar La SA3 123 A8
Sweet Water Pk CF48 10 B2
Sweetwells Cotts CF32 129 F7
Sweldon Cl CF5 193 B3
SWFFRYD 60 B2
Swift Bsns Ctr The CF24 195 D5
Swift Cl CF3 179 B7
Swinburne Cl NP19 144 A5
Swinton St CF24 195 E6
Swn Cloch Yr Eglwys CF31 168 D6
Swn-Y-Mor
Barry / Y Barri CF62 214 A3
Port Talbot SA12 98 D1
Swn Y Mor CF32 185 A1
Swn-y-Nant
Abergwynfi SA13 76 B6
Church Village CF38 135 E1
Crynant / Creunant SA10 226 A8
Cwm-twrch Isaf SA9 1 B2
Pencoed CF35 152 C1
Swn Yr Adar CF31 168 D8
Swn Yr Aderyn CF33 148 D2
Swn-yr-Afon
Aberdulais SA10 49 C4
Cefn Coed / Cefn-coed-y-cymmer CF48 10 B4
Gilfach Goch CF39 132 B7
Pyle / Y Pîl CF33 148 E3
Ton Pentre CF41 79 B3
Swn Yr Afon CF42 78 E5
Swn yr Eos SA9 2 E7
Swn-yr-Nant CF82 84 D7
Swyn Y Nant CF39 133 A2
Sybil St SA6 46 E7
Sycamore Ave
Neath / Castell-Nedd SA11 72 A6
Newport / Casnewydd NP19 144 B4
Porthcawl CF36 183 D8
Pyle / Y Pîl CF33 148 C2
St Athan / Sain Tathan CF62 211 B7
Swansea / Abertawe, Tircanol SA6 46 D2
Tredegar NP22 6 D1
Sycamore Cl
Aberdare / Aberdâr CF44 28 D3
Bridgend / Pen-y-Bont ar Ogwr CF31 168 F8
Dinas Powis / Dinas Powys CF64 206 B2
Sycamore Cl *continued*
Llandough / Llandochau CF64 206 E6
Miskin / Meisgyn CF72 173 D7
Swansea / Abertawe SA2 94 A7
Sycamore Cres
Baglan SA12 98 D7
Barry / Y Barri CF62 215 A7
Risca / Rhisga NP11 115 B1
Trefechan CF48 10 B6
Sycamore Cross CF5 191 D1
Sycamore Ct
Bargoed / Bargod CF81 57 E2
Blackwood / Coed-Duon NP12 85 F6
Sycamore Ct / Cwrt Sycanor NP44 115 F8
Sycamore Ct / Llys Sycamorwydden SA12 98 D7
Sycamore Dr CF40 107 A5
Sycamore Ho CF14 176 E6
Sycamore Pl 1 CF5 193 D8
Sycamore Pl / Maes Sycamorwydden NP44 89 B6
Sycamore Rd
Llanharry CF72 172 C5
Merthyr Tydfil / Merthyr Tudful CF47 10 E4
Pontypool / Pont-y-pwl NP4 62 D2
The Mumbles / Y Mwmbwls SA3 123 A8
Sycamore Rd S NP4 62 D1
Sycamore Rise CF42 51 A1
Sycamore St
Rhydyfelin CF37 136 A5
Taffs Well / Ffynnon Taf CF15 158 A4
Sycamore Terr NP11 87 B4
Sycamore Tree Cl CF15 176 A6
Sychbant Ave CF34 102 A1
Sydney Ct NP12 85 C6
Sydney St SA5 68 C4
Sylvan Cl
Cardiff / Caerdydd CF5 176 E1
Newport / Casnewydd NP20 117 B3
Sylvan Way SA2 94 C7
Sylvia Terr SA5 68 C4
Symmons St SA1 68 C1
Syndicate Terr NP11 113 A4
Syon Park Cl CF3 180 A7
Syphon St CF39 107 F3
Syr Dafydd Ave NP12 59 B2
Syr David's Ave CF5 194 B7
Syr David's Ct CF5 194 B7
System St CF24 195 D6

T

Tabernacle Ct NP23 14 F2
Tabernacle Rd / Heol Tabernacle 2 SA18 220 A8
Tabernacle St
Neath / Castell-Nedd SA10 70 F7
Swansea / Abertawe SA1 68 D3
Tabernacle Terr 5 SA12 99 D5
Tabor Pl CF34 102 B3
Tabor Rd CF82 85 B2
Tabor St CF15 158 A4
Tabor Terr SA14 41 E6
Tacoma Sq CF10 195 C1
Tafarnaubach Ind Est NP22 6 A2
Taf Cl CF62 214 C6
Taff Bargoed Community Pk★ CF46 56 C3
Taff Bargoed Ctr★ CF46 56 C4
Taff Bsns Ctr CF37 136 C3
Taff Cl NP23 7 C4
Taff Cotts
Llantrisant CF72 155 E2
Tonypandy CF40 106 E8
Taff Ct NP44 89 A5
Taf Fechan Hos CF48 3 F4
Taff Emb CF11 195 A2
Taff Fawr Cl CF48 10 A4
Taff Fawr Ho CF48 10 A3
Taff Fechan Ho CF48 10 A3
Taff Fechan Nature Trail★ CF48 10 C8
Taff Glen View CF47 30 F8
Taff Gorge Countryside Ctr★ CF15 158 D2
TAFF MERTHYR GARDEN VILLAGE 56 D1
Taffs Fall Rd CF37 136 D2
Taffs Mead Emb CF11 232 A1
Taffs Mead Rd CF37 136 C2
Taff St
Cardiff / Caerdydd CF24 232 C2
Ferndale CF43 79 F7
Merthyr Vale / Ynysowen CF48 55 D3
Pontypridd CF37 109 C1
Tongwynlais CF15 158 C1
Treherbert CF42 50 F1
TAFFS WELL / FFYNNON TAF 158 B5
Taffs Well Sta CF15 158 A3
Taff Terr
Abercynon CF45 82 D1
Cardiff / Caerdydd CF11 195 A2
Radyr CF15 176 C5
Tonypandy CF40 106 C7
Treorchy / Treorci CF42 78 D6
Taff Vale CF46 82 F6
Taff Vale Ct CF47 10 E2
Taff Vale Flats CF37 135 C8
Taff Vale Prec 3 CF37 109 C1
Taff Vale Sh Ctr CF37 109 C1
Taff Workshops CF10 232 B1
Taf Olwg CF46 83 D3
Tafwys Wlk CF83 138 A3
Tai Ann CF37 109 F5
Tai Arfryn / Houses on the Hill 7 CF31 168 C3
TAIBACH 125 D7
Tai Bach
Ebbw Vale / Glyn Ebwy NP23 7 B4
Pentrebach CF48 31 A4
Taibah Sch CF24 195 C7
Tai Bank SA11 49 D3
Taicanol SA12 99 E6
Tai-Canol CF48 10 B1
Tai Cap Coch CF44 53 E5
Tai Cwm CF39 107 F3
Tai Derwen CF3 161 D6
Tai Duffryn CF15 158 A7
Tai Ebenezer / Ebenezer Cl CF46 83 D7
Tai Educational Ctr CF40 107 A4
Tai Gwalia SA9 221 C5
Tai Llanbedr CF5 191 E6
Taillwyd Rd
Neath Abbey SA10 71 B8
Neath / Castell-Nedd SA10 48 B1
Tai Mawr Rd CF48 10 A3
Tai Mesen / Acorn Villas NP23 14 E3
Tai Newydd
Rhydyfelin CF37 136 B4
Ynysybwl CF37 81 F2
Tai Penyard CF47 10 E2
Tai Penylan CF5 175 C5
Taipren CF37 135 C8
Tai'r Briallu CF44 27 F7
Tair Erw Rd CF14 177 D5
Tairfelin CF31 168 E7
Tai'r Felin SA10 49 C4
Tair Grawen 6 CF47 10 D2
TAIRGWAITH 220 F7
Tairgwaith Prim Sch SA18 220 E6
TAI'R-HEOL 83 D2
Tai'r-Heol CF82 84 D8
Tai'r Heol CF37 109 B6
Tair Onnen CF5 190 B1
Tai'r Twynau CF48 11 B7
Tair Waun Pl CF34 101 E4
Tai'r Ynys Fawr SA12 73 C1
TAI'R-YSGOL 69 E8
Tai Siriol CF46 83 D3
Tai-yr-Efail CF48 11 A7
Tai Ysgol Fach CF48 29 F8
Talana Terr CF34 75 A1
Talbot Cl CF72 155 C3
Talbot Gn SA4 66 C5
TALBOT GREEN 155 B3
Talbot Green Ret Pk / Parc Manwerthu Tonysgyboriau CF72 155 C2
Talbot Green Spec Sch CF72 155 C2
Talbot La NP20 143 C4
Talbot Rd
Llantrisant CF72 155 D3
Neath / Castell-Nedd, Mount Pleasant SA11 71 F5
Neath / Castell-Nedd, Pentreffynnon SA10 70 F6
Port Talbot SA13 125 C7
Pyle / Y Pîl CF33 148 D3
Talbot Green CF72 155 C2
Talbot Rd / Ffordd Talbot 10 SA18 219 B7
Talbot Sq
Merthyr Tydfil / Merthyr Tudful CF47 10 F3
Talbot Green CF72 155 B2
Talbot St
Cardiff / Caerdydd CF11 194 E6
Gowerton / Tre-gwyr SA4 66 B5
Llanelli SA15 40 D4
Maesteg CF34 102 A3
Talbot Terr
Maesteg CF34 102 A4
St Mary Church / Llan Fair CF71 201 A4
Talcennau Rd SA13 125 C7
Taldwyn Terr CF48 31 C2
Talfaen Cl NP4 38 C1
Talfan Rd SA1 69 B3
Talgarth Cl NP44 89 E2
Talgarth St CF34 102 C2
Taliesin NP44 89 E4
Taliesin Cl
Pencoed CF35 152 B1
Rogerstone NP10 142 B6
Taliesin Ct 9 CF10 195 B2
Taliesin Dr NP10 142 B6
Taliesin Pl SA4 42 E1
Taliesyn Rd SA1 95 A8
Talley Rd SA5 68 B5
Tallis Cl NP19 144 E5
Tallis St CF42 78 B5
TALLISTOWN 35 A6
Talworth St CF24 232 D4
Talybont Cl CF62 211 D7
Talybont Ct CF14 194 E8
Talybont Rd CF5 193 D5
Tal-y-bryn CF64 206 E2
Talyclun SA14 18 E2
Tal Y Coed SA4 18 F3
Talycopa Prim Sch SA7 69 F7
Talyfan CF72 154 A3
Talyfan Cl CF71 188 F1
Talygarn Cl CF72 172 F5
Talygarn Ct CF72 173 A5
Talygarn Dr CF72 172 F6
Talygarn Mews CF72 173 A5
Talygarn St CF14 177 F2
TALYWAIN 37 E5
Talywain Ho NP4 37 E5
Talywern SA14 42 B7
Tal-y-Wern SA13 125 D5
Tamar Cl
Bettws NP20 116 E2
Bryn NP12 85 D3
Tanglewood Cl CF14 160 A2
Tanglewood Dr NP13 15 F5
Tangmere Dr CF5 176 D2
Tan House Dr NP18 118 C2
Tank Farm Rd SA10 70 C3
Tank Farm Way CF64 215 E6
Tanlan Sq NP24 33 F2
Tansy Cl
Cardiff / Caerdydd CF14 159 D3
Pen-pedair-heol CF82 84 E6
Tanyard Pl CF44 53 B8
Tanybryn
Mountain Ash / Aberpennar CF45 81 F8
Risca / Rhisga NP11 141 C8
Tan-y-Bryn
Beddau CF38 156 A7
Brynna CF72 153 D4
Tan Y Bryn CF43 79 B8
Tan-y-Bryn
Pencoed CF35 152 F1
Porth CF39 107 D2
Rhymney / Rhymni NP22 13 A2
Senghenydd CF83 111 A1
Tanybryn Pl CF47 10 F4
Tanybryn St CF44 29 A1
Tanybryn Terr CF43 107 C8
Tan Y Bryn Terr SA11 227 B8
Tan-y-bryn Terr SA4 64 F4
Tan-y-Coed NP4 37 F1
Tanycoed Rd SA6 22 F1
Tanycoed St CF45 81 F8
Tanycoed Terr CF44 53 F4
Tanydarren SA8 221 B1
Tanyfan SA18 218 E6
Tan-y-Farteg SA9 2 C7
Tan-y-Fron
Barry / Y Barri CF62 214 B3
Treorchy / Treorci CF42 78 D5
Tanygarth SA9 222 C7
Tan-y-Gelli SA18 220 B8
Tan-y-Graig SA9 222 B7
Tanygraig Rd SA14 41 E4
Tan-y-Groes Pl SA13 125 D8
Tan-y-Groes St SA13 125 C8
Tan-y-Lan Terr SA6 68 F8
Tan-y-Llan Terr NP22 12 E4
Tan-y-Lon SA6 22 D1
Tan Y Marian CF43 79 B8
Tan Y Marian Rd SA1 95 B8
Tan-y-Pych CF42 50 D4
Tanyrallt
Abercrave / Abercraf SA9 222 C7
Clydach SA6 22 D1
Tan-yr-Allt CF72 155 E2
Tanyrallt Ave CF31 168 F7
Tan-y-Rhiw SA10 222 D3
Tanyrhiw Rd SA11 226 E5
Tanywaun SA9 222 B6
Tanywern La / Lon Tanywen SA9 2 B7
Tanyyrallt Ave CF31 168 F7
Tapley Cl CF5 193 C3
Taplow Terr SA1 68 F2
Tarddiad Goron / Crown Rise 5 NP44 90 B1
Tarragon Way CF23 160 E1
Tarran Workshops CF31 168 F3
Tarren Terr SA12 100 A7
Tarrws Cl CF5 205 A7
Tarwick Dr CF3 179 E6
Tasker Sq CF14 177 D7
Tatem Dr CF5 193 C7
Tathan Cres CF62 211 D5
Tath Gwaun CF64 206 E1
Taunton Ave CF3 179 C5
Taunton Cres CF3 179 C5
Taverner Trad Est NP18 118 B2
Tavern-y-Coed CF37 135 F3
Tavistock Cl SA2 94 E7
Tavistock Rd SA2 94 D7
Tavistock St CF24 232 C4
Tawe Ave SA1 68 E2
Tawe Bsns Village SA6 69 B5
Tawelfan
Nelson CF46 83 E4
Tircoed SA4 44 C5
Ystradgynlais SA9 1 F4
Tawel Fan SA14 41 A6
Tawelfryn CF48 225 F3
Tawe Pk SA9 2 F7
Tawe Pl SA6 46 E7
Tawe Rd SA7 69 E8
Tawe St SA6 69 A8
Tawe Terr SA8 23 E4
Tawe View Cres SA6 45 F1
Taylor Rd CF31 168 F7
Taylor's Row 2 SA11 71 D6
Taylor St NP11 114 F3
Taymuir Green Ind Pk CF24 195 F8
Taymuir Rd CF24 195 F7
Teal Cl CF36 182 E8
Tealham Dr CF3 180 B7
Teal St CF24 195 C7
Teamans Row CF15 176 B8
Teasel Ave CF64 206 E5
Techniquest★ CF10 195 B1
Technium Bsns Pk SA1 233 C3
Technium Two SA1 233 C3
Techno Ctr / Canolfan Technoleg CF24 195 D4
Technology Dr CF31 168 E1
Ted Davies Cl CF33 165 F8
Tedder Cl CF14 177 F7
Tees Cl NP20 116 F2
Tegfan
Caerphilly / Caerffili CF83 137 E3
Cardiff / Caerdydd CF11 194 D6
Ferndale CF43 79 D7
Pontyclun CF72 173 A6
Swansea / Abertawe SA7 69 F5
Tircoed SA4 44 C5
Teg Fan SA10 70 E6
Tegfan Cl CF14 177 E8
Tegfan Ct NP44 115 F8
Tegfan / Fairview CF32 104 F6
Tegid Rd SA1 233 A5
Teglan Pk SA18 218 F5
Teifi Dr CF62 214 C5
Teifi Pl CF5 193 D5
Teify Cres CF32 104 E7
Teilo Cres SA1 95 B8
Teilos Dr CF31 169 A5
Teilo St CF11 194 D7
Telelkebir Rd CF37 109 A2
Telford Cl
Pen-pedair-heol CF82 84 E7
Rogerstone NP10 142 B6
Telford Court Flats NP19 143 E4
Telford St
Cardiff / Caerdydd CF11 194 E5
Newport / Casnewydd NP19 143 E4
Telor-y-Coed CF83 112 A5
Telyn Aur SA6 45 E2
Temperance Ct CF15 157 B1
Temperance Hill 8 NP11 114 F3
Temperance La SA9 1 F1
Temperance Pl CF37 109 C1
Templar Parc CF24 195 C4
Temple St
Llanelli SA15 40 E5
Maesteg CF34 102 B3
Newport / Casnewydd NP20 143 D2
Swansea / Abertawe SA1 233 B3
Templeton Ave CF14 159 E1
Templeton Cl CF14 159 E1
Templeton Way SA5 67 F7
Ten Acre Wood SA13 126 B1
Tenby Cl
Dinas Powis / Dinas Powys CF64 206 C3
Newport / Casnewydd NP10 163 E5
Tenby Cl / Clos Dimbych-y-Pysgod 4 NP44 90 A3
Tenby Ct CF83 137 D4
Tenison Rd NP4 38 D1
Tennyson Ave NP18 145 A4
Tennyson Cl CF37 136 A6
Tennyson Dr CF31 168 D6
Tennyson Rd
Barry / Y Barri CF62 214 E8
Newport / Casnewydd NP19 144 A5
Penarth CF64 206 F4
Tennyson Terr NP24 33 F1
Tennyson Way
Llantwit Major / Llanilltud Fawr CF61 210 B5
Swansea / Abertawe SA2 93 F8
Tensing Cl CF14 159 F1
Tensing Terr 11 CF63 215 B6
Tenth Ave
Merthyr Tydfil / Merthyr Tudful CF47 10 F5
Swansea / Abertawe SA6 45 D2
Tent Vale / Pant Y Pebyll CF35 170 C8
Teras Abermorlais / Abermorlais Terr 2 CF47 10 D1
Teras Afon Llwyd / Afon Llwyd Terr 2 NP4 38 A1
Teras Brookland / Brookland Terr NP44 89 E6

Teras Brynhyfryd / Brynhyfryd Terr
Ebbw Vale / Glyn Ebwy NP23 14 F2
Seven Sisters / Blaendulais SA10 222 D4
Teras Brynteg / Bryn-Teg Terr 13 SA18 219 B7
Teras Caersalem / Caersalem Terr 2 SA15 40 D3
Teras Clifton / Clifton Terr 3 NP4 17 C7
Teras Gorsaf / Station Terr SA10 222 D3
Teras Graham / Graham Terr SA10 70 F7
Teras Jones / Jones' Terr SA18 219 F8
Teras Llsyg Falwen / Snail Creep Terr NP4 37 F8
Teras Maes Y Deri / Oakfield Terr 7 SA18 219 C7
Teras Maes-y-Gwanwyn / Springfield Terr SA12 99 A1
Teras Noel / Noel Teras CF48 55 C4
Teras Parc Bigyn / Bigyn Park Terr SA15 40 E4
Teras Rawlinson Isaf / Rawlinson Terr NP22 13 F5
Teras Rockingham / Rockingham Terr SA11 71 C2
Teras St Ioan / St John's Terr SA10 71 A7
Teras Tir Y Llys / Courtland Terr 8 CF47 10 E1
Teras Torfaen / Torfaen Terr 3 NP4 38 A1
Teras Trem Y Graig / Craig View Terr NP4 37 D6
Teras Tyisha / Tyisha Terr SA15 40 E8
Teras Waterloo / Waterloo Terr SA18 218 D6
Teras Y Ffynnon / Spring Terr NP4 62 D2
Teras Yr Arced / Arcade Terr 11 SA18 220 B8
Terfyn Ynysawdre CF32 150 E4
Terminus Ho SA10 71 A7
Tern Cl CF3 179 F8
Tern Ct NP44 89 A5
Tern Rd CF36 182 D8
Terrace Rd SA1 95 B7
Terrace Road Prim Sch SA1 95 B7
Terrace The
Creigiau CF15 174 E8
Rhymney / Rhymni NP22 12 E4
Terra Nova Way CF64 206 F5
Terry's Way CF72 153 F2
Tetbury Cl NP20 143 C7
Tewdric Ct NP44 90 B5
Tewdrig Cl CF61 209 F5
Tewends 11 NP44 89 B1
Tewkesbury Pl CF24 178 A2
Tewkesbury St CF24 178 A1
Tewkesbury Wlk 6 NP20 143 C6
Teynes NP44 89 B1
Thackeray Cres CF3 179 B7
Thames Cl
Bettws NP20 116 E1
Bryn NP12 85 D4
Tharsis Cl CF24 232 D2
Thaw Cl CF62 212 E1
THE HERBERTS 201 A4
THE KNAP 214 C1
THE MUMBLES / Y MWMBWLS 123 C4
Theobald Rd CF5 194 C5
Theodora St CF24 195 E7
Theodore Rd SA13 125 C7
THE QUAR 10 C3
Thesiger Ct 7 CF24 195 A8
Thesiger St CF24 195 A8
THE VILLAGE 144 C8
Third Ave
Caerphilly / Caerffili CF83 137 E3
Merthyr Tydfil / Merthyr Tudful CF47 10 E5
Swansea / Abertawe SA6 45 D1
Thirlemere Terr 1 CF44 53 E8
Thirlmere Pl 5 NP19 143 F8
Thirteenth Ave CF44 224 C1
THISTLEBOON 123 B3
Thistleboon Cvn Site SA3 123 C4
Thistleboon Dr SA3 123 C4
Thistleboon Gdns SA3 123 B3
Thistleboon Rd SA3 123 B4
Thistle Cl CF62 214 D6
Thistle Ct NP44 88 F2
Thistle Terr 1 CF40 106 E6
Thistle Way
Cardiff / Caerdydd CF5 194 A8
Risca / Rhisga NP11 115 B2
Thomas Cres CF33 166 A7
Thomas Davies Ct 3 CF3 179 B3
Thomas Ellis Way NP22 13 F7
Thomas Evans Ho SA1 67 F1
Thomas Fields NP22 12 F4
Thomas Gr 12 NP10 142 B4
Thomas Harris Ho SA3 123 A8
Thomas Jones Sq 6 CF48 31 C1
Thomas' Pl CF39 107 F2
Thomas Row SA1 233 B4
Thomas's Ct 11 SA11 71 E6
Thomas's Pl CF39 107 E7
Thomas St
Aberavon SA12 98 F1
Aberbargoed / Aberbargod CF81 58 B5
Aberdare / Aberdâr CF44 29 A3
Aberfan CF48 55 C4
Abertridwr CF83 137 A7
Bargoed / Bargod CF81 58 A2
Bedwas CF83 139 A6
Briton Ferry / Llansawel SA11 71 C1
Cardiff / Caerdydd CF11 194 F3
Hendreforgan CF39 132 C5
Llanbradach CF83 111 F1
Llanelli SA15 40 D6
Maerdy CF43 52 A1
Maesycwmmer CF82 85 B2
Mountain Ash / Aberpennar CF45 54 E1
Nelson CF46 83 E3
New Tredegar NP24 33 E3
Pontardawe SA8 23 E5
Pontypridd CF37 109 B1
Swansea / Abertawe SA1 233 C3
Tonypandy, Blaen Clydach CF40 106 D6
Tonypandy, Penygraig CF40 106 E4
Treharris CF46 83 B6
Treorchy / Treorci CF41 79 A5
Thomas Terr
Aberdare / Aberdâr CF44 53 C7
Dowlais CF48 11 A5
Resolven / Resolfen SA11 226 D5
Swansea / Abertawe SA6 68 E6
THOMASTOWN 133 A2
THOMAS TOWN 10 E1
Thomasville CF83 137 E5
Thompson Ave
Cardiff / Caerdydd CF5 194 A7
Newport / Casnewydd NP19 144 B3
Thompson Cl NP19 144 C3
Thompson Ct
1 Cardiff / Caerdydd CF5 194 C6
Gorseinon SA4 66 D8
Thompson Pl CF5 194 A7
Thompson St
Barry / Y Barri CF63 214 F4
Pontypridd CF37 109 A1
Ynysybwl CF37 109 A8
Thompson Villas CF37 109 A8
Thorburn Cl SA11 71 F8
Thorley Cl CF23 178 B4
Thornaby Ct CF10 232 C1
Thornbury Cl
Baglan SA12 98 E4
Cardiff / Caerdydd CF14 177 C5
Merthyr Tydfil / Merthyr Tudful CF48 225 F1
Thornbury Park Sh Ctr 15 NP10 142 B4
Thornbury Pk NP10 142 B4
Thornbush Hill / Bryn Dryslwyn CF31 168 C2
Thorncombe Rd NP12 85 F6
Thorne Ave NP11 86 F7
Thorne Way CF5 193 B3
Thorney Rd SA12 98 D7
Thorn Gr CF64 217 A8
THORNHILL
Cardiff 159 E2
Cwmbran 89 B4
Thornhill Cl
Brynmawr NP23 8 C5
Cwmbran / Cwmbrân NP44 89 B6
Thornhill Ct CF14 177 D8
Thornhill Gdns NP10 141 E7
Thornhill Prim Sch CF14 159 E3
Thornhill Rd
Capel Hendre SA14 218 C6
Cardiff / Caerdydd CF14 159 C3
Cwmbran / Cwmbrân NP44 89 B5
Thornhill St 9 CF5 194 C6
Thornhill Way NP10 141 E6
Thornleigh Rd NP11 59 F5
Thornton Cres CF32 103 F2
Thornwood CF46 83 B6
Thornwood Cl CF14 159 E3
Thornwood Pl CF46 83 B6
Three Arches Ave CF14 178 A6
Three Cliffs Dr SA3 121 A6
THREE CROSSES 65 E1
Three Elms Cl CF82 84 F4
Three Oaks Cl CF83 138 C7
Three Salmon St CF47 30 D8
Three Ships Ct SA3 123 C3
Threipland Dr CF14 177 D5
Thrush Cl 1 CF3 180 A6
Thurston Rd CF37 109 D2
Thurston St
Abercynon CF45 82 E3
7 Cardiff / Caerdydd CF5 194 D5
Tichbourne St SA3 123 B4
Tidal Sidings CF24 195 F5
Tide Fields Rd CF24 196 A5
Tidenham Ct CF5 193 D4
Tidenham Rd CF5 193 D4
Tillery Rd NP13 36 B7
Tillery St NP13 36 B6
Till Gr NP18 117 F3
Tillsland NP44 116 C8
Timber Pl / Man Y Coed 3 SA12 98 C2
Timbers Sq CF24 195 D8
Timber Yd The CF24 195 D4
Timothy Pl CF44 53 D8
Timothy Rees Cl CF5 176 D3
Tingle La CF35 186 A7
Tinkinswood Burial Chamber* CF5 204 A7
Tin St CF24 195 D6
Tintagel Cl CF14 159 D2
Tintern Cl
Cwmbran / Cwmbrân NP44 89 F2
St Athan / Sain Tathan CF62 211 C7
Tintern Ct 13 CF5 194 C6
Tintern St CF5 194 C6
Tippett Cl NP19 144 E5
Tir-Afon Ct CF72 173 B7
Tirbach Rd SA9 2 C7
Tir Bach Rd NP12 85 F1
Tir-Berllan NP12 59 B2
TIRCANOL 46 B2
Tir Capel SA14 41 A6
Tir Celyn SA13 148 A6
TIRCOED 44 C5
Tir Coed CF83 137 E5
TIRDEUNAW 68 B7
Tirdeunaw Cl SA5 68 C7
Tir Einon SA14 41 C4
Tirforgan SA14 41 A7
Tirfounder Rd CF44 53 E7
Tirgof SA14 42 B8
Tir John North Rd SA1 96 C8
Tir-mabellis Ho CF37 135 A1
Tir Meibion La CF72 155 D3
Tirmorfa / Moorlands SA10 223 A5
Tirmorfa Prim Sch / Ysgol Gynradd Tirmorfa SA12 98 B1
Tir Morfa Rd / Heol Tir Morfa SA12 98 B1
Tirmynydd SA4 43 B1
Tirmynydd Rd SA2, SA4 92 D8
TIR-NEST 69 B3
Tir Newydd
Llanelli SA14 41 D4
North Cornelly CF33 166 A8
TIRPENRY 46 A1
Tirpenry St SA6 46 A1
Tirpentwys Terr NP4 61 F8
TIR-PHIL 33 D3
Tir-Philkins NP12 86 B6
Tir-Phil Sta NP24 33 E3
Tirprys SA18 219 A5
Tirwaun SA14 218 B7
TIR-Y-BERTH 85 A6
Tir-y-Berth NP23 7 C3
Tir-y-berth Ind Est CF82 85 A6
Tir-y-berth Prim Sch CF82 85 A6
Tir-y-Berth St CF82 85 A6
Tir-y-coed CF38 157 A6
Tirycoed Rd / Heol Tir Y Coed 3 SA18 220 A8
Tir-y-Cwm La NP11 114 F1
Tir-y-Cwm Rd NP11 114 F1
Tir-y-Dail La / Lon Tir-y-Dail 11 SA18 219 B7
Tir Y Farchnad SA4 66 C5
Tir-y-Graig CF38 136 A2
Tirynys SA15 40 F8
Tir-y-Pwll Terr NP11 87 B7
Tir Yr Hen Ysgol SA14 41 F3
Tir Ysgol SA15 40 D6
Tir Y Waun SA9 222 A5
Titan Rd CF24 195 D4
Tiverton Dr CF3 179 A4
Toftingall Ave CF14 177 D5
Toft Pl SA15 40 E6
Toghill Dr CF15 158 B3
Tollgate Cl
Caerphilly / Caerffili CF83 138 D5
Cardiff / Caerdydd CF11 194 D1
Tollgate Rd SA13 125 E3
Tolpath NP44 89 A1
Tom Mann Cl NP19 144 E7
Tom Williams Ct SA1 233 B4
Ton-Bach St / Stryd Ton-Bach NP4 17 D6
TON-BREIGAM 171 E4
Tonclwyda SA11 226 B3
Ton-coch Terr CF45 54 B6
TON-DU 150 C5
Tondu Iron Pk* CF32 150 C6
Tondu Prim Sch / Ysgol Gynradd Tondu CF32 150 C4
Tondu Rd CF31 168 D6
Ton-du Sta CF32 150 D5
Tone Cl NP20 116 D2
Tone Rd NP20 116 D2
Tone Sq NP20 116 D2
Ton Glas
Bridgend / Pen-y-Bont ar Ogwr CF31 168 B5
Pyle / Y Pîl CF33 148 A2
TONGWYNLAIS 158 D2
Tongwynlais Prim Sch CF15 176 C8
Ton Hywel CF39 107 D1
Ton Inf Sch CF41 79 A3
TON-MAWR 73 C6
Ton-Mawr Ave NP4 17 D6
Tonmawr Bsns Pk SA12 73 B5
Ton-mawr Prim Sch SA12 73 C5
Ton-Mawr Rd
Pontrhydyfen SA12 72 F4
Ton-mawr SA12 73 B5
Ton-Mawr Rd / Ffordd Ton Mawr NP4 17 D6
Ton-mawr St NP4 17 D6
Tonna Hospl SA11 49 E3
Tonna Rd CF34 102 A7
TONNA / TONNAU 49 D2
Tonna Uchaf SA11 49 D3
Tonnau Prim Sch SA11 49 C2
TONNAU / TONNA 49 D2
TON PENTRE 79 A3
Ton Pentre Ind Est / Ystad Ddiwydiannol Ton Pentre CF41 79 A3
Ton Pentre Jun Sch CF41 78 F3
Ton Pentre Sta CF41 79 A3
Ton Rd / Heol Ton
Cwmbran / Cwmbrân NP44 89 B2
Cwmbran / Cwmbrân NP44 89 C1
Ton Rhosyn CF31 169 B5
Ton Row CF41 79 A3
TON-TEG 136 B1
Ton Teg CF35 170 D7
Tonteg Cl CF38 136 A2
Tonteg Hospl CF38 135 F2
Tonteg Rd CF37 136 B3
Ton The CF3 179 D7
Tontine St SA1 233 B4
Ton Tylluan / Owl Mdw CF31 168 D3
Ton View CF33 148 D2
Ton Y Felin CF37 136 A6
Ton-y-Felin Rd CF83 138 B3
Ton-y-Groes CF35 170 E7
TONYPANDY 106 D5
Tonypandy Comp Sch / Ysgol Gyfun Tonypandy CF40 106 E4
Tonypandy Ent Ctr / Canolfan Fentor Tonypandy CF40 106 E7
Tonypandy Prim Sch CF40 106 E5
Tonypandy Sta CF40 106 F5
TON-Y-PISTYLL 86 D5
Ton-y-Pistyll Rd NP11 86 D5
TONYREFAIL 133 C4
Tonyrefail Comp Sch / Ysgol Gyfun Tonyrefail CF39 133 A4
Tonyrefail Prim Sch / Ysgol Gynradd Tonyrefail CF39 133 C5
Tonyrefail Rd CF37 134 E5
Ton-Yr-Ywen Ave CF14 177 E5
Ton-yr-ywen Prim Sch CF14 177 E6
Tonysguboriau Prim Sch CF72 155 B2
Topaz St CF24 195 D6
Top Rd NP4 37 F6
Torbay Terr CF62 213 A1
Tordoff Way CF62 214 E6
Torfaen Bsns Ctr NP4 62 F4
Torfaen Terr / Teras Torfaen 3 NP4 38 A1
Tor Ho SA3 123 A3
Torlais St NP11 86 F6
Toronto Ave / Rhodfa Toronto 9 SA13 125 E4
Toronto Cl
Blackwood / Coed-Duon NP12 85 F8
Newport / Casnewydd NP20 142 D3
Torrens Dr CF23 178 B4
Torridge Rd NP20 116 C3
Torrington Rd
Cardiff / Caerdydd CF3 179 C7
Swansea / Abertawe SA5 68 A3
Tor View
Bedwas CF83 138 C7
Penmaen SA3 120 B5
Tor-y-Crug NP23 7 B5
Tor-y-Mynydd SA12 98 C7
Tothill St NP23 7 C1
Tower Cl CF31 169 A3
Tower Ct
Llansamlet SA6 69 B8
1 Newport / Casnewydd NP19 143 E5
Swansea / Abertawe SA1 94 F8
Tower Gdns SA1 67 F1
Tower Hill CF64 207 B3
Tower Hill Ave CF64 207 B3
Tower Rd
Gileston / Silstwn CF62 211 E1
Hirwaun CF44 27 C7
Tower St CF37 135 D7
Towers The NP44 89 F3
Tower Way CF64 215 E6
Town Bridge Bldgs NP4 62 C7
Towngate Bsns Ctr SA13 125 B8
Towngate Ind Est
Cwmbran / Cwmbrân, Two Locks NP44 89 E1
Cwmbran / Cwmbrân, Ty Coch NP44 116 E8
Town Hall Sq CF71 188 F2
TOWNHILL 95 A8
Townhill Com Prim Sch SA1 95 A8
Townhill Gdns SA2 94 F8
Townhill Rd SA2 95 A8
Town Mill Rd CF71 188 E1
Towyn Rd CF3 179 C4
Towyn Way CF38 136 A2
Towy Rd CF14 178 A7
Trade La CF10 195 A3
Trade St CF10 232 B1
Traeth Ffordd
Llanelli SA15 40 B4
Llanelli SA15 40 C4
Traethmelyn SA12 98 A3
Trafalgar Bldgs CF81 58 A3
Trafalgar Cl 3 NP23 8 C4
Trafalgar Ct 1 CF24 178 C1
Trafalgar Ho NP23 8 C5
Trafalgar Pl SA2 94 F5
Trafalgar Rd CF23 195 D8
Trafalgar St NP11 115 A1
Trafalgar Terr CF41 79 D2
Trahearne Ct SA10 71 C8
Traherne Dr CF5 192 F4
Trallwm Rd SA14 41 D5
TRALLWN
Pontypridd 109 D2
Swansea 69 F6
Trallwng Inf Sch CF37 109 D2
Trallwn Pl SA7 69 E6
Trallwn Prim Sch / Ysgol Gynradd Trallwn SA7 69 E7
Trallwn Rd SA7 69 E6
Tram La NP44 117 D7
Tramore Way CF23 161 A1
Tram Rd
Caerleon / Caerllion NP18 118 C2
Cwmbran / Cwmbrân NP44 89 B6
Pontllanfraith NP12 85 F4
Tram Rd Ind Est 5 NP12 85 F4
Tramroad La CF47 10 E3
Tramroadside
Ebbw Vale / Glyn Ebwy NP23 7 A4
Newbridge / Trecelyn NP11 86 F6
Tramroad Side
Heolgerrig CF48 10 A1
Merthyr Tydfil / Merthyr Tudful CF48 10 C1
Tram Road Side
Quakers Yard CF46 83 A4
Treharris CF46 83 A6
Tramroad Side N CF47 10 E1
Tramroad Side S CF47 30 E8
Tramroad Terr 4 CF47 10 E1
Tramway CF44 27 E7
Tramway Cl NP44 89 A1
Tramway Rd SA8 24 B5
Tramway Side SA11 223 E1
TRANCH 62 A6
Tranch Rd NP4 62 A6
Trannon Ct NP44 89 A4
Tranquil Pl NP44 89 E1
Trap Well CF83 138 D5
Traston Ave NP19 144 B1
Traston Cl NP19 144 B1
Traston La NP19 144 B1
Traston Rd
Newport / Casnewydd NP19 144 B1
Newport / Casnewydd NP19 164 F8
Travis Way CF36 165 E2
Trawler Rd SA1 233 B1
Trawsffordd SA9 2 E8
Traws Fynydd CF31 169 B4
Trawsmawr La NP20, NP44 116 E4
TREALAW 107 A5
Trealaw Prim Sch CF40 106 F5
Trealaw Rd CF40 106 F6
Treasure St CF42 78 D7
TRE-AUBREY 202 B5
Trebannws Prim Sch / Ysgol Gynradd Gymraeg Draddodiadol Trebannws SA8 23 C2
TREBANNWS / TREBANOS 23 B2

TREBANOG 107 D1
Trebanog Cl CF3 179 E6
Trebanog Cres CF3 179 E5
Trebanog Rd CF39 107 D1
Tre-banog Terr CF44 224 D2
TREBANOS / TREBANNWS 23 B2
Tre-Beferad CF61 210 C5
TREBEFERED / BOVERTON 210 C6
Treberth Ave NP19 144 E6
Treberth Cl NP19 144 E6
Treberth Cres NP19 144 E6
Treberth Ct NP19 144 E6
Treberth Dr NP19 144 E6
Treberth Gdns NP19 144 E6
Treberth Gr NP19 144 E6
Treberth Rise NP19 144 E6
Treberth Way NP19 144 E6
TRE-BOETH 68 B6
Treborth Rd CF3 179 E5
Trecastle Ave CF14 159 E1
TRECELYN / NEWBRIDGE 87 B7
TRECENYDD 137 F3
Trecenydd Ind Est CF83 137 F3
Trecinon Rd CF3 179 F5
TRECYNON 28 E3
TREDEGAR 13 E7
Tredegar Ave
  Ebbw Vale / Glyn Ebwy NP23 14 C7
  Llanharan CF72 153 F3
Tredegar Bsns Pk NP22 13 E7
Tredegar Cl CF72 153 F4
Tredegar Comp Sch NP22 13 E5
Tredegar Ct
  Abercarn NP11 114 B3
  Cardiff / Caerdydd CF14 176 F5
  Newport / Casnewydd NP20 143 C2
Tredegar Flats CF83 139 F7
Tredegar Gap NP23 14 D8
Tredegar General Hospl NP22 13 E6
Tredegar Ho★ NP10 163 D7
Tredegar House Ctry Pk★ NP10 163 D7
Tredegar House Dr NP10 163 E6
Tredegar Mews NP11 114 F1
Tredegar Park View NP10 142 C4
Tredegar Rd
  Ebbw Vale / Glyn Ebwy NP23 14 C7
  Gorseinon SA4 43 C1
  New Tredegar NP24 33 E3
Tredegar St
  Abercarn NP11 114 B4
  Bassaleg NP10 141 E4
  Cardiff / Caerdydd CF10 232 C2
  Newport / Casnewydd NP20 143 C3
  Risca / Rhisga NP11 114 F2
Tredegar Terr
  Aberbargoed / Aberbargod CF81 58 A4
  Abercarn NP11 114 B4
  Risca / Rhisga NP11 114 F1
Tredegarville CW Prim Sch CF24 232 D3
Tredelerch Rd CF3 179 A2
Trederwen NP23 14 B8
Trederwen / Home Of The Oak Tree CF33 148 D3
TRE-DODRIDGE 190 E7
TREDOGAN 213 C4
Tredogan Rd CF62 213 B4
TREDOMEN 84 D1
Tredomen Pk / Parc Tredomen CF82 84 D2
Tredomen Terr CF82 84 D1
Tredomen Villas CF82 84 D2
Tre-Edwards NP22 12 E5
Treehill Ct / Llys Bronwydd CF31 168 D3
Tree Tops Ave NP12 85 E8
Treetops Cl CF5 176 B1
Trefaser Cres CF3 179 E6
TREFECHAN 10 A6
Trefelin CF44 28 E4
Trefelin Cres SA13 99 C2
Trefelin St SA13 99 C2
TREFFLEMIN / FLEMINGSTON 201 D1
Trefforest Estate CF38 136 D1
Trefforest Prim Sch CF37 135 E7
Trefforest Sta CF37 135 E6
TREFIL 6 A6
Trefil Rd NP22 6 A4
TREFOREST 135 D7
Treforest Ct CF37 135 E6
Treforest Ind Est CF15 157 E8
Treforest Ind Est / Ystad Ddiwydiannol Trefforest CF37 136 C2
TREFORGAN / MORGANSTOWN 176 A8
Treforgan Rd
  Crynant / Creunant SA10 226 A8
Treforgan Rd *continued*
  Crynant SA10 222 A1
Treforis SA18 219 C6
TREFORYS / MORRISTON 45 E1
Trefrhiw Rd / Heol Trefrhiw SA18 219 A6
Tref-y-Rhyg Prim Sch / Ysgol Gynradd Tref-y-Rhyg CF39 133 D5
Tregare St NP19 143 D6
Tregarn Cl NP18 119 E2
Tregarn Ct NP18 119 F2
Tregarne Cl SA6 45 F4
Tregarn Rd NP18 119 F2
Tregaron Cl NP12 85 F4
Tregaron Ho SA13 125 E3
Tregaron Rd CF5 193 B5
Tregarth Cl CF15 174 D8
Tregarth Ct CF15 174 D8
Tregelles Ct
  Cwmrhydyceirw SA6 46 A4
  Swansea / Abertawe SA6 45 F3
Tregelles Rd SA10 48 B1
TRE-GIBBON 28 E7
TREGOLWYN / COLWINSTON 187 A4
Tre Gwilym CF44 53 E8
Tregwilym Cl NP10 142 B4
Tregwilym Ind Est NP10 142 A4
Tregwilym Rd
  Rogerstone NP10 142 A4
  Rogerstone / Ty-du NP10 141 F5
Tregwilym Wlk NP10 142 B4
TRE-GWYR / GOWERTON 66 B4
Tregwyr Inf Sch SA4 66 B5
Tregwyr Jun Sch SA4 66 B5
TREHAFOD 108 D3
Trehafod Rd CF37 108 D2
Trehafod Sta CF37 108 C3
Treharne Cotts CF34 102 B3
Treharne Ct CF39 107 E2
Treharne Dr CF31 150 D1
Treharne Flats CF37 136 B5
Treharne Pk CF46 82 F6
Treharne Rd
  Barry / Y Barri CF63 215 A7
  Maesteg CF34 75 B1
  Swansea / Abertawe SA6 45 F1
  Treharris CF46 82 F6
Treharne Row
  Maesteg CF34 102 A4
  Pont-y-rhyl CF32 129 E8
Treharne St
  Merthyr Vale / Ynysowen CF48 55 D5
  Treorchy / Treorci CF41 78 F4
  Treorchy / Treorci, Cwmparc CF42 78 B4
Treharne Terr CF46 82 F6
TREHARRIS 83 B8
Treharris Com Coll CF46 83 B6
Treharris St CF24 232 D4
TREHERBERT 50 E1
Treherbert Ind Est / Ystad Ddiwydiannol Treherbert CF42 78 A8
Tre-Herbert Rd NP44 90 D6
Treherbert St CF24 194 F8
Treherbert Sta CF42 50 F1
TREHILL 191 E1
Trehopcyn Prim Sch CF37 109 A2
TRE-IFOR 28 E8
Tre-Ifor CF44 28 E7
Trelai Ct CF5 193 C3
TRE-LAI / ELY 193 D6
Trelai Prim Sch CF5 193 E5
TRELALES / LALESTON 167 F5
Trelales Prim Sch CF32 167 E4
Trelawney Ave 1 CF3 179 B3
Trelawney Cres 2 CF3 179 B3
Trelech Cl NP44 89 F2
TRELEWIS 83 D7
Trelewis Prim Sch CF46 83 D7
Tre-Lyn La NP12 85 A6
Trelys Cl NP12 85 A5
TREMAINS 169 A4
Tremains Ct CF31 169 B4
Tremains Inf Sch CF31 169 C5
Tremains Jun Sch CF31 169 C5
Tremains Rd CF31 168 F4
Trem Craigddu / Craigddu View NP4 37 E7
Trem Dan-y-Parc / Dan-y-Parc View CF47 10 F1
Trem Echni CF62 213 B1
Tremgarth CF31 168 E6
Trem Mapgoll CF63 205 B1
TREMORFA 195 F6
Tremorfa Ind Est CF24 195 F4
Trem Penallta CF82 84 F3
Trem Powys CF63 215 C8
Trem Twry Drwm / Drum Tower View CF83 137 D2
Trem Twynbarlwm NP44 89 D1
Trem Y Bryn CF31 168 E7
Trem Y Castell CF83 137 D1
Trem Y Coed CF63 205 B1
Trem-y-Cwm 3 CF38 156 A6
Trem Y De / South View CF32 103 F4
Trem-y-Don CF62 214 B2
Trem-y-Duffryn / Valley View 2 CF31 168 C3
Trem-y-Dyffryn / Valley View SA11 226 C4
Trem-y-Fforest CF72 172 C4
Trem-y-Garth CF72 172 D5
Trem-y-Glyn CF39 107 D1
Trem Y Goedlan / Woodland View NP4 37 E7
Trem Y Goron NP12 85 D3
Trem-y-Mor CF31 169 B4
Trem Y Mor SA4 64 B2
Trem-y-Mynydd NP4 17 D6
Trem Y Mynydd CF42 50 F1
Trem Y Mynydd / Mynydd View NP4 62 C4
Trem-y-parc / Park View 1 NP4 38 A1
Trem Y Parc / Parkview Terr SA15 40 C5
Trem-yr-Efail CF82 111 E7
Trenant
  Ebbw Vale / Glyn Ebwy NP23 14 C8
  Hirwaun CF44 27 F7
Trenchard Dr CF14 177 F6
Treneol CF44 53 B5
Tre Newydd
  Ebbw Vale / Glyn Ebwy NP23 7 E1
  Pyle / Y Pîl CF33 148 D2
Trenewydd Rise SA11 71 F6
Trenos Gdns CF72 153 D2
Trenos Pl CF72 153 E2
Trent Rd NP20 116 D3
Treochy Sta CF42 78 D5
Treoda Ct 3 CF14 177 B5
TREOES 170 B1
Treoes Rd CF35 169 F3
Treorchy Comp Sch CF42 78 D6
Treorchy Ent Ctr CF42 78 E5
Treorchy Ind Est / Ystad Ddiwydiannol Treorchy CF42 78 E5
Treorchy Prim Sch CF42 78 D6
TREORCHY / TREORCI 78 E7
TREORCI / TREORCHY 78 E7
Treorky St 4 CF24 195 A8
TREOWEN 86 F8
Treowen Ave NP12 85 E4
Treowen Rd NP11 59 F1
Tre-Pit Rd CF71 198 B5
TRERHYNGYLL 189 B7
Trerobart Prim Sch CF37 109 A8
Treseder Way CF5 193 E5
Tresigin Rd CF3 179 E6
TRESIGIN / SIGINGSTONE 200 A4
Tresilian Cl CF61 209 F5
Tresillian Terr CF10 232 B1
Tresillian Way / Fford Tresillian CF10 232 B1
Tresillian Way Ind Est CF10 232 B1
TRESIMWN / BONVILSTON 191 B1
Tressilian Pl CF45 82 D2
Tre Telynog CF44 53 E8
TRETHOMAS 139 B6
Tretower Ct NP44 90 B3
Tre Uchaf Prim Sch SA4 42 F1
Trevallen Ave SA11 72 A5
Trevelyan Ct
  Caerphilly / Caerffili CF83 138 C3
  Llantwit Major / Llanilltud Fawr CF61 210 B7
Trevethick Ho 6 CF47 30 D8
Trevethick St
  Cardiff / Caerdydd CF11 194 E5
  Merthyr Tydfil / Merthyr Tudful CF47 10 E2
TREVETHIN 38 C1
Trevethin Com Sch NP4 62 C7
Trevine Path NP44 89 C2
Trevithick Cl NP20 116 F3
Trevithick Gdns CF47 30 E8
Trevor Cl / Clos Trefor CF48 11 B7
Trevor St
  Aberdare / Aberdâr CF44 29 A1
  Treorchy / Treorci CF42 78 D7
TREWALLTER / WALTERSTON 203 B3
Trewartha Ct 7 CF14 177 B5
Trewaun CF44 27 E7
Trewen Rd
  Birchgrove SA7 47 A1
  Swansea / Abertawe SA7 70 A8
Trews Field Ind Site CF31 168 E6
Trewyddfa Comm SA6 68 F6
TREWYDDFA FACH 68 E7
Trewyddfa Gdns SA6 68 F6
Trewyddfa Rd SA6 68 E6
Trewyddfa Terr SA6 68 E6
Tre-York St NP22 12 E4
Triangle
  Barry / Y Barri CF62 214 F2
  Cefn Coed / Cefn-coed-y-cymmer CF48 10 A4
Triangle Bsns Pk / Parc Busnes y Triongl CF48 30 F5
Triangle The
  Bridgend / Pen-y-Bont ar Ogwr CF31 169 B4
  Mountain Ash / Aberpennar CF45 54 D4
Tribute Ave NP11 114 C8
Trident Ct CF24 195 C4
Tridwr Rd CF83 136 F7
Trigfan Dawi SA12 99 D6
TRINANT 59 F5
Trinant Prim Sch NP11 59 F6
Trinant Terr NP11 59 F6
Trinity Cl
  Pontarddulais SA4 19 C3
  The Mumbles / Y Mwmbwls SA3 123 A5
  Ystrad Mynach CF82 84 E1
Trinity Ct
  Cardiff / Caerdydd CF24 232 D3
  Newport / Casnewydd NP20 143 D2
  Port Talbot SA12 98 D2
  Risca / Rhisga NP11 114 F2
  2 Swansea / Abertawe SA1 233 A3
Trinity Fields Specl Sch CF82 84 E1
Trinity Hill NP11 114 C6
Trinity La
  Caerleon / Caerllion NP18 117 F3
  Pen-clawdd SA4 64 D4
Trinity Pl
  Newport / Casnewydd NP20 143 D2
  Pontarddulais SA4 19 C3
  Swansea / Abertawe SA1 233 B3
Trinity Rd
  Llanelli SA15 40 E3
  Tonypandy CF40 106 F5
Trinity Rd / Ffordd Drindod NP44 89 D5
Trinity St
  Barry / Y Barri CF62 214 D4
  Cardiff / Caerdydd CF10 232 B2
  Gorseinon SA4 43 C1
Trinity Terr SA15 40 D3
Trinity View NP18 117 E3
Trip Terr CF41 79 A5
Triscombe Dr CF5 176 E1
Tristram Cl CF14 159 D2
Troedpennar Terr CF45 82 E3
Troedrhiw-gwair NP22 14 B2
TROEDRHIW-TRWYN 108 F3
Troedrhiw-trwyn CF37 108 F2
Troed-y-bryn
  Abercrave / Abercraf SA9 222 E7
  Blaina / Blaenau NP13 15 E6
  Caerphilly / Caerffili CF83 137 E5
Troed-y-Garth CF15 157 B1
TROEDYRHIW 31 C1
Troedyrhiw CF82 111 E8
Troed-y-Rhiw
  Abercarn NP11 87 A3
  Abercrave / Abercraf SA9 222 B7
Troed Y Rhiw CF14 159 A1
Troed-y-Rhiw SA7 69 F6
Troedyrhiw Inf Sch / Ysgol Plant Bach Troed-y-rhiw CF48 31 C1
Troedyrhiw Jun Sch / Ysgol Plant Lau Troed-y-rhiw CF48 31 C2
Troedyrhiw Rd CF39 107 E4
Troed-y-Rhiw Rd
  Cwmfelinfach NP11 113 E4
  Mountain Ash / Aberpennar CF45 54 E3
Troed-y-Rhiw Sta CF48 31 C1
Troedyrhiw Terr CF42 78 E6
Tro Rhymni / Rumney Wlk NP44 90 B3
Troserch Rd / Heol Troserch SA14 18 B2
Tros- Maen SA14 40 F8
TROSNANT 62 D6
Trosnant Cres CF82 84 D5
Trosnant St NP4 62 C6
Trosnant Villa NP4 62 C6
Trostre Ind Pk SA14 41 A3
Trostre Rd
  Llanelli SA14, SA15 40 F3
  Llanelli SA15 40 F4
Trostre South Ret Pk SA14 41 A4
Trostrey NP44 116 C8
Trostrey Cl NP4 63 B4
Trostrey St NP19 143 D6
Tro Tircoed SA4 44 C4
Trotman Dickenson Pl CF14 177 E1
Tro Tref Y Cernyw / Dorstone Wlk NP44 90 A3
TROWBRIDGE 179 F5
Trowbridge Gn CF3 179 E6
Trowbridge Inf Sch CF3 179 E5
Trowbridge Jun Sch CF3 179 E5
Trowbridge Rd CF3 179 D4
Troy Rd NP13 60 B7
Trum Hyfryd / Pleasant Hts CF39 107 E5
Trussel Rd / Heol Trussel 1 NP44 89 E4
Tucker St SA11 71 C3
Tuckers Villas NP12 85 E7
Tudno Pl SA5 68 A5
Tudor Ave CF44 27 D8
Tudor Cl
  Cardiff / Caerdydd CF5 193 D7
  Ebbw Vale / Glyn Ebwy NP23 7 B5
  Penarth CF64 207 A1
Tudor Cl / Clos Tudur CF48 55 D4
Tudor Cres
  8 Brynmawr NP23 8 B4
  Rogerstone NP10 142 C4
Tudor Ct
  Aberbargoed / Aberbargod CF81 58 B4
  Bishopston SA3 122 A6
  Cardiff / Caerdydd CF14 177 D5
  Llanedi SA4 218 D1
Tudor Dr CF32 129 E1
Tudor Est CF34 75 A1
Tudor Gdns
  Machen CF83 139 F6
  Neath / Castell-Nedd SA10 48 C1
Tudor Gr / Gelli Tudur SA13 125 F3
Tudor La CF11 232 A1
Tudor Mews CF72 173 D7
Tudor Pl
  Aberdare / Aberdâr CF44 53 C8
  Llantwit Major / Llanilltud Fawr CF61 210 A5
Tudor Rd
  Cwmbran / Cwmbrân NP44 89 E3
  Newport / Casnewydd NP19 143 E8
  Swansea / Abertawe SA5 68 C5
  Ton Pentre CF41 79 A2
Tudor St / Heol Tudor SA9 2 E7
Tudor St
  Cardiff / Caerdydd CF11 194 F4
  Ferndale CF43 79 F6
  Hawthorn CF37 136 A4
  Merthyr Tydfil / Merthyr Tudful CF47 10 D2
  1 Port Talbot SA13 99 B1
Tudors The CF23 178 D1
Tudor Terr
  Aberdare / Aberdâr CF44 28 F3
  Merthyr Tydfil / Merthyr Tudful CF47 10 D2
Tudor Way
  Bishopston SA3 122 B7
  Llantwit Fadre / Llanilltud Faerdref CF38 156 D6
Tudor Woods NP44 90 B2
Tulip Wlk NP10 141 D6
Tulloch St 4 CF24 178 C1
Tummel Cl CF23 178 C5
Tumulus Way CF71 199 D4
Tunnel Rd SA15 40 E5
Tunnel Row NP11 86 E6
Tunnel Terr NP20 143 B4
Turberville Cres CF31 150 F1
Turberville Pl CF11 194 D6
Turberville Rd
  Cwmbran / Cwmbrân NP44 89 E4
  Porth CF39 107 E5
Turberville St
  Maesteg CF34 102 C2
  Tonypandy CF40 79 F1
Turberville Terr 5 CF40 106 F4
Turbine Annexe Rd CF62 211 E1
Turkey St CF61 209 F7
Turner House Gallery★ CF64 207 B3
Turner Rd CF5 194 B6
Turners End NP44 89 B1
Turner St NP19 143 D6
Turnham Gn CF23 178 E2
Turnpike Cl
  Dinas Powis / Dinas Powys CF64 206 B4
  Pontypool / Pont-y-pwl NP4 62 F6
Turnpike Rd NP44 90 B1
Turnpike Rdbt NP44 90 B3
Turnstiles The NP20 143 C7
Turnstone Ct SA12 98 C1
Turnstone Rd CF36 165 E1
Tuscan Cl CF64 206 D7
TUTT 123 D3
Twchwyn Garth CF35 187 E8
Tweedsmuir Rd CF24 195 F7
Tweedy La NP19 143 F5
Twelfth Ave CF47 10 F5

Twinings The 8 NP44 89 B3
Twissell's Rd NP4 62 A6
Twll-yn-y-Wal Rd 5 SA13 125 E4
Twm Barlwm Cl NP11 115 C2
Twmbarlwm Rise NP44 88 E1
Twm Barlwm View NP44 90 B2
Twmpath Gdns NP4 62 B6
TWMPATH-MAWR 102 A5
TWO LOCKS 89 E1
Two Locks Rd / Heol Dwy Loc NP44 89 D1
Two Stones Cres CF33 148 D2
Twympath Rd NP4 62 B6
Twyn NP12 85 A5
Twyn Bedw CF39 107 E1
Twyn Bedw Rd SA6 46 D7
Twyncarmel CF48 225 F1
Twyn Carno NP22 12 E5
Twyncarn Rd NP11 114 B6
Twyncyn CF64 205 F3
Twyncynghordy NP23 8 A4
Twyncynghordy Pl NP23 8 A4
Twyncynghordy Rd
- Brynmawr NP23 8 A4
- Ebbw Vale / Glyn Ebwy NP23 7 F4
TWYN CYNHORDY 8 A3
Twynderwyn Flats NP23 8 D2
Twyn Gdns NP12 85 C7
Twyn-gwyn Rd NP11 113 A5
Twyn Gwyn Rd CF40 107 B4
Twyn-gwyn Terr NP11 86 E6
Twyniago SA4 19 D4
Twyni Teg SA2 93 E8
Twyn Oaks NP18 118 D3
Twynpandy SA12 73 A2
Twyn Pl NP11 87 C3
Twyn Prim Sch CF83 138 B2
Twyn Rd
- Abercarn NP11 87 B3
- Ystrad Mynach CF82 111 E7
Twynrefail Pl SA18 220 D6
Twyn Star / Seren Twyn NP22 6 D1
Twyn Teg SA10 48 D1
Twyn The CF83 138 B2
Twyn-y-Fedwen CF14 177 D3
Twynyffald Rd NP12 85 D8
Twynygarreg CF46 83 B7
Twyn-y-Gored SA12 100 A7
Twyn Yr Eglwys CF71 186 F3
Twyn-yr-Eos CF42 51 A1
TWYNYRODYN 30 E8
TWYN-YR-ODYN 204 F8
Twynyrodyn Com Sch
- Merthyr Tydfil / Merthyr Tudful CF47 10 F1
- Troedyrhiw CF47 30 F8
Twynyrodyn Rd 11 CF47 30 E8
Twyn-Yr-Ynys SA12 100 A7
Twyn-yr-Ysgol SA9 2 B7

Ty = house

Ty Alban CF40 106 E7
Ty Beddoe SA1 96 B7
Ty Bedwellty NP12 85 D7
Ty Bethania CF42 78 D6
Ty Box Cl NP44 89 D5
Ty Box Rd / Heol Ty Bocs NP44 89 D5
Ty Brachty Terr NP11 59 D2
Ty Bruce La CF44 27 E8
Ty Brunel 8 SA11 71 C1
Ty Bryn
- Aberbargoed / Aberbargod CF81 58 A5
- Tredegar NP22 13 E7
Ty Bryncoch CF15 158 A4
Ty Bryn Ct NP13 36 A6
Ty Bryngoleu CF48 55 C3
Ty Bryn Rd NP13 36 A6
Tybryn Terr CF35 170 B8
Ty-Bwmpyn Rd NP4 61 D7
Ty Caitlin 5 SA1 233 A3
Ty Camlas 3 CF63 214 F4
TY CANOL 88 E2
Ty Canol CF36 165 F1
Ty-Canol Ct NP44 89 A1
Ty-Canol La CF83 139 A8
Ty Canol La CF83 139 F7
Ty-Canol Row NP44 89 A1
Ty Canol Way NP44 88 F2
Ty-capel CF15 158 A3
Ty Capel Zion CF43 80 B2
Ty Capstan 9 CF63 214 F4
Ty-Cefn Rd CF5 193 D6
Ty Celyn Mews CF14 176 F7
Ty Cerrig
- 5 Barry / Y Barri CF63 215 B7
- Cardiff / Caerdydd CF23 178 E8
Ty Charlotte CF64 207 A6
Ty Cheriog SA12 99 E5
TY-COCH 94 C8
TY COCH 116 E8
Ty Coch NP22 12 E6
Ty-Coch Cl NP10 141 F2
Ty Coch Distribution Ctr NP44 116 E7
Ty Coch Ind Est NP44 89 E1
Ty-Coch La NP44 116 E8
Ty-Coch La / Llwybr Ty Coch NP44 116 F6
Ty-coch Maisonettes SA2 94 D7
Tycoch Rd SA2 94 D7
Ty-Coch Rd CF5 193 C5
Ty-Coch Terr NP44 116 E8
Ty Coch Way / Ffordd Ty Coch NP44 116 E8
Ty-Coed NP44 89 B5
Ty Copa CF72 155 D3
Ty Cornel CF81 58 A5
Tycribwr Hill
- Aberkenfig / Abercynffig CF32 150 A3
- Cefn Cribwr CF32 149 F2
TYCROES 218 F5
Tycroes Rd / Heol Tycroes
- Ammanford / Rhydaman SA18 219 A5
- Tycroes SA18 218 F5
Ty Crwyn CF38 156 E8
Ty Cwmpas 8 CF63 214 F4
Ty Cyan SA12 99 E5
Ty Cydwel 10 SA15 40 D4
Ty-Dan-y-Wal NP13 16 B1
Ty-Dan-y-Wal Rd NP13 36 A7
Ty Dawel CF39 133 C5
Ty Ddewi CF41 79 A2
Tyddyn Gwaun CF32 167 E4
Tydeg Anerys NP12 85 E7
Ty Devonia CF64 206 F6
Ty Dewi-Sant SA12 99 E5
Ty Dewi Sant SA5 67 E3
Tydfil Cl CF46 83 E6
Tydfil Ho CF41 78 F5
Tydfil Pl CF23 178 B2
Tydfil Rd CF83 138 D7
Tydfil St CF63 215 B6
Tydfil's Terr 2 CF47 10 D2
TYDFIL'S WELL 10 D3
Tydfil Terr CF48 31 C2
Tydfil Villas CF48 11 B7
Tydies NP44 116 B8
TY-DRAW 69 C2
Ty Draw CF38 135 E1
Ty-Draw
- Llandow / Llandw CF71 199 A7
- Penperlleni NP4 39 E3
Ty Draw CF72 155 A5
Tydraw Cres CF33 166 B8
Ty-Draw Cres SA1 69 B2
Ty-Draw Hill SA13 99 C1
Ty Draw La
- Penperlleni NP4 39 E3
- South Cornelly CF33 165 F6
Ty-draw Pl
- Aberdare / Aberdâr CF44 29 C2
- Cardiff / Caerdydd CF23 178 C1
- Port Talbot SA13 125 B8
- Swansea / Abertawe SA1 69 B2
Ty-Draw Rd
- Aberdare / Aberdâr CF44 29 C2
- Cardiff / Caerdydd, Pentwyn CF23 160 E1
- Cardiff / Caerdydd, Pen-y-lan CF23 178 B2
- Swansea / Abertawe SA1 69 C2
Ty-Draw St / Stryd Tydraw 1 SA13 125 B8
Ty-Draw St 5 SA13 99 B1
Tydraw Terr CF42 50 D3
Ty Du Rd CF46 83 E2
TY-DU / ROGERSTONE 141 F6
Tydu View NP10 142 B4
Ty Ebenezer CF43 80 C3
Ty Elizabeth 6 SA15 40 D4
Ty Fforest 3 SA6 46 A1
Ty Ffynnon CF62 214 F8
Tyfica Cres CF37 109 C1
Tyfica Rd CF37 109 C1
Ty Florence Asher SA6 22 E1
Ty Fry CF44 28 F1
Ty-Fry Ave CF3 179 B3
Ty Fry Cl NP4 17 D7
Ty-Fry Cl
- Brynmenyn CF32 150 F7
- Cardiff / Caerdydd CF3 179 C4
Ty-Fry Gdns CF3 179 C4
Ty Fry Rd CF81 58 B4
Ty-Fry Rd CF3 179 B4
Ty Fry Rd CF32 149 A2
Ty-fry Rd / Heol Ty Fry SA13 125 E4
Ty Gambig CF62 214 F1
Ty-Glas Ave CF14 177 F8
Ty Glasfryn CF43 80 B3
Ty-Glas Rd CF14 177 E8
Ty Glas Sta CF14 177 E6
Ty Gnoll Newydd SA11 71 F7
Ty Gwalia CF64 206 F6
Ty Gwaunfarren CF47 10 C6
Ty Gwendollen CF64 207 A6
Ty Gwenfo CF63 215 C6
Ty-Gwyn NP44 89 A2
Ty Gwyn SA4 66 C5
Ty-Gwyn Ave CF23 178 C2
Ty Gwyn Cl CF35 152 B5
Ty-Gwyn Cres CF23 178 C3
Ty Gwyn Dr CF31 169 D4
Tygwyn Rd
- Church Village CF38 135 F1
- Clydach SA6 46 E8
- Pontypridd CF37 109 E1
Ty-Gwyn Rd
- Cardiff / Caerdydd, Pen-y-lan CF23 178 C2
Ty-Gwyn Rd *continued*
- Cardiff / Caerdydd, Rhydwaedlyd CF14 177 C7
Ty Gwyn Rd NP4 39 E3
Ty-Gwyn Rd / Heol Ty Gwyn NP4 37 E7
Ty Gwyn Rd / Heol Ty Gwyn NP44 89 B3
Ty Gwyn Specl Sch CF23 178 C3
Tygwyn St CF47 10 F3
Ty Gwyn Way NP44 89 A2
Ty Heddlu 6 CF42 51 A1
Ty Hedd-wyn 1 SA12 99 D5
Ty Hermon SA6 68 E5
Ty-Heulwen NP23 8 C2
Ty Horeb SA6 45 F1
Ty Howard 7 SA15 40 D4
Ty Ifor 4 SA11 71 E7
TY-ISAF 40 E3
Ty-Isaf CF83 137 D5
Ty Isaf CF72 172 B5
Ty-Isaf Complex NP11 141 B8
Ty-Isaf Cres NP11 141 B8
Ty Isaf Inf Sch NP11 115 B1
Ty-Isaf Park Ave NP11 141 C8
Ty-Isaf Park Circ NP11 141 C8
Ty-Isaf Park Cres NP11 141 B8
Ty-Isaf Park Rd NP11 141 C8
Ty-Isaf Park Villas NP11 141 B8
Tyisaf Rd CF41 79 B3
Ty-Isaf Rd CF32 149 B1
Tyisha Rd SA15 40 E4
Ty-Isha Terr NP12 85 D8
Tyisha Terr / Teras Tyisha SA15 40 E8
Tylacelyn Rd CF40 106 F4
Tylacoch CF72 172 B5
Tylacoch Pl CF42 78 C6
Tylagarw Terr CF72 172 F8
Tyla Glas CF83 158 F8
Tyla Gwyn CF15 157 F7
Tyla-Gwyn CF82 84 D8
Tyla La CF3 162 A3
Tyla Moes SA10 48 C2
Tyla Rd SA11 71 C3
Tyla Rhosyr CF71 188 D2
Tyla Teg CF14 176 F8
Tylcha Fach CF39 133 D2
Tylcha Fach Cl CF39 133 D2
Tylcha Fach Terr CF39 133 D2
Tylcha Ganol CF39 133 C2
Tylcha Isaf CF39 133 D2
Tylcha Wen Cl CF39 133 B3
Tylcha Wen Terr CF39 133 B3
Tyle-Fforest CF42 51 A1
Tyle Garw CF72 172 F8
Tyle Glas
- Glanaman SA18 220 C7
- North Cornelly CF33 166 A8
Tyle House Cl CF61 210 B8
Tyle Mali CF71 187 E1
Tyle-Rackland CF71 198 B7
Tyle'r Hendy CF72 173 C7
Tyleri Gdns NP13 36 B6
Tyler St CF24 195 E7
Tyle Teg SA6 46 C7
Ty Levant 7 CF63 214 F4
Ty-Llansawel 6 SA11 71 C1
Ty Llunfan CF39 132 C7
Tyllwyd SA10 48 B6
Ty-Llwydd Pl NP11 86 F6
Ty Llwyd Parc CF46 83 C5
Tyllwyd Rd NP20 142 F4
Tyllwyd St CF47 10 F3
Ty-Llwyd Wlk CF81 58 B5
TY LLWYN 14 F6
Tylors Ct CF43 80 C4
TYLORSTOWN 80 C3
Tylorstown Prim Sch / Ysgol Gynradd Pendyrus CF43 80 C3
Ty Lowri SA2 94 D8
Tymaen Cres SA12 99 F6
Tymaen Terr 3 SA12 99 F6
Ty-mawr SA8 23 E4
Ty Mawr 2 SA1 95 B7
Ty-Mawr Ave CF3 179 A2
Tymawr Cl CF3 179 A2
Ty mawr Cl CF71 189 C8
Ty Mawr La CF3, NP10 162 F1
Ty Mawr Parc CF37 108 F2
Tymawr Rd CF37 108 F2
Ty-Mawr Rd
- Cardiff / Caerdydd, Rumney / Rhymni CF3 179 A2
- Cardiff / Caerdydd, Whitchurch / Yr Eglwys Newydd CF14 176 E4
Tymawr St SA1 96 B7
Tymawr Terr CF37 109 A2
Ty Mawr Uchaf CF37 108 F2
Tymeinwr Ave CF32 103 E5
Ty Melin NP11 59 D1
Ty Merchant CF35 152 F1
Ty Meriel 8 SA15 40 D4
Ty Mynydd
- Blaenavon NP4 17 D6
- Cwmbran / Cwmbrân NP44 89 E5
Tymynydd Cl CF15 176 B7
Ty Mynyddislwyn NP12 85 F3
Ty-myrtwydd SA4 65 E8
TYNANT 156 B7
Tynant CF14 177 B4
Ty Nant
- Bridgend / Pen-y-Bont ar Ogwr CF31 168 C5
- Caerphilly / Caerffili CF83 137 E4
Ty-Nant CF82 84 D8
Ty Nant Ct CF15 158 B1
Tynant Rd
- Beddau CF38 156 A7
- Creigiau CF15 174 D7
Ty-Nant Rd CF15 176 B7
Ty-Nant St CF11 194 E3
Tyndall St CF10 232 D1
Tyndall Street Ind Est CF10 232 C1
Tyne Cl NP20 116 D1
Tyneside Rd CF10 195 D2
TYNEWYDD
- Seven Sisters 222 D4
- Tredegar 6 B3
Tynewydd
- Cardiff / Caerdydd CF14 177 B4
- Tredegar NP22 6 B3
Ty Newydd
- Cardiff / Caerdydd CF14 177 A4
- Machen CF83 139 D5
- Pontardawe SA8 24 A7
- Seven Sisters / Blaendulais SA10 222 D4
Tynewydd Ave NP44 89 E6
Ty-Newydd Ct NP44 89 E5
Tynewydd Dr CF3 162 C3
Tynewydd Farm Cl NP44 89 E6
Tynewydd Gn / Glaslawr Tynewydd NP44 89 E6
Ty-Newydd Ho 5 NP44 89 E5
Tynewydd North Cl NP44 89 E6
Ty-Newydd Rd
- Barry / Y Barri CF62 214 F6
- Cwmbran / Cwmbrân NP44 89 E5
Tynewydd Row CF32 104 E2
Tynewydd South Cl NP44 89 E6
Tynewydd Sq CF39 107 E4
Tynewydd St CF81 32 F8
Tynewydd Terr NP11 86 F6
Ty Newydd Terr SA14 218 B8
Tyntaldwyn Rd 2 CF48 31 C1
TYNTETOWN 82 B5
Tynton Rd CF31 168 E5
Tyntyla Ave CF40 79 E2
Tyntyla Pk CF40 79 F1
Tyntyla Rd CF40 79 E2
Tyntyla Terr CF41 79 D3
Tyn-y-Banwen Rd CF46 82 F6
Tynybedw Cl CF42 78 E6
Tynybedw St CF42 78 E6
Tynybedw Terr CF42 78 E6
Tyn-y-berllan SA6 22 C6
Tyn-y-Bettws Cl CF32 129 E1
Ty'n-y-Bonau Rd SA4 19 C5
Ty'n-y-brwyn NP10 162 F4
TY'N-Y-BRYN 133 A3
Tynybryn Rd CF39 133 B4
Tyn-y-Cae SA8 23 F3
TY'N-Y-CAEAU 71 F8
Tyn-y-Caeau La CF36 166 C1
Ty'n-y-Cae Gr CF14 177 C6
Ty'n-y-Cae Rd SA7 69 D7
Tynycai Pl CF40 106 F3
Tyn-y-Coed CF82 84 E1
Ty'n-y-coed NP44 89 B2
Tyn-y-Coedcae CF42 51 A1
Ty'n-y-coedcae CF83 139 D5
Tynycoed Cres NP12 85 C8
Ty'n-y-Coed La CF24 178 B1
Ty'n-y-Coed Pl CF24 178 B1
Tyn-y-Coed Rd CF15 157 B1
Tynycoed Terr CF47 10 F3
Ty'n-y-Coed Terr CF32 150 E4
TYN-Y-CWM 20 D2
Tyn-y-Cwm Rd NP11 141 C8
Tynycymmer Cl CF39 107 E3
TY'N-Y-GARN 150 D2
Ty'n-y-graig SA10 25 F5
Ty'n-y-Graig Rd CF83 111 F1
Tynygraig Terr 1 CF83 111 F1
Ty'n-y-Pant Rd SA8 23 C5
Ty'n Y Parc CF83 136 F8
Ty'n-y-parc Rd
- 2 Cardiff / Caerdydd CF14 177 B5
- Cardiff / Caerdydd CF14 177 B6
Ty'n-y-Pwll Rd CF14 177 A5
Ty'n Yr Haul CF32 150 E6
Tynyrheol Flats SA11 72 A5
Tynyrheol Prim Sch CF32 130 B4
Ty'n-yr-Heol Rd SA10 48 C3
Tyn-y-twr SA12 98 F6
Tynywaun CF41 79 D3
Tyn-y-Waun CF32 129 E3
Tyn y Waun Rd CF83 140 A7
Tyn-y-Waun Rd SA7 69 E6
Ty'n Y Wern CF39 133 C2
Tyn-y-Wern Ct CF83 139 A6
Tyn-y-Wern Prim Sch CF83 139 A6
Tynywern Terr CF83 139 A7
Ty Parc Cl CF5 176 D3
Ty Penderyn CF48 10 A4
Ty Penry Thomas NP23 14 D7
Typica Cotts CF37 108 F2
Ty-Pica Dr CF5 205 A7
Ty Pontrhun CF48 31 B2
Ty Pucca Cl CF83 140 A6
Ty Pwca Pl NP44 89 C6
Ty Pwca Rd NP44 89 C6
Ty'r Felin SA5 67 F6
Tyr Felin St CF45 81 E8
TYRFRAN 40 E7
Ty'r Fran SA7 47 A2
Ty'rfran Ave SA15 40 E7
Ty'r-Groes Dr SA13 125 F3
Tyr Halen Row SA12 98 D6
Ty Rhiannon SA2 94 E5
TY-RHIW 158 C4
Ty Rhiw CF15 158 B4
Ty'r Holl Saint 5 CF24 195 C5
Tyrisha Ave SA4 43 C6
Tyrisha Ct SA4 43 C6
Tyrisha Rd SA4 43 C6
Ty'r Maes SA5 67 F6
Tyr-Meddyg NP23 7 E2
Tyr Onen SA12 98 D6
Ty-Rosser-Gwyn NP4 37 E7
Ty'r-Owen Row SA12 99 D5
Ty'r-Owen Terr 6 SA12 99 D5
Ty'r Person CF38 135 E1
Ty'r Pobydd 4 SA11 71 E6
Ty'r Sianel 4 CF63 214 F4
Ty'r Waun CF15 158 B8
Tyrwhitt Cres CF23 178 A5
Tyr Winch Rd CF3 179 D8
Tyr-y-Sarn Rd CF3 179 B2
Ty'r Ysgol 4 CF24 195 C5
Ty-segur SA11 71 E5
Ty Seion 6 CF45 54 D3
TY-SIGN 115 C2
Ty Sign Prim Sch NP11 115 A2
Ty Sivertsen SA1 95 B6
Ty Stafford 9 SA15 40 D4
Tytalwyn Ave CF33 148 C2
TYTHEGSTON 167 B2
Tythegston Cl / Clos Llanduowg CF36 165 F2
Tytherley CF64 206 A2
Ty-to-Maen CF62 202 E2
Ty-To-Maen Cl CF3 179 E8
Ty Trappa NP44 89 C6
Ty Trappa Pl 1 NP44 89 C6
Ty Tudor NP44 89 E3
Ty Twyn CF38 135 D1
Ty Twyn Teg SA10 48 D1
Ty Uchaf CF64 206 E2
Ty Vaynor CF48 10 A4
Ty-Verlon Ind Est CF63 215 E7
Ty-Wern Ave CF14 177 C6
Ty-Wern Rd CF14 177 C6
Ty Westonia CF64 206 F6
Ty Windsor CF64 207 A6
Tywith Cotts CF34 102 A7
Tywod Vale / Pant Tywod CF35 170 C8
Tywyn Cl SA12 124 E8
Tywyn Cres SA12 124 D8
Tywyn Prim Sch SA12 124 D7
Ty Ystradfellte CF48 10 A4

U

Ullswater Ave CF23 178 A3
Ullswater Cres SA6 68 E7
Under Cardiff Rd CF81 58 A3
Underhill Dr CF38 136 A1
Underhill La SA3 231 B4
Underhill Mans 3 CF14 176 F6
Underhill Villas CF44 53 B8
UNDERWOOD 145 E6
Underwood CF83 138 B1
Underwood Ave CF82 85 A1
Underwood Pl / Maes Tanrallt CF31 169 C4
Underwood Rd
- Blackwood / Coed Duon NP12 86 A8
- Tonna / Tonnau SA10 49 A3
Underwood Terr
- Abertridwr CF83 137 B7
- Pontypridd CF37 109 A2
Union Bldgs SA15 40 D7
Union Pl
- Merthyr Tydfil / Merthyr Tudful CF47 10 E1
- Tylorstown CF43 80 B4
Union St / Stryd Yr Undeb NP4 37 F3
Union St
- Aberdare / Aberdâr CF44 28 F4
- 1 Ammanford / Rhydaman SA18 219 C7
- Ferndale CF43 79 F6
- Maesteg CF34 101 F5
- Merthyr Tydfil / Merthyr Tudful CF47 10 E1
- 5 Mountain Ash / Aberpennar CF45 54 D3
- Pontlottyn CF81 12 F1

Union St *continued*
Pontypridd CF37 ... 135 C8
Swansea / Abertawe SA1 ... 233 A2
Ton Pentre CF41 ... 79 B3
Tredegar NP22 ... 13 D6
Union Terr [6] CF47 ... 10 E1
United World Coll of the Atlantic CF61 ... 208 H5
Unity St CF44 ... 28 F1
Univ Coll of Wales / Coleg Brifysgol Cymru NP18 ... 118 A3
Universal St CF11 ... 232 A1
University Pl CF24 ... 195 E6
Univ Hospl of Wales / Ysbyty Athrofoal Cymru CF14 ... 177 F3
Univ of Glamorgan / Prifysgol Morgannwg CF37 ... 135 E6
Univ of Wales Coll Newport NP20 ... 142 F5
Univ of Wales Coll of Medicine CF14 ... 177 F3
Univ of Wales Dental Sch CF14 ... 177 E3
Univ of Wales Inst Cardiff
Cardiff / Caerdydd, Adamsdown CF24 ... 232 D3
Cardiff / Caerdydd CF23 ... 178 D4
Univ of Wales Inst Cardiff (Colchester Ave Campus) CF23 ... 178 E1
Univ of Wales Inst, Cardiff (Llandaff Campus) CF5 ... 177 B1
Univ of Wales Swansea / Prifysgol Cymru Abertawe SA2 ... 94 D4
Uphill Cl CF64 ... 216 B6
Uphill Rd CF3 ... 179 B5
Upland Dr NP4 ... 38 B1
Upland Rd
Neath / Castell-Nedd SA11 ... 71 F6
Pontllanfraith NP12 ... 86 B4
UPLANDS ... 94 F6
Uplands
Gowerton / Tre-gwyr SA4 ... 66 B5
Gwaun-Cae-Gurwen SA18 ... 220 D5
Newbridge / Trecelyn NP11 ... 86 F7
Ton Pentre CF41 ... 79 B3
Uplands Cres
Llandough / Llandochau CF64 ... 206 E6
Swansea / Abertawe SA2 ... 94 F6
Uplands Ct
[3] Newport / Casnewydd NP19 ... 143 F6
Rogerstone / Ty-du NP10 ... 141 F6
Uplands Dr CF34 ... 101 F5
Uplands Rd
Cardiff / Caerdydd CF3 ... 179 A2
Pontardawe SA8 ... 23 D4
Uplands Terr
Cwmbran / Cwmbrân NP44 ... 89 C3
Swansea / Abertawe, Graig Trewyddfa SA6 ... 68 F8
Swansea / Abertawe, Uplands SA2 ... 94 F6
Uplands The
Newbridge / Trecelyn NP11 ... 86 F7
Pontrhydyfen SA12 ... 73 A1
Port Talbot SA13 ... 99 C1
Radyr CF15 ... 176 C6
Rogerstone / Ty-du NP10 ... 141 F6
Upper Adare St CF32 ... 103 E4
Upper Alma Pl CF41 ... 78 F5
Upper Alma Terr CF37 ... 135 D8
Upper Arail St NP13 ... 36 B3
Upper Banks Sta* SA1 ... 69 A4
UPPER BOAT ... 136 E2
Upper Boat Ind Pk CF37 ... 136 C3
Upper Bridge St NP4 ... 62 C6
Upper Brynhyfryd Terr CF83 ... 110 F3
Upper Canning St CF41 ... 78 F3
Upper Capel St CF81 ... 57 F4
Upper Church Pk SA3 ... 123 B4
Upper Church St
Bargoed / Bargod CF81 ... 57 F4
[1] Pontypridd CF37 ... 109 C1
UPPER CHURCH VILLAGE ... 135 D2
Uppercliff Cl CF64 ... 207 C5
Uppercliff Dr CF64 ... 207 C5
Upper Clifton St [3] CF24 ... 195 D7
UPPER COEDCAE
Blaenavon ... 17 E7
Nantyglo ... 15 D8
Upper Coedcae Rd NP4 ... 17 D6
Upper Colbren Rd SA18 ... 220 D6
Upper Colliers' Row CF48 ... 10 B1
Upper Cosmeston Farm CF64 ... 217 A7
Upper Court Terr NP13 ... 60 B6
Upper Cross Rd SA15 ... 40 F5
Upper Cross St NP24 ... 33 D3
UPPER CWMBRAN ... 89 B6
Upper Cwmbran Inf Sch NP44 ... 89 C6
Upper Cwmbran Rd NP44 ... 89 B6
Upper Dock St NP20 ... 143 C5
Upper Edward St [19] CF47 ... 10 D2
Upper Elizabeth St CF48 ... 11 A4
Upper Fforest Way
Llansamlet SA6 ... 46 B1
Swansea / Abertawe SA6 ... 69 B8
Upper Forest Level CF45 ... 54 E2
UPPER FORGE ... 46 D8
Upper Francis St CF83 ... 136 F7
Upper Garn Terr NP4 ... 16 F8
Upper Gendros Cres SA5 ... 68 A3
Upper Gertrude St CF45 ... 82 E2
Upper Glantorvaen Terr NP4 ... 17 B6
Upper Glyn Gwyn St CF83 ... 139 A7
Upper Griffin St NP13 ... 36 C3
Upper Gwastad Terr NP13 ... 36 C8
Upper Gwyddon Rd NP11 ... 87 B2
Upper Gynor Pl CF39 ... 107 E5
Upper Heathfield Rd SA8 ... 23 E6
Upper High St
Bargoed / Bargod CF81 ... 58 A4
Bedlinog CF46 ... 56 A7
Merthyr Tydfil / Merthyr Tudful CF48 ... 225 F3
Rhymney / Rhymni NP22 ... 12 E6
Upper Hill St NP4 ... 17 D6
Upper Inkerman St [9] SA15 ... 40 D5
Upper James St NP12 ... 58 F4
UPPER KILLAY ... 93 A5
Upper Kincraig St CF24 ... 195 C8
Upper King's Head Rd SA5 ... 67 F4
Upper Mdw CF5 ... 193 B3
Upper Mill SA15 ... 40 E6
Upper Mill Rd SA4 ... 19 D4
Upper Mount Pleasant [7] CF48 ... 31 C1
Upper North Rd CF81 ... 57 F5
Upper Ochrwyth NP11 ... 140 F7
Upper Park St [5] SA15 ... 40 D5
Upper Park Terr NP4 ... 62 C6
Upper Power St NP20 ... 143 B7
UPPER RACE ... 62 B3
Upper Rd NP24 ... 34 A1
Upper Regent St [10] CF44 ... 29 A1
Upper Rhymney Prim Sch NP22 ... 12 E5
Upper Robinson St [11] SA15 ... 40 D5
Upper Row CF48 ... 11 B5
Upper Royal La NP13 ... 36 A6
Upper St Alban's Rd CF42 ... 50 D3
Upper Salisbury St NP22 ... 13 E6
Upper St CF34 ... 101 F3
Upper Stanley Terr NP24 ... 33 F2
Upper Station Rd / Heol Uchaf Yr Orsaf [9] SA18 ... 220 B8
Upper Strand SA1 ... 233 B5
Upper Taff St CF42 ... 50 F1
Upper Tennyson Rd NP19 ... 144 A5
Upper Terr CF43 ... 80 C2
Upper Thomas St [3] CF47 ... 10 E1
Upper Tribute Ave NP11 ... 114 C8
Upper Trosnant St NP4 ... 62 C6
Upper Ty' n-y-parc Terr CF14 ... 177 B6
Upper Union St CF48 ... 11 B4
Upper Vaughan St [7] CF37 ... 109 B1
Upper Vaynor Rd CF48 ... 10 A5
Upper Viaduct Terr NP11 ... 60 A2
Upper Waun St NP4 ... 17 C7
Upper West End [2] SA13 ... 125 C6
Upper William St [1] SA15 ... 40 E5
Upper Woodland St NP4 ... 17 D7
Upper Wood St CF81 ... 57 F3
Uppingham Ct [3] CF5 ... 193 E6
Upton La NP20 ... 142 F4
Upton Pl CF38 ... 156 A6
Upton Rd NP20 ... 142 F4
Upton St
Blaengwynfi SA13 ... 76 C6
Upton St *continued*
Porth CF39 ... 107 E4
Tonypandy CF40 ... 106 E4
Upton Terr SA1 ... 96 A7
Urban St CF47 ... 10 F4
Usk Ct
[8] Cardiff / Caerdydd CF14 ... 177 A6
Cwmbran / Cwmbrân NP44 ... 89 B4
Uskley Ct CF3 ... 179 E6
Usk Pl
Cwmrhydyceirw SA6 ... 46 A5
Ebbw Vale / Glyn Ebwy NP23 ... 7 C5
Usk Rd
Bargoed / Bargod CF81 ... 57 F5
Caerleon / Caerllion NP18 ... 118 C3
Cardiff / Caerdydd CF14 ... 178 A8
Pontypool / Pont-y-pwl NP4 ... 63 B8
Usk St NP19 ... 143 D6
Usk Vale Cl NP18 ... 118 B3
Usk Vale Ct NP4 ... 62 F6
Usk Vale Dr NP18 ... 118 B3
Usk Vale Mews NP18 ... 118 B3
Usk Way
Barry / Y Barri CF62 ... 214 C6
Newport / Casnewydd, Pillgwenlly NP20 ... 143 D1
Newport / Casnewydd, St Woolos NP20 ... 143 D4
Uxilla Terr CF31 ... 169 A3

V

Vachell Ct CF61 ... 210 B6
Vachell Rd CF5 ... 193 D5
Vaendre Cl CF3 ... 162 A1
Vaendre Ct CF3 ... 179 F8
Vaendre La
Cardiff / Caerdydd CF3 ... 179 F8
Cardiff / Caerdydd CF3 ... 180 A8
Vaindre Cl [5] CF3 ... 180 A8
Vaindre Dr [6] CF3 ... 180 A8
Valarian Cl CF3 ... 180 B6
Vale Bsns Pk CF71 ... 199 D5
Vale Ct
Cowbridge / Y Bont-Faen CF71 ... 189 A1
Dinas Powis / Dinas Powys CF64 ... 206 B3
Swansea / Abertawe SA1 ... 68 E3
Vale Ent Ctr CF64 ... 215 F5
Valegate Ret Pk CF5 ... 192 F2
Vale Gdns CF37 ... 109 B2
Valentine Rd NP4 ... 38 A3
Vale Of Neath Bsns Pk SA10 ... 48 E1
Vale Of Wern Terr SA1 ... 96 B7
Vale Pk / Parc Glyn CF31 ... 168 D3
Vale Rd CF24 ... 195 E7
Vale Reach CF35 ... 152 E2
Vale St CF62 ... 214 C3
Vale Terr NP22 ... 13 F5
Vale View
Bargoed / Bargod CF81 ... 57 F2
Barry / Y Barri CF62 ... 214 D8
Bridgend / Pen-y-Bont ar Ogwr CF31 ... 169 C6
Ebbw Vale / Glyn Ebwy NP23 ... 7 E4
Llanharan CF72 ... 153 F3
Maesycwmmer CF82 ... 85 A1
Newport / Casnewydd NP19 ... 144 A7
Pontneddfechan SA11 ... 223 F2
Risca / Rhisga NP11 ... 115 A2
Sarn CF32 ... 150 E3
Tonypandy CF40 ... 107 A3
Tredegar NP22 ... 14 A4
Vale View Cl CF64 ... 206 D6
Vale View Cres CF64 ... 206 D6
Vale View Rd NP12 ... 85 F6
Valeview Terr CF32 ... 104 F7
Vale View Terr CF45 ... 81 E8
Vale View Villas CF32 ... 130 E8
Valley Enterprise CF83 ... 138 D6
Valley Inheritance Mus The* NP4 ... 62 C7
Valley Rd NP23 ... 7 D1
Valley View
Abertillery / Abertyleri NP11 ... 59 F6
Bryn NP12 ... 85 E3
Cardiff / Caerdydd CF3 ... 179 E4
Cefn Hengoed CF82 ... 84 F5
Neath / Castell-Nedd SA11 ... 72 A5
Swansea / Abertawe SA2 ... 94 B5
Valley View Rd NP13 ... 36 B6
Valley View St CF44 ... 53 C6
Valley View / Trem-y-Duffryn [2] CF31 ... 168 C3
Valley View / Trem-y-Dyffryn SA11 ... 226 C4
Valley Way SA6 ... 69 A6
Vanbrugh Cl NP10 ... 142 B6
Vanbrugh Gdns NP20 ... 142 E1
Vancouver Dr
Blackwood / Coed-Duon NP12 ... 85 F8
Vancouver Dr *continued*
Blackwood / Coed Duon NP12 ... 86 A8
Newport / Casnewydd NP20 ... 142 D3
Van Dyke Cl NP19 ... 143 F7
Vanewood Ct SA3 ... 123 C3
Vanfield Cl CF83 ... 138 C2
Vanguard Way CF24 ... 195 E4
Van Rd CF83 ... 138 C2
Van St CF11 ... 194 E3
Van Terr CF83 ... 138 D2
Vardre Rd SA6 ... 46 E8
Varna Terr SA13 ... 125 D7
VARTEG ... 17 E1
Varteg Pl NP22 ... 6 E1
Varteg Rd
Blaenavon NP4 ... 17 E3
Ystalyfera SA9 ... 2 B5
Varteg Rd / Heol Varteg NP4 ... 37 E8
Varteg Row SA13 ... 100 F5
Vartes Hill / Mynydd Y Farteg SA9 ... 2 F6
Vaughan Ave
Cardiff / Caerdydd CF5 ... 194 A8
Resolven / Resolfen SA11 ... 226 D5
Vaughan Cl [1] SA12 ... 99 A1
Vaughan Pl SA4 ... 42 E1
Vaughan St
Dowlais CF48 ... 11 A4
Llanelli SA15 ... 40 D5
[6] Pontypridd CF37 ... 109 B1
Vaughan Terr CF45 ... 82 A7
Vaughan Williams Dr NP19 ... 144 C5
Vauxhall Rd SA15 ... 40 D5
VAYNOR / FAENOR ... 3 D1
Vaynor La CF48 ... 10 A5
Vaynor St CF39 ... 107 E4
Vaynor Villas CF48 ... 10 A5
VELINDRE ... 99 B2
Velindre Ct CF14 ... 176 F5
Velindre Hospl / Ysbyty Felindre CF14 ... 176 F5
Velindre Pl CF14 ... 176 F5
Velindre Rd CF14 ... 176 F5
Velindre St SA13 ... 99 B2
Vellacott Cl / Clos Vellacott CF10 ... 232 C1
Venables Cl SA5 ... 67 D2
Vennaway La SA3 ... 121 D7
Vennwood Cl CF5 ... 205 A6
Venosa Trad Est CF83 ... 138 C4
Vensland SA3 ... 122 A6
Ventnor Pl CF14 ... 177 D2
Ventnor Rd NP44 ... 89 E2
Verallo Dr CF11 ... 194 B5
Verandah St SA1 ... 233 A3
Vera Rd SA6 ... 46 E8
Verbena Cl CF3 ... 180 A8
Verdi Rd / Heol Verdi SA12 ... 98 B2
Vere Pl CF81 ... 58 A1
Vere St
Bargoed / Bargod CF81 ... 58 A1
Barry / Y Barri CF63 ... 215 C6
Cardiff / Caerdydd CF24 ... 232 D4
Verig St SA5 ... 68 C3
Verland Cl CF5 ... 194 A8
Verland Ct CF35 ... 170 C8
Verlands The CF71 ... 188 D2
Verland Way CF35 ... 170 C8
Verlon Cl CF63 ... 215 E7
Vermeer Cres NP19 ... 144 A7
Vernon Cl
Merthyr Tydfil / Merthyr Tudful CF47 ... 10 F2
Pontlliw SA4 ... 44 A5
Vernon Ho CF31 ... 169 A5
Vernon Pl
Blackwood / Coed Duon NP11 ... 59 D1
Briton Ferry / Llansawel SA11 ... 71 B1
Vernon Rd CF36 ... 183 A7
Vernon St / Stryd Vernon SA11 ... 71 C2
Vernon St
Bridgend / Pen-y-Bont ar Ogwr CF31 ... 169 A5
Swansea / Abertawe SA1 ... 233 B5
Verona Ho CF10 ... 232 C1
Verona Pl CF63 ... 215 C7
Veronica Cl NP10 ... 142 B3
Versil Terr SA4 ... 65 F8
Vervain Cl CF5 ... 193 A5
Verwey Rd NP23 ... 15 D8
Viaduct Ct NP4 ... 62 D5
Viaduct Rd
Abersychan NP4 ... 37 E5
Barry / Y Barri CF63 ... 215 B4
Taffs Well / Ffynnon Taf CF15 ... 158 A2
Viaduct Terr NP11 ... 60 A2
Vibernum Rise CF38 ... 156 C5
Vicarage Cl
Bargoed / Bargod CF81 ... 57 F4
Bassaleg NP10 ... 142 B2
[1] Tonypandy CF40 ... 107 A4
Ystrad CF41 ... 79 D3
Vicarage Ct
Church Village CF38 ... 135 F2
Marshfield CF3 ... 162 D2
Vicarage Dr SA8 ... 23 F6
Vicarage Gdns
Marshfield CF3 ... 162 D1
Rogerstone / Ty-du NP10 ... 141 F6
Vicarage Hill NP20 ... 143 B4
Vicarage La
Abersychan NP4 ... 37 F5
Bargoed / Bargod CF81 ... 57 F4
Hengoed CF82 ... 85 A2
Llangennith SA3 ... 228 C2
Pontllanfraith NP12 ... 86 B4
Pontlottyn CF81 ... 32 F8
Swansea / Abertawe SA5 ... 68 A2
Vicarage Rd
Porth CF39 ... 107 E5
Swansea / Abertawe, Clun-Du SA6 ... 68 E8
Swansea / Abertawe, Morriston / Treforys SA6 ... 45 F2
Tonypandy CF40 ... 107 A4
Tonypandy CF40 ... 107 B4
Tredegar NP22 ... 6 E1
Vicarage Rd / Heol Ficerei [7] SA18 ... 220 B8
Vicarage Terr
Abersychan NP4 ... 38 A5
Maesteg CF34 ... 101 F3
Swansea / Abertawe SA1 ... 233 C3
Treorchy / Treorci CF42 ... 78 B5
Viceroy Ct [14] CF10 ... 195 B2
Viceroy Mans [13] CF10 ... 195 B2
Vickery Ho [10] SA12 ... 98 F1
VICTORIA ... 14 E3
Victoria Ave
Cardiff / Caerdydd CF5 ... 194 B6
Ebbw Vale / Glyn Ebwy NP23 ... 14 E3
Newport / Casnewydd NP19 ... 143 F6
Penarth CF64 ... 207 A3
Porthcawl CF36 ... 182 E6
Swansea / Abertawe SA1 ... 95 A5
The Mumbles / Y Mwmbwls SA3 ... 123 A5
Victoria Bldgs
Abercarn NP11 ... 87 A2
Coytrahen CF32 ... 150 C8
[1] Troedyrhiw CF48 ... 31 C1
Victoria Bridge CF64 ... 207 A4
Victoria Cl [7] NP20 ... 143 C4
Victoria Cres NP20 ... 143 B4
Victoria Ct
[7] Cardiff / Caerdydd CF5 ... 194 B7
Newport / Casnewydd NP19 ... 143 E5
The Mumbles / Y Mwmbwls SA3 ... 122 D4
Victoria Gdns SA11 ... 71 E7
Victoria Hall CF10 ... 194 F8
Victoria La NP19 ... 143 F6
Victoria Mews
[3] Cardiff / Caerdydd CF14 ... 177 E2
Pontyclun CF72 ... 173 B8
VICTORIA PARK ... 194 A6
Victoria Park Rd CF63 ... 215 C7
Victoria Park Rd E CF5 ... 194 B6
Victoria Park Rd W CF5 ... 194 A6
Victoria Pl
Abersychan NP4 ... 37 F5
Bargoed / Bargod CF81 ... 58 A2
[6] Newport / Casnewydd NP20 ... 143 C4
Victoria Prim Sch
Abersychan NP4 ... 37 F4
Penarth CF64 ... 206 F4
Victoria Quay SA1 ... 233 B2
Victoria Rd
[13] Aberavon SA12 ... 124 F8
Abersychan NP4 ... 37 F5
Abertillery / Abertyleri NP13 ... 36 B1
Barry / Y Barri CF62 ... 214 C3
Cardiff / Caerdydd CF14 ... 177 A5
Ebbw Vale / Glyn Ebwy NP23 ... 14 D5
Fleur-de-lis NP12 ... 85 B4
Gowerton / Tre-gwyr SA4 ... 66 B7
[8] Newport / Casnewydd NP20 ... 143 C4
Penarth CF64 ... 207 A3
Pen-clawdd SA4 ... 64 E3
Pontypool / Pont-y-pwl NP4 ... 62 D5
Port Talbot SA12 ... 124 E8
Pyle / Y Pîl CF33 ... 148 D3
Rhymney / Rhymni NP22 ... 12 E4
Swansea / Abertawe SA1 ... 233 B2
Waunarlwydd SA5 ... 66 E3
Victoria Row SA4 ... 64 E4
Victoria St / Heol Buddug NP44 ... 89 E2
Victoria Sq
Aberdare / Aberdâr CF44 ... 29 A2
Penarth CF64 ... 207 A3
Victoria St
Abertillery / Abertyleri NP13 ... 36 A6
Blaina / Blaenau NP13 ... 15 D4

Victoria St *continued*
Briton Ferry / Llansawel SA11 71 B1
Dowlais CF48 11 A4
Llanbradach CF83 112 A3
Maesteg CF34 75 B2
Merthyr Tydfil / Merthyr Tudful CF47 10 D1
Merthyr Vale / Ynysowen CF48 55 D5
Mountain Ash / Aberpennar CF45 54 E1
Pontycymer CF32 103 E4
Pontypool / Pont-y-pwl NP4 62 E3
Swansea / Abertawe SA2 94 F7
Ton Pentre CF41 79 A3
Tonypandy CF40 107 A5
3 Treharris CF46 83 B6
Treherbert CF42 50 F2
Ystrad CF41 79 D3
Victoria Terr
Abertillery / Abertyleri NP13 60 B6
3 Cwmavon / Cwmafan SA12 99 D5
Newbridge / Trecelyn NP11 86 F6
Pyle / Y Pîl CF33 148 B1
Quakers Yard CF46 83 B5
Swansea / Abertawe SA1 95 A5
Tredegar NP22 13 F6
Wattstown CF39 107 D8
Victor Rd NP13 36 B6
Victor St CF45 54 C2
Victory Ave CF39 107 E4
Vienna Ho 19 CF10 195 B2
View Rd SA6 46 D7
Viking Ct SA1 69 C6
Viking Pl CF10 195 F2
Viking Way SA1 69 D6
Village Cl SA10 48 D3
Village Ct
Blackwood / Coed Duon NP12 59 B1
Pyle / Y Pîl CF33 148 C1
Village Dr SA4 43 C1
Village Farm CF5 191 B1
Village Farm Ind Est
North Cornelly CF33 166 C8
Pyle / Y Pîl CF33 148 C1
Village Farm Rd
North Cornelly CF33 166 C8
Pyle / Y Pîl CF33 166 C8
Village Farm Starter Units
North Cornelly CF33 166 C8
Pyle / Y Pîl CF33 148 C1
Village Gdns SA12 98 C4
Village La
Ebbw Vale / Glyn Ebwy NP23 14 E2
The Mumbles / Y Mwmbwls SA3 123 B4
Village Way CF15 176 E8
Villas The
Markham NP12 58 D7
Newbridge / Trecelyn NP11 86 E6
Villa Terr SA5 68 C5
Villiers Ct
Briton Ferry / Llansawel SA11 71 B1
7 Port Talbot SA13 99 B1
Villiers Rd
Blaengwynfi SA13 76 C6
Skewen / Sclwen SA10 71 A7
Villiers Rd / Ffordd Villiers SA18 219 B6
Villiers St
Briton Ferry / Llansawel SA11 71 C1
Port Talbot SA13 99 C1
Swansea / Abertawe SA1 233 B5
Vincent Ave NP23 8 D1
Vincent Cl CF63 215 C7
Vincent Ct CF5 193 E5
Vincent Pl CF47 10 D2
Vincent Rd CF5 193 E5
Vincent St
7 Blaenavon NP4 17 C7
Swansea / Abertawe SA1 95 B6
Vine Pl 7 NP19 143 E6
Vine Row SA9 2 A6
Vine St NP11 87 B3
Vines The CF71 186 F3
Vintin La CF36 183 A7
Vintin Terr CF36 183 A7
Viola Rd / Heol Fiola SA12 98 C2
Violet Pl CF14 177 D4
Violet Row CF24 195 B8
Violet St CF44 53 B8
Violet Wlk NP10 141 D7
Virgil Ct CF11 194 E3
Virgil St CF11 194 E3
Virginia Cl CF83 138 B4
Virginia View CF83 138 B4
Viscount Ct 4 SA11 71 C1
Viscount Evan Dr NP10 163 F7
Vishwell Rd
Cardiff / Caerdydd CF5 194 B7
Wenvoe / Gwenfo CF5 205 A5
Vista Ct 3 CF64 207 B5
Vista Rise CF5 176 D2
Vivian Cotts NP13 36 C3
Vivian Ct
Aberavon SA12 124 F8
Swansea / Abertawe SA2 94 D7
Vivian Ho SA3 94 B2
Vivian Mans SA2 94 D7
Vivian Park Dr / Rhodfa Parc Vivian SA12 98 D2
Vivian Rd
Newport / Casnewydd NP19 143 E4
Swansea / Abertawe SA2 94 D7
Vivians Row SA6 45 D4
Vivian St
Abertillery / Abertyleri NP13 36 B4
Swansea / Abertawe SA1 68 D2
Tylorstown CF43 80 B3
Vivian Terr SA12 98 F1
Volunteer St CF41 78 F5
Voss Park Cl CF61 210 B6
Voss Park Dr CF61 210 B6
Voylart Cl SA2 93 C8
Voylart Rd SA2 93 C8
Voysey Pl CF5 193 C7
Vulcan Rd CF47 10 D2

W

Wade Ave SA9 2 B6
Wades The 13 NP44 89 B1
Waen Fawr NP23 8 B2
Waengron NP13 15 E5
Wagner Rd / Heol Wagner 10 SA12 98 B3
Wagtail Rd CF62 210 E6
Wain Cl CF23 161 B1
WAINFELIN 62 A7
Wainfelin Ave NP4 62 B7
Wainfelin Rd NP4 62 B7
Wakehurst Pl CF3 179 F7
Wakelin Cl CF38 156 E8
Walden Grange Cl NP19 144 B5
Waldhof Ct SA5 67 E7
Waldsassen Rd / Heol Waldsassen CF35 170 D6
Wales Millennium Ctr / Canolfan Mileniwm Cymru CF10 195 C2
Walford Davies Dr NP19 144 C5
Walford Pl CF11 194 D5
Walford St NP20 143 B7
Walkdens 2 NP44 89 B1
Walker Rd
Barry / Y Barri CF62 214 E5
Cardiff / Caerdydd CF24 195 E5
Walker's Terr CF48 31 B4
Walk Farm Dr CF3 162 C4
Walk The
Aberdare / Aberdâr CF44 29 B3
Cardiff / Caerdydd, Cathays CF24 232 C3
Cardiff / Caerdydd, Rumney / Rhymni CF3 179 A3
Ebbw Vale / Glyn Ebwy NP23 14 D7
Merthyr Tydfil / Merthyr Tudful CF47 10 D2
Nantyglo NP23 15 D8
Pontypool / Pont-y-pwl NP4 63 A4
Ystrad Mynach CF82 84 F2
Wallace Rd
Neath / Castell-Nedd SA11 71 E6
Swansea / Abertawe SA1 95 F7
Wallasey Rd / Heol Wallasey SA18 219 C7
Wallhead Rd CF47 30 F8
Wallis Dr CF82 84 E7
Wallis St NP20 143 D2
Wall St NP23 14 D8
WALLSTON 204 F7
Walmer Rd NP19 143 F5
Walnut Cl
Miskin / Meisgyn CF72 173 D8
The Mumbles / Y Mwmbwls SA3 122 E7
Walnut Dr NP18 117 E2
Walnut Gr CF62 211 B7
Walnut Tree Cl CF15 176 A7
Walnut Way CF47 10 E4
Walpole Cl CF3 179 C8
Walsall St NP19 143 E4
Walsh St CF45 82 B6
Walston Cl CF5 205 A7
Walston Rd CF5 204 F7
Walter Conway Ave NP22 13 D5
Walter Rd SA1 95 B6
Walter Rd / Ffordd Walter 9 SA18 219 C7
Walters Ave NP11 60 B2
Walters Cres SA3 123 A5
Walters La SA3 228 C2
Walters Rd
Bridgend / Pen-y-Bont ar Ogwr CF31 168 D4
Cwmllynfell SA9 221 B7
Llansamlet SA7 46 E1
Ogmore Vale CF32 130 E8
Pontypridd CF37 135 B7
Swansea / Abertawe SA7 69 D8
Walter's Rd
Llanelli SA15 40 E4
Neath / Castell-Nedd SA11 71 D5
Walters Row SA2 93 C8
Walters St SA5 68 C3
Walter St
Abercynon CF45 82 E2
Abertillery / Abertyleri NP13 36 B6
Abertysswg NP22 33 B8
Dowlais CF48 11 A5
Ferndale CF43 79 F7
Tredegar NP22 13 F4
Walter's Terr
Aberfan CF48 55 C4
Merthyr Tydfil / Merthyr Tudful CF47 30 F8
WALTERSTON / TREWALLTER 203 B3
Waltham Cl SA6 68 D7
Walton Cl NP19 144 C4
Walton Pl CF11 194 D3
Waltwood Park Dr NP18 145 F7
Waltwood Rd NP18 145 E6
Walwyn Pl CF3 180 A5
Wanderers Cres CF5 193 A4
Warborough Cl SA15 40 C6
Warborough Rd SA15 40 C7
Ward Cl NP19 144 A7
Ware Rd CF83 137 E1
Warlock Cl NP19 144 F5
Warlow Cl CF62 211 D4
Warlow St CF47 30 E8
Warmington Pl NP22 12 E5
Warner Pl SA15 40 E7
Warne St NP2 85 B6
Warn's Terr NP22 33 B8
Warren Cl
Bridgend / Pen-y-Bont ar Ogwr CF31 169 C4
Pontypridd CF37 135 F5
Rhydyfelin CF37 136 A5
Warren Cl / Clos Warren SA11 71 D4
Warren Ct NP12 86 A3
Warrendale NP44 89 B1
Warren Dr CF83 138 B1
Warren Evans Ct 1 CF14 177 B4
Warren Hill SA11 71 B1
Warren Mill Farm Park* CF71 190 E4
Warren Terr CF46 83 D6
Warwick Cl
Cwmbran / Cwmbrân NP44 89 A3
Pontypool / Pont-y-pwl NP4 63 A2
Warwick Cres CF36 182 E8
Warwick Ho CF10 232 A2
Warwick La 2 NP19 144 A5
Warwick Pl
1 Cardiff / Caerdydd CF11 194 F3
The Mumbles / Y Mwmbwls SA3 123 A8
Warwick Rd
Brynmawr NP23 8 B3
Newport / Casnewydd NP19 144 A5
Swansea / Abertawe SA2 94 B4
Warwick St CF11 194 F3
Warwick Way CF62 214 F6
Wasdale Cl CF23 178 B2
Washford Ave CF3 179 C7
Washington Bldgs 8 CF64 207 A4
Washington Flats 7 CF64 207 A4
Washington Shops CF64 207 B4
Washington St SA1 68 D3
Watchet Cl CF3 179 B5
Watch House Par NP20 143 C1
Water Avens Cl CF3 180 B6
Waterfall Cl SA11 226 D5
Waterfall Cotts SA13 125 D6
Waterfall Mews CF61 210 A4
Waterfall Rd SA11 226 D4
Waterfall Terr SA11 226 D4
Waterford Cl CF11 194 E4
Waterhall Rd
Cardiff / Caerdydd CF5 176 D2
Pyle / Y Pîl CF33 148 C3
Waterhouse Dr CF11 194 E3
Water La SA6 69 A7
WATERLOO
Abersychan 37 E4
Caerphilly 139 D5
Waterloo NP12 59 B2
Waterloo Cl 6 CF23 178 E1
Waterloo Ct NP4 62 E1
Waterloo Gdns CF23 195 D8
Waterloo Pl
Aberdare / Aberdâr CF44 28 F4
Abersychan NP4 37 E4
Machen CF83 139 D5
Swansea / Abertawe SA2 94 F5
Waterloo Rd
Cardiff / Caerdydd CF23 178 D1
Newport / Casnewydd NP20 143 A3
Waterloo Rd / Heol Waterloo
Abersychan NP4 37 F4
Pen-y-groes SA14, SA18 218 D7
Waterloo St
Aberdare / Aberdâr CF44 29 F1
Llanelli SA15 40 D4
Waterloo Terr CF81 32 F8
Waterloo Terrace Rd CF83 139 D5
Waterloo Terr / Teras Waterloo SA18 218 D6
Waterside Bsns Pk SA6 69 A6
Waterside Cl NP10 142 A7
Waterside Ct NP20 143 C8
Waterside Ct / Cwrt Glandwr 5 NP44 89 E2
Waterside Wlk W NP10 142 A6
Waters La NP20 143 C5
Water St
Aberavon SA12 125 A8
Bridgend / Pen-y-Bont ar Ogwr CF31 168 E4
Gwaun-Cae-Gurwen SA18 220 D6
Llanelli SA15 40 D6
Margam SA13 147 C4
Monknash / Yr As Fawr CF71 198 C2
Neath / Castell-Nedd SA11 71 E8
Ogmore Vale CF32 130 E8
Pontarddulais SA4 19 B4
Pontarddulais SA4 19 C4
Waterston Rd CF14 177 B2
WATERTON 169 D1
Waterton Cl CF31 169 E2
Waterton Cross CF31 169 B2
Waterton Cross Bsns Pk CF31 169 B2
Waterton Ind Est CF31 169 F2
Waterton La CF31 169 E2
Waterton Pk / Parc Tredwr CF31 169 E2
Waterton Rd
Bridgend / Pen-y-Bont ar Ogwr CF31 169 D2
Bridgend / Pen-y-Bont ar Ogwr, Coychurch / Llangrallo CF35 169 F3
Water Wheel Dr SA6 46 C2
Waterworks La NP4 38 A5
Watery La CF71 189 D5
Watford Cl CF83 137 F1
WATFORD PARK 137 F1
Watford Rd
Caerphilly / Caerffili CF83 158 F8
Cardiff / Caerdydd CF24 195 F8
Watford Rise CF83 138 A1
Watkins La 2 NP20 142 F4
Watkins Sq CF14 177 D7
Watkin St SA1 233 A4
Watkins Terr SA9 222 B6
Watkins Wlk 5 NP10 142 B4
Watson Rd CF14 177 A2
Watson Row CF81 57 B8
Watson St CF63 215 A5
Watton Cl CF14 177 E8
Watts Cl NP10 142 B6
WATTSTOWN 107 E8
WATTSVILLE 113 F3
WAUNARLWYDD 66 E4
Waunarlwydd Prim Sch SA5 66 D3
Waunarlwydd Rd SA2, SA5 67 B2
Waun Ave SA13 227 C1
Waunbant Ct CF48 225 F2
Waun Bant Rd CF33 148 D2
Waun Borfa Rd NP12 85 C8
Waunceirch Prim Sch / Ysgol Gynradd Waunceirch SA10 48 C2
Waun Cl SA4 65 F8
Waun Daniel SA8 24 B2
Waunddu NP4 61 F8
Waun Ddyfal CF14 177 D6
WAUNDEG 6 B2
Waundeg NP22 6 B2
Waun Dew NP23 7 F4
Waun-Ebbw Bglws NP23 8 B2
Waun-Ebbw Rd NP23 8 B2
Waun Erw CF83 138 B5
Waunfach CF32 129 E3
Waun Fach CF23 178 E7
Waunfach Flats CF83 138 A4
Waunfach St CF83 138 A4
Waun Fach Terr CF32 104 F5
Waunfain CF83 137 F6
Waunfarlais Rd SA18 219 A8
Waunfawr SA18 219 A7
Waun Fawr NP23 7 B4
Waunfawr Gdns NP11 114 D4
Waunfawr Ho NP11 114 C3
Waunfawr Park Rd NP11 114 C4
Waunfawr Prim Sch NP11 114 C4
Waunfawr Rd NP11 114 C4
Waun-Fawr Rd CF14 177 D6
Waunfawr Terr NP11 114 C4
Waun Ganol CF64 206 E1
Waun Ganol St CF83 138 B4
Waun Goch CF82 84 E5
Waun Goch District NP23 7 D4
Waungoch Rd NP12 59 C1
Waun Goch Terr
Ebbw Vale / Glyn Ebwy NP23 7 D4
Nant-y-Moel CF32 104 F5
WAUNGRON 19 C1
WAUN-GRON 68 D6
Waungron
Bettws CF32 129 E3
Glyn-neath / Glyn-nedd SA11 223 D1
Waun Gron
Llantwit Major / Llanilltud Fawr CF61 210 A7
Pontardawe SA8 23 D6
Waun-Gron Cl SA5 68 C6
Waun-gron Park Halt CF5 193 F7
Waungron Rd SA6 46 D8
Waun-Gron Rd
Cardiff / Caerdydd CF5 194 A7
Swansea / Abertawe SA5 68 C6
Waun-Gron Rd / Ffordd Waun-Gron SA18 219 D6
Waun Gyrlais SA9 222 A6
Waunhafog Rd SA18 219 A8
Waunheulog NP23 8 A3
Waun Hir CF38 156 F5
Waun Hywel Rd / Ffordd Gwaun Hywel 6 NP44 89 C6
Waunlanyrafon SA15 40 C5
Waun Las SA10 48 C1
Waun Lee Ct CF23 178 E8
Waunleision SA18 220 D7
Waunllapria NP7 9 C5
Waunllwyd CF44 28 A6
Waunllwyn Cres NP12 85 D7
Waunlon CF36 183 C8
WAUN-LWYD 14 F3
Waunlwyd Prim Sch NP23 14 F3
Waun Lwyd Terr CF32 104 F5
Waun-marsley NP23 15 D8
Waun Newydd CF35 152 B5
Waun Penlan SA8 23 D7
Waun Rd
Cwmbran / Cwmbrân NP44 89 C1
Llanelli SA15 40 E7
Loughor SA4 65 F8
Swansea / Abertawe SA6 45 F2
Tonypandy CF40 106 D6
Waun Rhydd CF82 84 D6
Waunrhydd Rd CF39 133 B5
Waun Row CF44 28 F6
Waunscil Ave CF31 169 A4
Waun St SA13 76 C5
Waun Sterw SA8 23 D7
Wauntreoda Rd CF14 177 C4
Waunwaelod Way / Ffordd Waunwaelod CF83 158 F7
Waun Wen
Cwmavon / Cwmafan SA12 99 F6
Porth CF39 133 D8
Waun Wen Prim Sch SA1 68 C2
Waun-Wen Rd SA1 233 A5
Waun Wen Terr CF32 104 F5
Waun-wen Terr SA1 68 C1
Waun Y Felin SA4 65 A4
Waun-y-Groes Ave CF14 177 D7
Waun-y-Groes Rd CF14 177 D7
Waun-y-Pistyll SA5 68 C5
Waun-y-Pound Ind Est NP23 7 A2
Waun-y-Pound Rd NP23 7 B2
Wavell Cl CF14 177 F6
Wavell Dr NP20 117 A3
Waveney Cl NP20 116 C2
Waverley Cl CF64 206 E6
Waverley Ct CF63 215 A4
Waverley Dr SA3 123 A5
Waverley Sq CF10 195 B1
Waverley St SA6 46 D7
Waverly Cl SA6 46 F8
Waverly Pk SA6 46 F8
Waycock Cross CF62 214 B6
Waycock Rd CF62 214 A6
Wayfield Cres NP44 89 E5
Wayne Cotts CF44 53 C7
Wayne St
Aberdare / Aberdâr CF44 28 F3
Porth CF39 107 E4
Trehafod CF37 108 C2
Wayside Cotts CF64 206 C4
Weare Cl NP20 116 C2
Weatheral St 4 CF44 29 A2
Weaver Rd / Heol-y-Gwaudd SA9 222 A4
Weavers Ho 7 SA1 233 C2
Weavers Mill 5 SA5 68 C4
Webbons Way SA1 67 F2
Webb Pl / Man Webb SA12 124 E7
Webley Cl NP18 118 A4
Webley Gdns NP18 118 A4
Webster St CF46 83 B7

Wedal Rd CF14 . . . . 178 A2
Wedgewood Ct CF83 . . . . 138 D3
Wedmore Rd CF11 . . . . . . 194 E4
Wednesbury St NP19 . . . . 143 F4
Weekes Cl CF3 . . . . 179 D7
Weig Fach La SA5 . . . . 67 D3
Weig Gdns SA5 . . . . 68 A4
Weig La SA5 . . . . 67 F3
Weig Rd SA5 . . . . 67 F3
Welby La 5 CF5 . . . . 194 D5
Welby Rd 4 CF5 . . . . 194 D5
Welch Regiment Mus★ CF10 . . . . 232 B3
Welcome La SA1 . . . . 233 B3
Weldon Cl NP44 . . . . 90 B5
Welfare Ave SA13 . . . . 100 E5
Welford St CF62 . . . . 214 D3
Welland Circ NP20 . . . . . . 116 C2
Welland Cres NP20 . . . . . 116 C2
Wellfield
Beddau CF38 . . . . 156 A8
Bishopston SA3 . . . . 121 F6
Melincourt SA11 . . . . 226 D4
Well Field SA2 . . . . 93 E8
Wellfield Ave
Neath / Castell-Nedd SA11 . . . . 71 F6
Porthcawl CF36 . . . . 183 A7
Wellfield Cl SA4 . . . . 43 B1
Wellfield Cres CF36 . . . . . 183 A7
Wellfield Ct
Barry / Y Barri CF63 . . . . . 205 B1
Church Village CF38 . . . . . 135 E1
Marshfield CF3 . . . . 180 D8
Wellfield La NP4 . . . . 62 D1
Wellfield Mews CF38 . . . . 156 A8
Wellfield Pl 2 CF24 . . . . . 195 C8
Wellfield Rd
Aberavon SA12 . . . . 99 A2
Cardiff / Caerdydd CF24 . . 178 C1
Marshfield CF3 . . . . 180 E8
Wellfield Sq SA11 . . . . 71 E6
Wellington Ct 3 CF11 . . . 194 E5
Wellington Dr NP44 . . . . . . 89 A3
Wellingtonia Cl CF47 . . . . . 10 D6
Wellington La NP4 . . . . 62 A6
Wellington Mews 4 CF11 . . . . 194 E5
Wellington Pl 11 SA12 . . . 124 F8
Wellington Rd NP20 . . . . . 142 D3
Wellington Rd / Ffordd Wellington NP4 . . . . 37 E4
Wellington St
Aberdare / Aberdâr CF44 . . . . 29 A3
Cardiff / Caerdydd CF11 . . 194 E5
Swansea / Abertawe SA1 . . . . 233 A2
Tongwynlais CF15 . . . . 158 C1
Wellington Terr NP24 . . . . 33 F1
Wellington Way NP22 . . . . 12 F2
Well La CF5 . . . . 191 F2
Wellpark SA3 . . . . 228 C2
Well Pl CF44 . . . . 53 D8
Well Rd CF62 . . . . 212 A2
Wells Cl
Baglan SA12 . . . . 98 E5
Newport / Casnewydd NP20 . . . . 142 E1
Wellspring Terr NP11 . . . 115 A1
Wells Rd SA12 . . . . 98 E5
Wells St CF11 . . . . 194 E5
Wells Street La 15 CF11 . . . . 194 E5
Well St
Abercynon CF45 . . . . 82 D2
Brynmawr NP23 . . . . 8 B4
Cefn Coed / Cefn-coed-y-cymmer CF48 . . . . 10 B4
Laleston / Trelales CF32 . . . . 167 F4
Merthyr Tydfil / Merthyr Tudful CF47 . . . . 10 D2
Porthcawl CF36 . . . . 182 F6
Well The CF32 . . . . 167 E4
Well Wlk CF62 . . . . 214 C2
Wellwood CF23 . . . . 178 E3
Well Wood Cl CF23 . . . . . . 178 E2
Wellwood Dr CF64 . . . . . . 206 A2
Wellwood Ho NP19 . . . . . . 144 E5
Wellwright Rd CF5 . . . . . . 193 D7
Welsh Assembly Government CF10 . . . . . . 232 A4
Welsh Coll of Music & Drama / Coleg Cerdd a Drama Cymru CF10 . . . . 232 A3
Welsh Comp Sch Glantaf The / Ysgol Gyfun Gymraeg Glantaf CF14 . . . . 176 F2
Welsh Hawking Ctr★ CF62 . . . . 214 A7
Welsh Ind & Maritime Mus★ CF10 . . . . 195 C1
Welsh Inst of Sport / Athrofa Chwaraeon Cymru CF11 . . . . 194 E7
Welsh Miners Mus★ SA13 . . . . 74 A3
Welsh Mus of Public Road Transport★ SA1 . . . . 69 A4
Welsh National Tennis Ctr CF24 . . . . 195 D4
Welsh National Velodrome NP19 . . . . 144 B2
WELSH ST DONATS / LLANDDUNWYD 189 F5
Welwyn Rd CF14 . . . . 177 C5
Wembley SA11 . . . . 71 D4
Wembley Ave SA10 . . . . . 222 F5
Wembley Rd
Cardiff / Caerdydd CF5 . . . . 194 C5
Ystalyfera SA9 . . . . 2 A6
Wenallt Ct
Aberdare / Aberdâr CF44 . . . . 29 C2
Cardiff / Caerdydd CF14 . . 177 B8
Wenallt Rd
Aberdare / Aberdâr CF44 . . . . 29 B3
Cardiff / Caerdydd CF14, CF83 . . . . 159 A3
Tonna / Tonnau SA11 . . . . . 49 D2
Wengraig Rd CF40 . . . . . . 106 F5
Wenham Pl / Lle Wenham SA11 . . . . 71 F7
Wentlloog Rd CF3 . . . . . . 179 D3
Wentloog Ave CF3 . . . . . . 179 C2
Wentloog Cl
Cardiff / Caerdydd CF3 . . . . 179 B3
Cwmbran / Cwmbrân NP44 . . . . 89 E3
Wentloog Corporate Ind Pk CF3 . . . . 179 F4
Wentloog Ct CF3 . . . . 179 B3
Wentloog Rd
Cardiff / Caerdydd CF3 . . . . 179 B3
Peterstone Wentlooge / Llanbedr Gwynllwg CF3 . . . . 180 C3
Wentloog Rise CF83 . . . . . 162 C3
Wentsland Cres NP4 . . . . . 62 A6
Wentsland Rd NP4 . . . . 62 A6
Wentwood Cl NP44 . . . . . . 89 C6
Wentwood Pl NP11 . . . . . 115 C1
Wentwood Rd NP18 . . . . . 117 E2
Wentworth Cl
Bassaleg NP10 . . . . 141 F3
4 Cardiff / Caerdydd CF3 . . . . 180 A8
Wentworth Cres SA3 . . . . . 93 E1
Wentworth La CF3 . . . . . . 180 A8
Wenvoe Cl CF5 . . . . 205 A6
Wenvoe Ct 13 CF5 . . . . . . 193 C4
WENVOE / GWENFO 205 A6
Wenvoe Terr CF62 . . . . . . 214 D4
Weobley Castle★ SA3 . . . 229 B3
Weobley Ct SA5 . . . . 67 F6
Werfa Cl CF44 . . . . 29 D4
Werfa La CF44 . . . . 29 D3
Werfa St CF23 . . . . 178 B1
WERN 40 D4
Wern Bank SA11 . . . . 71 B2
WERNBWLL 65 A2
Wern Cres
Neath / Castell-Nedd SA10 . . . . 70 E5
Nelson CF46 . . . . 83 F4
Wern Ddu CF32 . . . . 150 D3
Wernddu Ct CF83 . . . . 138 D2
Wern-Ddu Rd / Ffordd Wern-Ddu SA18 . . . . 219 D8
Wern-Ddu Row CF83 . . . . 138 E1
Wern Deg CF35 . . . . 170 D8
Wern Fach CF82 . . . . 85 A3
Wern Fach Ct / Cwrt Wern Fach NP44 . . . . 115 F8
Wern Fawr La CF3 . . . . . . 179 E8
Wern Fawr Rd
Pencoed CF35 . . . . 152 E5
Swansea / Abertawe SA1 . . 96 C7
WERNFFRWD 229 F5
Wern Fraith SA10 . . . . 48 C1
Wern Gethin La CF3 . . . . . 179 F6
Wern Goch E CF23 . . . . . . 178 E6
Werngoch Rd CF23 . . . . . . 178 C6
Wern Goch W CF23 . . . . . 178 D6
Wern Hill NP4 . . . . 62 B6
Wern Ind Est
Rogerstone NP10 . . . . 142 A5
Rogerstone / Ty-du NP10 . . . . 141 F5
Wern Isaf CF48 . . . . 11 C5
Wern La CF48 . . . . 30 C8
Wernlys Rd CF31 . . . . 150 D1
Wern Migna CF5 . . . . 175 E5
WERN-OLAU 65 D4
Wern Olau SA10 . . . . 49 B6
Wernoleu Rd SA18 . . . . . . 219 D7
Wern Rd
Cefn Coed / Cefn-coed-y-cymmer CF48 . . . . 10 A4
Glanaman SA18 . . . . 220 B8
Llanelli SA15 . . . . 40 E5
Llanmorlais SA4 . . . . 64 C1
Margam SA13 . . . . 125 E4
Pontypool / Pont-y-pwl NP4 . . . . 62 E1
Swansea / Abertawe SA1 . . 68 D4
Tonypandy CF40 . . . . 106 E5
Ystalyfera SA9 . . . . 2 B6
Wern Rd / Heol Wern SA10 . . . . 70 E7
Wern Row CF44 . . . . 28 F3
Wern School Cl NP4 . . . . . 62 E1
Wern St
Dowlais CF48 . . . . 11 B5
Tonypandy CF40 . . . . 106 B7
Wern Tarw Hos CF35 . . . . 152 F5
Wern Terr
Ammanford / Rhydaman SA18 . . . . 219 D6
Cymmer / Cymer SA13 . . . . 75 D4
Pontypool / Pont-y-pwl NP4 . . . . 62 B6
Rogerstone / Ty-du NP10 . . . . 141 F6
Swansea / Abertawe SA1 . . 96 C7
Wern View SA12 . . . . 73 A2
Wernwood Rd SA9 . . . . 2 B6
Wesleyan Church NP13 . . . 60 B6
Wesleyan Cotts CF37 . . . . 109 A8
Wesleyan Flats CF39 . . . . 107 F4
Wesleyan Pl NP23 . . . . 7 D4
Wesleyan Row NP23 . . . . . . 7 D1
Wesley Ave CF62 . . . . 212 F1
Wesley Bldgs NP23 . . . . 8 C2
Wesley Cl NP44 . . . . 89 D2
Wesley Ct
Cardiff / Caerdydd CF3 . . . . 179 C5
Dinas Powis / Dinas Powys CF64 . . . . 206 A3
Wesley Hill CF83 . . . . 139 F7
Wesley Ho 6 NP23 . . . . 8 C4
Wesley La CF10 . . . . 232 C2
Wesley Pl
6 Neath / Castell-Nedd SA11 . . . . 71 E7
15 Newport / Casnewydd NP20 . . . . 143 B4
Risca / Rhisga NP11 . . . . . 114 F1
Treorchy / Treorci CF41 . . . 79 A4
Wesley Pl / Mars Wesley CF48 . . . . 55 D4
Wesley Rd
Blackwood / Coed-Duon NP12 . . . . 85 E7
Caerphilly / Caerffili CF83 . . . . 137 D1
Wesley St / Stryd Wesley NP44 . . . . 89 D2
Wesley St
Abercynon CF45 . . . . 82 D2
Llantwit Major / Llanilltud Fawr CF61 . . . . 209 F6
Maesteg CF34 . . . . 75 B1
Wesley Terr
Abertillery / Abertyleri NP11 . . . . 59 F4
Llanelly Hill NP7 . . . . 9 C4
Pontardawe SA8 . . . . 23 E4
Pontypool / Pont-y-pwl NP4 . . . . 61 D7
Wessex Pl CF62 . . . . 214 C2
Wessex St CF5 . . . . 194 B6
WEST ABERTHAW 211 F2
West Acre CF61 . . . . 210 B8
West Ave
Caerphilly / Caerffili CF83 . . . . 137 E3
Cefn Cribwr CF32 . . . . 149 B2
Maesycwmmer CF82 . . . . . . 85 B2
Pontypool / Pont-y-pwl NP4 . . . . 62 D1
West Bank
Abertillery / Abertyleri NP13 . . . . 36 B8
Llanyrafon NP44 . . . . 90 B2
West Bank Ct 17 NP4 . . . . . 38 A1
West Bk / Glan y Gorllewin 12 NP44 . . . . 90 B2
Westbourne Cres
CF14 . . . . 176 F4
Westbourne Ct
Cardiff / Caerdydd CF3 . . . . 179 C2
Penarth CF64 . . . . 207 A1
Porthcawl CF36 . . . . 182 E7
Westbourne Gr SA2 . . . . . . 94 C7
Westbourne Pl
Merthyr Tydfil / Merthyr Tudful CF47 . . . . 30 E7
Porthcawl CF36 . . . . 182 F7
The Mumbles / Y Mwmbwls SA3 . . . . 123 B4
4 Troedyrhiw CF48 . . . . 31 B1
Westbourne Prim Sch CF64 . . . . 207 A3
Westbourne Rd
Cardiff / Caerdydd CF14 . . . . 176 F4
Penarth CF64 . . . . 207 A2
Penrhiwtyn SA11 . . . . 71 C4
Swansea / Abertawe SA2 . . 94 C7
Westbourne Sch CF64 . . . 207 A4
Westbourne Terr CF72 . . . 153 E2
Westbury Bglws SA15 . . . . 40 E3
Westbury Cl CF63 . . . . 215 B7
Westbury La SA1 . . . . 95 A6
Westbury St
Llanelli SA15 . . . . 40 E3
Swansea / Abertawe SA1 . . 95 A6
Westbury Terr CF5 . . . . . . 194 B7
West Bute St CF10 . . . . . . 195 C2
West Canal Wharf / Glanfa Gorllewin Y Gamlas CF10 . . . . 232 B1
West Cl / Clos Y Gorllewin 10 CF10 . . . . 195 B2
Westcliff SA3 . . . . 123 C3
West Cliff SA3 . . . . 121 A3
Westcliff Mews SA3 . . . . . 123 C3
WEST CROSS 123 A7
Westcross Ave SA3 . . . . . 123 A6
Westcross La SA3 . . . . 122 F7
West Crossways SA8 . . . . . 23 D6
West Ct 2 CF64 . . . . 207 A4
Westdale Rd SA5 . . . . 67 D7
West Dr
Porthcawl CF36 . . . . 182 E6
St Donat's / Sain Dunwyd CF61 . . . . 208 H5
WEST END 87 A3
West End
Llanelli SA15 . . . . 40 C6
Pen-clawdd SA4 . . . . 64 D4
Port Talbot SA13 . . . . 125 C6
West End Ave CF36 . . . . . 165 F1
West End Ave / Coedlan-y-West End NP4 . . . . 37 F2
West End Terr
Ebbw Vale / Glyn Ebwy NP23 . . . . 14 D8
Llantwit Major / Llanilltud Fawr CF61 . . . . 209 E6
Western Arc CF62 . . . . 214 E1
Western Ave
Bridgend / Pen-y-Bont ar Ogwr CF31 . . . . 169 C3
Brynmawr NP23 . . . . 8 A4
Cardiff / Caerdydd CF14 . . 177 C1
Newport / Casnewydd NP20 . . . . 142 C3
Western Ave N CF14 . . . . 177 C2
Western Ave / Rhodfa Gorllewin SA12 . . . . 98 C2
Western Bsns Ctr CF5 . . . 193 F6
Western Cl SA3 . . . . 123 B4
Western Cres NP22 . . . . . . 13 D7
Western Ct
10 Barry / Y Barri CF63 . . . . 215 B6
Bridgend / Pen-y-Bont ar Ogwr CF31 . . . . 168 D4
1 Cardiff / Caerdydd CF11 . . . . 194 D7
Western Ctyd CF72 . . . . . . 173 A5
Western Dr
Bargoed / Bargod CF81 . . . 57 E2
Cardiff / Caerdydd CF14 . . 177 C2
Western Ind Est
Caerleon / Caerllion NP18 . . . . 118 B4
Caerphilly / Caerffili CF83 . . . . 137 E2
Western La SA3 . . . . 123 B4
Westernmoor Rd SA11 . . . 71 F6
Western Rd
Clydach SA6 . . . . 46 C6
Pontardawe SA8 . . . . 23 D4
Western St
Swansea / Abertawe SA1 . . . . 95 B6
Trehafod CF37 . . . . 108 D2
Western Terr
Abercarn NP11 . . . . 114 B5
Blaengwynfi SA13 . . . . 76 C5
Cwmfelinfach NP11 . . . . . . 113 A4
Ebbw Vale / Glyn Ebwy NP23 . . . . 7 D1
Swansea / Abertawe SA1 . . 68 D3
Western Valley Rd NP10 . . . . 142 C3
Westfa Rd SA2 . . . . 94 F7
West Farm Cl CF32 . . . . . . 184 D2
West Farm Rd CF32 . . . . . 184 E2
Westfield Ave
Bridgend / Pen-y-Bont ar Ogwr CF31 . . . . 168 D5
Cardiff / Caerdydd CF14 . . 177 C5
Newport / Casnewydd NP20 . . . . 117 A2
Westfield Cl NP18 . . . . 117 F4
Westfield Cres CF36 . . . . 165 F2
Westfield Ct CF72 . . . . 155 E2
Westfield Dr
Newport / Casnewydd NP20 . . . . 117 A2
Penarth CF64 . . . . 206 E2
Westfield Rd
Caerleon / Caerllion NP18 . . . . 117 F3
Cardiff / Caerdydd CF14 . . 177 C4
Newport / Casnewydd NP20 . . . . 143 A5
Pontypridd CF37 . . . . 109 C5
Waunarlwydd SA5 . . . . 66 D4
Westfield Way NP20 . . . . 117 A2
Westgate CF71 . . . . 188 E2
Westgate Cl CF36 . . . . 165 F1
Westgate Ct NP18 . . . . 118 B2
Westgate St / Heol Y Porth CF10 . . . . 232 B2
Westgil Pen Ffordd NP12 . . . . 85 D6
West Gr
Cardiff / Caerdydd, Cathays CF24 . . . . 232 C3
Cardiff / Caerdydd, Culverhouse Cross CF5 . . . . 192 F2
Merthyr Tydfil / Merthyr Tudful CF47 . . . . 10 D3
Westgrove Ct SA4 . . . . 43 B4
West Grove Ct CF24 . . . . . 232 C3
West Hall CF62 . . . . 211 E2
West Hill NP22 . . . . 13 D7
Westhill Dr CF72 . . . . 155 E2
West Hill Rd NP4 . . . . 38 B1
Westhill St CF61 . . . . 209 F6
West House Rd CF31 . . . . 168 D4
Westland Ave SA3 . . . . . . 122 E7
Westland Cl
Cardiff / Caerdydd CF24 . . . . 196 A7
Loughor SA4 . . . . 42 E1
Westlands SA12 . . . . 98 D4
West Lee CF11 . . . . 194 E6
West Luton Pl 2 CF24 . . 195 C5
West Market St
9 Newport / Casnewydd NP20 . . . . 143 C3
Newport / Casnewydd NP20 . . . . 143 D3
Westminster Cres
CF23 . . . . 178 C7
Westminster Dr
Cardiff / Caerdydd CF23 . . . . 178 C8
Sully CF64 . . . . 216 B5
Westminster Way
CF31 . . . . 168 C6
West Monmouth Comp Sch NP4 . . . . 62 C5
Westmoor Cl NP19 . . . . . . 144 C3
Westmoreland St CF5 . . . 194 C5
West Mound Cres
CF38 . . . . 136 A1
Weston Ave CF64 . . . . 216 B4
Westonbirt Cl CF3 . . . . . . 179 F6
Weston Rd
Cardiff / Caerdydd CF3 . . . . 179 B5
Tonypandy CF40 . . . . 107 B1
Weston Sq CF63 . . . . 215 C6
Weston St 7 CF63 . . . . . . 215 B6
Weston Terr
Porth CF39 . . . . 107 E6
Treorchy / Treorci CF42 . . . . 78 B4
West Orchard Cres
CF5 . . . . 194 A7
West Park Dr CF36 . . . . . . 165 E1
West Park La 1 NP20 . . . 142 F4
West Park Prim Sch CF36 . . . . 165 F1
West Park Rd NP20 . . . . . 142 F4
West Point Ind Est CF11 . . . . 206 D8
WEST PONTNEWYDD 89 C5
Westport Ave SA2 . . . . 94 A2
WESTRA 205 E2
Westra CF64 . . . . 205 E2
Westra Ct 2 CF5 . . . . 194 B7
Westray Cl NP19 . . . . 143 F7
West Rd
Bridgend / Pen-y-Bont ar Ogwr CF31 . . . . 168 D4
Cardiff / Caerdydd CF14 . . 176 F3
Penybryn CF82 . . . . 84 D5
Porthcawl CF36 . . . . 165 E2
West Rhondda CF32 . . . . . 129 F7
West Rise CF14 . . . . 178 A8
West Roedin NP44 . . . . . . 116 C8
WEST SIDE 15 D4
Westside Rd CF83 . . . . 110 E2
West St
Abercynon CF45 . . . . 82 E3
Aberkenfig / Abercynffig CF32 . . . . 150 C4
Bargoed / Bargod CF81 . . . 57 F4
Gorseinon SA4 . . . . 43 B1
Llantwit Major / Llanilltud Fawr CF61 . . . . 209 F6
Maesteg CF34 . . . . 102 A2
Monknash / Yr As Fawr CF71 . . . . 198 C3
Newport / Casnewydd NP20 . . . . 143 B4
Pontypridd CF37 . . . . 109 D2
West Taff St CF39 . . . . 107 F3
West Terr CF64 . . . . 207 A4
West View
Bettws CF32 . . . . 129 E1
Newbridge / Trecelyn NP11 . . . . 86 F6
Taffs Well / Ffynnon Taf CF15 . . . . 158 B4
West View Cres
Blackwood / Coed Duon NP12 . . . . 59 A1
Trelewis CF46 . . . . 83 D6
Westview Terr
Abertillery / Abertyleri NP13 . . . . 36 C2
Caerphilly / Caerffili CF83 . . . . 138 D5
West View Terr
Blaenavon NP4 . . . . 17 B7
Ebbw Vale / Glyn Ebwy NP23 . . . . 14 E6
West View Villas CF81 . . . . 58 A4
WEST VILLAGE 188 D2
Westville NP22 . . . . 33 B7
Westville Rd
Cardiff / Caerdydd CF23 . . . . 178 D1
9 Newport / Casnewydd NP20 . . . . 142 F4
Westville Wlk CF23 . . . . . 178 C1
Westward Cl
Bridgend / Pen-y-Bont ar Ogwr CF31 . . . . 168 B6
The Mumbles / Y Mwmbwls SA2 . . . . 94 A1
Westward Pl CF31 . . . . . . 168 B6
Westward Rise CF62 . . . . 214 B3
West Way / Ffordd Y Gorllewin SA1 . . . . 233 A2
West Way Rd NP20 . . . . . . 143 B1
Westwinds SA3 . . . . 122 E3

Westwinds Cl SA5 .... 66 E3
West Winds Ind Est CF35 .... 187 F8
West Wlk CF62 .... 214 D6
Westwood Ct 9 CF64 ... 207 A4
Westwood Dr CF46 ...... 83 A6
Wexford Ct CF23 .... 161 A2
Wharfedale Rd CF23 .... 178 F8
Wharf La 5 NP19 .... 143 E5
Wharf Rd NP19 .... 143 E5
Wharton Cl CF62 .... 212 E1
Wharton St / Heol y Cawl CF10 .... 232 B2
Wheate Cl The CF62 ..... 213 A2
Wheatfield Terr SA1 .... 233 A5
Wheatley Ave / Rhodfa Wheatley 2 SA12 ..... 124 E8
Wheatley Pl
Blackwood / Coed-Duon NP12 .... 85 D8
Merthyr Tydfil / Merthyr Tudful CF47 .... 30 F7
Wheatley Rd
Cardiff / Caerdydd CF5 .... 193 C5
Neath / Castell-Nedd SA11 .... 71 D4
Wheatsheaf Dr SA6 ...... 46 A4
Wheatsheaf La CF47 ..... 10 D1
Wheeler Ct CF24 .... 195 E6
Wheeler St NP20 .... 143 C6
Whimbrels The CF36 .... 182 D8
Whinberry Way CF5 ..... 193 A5
Whinchat Cl 8 CF3 ..... 180 A7
Whistle Halt* NP4 .... 9 D1
Whistler Cl NP19 .... 143 F7
Whistle Rd NP4 .... 9 D1
Whitaker Rd CF24 .... 196 A8
Whitby Pl NP19 .... 143 D6
WHITCHURCH 177 A4
Whitchurch High Sch (Lower) CF14 .... 177 B5
Whitchurch High Sch / Ysgol Uwchradd Yr Eglwys Newydd CF14 .... 177 A5
Whitchurch Hospl / Ysbyty Eglwys Newydd CF14 .. 176 F6
Whitchurch Pl 1 CF24 .... 178 A1
Whitchurch Rd CF14 ..... 177 F2
Whitchurch Sta CF14 .... 177 A6
WHITCHURCH / YR EGLWYS NEWYDD 176 E5
Whitcliffe Dr CF64 ...... 217 B8
Whitcombe St 3 CF44 ... 29 A2
Whiteacre Cl CF14 ...... 159 F2
White Ash Glade NP18 .. 117 F2
White Ave NP10 .... 163 E5
White Barn Rd CF14 ..... 177 D8
Whitebeam Cl CF47 ...... 10 D6
Whitebrook Way / Ffordd Whitebrook NP44 ...... 89 F2
White Cairn / Carn Wen CF31 .... 168 C2
White City Rd SA5 .... 67 D4
White Cl SA12 .... 98 B3
White Cross La CF83 .... 137 E4
Whitefield Cl SA11 ...... 223 C1
Whitefield Rd CF14 ..... 177 A2
Whitefield St CF41 .... 78 F3
Whiteford Bay L Pk SA3 .... 228 C4
Whiteford Rd SA5 .... 67 F6
Whitegates SA2 .... 94 A1
White Gates Ct SA10 ..... 71 A7
White Gr SA3 .... 122 E7
White Gr / Gelli Wen CF31 .... 168 C3
Whitehall Ave CF3 ...... 179 B3
Whitehall Cl CF5 .... 204 F7
White Hall La / Lon y Neuado Wen 10 NP44 ... 90 B1
Whitehall Par CF3 ...... 179 B3
Whitehall Pl CF3 .... 179 A3
Whitehall Rd CF5 .... 176 F1
White Hart Cotts CF83 ... 139 E7
White Hart Dr CF83 ..... 139 E7
Whitehart La NP18 ...... 118 C1
White Ho CF62 .... 214 C1
White Hollow / Pant Gwyn CF31 .... 168 B3
White Horse Ct NP13 ..... 36 B7
White House Cl CF61 .... 209 F5
White House Rd NP44 .... 90 A5
White Lion Cotts / Bythynnod Y Llew Gwyn NP22 .... 6 C2
White Lodge / Llety Gwyn CF31 .... 168 E7
White Mdw / Maes Gwyn CF31 .... 168 D3
White Oaks Dr CF3 ...... 179 E8
WHITEROCK 168 F2
Whiterock Ave CF37 .... 109 B2
Whiterock Cl CF37 ...... 109 B2
Whiterock Dr CF37 ...... 109 B2
White Rose Prim Sch NP24 .... 33 F2
White Rose Way NP24 .... 33 F2
Whitesands Rd CF14 .... 159 D1
Whiteshell Dr SA3 ...... 122 E4
White St
Caerphilly / Caerffili CF83 .... 138 B2
Dowlais CF48 .... 11 A5
Swansea / Abertawe SA1 .. 95 B7
Whitestone Ave SA3 .... 122 A5
Whitestone Cl SA3 ...... 122 F8
Whitestone La SA3 ...... 122 E5
Whitestone Prim Sch SA3 .... 122 E7
Whitestone Rd SA3 ..... 122 A5
Whitethorn Ct SA5 .... 67 F5
Whitethorn Dr CF31 ..... 169 B4
Whitethorne St NP11 ..... 60 A1
Whitethorn Pl SA2 .... 94 B6
Whitethorn Way CF3 .... 180 E8
White Walls SA1 .... 233 B2
Whiteways CF61 .... 210 B7
Whitewell Dr CF61 ...... 210 A5
Whitewell Rd CF62 ...... 214 E7
Whitland Cl
Cardiff / Caerdydd CF5 .... 176 D1
Swansea / Abertawe SA5 .. 67 F6
Whitland Cres CF5 ...... 176 E1
Whitland Ho CF14 .... 177 A4
Whitley Rd SA4 .... 42 F1
Whitmore Park Dr CF62 .... 214 C7
Whitmuir Rd CF24 ...... 195 F7
Whitstone Rd NP19 ..... 144 B6
Whittan Cl CF62 .... 212 E1
Whitting St SA11 .... 223 D1
Whitting Terr CF39 ...... 107 E5
Whittington St
Neath / Castell-Nedd SA11 .... 71 E6
Tonna / Tonnau SA11 ..... 49 D3
Whittington Terr SA4 .... 43 D2
Whittle Ct 1 NP20 ...... 117 A3
Whittle Dr NP20 .... 117 A3
Whittle Rd CF11 .... 194 D3
Whitworth Ct CF11 ...... 194 F4
Whitworth Sq CF14 ..... 176 E7
Whitworth Terr NP22 .... 13 F5
Wholesale Fruit Ctr CF11 .... 194 D2
Wicken Cl CF3 .... 180 A7
Wicklow Cl CF23 .... 161 A1
Wick Marcross CW Prim Sch CF71 .... 198 C5
Wick Rd
Corntown / Corntwn CF35 .... 186 B4
Ewenny / Ewenni CF35 ... 185 F7
Llantwit Major / Llanilltud Fawr CF61 .... 209 E7
St Brides Major / Saint-y-Brid CF32 .... 185 D1
St Brides Major / Saint-y-Brid CF32 .... 197 F8
Wick / Y Wig CF61, CF71 .... 199 B2
WICK / Y WIG 198 D5
Widecombe Dr CF3 ..... 179 A3
Widgeon Cl CF36 .... 165 E1
Wigan Terr CF32 .... 151 A5
Wigmore Cl CF14 .... 159 E2
Wildbrook SA13 .... 125 D8
Wilde Ct CF15 .... 176 D4
Wilden Ave / Rhodfa Wilden 3 SA13 .... 125 D5
Wild Gardens Rd CF23 .. 178 B5
WILD MILL 168 E7
Wild Mill La CF31 .... 168 E7
Wildmill Sta CF31 .... 168 E7
Wilfred Brook Ho CF11 .... 194 F2
Wilfred St CF63 .... 215 B5
Wilfried Way CF39 ...... 132 E4
Wilkinson Cl CF24 ...... 195 D5
Wilkins Terr CF83 .... 138 A6
Wilks Row SA1 .... 233 A4
Willenhall St NP19 ...... 143 E4
Willesden Rd CF31 ...... 168 C6
Willet Cl SA11 .... 71 F8
William Adams Ct 7 NP23 .... 14 D8
William Belcher Dr CF3 .... 180 A5
William Bowen Cl SA4 ... 66 A5
William Brown Cl NP44 .... 117 A7
William Ct
Swansea / Abertawe SA1 .... 233 A2
Ystrad CF41 .... 79 C3
William Dennis Ave SA4 .... 66 A8
William Forbes Bglws CF81 .... 58 A6
William Gammon Dr SA3 .... 123 C3
William Harris Bglws CF83 .... 137 A7
William Lovett Gdns 1 NP20 .... 143 B4
William Morris Dr NP19 .... 144 D6
William Morris Gdns SA1 .... 96 B7
William Nicholls Dr CF3 .... 179 E8
Williams Ave SA11 ...... 226 D5
Williams Cl
Hawthorn CF37 .... 136 C3
28 Newport / Casnewydd NP20 .... 143 C3
Williams Cres
Barry / Y Barri CF62 ..... 214 E5
Sarn CF32 .... 150 F5
Williams Pl
Hawthorn CF37 .... 136 C3
Williams Pl *continued*
Merthyr Tydfil / Merthyr Tudful CF47 .... 10 F3
Porth CF39 .... 107 E3
Williams St
Blackwood / Coed-Duon NP12 .... 85 F7
Brynna CF72 .... 153 C3
Pontarddulais SA4 .... 19 C4
Tonypandy CF40 .... 106 F8
William's St NP12 .... 34 D4
William St
Aberbargoed / Aberbargod CF81 .... 58 B4
Abercwmboi CF44 .... 53 E4
Abercynon CF45 .... 82 E2
Abertridwr CF83 .... 137 A7
Bargoed / Bargod CF81 ... 58 A2
Bedwas CF83 .... 139 A6
Cardiff / Caerdydd CF11 .... 194 D7
Cwmfelinfach NP11 ..... 113 B3
Cwm NP23 .... 35 A7
Fleur-de-lis NP12 .... 85 B5
13 Merthyr Tydfil / Merthyr Tudful, Cae-Pant Tywll CF47 .... 10 D2
19 Merthyr Tydfil / Merthyr Tudful, Twynyrodyn CF47 .... 30 E8
Newbridge / Trecelyn NP11 .... 59 F1
Pontardawe SA8 .... 23 B1
Pontycymer CF32 .... 103 E3
Pontypridd CF37 .... 109 F5
Porth CF39 .... 107 F6
Swansea / Abertawe SA1 .... 233 A2
The Mumbles / Y Mwmbwls SA3 .... 123 A5
Tir-Y-Berth CF82 .... 85 A6
Treherbert CF42 .... 50 F2
Ystrad CF41 .... 79 C3
Ystradgynlais SA9 .... 2 E7
Williams Terr
Brynmenyn CF32 .... 150 E6
5 Merthyr Tydfil / Merthyr Tudful CF47 .... 30 F8
Treharris CF46 .... 83 B7
WILLIAMSTOWN 107 B2
Williamstown CF47 ...... 10 C2
Williamstown Prim Sch CF40 .... 107 A2
Williams Way CF10 ..... 195 A3
Willie Seager Cotts CF23 .... 178 D1
Willins NP44 .... 116 B8
Williton Rd CF3 .... 179 C7
Willow Bank SA4 .... 66 D3
Willowbrook Dr CF3 .... 179 E6
Willowbrook Gdns
Cardiff / Caerdydd CF3 .... 179 F7
The Mumbles / Y Mwmbwls SA3 .... 93 F1
Willowbrook Prim Sch CF3 .... 180 A6
Willow Cl
Beddau CF38 .... 155 F5
Bridgend / Pen-y-Bont ar Ogwr CF35 .... 169 F3
Ebbw Vale / Glyn Ebwy NP23 .... 7 C1
Newport / Casnewydd NP19 .... 144 B2
Penarth CF64 .... 206 E3
Porthcawl CF36 .... 183 E8
Willow Ct
Bishopston SA3 .... 122 C7
7 Cardiff / Caerdydd CF24 .... 195 C7
Newbridge / Trecelyn NP11 .... 87 C8
Tredegar NP22 .... 6 C2
Willowdale Cl CF5 ...... 193 C8
Willowdale Rd CF5 ..... 193 C8
Willowdene Way CF3 ... 180 A8
Willow Dr
Blackwood / Coed-Duon NP12 .... 85 F6
Underwood NP18 .... 145 E6
Willowfield Ct CF23 .... 178 C6
Willowford CF15 .... 157 E8
Willow Gn NP18 .... 117 F3
Willow Gr
Aberdare / Aberdâr CF44 .... 28 E2
Cardiff / Caerdydd CF3 ... 180 A8
Willow Gr / Llwyn Helyg SA12 .... 98 E6
Willow Herb Cl CF3 .... 180 B6
Willowmere CF64 .... 206 D7
Willow Pk NP11 .... 59 D1
Willow Rd
Blackwood / Coed Duon NP11 .... 59 D3
Llanharry CF72 .... 172 C5
Merthyr Tydfil / Merthyr Tudful CF47 .... 10 D5
Willow Rise CF82 .... 84 D7
Willows Ave CF24 .... 195 F6
Willows Cres CF63 ...... 215 A7
Willows High Sch CF24 .... 196 A6
Willows Pl SA1 .... 233 A3
Willow St CF37 .... 136 A5
Willows The
Abertillery / Abertyleri NP13 .... 36 C4
Bedwas CF83 .... 138 E7
Bridgend / Pen-y-Bont ar Ogwr CF31 .... 169 A4
Croesyceiliog NP44 ...... 90 A5
Cwmdare CF44 .... 28 D3
Laleston / Trelales CF32 .... 167 E4
Llanelli SA15 .... 40 C7
St Athan / Sain Tathan CF62 .... 211 D4
Willows The / Yr Helys CF35 .... 152 B6
Willow Terr
Mountain Ash / Aberpennar CF45 .... 81 F8
Troedyrhiw CF48 .... 31 B2
WILLOWTOWN 7 C1
Willowtown Prim Sch NP23 .... 14 C8
Willow Tree Cl CF15 .... 175 F6
Willowturf Ct CF32 ...... 150 E4
Willow Way SA12 .... 98 D6
Willow Wlk
Cimla SA11 .... 72 C6
Cowbridge / Y Bont-Faen CF71 .... 188 F2
Rogerstone / Ty-du NP10 .... 141 D7
Will Paynter Wlk NP19 .... 144 D7
Wills Row 1 NP10 ...... 142 B4
Wilmot St 5 SA11 .... 71 E6
Wilson Ct 2 CF47 .... 30 D8
Wilson Pl
Cardiff / Caerdydd CF5 .... 193 C4
Maerdy CF43 .... 52 A1
Wilson Rd
Cardiff / Caerdydd CF5 .... 193 B5
Newport / Casnewydd NP19 .... 144 A7
Wilson St
Cardiff / Caerdydd CF24 .... 195 E7
Newport / Casnewydd NP20 .... 143 D2
Wimblewood Cl SA3 .... 123 A7
Wimborne Bldgs CF63 ... 215 C4
Wimborne Cres CF64 .... 216 B5
Wimborne Rd
Barry / Y Barri CF63 ..... 215 C5
Pencoed CF35 .... 152 E1
Wimborne Rise NP44 ..... 89 C5
Wimborne St CF48 .... 11 A5
Wimbourne Cl CF61 ..... 209 F5
Wimbourne Cres CF35 .. 152 E1
Wimbourne Terr CF82 .... 57 A1
Wimmerfield Ave SA2 .... 93 E7
Wimmerfield Cl SA2 ..... 93 E7
Wimmerfield Cres SA2 ... 93 E7
Wimmerfield Dr SA2 ..... 93 F7
Winchester Ave CF23 ... 178 D2
Winchester Cl
Barry / Y Barri CF62 ..... 214 D5
Newport / Casnewydd NP20 .... 143 A1
WINCHESTOWN 8 A2
Winch Fawr Ho CF48 .... 10 A3
Winch Fawr Pk CF48 .... 225 F1
Winch Fawr Rd
Heolgerrig CF48 .... 10 A1
Merthyr Tydfil / Merthyr Tudful CF48 .... 29 F8
Merthyr Tydfil / Merthyr Tudful CF48 .... 225 F1
WINCH-WEN 69 C5
Winch Wen Ind Est SA1 .. 69 C6
Windermere Ave CF23 .. 178 A3
Windermere Cl CF44 ..... 29 D1
Windermere Rd SA6 ..... 68 E7
Windermere Sq 4 NP19 .... 143 E8
Windflower Cl 7 CF3 ... 180 A7
Windhover Cl 3 CF3 .... 180 A6
Windlass Ct CF10 .... 195 C3
Windmill Cl
Cardiff / Caerdydd CF14 .... 159 E2
Llantwit Major / Llanilltud Fawr CF61 .... 210 A7
Wick / Y Wig CF71 ...... 198 D5
Windmill Ind Area CF64 .... 215 D4
Windmill La
Llanblethian / Llanfleiddan CF71 .... 188 E1
Llantwit Major / Llanilltud Fawr CF61 .... 210 A7
Windmill Sq 7 NP20 .... 143 C3
Windmill Terr SA1 ...... 233 C4
Wind Rd SA9 .... 2 D7
Windrush Cl NP20 ...... 116 E2
Windrush Pl 6 CF5 ..... 193 D8
Wind St / Stryd-y-Gwynt SA18 .... 219 B7
Windsberry Ct SA18 ..... 219 A6
Windsor Arc 3 CF64 .... 207 B4
Windsor Ave
Newbridge / Trecelyn NP11 .... 86 F6
Radyr CF15 .... 176 B6
Windsor Cl
Llantwit Major / Llanilltud Fawr CF61 .... 210 B6
Windsor Cl *continued*
Radyr CF15 .... 176 B6
Windsor Clive Dr CF5 ... 175 E5
Windsor Clive Inf Sch CF5 .... 193 C5
Windsor Clive Jun Sch / Ysgol Iau Windsor Clive CF5 .... 193 C5
Windsor Cres CF15 ..... 176 C5
Windsor Ct
Cardiff / Caerdydd CF24 .... 232 D3
10 Neath / Castell-Nedd SA11 .... 71 E7
Penarth CF64 .... 207 B3
Pontyclun CF72 .... 173 B8
2 Radyr CF15 .... 176 B6
3 Swansea / Abertawe SA1 .... 233 A3
Ynysybwl CF37 .... 81 F1
Windsor Dr CF72 .... 173 D7
Windsor Espl CF10 ...... 195 B1
Windsor Gdns
Beddau CF38 .... 156 A8
2 Cardiff / Caerdydd CF5 .... 193 E6
Windsor Gn CF5 .... 193 E6
Windsor Gr CF15 .... 176 B6
Windsor Ho CF10 .... 232 A2
Windsor La
Cardiff / Caerdydd CF10 .... 232 C3
Penarth CF64 .... 207 A5
Windsor Mews 3 CF24 .... 195 C5
Windsor Pl
Abertillery / Abertyleri NP13 .... 59 F7
Abertridwr CF83 .... 136 F7
Merthyr Vale / Ynysowen CF48 .... 55 D4
Pant CF48 .... 11 B6
1 Penarth CF64 .... 207 A4
4 Rogerstone NP10 ..... 142 B4
Senghenydd CF83 ...... 110 F2
The Mumbles / Y Mwmbwls SA3 .... 123 B5
Treharris CF46 .... 83 B6
Treorchy / Treorci CF41 .... 78 F4
Ynysybwl CF37 .... 81 F1
Windsor Pl / Plas Windsor CF10 .... 232 C3
Windsor Rd
Abertillery / Abertyleri NP13 .... 36 C3
Barry / Y Barri CF62 ..... 214 D3
Brynmawr NP23 .... 8 A4
Cardiff / Caerdydd CF24 .. 195 C5
Mountain Ash / Aberpennar CF45 .... 54 D1
Neath / Castell-Nedd SA11 .... 71 E7
Newport / Casnewydd NP19 .... 143 F5
Penarth CF64 .... 206 F5
Pontypool / Pont-y-pwl NP4 .... 62 E3
Pontypridd CF37 .... 135 E7
Porthcawl CF36 .... 182 E7
Radyr CF15 .... 176 C5
Treharris CF46 .... 82 F6
Windsor Rd / Heol Windsor NP44 .... 89 B2
Windsor St
Aberdare / Aberdâr CF44 .... 28 E4
Caerphilly / Caerffili CF83 .... 138 B2
Swansea / Abertawe SA2 .. 94 F7
Treherbert CF42 .... 50 F2
Treorchy / Treorci CF41 .... 78 F5
Treorchy / Treorci CF42 .... 78 C6
Troedyrhiw CF48 .... 31 B1
Windsor Terr
Aberdare / Aberdâr CF44 .... 29 C3
Abertillery / Abertyleri NP13 .... 59 F7
Cardiff / Caerdydd CF10 .. 195 B1
Gorseinon SA4 .... 43 D2
6 Merthyr Tydfil / Merthyr Tudful CF47 .... 30 E8
2 Newport / Casnewydd NP20 .... 143 B4
Penarth CF64 .... 207 B4
Windsor Terrace La CF64 .... 207 B4
Windsor Village SA12 .... 98 D3
Wind St
Aberdare / Aberdâr CF44 .... 29 A1
Ferndale CF43 .... 80 A7
Laleston / Trelales CF32 .... 167 E5
Neath / Castell-Nedd SA11 .... 71 E8
Porth CF39 .... 107 E6
Swansea / Abertawe SA1 .... 233 B2
Windway Ave CF5 ...... 194 A7
Windway Rd CF5 .... 194 A7
Windyridge CF64 .... 206 C2
Wine St
Llantwit Major / Llanilltud Fawr CF61 .... 209 F6

Wine St continued
Pontlottyn CF81 . . . 12 F1
Wingate Dr CF14 . . . 177 F6
Wingate St NP20 . . . 143 C1
Wingfield Ave CF38 . . . 155 F7
Wingfield Cl CF37 . . . 109 E1
Wingfield Cres CF83 . . . 112 A3
Wingfield Rd CF14 . . . 177 A4
Wingfield Rise CF46 . . . 83 B5
Wingfield St / Stryd Wingfield CF48 . . . 55 C5
Wingfield Terr CF46 . . . 83 B5
Winifred Ave CF62 . . . 214 E8
Winifred Rd / Heol Winifred SA10 . . . 70 E7
Winifred St
Dowlais CF48 . . . 11 A5
3 Mountain Ash / Aberpennar CF45 . . . 81 F8
Winifred Terr NP13 . . . 36 B8
Winnipeg Dr CF23 . . . 178 C5
Winsford Rd CF64 . . . 216 C4
Winslade Ave CF39 . . . 133 C6
Winston Ave CF5 . . . 193 A2
Winstone Cotts NP4 . . . 37 F5
Winstone Rd NP4 . . . 38 B1
Winston Rd CF62 . . . 214 E8
Winston St SA1 . . . 233 A4
Wisley Pl CF23 . . . 160 E1
Wistaria Cl NP20 . . . 117 B3
Wiston Path NP44 . . . 89 B2
Witham St NP19 . . . 143 E4
Witherdene Rd CF43 . . . 80 C2
Withycombe Rd CF3 . . . 179 C7
Withy Pk SA3 . . . 122 A6
Witla Court Rd CF3 . . . 179 C5
Witts End CF72 . . . 153 F2
Wolfe Cl
Barry / Y Barri CF63 . . . 215 C7
Cowbridge / Y Bont-Faen CF71 . . . 188 D2
Wolfs Castle Ave CF14 . . . 159 E1
Wolseley Cl NP20 . . . 143 C1
Wolseley St NP20 . . . 143 C1
Womanby St / Stryd Womanby CF10 . . . 232 B2
Woodbine Cotts SA11 . . . 226 C4
Woodbine Rd NP12 . . . 85 E7
Woodburn Dr SA3 . . . 123 A6
Wood Cl
Cardiff / Caerdydd CF14 . . . 160 B1
Llanyrafon NP44 . . . 90 B1
Neath / Castell-Nedd SA11 . . . 71 D4
Rogerstone NP10 . . . 142 A7
Woodcock St CF24 . . . 195 C7
Woodcote SA2 . . . 93 D6
Woodcote Gn SA4 . . . 43 C7
Wood Cres NP10 . . . 142 A7
Wood End Mdw / Maes Tal Coed 6 CF31 . . . 168 C3
Woodend Rd SA15 . . . 40 E6
Woodfield Ave
Pontlliw SA4 . . . 44 A5
Radyr CF15 . . . 176 C4
Woodfield Bldgs CF39 . . . 107 F4
Woodfield Cl CF3 . . . 180 E8
Woodfield Cross NP22 . . . 13 F4
Woodfield Park Cres NP12 . . . 85 F6
Woodfield Rd
Cwm NP23 . . . 35 B8
Pontypool / Pont-y-pwl NP4 . . . 63 A4
Talbot Green CF72 . . . 155 A2
Tredegar NP22 . . . 13 F5
WOODFIELDSIDE . . . 85 F7
Woodfieldside Bsns Pk NP12 . . . 86 A5
Woodfield St
Bryncae CF72 . . . 153 E2
Pontllanfraith NP12 . . . 86 A6
7 Port Talbot SA13 . . . 125 C6
Swansea / Abertawe SA6 . . 68 F8
Woodfield Terr
Ammanford / Rhydaman SA18 . . . 219 D7
Mountain Ash / Aberpennar CF45 . . . 81 F8
Pontllanfraith NP12 . . . 86 A6
Porth CF39 . . . 107 F4
Tir-Y-Berth CF82 . . . 84 F6
Trehafod CF37 . . . 108 C2
Woodford Cl CF5 . . . 176 E1
Woodford Rd SA5 . . . 67 E7
Woodham Cl CF62 . . . 214 D6
Woodham Halt* CF62 . . . 214 E4
Woodham Pk CF62 . . . 214 D6
Woodham Rd CF63 . . . 215 A4
Woodland Ave
1 Margam SA13 . . . 125 E4
Pencoed CF35 . . . 170 D8
Porthcawl CF36 . . . 183 B8
The Mumbles / Y Mwmbwls SA3 . . . 122 F7
Woodland Cl
Bettws CF32 . . . 129 E1
Neath / Castell-Nedd SA10 . . . 70 E8
Woodland Cotts
Bedlinog CF46 . . . 56 A7
Quakers Yard CF46 . . . 83 B6
Woodland Cres
Abercynon CF45 . . . 82 F3
Woodland Cres continued
Cardiff / Caerdydd CF23 . . 178 C4
Creigiau CF15 . . . 174 E8
Woodland Ct
Abercynon CF45 . . . 82 F3
Croesyceiliog NP44 . . . 90 A4
Swansea / Abertawe SA2 . . 94 A6
Woodland Dr
Aberfan CF48 . . . 55 C3
Abertillery / Abertyleri NP11 . . . 59 F5
Bassaleg NP10 . . . 141 F3
Newbridge / Trecelyn NP11 . . . 87 A6
Penarth CF64 . . . 207 A4
Rogerstone / Ty-du NP10 . . . 141 E7
Woodland Flats 4 CF83 . . . 111 F1
Woodland Park Rd NP19 . . . 143 F6
Woodland Park View 5 NP19 . . . 143 F6
Woodland Pk
Glyn-neath / Glyn-nedd SA11 . . . 223 D1
Penderyn CF44 . . . 224 D2
Pontypool / Pont-y-pwl NP4 . . . 62 A5
Ynystawe SA6 . . . 46 B5
Woodland Pl
Bargoed / Bargod CF81 . . . 58 A1
Bedlinog CF46 . . . 56 B7
1 Cardiff / Caerdydd CF24 . . . 195 C7
Cefn Hengoed CF82 . . . 84 F4
10 Merthyr Tydfil / Merthyr Tudful CF47 . . . 10 E1
North Cornelly CF33 . . . 166 A7
Penarth CF64 . . . 207 A4
Pengam NP12 . . . 85 B7
Woodland Rd
Beddau CF38 . . . 156 B6
Cardiff / Caerdydd CF14 . . 176 F4
Croesyceiliog NP44 . . . 90 A4
Crynant / Creunant SA10 . . . 226 A7
Glyncorrwg SA13 . . . 227 C2
Mountain Ash / Aberpennar CF45 . . . 54 C3
Neath / Castell-Nedd, Skewen / Sciwen SA10 . . . 70 E8
Neath / Castell-Nedd, Ty'n-y-Caeau SA11 . . . 71 F7
Newport / Casnewydd NP19 . . . 143 F6
Pontllanfraith NP12 . . . 86 A4
Pontygwaith CF43 . . . 80 B2
Underwood NP18 . . . 145 E6
Woodland Rd / Heol Tir Y Coed SA9 . . . 221 C7
Woodland Rise
Deri CF81 . . . 33 A1
Pen-y-fai CF31 . . . 150 D1
Woodland Row SA12 . . . 99 D6
Woodlands
Beddau CF38 . . . 156 B7
Gowerton / Tre-gwyr SA4 . . 66 C5
Tredegar NP22 . . . 6 C1
Woodlands Ave
Clydach SA6 . . . 46 F8
Treharris CF46 . . . 83 B6
Woodlands Bsns Pk / Parc Busnes Coed Cedwyn SA9 . . . 2 D7
Woodlands Cl CF71 . . . 188 D2
Woodlands Cres CF46 . . . 83 B5
Woodlands Ct 4 CF62 . . 214 F5
Woodlands Cvn Pk CF46 . . . 83 B5
Woodlands Dr NP20 . . . 117 A4
Woodlands Gr CF32 . . . 104 E6
Woodlands High Sch / Ysgol Uwchradd Woodlands CF5 . . . 193 E5
Woodlands Jun & Inf Schs NP44 . . . 89 B5
Woodlands La SA18 . . . 219 C6
Woodlands Park Dr
Cardiff / Caerdydd CF5 . . . 193 C3
Neath / Castell-Nedd SA10 . . . 48 E1
Woodlands Pk
Pencoed CF35 . . . 170 C8
Pyle / Y Pîl CF33 . . . 148 D1
Woodlands Pk / Parc Tir-y-Coed SA18 . . . 219 C6
Woodlands Rd
Barry / Y Barri CF62 . . . 214 F5
Loughor SA4 . . . 42 F1
Woodlands Rise CF31 . . . 168 C4
Woodlands St CF32 . . . 104 E3
Woodland St
Blaenavon NP4 . . . 17 D7
Cwmbran / Cwmbrân NP44 . . . 89 D4
Mountain Ash / Aberpennar CF45 . . . 54 C3
Pontardawe SA8 . . . 23 F5
Woodlands Terr
Cross Hands SA14 . . . 218 B7
Maesteg CF34 . . . 75 A1
Resolven / Resolfen SA11 . . . 226 E5
Swansea / Abertawe SA1 . . 95 B7
Woodlands The
Abersychan NP4 . . . 37 E5
Woodlands The continued
Bridgend / Pen-y-Bont ar Ogwr CF31 . . . 169 C5
Cardiff / Caerdydd CF14 . . 160 B2
Pontypool / Pont-y-pwl NP4 . . . 62 D7
Woodlands Workshop Ctr CF72 . . . 155 A1
Woodland Terr
Abercarn NP11 . . . 87 A3
Aberdare / Aberdâr CF44 . . 53 C6
Abertillery / Abertyleri, Cwmtillery / Cwmtyleri NP13 . . . 36 B8
Abertillery / Abertyleri, St Illtyd / Llanhiledd NP13 . . 36 A1
Abertridwr CF83 . . . 136 F7
Argoed NP12 . . . 58 F4
Merthyr Tydfil / Merthyr Tudful CF47 . . . 10 E1
Mountain Ash / Aberpennar CF45 . . . 54 C3
Nantyglo NP23 . . . 8 C1
Neath / Castell-Nedd SA10 . . . 48 F2
New Tredegar NP24 . . . 33 D5
Pant-yr-awel CF32 . . . 130 D4
Pontyclun CF72 . . . 172 F8
Pontypool / Pont-y-pwl NP4 . . . 61 F8
Pontypridd CF37 . . . 135 B8
Senghenydd CF83 . . . 110 F3
Treorchy / Treorci, Cwmparc CF42 . . . 78 B4
Treorchy / Treorci, Ynys-wen CF42 . . . 78 C7
Woodland Vale CF42 . . . 78 D7
Woodland View
Church Village CF38 . . . 156 D8
Cwmfelinfach NP11 . . . 113 F3
Pontypool / Pont-y-pwl NP4 . . . 62 B8
Woodland View / Golygfa'r Goedwig 4 NP44 . . . 90 A5
Woodland View / Trem Y Goedlan NP44 . . . 37 E7
Woodland Villa CF72 . . . 172 F8
Woodland Way
Merthyr Tydfil / Merthyr Tudful CF48 . . . 30 A8
Sarn CF32 . . . 150 E3
Woodland Wlk NP13 . . . 15 F5
Woodlawn Way CF14 . . . 159 E2
Woodley Ct CF5 . . . 176 D2
Woodmans Terr SA9 . . . 2 B6
Woodmill / Allt Y Felin SA10 . . . 48 C1
Wood Path NP44 . . . 90 A6
Woodpecker Sq CF62 . . . 210 E6
Wood Rd
Abercynon CF45 . . . 82 E2
Pontypridd CF37 . . . 135 D7
Woodridge Ct SA3 . . . 122 F4
Woodruff Way CF14 . . . 159 D3
Wood St / Stryd Y Coed SA13 . . . 125 D6
Woodside
Newport / Casnewydd NP10 . . . 163 E7
Tir-Y-Berth CF82 . . . 84 F6
Tonna / Tonnau SA10 . . . 49 A3
Woodside Ave
Bridgend / Pen-y-Bont ar Ogwr CF31 . . . 168 F8
Neath / Castell-Nedd SA11 . . . 71 F7
Swansea / Abertawe SA2 . . 93 E6
Woodside Cl
Bishopston SA3 . . . 122 A5
Swansea / Abertawe SA2 . . 93 E6
Woodside Cres
Clydach SA6 . . . 46 C8
Ebbw Vale / Glyn Ebwy NP23 . . . 14 D6
Woodside Ct CF14 . . . 160 A1
Woodside Rd
Cwmbran / Cwmbrân NP44 . . . 89 E4
Pontypool / Pont-y-pwl NP4 . . . 38 B2
Woodside Terr
Abertillery / Abertyleri NP13 . . . 60 B6
Newbridge / Trecelyn NP11 . . . 60 B2
Woodside Way NP44 . . . 89 C4
Woodside Wk NP11 . . . 113 E3
Wood St
Abercarn NP11 . . . 114 B8
Bargoed / Bargod CF81 . . . 58 A4
Cardiff / Caerdydd CF10 . . 232 B1
Ferndale CF43 . . . 79 F7
Gilfach Goch CF39 . . . 132 B5
Maerdy CF43 . . . 52 A2
Maesteg CF34 . . . 102 B2
Penarth CF64 . . . 207 A4
Pontycymer CF32 . . . 103 F4
Pontypridd CF37 . . . 109 F5
Woodstock Cl CF62 . . . 214 D5
Woodstock Gdns CF35 . . 152 D1
Woodstock Mews CF71 . . . 188 E2
Woodsy Cl CF23 . . . 161 A2
Woodvale Ave CF23 . . . 178 D7
Woodview
Brynna CF72 . . . 153 C3
Gowerton / Tre-gwyr SA4 . . . 66 D4
Wood View
Cimla SA11 . . . 72 B6
Newbridge / Trecelyn NP11 . . . 59 F2
Wood View Cl / Clos Golwg Y Coed 2 SA11 . . . 71 C1
Wood View Cres NP11 . . 115 A1
Woodview Ct NP4 . . . 62 B6
Woodview Pl SA5 . . . 67 E6
Wood View Rd NP11 . . . 115 A2
Woodview Terr
Bryn-côch SA10 . . . 48 C4
Pontypool / Pont-y-pwl NP4 . . . 62 B6
Woodville Ct 6 CF24 . . . 195 A8
Woodville Pl
1 Ebbw Vale / Glyn Ebwy NP23 . . . 14 D6
Ferndale CF43 . . . 79 F7
Woodville Rd
3 Cardiff / Caerdydd CF24 . . . 178 A1
Cardiff / Caerdydd CF24 . . 195 A8
Newport / Casnewydd NP20 . . . 142 F4
The Mumbles / Y Mwmbwls SA3 . . . 123 A4
Woodville St SA4 . . . 19 C5
Woodville Terr NP12 . . . 58 F5
Woodward Ave NP11 . . . 114 B4
Woodward Rd NP11 . . . 114 C4
Woolacombe Ave CF3 . . . 179 C6
Woolaston Ave CF23 . . . 178 C5
Woollacott Dr SA3 . . . 122 D5
Woollacott Mews SA3 . . . 122 D5
Wooller Ho 9 SA12 . . . 98 F1
Woolmer Cl CF5 . . . 176 D2
Woolpitch NP44 . . . 89 B3
Woosnam Cl CF23 . . . 178 E1
Worcester Cl
Cardiff / Caerdydd CF11 . . . 194 F2
Heolgerrig CF48 . . . 10 A1
Worcester Cl / Clos Caerwrangon 8 NP44 . . 90 A3
Worcester Cres NP19 . . . 144 A8
Worcester Ct CF11 . . . 194 F1
Worcester Ct SA7 . . . 69 C7
Worcester Dr SA3 . . . 123 B4
Worcester Ho CF23 . . . 178 C3
Worcester Path / Llwybr Caerwrangon 3 NP44 . . 90 A3
Worcester Pl SA1 . . . 233 B3
Worcester Rd SA3 . . . 123 B4
Worcester St
Brynmawr NP23 . . . 8 C4
Cardiff / Caerdydd CF11 . . 194 F2
Wordsworth Ave
Bridgend / Pen-y-Bont ar Ogwr CF31 . . . 168 C6
Cardiff / Caerdydd CF24 . . 195 C7
Penarth CF64 . . . 206 F4
Wordsworth Cl
Ebbw Vale / Glyn Ebwy NP23 . . . 14 B8
Llantwit Major / Llanilltud Fawr CF61 . . . 210 B6
Wordsworth Cl / Clos Wordsworth 6 NP44 . . . 89 D2
Wordsworth Gdns CF37 . . . 136 B6
Wordsworth Rd NP19 . . . 144 A5
Wordsworth St
Cwmaman CF44 . . . 53 A4
Swansea / Abertawe SA1 . . . 233 A4
Working St CF10 . . . 232 B2
Works Rd SA8 . . . 23 E4
Worle Ave CF3 . . . 179 B5
Worle Pl CF3 . . . 179 B5
Worrells Pl CF5 . . . 193 B2
Wren Ave SA11 . . . 72 B5
Wren Cl
Bridgend / Pen-y-Bont ar Ogwr CF31 . . . 169 C4
Cardiff / Caerdydd CF3 . . 180 A6
Wrenford Ct 21 NP20 . . . 143 C4
Wren Hollow / Pant Y Dryw CF31 . . . 168 D3
Wren Rd CF62 . . . 210 E6
Wrenwood / Coed Y Dryw SA10 . . . 48 C1
Wrexham Ct CF3 . . . 179 E5
Wrgant Pl CF43 . . . 52 A2
Wright Cl NP19 . . . 144 B3
Wroughton Pl CF5 . . . 193 E6
Wychtree St SA6 . . . 69 A7
Wychwood Cl SA3 . . . 123 A4
Wye Cl
Barry / Y Barri CF62 . . . 214 C6
Swansea / Abertawe SA1 . . 69 B3
Wye Cres NP20 . . . 116 E2
Wye Ct / Cwrt Gwt NP44 . . . 89 B4
Wyeverne Rd
Cardiff / Caerdydd CF24 . . . 195 A8
1 Newport / Casnewydd NP19 . . . 144 A5
Wyfan Pl CF14 . . . 177 D2
WYLLIE . . . 85 F1
Wyncliffe Rd CF23 . . . 179 A8
WYNDHAM . . . 104 E3
Wyndham Arc CF10 . . . 232 B2
Wyndham Cl
Bridgend / Pen-y-Bont ar Ogwr CF31 . . . 169 C6
Wyndham Cl continued
Pontarddulais SA4 . . . 19 C3
Wyndham Cres
7 Aberdare / Aberdâr CF44 . . . 53 D7
Bridgend / Pen-y-Bont ar Ogwr CF31 . . . 168 F2
Cardiff / Caerdydd CF11 . . . 194 D6
Wyndham Ct SA6 . . . 69 C8
WYNDHAM PARK . . . 191 F5
Wyndham Park Way CF5 . . . 191 E5
Wyndham Pl CF11 . . . 194 E5
Wyndham Rd CF11 . . . 194 D6
Wyndham St / Stryd Wyndham CF31 . . . 168 F4
Wyndham St
Barry / Y Barri CF63 . . . 215 A5
Bryncae CF72 . . . 153 E2
Cardiff / Caerdydd CF11 . . 194 E5
Dowlais CF48 . . . 11 A4
Evanstown CF39 . . . 132 B8
Machen CF83 . . . 140 A7
Newport / Casnewydd NP20 . . . 143 C6
Ogmore Vale CF32 . . . 104 E4
Porth CF39 . . . 107 F2
6 Port Talbot SA13 . . . 125 C7
Swansea / Abertawe SA1 . . 95 B6
Tongwynlais CF15 . . . 158 C1
Ton Pentre CF41 . . . 79 A2
Tonypandy CF40 . . . 106 F4
Treherbert CF42 . . . 50 E2
Troedyrhiw CF48 . . . 31 C1
Wyndham Terr
Cardiff / Caerdydd CF14 . . . 178 A8
Risca / Rhisga NP11 . . . 115 B1
Wynd St CF63 . . . 215 B6
Wyngarth SA1 . . . 69 D5
Wynnstay Cl CF11 . . . 194 E3
Wynter Ct SA5 . . . 68 C6
Wyon Cl CF5 . . . 176 D3
Wyvern Ave / Rhodfa Gwifir 2 SA12 . . . 98 C2
Wyvern Ho 1 SA12 . . . 98 C2

Y

Yalton SA3 . . . 122 F7
Yard Coal Rise NP11 . . . 59 C3
Yard Row NP23 . . . 7 D3
Yarrow Cl CF5 . . . 193 A5
Y Banwen / Banwen Pl SA18 . . . 220 D8
Y BARRI / BARRY . . . 214 E3
Y Berllan
Cimla SA11 . . . 72 B6
Dunvant SA2 . . . 93 D7
Swansea / Abertawe SA6 . . 45 C2
Ystradgynlais SA9 . . . 2 D7
Y BONT-FAEN / COWBRIDGE . . . 188 C2
Y Bont Faen Prim Sch CF71 . . . 188 E1
Y Bwthyn SA15 . . . 40 E4
Y Cedrwydden NP12 . . . 85 D5
Y Cilffordd CF83 . . . 137 F4
Y Cilgant CF83 . . . 137 E6
Y Cilgant / The Crescent NP44 . . . 89 D1
Y Clos
Cwmllynfell SA9 . . . 221 B7
Llanelli SA15 . . . 41 A5
Y Clos / Close The 1 NP44 . . . 116 F8
Y Closs Craig CF81 . . . 57 F5
Y Craig CF32 . . . 184 D3
Y Cyswllt SA4 . . . 44 C5
Y Dderwen CF34 . . . 128 D7
Y Dderwen / Oaks The NP44 . . . 90 B5
Y Deri CF38 . . . 156 C6
Y Dolau SA6 . . . 45 C2
Y Dolydd CF83 . . . 137 F1
Y Dolydd / The Paddocks SA11 . . . 49 B2
Y Drenewydd / Newtown SA18 . . . 219 A7
Yellow Row NP22 . . . 6 E2
Yeo Cl NP20 . . . 116 E1
Yeo Rd NP20 . . . 116 E1
Yeo St SA11 . . . 226 D5
Yewberry Cl NP20 . . . 117 B2
Yewberry La
Newport / Casnewydd NP20 . . . 117 B2
Newport / Casnewydd NP20 . . . 117 C1
Yew Cl CF47 . . . 10 D5
Yew Gr
Blackwood / Coed-Duon NP12 . . . 85 F6
Pontllanfraith NP12 . . . 86 A6
Yew St
Aberbargoed / Aberbargod CF81 . . . 58 B5
Merthyr Tydfil / Merthyr Tudful CF47 . . . 30 E8
Taffs Well / Ffynnon Taf CF15 . . . 158 A4
Troedyrhiw CF48 . . . 31 C1
Yewtree Cl
Cardiff / Caerdydd CF5 . . . 193 C8

Yewtree Cl *continued*
The Mumbles / Y Mwmbwls SA3 ... 122 F8
Yew Tree Cl CF71 ... 187 B4
Yew Tree Ct
Barry / Y Barri CF62 ... 214 C3
Cardiff / Caerdydd CF23 .. 178 C2
Yewtree Gr CF62 ... 211 B7
Yew Tree La NP18 ... 118 B3
Yewtree Rd NP11 ... 87 A7
Yew Tree Terr
Croesyceiliog NP44 ... 90 A5
Cwmbran / Cwmbrân NP44 ... 89 D2
Y Faenor / Manor The NP44 ... 117 A5
Y-fan SA14 ... 41 C5
Y Fawydd / The Beeches 8 NP44 ... 89 D2
Y Felin Ffrwd CF83 ... 137 F4
Y Fron SA14 ... 218 A8
Y-Gaer SA14 ... 41 A8
Y Ganolfan CF48 ... 11 A4
Y Garn SA4 ... 44 A2
Y Garreg Llwyd SA4 ... 218 D2
Y Garth CF44 ... 28 C4
Y Gefnen SA7 ... 69 F6
Y Gelli / The Grove CF48 ... 55 C6
Y Gilfach SA9 ... 2 B7
Y Gilwern SA9 ... 2 B6
Y Glyn
Cefneithin SA14 ... 218 A8
Dunvant SA2 ... 93 D7
Maesycwmmer CF82 ... 85 A1
Y Goedlan
Cwmfelin CF34 ... 128 C8
Cwm-twrch Uchaf SA9 ... 221 C6
Y Goedwig CF14 ... 177 A8
Y Gorlan SA2 ... 93 D7
Y Gorsedd 7 SA18 ... 219 B7
Y Graig CF48 ... 11 A7
Y Graw / Garw The NP44 ... 90 B5
Y Groes
Cardiff / Caerdydd CF14 ... 177 B7
Sarn CF32 ... 150 F3
Y Gwernydd SA7 ... 46 F6
Y Gwter / Golate CF10 ... 232 B2
Y Lan CF35 ... 152 F1
Y Llanerch SA4 ... 44 A7
Y Llest CF31 ... 150 C1
Y Llwyn SA15 ... 41 A5
Y Llwyni SA6 ... 45 C2
YMCA Bldgs 10 CF62 ... 214 F5
YMCA Wales Com Coll CF14 ... 177 F7
Y MWMBWLS / THE MUMBLES ... 123 C4
Ymyl-yr-Afon SA10 ... 49 C4
Yniscedwyn Rd / Heol Ynyscedwyn SA9 ... 2 E8
Ynisderw Rd SA8 ... 23 E4
Ynisisaf Cotts SA9 ... 222 A6
Ynysallan Rd SA6, SA7 ... 46 D3
Ynysangharad Rd CF37 ... 109 D1
Ynys-arwed Cotts / Bythynod Ynys-Arwed SA11 ... 226 B4
Ynysawdre Comp Sch / Ysgol Ynysawdre CF32 ... 150 E5
YNYSBOETH ... 82 C5
Ynysboeth Inf Sch CF45 .. 82 C6
Ynysboeth Jun Sch CF45 ... 82 C5
Ynys Bridge Ct CF15 ... 158 B2
Ynysbryn Cl CF72 ... 155 C3
Ynys-bydafau SA9 ... 222 B7
Ynys Cadwyn SA11 ... 227 C8
Ynyscedwyn Ent Pk / Parc Menter Ynyscedwyn SA9 ... 2 E8
Ynys-Cedwyn Lodge SA9 ... 2 D7
Ynys Cl CF37 ... 135 F6
Ynyscorrwg Rd CF37 ... 136 B4
Ynys Ct SA13 ... 227 C1
Ynys Ct SA6 ... 69 B7
Ynyscynon Rd CF40 ... 106 F7
Ynyscynon St CF44 ... 29 D1
Ynyscynon Terr CF44 ... 29 D1
YNYSDDU ... 113 B5
Ynysddu
Pontyclun CF72 ... 173 A8
Talbot Green CF72 ... 155 A1
Ynysddu Prim Sch NP11 ... 113 A5
Ynysderw Ho SA8 ... 23 D4
YNYS-FACH ... 30 C8
Ynys Fach Ave SA11 ... 226 E5
Ynysfach Iron Heritage Mus★ CF48 ... 10 D1
Ynysfach Prim Sch SA11 ... 226 E5
Ynys Fawr Ave SA11 ... 226 E5
Ynysfeio Ave CF42 ... 51 B1
Ynysfeio Cl CF42 ... 78 B8
YNYSFORGAN ... 46 C4
Ynysgau St CF41 ... 79 C3
Ynys Glyd St CF82 ... 111 F7
Ynys-Gyfeillon Rd CF37 ... 109 C2
YNYSHIR ... 107 E6
Ynys Hir CF37 ... 109 D7
Ynyshir Ind Est CF39 ... 107 F5
Ynyshir Inf Sch CF39 ... 107 E6
Ynyshir Jun Sch CF39 ... 107 F6
Ynyshir Rd CF39 ... 107 E7
Ynys Hywel Visitor Ctr★ NP11 ... 113 B3
Ynys La NP44 ... 90 A5
Ynyslas CF36 ... 183 B8
Ynys-Las SA14 ... 41 C5
Ynys Las CF46 ... 83 D4
Ynyslas Cres SA11 ... 223 D1
Ynys-Lee SA12 ... 99 E4
Ynys Llwyd Cl CF44 ... 53 B8
Ynys-Lwyd Rd CF44 ... 53 C8
Ynys-Lwyd St CF44 ... 29 A1
Ynyslyn Rd CF37 ... 136 B4
YNYSMAERDY
71 D2
155 A5
Ynysmaerdy Prim Sch SA11 ... 71 C2
Ynysmaerdy Terr CF72 ... 155 A5
YNYSMEUDWY ... 24 B8
Ynys-Meudwy Rd SA8 ... 24 B8
Ynysmeurig Rd CF45 ... 82 E2
Ynys Nedd SA11 ... 226 E5
Ynys Newydd Rd SA2 ... 94 B4
Ynysowen Fach CF48 ... 55 C6
YNYSOWEN / MERTHYR VALE ... 55 D4
Ynysowen Prim Sch CF48 ... 55 C4
Ynys Park Cotts CF41 ... 79 A3
Ynys-Penllwch Rd SA6, SA7 ... 46 F7
Ynys St
Porth CF39 ... 107 F7
Port Talbot SA13 ... 99 C1
YNYSTAWE ... 46 B6
Ynystawe Prim Sch SA6 ... 46 C5
Ynysteg CF32 ... 150 E5
Ynys Terr CF37 ... 135 F5
YNYSWEN ... 222 E8
YNYS-WEN ... 78 C8
Ynyswen
Abercrave / Abercraf SA9 ... 222 E8
Llanelli SA14 ... 41 A8
Pontllanfraith NP12 ... 86 A3
Ynyswen Ind Est / Ystad Ddiwydiannol Ynyswen CF42 ... 78 B8
Ynyswen Inf Sch CF42 ... 78 B7
Ynyswen Rd CF42 ... 78 C7
Ynyswen Sta CF42 ... 78 B7
Ynyswen Terr SA10 ... 222 A1
Ynyswerdd SA4 ... 44 B2
YNYSYBWL ... 81 F1
Ynysybwl Rd CF37 ... 109 D6
Ynys-y-Coed NP12 ... 86 B8
Ynys Y Coed CF5 ... 194 A8
Ynys Y Cwm Rd SA15 ... 40 C7
Ynysydarren Rd / Heol Ynysydarren SA9 ... 2 B6
Ynysygerwn Ave SA10 ... 49 D4
Ynysygerwn Cres SA10 ... 49 D4
Ynys Y Gored SA13 ... 99 C2
Ynysygored Rd / Heol Ynysyored CF48 ... 55 C6
Ynysygwas Hill SA12 ... 99 E4
Ynysygwas Terr SA12 ... 99 E4
Ynys-y-gwial SA9 ... 1 F5
Ynysymaerdy Rd SA11 ... 71 D3
Ynys-y-Mond Rd
Glais SA7 ... 47 B7
Pontardawe SA8 ... 23 E2
Ynys-y-Nos Ave SA11 ... 223 E1
Ynys Y Plant SA3 ... 123 A7
Ynys-yr-Afon SA11 ... 226 B3
Yorath Rd CF14 ... 177 B5
York Ave
Blackwood / Coed Duon NP12 ... 59 B1
Ebbw Vale / Glyn Ebwy NP23 ... 14 D4
York Cl
Cwmbran / Cwmbrân NP44 ... 89 A3
Heolgerrig CF48 ... 10 A1
York Ct
Cardiff / Caerdydd CF10 ... 232 D1
5 Radyr CF15 ... 176 B6
Swansea / Abertawe SA1 ... 233 B2
York Dr CF38 ... 156 D6
York Mans 7 CF14 ... 176 F6
York Pk CF31 ... 169 B2
York Pl
Abercarn NP11 ... 114 A8
Barry / Y Barri CF62 ... 214 D3
Cardiff / Caerdydd CF11 .. 194 F1
Newport / Casnewydd NP20 ... 143 B4
Port Talbot SA13 ... 125 C8
5 Risca / Rhisga NP11 .. 114 F3
York Rd
Bridgend / Pen-y-Bont ar Ogwr CF31 ... 169 B2
Newport / Casnewydd NP19 ... 143 E7
York St
Aberdare / Aberdâr CF44 ... 53 C6
Abertillery / Abertyleri NP13 ... 36 A5
York St *continued*
Cardiff / Caerdydd CF5 ... 194 C5
Mountain Ash / Aberpennar CF45 ... 54 D1
Porth CF39 ... 107 F3
Swansea / Abertawe SA1 ... 233 B2
York Terr
Cwm NP23 ... 35 B7
Tredegar NP22 ... 13 F6
Youghal Cl CF23 ... 161 A2
Youldon Ho CF64 ... 206 B3
Young Bsns Ctr SA12 ... 98 A3
Y Pant Comp Sch / Ysgol Gyfun Y Pant CF72 ... 155 C1
Y PARC ... 102 A2
Y Parc CF72 ... 174 B7
Y PÎL / PYLE ... 148 A2
Y Poplys / Poplars SA12 ... 98 E1
Y Porth / Gateway The CF14 ... 177 E3
Yr Aelwyd CF37 ... 109 A7
Yr Aes / The Hayes CF10 ... 232 B2
Yr Allt
Llangennech SA14 ... 18 B1
Llantrisant CF72 ... 155 D3
Yr Aran SA2 ... 66 D1
YR AS FAWR / MONKNASH ... 198 C2
Yr Efail CF35 ... 170 B1
YR EGLWYS NEWYDD / WHITCHURCH ... 176 E5
Yr Elain SA2 ... 93 D8
Yr Hafan CF32 ... 103 F1
Yr Hafod
Llanelli SA15 ... 40 E7
Saron SA18 ... 218 F7
Swansea / Abertawe SA6 .. 45 C2
Y RHATH / ROATH ... 195 C8
Yr Helys / Willows The CF35 ... 152 B6
Yr Hendre
Nantgarw CF15 ... 158 A8
Pyle / Y Pîl CF33 ... 148 D3
Yr Hen Dy CF5 ... 177 A1
Yr Hen Laethdy CF48 ... 55 C3
Yr-Hen-Lawnt CF40 ... 106 F3
Yr Hen Ysgol CF44 ... 28 F3
Yr Hirgylch / Ellipse The NP4 ... 62 D1
Y Rhodfa CF62, CF63 ... 214 F4
Y Rhodfa / The Drive SA10 ... 71 B8
Y Rhos SA15 ... 40 F7
Y RHWS / RHOOSE ... 213 B1
Yr Ynys CF33 ... 148 A1
Yr Ysfa CF34 ... 102 A2
Ysbryd-y-coed CF31 ... 168 D8
Ysbryd Y Mor SA12 ... 98 B1
Ysbuty'r Santes Tudfil / St Tydfils Hospl CF47 ... 10 E1

Ysbyty = hospital

Ysbyty Athrofol Cymru / Univ Hospl of Wales CF14 ... 177 F3
Ysbyty Castell Nedd Port Talbot / Neath Port Talbot Hospl SA12 ... 98 E1
Ysbyty Eglwys Newydd / Whitchurch Hospl CF14 ... 176 F6
Ysbyty Fairwood / Fairwood Hospl SA2 ... 93 A6
Ysbyty Felindre / Velindre Hospl CF14 ... 176 F5
Ysbyty Frenhinol Morgannwg / Royal Glamorgan Hospl CF72 ... 155 B5
Ysbyty George Thomas CF42 ... 78 E5
Ysbyty Llandochau / Llandough Hospl CF64 ... 206 C6
Ysbyty Maesgwyn / Maesgwyn Hospl CF32 ... 151 A6
Ysbyty Sant Mair / St Mary's Day Hospl CF64 ... 206 C6
Ysbyty Treforys / Morriston Hospl SA6 ... 45 E5
Ysbyty Twysog Siarl / Prince Charles Hospl CF47 ... 10 C5
Ysbyty Tywysoges Cymru / Princess of Wales Hospl CF31 ... 169 A6
Ysgal Plant Bach Clydach / Clydach Inf Sch SA6 ... 46 D7
Ysgal Plant Bach Clydach / Clydach Jun Sch SA6 ... 46 D8
Ysgfol Uwchradd Duffryn / Duffryn High Sch NP10 ... 163 F6

Ysgol = school

Ysgol Babanod Llwyncelyn / Llwyncelyn Inf Sch CF39 ... 108 A3
Ysgol Babanod New Inn / New Inn Inf Sch NP4 ... 63 B4
Ysgol Bro Eirwg CF3 ... 179 A4
Ysgol Bro Morgannwg CF62 ... 214 D7
Ysgol Bro Sannan CF81 .. 58 B4
Ysgol Bryn Castell CF31 ... 168 D5
Ysgol Bryn Onnen NP4 ... 37 F8
Ysgol Cefnbrynbrain SA9 ... 221 B8
Ysgol Crug Glas SA1 ... 233 B4
Ysgol Cynlais Cty Prim Sch SA9 ... 1 F2
Ysgol Cynwyd Sant CF34 ... 102 A2
Ysgol Erw'r Delyn CF64 ... 206 D3
Ysgol Esgob Gore / Bishop Gore Sch SA2 ... 94 C6
Ysgol Fabanod Blaenllechchau / Blaenllechchau Inf Sch CF43 ... 79 F8
Ysgol G.G.Ynyswen CF42 ... 78 B7
Ysgol Golwg-y-Mor / Sea View Com Prim Sch SA1 ... 233 A4
Ysgol Grynradd Maes-y-Coed / Maes-y-Coed Prim Sch CF37 ... 135 B8
Ysgol Grynradd Parcyrhun SA18 ... 219 B6
Ysgol Gwaun-y-Nant / Oak Field Prim Sch CF62 ... 214 F7
Ysgol Gyfun Aberpennar / Mountain Ash Comp Sch CF45 ... 54 C4
Ysgol Gyfun Blaen-Gwawr / Blaengwawr Comp Sch CF44 ... 53 B8
Ysgol Gyfun Bryn Celynnog / Bryn Celynnog Comp Sch CF38 ... 155 F7
Ysgol Gyfun Bryn Tawe SA5 ... 68 A6
Ysgol Gyfun Brynteg (Isaf) / Brynteg Comp (Lower) Sch CF31 ... 168 E2
Ysgol Gyfun Brynteg (Uchaf) / Brynteg Comp (Upper) Sch CF31 ... 168 F2
Ysgol Gyfun Bryntirion / Bryntirion Comp Sch CF31 ... 168 C7
Ysgol Gyfun Cwm Rhymni NP12 ... 85 C5
Ysgol Gyfun Cwmtawe / Cwmtawe Comp Sch SA8 ... 23 E3
Ysgol Gyfun Cymer Rhondda CF39 ... 107 E2
Ysgol Gyfun Cynffig / Cynffig Comp Sch CF33 ... 148 D1
Ysgol Gyfun Gatholig Joseff Sant / St Joseph's RC High Sch NP10 ... 163 E6
Ysgol Gyfun Gatholig Sant Ioan Llwyd / St John Lloyd RC Comp Sch SA14 ... 41 B6
Ysgol Gyfun Glyncoed / Glyncoed Comp Sch NP23 ... 7 C3
Ysgol Gyfun Gwynllyw NP4 ... 38 C1
Ysgol Gyfun Gwyr SA4 ... 66 C5
Ysgol Gyfun Gymraeg Glantaf / The Welsh Comp Sch Glantaf CF14 ... 176 F2
Ysgol Gyfun Gymraeg Plasmawr / Plasmawr Welsh Comp Sch CF5 ... 176 C1
Ysgol Gyfun Heolddu / Heolddu Comp Sch CF81 ... 57 E4
Ysgol Gyfun Lewis I Ferched / Lewis Girls' Comp Sch CF82 ... 84 F1
Ysgol Gyfun Llanhari CF72 ... 172 A5
Ysgol Gyfun Maes Yr Yrfa SA14 ... 218 A8
Ysgol Gyfun Ogwr / Ogmore Comp Sch CF32 ... 151 A6
Ysgol Gyfun Rhydfelen CF37 ... 135 F5
Ysgol Gyfun Rhydyfelin CF37 ... 136 A5
Ysgol Gyfun Rhydywaun CF44 ... 27 F7
Ysgol Gyfun Sant Cenydd / St Cenydd Comp Sch CF83 ... 137 D4
Ysgol Gyfun Tonypandy / Tonypandy Comp Sch CF40 ... 106 E4
Ysgol Gyfun Tonyrefail / Tonyrefail Comp Sch CF39 ... 133 A4
Ysgol Gyfun Uchaf Bryn Hafren / Bryn Hafren Comp Sch CF62 ... 204 F1
Ysgol Gyfun Y Merched Aberdar / Aberdare Girls Comp Sch CF44 ... 29 B2
Ysgol Gyfun Y Pant / Y Pant Comp Sch CF72 ... 155 C1
Ysgol Gyfun Ystalyfera SA9 ... 2 C6
Ysgol Gyfun Y Strade SA15 ... 40 A6
Ysgol Gymradd Y Rhos / Rhos Prim Sch SA8 ... 24 B3
Ysgol Gymraeg Abercynon CF45 ... 82 E4
Ysgol Gymraeg Bro Allta CF82 ... 84 E1
Ysgol Gymraeg Bro Ogwr CF31 ... 169 A6
Ysgol Gymraeg Brynmawr Jun & Inf Schs NP23 ... 8 B4
Ysgol Gymraeg Brynsierfel SA14 ... 41 D5
Ysgol Gymraeg Caerffili CF83 ... 138 B4
Ysgol Gymraeg Casnewydd NP18 ... 144 E4
Ysgol Gymraeg Coed-y-gof CF5 ... 176 C1
Ysgol Gymraeg Cwmbran NP44 ... 89 D2
Ysgol Gymraeg Cwm Gwyddon NP11 ... 87 B2
Ysgol Gymraeg Cwmtwrch SA9 ... 1 B1
Ysgol Gymraeg Dewi Sant SA14 ... 40 F7
Ysgol Gymraeg Llantrisant / Llantrisant Welsh Prim Sch CF72 ... 155 D3
Ysgol Gymraeg Melin Gruffydd Sch CF14 ... 177 A4
Ysgol Gymraeg Mynachlog Nedd / Mynachlog Nedd Jun Sch SA10 ... 71 A7
Ysgol Gymraeg Pontybrenin SA4 ... 66 B8
Ysgol Gymraeg Pwll Coch CF11 ... 194 C4
Ysgol Gymraeg Trelyn NP12 ... 85 A7
Ysgol Gymraeg Ynysgedwyn SA9 ... 2 F8
Ysgol Gymraeg Y Wern SA9 ... 2 B6
Ysgol Gymunedol Abercanaid / Abercanaid Com Sch CF48 ... 31 A4
Ysgol Gymunedol Cwmamman Com Sch SA18 ... 220 A8
Ysgol Gynradd Blaenau SA18 ... 218 F8
Ysgol Gynradd Blaentillery / Blaentillery Prim Sch NP13 ... 36 B8
Ysgol Gynradd Bryncethin / Bryncethin Prim Sch CF32 ... 151 A4
Ysgol Gynradd Brynmenyn / Brynmenyn Prim Sch CF32 ... 150 E6
Ysgol Gynradd Brynnau / Brynnau Prim Sch CF72 ... 153 D3
Ysgol Gynradd Bynea / Bynea Prim Sch SA14 ... 41 F3
Ysgol Gynradd Cae-draw / Caedraw Prim Sch CF47 ... 30 D8
Ysgol Gynradd Capcoch / Capcoch Prim Sch CF44 ... 53 E5
Ysgol Gynradd Catholig Sant Roberts / St Robert's RC Prim Sch CF32 ... 150 C3
Ysgol Gynradd Coed y Dderwen CF48 ... 10 A3
Ysgol Gynradd Coed-yr-Esgob / Coed-yr-Esgob Prim Sch CF72 ... 155 D4
Ysgol Gynradd Coety / Coety Prim Sch CF35 ... 169 D8
Ysgol Gynradd Corneli / Corneli Prim Sch CF33 ... 165 F8
Ysgol Gynradd Creigiau / Creigiau Prim Sch CF15 ... 174 D8
Ysgol Gynradd Crymlyn / Crymlyn Prim Sch SA10 ... 70 C1
Ysgol Gynradd Ffynnon-yr-Eryr / Eagleswell Prim Sch CF61 ... 210 B7
Ysgol Gynradd Gatholig Padrig Sant / St Patrick's RC Primary Sch NP19 ... 144 A4
Ysgol Gynradd Gatholig Y Santes-Fair / St Mary's RC Prim Sch CF47 ... 30 D8
Ysgol Gynradd Gelli / Gelli Prim Sch CF41 ... 79 B3

Ysgol Gynradd Glan-yr-Afon / Glan-yr-Afon Prim Sch CF3 179 B7
Ysgol Gynradd Glyncoed / Glyncoed Prim Sch NP23 7 D3
Ysgol Gynradd Gorslas / Gorslas Com Prim Sch SA14 218 B8
Ysgol Gynradd Graig-y-Rhacca / Graig-y-Rhacca Prim Sch CF83 139 C6
Ysgol Gynradd Gwaelod-y-garth CF15 157 F4
Ysgol Gynradd Gymraed Garth Olwg CF38 156 E8
Ysgol Gynradd Gymraeg Aberdar
Aberdare / Aberdâr CF44 29 B1
Cwmdare CF44 28 D3
Ysgol Gynradd Gymraeg Bodringallt CF41 79 D3
Ysgol Gynradd Gymraeg Bronllwyn CF41 79 A2
Ysgol Gynradd Gymraeg Bryniago SA4 19 D4
Ysgol Gynradd Gymraeg Bryn-y-mor SA2 94 F5
Ysgol Gynradd Gymraeg Castellau CF38 155 F7
Ysgol Gynradd Gymraeg Castell Nedd SA11 71 F7
Ysgol Gynradd Gymraeg Cwm Garw CF32 103 E4
Ysgol Gynradd Gymraeg Cwmnedd SA11 223 D1
Ysgol Gynradd Gymraeg Draddodiadol Rhiwfawr SA9 221 B5
Ysgol Gynradd Gymraeg Draddodiadol Trebannws / Trebannws Prim Sch SA8 23 C2
Ysgol Gynradd Gymraeg Draddodianol Cwmllynfell SA9 221 B7
Ysgol Gynradd Gymraeg Draddodiaol Cwmgors SA18 220 D5
Ysgol Gynradd Gymraeg Draddodiaol Glyn SA18 220 D8
Ysgol Gynradd Gymraeg Evan James CF37 109 B1
Ysgol Gynradd Gymraeg Felindre SA5 20 F2
Ysgol Gynradd Gymraeg Garnswllt SA18 219 B3
Ysgol Gynradd Gymraeg Gellionnen SA6 46 E8
Ysgol Gynradd Gymraeg Gilfach Fargoed CF81 58 A1
Ysgol Gynradd Gymraeg Gwaun Cae Gurwen SA18 220 D7
Ysgol Gynradd Gymraeg Llwyncelyn CF39 108 A3
Ysgol Gynradd Gymraeg Llwynderw SA2 94 D6
Ysgol Gynradd Gymraeg Llyn-y-Forwyn CF43 79 F6
Ysgol Gynradd Gymraeg Lonlas SA7 69 D8
Ysgol Gynradd Gymraeg Pontardawe SA8 23 E6
Ysgol Gynradd Gymraeg Pont Sion Norton CF37 109 E3
Ysgol Gynradd Gymraeg Tonyrefail CF39 133 C5
Ysgol Gynradd Gymraeg Tyle'r Ynn SA11 71 B4
Ysgol Gynradd Gymraeg Y Castell CF83 138 A2
Ysgol Gynradd Gymraeg Y Login Fach SA5 66 F3
Ysgol Gynradd Gymunedol Gymraeg Llantrisant CF72 173 C8
Ysgol Gynradd Hendreforgan / Hendreforgan Prim Sch CF39 132 C5
Ysgol Gynradd Heolycyw / Heolycyw Prim Sch CF35 152 B5
Ysgol Gynradd Hillside / Hillside Prim Sch NP4 17 D7
Ysgol Gynradd Llandochau / Llandough Prim Sch CF64 206 D7
Ysgol Gynradd Llanedi SA4 218 D2
Ysgol Gynradd Llanilltud Faerdref / Llanilltud Faerdref Prim Sch CF38 135 F1
Ysgol Gynradd Machen / Machen Prim Sch CF83 139 F7
Ysgol Gynradd Maes-glas / Greenmeadow Prim Sch NP44 89 A3
Ysgol Gynradd Maes-y-Bryn / Maes-y-Bryn Prim Sch CF38 156 D7
Ysgol Gynradd Parc Hendredenni / Hendredenny Park Prim Sch CF83 137 D4
Ysgol Gynradd Pendyrus / Tylorstown Prim Sch CF43 80 C3
Ysgol Gynradd Pentrechwyth / Pentrechwyth Prim Sch SA1 69 A3
Ysgol Gynradd Penygawsi / Penygawsi Prim Sch CF72 155 D2
Ysgol Gynradd Plasmarl / Plasmarl Prim Sch SA6 68 E5
Ysgol Gynradd Plasnewydd / Plasnewydd Prim Sch CF34 102 A3
Ysgol Gynradd Pontlottyn / Pontlottyn Cty Prim Sch CF81 32 F8
Ysgol Gynradd Pontyclun / Pontyclun Prim Sch CF72 173 B7
Ysgol Gynradd Pont-y-moel / Pontymoile Prim Sch NP4 62 D5
Ysgol Gynradd RC Crist y Brenin / Christ The King RC Prim Sch CF14 160 A1
Ysgol Gynradd Rhiwbeina / Rhiwbina Prim Sch CF14 177 B7
Ysgol Gynradd Sain Alban / St Albans RC Prim Sch CF24 195 F7
Ysgol Gynradd St Illtyd's / St Illtyd's Prim Sch / NP13 60 B6
Ysgol Gynradd Saint-y-Brid / St Brides CW Prim Sch CF32 185 C2
Ysgol Gynradd Sant Cuthbert / St Cuthberts RC Prim Sch CF10 195 C3
Ysgol Gynradd Saron SA18 218 E6
Ysgol Gynradd Sgeti / Sketty Prim Sch SA2 94 C8
Ysgol Gynradd Stebonheath / Stebonheath Prim Sch SA15 40 F5
Ysgol Gynradd Tirllydan / Broadlands Prim Sch CF31 168 B3
Ysgol Gynradd Tirmorfa / Tirmorfa Prim Sch SA12 98 B1
Ysgol Gynradd Tondu / Tondu Prim Sch CF32 150 C4
Ysgol Gynradd Tonyrefail / Tonyrefail Prim Sch CF39 133 C5
Ysgol Gynradd Trallwn / Trallwn Prim Sch SA7 69 E7
Ysgol Gynradd Treforys / Morriston Prim Sch SA6 69 A8
Ysgol Gynradd Tref-y-Rhyg / Tref-y-Rhyg Prim Sch CF39 133 D5
Ysgol Gynradd Tycroes SA18 218 F5
Ysgol Gynradd Waunceirch / Waunceirch Prim Sch SA10 48 C2
Ysgol Gynradd y Crwys / Crwys Prim Sch SA4 65 E1
Ysgol Gynradd Y Gnoll / Gnoll Prim Sch SA11 71 F7
Ysgol Gynradd Y Mileniwm Roseheyworth / Roseheyworth Millennium Prim Sch NP13 35 F7
Ysgol Gynradd yr Eglwys Yng Nghymru Tref Aberdar / Aberdare Town CW Prim Sch CF44 29 B1
Ysgol Gynradd Y Sir Pontybrenin / Pontybrenin Prim Sch SA4 43 B1
Ysgol Gynradd Ystradowen SA9 221 C7
Ysgol Gynrodd Llwydcoed / Llwydcoed Prim Sch CF44 28 E6
Ysgol Hendre Specl Sch SA10 48 C5
Ysgol Heol Goffa SA15 40 E7
Ysgol Heol-y-Celyn / Heol-y-Celyn Prim Sch CF37 136 A5
Ysgol Iau & Babanod Fairwater / Fairwater Jun & Inf Sch NP44 89 C2
Ysgol Iau Greenlawn / Greenlawn Jun Sch NP4 63 B4
Ysgol Iau Llangewydd / Llangewydd Jun Sch CF31 168 C5
Ysgol Iau Sant Helen / St Helens RC Jun Sch CF62 214 F6
Ysgol Iau Windsor Clive / Windsor Clive Jun Sch CF5 193 C5
Ysgol Ifor Bach CF83 110 F3
Ysgol Iolo Morganwg CF71 188 F1
Ysgol Llanilltud Fawr / Llantwit Major Sch CF61 210 A5
Ysgol Maes Dyfan CF63 215 A7
Ysgol Maes-y-Dderwen SA9 2 E7
Ysgol Mynydd Bychan CF14 177 F2
Ysgol Pencae CF5 176 F2
Ysgol Pentrehafod / Pentrehafod Sch SA1 68 D3
Ysgol Pen-y-Garth CF64 206 D5
Ysgol Plant Bach Bracla / Brackla Inf Sch CF31 169 B5
Ysgol Plant Bach Cwm-bach / Cwmbach Inf Sch CF44 53 E8
Ysgol Plant Bach Glanffrwd / Glanffrwd Inf Sch CF37 81 E2
Ysgol Plant Bach Llanfabon / Llanfabon Inf Sch CF46 83 E3
Ysgol Plant Bach Troed-y-rhiw / Troedyrhiw Inf Sch CF48 31 C1
Ysgol Plant Iau Bracla / Brackla Jun Sch CF31 169 B5
Ysgol Plant Lau Troed-y-rhiw / Troedyrhiw Jun Sch CF48 31 C2
Ysgol Plent Bach Ferndale / Ferndale Inf Sch CF43 79 F7
Ysgol Pl / Maes Yr Ysgol NP44 89 C6
Ysgol Sant Curig CF62 214 E5
Ysgol St SA1 96 B7
Ysgol Thomas Stephens SA11 223 F3
Ysgol Ty Coch CF38 136 B1
Ysgol Uwchradd Glyn Derw / Glyn Derw High Sch CF5 193 E4
Ysgol Uwchradd Hawthorn / Hawthorn High Sch CF37 136 B3
Ysgol Uwchradd Woodlands / Woodlands High Sch CF5 193 E5
Ysgol Uwchradd Yr Eglwys Newydd / Whitchurch High Sch CF14 177 A5
Ysgol Y Babanod Felinfoel SA14 41 A8
Ysgol y Berllan Deg CF23 178 E4
Ysgol Y Ferch O'r Sger CF33 165 F8
Ysgol-y-Graig Prim Sch CF48 10 A5
Ysgol y habanod Litchard / Litchard Inf Sch CF31 168 F8
Ysgol Y Lawnt NP22 12 E3
Ysgol-y-llys / The Court Specl Sch CF14 160 A1
Ysgol Ynysawdre / Ynysawdre Comp Sch CF32 150 E5
Ysgol yr Eos Prim Sch CF40 107 A3
Ysgol-Y-Wern CF14 159 E1
Ysgubor Fach CF83 139 F7
Ysgubor Fach St SA1 68 C2
YSGUBOR NEWYDD 30 F8
Ysguborwen NP22 6 F1
Ysguthan Rd SA12 124 F8
Ysgwyddgwyn CF81 57 B8
YSPITTY 42 B2
Yspitty Rd SA14 42 B1

Ystad = estate

Ystad Celyn CF34 102 A1
Ystad Ddiwdiannol Graddfa / Graddfa Ind est CF83 111 F2
Ystad Ddiwydiannol Abergorki / Abergorki Ind Est CF42 78 C7
Ystad Ddiwydiannol Cae Mawr / Cae Mawr Ind Est CF42 78 E5
Ystad Ddiwydiannol Cwmtyleri / Cwmtillery Ind Est NP13 36 B7
Ystad Ddiwydiannol Cyfarthfa / Cyfarthfa Ind Est CF47 10 C2
Ystad Ddiwydiannol Ferndale / Ferndale Ind Est CF43 79 D8
Ystad Ddiwydiannol Gelli / Gelli Ind Est CF41 79 C2
Ystad Ddiwydiannol Highfield / Highfield Ind Est CF43 79 E8
Ystad Ddiwydiannol Hirwaun / Hirwaun Ind Est CF44 224 C1
Ystad Ddiwydiannol Maerdy Road / Maerdy Road Ind Est CF43 79 D8
Ystad Ddiwydiannol Ton Pentre / Ton Pentre Ind Est CF41 79 A3
Ystad Ddiwydiannol Trefforest / Treforest Ind Est CF37 136 C2
Ystad Ddiwydiannol Treherbert / Treherbert Ind Est CF42 78 A8
Ystad Ddiwydiannol Treorchy / Treorchy Ind Est CF42 78 E5
Ystad Ddiwydiannol Ynyswen / Ynyswen Ind Est CF42 78 B8
Ystad Deri NP22 6 E2
Ystadwaun CF35 152 C1
YSTALYFERA 2 A6
Ysticlau Rd SA10 222 D4
Ysticl-Garu CF71 199 F8
YSTRAD 79 D3
Ystradbarwig Terr CF38 156 C6
Ystrad Bldgs CF83 139 A6
Ystrad Cl CF3 180 A7
Ystrad Einon SA4 43 B1
YSTRAD FAWR 168 D5
Ystrad Fawr CF31 168 D5
Ystrad-Fawr Villas SA9 222 A5
YSTRADFELLTE 224 B8
Ystradfellte Rd SA11 223 F3
YSTRADGYNLAIS 222 A5
Ystradgynlais Com Hospl SA9 2 E7
Ystradgynlais Workshops SA9 2 E8
YSTRAD MYNACH 84 F1
Ystrad Mynach Coll CF82 111 E8
Ystrad Mynach Coll (Rhymney Campus) NP22 12 E3
Ystrad Mynach Hospl CF82 111 E8
Ystrad Mynach Prim Sch CF82 84 E1
Ystrad Mynach Sta CF82 84 E1
YSTRADOWEN
Cowbridge 189 D8
Ystalyfera 221 C7
Ystrad Rd
Swansea / Abertawe SA5 67 B4
Ton Pentre CF41 79 B3
Ystrad Rhondda Sta CF41 79 D2
Ystrad St CF11 195 A2
Ystrad Terr
Abercarn NP11 87 C4
Ton Pentre CF41 79 B3
Ystruth Prim Sch NP13 15 E5
Ystwyth Pl SA6 45 D1
Y Waun CF37 81 F2
Y Waun Fach SA6 45 B2
Y Waun / Meadows The SA10 70 E7
Y Wern CF32 129 E3
Y-Wern SA6 45 B2
Y WIG / WICK 198 D5

Z

Zammit Cres SA15 41 A5
Zephaniah Way NP13 15 D5
Zig-Zag La CF36 166 B2
Zinc St CF24 195 D6
Zion Cl 12 CF48 31 C1
Zion Ct CF38 156 A7
Zion Pl 4 NP23 14 D6
Zion Row SA15 40 E6
Zion St NP23 14 D6
Zion Terr CF40 106 E6
Zoar Ave CF34 102 A4
Zoar Pl CF34 102 A4
Zoar Rd
5 Neath / Castell-Nedd SA11 71 E8
Ystalyfera SA9 2 B6
Zoar Terr CF46 83 A5
Zouch St SA5 68 C3

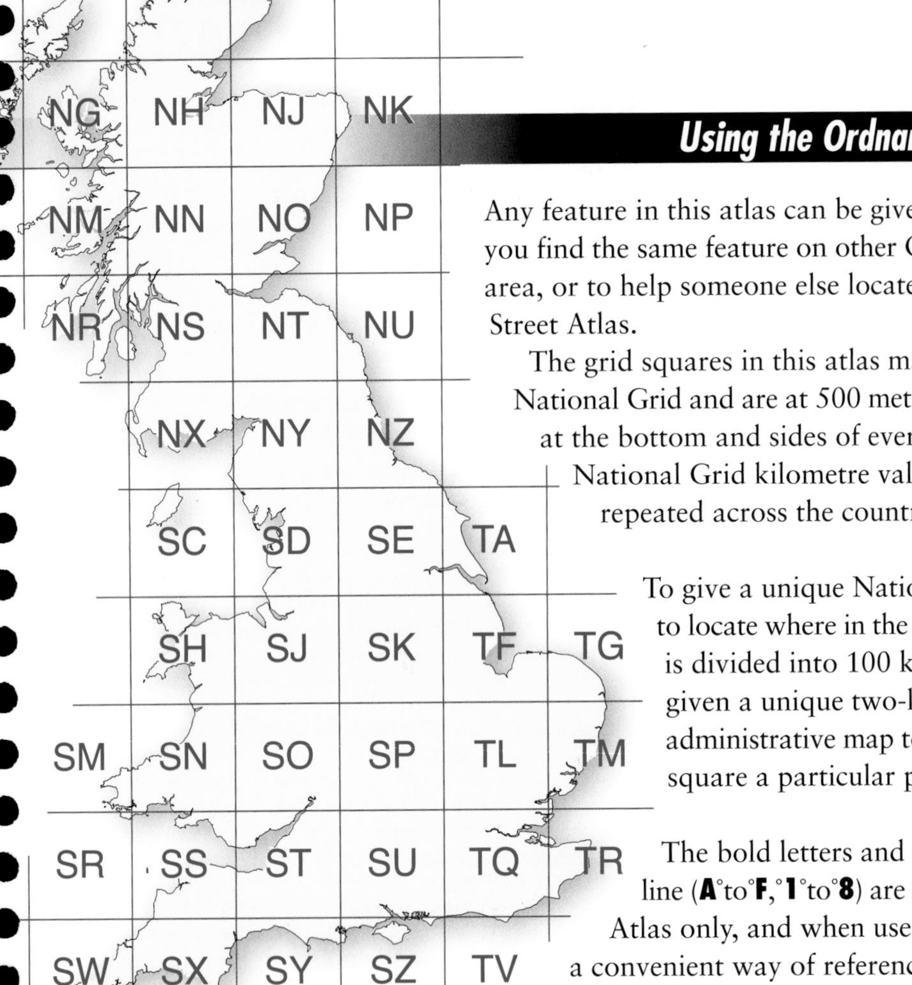

Using the Ordnance Survey National Grid

Any feature in this atlas can be given a unique reference to help you find the same feature on other Ordnance Survey maps of the area, or to help someone else locate you if they do not have a Street Atlas.

The grid squares in this atlas match the Ordnance Survey National Grid and are at 500 metre intervals. The small figures at the bottom and sides of every other grid line are the National Grid kilometre values (**00** to **99** km) and are repeated across the country every 100 km (see left).

To give a unique National Grid reference you need to locate where in the country you are. The country is divided into 100 km squares with each square given a unique two-letter reference. Use the administrative map to determine in which 100 km square a particular page of this atlas falls.

The bold letters and numbers between each grid line (**A** to **F**, **1** to **8**) are for use within a specific Street Atlas only, and when used with the page number, are a convenient way of referencing these grid squares.

Example The railway bridge over DARLEY GREEN RD in grid square B1

Step 1: Identify the two-letter reference, in this example the page is in **SP**

Step 2: Identify the 1 km square in which the railway bridge falls. Use the figures in the southwest corner of this square: Eastings **17**, Northings **74**. This gives a unique reference: **SP 17 74**, accurate to 1 km.

Step 3: To give a more precise reference accurate to 100 m you need to estimate how many tenths along and how many tenths up this 1 km square the feature is (to help with this the 1 km square is divided into four 500 m squares). This makes the bridge about **8** tenths along and about **1** tenth up from the southwest corner.

This gives a unique reference: **SP 178 741**, accurate to 100 m.

Eastings (read from left to right along the bottom) come before Northings (read from bottom to top). If you have trouble remembering say to yourself Along the hall, THEN up the stairs !

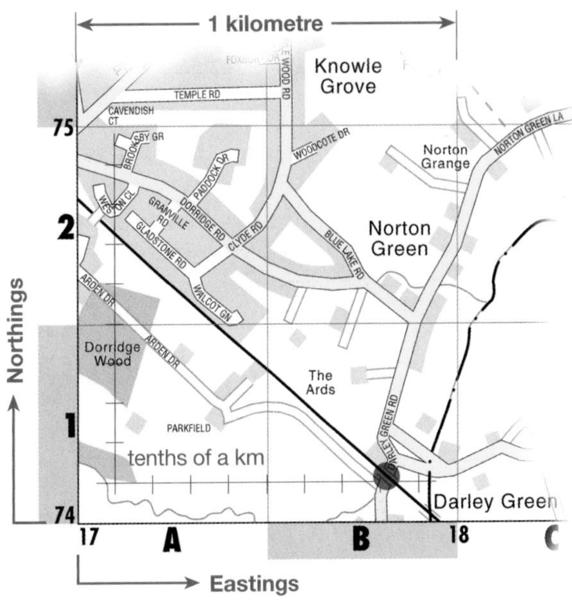